The Pillar New Testament Commentary

General Editor

D. A. CARSON

The Acts of the Apostles

David G. Peterson

WILLIAM B. EERDMANS PUBLISHING COMPANY
GRAND RAPIDS, MICHIGAN / CAMBRIDGE, U.K.

APOLLOS
NOTTINGHAM, ENGLAND

Published 2009 in the United States of America by
Wm. B. Eerdmans Publishing Co.
2140 Oak Industrial Drive N.E., Grand Rapids, Michigan 49505 /
P.O. Box 163, Cambridge CB3 9PU U.K.
www.eerdmans.com

and in the United Kingdom by
APOLLOS
Norton Street, Nottingham,
England NG7 3HR

Printed in the United States of America

20 19   8 7 6 5 4

Library of Congress Cataloging-in-Publication Data

Peterson, David, 1944-
The Acts of the Apostles / David G. Peterson.
p.   cm.   — (The Pillar New Testament commentary)
Includes bibliographical references and index.
ISBN 978-0-8028-3731-8 (cloth: alk. paper)
1. Bible. N.T. Acts — Commentaries.   I. Title.
BS2625.53.P43   2009
226.6'07 — dc22

                              2009009271

British Library Cataloguing in Publication Data

A catalogue record for this book is available from the British Library.
Apollos ISBN 978-1-84474-386-5

Contents

COMMENTARY

Editor's Preface

Commentaries have specific aims, and this series is no exception. Designed for serious pastors and teachers of the Bible, the Pillar commentaries seek above all to make clear the text of Scripture as we have it. The scholars writing these volumes interact with the most important informed contemporary debate, but avoid getting mired in undue technical detail. Their ideal is a blend of rigorous exegesis and exposition, with an eye alert both to biblical theology and the contemporary relevance of the Bible, without confusing the commentary and the sermon.

The rationale for this approach is that the vision of "objective scholarship" (a vain chimera) may actually be profane. God stands over against us; we do not stand in judgment of him. When God speaks to us through his Word, those who profess to know him must respond in an appropriate way, and that is certainly different from a stance in which the scholar projects an image of autonomous distance. Yet this is no surreptitious appeal for uncontrolled subjectivity. The writers of this series aim for an even-handed openness to the text that is the best kind of "objectivity" of all.

If the text is God's Word, it is appropriate that we respond with reverence, a certain fear, a holy joy, a questing obedience. These values should be reflected in the way Christians write. With these values in place, the Pillar commentaries will be warmly welcomed not only by pastors, teachers, and students, but by general readers as well.

*   *   *

Anyone writing a commentary on the Acts of the Apostles faces several challenges unique to this book. On the face of it, this is volume 2 of a two-part work, and the first part is the Synoptic Gospel we call Luke — so suddenly the relationships Acts sustains with the life and times of Jesus become rich and intricate. Acts is also the only source we have that directly tells part of the history of the earliest decades of the church — and that means it be-

xiv

comes imperative to think through the relationships this book has with the New Testament letters written during the same period. In particular, Acts devotes more than half its length to the ministry of the apostle Paul, a fact that invites interaction with the sheaf of letters Paul has left us in the New Testament corpus. And finally, Acts is, by New Testament standards, a long book, so a commentator, while tackling the whole, must judiciously avoid exploring tangential warrens that seem excusable when writing on short books like, say, Galatians or Jude. That means that the commentator must first and foremost devote attention to Acts itself and not to all of the many relationships this book has with much of the rest of the New Testament — which of course puts severe limitations on how much space can be fairly devoted to the features of Acts I've already mentioned.

All these challenges David Peterson has met superbly. His commentary focuses on what the text actually says, and his judgments are invariably sane, even-handed, judicious. While unpacking exegetical details, Peterson is careful to keep scanning the horizon so as to establish the larger vision. Moreover, his own commitments as a churchman, lecturer in New Testament, and long-time Principal of Oak Hill Theological College mean that he knows what kinds of information pastors and students want and need. So it is a great pleasure to add this commentary to the Pillar series.

D. A. CARSON

Author's Preface

It is an extraordinary privilege to live and work with any biblical book over an extended period of time, reading and re-reading the text many times, interacting with commentaries, articles, and monographs, while teaching and discussing the issues that arise with colleagues and students in a fellowship of learning and prayer. My most recent journey with Acts has lasted more than fifteen years. After teaching the book to a generation of theological students in Sydney, I was encouraged by the editor of this series to begin work on a commentary. Coincidentally, I was invited to contribute to the first volume of The Book of Acts in Its First-Century Setting (1993-96). In a rewarding partnership with Howard Marshall, I then became the editor of a book of essays on the theology of Acts, entitled *Witness to the Gospel* (1998). Working with Howard and the gifted contributors to that volume forced me to think in new ways about Luke's theological method and intentions. The writing of the commentary slowed down as I engaged in these tasks, though inevitably the whole project was enriched by such opportunities for scholarly encounter.

In the midst of all this, I was appointed Principal of Oak Hill Theological College in London (1996), where I also taught New Testament for eleven years. This volume is consequently dedicated to the faculty, support staff, and students, who played such a formative role in its production. As well as teaching Acts in undergraduate and graduate classes, I managed to preach through much of the book in the College Chapel. I am greatly indebted to those who responded in various ways, with comments, suggestions, and criticisms, allowing me to benefit from their insights. I am particularly grateful to Chris Green and Matthew Sleeman, who have published their own helpful contributions to the study of Acts, and to Alistair Seabrook, who acted as my research assistant for a year.

In recent years, the Acts of the Apostles has attracted the interest of many scholars and preachers, and the number of relevant publications one could consult is enormous and growing steadily! I regret not being able to read or refer to them all. Some commentaries major on textual issues, some on matters of historical and social context, some on theology and application. My own contribution attempts to be as comprehensive as possible, but with a bias towards theological analysis and an exploration of hermeneutical issues. The reason for this is twofold. First of all, monographs and articles on the theology of Acts are not normally accessible to the general reader. Wherever possible, I have tried to distil the insights of valuable scholarly work for the benefit of a wider public. Secondly, as I will argue, Acts was written primarily for the edification of the church and for the encouragement of gospel ministry. How, then, is this book to be understood and used with reference to the life and witness of contemporary believers? Many pastors and teachers are uncertain about the way to preach from biblical narratives, but recent developments in the field of narrative criticism have offered important guidelines for interpretation. Luke has offered us more clues for understanding the purpose and meaning of various elements in his work than may first appear.

The problem of application is particularly acute with respect to Acts because of the divisions that exist among Christians over matters such as the ministry of the Holy Spirit, divine guidance, miracles, the nature of the gospel, priorities for mission, the character and purpose of Christian gatherings, the relevance of the Old Testament, and Christian attitudes towards Jews. These are just a few of the topics that surface in any evaluation of Acts, all of which are matters of great importance for the contemporary life and witness of believers. A number of these receive special attention in the section on the theology of Acts. Those who lead churches, teach the Bible regularly in any context, or engage in missionary activity are challenged to reevaluate their understanding of such matters through a fresh examination of Luke's work. This commentary, incorporating the insights of so many others, is offered as an aid to this task.

I have followed the pattern of recent volumes in this series by using Today's New International Version as the basis of the exposition. Where appropriate, I have offered a more literal translation or suggested a better way of expressing the Greek. Readers who are familiar with New Testament Greek will find relevant words and phrases transliterated in parentheses or footnotes, sometimes with comments about the grammatical and syntactical significance. Where appropriate, I have also compared different English translations. Sometimes these vary because they rely on alternative textual traditions. I have tried to summarise the issue briefly at the end of my Introduction, but detailed discussion of textual variants is provided in the body of the commentary when they give rise to different translations.

It is no formality to conclude this preface with an expression of profound thanks to my wife, Lesley. Her loving care has sustained me through the years in which this work has been an absorbing commitment alongside many other responsibilities that we have shared. She has never ceased to encourage me and to maintain personal interest in the project. Readers should be aware of the significant role she has played! But together we would want to praise our heavenly Father for his constant provision, guidance, and enabling, which is the ultimate explanation for the successful completion of this endeavour.

DAVID G. PETERSON

Abbreviations

I. Modern Works

AB	Anchor Bible
AnBib	Analecta Biblica
ANRW	*Aufstieg und Niedergang der römischen Welt*, ed. W. Haase
ASNU	Acta Seminarii Neotestamentici Upsaliensis
BAGD	*A Greek-English Lexicon of the New Testament and Other Early Christian Literature*, by W. Bauer, W. F. Arndt, F. W. Gingrich, and F. W. Danker (2nd ed.; Chicago: University of Chicago, 1979)
BAR	*Biblical Archaeological Review*
BDAG	*A Greek-English Lexicon of the New Testament and Other Early Christian Literature*, by W. Bauer, F. W. Danker, W. F. Arndt, and F. W. Gingrich (3rd ed.; Chicago: University of Chicago, 2000)
BECNT	Baker Exegetical Commentary on the New Testament
BETL	Bibliotheca Ephemeridum Theologicarum Lovaniensium
BJRL	*Bulletin of the John Rylands Library*
BNTC	Black's New Testament Commentary
BST	The Bible Speaks Today
BTB	*Biblical Theology Bulletin*
CBQ	*Catholic Biblical Quarterly*
CGNTC	Cambridge Greek New Testament Commentary
DNTB	*Dictionary of New Testament Background*, ed. C. A. Evans and S. E. Porter (Downers Grove/Leicester: InterVarsity, 2000)
DPL	*Dictionary of Paul and his Letters*, (ed.) G. F. Hawthorne and R. P. Martin (Downers Grove/Leicester: Inter-Varsity, 1993).
EphThLov	*Ephemerides Theologicae Lovanienses*
EQ	*Evangelical Quarterly*
ESV	English Standard Version
EVV	English versions

ExpT	*Expository Times*
GNC	Good News Commentaries
HSM	Harvard Semitic Monographs
HTS	Harvard Theological Studies
HTR	*Harvard Theological Review*
IBD	*The Illustrated Bible Dictionary,* 3 vols.; ed. J. D. Douglas and N. Hillyer (Leicester: Inter-Varsity, 1980)
IBS	*Irish Biblical Studies*
ICC	International Critical Commentary
Int	*Interpretation*
ISBE	*International Standard Bible Encyclopedia,* 4 vols.; ed. G. W. Bromiley (Grand Rapids: Eerdmans, 1979-88)
JB	Jerusalem Bible
JBL	*Journal of Biblical Literature*
JBLMS	Journal of Biblical Literature Monograph Series
JBP	J. B. Phillips
JETS	*Journal of the Evangelical Theological Society*
JPT	*Journal of Pentecostal Theology*
JPTSS	Journal of Pentecostal Theology Supplement Series
JSNT	*Journal for the Study of the New Testament*
JSNTSS	Journal for the Study of the New Testament Supplement Series
JSOT	*Journal for the Study of the Old Testament*
JSOTS	Journal for the Study of the Old Testament Supplement
JSS	*Journal of Semitic Studies*
JTS	*Journal of Theological Studies*
KJV	King James Version
NASB	New American Standard Bible
NCB	New Century Bible
ND	*New Documents Illustrating Early Christianity,* ed. G. H. R. Horsley and S. Llewelyn (North Ryde, NSW: Ancient History Documentary Research Centre, 1976-)
NEB	New English Bible
NKJV	New King James Version
NICOT	New International Commentary on the Old Testament
NICNT	New International Commentary on the New Testament
NIDNTT	*New International Dictionary of New Testament Theology,* 3 vols.; ed. C. Brown (Exeter: Paternoster/Grand Rapids: Zondervan, 1975-78)
NIDOTTE	*New International Dictionary of Old Testament Theology and Exegesis,* 5 vols.; ed. Willem VanGemeren (Exeter: Paternoster/Grand Rapids: Zondervan, 1997-2002)
NIGTC	New International Greek Testament Commentary
NIV	New International Version
NovT	*Novum Testamentum*
NovTSup	Supplement to Novum Testamentum

NRSV	New Revised Standard Version
NTG	New Testament Guides
NTS	*New Testament Studies*
NTTS	New Testament Tools and Studies
RB	*Revue Biblique*
RSV	Revised Standard Version
RTR	*Reformed Theological Review*
SBK	*Kommentar zum Neuen Testament aus Talmud und Midrasch,* by H. L. Strack and P. Billerbeck, 6 vols. (Munich: Beck, 1922-61)
SBLAB	Society for Biblical Literature Academia Biblica
SBLDS	Society for Biblical Literature Dissertation Series
SBLMS	Society for Biblical Literature Monograph Series
SBLSBL	Society for Biblical Literature Studies in Biblical Literature
SBT	Studies in Biblical Theology
SJLA	Studies in Judaism in Late Antiquity
SJT	*Scottish Journal of Theology*
SNTSMS	Society for New Testament Studies Monograph Series
SNTSU	Studien zum Neuen Testament und seiner Umwelt
TNIV	Today's New International Version
TDNT	*Theological Dictionary of the New Testament,* 10 vols.; ed. G. Kittel and G. Friedrich; trans. G. W. Bromiley (Grand Rapids: Eerdmans, 1964-76)
TNTC	Tyndale New Testament Commentary
TrinJ	*Trinity Journal*
TynB	*Tyndale Bulletin*
VE	*Vox Evangelica*
WTJ	*Westminster Theological Journal*
WUNT	Wissenschaftliche Untersuchungen zum Neuen Testament
ZNW	*Zeitschrift für die neutestamentliche Wissenschaft*

II. Biblical Books

		2 Chr.	2 Chronicles
		Ezr.	Ezra
Gn.	Genesis	Neh.	Nehemiah
Ex.	Exodus	Est.	Esther
Lv.	Leviticus	Jb.	Job
Nu.	Numbers	Ps(s).	Psalm(s)
Dt.	Deuteronomy	Pr.	Proverbs
Jos.	Joshua	Eccl.	Ecclesiastes
Jgs.	Judges	Song	Song of Solomon
Ru.	Ruth	Is.	Isaiah
1 Sa.	1 Samuel	Je.	Jeremiah
2 Sa.	2 Samuel	Lam.	Lamentations
1 Ki.	1 Kings	Ezk.	Ezekiel
2 Ki.	2 Kings	Dn.	Daniel
1 Chr.	1 Chronicles	Hos.	Hosea

Jl.	Joel	Gal.	Galatians
Am.	Amos	Eph.	Ephesians
Ob.	Obadiah	Phil.	Philippians
Jon.	Jonah	Col.	Colossians
Mi.	Micah	1 Thes.	1 Thessalonians
Na.	Nahum	2 Thes.	2 Thessalonians
Hab.	Habakkuk	1 Tim.	1 Timothy
Zp.	Zephaniah	2 Tim.	2 Timothy
Hg.	Haggai	Tit.	Titus
Zc.	Zechariah	Phlm.	Philemon
Mal.	Malachi	Heb.	Hebrews
Mt.	Matthew	Jas.	James
Mk.	Mark	1 Pet.	1 Peter
Lk.	Luke	2 Pet.	2 Peter
Jn.	John	1 Jn.	1 John
Acts	Acts	2 Jn.	2 John
Rom.	Romans	3 Jn.	3 John
1 Cor.	1 Corinthians	Jude	Jude
2 Cor.	2 Corinthians	Rev.	Revelation

III. Other Jewish, Christian, and Greco-Roman Writings

A. Jewish Apocrypha

1 Esdr.	1 Esdras
Jdt.	Judith
1 Macc.	1 Maccabees
2 Macc.	2 Maccabees
Sir.	Sirach
Tob.	Tobit
Wis.	Wisdom of Solomon

B. Jewish Pseudepigrapha

4 Ezr.	4 Ezra
Jub.	Jubilees
3 Macc.	3 Maccabees
Ps. Sol.	Psalms of Solomon
Sib. Or.	Sibylline Oracles
Test. Ash.	Testament of Asher
Test. Ben.	Testament of Benjamin
Test. Jos.	Testament of Joseph
Test. Jud.	Testament of Judah
Test. Reu.	Testament of Reuben
Test. Sol.	Testament of Solomon

C. Dead Sea Scrolls
CD   Cairo copy of *Damascus Document*
1QS   *Rule of the Community*
1QSa   *Rule of the Congregation*

D. Josephus
Ant.   *Jewish Antiquities*
Life   *Life of Flavius Josephus*
War   *Jewish War*

E. Rabbinic Tractates and Related Literature
Prefixes indicate whether tractates are in the Babylonian Talmud (*b.*), the Mishnah (*m.*) or the Tosefta (*t.*).
Ber.   *Berakot*
Mak.   *Makkot*
Menaḥ.   *Menaḥot*
Mid.   *Middot*
Ohol.   *Oholot*
Sanh.   *Sanhedrin*

F. Early Christian Literature
Barn.   *Barnabas*
1 Clem.   *1 Clement*
Did.   *Didache*

Dio Cassius
Hist.   *Roman History*

Epictetus
Disc.   *Discourses*
Diss.   *Dissertations*

Hermas
Sim.   *Similitudes*
Vis.   *Vision*

Ignatius
Eph.   *To the Ephesians*
Magn.   *To the Magnesians*
Phil.   *To the Philadelphians*
Pol.   *To Polycarp*
Rom.   *To the Romans*
Smyrn.   *To the Smyrnaeans*

Irenaeus
Haer.   *Adversus Haereses*

G. Greek and Latin Works

Apuleius
Meta.   Metamorphoses

Aristotle
Pol.   Politics

Cicero
Ad Att.   Epistulae ad Atticum
Fam.   Epistulae ad Familiares

Dio Chrysostom
Or.   Orations

Eusebius
Hist Eccl.   Historia Ecclesiastica
Praep. Ev.   Praeparatio Evangelica

Herodotus
Hist.   Histories

Homer
Il.   Iliad

Horace
Od.   Odes

Juvenal
Sat.   Satires

Lucian
Alex.   Alexander (the False Prophet)

Philostratus
Apoll.   Vita Apollonii
Phaedr.   Phaedrus

Plato
Apol.   Apologia (of Socrates)
Gorg.   Gorgias
Phaed.   Phaedo
Pol.   Politicus

Pliny the Elder
Nat. Hist.   Naturalis Historia

Pliny the Younger
Ep.   Epistulae

Plutarch
Mor.   Moralia

Pyrrh.	*Pyrrhus*

Seneca

Ep. Mor.	*Epistulae Morales*Peloponnesian War

Strabo

Geog.	*Geography*

Suetonius

Claud.	*Claudius*

Tacitus

Ann.	*Annales*
Hist.	*Historiae*

Thucydides

Hist.	*History of the Peloponnesian War*

Bibliography

I. SELECTED COMMENTARIES ON ACTS

After initial citations in the opening chapters, commentaries are cited in the footnotes using the author-date method, followed by the page reference (e.g., Barrett 1994, 4).

Barrett, C. K.

1994   *A Critical and Exegetical Commentary on the Acts of the Apostles*, ICC, Vol. 1 (Edinburgh: Clark).

1998   *A Critical and Exegetical Commentary on the Acts of the Apostles*, ICC, Vol. 2 (Edinburgh: Clark).

Bock, D. L.

2007   *Acts*, BECNT (Grand Rapids: Baker Academic).

Bruce, F. F.

1988   *The Book of the Acts*, NICNT (rev. ed.; Grand Rapids: Eerdmans).

1990   *The Acts of the Apostles: The Greek Text with Introduction and Commentary* (3rd rev. and enl. ed.; Grand Rapids: Eerdmans; Leicester: Apollos).

Calvin, J.

1965-96 *Calvin's Commentaries: The Acts of the Apostles*, 2 vols.; ed. D. W. Torrance and T. F. Torrance (Grand Rapids: Eerdmans).

Dunn, J. D. G.

1993   *The Acts of the Apostles* (Peabody: Hendrickson).

Gaventa, B. R.

2003   *The Acts of the Apostles*, Abingdon New Testament Commentaries (Nashville: Abingdon).

Gooding, D.

1990   *True to the Faith: A Fresh Approach to the Acts of the Apostles* (London: Hodder & Stoughton).

Green, C.

2005   *The Word of His Grace: A Guide to Teaching and Preaching from Acts* (Leicester: Inter-Varsity).

Haenchen, E.

1971   *The Acts of the Apostles: A Commentary* (ET, Oxford: Blackwell).

Hanson, R. P. C.

1967   *The Acts*, New Clarendon Bible (Oxford: Clarendon).

Johnson, L. T.

1992   *The Acts of the Apostles*, Sacra Pagina 5 (Collegeville: Liturgical).

Krodel, G. A.

1986   *Acts*, Augsburg Commentary on the New Testament (Minneapolis: Augsburg).

Larkin, W. J., Jr.

1995   *Acts*, The IVP New Testament Commentary Series (Downers Grove/ Leicester: InterVarsity).

Longenecker, R. N.

1981   'The Acts of the Apostles', in *The Expositor's Bible Commentary*, Vol. 9: *John-Acts*, ed. F. E. Gaebelein (Grand Rapids: Zondervan).

2007   'Acts', in *The Expositor's Bible Commentary, Revised Edition*, Vol. 10: *Luke-Acts*, ed. T. Longman III and D. E. Garland (Grand Rapids: Zondervan).

Marshall, I. H.

1980   *The Acts of the Apostles: An Introduction and Commentary*, TNTC (Leicester: Inter-Varsity; Grand Rapids: Eerdmans).

Page, T. E.

1886   *The Acts of the Apostles: The Greek Text . . . with Explanatory Notes* (London: Macmillan).

Polhill, J. B.

1992   *Acts*, New American Commentary 26 (Nashville: Broadman).

Spencer, F. S.

1997   *Acts* (Sheffield: Sheffield Academic).

Stott, J. R. W.

1990   *The Message of Acts: To the Ends of the Earth*, BST (Leicester/Downers Grove: Inter-Varsity).

Talbert, C. H.

1997   *Reading Acts: A Literary and Theological Commentary on the Acts of the Apostles* (New York: Crossroad).

Tannehill, R. C.

1990   *The Narrative Unity of Luke-Acts: A Literary Interpretation*, Vol. 2: *The Acts of the Apostles* (Minneapolis: Fortress).

Williams, D. J.

1985   *Acts*, GNC (San Francisco: Harper).

Witherington III, B.

1998   *The Acts of the Apostles: A Socio-Rhetorical Commentary* (Grand Rapids/ Cambridge: Eerdmans; Carlisle: Paternoster).

II. OTHER BOOKS AND ARTICLES

After initial citations, these works are cited using the author's surname, an abbreviated title, and the page reference (e.g., Alexander, *Preface*, 6).

Alexander, L. C. A.

1993a   *The Preface to Luke's Gospel: Literary Conventions and Social Context in Luke 1:1-4 and Acts 1:1*, SNTSMS 78 (Cambridge: Cambridge University).

1993b   'Acts and Ancient Intellectual Biography', in Winter and Clarke (eds.) 1993, 31-63.

Allen, O. W., Jr.

1997   *The Death of Herod: The Narrative and Theological Function of Retribution in Luke-Acts*, SBLDS 158 (Atlanta: Scholars).

Alon, G.

1977   *Jews, Judaism, and the Classical World: Studies in Jewish History in the Times of the Second Temple and the Talmud* (Jerusalem: Magnes).

Andersen, T. D.

1988   'The Meaning of ECHONTES CHARIN PROS in Acts 2:47', *NTS* 34, 604-10.

Anderson, K. L.

2006   'But God Raised Him from the Dead': The Theology of Jesus' Resurrection in Luke-Acts* (Milton Keynes: Paternoster).

Archer, G. L.

1982   *Encyclopedia of Bible Difficulties* (Grand Rapids: Zondervan).

Arnold, C. E.

1989   *Ephesians: Power and Magic. The Concept of Power in Ephesians in the*

Light of Its Historical Setting, SNTSMS 63 (Cambridge: Cambridge University).

Aune, D.
1980   'Magic in Early Christianity', *ANRW* 2.23.2.
1987   *The New Testament in Its Literary Environment* (Philadelphia: Westminster).

Barnes, T. D.
1969   'An Apostle on Trial', *JTS* n.s. 20, 407-19.

Barnett, P. W.
1980-81 'The Jewish Sign Prophets, AD 40-70', *NTS* 27, 679-97.
1997   *The Second Epistle to the Corinthians*, NICNT (Grand Rapids/ Cambridge: Eerdmans).

Barrett, C. K.
1956   *The New Testament Background: Selected Documents* (London: SPCK).
1964   'Stephen and the Son of Man', in W. Eltester and F. H. Kettler (eds.), *Apophoreta: Festschrift für Ernst Haenchen* (Berlin: de Gruyter), 32-38.
1984   'Apollos and the Twelve Disciples of Ephesus', in W. C. Weinrich (ed.), *The New Testament Age: Essays in Honor of Bo Reicke*, Vol. 1 (Macon: Mercer University), 29-39.
1985   'Faith and Eschatology in Acts 3', in E. Grässer and O. Merk (eds.), *Glaube und Eschatologie: Festschrift für W. G. Kümmel zum 80. Geburtstag* (Tübingen), 1-17.
1992   'The Third Gospel as a Preface to Acts? Some Reflections', in F. Van Segbroeck, C. M. Tuckett, G. Van Belle, and J. Verheyden (eds.), *The Four Gospels 1992: Festschrift Frans Neirynck*, 3 vols., BETL 100 (Leuven: Leuven University), 1451-66.

Bauckham, R.
1979   'Barnabas in Galatians', *JSNT* 2, 61-70.
1993   'The *Acts of Paul* as a Sequel to Acts', in Winter and Clarke (eds.) 1993, 105-52.
1995a 'James and the Jerusalem Church', in Bauckham (ed.) 1995b, 415-80.
1996   'James and the Gentiles (Acts 15:13-21)', in B. Witherington III (ed.), *History, Literature and Society in the Book of Acts* (Cambridge: Cambridge University), 154-84.

Bauckham, R. (ed.)
1995b *The Book of Acts in Its First-Century Setting*, Vol. 4: *Palestinian Setting* (Grand Rapids: Eerdmans; Carlisle: Paternoster).

Bayer, H. F.
1998   'The Preaching of Peter in Acts', in Marshall and Peterson (eds.) 1998, 257-74.

Beale, G. K., and D. A. Carson (eds.)

2007   *Commentary on the New Testament Use of the Old Testament* (Grand Rapids: Baker Academic; Nottingham: Apollos).

Beasley-Murray, G. R.

1972   *Baptism in the New Testament* (Exeter: Paternoster).

Bechard, D. P.

2000   *Paul outside the Walls: A Study of Luke's Socio-Geographical Universalism in Acts 14:8-20*, AnBib 143 (Rome: Pontifical Biblical Institute).

Bird, M. F.

2007   'The Unity of Luke-Acts in Recent Discussion', *JSNT* 29, 425-48.

Blackman, P. (ed.)

1990   *Mishnayoth II: Order Moed* (2nd ed.; Gateshead: Judaica).

Blomberg, C. L.

1998   'The Christian and the Law of Moses', in Marshall and Peterson (eds.) 1998, 397-416.

Blue, B.

1994   'Acts and the House Church', in Gill and Gempf (eds.) 1994, 119-222.

Bock, D. L.

1987   *Proclamation from Prophecy and Pattern: Lucan Old Testament Christology*, JSNTSS 12 (Sheffield: JSOT).

1998   'Scripture and the Realisation of God's Promises', in Marshall and Peterson (eds.) 1998, 41-62.

Bockmuehl, M.

2000   *Jewish Law in Gentile Churches: Halakah and the Beginning of Christian Public Ethics* (Edinburgh: Clark).

Bolt, P. G.

1998   'Mission and Witness', in Marshall and Peterson (eds.) 1998, 191-214.

Bovon, F.

1987   *Luke the Theologian: Thirty-three Years of Research (1950-1983)*, trans. K. McKinney (Allison Park, PA: Pickwick).

Bowker, J. W.

1967   'Speeches in Acts: A Study in Proem and Yelammedenu Form', *NTS* 14, 96-111.

Brawley, R. L.

1987   *Luke-Acts and the Jews: Conflict, Apology and Conciliation*, SBLMS 33 (Atlanta: Scholars).

Brown, R. E., K. P. Donfried, and J. Reumann
1973   *Peter in the New Testament: A Collaborative Assessment by Protestant and Roman Catholic Scholars* (London: Geoffrey Chapman).

Bruce, F. F.
1944   *The Speeches in the Acts of the Apostles*, Tyndale New Testament Lecture 1942 (London: Tyndale).
1971   *New Testament History* (2nd ed.; London/Garden City, NY: Doublday).
1973   'The Holy Spirit in the Acts of the Apostles', *Int* 27, 170-71.
1974   'The Speeches in Acts — Thirty Years After', in R. Banks (ed.), *Reconciliation and Hope: Festschrift for L. Morris* (Grand Rapids: Eerdmans).
1993   'Paul in Acts and Letters', in *DPL*, 679-92.

Buckwalter, H. D.
1996   *The Character and Purpose of Luke's Christology*, SNTSMS 89 (Cambridge: Cambridge University).
1998   'The Divine Saviour', in Marshall and Peterson (eds.) 1998, 107-23.

Burrell, B., K. Gleason, and E. Netzer
1993   'Uncovering Herod's Seaside Palace', *BAR* 19, 50-57, 76.

Burridge, R. A.
1992   *What Are the Gospels? A Comparison with Greco-Roman Biography*, SNTSMS 70 (Cambridge: Cambridge University).

Cadbury, H. J.
1920   *The Style and Literary Method of Luke*, Vol. 1: *The Diction of Luke and Acts*, HTS 6 (Cambridge, MA: Harvard University).
1927   *The Making of Luke-Acts* (Naperville: Allenson, 1927; 2nd ed.; London: SPCK, 1958).

Caird, G. B.
1995   *The Apostolic Age* (London: Duckworth).

Campbell, W. S.
2007   *The 'We' Passages in the Acts of the Apostles: The Narrator as Narrative Character*, SBLSBL 14 (Atlanta: SBL; Leiden: Brill).

Capper, B. J.
1983   'The Interpretation of Acts 5.4', *JSNT* 19, 117-31.
1998   'Reciprocity and the Ethic of Acts', in Marshall and Peterson (eds.) 1998, 499-518.

Carson, D. A.
1981   *Divine Sovereignty and Human Responsibility: Biblical Perspectives in Tension* (London: Marshall).
1988   *Showing the Spirit: A Theological Exposition of 1 Corinthians 12–14* (Homebush West, Sydney: Lancer; Grand Rapids: Baker).

1990   *Teach us to Pray: Prayer in the Bible and the World* (Grand Rapids: Baker;
        Exeter: Paternoster).
1991   *The Gospel according to John* (Grand Rapids: Eerdmans; Leicester: Inter-
        Varsity).
1998   *The Inclusive-Language Debate: A Plea for Realism* (Grand Rapids:
        Baker).

Carson, D. A., and J. D. Woodbridge (eds.)
1986   *Hermeneutics, Authority and Canon* (Grand Rapids: Zondervan).

Carson, D. A., D. J. Moo, and L. Morris (eds.)
1992   *An Introduction to the New Testament* (Grand Rapids: Zondervan).

Cassidy, R.
1987   *Society and Politics in the Acts of the Apostles* (Maryknoll: Orbis).

Cato, S.
2006   'A Critical Analysis of the Present State of Synagogue Research and
        Its Implications for the Study of Luke-Acts', *TynB* 57, 313-15.

Cheung, A. T. M.
1993   'A Narrative Analysis of Acts 14:27–15:35: Literary Shaping in Luke's
        Account of the Jerusalem Council', *WTJ* 55, 137-54.

Childs, B. S.
1974   *Exodus: A Commentary* (London: SCM).

Clark, A. C.
1989   'Apostleship: Evidence from the New Testament and Early Christian
        Literature', *VE* 19, 65-69.
1998   'The Role of the Apostles', in Marshall and Peterson (eds.) 1998, 169-
        90.
2001   *Parallel Lives: The Relation of Paul to the Apostles in the Lucan Perspective*
        (Carlisle: Paternoster).

Clarke, A. D.
1994   'Rome and Italy', in Gill and Gempf (eds.) 1994, 455-81.

Co, M. A.
1992   'The Major Summaries in Acts: Acts 2,42-47; 4,32-35; 5,12-16.
        Linguistic and Literary Relationship', *EphThLov* 68, 49-85.

Cohen, S. J. D.
1986   'Was Timothy Jewish? Patristic Exegesis, Rabbinic Law, and
        Matrilineal Descent,' *JBL* 105, 251-68.

Conzelmann, H.
1960   *The Theology of St. Luke*, trans. G. Buswell (New York: Harper & Row).

Cullmann, O.
1953   *Peter: Disciple-Apostle-Martyr: A Historical and Theological Study* (ET, London: SCM).
1959   *The Christology of the New Testament*, trans. S. C. Guthrie and C. A. M. Hall (London: SCM).

Cunningham, S.
1997   *'Through many tribulations': The Theology of Persecution in Luke-Acts*, JSNTSS 142 (Sheffield: Sheffield Academic).

Danker, F. W.
1983   'Reciprocity in the Ancient World and in Acts 15:23-29', in R. J. Cassidy and P. J. Sharper (eds.), *Political Issues in Luke-Acts* (Maryknoll: Orbis), 49-58.

Daube, D.
1956   *The New Testament and Rabbinic Judaism* (London: Athlone).
1990   'On Acts 23: Sadducees and Angels', *JBL* 109, 493-97.

Davies, G. N.
1987   'When Was Cornelius Saved?', *RTR* 46, 43-49.

Davis, J.
1994   'Biblical Precedents for Contextualisation', *Asia Theological Association Journal* 2, 21.

Derrett, J. D. M.
1977   'Ananias and Sapphira and the Right of Property', in *Studies in the New Testament* (Leiden: Brill), 193-201.

de Silva, D.
1987   'The Meaning and Function of Acts 7:46-50', *JBL* 106, 261-75.

de Waard, J. A.
1965   *A Comparative Study of the Old Testament Texts in the Dead Sea Scrolls and in the New Testament* (Leiden: Brill).

Dibelius, M.
1956   *Studies in the Acts of the Apostles*, ed. H. Greeven; trans. M. Ling (London: SCM).

Dodd, C. H.
1936   *The Apostolic Preaching and Its Developments* (London: Hodder).
1952   *According to the Scriptures: The Sub-Structure of the New Testament* (London: Nisbet).
1953   *New Testament Studies* (Manchester: Manchester University).

Doyle R. C. (ed.)
1987   *Signs and Wonders and Evangelicals: A Response to the Teaching of John Wimber* (Homebush West, Sydney: Lancer).

Dumbrell, W. J.

1984 *Covenant and Creation: An Old Testament Covenantal Theology* (Exeter: Paternoster).

Dunn, J. D. G.

1970 *Baptism in the Holy Spirit: A Re-examination of the New Testament Teaching on the Gift of the Spirit in Relation to Pentecostalism Today*, SBT (Second Series) 15 (London: SCM).

1975 *Jesus and the Spirit: A Study of the Religious and Charismatic Experience of Jesus and the First Christians as Reflected in the New Testament* (London: SCM).

1977 *Unity and Diversity in the New Testament: An Inquiry into the Character of Earliest Christianity* (London: SCM).

1993a 'Baptism in the Spirit: A Response to Pentecostal Scholarship on Luke-Acts', *JPT* 3, 3-27.

1993b *The Theology of Paul's Letter to the Galatians* (Cambridge: Cambridge University).

Dupont, J.

1973 'Ascension du Christ et don de l'Ésprit d'après Actes 2:35', in B. Lindars and S. S. Smalley (eds.), *Christ and Spirit in the New Testament: In Honour of C. F. D. Moule* (Cambridge: Cambridge University).

1985 'La structure oratoire du discours d'Étienne (Actes 7)', *Biblica* 66, 153-67.

Ehrhardt, A.

1969 *The Acts of the Apostles* (Manchester: Manchester University).

Eichrodt, W.

1967 *Theology of the Old Testament*, 2 vols. (ET, London: SCM, 1961, 1967).

Ellis, E. E.

1999 *The Making of the New Testament Documents* (Leiden: Brill).

Epp, E. J.

1966 *The Theological Tendency of Codex Bezae Cantabrigiensis in Acts*, SNTSMS 3 (Cambridge: Cambridge University).

Esler, P. F.

1987 *Community and Gospel in Luke-Acts: The Social and Political Motivations of Lucan Theology*, SNTSMS 57 (Cambridge: Cambridge University).

Estrada, N. P.

2004 *From Followers to Leaders: The Apostles in the Ritual of Status Transformation in Acts 1–2*, JSNTSS 255 (London/New York: Clark International).

Evans, C. A.

1993   'Prophecy and Polemic: Jews in Luke's Scriptural Apologetic', in C. A. Evans and J. A. Sanders, *Luke and Scripture: The Function of Sacred Tradition in Luke-Acts* (Minneapolis: Fortress).

Evans, C. A., and S. E. Porter (eds.)

2000   *Dictionary of New Testament Background* (Downers Grove/Leicester: InterVarsity, 2000).

Falk, D. K.

1995   'Jewish Prayer Literature and the Jerusalem Church in Acts', in Bauckham (ed.) 1995b.

Findlay, J. A.

1934   *The Acts of the Apostles* (London: SCM).

Finegan, J.

1969   *The Archaeology of the New Testament: The Life of Jesus and the Beginning of the Early Church* (Princeton: Princeton University).

Fitzmyer, J. A.

1971   *Essays on the Semitic Background of the New Testament* (London: Chapman).

1972   'David, Being Therefore a Prophet . . . (Acts 2:30)', *CBQ* 34, 332-39.

Flender, H.

1967   *St. Luke — Theologian of Redemptive History* (London: SPCK).

Foakes Jackson, F. J., and K. Lake (eds.)

1920-33 *The Beginnings of Christianity*, Part I, Vols. 1-5 (London: Macmillan).

France, R. T.

1971   *Jesus and the Old Testament* (London: Tyndale).

Franklin, E. R.

1975   *Christ the Lord: A Study in the Purpose and Theology of Luke-Acts* (London: SPCK).

Gapp, K. S.

1935   'Notes: The Universal Famine under Claudius', *HTR* 28, 258-65.

Garnsey, P.

1970   *Social Status and Legal Privilege in the Roman Empire* (Oxford: Oxford University).

Garrett, S.

1989   *The Demise of the Devil: Magic and the Demonic in Luke's Writings* (Minneapolis: Fortress).

Gärtner, B.

1955   *The Areopagus Speech and Natural Revelation* (Lund: Gleerup).

Gasque, W. W., and R. P. Martin (eds.)
1970   *Apostolic History and the Gospel: Biblical and Historical Essays Presented to F. F. Bruce* (Exeter: Paternoster).

Gaventa, B. R.
1985   'The Overthrown Enemy: Luke's Portrait of Paul', in *Society of Biblical Literature 1985 Seminar Papers*, ed. K. H. Richards (Atlanta: Scholars), 439-49.
1986   *From Darkness to Light: Aspects of Conversion in the New Testament*, Overtures to Biblical Theology 20 (Philadelphia: Fortress).
2004   'Theology and Ecclesiology in the Miletus Speech: Reflections on Content and Context', *NTS* 50, 36-50.

Gempf, C.
1993   'Public Speaking and Published Accounts', in Winter and Clarke (eds.) 1993, 259-303.

Gerhardsson, B.
1964   *Memory and Manuscript: Oral Tradition and Written Transmission in Rabbinic Judaism and Early Christianity*, ASNU 22 (Lund: Gleerup).

Giles, K. N.
1985   'Luke's Use of the Term *ekklēsia* with Special Reference to Acts 20.28 and 9.31', *NTS* 31, 135-42.
1995   *What on Earth Is the Church? A Biblical and Theological Enquiry* (London: SPCK).

Gill, D. W. J.
1994a   'Macedonia', in Gill and Gempf (eds.) 1994, 397-417.
1994b   'Achaia', in Gill and Gempf (eds.) 1994, 433-53.

Gill, D. W. J., and C. Gempf (ed.)
1994   *The Book of Acts in Its First-Century Setting*, Vol. 2: *Graeco-Roman Setting* (Grand Rapids: Eerdmans; Carlisle: Paternoster).

Gordon, A. B.
1971   'The Fate of Judas according to Acts 1:18', *EQ* 43, 97-103.

Grässer, E., and O. Merk (eds.)
1985   *Glaube und Eschatologie: Festschrift für Werner Georg Kümmel zum 80 Geburtstag* (Tübingen: Mohr).

Green, J. B.
1990   'The Death of Jesus, God's Servant', in Sylva (ed.) 1990, 1-28.
1997   *The Gospel of Luke*, NICNT (Grand Rapids/Cambridge: Eerdmans).
1998   '"Salvation to the end of the earth" (Acts 13:47): God as Saviour in the Acts of the Apostles', in Marshall and Peterson (eds.) 1998, 83-106.
2001   'Persevering Together in Prayer: The Significance of Prayer in the Acts

of the Apostles', in R. N. Longenecker (ed.), *Into God's Presence: Prayer in the New Testament* (Grand Rapids: Eerdmans), 183-202.

Grumm, M. H.
1985   'Another Look at Acts', *ExpT* 96, 335-36.

Haacker, K.
1985   'Das Bekenntnis des Paulus zur Hoffnung Israels nach der Apostelgeschichte des Lukas', *NTS* 31, 437-51.

Hansen, G. W.
1998   'The Preaching and Defence of Paul', in Marshall and Peterson (eds.) 1998, 295-324.

Harlé, P.
1977-78 'Un "private-joke" de Paul dans le livre des Actes (xxxvi.28-29)', *NTS* 24, 527-33.

Hartman, L.
1973-74 'Into the Name of Jesus', *NTS* 20, 432-40.

Haubeck, W., and M. Bachmann (eds.)
1980   *Wort in der Zeit: Neutestamentliche Studien. Festgabe für H. Rengstorf* (Leiden: Brill).

Hay, D. M.
1973   *Glory at the Right Hand: Psalm 110 in Early Christianity*, SBLMS 18 (Nashville/New York: Abingdon).

Head, P.
1993   'Acts and the Problem of Its Texts', in Winter and Clarke (eds.) 1993, 415-44.

Hedrick, C. W.
1981   'Paul's Conversion/Call: A Comparative Analysis of the Three Reports in Acts', *JBL* 100, 415-32.

Hemer, C. J.
1973-74 'Paul at Athens: A Topographical Note', *NTS* 20, 341-50.
1975   'Euraquilo and Melita', *JTS* n.s. 26, 100-111.
1985   'First Person Narrative in Acts 27–28', *TynB* 36, 79-109.
1989   *The Book of Acts in the Setting of Hellenistic History*, (ed.) C. Gempf, WUNT 49 (Tübingen: Mohr; reprinted Winona Lake: Eisenbrauns, 1990).

Hengel, M.
1979   *Acts and the History of Earliest Christianity* (Philadelphia: Fortress).
1983   *Between Jesus and Paul: Studies in the Earliest History of Christianity*, trans. J. Bowden (London: SCM; Philadelphia: Fortress).
1995   'The Geography of Palestine in Acts', in Bauckham (ed.) 1995b, 27-78.

Hesselgrave, D., and E. Rommen

1989   *Contextualisation, Meanings, Methods and Models* (Grand Rapids: Baker).

Higgins, A. J. B.

1970   'The Preface to Luke and the Kerygma in Acts', in *Apostolic History and the Gospel*, 78-91.

Hill, D.

1984   'The Spirit and the Church's Witness: Observations on Acts 1:6-8', *IBS* 6, 16-17.

Hock, R. F.

1978   'Paul's Tent-Making and the Problem of His Social Class', *JBL* 97, 555-64.

1980   *The Social Context of Paul's Ministry: Tentmaking and Apostleship* (Philadelphia: Fortress).

Horsley, G. H. R.

1986   'Speeches and Dialogue in Acts' *NTS* 32, 609-14.

1994   'The Politarchs', in Gill and Gempf (eds.) 1994, 419-31.

Hort, F. J. A.

1897   *The Christian Ecclesia* (London: Macmillan).

House, P. R.

1990   'Suffering and the Purpose of Acts', *JETS* 33, 317-30.

Hubbard, B. J.

1977   'Commissioning Stories in Luke-Acts: A Study of Their Antecedents, Form and Content', *Semeia* 8, 103-26.

1978   'The Role of the Commissioning Accounts in Acts', in C. H. Talbert (ed.), *Perspectives on Luke-Acts*, Perspectives in Religious Studies Special Studies Series 5 (Danville: Association of Baptist Professors of Religion), 187-98.

Hur, J.

2001   *A Dynamic Reading of the Holy Spirit in Luke-Acts*, JSNTSS 211 (Sheffield: Sheffield Academic).

Hurtado, L. W.

1988   *One God, One Lord: Early Christian Devotion and Ancient Jewish Monotheism* (Minneapolis: Fortress; London: SCM).

1993   'Son of God', in *DPL*, 900-906.

Jeremias, J.

1960   *Infant Baptism in the First Four Centuries*, trans. D. Cairns (London: SCM).

1966   *The Eucharistic Words of Jesus*, trans. N. Perrin (London: SCM).

1969   *Jerusalem in the Time of Jesus: An Investigation into Economic and Social*

Conditions during the New Testament Period, trans. F. H. and C. H. Cave
(London: SCM).

Jervell, J.
1972 *Luke and the People of God* (Minneapolis: Augsburg).
1984 *The Unknown Paul* (Minneapolis: Augsburg).
1996 *The Theology of the Acts of the Apostles,* New Testament Theology
(Cambridge: Cambridge University).

Johnson, L. T.
1977 *The Literary Function of Possessions in Luke-Acts,* SBLDS 39 (Missoula:
Scholars).
1983 *Decision Making in the Church: A Biblical Model* (Philadelphia: Fortress).
1991 *The Gospel of Luke,* Sacra Pagina 3 (Collegeville: Liturgical).

Jones, D. L.
1984 'The Title "Servant" in Luke-Acts', in C. H. Talbert (ed.), *Luke-Acts:
New Perspectives from the Society of Biblical Literature Seminar* (New
York: Crossroad), 148-65.

Judge, E. A.
1971 'The Decrees of Caesar at Thessalonica', *RTR* 30, 1-7.

Judge, E. A., and G. S. R. Thomas
1966 'The Origins of the Church at Rome: A New Solution?', *RTR* 25, 81-94.

Kaiser, W. C., Jr.
1985 *The Uses of the Old Testament in the New* (Chicago: Moody).

Kearsley, R. A.
1994 'The Asiarchs', in Gill and Gempf (eds.) 1994, 363-76.

Keck, L. E., and J. L. Martyn (eds.)
1968 *Studies in Luke-Acts: Essays Presented in Honor of Paul Schubert*
(Nashville: Abingdon, 1966; London: SPCK).

Kennedy, G. A.
1984 *New Testament Interpretation through Rhetorical Criticism* (Chapel Hill:
University of North Carolina).

Kern, P. H.
2003 'Paul's Conversion and Luke's Portrayal of Character in Acts 8–10',
TynB 54, 63-80.

Kim, S.
1982 *The Origin of Paul's Gospel* (Grand Rapids: Eerdmans, 1982; first
published as WUNT 4 [Tübingen: Mohr], 1981).
1983 *'The "Son of Man"' as the Son of God,* WUNT 30 (Tübingen: Mohr).

Klutz, T.
2004   *The Exorcism Stories in Luke-Acts: A Sociostylistic Reading*, SNTSMS 129 (Cambridge/New York: Cambridge University).

Klutz, T. (ed.)
2003   *Magic in the Biblical World: From the Rod of Aaron to the Ring of Solomon*, JSNTSS 245 (Sheffield: Sheffield Academic).

Kodell, J.
1974   '"The Word of God Grew" — The Ecclesial Tendency of *Logos* in Acts 6:7; 12:24; 19:20', *Biblica* 55, 505-19.

Koenig, J.
1985   *New Testament Hospitality: Partnership with Strangers as Promise and Mission*, Overtures to Biblical Theology (Philadelphia: Fortress).

Kraft, C.
1979   *Christianity in Culture: A Study in Dynamic Biblical Theologizing in Cross-Cultural Perspective* (Maryknoll: Orbis).

Ladouceur, D.
1980   'Hellenistic Preconceptions of Shipwreck and Pollution as a Concept for Acts 27–28', *HTR* 73, 435-49.

Lampe, G. W. H.
1957   'The Holy Spirit in the Writings of St. Luke', in D. E. Nineham (ed.), *Studies in the Gospels: Essays in Memory of R. H. Lightfoot* (Oxford: Blackwell).
1967   *The Seal of the Spirit* (London: SPCK).
1969   *St. Luke and the Church of Jerusalem* (London: Athlone).

Larkin, W. J.
1977   'Luke's Use of the Old Testament', *JETS* 20/4, 326-36.

Légasse, S.
1995   'Paul's Pre-Christian Career according to Acts', in Bauckham (ed.) 1995b, 365-90.

Lentz, J. C., Jr.
1993   *Luke's Portrait of Paul*, SNTSMS 77 (Cambridge: Cambridge University).

Levinskaya, I.
1996   *The Book of Acts in Its First-Century Setting*, Vol. 5: *Diaspora Setting* (Grand Rapids: Eerdmans/Carlisle: Paternoster).

Liddell, H. G., and R. Scott
1940   *A Greek-English Lexicon*, New Edition, ed. H. S. Jones and R. McKenzie (Oxford); Supplement, ed. E. A. Barber (Oxford, 1968).

Lincoln, A. T.

1984-85 'Theology and History in the Interpretation of Luke's Pentecost', *ExpT* 96, 204-9.

Lindars, B.

1961 *New Testament Apologetic: The Doctrinal Significance of the Old Testament Quotes* (London: SCM).

Lindars, B., and S. S. Smalley (eds.)

1973 *Christ and Spirit in the New Testament: In Honour of C. F. D. Moule* (Cambridge: Cambridge University).

Litwak, K.

2006 'One or Two Views of Judaism: Paul in Acts 28 and Romans 11 on Jewish Unbelief', *TynB* 57, 229-49.

Longenecker, R. N.

1970 *The Christology of Early Jewish Christianity* (London: SCM).

1975 *Biblical Exegesis in the Apostolic Period* (Grand Rapids: Eerdmans).

Lull, D. J.

1986 'The Servant-Benefactor as a Model of Greatness (Luke 22.24-30)', *NovT* 28, 305.

Macdonald, J.

1964 *The Theology of the Samaritans* (London: SCM).

MacRae, G. W.

1973 'Whom Heaven Must Receive Until the Time', *Int* 27, 151-65.

McIntosh, J.

2002 '"For it seemed good to the Holy Spirit", Acts 15:28: How Far Did the Members of the Jerusalem Council *Know* This?', *RTR* 61, 131-47.

McKelvey, R. J.

1969 *The New Temple: The Church in the New Testament* (London/New York: Oxford University).

McMahan, C. T.

1987 'Meals as Type-Scenes in the Gospel of Luke', Ph.D diss., Southern Baptist Theological Seminary.

Maddox, R.

1982 *The Purpose of Luke-Acts* (Edinburgh: Clark).

Maile, J. F.

1986 'The Ascension in Luke-Acts', *TynB* 37, 29-59.

Malherbe, A.

1989 *Paul and the Popular Philosophers* (Minneapolis: Fortress).

Malina, B. J., and J. H. Neyrey

1991   'Conflict in Luke-Acts: Labelling and Deviance Theory', in J. H.
        Neyrey (ed.), *The Social World of Luke-Acts: Models for Interpretation*
        (Peabody: Hendrickson), 97-122.

Marguerat, D.

1993   'La mort d'Ananias et Sapphira (Ac 5.1-11) dans la stratégie narrative
        de Luc', *NTS* 39 (1993), 209-26.

2000   'The God of the Book of Acts', in G. J. Brooke and J.-D. Kaestli (eds.),
        Narrative in Biblical and Related Texts (Leuven: Leuven University), 159-
        81.

2002   *The First Christian Historian: Writing the 'Acts of the Apostles'*, SNTSMS
        121, trans. K. McKinney, G. J. Laughery, and R. Bauckham
        (Cambridge: Cambridge University).

2003   'Magic and Miracles in the Acts of the Apostles', in T. Klutz (ed.),
        Magic in the Biblical World: From the Rod of Aaron to the Ring of Solomon,
        JSNTSS 245 (Sheffield: Sheffield Academic), 100-124.

Marguerat, D., and Y. Bourquin

1999   *How to Read Bible Stories: An Introduction to Narrative Criticism*, trans.
        J. Bowden (London: SCM).

Marshall, I. H.

1970   *Luke: Historian and Theologian* (Exeter: Paternoster).

1977   'The Significance of Pentecost', *SJT* 30, 347-69.

1978   *The Gospel of Luke: A Commentary on the Greek Text*, NIGTC (Exeter:
        Paternoster).

1992   *The Acts of the Apostles*, NTG (Sheffield: JSOT).

1993   'Acts and the "Former Treatise"', in Winter and Clarke (eds.) 1993,
        163-82.

1998   'How Does One Write on the Theology of Acts?', in Marshall and
        Peterson (eds.) 1998, 3-16.

Marshall, I. H., and D. Peterson (eds.)

1998   *Witness to the Gospel: The Theology of Acts* (Grand Rapids/Cambridge:
        Eerdmans).

Mason, S.

1995   'Chief Priests, Sadducees, Pharisees and Sanhedrin in Acts', in
        Bauckham (ed.) 1995b, 115-77.

Matera, F. J.

1990   'Responsibility for the Death of Jesus according to the Acts of the
        Apostles', *JSNT* 39, 77-93.

Mays, J. L.

1969   *Amos: A Commentary* (London: SCM).

Mealand, D. L.

1990   'The Close of Acts and Its Hellenistic Greek Vocabulary', *NTS* 36, 584-87.

1991   'Hellenistic Historians and the Style of Acts', *ZNW* 82, 42-66.

Menzies, R. P.

1991   *The Development of Early Christian Pneumatology with Special Reference to Luke-Acts*, JSNTSS 54 (Sheffield: JSOT).

1993   'Spirit and Power in Luke-Acts: A Response to Max Turner', *JSNT* 49, 11-20.

1994   *Empowered for Witness: The Spirit in Luke-Acts* (Sheffield: JSOT; repr. London: Clark International, 2004).

Metzger, B. M.

1968a   'The Ascension of Jesus Christ', in *Historical and Literary Studies Pagan, Jewish and Christian*, NTTS 8 (Leiden: Brill), 77-87.

1968b   'The Christianization of Nubia and the Old Nubian Version of the New Testament', in *Historical and Literary Studies Pagan, Jewish and Christian*, NTTS 8 (Leiden: Brill), 111-22.

1980   'Ancient Astrological Geography and Acts 2:9-11', in *New Testament Studies: Philological, Versional and Patristic*, NTTS 10 (Leiden: Brill), 46-56.

1994   *A Textual Commentary on the Greek New Testament: A Companion Volume to the United Bible Societies' Greek New Testament (Fourth Revised Edition)* (2nd ed.; Stuttgart/New York: United Bible Societies).

Miles, G. B., and G. Trompf

1976   'Luke and Antiphon: The Theology of Acts 27–28 in the Light of Pagan Beliefs about Divine Retribution, Pollution, and Shipwreck', *HTR* 69, 259-67.

Mitchell, A. C.

1992   'The Social Function of Friendship in Acts 2:44-47 and 4:32-37', *JBL* 111, 255-72.

Moessner, D. P.

1986   '"The Christ Must Suffer": New Light on the Jesus-Peter, Stephen, Paul Parallels in Luke-Acts', *NovT* 28, 220-56.

Moo, D. J.

1983   *The Old Testament in the Gospel Passion Narratives* (Sheffield: Almond).

1986   'The Problem of Sensus Plenior', in D. A. Carson and J. D. Woodbridge (eds.), *Hermeneutics, Authority and Canon* (Grand Rapids: Zondervan), 179-211.

Moore, G. F.

1927   *Judaism in the First Centuries of the Christian Era: The Age of Tannaim* (Cambridge: Harvard University).

Moule, C. F. D.

1953   *An Idiom Book of New Testament Greek* (Cambridge: Cambridge
        University).

1961   *Worship in the New Testament,* Ecumenical Studies in Worship 9
        (London: Lutterworth).

1966,   'The Christology of Acts', in L. E. Keck and J. L. Martyn (eds.), *Studies*
1976   *in Luke-Acts: Essays Presented in Honor of Paul Schubert* (Nashville:
        Abingdon 1966; London: SPCK, 1976), 159-85.

Müller, P. G.

1973   *CHRISTOS ARCHĒGOS: Der religionsgeschichtliche und theologische*
        Hintergrund einer neutestamentlichen Christusprädikation, Europäische
        Hochschulschriften Reihe 23, Vol. 28 (Frankfurt/Bern: Lang).

Murphy-O'Connor, J.

1983   *St. Paul's Corinth: Texts and Archaeology,* Good News Studies 6
        (Wilmington: Michael Glazier).

Neudorfer, H.-W.

1998   'The Speech of Stephen', in Marshall and Peterson (eds.) 1998, 275-94.

Neusner, J.

1971   *The Rabbinic Tradition about the Pharisees before 70,* Vols. 1-3 (Leiden:
        Brill).

Neyrey, J.

1984   'The Forensic Defense Speech and Paul's Trial Speeches in Acts 22–26:
        Form and Function', in C. H. Talbert (ed.), *Luke-Acts: New Perspectives*
        from the Society of Biblical Literature Seminar (New York: Crossroad),
        210-24.

Nobbs, A.

1994   'Cyprus', in Gill and Gempf (eds.) 1994, 279-89.

Nock, A. D.

1972   *Essays on Religion and the Ancient World I and II* (Cambridge, MA:
        Harvard University).

Nolland, J.

1980-81 'A Fresh Look at Acts 15.10', *NTS* 27, 105-15.

1989   *Luke 1–9:20,* Word Biblical Commentary 35A (Dallas: Word).

1998   'Salvation-History and Eschatology', in Marshall and Peterson (eds.)
        1998, 63-81.

Noorda, S. J.

1979   'Scene and Summary', in J. Kremer (ed.), *Les Actes des Apôtres:*
        Traditions, Rédaction, Théologie, BETL 48 (Louvain: Leuven University),
        475-83.

O'Brien, P. T.
1973   'Prayer in Luke-Acts', *TynB* 24, 111-27.
1982   *Colossians, Philemon*. Word Biblical Commentary 44 (Waco: Word).

O'Neill, J. C.
1970   *The Theology of Acts in Its Historical Setting* (2nd ed.; London: SPCK).

O'Reilly, L.
1987   *Word and Sign in the Acts of the Apostles: A Study in Lucan Theology*, Analecta Gregoriana 243 (Rome: EPUG).

Oster, R. E.
1990   'Ephesus as a Religious Center under the Principate, I. Paganism before Constantine', *ANRW* 2.18.3, 1661-1728.

O'Toole, R. F.
1979   'Luke's Understanding of Jesus' Resurrection-Ascension-Exaltation', *BTB* 9, 106-14.
1981   'Activity of the Risen Jesus in Luke-Acts', *Biblica* 62, 471-98.

Palmer, D. W.
1987   'The Literary Background of Acts 1.1-14', *NTS* 33, 427-38.
1993a   'Acts and the Ancient Historical Monograph', in Winter and Clarke (eds.) 1993, 1-29.
1993b   'Mission to Jews and to Gentiles in the Last Episode of Acts', *RTR* 52, 62-73.

Pao, D. W.
2002   *Acts and the Isaianic New Exodus*, WUNT 2, no. 130 (Tübingen: Mohr, 2000; repr. Grand Rapids: Baker Academic, 2002).

Parsons, M. C.
1987   *The Departure of Jesus in Luke-Acts: The Ascension Narratives in Context*, JSNTSS 21 (Sheffield: JSOT).
1990   'Christian Origins and Narrative Openings: The Sense of a Beginning in Acts 1–5', *Review and Expositor* 87, no. 3, 404-22.
2007   *Luke: Storyteller, Interpreter, Evangelist* (Peabody: Hendrickson).

Parsons, M. C., and M. M. Culy
2003   *Acts: A Handbook on the Greek Text* (Waco: Baylor University).

Parsons, M. C., and R. I. Pervo
1993   *Rethinking the Unity of Luke and Acts* (Philadelphia: Fortress).

Penner, T.
2004   *In Praise of Christian Origins: Stephen and the Hellenists in Lukan Apologetic Historiography*, Emory Studies in Early Christianity 10 (New York/London: Clark International).

Penney, J. M.

1997   *The Missionary Emphasis of Lukan Pneumatology* (Sheffield: Sheffield Academic, 1997).

Pereira, F.

1983   *Ephesus: Climax of Universalism in Luke-Acts. A Redactional Study of Paul's Ephesian Ministry (Acts 18:23–20:1)*, Jesuit Theological Forum 10.1 (Anand: Gujarat Sahitya Prakash).

Pervo, R. I.

1987   *Profit with Delight: The Literary Genre of the Acts of the Apostles* (Philadelphia: Fortress).

2006   *Dating Acts: Between the Evangelists and the Apologists* (Santa Rosa, CA: Polebridge)

Peterson, D. G.

1982   *Hebrews and Perfection: An Examination of the Concept of Perfection in the 'Epistle to the Hebrews'*, SNTSMS 47 (Cambridge: Cambridge University).

1986   'The Ministry of Encouragement', in P. T. O'Brien and D. G. Peterson (eds.), *God Who Is Rich in Mercy: Essays Presented to Dr. D. B. Knox* (Sydney: ANZEA), 235-53.

1992   *Engaging with God: A Biblical Theology of Worship* (Leicester: Apollos; Grand Rapids: Eerdmans).

1993   'The Motif of Fulfilment and the Purpose of Luke-Acts', in Winter and Clarke (eds.) 1993, 83-104.

1995   *Possessed by God: A New Testament Theology of Sanctification and Holiness* (Leicester: Apollos; Grand Rapids: Eerdmans).

1998a   'The Worship of the New Community', in Marshall and Peterson (eds.) 1998, 373-95.

1998b   'Luke's Theological Enterprise: Integration and Intent', in Marshall and Peterson (eds.) 1998, 521-44.

2004   'Atonement Theology in Luke-Acts: Some Methodological Reflections', in P. J. Williams, A. D. Clarke, P. M. Head, and D. Instone-Brewer (eds.), *The New Testament in Its First-Century Setting: Essays on Context and Background in Honour of B. W. Winter on His 65th Birthday* (Grand Rapids/Cambridge: Eerdmans), 56-71.

2006   'Kerygma or Kerygmata: Is There Only One Gospel in the New Testament?', in C. Green (ed.) *God's Power to Save: One Gospel for a Complex World?* (Leicester: Apollos), 155-84.

Pfitzner, V. C.

1980   '"Pneumatic" Apostleship? Apostle and Spirit in the Acts of the Apostles', in W. Haubeck and M. Bachmann (eds.), *Wort in der Zeit: Neutestamentliche Studien, Festgabe für H. Rengstorf* (Leiden: Brill), 210-35.

Pinnock, C. H.

1992   *A Wideness in God's Mercy: The Finality of Jesus Christ in a World of Religions* (Grand Rapids: Eerdmans).

Plymale, S. F.

1991   *The Prayer Texts of Luke-Acts* (New York: Lang).

Porter, S. E.

1994   *Idioms of the Greek New Testament* (2nd ed.; Sheffield: Sheffield Academic).

2001   *Paul in Acts* (Peabody: Hendrickson), a reprint of *The Paul of Acts: Essays in Literary Criticism, Rhetoric, and Theology*, WUNT 115 (Tübingen: Mohr, 1999).

Powell, M. A.

1990   *What Is Narrative Criticism? A New Approach to the Bible* (Minneapolis: Augsburg Fortress).

Praeder, S. M.

1984   'Acts 27:1–28:16: Sea Voyages in Ancient Literature and the Theology of Luke-Acts', *CBQ* 46, 683-706.

Ramsay, W. M.

1893   *The Church in the Roman Empire before AD 170* (London: Hodder & Stoughton).

1895   *St Paul the Traveller and the Roman Citizen* (London: Hodder & Stoughton).

1907   *The Cities of St. Paul: Their Influence on His Life and Thought* (London: Hodder & Stoughton).

Rapske, B.

1994a   'Acts, Travel, and Shipwreck', in Gill and Gempf (eds.) 1994, 1-47.

1994b   *The Book of Acts in Its First Century Setting*, Vol. 3: *The Book of Acts and Paul in Roman Custody* (Grand Rapids: Eerdmans; Carlisle: Paternoster).

1998   'Opposition to the Plan of God and Persecution', in Marshall and Peterson (eds.) 1998, 235-56.

Read-Heimerdinger, J.

2003   *The Bezan Text of Acts: A Contribution of Discourse Analysis to Textual Criticism* (Sheffield: Sheffield Academic).

Reimer, I. R.

1995   *Women in the Acts of the Apostles: A Feminist Liberation Perspective*, trans. L. M. Maloney (Minneapolis: Fortress).

Resseguie, J. L.

2005   *Narrative Criticism of the New Testament* (Grand Rapids: Baker Academic).

Richard, E.

1978   *Acts 6:1–8:4: The Author's Method of Composition*, SBLDS 41 (Missoula: Scholars).

1984   'The Divine Purpose: The Jews and the Gentile Mission (Acts 15)', in C. H. Talbert (ed.), *Luke-Acts: New Perspectives from the Society of Biblical Literature Seminar* (New York: Crossroad), 188-209.

Ricoeur, P.

1995   *La critique et la conviction* (Paris: Calmy-Lévy).

Riesner, R.

1995   'Synagogues in Jerusalem', in Bauckham (ed.) 1995b, 179-212.

Robbins, V. K.

1978   'By Land and by Sea: The We-Passages and Ancient Sea Voyages', in C. H. Talbert (ed.), *Perspectives in Luke-Acts* (Edinburgh: Clark), 215-42.

Robinson, J. A. T.

1962   *Twelve New Testament Studies*, SBT 34 (London: SCM).

1975   *Redating the New Testament* (London: SCM).

Rosner, B. S.

1993   'Acts and Biblical History', in Winter and Clarke (eds.) 1993, 65-82.

1998   'The Progress of the Word', in Marshall and Peterson (eds.) 1998, 215-33.

Rowley, H. H.

1967   *Worship in Ancient Israel* (London: SPCK).

Sanders, J. T.

1987a   'The Prophetic Use of the Scriptures in Luke-Acts', in C. A. Evans and W. F. Stinespring (eds.), *Early Jewish and Christian Exegesis* (Atlanta: Scholars), 191-98.

1987b   *The Jews in Luke-Acts* (London, SCM).

Satterthwaite, P. E.

1993   'Acts against the Background of Classical Rhetoric', in Winter and Clarke (eds.) 1993, 337-79.

Schubert, P.

1968   'The Place of the Areopagus Speech in the Composition of Acts', in J. C. Rylaarsdam (ed.), *Transitions in Biblical Scholarship* (Chicago: University of Chicago), 235-61.

Schürer, E.

1973-87 *The History of the Jewish People in the Age of Jesus Christ (175 B.C.–A.D. 135)*, Vols. 1–3.2 trans. T. A. Burkill and others; rev. and ed. G. Vermes, F. Millar, P. Vermes, and M. Black (Edinburgh: Clark).

Schwartz, D. R.

1983   'Non-Joining Sympathizers (Acts 5,13-14)', *Biblica* 64, 550-53.

1992   'On Sacrifice by Gentiles in the Temple of Jerusalem', in D. R. Schwartz, *Studies in the Jewish Background of Christianity* (WUNT 60; Tübingen: Mohr), 102-16.

Seccombe, D. P.

1981   'Luke and Isaiah', *NTS* 27, 252-59.

1983   *Possessions and the Poor in Luke-Acts,* SNTSU (Linz: Fuchs).

1998   'The New People of God', in Marshall and Peterson (eds.) 1998, 349-72.

Shelton, J.

1991   *Mighty in Word and Deed: The Role of the Holy Spirit in Luke-Acts* (Peabody: Hendrickson).

2000   'Epistemology and Authority in the Acts of the Apostles: An Analysis and Test Case Study of Acts 15:1-29', in *The Spirit and Church* 2/2, 231-47.

Shepherd, W. H., Jr.

1994   *The Narrative Function of the Holy Spirit as a Character in Luke-Acts,* SBLDS 147 (Atlanta: Scholars).

Sherwin-White, A. N.

1963   *Roman Society and Roman Law in the New Testament* (Oxford: Clarendon).

Shipp, B.

2005   *Paul the Reluctant Witness: Power and Weakness in Luke's Portrayal* (Eugene: Cascade).

Simon, M.

1958   *St. Stephen and the Hellenists in the Primitive Church* (London: Longmans).

1979   'From Greek Hairesis to Christian Heresy', in W. R. Schoedel and R. L. Wilken (eds.), *Théologie Historique* 53 (Paris), 101-16.

Sizer, S.

2004   *Christian Zionism: Road-map to Armageddon?* (Leicester: Inter-Varsity).

Skinner, M. L.

2003   *Locating Paul: Places of Custody as Narrative Settings in Acts 21–28,* SBLAB 13 (Atlanta: SBL).

Sleeman, M.

2007   'The Ascension and the Heavenly Ministry of Christ', in S. Clark (ed.), *The Forgotten Christ: Exploring the Majesty and Mystery of God Incarnate* (Nottingham: Apollos), 140-90.

Smith, L.

1880   *The Voyage and Shipwreck of St. Paul* (4th ed.; London: Longman, Brown, Green & Longmans).

Smith, P.

1993   *Is It Okay to Call God 'Mother'? Considering the Feminine Face of God* (Peabody: Hendrickson).

Soards, M.

1994   *The Speeches in Acts: Their Content, Context and Concerns* (Louisville: Westminster/John Knox).

Spencer, F. S.

1993   'Acts and Modern Literary Approaches', in Winter and Clarke (eds.) 1993, 381-414.

Squires, J. T.

1993   *The Plan of God in Luke-Acts*, SNTSMS 76 (Cambridge: Cambridge University).

1998   'The Function of Acts 8:4–12:25', *NTS* 44, 608-17.

1998b   'The Plan of God in the Acts of the Apostles', in Marshall and Peterson (eds.) 1998, 19-39.

Stanley, D. M.

1953   'Why Three Accounts?', *CBQ* 15, 315-18.

Stanton, G. N.

1974   *Jesus of Nazareth in New Testament Preaching* (Cambridge: Cambridge University).

1980   'Stephen in Lucan Perspective', in *Studia Biblica 1978*, Vol. 3: *Papers on Paul and Other New Testament Authors*, JSNTSS 3 (Sheffield: Sheffield Academic), 345-60.

Stendahl, K.

1963   'The Apostle Paul and the Introspective Conscience of the West', *HTR* 56, 199-215.

1976   *Paul among Jews and Gentiles — and Other Essays* (Philadelphia: Fortress).

Stenschke, C.

1998   'The Need for Salvation', in Marshall and Peterson (eds.) 1998, 125-44.

1999   *Luke's Portrait of Gentiles prior to Their Coming to Faith*, WUNT 2, no. 108 (Tübingen: Mohr).

Sterling, G. E.

1992   *Historiography and Self-Definition: Josephus, Luke-Acts and Apologetic Historiography* (Leiden: Brill).

Sternberg, M.

1985   *The Poetics of Biblical Narrative: Ideological Literature and the Drama of*

Reading, Indiana Literary Biblical Series (Bloomington: Indiana University).

Stewart, R. A.
1971   'The Synagogue', *EQ* 43, 41-56.

Stoops, R. F.
1989   'Riot and Assembly: The Social Context of Acts 19:23-41', *JBL* 108, 73-91.

Strange, D.
2001   *The Possibility of Salvation among the Unevangelised: An Analysis of Inclusivism in Recent Evangelical Theology* (Carlisle: Paternoster).

Strack, H. L., and P. Billerbeck
1922-61 *Kommentar zum Neuen Testamentum aus Talmud und Midrasch,* 6 vols. (München: Beck).

Streeter, B. H.
1924   *The Four Gospels* (London: Macmillan).

Sweeney, J. P.
2002   'Stephen's Speech (Acts 7:2-53): Is It as "Anti-temple" as Is Frequently Alleged?', *TrinJ* 23, n.s., 185-210.

Sylva, D. D. (ed.)
1990   *Reimaging the Death of the Lukan Jesus* (Frankfurt: Anton Hain).

Tajra, H. W.
1989   *The Trial of St. Paul: A Juridical Exegesis of the Second Half of Acts,* WUNT 2, no. 35 (Tübingen: Mohr).
1994   *The Martyrdom of St. Paul: Historical and Judicial Contexts, Traditions and Legends,* WUNT 2, no. 67 (Tübingen: Mohr).

Talbert, C. H.
1974   *Literary Patterns, Theological Themes, and the Genre of Luke-Acts,* SBLMS 20 (Missoula: Scholars).
1982   'The Fulfillment of Prophecy in Luke-Acts', in C. H. Talbert, *Reading Luke: A Literary and Theological Commentary on the Third Gospel* (New York: Crossroad), 234-40.
1983   'Martyrdom and the Lukan Social Ethic', in R. J. Cassidy and P. J. Scharper (eds.), *Political Issues in Luke-Acts* (Maryknoll: Orbis), 99-110.
1984   *Luke-Acts: New Perspectives from the Society of Biblical Literature Seminar* (New York: Crossroad).

Tannehill, R. C.
1986   *The Narrative Unity of Luke-Acts: A Literary Interpretation,* Vol. 1: *The Gospel of Luke* (Minneapolis: Fortress).
1990   'Narrative Criticism', in R. J. Coggins and J. L. Houlden (eds.),

Dictionary of Biblical Interpretation (London, SCM; Philadelphia: Trinity).

2005   *The Shape of Luke's Story: Essays on Luke-Acts* (Eugene: Cascade).

Teeple, H. M.

1957   *The Mosaic Eschatological Prophet*, JBLMS 10 (Philadelphia: JBL).

Thiede, C. P.

1986   *Simon Peter: From Galilee to Rome* (Exeter: Paternoster).

Thiselton, A. C.

2000   *The First Epistle to the Corinthians: A Commentary on the Greek Text*, NIGTC (Grand Rapids/Cambridge: Eerdmans; Carlisle: Paternoster).

Tiede, D. L.

1980   *Prophecy and History in Luke-Acts* (Philadelphia: Fortress).

1986   'The Exaltation of Jesus and the Restoration of Israel in Acts 1', *HTR* 79, 278-86.

Thomas, J. C.

1994   'Women, Pentecostals and the Bible: An Experiment in Pentecostal Hermeneutics', *JPT* 5, 41-56.

2000   'Reading the Bible from within Our Traditions: A Pentecostal Hermeneutic as a Test Case', in J. Green and M. Turner (eds.), *Between Two Horizons: Spanning New Testament Studies and Systematic Theology* (Grand Rapids: Eerdmans), 108-22.

Thompson, R. P.

2006   *Keeping the Church in Its Place: The Church as Narrative Character in Acts* (New York/London: Clark).

Towner, P. H.

1998   'Mission Practice and Theology under Construction', in Marshall and Peterson (eds.) 1998, 417-36.

Tracey, R.

1994   'Syria', in Gill and Gempf (eds.) 1994, 223-78.

Trebilco, P. R.

1991   *Jewish Communities in Asia Minor*, SNTSMS 69 (Cambridge: Cambridge University).

1994   'Asia', in D. W. J. Gill and C. Gempf (eds.) 1994, 291-62.

2007   *The Early Christians in Ephesus from Paul to Ignatius* (Grand Rapids: Eerdmans).

Trites, A. A.

1977   *The New Testament Concept of Witness*, SNTSMS 31 (Cambridge: Cambridge University).

1978   'The Prayer-Motif in Luke-Acts', in C. H. Talbert (ed.), *Perspectives on Luke-Acts* (Edinburgh: Clark), 168-86.

Turner, M. M. B.
1981a   'Jesus and the Spirit in Lucan Perspective', *TynB* 32, 3-42.
1981b   'Spirit Endowment in Luke-Acts: Some Linguistic Considerations', *VE* 12, 45-63.
1981c   'The Significance of Receiving the Spirit in Luke-Acts: A Survey of Modern Scholarship', *TrinJ* 2, 131-58.
1985   'Spiritual Gifts Then and Now', *VE* 15, 7-64.
1990   'Prayer in the Gospels and Acts', in D. A. Carson (ed.), *Teach Us to Pray: Prayer in the Bible and the World* (Grand Rapids: Baker; Exeter: Paternoster), 58-83.
1991   'The Spirit and the Power of Jesus: Miracles in the Lucan Conception', *NovT* 33, 124-52.
1996   *Power from on High: The Spirit in Israel's Restoration and Witness in Luke-Acts*, JPTSS 9 (Sheffield: Sheffield Academic).
1998   'The "Spirit of Prophecy" as the Power of Israel's Restoration and Witness', in Marshall and Peterson (eds.) 1998, 327-48.
2004   'The Spirit and Salvation in Luke-Acts', in G. N. Stanton, B. W. Longenecker, and S. C. Barton (eds.), *The Holy Spirit and Christian Origins* (Grand Rapids: Eerdmans).

Turner, N.
1965   *Grammatical Insights into the New Testament* (Edinburgh: Clark).

Tyson, J. B. (ed.)
1988   *Luke-Acts and the Jewish People: Eight Critical Perspectives* (Minneapolis: Augsburg).

van der Horst, P. W.
1976-67 'Peter's Shadow: The Religio-Historical Background of Acts 5:15', *NTS* 23, 204-12.

van Stempvoort, P. A.
1958-59 'The Interpretation of the Ascension in Luke and Acts', *NTS* 5, 30-42.

van Unnik, W. C.
1961-62 'The Christian's Freedom of Speech in the New Testament', *BJRL* 44, 466-88.

Verheyden, J.
1999   *The Unity of Luke-Acts*, BETL 142 (Leuven: Leuven University).

Vielhauer, P.
1966   'On the "Paulinism" of Acts', in L. E. Keck and J. L. Martyn (eds.), *Studies in Luke-Acts: Essays Presented in Honor of Paul Schubert* (Nashville: Abingdon, 1966; London: SPCK, 1976), 33-50 (first published in *Evangelische Theologie* 10 [1950-51]).

Viviano, B. T., and J. Taylor
1992   'Sadducees, Angels, and the Resurrection', *JBL* 111, 496-98.

Walaskay, P. W.
1983   *'And so we came to Rome': The Political Perspective of St. Luke*, SNTSMS
        49 (Cambridge: Cambridge University).

Wall, R.
1998   'Israel and the Gentile Mission in Acts and Paul: A Canonical
        Approach', in Marshall and Peterson (eds.) 1998, 437-57.
2000   'Canonical Context and Canonical Conversations', in J. Green and
        M. Turner (eds.), *Between Two Horizons: Spanning New Testament Studies
        and Systematic Theology* (Grand Rapids: Eerdmans), 165-82.

Wallace, D. B.
1996   *Greek Grammar beyond the Basics: An Exegetical Syntax of the New
        Testament* (Grand Rapids: Zondervan).

Walton, S.
2000   *Leadership and Lifestyle: The Portrait of Paul in the Miletus Speech and
        1 Thessalonians*, SNTSMS 108 (Cambridge: Cambridge University).

Watson, F.
1986   *Paul, Judaism and the Gentiles*, SNTSMS 56 (Cambridge: Cambridge
        University).

Wenham, D.
1993   'Acts and the Pauline Corpus, II. The Evidence of the Parallels', in
        Winter and Clarke (eds.) 1993, 215-58.

Wenham, G. J.
1987   *Genesis 1–15*, Word Biblical Commentary 1 (Waco: Word).

Wenk, M.
2000   *Community-Forming Power: The Socio-Ethical Role of the Spirit in Luke-
        Acts* (Sheffield: Sheffield Academic).

Wiarda, T.
2003   'The Jerusalem Council and the Theological Task', *JETS* 46, no. 2, 233-
        48.

Wilson, S. G.
1973   *The Gentiles and the Gentile Mission in Luke-Acts*, SNTSMS 23
        (Cambridge: Cambridge University).
1983   *Luke and the Law*, SNTSMS 50 (Cambridge: Cambridge University).

Wimber, J.
1985   *Power Evangelism: Signs and Wonders Today* (London: Hodder).

Winter, B. W.
1993   'Official Proceedings and the Forensic Speeches in Acts 24–26', in
        Winter and Clarke (eds.) 1993, 305-36.
1994   'Acts and Food Shortages', in Gill and Gempf (eds.) 1994, 59-78.

1996   'On Introducing Gods to Athens: An Alternative Reading of Acts
        17:18-20', *TynB* 47, 71-90.
2005   'Introducing the Athenians to God: Paul's Failed Apologetic in Acts
        17?', in R. Chia and M. Chan (eds.), *A Graced Horizon: Essays in Gospel,
        Culture and Church in Honour of the Reverend Dr. Choong Chee Pang*
        (Singapore: Genesis), 65-84.
2006   'Rehabilitating Gallio and His Judgement in Acts 18:14-15', *TynB* 57,
        291-308.

Winter, B. W., and A. D. Clarke (eds.)
1993   *The Book of Acts in Its First-Century Setting*, Vol. 1: *Ancient Literary
        Setting* (Grand Rapids: Eerdmans; Carlisle: Paternoster).

Witherington, B., III
1984   'The Anti-Feminist Tendencies of the Western Text in Acts', *JBL* 103,
        82-84.
1988   *Women in the Earliest Churches* (Cambridge: Cambridge University).
1993   'Christ', in *DPL*, 95-100.
1998b   'Salvation and Health in Christian Antiquity: The Soteriology of Luke-
        Acts in Its First-Century Setting', in Marshall and Peterson (eds.) 1998,
        145-66.

Witherup, R. D.
1993   'Cornelius Over and Over Again: "Functional Redundancy" in the
        Acts of the Apostles', *JSNT* 49, 45-66.

Ziesler, J. A.
1979   'The Name of Jesus in the Acts of the Apostles', *JSNT* 4, 28-32.

Zwiep, A. W.
1997   *The Ascension of the Messiah in Lukan Christology*, NovTSup 87 (Leiden:
        Brill).
2004   *Judas and the Choice of Matthias: A Study on Context and Concern of Acts
        1:15-26* (Tübingen: Mohr).

Introduction

I. AUTHORSHIP AND DATE

A. Authorship

Early Christian tradition identifies the author of the Third Gospel and Acts as Luke, 'the beloved physician' mentioned in Colossians 4:14 (TNIV 'our dear friend Luke, the doctor'), who was an occasional participant in the Pauline mission and was with Paul during his imprisonment in Rome (cf. Phlm. 24; 2 Tim. 4:11). The earliest extant manuscript of the Gospel (Papyrus 75), which is dated between AD 175 and 225, has at its end the ascription 'Gospel according to Luke' (*Euangelion kata Loukan*). The Muratorian Canon, which lists the books recognised as Scripture in the Roman Church in about AD 170-180, describes the author of the Gospel and Acts as 'Luke the physician' and companion of Paul, who 'wrote in his own name but in accordance with [Paul's] opinion'.[1] Luke's authorship of both the Gospel and Acts is also confirmed by the so-called Anti-Marcionite Prologue to the Third Gospel, which is of uncertain date, but possibly belongs to the end of the second century. This document describes Luke as 'an Antiochene of Syria, a physician by profession'.[2] About this time also, Irenaeus (*Against Heresies* 3.1.1; 3.14.1) mentions Luke 'the follower of Paul'

---

1. Translation of F. F. Bruce, *The Acts of the Apostles: The Greek Text with Introduction and Commentary* (3rd ed.; Grand Rapids: Eerdmans; Leicester: Apollos, 1990), 1. Bruce takes this last expression to mean that Luke's writings are 'endowed with apostolic authority although they do not appear under the apostle's name' (p. 2).

2. Translation of Bruce 1990, 8, who notes that Luke's Antiochene origin is also mentioned by Eusebius and Jerome. C. K. Barrett, *A Critical and Exegetical Commentary on the Acts of the Apostles*, ICC, Vol. 1 (Edinburgh: Clark, 1994), 31-32, gives a full translation of the relevant lines from Eusebius and Jerome. Bruce 1990, 9, observes that the Western text of Acts 11:28 appears to reflect this tradition, which means that it must date from 'not later than the middle of the second century'.

as the author of both works and attaches Paul's authority to Luke's writing.[3] Witherington observes that the unanimity of this external evidence is striking when it is considered that 'no one was contending that Luke was either an apostle or an eyewitness of much of what he records'.[4]

From the preface in Luke 1:1-4 it appears that the author was a second-generation Christian who was not personally involved in the ministry of Jesus, but who had contact with 'those who from the first were eyewitnesses and servants of the word'. His native tongue was Hellenistic Greek, and he seems to have progressed 'to the higher levels of Greco-Roman education'.[5] At the same time, from the beginning of his narrative he betrays a great interest in Judaism, a knowledge of the Jewish Scriptures in their Greek translation (the so-called LXX), and some Semitisms in his Greek writing. When he refers to 'the things that have been fulfilled among us' (1:1) and the handing down of the testimony 'to us' (1:2), the implied author claims membership of the believing community formed around these events. When he describes himself as having 'carefully investigated everything from the beginning' (1:3), he could be claiming something more — at least some personal involvement in the events recorded in his second volume.[6] The most important internal evidence in this connection is the use of the first-person plural at significant points in the narrative of Acts (16:10-17; 20:5-15; 21:1-18; 27:1–28:16). Although some scholars have questioned whether these were actually the author's firsthand account, the style, grammar, and vocabulary of the 'we' passages are very much the same as that found elsewhere in Luke-Acts.[7]

---

3. Bruce 1990, 2-3, details the evidence also from other writers at the end of the second century, showing how consistent was the testimony by that time. R. Maddox, *The Purpose of Luke-Acts* (Edinburgh: Clark, 1982), 7, observes that it is possible that this is a reliable tradition, but it is also possible that ancient scholars worked from the 'we' passages in Acts and settled on Luke as the most likely contender. Maddox offers a third possibility, 'that there was indeed a sound tradition which named the author as "Luke", but that it was only later supposition which identified him with "the beloved physician"'.

4. B. Witherington III, *The Acts of the Apostles: A Socio-Rhetorical Commentary* (Grand Rapids/Cambridge: Eerdmans; Carlisle: Paternoster, 1998), 56.

5. Witherington 1998, 52. He notes the author's acquaintance with Greco-Roman rhetorical practices and historical conventions.

6. The participle *parakolouthēkoti* in Lk. 1:3 could mean 'follow, accompany, attend', 'follow with the mind, understand, make one's own' or 'follow a thing, trace or investigate a thing' (BAGD). Maddox, *Purpose*, 4-5, argues that this verb cannot be taken to mean historical research from some distance. However, J. Nolland, *Luke 1–9:20*, Word Biblical Commentary 35A (Dallas: Word, 1989), 9, notes that the meaning 'investigated' can be argued by comparison with Josephus, *Life* 357; Nicomachus, *Comicus* 1.20.

7. Barrett 1994, xxv-xxx, takes up three ways of looking at the evidence. S. E. Porter, *Paul in Acts* (Peabody: Hendrickson, 2001), 10-46, argues that the author of Acts used a previously written and continuous 'we' source that was not his own eyewitness account. However, Witherington 1998, 53-54, 480-86, convincingly argues that the 'we' passages are the author's own record of events. Cf. C. J. Hemer, *The Book of Acts in the Setting of Hellenistic History*, ed. C. Gempf, WUNT 49 (Tübingen: Mohr, 1989; repr. Winona Lake: Eisenbrauns, 1990), 312-34; W. S. Campbell, *The 'We' Passages in the Acts of the Apostles: The Narrator as Narrative Charater*, SBLSBL 14 (Atlanta: SBL; Leiden: Brill, 2007).

'Their most natural explanation is that the author himself was present during those phases of his story which he records in the 1st pers. — that the "we" of those sections includes the "I" of 1:1.'[8] The 'we' passages reveal the occasions on which the author was the companion of Paul in his missionary activity and in the period of his imprisonment and trials.

Other characters are named in the text of Acts as travel companions of Paul at various stages of his ministry (Silas, Timothy, Sopater, Aristarchus, Secundus, Gaius, Tychicus, Trophimus). All except Silas and Timothy appear to have joined Paul after the period covered by the first 'we' passage (16:10-17). Significantly, Luke is not named in the text of Acts, even though the letters identify him among those present with Paul in the period of his imprisonment (Col. 4:14; Phlm. 24; cf. 2 Tim. 4:11). This lack of reference in Acts to one of the serious candidates for authorship is actually a strong pointer to Luke. Although reticent about naming himself, the author of the 'we' passages was with Paul on his final journey to Rome (Acts 27:1–28:16) and then presumably during his captivity there (28:17-31). However, since scholars are divided about whether the 'captivity letters' were actually written from Ephesus, Caesarea, or Rome, the argument linking Luke with Paul's Roman imprisonment in this way is disputed.

It has sometimes been argued that there is distinctive medical language in Luke-Acts that supports the case for authorship by 'the beloved physician'. However, Cadbury's careful study concluded that the medical element in the language of these volumes is no greater than that which is found in the writings of educated first-century Greeks more generally.[9] On the negative side, some commentators have argued that the differences between Acts and the letters of Paul are such that the author of Acts can hardly have been a regular Pauline travel companion.[10] This issue is addressed below under the heading 'Sources'.

Looking more broadly at what can be gleaned from Luke-Acts about the author's social location, Witherington concludes:

> Our author is a well-traveled retainer of the social elite, well educated, deeply concerned about religious matters, knowledgeable about Judaism, but no prisoner of any subculture in the Empire. Rather, he is a cosmopolitan person with a more universalistic vision of the potential

---

8. Bruce 1990, 4. Lk. 1:3 (*kamoi*, 'I myself' [TNIV]).

9. H. J. Cadbury, *The Style and Literary Method of Luke*, Vol. 1: *The Diction of Luke and Acts*, HTS 6 (Cambridge, MA: Harvard University, 1920). Cf. Bruce 1990, 6-7. Note, however, that L. C. A. Alexander, *The Preface to Luke's Gospel: Literary Conventions and Social Context in Luke 1:1-4 and Acts 1:1*, SNTSMS 78 (Cambridge: Cambridge University, 1993), argues that the author of Luke-Acts was familiar with some ancient scientific writings and the conventions for writing prefaces to such works.

10. Cf. C. K. Barrett, *A Critical and Exegetical Commentary on the Acts of the Apostles*, ICC, Vol. 2 (Edinburgh: Clark, 1998), xliv-xlv. Witherington 1998, 58-60, and D. L. Bock, *Acts*, BECNT (Grand Rapids: Baker Academic, 2007), 16-19, offer cautious responses to this critical line of argument.

scope of impact of his faith, both up and down the social ladder, and also across geographical, ethnic, and other social boundaries.[11]

Considering the strong, early Christian evidence for Luke as the author of the Third Gospel and Acts, and the appropriateness of this tradition with reference to the internal data of the NT itself, there are good reasons for concluding that the traditional solution is reliable and true.

B. Date

Although Acts cannot be proved by quotation or allusion in other writings to have existed before about AD 150, 'its circulation in the churches from the second half of the second century onward is amply attested'.[12] Moreover, a first-century date for its composition can be argued from the evidence of the work itself. For example, Barrett observes that the book appears to have been written 'at a time of both inward and outward peace, and there is evidence in remarks about Roman provincial administration and provincial officers that suggests a date within the first century'.[13] He then follows a fairly standard line, dating Luke's two volumes in the late 80s or early 90s. However, there are two problems associated with this conclusion. First, if the 'we' passages were written by a travel companion of Paul, Luke-Acts could not have been composed much later than the early 80s, unless the author was quite young at the time when he first met Paul. Secondly, it is difficult to explain the end of Acts, which describes only Paul's two-year imprisonment and ministry in Rome (28:30-31), if a late date is proposed. Why does the author not take the story up to the point of Paul's trial or death? The longer the time gap, the more the need to fill in the details for the next generation of believers.

Barrett acknowledges that the simplest solution is to insist that the work was written earlier and that it tells no more of Paul because there was no more for Luke to tell. Like many scholars, however, Barrett considers this to be an unconvincing argument. He contends that Luke used Mark as a source for his Gospel and that Mark was written about AD 70. Furthermore, Luke 21:20-24 is said to imply the fall of Jerusalem, which took place in that year.[14] But even if these presuppositions are accepted, it is not diffi-

---

11. Witherington 1998, 56. Witherington, 63-65, evaluates the presumed audience of Acts by considering Theophilus as Luke's patron, who might publish the work for those from a similar background. Theophilus is regarded as a fairly recent convert to Christianity from a synagogue context. At the same time, Luke's method of writing suggests 'an audience with a Hellenistic education in at least some rhetoric and Greek history prior to coming to Christian faith, and surely prior to becoming a synagogue adherent as well'.

12. Bruce 1990, 11-12. Like Bruce, Barrett 1994, 34-38, lists traces of the knowledge and use of Acts in various early sources.

13. Barrett 1994, xlii. Cf. Bruce 1990, 17-18; R. I. Pervo, *Dating Acts: Between the Evangelists and the Apologists* (Santa Rosa, CA: Polebridge, 2006).

14. Barrett 1998, xliii. However, J. A. T. Robinson, *Redating the New Testament* (Lon-

cult to imagine that Luke published his work in the mid 70s. He could well have been at work consulting witnesses, assembling his sources, and writing them up when he first came into contact with Mark's Gospel. Knowing that he had more to offer and having his own distinctive purpose in writing, Luke could have achieved his goal in only a few years. Why must there have been more than a decade between the publication of Mark and the appearance of Luke-Acts? A date in the 70s seems entirely reasonable and consistent with the evidence from the documents themselves.[15] However, a good case can be made for a date as early as 62-64, given Luke's apparent ignorance of the letters of Paul, his portrayal of Judaism as a legal religion, and his omission of any reference to the Neronian persecution of Christians, let alone his failure to say anything about the outcome of Paul's imprisonment in Rome.[16]

II. GENRE

Genre can be defined in terms of the content, form, and function of a particular text. Considering the genre of a book can be an important preliminary in the process of interpretation. With regard to the Acts of the Apostles, it is first necessary to investigate the relationship between this work and the Third Gospel. It is then instructive to consider the character of Acts itself, in comparison with other forms of literature in the ancient world. A Christian writer with a desire to influence people in the first-century, Greco-Roman environment may well have reflected some of its literary trends, though the critical question is 'how closely or consciously'.[17] A great deal of scholarly work has taken place in this area in recent decades, and there are conflicting views which need to be examined and assessed.

---

don: SCM, 1975), 86-92, argues that there are no allusions to the fall of Jerusalem in Luke-Acts and that the work was written before AD 70. Cf. Bruce 1990, 15-17.

15. Bruce 1990, 17-18, argues for the publication of both Luke and Acts 'in the period following AD 70'. In support, he notes the attention to subjects in Acts which were of urgent importance before AD 70, but which were of lesser moment after that date, the fact that Acts is true to its 'dramatic' date (the date of the events and developments which it relates), political, geographical, and social references appropriate to the pre-70 era, and the authorial perspective of one who was involved in the events but reviews them from some temporal distance. Witherington 1998, 61-62, agrees with this conclusion.

16. Cf. D. A. Carson, D. J. Moo, and L. Morris, *An Introduction to the New Testament* (Grand Rapids: Zondervan, 1992), 190-94. Bock 2007, 27, favours a date just before AD 70; R. N. Longenecker, 'Acts', in *The Expositor's Bible Commentary, Revised Edition*, Vol. 10: *Luke-Acts*, ed. T. Longman III and D. E. Garland (Grand Rapids: Zondervan, 2007), 701, suggests AD 64 as the date of composition.

17. Hemer, *Book of Acts*, 34. Hemer's cautions about seeking to establish the genre of Acts are salutary.

A. The Unity of Luke and Acts

Many contemporary scholars would agree with Cadbury's proposal that 'Acts is neither an appendix nor an afterthought. It is probably an integral part of the author's original plan and purpose.'[18] Since Cadbury's foundational work, a variety of publications regarding the generic, narrative, and theological unity of Luke-Acts has emerged. However, Parsons and Pervo have offered a significant challenge to this approach. Acknowledging the common authorship of the two volumes, they insist that it is neither necessary nor helpful to force one to fit the pattern of the other. Indeed, Luke and Acts are sufficiently different to suggest *two distinct genres*.[19] Parsons and Pervo examine various contemporary proposals for the generic unity of Luke and Acts and find them wanting.

If Mark was one of his sources, Luke clearly modified the Gospel form by more than doubling its length and increasing the time span of the story. But his first volume still broadly resembles the other Synoptic Gospels in structure, character, and style.[20] The Gospel genre was a unique creation of Christian writers, determined partly by the realities of Jesus' life and ministry and partly by the exigencies of the Christian mission. Structurally, Luke's Gospel provides an 'episodic series of events punctuated by numerous aphorisms and parables of Jesus', whereas Acts 'unfolds more smoothly as a continuous narrative featuring extended journeys and developed discourse by Jesus' followers'.[21] After its introductory chapters (1–3), the Gospel focuses on the public ministry of Jesus (4:1–9:50), his final journey to Jerusalem (9:51–19:44), and then the events of his last week in Jerusalem, culminating in his death and resurrection (19:45–24:53). It covers a limited period of time and portrays Jesus moving from Galilee, through Samaria, to Judea and Jerusalem. Acts deals with the expanding geographical and cultural outreach of 'the word' about Jesus, in an outward movement from Jerusalem corresponding to the prediction in 1:8. The gospel is first proclaimed by the apostles Peter and John in Jerusalem (1–5), and then by prophetic figures such as Stephen, Philip, and Paul, in Judea, Samaria, and 'to the ends of the earth' (6–20). The final section focuses on the trials of

18. H. J. Cadbury, *The Making of Luke-Acts* (Naperville: Allenson, 1927; 2nd ed., London: SPCK, 1958), 8-9. Cadbury's arguments for the unity of Luke-Acts have been influential since they were first advanced. Cf. Maddox, *Purpose*, 3-6; J. Verheyden, *The Unity of Luke-Acts*, BETL 142 (Leuven: Leuven University, 1999).

19. M. C. Parsons and R. I. Pervo, *Rethinking the Unity of Luke and Acts* (Philadelphia: Fortress, 1993), 37-40. They tend to exaggerate the differences to establish their point. I find it difficult, however, to agree with Witherington 1998, 18-24, that both Luke and Acts can be similarly classified as historical monographs.

20. Against J. B. Green, *The Gospel of Luke*, NICNT (Grand Rapids/Cambridge: Eerdmans, 1997), 1, 7, just because Luke appears to categorize his work as a narrative (Lk. 1:1, *diēgēsis*) does not mean that the category of 'Gospel' is not also applicable to his first volume. It is a narrative with a particular shape and purpose.

21. F. S. Spencer, *Acts* (Sheffield: Sheffield Academic, 1997), 14.

Paul and his journey to Rome as a prisoner (21–28). Acts appears to be a highly selective history, carried forward by a number of significant speeches from some of the main characters, covering a period of thirty or more years after Jesus' resurrection and ascension. Luke's innovation is to show that 'the gospel-story is incomplete without the church-story'.[22]

Analysing Luke and Acts from a literary perspective, Parsons and Pervo first conclude that, at the discourse level, it is inappropriate to speak of a narrative unity. 'The two works are independent narratives with distinct narration, that is, they each tell the story *differently*.'[23] The narrative unity exposed by writers such as Tannehill is said to be almost exclusively at the level of the story and 'does not reckon adequately with the disunity at the discourse level'.[24] But Tannehill's approach has been poorly assessed by Parsons and Pervo, and its implications inadequately considered. More will be said about this below. Even more questionable is their glib treatment of the theological coherence between Luke and Acts.[25] They rightly suggest that, where theological unity between Luke and Acts can be established, it should not be 'a brush with which to efface particularity'.[26] They also rightly argue that Acts is a *sequel* to the Gospel rather than a simple continuation. But they obscure the literary, stylistic, and thematic links between the two volumes. In short, Parsons and Pervo have offered an important caution in the ongoing debate about the relationship between Luke and Acts, but they have overstated their case. These two volumes may be different in genre, structure, and style, but it is necessary to explain the links between them at the level of story, themes, and theology.

Assessing a variety of theories about the relationship between the Gospel and Acts, Marshall notes that the options commanding the most serious scholarly support are that they were either two separate works by the same author or a two-part work (whatever the process by which this two-volume work came to its present form).[27] Marshall's preference for the latter alternative is based on three lines of argument. There is first the evi-

22. Maddox, *Purpose*, 10.

23. Parsons and Pervo, *Rethinking*, 82.

24. Parsons and Pervo, *Rethinking*, 83. Cf. R. C. Tannehill, *The Narrative Unity of Luke-Acts: A Literary Interpretation*, Vol. 1: *The Gospel of Luke* (Minneapolis: Fortress, 1986) and *The Narrative Unity of Luke-Acts: A Literary Interpretation*, Vol. 2: *The Acts of the Apostles* (Minneapolis: Fortress, 1990).

25. For example, Parsons and Pervo, *Rethinking*, 84-114, seriously misread the anthropology of Acts by identifying it with contemporary Greco-Roman perspectives. Luke is said to use 'elements of a common Greco-Roman anthropology as a means for forging unity between God and humankind, the histories of Israel, Jesus, and the Church, and thus between Jews and Gentiles' (125).

26. Parsons and Pervo, *Rethinking*, 126.

27. I. H. Marshall, 'Acts and the "Former Treatise"', in B. W. Winter and A. D. Clarke (eds.), *The Book of Acts in Its First-Century Setting*, Vol. 1: *Ancient Literary Setting* (Grand Rapids: Eerdmans; Carlisle: Paternoster, 1993), 163-82. Cf. Maddox, *Purpose*, 3-6, 9-12; C. K. Barrett, 'The Third Gospel as a Preface to Acts? Some Reflections', in F. Van Segbroeck (ed.), *The Four Gospels 1992: Festschrift for Frans Neirynck* (Leuven: Leuven University, 1992), 1451-66.

dence of the two prologues (Lk. 1:1-4; Acts 1:1), linking the works in terms of subject matter and purpose. Secondly, some material in the Gospel appears to have been either adapted or excluded because of what is found in Acts (e.g., Mt. 15:1-28/Mk. 7:1-30 finds no parallel in Luke, presumably because the theme of true purity and healing/salvation for Gentiles is addressed so fully in Acts 10–11). Thirdly, the overlap between the ending of the Gospel and the beginning of Acts is significant (Lk. 24:36-52 is recapitulated in Acts 1:1-14 and its predictions are shown to be fulfilled in subsequent narratives). Marshall concludes that 'Luke's justification for his fresh attempt to give an account of "the things that have taken place among us" was in the fact that his predecessors had treated only the material contained in the Gospel and not gone on to present the other, comparably important material about the spread of the gospel. Their story was incomplete.'[28] His approach is persuasive and suggests that Acts is best interpreted as the intended sequel to the Gospel. Witherington similarly concludes his assessment of the evidence by saying, 'Luke planted some seeds in his Gospel that he did not intend to fully cultivate and bring to harvest before his second volume. In short, the first volume was likely written with at least one eye already on the sequel.'[29]

B. Ancient Literary Models for Acts

1. *Historical Monograph*

The term 'historical monograph' is a modern one, 'commonly applied to ancient historical writings which deal with a limited issue or period without regard to the length of the books themselves'.[30] The Greek historian Polybius (2nd cent. BC) distinguished between a universal history and a particular history, but prior to the work of the Roman writer Sallust (1st cent. BC), 'single-volume historical monographs were rare, if they existed at all'.[31] Sallust's contemporary, Cicero, had 'no specific *term* for the historical mono-

28. Marshall, 'Acts and the "Former Treatise"', 176-77.

29. Witherington 1998, 8. M. F. Bird, 'The Unity of Luke-Acts in Recent Discussion', *JSNT* 29 (2007), 425-48, surveys a number of scholarly responses to Parsons and Pervo, concluding that they have failed to convince the majority due to 'the success of Cadbury, and others like Tannehill, who have constructed arguments that are both persuasive on the textual level and that resonate with the current interests of scholarship in literary-critical studies' (435). However, Bird goes on to discuss challenges to the consensus raised by 'reception history', namely the way Luke and Acts were received and circulated in the second century AD.

30. D. W. Palmer, 'Acts and the Ancient Historical Monograph', in Winter and Clarke, *Ancient Literary Setting*, 4.

31. Palmer, 'Monograph', 14. Palmer, 26, concludes that 'the fragmentary evidence for numerous Greek monographs and one in Latin confirms the existence of the genre, but does not give a picture of what an individual example looked like'.

graph; but his correspondence provides evidence for his *concept* of various features of the genre'.[32] Palmer contends that, 'while Acts may be allowed an implicit function of apology or self-definition, its length, scope, focus and formal features fit the pattern of a short historical monograph'.[33] Palmer also discusses Hellenistic Jewish historiography and concludes that 1 Esdras (2nd cent. BC) and 1 and 2 Maccabees (1st cent. BC) share many of the features of Greek and Roman historical monographs, though their religious perspective is influenced by earlier Jewish writings. In many ways, they correspond to the theory and practice of Cicero and Sallust. They are earlier than these writers, 'but they perhaps point to the Graeco-Roman heritage which lies behind Cicero and Sallust on the one hand and to the milieu of "biblical history" on the other. Indeed, they provide a link between this double background in the past and the future composition of Acts.'[34]

Witherington argues from the preface found in Luke 1:1-4 that Luke intended both his volumes 'to be compared to other ancient works of Greco-Roman historiography'.[35] However, reviewing various Greek and Roman models, Witherington argues that 'Luke's work stands much closer to Greek historiography than to the Roman sort'.[36] A particular hallmark of true history for the Greeks was 'personal observation *(autopsia)* and participation in events, travel inquiry, the consultation of eyewitnesses'.[37] Acts also has a broad ethnographical and geographical scope, which is the pattern of the Greek histories, with a message about salvation for the nations being announced in the earliest chapters of the Gospel (Lk. 2:29-32; 3:1-6). Luke's presentation of the impact of Christianity on the ancient world contains a surprising lack of 'broadscale polemics against either Jews or Romans, though both are portrayed as persecuting or causing problems for Christians at various points in the narrative'.[38]

32. Palmer, 'Monograph', 11. Palmer, 11-13, cites the evidence from Cicero's letters.

33. Palmer, 'Monograph', 18. Palmer includes the notions of apology and self-definition in his evaluation because he has compared Acts with the *Jewish Antiquities* of Josephus.

34. Palmer, 'Monograph', 27. See below for comments on 'Acts and Biblical Histories'.

35. Witherington 1998, 381. Witherington, 4-24, discusses the prefaces at some length and suggests that Luke is 'closer to Polybius than to various other ancient historians in his understanding that his job is to instruct and reassure Theophilus about the nature and meaning of the events (both words and deeds) that had happened "among us"' (11).

36. Witherington 1998, 27. He notes that Josephus, 'by limiting himself to the chronicling of developments among one people (the Jews rather than the Romans) and attempting a "universal history" of this one people, much more closely approximates some of his Roman predecessors and contemporaries.'

37. Witherington 1998, 27. Cadbury, *Making*, 220, concluded from the style of Luke-Acts that the author must have been 'for his time and station a gentleman of ability and breadth of interest, whatever his past reading and training may have been'. D. Mealand, 'Hellenistic Historians and the Style of Acts', *ZNW* 82 (1991), 59, concluded that Luke 'is a skilful literary artist who can use varieties of style for effect'.

38. Witherington 1998, 29. 'Were Luke-Acts a Roman apologetic work, we might ex-

Witherington contends that Luke's work is most like that of Polybius, and, to a lesser degree, that of Thucydides.[39] However, Luke differs from these Greek historians in at least two significant ways. First, he is 'not in the main concerned about the political or military history of the larger culture, but about the social and religious history of a particular group or subculture within the Empire. Luke believes it is a group which can and should continue to have a growing and ever broader impact, for they proclaim a universal savior and salvation.'[40] Second, Luke includes many visions, prophecies, and amazing events in his narrative, to highlight God's involvement in the story, whereas Polybius can only write about 'the operations of the laws of Fortune' (1.1-4) on the events he records. However, Luke does not present the amazing and the supernatural in a way that suggests any immunity from historical scrutiny, 'unlike some of the literature about the "fabulous" in antiquity'.[41]

Witherington further observes a notable similarity between Acts and the work of the historian Ephorus with respect to the arrangement and presentation of his material. In a given book or section, Ephorus would 'only deal with matters in a particular geographical or major cultural region, usually proceeding with it in a chronological order'.[42] In Acts, the geographical movement from one region to another is culturally and theologically significant in terms of the prediction made in 1:8. Geographical advance is broadly linked to chronological development in the unfolding of Luke's story, which only selectively records the ministry of the apostles and other early Christian leaders. Moreover, a number of theological agendas influence the way the narrative is constructed and presented. Although there is much evidence pointing to Luke's accuracy as a historian, the work demonstrates a literary artistry and rhetorical style that makes it more than a chronicle of remarkable events.[43]

---

pect a quiet omission or even in some cases a glossing over of stories that portray Christians or Romans in a negative light and others in a positive one.'

39. Witherington 1998, 32. Polybius 1.1-4 proclaims the uniqueness and importance of the events he records, believing that they have come about because of some larger guiding force or Being. He criticises those who invent speeches, contending that it is important for them to be accurately recorded and used as 'summaries of events and as the unifying element in historical writing' (12.25a-b; cf. 36.1). Cf. M. Soards, *The Speeches in Acts: Their Content, Context and Concerns* (Louisville: John Knox/Westminster, 1994), 199ff. Polybius 36.12 also highlights his own personal involvement in the story from a certain point by using the first-person narrative form.

40. Witherington 1998, 31.

41. Witherington 1998, 32. Witherington, 31, compares Luke's style to that of Herodotus, 'the so-called father of Greek historiography, who wrote what can rightly be called a form of theological historiography'.

42. Witherington 1998, 34. Ephorus's method became standard for Greek historians after him, and Witherington submits that Luke followed his approach.

43. P. E. Satterthwaite, 'Acts against the Background of Classical Rhetoric', in Winter and Clarke, *Ancient Literary Setting*, 337-79, discusses Luke's use of classical rhetorical techniques. Cf. Witherington 1998, 39-51.

2. Biography

Talbert proposed that 'Luke-Acts, to some extent, must be regarded as be-longing to the genre of Greco-Roman biography, in particular, to that type of biography which dealt with the lives of philosophers and their succes-sors'.[44] More recently, Alexander has argued that Acts cannot be forced into a biographical mould, but she insists that 'the reader of Acts has much to learn from the study of ancient biography; and Talbert's proposal makes a good starting-point in a number of ways'.[45] She notes the succes-sion structure of Luke's double work: the narrative of Acts is focussed on the ministry of a number of key disciples who carry on the work of Jesus, with Paul being the dominant figure in the latter half of the book. 'Acts is not just a biography of Paul but it *contains* a Pauline biography in the same way that the books of Samuel contain the Davidic "succession narrative", or Genesis contains the story of Joseph.'[46] Alexander then explores a par-ticular comparison with ancient 'intellectual biography', namely 'biogra-phy of individuals distinguished for their prowess in the intellectual field (philosophers, poets, dramatists, doctors) rather than in the political or military arena (kings, statesmen, generals)'.[47] She argues that 'if we broaden our definition of biography to include not only the fully-fledged biographical texts but also the underlying traditions and patterns of thought, it is not difficult to see many points of interest for Acts'.[48] She fi-nally sketches a Socratic paradigm, which does not exist in any known bi-ography of Socrates but was 'a narrative pattern familiar to a wide range of writers in the first century AD'.[49] At this point, however, the discussion

44. C. H. Talbert, *Literary Patterns, Theological Themes, and the Genre of Luke-Acts,* SBLMS 20 (Missoula: Scholars, 1974), 134. Talbert, 125-34, argued that Diogenes Laertius's *Lives of the Philosophers,* although dated in the early third century AD, attested to a long tradi-tion of writing up the lives of philosophers and their successors in a similar fashion. L. C. A. Alexander, 'Acts and Ancient Intellectual Biography', in Winter and Clarke, *Ancient Literary Setting,* 35, employs Talbert's fivefold classification of biography according to social func-tion.

45. Alexander, 'Biography', 33.

46. Alexander, 'Biography', 34. R. A. Burridge, *What Are the Gospels? A Comparison with Greco-Roman Biography,* SNTSMS 70 (Cambridge: Cambridge University, 1992), 245, has argued against making rigid genre distinctions between biography and other sorts of an-cient history writing, contending that 'they are only differentiated by internal features such as subject or focus'. The Third Gospel is best viewed as an ancient biography because of the way it reveals the character of Jesus. Witherington 1998, 16-24, disagrees, insisting that nei-ther Luke nor Acts is truly biographical, and that both together must be seen as 'some sort of two-volume historiographical work'.

47. Alexander, 'Biography', 34. Alexander, *Preface,* 1-206, argues that the prefaces of Luke and Acts are most similar to those of ancient scientific or technical treatises, classifying ancient biographies as part of that tradition. Palmer, 'Monograph', 21-26, and Witherington 1998, 14-15, both offer brief critiques of Alexander in this respect.

48. Alexander, 'Biography', 56.

49. Alexander, 'Biography', 63. She suggests that 'this Socratic paradigm was avail-able to Luke's readers and offered them the possibility of fitting Paul's story — and by im-

has clearly moved beyond any proposal for a specific genre or literary model for Acts.

Ancient histories contained biographical elements or passages, but the purpose was not characterization for some didactic or moral purpose, as in biographies. Ancient historiography 'focussed on events *more* than on persons and personalities, and was concerned not only to record significant happenings but to probe and if possible explain the causes of these happenings'.[50] This agenda can be discerned in Luke-Acts, where there is a regular stress on the fulfillment of Scripture and an interpretation of the events in terms of the fulfillment of God's will and plan.[51] There are certainly ways in which key figures in Acts are presented as model disciples, but it is not helpful to classify Acts as a form of biography, nor to view Luke-Acts primarily in terms of the succession model. Theological and apologetic concerns are prominent in the narrative of Acts, where the progress of 'the word' in the face of various forms of resistance and opposition is a major interest for the author.

Even in the last chapters of Acts, Luke's concern is to chart the progress of the gospel, not to complete a character study of his hero. Paul's penultimate speech to the Jews of Rome (28:17-20) recalls events in the preceding narratives and concludes with the claim that it is because of 'the hope of Israel' that he is in chains. His final speech (28:23-28) reiterates the pattern of teaching to Jews evidenced earlier in the book, bringing a challenge about Isaiah's prophecy being fulfilled in their stubborn resistance, and proclaiming that 'God's salvation has been sent to the Gentiles, and they will listen'. Luke's editorial conclusion (28:30-31) leaves the reader with little indication of the outcome for Paul personally. The focus is on his continuing ministry of the gospel 'with all boldness and without hindrance'. In effect, Luke makes another statement about the word of God increasing and spreading, despite the opposition or difficulties encountered (cf. 6:7; 12:24; 19:20). In other words, Acts 28 is a significant indicator of Luke's purpose in writing, and it suggests that his interest is historical and theological rather than strictly biographical.

---

plication their own — into "a story they already knew", one which could work alongside the paradigm of the prophet which Luke employs to such good effect in the Gospel and in the first half of Acts'.

50. Cf. Witherington 1998, 17. Witherington, 11-13, argues that Luke's interest in certain *events* and their significance (Lk. 1:1-4), rather than in personalities and the details of their life stories, suggests a historical rather than a biographical concern, even in the Gospel narratives about Jesus.

51. Cf. J. T. Squires, *The Plan of God in Luke-Acts*, SNTSMS 76 (Cambridge: Cambridge University, 1993); D. G. Peterson, 'The Motif of Fulfilment and the Purpose of Luke-Acts', in Winter and Clarke, *Ancient Literary Setting*, 83-104.

3. *Historical Novel*

More controversial is the evaluation of Acts as a type of historical novel, involving both history and fiction, and following the conventions of certain ancient romances. This approach is championed by Pervo, who attempts to broaden the literary classification of novel to fit the case, and who likens canonical Acts to the apocryphal Acts in this connection.[52] Witherington, however, raises a number of serious objections, including the fact that there is no romance in Acts properly defined, the book is not a tale of two parties long separated and then reunited, there is no happy ending since Paul's fate is left untold, and the book is full of speeches, which is not characteristic of ancient romances.[53] At the same time, Witherington says, 'Pervo is right to point out that the humor, wit, irony, and pathos in Acts have been underappreciated by scholars. These features, however, are often found in historiographical works during the Empire *due to the influence of Greco-Roman rhetoric* on the genre, not due to the influence of the novel.'[54]

C. Acts and Biblical Histories

Rosner has argued that Acts is 'consciously modelled on accounts of history found in the Old Testament'.[55] It has long been recognised that there is a Semitic colouring to some of Luke's language, particularly in Acts 1–15, though scholars debate the extent to which this is the result of deliberately imitating the Septuagint (LXX). Thematically, Acts shows a close relationship with the OT in dealing with matters such as promise and fulfillment, Jerusalem, the law, and the Jewish people. Characters such as Peter, Stephen, and Paul are presented to some extent as prophetic figures, following OT models. Furthermore, certain narratives in Acts appear to be patterned on biblical precedents. Together, these characteristics suggest that the author intended to create 'a "biblical effect" for those readers familiar with the Bible'.[56]

52. Cf. R. I. Pervo, *Profit with Delight: The Literary Genre of the Acts of the Apostles* (Philadelphia: Fortress, 1987), and the critique by Witherington 1998, 376-81, 755-77. R. Bauckham, 'The *Acts of Paul* as a Sequel to Acts', in Winter and Clarke, *Ancient Literary Setting*, 105-52, compares canonical Acts with the apocryphal *Acts of Paul and Thecla*, showing that the latter is much more akin to the category of historical novel or romance.

53. Witherington 1998, 377.

54. Witherington 1998, 378. Witherington, 756, thinks that Pervo is right to propose that Luke 'as a rhetorical historian had some interest in giving his audience pleasure as well as information'. However, 'this was as a secondary interest and not the one that determined the genre or historical substance of the work'. Witherington, 39-51, discusses the influence of ancient rhetorical conventions on Luke-Acts.

55. B. S. Rosner, 'Acts and Biblical History', in Winter and Clarke, *Ancient Literary Setting*, 68. Cf. J. Jervell, *The Theology of the Acts of the Apostles*, New Testament Theology (Cambridge: Cambridge University, 1996), 104-26.

56. Rosner, 'Biblical History', 73. Rosner argues that Luke is not inventing material to

A number of literary techniques found especially in the so-called Deuteronomistic history (Deuteronomy–2 Kings) have parallels in Acts. Rosner observes the repetition of verbal formulas to mark the end of one section of narrative and the beginning of another (he compares Acts 6:7; 9:31; 12:24; 16:5; 19:20; 28:31, to 1 Ki. 14:19-20, 31; 15:8, 24, etc.). Speeches by major characters or editorial comments are used to introduce or sum up the theme of a unit (he compares the literary function of prayer in Acts 4:24-30 and 1 Ki. 8:22-53). The narrative of Acts progresses by telling the stories of key characters, using a technique found in the Pentateuch and the Deuteronomistic history. Rosner notes that 'caution must be exercised in assessing the significance of these common features', since 'such literary devices were widely used both in the ancient near East generally and in early Greek prose, not to mention Greek historiography contemporary with Luke'.[57] However, there are good reasons for seeing the LXX as a primary influence on the style and character of Acts.

Rosner finally investigates the extent to which the OT may have provided Luke with his understanding of the nature of history. As in those biblical precedents, God is in control — despite human wickedness and rebellion — with key terms being used to draw attention to the will and purpose of God and his direction of human history. Events are narrated as the action of God, and there is great stress on the fulfillment of divine promises in what is recorded, sometimes using specific quotations from Scripture to make the point. The LXX thus appears to have influenced the language, form, content, and presuppositions of Luke's work. Rosner concludes that Luke was consciously writing a history following biblical precedents, and he agrees with Sterling that 'our author conceived of his work as the *continuation* of the LXX'.[58] Luke was concerned to reflect upon sacred history for the benefit of the believing community, drawing a link between the time of Israel, the time of Jesus, and the time of the early church.

Witherington acknowledges the strength of some of these arguments, but he contends that 'the *sort* of history Luke chooses to write about is different in crucial respects from the sort found in the OT, or in the Maccabean literature, or in the Hellenistic Jewish historians'.[59] Luke is writing about *salvation* history and the fulfillment of God's purposes through preaching rather than through political and military means. He is writing a sequel to the OT not merely in terms of historical development, but in terms of 'the dramatic and surprising intervention of God in Jesus'.[60] Luke's view of the people of

---

fit the pattern, but rather he is making important theological links by his use of OT language and allusion.

57. Rosner, 'Biblical History', 77.

58. Rosner, 'Biblical History', 81, citing G. E. Sterling, *Historiography and Self-Definition: Josephus, Luke-Acts and Apologetic Historiography* (Leiden: Brill, 1992), 363 (Sterling's emphasis).

59. Witherington 1998, 37.

60. Witherington 1998, 38.

God is also 'much more inclusive and universal than one finds in the LXX or in early Hellenistic Jewish historiography'.[61] Witherington therefore concludes that Luke-Acts should be 'evaluated on its own terms as a two-volume historical work about a particular religious and social movement'.[62]

D. Conclusion about Genre

Having surveyed the options, I find myself largely in agreement with Witherington's conclusion:

> Luke-Acts bears some strong resemblances to earlier Greek historiographic works in form and method and general arrangement of material, as well as some similarities to Hellenized Jewish historiography in content and general apologetic aims. Furthermore, the echoes and quotes of the OT in Luke-Acts as well as the stress on fulfillment reveal a vital link to the biblical promises and prophecies of the past. Luke's work follows no one model, but clearly enough it would not have been seen as a work like Roman historiography, Greek biography, or Greek scientific treatises. It would surely, however, have been seen as some sort of Hellenistic historiography, especially by a Gentile audience.[63]

However, I find it difficult to put the Third Gospel into exactly the same category as Acts, as Witherington does. Comparison with the other Synoptics shows how Luke used the gospel genre to fulfill his purpose. He included certain historiographical features such as synchronism with events in the wider world (cf. Lk. 2:1-3; 3:1-2), but these are not sufficient to warrant a classification of the Third Gospel as a historical monograph like Acts. Witherington tends to play down the differences between Luke's two volumes in form, style, and function. Two distinct genres are developed by Luke, and these are linked together in textual and thematic ways to achieve a remarkable degree of narrative unity. Although there are other ancient examples of literary compositions in two parts, Marshall observes that even within the Christian context there is nothing corresponding to it: 'Christians produce apocryphal Gospels and apocryphal Acts, but not apocryphal Gospels-cum-Acts'.[64]

61. Witherington 1998, 38. Each volume of Luke-Acts begins with a strong Semitic flavour and then becomes more cosmopolitan in scope. Acts makes it clear that Gentiles are incorporated into the people of God on the law-free basis of grace and faith.

62. Witherington 1998, 38.

63. Witherington 1998, 39. D. Marguerat, *The First Christian Historian: Writing the 'Acts of the Apostles'*, SNTSMS 121, trans. K. McKinney, G. J. Laughery, and R. Bauckham (Cambridge: Cambridge University, 2002), 34, identifies Acts as a work of apologetic historiography, specifically a 'narrative of beginnings'. Bock 2007, 2-3, agrees that it is 'a "historical monograph" in the ancient sense of the term'.

64. Marshall, 'Former Treatise', 180. He concludes that 'the whole work demonstrates

III. SOURCES, RHETORIC, AND
HISTORICAL RELIABILITY

A. Sources

As already indicated, it is likely that the Prologue in Luke 1:1-4 applies to both volumes of this work, though some of its claims may have a more direct reference to the Gospel. The author first speaks about the many who have 'undertaken to draw up an account of the things that have been fulfilled among us'. The expression *anataxasthai diēgēsin* (TNIV 'to draw up an account') implies a completed narrative rather than a loose collection of sayings or stories. It presumably included Mark's Gospel, which appears to have been a major source for Luke's first volume. The accounts that the author mentions were themselves based on evidence transmitted by 'those who from the first were eyewitnesses and servants of the word'. So he does not denigrate his predecessors or question their reliability, but he still feels the need to offer more to Theophilus, to give him appropriate 'certainty' *(asphaleia)* or assurance about the things he has been taught.[65] Doubtless there were other sources in more fragmentary form that he discovered and wanted to incorporate in his first volume (special Lukan material that appears in no other Gospel, as well as some material in common with Matthew, but not Mark). Nevertheless, having himself 'carefully investigated everything from the beginning', he also wished to write about events subsequent to the life, death, and resurrection of Jesus, and to tell about the people who were involved in those events. Luke mentions 'servants of the word' *(hypēretai tou logou)* and summarizes their subject matter in 'fulfillment' terms *(tōn peplērophorēmenōn en hēmin pragmatōn*, 'the things that have been fulfilled among us'). By implication, Luke will also present a theological way of viewing things.[66]

When he claims to write 'in order' *(kathexēs*; TNIV 'an orderly account'), the reference could be to chronological, geographical, or logical order, incorporating the diverse and extensive material in Acts to give a more complete and convincing picture of 'the things that have been fulfilled among us'.[67] The use of similar terminology in Acts 11:4 might suggest that

---

affinities both to historical monographs and to biographies, but it appears to represent a new type of work, of which it is the only example'.

65. Hemer, *Book of Acts,* 327, wisely observes that 'the thrust of the clauses in this carefully structured sentence is cumulative rather than antithetical'. Against the view that *katēchēthēs* ('instructed') implies hostile misinformation and that Theophilus was an influential non-Christian, Hemer, 325, says that this is 'a nuance that is due more to modern arguments about the purpose of Acts than it is to the first-century usage of the term'. Maddox, *Purpose,* 12-15, considers different ways of interpreting Luke 1:1-4

66. Cf. Peterson, 'Fulfillment', 83-104. As 'servants of the word', the eyewitnesses presumably became interpreters of the events they reported.

67. Witherington 1998, 50, rightly observes that 'Luke's concern is with a community's history; it is microhistory, not macrohistory, for it is about what has happened

he means 'an account written in such a fashion and order that one can make sense of or discern the truth in the maze of events'.[68] As noted above, Luke's Gospel seems to have been written so as to anticipate and prepare for the wider perspective presented in Acts. While the latter follows a certain chronological and geographical order, there are gaps and dislocations because the author is to some extent driven by a desire to order his material thematically. So logical, thematic, or theological order may be the primary meaning of the expression in Luke 1:3.

Luke draws attention to his own eyewitness material by casting it in the first person plural. Although some have doubted the authenticity of the 'we' passages, most scholars view these as evidence of the author's participation in the events recorded.[69] Apart from these passages and Luke's possible contact with Paul's mission companions in other places, what might have been his sources for the rest of Acts? Meeting Philip the Evangelist in Caesarea (21:8) presumably gave Luke the opportunity to hear stories about his early ministry and that of his fellow worker Stephen (6:5-6), providing the basis for the material in Acts 6–8.[70] Other Christians in Caesarea could also have told Luke about the strategic visit of Peter to the household of Cornelius and the spread of the gospel in that region (10:1–11:18). Acts 21:10-11 further mentions that Luke met the prophet Agabus in Caesarea, who could have given him information about the early life of the churches of Judea and Antioch (11:27-30). On the way to Jerusalem, Luke stayed with Paul and his team in the house of Mnason (21:16), 'a man from Cyprus and one of the early disciples', who could have been another source of vital information. Contact with the believers in Jerusalem and then with James and the elders is recorded in 21:17-25. Such people must have been able to supply Luke with information about the growth and development of that church from the beginning. Barrett argues in connection with 11:19–15:35 that 'it is certain that Luke received traditional material from Antioch, and that the account that the Antiochenes gave of the origin of their church included the claim that almost from the beginning the Gentiles had been included'.[71] Bruce also suggests that if John Mark of Jerusalem is identical

----

"among us", though it has universal significance and implications as it potentially includes all kinds and races of people'.

68. Witherington 1998, 50. TNIV translates *kathexēs* in Acts 11:4 'the whole story', but the context implies 'in order' from Peter's perspective. The same word is used for chronological order in 3:24, and for geographical order in 18:23.

69. This is discussed above under 'Authorship', with a reference to alternative viewpoints in note 7.

70. Bruce, 1990, 41-42, argues that a change of source is not difficult to discern between chapters 5 and 6. Hemer, *Book of Acts*, 335-64, discusses possible sources for both Luke and Acts in some detail and considers some of the scholarly arguments in this connection. Hemer, 354-55, summarizes the way he thinks Luke went about researching and writing his two-volume work.

71. Barrett 1994, 51. Ancient tradition (e.g., Jerome, *De Viris Illustribus* 7) made Luke a native of Antioch, which may or may not be true. Barrett, 54-56, goes on to argue against the

with the second Evangelist and Luke had direct contact with him (cf. Col. 4:10, 14), 'then perhaps it was not only to his Gospel that Luke was indebted for information, but also to his spoken recollection'.[72]

Ellis contends that the evidence points to a cooperative relationship between Luke and 'colleagues involved with the Jacobean mission based in Jerusalem; with the Petrine mission which was active in Caesarea and with which Mark was associated; and with the Johannine mission, which before AD 66 was also active in Judea'.[73] Somewhat speculatively, Ellis describes the situation in the fifties and sixties of the first century, when Luke was gathering his information, as follows:

> At that time, the four apostolic missions of James, Paul, Peter and John worked cooperatively, though not without tensions, to promote the messianic person and teaching of Jesus. Each mission made available its respective traditions for the use of others, and all four showed in other ways a unity in the midst of the diversity that characterized this major sector of first-century Christianity from which our New Testament came forth. Each mission produced a Gospel, initially for use in its own congregations. Luke's Gospel and Acts were published initially for use in the congregations of the Pauline (Gentile) mission, as the structure and development of Luke-Acts show.[74]

If Luke was a companion of Paul on some of his journeys, he doubtless learned much from him personally about his conversion and early ministry, and even possibly gained something of Paul's perspective on the development of Christianity in Jerusalem before he was converted. One of the most vexed questions for many scholars, however, concerns the degree to which the Paul of Acts differs from the Paul revealed in his letters, especially with reference to key theological issues. How well did Luke know Paul, and how well did he represent him and his teaching when writing Acts? Allied to this, there are questions about whether Luke used any of Paul's letters as source material, and whether the chronology of Acts can be reconciled with evidence from the letters about Paul's movements. Where conflict between Acts and the letters is discerned, how should this be resolved?

Wenham has shown how frequently the Pauline letters and Acts intersect. But he concludes that 'much of the story of Paul in Acts has no basis in the letters and some of the strongly emphasized features of the letters are

---

view that there was a written Antiochian source, though he suggests that written inquiries to the great centres of Christian growth may have supplied Luke with written replies.

72. Bruce 1990, 45. Longenecker 2007, 681-86, considers the possible sources of Acts in some detail.

73. E. E. Ellis, *The Making of the New Testament Documents* (Leiden: Brill, 1999), 401-2. He discusses the sources of Acts more specifically on pp. 403-4.

74. Ellis, *Making*, 404-5.

not in Acts (e.g. the collection), so that it is highly probable that Luke had other sources of information about Paul (as may in any case be inferred from the "we" sections of Acts)'.[75] Although there are many points of contact — and there is value in comparing the evidence of Acts with the letters where possible — Luke offers a different perspective on Paul's ministry. Some have taken this to mean that Luke was misinformed, or deliberately misleading, or presenting an ideal or legendary Paul. But it is important to remember the occasional nature of Paul's letters, the limited scope of Luke's description of Paul, and his own distinctive agenda in writing. Witherington has rightly suggested that 'if Luke's account is tendentious and apologetic in character, Paul's letters, especially in the biographical remarks are equally so'.[76] Both sources must be read critically and consulted carefully to make a proper evaluation of all the evidence. Luke's interests are not primarily biographical but historical, 'and so he chronicles the part Paul plays in the advance of the gospel from Jerusalem to Rome, his roles as evangelist, teacher, preacher, rhetorician, and missionary, giving only brief mention to his pastoral roles'.[77] Bruce concludes his examination of the issues by claiming that the Paul whose portrait Luke paints is nevertheless the real Paul. 'It is the real Paul viewed in retrospect by a friend and admirer, whose own religious experience was different from Paul's, who expresses a distinctive theological outlook, who writes for another constituency than that for which Paul wrote his letters.'[78]

B. Rhetoric

'Rhetoric has to do with persuasion, specifically the persuasive powers of words, spoken or written.'[79] In the first century AD, some works which claimed to be history 'often owed more to declamation and Greco-Roman rhetoric than to careful historical study of sources and consulting of wit-

75. D. Wenham, 'Acts and the Pauline Corpus, II: The Evidence of the Parallels', in Winter and Clarke, *Ancient Literary Setting*, 257. Hemer, *Book of Acts*, 181-90, gives an extensive list of possible links between Acts and the letters attributed to Paul.

76. Witherington 1998, 431. On pp. 77-97 he examines issues of chronology, comparing Acts with Paul's letter to the Galatians. On pp. 432-38, he deals with the charge that Luke has distorted the social status and abilities of Paul and distorted his theology. He takes particular issue with the arguments of P. Vielhauer, 'On the "Paulinism" of Acts', in L. E. Keck and J. L. Martyn (eds.), *Studies in Luke-Acts: Essays Presented in Honor of Paul Schubert* (Nashville: Abingdon, 1966; London: SPCK, 1976), 33-50, and Barrett. Cf. J. Jervell, *The Unknown Paul* (Minneapolis: Augsburg, 1984), 68-76; Bock 2007, 16-18.

77. Witherington 1998, 438. Cf. F. F. Bruce, 'Paul in Acts and Letters', in *DPL*, 679-92, for a fuller comparison of the Paul in Acts and in the letters.

78. Bruce 1990, 59.

79. Satterthwaite, 'Classical Rhetoric', 338. He distinguishes between 'primary rhetoric', which was the art of persuasive public speech, and 'secondary rhetoric', which was 'the use of "primary" rhetoric in literature whose main focus was not a public speech; for example, historical accounts, philosophical treatises, drama and poetry'.

nesses'.[80] There was actually a debate among historians about how much rhetorical material should be included in their writings, with a special concern about the use of speeches. The debate was specifically over 'whether distortion or free invention was allowable in a historical work in the service of higher rhetorical aims'.[81] Luke appears to be on the side of those who were cautious about the use of rhetorical techniques. Even in the speeches, his concern for style seems to have been subordinated to his concern for faithfulness to his sources.[82] However, given that ancient historical works were meant to be *heard* primarily and read only secondarily, 'if Luke wished for Theophilus to give *ear* to the case he was making, he would almost certainly have had to give attention to the rhetorical properties and potentialities of his composition'.[83]

Ancient historians did not record speeches in their works as mere commentary on events, nor simply as transcripts or accompaniments to events. Gempf insists that 'speeches must be seen *as* events in their own right'.[84] Since these historians regularly used their own vocabulary and style in recording speeches, the question about the authenticity of the process has often been raised. Gempf acknowledges that 'the write-up of a speech in an ancient history *does call* for rhetorical skill simply because the author must, while being faithful to the main lines of the historical "speech-event", adapt the speech to make it "speak to" a new audience in a different situation'.[85] But he contends that, 'just as a writer was expected to represent faithfully the strategies, tactics and results of a battle, but not necessarily all the fine movements of each combatant, so a writer was expected to represent faithfully the strategies, tactics and results of a speech, without necessarily recording the exact words used on the day'.[86] Just because a speech is in line

---

80. Witherington 1998, 40. He cites Livy and Tacitus as two different examples and says that 'some ancients even considered history and history writing a subset or part of the science of rhetoric'.

81. Witherington 1998, 41.

82. Cf. F. F. Bruce, *The Speeches in the Acts of the Apostles*, Tyndale New Testament Lecture 1942 (London: Tyndale, 1944); 'The Speeches in Acts — Thirty Years After', in R. Banks (ed.), *Reconciliation and Hope*, Festschrift for L. Morris (Grand Rapids: Eerdmans, 1974), 53-68; Hemer, *Book of Acts*, 41-42, 415-27.

83. Witherington 1998, 42.

84. C. Gempf, 'Public Speaking and Published Accounts', in Winter and Clarke, *Ancient Literary Setting*, 261. D. Aune, *The New Testament in Its Literary Environment* (Philadelphia: Westminster, 1987), 125, argues that 'in Thucydides speeches function as a commentary on events. In Luke-Acts, speeches are an essential feature of the action itself, which is the spread of the word of God'. Satterthwaite, 'Classical Rhetoric', 356-57, outlines the various ways in which speeches in Acts are used in relation to narratives.

85. Gempf, 'Public Speaking', 264. Gempf, 265, insists that speeches had to fit in stylistically and thematically with the author's work, but they also had to fit 'the speaker and the reported historical situation'. This, of course, does not establish the historicity of a given speech unless sources were faithfully used. Gempf, 291-94, critiques the scepticism of Cadbury and Dibelius regarding the historical dimension of the speeches in ancient histories and in Acts.

86. Gempf, 'Public Speaking', 264. Gempf, 266-85, goes on to discuss the practices

with what the author of a book is known to believe is not sufficient ground for dismissing the record of that speech as invention. Gempf concludes:

> In determining historical *faithfulness*, the most important clues are likely to come in weighing whether a speech shows 1. traces of the alleged situation into which it was purported to have been delivered and 2. traces of the personality and traits of the alleged speaker. If discontinuities appear, then there is reason for questioning the faithfulness of the speech to the event.[87]

But there may be more than 'traces' in Luke's work. Witherington is convinced that 'Luke's use of the art of persuasion is more like that of the serious earlier Greek historians such as Polybius than it is of a Livy or a Dionysius of Halicarnassus'.[88] Luke's Greek style does not involve an indulgence in rhetorical excess. He even varies his style to be more Semitic in the early chapters of the Gospel and Acts, where the focus is on Jerusalem and the temple. There are obvious stylistic differences between narrative and speeches, with Luke's rhetorical skills 'more in evidence in the preface and speeches than elsewhere in Luke-Acts'.[89] Witherington notes few moralizing asides or other sorts of intrusions or digressions in Acts. Apart from a few aspects of the final travel narrative, most of the narrative 'could not be said to be intended for entertainment. The tone and purpose of the account seem far too serious for that.'[90]

Nevertheless, Luke's choice and arrangement of his material shows him to be operating 'according to conventions similar to those outlined in classical rhetorical treatises'.[91] Satterthwaite evaluates Luke's narrative method in the light of a proposed apologetic aim: 'to show that Jesus and the church he founded were God's fulfillment of his promises to Israel, thereby assuring both Jewish and Gentile believers of the reliability of the message they have heard, and of God's faithfulness'.[92] He notes that there

---

and views of several famous Greek and Roman historians. He then deals with Jewish practice and precedents in history writing.

87. Gempf, 'Public Speaking', 301.

88. Witherington 1998, 43. Polybius 2.56.1-13 was notably cautious in proposing that 'it was the task of the historian to teach and persuade, but to do so by a selection of events and speeches that record what really happened or really was said, however commonplace'. (Witherington, 42). Witherington, 46-49, goes on to discuss the approach of Thucydides to the recording of speeches in historical narrative settings.

89. Witherington 1998, 44.

90. Witherington 1998, 45. However, see R. P. Thompson, *Keeping the Church in its Place: The Church as Narrative Character in Acts* (New York/London: Clark, 2006), 9-17, on ancient narrative texts, readers, and the reading process.

91. Satterthwaite, 'Classical Rhetoric', 378. Cf. B. W. Winter, 'Official Proceedings and the Forensic Speeches in Acts 24–26', in Winter and Clarke, *Ancient Literary Setting*, 305-36, on rhetoric and legal proceedings in Acts 24–26.

92. Satterthwaite, 'Classical Rhetoric', 347. Cf. Maddox, *Purpose*, 31-56, 182-87; L. T. Johnson, *The Acts of the Apostles*, Sacra Pagina 5 (Collegeville: Liturgical, 1992), 7-9; Peterson, 'Fulfillment', 100-104.

are patterns and themes that run through Acts and unify it. The book falls into four sections of roughly equal length, each of which records a further spread of the gospel message and of the community of believers. Luke arranges the proportions of his narrative within this broader framework, so as to underscore his theological themes. His repetition and amplification of certain events is entirely in line with classical rhetorical ideals, not simply by multiplying words but by using 'heightened diction and striking presentation of events'.[93]

In addition to the summarising comments and evaluations of people and events which occur in the narrative of Acts, Satterthwaite further observes what he calls 'implicit commentary'. Techniques such as simple juxtaposition of events, analogical patterning of events, and interplay between narration and dialogue are used to give meaning and significance to the developing narrative, following the practices of classical writers.[94] Such writers also had much to say about style. Luke's word usage, sentence construction, and verbal artistry are compared with ancient discussions on these matters, showing the extent to which his narrative conforms to classical requirements.[95]

Satterthwaite concludes his very helpful comparison of Acts with the rhetorical treatises of the Greco-Roman world by drawing attention to the persuasive qualities of Acts. In some contexts there is *overt persuasion*, as in the speeches, recurring summaries, and explicit evaluative or interpretative comments (e.g., 10:2; 11:24; 12:23; 13:48; 16:14; 17:11). *Covert persuasion* comes with the presentation of the character and behaviour of apostles and other believers in a positive light. Those who oppose them emerge in a less favourable light.[96] Then there is the *treatment of opposing viewpoints* (e.g., 5:34-39; 6:13-14; 16:19-21; 17:6-7; 18:12-13; 19:35-40; 24:5-8), where readers are challenged to compare these views with the recorded events and the beliefs of Luke's main characters. Luke appears to have been given 'the kind of (rhetorical) education one would expect in a Graeco-Roman writer of this period who embarked on a work of this sort'.[97] However, he was no slave to classical conventions, as his use of the OT and Semitic patterns of speech would indicate. A reader with some rhetorical appreciation would be alert to the significance of many of the techniques highlighted above. Such a reader might therefore be impressed by 'the care with which Luke

93. Satterthwaite, 'Classical Rhetoric', 353. Summary statements and other linking devices are used to demonstrate progress and development in the narrative. Cf. 'Literary Approaches to Acts' and 'Some Editorial Techniques with Thematic Implications' below.

94. Satterthwaite, 'Classical Rhetoric', 360-67. Recent scholarship has highlighted such techniques in OT narratives as well, so that Satterthwaite is prepared to conclude that Luke may have been influenced by either or both of these bodies of literature.

95. Cf. Satterthwaite, 'Classical Rhetoric', 367-75.

96. Cf. Satterthwaite, 'Classical Rhetoric', 376-67. Thompson, *Church*, 17-28, discusses more fully the importance and function of characters in ancient narratives.

97. Satterthwaite, 'Classical Rhetoric', 378.

presents his account, and the seriousness with which he takes possible objections'.[98]

C. Historical Reliability

For a variety of reasons, many writers have expressed distrust in Luke's historical method and scepticism about the historical value of Acts. Some of the reasons have already been listed or implied: uncertainty about Luke's sources and the freedom with which he handled them; doubts about Luke's knowledge of Paul, his letters, his theology, and details of his ministry; and concern about the degree to which Luke's theological and apologetic agenda has distorted his constructing of speeches and narratives. Hemer contends that 'opinion about the book of Acts has become polarized, and often between those who differ profoundly on the matter of historicity, but this aspect of their disagreement is often implicit rather than explicit'.[99]

Hemer has provided the most comprehensive recent study of these issues, arguing that it is important 'to judge Luke by the standards of his own day, whether or not we conclude that he was consciously influenced by them or measured himself by them'.[100] The sources for Hemer's contextual study of Acts are literary works which are roughly contemporary with Luke's publication, together with inscriptions and other archaeological evidence. Comparing Luke's work with the practices of ancient historians and their views about the historian's task, he observes among them 'the existence of a distinctive and rigorous theory of historiography'.[101] This involved a stress on the value of eyewitness participation and the importance of interviewing eyewitnesses; 'the limitation of coverage to material where the writer has privileged access to evidence of guaranteed quality'; mention of the value of travel to the scene of events; 'the prospect then (and for us) of checking details with contemporary documents'; 'the occasional in-

---

98. Satterthwaite, 'Classical Rhetoric', 379.

99. Hemer, *Book of Acts*, 1. He goes on to give a brief overview of scholarship on the historicity of Acts in the century before he himself writes and considers why it is important to revisit the issue (pp. 3-29). Later he provides a brief selection of opposing views on Luke's historical reliability (pp. 101-2). Cf. Marguerat, *First Christian Historian*, 1-5.

100. Hemer, *Book of Acts*, 43. Hemer, 47, therefore seeks to establish 'whether Luke is habitually and in general a trustworthy source by the standards of his day, whether he exhibits accuracy or inaccuracy of mind, a general conscience for, or a general disregard of, historical fact'.

101. Hemer, *Book of Acts*, 100, summarising the findings of his chapter on ancient historiography. Bruce 1990, 29-31, specifically discusses Luke's method in relation to the views of Lucian of Samosata on the writing of history. Cf. Marguerat, *First Christian Historian*, 13-25. Bruce contends that, by the exacting standards of some who wrote about the requirements of good historiography in the Greco-Roman world, Luke's work shapes up well.

sistence on the use of sources for speeches'; and 'the vigour of the concept of "truth" in history "as it actually happened"'.[102]

Hemer explores in some detail the types of knowledge displayed in Acts. This involves the correlation of external, especially documentary, sources with inconsequential details in Acts, where the issue of theological bias can hardly be raised. He first investigates 'items of geographical detail and the like which may be assumed to have been generally known'.[103] He then goes on to consider 'more specialized details, which may still have been widely known to those who possessed relevant experience: titles of governors, army units, major routes, etc., which may have been accessible to those who travelled or were involved in administration, but perhaps not to those without such backgrounds'.[104] After this he turns to 'specifics of local routes, boundaries, titles of city magistrates, and the like, which may not be closely controllable in date, but are unlikely to have been known except to a writer who had visited the districts'.[105] The latter two categories of evidence suggest that the author of Acts had at least travelled to many of the places mentioned in his narrative.

Hemer then attempts a correlation of the dates of known kings and governors with 'the ostensible chronology of the Acts framework'.[106] This is followed by a study of details in the narrative of Acts which are broadly suggestive of date, correlations between Acts and the letters attributed to Paul, latent internal correlations within Acts, details involving differences between Alexandrian and Western texts of Acts, unstudied allusions in Acts to geographical and other factors, together with several other categories of research.[107]

Hemer admits that 'there is no simple correspondence between the confirmation of individual details and the overall historicity of a book'.[108] After all, it is possible to have a fictional narrative with accuracies of locality and background included! However, his research shows how strikingly careful Luke was about such details, and he contrasts the carelessness of the Jewish historian Josephus in this regard. To suggest that 'the historical components are there to give topicality or verisimilitude to Paul as a lay-figure of Lukan theology seems forced beyond all probability.

102. Hemer, *Book of Acts*, 100. Bruce 1990, 34, concludes that Luke's purpose was didactic and religious, but this necessitated 'no falling away from the standards expected in ancient historians'. He notes that history writing in antiquity had a confessedly didactic quality and purpose that could 'co-exist with the strictest canons of accuracy'.

103. Hemer, *Book of Acts*, 104. These are itemised on p. 107.

104. Hemer, *Book of Acts*, 104. These are itemised on p. 108.

105. Hemer, *Book of Acts*, 104. These are itemised on pp. 108-58 and form a considerable list, even though the comparisons are drawn exclusively from Acts 13–28. Many of the contextual items have only recently come to light with the publication of new collections of papyri and inscriptions from the Greco-Roman world of the first century AD.

106. Hemer, *Book of Acts*, 104. These are itemised on pp. 159-75.

107. Cf. Hemer, *Book of Acts*, 175-218, and subsequent chapters.

108. Hemer, *Book of Acts*, 219.

Even to treat Acts as a theological treatise or polemical document which incorporates historical traditions from a diary or itinerary-source seems to risk making a difficult mixture of a book which appears to have a more integrated unity of character.'[109] Hemer rightly concludes that a more satisfactory view must explore how history and theology work together in Acts.

Marguerat begins his helpful discussion of Luke's historical method by saying that it is not to be judged on its conformity to so-called 'brute facts', but 'according to the *point of view of the historian* which controls the writing of the narrative, *the truth* that the author aims to communicate and *the need for identity* to which the historian responds'.[110] He follows Ricoeur in identifying three types of historiography: there is *documentary* history, which seeks to establish the verifiable facts, *explicative* history, which evaluates events from a social, economic, or political perspective, and *poetic* history, whose truth lies in 'the interpretation it gives to the past and the possibility it offers to a community to understand itself in the present'.[111] Acts is sometimes documentary and sometimes 'poetic', meaning in this case that there is a theological dimension to the story, whereby God is constantly presented as intervening, saving, or consoling his people.

A documentary approach is evident in the extraordinary attention Acts gives to topographical and sociopolitical details, as noted above. However, this documentary realism is not simply 'the narrative clothing of a fiction created by the author'.[112] All historical work is driven by 'a choice of plot, a narrative setting and the effects of (re)composition. Once the necessary subjectivity of the historian in the construction of the plot of the narrative is recognized, we must abandon the factual/fictional duality as the product of unhealthy rationalism.'[113] Marguerat concurs with the sort of conclusion reached above, that 'Luke is situated precisely at the meeting point of Jewish and Greek historiographical currents. His narrative devices are heavily indebted to the cultural standard in the Roman Empire, that is, history as the Greeks wrote it. However, contrary to the ideal of objectivity found in Herodean and Thucydidean historiography, Luke recounts a confessional history.'[114]

---

109. Hemer, *Book of Acts*, 220.

110. Marguerat, *First Christian Historian*, 6-7 (his emphasis).

111. Marguerat, *First Christian Historian*, 8. Cf. P. Ricoeur, *La Critique et la Conviction* (Paris: Calmy-Lévy, 1995), 131-32.

112. Marguerat, *First Christian Historian*, 11. Marguerat, 10, 238, 249-53, notes that the apocryphal *Acts of Apostles* abandon the historical realism of canonical Acts.

113. Marguerat, *First Christian Historian*, 12. Bock 2007, 4-5, is unhappy with Marguerat's approach, but he does acknowledge that 'it is possible for ideology and historical data to be combined in a way that reflects an appropriate historical perspective'. Cf. Bock, 10-12, on creativity in Acts and other ancient historical works.

114. Marguerat, *First Christian Historian*, 25. Cf. Palmer, 'Monograph', 27; Witherington 1998, 39.

IV. CHARACTER, STRUCTURE, AND PURPOSE

A. Character

1. A Theological History

In broad terms, the narrative of Acts unfolds *geographically* and focuses on the ministry of key *individuals* within each context. The prediction of Jesus about the apostolic witness moving from Jerusalem to Judea, Samaria, and 'to the ends of the earth' (1:8) is shown to be progressively fulfilled.[115] However, this geographical advance is illustrated selectively, and the twelve apostles appointed by Jesus (1:12-26 includes Matthias as a replacement for Judas Iscariot) are not always the ones who take the gospel to the places identified.[116] In the first geographical outreach from Jerusalem (8:5-40), the apostolic witness to the risen Lord Jesus is carried by Philip 'the evangelist' (21:8), with Peter and John having a confirmatory function. Peter then plays a foundational role in preaching the gospel to the Gentiles in Caesarea (10:1–11:18). The outreach to Phoenicia, Cyprus, and Syrian Antioch is significantly extended by a wider group of disciples who were scattered from Jerusalem because of the persecution against the church in that city (11:19-21; cf. 8:1-4). The first half of the book concludes with a further narrative about the suffering of the church in Jerusalem and records the third imprisonment and miraculous release of Peter (12:1-19; cf. 4:1-22 [with John]; 5:17-42 [among the apostles]).

The next main section of the book is occupied with the extension of the gospel from Antioch to Cyprus, Asia Minor, and Greece by Paul and his associates. It is remarkable that Paul is only incidentally called an apostle (14:4, 14) and that Barnabas is included in these references, suggesting a use of the term that differs from the one in 1:12-26. Mostly, Paul is presented as a prophetic figure, whose divinely given role is to complete the task of the Servant of the Lord portrayed by Isaiah, to bring Israel back to God and to take the messianic salvation to the Gentiles (Acts 13:47, citing Is. 49:6; cf. 9:15-16; 22:14-21; 26:15-23; 28:25-28). Although Luke seems to be at pains to point out the parallels between Paul's ministry and that of the Twelve, particularly Peter, there are differences in their calling and the na-

---

115. Witherington 1998, 69, observes that Luke-Acts is interested in 'the universal spread of the good news not only up and down the social scale but geographically outward to the world'. However, it is an oversimplification to say that 'the Gospel focuses on the vertical (up and down the social scale) universalization of the gospel, while Acts focuses on its horizontal universalization (to all peoples throughout the Empire)'. Both agendas are to some extent present in both parts of Luke-Acts.

116. Narrative selectivity is obvious, for example, when we are merely told in a summary statement about the growth of the church in Galilee (9:31) or about the gospel being planted in Cyprus and Phoenicia (11:19). Contrastingly, there are developed narratives about the foundation of the church in Syrian Antioch (11:20-26), Pisidian Antioch (13:13-52), Philippi (16:12-40), and other strategic centres in the Greco-Roman world.

ture of the witness they provide.[117] Acts concludes with the story of Paul's imprisonment in Jerusalem, Caesarea, and Rome, recording the trials he endured and the opportunities he had to testify to Christ (21:27–28:31).

This highly selective history is about *some* acts of *some* apostles, but more broadly about a range of people used by God to take the apostolic witness to Jews and Gentiles in various centres of the Roman Empire.[118] There is a major focus on Paul and his contribution to this work in the second half of the book, where the issue of Jews and Gentiles in the plan of God continues to surface in various ways. Indeed, there is a concern throughout the book about Jewish unbelief and opposition, accompanied by various assertions about the hope of Israel being found in Jesus and his resurrection (e.g., 4:1-2, 11-12; 13:16-41; 17:1-3; 23:6; 24:14-16, 21; 26:6-8, 19-23). This climaxes in Paul's encounter with the Jews of Rome and his final pronouncement on the subject (28:17-28, citing Is. 6:9-10). From beginning to end, however, the ascended Lord is shown to be sovereign over everything that happens, furthering his purpose in the world through his word and his Spirit. Working through those who call upon his name, he continues to bring Jews and Gentiles to himself and to unite them in the fellowship of his church. Acts is a theological history in the sense that it records God's activity in fulfillment of Scripture and other forms of revelation noted by Luke, such as visions and dreams.[119] Every major event is viewed in the light of this outworking of God's plan.

2. A Narrative Dominated by Speeches

Acts contains a surprising number of speeches, which convey theological perspectives on reported events and carry the narrative forward.[120] These include addresses by *Christians* to groups of believers about community issues (1:15-22 [Peter]; 6:2-4 [the Twelve]; 11:4-17 [Peter]; 15:7-21 [Peter and James]; 20:18-35 [Paul]), and speeches by *unbelievers* concerning the beliefs and behaviour of Christians (5:35-9 [Gamaliel]; 19:25-27 [Demetrius the silversmith]; 19:35-40 [the city clerk in Ephesus]; 24:2-8 [the lawyer Tertullus];

---

117. A. C. Clark, *Parallel Lives: The Relation of Paul to the Apostles in the Lucan Perspective* (Carlisle: Paternoster, 2001), explores the extensive parallels between Peter and Paul in the narrative of Acts and considers the implications. A. C. Clark, 'The Role of the Apostles', in I. H. Marshall and D. Peterson (eds.), *Witness to the Gospel: The Theology of Acts* (Grand Rapids/Cambridge: Eerdmans, 1998), 169-90, examines the apostleship of Paul in relation to that of the Twelve. Cf. Maddox, *Purpose*, 66-82.

118. Cf. P. G. Bolt, 'Mission and Witness', in Marshall and Peterson, *Witness to the Gospel*, 191-214.

119. See the section on Acts as a narrative of fulfillment below.

120. Cf. H. F. Bayer, 'The Preaching of Peter in Acts', in Marshall and Peterson, *Witness to the Gospel*, 257-74; H.-W. Neudorfer, 'The Speech of Stephen', in Marshall and Peterson, 275-94; G. W. Hansen, 'The Preaching and Defence of Paul', in Marshall and Peterson, 295-324.

25:14-21, 24-27 [Governor Festus]).[121] Some speeches are *defences* by Christians on trial before various authorities, quite often with an evangelistic edge to them (4:8-12; 5:29-32; 7:2-56; 22:1-21; 24:10-21; 26:2-23; 28:17-20). Mostly, however, speeches by Christians to Jewish or Gentile audiences are explicitly *evangelistic* and are designed to persuade them to believe and turn to Christ (2:14-39; 3:12-26; 10:34-43; 13:16-41, 46-47; 14:15-17; 17:22-31; 27:21-26; 28:23-38).[122]

Ancient historians recorded speeches in their writings for various reasons. Generally, they were designed to lighten the narrative and please the reader.[123] More specifically, they were meant to give insight into the total situation from different angles, to give meaning to specific events, to reveal the character of speakers, to convey general ideas concerning particular events, and to further the action of the narrative.[124] In Acts, the numerous speeches unify and illuminate diverse elements of the story. One reason why there is such a large proportion of speeches (about one-third of the text) is that 'Luke is chronicling a historical movement that was carried forward in the main by evangelistic preaching'.[125] The phenomenon of repetition in the mission speeches brings readers back to a common point of reference, namely the main message being communicated by the major characters.[126] Some of the speeches reveal the way the gospel was conveyed

121. This list could be extended to include various dialogue situations in which unbelievers either engage with Christians or express their opinions about Christians to others (e.g., 4:16-17; 17:6-7). It could also include brief addresses by Christians to individuals (e.g., 8:20-23; 21:20-25) or reported addresses by the Lord to believers (e.g., 9:10-16; 18:9), but I have taken 'speeches' to mean more formal, generally public monologues. The boundaries are fluid in some cases (e.g., the apparently private address to Paul by James and the elders in 21:20-25 may also have had a public function). There are also reported speeches in Acts (e.g., 14:22; 15:12; 17:2-3; 24:24-25), which reveal indirectly what the characters said in particular contexts.

122. The kerygmatic character of so many speeches suggests something of a kerygmatic aim for Acts, though not directly, as if it were an evangelistic tract to be handed to unbelievers to persuade them. Luke is developing a theology of the gospel to assure Theophilus and those he represents of the certainty of the things they have been taught (Lk. 1:1-4). There are apologetic issues involved in this presentation, concerning the way in which the apostolic message fulfills OT expectations and forms a church consisting of believing Jews and Gentiles. In addition to this, Luke presents a challenge to Christian readers about faithfulness to the gospel and zeal for gospel growth in the face of suffering, opposition, and conflict among believers. These matters will be explored further below in the section about the purpose of Acts.

123. Cf. G. H. R. Horsley, 'Speeches and Dialogue in Acts', *NTS* 32 (1986), 613.

124. Cf. M. Dibelius, *Studies in the Acts of the Apostles*, ed. H. Greeven; trans. M. Ling (London: SCM, 1956), 139-40.

125. Witherington 1998, 118. Horsley, 'Speeches and Dialogue', 612-13, contrasts the high density of speeches in Acts with the pattern in the works of other ancient historians. Witherington 1998, 39-49, 116-20, deals with the historicity of the speeches in Acts.

126. Cf. Soards, *Speeches*, 189. This is particularly so in connection with the evangelistic or mission addresses. Diversity and repetition in the speeches made it possible for Luke to articulate more fully a message that could not be adequately explained in a single address.

to outsiders, and some portray the way it was misunderstood and opposed. Speeches are part of the action, often being instrumental in precipi-
tating important events (e.g., 1:15-22 leads to the appointment of another
apostle; 2:14-39 brings a large crowd of people to experience the salvation
offered; 6:2-4 initiates a new pattern of ministry and gospel growth in Jerusalem; and 7:2-56 leads to the martyrdom of Stephen, the scattering of
Christians from Jerusalem, and the progress of the gospel in new areas).

Most of the numerous quotations from the OT that appear in Acts are
found in the speeches, notably in chapters 1–15 and 28.[127] There are also important scriptural allusions scattered throughout the speeches and the narrative of Acts more generally. Bock notes how five scriptural themes are developed: the theme of covenant and realized promise for Israel; the role of
Jesus as Messiah in the fulfillment of the divine plan; community mission
or community guidance; the commission to include Gentiles in the promised salvation; and challenge and warning to unbelieving Israel.[128] He concludes that the use of Scripture in Acts 'supports the new community's
claim to the heritage of God revealed in Moses and the prophets' and allows the community to appreciate that her current suffering is 'rooted in
the way of Jesus, who had travelled a similar road'.[129]

3. A Narrative of Fulfillment

The terminology of fulfillment is used extensively throughout Luke-Acts,
and there are also several references to the *plan of God* (Lk. 7:30; Acts 2:23;
4:28; 5:38-39; 13:36; 20:27) or the *will of God* (Lk 11:2; 22:42; Acts 21:14;
22:14). Other expressions similarly indicate God's sovereignty over the
events narrated (e.g., Lk. 22:22; Acts 1:7; 10:42; 17:31; 22:14; 26:16).[130] The
motif of fulfillment is signalled from the beginning of Luke's work (1:1, 20,
45, 46-55), where some of the main themes of the Gospel are introduced.
Here there is a transition from the story of Israel to the story of Jesus, with
godly characters proclaiming the realization of Israel's hopes with the birth
of John the Baptist and Jesus the Messiah. Angelic revelations (1:11-20, 26-
37; 2:9-14) combine with prophetic declarations by those 'filled with the
Holy Spirit' (1:41-45, 46-55, 67-79; 2:25-35, 36-38; 3:1-18) to explain the significance of the great events to follow. These chapters parallel in some respects the Spirit-inspired interpretation of Jesus and his ministry found in

127. Cf. R. N. Longenecker, *Biblical Exegesis in the Apostolic Period* (Grand Rapids:
Eerdmans, 1975), 86-87.
128. D. L. Bock, 'Scripture and the Realisation of God's Promises', in Marshall and
Peterson, *Witness to the Gospel*, 49-62.
129. Bock, 'Scripture and the Realisation of God's Promises', 62.
130. A fuller version of the argument presented in this section may be found in Peterson, 'Fulfillment', 83-104, where all the terminology used to convey these ideas is discussed.
Cf. Marguerat, *First Christian Historian*, 38-40, 85-108, on the providence of God in Acts.

the speeches of Acts. In a variety of ways, Luke 1–2 uses OT prophecy to proclaim the messiahship of Jesus, but not in the manner of a simple 'proof from prophecy' apologetic.[131]

Jesus' sermon in the synagogue at Nazareth, with its proclamation of the fulfillment of prophecy (4:16-30, citing Is. 61:1-2 with 58:6), becomes a paradigm of what he says and does throughout his ministry. The opposition he receives anticipates the events leading to his crucifixion. His Galilean ministry is climaxed by the revelation that he must 'suffer many things, and be rejected by the elders, the chief priests and the teachers of the law, and he must be killed, and on the third day be raised to life' (9:22). In various ways he is then portrayed as the consummator of redemptive history (e.g., 9:31, 51; 12:50; 18:31; 22:15-22, 37).

Parallel incidents in Luke 24 leave the reader with the impression that a global view of the OT and its promises is necessary for understanding the eschatological plan and purpose of God (vv. 25-27, 44-49). Far from disqualifying Jesus as the Messiah of Israel and Saviour of all, his death and resurrection make it possible for repentance and forgiveness of sins to be 'preached in his name to all nations, beginning at Jerusalem'. With this last clause, the mission that is committed to the disciples is also related to the fulfillment of Scripture.[132] The unfolding of events in Luke's second volume is thus meant to be viewed against the background of OT expectations and Jesus' own predictions.

Acts 1:8 reiterates God's plan to bless the nations through the witness of the apostles, in a geographical outreach from Jerusalem. The rest of the book shows how that happened, with the selection of events illustrating the way Jesus' promise was fulfilled.[133] Peter is the first to use the actual language of fulfillment in Acts, asserting that 'the Scripture had to be fulfilled, in which the Holy Spirit spoke long ago through David concerning Judas, who served as guide for those who arrested Jesus' (1:16). Two citations from Psalms are used to explain the judgment served on Judas and the need to replace him as an apostle. Peter's Pentecost discourse and its sequel (Acts 2:14-41) is then programmatic for the rest of the book, just as the preaching of Jesus in Luke 4:16-30 is foundational for understanding his ministry in the Third Gospel. Peter interprets the coming of the Holy Spirit as the fulfillment of Joel 2:28-32, and links this extraordinary event

---

131. Cf. D. L. Bock, *Proclamation from Prophecy and Pattern: Lucan Old Testament Christology*, JSNTSS 12 (Sheffield: JSOT, 1987), 55-90.

132. Squires, *Plan of God*, 154, rightly observes that 'the two crucial events of Luke's history, namely the passion of Jesus and the mission to the Gentiles, are each authorized and guided by prophecies given in both written and oral forms.'

133. The phrase 'to the ends of the earth' in 1:8 appears to be an allusion to Is. 49:6. This text is actually quoted by Paul in Acts 13:47 as a justification for his pattern of preaching to the Jews first and then turning to the Gentiles. Thus it is implied that there are aspects of the ministry of the Servant of the Lord that must be completed by the disciples of Jesus. His 'fulfillment' of the Servant's role in his death and resurrection does not exhaust the meaning and application of the Servant Songs for the messianic era.

with the resurrection and ascension of Christ, using citations from Psalms 16:8-11; 110:1 to develop his argument.[134] Peter's call for repentance and baptism in the name of Jesus implies the fulfillment of OT promises about an eschatological gift of forgiveness and renewal by the Holy Spirit (2:38; cf. Je. 31:34; Ezk. 36:25-27).

Peter's sermon in the temple precincts (3:12-26) makes another significant claim about the fulfillment of Scripture, maintaining that the pattern of Christ's rejection and suffering is to be found in many parts of the prophetic Scriptures (cf. 4:24-28, citing Pss. 2:1-2; 8:32-35, citing Is. 53:7-8). This sermon also introduces a pattern of argument from Scripture that is reflected in later speeches to Jewish audiences. Peter presents a theological overview of Israel's history, beginning with the declaration of God's saving purpose to Abraham (3:25, citing Gn. 12:3; 22:18). The testimony of the prophets from Moses onward was that God's ultimate plan for Israel and the nations would be fulfilled in the raising up of a particular individual, here identified as a prophet like Moses (3:22-24, citing Dt. 18:15-16). In Stephen's speech the picture is filled out, especially in connection with the role of Moses and the bearing his story has on the rejection of Jesus and his representatives in the messianic era (7:1-53). Sacred history is used to make sense of present-day events. Scripture is used in a polemical way against opponents of the gospel, as well as in a positive way, to expound the significance of Jesus and his saving work (cf. 13:15-41, where this approach is illustrated in Paul's preaching).

Scripture quotations and affirmations of fulfillment are largely confined to the early chapters of Acts and to encounters with Jewish audiences. Nevertheless, the claim that Israel's hopes are fulfilled in the resurrection of the Messiah becomes a dominant note in Paul's trial speeches (23:6; 24:14-15; 26:22-23). Here Paul's defence of his call and missionary activity is also part of a wider apology for the Gentile mission. The concluding chapters are presented as the outworking of Paul's divinely led aspiration to visit Rome (19:21) and the Lord's confirming promise (23:11).[135] Once again the effect is to show how everything occurred in accordance with God's plan. Luke-Acts ends where it began, with a declaration of the fulfillment of Scripture in the events recorded (28:23-28). Above all, the author sees 'the worldwide extension of the gospel as the fulfillment of God's self-revelation progressively imparted in earlier days through mighty work and prophetic word, as recorded in the Hebrew scriptures'.[136]

Luke's focus on the divine control or guidance of history would have been familiar to those who knew the Jewish Scriptures. But in Mediterra-

---

134. In the flow of the narrative, Pentecost also appears to be the fulfillment of the prediction of Jesus in Acts 1:4-5, which is itself based on what the Father promised in Scripture.

135. Paul himself acts as a prophet in Acts 20:22-25, 28-31; 27:21-26, and various aspects of the narrative are used to show the fulfillment of these predictions.

136. Bruce 1990, 63-64.

nean antiquity more generally the belief was also widespread that a divine necessity controls human history. Providence was a central theme in Hellenistic historiography, where it often had an apologetic or religious application.[137] Allied to this was the concept of history's fulfilling oracles, whether written or oral. So, 'whether Luke's community was composed of former Jews or pagans — or both — his original readers would have found no surprises in the theme of history's course being determined by the fulfillment of oracles/prophecies'.[138]

In the Hellenistic age it was common for a people to try to trace its own origins back to the remotest antiquity (e.g., Josephus, *Against Apion* 2.152; Diodorus 1.44.4; 1.96.2). So it is likely that Luke emphasized the OT roots of Christianity and the fulfillment of Scripture in the events that he records for more than religious reasons. His approach would have given Greek-speaking Christians the chance to appeal to an argument from antiquity, allowing them to feel 'not the least bit inferior to pagans with their cultural and religious claims allegedly rooted in antiquity'.[139] At one level, therefore, the theme of the fulfillment of prophecy is 'a legitimation device' in the Lukan narrative, just as it was in Mediterranean antiquity generally. In a social context where such matters were considered important, it offered Christians a confident basis from which to address their contemporaries. However, at a theological level, it also offered a profound explanation and justification for the great events being narrated, thus providing assurance for Christians with regard to their own faith and identity.

B. Structure

1. *The Progress of 'the Word'*

There are many references to evangelism in Acts, using a variety of terms, and there are many examples of evangelism in action. Evangelistic speeches convey the contents of the message presented by different characters in different situations. In this gospel-centred framework, Luke regularly uses the Greek noun *logos* ('word') to describe the actual message proclaimed by Jesus and his followers.[140] When it is called 'the word of God'

137. Cf. Squires, *Plan of God*, 36; J. T. Squires, 'The Plan of God in the Acts of the Apostles', in Marshall and Peterson, *Witness to the Gospel*, 37-39.

138. C. H. Talbert, 'The Fulfillment of Prophecy in Luke-Acts', in *Reading Luke: A Literary and Theological Commentary on the Third Gospel* (New York: Crossroad, 1982), 238. Cf. C. H. Talbert, *Luke-Acts: New Perspectives from the Society of Biblical Literature Seminar* (New York: Crossroad, 1984), 91-103.

139. Talbert, 'Fulfillment', 240. However, such views need to be weighed against the argument of Marguerat, *First Christian Historian*, 31-34, that Acts is 'a narrative of beginnings'. There is a newness about what Luke records, but it has profound links with what was revealed beforehand in the Scriptures of Israel.

140. The word 'gospel' (*euangelion*) occurs only twice in Acts (15:7; 20:24). However,

(4:31; 6:2, 7; 8:14; 11:1; 12:24; 13:5, 7, 44, 46, 48; 16:32; 17:13; 18:11) or 'the word of the Lord' (8:25; 13:49; 15:35, 36; 19:10, 20), the divine origin and authority of the gospel are being asserted. Consistent with certain OT reflections on the nature and power of the word of God (e.g., Ps. 33:6-11; Is. 55:10-11; Je. 1:9-12; 23:21-29), the gospel is presented as a dynamic force at work in the world (6:7; 12:24; 19:20), transforming the lives of those who receive it (2:41; 8:14; 11:1; 17:11), as it spreads (13:49), and is praised or honoured by those who believe it (13:48). Marguerat suggests that the leading theme of Acts is 'neither the history of the Church, nor the activity of the Spirit, but the expansion of the Word. The real hero of the Acts of the Apostles is the *logos*, the Word.'[141] However, when I discuss characterisation later in this chapter, I conclude that the ascended Lord Jesus is the central figure in the narrative, and that he employs his word and his Spirit to advance his purpose through human agents in the world.

The growth of the word is clearly coextensive with the growth of the church. The same Greek verb *plēthynein* is used for the 'increase' in the number of disciples (6:1; 9:31) and for the increase of the word (6:7; 12:24). This recalls the use of such language in the OT to express 'the promise and realization of the growth and expansion of God's covenant People'.[142] These texts are part of a series of eight summaries of church growth in Acts (2:47; 5:14; 6:7; 11:21, 24; 12:24; 16:5; 19:20). Luke also uses the verb to 'grow' in connection with 'the word' (6:7; 12:24; 19:20, *auxanein*), recalling Jesus' parable about the seed of the word of God being sown in good soil and yielding an amazing crop (Lk. 8:4-15).[143] This unusual application of the language of increase and growth signifies *the advance of the gospel and the movement it creates*. Each of the key editorial markers (6:7; 12:24; 19:20) climaxes a section of the narrative recording the resolution of some conflict or the cessation of opposition and persecution. The gospel is shown to pros-

---

the related verb 'evangelise', or 'preach the gospel' *(euangelizomai)*, is used extensively throughout Luke-Acts, together with other terms of proclamation and persuasion. *Ta rhēmata tauta* ('these words') refers to the gospel in 10:44; 13:42 (cf. *ta rhēmata tēs zōēs tautēs*, 'the words of this life', 5:2), and in Lk. 3:2 *rhēma theou* ('the word of God') refers to the message which came to John the Baptist from God.

141. Marguerat, *First Christian Historian*, 37. Cf. B. S. Rosner, 'The Progress of the Word', in Marshall and Peterson, *Witness to the Gospel*, 215-33; D. W. Pao, *Acts and the Isaianic New Exodus*, WUNT 2, no. 130 (Tübingen: Mohr, 2000; repr. Grand Rapids: Baker Academic, 2002), 49, 147-79.

142. J. Kodell, '"The Word of God Grew" — The Ecclesial Tendency of *Logos* in Acts 6:7; 12:24; 19:20', *Biblica* 55 (1974), 511. The language of the creation mandate (Gn. 1:22, 28; 8:17; 9:1, 7) becomes the basis for the promise that God will grow and multiply his chosen people (Gn. 28:3; 35:11; 47:27; 48:4; Ex. 1:7; Lv. 26:9; Je. 3:16; 23:3). Luke takes up this formula from the LXX 'to fit his presentation of the growth and expansion of the New Testament People of God'. Cf. Pao, *New Exodus*, 155-58, 168-69, 176, on the OT background to this word usage.

143. Kodell, 'The Word of God Grew', 517, observes that 'the flourishing of the early Christian community was proof positive for Luke that the word had fallen on good soil and was bearing fruit'.

per in spite of, and even because of, suffering. By implication, 'nothing can stop the gospel but its spread still causes grief and loss'.[144] Four major sections of Acts are suggested by these texts:[145]

> **1:1–6:7   Development of the church in Jerusalem under the leadership of the Twelve.** The transitional summary in 6:7 indicates that growth of the word followed the satisfactory resolution of conflict in the church with the appointment of the Seven (cf. 6:1-6).
>
> **6:8–12:24   Spontaneous expansion to Judea, Samaria, and Gentile areas, with a widening of ministry to include the Seven and others scattered because of the persecution in Jerusalem.** The transitional summary in 12:24 indicates that growth of the word followed the release of Peter from prison and the death of Herod, the persecutor of the church (cf. 12:1-23).
>
> **12:25–19:20   Planned geographical expansion into Asia Minor and Europe, under the leadership of Paul, emanating from Antioch in Syria.** The transitional summary in 19:20 indicates that growth of the word in Ephesus was specifically related to the overcoming of demonic opposition and the power of magic (cf. 19:11-19).
>
> **19:21–28:31   The word of the Lord continues to grow and prevail, even though Paul is persecuted and arrested.** The focus is on Paul's testimony to the gospel when he is on trial, climaxing with the statement about his freedom to preach when under arrest in Rome (28:30-31). At the same time, various travel companions are mentioned and supportive groups of believers are encountered in his journey, suggesting that the progress of the word will continue through such as these, no matter what happens to Paul.

2. Further Indications of Expansion and Church Growth

The four 'panels' of Acts noted above can be subdivided into six, if the significance of two related editorial markers is noted.[146] A reference to the

---

144. P. R. House, 'Suffering and the Purpose of Acts', *JETS* 33 (1990), 323. Cf. S. Cunningham, *'Through many tribulations': The Theology of Persecution in Luke-Acts*, JSNTSS 142 (Sheffield: Sheffield Academic, 1997); B. Rapske, 'Opposition to the Plan of God and Persecution', in Marshall and Peterson, *Witness to the Gospel*, 235-56.

145. Cf. M. H. Grumm, 'Another Look at Acts', *ExpT* 96 (1985), 335-36. The growth and progress of the word are what Grumm calls 'the *cantus firmus* of the message of Acts' (336). He observes a 'natural' growth of the word as well as a growth stemming directly from opposition and persecution.

146. Longenecker 1981, 233-34; 2007, 695-96, takes Acts 1:1–2:41 to be the Introduc-

church throughout Judea, Galilee, and Samaria enjoying peace and encouragement, and increasing in numbers (9:31, using the verb *plēthynein*), comes immediately after the record of Saul's conversion, signifying an end to the persecution he promoted (cf. 9:1-30). Here the growth of the church is linked to the cessation of opposition from unbelieving outsiders. A reference to the South Galatian churches being strengthened in the faith, so that they 'grew daily in numbers' (16:5, using the verb *perisseuein*), is related to Paul's second visit to that area, delivering the decisions reached by the council in Jerusalem (cf. 15:36–16:4). As in 6:1-7, church growth is once more linked to the cessation of conflict among believers.

A further subdivision acknowledges the extraordinary importance of Paul's Ephesian ministry in Luke's narrative (18:23–20:38). Although this segment does not begin or end with the sort of markers previously noted, it is preceded by a reference to the difficulties experienced by Paul in Corinth (18:12-17), followed by indications of successful ministry in several places (18:18-22). It concludes with Paul's speech about ministry in the face of opposition and with a scene of tender farewell, implying resolution and progress (20:17-38). The Ephesian narratives effectively contain two significant statements about church growth through conflict (19:10, 20), and this theological perspective is reinforced in Paul's farewell speech. This whole section thus forms a summary-conclusion to Luke's total presentation of Paul's mission campaigns.[147] What follows in the travel and trial scenes (21:1–28:31) is a portrayal of Paul in generally more restricted circumstances, making a personal defence for his gospel and ministry.

3. *An Expositional Outline*

Following the pattern suggested by editorial references to growth in the text of Acts, and acknowledging the distinctive importance of the section about Ephesus, the following outline also recognises the need to separate the Introduction (1:1-14) from the beginning of the narrative about the growth of the word in Jerusalem. A more detailed version of this outline appears in the Contents. It is defended at various points in the commentary, as exegetical and theological observations suggest ways in which the narrative is constructed and should be expounded.

I. Introduction and Recapitulation: The Mission Plan of the Risen Lord (1:1-14)
II. The Word in Jerusalem (1:15–6:7)

---

tion and divides the rest of the book into six 'panels', each concluding with a summary statement about growth and progress (6:7; 9:31; 12:24; 16:5; 19:20; 28:31).

147. Tannehill 1990, 230, has helpfully identified the section about Ephesus as the 'climax of Paul's mission as a free man'.

C. Purpose

The previous discussion about the unity of Luke and Acts needs to be kept in mind as the issue of purpose is considered. It really makes a difference if Acts is considered together with the Third Gospel. Although Luke's two-volume work may employ different literary genres, there are sufficient grounds for considering it as one project with a common aim.[148] Focussing particularly on Acts, Bruce wrote that Luke deserves to be called 'the first Christian apologist':

> The great age of Christian apologetic was the second century, but of the three main types of defense represented among the second century Christian apologists, Luke provides first-century prototypes: defense against pagan religion (Christianity is true; paganism is false), defense against Judaism (Christianity is the fulfillment of true Judaism), defense against political accusations (Christianity is innocent of any offense against Roman law).[149]

In fact, the view that Luke-Acts as a whole is an apologetic history has had a number of supporters in recent decades. However, the apologetic aim has been differently understood. For example, O'Neill argues that 'Luke-Acts was primarily an attempt to persuade an educated reading public to become Christians; it was an "apology" in outward form but, like all true apologies, it had the burning inner purpose of bringing men to the faith'.[150]

---

148. Maddox, *Purpose*, 4, rightly observes that we can speak confidently of 'the purpose of Luke-Acts' only if Luke planned the whole work as a unity, though in two volumes.

149. Bruce 1990, 22. Bruce argues that Acts contains a defence against paganism (e.g., 14:15-18) and a defence against Judaism (e.g., 7:2-53; 21:39–28:28). Bruce, 23-25, does not agree with the view that Luke-Acts was written to provide material for Paul's defence at his trial, but he nevertheless discerns a political apologetic throughout. This concerns the innocence of Christianity in relation to Roman law. Bruce offers qualified support to the argument of P. W. Walaskay, *'And so we came to Rome': The Political Perspective of St. Luke*, SNTSMS 49 (Cambridge: Cambridge University, 1983), that Luke also wrote to commend the Roman Empire to Christians. Bruce, 25-27, further notes that there is a sense in which Acts has an apologetic intention with reference to some sections of the church.

150. J. C. O'Neill, *The Theology of Acts in Its Historical Setting* (2nd ed.; London: SPCK, 1970), 176. He acknowledges the need to demonstrate 'the innocence of the Christians of

He rightly opposes the view that it was designed to gain recognition for Christianity by Roman officials, arguing that large portions of Luke-Acts would be irrelevant to such a narrowly defined aim.[151] He rightly highlights the evangelistic dimension of the speeches in Acts and Luke's interest in the progress of the word from Jerusalem to Rome. However, he assumes that Theophilus and those he represents were outsiders who were wrongly or inadequately instructed about Christianity, and needed to be corrected and persuaded about the true significance of what was being proclaimed. But was Luke-Acts published for the benefit of unbelievers or was it designed to help Christians in their engagement with unbelievers? Maddox draws attention to the fact that the work ends with a long section about the imprisonment and trials of Paul, which 'blunts the edge of any suggestion that Luke's aim was evangelistic'.[152]

Acknowledging the presence of apologetic elements in Luke's narrative, Marguerat wisely cautions that this does not yet say what might be 'the apologetic aim of the *narrative itself*'.[153] The decisive question seems to be one of audience.

> It is neither the Synagogue (that bristled at the degradation of the figure of "Jews" on every page), nor the Gentiles ignorant of Christianity (who got lost incessantly in the reminiscences of the LXX). The language of Acts is *a language for the initiated*. The implied reader is the Christian or an interested sympathizer, as, for example, the most excellent Theophilus (Luke 1.3-4; Acts 1.1). Luke's apologetic is addressed to Christian 'insiders' of the movement and a circle which gravitates around it.[154]

Marguerat links Acts with ancient apologetic histories which were designed to 'unfold the identity of a movement by exposing its native traditions, by revealing its cultural dignity and the antiquity of its origins'.[155] He believes that Esler has given a sociological foundation to this view by

---

any revolutionary political tendencies' (p. 179), but insists that this was a subsidiary aim. Cf. Marguerat, *First Christian Historian*, 27-28. O'Neill, 181-85, goes on to consider a number of specific warnings to the church which flow from Luke's apologetic and evangelistic material.

151. Maddox, *Purpose*, 20-21, 91-99, more fully discusses the question of whether Luke-Acts can in any sense be understood as a political apology for Christianity.

152. Maddox, *Purpose*, 181. Maddox, 12-15, considers the options carefully and concludes that there are 'good reasons for doubting that Luke was writing for an audience outside the Christian fellowship'.

153. Marguerat, *First Christian Historian*, 29.

154. Marguerat, *First Christian Historian*, 30. He defines the implied reader as 'the image of the recipient of the narrative, as the text makes him appear (his presupposed knowledge) and as the narrative constructs him (his cooperation in reading the text)'. Cf. D. Marguerat and Y. Bourquin, *How to Read Bible Stories: An Introduction to Narrative Criticism*, trans. J. Bowden (London: SCM, 1999), 14-15.

155. Marguerat, *First Christian Historian*, 30.

describing Luke's programme as a 'sophisticated attempt to explain and
justify Christianity to the members of his community at a time when they
were exposed to social and political pressures which were making their allegiance waver'.[156] The danger with such an approach is to lose the evangelistic dimension entirely. If Luke-Acts was not addressed directly to unbelievers, it must surely have been intended to motivate and equip believers
to bear faithful witness to the apostolic gospel. Marguerat allows for this
when he argues that Luke wanted to help his readers 'to understand and
speak of themselves (to others, to the Jews and the Gentiles)'.[157] Maddox
does the same when he concludes that Luke writes 'to reassure the Christians of his day that their faith in Jesus is no aberration, but the authentic
goal towards which God's ancient dealings with Israel were driving'.[158]
With this reassurance, 'Luke summons his fellow-Christians to worship
God with whole-hearted joy, to follow Jesus with unwavering loyalty, and
to carry on with zeal, through the power of the Spirit, the charge to be his
witnesses to the end of the earth'.[159]

Other recent scholars have also identified Luke-Acts an apologetic
work for a Christian readership. Johnson compares Jewish apologetic literature at the time, which had the dual function of seeking to defend
Jews against misunderstanding and persecution by outsiders, while aim-
ing to help them understand their own traditions within a pluralistic
context.[160] Luke wrote to give his Christian readers 'full confidence' by
the way he told his story 'in sequence' (Lk. 1:3-4). In the broadest sense,
his approach was to write a 'theodicy', defending God's activity in the
world:

> Luke-Acts ostensibly addresses a wider audience in the clothing of
> Greek literature; but its main interest is to construct a continuation of
> the biblical story for Gentile believers in order to help them come to
> grips with the profound puzzle generated by their own recent experi-
> ence.[161]

156. P. F. Esler, *Community and Gospel in Luke-Acts: The Social and Political Motivations of Lucan Theology*, SNTSMS 57 (Cambridge: Cambridge University, 1987), 222. Maddox, *Purpose*, 21-23, 182-83, reviews and critiques four theories concerning issues of faith that Luke may have been addressing in the church of his day. The dominant themes of Luke-Acts are identified as ecclesiology (with special reference to Israel and the promises of the OT) and eschatology (pp. 183-86).

157. Marguerat, *First Christian Historian*, 31 (my emphasis). However, it limits the scope and intent of Luke's work to describe it as 'a tool of self-understanding'. Cf. Longenecker 2007, 676-78, on the kerygmatic purpose of Luke-Acts.

158. Maddox, *Purpose*, 187.

159. Maddox, *Purpose*, 187.

160. L. T. Johnson, *The Gospel of Luke*, Sacra Pagina 3 (Collegeville: Liturgical, 1991), 9. Such literature could provide security or reassurance to Jewish readers 'by demonstrating within a pluralistic context the antiquity and inherent value of their traditions'.

161. Johnson, 7.

Johnson believes that the success of the Gentile mission created 'a serious problem of confidence in the very God who accomplished it'.[162] The failure of many Jews to believe and experience the blessings of the messianic salvation raised questions about the faithfulness of God and his ability to sustain Gentiles in their faith. Luke aims to assure his readers by setting forth 'the sequence of events in the story', showing how God has fulfilled his promises. For all its strengths, Johnson's approach does not sufficiently highlight the problem of persecution from Jewish quarters nor the need to help Christians communicate effectively with Jewish and Gentile opponents. However, Green incorporates these emphases when he proposes that 'the purpose of Luke-Acts would have been to strengthen the Christian movement in the face of opposition by (1) ensuring them in their interpretation and experience of the redemptive purpose and faithfulness of God and by (2) calling them to continued faithfulness and witness in God's salvific project'.[163]

Squires similarly concludes that Luke's work is a kind of cultural 'translation', an attempt to explain and defend Christianity to hellenized Christians. Various techniques familiar to educated readers from contemporary histories are embedded in the story of Luke-Acts to show how the gospel related to their thought-world. Luke's appeal is to 'insiders', using the categories provided by 'outsiders'. Although the primary audience for which Luke writes is the Christian community, his apologetic method offered Christians a 'missionary tool', to assist them in evangelism. Even the prominence of the Hebrew Scriptures and the insistently Jewish practices of Jesus and the earliest Christians in Luke-Acts 'reinforce the notion (essential in the hellenistic context) that Christianity was "no mere novelty", but was able to claim a long antiquity in Israel'.[164] Luke's attempt to outline the continuity between Christians and Israel and between the events of Jesus' career and OT prophecies was an important aspect of his response to criticisms of Christianity that may have been made, both by Jews and by pagans.

V. INTERPRETIVE ISSUES

A. Literary Approaches to Acts

The study of Luke-Acts has been enriched in recent decades as scholars have begun to adopt various literary-critical approaches to the text. Inevitably, the relationship with more conventional historical-critical ap-

---

162. Johnson 1992, 8.

163. Green, *Luke*, 21-22. Green believes that the genre of Luke-Acts suggests that the Evangelist's concern with 'legitimation and apologetic'.

164. Squires, *Plan of God*, 191. Note the way Squires, 192-94, develops the argument that Luke's apology was directed to hellenized Christians.

proaches has become 'uncertain, uneasy and at times antagonistic'.[165] There
has been a movement away from redaction-critical studies, with their reliance on source- and form-critical assumptions, towards 'a more comprehensive, holistic literary reading of the final form of Luke's two-volume
work'.[166] In this process, some scholars have turned for help to secular theories, seeking an integrated model of literary analysis which can be applied
to any text.

Tannehill's work on Luke-Acts has been the most prodigious and
helpful in this field. It has considerably influenced my own approach to
Acts, though I have sought to be more eclectic in writing this commentary,
drawing also on the insights of other interpreters who have different concerns. Tannehill practices a conservative form of narrative criticism, approaching the biblical narrative as 'an interactive whole, with harmonies
and tensions that develop in the course of narration'.[167] Narrative critics
trace these developments by paying attention to 'plot lines, gaps and re-
dundancies, character roles, points of view, foreshadowing, irony and
other literary features associated with the study of modern novels, short
stories and films'.[168] Tannehill is wary of abstracting dogmatic propositions
from narrative, but he finds evidence for Lukan theology in four particular
types of narrative material:

> (1) previews of ensuing events (e.g. birth stories) and reviews of past
> action (e.g. Acts summaries and speeches); (2) repeated or accentuated
> scriptural citations or allusions (e.g. key Isaianic references); (3) com-
> missioning instructions (e.g. Lk. 24; Acts 9–11); and (4) interpretive
> comments by trustworthy characters (e.g. Jesus, Peter, Stephen,
> Paul).[169]

165. F. S. Spencer, 'Acts and Modern Literary Approaches', in Winter and Clarke, *Ancient Literary Setting*, 382. Longenecker 2007, 666-71, gives a brief overview of the history of
criticism as it applies to the study of Acts.

166. Spencer, 'Modern Literary Approaches', 390. Spencer, 383-91, discusses some of
the key contributions to this development. Cf. Thompson, *Church*, 7-28.

167. R. C. Tannehill, 'Narrative Criticism', in R. J. Coggins and J. L. Houlden (eds.),
Dictionary of Biblical Interpretation (London, SCM; Philadelphia: Trinity, 1990), 488. R. C.
Tannehill, *The Shape of Luke's Story: Essays on Luke-Acts* (Eugene: Cascade, 2005), offers a convenient republication of articles in which he has demonstrated his methodology over several years. M. A. Powell, *What Is Narrative Criticism? A New Approach to the Bible* (Minneapolis: Augsburg Fortress, 1990), 20, proposes that 'the goal of narrative criticism is to read the
text as the implied reader'. It is concerned with uncovering the strategies employed by the
implied author to guide the implied reader. Cf. Marguerat and Bourquin, *Bible Stories;* J. L.
Resseguie, *Narrative Criticism of the New Testament* (Grand Rapids: Baker Academic, 2005).

168. Spencer, 'Modern Literary Approaches', 393. Spencer, 393-94, notes the extent to
which Tannehill's work is dependent on the insights of secular narratologists, though his
commentary is by and large free of technical literary jargon. Tannehill, *Luke*, 1, vows not to
be concerned with 'developing narrative theory'.

169. Spencer, 'Modern Literary Approaches', 394. Cf. Tannehill, *The Shape of Luke's
Story*, for reflections on his own use of narrative criticism in a series of case studies.

In the following section, I outline ways in which I think Luke's narrative method may be further examined for its thematic and theological implications.

Spencer notes that Tannehill has not demonstrated a correspondingly high degree of interest in historical analysis: 'this is not to say he has been hostile to such analysis or ignored it altogether but simply that for the most part he has bracketed out historical queries'.[170] More recent studies of Luke-Acts have attempted to blend narrative criticism and historical analysis. Spencer outlines and critiques five of these, covering a wide range of literary issues and historical concerns, and concludes that narrative criticism is not essentially 'ahistorical' or 'antihistorical'.[171] 'Although modern literary approaches have neither called for nor brought about the total collapse of the historical-critical paradigm, they have instigated a substantial shift in focus from *author* and *event* (major concerns of historical criticism) to *text* and *reader*.'[172] Spencer goes on to consider the implications of this shift for the study of Acts.

Narrative criticism takes a cautious approach to *authorial* issues, though it accepts the fact that clues about the author's identity and function may be helpful in the process of interpretation. Whatever the conclusion reached from these clues (e.g., about Luke's involvement in certain activities he records), the canonical form of the text in its overall narrative context must be 'the first and final arbiter of exegesis'.[173] Spencer contends that narrative critics have played a useful role in calling historical critics back to the priority of examining *narrative events* before moving on to consider more elusive background events. But he holds that some have become 'so absorbed in "poetic" features that "referential" matters are scarcely given their due even as secondary concerns.'[174]

With regard to *textual issues*, Spencer argues that narrative critics have sometimes been neglectful of important text-critical matters. Moreover, their commitment to view Luke-Acts as a single, continuous, unified story can cause them to disregard different patterns of narrative rhetoric, and to gloss over questions regarding 'the constraints of variable *source* material and *generic* models on the final composition of each volume'.[175] Finally, with respect to *readers* and their response to the text, Spencer is critical of some of the expectations of both historical and narrative critics. He draws attention to the fact that Acts would typically have been read aloud and not pored

170. Spencer, 'Modern Literary Approaches', 394. He goes on to illustrate the way Tannehill ventures into historical-critical territory in his treatment of the Stephen speech in Acts 7.

171. Spencer, 'Modern Literary Approaches', 396-405 (406).

172. Spencer, 'Modern Literary Approaches', 406.

173. Spencer 'Modern Literary Approaches', 407.

174. Spencer, 'Modern Literary Approaches', 409.

175. Spencer, 'Modern Literary Approaches', 411. Spencer rightly argues that 'Acts has a literary and historical life of its own which must be respected'. See my comments above on the unity of Luke and Acts. Spencer, 411-12, also critiques those who allow literary theory to triumph over common sense in examining texts.

over in a written form as we might today. The hearer would typically move 'in a steady rhythm and sequential order from beginning to end, without the opportunity afforded to the reader-scholar for reflective pausing and cross-referencing back and forth through the text'.[176] Nevertheless, an alert audience must surely have been influenced by the literary techniques and rhetorical properties of Luke's work as the text was read to them.

B. Some Editorial Techniques with Thematic Implications

Tannehill's way of finding evidence for Lukan theology in narrative material can be expanded and augmented in various ways. Moreover, it can be suggested that certain literary and rhetorical devices in Luke-Acts have hortatory implications for auditors or readers in different contexts.[177]

1. Editorial Summaries

There are transitional verses in Acts, marking the end of one section of the narrative and setting the scene for what follows (e.g., 1:12-14; 2:42-47; 4:32-37; 6:7; 9:31; 12:24; 16:5; 19:20). Some of these contain personal details (e.g. 1:13-14; 4:36-37; 28:30-31), though most are generalisations about developments since the last summary. Most share themes with at least one other summary (e.g., the community of believers gather for prayer in 1:12-14; 2:42-47; the believers generously care for one another in 2:42-47; 4:32-37; 'the word' continues to grow in 6:7; 12:24; 19:20). Many speak of growth and progress after the resolution of some conflict in the church or after the cessation of a season of persecution from unbelievers (4:32-37; 6:7; 9:31; 12:24; 16:5; 19:20; 28:30-31), giving a perspective on suffering that is explicitly commended to all believers in 14:22. Such themes are interconnected and contribute to Luke's overall picture of how the church grows in size and maturity. These explanatory summaries highlight themes otherwise presented in particular narratives or collections of narratives.

2. Inclusions

Some sections of narrative are marked off by the use of similar terms at the beginning and the end, although this is not always made clear in English

---

176. Spencer, 'Modern Literary Approaches', 414. 'Consequently, the hearer's responses to the text are likely to be more impressionistic than scientific, more dynamic than static, more like a participant in a communication event than an examiner of linguistic detail.' Cf. Witherington 1998, 42.

177. Compare what is said above under 'Rhetoric'. Such factors offer important hermeneutical clues for those who would expound Acts and apply its message today.

versions (e.g. *anelēmphthē* ['taken up'], 1:2, 11; *hyparchontōn* ['possessions', 4:32] and *hyparchontos* ['possessing', 4:37]; *anastas* ['stood up', 5:17, 34], indicating new developments in the narrative; *plēthynontōn* ['increasing', 6:1] and *eplēthyneto* ['increased', 6:7]). Such inclusions suggest the theme or setting of a passage that is demarcated in this way. Larger inclusions are formed by the use of editorial summaries (e.g., 2:42-47 and 4:32-37, marking off a section about the Jerusalem church) or by the repetition of key terms (e.g., compare 8:1 and 9:31, indicating expansion into Judea and Samaria with persecution, suggesting a new, more dispersed understanding of 'church' in 9:31)

3. Use of Key Terms, Often in Contextually Limited Ways

Acts is full of key terms, which are repeated in various contexts, indicating ongoing thematic significance (e.g., witness, prayer, word, Spirit, salvation, resurrection, faith, repentance, baptism, signs and wonders, the jealousy of the Jews, persecution, exhortation, visions). Several of these themes are expounded in the following chapter on the theology of Acts. Sometimes related terms occur with surprising frequency in a particular context, indicating that this is a theological focus of the section, where Luke may also be explaining and commending certain behaviour to his readers (e.g., sharing of possessions [2:44-45; 4:32–5:11]; evangelism [8:4-40]; responding to divine guidance [10:1–11:18]; suffering and faith [14:1-28]; resurrection and the hope of Israel [23:6; 24:15, 21; 25:19; 26:6-8, 22-23; 28:20]).[178]

4. Use of Scripture

As already noted, characters in the narrative cite Scripture at strategic points in the argument to explain and justify what has been happening in terms of God's plan (e.g., Peter [1:15-20; 2:14-36; 3:12-26; 4:8-12]; unspecified believers [4:25-26]; Stephen [7:1-53]; Philip [8:32-38]; Paul [13:16-48]; James [15:13-18]; Paul [28:25-29]). Such quotations do not occur in Acts 16–27, though there are many allusions to Scripture here, as in earlier chapters. Significantly, Acts virtually concludes with a challenging citation from Scripture as part of Paul's dialogue with the Jews in Rome (28:25-29). Scriptural allusions are important for the exposition of theological themes in passages such as 10:34-36; 17:24-31, where the gospel is being applied to new situations, or in a passage such as 26:16-18, where there is a theological explanation of what has been happening in the preceding narratives con-

---

178. However, Witherington 1998, 98, discussing 'Acts and Hermeneutics', rightly cautions that 'what was *normal* for the earliest church might not be seen by Luke as a *norm* for his own or other churches'.

cerning Paul's mission. Those familiar with the LXX would have heard biblical echoes that gave them a framework for understanding what was being recounted.

5. Speeches, with Patterns of Repetition

The speeches in Acts are framed in a way that suits their context, and each has distinctive elements that could be identified with the speaker concerned.[179] There are also common features in the mission speeches to Jewish audiences, which include the fulfillment of scriptural promises regarding God's covenant promises and Davidic kingship (2:25-36; 3:13, 18-26; 10:36, 43; 13:32-41), the saving significance of Jesus' life, death, and resurrection-ascension (2:22-24; 3:14-17; 4:10-12; 5:30-32; 10:37-42; 13:23-31), and a call to turn to Jesus with faith (or to repent), and receive the benefits (2:37-41; 3:19-20; 10:43; 13:38-41). This common core of apostolic preaching before Jewish audiences is essentially what Luke means by 'the word' or 'the gospel' (15:7; 20:24). Even in Samaria, Philip is said to proclaim the Messiah (8:5) or to proclaim the good news of the kingdom of God and the name of Jesus Christ (8:12). Peter's message to Cornelius (10:34-43), who was a Gentile with a synagogue connection, ends up being very similar in structure and emphasis to his Pentecost discourse.

Luke's two specific examples of preaching to pagan audiences (14:15-17; 17:22-31) begin by asserting a doctrine of creation in opposition to a polytheistic and idolatrous worldview. Only the second message makes a claim about the significance of Jesus and the need to respond to him with repentance and faith (17:30-31). But Luke gives other narrative indications of the way gospel perspectives were introduced to those unfamiliar with biblical teaching (e.g., 17:18; 24:24-25; 27:22-26). Although only a preliminary challenge is offered in some contexts, the proclamation of Jesus and his resurrection seems to be the goal towards which these encounters were pressing. The messianic kingship of Jesus and its implications remains the core of the message to pagan audiences, though the terminology and approach are very different from the preaching to Jews or Gentiles who were familiar with the Jewish Scriptures.

6. Narrative Repetition

The story of Saul's conversion and commissioning occurs three times. The first account is from Luke's perspective as narrator and gives a prominent role to Ananias (9:1-19). The second account is from Paul's own perspective and gives a lesser role to Ananias, while including a subsequent vision in

179. Cf. Witherington 1998, 46-51, 116-23.

the temple (22:6-21). The third account is again from Paul's perspective and makes no mention of Ananias, but expands the words of commissioning in terms of scriptural allusions (26:12-18). Each account reinforces the same central claims about the Lord's sovereign intervention in his life and highlights Paul's significance within the plan of God for Israel and the nations. Within the wider framework of Acts, these narratives illustrate the transformative power of the risen Jesus and validate Paul's ministry as his witness and servant, with a special prophetic commission. They also explain why he has to suffer as much as he does.[180]

The narrative of Peter's visit to the house of Cornelius and his preaching to the Gentiles there is first told from Luke's perspective in Acts 10 and then from Peter's perspective (11:1-18), as he seeks to justify his actions before 'the circumcised believers' in Jerusalem. Peter gives a third account in 15:7-11 in the context of the Jerusalem Council, which is even richer in theological interpretation. Such narrative repetition draws attention to the significance of the event from different angles, progressively exposing the full meaning of the event for the characters and for the readers.

Although the trial scenes in Acts 22–26 vary in terms of location, audience, and legal significance, they illustrate the fulfillment of the Lord's promise in 9:15 about Paul proclaiming Christ 'to the Gentiles and their kings and to the people of Israel'. Moreover, they portray him as a faithful Jew, announcing the fulfillment of Israel's hope of a resurrection from the dead (23:6; 24:15, 21; 25:19; 26:6-8, 22-23; 28:20). This form of narrative repetition highlights the central issue of the trials from Paul's perspective and shows how he uses the message about resurrection to challenge both Jewish and Gentiles audiences. In particular, he seeks to justify foundational Christian claims in the face of Jewish indifference or opposition.

7. Parallel Accounts

Significant parallels are drawn between Peter and Paul in Acts, with respect to their teaching, miracles, and ministerial experiences. Although these links have been interpreted in different ways, they are best evaluated within the wider framework of a 'prophetic patterning', involving Jesus, Peter, Stephen, Philip, and Paul, and illustrating both continuity and development.[181] The main purpose of the Peter-Paul parallels is 'to highlight the

180. B. Shipp, *Paul the Reluctant Witness: Power and Weakness in Luke's Portrayal* (Eugene: Cascade, 2005), reviews a number of studies considering the threefold presentation of the Damascus road incident in Acts. His own thesis is that the first account in Acts 9 presents a picture of Paul's transformation from '[a] resisting enemy to [b] overcome enemy to [c] empowered witness' (22). The successive accounts portray Paul on different points of this three-stage transformation.

181. Cf. Clark, *Parallel Lives*, 320-41. Johnson 1992, 12-14, sees a broad prophetic structure for Luke-Acts, involving Moses as the starting point.

themes of continuity in salvation history, and the unity of the Jewish and Gentile missions'.[182] Paul does not share 'the symbolic and authenticating roles of the twelve apostles which are peculiar to them. Luke does portray him, however, as similar to Peter as a witness to the resurrection, as a strengthener of the church, and as a key figure in the development of the Gentile mission.'[183]

Stephen and Philip share certain prophetic functions with Paul, though Paul's peculiar significance in the plan of God is highlighted by the narratives concerning his calling, and the application of Isaiah 49:6 to his ministry in Acts 13:47. Peter, Stephen, and Paul each share to some extent in the pattern of rejection and suffering experienced by Jesus, but Paul is particularly viewed as fulfilling the Servant's role in bringing light and salvation to Israel and to the Gentiles, and being persecuted as a consequence (cf. 26:16-18).

8. Contrasting Accounts

If parallel accounts expose something of Luke's theological agenda, so do contrasting accounts. The first example of the latter is the juxtaposition of the story about the generosity of Barnabas (4:36-37) and the story about the deceit of Ananias and Sapphira (5:1-11). Their outward behaviour is similar, but this only serves to highlight the differences in their understanding and motivation. Another example is the contrast between the response of the Jews in Thessalonica to the gospel (17:1-9, 13-15) and the response of the Berean Jews (17:10-12). This highlights the differences in their attitude to the Scriptures and willingness to be challenged by new insights and claims of fulfillment.

A third example is the contrast between Apollos, who 'taught about Jesus accurately, though he knew only the baptism of John', and who needed to have 'the way of God' explained to him more accurately (18:24-28), and the Ephesian 'disciples' (19:1-7). The latter also knew the baptism of John, but are shown by comparison to be further back than Apollos in their understanding and experience. The second narrative recalls Peter's foundational call for baptism 'into the name of the Lord Jesus' in order to enjoy the spiritual blessings of the messianic age (cf. 2:38-39), and applies this to a group of seekers in a very different context.

9. Significant Geographical, Cultural, and Social Indicators

Some contextual features are more than incidental to the narratives in which they are found. They appear to have a theological, as well as geo-

182. Clark, *Parallel Lives*, 325.
183. Clark, *Parallel Lives*, 320.

graphical, cultural, or social significance. For example, in geographical terms, the promise of Jesus' return is given on the Mount of Olives (1:11-12), 'Jews from every nation under heaven' are present in Jerusalem to witness the coming of the Spirit (2:5-12), the first Christians continued to meet together in the temple courts as well as in homes (2:46-47), and the gospel goes throughout the extent of ancient Israel ('Judea, Galilee and Samaria', 9:31) before being taken to the Gentiles.

In cultural and social terms, there is an emphasis on the place of women in the church from the beginning (1:14), sometimes with special mention of their conversion, but mostly with reference to their ministries (e.g., Tabitha [9:36-42], Rhoda [12:12-15], Lydia [16:13-15, 40], Priscilla [18:1-3, 18, 26]).[184] Luke also shows a special interest in the way the gospel impacted the lives of those at different levels in society, from slaves and jailers (16:16-36) to proconsuls (13:6-12) and kings (26:25-32).[185] Such narratives present implicit challenges about the universal relevance of the message and the need to offer it persuasively to all.

C. Characterisation

Two significant elements are usually identified by narrative critics in assessing a literary work such as Acts: the creative arrangement or plot and the artistic techniques used in presenting the plot.[186] Thompson observes that 'through a combination of literary patterns and the creative episodic arrangement, a historical narrative such as Acts escorts its reader to a potential point of final judgment and response'.[187] In ancient history writing, the characters of the story are critical to the presentation and its potential readings. Character depiction takes place by various direct and indirect methods.[188]

Thompson uses such observations to develop and appraise the character of the church in the narrative of Acts. Thompson argues that 'any attempt to understand the church in Acts must keep the church in its narrative place'.[189] Luke progressively invites the reader 'to identify the Christian church as the people of God that is not distinguished by traditional Jewish boundaries but by divine activity and a strong, communal

184. Cf. Witherington 1998, 334-39.

185. Cf. Witherington 1998, 210-13.

186. Thompson, *Church*, 10, observes that 'the consistency and unity of the historical narrative depend on a synthesis of selected events and persons'.

187. Thompson, *Church*, 12. Thompson, 17, argues that the text 'leads, summons and coaxes the reader along the way with various literary elements'. However, no text provides all the necessary clues and information for a consistent reading. The reader must fill in 'textual indeterminancies in ways that are consistent with what the text states or describes'.

188. Thompson, *Church*, 18-28.

189. Thompson, *Church*, 241.

bond among those who are believers in the gospel message'.[190] Although there are some valuable insights in Thompson's work, I am not persuaded that 'the church' as a unified and comprehensive entity is as much in focus as he suggests. He rightly draws attention to the narrative significance of particular churches, but Luke's presentation of the church in a wider sense emerges slowly and hardly functions as a central character in relation to other potential claimants.[191]

Other scholars have drawn attention to the importance of the Holy Spirit as a literary character in the narrative of Acts. Shepherd, for example, argues that the Holy Spirit is God's onstage representative throughout, with the crucial role of providing 'narrative-reliability' for the reader.[192] Hur goes on to explore the narrative function of the Spirit more in terms of the plot of Luke-Acts and 'the immediate narrative effect of the Spirit in relation to the reader'.[193] Hur thus provides a more holistic and dynamic reading of the Spirit as a character in Luke-Acts.

Sleeman has drawn attention to the narrative significance of the ascended and enthroned Lord Jesus. The ascension creates for Jesus the possibility of an altogether different form of presence. The heavenly Christ influences Luke's story at pivotal points, sending the Spirit (2:33), inspiring preachers (7:55-56), calling and commissioning his witnesses (9:5-6; 22:14-15, 17-21), healing the sick (9:34), and using his servants to accomplish his saving purpose in the world (26:16-18). The cumulative effect of such references is that 'the heavenly Christ is a key character within the book of Acts'.[194]

As noted above, 'the word' is also personified in certain texts and appears as a chief character in the narrative of Acts as a whole.[195] But how is the word to be evaluated in relation to the ministry of the Holy Spirit and the sovereign direction of the ascended Lord Jesus? Word and Spirit are presented as the primary agents of the reigning Lord in forming and growing his church. Human characters have an important role to play in the

190. Thompson, *Church*, 246. The reader thus discovers that these issues regarding the nature of the church are not minor themes or insignificant elements on the book.

191. See my argument in THE THEOLOGY OF ACTS: X. THE CHURCH (pp. 92-97).

192. Cf. W. H. Shepherd Jr., *The Narrative Function of the Holy Spirit as a Character in Luke-Acts*, SBLDS 147 (Atlanta: Scholars, 1994), 101, 247, 255.

193. J. Hur, *A Dynamic Reading of the Holy Spirit in Luke-Acts*, JSNTSS 211 (Sheffield: Sheffield Academic, 2001), 31.

194. M. Sleeman, 'The Ascension and the Heavenly Ministry of Christ', in S. Clark (ed.), *The Forgotten Christ: Exploring the Majesty and Mystery of God Incarnate* (Nottingham: Apollos, 2007), 158.

195. Note particularly Marguerat, *First Christian Historian*, 37; Pao, *New Exodus*, 49, 147-79. In 'Luke's Theological Enterprise: Integration and Intent', in Marshall and Peterson, *Witness to the Gospel*, 541, I too assert that 'the word is the real "hero" of Luke's narrative.' However, I am now persuaded that, although the narrative is emphatically about the progress of the word, the central role of the ascended Lord in relation to the word and the Spirit must be considered.

story, as those who have encountered the heavenly Christ and who act as Spirit-empowered proclaimers of his word. Acts implies that the Lord Jesus will continue to fulfill his purpose in the world, even in the absence of apostles and prophetic figures such as Stephen, Philip and Paul (cf. 20:28-32). The same word on the lips of Spirit-directed believers is able to reach new people groups and break through cultural and religious barriers to grow the church in ever-widening circles (e.g., 8:4; 11:19-21).[196]

VI. TEXTUAL MATTERS

There are certain textual issues that the interpreter of Acts must regularly face. In the first place, there are variants in the Greek text of the so-called Byzantine tradition that are found in the KJV and NKJV, but not in most contemporary English versions. Secondly, there are variants in the so-called Western text that are sometimes represented in the footnotes of English versions. Debate continues about the reliability of these textual traditions in relation to what is called the Alexandrian text. It is important to be aware of some of the factors involved in making judgments about these issues.

In general terms, 'the original text of the NT must be recovered as far as possible by a critical comparison of the various types of text current in the early Christian centuries, as these have been preserved in manuscripts, ancient versions, and quotations in early Christian writers'.[197] The evidence is normally classified in terms of the geographical location of the main text types.

The Byzantine textual tradition is a revision and amalgamation of earlier texts, carried out from the fourth century AD and propagated from Byzantium (Constantinople). This is sometimes called 'the majority text' because it increasingly superseded other textual forms. Indeed, 'the great mass of later MSS and versions from the fifth century on is Byzantine in character'.[198] It also became known as the *Textus Receptus,* or 'Received Text', when it was published in the first printed editions of the Greek New Testament (from 1516). This text then became the basis of Reformation translations, including the English Authorized or King James Version (1611). The New King James Version is largely reliant on the same textual tradition.

The Byzantine text is characterized chiefly by 'lucidity and com-

196. Rosner, 'Progress of the Word', 229-33, offers important comments about the way Luke seeks to involve readers in the continuing progress of the word.

197. Bruce 1990, 69.

198. Bruce 1990, 70. The Byzantine text of Acts is exhibited by the uncial MSS H L P S and by most minuscule MSS. It is sometimes called the Syrian or Antiochene text, because it is believed that the revision was initiated by Lucian of Antioch.

pleteness'.[199] However, Bruce concludes that 'the circumstances under which this text seems to have originated, the fact that it is not represented in quotations in writers of the first three centuries AD, and the secondary relation which it appears to bear to other early forms of NT text suggest that, where it differs from those earlier texts, the earlier are usually to be preferred'.[200]

A number of important early manuscripts of the NT were discovered in the nineteenth and twentieth centuries, exhibiting common characteristics. These witnesses are classified as Alexandrian, because it is believed that they represent the textual tradition associated with that ancient centre of Christian scholarship.[201] Westcott and Hort published a new edition of the Greek NT in 1881 that was considerably influenced by the major witnesses in this tradition. Most editions of the Greek since then have treated the Alexandrian text as best preserving the original, since 'it is generally shorter than the text of other forms, and it does not exhibit the degree of grammatical and stylistic polishing that is characteristic of the Byzantine type of text'.[202] Most recent English versions favour Alexandrian readings where variants occur, including the TNIV on which this commentary is based.

The third manuscript tradition that is important for establishing the text of Acts is called Western, because it was widely current in Italy, Gaul, and North Africa.[203] Metzger describes the character of this text in comparison with the Alexandrian as follows:

> Words, clauses, and even whole sentences are freely changed, omitted, or inserted. Sometimes the motive appears to have been harmonization, while at other times it was the enrichment of the narrative by the

199. B. M. Metzger, *A Textual Commentary on the Greek New Testament: A Companion Volume to the United Bible Societies' Greek New Testament (Fourth Revised Edition)* (2nd ed.; Stuttgart/New York: United Bible Societies, 1994), 7. Metzger says that 'the framers of this text sought to smooth away any harshness of language, to combine two or more divergent readings into one expanded reading (called conflation), and to harmonize divergent parallel passages'.

200. Bruce 1990, 70. Witherington 1998, 65-66, offers further arguments against those who would advocate the originality of the *Textus Receptus* (Received Text).

201. The most important witnesses of the Alexandrian text of Acts are the uncials ℵ A B C, Papyri 45, 50, 56, 57 58, 74, and the minuscules 33, 81, 104, 326, 1175, and 1739. The uncials date from about the middle of the fourth century, but several of the papyri were copied at the end of the second or the beginning of the third century. This means that the archetype of the Alexandrian text can be dated early in the second century.

202. Metzger, *Textual Commentary*, 5.

203. The chief witness of the Western text of Acts is the Greek and Latin Codex D (Codex Bezae), which is commonly thought to have been copied in the fifth century in some part of Western Europe. Bruce 1990, 71-72, lists also the ancient versions that represent this text type (particularly Old Latin and Syriac) and discusses two papyrus fragments dating from the third and fourth centuries that manifest a 'Western' character. Bruce, 76-77, discusses the possible relevance of the Caesarean text for the study of Acts.

inclusion of traditional or apocryphal material. Some readings involve quite trivial alterations for which no special reason can be assigned.[204]

The Western text presents particular problems for the interpreter of Acts, since it is nearly 10 percent longer than the Alexandrian text. Some scholars have argued that Luke produced two editions of his work, pruning a longer first edition to create a shorter second version. Critics, however, 'have found it difficult to understand the motives of the author in choosing to omit certain details found in the presumed earlier account; the gain in space is small and the loss in information and descriptiveness is sometimes great'.[205] Other scholars have suggested that the Western text arose from annotations to the original left by Luke himself and then incorporated by someone else in a longer version. Most would regard the Western text as having arisen from glosses based on oral tradition that were added in a context where the text of Acts was not regarded as fixed.[206]

Bruce insists that the Western text cannot be lightly dismissed as a trustworthy witness to the original:

> Its manuscript attestation is very ancient, and it can be traced in versions as apparently independent of each other as the Old Latin and the Old Syriac, both of which go back to the later decades of the second century. It appears in patristic citations earlier than (the Alexandrian text) does. Internal evidence, however, makes it unlikely that it is a more reliable witness than (the Alexandrian text).[207]

Bruce goes on to argue that if the Western text is indeed secondary, some explanation must be offered for the fact that its Greek embodies a significant amount of Semitic colouring. Metzger lists various theories designed to account for this linguistic problem and concludes that none offers help in explaining how the Western text of Acts became nearly one-tenth longer than the Alexandrian text.[208]

---

204. Metzger, *Textual Commentary*, 6.

205. Metzger, *Textual Commentary*, 225. Metzger, 223-27, lists the influential scholars who have argued for two editions emanating from Luke himself, some proposing that the second edition was a deliberate expansion of the first.

206. Cf. Metzger, *Textual Commentary*, 228-29. P. Head, 'Acts and the Problem of Its Texts', in Winter and Clarke, *Ancient Literary Setting*, 417-20, gives a historical survey showing how a consensus emerged that the Western text represents 'a later form of the text which arose from paraphrasing interpolations to the shorter (Alexandrian) original'. Head, 420-28, then outlines the position of those who have challenged this consensus, who have argued that the Western text is original in one way or another.

207. Bruce 1990, 72. He argues that the longer readings in the Western text are generally secondary in character. Nevertheless, he regards some of the peculiar Western readings as attractive because 'they make an already colorful narrative even more colorful'. Bruce, 75-76, outlines some of the characteristics of the Western text and his own approach to the two textual traditions.

208. Metzger, *Textual Commentary*, 230-32. Metzger summarizes the research of Yoder,

A significant factor in evaluating Western readings is the theological agenda that appears in several ways. Head notes the addition or expansion of honorific titles of Jesus, additional references to the work of the Holy Spirit, an emphasis on the wisdom, authority, and power of the apostolic figures, and modifications to the Apostolic Decree (15:20, 29; 21:25) to make it a more decisive statement about Gentile freedom from the law of Moses.[209] Witherington adds that there are antifeminist tendencies in the Western text that suggest the influence of debates in the church from the second century onwards.[210]

No hypothesis thus far proposed to explain the relation of the Western and the Alexandrian texts of Acts has gained anything like general assent. Many textual critics would therefore agree with the eclectic approach of the committee responsible for the United Bible Societies Greek NT, 'judging that neither the Alexandrian nor the Western group of witnesses always preserves the original text, but that in order to attain the earliest text one must compare the two divergent traditions point by point and in each case select the reading that commends itself in the light of transcriptional and intrinsic probabilities'.[211] In practice, this means that the shorter Alexandrian text is mostly preferred, and that the information incorporated in certain Western expansions is sometimes regarded as factually accurate, though not deriving from Luke himself.

---

who concluded that the net increase in Semitisms in Codex Bezae compared with other Greek witnesses is sometimes inconsequential. Indeed, sometimes this MS reveals fewer Semitisms than the Alexandrian text. Semitisms are concentrated in limited areas of Codex Bezae.

209. Head, 'Acts and the Problem of Its Texts', 428-44, concluding that these modifications appear to have arisen in reaction to the Alexandrian tradition rather than vice versa. Cf. Bruce 1990, 75-76; Witherington 1998, 66-68.

210. Witherington 1998, 67 note 231. Cf. B. Witherington III, 'The Anti-Feminist Tendencies of the Western Text in Acts', *JBL* 103 (1984), 82-84.

211. Metzger, *Textual Commentary*, 235. Cf. Bruce 1990, 75-76. J. Read-Heimerdinger, *The Bezan Text of Acts: A Contribution of Discourse Analysis to Textual Criticism* (Sheffield: Sheffield Academic, 2003), has used discourse analysis to reassess how variant readings have arisen and concludes that the Bezan or Western text is earlier than the Alexandrian. She has begun to publish a series of commentaries comparing the two textual traditions of Acts. However, to date, this approach had not received much scholarly endorsement.

The Theology of Acts

In the Introduction it was argued that Luke-Acts 'bears some strong resemblances to earlier Greek historiographic works in form and method and general arrangement of material, as well as some similarities to Hellenized Jewish historiography in content and general apologetic aims'.[1] In particular, OT allusions and quotations, together with a stress on fulfillment, link the narratives to biblical promises and prophecies. Moreover, certain narratives in Acts appear to be patterned on biblical precedents and employ literary techniques familiar from OT histories. Indeed, Luke uses a variety of rhetorical techniques in the construction of his narrative and the presentation of speeches to achieve the suggested aim of showing 'that Jesus and the church he founded were God's fulfillment of his promises to Israel, thereby assuring both Jewish and Gentile believers of the reliability of the message they have heard, and of God's faithfulness'.[2] Acts was described as a 'theological history' in the sense that it records God's activity in fulfilling his promises and working out his purpose for humanity. At the same time, it was maintained that Luke is a reliable historian, who has not allowed his theological and apologetic agenda to distort the facts.

It was further proposed that although the Gospel and Acts represent two different literary genres, Acts is the intended sequel to the Gospel and there is a coherence between the two volumes at the level of story, themes, and theology. As much as possible, therefore, this chapter will examine the

---

1. B. Witherington III, *The Acts of the Apostles: A Socio-Rhetorical Commentary* (Grand Rapids/Cambridge: Eerdmans; Carlisle: Paternoster, 1998), 39. D. Marguerat, *The First Christian Historian: Writing the 'Acts of the Apostles'*, SNTSMS 121, trans. K. McKinney, G. J. Laughery, and R. Bauckham (Cambridge: Cambridge University, 2002), 20, observes, 'Luke, situated at the crossroads of Hellenistic and Jewish historiography, opts for the Jewish line as far as subject matter is concerned'.

2. P. E. Satterthwaite, 'Acts against the Background of Classical Rhetoric', in B. W. Winter and A. D. Clarke (eds.), *The Book of Acts in Its First-Century Setting*, Vol. 1: *Ancient Literary Setting* (Grand Rapids: Eerdmans; Carlisle: Paternoster, 1993), 347.

themes of Acts in relation to the theology of Luke's Gospel, illustrating similarities and developments. There are various ways to construct a theology
of Acts, and Marshall concludes that 'the study of themes is manifestly legitimate, provided that we pay attention to the intricate interplay of numerous themes and do not hitch our wagon to a single star'.[3] What follows
is not a comprehensive approach, since certain themes are not explored.
There is limited interaction with alternative views and no examination of
theories about the evolution of Luke's theology. Under various headings,
an attempt is made to summarize and systematize some of the conclusions
reached in the Commentary about major theological themes.

I. GOD AND HIS PLAN

God makes known his powerful presence and purpose in the narrative of
Acts by direct action and speech (e.g., 1:24-26; 2:1-4, 37-47; 3:1-10; 4:23-31;
5:1-11; 8:29, 39; 9:1-18), and through angelic or human messengers (e.g.,
1:15-23; 2:14-36; 3:11-26; 4:7-12; 8:12; 10:1-48), with the latter regularly using
Scripture to proclaim the character and will of God.[4] Foundationally, God is
presented in three key speeches as the creator and sustainer of all life (4:24;
14:15, 17; 17:24-25), the disposer of time and space (14:16; 17:26-27), and the
judge of all (17:29-31; cf. 10:42). Although Scripture is not explicitly cited to
make these points, a biblical-theological perspective is presented in which
God's creation of humanity and provision for humanity's needs are highlighted. God's fundamental purpose for human beings is that 'they would
seek him and perhaps reach out for him and find him' (17:27). Although
this last point is not articulated until Paul addresses the meeting of the
Areopagus in Athens, it is the implied basis of everything that is said in
Acts about God's intention to engage with Jews and Gentiles on the same
basis, and draw them into a relationship with himself through Jesus Christ.

Ironically, the challenge to Jews through Stephen and to Gentiles
through Paul is similar: not to treat God as inhabiting material structures
(7:48-50; 17:24), nor to imagine that he can be served by means of idolatry
or any humanly devised pattern of worship (7:39-43; 14:15; 17:25-29). Posi-

---

3. I. H. Marshall, 'How Does One Write on the Theology of Acts?' in I. H. Marshall
and D. Peterson (eds.), *Witness to the Gospel: The Theology of Acts* (Grand Rapids/Cambridge:
Eerdmans, 1998), 13. This volume sought to cover many of the topics that would properly
find their way into an account of the theology of Acts. It was far from complete, and some
integration of the themes was attempted only in the last chapter. F. Bovon, *Luke the Theologian: Thirty-three Years of Research (1950-1983)*, trans. K. McKinney (Allison Park: Pickwick,
1987), offers a survey of thirty-three years of research on the theology of Luke-Acts,
critiquing different methods of approach.

4. Cf. D. Marguerat, 'The God of the Book of Acts', in G. J. Brooke and J.-D. Kaestli
(eds.), *Narrative in Biblical and Related Texts* (Leuven: Leuven University, 2000), 159-81.

tively, the challenge to Jews is to recognise the implications of the covenant God made with the patriarchs, beginning with Abraham in Genesis 12:1-3, forming the basis of his historic relationship with that people (3:25-26; cf. Lk. 1:54-55, 70-75). Remarkably, however, the verse quoted by Peter contains the promise that 'all peoples on earth will be blessed' through Abraham's offspring. This is the intention of 'the plan' of God (*boulē*, 2:23; 4:28; 5:38-39; 13:36; 20:27; cf. Lk. 7:30),[5] which necessitated the death and resurrection of Jesus, making salvation possible for Jews and Gentiles alike. In cosmic terms, this plan involves the return of Jesus and the restoration of all things, as God promised 'long ago through his holy prophets' (3:20-21; cf. Lk. 9:26-27; 12:40; 13:28-30; 18:29-30; 22:29-30).

In the story of Acts, the gospel comes to the Jews first, to enable them to turn to Jesus as their Messiah, and then to be the source of light and life for Gentiles. Stephen and Paul outline the first stages in the fulfillment of the divine plan with the salvation of Israel from Egypt and the establishment of the nation in Canaan (7:2-38; 13:17-21). Peter and Paul focus on the particular significance of David in the unfolding plan of God, both with respect to his appointment as king of Israel and his prophetic role, pointing to Jesus and the gospel events (2:25-31, 34-35; 4:25-26; 13:22-23, 32-37). But the revelation of God's eschatological will and purpose comes more broadly through Moses (3:22-23; 7:37) and the prophets (2:16-21; 3:18-21, 24; 8:32-35; 13:40-41, 47; 15:15-18; 26:22-23; 28:25-27; cf. Lk. 24:25-27, 45-47). Through these divine messengers the different dimensions and full extent of the plan of salvation are made known and regularly expounded by Christian preachers in Luke's narrative.

Acts 1 sets the scene by indicating that 'the Spirit will guide, angelic figures will lead, a certain necessity will drive events as they occur, and these events can be understood as fulfilling scriptural prophecy'.[6] Peter's Pentecost preaching and subsequent speeches then make it clear how the story of Jesus and of the church in Jerusalem is to be understood within the framework of the divine plan (Acts 2–7). The movement into the wider Hellenistic world (Acts 8–12) is similarly validated by miracles, divine agents, the work of the Spirit, and explicit statements of God's plan. In various ways, human characters are portrayed as 'acting out the drama of

---

5. Note that 'the will' of God functions somewhat similarly in some contexts (*thelēma*, 13:22; 21:14; 22:14). Other expressions speak of God's having predetermined the things that have taken place (10:42; 17:31; 22:14; 26:16). God's sovereignty and the fulfillment of his plan of salvation are further stressed by the extensive use of *dei* or *edei* ('it is/was necessary') in 1:16, 21; 3:21; 4:12; 5:29; 9:6, 16; 14:22; 15:5; 16:30; 17:3; 19:21; 20:35; 23:11; 24:19; 25:10; 27:24. J. T. Squires, *The Plan of God in Luke-Acts*, SNTSMS 76 (Cambridge: Cambridge University, 1993), 1-10, shows how this terminology is used in Luke's Gospel also.

6. J. T. Squires, 'The Plan of God in the Acts of the Apostles', in Marshall and Peterson, *Witness to the Gospel*, 23. Squires argues that the plan of God functions as 'the foundational theological motif' for Luke-Acts. Cf. D. L. Bock, 'Scripture and the Realisation of God's Promises', in Marshall and Peterson, *Witness to the Gospel*, 41-62, and my section in the Introduction, 'A Narrative of Fulfillment'.

God's providence'.[7] The same pattern of divine validation is found in the narrative about Paul's missionary endeavours (Acts 13–21). The final section in Acts 22–28, focussing on Paul's trials and journey to Rome, has fewer explicit references to the theme of providential guidance, though there are dramatic rescues, divine revelations, miracles, and confirming statements about Paul's role in the plan of God. The overall function of Luke's interpretation of events within the framework of the divine plan is,

> to offer encouragement to his readers as they live out their faith in a post-apostolic situation; to offer them a theological grounding for their missionary activity (it is an integral part of the divine plan); and to present ways by which potential criticisms can be defended by respectable means (using the language of historians who depicted history in this fashion).[8]

II. JESUS AS MESSIAH AND LORD

Christology is a topic demanding some assessment of the way Luke's Gospel prepares for the presentation in Acts.[9] The angelic announcements and prophecies of the opening chapters introduce him as 'the Son of the Most High' (1:32) and 'the Son of God' (1:35). The uniqueness of his relationship with God is highlighted by the nature of his conception (1:35), the way in which the child develops (2:40-52), and the declaration at his baptism (3:21-22; cf. 9:35). But the focus of these early chapters is particularly on his messianic status and calling (1:32-33, 68-75; 2:11, 26-32), and the preparatory role of John the Baptist in the fulfillment of the divine plan of salvation (1:76-80; 3:1-20). Moreover, the divine sonship of Jesus remains largely hidden to the participants in the narratives that follow. It is privately challenged during his testing in the wilderness (4:1-13), and is occasionally exposed by demonic forces throughout his public ministry (4:41; 8:28; cf. 4:33-34). It becomes the focus of an important claim by Jesus about the revelation that has been given to the disciples throughout his ministry (10:21-24), and is hinted at in the parable of the tenants (20:13).

Jesus' Davidic sonship is confessed privately by the disciples (9:20) and proclaimed publicly by a blind beggar (18:38, 39), but he does not actually confirm this identity. He challenges his opponents about the Messiah's relationship to God and to David in connection with the interpretation of Psalm 110:1 (20:41-44). But when he is asked at his trial, 'Are you then the

---

7. Squires, 'Plan of God', 31.
8. Squires, 'Plan of God', 39.
9. Cf. C. F. D. Moule, 'The Christology of Acts', in L. E. Keck and J. L. Martyn (eds.), *Studies in Luke-Acts: Essays Presented in Honor of Paul Schubert* (Nashville: Abingdon, 1966; London: SPCK, 1976), 159-85.

Son of God?' he only responds, 'You say that I am' (22:70-71). Jesus' relationship to God as Father appears to be more than functional, though it is certainly expressed in the carrying out of his messianic role.

Preaching in the synagogue at Nazareth, Jesus identifies himself as the Spirit-anointed messenger of Isaiah 61:1-2, sent to proclaim release and salvation to Israel (Lk. 4:16-21). Faced with unbelief in his hometown, he suggests that he might be better accepted by Gentiles, and is met with furious rejection (4:22-30). Luke's portrait of Jesus is very much that of 'a prophet, powerful in word and deed before God and all the people' (24:19; cf. 7:16; 9:19), regarded by some as the hoped-for redeemer of Israel (24:20-21; cf. 2:25, 34-35, 38) but, like so many prophets before him, destined to die in Jerusalem (13:31-34). As in the other Synoptic Gospels, his preferred method of self-designation is indirect, as 'the Son of Man' (e.g., 5:24; 6:5, 22; 7:34). This title is used to highlight his eschatological destiny, to be the world ruler and judge of everything anticipated in the prophecy of Daniel 7:13-14. Paradoxically, this title is used in connection with his suffering, death, and resurrection (e.g., 9:22, 26, 44), to indicate the way in which he is enabled to fulfill that eschatological role. The redemptive character of his death is further signalled in the Passover context of the Last Supper (22:1-19), where he indicates that he will inaugurate a new covenant in his blood (22:20), and declares that Isaiah 53:12 and the associated oracle must be fulfilled in him (22:37). His role as the suffering Servant of the Lord is discussed below in relation to his atoning work.

These diverse strands are brought together and interrelated in the presentation of the person and work of Jesus in Luke's second volume.[10] First, there is the insistence that the same Jesus is 'alive' and continuing to minister to the disciples after his death and resurrection (1:1-3). With his ascension and the pouring out of the Spirit, he maintains a different kind of presence in the narrative. Emphatically, however, it is the resurrected and ascended Jesus who continues to work through his earthly agents, as they proclaim his word and minister in the power of his Spirit.[11] Indeed, Acts depicts the exalted Jesus as 'present within the church in the same way that the OT describes transcendent Yahweh as immanently involved with Israel'.[12]

---

10. D. L. Bock, *Proclamation from Prophecy and Pattern: Lucan Old Testament Christology*, JSNTSS 12 (Sheffield: JSOT, 1987), 262, 265, argues that Luke first uses OT quotations and allusions to make 'the foundational declaration of Jesus as regal Messiah-Servant', but then shifts his focus to OT elements suggesting that Jesus is 'a more than Messiah figure', to make 'the climactic declaration that Jesus is Lord'.

11. Cf. R. F. O'Toole, 'Luke's Understanding of Jesus' Resurrection-Ascension-Exaltation', *BTB* 9 (1979), 106-14; M. Sleeman, 'The Ascension and the Heavenly Ministry of Christ', in S. Clark (ed.), *The Forgotten Christ: Exploring the Majesty and Mystery of God Incarnate* (Nottingham: Apollos, 2007), 140-90. J. Hur, *A Dynamic Reading of the Holy Spirit in Luke-Acts*, JSNTSS 211 (Sheffield: Sheffield Academic, 2001), 141-44, examines the relationship between the Spirit and the risen Jesus in Acts.

12. H. D. Buckwalter, 'The Divine Saviour', in Marshall and Peterson, *Witness to the*

One particular way in which this similarity is shown is through the use of the title 'Lord'. The disciples address Jesus as 'Lord' (1:6) during his resurrection appearances (cf. 'the Lord' in Lk. 24:34), and again immediately after the ascension in a prayer for him to choose a successor to Judas (1:24-25; cf. 7:59, 60). This is followed by three references to the God of Israel as 'the Lord' in scriptural citations (Jl. 2:32 in Acts 2:20-21; Ps.16:8 in 2:25; Ps. 110:1 in 2:34), and then Peter's stunning declaration that 'God has made this Jesus, whom you crucified, both Lord and Messiah' (2:36).[13] He is called 'the Lord Jesus' in some contexts (1:21; 4:33) and 'the Lord' in others (5:14). The 'name' of the Lord Jesus becomes powerful to heal and to save (2:38-41; 3:6, 16; 4:9-12, 17, 30; 5:28, 40-41; 8:16) because of what it represents.[14] It is the Lord Jesus who confronts Saul on the Damascus road (9:3-6; cf. v. 17) and who speaks to Ananias in a vision about his plans for Saul (9:10-16). The divine designation 'the Lord' is applied to the risen and ascended Jesus in contexts where he is shown to be active in bringing people to faith (9:35, 42; 16:14), initiating new missionary endeavours (10:13-15; 11:20-21, 24), confirming the message of his grace by enabling his messengers to perform signs and wonders (14:3), and encouraging them to persevere in the face of opposition and disappointment (18:9-10; 23:11; cf. 22:17-21).[15]

Jesus' messiahship is the primary focus of preaching to audiences who know the Scriptures. The events of his public ministry are sometimes briefly recalled as an indication of his divine attestation (2:22; 10:37-38; 13:24-25), before his betrayal and death are recounted (2:23; 10:39; 13:27-29). In 3:13-15, 17, his messiahship is presented in terms of the Isaianic Suffering Servant (see also 4:25-30; 8:32-35), echoing some of the perspectives of Jesus himself in the Gospel material.[16] But the ultimate indications of his true identity are

Gospel, 113. Buckwalter, 113-19, compares ways in which God's presence with Israel is signified in the OT with Luke's presentation of Jesus and his Spirit in Acts, the visionary appearances of the exalted Lord, and the way the name of Jesus is understood and used.

13. Witherington 1998, 147-48, observes that the term 'Lord' is Luke's most frequently used Christological title and details the way it is employed in Acts. The title 'Son of God' is found only in Acts 9:20, in a report of Paul's early preaching (though cf. 13:33). 'Messiah' and 'Lord' are the terms regularly used in the sermons in Acts to convey what is implied by divine sonship in the early chapters of Luke's Gospel. Jesus is also called 'the Holy and Righteous One' (3:14; cf. 7:52; 22:14), 'the author of life' (3:15), and 'Prince and Saviour' (5:31), which appear to be messianic titles with different implications.

14. Cf. J. A. Ziesler, 'The Name of Jesus in the Acts of the Apostles', *JSNT* 4 (1979), 28-32. F. F. Bruce, *The Acts of the Apostles: The Greek Text with Introduction and Commentary* (3rd ed.; Leicester/Grand Rapids: Apollos/Eerdmans, 1990), 60, observes that 'the name of Jesus is sometimes given almost hypostatic status (3:16; 4:30; 26:9), like the name of Yahweh in the deuteronomic writings of the OT (e.g., Dt. 12:5, 11), especially when Jesus is represented as still powerfully at work through his witnesses'.

15. Buckwalter, 'The Divine Saviour', 117, says that 'the exalted Jesus behaves towards Paul here as deity supreme in power and knowledge and as one who is personally present.'

16. Cf. Lk. 9:21-22, 44; 18:31-3; 22:20-22, 37. In Acts 17:3, a specific apologetic with a

his resurrection and ascension to God's right hand, understood from a scriptural perspective (2:24-36, citing Pss. 16:8-11; 110:1 [as in Lk. 20:41-44]; 3:13, 15; 10:40-43; 13:30-37, citing Pss. 2:7; 16:10; Is. 55:3). These events place him in the position of eternal power and universal authority that David himself predicted would be given to one of his descendants (cf. Ps. 118:22 in 4:10-12, as in Lk. 20:17). As the Messiah who is enthroned in heaven, he is 'Lord of all' (10:36), and 'the one whom God appointed as judge of the living and the dead' (10:41; cf. 17:31).[17] As the heavenly Messiah, he is able to provide forgiveness and the gift of the Holy Spirit to all who turn to him in repentance and faith (2:38; 3:19-20; 5:31; 10:43; 13:38-39). The restoration of 'all things' is associated with his promised return (3:20-21; cf. 1:11). Indeed, salvation in all its dimensions 'is found in no one else, for there is no other name given under heaven by which we must be saved' (4:12).

Thus, many passages focussing on the messiahship of Jesus imply that he is a divine figure. Luke's Christology is not confined to the titles given to Jesus,[18] but is revealed in significant narrative presentations. Most importantly, in various ways, 'the exalted Jesus conspicuously behaves in Acts as does Yahweh in the OT.'[19] Some scholars have argued on the basis of Acts 2:36 that Luke has an adoptionist Christology, meaning that Jesus became Lord over all and universal Messiah only because God raised him from death and exalted him to a new status and role.[20] But the preceding verses insist that Jesus is raised from death and exalted to God's right hand because he *is* the Messiah and has accomplished the Messiah's work on earth (2:22-35). Moreover, Acts 10:38 indicates that he did that work as one already anointed 'with the Holy Spirit and power' (cf. 4:27). 'Jesus is enthroned as Lord and Messiah for Israel, to fulfill all the promises made to it. This newly enthroned ruler will also offer salvation to the world, having been granted universal power to rule and judge.'[21] Luke may not articulate

---

synagogue audience involves proving from the Scriptures that 'the Messiah had to suffer and rise from the dead' (cf. Lk. 24:25-27, 45-46; Acts 13:27-30; 26:22-23).

17. Jesus is identified as 'the Son of Man' only in Stephen's vision (7:55-56), where the Christology is expressed differently from the Gospel because of Jesus' ascension and presence at the Father's right hand. Cf. Witherington 1998, 151-52.

18. Bruce 1990, 60, insists that there are no distinct 'christologies' associated with these various titles. Contrast Witherington 1998, 153.

19. Buckwalter, 'The Divine Saviour', 119. Buckwalter, 120-22, goes on to show that in his heavenly reign, as in his earthly ministry, his divine lordship continues to be expressed towards his people through acts of service.

20. Cf. C. K. Barrett, *A Critical and Exegetical Commentary on the Acts of the Apostles*, ICC, Vol. 1 (Edinburgh: Clark, 1994), 140-41, 151-52.

21. R. C. Tannehill, *The Narrative Unity of Luke-Acts: A Literary Interpretation*, Vol. 2: *The Acts of the Apostles* (Minneapolis: Fortress, 1990), 39. R. N. Longenecker, 'Acts', in *The Expositor's Bible Commentary: Revised Edition, Volume 10 (Luke-Acts)*, ed. T. Longman III and D. E. Garland (Grand Rapids: Zondervan, 2007), 746, argues that Peter is proclaiming 'not an adoptionist Christology but a functional one with ontological overtones'. Cf. M. M. B. Turner, *Power from on High: The Spirit in Israel's Restoration and Witness in Luke-Acts*, JPTSS 9 (Sheffield: Sheffield Academic, 1996), 294-97; Witherington 1998, 147-53.

belief in a preexistent Son of God, as in John 1:1-18, Philippians 2:6-11, or Hebrews 1:3-4, but such a belief could be regarded as the logical implication of his total Christological presentation.[22]

III. THE HOLY SPIRIT

Luke's special interest in the Holy Spirit is indicated by the fifty-seven occurrences of the noun *pneuma* ('Spirit') in Acts alone. Before and after Pentecost, the Spirit is identified as the one who 'spoke long ago' through prophetic figures in Scripture (1:16; 4:25; 28:25; cf. 7:51-52). But Peter acknowledges having recently experienced the Spirit of God at work in a new way, in the ministry of Jesus (10:37-38; cf. 2:22). Readers of Luke's Gospel know that the Spirit descended on Jesus at his baptism (Lk. 3:22), so that he was 'full of the Spirit' and 'led by the Spirit' in all that he did (4:1; cf. 4:14, 18-19; 10:21).[23] Moreover, Jesus had spoken about the Father giving the Holy Spirit to those who would ask him (11:13), and had promised that the Spirit would teach disciples what to say when on trial for their faith (12:11-12).

In Acts 1, the risen Jesus makes two further, but related promises which are critical for understanding the narratives to follow. First, he reiterates in an abbreviated fashion the Baptist's claim that the one coming after him would *baptise with the Holy Spirit*, applying the promise directly to the disciples and saying that it would be fulfilled in Jerusalem 'in a few days' (1:4-5; cf. Lk. 3:16; 24:49, 'clothed with power from on high'). Jesus calls the Spirit 'the gift of my Father', but true to the Baptist's prediction, Peter later declares that *the ascended Lord Jesus* has 'received from the Father the promised Holy Spirit and has poured out what you now see and hear' (2:33).[24] Secondly, the risen Lord promises that his disciples will receive power when the Holy Spirit comes on them, enabling them to be *his witnesses*, 'in Jerusalem, and in all Judea and Samaria, and to the ends of the earth' (1:8; cf. Lk. 24:48-49).

Several things are immediately obvious from these pronouncements.

---

22. Bovon, *Luke the Theologian*, 197, says that 'for Luke, the word of God was made flesh in Jesus, but not in John's manner: it is the word of God, in the past addressed to *the prophets* and not pre-existent in heaven, which took on a body in Jesus (Acts 10:36f.)'. But this fails to deal adequately with the material in Luke 1–2, the implications of the Father-Son language at various points in Luke-Acts, and the presentation in Acts of the exalted Jesus as co-equal with God.

23. Cf. Turner, *Power from on High*, 336-37. In the opening chapters of the Gospel, the Holy Spirit enables the virginal conception of Jesus (1:35) and fills prophetic figures such as John the Baptist (1:15, 17), Elizabeth (1:41), Zechariah (1:67), and Simeon (2:25-27), who recognise and proclaim the significance of what is happening. Thus, Luke signals the dawn of the eschatological era in which the Spirit will play a key role, and anticipates the outpouring of the Spirit 'on all people' at Pentecost.

24. Although Luke does not articulate a doctrine of God as trinity, a passage such as Acts 2:32-36 demands such a theological resolution and explication.

First, the giving of the Spirit is in some sense the giving of God himself to believers (cf. 16:7, 'the Spirit of Jesus'), with the implication that this effects a new relationship between God and his people, in fulfillment of his ancient promises (e.g., Is. 32:15; 59:21; Ezk. 36:26-27; Jl. 2:28-32; cf. Je. 31:31-34).[25] Secondly, the eschatological coming of the Spirit can be described in terms of clothing (Lk. 24:49), baptism (Acts 1:5; 11:16), coming upon (1:8; 19:6), falling upon (8:16; 10:44; 11:15), pouring out (2:17-18, 33; 10:45), reception (1:8; 2:38; 8:15, 17, 19; 10:47; 19:2), and filling (2:4; 9:17).[26] These are complementary metaphors, used interchangeably in some contexts, and designed to express different aspects of the same experience. One should not be elevated above the others as an interpretive key to the rest. Thirdly, the Spirit's empowering of Christ's witnesses implies some sort of prophetic enabling, as the narrative in Acts 2:1-37 indicates. However, the witness of the Spirit involves more than inspired speech.[27] The gift of the Spirit to those who believe in 2:38-47 brings a new knowledge of the ascended Lord Jesus, and an experience of salvation among the fellowship of believers. Indeed, the Spirit's work to restore God's people and mould the inner life of the church reverberates throughout the Acts narrative.[28]

Luke is the only NT writer to describe the coming of the Spirit at Pentecost and portray this as a decisive event in salvation history. In one sense, each subsequent reference to the Spirit in Acts must be interpreted in the light of it. But Hur also notices that as the plot of Luke-Acts develops, so do the functions of the Holy Spirit:

> on the one hand, references to the Spirit function to verify group characters as incorporated into God's people; and on the other, the Spirit is

25. D. W. Pao, *Acts and the Isaianic New Exodus*, WUNT 2, no. 130 (Tübingen: Mohr, 2000; repr. Grand Rapids: Baker Academic, 2002), 112-42, has argued that Luke evokes Isaiah's new exodus programme throughout Acts. The postexilic picture of salvation described by Isaiah (and shared by Jeremiah, Ezekiel, and Joel) indicates that before God's people can be a light to the nations, they must be transformed into a people of righteousness.

26. 'Filling' can refer to the initial endowment of the Spirit, or to the special inspiration of a person for prophetic utterance, for preaching, or for testimony to Christ in some other way (4:8, 31; 13:9, 52). Someone who is already filled with or full of the Spirit can receive a further filling or enabling for a particular ministry (4:31).

27. Cf. 5:32 note. Turner, *Power from on High*, 330, outlines different ways in which the narrative of Acts associates the Spirit with witness.

28. Cf. M. Wenk, *Community-Forming Power: The Socio-Ethical Role of the Spirit in Luke-Acts* (Sheffield: Sheffield Academic Press, 2000); Turner, *Power from on High*, 341-43. Luke makes this point in various ways. The lying of Ananias and Sapphira to the believing community is a sin against the Holy Spirit (5:1-9). The Spirit is instrumental in building or strengthening the church on a wide scale (9:31), enabling it to live in the fear of the Lord and go forward with encouragement and comfort. The Spirit endows and equips various individuals for ministry within and between the churches (6:3; 11:28; 20:28). The Spirit guides the Jerusalem Council to make a decision that will enable Jews and Gentiles to live and work together in the churches (15:28-29). The Spirit's work may therefore be assumed in summaries of church life and ministry such as 2:42-47; 4:32-37. Turner rightly acknowledges secondary missiological effects from these activities.

employed in relation to the life-situations of believers in settled communities by granting them charismatic gifts, or comforting and encouraging them or initiating forms of patriarchal leadership.[29]

Pentecostal scholarship has tended to regard the Spirit's coming upon
the disciples at Pentecost, and then upon the Samaritans (8:14-17), the
Gentiles in the house of Cornelius (10:44-8), and twelve 'disciples' in
Ephesus (19:1-7), as providing a paradigm for everyone to experience
Spirit-baptism in addition to conversion. The aim of such an experience is
essentially empowerment for mission.[30] However, Turner has argued extensively for a broader, soteriological view of the Spirit's work in Acts, so
that with the ascension of Christ, the gift of the Spirit becomes 'the key to
the ongoing presence and intensification of the salvation/kingdom of God
which the disciples began to experience through Jesus' ministry'.[31] The
Spirit is given as much to create life in the kingdom — conversion, transformation, and relationship building — as for the numerical growth of the
kingdom — through prophetic ministry and missionary outreach.[32]

According to Luke's Gospel, the disciples had recognized, enjoyed,
and preached the inbreaking kingdom of God in the ministry of Jesus (9:1-
6; cf. 10:1-24). They experienced God's rule in following Jesus and under
the influence of the Spirit working through him. But his death and then his
ascension posed the problem of how they would continue to experience the
powers of the new age shaping their existence. Acts 2 indicates that the answer to their needs was the gift of the Spirit at Pentecost, viewed in terms
of Joel's prophecy. But the outcome was not simply ecstatic speech, inspired preaching, or predictive prophecy. The Spirit is more fundamentally

---

29. Hur, *Dynamic Reading*, 281.

30. Cf. R. P. Menzies, *Empowered for Witness: The Spirit in Luke-Acts* (Sheffield: JSOT,
1994; repr. London: Clark International, 2004). J. M. Penney, *The Missionary Emphasis of
Lukan Pneumatology* (Sheffield: Sheffield Academic, 1997), presents a modified Pentecostal
view.

31. M. M. B. Turner, 'The Spirit and Salvation in Luke-Acts', in G. N. Stanton, B. W.
Longenecker, and S. C. Barton (eds.), *The Holy Spirit and Christian Origins* (Grand Rapids:
Eerdmans, 2004), 115, reflecting the argument of some of his previous works. D. A. Carson,
Showing the Spirit: A Theological Exposition of 1 Corinthians 12–14 (Homebush West, Sydney:
Lancer; Grand Rapids: Baker, 1988), 152-58, largely endorses Turner's approach, but he
rightly warns against jeopardizing the structure of NT eschatology by a failure to assert the
difference that the coming of the Spirit made for the experience of believers. R. P. Menzies,
The Development of Early Christian Pneumatology with Special Reference to Luke-Acts, JSNTSS 54
(Sheffield: JSOT, 1991), 205-79, offers an extensive criticism of Turner's approach. The weak-
est part of Menzies' argument is his treatment of Acts 2:38-39.

32. Acts 15:8-11 is a critical passage for understanding the transforming work of the
Spirit in individuals. Peter links the giving of the Spirit to Gentiles through his preaching of
the gospel with the purifying of their hearts by faith (cf. 10:44-48; 11:15-17). This is further
explained in terms of their being saved by grace through explicit faith in the Lord Jesus. In
other words, the Spirit is not simply given in response to faith, but he enables saving faith.
There is a prevenient and regenerative work of the Spirit, as indicated in Jn. 3:3-8; 2 Thes.
2:13-14; Tit. 3:4-7.

portrayed by Luke in terms of Jewish thinking about the 'Spirit of prophecy' being the organ of communication between God and his people.[33]

As in the OT, the Spirit's presence is associated in Acts with dreams, visions, ecstatic speech, prayer and praise, and words that formed the basis of prophetic utterance and preaching. All of these things belong to the category of what Turner calls 'prophetism'. Joel's emphasis on seeing visions and dreaming dreams was a way of predicting what Jeremiah 31:31-34 also anticipated. In the last days God would enable all his people ('from the least of them to the greatest') to *know* him as Moses and the prophets knew him.[34] There would be a 'democratisation' of access to God, making it possible for all to call on the Lord for salvation and to enjoy his deliverance (cf. Jl. 2:32; Acts 2:38-39). Prophesying, in its various manifestations, would be the means of *giving expression* to that relational knowledge of God made possible through the Spirit. It would involve bringing others to the same experience of God, through bold and effective proclamation of Christ. It would also make possible the edification of the church.[35]

In Acts 2:38-39, the gift of the Spirit is promised to all whom the Lord our God will call to himself, who respond to the preaching of the gospel by repenting and being baptised in the name of Jesus Christ. The purpose of such baptism is to receive the new covenant promise of the forgiveness of sins *and* the gift of the Holy Spirit. The Spirit works through the preaching of the gospel to bring people to faith,[36] and in turning to the Lord Jesus for salvation they receive the fullness of the Spirit, as promised. Acts 2:28-29 establishes the normal expectation of the apostles for those who believe the gospel. Their own experience of being Jesus' disciples for several years and subsequently receiving the Spirit is now set forth as the pattern for others. It is as if the two elements of Jeremiah 31:34 are being offered together: a definitive forgiveness of sins and a profound transformation of Israel's relationship with God, made possible by the gift of his Spirit (cf. Ezk. 36:26-27).[37]

33. Cf. M. M. B. Turner, 'The "Spirit of Prophecy" as the Power of Israel's Restoration and Witness', in Marshall and Peterson, *Witness to the Gospel,* 330-37. Luke evidently regards 'the promise' made to believers (2:38-39) to be 'a christianised version of Joel's "Spirit of prophecy"' (p. 335). Turner thus concludes that Luke does not synthesise some more composite 'promise of the Spirit' by adding other OT prophecies of the eschatological Spirit. However, see my comments on the echoes of Je. 31:31-34 in this text.

34. In the OT, prophetic gifting is the privilege of the few who mediate the knowledge of the Lord to the people (e.g., Nu. 11:16-30; 1 Sa. 10:6; 19:20; 2 Sa. 23:2; 1 Chr. 12:18; 2 Chr. 15:1; 20:14; 24:20). Joel transforms Moses' wish that 'all the LORD's people were prophets' (Nu. 11:29) into a formal prediction.

35. Equivalent possession of the Spirit of prophecy does not necessitate equivalent roles for everyone. Only some are designated as 'prophets' in Acts (11:27; 13:1; 15:32; 21:9, 10), though the Spirit enables a wide range of people to engage in different types of prophetic ministry (e.g., Stephen and Philip [6:5, 8-10; 8:5-8]; ordinary believers engaged in evangelistic outreach [8:4; 11:19-21]). Paul is different from Agabus (11:28) in his level of prophetic authority and significance, as is Peter when compared with Judas and Silas (15:7-11, 32).

36. See note 32 above.

37. Menzies, *Early Christian Pneumatology,* 225-26, argues that it is inappropriate to

The advent of 'the Spirit of prophecy' does not create a special class of spiritually gifted or empowered Christians over against others:

> Rather, it brings to *each* the means of receiving not only 'communion with the Lord' viewed generally, but also the same concretely specified in charismata of heavenly wisdom and knowledge. These may inform the teacher, guide the missionary, lead in individual decisions, give diagnosis to the pastor, 'irresistible wisdom' and power to the preacher, or be related as prophecy to the congregation or other individuals. The 'power' received by the apostles (cf. Acts 1:8) was not something *in addition to* Joel's promised gift, but precisely *an intense experience of* some of the charismata which are part and parcel of the operation of the Spirit as Joel's promised Spirit of prophecy.[38]

The particular displays of charismata at Pentecost and when the Spirit was received by the Samaritans (8:14-17), the Gentiles (10:44-46), and the twelve Ephesian disciples (19:1-7) were 'appropriate divine attestations of the beginning of the whole post-ascension Christian work of the Spirit'.[39] These events were critical moments in the unfolding of God's saving purposes, involving a movement outwards from Jerusalem to new people groups, as predicted and outlined in Acts 1:8. They cannot be taken as universal paradigms for individual experience.[40] Nevertheless, Acts implies that the benefits of Pentecost must be appropriated by every single believer. This happens when people turn to Jesus as Saviour and Lord and become members of the body that the Spirit brought into being at Pentecost. In so doing, they take to themselves the birthright of Christ's body, which is the Spirit himself.[41]

In summary, the Spirit fundamentally communicates the blessings of a relationship with God through faith in Christ. The Spirit then works through those who have turned to the Lord Jesus, enabling them to com-

---

link the prophecies of Joel, Jeremiah, and Ezekiel because this was rarely done in Jewish literature. However, NT interpreters are bound to relate such eschatological prophecies when the context allows for it and other NT writings point to the appropriateness of such a link. Cf. J. D. G. Dunn, *Baptism in the Holy Spirit: A Re-examination of the New Testament Teaching on the Gift of the Spirit in Relation to Pentecostalism Today*, SBT (Second Series) 15 (London: SCM, 1970), 47-49.

38. M. M. B. Turner, 'Spiritual Gifts Then and Now', *VE* 15 (1985), 51.

39. Turner, 'Spiritual Gifts', 52. The historical and contextual reasons for these events are discussed in the Commentary as each passage is interpreted.

40. Turner, 'Spirit of Prophecy', 338-39, points out that 'the only passage which postpones the gift of the Spirit to a point discernibly later than Christian baptism is Acts 8:12-17, and 8:16 implies that this was exceptional (the notice would be redundant if the Spirit were normally given subsequent to baptism)'. Water baptism and the gift of the Spirit are then linked together again in the narrative of Saul's conversion (9:17-18; cf. 2:38-39).

41. D. J. Williams, *Acts*, GNC (San Francisco: Harper, 1985), 26, rightly observes that, 'when we become Christians, we participate in the baptism with the Spirit that uniquely took place on that day so long ago'.

municate salvation to unbelievers and to make disciples. Believing communities are established by the Spirit; in them gifted individuals minister to one another to edify the church and make it grow. Together with angels, heavenly voices, and visions, the Spirit initiates new phases of mission and oversees the direction of mission (8:29, 39; 10:19, 44; 13:2-4; 16:6-10). The Spirit establishes and preserves unity between different racial and cultural groups in the church (8:14-17; 11:12, 15-18),[42] providing guidance in important ecclesial and personal decisions (6:1-7; 15:12, 28-29, 32; 20:22-24, 28). As the Spirit imparts wisdom and knowledge of the risen Lord, he effects changes in the lives of believers on a communal as well as on an individual level.

IV. SALVATION

Salvation is a central concept in Luke's theology, playing a key role in both volumes of his work. The terminology is more frequently used by Luke than by any other Gospel writer, and with a wider application.[43] An initial reference to God as 'my Saviour' occurs in Mary's Song (1:46-55), where Mary links the fulfillment of the promise made to her about the birth of a son (1:29-37) with God's consistent pattern of rescuing and restoring 'his servant Israel'. Zechariah also employs the terminology, as he blesses God for raising up 'a horn of salvation' for his people 'in the house of his servant David' (1:68-70). The messianic salvation is first portrayed in terms of rescue from enemies, in faithfulness to God's covenant promises, to enable his people 'to serve him without fear in holiness and righteousness' (1:71-75).[44] Zechariah then predicts that his son John will prepare the way for the Lord himself, 'to give his people the knowledge of salvation through the forgiveness of their sins' (1:76-77; cf. Is. 40:3-8). John's offer of 'a baptism of repentance for the forgiveness of sins' is soon identified as the fulfillment of this expectation (3:3-6). He warns about 'the wrath to come' (3:7-14), and employs images of separation and judgment when describing the imminent arrival of the Messiah (3:15-18).

The promise that God is coming to save his people merges in Luke 1 with the idea that salvation will be accomplished by the Son of David

42. Hur, *Dynamic Reading*, 283, observes that 'the Spirit's direct speeches and actions are noticeably highlighted in relation to the witness-mission to non-Jews'. Cf. 8:29, 39; 10:19; 11:12; 13:2-4; 15:28; 16:6-7.

43. I. H. Marshall, *Luke: Historian and Theologian* (Exeter: Paternoster, 1970), 94-102, gives a brief overview of Luke's concept of salvation, based on a preliminary survey of the use of the terminology.

44. J. B. Green, '"Salvation to the End of the Earth" (Acts 13:47): God as Saviour in the Acts of the Apostles', in Marshall and Peterson, *Witness to the Gospel*, 92-94, considers ways in which the promise of deliverance from enemies is fulfilled in the narrative of Luke-Acts.

promised to Mary. Moreover, broader categories of salvation familiar from OT prophetic literature merge with the specific prospect of salvation through *the forgiveness of sins* (cf. Is. 43:25; 44:22; Je. 31:34).[45] Salvation is also associated in 1:78-79 with the shining of divine *light* on those 'living in darkness and in the shadow of death' (cf. Is. 9:2; 42:6-7, 16; Lk. 2:28-32; 4:18-21), and guidance 'into the path of *peace*' (cf. Is. 9:6; 59:8; Lk. 2:14, 29). Luke's opening chapter thus indicates both continuity and discontinuity with OT teaching on the subject. There are significant Jewish roots to this theology, although it is not sufficient to see it as merely 'an extension of the concepts found in the Hebrew Scriptures'.[46]

Luke alone records the angelic ascription of the title 'Saviour' to Jesus (2:11), and this is later echoed in the preaching of Peter (Acts 5:31) and Paul (13:23).[47] Simeon proclaims that the promised salvation has become visible in the person of Jesus (Lk. 2:28-32), but he also warns of the division that 'the Lord's Messiah' (2:26) will bring within Israel, provoking antagonism against himself (2:33-35). Thus, the achievement of salvation is associated from the beginning of Luke's work with the rejection and suffering of the Messiah (cf. Lk. 9:22, 44-45; 12:49-53; 13:32-33; 18:31-34; 22:20-23, 35-37; 24:26, 46).

Jesus begins his public ministry by proclaiming the fulfillment of Isaiah 61:1-2 (Lk. 4:16-21). The terminology of salvation is not used in this passage, though the words cited indicate the gracious, saving character of his message.[48] Jesus' quotation from Isaiah finishes with the proclamation of the year of the Lord's favour, and does not include the words 'and the day of vengeance of our God'. By implication, his ministry will delay the final

45. B. Witherington III, 'Salvation and Health in Christian Antiquity: The Soteriology of Luke-Acts in Its First-Century Setting', in Marshall and Peterson, *Witness to the Gospel*, 156, argues that when the later prophets refer to God's future salvation of his people, the subject is often 'a final temporal deliverance into the Holy land, not forgiveness of sins, not conversion, not a heavenly reward, not a final resurrection'. But promises of forgiveness, spiritual renewal, and the resurrection of Israel are part of the wider OT prophetic agenda, not always specifically linked to the language of salvation.

46. Witherington, 'Salvation and Health', 155. Witherington prefers to speak of a final fulfillment in Christ of God's promises, rather than a continuum or extension of the salvation referred to in the OT. R. C. Tannehill, *The Shape of Luke's Story: Essays on Luke-Acts* (Eugene: Cascade, 2005), 50, notes how the scene of Jesus' arrival in Jerusalem (Lk. 19:37-44) looks back to the birth narratives, and 'indicates that these hopes will not now be fulfilled for Jerusalem because of its blindness'. Luke-Acts is concerned with 'transformed expectations' for Israel, but also 'persistent hopes'.

47. The language of salvation was an important feature of the veneration of the Roman Emperor Caesar Augustus, who was referred to as 'saviour'. Green, 'Salvation to the end of the earth', 87-88, says that this conveyed the notion of 'beneficent power for the provision of a variety of blessings'. Witherington, 'Salvation and Health', 148, argues that Luke's presentation was implicitly a challenge to contemporary religious, social, and political views of salvation.

48. Tannehill, *Shape of Luke's Story*, 26-27, points out that 'gracious words' in Lk. 4:22 refers 'not simply to the form of Jesus' words or to the impression which they made, but to their content.'

judgment and provide people with the opportunity to be reconciled to God. The Spirit-anointed Messiah is sent by God 'to proclaim good news to the poor' (*euangelizomai* ['evangelise'], as in 1:19; 2:10; 3:18; 4:43; 7:22; 8:1; 9:6; 16:16: 20:1). This involves proclaiming 'freedom for the prisoners' (*aphesis* ['release' or 'forgiveness'], as in 1:77; 3:3; 24:47) and 'recovery of sight for the blind'.[49]

In the following scenes, there is narrative and parabolic development of the themes of forgiveness and repentance (e.g., 5:17-32; 7:36-50; 15:1-32). 'Repentance and forgiveness together refer to the transformation in human lives that results from God's saving action in fulfilling the promises of salvation through Israel's Messiah.'[50] Through the preaching of the gospel, God grants both the opportunity and the incentive for repentance (e.g., Lk. 1:16-17; 3:18; 5:32; 24:47; Acts 5:31; 14:15; 20:20-21). Salvation is offered in advance of the anticipated coming of 'the Son of Man' and final judgment (5:24; 11:29-32; 12:4-10, 40-46; 13:1-9, 22-30; 17:22-37; 18:7-8; 21:25-36).

As in the other Gospels, the verb *sōzein* ('save') is employed with reference to the saving of life by healing or by rescue from some other plight.[51] As also in the other Gospels, this verb is used with reference to entering the kingdom of God or enjoying eternal life.[52] In various healing incidents, a picture is painted of how to receive eschatological salvation through faith in Jesus (e.g., 5:17-26; 8:43-48; 17:15-19; 18:35-43). However, the narrative describing the restoration of a woman 'who lived a sinful life' (7:36-50, Luke only) involves no physical healing. It concludes with the statement 'your faith has saved you' (physical healing is intended by the same expression in 8:48; 17:19; 18:42). In the context, this is clearly related to her repentance and Jesus' declaration that her sins are forgiven.

This last incident, together with the story of Zacchaeus (19:1-10, Luke only), best illustrates what the reception of salvation means in the period of Jesus' public ministry.[53] In the encounter with Zacchaeus, as Jesus approaches Jerusalem for the last time, there are two important references to salvation that are not recorded in any other Gospel. Jesus first declares that 'salvation has come to this house' (v. 9), because Zacchaeus has welcomed the Messiah gladly (v. 6) and expressed genuine repentance for his sins

---

49. Although Jesus heals those who are physically blind (7:21-22; 18:35) — and this message could be taken as a pointer to such miracles — both the original prophecy and the miracles of restoration point to the spiritual enlightenment and renewal needed by Israel as a nation (cf. 1:78-79; Is. 9:2; 42:6-7, 16).

50. Tannehill, *Shape of Luke's Story*, 88. Tannehill, 84-101, observes how frequently the language of turning or repenting occurs in Luke-Acts, in conjunction with the emphasis on forgiveness through Christ. He rightly argues that repentance is a human action with ethical implications, but that, theologically discerned, it is also 'divine action in individuals and societies' (p. 89).

51. Lk. 6:9; 8:36, 48, 50; 17:19; 18:42; 23:35, 37, 39.

52. Lk. 8:12 (in the light of 8:10); 9:23-25; 13:23; 18:24-30; 19:10 (cf. 15:32, where 'lost-found' is paired with 'dead-alive').

53. Cf. Marshall, *Historian and Theologian*, 116-56.

(v. 8). Then Jesus identifies the purpose of his coming more generally by saying, 'the Son of Man came to seek and to save what was lost' (v. 10).[54] Salvation is thus portrayed as a new or renewed relationship with God, established through repentance and faith on the one hand, and the reception of divine forgiveness on the other. It is losing one's life to Jesus in order to enter the kingdom of God and experience eternal life (cf. 9:23-26; 18:26-30). It is the enjoyment in the present of the eschatological salvation that the Messiah came to achieve for his people.

This concept is developed in Acts with reference to faith in the crucified and glorified Jesus, the gift of the Holy Spirit, and the sharing of this salvation with the nations.[55] The word *sōtēria* ('salvation') occurs six times (4:12; 7:25; 13:26, 47; 16:17; 27:34), with the neuter form of the adjective *sōtērion* being used as a substitute once (28:28). The verb *sōzein* ('save') is employed thirteen times (2:21, 40, 47; 4:9, 12; 11:14; 14:9; 15:1, 11; 16:30, 31; 27:20, 31), and the noun *sōtēr* ('saviour') twice (5:31; 13:23). Sometimes the verb is employed in the sense of rescue from danger (e.g., 7:25; 27:20, 31, 34) or deliverance from sickness (e.g., 4:9; 14:9), though this usage is less common in Luke's second volume.[56]

Witherington observes that Luke never uses the terms *sōtēr*, *sōtēria*, or *sōtērion* when he relates stories about the healing of the sick or the raising of the dead. It is as though he has 'reserved these nouns to refer to something of more enduring and eternal significance'.[57] However, the verb *sōzein* may be used in 4:9 to suggest that healing in the name of Jesus points to his ability to provide the salvation offered in the gospel (cf. 3:12-26; 4:8-12). More fundamentally, the terminology in Acts 27–28 highlights the fact that God alone is able to deliver from death.[58]

The need for eschatological salvation is first emphasised in Acts 2:16-21, when Peter quotes from Joel 2:38-32. This programmatic prophecy talks about salvation from God's judgment on the coming 'day of the Lord', and ends with the promise that 'whoever calls on the name of the Lord will be

---

54. The question of how a son of Abraham can be lost and in need of salvation is variously addressed throughout Luke's Gospel, as Jesus encounters people in need of rescue and restoration, and as he teaches about the need for repentance, as in the parables of Luke 15.

55. Cf. Marshall, *Historian and Theologian*, 157-215.

56. Witherington, 'Salvation and Health', 146, shows that 'the "salvation" most ancients looked for was from disease, disaster, or death in this life, and the "redemption" many pagans cried out for was redemption from the social bondage of slavery, not from the personal bondage to sin'. Witherington, 155, notes that the LXX and the Hebrew Scriptures reveal a use of the terminology for 'material deliverance attended by spiritual blessings'.

57. Witherington, 'Salvation and Health', 154. He rightly points out that 'healing' itself is not portrayed in Luke-Acts 'as either a necessary or sufficient description of what "salvation" in Christ entails' (p. 150).

58. The verbs *sōzō* (27:20, 31) and *diasōzō* (27:43, 44; 28:1, 4) are used in conjunction with the noun *sōtēria* (27:34). In a narrative sense, this whole sequence is a reminder to readers of their need for divine salvation in the fullest sense.

saved'. Peter proclaims that, as a result of his death, resurrection, and ascension, Jesus is the Lord upon whom to call for such salvation (2:36-40). Repentance and baptism 'in the name of Jesus Christ' are necessary for the forgiveness of sins and reception of the Holy Spirit. With Jesus physically absent, ultimate salvation is secured by taking hold of the present benefits offered in his name. Reconciliation with God in the present is a preliminary to rescue from the coming judgment and the enjoyment of life in a renewed creation, as promised by the prophets (3:19-21; cf. Is. 35:1-10; 65:17-25; Ezk. 47:1-12).

Rescue from divine judgment is needed because of human rebellion against God in various forms: moral failure (Lk. 3:7-17; Acts 24:25), refusal to recognise and receive God's messengers past and present (Lk. 13:33-35; 19:41-44; Acts 7:51-53), betrayal of the Lord's Messiah (Acts 2:23; 3:13-15), idolatry, and false religion (Acts 17:29-31).[59] Forgiveness is related to rescue from 'this corrupt generation' in Acts 2:40, but the need for salvation should not be simply linked with the recent events in Jerusalem. Forgiveness and repentance need to be preached to all nations (Lk. 24:47; Acts 10:42-43; 26:17-20), because sin is regarded as a universal problem. Stenschke argues that people need to be saved 'because they are part of one of the many generations that have failed or is presently failing before God and thus constitute corrupt humanity'.[60] He concludes that 'people need to be saved because of their alienation from God, which shows itself in their attitude towards him, towards themselves and their fellow people, and which culminated in the rejection of Jesus'.[61]

There is a progression in Luke-Acts in the way salvation is experienced, and this is explained by the events of Good Friday, Easter, and Pentecost:

> In Luke's way of thinking salvation in the fuller and more spiritual sense comes about because of Christ's death and resurrection, and the means of receiving the benefits of these climactic events is through the Holy Spirit, who is not sent before Pentecost to be and convey God's soteriological blessing.[62]

59. Cf. C. Stenschke, 'The Need for Salvation', in Marshall and Peterson, *Witness to the Gospel*, 130-32. Stenschke, 126-29, discusses several scholarly approaches to Luke's anthropology and re-examines the evidence for himself. Both Jews and Gentiles are presented by Luke as being in darkness, and captive to sin and its consequences.

60. Stenschke, 'The Need for Salvation', 140. Stenschke, 135-40, reviews the use of 'generation' language in Luke-Acts (Lk. 7:31-35; 9:41; 11:29-32, 50-52; 17:25-29; 21:32; Acts 2:40) and discusses OT parallels. He concludes that this terminology is used to reveal that 'people have a deeper problem in their relationship with God than what could be termed moral-ethical' (p. 139).

61. Stenschke, 'The Need for Salvation', 144. Green, 'Salvation to the End of the Earth', 91-92, makes the point that salvation involves being incorporated into the community of those who have turned to Christ (Acts 2:47).

62. Witherington, 'Salvation and Health', 154.

The salvation that Luke describes is not something that humans can attain for themselves, but is the gift of God.[63] This is related to Luke's understanding of the role of the Holy Spirit as the agent of the exalted Lord Jesus in applying the blessings of salvation to individuals (Acts 2:33-38, 47; 10:15-18).[64] But it is also related to the achievement of the cross, which is discussed below in connection with the theology of atonement in Luke-Acts.

Another significant point of progression from the Gospel to Acts is the offering of salvation to the nations (cf. Lk. 24:46-49; Acts 1:8; 8:4-40; 9:15; 10:34-43; 13:46-48; 22:21; 28:25-29).[65] In Acts 4:12 Peter declares that salvation can be found only in Jesus Christ, 'for there is no other name under heaven given among mortals by which we must be saved'. The gospel has a universal scope and is the message of salvation for all peoples (10:34-36, 42-43; 15:7-11; 26:17-18, 22-23). But it is a message for Israel first, not simply because of the ancient promises made by God, but also because those who rejected and crucified Jesus need the forgiveness he has made possible for them (3:13-15, 17-20; 5:30-31).

The resurrection of Jesus is presented as a pointer to his role in the judgment to come (2:31-35; 10:39-42; 17:31), but also as a guarantee of the general resurrection of the dead (4:2; 26:23). The resurrection hope of Israel has been realised already in God's raising Christ from the dead (cf. 23:6; 24:24; 26:6-8; 28:20), although it remains thus far unrealised for believers. However, 'its realising in the raising of Christ is the guarantee of its coming fulfillment for others'.[66]

V. THE GOSPEL

In contrast with the other Synoptics, Luke does not contain the word 'gospel' *(euangelion),* and this important term occurs only twice in Acts (15:7, 'the word of the gospel'; 20:24, 'the gospel of the grace of God'). However, the related verb 'evangelise', or 'preach the gospel' *(euangelizomai),* is extensively used throughout Luke-Acts,[67] together with other terms of proclamation and persuasion. This suggests Luke's concern to highlight the im-

---

63. Cf. Marshall, *Historian and Theologian,* 188-92.

64. Witherington, 'Salvation and Health', 158. Cf. Marshall, *Historian and Theologian,* 199-202.

65. However, B. S. Rosner, 'The Progress of the Word', in Marshall and Peterson, *Witness to the Gospel,* 220, lists six ways in which Luke's Gospel points forward to the universal perspective of Acts.

66. F. F. Bruce, *The Book of the Acts,* NICNT (Grand Rapids: Eerdmans, 1954; rev. ed. 1988), 59.

67. Lk. 1:19; 2:10; 3:18; 4:18, 43; 7:22; 8:1; 9:6; 16:16; 20:1; Acts 5:42; 8:4, 12, 25, 35, 40; 10:36; 11:20; 13:32; 14:7, 15, 21; 15:35; 16:10; 17:18. On the resurrection in Acts, see p. 188 n. 9 below.

portance of the *activity* by which God addresses people and draws them to himself. However, the message itself is clearly the key to this divine engagement. Luke regularly uses the Greek noun *logos* in various combinations to describe the 'word' proclaimed by Jesus (Lk. 4:32; 10:39 ['his message']; 5:1; 8:11, 21; 11:28 ['the word of God']; 9:26; 21:33; 24:44 ['my words']) and by his disciples (Acts 2:41 [Peter's message]; 4:4; 8:4; 10:44; 16:6; 18:5 ['the word']; 4:31; 6:2, 7; 8:14; 11:1; 12:24; 13:5, 7, 44, 46, 48; 16:32; 17:13; 18:11 ['the word of God']; 8:25; 13:49; 15:36; 19:10, 20 ['the word of the Lord']; 13:26 ['the message of this salvation']; 14:3; 20:32 ['the message of his grace']). This linguistic choice suggests the continuity of the Christian message with the prophetic scriptures and the divine origin and authority of the gospel as 'the word of God'. When it is called 'the word of the Lord', it is likely that the stress is specifically on Jesus as the source of the apostolic message. When other qualifiers are used ('message of this salvation', 'the message of his grace'), the focus is on the content of the revelation received and communicated.[68] But what is that word?

Much scholarly research has taken place on the evangelistic sermons in Acts, with respect to their structure, contents, theology, and rhetorical style.[69] Dodd was a pioneer in this field. Although he did not believe that the speeches attributed to Peter in Acts 2:14-36, 38-39; 3:12-26; 4:8-12; 10:34-43 are actual records of what Peter said, he proposed that they are 'based upon material which proceeded from the Aramaic-speaking Church at Jerusalem, and was substantially earlier than the period at which the book was written'.[70] Noting how these speeches supplement one another, he concluded that, 'taken together they afford a comprehensive view of the content of the early *kerygma*'.[71] In summary, they proclaim that the age of fulfillment has dawned; this has taken place through the ministry, death, and resurrection of Jesus; by virtue of his resurrection Jesus has been ex-

68. Note also *ta rhēmata* ('words') with reference to the gospel in Acts 5:2; 10:44; 13:42, and *rhēma theou* ('the word of God') in Lk. 3:2, with reference to John's message. Cf. my INTRODUCTION TO ACTS: IV.B.1. The Progress of 'the Word' (pp. 32-34).

69. Cf. M. Soards, *The Speeches in Acts: Their Content, Context and Concerns* (Louisville: John Knox/Westminster, 1994). H. F. Bayer, 'The Preaching of Peter in Acts', in Marshall and Peterson, *Witness to the Gospel*, 257-74, offers a review of the work done on the Petrine speeches; H.-W. Neudorfer, 'The Speech of Stephen', in Marshall and Peterson, 275-94, gives special attention to the speech of Stephen; and G. W. Hansen, 'The Preaching and Defence of Paul', in Marshall and Peterson, 295-324, considers the preaching and defence speeches of Paul in Acts. In the Introduction, I discuss the authenticity and style of these speeches under 'Rhetoric' and 'Character, Structure and Purpose' (pp. 19-23, 27-29).

70. C. H. Dodd, *The Apostolic Preaching and Its Developments* (London: Hodder, 1936), 20.

71. Dodd, *Apostolic Preaching*, 21, rightly took the Greek word *kerygma* to mean '*what* is preached', whereas others have taken it to refer to 'the *act* of preaching'. Although God clearly encounters people through the act of proclamation, the actual content of the message is critical for Luke and the preachers in Acts. Dodd's hard-and-fast distinction between preaching and teaching (pp. 7-9) cannot be sustained when a careful study of the terminology and content of Christian communication in Acts is undertaken.

alted at the right hand of God, as the messianic head of the new Israel; the Holy Spirit in the church is the sign of Christ's present power and glory; the Messianic Age will shortly reach its consummation in the return of Christ; repentance is necessary in order to receive the offer of forgiveness and the Holy Spirit, and the promise of 'salvation' (i.e., 'the life of the Age to Come') to those who enter the elect community.

Dodd went on to show the links between the sermon attributed to Paul in Acts 13:16-41 and the Petrine *kerygma*.[72] Moreover, a comparison of the Pauline letters with the speeches in Acts led Dodd to discover 'a fairly clear and certain outline sketch of the preaching of the apostles'.[73] Dodd recognised that, within the NT, there is 'an immense range of variety in the interpretation that is given to the *kerygma*', but he was convinced that 'in all such interpretation, the essential elements of the original *kerygma* are steadily kept in view'.[74] Despite the diversity that he saw, he believed that there was one gospel, which could be discerned in the NT as a whole.

Although disagreeing with Dodd in certain respects, Dunn acknowledges that we can recognise within the different sermons reproduced in Acts a regular outline which may be said to provide a solid core which we can call the basic *kerygma* of the earliest church.[75] For Dunn, the most regular and foundational elements are proclamation of the resurrection of Jesus; the call for a response to this proclamation for repentance and faith in this Jesus; and the promise of forgiveness, salvation, and the Spirit to those who so respond.

However, the very simplicity of this outline is problematic when Dunn seeks to compare this *kerygma* with the preaching of Jesus and the *kerygma* of Paul's letters. For example, Dunn expresses a widely held view when he says, 'Jesus proclaimed the kingdom; the sermons in Acts *proclaim Jesus*. Jesus has become the content of the message; the proclaimer has become the proclaimed'.[76] But the kingdom of God remains a key for understanding the gospel in Acts. It is mentioned at significant points in the narrative as a way of describing the preaching of the gospel, and it is clearly the theological context or framework in which Jesus was proclaimed as

---

72. Dodd, *Apostolic Preaching*, 29-30.

73. Dodd, *Apostolic Preaching*, 31.

74. Dodd, *Apostolic Preaching*, 74.

75. J. D. G. Dunn, *Unity and Diversity in the New Testament: An Inquiry into the Character of Earliest Christianity* (London: SCM, 1977), 11-32, is really an extended critique of Dodd's position. I have engaged more fully with Dunn's argument in D. G. Peterson, 'Kerygma or Kerygmata: Is There Only One Gospel in the New Testament?', in C. Green (ed.), *God's Power to Save: One Gospel for a Complex World?* (Leicester: Apollos, 2006), 155-84.

76. Dunn, *Unity and Diversity*, 17. Dunn thinks it is striking that the actual sermons in Acts contain remarkably few echoes of Jesus' own message and teaching. He also argues that there is hardly any concern shown for the historical Jesus, but then immediately qualifies this by referring to 2:22 and 10:36-39. A difference of emphasis does not establish a discontinuity between Jesus' proclamation of the kingdom and the apostolic proclamation of Jesus and the kingdom in Acts.

Lord and Christ (Acts 19:8-10; 20:21-27; 28:23, 31; cf. 1:3). Sometimes it is simply stated that the early Christian preachers proclaimed the kingdom (8:12; 19:8; 20:25; cf. 14:22), and sometimes it appears that the preaching was exclusively Christological (e.g., 2:14-41; 3:12-26; 4:8-12). Although Jesus has become more explicitly the content of the message in Acts, his teaching in the Gospel progressively reveals how central he is to the fulfillment of God's kingdom purpose (e.g., Lk. 4:16-27; 5:22-24, 27-32; 9:18-27).

The following paragraphs expand Dodd's outline of the Petrine speeches and incorporate key points from the sermon preached by Paul in the synagogue at Pisidian Antioch. Context undoubtedly influenced the shape and focus of these different speeches, but it is remarkable that certain themes regularly emerge in them all. Paul's Athenian address (17:22-31) is a special case, though there are some points of overlap with his preaching to Jewish audiences (cf. 17:17-18).[77]

The age of fulfillment theme appears first in 2:15-21, where Peter uses Joel 2:28-32 to explain the Pentecost event. However, the note of fulfillment is sounded again when 'God's deliberate plan and foreknowledge' is mentioned in connection with Jesus' betrayal and death (2:23), and the meaning of his resurrection and ascension is explored in terms of other scriptural texts (2:24-36). Peter's second sermon is driven by the need to explain the healing of the man who was lame and to highlight the authority of the 'name' of Jesus in the process (3:16).[78] However, even this occasional setting moves Peter to begin with a reference to 'the God of Abraham, the God of Isaac, and the God of Jacob, the God of our fathers' (3:13) and to conclude with a reference to the fulfillment of the promise to Abraham in the sending of Jesus to Israel (3:25-26). Other important scriptural allusions in this sermon occur in relation to the glorification of Jesus as the rejected Servant of the Lord (3:13-15, 18; cf. Is. 52:13–53:12) and the promised restoration of all things (3:20-21; cf. Is. 65:17-25). The fulfillment theme appears only briefly at the climax of the message preached to Cornelius and his household (10:42-43), and only by allusion to scriptural themes in the brief response to the Sanhedrin in 5:30-32. Yet it constitutes the basis of the first main portion of Paul's sermon in the synagogue at Pisidian Antioch (13:16-25) and reappears as an essential part of his Christological exposition (13:32-37) and warning to the hearers (13:40-41).

77. The theme of fulfillment, which would have been less appropriate for such an audience, is replaced in Acts 17 by a biblical perspective on creation, God's character, and his purpose for humanity in the created order. Luke's brief record of this address nevertheless concludes with the proclamation of Jesus' resurrection, the coming judgment, and the need for repentance. Key elements in Paul's gospel are preceded by a biblical apologetic, based more on the early chapters of Genesis than prophetic expectations.

78. This 'name of Jesus' theology emerges again in a further defence of the healing of the lame man (4:8-12), where the fulfillment aspect of the *kerygma* is expressed in terms of Ps. 118:22, and the death and resurrection of Jesus are said to achieve the salvation which has been expounded in the two preceding sermons.

The ministry, death, and resurrection of Jesus are fundamental to every gospel proclamation, but with different degrees of emphasis. The fullest accounts are found in 2:22-24; 10:36-42; 13:26-31 (even preceded by details about the significance of the ministry of John the Baptist in 13:24-25). The focus in 3:13-15; 4:10-12; 5:30-31 is rather more on the betrayal, death and glorification of Jesus as the Lord's servant. This focus is specifically linked to an appeal for repentance on the part of those who crucified Jesus and is accompanied by the offer of forgiveness and salvation (though this offer is not confined to such contexts). Exclusive reference to the resurrection of Jesus and its implications is found only in 17:30-31. It is important to notice how normally the cross and resurrection are closely linked in the apostolic preaching.

The exaltation of Jesus at the right hand of God, as the messianic head of the new Israel, is explicitly mentioned in 2:33-36, where it is closely linked with the theme of *the Holy Spirit in the Church as the sign of Christ's present power and glory.* In this programmatic sermon, Jesus is proclaimed as 'both Lord and Messiah', with the first title indicating his identity in relation to the prophecy of Joel 2:32 and the second in relation to the prediction of Psalm 110:1. Peter's second sermon is much more focussed on explaining a healing in the name of Jesus and offering forgiveness and a share in the messianic restoration of all things to those who 'killed the author of life'. His exaltation is more specifically as the rejected Servant of the Lord in 3:13-15, and the Holy Spirit is possibly alluded to in the promise of 'times of refreshing' before the return of the Messiah and the ultimate restoration (3:20-21). The heavenly exaltation is not explicitly mentioned in 4:10-12, though it could be implied from the use of Psalm 118:22. Exaltation to the right hand of God to be 'Prince and Saviour' is stressed in 5:31, and the promise of the Holy Spirit is closely linked with this proclamation in 5:32. The exaltation of Jesus may be implied from the description of him as 'Lord of all' in 10:36 and the declaration that he is 'the one whom God appointed as judge of the living and the dead' (10:42). The Holy Spirit is not offered to the household of Cornelius, though the text implies that the preacher was interrupted by the actual coming of the Spirit on those who heard (10:44-46; cf. 10:38, where Jesus himself is anointed with the Holy Spirit for his earthly ministry). The messianic kingship of Jesus is emphasised in 13:23, 32-37, though the ascension as a sequel to the resurrection is not mentioned. Here again the Holy Spirit is not mentioned and, as in 3:17-21; 4:11-12; 10:43, the focus is on the offer of forgiveness or participation in eschatological salvation through Jesus.

The idea that *the Messianic Age will shortly reach its consummation in the return of Christ* is most fully explained in 3:20-21, where it is part of a sequence explaining how the present experience of healing and forgiveness is an anticipation of the promised restoration of all things. Peter introduces the theme of Jesus as 'the one appointed by God to be judge of the living and the dead' (10:42) without linking this to any promise of his return. In the narrative of Acts, Stephen's vision of Jesus as the Son of Man (7:56) and Paul's proclamation of Jesus as the judge (17:31) help to confirm the view that the salvation so often mentioned means rescue from the coming judgment of God (cf. 2:20-21, where this theological context is established, and 3:23, where it is indicated in a different way). The offer of forgiveness is similarly to be understood within that eschatological or kingdom-of-God framework.

Repentance is necessary in order to receive the offer of forgiveness and the Holy Spirit, and the promise of 'salvation' (i.e., 'the life of the Age to Come') to those who enter the elect community. In one way or another, this is made clear in all the recorded sermons (2:37-39; 3:17-21; 4:12; 5:31; 10:43; 13:38-39). The precise way in which salvation is offered varies with the context, as does the presentation of the person and work of Christ. But the reader of Acts is surely meant to discern the interconnections and gain a cumulative but consistent picture of what was proclaimed and promised.[79]

VI. THE ATONING WORK OF JESUS

Many scholars see no atoning significance in Luke's presentation of the death of Jesus and no connection with the forgiveness of sins.[80] Even the citation from Isaiah 53 in Acts 8:32-33 is said to demonstrate that Luke is interested 'not in the atoning death of Jesus but in the fulfillment of scripture in the obedient passion (silence), death (humiliation), and resurrection (taking up from the earth) of the Servant'.[81]

Nevertheless, in a Passover context, Jesus speaks at the Last Supper of inaugurating 'the new covenant in my blood, which is poured out for you' (Lk. 22:19-20). Alluding to Jeremiah 31:34, he implies that his death will make possible a definitive forgiveness of sins (cf. Mt. 26:28; Mk. 14:24; 1 Cor. 11:25). There can be no doubt that Jesus' eucharistic words 'root human salvation in the death of Jesus'.[82] In narrative terms, they introduce a

79. It is this 'word' which grew the church in apostolic times and which Luke implicitly commends to his readers as the continuing means by which God grows his people in the world and sustains them for the inheritance he has prepared for them (20:32).

80. H. Conzelmann, *The Theology of St. Luke*, trans. G. Buswell (New York: Harper & Row, 1960), 200-201, was very influential in promoting this view. D. D. Sylva (ed.), *Reimaging the Death of the Lukan Jesus* (Frankfurt: Anton Hain, 1990), records a variety of ways in which the death of Jesus in Luke-Acts has been understood.

81. Sylva, *Reimaging*, 146. In D. G. Peterson, 'Atonement Theology in Luke-Acts: Some Methodological Reflections', in P. J. Williams, A. D. Clarke, P. M. Head, and D. Instone-Brewer (ed.), *The New Testament in Its First-Century Setting: Essays on Context and Background in Honour of B. W. Winter on His 65th Birthday* (Grand Rapids/Cambridge: Eerdmans, 2004), 56-71, I review and critique a number of these views.

82. J. B. Green, 'The Death of Jesus, God's Servant', in Sylva, *Reimaging*, 3-4. However, Green inadequately concludes that 'Luke has neither exploited the redemptive themes

telling sequence of sayings and events in Luke's Gospel. Jesus goes on to cite Isaiah 53:12, preceded by an emphatic insistence that this Scripture must be fulfilled in him, and followed by the affirmation, 'what is written about me is reaching its fulfillment' (22:37). Although there is debate about whether the specific reference ('and he was numbered with the transgressors') means that the whole passage from Isaiah 53 is in view, this seems most likely from the unfolding of Luke's passion narrative.[83] In essence, the phrase 'he was numbered among the transgressors' shows that 'he was occupied with the fact that he, who least deserved it, was to be punished as a wrongdoer'.[84] The crucifixion scene suggests the fulfillment of Isaiah 53 as a whole, with the penitent thief acknowledging the injustice of the sentence against Jesus and asking to be remembered when he comes into his kingdom (23:32-43). The scriptural necessity of Messiah's death and resurrection is then reaffirmed in Luke 24:26, 44-46, and made the basis for the challenge to preach 'repentance for the forgiveness of sins' in Jesus' name 'to all nations, beginning from Jerusalem' (24:47). Salvation is clearly linked to the shedding of Christ's blood and his subsequent resurrection at the end of Luke's first volume.

Several texts in Acts reveal how the death of Christ was salvific and how this was explained by the earliest Christians to 'outsiders'. In 5:30-32, Jesus' resurrection and exaltation to the right hand of God as 'Prince and Saviour' make it possible for him to offer repentance and forgiveness of sins to Israel (cf. 2:38; 3:19-20, 26; 11:18). Jesus was killed by 'hanging him on a tree' (5:30; cf. 10:39; 13:29; 1 Pet. 2:24, where similar language is found). This unusual way of describing his crucifixion seems to be an allusion to Deuteronomy 21:22-23, suggesting that Jesus was under the curse of God. The raising of Jesus in this sequence of thought proclaims his vindication and ability to save from God's judgment even those who condemned him to death. While there may not be an articulated theology of Christ becoming a curse for us here (cf. Gal. 3:13-14), a penal and substitutionary dimension to his death may be assumed from the cumulative effect of the argument in 5:30-31. 'These allusions serve to locate Jesus' death firmly in the

---

of the Last Supper nor made this material his own by integrating it more fully into his narrative.' B. M. Metzger, *A Textual Commentary on the Greek New Testament: A Companion Volume to the United Bible Societies' Greek New Testament (Fourth Revised Edition)* (2nd ed.; Stuttgart/ New York: United Bible Societies, 1994), 148-50, discusses the textual difficulties associated with Lk. 22:19-20.

83. Green, 'The Death of Jesus', 22-23, actually makes this point, but he does not satisfactorily incorporate this insight into his overall argument. W. J. Larkin, 'Luke's Use of the Old Testament as a Key to His Soteriology', *JETS* 20 (1977), 325-35, shows how Luke's passion narrative indicates the fulfillment of Isaiah 53 more extensively.

84. R. T. France, *Jesus and the Old Testament* (London: Tyndale, 1971), 115. The quotations from Isaiah 53 in Lk. 22:37; Acts 8:32-23 do not make explicit reference to vicarious atonement. However, they draw attention to the *key aspects* of Jesus' suffering (the innocent one suffering the death of a transgressor, led like a sheep to the slaughter), suggesting that these events should be understood in terms of Isaiah's redemptive theology.

necessity of God's purpose. The ultimate disgrace, the curse from God, is antecedent to exaltation.'[85]

Green notes that the witness of Acts 10:43 is less direct, but quite similar. Jesus' ability to forgive sins in this verse is said to be in accordance with the testimony of 'all the prophets'. He argues that the solution to this puzzling allusion to the prophets is 'Luke's consistent view that at his exaltation Jesus received the title "Lord" and with it the divine prerogative to offer salvation'.[86] That may indeed be so in the case of 2:33, which is the third text to which Green draws attention and which in its context is showing how the prophecy from Joel cited in 2:21 is fulfilled by the exalted Lord Jesus Christ. However, it is necessary to ask what Scriptures could be included in the testimony of 'all the prophets' other than those with strictly Christological significance, such as we find in the sermons in Acts 2 and 13.

Peter's sermon on the occasion of the healing of the lame man complements his Pentecost message in significant ways. The healing 'in the name of Jesus Christ' (3:6, 16) is a further sign of the messianic salvation. Peter offers forgiveness of sins once more to the crowd (3:19), and possibly also the Holy Spirit in terms of 'times of refreshing' from the presence of the Lord (3:20), paralleling the twofold offer of 2:38. However, the miracle appears to point more broadly to the renewal of all things contingent upon Christ's return (3:20-21). Even the offer of forgiveness is couched in different terms: 'so that your sins may be wiped out'.[87] This is linked to a simple statement that God has fulfilled 'what he had foretold through all the prophets, saying that his Messiah would suffer' (3:17). Here the focus is on *Christ's death alone*, though the resurrection has been previously mentioned (3:13, 15). Many commentators have suggested a deliberate echo of Isaiah 52:13 in the wording of v. 13 (God has 'glorified his servant Jesus'). An echo of the same theology can be found in v. 26, where Peter speaks about God having 'raised up his servant'. Although 'his servant' and the parallel expressions in 4:27, 30 are not necessarily pointers to the full Servant theology of Isaiah 52:13–53:12, use of the word 'glorified' suggests a deliberate allusion to that passage in 3:13-18. Peter begins where the fourth Servant Song begins, with the exaltation of the Servant. However, his emphasis is also on the unjust suffering by which Jesus became the Saviour able to offer a definitive forgiveness of sins and all the promised blessings of eschatological salvation.[88]

---

85. Green, 'Salvation to the End of the Earth', 101.

86. Green, 'The Death of Jesus', 9. Green expounds this 'exaltation-soteriology' on pp. 9-11 and then seeks to relate this to a number of other NT texts where the salvific character of Jesus' resurrection in tandem with the cross is highlighted (pp. 11-12). He then shows parallels with the literature of Late Judaism, where exalted human beings carry out soteriological functions (pp. 12-18).

87. In Acts 3:19 the meaning of the verb *exaleiphein* is similar to Ps. 51 (LXX 50):9 ('blot out all my iniquity'; cf. Ps. 109 [LXX 108]:14) and Is. 43:25 ('I am he who blots out your transgressions'; cf. Je. 18:23).

88. The suffering of an innocent person like this could only bring forgiveness of sins to others if it were penal and substitutionary, in the pattern of Isaiah 53.

It is reasonable to conclude that Isaiah 52:13–53:12 is the basis of Peter's thinking in Acts 3:13-15, 17-19, and that Jesus is envisaged as fulfilling the pattern of redemptive suffering set out in that prophecy. In terms of the overall flow of Luke's narrative, the announcement of its imminent fulfillment in Luke 22:37 shows us how we are to understand the events in the passion narrative. Then, in Peter's second sermon, there is an explicit interpretation of these events and their outcome in language echoing that specific prophecy.[89] Acts 8:26-38 shows us how the fourth Servant Song could be used evangelistically and reinforces the view that this passage is the primary reference when Peter says, 'this is how God fulfilled what he had foretold through all the prophets, saying that his Messiah would suffer' (3:18).[90] Mention of God's servant being sent first to Israel, 'to bless you by turning each of you from your wicked ways' (3:26), is reminiscent of Isaiah 49:5-6. Servant Christology is at the heart of this sermon and, consistent with the Isaianic Songs, the Servant's ministry is linked to the notion of covenant renewal, so that God's salvation can reach the end of the earth. At the heart of that renewal, according to Isaiah 53, is the atoning work accomplished by the death of the Servant himself.

There are several similarities between the sermon attributed to Paul in Acts 13:16-41 and Peter's Pentecost sermon, including the offer of forgiveness of sins through Jesus (v. 38). However, Paul goes beyond Peter in explaining that 'through him, everyone who believes is set free from every sin, a justification you were not able to obtain under the law of Moses' (v. 39). This could mean that the law of Moses offered forgiveness and freedom from the penalty for sin in some cases, but Jesus provides complete salvation from sin. If this is so, the reference will be to the sacrifices which could atone for sins committed inadvertently, but could not deal with deliberate sin.[91] More likely, it means that Jesus sets people free from the consequence of all sin, in a way that the law could not. Either way, the contrast points to the inability of the law to deal with sin in the way that Jesus has, through his death and resurrection.

Acts 20:28-32 contains the fullest expression of atonement theology and its implications in Paul's pastoral discourse at the end of his missionary journeys. Paul warns the Ephesian elders to be faithful shepherds of 'the church of God which he bought with his own blood' (v. 28).[92] In addition to a reference to the Messiah's 'blood', 'the specifically covenantal language employed in 20:28 (*peripoieomai*, 'to acquire'; cf. Exod. 19:5; Isa. 43:21)

89. Rejection of Jesus as 'the Holy and Righteous One' could be a deliberate allusion to Is. 53:11.

90. Green, 'The Death of Jesus', 19, similarly argues that 'the Servant-theme makes up something of the sub-structure of Luke's two-part narrative'.

91. Cf. Witherington 1998, 413.

92. Metzger, *Textual Commentary*, 425-27, discusses the textual variants of this verse. In the Commentary, I argue that it may be best to read *tou idiou* as a reference to Jesus Christ as God's 'own' (NRSV 'the blood of his own Son').

and 20:32; 26:18 (*hagiazō*, 'to sanctify'; cf. Deut. 33:3) reminds us of Luke's record of Jesus' last meal with his disciples wherein he grounds the "new covenant" in his own death (Luke 22:19-20)'.[93] Like Jesus' words at the Last Supper, this speech offers a significant challenge and encouragement to believers about the future of God's people, linked to a covenantal and sacrificial understanding of the death of the Messiah.

The shedding of Messiah's blood is the means by which the New Covenant is inaugurated and Messiah's people are sanctified for their share with him in his eternal inheritance. This is the heart of 'the message of his grace' (v. 32), which is able to sustain the church in the face of persecution and false teaching. In other words, atonement theology here, as in Luke 22, is not simply the basis for proclaiming the forgiveness of sins, but also for understanding how God establishes and maintains the church.

VII. WITNESS AND MISSION

Luke begins his Gospel by announcing his dependence on 'those who from the first were eyewitnesses (*autoptai*) and servants of the word' (1:2). He concludes his first volume with Jesus' declaration that 'the Eleven and those with them' (24:33) are to be 'witnesses of these things' (24:48, *martyres*). Their role as witnesses is specifically related to the fulfillment of three scriptural necessities: 'the Messiah will *suffer* and *rise* from the dead on the third day, and repentance for the forgiveness of sins will be *preached* in his name to all nations, beginning at Jerusalem' (24:45-47). As Jesus ascends into heaven, only the third element in that scriptural agenda remains to be completed. Throughout the course of his public ministry, Jesus had prepared them for this role, but only after the resurrection did he clarify his intentions for them, and promise the Spirit's empowerment for their task (24:49).[94]

So important is this commissioning event that Luke repeats it in a slightly different form at the beginning of Acts. Jesus appears to the apostles 'over a period of forty days', giving them 'many convincing proofs'

93. Green, 'Salvation to the End of the Earth', 99. Green, 'The Death of Jesus', 7, suggests that Luke is 'parrotting' the phraseology of others here: 'he has not developed this motif. He has not "owned" it.' His later article is more positive in showing links with earlier texts in Luke-Acts, but he still concludes that the salvific effect of the cross is 'not woven fully into the fabric of Luke's theology of the cross.'

94. Lk. 21:12-15 contains important teaching about being persecuted, arrested, and bearing 'witness' to Christ before kings and governors (v. 13, *martyrion*). This passage contains the promise of 'words and wisdom' being given by Jesus in such circumstances. It prepares for various narratives in Acts, particularly the trials of Peter, Stephen, and Paul. The terminology of 'witness' is also applied in Luke's Gospel to the synagogue congregation who heard Jesus (4:22, *emartyroun*), to the witness of the Pharisees (11:48, *martyres*), and to Jesus' self-witness at his trial (22:71, *martyrias*). Cf. 5:14; 9:5 (*martyrion*).

and continuing to teach them 'about the kingdom of God' (1:3). Before his ascension, he promises, 'you will receive power when the Holy Spirit comes on you; and you will be my witnesses in Jerusalem, and in all Judea and Samaria, and to the end of the earth' (1:8). This is a prediction rather than a command (contrast Mt. 28:18-20). The expression 'my witnesses' could mean witnesses belonging to the ascended Lord, but in view of Luke 24:46-8, the meaning is more likely to be witnesses who proclaim him as the content of their testimony. Here the sphere of their witness is more clearly delineated, with the Spirit directing them outwards from Jerusalem, to the borders of ancient Israel and 'the end of the earth'.[95] However, as Acts goes on to show, their role as witnesses does not mean that they must together take the gospel to every geographical context.

The terminology of witness is more frequently used in Luke's second volume than in his first.[96] The distinctive role of the Twelve is reinforced when a replacement for Judas is chosen (1:21-26). Peter declares that this person must become 'a witness with us of his resurrection', but this entails having been 'with us the whole time the Lord Jesus went in and out among us, beginning from John's baptism to the time when Jesus was taken up from us' (vv. 21-22). As in Luke's Gospel, Jesus' chosen witnesses can only be those who have experienced the totality of his public ministry and have understood the significance of what they saw and heard in the light of his teaching from the Scriptures (cf. 10:39-41).

Since the claims of the apostles about Jesus were so hotly disputed, a legal and a religious dimension to their testimony emerges in Acts. 'After the resurrection the trial of Jesus, in effect, is reopened and fresh evidence is presented by the apostles to get the Jews to change their verdict.'[97] Beyond the opening chapter, the Twelve are specifically identified as witnesses to 'the people' of Israel (2:32; 3:15; 5:32; 10:39, 41; 13:31). But Paul is also chosen to be a 'witness to all' of what he has seen and heard of the risen Christ (22:14-15; 26:16; cf. 22:18; 23:11). The uniqueness of his calling is highlighted three times in Acts, in the records of his encounter with Christ on the Da-

---

95. Rosner, 'Progress of the Word', 217-19, rightly argues that 'the end of the earth' is not a reference to Rome but is an allusion to Is. 49:6 (cf. Acts 13:47): 'the phrase takes in the whole of the inhabited world, denoting the ultimate limits of civilisation'. Acts 1:8 anticipates the progress of the word throughout Acts and beyond.

96. The noun *martys*, describing a person as a 'witness', is found in 1:8, 22; 2:32; 3:15; 5:32; 6:13; 7:58; 10:39, 41; 13:31; 22:15, 20; 26:16. The nouns *martyria* and *martyrion*, describing the 'testimony' or 'witness' given by someone, are found in 4:33; 7:44; 22:18. The verb *martyrein*, 'to witness, testify', is used in 6:3; 10:22, 43; 13:22; 14:3; 15:8; 16:2; 22:5, 12; 23:11; 26:5, and *martyromai* in 20:26; 26:22.

97. A. A. Trites, *The New Testament Concept of Witness*, SNTSMS 31 (Cambridge: Cambridge University, 1977), 129. 'Luke has taken the original notion of bearing witness before a law court and adapted it to the conditions of the Messianic Age' (p. 133). Examining the importance of Isaiah 40–55 for the NT concept of witness, Trites notes how it is the task of God's witnesses 'not only to attest the facts but also to convince the opposite side of the truth of them' (p. 46). This is certainly the pattern we see operating in Acts.

mascus road and his commissioning to be Christ's witness among the nations (9:1-16; 22:6-21; 26:12-18). In one synagogue context, Paul defers to the uniquely compelling witness of the Twelve in his testimony about Jesus (13:31), but he mostly offers his own distinctive witness to the risen Christ. The legal and religious dimension to his testimony is particularly stressed in the trial scenes in chapters 22–26, where he becomes the 'prisoner witness'.[98]

Paul himself describes Stephen as the Lord's witness (22:20), perhaps because of Stephen's singular vision of the glorified Son of Man during his trial (7:55-56), but more likely in the context because he shed his blood in bearing witness to Jesus.[99] The noun 'witness' *(martys)* is not applied to anyone else in Acts, except the false witnesses mentioned in 6:13 and those who participated in the stoning of Stephen (7:58). But it soon becomes clear that gifted individuals like Stephen and Philip share the apostolic task of testifying to Christ in a variety of situations. Their preaching and teaching is derived from the primary witness of the apostles, but it is no less effective in spreading the message about Jesus far and wide. Even more generally, there are unnamed believers who take the apostolic gospel to new places and plant churches (e.g., 8:4; 11:19-21).

The apostles are shown to be distinctive witnesses to Christ in at least three senses.

> First, they are witnesses to the *fact*, for they can testify to the facts of the public ministry of Jesus, as is clear from the speeches in Acts 1, 2 and 10. Second, they are witnesses to *character* (cf. 3 Jn. 12), for they can testify to the holiness and righteousness of the life of Jesus (3:14) and can point to the positive works of healing and benevolence which flowed from it (10:38). Third, they are witnesses to the *Christian faith;* their testimony is not simply a testimony of fact, but a testimony to lead the Jews, and later the Gentiles, to faith in Christ.[100]

This last point ties in with what is said below about the witness of the Holy Spirit. A further point of interest is the degree to which the Scriptures are used by the apostles in their witness to Jewish audiences. 'All the prophets' are said to testify about Jesus (10:43). Scripture is thus used to explain and interpret the life, death, and resurrection of Jesus and to confirm the testimony of the apostles (e.g., 2:22-36; 13:16-41).[101]

---

98. P. G. Bolt, 'Mission and Witness', in Marshall and Peterson, *Witness to the Gospel*, 192. Bolt believes that Paul may be regarded as the thirteenth witness in Acts, even though he could not qualify in the sense outlined in 1:21-22.

99. Bolt, 'Mission and Witness', 193, observes that, unlike Paul, Stephen receives no specific choice from the Lord and his speech is different in content and purpose from those of the designated witnesses of Jesus. Bruce 1990, 459, argues that this particular use of the term 'witness' is 'a step in the direction of the later meaning "martyr" (cf. Rev. 2:13; 17:6).'

100. Trites, *Witness*, 144 (my emphasis). All three senses in which the apostles serve as witnesses are illustrated in 10:39-43.

101. Cf. Bock, 'Scripture', 41-62.

When the Holy Spirit is described as a 'witness' of the things that the apostles proclaim (5:32), there may be two levels of meaning. First of all, the actual giving of the Spirit to those who obey Jesus is an indication that he is the eschatological 'Prince and Saviour' of Israel, exalted at God's right hand (cf. 2:33). Peter points to the evidence of the Spirit at work in the infant church as a sign that the apostolic claims about Jesus are correct. God himself then testifies that offering salvation to Gentiles was his will by giving the Holy Spirit to them (15:8; cf. 11:17). God further testifies to the message of his grace among the Gentiles by enabling Paul and Barnabas to do miraculous signs and wonders (14:3; cf. 15:12), just as the apostles did in Jerusalem (2:43; 5:12) and beyond (9:32-43). These events play a part in encouraging certain people to trust in Jesus (5:12-14; 9:35, 42; 13:12). Secondly, the Spirit's witness is also to be observed in the boldness that characterizes the testimony of the apostles and others to Jesus (4:8-12, 31; 7:55-56; cf. Lk. 12:11-12; 21:14-15). Although Luke does not make it explicit, the implication is that the Spirit makes possible the complete change of values and lifestyle illustrated in passages such as 2:42-47; 4:32-37; 11:29-30. The Spirit's testimony to Jesus and his saving power must include this individual and ecclesial transformation, with its spiritual and ethical dimensions.

Luke does not imply that others can be witnesses in the same foundational sense that the apostles could. Christians in general are neither eyewitnesses nor earwitnesses in the way that they were. On the other hand, Luke shows how those who were converted through the testimony of the apostles came to share in the task of testifying to Jesus and the fulfillment of God's saving plan in him.[102] 'For Luke the idea of witness is a living metaphor. Christians take Christ's side in real courts of law when his claims are in dispute and when their loyalty is tested by persecution. The witness is Messianic, juridical and religious.'[103] For readers of Luke-Acts, the authoritative witness of the apostles should be the inspired basis and guide for witness in their own time and place. The apostolic witness is available to us in Luke's record — particularly in summaries of the apostolic preaching — and in the other NT writings that come to us in their names. Authentic Christian witness cannot simply be a matter of sharing one's subjective experience of Christ or personal insights on religious matters. Furthermore, it is not simply the corporate or ecclesial testimony of vibrant Christian faith issuing in good works, important though this may be in convincing unbelievers about the truth of Christianity. Fundamentally, it involves proclaiming the kingdom of God and teaching about the Lord Jesus Christ as the

---

102. Bolt, 'Mission and Witness', 212, makes the point that 'the reader is not amongst the witnesses, but amongst those who hear and then proclaim their witness'.

103. Trites, *Witness*, 153. Bolt, 'Mission and Witness', 211, rightly argues that it is not the unique commission of the apostolic witnesses but 'the message which resulted from that commission that was preached beyond their circle and, by virtue of Luke's endeavours, . . . has now become the property of his readers'. Acts records the message of the original witnesses and so keeps their testimony alive.

apostles did. It means using the apostolic witness to persuade people of the need to turn to Jesus, relying upon God to provide his own confirming witness to the proclamation of this message through the work of his Spirit in believers.

Bolt concludes that Acts 'does not provide the readers with a mission, in the sense of them being divinely commissioned for a particular task, but instead it presents God's mission'.[104] The sending of the Messiah to fulfill the plan of salvation set out in the Scriptures is foundational to the divine mission. This makes possible the sending of the Spirit, to enable his chosen witnesses to proclaim the crucified and resurrected Christ, and to enable others to receive their testimony and enjoy the fruit of his victory. As the apostolic testimony is received and believed, the Spirit continues to equip and motivate disciples to share the message with still more people, urging them to respond with repentance and faith.

VIII. MIRACLES

'Signs and wonders' *(sēmeia kai terata)* are mentioned in Acts 4:30 (together with healing, *iasis*); 5:12; 14:3; 15:12. The expression 'wonders and signs' is found in 2:19 (an adaptation of Joel 2:30); 2:22 (with 'miracles'; *dynameis,* [lit.] 'powers'); 2:43; 6:8; 7:36. 'Great signs and miracles' *(sēmeia kai dynameis megalas)* are recorded in 8:13, and 'signs' alone in 8:6. This linguistic usage is interesting when compared with Luke's Gospel. There the word 'sign' *(sēmeion),* mostly in the singular, refers to specific events associated with the coming of the Messiah or with the end of the age (2:12, 34; 11:16, 29, 30; 21:7, 11 [plural], 25 [plural]; 23:8), and the word 'wonder' does not occur at all.[105] Luke's preferred term is *dynamis,* which is used for the 'power' given to Jesus to heal and to exorcise (4:14, 36; 5:17; 6:19; 8:46; 10:13 [plural]; 19:37 [plural]), the 'power' given to disciples in this connection (9:1; 10:19; 24:49 [preparing for Pentecost]), and the shaking of 'the heavenly powers' when the Son of Man comes with power and great glory (21:26-27; 22:69).

Luke-Acts as a whole presents the idea that the power of the Holy Spirit enabled Jesus to do mighty works, which were signs of who he was and of the nearness of the end of the age. That power was to some extent shared with the disciples before Pentecost, but the exaltation of Jesus to God's right hand made possible the outpouring of the Spirit at Pentecost in such a way that 'signs and wonders' were abundantly present. Although some miracles are not designated in this way, it would appear from Luke's

---

104. Bolt, 'Mission and Witness', 214. Bolt, 194-95, discusses the terminology that is used in Acts to highlight God's 'sending' of various individuals for the 'work' that he is accomplishing.

105. The singular *sēmeion* is used in Acts 4:16, 22, as in Luke's Gospel, but with specific reference to the healing mentioned in Acts 3.

use of such terminology in the earliest chapters of Acts that he wished his readers to view them all in such terms. The first use is associated with Joel's prophecy (Acts 2:19; 22), though Joel's own usage probably reflects an earlier biblical employment of such words.

Extraordinary events which foreshadowed the coming of great moments in history were often described by Hellenistic writers as wonders and signs.[106] Jewish literature sometimes reflected the same perspective, but also spoke about miracles whose function was to demonstrate the divine origin of a word or revelation which accompanied them. This was particularly exemplified in the biblical narratives about Moses and the exodus.[107] Luke's awareness of this Mosaic tradition is especially highlighted in Acts 7:35-38. Stephen characterises Moses as the God-ordained deliverer of his people, authenticated by God with signs and wonders, but repudiated by Israel. Allusion to the prophecy of Deuteronomy 18:18 in Acts 7:37 suggests that Moses was a type of Christ (cf. 3:22-23), who was the last and greatest of the prophets to be accredited by God with 'miracles, wonders and signs' (2:22; cf. Lk. 24:19), but who was rejected and ultimately put to death. The crucifixion of Jesus is thus portrayed as the climax of Israel's history of resisting the Holy Spirit in the person of his messengers (7:51-53). But Stephen is also linked with the figure of Moses and the fate of Jesus in this context. He is introduced as 'a man full of faith and of the Holy Spirit' (6:5) and as one 'full of God's grace and power', who 'performed great wonders and miraculous signs among the people' (6:8). His prophetic status is further indicated by the observation that his opponents 'could not stand up against the wisdom the Spirit gave him as he spoke' (6:10). Empowered and led by God's Spirit, he also died as a prophet, much as Jesus did (7:54-60).

In the sequence of Acts, the Twelve are the first to be presented as prophetic successors of Jesus. The Spirit empowers them to preach with great boldness and turn many to Jesus as Lord and Christ (2:1-41). Closely associated with this activity, 'many wonders and signs' were done by the apostles (2:43; cf. 4:29-31, 33). For them, the baptism of the Spirit at Pentecost was preeminently 'a prophetic anointing for a ministry of preaching and healing, a ministry characterized by powerful word and mighty deed'.[108] The

---

106. L. O'Reilly, *Word and Sign in the Acts of the Apostle: A Study in Lucan Theology*, Analecta Gregoriana 243 (Rome: EPUG, 1987), 170-71; Witherington 1998, 220-24.

107. O'Reilly, *Word and Sign*, 171-74. The signs that Moses was enabled to perform in the presence of the Israelites were designed to show that God had appeared to him and spoken to him (Ex. 4:1-9; cf. 19:9). The signs and wonders performed by Moses in Pharaoh's court were acts of judgment against the Egyptians and the means by which God also secured the release of the Israelites from captivity (Exodus 7–12). Deuteronomy contains the greatest number of references to 'signs and wonders' in the OT. There the terminology is used to describe the saving actions of God in bringing the Israelites out of Egypt and leading them into the promised land (4:34; 6:22; 7:19; 11:3; 13:2, 3; 26:8; 29:3; 34:11). In Dt. 34:10-12, Moses is identified as the agent of God in this regard.

108. O'Reilly, *Word and Sign*, 43. Menzies, *Early Christian Pneumatology*, 122-28, de-

healing of the crippled beggar in Acts 3 is the most detailed example of the way signs and wonders operated in their ministry. This miracle was performed 'in the name of Jesus Christ of Nazareth' (3:6), and the sermon that followed proclaimed the significance of that name, offering the astonished bystanders forgiveness and a share in his resurrection life (3:12-26). In a sense, the miracle itself was a proclamation that Jesus is Lord and a pointer to the saving power of Jesus in the widest sense (cf. 3:16; 4:10-12).[109] But the passage shows the need for a careful interpretation of the sign in the light of Scripture and the mighty work of God in raising Jesus from death. Even the great miracle of the resurrection needed to be explained, so that the full significance of the event could be grasped and understood (cf. Lk. 24:4-8, 25-27, 44-49). A segment like Acts 5:12-16, therefore, with its concentration on the signs and wonders performed by the apostles, cannot be taken to mean that people believed in Jesus apart from some ministry of the word.

A close connection between word and sign is maintained in the record of Philip's ministry in Samaria (8:5-6, 12-13), but the dominant note is that of Philip's preaching about Jesus. Again, the narrative about the work of Paul and Barnabas in Cyprus focuses on the desire of the proconsul to 'hear the word of God' that they were proclaiming (13:7). The extraordinary blinding of the sorcerer Elymas was a real factor in the conversion of the proconsul, but Luke concludes this account with the observation that 'he believed, for he was amazed at the teaching about the Lord' (13:12). Paul's ministry in Ephesus is characterized as an intensive period of preaching and teaching (19:8-10; 20:17-35). Nevertheless, a series of remarkable events is recorded in 19:11-20 as a way of demonstrating how 'the word of the Lord spread widely and grew in power' (v. 20). There was a close connection between such signs and wonders and the progress of the gospel, but Luke makes it clear that it was the message about Jesus that actually brought people to faith.

In continuity with the miracles of Jesus, signs and wonders in Acts validate the messengers and their message.[110] They herald the nearness of the kingdom that Jesus proclaimed and point to the salvation he brings. They demonstrate the breaking of the power of Satan, sin, and death, and portray the restoration of relationships between humanity and God that the gospel offers all who repent and believe. In OT prophetic expectation,

---

scribes the gift of the Spirit exclusively in terms of power for effective witness and distances the Spirit from miracles performed either by Jesus or the apostles. This position is critiqued by M. M. B. Turner, 'The Spirit and the Power of Jesus: Miracles in the Lucan Conception', *NovT* 33 (1991), 124-52. Menzies, 'Spirit and Power in Luke-Acts: A Response to Max Turner', *JSNT* 49 (1993), 11-20, responds to Turner.

109. The resurrection of Jesus was the outstanding manifestation of God's power. Apostolic miracles done in the name of the risen Lord 'recall and reactualize the resurrection as the event in which Jesus was made Lord and Christ, and hence the miracles are a proclamation of the name of Jesus as Lord' (O'Reilly, *Word and Sign*, 140).

110. It is important to note, however, that Jesus had the power to do signs and wonders in his own right, whereas the apostles and others performed miracles *in his name.*

this salvation ultimately involves the perfection of life in a renewed creation (e.g., Is. 11:6-9; 65:17-23). The miracles in the NT, therefore, anticipate that resurrection wholeness of body, mind, and spirit, though they do so in a piecemeal and temporary fashion. Together with the gospel message they accompany, apostolic signs and wonders point forward to the restoration of all things that the returning Lord Jesus will bring (cf. Acts 3:20-21 note).

Although the Spirit brought to all believers the means of knowing God and communicating that knowledge to others in different ways, Acts illustrates that not all are teachers and not all work miracles (cf. 1 Cor. 12:28-30). Despite the fact that God's Spirit was poured out on all his New Covenant people alike, only certain individuals are specifically identified as prophets (e.g., Acts 11:27-28; 13:1; 15:22; 21:9, 10-11). Others, such as the apostles, are portrayed as exercising the prophetic-type ministry of receiving and communicating divine revelation, having knowledge of people's hearts, preaching with convicting power, and working miracles. Indeed, key figures such as Peter and Paul combined the roles of apostle, teacher, and prophet.

In conclusion it may be said that the terminology of signs and wonders is used in Acts to link miraculous activity with OT precedents, especially with Moses and the exodus redemption. Signs and wonders establish the credentials of a prophet before all the people and authenticate or verify the prophet's message by actually conveying a partial realization of the salvation proclaimed. In the case of Jesus and the apostles, signs and wonders signal a salvation that is even more wonderful than the redemption achieved under Moses. By his death and resurrection, Jesus reconstituted the people of God under the terms of a New Covenant, bringing them into the ultimate inheritance of God's eschatological kingdom. Within this framework of thought, Luke highlights the prophetic succession from Jesus to the twelve apostles and then to other specially selected individuals such as Stephen, Philip, and Paul. He does not suggest that signs and wonders were done by all the earliest preachers of the gospel. He does not even suggest that signs and wonders were a necessary aspect of the progress of the word in every context. Signs and wonders seem to accompany the planting of the gospel in new situations for a time, but Luke leaves us with the lasting impression that the work of God is advanced in the world essentially by proclaiming the kingdom of God and teaching about the Lord Jesus Christ (28:31).

Although we should be open to the possibility that God can work miracles in any age, it is important to understand the reason for signs and wonders in the NT being especially associated with the ministry of Jesus and the apostles. We should not expect God to do the same things today, envisaging them as an aspect of 'the normal Christian life'.[111] Nor should

---

111. J. Wimber, *Power Evangelism: Signs and Wonders Today* (London: Hodder, 1985), 117. Note the critique of Wimber's position by J. R. W. Stott, *The Message of Acts: To the Ends*

it be expected that signs and wonders will necessarily have an important role in contemporary evangelism, overcoming resistance to the gospel and making people more receptive to its claims.[112] After the exodus event, the signs and wonders that mattered for faith in OT times were not contemporary miracles but the signs and wonders that *accomplished the historical act of redemption for Israel*.[113] The same can be said for the miracles of the NT, particularly the miracles of Jesus and his resurrection by God, which are an aspect of the message we preach (cf. Jn. 20:30-31). Evangelism without accompanying signs and wonders is in no sense incomplete. The gospel alone is fully sufficient to lead to faith in Christ and the salvation he has won for us.

IX. MAGIC AND THE DEMONIC

Jesus' overcoming of Satan and the powers of evil is an important theme in Luke's Gospel. This is developed in Acts when key characters prevail in encounters with the practitioners of magic (Simon [8:9-24]; Bar-Jesus [13:4-12]; many in Ephesus [19:13-20]), or when people are exorcised 'in the name of Jesus Christ' (16:16-18; cf. 5:16; 8:7). In this confrontation with magic and the demonic, the conflict between the devil and the exalted Christ continues. As the gospel moves out into the Gentile world, many are released from spiritual oppression and its social and economic consequences.

In Luke 4:1-13, the devil presents himself as the ruler of all the kingdoms of the world and offers them to Jesus in return for his worship, but Jesus resists, so that the devil leaves him 'until an opportune time'. Later in the Gospel, Luke depicts Satan as the ruler of demonic forces (11:15, 18) and as a strong man fully armed against attack (11:21-22). But Jesus claims to be driving out demons 'by the finger of God', and gives this as evidence that 'the kingdom of God has come upon you' (11:20). He is stronger than the strong man and is in the process of overpowering him and seizing his possessions.

At Jesus' first exorcism (4:33-37), the man possessed by a demonic spirit identifies Jesus as 'the Holy One of God' and cries, 'Have you come to destroy us?' This suggests that every subsequent reference to exorcism ought to be interpreted as an earthly, visible sign of Jesus Christ's victory over his spiritual enemy, the devil.[114] Most significant of all are Jesus' com-

---

of the Earth, BST (Leicester/Downers Grove: Inter-Varsity, 1990), 100-104, and R. C. Doyle (ed.), *Signs and Wonders and Evangelicals: A Response to the Teaching of John Wimber* (Homebush West, Sydney: Lancer, 1987).

112. Cf. Wimber, *Signs and Wonders,* 44-60.

113. Doyle, *Response,* 22. Cf. Dt. 7:21-22; Pss. 77:11, 15; 78:11-12.

114. Jesus and his followers were vulnerable in their time to charges of practising

ments in Luke 10:18-20, where he describes a vision of Satan falling from heaven like lightning and indicates that the disciples share his authority over 'all the power of the enemy'. Their experience of the demons submitting to them in the name of Jesus is a foretaste of the ultimate overthrow of Satan. Finally, Satan is portrayed as playing a role in the betrayal of Jesus and attempting to defeat his mission (22:3, 31-32), but Jesus is resurrected and Satan is not able to stop the disciples from following him and proclaiming his victory. In Acts, magic appears to be a specific way in which satanic power continues to be actualised and encountered.[115]

There have been a number of scholarly attempts to understand the role of magic in Greco-Roman society. David Aune reviewed the results of various anthropological studies and argued that religion and magic are 'so closely intertwined that it is virtually impossible to regard them as discrete socio-cultural categories'.[116] Noting that magic exists in the context of religious traditions, he proposed that studies into deviant behaviour may help in the understanding of magic owing to its illicit nature.[117] These observations contributed to Aune's definition:

> Magic is defined as that form of religious deviance whereby individual or social goals are sought by means alternate to those normally sanctioned by the dominant religious institution. . . . Religious activities which fit this first and primary criterion must also fit a second criterion: goals sought within the context of religious deviance are magical when attained through the management of supernatural powers in such a way that results are virtually guaranteed.[118]

Aune further observed that people used magic irregularly, when the normal religious rituals were unable to deal adequately with an unexpected situation or crisis. He also noted that magic was more popular among the members of the lower socio-economic groups. Aune is critical of attempts by contemporary commentators to distinguish between magic and biblical miracles.[119] However, such a distinction is imperative if it is ac-

---

magic (cf. Mt. 10:25; Mk. 3:22-27; Jn. 7:20; 8:48-52). Jesus did not deny the external similarity of his deeds to those done 'by the power of Beelzebul', but argued that a proper understanding of his activity depended on factors not apparent to the human eye (cf. Mk. 3:22-27; Jn. 8:48-52).

115. S. Garrett, *The Demise of the Devil: Magic and the Demonic in Luke's Writings* (Minneapolis: Fortress, 1989), 60.

116. D. Aune, 'Magic in Early Christianity', *ANRW* 2.23.2 (1980), 1516. Garrett, *Demise*, 11-36, provides a briefer survey of magic in the Greco-Roman world and assesses a number of studies in this area.

117. Aune, 'Magic', 1516, further argues that 'magic appears to be as universal a feature of religion as deviant behavior is of human societies'.

118. Aune, 'Magic', 1515. Aune, 1518, says that the goals of Greco-Roman magic were generally the same as those of contemporary religions: 'protection, healing, success and knowledge for magic practitioners and their clients, and harm for their opponents'.

119. Aune, 'Magic', 1521-22. Aune's scepticism about the miracles attributed to Jesus

cepted that God was actually responsible for the 'mighty works' attributed to Jesus and his representatives. Marguerat has more helpfully proposed that Luke, conscious of the risk of confusion with magic, has developed 'a hermeneutic of miracle which is closely related to his Christology. He has established, between healing and faith, a dialectical relation where the word of the witness plays a decisive role.'[120]

Noting the use of the name of Jesus in the performance of healings and exorcisms in Acts (3:6, 16; 4:7, 10, 30; 16:18; cf. 9:34; 19:13), Aune surmised that it 'must surely have appeared to Jewish and pagan observers that early Christian wonderworkers were practising necromancy'.[121] However, he goes on to show how contemporary Jewish exorcists used *the name of God* in exorcisms, without drawing the obvious conclusion that, by using the name of Jesus as they did, the early Christians were making an implied claim about the divinity of Christ and his continuing control over events.[122]

Subsequent scholarship has taken issue with Aune's insistence that it is impossible to regard magic and religion as discrete, sociocultural categories. Klutz, for example, proposes that magic '(if it is to be spoken of at all) should be seen as more manipulative, illogical, primitive, individualistic, private and clandestine than what is usually recognized as "religion"'.[123] Garrett considers the references to magic in Luke-Acts from a literary and theological perspective, proposing that 'magicians — viewed as diabolical agents — are the perfect vehicle for Luke to illustrate Satan's impotence in the period after Jesus' exaltation to glory'.[124]

The first encounter with a magician in Acts involves the Samaritans, who are said to have been enthralled by Simon because of his magic (8:9-11). This apparently predisposed them to pay attention to the miraculous signs performed by Philip when he preached the message that Jesus of Nazareth was the Christ (8:6-7). Having heard the preaching and seen the accompanying signs and wonders, many repented of their sins and claimed forgiveness (8:12). Although Simon submitted to baptism, his

---

is outlined on pp. 1524-26. On pp. 1527-39, he considers Jesus' wonderworking within the context of a millennial movement as 'essentially magical', though he will not finally categorize Jesus as a magician, but as the 'messianic prophet'. Cf. Garrett, *Demise*, 22-26.

120. D. Marguerat, 'Magic and Miracles in the Acts of the Apostles', in T. Klutz (ed.), *Magic in the Biblical World: From the Rod of Aaron to the Ring of Solomon*, JSNTSS 245 (Sheffield: Sheffield Academic, 2003), 101.

121. Aune, 'Magic', 1545.

122. Marguerat, 'Magic and Miracles', 103, observes that use of the name of Jesus in healing signifies 'an actualisation of his power'. Garrett, *Demise*, 13-17, discusses magic in the context of first-century Judaism and shows how important this is as a background for studying Luke-Acts. There is a close association between magic, false prophecy, and Satan in much Jewish literature of the time.

123. Klutz, *Magic in the Biblical World*, 3.

124. Garrett, *Demise*, 2. Garrett, 35, rightly argues that 'because Luke's "discussion" of magic consists of a series of stories set within a narrative framework, the primary context for interpretation must be the narrative world'.

magical worldview continued to control his life. This is particularly illustrated by his desire to purchase the power of God with money and to use it
for his own advantage (8:13-19). Luke highlights the *moral difference* between magic and Christian works of supernatural power, as well as revealing the differences in *belief patterns*. Peter exposes Simon's wickedness, and
his submission shows that Jesus Christ's servants have authority over Simon's master the devil (8:20-24). Luke exploits the outward similarity between Christian signs and magic by constructing his narrative so as to suggest that Simon mistook the former for the latter. The real power lies not in
magic or magicians 'but in God and God's emissaries, such as Peter and
Paul'.[125] Against any who would malign the Christian's source of power,
Luke insists that believers are authorised by God. Any similarity to magic
is therefore entirely superficial. Garrett concludes that 'at the unseen spiritual level Christian "signs and wonders" and "magic" are worlds apart'.[126]

The next encounter is with Bar-Jesus, who opposed Paul and Barnabas in Cyprus, 'and tried to turn the proconsul from the faith' (13:6-8). Bar-
Jesus is introduced as 'a Jewish sorcerer and false prophet', but Paul goes
further and identifies him as 'a child of the devil and an enemy of everything that is right' (13:10).[127] When Paul invokes the hand of the Lord and
blindness falls on Bar-Jesus, the weakness of the devil is demonstrated
(13:11). The irony of this incident is that Paul had also been struck blind by
God when he attempted to hinder the spread of the gospel. The devil's one-
time helper is now depicted by Luke as his foe. 'By depicting Paul's success
in cursing this "enemy of all righteousness," Luke aimed to show that Paul
was conquering magical-satanic powers.'[128] The end of the narrative connects this incident with the theme of the progress of the word: 'When the
proconsul saw what had happened, he believed, for he was amazed at the
teaching about the Lord' (v. 12). 'Luke is careful to marginalize the miraculous . . . and to draw attention to the kerygma, which remains the basis and
goal of every action.'[129]

In Philippi, the missionaries encounter a slave girl with 'a spirit by
which she predicted the future' (16:16; *pneuma pythōna*, 'a pythonic spirit'
or 'a spirit of divination').[130] With this gift, 'she earned a great deal of

---

125. Witherington 1998, 578. Marguerat, 'Magic and Miracles', 119-20, highlights the
differences between Simon and Philip in Acts 8 and concludes that what separates them is
'neither the belief in supernatural powers, nor in charismatic performance, but the positioning of human being(s) before God'.

126. Garrett, *Demise*, 78. Marguerat, 'Magic and Miracles', 100-124, shows how Luke
differentiates between magic and miracles in specifically observable ways in his narrative.

127. Marguerat, 'Magic and Miracles', 115-17, highlights two uses of the word 'magician' in antiquity, one functional and the other pejorative. He rightly argues that reference
to Bar-Jesus as a false prophet means that Luke is clearly using the description 'magician'
negatively.

128. Garrett, *Demise*, 86.

129. Marguerat, 'Magic and Miracles', 122, citing Christine Prieto.

130. Luke means that the girl was possessed by an underworld spirit, who spoke

money for her owners by fortune-telling' (*manteuomenē*, 'by giving oracles'), which is a practice prohibited in the OT.[131] The girl's perception of who the missionaries are and what their task is recalls the recognition of Jesus by the demon-possessed in the course of his ministry (e.g., Lk. 4:33-34; 8:27-28). Marguerat observes:

> The mortal danger of this undesirable publicity of the pythoness of Philippi is that it synthesizes the preaching of the missionaries with the ambient syncretism; the God that Paul and Silas announce could be Sabazinus or Zeus as well as Yahweh Sabaoth. The exorcism puts an end to this confusion.[132]

Paul exorcises her 'in the name of Jesus Christ', and the economic and social implications of her liberation from the powers of evil come back into focus: 'When her owners realized that their hope of making money was gone, they seized Paul and Silas and dragged them into the marketplace to face the authorities' (16:19).[133]

In Ephesus, the most spectacular conflict with the demonic and the power of magic takes place (19:11-20). After Paul's successful ministry in that city, some Jewish exorcists, including the seven sons of a chief priest, tried to imitate what they supposed to be Paul's magical technique, but without success. The refusal of the demons to be cast out makes it clear that the name of Jesus is not a magical incantation to be used at will. Their invocation of the name of Jesus fails because the demon does not acknowledge the authority of the exorcists to do so. They are authorised only by the devil, and his authority has been taken away by Jesus Christ. Paradoxically, then, 'the demon's apparent victory is actually a defeat of the devil'.[134] Both the demons and the exorcists are on the same side. Satan's kingdom has been divided, as Jesus predicted in Luke 11:18, and it will soon collapse. From now on, only Jesus or his followers will be obeyed by the demons, making magic impotent. The inhabitants of Ephesus understood this and believed the message that Paul preached. They repented of magical practices and burned their books to demonstrate the end of the devil's control and influence. Christianity is thus presented as an alternative to 'popular' religion, 'the religion of magic and mysteries, the religion of astrology and fate'.[135] The devil is shown to be defeated.

---

through her. Cf. L. T. Johnson, *The Acts of the Apostles*, Sacra Pagina 5 (Collegeville: Liturgical, 1992), 293-94; C. K. Barrett, *A Critical and Exegetical Commentary on the Acts of the Apostles*, ICC, Vol. 2 (Edinburgh: Clark, 1998), 784-85.

131. Cf. Dt. 18:10; 1 Sa. 28:8; 2 Ki. 17:17; Je. 27 (LXX 34):9; Ezk. 12:24.

132. Marguerat, 'Magic and Miracle', 112.

133. In Acts 8:4-24; 16:16-19; 19:11-41, Luke demonstrates a close connection between 'magic, pagan or false religion, and the profit motive of humans' (Witherington 1998, 494). Cf. Marguerat, 'Magic and Miracle', 113-15.

134. Garrett, *Demise*, 98.

135. Witherington 1998, 578.

By portraying Christian leaders as staunch opponents of magicians and therefore the devil, Luke refutes the notion that they were themselves practitioners of magic. Luke's anti-magic apology has a sharp polemical edge since, on two out of three occasions in Acts, the magicians are identified as Jewish. This reflects Aune's observation that 'during the first century AD, magic was a phenomenon which pervaded the various Greco-Roman cults, Judaism and Christianity'.[136] As the followers of Jesus spread the Christian message throughout the ancient world, they encountered 'noble' Jews (cf. 17:11), as well as vigorous opponents to their message (e.g., 17:5-9, 13). But they also encountered the corruption of Judaism by syncretistic associations and practices. Luke is turning the tables on those who accused Christians falsely and demonstrating the defeat of the devil and the victory of Jesus Christ. He is also demonstrating the power of the gospel to liberate people from the oppression imposed by magical beliefs and practices.

X. THE CHURCH

The church is not mentioned by name in Luke's Gospel (cf. Mt. 16:18; 18:17). However, it is clear from Jesus' calling of various disciples (e.g., 5:1-11, 27-32), and from his distinctive way of identifying them (e.g., 6:20-26; 8:19-21; 9:23-27; 10:21-24; 12:32; 22:14-32), that he was engaged in drawing out the community of the faithful from Israel and preparing them for the kingdom of God. Although Acts begins with a special focus on the ministry of the risen Lord to the apostles (1:1-11), there is soon mention of a wider group of disciples 'numbering about a hundred and twenty' (1:15). Those who remained faithful after his crucifixion are described as 'the brothers' (TNIV 'the believers'), though women are clearly present (1:14). Luke emphasises that 'they all joined together constantly in prayer', and that they were 'together' (2:1, *epi to auto*) when the Spirit was poured out on the Day of Pentecost. They form the nucleus of the community baptised in the name of Jesus Christ when Peter preaches to Jews from every nation under heaven (2:5-41). The life of this new messianic fellowship in Jerusalem is described in glowing terms (2:42-47), but the word 'church' *(ekklēsia)* is not used until 5:11.

Luke introduces the term without explanation, apparently assuming that his readers will know what is meant by 'the whole church' *(holēn tēn ekklēsian)*. Moreover, the preceding chapters have given a theological context to explain the significance of this term.[137] The new Israel has been

---

136. Aune, 'Magic', 1519.

137. The noun *ekklēsia* is employed in its ordinary secular sense in Acts 19:32, 41, with reference to the gathering of the citizens of Ephesus to accuse Paul and his companions, and in 19:39, with reference to 'the regular assembly' where charges are properly brought. Cf.

emerging from the midst of the old (cf. 2:36-47; 3:17-26; 4:32-37). Other expressions have been used to describe those drawn to faith in Jesus as Lord and Messiah by the preaching of the gospel, such as 'those who accepted his message' (2:41), 'all the believers' (2:44; 4:32), and 'those who were being saved' (2:47).[138] God has been gathering to himself the end-time community of those who believe in Jesus as Lord and Christ. The judgment of Ananias and Sapphira exposes those who do not truly belong to this new community, where the Holy Spirit of God is present (5:3-4, 9; cf. the challenge of 3:22-23).

This theological dimension is confirmed by the use of *ekklēsia* in Stephen's speech, referring to 'the congregation' of the Israelites in the desert with Moses (7:38, alluding to passages such as Dt. 9:10). A link between these entities has been suggested by the progression of the narrative. Indeed, Seccombe argues that Luke has avoided the word *ekklēsia* in the early part of Acts because he wanted first to establish its true significance.[139] The nascent community of believers in Jerusalem is the new Israel, gathered together by the heavenly Messiah, through the agency of his Spirit-directed messengers.[140] Although it meets in the temple courts and in homes, its true locus is not Jerusalem but heaven, where the glorified Jesus reigns (2:32-36; cf. Gal. 4:21-31; Eph. 2:6, 19-22; Heb. 12:22-24).[141] 'Having established its true connection Luke proceeds to use *ekklēsia* without restraint throughout the rest of Acts.'[142]

Thompson argues that the narrative in 1:1–8:3 creates two contrasting paradigms for those who claim to be God's people: 'these contrasts func-

---

K. L. Schmidt, *TDNT* 3:505, 513-14. Although *ekklēsia* consistently has a Christian reference in every preceding text except 7:38, the root meaning of gathering, assembly, or congregation remains fundamental to every application.

138. K. N. Giles, *What on Earth Is the Church? A Biblical and Theological Enquiry* (London: SPCK, 1995), 79-82, surveys other collective titles for Christians in Acts, such as 'brothers', 'disciples' and 'saints'. He rightly points out that the Jesus community has its beginning with the call of the disciples during the ministry of Jesus and that Acts speaks only of the birthday of the post-Easter church.

139. D. P. Seccombe, 'The New People of God', in Marshall and Peterson, *Witness to the Gospel*, 358. Seccombe exposes what can be learned about the doctrine of the church in Acts by observing the progression of the narrative.

140. Giles, *Church*, 83-84, 230-40, rightly argues from Acts 7:38 for a Moses-Jesus typology associated with the *ekklēsia* in the wilderness and the *ekklēsia* of the eschatological age. However, he fails to highlight the significant differences. Jesus gathers his *ekklēsia* to himself, whereas Moses summons Israel to enter into an exclusive covenant with the Lord. The place of assembly for Christians is not Sinai or Jerusalem or any other earthly location. Those on earth must call upon Jesus as Lord in heaven for the salvation and daily direction they need (2:36-41).

141. I am not suggesting that Luke articulates the concept of a heavenly church in Acts such as we find it in Heb. 12:22-24. However, Acts does teach that the ascended Christ calls, sustains, and rules over his church from heaven in a variety of ways. Against Giles, *Church*, 83, it is not sufficient to make a simple dichotomy between Christ in heaven and the Christian community on earth, based on Luke's alleged 'absentee Christology'.

142. Seccombe, 'People of God', 358.

tion rhetorically to assist the reader in identifying potentially the church or Christian community rather than its opponents (the Jewish leaders and finally the Jewish people) as a people that belongs to God, *hē ekklēsia*'.[143] 'The church in Jerusalem' in 8:1 means the community of believers in that city subjected to persecution (cf. 8:3). This expression is equivalent to 'the whole church' in 5:11. In both cases, it is unlikely that the reference is to a congregation actually gathered for corporate worship and edification, since we know that the Jerusalem Christians met in various house groups. Having grown in numbers to exceed 5,000 'men' (4:4) — possibly with women and children in addition to that — it would have been difficult for all the believers to have continued meeting in the temple courts together.[144]

There is a particular focus in Acts 9 on how the church emerged from its Jewish roots and came to identify itself as a distinct entity. As this chapter progresses, various terms help identify the character of the church ('the Lord's disciples' [v. 1]; those 'who belonged to the Way' [v. 2]; 'your saints' [v. 13], 'all who call on your name' [v. 14], 'brother[s]' [vv. 17, 30]). The words of the risen Christ to Saul (vv. 4, 5) throw further light on this, intimately linking the body of believers with the exalted Lord Jesus. Acts 9:31 then signifies that 'the church' now encompasses disciples 'throughout Judea, Galilee and Samaria'.[145] Luke has not previously mentioned a Galilean mission, having been selective in recording how the work of the gospel proceeded. The church in Galilee could refer to those members of the Jerusalem church who were scattered there because of the persecution and who soon added others to their number.[146] However, Acts 8 has shown how a church was planted in Samaria as a result of Philip's ministry, with no core group from Jerusalem. Once this pattern of new plants multiplied,

143. R. P. Thompson, *Keeping the Church in Its Place: The Church as Narrative Character in Acts* (New York/London: Clark, 2006), 115. Unbelieving Jews are depicted as those who reject God's purpose and whose actions place them outside the realm of God's saving activity.

144. Bruce 1990, 62-63, discusses the conditions of church membership, the pattern of church meetings, and the administration of the churches in Acts. Cf. D. G. Peterson, 'The Worship of the New Community', in Marshall and Peterson, *Witness to the Gospel*, 373-95.

145. The plural *hai ekklēsiai*, followed by plural verbs and participles, is found in some Western and Byzantine readings. The range and age of the witnesses that read the singular are superior, but K. N. Giles, 'Luke's Use of the Term *ekklēsia* with Special Reference to Acts 20.28 and 9.31', *NTS* 31 (1985), 135-42, argues that the plural could be the original on the ground that Luke normally uses the singular *ekklēsia* of a local congregation of Christians. Giles dismisses 20:28 as Paul's theology and not Luke's, but Luke could easily have been influenced by this wider view of the church while maintaining a local view. There is a twofold use of the terminology in Paul's letters, with reference to local churches and with reference to the heavenly gathering of believers around Christ. Cf. P. T. O'Brien, *Colossians, Philemon*, Word Biblical Commentary 44 (Waco: Word, 1982), 57-61.

146. Giles, 'Luke's Use', 139-40, argues this case with reference to those textual variants that have the singular *ekklēsia* and plural verbs (E H L P S 049 056 0142 etc.). But the same case could be argued with reference to texts that use the singular noun with singular verbs.

there were doubtless many congregations in the region claiming to be churches of Christ (cf. 11:26). Indeed, from this point in the narrative Luke begins to use the word *ekklēsia* of any local congregation of Christians (e.g., 13:1; 14:23, 27). So a term which at first is applied to the new Israel in Jerusalem is soon used to describe any gathering of believers in the Messiah.

Giles argues that 'Luke does not have in mind in 9.31 either the "catholic church" in Judaea, Galilee and Samaria, nor the local churches of each of these locations but the one congregation, the church of Jerusalem, which has been dispersed because of persecution'.[147] He rightly opposes the idea that this verse evidences the beginning of a centralised, organized, and interconnected series of congregations, forming a united whole under apostolic leadership. However, as already noted, the notion that Luke refers to 'the one congregation, the church of Jerusalem, which has been dispersed because of persecution' fits ill with the story of how Christianity was planted in Samaria. At the same time, the church that extends beyond the walls of Jerusalem in 8:4–12:25 is portrayed in a way that links it clearly with that original community in terms of unanimity, fellowship, and gospel witness — all made possible by the divine presence and blessing.[148]

Acts 8–15 bears witness to the divine initiative in incorporating Samaritans and Gentiles with believing Jews in the Christian fellowship. Luke shows little interest in the development of ecclesiastical systems of government and discipline, though he does highlight the efforts that were made to maintain links between the new churches and the original Jerusalem church. The Jerusalem Council provides the opportunity to reflect on the way God has formed and maintained an international movement consisting of Jews and Gentiles through the preaching of the gospel of grace and the work of the Holy Spirit (15:7-12). Scripture is also cited to explain how God has been faithful to Israel through the raising up of the Messiah and has also 'intervened to choose a people for his name from the Gentiles' (15:13-18, citing Amos 9:11-12). At a practical level, Acts 15 dwells on the importance of facilitating table fellowship between Jewish and Gentile Christians, 'which was such a sticking point for many Jews, but which underlined the reality of the unity of these people in the one people of God'.[149]

The church at Antioch has a significant role in Luke's narrative, being presented as something of a model.[150] Founded by unnamed believers who were 'scattered by the persecution that broke out when Stephen was killed', it was nurtured by the outstanding ministries of Barnabas and Saul (11:19-26). Jews and Gentiles were united for the first time in the fellowship

---

147. Giles, 'Luke's Use', 139. Cf. F. J. A. Hort, *The Christian Ecclesia* (London: Macmillan, 1897), 55-56.

148. Cf. Thompson, *Church*, 116-60.

149. Seccombe, 'People of God', 372. Acts 21:17-26 gives the impression that there were believers in Jerusalem who continued to focus on ethnic, social, and religious issues in identifying the people of God.

150. Cf. Thompson, *Church*, 147-54, 163-67, 178-200.

at Antioch, with no apparent tension or difficulties. Practical help was will-ingly given to distressed believers in Judea (11:27-30), but when certain in-dividuals came from Judea with a demand for Gentiles to be circumcised, the church sent a delegation back to Jerusalem to put this issue before the apostles and elders (15:1-5), thus instigating the Jerusalem Council. In re-sponse to the Spirit's initiative, Barnabas and Saul were earlier released by this church to take the gospel elsewhere among the nations (13:1-5). At the end of their first campaign, the missionaries returned to this fellowship and reported what God had done through them, particularly noting how God had 'opened a door of faith to the Gentiles' (14:26-28). The issue of Jews and Gentiles being united in Christ was clearly significant for this church.

In the second half of Acts (13:1–28:31), three general developments contribute significantly to the characterization of 'the church' in these chapters: the success of the Christian mission among both Jews and Gentiles; the identification of Jewish and Gentile believers together as the people of God; and the increasing separation of the Christian community from Judaism. 'The Lukan characterization of the Christian community thereby shifts the focus of the believers' identity as the people of God from issues of Jewishness to "typical" signs of divine blessing and possession.'[151] The narrator 'implicitly identifies the unanimity that transcends ethnic and cultural boundaries as characteristic of the Christian church or those who belong to God'.[152]

When Luke speaks of Christian congregations in different locations he uses the plural 'churches' (e.g., 15:41; 16:5). Schmidt observes:

> It is not that the *ekklēsia* divides up into *ekklēsiai*. Nor does the sum of the *ekklēsiai* produce the *ekklēsia*. The one *ekklēsia* is present in the places mentioned, nor is this affected by the mention of *ekklēsiai* alongside one another. We must always understand and translate either 'congrega-tion' and 'congregations' or 'Church' and 'churches'.[153]

A profound theological statement about the church in Acts is found in Paul's challenge to the Ephesian elders to shepherd 'the church of God, which he bought with his own blood' (20:28). The epithet 'of God' suggests that God assembles and owns this entity.[154] The church in Ephesus is

151. Thompson, *Church*, 240. Thompson, 161-240, explores in detail 'the churches in the Roman Empire as narrative characters'. Thompson, 247, concludes that 'the progressive nature of the Acts narrative indicates that the replacement of the Jewish people is *not* the critical issue. Rather, Luke assists the reader in wrestling with the issue of the identity of a church *in its own situations*.'

152. Thompson, *Church*, 244.

153. K. L. Schmidt, *TDNT* 3:505. Schmidt observes that the only epithet applied to *ekklēsia* in Acts is *tou theou* (20:28, 'of God'), though see note 154 below. He argues that 'the congregation or Church of God always stands in contrast and even in opposition to other forms of society'.

154. Metzger, *Textual Commentary*, 425-27, discusses the variants 'church *of the Lord*'

viewed as a manifestation or expression of the entire community of the redeemed for whom Christ died. God's assembly, whether local and particular or heavenly and ultimate, depends for its existence on the one who has
called and purchased it.[155] It has been argued that the doctrine of the
church in this verse and the interpretation of the death of Christ in redemptive terms set it apart from anything else in Acts, and that it does not represent Luke's theology.[156] However, Acts has presented a picture of the
church being called into existence by the risen Christ wherever the gospel
is heard and obeyed, and constituted by the saving work of Jesus. Even if
Acts 20:28 represents an ecclesiology and soteriology more familiar to us
from the Pauline letters, the narrator allows Paul to make the climactic declaration about the true nature of the church and its divine purpose.[157]
Paul's words articulate and explain more fully the significance of what has
been progressively revealed about the church in Acts. In this context, a
challenge is offered about the ongoing need for faithful leadership in 'the
church of God', to preserve it from error and division (20:18-35).

Luke develops a doctrine of the church by various narrative means,
including key speeches by Stephen in Acts 7, the leading figures at the Jerusalem Council in Acts 15, and Paul in Acts 20. These speeches give a theological framework for Luke's use of various terms to describe the new people of God throughout his narrative. Although I have disagreed with the
argument of Giles at various points, I concur with his conclusion:

> The Lucan writings bear witness to a point in history where the Chris-
> tians are coming to see themselves as a distinct new entity, having their
> roots in Israel, but now independent of Israel. They are the community
> of salvation, the 'church of God'. Entry is through faith in Christ, not
> through descent from Abraham or by keeping the law; however, time-
> honoured titles for Israelites such as 'brethren' or 'the people of God'
> are not denied to Jews as yet, but they are being taken over by Chris-
> tians.[158]

---

and 'church *of the Lord and God*', arguing that the latter is obviously conflate, and therefore
secondary. The reading 'church *of God*' is more likely to have been altered to 'church *of the
Lord*' than vice versa.

155. K. L. Schmidt, *TDNT* 3:505, notes that 'it is in being when God gathers his own'.
Giles, *Church*, 135, misses this point when he puts the emphasis on human initiative: 'those
who assemble together in Christ's name form a community'.

156. See my discussion of this passage above, in connection with the atoning work of
Jesus, and Giles, 'Luke's Use', 136-37.

157. Similarly, Stephen's use of *ekklēsia* in Acts 7:38 makes a significant contribution
to Luke's narrative presentation of a doctrine of the church.

158. Giles, *Church*, 92.

Commentary

I. INTRODUCTION AND RECAPITULATION: THE MISSION PLAN OF THE RISEN LORD (1:1-14)

Acts begins with a long, programmatic sentence in Greek (vv. 1-5), which looks back in summary fashion to the concluding scenes of Luke's Gospel and prepares for the great events soon to be narrated. The resurrected Jesus teaches and commissions his apostles before ascending to heaven. Most importantly, he prepares them for the promised baptism with the Holy Spirit. In this way, the two volumes of Luke's work are closely linked together. Although some interpreters have argued that the introduction ends at v. 5, there are good reasons for concluding that it extends to v. 14. 'The whole of vv. 1-14 is paralleled in the gospel and is best regarded as a résumé of what the reader may be supposed to have already read.'[1] Moreover, four literary forms are woven together into a continuous whole (prologue, appearance narrative, farewell scene, and assumption narrative), prefacing everything that follows.[2] Editorial comment in the first person soon flows into narra-

---

1. C. K. Barrett, *A Critical and Exegetical Commentary on the Acts of the Apostles*, ICC, Vol. 1 (Edinburgh: Clark, 1994), 61. Barrett notes the possibility that vv. 15-26 could be included in the introduction, but argues that 'the appointment of Matthias breaks fresh ground, having no parallel in Lk'. I. H. Marshall, *The Acts of the Apostles: An Introduction and Commentary*, TNTC (Leicester: Inter-Varsity; Grand Rapids: Eerdmans, 1980), 55, views vv. 1-5 as the Prologue, but observes that 'the introduction is not sharply distinguished from the following narrative, and the latter flows out of the former'. F. F. Bruce, *The Acts of the Apostles: The Greek Text with Introduction and Commentary* (3rd ed.; Grand Rapids: Eerdmans; Leicester: Apollos, 1990), 97, limits the introduction to vv. 1-5. B. Witherington III, *The Acts of the Apostles: A Socio-Rhetorical Commentary* (Grand Rapids/Cambridge: Eerdmans; Carlisle: Paternoster, 1998), 105-14, argues for vv. 1-14 to be considered 'Prologue and Recapitulation'.

2. D. W. Palmer, 'The Literary Background of Acts 1.1-14', *NTS* 33 (1987), 428, notes that Luke's shifting mode of expression in vv. 1-14 'corresponds to the gradual transition from retrospective to prospective summary'. He goes on to establish most convincingly that vv. 1-14 is the intended introduction.

tive (vv. 1-3), leading to teaching from Jesus about the role of the Holy
Spirit in the outworking of God's purposes (vv. 4-5). Themes raised in vv. 1-
5 are developed in vv. 6-8, as Luke's summary of Jesus' appearances focuses on his last encounter with the apostles.[3] Following Jesus' ascension
into heaven (v. 9), there is angelic comment on the significance of the event
(vv. 10-11), and mention of the impact on those left behind (vv. 12-14). References to Jesus' ascension in v. 2 and v. 11 form an inclusion or bracket
around the intervening material, suggesting that the introduction reaches
its climax with the ascension narrative. But the opening paragraph extends
to v. 14 and includes the response of the eleven apostles to Jesus' farewell
promises and commands. A new episode begins in v. 15, on a different occasion ('in those days'), and with a larger audience ('a group numbering
about a hundred and twenty').

What links these diverse elements together is the preparation of the
apostles to be witnesses of the risen and ascended Lord Jesus. We are first
told about his instructions through the Holy Spirit (v. 2) and his speaking to
them about the kingdom of God (v. 3). More specifically, his instruction is
the command to wait in Jerusalem for the gift of the Spirit (vv. 4-5). The
themes of kingdom, Spirit, and witness are developed and interconnected
in vv. 6-8, where the ground plan for the book is laid out. The ascension
confirms Jesus' heavenly enthronement as Messiah, guaranteeing that he
will remain sovereign over the life and witness of his people. The manner
of his departure also foreshadows his return to consummate God's saving
plan (vv. 9-11). In effect, the introduction lays down 'the eschatological
framework within which the Christian story is to unfold'.[4] The church lives
between Jesus' exaltation into heaven and his return, and its life is determined by these boundary markers.

Some scholars see very little role for the ascended Christ in the outworking of Luke's narrative. Yet the risen Lord acts and is present to the
whole life of his church in Acts.[5] He gives his followers their mission and
directs them in various ways throughout the narrative. 'When they are persecuted, he encourages, supports, and protects them. His power enables
them to perform miracles. When they preach, he preaches; when they are
heard, he is heard. Their salvation, a present experience and reality, comes

3. Some of the typical features of a Jewish farewell scene control this section. Cf.
Palmer, 'Literary Background', 430-31.

4. Barrett 1994, 63. Cf. J. Nolland, 'Salvation-History and Eschatology', in I. H. Marshall and D. Peterson (eds.), *Witness to the Gospel: The Theology of Acts* (Grand Rapids/Cam-
bridge: Eerdmans, 1998), 63-81, on salvation history and eschatology in Acts.

5. G. W. MacRae, 'Whom Heaven Must Receive Until the Time', *Int* 27 (1973), 160-65,
considers the mode of Christ's continuing presence with his disciples in Acts. J. D. G. Dunn,
Unity and Diversity in the New Testament: An Inquiry into the Character of Earliest Christianity
(London: SCM, 1977), 19, is representative of those who argue for an absentee Christology
in Acts. A. W. Zwiep, *The Ascension of the Messiah in Lukan Christology*, NovTSup 87 (Leiden:
Brill, 1997), 1-35, 200-215, summarizes and assesses the different approaches to the ascension in literature on Acts up to 1996.

only from him.'[6] Jesus' ascension is essentially the context in which there is a transfer of prophetic responsibility to the apostles, with the promise of enabling power to come. In this way, the introduction draws attention to the specific significance of the apostles in the outworking of God's plan for Israel and the nations. Even so, the final scene is of the apostles and *others* waiting for the gift of the Holy Spirit (vv. 12-14). This passage therefore raises a question about the extent to which the apostolic task is to be shared by others. Discerning readers will discover that this question is answered in various ways throughout the rest of Acts.

A. The Promise of the Spirit (1:1-5)

Commenting briefly on his writing task (vv. 1-2; cf. Lk. 1:1-4), Luke moves easily to a summary of the ministry of the resurrected Jesus (v. 3), and then to a specific statement by Jesus about the gift of the Holy Spirit (vv. 4-5; cf. Lk. 24:49). 'By this time we are no longer attending to an author's comments on writing; we are attending to Jesus, a character internal to the narrative.'[7] Jesus' words about the coming of the Spirit point beyond the ascension to what is about to happen in Acts 2, and emphasize the significance of that gift by presenting it in terms of 'a divine promise transmitted by two prophetic spokesmen, himself and John'.[8] The paragraph as a whole implies that the risen Christ will continue to act and to teach through the promised Holy Spirit.

1 The first few words of Acts are meant to recall the opening verses of Luke's Gospel and indicate the author's intention to begin a second volume linked to his *former book (prōton logon)*.[9] Such an arrangement, with a common preface in the first volume and then brief introductions to subsequent volumes, was not uncommon in the ancient world.[10] A particular

6. R. F. O'Toole, 'Activity of the Risen Jesus in Luke-Acts', *Biblica* 62 (1981), 498. Cf. R. F. O'Toole, 'Luke's Understanding of Jesus' Resurrection-Ascension-Exaltation', *BTB* 9 (1979), 106-14; M. Sleeman, 'The Ascension and the Heavenly Ministry of Christ', in S. Clark (ed.), *The Forgotten Christ: Exploring the Majesty and Mystery of God Incarnate* (Nottingham: Apollos, 2007), 140-90. J. Hur, *A Dynamic Reading of the Holy Spirit in Luke-Acts*, JSNTSS 211 (Sheffield: Sheffield Academic, 2001), 141-44, helpfully examines the relationship between the Spirit and the risen Jesus in the narrative of Acts.

7. R. C. Tannehill, *The Narrative Unity of Luke-Acts: A Literary Interpretation*, Vol. 2: *The Acts of the Apostles* (Minneapolis: Fortress, 1990), 9. A preview of the book that Luke is writing thus appears as part of Jesus' speech, both here and in v. 8.

8. Tannehill 1990, 12.

9. Barrett 1994, 64, notes that *logos* may mean 'a historical work' or 'one section of such a work'. Strictly speaking, *ton prōton* means 'the first' of more than two, but failure to use the comparative form of this adjective does not necessarily imply that Luke intended to write a third volume.

10. Cf. Tannehill 1990, 5-8; L. C. A. Alexander, *The Preface to Luke's Gospel: Literary Conventions and Social Context in Luke 1:1-4 and Acts 1:1*, SNTSMS 78 (Cambridge: Cambridge University, 1993). Witherington 1998, 105-8, shows how Luke is following the rhetorical convention of retelling some of the story from the first volume in a different style.

parallel is provided by the twofold address of the Jewish historian Josephus to his patron at the beginning of both parts of his work *Against Apion* (1.2; 2.1). The first volume is addressed to 'Epaphroditus, most excellent of men', and the second is introduced with the words: 'By means of the former volume, my most honored Epaphroditus'.[11] In Christian circles, however, Luke was doing something novel, writing a second book as a sequel to his Gospel, making it clear that the story of Jesus is not completed by telling about his ministry, death, and resurrection. *Theophilus*, meaning 'friend of God' or 'loved by God', was an ordinary Greek name, well attested from the third century BC onward. The title 'most excellent' *(kratiste)* is given to him in Luke 1:3, but not here. It may signify that Theophilus was a person of some rank (cf. the use of the term for provincial governors in Acts 23:26; 24:3; 26:25), though there is no ground for saying that Luke wished to mask the identity of some well-known Roman official.[12] Whatever his status, Theophilus needs clarification and assurance about the understanding of Christianity he has so far received (Lk. 1:4). But Luke presumably also hoped that Theophilus would act as a patron or sponsor in bringing his work to a wider audience. Luke's 'intended readers' are people needing the same clarification and assurance as Theophilus. *All that Jesus began to do and to teach until the day he was taken up to heaven* summarizes the contents of Luke's *former book.* Jesus is presented in the Gospel as being 'powerful in word and deed before God and all the people' (Lk. 24:19), and the narrative ends with his ascension (24:51). The opening verses of Acts suggest that Luke is about to narrate what Jesus continued *to do and to teach* after his ascension, through his Spirit and the ministry of his followers.[13]

2   The words *to heaven* do not occur in the Greek of v. 2, and some scholars have proposed that the verb *anelēmphthē (taken up)* refers to Jesus' crucifixion. Thus, the sequence is thought to be ministry (v. 1), death (v. 2), and resurrection appearances (v. 3).[14] However, since the same verb is

---

11. D. W. Palmer, 'Acts and the Ancient Historical Monograph', in B. W. Winter and A. Clarke (eds.), *The Book of Acts in Its First-Century Setting*, Vol. 1: *Ancient Literary Setting* (Grand Rapids: Eerdmans; Carlisle: Paternoster, 1993), 21-26, notes also the use of a purely retrospective prologue by the Greek writers (pseudo-)Xenophon, Polybius, and Herodian. Some ancient writers used prospective summaries only, and some employed a second preface that was both retrospective and prospective.

12. B. H. Streeter, *The Four Gospels* (London: Macmillan, 1924), 534-39, argued that Theophilus was really Titus Flavius Clemens, cousin of Emperor Domitian. Barrett 1994, 66, argues that the use of *kratiste* in Lk. 1:3 counters the possibility that Theophilus is merely 'a cypher intended to represent the Christian (or Christian inquirer)'. Barrett thinks that he could have been 'an inquirer, a catechumen, a Christian seeking further information about the origins of his faith and the early history of the church, or a Roman magistrate'.

13. *ērxato* ('began') is emphatic here and 'should not be regarded merely as a semitizing auxiliary' (Bruce 1990, 98; cf. Barrett 1994, 66-67). The idea that Jesus continues to work through his Spirit is especially suggested by Acts 2:33; 16:7. Other texts speak more generally of the risen Lord's continuing guidance, protection, and provision for his people (e.g., 9:4-17; 16:14-15; 18:9-10; 23:11). Cf. Sleeman, 'Heavenly Ministry,' 140-90.

14. Cf. P. A. van Stempvoort, 'The Interpretation of the Ascension in Luke and Acts',

used in v. 11 with the words *to heaven (eis ton ouranon)*, it is better to see v. 2 as a shorthand way of referring in advance to Jesus' ascension. The ascension is the climax of the Gospel narrative, but here it signifies a new beginning. Central to Luke's purpose is the indication that Jesus' ascension took place *after giving instructions through the Holy Spirit.* The Greek participle *enteilamenos* literally means 'having given commandment'.[15] TNIV apparently takes this as a general reference to all the teaching imparted by Jesus throughout his resurrection appearances (so also KJV, NRSV, ESV). But it is more likely that a single command is in view and that this is detailed in v. 4, where a synonym is employed (*parēngeilen*, 'he commanded'). Jesus' command to wait in Jerusalem for the gift of the Spirit was an essential preliminary to his commissioning of the apostles as his witnesses in vv. 6-8. TNIV rightly relates the expression *through the Holy Spirit (dia pneumatos hagiou)* to the verb 'having given commandment', suggesting that Jesus himself was 'full of the Holy Spirit' (Lk. 4:1) and empowered by the Holy Spirit (Lk. 4:14) in this, as in other aspects of his ministry. Luke-Acts emphasizes that the one who was himself especially endowed with the Spirit became the one who eventually poured out the same Spirit at Pentecost (Acts 2:33).[16] Jesus' instruction to the apostles to wait in Jerusalem for this gift (Lk. 24:49) is closely linked with his missionary plan in Luke 24:47-49. With such repetition, we are not meant to miss the importance of this command with its associated promise!

Although others may have been present at the time, the command is especially directed to *the apostles he had chosen.* The apostles are the Twelve whom Jesus appointed from among a wider group of disciples (cf. Lk. 6:13) in the early stages of his public ministry. They are named in Luke 6:14-16 and are then 'sent out' (Lk. 9:2), to preach the kingdom of God and to heal. Since others were sent out to share the missionary task and were not called apostles

---

NTS 5 (1958-59), 30-42; Tannehill 1990, 10-11. M. C. Parsons, *The Departure of Jesus in Luke-Acts: The Ascension Narratives in Context*, JSNTSS 21 (Sheffield: JSOT, 1987), 130-33, modifies the thesis by taking *anelēmphthē* as a reference to 'Jesus' entire journey back to God (burial, resurrection, exaltation)'. B. M. Metzger, *A Textual Commentary on the Greek New Testament: A Companion Volume to the United Bible Societies' Greek New Testament (Fourth Revised Edition)* (2nd ed.; Stuttgart/New York: United Bible Societies, 1994), 236-41, and Barrett 1994, 67-69, discuss textual variants involving differences of word order and content in v. 2, arguing in favor of the text translated by TNIV.

15. *entellomai* can mean 'command' or 'commission' (cf. Mt. 4:6; 17:9; 19:7; 28:20; G. Schrenk, *TDNT* 2:544-45). In Acts 13:47 it is used of the missionary command according to Is. 49:6. Acts 1:2 should be translated 'until the day when he commissioned through the Holy Spirit the apostles whom he had chosen and ascended'.

16. So Barrett 1994, 69, against E. Haenchen, *The Acts of the Apostles: A Commentary* (ET, Oxford: Blackwell, 1971), 139. Marshall 1980, 57, proposes that 'through the Holy Spirit' relates to *exelexato* ('chose'). Following L. T. Johnson, *The Acts of the Apostles*, Sacra Pagina 5 (Collegeville: Liturgical Press, 1992), 12-14, Hur, *Dynamic Reading*, 189, argues that Jesus offers himself as the 'model of prophetic witness' for his witnesses in Acts, and, 'at the same time, he becomes the core of the message that his witnesses are represented proclaiming to the ends of the earth (Acts 1:8; cf. Lk. 24:46-48)'.

(Lk. 10:1-20), there must have been something more distinctive about the role of the Twelve. The number 'twelve' suggests that Jesus intended them to be patriarchs or leaders of a restored and renewed Israel (cf. Lk. 22:14-30, especially v. 30). Apostles are mentioned twenty-eight times in the narrative of Acts 1–16, after which the term is no longer employed. Presumably, this is because the focus is then on Paul and his ministry. Luke does not normally identify Paul as an apostle, although in Acts 14:4, 14 the title is unexpectedly applied to both Paul and Barnabas. Here Luke betrays an awareness of a wider usage of the term in early Christian circles. Moreover, his threefold presentation of Paul's encounter with the risen Christ shows that Paul fulfilled the basic requirement of apostleship, being a witness of the resurrection, with a special commission of his own in God's eschatological plan (9:1-19; 22:1-21; 26:2-18). 'In short, the picture that Acts paints is not that Paul was not an apostle, but that he was an apostle extraordinary, which is consonant with Paul's own account (1 Cor. 9:1ff.; 15:5-9; Gal. 1:12-17).'[17] There is no suggestion in Luke-Acts that apostleship is an office that is somehow transferable to others in a historical succession (see further on 1:21-26).

3   Further overlap between Luke 24 and Acts 1 is provided by a reference to resurrection appearances in and around Jerusalem. The Greek says literally: 'to them also he presented himself alive *(parestēsan heauton zōnta)* after he suffered'. Luke 24 records only three such appearances and links them so that they all seem to have happened on Easter Day. The first was to Cleopas and his companion, who were not apostles (vv. 13-33), the second was to Simon (v. 34), and the third to the Eleven and 'those with them' (vv. 36-51). Acts 1 tells us that there were other such appearances and that they took place *over a period of forty days (di' hēmerōn tesserakonta;* cf. 13:31; 1 Cor. 15:5-7).[18] One of the aims of these encounters was to demonstrate the physicality of Jesus' resurrection *with many convincing proofs (en pollois tekmēriois).*[19] So we are told that Jesus invited them to touch him and that he ate and drank in their presence (cf. Lk. 24:36-43; Acts 10:41). He was

---

17. C. Brown, *NIDNTT* 1:136. Brown's article gives a helpful survey of the scholarly debate regarding the origin and meaning of apostleship in the NT. Cf. also S. G. Wilson, *The Gentiles and the Gentile Mission in Luke-Acts,* SNTSMS 23 (Cambridge: Cambridge University, 1973), 113-20; A. C. Clark, 'Apostleship: Evidence from the New Testament and Early Christian Literature', *VE* 19 (1989), 65-69; A. C. Clark, 'The Role of the Apostles', in Marshall and Peterson, *Witness to the Gospel,* 169-90.

18. *di' hēmerōn tesserakonta* (with the genitive) implies that Jesus appeared to them 'in the course of forty days', but not continuously. There is no ground for the assertion that the space of time was a Lukan invention, influenced by the 'sacred' number of forty days (cf. Haenchen 1971, 141), or by the need to fill in the fifty-day gap before Pentecost (cf. Wilson, *Gentiles,* 98-100). F. S. Spencer, *Acts* (Sheffield: Sheffield Academic, 1997), 25, suggests something of a parallel with Moses in Ex. 24:18; 34:27-28; Dt. 9:9-11; 10:10.

19. *tekmērion* means 'strict proof' or 'a compelling sign'. Witherington 1998, 108, notes that 'many proofs' is an expression found almost exclusively in Greek historiographical works. The word *tekmērion* occurs only here in the NT. Luke could not have chosen a stronger term to convey the sense of proof beyond doubt.

no phantom, and their experience was not simply visionary or spiritual. In the contemporary scene, where doubt is often cast on the resurrection narratives by scholars and church leaders alike, we do well to remember that Luke himself was utterly convinced of the historical reliability of the evidence he received from 'eyewitnesses' (Lk. 1:2, *autoptai*), to whom Jesus *appeared* (Acts 1:3, *optanomenos*, 'appearing'). Furthermore, he wrote in such terms for people in the Greco-Roman world, where belief in the physical resurrection of Jesus was just as difficult as it is for skeptics today (cf. Acts 17:32; 26:8).

Jesus spent this time speaking to the apostles about *the kingdom of God,* which had been the central theme of his teaching in the Gospel (e.g., Lk 4:43; 6:20; 8:1, 10; 9:2, 11; 11:20; 17:20-21; 18:16-17, 24-25; 21:31; 22:16). Related Hebrew or Aramaic terms were used in Jewish literature to describe God acting in his kingly power or exercising his sovereignty (e.g., Pss. 103:19; 145:11-13; Dn. 4:3). This terminology came to be particularly associated with Israel's hope for an ultimate and decisive manifestation of God's rule in human history (e.g., Is. 24:23; Dn. 2:44; 7:13-14; Ob. 21; Zc. 14:9).[20] Since a variety of eschatological perspectives emerged in the OT and inter-testamental writings, it was important for Jesus to reveal how his own coming was significant for the fulfillment of kingdom expectations. The parallel passages in Luke 24:25-27, 44-49, indicate that he was specifically teaching his apostles how to interpret his death and resurrection in the light of Scripture, demonstrating that these events were to be the means by which he entered his glory as Messiah and fulfilled God's saving plan for Israel and the nations. They were shown how to understand and explain Jesus and his ministry within the light of OT revelation as a whole ('the Law of Moses, the Prophets and the Psalms', Lk. 24:44). Put another way, they were being taught how to interpret the Scriptures christologically, but also in terms of kingdom expectations. The kingdom of God is mentioned at strategic points in Acts (8:12; 14:22; 19:8; 20:25; 28:23, 31), indicating that this remains an important way to represent the message of the gospel. It is a comprehensive term used to describe the salvation already accomplished by Christ and available to be received in the present (8:12). However, when there is mention of entering the kingdom 'through many hardships' (14:22), the reference is to enjoyment of the ultimate blessing of a restored creation (cf. 3:19-21). On one occasion, 'preaching the kingdom' (20:25) is actually equated with declaring 'the whole counsel' or plan of God (20:27). But even where the terminology is not specifically used, the kingdom is proclaimed whenever Jesus and his resurrection is preached with reference to biblical prophecy (cf. Acts 2:14-36; 13:16-41; 20:20-21; 28:31).[21] The reign of God and the future of God's people

---

20. Cf. B. Klappert, *NIDNTT* 2:372-89, for a brief survey of OT background and NT usage, with bibliography.

21. C. H. Dodd, *The Apostolic Preaching and Its Developments* (London: Hodder, 1936), 46-47, rightly observes that, from the point of view of the apostolic speeches in Acts, 'the

are bound up with the heavenly rule of Jesus as Messiah. While it is true that other disciples heard Jesus expounding the Scriptures in the post-resurrection period (cf. Lk. 24:25-27, 33), and others who were not apostles soon began to preach the fulfillment of Scripture in the person and work of Jesus (cf. Acts 7:1-56; 8:30-35), Jesus' teaching of the apostles qualified them in a unique sense to be the authoritative interpreters of Scripture for the earliest Christian communities and for subsequent generations of believers (cf. 1:21-22 note).

4 TNIV has added the words *on one occasion* to highlight the fact that a particular encounter is now in view. It was *while he was eating with them* (*synalizomenos*; cf. Lk. 24:41-43; Acts 10:41)[22] that he specifically commanded them *(parēngeilen autois)* not to leave Jerusalem, *'but wait for the gift my Father promised'*. The promise associated with the command is literally 'the promise of the Father' *(tēn epangelian tou patros)*, and it is clear from v. 5 that the gift of the Holy Spirit is in view (cf. 2:33). According to Luke 24:49, this meant being 'clothed with power from on high'. Joel 2:28-32 immediately comes to mind as 'the promise' in view because of its prominence in the preaching of Peter in Acts 2. However, it would be a mistake to limit the significance of the Spirit's coming to that text.[23] Passages like Isaiah 32:15; 44:3-5 and Ezekiel 11:19-20; 36:25-27 give a broader picture of God's intention to renew his people and his relationship with them through the gift of his Spirit in the end time. The link between Joel's more specific prophecy and other OT predictions will be discussed in connection with Peter's Pentecost sermon. Empowering for proclamation as Christ's witnesses is clearly implied in Luke 24:47-49; Acts 1:8, but that is not the only import of the gift of the Spirit in Acts.[24] The Father's promise was given in the Scrip-

---

Kingdom of God is conceived as coming in the events of the life, death, and resurrection of Jesus, and *to proclaim these facts, in their proper setting,* is to preach the gospel of the Kingdom of God'. Cf. THE THEOLOGY OF ACTS: V. THE GOSPEL (pp. 70-75).

22. Some EVV understand the present participle *synalizomenos* to be a passive form of *synalizō*, meaning 'being gathered together with (them)' (so KJV, NEB). Others take it as a variant of *synaulizomenos*, 'while staying with (them)' (so NRSV, ESV). But if the verb is derived from *halas* ('salt'), and means literally 'eating salt with them', TNIV has rightly taken it to mean that Jesus was eating an evening meal with them (so also NRSVmg., ESVmg.). Cf. Bruce 1990, 101; Metzger, *Textual Commentary*, 241-42; Barrett 1994, 71-72; D. L. Bock, *Acts*, BECNT (Grand Rapids: Baker Academic, 2007), 59.

23. This is a weakness in the argument of R. P. Menzies, *The Development of Early Christian Pneumatology with Special Reference to Luke-Acts*, JSNTSS 54 (Sheffield: JSOT, 1991), 203-4, and others who propose that the Spirit is given only for the renewal of Israel's prophetic vocation, equipping the disciples for mission. Contrast J. D. G. Dunn, *Baptism in the Holy Spirit: A Re-examination of the New Testament Teaching on the Gift of the Spirit in Relation to Pentecostalism Today*, SBT (Second Series) 15 (London: SCM, 1970), 47-48; F. F. Bruce, 'The Holy Spirit in the Acts of the Apostles', *Int* 27 (1973), 170-71; D. A. Carson, *Showing the Spirit: A Theological Exposition of 1 Corinthians 12–14* (Homebush West, Sydney: Lancer; Grand Rapids: Baker, 1988), 153-55; M. M. B. Turner, 'The "Spirit of Prophecy" as the Power of Israel's Restoration and Witness', in Marshall and Peterson, *Witness to the Gospel*, 1998, 327-48.

24. Cf. Tannehill 1990, 12-13; J. Shelton, *Mighty in Word and Deed: The Role of the Holy*

tures and confirmed by Jesus in his teaching *('which you have heard me speak about').*[25] The promise of John the Baptist, recalled in the next verse, makes it clear that Jesus as Messiah will be the one through whom the eschatological gift of the Spirit is experienced (cf. 2:33 note).

The apostles were to *wait* because Jesus' heavenly exaltation had to take place before the promised gift of the Spirit could be poured out (2:33). They were to wait in *Jerusalem* because of the historical and theological significance of that city in God's dealings with Israel. Jerusalem was especially associated with the promise of God to rule over his people and bless them through the kings of David's line (cf. 2 Sa. 7:1-29; 1 Ki. 8:1-21; Pss. 78:67-71; 132:11-18). So the city of David became a focal point of predictions about the future of the nation as a whole (e.g., Is. 40:1-2; 65:18-25; Zechariah 8). In the last days, people from many nations would be drawn to Zion to learn of Israel's God, and 'the word of the LORD' would go out from Jerusalem (Is. 2:3; Mi. 4:2). Luke's Gospel puts the focus on Jerusalem as the place where Jesus accomplished the great redemptive events that inaugurated the blessings of the New Covenant (e.g., Lk. 9:31, 51; 13:32-33; 19:11; 22:14-20; 24:18-21). As the nucleus of a renewed Israel, his disciples were called to be his witnesses in Jerusalem first (Lk. 24:47; Acts 1:8). It was there that they were to be empowered with the eschatological gift of the Spirit, as a community of expectant believers (cf. Acts 1:12-14). As we shall see, Luke regarded the apostles as representing that whole community of disciples when the promise was made to them.

5 John the Baptist provided further assurance that the promise of the Father would be fulfilled in their time. Those who received his baptism of repentance heard him say, 'I baptize you with water. But one who is more powerful than I will come, the thongs of whose sandals I am not worthy to untie. He will baptize you with the Holy Spirit and fire' (Lk. 3:16). John's water baptism prepared penitent Israelites to face the purging and transforming power of the Spirit that would characterize the messianic era (cf. Acts 2:3 note). *'Baptized with the Holy Spirit'* has been taken to mean being 'overwhelmed with' or 'immersed in Holy Spirit' *(en pneumati hagiō).* Thus Dunn argues that 'the idea of immersion in the river Jordan was itself one which was able to convey the ideas of both judgment and redemption, and the baptismal metaphor to describe the Coming One's ministry is obviously taken from the rite which most characterized John's ministry'.[26] But

Spirit in Luke-Acts (Peabody: Hendrickson, 1991), 125-56; M. M. B. Turner, *Power from on High: The Spirit in Israel's Restoration and Witness in Luke-Acts,* JPTSS 9 (Sheffield: Sheffield Academic, 1996), 343-47; THE THEOLOGY OF ACTS: III. THE HOLY SPIRIT (pp. 60-65).

25. There is an unusual change from indirect to direct speech here. Cf. Tannehill 1990, 12-13. Lk. 11:13 is an important example of Jesus' teaching on this subject, which finds echoes at various points in Acts. But Turner, *Power,* 341 note 66, argues that 'the promise of the Father' in Acts 1:4 is simply an anticipatory statement.

26. Dunn, *Baptism in the Holy Spirit,* 11. Dunn (11-14) discusses the metaphorical use of *baptizesthai* ('to be baptized') in literature and draws OT parallels. He notes that 'liquid'

Turner has argued that the Baptist 'forged his metaphor to affirm the stronger one to come would *cleanse* Israel (in accordance with the Isaianic oracles as they were currently understood), and that he would be able to do this because (as those oracles promised) God would mightily endow him with Spirit-and-power to accomplish that promised restoration'.[27] The addition of the words *'in a few days'* to Jesus' report of the Baptist's prophecy shows that, in the progress of the narrative, Pentecost is to be regarded as the occasion on which he provides that spiritual baptism (cf. 1:8; 2:4, 33).[28] Nevertheless, later recollection of this promise in connection with the giving of the Spirit to the Gentiles (11:16-17), and a further distinction between John's water baptism and the gift of the Holy Spirit (19:1-6), imply that the terminology of baptism in the Spirit 'relates to a process in which the Spirit progressively passes to new groups'.[29]

B. The Commissioning of the Apostles (1:6-8)

The timing of the restoration of the kingdom to Israel is a question that naturally arises out of Jesus' previous teaching (v. 3) and his announcement of the coming of the eschatological gift of the Spirit (vv. 4-5). But the apostles' attention is diverted by the risen Lord away from 'times' and 'dates', so that they might face the immediate challenge of being his witnesses. 'The resurrection revives the hope for the redemption of Israel but does not fulfill it.'[30] Acts makes it clear that the gospel about God's saving accomplishment in Jesus must be proclaimed and believed if people are to 'enter' God's kingdom and experience all its benefits (cf. 14:22). The Twelve are commissioned to fulfill a unique role, as the narrative in 1:15-26 makes clear. Nevertheless, allusions to Isaiah 43:10-12; 49:6 in 1:8 suggest that the apostles also function as the foundational core of the servant community appointed by the Lord Jesus to bring his salvation to Israel and the nations.

---

imagery is regularly used in the OT to describe the gift of the Spirit in the last days ('pour out', 'sprinkle'), making it easy for John to speak of the messianic gift of the Spirit 'in a metaphor drawn from the rite which was his own hall-mark'. The absence of 'fire' from Jesus' quotation of John's prophecy in Acts 1:5 is discussed by Dunn (43).

27. Turner, *Power*, 185, concluding a discussion about Luke's understanding of the Baptist's prediction. Turner argues on this basis that 'the Spirit is clearly in some sense "soteriologically necessary"' and is not simply given to empower disciples for mission.

28. *ou meta pollas tautas hēmeras* ('after not many days' [the demonstrative *tautas* appears to be redundant]) is the first example in Acts of a figure of speech called 'litotes', which makes a deliberate understatement, but TNIV has rightly indicated that the intention is to say *in a few days*. Luke uses litotes in 12:18; 14:17, 28; 15:2; 17:4, 12, 27; 19:11, 23-24; 20:12; 21:39; 26:19, 26; 27:20; 28:2. Cf. Barrett 1994, 74-75, for a discussion of various explanations of the grammatical form of the phrase in 1:5.

29. Tannehill 1990, 13.

30. Tannehill 1990, 14-15, draws a parallel with the premature hopes of those who expected that God's reign would appear immediately upon Jesus' arrival in Jerusalem (Lk. 19:11). Cf. Lk. 24:21, in the light of Lk. 1:32-33, 68-69; 2:29-32, 38.

6 Others were present with the apostles after the ascension (vv. 13-14), but the apostles alone appear to be addressed here. Jesus' final conversation with them (vv. 6-8) is clearly linked with what has gone before, even though Luke indicates the beginning of a new section with the opening words *so when they (hoi men oun)*.[31] Their question (*'Lord, are you at this time going to restore [apokathistaneis] the kingdom to Israel?'*) suggests that they were thinking of the immediate completion of the divinely ordered plan for the redemption of Israel and everything associated with that in biblical expectation (cf. Lk. 1:32-33, 46-55, 68-79; 2:29-32, 38). 'Restoration hopes were deeply rooted in classical prophecies of Israel's future and closely tied to the sacred space of Jerusalem/Zion.'[32] The apostles were expecting Jesus, as God's anointed king, to usher in the restoration to which many Jews looked forward, and of which Jesus himself had spoken.[33] Since the Spirit was connected with the end events in Jewish expectation (e.g., Jl. 2:28-32), they took it for granted that sovereignty was soon to be restored to Israel, so that God's ultimate purpose for the world might be fulfilled. The question was, would he act decisively *at this time (en tō chronō toutō)?*

It is often suggested that the apostles' question was misguided,[34] but this is not so. Jesus did not deny their expectation of the 'restoration'. He endorsed it, but interpreted it in terms of the gift of the Spirit and the fulfillment of prophecies about the restoration of Israel as a servant community, called to be God's 'witnesses' to the nations (Is. 43:10, 12 and 44:8). The end-time restoration would begin with the pouring out of the promised

31. This is 'a favorite formula in Acts for opening a new section of the narrative, connecting it with the preceding section' (Bruce 1990, 102). From 1:12 we learn that this conversation took place on the Mount of Olives.

32. Spencer 1997, 25-26. This included the hope that Jewish exiles and many Gentiles would be drawn to Zion, to share in the blessings bestowed on restored Israel. Cf. Is. 2:2-4; Mi. 4:1-8; Zc. 8:20-23.

33. *apokathistaneis* is a futuristic present here ('will you restore'). The same verb is used in Mt. 17:11; Mk. 9:12 in a technical sense, to refer to the restoration of all things, as anticipated in OT prophecy and in some strands of Jewish intertestamental literature. Cf. *apokatastasis* ('restoration') in Acts 3:21. Mt. 19:28 uses another technical term, *palingenesia* (lit. 'the regeneration' or 'the restoration'), to describe the situation in which the apostles will judge the twelve tribes of Israel (NRSV 'at the renewal of all things'; ESV 'in the new world'). This parallels Lk. 22:29-30, where kingdom language is employed. The 'consolation of Israel' or 'the redemption of Jerusalem' is on the agenda from the beginning of the Gospel (cf. Lk. 2:25, 38). Cf. Tannehill 1990, 15-16.

34. E.g., D. Hill, 'The Spirit and the Church's Witness: Observations on Acts 1:6-8', *IBS* 6 (1984), 16-17; F. F. Bruce, *The Book of the Acts*, NICNT (Grand Rapids: Eerdmans, 1954, rev. ed. 1988), 36; and J. R. W. Stott, *The Message of Acts: To the Ends of the Earth*, BST (Leicester: Inter-Varsity, 1990), 40-5. Jesus' response is said to challenge the narrow expectation of the apostles, which limits the restoration of the kingdom and its blessings to Israel. This popular line of interpretation is ably challenged by D. L. Tiede, 'The Exaltation of Jesus and the Restoration of Israel in Acts 1', *HTR* 79 (1986), 278-86; D. Gooding, *True to the Faith: A Fresh Approach to the Acts of the Apostles* (London: Hodder & Stoughton, 1990), 34-41; Tannehill 1990, 14-17; D. Pao, *Acts and the Isaianic New Exodus*, WUNT 2, no. 130 (Tübingen: Mohr [Siebeck], 2000; repr. Grand Rapids: Baker Academic, 2002), 95-96.

Spirit and the bringing of God's salvation, first to Israel and then 'to the ends of the earth' (Is. 49:6; cf. Is. 42:6-7). It would be consummated when Jesus returned (cf. 1:11; 3:20-21). Through the witness of Jesus' apostles, 'the kingdom' would be restored to Israel, but not in nationalistic or political terms, nor immediately in the full and final sense outlined in biblical prophecy (cf. 3:19-26).

7 The first part of Jesus' response takes up the matter of timing, which was central to the apostles' question. Any attempt to compute *'times or dates' (chronous ē kairous)* must be put aside (cf. Mt. 24:36; Mk 13:32).[35] This is because *the Father* has already *set* or determined these *'by his own authority' (etheto en tē idia exousia,* 'placed within his own authority'). This is confirmed by the use of similar terminology in 3:19-21 *(kairoi . . . chronōn)* to explain the way God's eschatological plan will be fulfilled. Since such matters are in his hands, his disciples are in no position to predict the time of the end, and it should not concern them. How foolishly this warning has been ignored across the centuries! What should preoccupy believers is the mission plan that Jesus goes on to reveal. By this means he gives his own distinctive meaning and purpose to the critical age in which we live. The period between the ascension of Jesus and his return (v. 11) is to be marked by the presence and power of the Holy Spirit ('times of refreshing from the Lord'; cf. 3:19 note).

8 The first element of the risen Lord's promise is *'you will receive power' (lēmpsesthe dynamin),* and the qualifying clause explains that this will happen *'when the Holy Spirit comes on you' (epelthontos tou hagious pneumatos eph' hymas;* cf. Lk. 24:49). The Holy Spirit's 'coming' is not continuous but definitive (the context so delimits the aorist participle *epelthontos* to show that the meaning is temporal and punctiliar here), though clearly the Spirit is available at any time after Pentecost for those who repent and are 'baptized in the name of Jesus Christ' (2:38). In the light of v. 5, this coming of the Spirit upon the apostles must be equivalent to being *baptized with the Holy Spirit* (cf. 2:4 note). The word *dynamis (power)* is used with reference to miracles in 2:22; 3:12; 4:7; 8:13; 10:38; 19:11, but in 4:33; 6:8-10 it includes power to speak boldly. In view of what follows, the *power* that is promised in 1:8 is essentially related to the task of being Christ's *witnesses,* though this is not all that Acts teaches about the role of the Spirit in believers. Jesus himself was anointed with the Spirit as God's chosen Servant (Lk. 3:21-22; cf. Is. 42:1; Lk. 4:18-21, cf. Is. 61:1-2), and now he promises that his apostles will shortly be empowered by the same Spirit to share the Servant's ministry. The promise of the Spirit here specifically recalls Isaiah 32:15, which speaks of the desolation of Israel that continues until 'the Spirit is poured on us from on high' (LXX, 'upon

---

35. Barrett 1994, 78, says that it is hardly possible in this verse to make a clear distinction between *chronous* and *kairous,* though one might think of the latter as 'unspecified points of time' and the former as 'unspecified intervals' separating the times.

you', *epelthē eph' hymas*).[36] The gift of the Holy Spirit is a sign that God's end-time restoration has begun, but since the Spirit is specifically given for the worldwide mission envisaged in v. 8, the 'day of the Lord' and all that it entails is delayed (cf. 2:17-21 note).[37] Christians have to live with the tension of knowing that the work of the gospel is central to God's eschatological plan, but never being able to calculate the exact date of the end.

The second element of the risen Lord's promise is *'you will be my witnesses' (esesthe mou martyres)*. This finds its closest parallel in Isaiah 43:10 (cf. 43:12, *hymeis emoi martyres*; 44:8). Isaiah envisages that the renewed people of God will be witnesses to the nations of the salvation of God when the new age arrives.[38] Jesus fulfills the divine function of appointing his own witnesses to the nations. The word 'witness' *(martys)* is almost exclusively applied to the Twelve in Acts (1:8, 22; 2:32; 3:15; 5:32; 10:39, 41; 13:31), though related terms are used in connection with the ministry of others.[39] There are two possible ways of understanding the Greek expression *mou martyres*: they will bear witness to the significance of Jesus and his ministry (objective genitive), and they will do so as those who belong to him (possessive genitive) — as his authorized representatives. The parallel passage in Luke 24:44-48 suggests that the former is primarily intended. In both passages, the implication is that the apostles have observed Christ's suffering and resurrection and can now uniquely 'give testimony' (cf. 4:33, *apedidoun martyrion*) or 'bear witness' (cf. 10:42, *diamartyrasthai*) to those events and their significance in the light of Jesus' teaching, especially his explanation from the OT of the way the kingdom of God is realized. We first see Peter doing this in Acts 2, when the Spirit comes as promised. The

---

36. Pao, *New Exodus*, 92, points out that the part of Is. 32:15 that does not appear in Acts 1:8 (*aph' hypsēlou*, 'from on high') can be found in the parallel passage in Lk. 24:49 in a similar phrase *(ex hypsous)*. Pao emphasizes that the coming of the Spirit in Is. 32:15 signifies the dawn of the 'new exodus' that is so much the theme in Isaiah 40–55.

37. This is not to say that 'Luke is reconciled to the prospect of a long time-gap' (Hill, 'Church's Witness', 21, following H. Conzelmann, *The Theology of St. Luke*, trans. G. Buswell (New York: Harper & Row, 1960), and others. From Luke's point of view, much of the missionary plan of Acts 1:8 had already been carried out when he completed his book. Why is it necessary to suppose that he envisaged such a long time-gap? Cf. J. Nolland, 'Salvation-History and Eschatology', in Marshall and Peterson, *Witness to the Gospel*, 63-81.

38. Pao, *New Exodus*, 93, observes that the people of Israel are portrayed in Is. 42:18-25 as being deaf and blind. The promise in 43:10-12 'therefore signifies the presence of a reversal, one that is possible through the introduction of the new work of the God of Israel'.

39. Cf. THE THEOLOGY OF ACTS: VII. WITNESS AND MISSION (pp. 79-83). In secular Greek literature, witness terminology appeared frequently in legal contexts and in histories that were concerned to establish certain facts. The Greeks also had a place for 'witnesses to convictions' (A. A. Trites, *The New Testament Concept of Witness*, SNTSMS 31 [Cambridge: Cambridge University, 1977], 4-15). The legal use of this terminology is found regularly in the LXX. The NT use of witness terminology rests squarely on the OT concept of justice. In the OT the lawsuit or controversy theme grows out of the legal assembly and plays an important part (Trites, 20-65). Cf. P. G. Bolt, 'Mission and Witness', in Marshall and Peterson, *Witness to the Gospel*, 191-214.

Twelve occupy a unique place in history as witnesses of Christ because of the time they spent with him — especially after his resurrection — and because of their commissioning by him (cf. 1:21-26 note). As 'eyewitnesses' (Lk. 1:2; cf. Acts 1:3a), they guarantee the historicity of the major events in Jesus' life, and as those uniquely instructed by him (Lk. 24:44-48; Acts 1:3b-5), they pass on Jesus' own understanding of his person and work. Even though Paul is called 'a witness' by the risen Christ (22:15; 26:16), Luke makes it clear that his experience and calling are different from that of the Twelve. Other characters in Acts are witnesses to Christ only in a secondary or derived sense, sharing with unbelievers the testimony of the apostles that they have come to believe for themselves. In terms of Isaiah 43:10-12; 49:6, Jesus calls the apostles to be the nucleus of the servant community that he will use to bring the message of salvation to Israel and to the Gentiles. Acts then shows how the apostles inform and enable others to be part of that community and to share in the task of bringing others to Christ. In the final analysis, Luke indicates that effective Christian witness involves both a sharing of the apostolic testimony to Jesus and a demonstration of spiritual and moral transformation arising from personal commitment to the risen Lord (cf. 5:32 note; 6:3, 10).

The sphere of the apostolic witness was to be *'in Jerusalem, and in all Judea and Samaria, and to the ends of the earth'*. Jesus echoes the words and concepts of Isaiah 49:6, especially with the phrase *to the ends of the earth*. 'Rather than sinking roots in Jerusalem and waiting for the world to flood *in*, Jesus' followers are to move *out* from Jerusalem, through Judea and Samaria, and ultimately *"to* the ends of the earth".'[40] More of this text is quoted in Acts 13:47, as a justification for Paul's ministry among the Gentiles, and it is alluded to in Luke 2:32; Acts 26:23, and possibly Acts 28:28. 'The promise of God's reign is not simply the restoration of the preserved of Israel, but the renewal of the vocation of Israel to be a light to the nations to the ends of the earth.'[41] Acts 1:8 is a prediction and promise of the way this divine plan will be fulfilled, rather than a command. The rest of the book shows how it happened, first *in Jerusalem* (chaps. 2–7), then *in all Judea and Samaria* (chaps. 8–12), and then *to the ends of the earth* (chaps. 13–28). However, Rome is not the ultimate goal of this mission, even though Acts finishes with Paul's ministry in that city. Pao argues that the programmatic statement in 1:8 should be understood, not merely in terms of physical geography, but in 'theopolitical' terms. There are three stages in the outworking of 'the new exodus' foretold by Isaiah: the dawn of sal-

40. Spencer 1997, 26, reflecting on the expectations in texts like Is. 2:2-4; Mi. 4:1-8; Zc. 8:20-23.

41. Tiede, 'Exaltation of Jesus', 286. Although the phrase 'to the ends of the earth' has a general reference (e.g., Is. 48:20; Je. 10:13), Barrett 1994, 80, argues that the city of Rome functions as 'representative of the whole world' in the structure of Acts. This is true from a narrative perspective, but the promise of Jesus is not to be limited in its scope to Rome. Cf. Pao, *New Exodus*, 93-94.

vation in Jerusalem, the reconstitution and reunification of Israel (signified here by *in all Judea and Samaria*), and the inclusion of the Gentiles
within the people of God.[42] In Acts 13–28, Paul's activity as a witness 'before the Gentiles and their kings and before the people of Israel' is highlighted, in accordance with the commission he receives (9:15; cf. 22:15;
23:11; 26:16). As noted in connection with 1:2, there are differences between the apostleship of Paul and of the Twelve, but Luke presents Paul as
an authorized witness in his own right. In his ministry the plan of 1:8 is
dramatically advanced. Nevertheless, Acts provides only selected illustra-
tions of the way God's purpose was advanced in the first few decades,
and the narrative concludes with the task uncompleted. Readers are left
with an implied challenge to continue the work of worldwide testimony
to Jesus.[43]

C. The Ascension of Christ and Its Aftermath (1:9-14)

Jesus' ascension appears in this context as the necessary condition for the
transfer of prophetic power to his disciples, as in the stories of Moses (Dt.
34:9) and Elijah (2 Ki. 2:9-22). He had to be removed from the scene before the
Spirit could be poured out on his 'successors' (2:33; 3:21; cf. Jn. 16:5-15), and
they could function as his witnesses. The angelic challenge is to believe his
promise and obey his commands, which included the specific instruction to
wait in Jerusalem for the promised gift of the Spirit (1:4-5; cf. Lk. 24:49). In
Luke 24:50-53 the departure scene brings the narrative to temporary closure,
but in Acts 1:9-14 it functions as a narrative beginning, pointing forward to
future events and moving the disciples to action.[44] The final section of the introduction (vv. 12-14) identifies eleven apostles as the core of the messianic
community, waiting expectantly for the risen Lord Jesus to act. It contains the
first of several summaries highlighting the unity and devotion of the first believers (cf. 2:42-47; 4:32-37; 9:31). In particular, the apostles are supported and
endorsed in their leadership by the women and Jesus' family, who were significant disciple groups among the 120 believers mentioned in v. 15.[45]

---

42. Pao, *New Exodus*, 95. Pao rightly notes that the phrase *en pasē tē (in all)* links Judea
and Samaria grammatically and evokes 'the theopolitical connotation of the two regions'. In
other words, this expression broadly relates to the area formerly occupied by the southern
and northern kingdoms of Israel. Barrett 1994, 80, says, 'Luke has no stories to tell about
Galilee and therefore does not include it in this programmatic verse', but cf. 9:31 note. Bock
2007, 64-65, concludes that 'the end of the earth' is 'geographic and ethnic in scope, inclusive of all peoples and locales'.

43. Cf. B. S. Rosner, 'The Progress of the Word', in Marshall and Peterson, *Witness to
the Gospel*, 229-33.

44. Tannehill 1990, 18. Tannehill notes that the angelic words in 1:11 'remind us that
the Jesus story has a future dimension that stretches beyond the end of Acts'.

45. Cf. N. P. Estrada, *From Followers to Leaders: The Apostles in the Ritual of Status Transformation in Acts 1–2*, JSNTSS 255 (London/New York: Clark International, 2004), 104-50, 234-35.

9 The words *after he said this (tauta eipōn)* closely link the mission
agenda of Jesus with his ascension and the angelic words that follow.
'Luke's point is that the missionary activity of the early church rested not
only on Jesus' mandate but also on his living presence in heaven and the
sure promise of his return.'[46] Although the ascension of Jesus is distinguished from his resurrection in meaning and significance elsewhere in the
NT (e.g., Jn. 20:17; Eph. 4:8-10; 1 Tim. 3:16; Heb. 4:14; 6:19-20; 9:11, 24; 13:20;
1 Pet. 3:21-22), only Luke gives a description of it as a separate historical
event, forty days after Easter (cf. Mk. 16:19 for another brief account in
some ancient MSS). There is textual uncertainty about Luke 24:51, but it appears that Luke wrote two accounts, the more detailed one being in Acts
1:9-11.[47] The description of Jesus' ascension is nevertheless quite brief in
Acts. A supernatural act of God is implied by the passive verb *he was taken
up (epērthē)*. The fourfold use of the phrase *eis ton ouranon* ('into the sky/
heaven') in vv. 10-11 further emphasizes the notion of going 'up'. Although
this language should not be taken to mean that heaven is a physical reality,
somewhere out in space, it should not be dismissed as purely symbolic or
pictorial.[48] 'A bodily ascension fits the Jewish background, especially after
a physical resurrection.'[49] The story is told from the point of view of the
spectators on earth. As experienced by the witnesses *(before their very
eyes)*,[50] the physical departure of Jesus on this occasion was different from
his disappearances during the preceding forty days of resurrection appearances (cf. Lk. 24:31). There was something final and decisive about his going this time. The resurrection appearances, 'in which he condescended to
his disciples' temporal conditions of life, were visitations from the eternal
order to which his "body of glory" now belonged. What happened on the
fortieth day was that this series of intermittent visitations came to an end,

46. R. N. Longenecker, 'The Acts of the Apostles', in *The Expositor's Bible Commentary,
Volume 9 (John-Acts)*, ed. F. E. Gaebelein (Grand Rapids: Zondervan, 1981), 258. Longenecker
rightly argues that, far from being a stopgap measure for the unrealized hope of the kingdom of God, Luke's position is that mission is an essential element in the eschatological divine plan of salvation.

47. Luke 24 gives the impression that the resurrection appearances and the ascension
all took place on the one day. The evangelist could afford to be vague in his chronology at
this point because he was simply recording the triumphant conclusion to Jesus' ministry.
But when he came to give an account of the origins of the Christian movement in Acts, he
had to be more precise in his chronology. Cf. note 18 above on the 'forty days'.

48. Marshall 1980, 60, unnecessarily speaks of 'the symbolism of "ascension"', but
rightly describes this supernatural event as expressing 'the way in which the physical presence of Jesus departed from this world, to be replaced by his spiritual presence'. Cf. B. M.
Metzger, 'The Ascension of Jesus Christ', in *Historical and Literary Studies: Pagan, Jewish and
Christian*, NTTS 8 (Leiden: Brill, 1968), 77-87; Stott 1990, 45-49.

49. Bock 2007, 68. A spiritual ascension or 'the mere ascent of a soul' would deny the
physicality of the resurrection that Luke has been keen to emphasize (Lk. 24:30, 37-43; Acts
1:3-4).

50. The genitive absolute with the present tense in Greek *(blepontōn autōn)* literally
means 'while they were watching' (cf. KJV, NRSV, ESV).

with a scene which brought home to the disciples the heavenly glory of their risen Lord.'[51] The ascension was not the beginning of his heavenly exaltation. It was the ultimate confirmation of the status that had been his from the moment of his resurrection. The *cloud* which *hid him from their sight* indicated to them his total envelopment in God's presence and glory. Perhaps they recalled the cloud as the visible token of God's glory associated with the tabernacle in the wilderness (e.g., Ex. 40:34-35). Certainly they must have remembered the cloud covering Jesus on the Mount of Transfiguration, when three of their number were given a revelation of the glory that was to be his after his suffering (cf. Lk. 9:31 ['his departure'], 34).

10-11 More attention is paid in this narrative to the response of the apostles and the words of the angelic messengers than to the details of the ascension itself. The awesome nature of the experience left the apostles *looking intently up into the sky as he was going.*[52] Maybe they expected the cloud to dissolve and Jesus to appear again as he had on the mountain in Galilee (cf. Lk. 9:28-36). *Suddenly two men dressed in white stood beside them.*[53] Their appearance and their function resembled that of the two men who met the women at the tomb of Jesus (Lk. 24:4-7). Supernatural beings attend both the resurrection and the ascension events.[54] Here, as at the empty tomb, a challenge (*'why do you stand here looking into the sky?'*) is followed by a correction (*'This same Jesus, who has been taken from you into heaven, will come back in the same way you have seen him go into heaven'*).[55] Such gazing into heaven was inappropriate because of Jesus' instructions and his promise about the Spirit. Since Jesus had been *taken* (*analēmphtheis*; cf. v. 2) from them so obviously *into heaven*, they would not see him again until he returned. By implication, they were to believe his promise and obey his command, returning to the city to wait for empowerment by the Spirit. In the promise of Jesus' second coming, at an unspecified time, there lies a further incentive for engaging in his mission, for the master will return and call his servants to account (cf. Lk. 12:35-48; 19:11-27; Acts 3:19-21). In the face of possible doubts and disappointments among his readers, Luke insists that

51. Bruce 1990, 103. Cf. J. F. Maile, 'The Ascension in Luke-Acts', *TynB* 37 (1986), 29-59; Zwiep, *Ascension*, 1-35, 200-215, for reviews and critiques of various assessments of the ascension. Western texts of v. 9 have Jesus enveloped by a cloud on earth before his ascension and say nothing about the disciples watching the event. MSS in this tradition also omit the second 'into heaven' from v. 11. But these readings are secondary.

52. *atenizontes ēsan* (*they were looking intently*) is a periphrastic imperfect, stressing that they continued to look, and the genitive absolute in the present tense *poreuomenou autou* (*as he was going*) highlights the continuous process by which he went into heaven.

53. The pluperfect *pareistēkeisan* (*stood beside*) is used with the meaning of the imperfect, suggesting a sudden appearance of the angels, while the apostles were gazing upward. Cf. Barrett 1994, 83.

54. Barrett 1994, 83, suggests that 'the whiteness of the clothes helps to identify the "men" as angels' (cf. 2 Macc. 11:8; Mk. 9:3; 16:5; Jn. 20:12; Hermas, *Vis.* 2.1; 3.5; *Sim.* 8.2.3).

55. Tannehill 1990, 19-20, compares the 'vision of angels' given to the women in Luke 24 with the angelic appearance to the 'men of Galilee' here.

the ascension of Christ is a guarantee that the end will come and all God's purposes will be fulfilled.[56] But we should not press the words *in the same way* too restrictively.[57] Jesus himself predicted that his second coming would be personal, glorious, and powerful, 'in a cloud with power and great glory' (Lk. 21:27). But it will not be as private as his ascension was. When he returns, 'every eye will see him' (Rev. 1:7), and he will not be alone (Lk. 9:26; 1 Thes. 4:14-17; 2 Thes. 1:7). As the lightning 'lights up the sky from one end to the other' (Lk. 17:25), so his second coming will somehow be obvious to people everywhere. The angelic promise effectively corresponds to Jesus' statement in Mark 13:10 that 'the gospel must first be preached to all nations' before the end comes.

12 The first response of the Eleven was to return to *Jerusalem*, to await 'the promise of the Father' (vv. 4-5). Mention of *the hill called the Mount of Olives* as the place of the ascension should not be taken to contradict Luke 24:50, which speaks more generally of Jesus leading them out 'to the vicinity of Bethany' *(heōs pros Bēthanian)*. Bethany was on the eastern slope of the mountain, and according to John 11:18 was about fifteen stadia from Jerusalem (about two miles or three kilometers). The summit of *the Mount of Olives* was *a Sabbath's day's walk from the city*, which was calculated in rabbinic sources to be 2,000 cubits (0.7 miles or 1,120 meters).[58] It is likely that Jesus would have led them into open country, rather than close to the village of Bethany, to witness his ascension. In Zechariah 14:1-5, the Mount of Olives is associated with the Lord's coming in judgment against the nations that fight against his people. However, here it is the place of the Lord's departure, from where his apostles must go and bear witness to Israel and the nations of his saving grace, 'before the coming of the great and glorious day of the Lord' (Jl. 2:31, cited in Acts 2:20).[59]

13 When Luke speaks of them going *upstairs to the room (hyperōon) where they were staying*, it is possible that he means the room where the Last Supper was held (although *anagaion* is used to describe this in Lk. 22:12; Mk. 14:15; *katalyma* in Lk. 22:11).[60] It may also have been the room where

---

56. Cf. Wilson, *Gentiles*, 106, arguing against those who see Luke addressing a community expecting an imminent end.

57. The promise is literally, 'so he shall come *(houtōs eleusetai)* in the way that you saw him going into heaven *(hon tropon theasasthe auton poreuomenon eis ton ouranon)*'. Cf. Barrett 1994, 84.

58. Cf. Barrett 1994, 85-86; Bock 2007, 76. The distance of the Mount of Olives from Jerusalem falls between five and six stadia in the writings of Josephus.

59. Spencer 1997, 28, points to Acts 21:38 and the abortive attempt to overthrow the Romans which began on the Mount of Olives, according to Josephus *(Ant.* 20.169-71; *War* 2.261-3). But I think Spencer's identification of the Mount of Olives as a place of opposition to the Jewish establishment, based on Lk. 19:28-48, is forced.

60. The periphrastic imperfect *ēsan katamenontes (were staying)* stresses that they habitually met there. Barrett 1994, 87, rightly observes: 'We can hardly suppose that all the persons mentioned were *residing* in one room.' Bock 2007, 77, argues that the size of the room required for such a large number to meet 'suggests a locale in a wealthy area'.

some resurrection appearances took place (cf. Lk. 24:33, 36; Jn. 20:19, 26). On the other hand, the various meetings recorded in Acts 1:13; 2:1-4; 4:23-31; 12:12-17 could all have been in different locations. There is not enough evidence to be certain. The names of the apostles are repeated, with a slight variation in order from Luke 6:14-16, and without Judas Iscariot.[61] The list thus forms a link with the account of their initial commissioning by Jesus. In both contexts, those whom he designated apostles have a particular mandate from Jesus to fulfill. Since only eleven are listed here, this prepares for the next section of the narrative, where the need for a twelfth is explained (1:15-26). From Acts 1:12-15 it is clear that these men formed the nucleus of a larger community that Jesus had gathered to himself. Only Peter, James, and John are mentioned again by name.

14 Those linked with the apostles at this stage are specifically *the women, Mary the mother of Jesus,* and *his brothers.* Doubtless the women were those who had gone up to Jerusalem from Galilee with Jesus. They supported him out of their personal incomes and were the first witnesses of his resurrection (cf. Lk. 8:2-3; 23:55–24:10).[62] Jesus' mother, Mary, who figured so significantly in the outworking of God's redemptive plan and who is presented in Luke 1–2 as a model of trust and submission to God's will, is mentioned for the last time. The disbelief of Jesus' brothers is recorded in Mark 3:21-35 and John 7:2-10. Perhaps Jesus' resurrection appearance to James (1 Cor. 15:7) was responsible for the conversion of Joses, Judas, and Simon also (cf. Mk. 6:3). James became the leader of the Jerusalem church (cf. 12:17; 15:13-21; 21:18), and 'the Lord's brothers' were acknowledged alongside the apostles as a distinctive group in the Christian community (cf. 1 Cor. 9:5).[63] Luke's description of the activity of the apostles and those with them at this stage *(they all joined together constantly in prayer)* is quite emphatic in Greek *(houtoi pantes ēsan proskarterountes homothymadon tē proseuchē).*[64] As they con-

---

61. The lists of the Twelve in Mk. 3:16-19 and Mt. 10:2-4 differ from Luke's lists mainly by putting Thaddaeus where Luke has Judas son of James and in the order of the names. It is possible that Thaddaeus (or Lebbaeus in some MSS) was a nickname for this Judas. Simon the Zealot (Lk. 6:15; Acts 1:13) appears to be another name for Simon the Cananaean (Mt. 10:4; Mk. 3:18). Cf. H.-C. Hahn, *NIDNTT* 3:1167. The use of the title 'the Zealot' does not automatically mean that he had been a member of the Zealot party. Such terminology can be used less technically (cf. 21:20; 22:3; Gal. 1:14). Cf. Barrett 1994, 87-88.

62. B. R. Gaventa, *The Acts of the Apostles*, Abingdon New Testament Commentaries (Nashville, Abingdon, 2003), 68, correctly opposes the view represented in Codex D that these women were wives of the apostles rather than being disciples and witnesses in their own right.

63. According to Bruce 1990, 106-7, the burden of proof lies on those who would understand 'the brothers of Jesus' to be other than 'uterine brothers' in the normal sense. Barrett 1994, 89-90, observes that 'the earthly family of Jesus is now taken up into his spiritual family (cf. Mk. 3:31-35)'.

64. The periphrastic imperfect *(ēsan proskarterountes homothymadon)* emphasizes the continuous nature of this activity. Luke uses the verb *proskartereō* six times in Acts with the sense of 'devotion or adherence to' a person (8:13; 10:7) or an activity such as prayer or teaching (1:14; 2:42, 46; 6:4). The adverb *homothymadon* ('of one mind, together') is used ten

tinually devoted themselves to prayer, they did so *together (homothymadon)*, as a fellowship of like-minded believers. If this narrative is read in the light of 1:15-26, it could be argued that the leadership status and authority of the apostles needed confirming after the betrayal of Judas. Luke highlights the unanimity of the Eleven with the women and Jesus' family because they were significant disciple groups among the believers in those early days.[65]

The context suggests that they focused their prayers on what they had heard and seen in recent days and asked for the fulfillment of Jesus' predictions. 'As they patiently wait on God's timing, the disciples are praying and readying themselves for their task as a group.'[66] Luke 24:53 also makes the point that after the ascension they 'stayed continually at the temple, praising God'. It is striking that at almost every important turning point in the narrative of God's redemptive action in Acts we find a mention of prayer (e.g., 1:24; 8:14-17; 9:11-12; 10:4, 9, 30; 13:2-3). Turner observes:

> This portrayal is never in danger of suggesting that the true initiative in salvation-history lies in believers, in their determination to pray for specific events to come to pass. God is only fulfilling what he long before promised. Such decisive acts of God as (e.g.) the descent of the Spirit on Jesus, on the disciples at Pentecost, and at Cornelius's home, take place in a context of prayer, but not obviously as an immediate response to a specific request for the same. Nevertheless, without answering questions of cause and effect, the whole tableau gives a unified picture of the close relationship between prayer and God's decisive acts of salvation, right up to the parousia (Lk. 18:1ff.).[67]

II. THE WORD IN JERUSALEM (1:15–6:7)

In this first major section of the narrative after the introduction, Luke demonstrates God's faithfulness to his promises by showing how he began the eschatological restoration of Israel in Jerusalem. This took place through the preaching of the gospel and the ministry of the Holy Spirit. The first hint of this restoration is given in the election of a twelfth apostle to replace Judas (1:15-26). A link between the reception of the Spirit by the apostles and their empowerment to be Christ's witnesses was signaled in 1:6-8.

times, to highlight the exemplary unity of Christians (1:14; 2:1, 46; 4:24; 5:12; 15:25; cf. 8:6), but also the unanimity of their opponents (7:57; 18:12; 19:29; cf. 12:20).

65. Cf. Estrada, *Followers*, 104-50, 234-35.

66. Bock 2007, 79.

67. M. M. B. Turner, 'Prayer in the Gospels and Acts', in D. A. Carson (ed.), *Teach Us to Pray: Prayer in the Bible and the World* (Grand Rapids: Baker; Exeter: Paternoster, 1990), 74-75. Cf. P. T. O'Brien, 'Prayer in Luke-Acts', *TynB* 24 (1973), 111-27; A. A. Trites, 'The Prayer-Motif in Luke-Acts', in C. H. Talbert (ed.), *Perspectives on Luke-Acts* (Edinburgh: Clark, 1978), 168-86; S. F. Plymale, *The Prayer Texts of Luke-Acts* (New York: Lang, 1991).

When the Spirit comes (2:1-4), Peter is enabled to proclaim to Jews 'from every nation under heaven' salvation through Jesus as Lord and Messiah (2:5-39). The Spirit brings many to repentance and faith, expanding the number of disciples dramatically and equipping them as a community for their prophetic role to others in the city (2:40-47). The first healing in Jerusalem provides a further opportunity for the apostles to offer the messianic salvation to any Israelite who will turn to Jesus, with a warning that those who refuse will be cut off from 'the people' (3:1-26). The trial scenes in Acts 4–5 show how the prophetic status of the apostles and the authority of their message become critical issues for the traditional leaders of Judaism. Despite the mounting opposition they experience, the apostles continue to proclaim the messiahship of Jesus in Jerusalem, and God blesses their endeavors. It seems as though the future of Israel lies in their hands. However, the particular role of 'the word of God' in growing the church is stressed as the ministry of the Seven is introduced (6:1-7).[68] This last passage is a bridge to a section in which the gospel begins to spread out from Jerusalem and people other than the apostles share in its progress.

A. Completion of the Apostolic Circle (1:15-26)

This subsection highlights the distinctive role and significance of the apostles as witnesses of the resurrection and guarantors of the traditions about Jesus' ministry. As the unfinished list of apostles in 1:13 shows, the circle of the Twelve had been broken. When the ascended Lord expresses his choice of Matthias as the apostle to succeed Judas, the context suggests that this was an essential preliminary to the giving of the Spirit.[69] There could be no witness 'to the ends of the earth' until the Messiah's claim on the whole house of Israel had been reiterated. So, 'it is first of all the restored Israel, represented by the Twelve, that receives the Holy Spirit at Pentecost'.[70]

---

68. 'The word' or 'the word of God', meaning the apostolic gospel, is explicitly mentioned in this section of Acts at 2:41; 4:4, 29, 31; 6:2, 4, 7. Luke also offers two major presentations of the gospel in 2:22-36 and 3:12-26 and records their impact. A briefer summary of the apostolic message is found in 4:8-12, followed by a significant prayer for boldness to continue preaching the word in the face of opposition (4:29-31; cf. 4:33; 5:42). In this way Luke introduces a theme that in various ways will dominate his narrative throughout. However, it is important to notice that 1:15–6:7 is designed to show the initial effect of gospel preaching on the people of Jerusalem, as a first step in the fulfillment of the prediction in 1:8. Cf. pp. 32-34, 70-75 above.

69. It is not correct, however, to say that this is a period without Jesus and without the Spirit (cf. A. W. Zwiep, *Judas and the Choice of Matthias: A Study on Context and Concern of Acts 1:15-26* [Tübingen: Mohr, 2004], 2, 129), since the language of v. 24 suggests that the ascended Lord appointed the new apostle just as he had chosen the Twelve in the first place (cf. Lk. 6:13; Acts 1:2). The Spirit's pre-Pentecost ministry is particularly obvious through Scripture (1:16).

70. Cf. V. C. Pfitzner, '"Pneumatic" Apostleship? Apostle and Spirit in the Acts of the

With its focus on witnessing to the resurrection, 1:21-22 prepares the reader to observe the centrality of that theme in the subsequent preaching of the apostles. Estrada argues that 'the apostles' leadership qualification was in serious question because of their association with Judas — the apostle who betrayed Jesus'.[71] Acts 1–2 is an apologetic narrative in which Luke seeks to promote the leadership integrity of the apostles, and this segment is at the heart of that approach. Zwiep takes a broader view of the apologetic significance of 1:15-26 and observes four ways in which readers are assured by it.[72] First, the language of necessity is used at the beginning (v. 16) and end (v. 21) of Peter's speech. Second, the betrayal of Jesus is shown to have been the tragic fulfillment of Scripture (v. 20), meaning that Jesus was not mistaken or caught off guard by events. Third, at this crucial point of transition in salvation history, the circle of the Twelve as the representatives of the new Israel was restored (vv. 21-26; cf. Lk. 22:28-30). Fourth, 'the fact that the circle of the Twelve was complete at Pentecost was a confirmation of Jesus' prophetic and messianic status and increased the credibility of his promise of the future role of the Twelve as the eschatological leaders of Israel. Matthias was not chosen because Judas had died, but because he had become an apostate.'[73]

1. The Fate of Judas (1:15-20)

This paragraph emphasizes the fulfillment of Scripture, which is a prominent theme in both volumes of Luke's work and is part of a wider emphasis on the plan of God being worked out in the events that are recorded.[74] Peter takes an important step in strengthening and encouraging the community of believers (cf. Lk. 22:32) when he follows the lead of Jesus and interprets the Scriptures for them. Judas is the first person in the plot of Acts to suffer

---

Apostles', in *Wort in der Zeit: Neutestamentliche Studien*, Festgabe für H. Rengstorf, ed. W. Haubeck and M. Bachmann (Leiden: Brill, 1980), 210-35 (218). He rightly argues that the founding of a central body of twelve apostles relates to 'the question of the mission of the church which begins with the gift of the Spirit', not to the establishment of an organizational structure.

71. Estrada, *Followers*, 231. Estrada, 151-88, deals with this theme particularly in relation to 1:15-26. See my criticism of Estrada in note 93 below.

72. Luke has stated his intention to provide for Theophilus and other potential readers 'certainty' about the things they have been taught (Lk. 1:4). But the defection of Judas Iscariot raises a big question about the divine control of salvation history.

73. Zwiep, *Judas*, 178-79. Cf. Johnson 1992, 38-40. Witherington 1998, 115, observes that Luke has shaped his source material 'into a form that a Gentile audience would recognize as rhetorically persuasive'. Witherington 116-20, gives a helpful extended note on the speeches in Acts and their historical reliability.

74. Cf. Witherington 1998, 123-24; D. L. Bock, 'Scripture and the Realisation of God's Promises', in Marshall and Peterson, *Witness to the Gospel*, 41-62; G. K. Beale and D. A. Carson (eds.), *Commentary on the New Testament Use of the Old Testament* (Grand Rapids: Baker Academic; Nottingham: Apollos, 2007), 513-606, on Luke's use of the OT.

divine punishment (cf. 5:1-11; 12:23; 13:6-12; 19:13-16). All the antagonists that Luke introduces 'attempt to derange the development of the plot but are removed from the scene by dramatic measures "from behind the scenes"'.[75] Readers may be perplexed about the apostasy of Judas and wonder whether this casts doubt on the ability of Jesus to fulfill his promise to pour out the Spirit and enable his witnesses to reach 'the ends of the earth' (1:6-8). However, the punishment of Judas, the fulfillment of certain prophecies, and the election of Matthias as successor to Judas demonstrate the sovereign hand of God at work in this situation. The risen Lord is not frustrated by human rebellion and will not allow even apostasy to hinder the fulfillment of his saving purpose.

15 The beginning of a new section is indicated with a general time reference (*in those days;* cf. Lk. 1:39; 6:12; Acts 6:1; 11:27),[76] namely between the ascension and Pentecost. No indication is given about the specific context, though somewhere in Jerusalem is suggested by vv. 12-14. The expression *epi to auto* ('together'), which is not translated by TNIV, suggests that the whole company of disciples was gathered together in the same place (cf. 2:1, 47).[77] TNIV rightly translates *en mesō tōn adelphōn* ('in the midst of the brothers') as *among the believers,* contrasting the socioreligious application of the term *adelphos* ('brother') here with its familial use at the end of v. 14.[78] Although women played an unusually important role in this 'brotherhood' (v. 14), *adelphos* is regularly used to include the feminine when a group of believers is in view (e.g., 1:15, 16; 6:3; 9:30; 11:1, 29).[79] Since this linguistic custom is not acceptable to many today, TNIV has used a more inclusive alternative. Although Peter denied Jesus three times (Lk. 22:54-62), Jesus had prayed that after his time of testing Peter would be used to strengthen his 'brothers' (Lk. 22:31-32). Peter now does that by becoming 'an interpreter of Scripture and of God's purpose for the church',[80] having learned how to do this from Jesus himself (cf. Lk. 24:44-49). Luke then re-

75. Zwiep, *Judas,* 177. Zwiep, 178, argues that 'in the narrative world of Acts, Judas plays the role of an absentee antagonist who tries to determine the plot even if he is not on stage'.

76. Bruce 1990, 108, notes that *kai en tais hēmerais tautais* ('in those days') indicates a more definite break in the narrative than *hoi men oun* ('they then'; cf. v. 6).

77. Cf. Bruce 1990, 108. 1 Cor. 15:6 says that there were over five hundred believers at this time, but Bruce suggests that most of these must have been in Galilee, hence the restricted number of *about a hundred and twenty* in Jerusalem.

78. Metzger, *Textual Commentary,* 247, notes that certain Western MSS substitute *mathētōn* ('disciples') for *adelphōn* ('brothers') in 1:15, presumably to avoid confusion with the brothers of Jesus mentioned in 1:14.

79. It should also be noted that *adelphos* is used in some contexts where Christians address fellow Jews (e.g., 2:29; 3:17; 7:2), or even where Jewish Christians are addressed by other Jews (e.g., 2:37). There is a Jewish 'brotherhood' (cf. 3:22, citing Dt. 18:15) and a Christian 'brotherhood'. In due course, the latter includes believing Gentiles (14:2; 15:1, 3, 32).

80. Tannehill 1990, 20. He observes the change that has taken place in Jesus' followers, even before the coming of the Spirit.

cords that a group of *about a hundred and twenty* was present,[81] thus preparing for 2:41; 4:4, where we are shown how quickly the number of disciples grew after Pentecost.

16-17 Peter's address to this group (*andres adelphoi*, lit. 'men, brothers'), is rendered *'brothers and sisters'* (NRSV 'friends'; ESV 'brothers') by TNIV. The word *andres* could be thought to make the whole expression in v. 16 even more explicitly masculine, but the context suggests that both *andres* and *adelphoi* refer to males and females together (but cf. 1:21 note).[82] Peter takes the lead among the believers by raising the important issue of a vacancy among the apostles and insisting that *'the Scripture had to be fulfilled in which the Holy Spirit spoke long ago through David concerning Judas'*. The Scripture in question is probably Psalm 69:25 (LXX 68:26), which is cited in v. 20 to highlight the need for a traitor like Judas to experience God's judgment (cf. Ps. 41:9 [LXX 40:10], which explicitly portrays betrayal by a close friend). A portion of Psalm 109:8 (LXX 108:8) is added to this, to emphasize the need for another to take his place. The language of fulfillment is extensively employed in Luke-Acts in connection with the filling up or completion of certain periods of time (e.g., Lk. 9:51; 21:24; Acts 2:1; 7:23, 30; 9:23; 24:27) or of key events and activities (e.g., Lk. 7:1; 9:31; 22:16; Acts 12:25; 13:25; 14:26; 19:21). Most important of all is Luke's reference to the completion or fulfillment of divine revelation in the person and work of Jesus and in the experience of those associated with him (Lk. 1:20, 45; 4:21; 18:31; 21:22; 22:37; 24:44; Acts 1:16; 3:18; 13:27, 29, 33).[83] Jesus included the Psalms in his teaching about the way Scripture 'must be fulfilled' (Lk. 24:44, *dei plērōthēnai*). Acts 1:16 says that the Scripture *had to be fulfilled*, using the imperfect tense *edei* (lit. 'it was necessary'). The first text had been fulfilled following the apostasy of Judas, while the second remained to be fulfilled with the appointment of his replacement. Luke regularly employs forms of this impersonal verb, along with other suitable terms, to indicate that the events he records are an unfolding of the predetermined plan or will of God.[84] The

---

81. *ochlos onomatōn* ('a crowd of names') is an unusual way of describing this group of people (cf. Barrett 1994, 96). Perhaps the expression is used because of the list of names in vv. 12-14, and Luke wishes to imply that the rest of the disciples were known by name to the risen Lord too. Marshall 1980, 64, suggests that the number (*about a hundred and twenty*) may be cited to indicate that this group was now large enough in Jewish law to establish a separate community with its own council. However, the company appears to contain women, which would challenge that argument.

82. The combination *andres adelphoi* is common in Acts (cf. 2:29, 37; 7:2; 13:15, 26, 38; 15:7, 13; 22:1; 23:1, 6; 28:17). Bruce 1990, 108, says that 'men' (*andres*) is a classical Greek idiom: 'the word is otiose, and does not necessarily exclude women.' Note the obvious inclusion of a woman among 'the men' (*andres*) in 17:34. D. A. Carson, *The Inclusive-Language Debate: A Plea for Realism* (Grand Rapids: Baker, 1998), 124-25, observes that the term is also likely to refer to males and females in Mt. 14:35; Jas. 1:20; 3:2.

83. Cf. D. G. Peterson, 'The Motif of Fulfillment and the Purpose of Luke-Acts', in Winter and Clarke, *Book of Acts*, 1:83-104; Bock, 'Scripture', 41-62.

84. *boulē* is the term used for the 'plan' or 'will' of God in Lk. 7:30; Acts 2:23; 4:28; 5:38-39; 13:36; 20:27; and *thelēma* in Lk 11:2; 22:42; Acts 21:14; 22:14 (cf. Acts 1:7). Other expressions

OT is the fundamental revelation of this plan of God since, through its human authors, *the Holy Spirit spoke long ago* (*proeipen,* 'spoke before') in a predictive fashion (cf. 2:16, 30; 3:18, 21; 4:25; 28:25). Various scriptures take on a particular meaning for the earliest Christians because of the way they point to the outworking of God's plan in their own time. As we shall see, the claim that the psalm citations in v. 20 were spoken by the Holy Spirit — literally, 'through the mouth of David' *(dia stomatos Dauid)* — is an important presupposition for understanding how they have been fulfilled in the messianic era. The Holy Spirit inspired prophetic leaders such as David in the OT era, before the pouring out of the Spirit at Pentecost on all the disciples of Jesus. This was God's way of directing and leading his people, making the scriptural record of that revelation foundational for Christians in every generation. David spoke, but it was the Holy Spirit who spoke through him, and so the psalms attributed to him were regarded as being inspired by God (cf. 2:25, 30; 4:25). When it is said that the verses in question were *concerning Judas,* the meaning is that they have their ultimate application to Judas in his betrayal of Jesus as the eschatological Son of David (cf. v. 20 note). There is an underlying, and frequently surfacing, Davidic Christology in Acts that makes it possible for passages related to David and his experiences to be applied to Jesus and his experiences (and so to Judas as his betrayer). The implication of this argument is that Jesus was not wrong to choose Judas, since such betrayal was a necessary part of the divine plan for the Messiah.

It was the defection of Judas and not simply his death that created the vacancy among the apostles. The tragedy of this is accentuated with two contrasting clauses: Judas *'served as guide for those who arrested Jesus'* (cf. Lk. 22:1-6, 39-48), but he was able to accomplish this betrayal so effectively only because *'he was one of our number'* (*katērithmēmenos ēn en hēmin,* 'he had been numbered among us' [periphrastic pluperfect]; cf. Lk. 6:12-16) *'and shared in our ministry'* (*elachen ton klēron tēs diakonias tautēs,* 'he was allotted his share in this ministry').[85] These last two expressions emphasize that being one of the Twelve and sharing in their ministry was Judas's gift from Jesus. Nevertheless, the Scripture had to be fulfilled, and he became the betrayer of Jesus. What he did conformed to a pattern revealed in certain OT texts, but he was not a puppet: Judas fell away because of his own deliber-

---

speak of God's having predetermined the things that have taken place (Lk. 22:22; Acts 10:42; 17:31; 22:14; 26:16). The note of God's sovereignty and of the fulfillment of his plan of salvation is further stressed by the extensive use of *dei* ('it is necessary') twenty-eight times in Luke-Acts. Cf. J. T. Squires, *The Plan of God in Luke-Acts,* SNTSMS 76 (Cambridge: Cambridge University, 1993), 1-10, 137-39; THE THEOLOGY OF ACTS: I. GOD AND HIS PLAN (pp. 54-56).

85. TNIV has not translated the *hoti* at the beginning of v. 17 (NRSV, ESV, 'for'), obscuring the link with the preceding verse. Zwiep, *Judas,* 140-45, discusses a number of ways of explaining the force of this *hoti.* I have taken it as an explicative conjunction, indicating how Judas could have served as a guide for those who arrested Jesus. *klēros* is used in its literal sense in v. 26 ('lot'), but in the expression *elachen ton klēron* in v. 17 it is used in a modified sense to mean 'he was allotted his share'. Cf. Johnson 1992, 35, on the significance of 'numbering' throughout this passage.

ate *wickedness* or unrighteousness (v. 18, *tēs adikias*). The interplay between God's sovereignty and human responsibility will be further explored in connection with 2:23; 3:13-15; 4:27-28, and later passages. The description of the apostolic role as 'service' in vv. 17 and 25 (*diakonia;* TNIV *ministry*) recalls the teaching of Jesus, especially at the Last Supper (Lk. 22:26-27), and implies that 'the early church now recognizes that its leadership must conform to Jesus' way of service'.[86]

18-19   These verses should not be taken as part of Peter's speech, since his audience scarcely needed to be told such things: *everyone in Jerusalem* is reported to have heard about the matters recalled by Luke. A parenthesis is provided for readers, to outline the fate of Judas and how he was judged by God. The people of Jerusalem are spoken about in the third person, and an explanation of the Aramaic term *Akeldama* is offered in Greek *(they called that field in their language Akeldama, that is, Field of Blood)*. Presumably it became known as *Field of Blood* 'not only because of Jesus' innocent blood which was sacrificed to buy it, but also Judas's own guilty blood which was spilt upon it'.[87] However, there are apparent difficulties in reconciling this account with the only other report of Judas's death in the NT. According to Matthew 27:3-10, the chief priests actually bought the field 'as a burial place for foreigners', using the thirty pieces of silver that Judas had returned with great remorse. If we accept the historicity of both accounts and seek to reconcile them, Luke's statement (*With the reward he got for his wickedness* [or 'with his unrighteous reward', *ek misthou tēs adikias*], *Judas bought a field*) can be understood in the light of Matthew's more detailed account. The chief priests actually purchased a field with the money that belonged to Judas (in his name, as it were). It became known as the *Field of Blood* because it was purchased with 'blood money' (Mt. 27:6). A major difficulty seems to be created by Matthew's statement that Judas went away from the temple and 'hanged himself', whereas Luke indicates that *he fell headlong, his body burst open and all his intestines spilled out.* TNIV's *there* is not in the original, but the context may be suggesting that he died in his own field. If this is so, the two narratives can be reconciled by assuming that Matthew has foreshortened the time reference and that the hanging did not take place until the chief priests had purchased the field. Luke's description of the gory end of Judas can be related to the tradition that he hanged himself if we imagine that his fall was the sequel to his hanging in some way, with his body rupturing as a consequence. There is also a possibility that the Greek expression *prēnēs genomenos* in v. 18 means 'swelling up' instead of 'falling headlong', in which case we can imagine his corpse becoming bloated in the heat and bursting open while still hanging.[88]

---

86. Tannehill 1990, 22.

87. Spencer 1997, 30. Cf. Barrett 1994, 92-93.

88. Cf. Bruce 1990, 109-10; A. B. Gordon, 'The Fate of Judas according to Acts 1:18', *EQ* 43 (1971), 97-103; A. Motyer, *NIDNTT* 1:93-94; Metzger, *Textual Commentary*, 247-48.

Whatever the precise meaning, the sense of the passage is that this was a form of divine retribution for his evil betrayal of Jesus (cf. 12:23 note).

20 Jesus' teaching about the plan of salvation in the OT and its fulfillment (Lk. 24:25-27, 44-47; Acts 1:3) was clearly decisive for the way the earliest Christians used the Scriptures. They did not disregard the context from which they took their citations but regularly employed texts to refer to whole passages and themes. Sometimes they used portions of Scripture that Jesus himself quoted. For example, Psalm 69:4 is cited by Jesus in John 15:25 and is said to have been fulfilled in the hatred of his enemies 'without reason'. This psalm of a righteous sufferer portrays the ordeal of David at the hands of false companions and others. Verses from the same psalm are variously used in John 2:17; Romans 11:9-10; 15:3. So Peter's quotation from Psalm 69:25 (LXX 68:26) is part of this exegetical tradition.[89] Things said of David or of righteous sufferers more generally in the psalms were interpreted as having their ultimate fulfillment in the life of Jesus as Son of David and Servant-Messiah. Consequently, the enemies of David or of the righteous sufferer could be seen as foreshadowing the enemies of Jesus, without implying that the primary reference of the psalm was to Judas himself.[90] Peter personalizes the text by turning the plural of the original into the singular: *'"May his place be deserted; let there be no one to dwell in it"'*.[91] This prayer for God's judgment was 'fulfilled' in what happened to Judas and his property (cf. 1:18-19). Having grasped certain principles of interpretation from Jesus, his disciples went on to discover other passages that expressed similar ideas. Hence, the addition of Psalm 109:8 (LXX 108:8), which is also attributed to David, calling for God's judgment upon his enemies. Part of this text is used with slight modification as a justification for replacing Judas as an apostle of Christ. The only thing fitting for such an opponent of God's Messiah was that another should *'"take his place of leadership"'* (*episkopēn* is used in a nontechnical sense here). This method of using the OT is not so culturally bound that it is invalid for Christians to-

---

89. C. H. Dodd, *According to the Scriptures: The Sub-Structure of the New Testament* (London: Nisbet, 1952), 61-108, argues that Psalm 69 was one of the major blocks of OT material used by the earliest Christians on the topic 'The Servant of the Lord and the Righteous Sufferer', and applied to Jesus the Christ, the Servant and the Righteous Sufferer par excellence. Cf. D. J. Moo, 'The Problem of Sensus Plenior', in D. A. Carson and J. D. Woodbridge (eds.), *Hermeneutics, Authority and Canon* (Grand Rapids: Zondervan, 1986), 179-211, for a discussion of the 'appropriation techniques' of the NT writers, as they interpreted and applied OT texts.

90. R. N. Longenecker, *Biblical Exegesis in the Apostolic Period* (Grand Rapids: Eerdmans, 1975), 97, argues that the Jewish exegetical rule *qal wahomer* ('light to heavy') is being applied here, 'allowing Peter to assert that what has been said of false companions and wicked men generally applies, *a minore ad majorem*, specifically to Judas, the one who proved himself uniquely false and evil'. I would add that the texts are particularly applicable to Judas because he betrays the eschatological Son of David.

91. Other verbal changes from the LXX do not appear to be exegetically significant. The word translated 'place' (*epaulis*) means 'homestead' (cf. *ND* 3 [1978], § 45), and cannot be taken to refer to his office, which obviously had to be filled. Cf. Bock 2007, 85-87.

day. If the apostolic principles of interpretation are carefully noted, and proper regard is paid to OT texts in their original context before a Christian application is attempted, the inspired preachers and authors of the NT will not lead us astray by their example.[92]

2. The Choice of Matthias (1:21-26)

The desire to make up the number of the Twelve was presumably related to the fact that Jesus intended them to be leaders of a restored Israel (cf. Lk. 22:14-30; Mt. 19:28). They could not be Messiah's witnesses unless they represented in their number the ideal of a reunited and renewed people of God, Israel in its fullness, not a remnant (cf. Je. 31:1-34; Ezk. 37:15-28; Rev. 21:12, 14).[93] Once the Spirit had been bestowed and the Twelve had been definitively constituted at the heart of this renewed Israel, there was no need to replace them when they died (cf. 12:1-2 note). Choosing a twelfth apostle at this time also implied 'acceptance of Jesus' commission to be his witnesses in the new situation following his death and resurrection'.[94]

21-22 With a resumptive *'therefore' (oun)* and another statement of necessity, the second part of Peter's speech begins. It was necessary that the Scripture be fulfilled (v. 16; imperfect tense, *edei*), and now *'it is necessary'* (present tense, *dei*) that a replacement for Judas be found. The Greek does not actually use the word *'choose'* at this point but reserves it until v. 24, where it is clear that the Lord himself must first choose and then demonstrate his choice. Peter simply declares that someone with the right qualification must *'become a witness with us of his resurrection'*. It is clear from the structure of the long sentence in vv. 21-22 that being a witness of the resurrection is the heart of the matter. Consequently, the resurrection assumes a central place in the apostolic preaching (e.g., Acts 2:24-36; 4:33; 13:30-37). In his own distinctive way, Paul could qualify for apostleship because he had seen the risen Lord (cf. 1 Cor. 9:1; 15:8-9). Yet he could not count himself as *'one of the men who have been with us the whole time the Lord Jesus went in and out among us, beginning from John's baptism to the time when Jesus was taken up from us'*.[95] In this respect the Twelve had a particular advantage and could

---

92. Cf. Bock, 'Scripture', 41-62; Beale and Carson, *Commentary*, 513-606.

93. I am not persuaded by the arguments put forward by Estrada, *Followers*, 172-78, against the view that Acts 1:15-26 is to be viewed as a fulfillment of Jesus' words in Lk. 22:30. Several commentators note the parallel in 1 QS 8:1, where twelve leaders appear to represent the Qumran community as the true or renewed Israel, final authority resting with a smaller body of two or three. Cf. Longenecker 1981, 265; Tannehill 1990, 22.

94. Tannehill 1990, 21. The next scene in Acts 2 presents the Twelve bearing witness to 'all Israel' (cf. 2:5, 36).

95. The period indicated here is the one covered in the apostolic preaching (e.g., Acts 10:37-42; 13:24-31). The expression in 1:22 cannot be pressed too literally, since it appears from Luke's Gospel that not all of the apostles were with Jesus from the very beginning. In

be guarantors of the whole Gospel tradition (cf. Lk. 1:2; Mt. 28:20; Acts 10:39-41). Their witness to the resurrection could be set within the framework of their wider experience of Jesus' ministry, with its teaching about the purpose of his death and subsequent exaltation (e.g., Lk. 9:21-36; 22:14-22; 24:44-49). Putting it another way, they could guarantee 'that it was the same Jesus who had led his disciples during his ministry that now led the Church as her exalted Lord.'[96] The word *andrōn* is rightly translated 'men' here (contrast v. 16), since the context shows the intention to replace Judas with one of two possible male candidates.[97]

23 Luke normally records the response of an audience to a speech (e.g., 2:37-41; 7:54-58; 13:42-45; 17:32-34; 22:22). The absence of any verbal response here suggests complete agreement. However, it is not clear whether the verb *estēsan (they proposed)* refers to the apostles or to the larger group of disciples assembled to make this appointment.[98] It is possible that the whole group put forward names, after some form of consultation (cf. 6:5-6). Only two candidates satisfied the criteria set out in vv. 21-22. *Joseph* is identified by his Aramaic name *Barsabbas* (which means 'son of the Sabbath' or 'son of Sabba') and by his Roman name *Justus.* The other nominee was simply known as *Matthias* (a shortened form of Mattathias).[99]

24-25 Before casting lots, the disciples united in prayer for the Lord to reveal his will. The *'Lord'* addressed here is almost certainly the Lord Jesus (cf. v. 21; 7:59-60).[100] Those who joined in this prayer believed that the Lord had already *chosen* the successor of Judas (*exelexō* is a perfective use of the aorist, implying a choice already made). Their confidence was presumably based on the fact that he had chosen the Twelve in the first place (cf. Lk. 6:13; Acts 1:2, where the same verb is found). In addition to having the qualifications mentioned in vv. 21-22, the twelfth apostle had to be designated in some obvious way by Christ himself. When the risen Jesus is addressed as the one who knows *'everyone's heart' (kardiognōsta pantōn),* the implication is that he shares a widely attested characteristic of God (cf. Dt.

simple terms, the candidates needed to have been with Jesus throughout the span of his ministry. Cf. Tannehill 1990, 23.

96. Wilson, *Gentiles,* 112-13. Zwiep, *Judas,* 155-56, argues that 'Luke's definition is in agreement with his stress on eyewitnesses'. Since Paul and Barnabas would not meet the strict Lukan criteria, Luke stresses the legitimacy of the Pauline mission 'by firmly anchoring Paul to the Twelve apostles in Jerusalem, who in turn had been commissioned by the risen Lord himself'. James the Lord's brother is apparently excluded from being one of the Twelve because he had not been a follower of Jesus before Easter (Jn. 7:5).

97. Carson, *Inclusive Language,* 153, describes this as the 'default' understanding of the noun *anēr.* Carson, 158, argues that 'one should assume the reference is to male human beings unless there is convincing contextual counter-evidence'.

98. Cf. Barrett 1994, 102. The Western reading is singular *(estēsen),* emphasizing the role of Peter in nominating the two persons. This tendency to enhance the significance of Peter is not supported by other textual traditions. Cf. Metzger, *Textual Commentary,* 249.

99. Zwiep, *Judas,* 160-63, discusses the meaning of their names and various issues relating to the identity of these two candidates.

100. Cf. Barrett 1994, 103.

8:2; 1 Sa. 16:7; 1 Ki. 8:39; Pss. 17:3; 44:21; 94:11; 139:2; Acts 15:8). An exalted Christology is thus implied in this address. Doubtless also the expression implies that certain inner qualities needed to be discerned for the office of apostleship, 'for the candidate's witness would be both to the historical facts of Jesus' life and to the transforming effect of his grace in the life of the believer'.[101] The defection of Judas made it essential to find someone who would be true to his calling this time! Since it was believed that the ascended Lord had already made his choice, it was simply a matter of asking him: *'Show us which of these two you have chosen to take over this apostolic ministry'* (*labein ton topon tēs diakonias tautēs kai apostolēs*, 'to take the place of this ministry and apostleship').[102] TNIV is a little tame when it translates the next clause, *'which Judas left to go where he belongs'*. Literally translated, the meaning is, 'from which Judas defected *(parebē)* to go to his own place *(eis ton topon ton idion)'*. Judas abandoned his 'place' among the apostles to go to 'his own 'place'. The last expression is a euphemism for his final destiny, most likely death and the judgment of God beyond that.[103] Without being specific about the details, Luke offers an implied warning to all apostates (cf. Heb. 6:4-8; 10:26-31).

26   The fact that they *cast lots* must be understood in the light of their confidence that the Lord knew the hearts of the candidates and had already made his choice. This was not a democratic election, with people casting votes.[104] It was a traditional way of determining God's will in Judaism (cf. Lv. 16:8; Nu. 26:55; Jon. 1:7-8; 1QS 5:3; 6:16). Here, specifically, it was a way of deciding between two equally qualified candidates, given the belief that 'the lot is cast into the lap, but its every decision is from the LORD' (Pr. 16:33). Even the fall of the dice is in the hands of the sovereign Lord.[105] In this context, *the lot fell to Matthias*, and that was taken to be the Lord's choice, *so he was added to* (*synkatepsēphisthē*, 'chosen [by a vote] together with', BDAG) *the eleven apostles*. It is important to observe that there are no

101. D. J. Williams, *Acts*, GNC (San Francisco: Harper, 1985), 15.

102. TNIV has taken *tēs diakonias tautēs kai apostolēs* to be a hendiadys *(this apostolic ministry)*, so that 'apostleship' defines more precisely the 'ministry' in question. As in v. 17, apostleship is first and foremost a service or ministry. Although the Received Text replaces *topon* ('place') with *klēron* ('lot'), the former reading is better attested. The latter was probably introduced under the influence of v. 17. Cf. Metzger, *Textual Commentary*, 249.

103. Zwiep, *Judas*, 166-68, opts for this view after considering a range of possibilities. Spencer 1997, 30, notes a play on the word 'place' *(topos)*: although Judas held an honourable 'place' among the Twelve (v. 20), he turned aside 'to his own place' (v. 25), 'a desolate, accursed spot where no one can survive'.

104. The Received Text reads *autōn* (KJV 'they cast *their* lots'). Together with the verb *edōkan* ('they gave'), instead of *ebalon* ('they cast'), this could mean that the matter was put to a vote. But the better-attested and harder reading is *autois* (NRSV, ESV 'they cast lots *for them'*). Cf. Metzger, *Textual Commentary*, 250. TNIV does not translate *autois*.

105. Cf. Barrett 1994, 94, 104-5; J. Eichler, *NIDNTT* 2:295-303; Zwiep, *Judas*, 168-70. Presumably here two stones were shaken together in a container, on each of which was written one name (cf. 1 Sa. 10:20-21; 14:41-42), until one stone tumbled out, revealing the name of the one chosen by the Lord (cf. 1 Chr. 26:13-16).

further examples of such decision making in the NT. As those who were about to enjoy the benefits of the New Covenant, the apostles were using a practice that was sanctioned by God but belonged to the old era. It took place before Pentecost, when the Spirit was poured out in a way that signified a new kind of relationship between God and his people. From Luke's later emphasis on the Spirit's role in giving wisdom, guidance, and direction, it would appear that the apostolic example on this occasion is not to be followed by Christians today.[106] Rather, we are to recognize and respond to the mind of the Spirit among the people of God, in ways that will be explored in connection with 5:3, 9; 13:1-2; 15:28; 16:6-10, and other passages.

B. The Restoration of Israel Begins (2:1-40)

As promised in Acts 1:4-5, 8, the Holy Spirit is poured out on the disciples of Jesus, to begin his work of renewal in Jerusalem and make it possible for his salvation to reach 'to the ends of the earth' (cf. Is. 49:10).[1] Dramatically and theologically, Acts 1 has prepared the reader to appreciate the significance of what is recounted in Acts 2. But Luke's description of the coming of the Spirit is remarkably brief (vv. 1-4). A longer section is devoted to the response of the observers (vv. 5-13), making the point that this critical event took place in the presence of Jews from many nations. 'Just as the Twelve represent the nucleus of the people that is being restored, so does this audience represent all the lands to which the Jews had been dispersed.'[2] Their reactions demonstrate the need for Peter's explanatory sermon, which follows. The apostle first defines what has happened and explains its cause. He proclaims the coming of the Spirit as an eschatological event, fulfilling God's ancient promise through the prophet Joel (vv. 14-21). Indeed, Peter speaks as a prophet himself — as one who has been filled with the Spirit — insisting that what has happened to the disciples must be related to what happened to Jesus. The real cause of this event is the resurrection and ascension of the Messiah to the right hand of God (vv. 22-35). Jesus is presented as the exalted Davidic ruler and as 'a greater Moses who ascends to God in order to grant a foundational gift to Israel'.[3] Peter therefore challenges his hearers to change their perception of Jesus and

106. There is no basis for the claim that the apostles were wrong to select Matthias and that they should have awaited God's choice of Paul to fill the vacancy (cf. Longenecker 1981, 267; Zwiep, *Judas*, 174).

1. Spencer 1997, 23-24, notes some important links between the ascension of Jesus in Jerusalem and the coming of the Spirit in Jerusalem, with special reference to 'the journey through Acts' which is about to begin.

2. Johnson 1992, 47.

3. M. M. B. Turner, *Power from on High: The Spirit in Israel's Restoration and Witness in Luke-Acts*, JPTSS 9 (Sheffield: Sheffield Academic, 1996), 267. Turner, 268, significantly concludes that the gift of the Spirit is portrayed in Acts 2 as 'the power of Israel's covenant renewal'.

to share the convictions of his followers and their experience of the Holy
Spirit (vv. 36-40). Although charged with rejecting the Messiah, who is
Lord of the Spirit, the Jerusalem crowd is given another chance to share in
the salvation promised to them, and previously offered to them in the
preaching of Jesus himself.

There are certain parallels between the experience of Jesus in Luke's
Gospel and the experience of Peter and the other disciples in Acts. When
Jesus was baptized by John, and the Holy Spirit 'descended on him' (Lk.
3:21-22), he soon went to Nazareth and made a programmatic proclamation concerning the nature and purpose of his mission (Lk. 4:16-30). When
Peter was baptized with the Holy Spirit, he too preached a sermon that was
programmatic for understanding the nature of authentic Christian mission
and ministry.[4] His witness as a Spirit-empowered apostle clarifies who Jesus really is and articulates the nature of the salvation he has made possible
for all who repent and are baptized in his name.

1. The Coming of the Spirit (2:1-13)

The NT signifies the central importance of the Holy Spirit for Christian life
and ministry in various ways (e.g., Rom. 5:5; 7:6; 8:1-16; 1 Cor 2:10-16; 12:1-
13; 14:1-40; Gal. 5:16-26; Tit. 3:5-6). However, apart from Acts 2:1-41; 10:47;
11:15-17, only John 20:22 is an independent witness to the Pentecost event
portrayed in Acts 2.[5] The progress of the gospel is marked by further dramatic endowments of the Spirit elsewhere in Acts, paralleling the foundational experience of Pentecost in some respects (Acts 8:14-17; 10:44-46; 19:1-
7), but Luke is concerned to show how 'the Jerusalem Pentecost was deter-
minative for the growth of Christianity as a whole'.[6] The first paragraph
(vv. 1-4) outlines the unique, supernatural occurrences of that day. A considerable portion of the next paragraph (vv. 5-13) is devoted to listing the
places represented by those who witnessed this event and describing their
reactions. While highlighting the miraculous nature of the communication

---

4. Cf. Tannehill 1990, 29-30; Witherington 1998, 128-29.

5. Jesus' exhalation with the words 'receive the Holy Spirit' in Jn. 20:22 is best understood as 'symbolic of the enduement *that is still to come*' (D. A. Carson, *The Gospel according to
John* [Grand Rapids: Eerdmans; Leicester: Inter-Varsity, 1991], 653). Note Carson's arguments against identifying this event as a 'Johannine Pentecost'. Jesus' prophetic-like action
is meant to assure the disciples that his prior teaching about the coming of the Spirit is
about to be fulfilled in some decisive fashion. Cf. Witherington 1998, 140 note 51.

6. J. D. G. Dunn, *Jesus and the Spirit: A Study of the Religious and Charismatic Experience
of Jesus and the First Christians as Reflected in the New Testament* (London: SCM, 1975), 139.
Barrett 1994, 108, describes it as the 'founding' gift of the Holy Spirit. Against those who
propose that the narrative was a theological creation by Luke, the essential historicity of
Acts 2 is argued by Dunn, 136-46; I. H. Marshall, 'The Significance of Pentecost', *SJT* 30
(1977), 360-65. A. T. Lincoln, 'Theology and History in the Interpretation of Luke's Pentecost', *ExpT* 96 (1984-85), 204-9, and Barrett 1994, 109-10, are less certain.

taking place, this passage also signifies that the blessings of the messianic kingdom are now available for 'all Israel' to receive.[7]

1 Luke introduces this critical moment in salvation history with an impressive note of fulfillment. The first clause literally reads 'when the day of Pentecost was being fulfilled' *(en tō symplērousthai)*, suggesting the end of a period of preparation and anticipation. Luke could simply mean that the fifty-day interval between Passover and Pentecost 'approached completion'.[8] But the same expression is used in Luke 9:51 with reference to the fulfillment of 'the days' when Jesus would be 'taken up' *(en tō symplērousthai tas hēmeras tēs analēmpseōs autou)*, presumably through his death, resurrection, and ascension. Both passages mark the beginning of a new stage in the outworking of God's purposes with similar terminology.[9] The Jewish festival known in Greek as *Pentecost* ('fiftieth') is the same as the 'Feast of Weeks' in Leviticus 23:15-21 (cf. Ex. 34:22; Nu. 28:26-31; Dt. 16:9-12). This was celebrated with sacrifices and feasting seven weeks and a day after the firstfruits of the grain harvest had been offered. It was one of three great agricultural festivals, held annually to acknowledge God's goodness in the cycle of the seasons and the fruitfulness of the earth. Although the date may originally have been a movable one, by NT times the fifty days were calculated from the Feast of the Passover.[10] Some Jewish sources associate Pentecost with God's renewal of the covenant, three months after the original Passover and the exodus redemption from Egypt (cf. Ex. 19:1). Although this tradition is unlikely to have influenced Luke's presentation directly,[11] some link between the giving of the law on Sinai and the coming of the Spirit at Pentecost may be implied by the use of wind and fire imagery (vv. 2-3). More significantly, Jesus reinterprets the Passover to signify the inauguration of a new covenant in his blood (Lk. 22:15-20; cf. Je. 31:31-34), and the promised renewal of God's relationship with Israel is experienced fifty days later through the gift of his Spirit, as a direct result of Jesus' redemptive death and resurrection. Some re-

7. Cf. THE THEOLOGY OF ACTS: III. THE HOLY SPIRIT (pp. 60-65).

8. Barrett 1994, 110; Barrett, 106, translates 'when the Day of Pentecost had at length come' (KJV 'was fully come'; NKJV 'had fully come'). TNIV does not capture the full significance of the present passive infinitive, which implies a process of fulfillment.

9. Tannehill 1990, 26, says, 'In both cases the fulfillment of a time is emphasized because the days in question bring the fulfillment of prophecy'. Cf. D. G. Peterson, 'The Motif of Fulfilment and the Purpose of Luke-Acts', in B. W. Winter and A. D. Clarke (eds.), *The Book of Acts in Its First-Century Setting*, Vol. 1: *Ancient Literary Setting* (Grand Rapids: Eerdmans; Carlisle: Paternoster, 1993), 83-104.

10. Cf. *IBD* 3:1188; Marshall, 'Significance', 347-50.

11. Barrett 1994, 111, notes that the Jewish sources connecting Pentecost with the giving of the law are second century AD and challenges the view that Luke was seeking to present the Christian Pentecost as 'the new revelation through the Holy Spirit, based upon the new act of redemption and deliverance'. Cf. R. P. Menzies, *The Development of Early Christian Pneumatology with Special Reference to Luke-Acts*, JSNTSS 54 (Sheffield: JSOT, 1991), 229-44. But Johnson 1992, 46; Turner, *Power*, 280-85; Witherington 1998, 131; and J. Hur, *A Dynamic Reading of the Holy Spirit in Luke-Acts*, JSNTSS 211 (Sheffield: Sheffield Academic, 2001), 223 note 130, are more positive about possible Jewish influences on Acts 2.

flection of the pattern of salvation and covenant renewal in Exodus is thus reflected in Luke-Acts.[12] When Luke says *they were all together in one place*, the collection of terms, reminiscent of 1:14-15, is quite emphatic *(pantes homou epi to auto).*[13] From v. 2 it appears that they were once again gathered in a house rather than in the temple precincts. But their outburst of inspired utterance soon brought them into a more public arena (vv. 6ff.). Despite the prominence of the Twelve in the preceding chapter, it is likely that those gathered together included the 120 disciples mentioned in 1:15.

2   The coming of the Spirit on this occasion was a sudden, unique, supernatural event. No such signs are associated with endowments of the Spirit recorded elsewhere in Acts. Only the phenomenon of inspired speech (v. 4) is paralleled later, though with apparent differences. In the foundational experience of Pentecost, audible signs (v. 2) were accompanied by visible phenomena (v. 3). *Suddenly a sound like the blowing of a violent wind came from heaven*, suggesting the powerful presence of God (cf. 1 Ki. 19:11), as it *filled the whole house where they were sitting*. There was no actual wind, but it sounded like wind, and the *sound (ēchos)* filled the room. In Scripture, wind *(pnoēs)* is an emblem for the Spirit or creative breath *(pneuma)* of God (e.g., 2 Sa. 22:16; Ps. 33:6; Ezk. 37:9-10; Jn. 3:8). This was a sign that God was about to accomplish a mighty work of renewal. Isaiah encountered the glory of the Lord filling the temple when he received his calling (Is. 6:1-4). Here, however, the witnesses of Jesus experienced the awesome presence of God in a private residence, as they were empowered for prophetic ministry.[14] Given the focus in 1:9-11 on Jesus' departure 'into heaven' *(eis ouranon)*, this wind *from heaven (ek tou ouranou)* could be understood as a specific demonstration of his intrusion into their midst again. Peter certainly makes it clear in v. 33 that the exalted Lord Jesus has poured out the promised Spirit.

3   There also appeared to them *what seemed to be tongues of fire (glōssai hōsei pyros, 'tongues as of fire')*. Fire is another symbol of God's presence in Scripture (cf. Ex. 19:18; Is. 66:15), sometimes specifically associated with purification or judgment (e.g., Is. 4:4; Je. 7:20; Jl. 2:30-31; Mal. 3:2-4; 4:1). John the Baptist had prophesied that when the Messiah came he would baptize

---

12. Longenecker 1981, 269, argues that the Spirit's coming is shown to be in continuity with God's purpose in giving the law to Israel and yet it signals the difference between the eras: life under the New Covenant is to be 'Christ centred and Spirit directed'. Cf. J. D. G. Dunn, *Baptism in the Holy Spirit: A Re-examination of the New Testament Teaching on the Gift of the Spirit in Relation to Pentecostalism Today*, SBT (Second Series) 15 (London: SCM), 48-49; THE THEOLOGY OF ACTS: IV. SALVATION (pp. 65-70).

13. *homou* can mean 'together in the same place' or 'together at the same time' (BDAG), and recalls the use of *homothymadon* ('together') in 1:14. *epi to auto* is also employed, as in 1:15; 2:44, 47; 4:26, to convey the idea of being in the same place at the same time. Cf. Barrett 1994, 112-13, for the different form of 2:1-2 in Codex D.

14. Spencer 1997, 32, makes too much of what he calls 'this critical spatial distinction', arguing that 'the Spirit/glory of God now finds a more receptive home in an ordinary dwelling than in Israel's sacred cultic center'. The great outpouring of the Spirit implied in 2:41 is likely to have taken place in the temple precincts.

Israel 'with the Holy Spirit and with fire' (Lk. 3:16; Mt. 3:11). John used the imagery of fire in connection with his preaching of imminent judgment and wrath (Lk. 3:17; Mt. 3:12), so that Spirit-and-fire together in his prediction probably meant 'one purgative act of messianic judgment which both repentant and unrepentant would experience, the former as a blessing, the latter as destruction'.[15] But it is doubtful that the tongues 'like fire' *(hōsei pyros)* in Acts 2:2 are to be related to John's prophecy, especially since the element of fire was excluded from Jesus' report of John's words in 1:5. In the perspective of Acts, the messianic judgment is mercifully delayed, giving the Spirit-filled disciples the chance to preach repentance and offer the hope of salvation to all (e.g., 3:19-21; 10:42-43; 17:30-31).[16] Again, it is unlikely that these tongues are meant to represent the *other tongues (heterais glōssais)* with which they began to speak (v. 4). This visionary experience is best understood against the background of passages like Exodus 3:2-5; 19:18; 24:17; 40:38, where fire symbolizes the presence of the Holy One to communicate with his people and guide them. The Pentecostal gift is God's empowering presence with his people in a new and distinctive way, revealing his will and leading them to fulfill his purposes for them as the people of the New Covenant. When Luke says the tongues like fire *separated and came to rest on each of them,* the implication is that the blessing of God's Spirit was for each individual member of the believing community.[17] The Spirit's work in binding them together as the nascent church is illustrated in 2:41-47.

4 The essential experience on that day was that *all of them were filled with the Holy Spirit.* Luke uses the verb 'fill' *(pimplēmi)* in a variety of ways, but mostly to describe filling with certain emotions or qualities (Lk. 4:28; 5:26; 6:11; Acts 3:10; 5:17; 13:45; 19:29) or filling with the Holy Spirit (Lk. 1:15, 41, 67; Acts 2:4; 4:8, 31; 9:17; 13:9).[18] It can refer to the initial endow-

---

15. Dunn, *Baptism*, 11. Dunn (43) argues with respect to Acts 1:5 that 'in some sense Jesus has exhausted the fire that was kindled on him, just as he drained the cup of wrath, so that the means of entry into the New Age is now only a baptism in the Spirit of Jesus'. However, note the critical response of Turner, *Power*, 298 note 87.

16. It is possible, however, that Luke understood the Pentecostal bestowal of the Spirit to be the means by which the righteous remnant in Israel would be separated from the chaff, in fulfillment of the Baptist's prophecy. The sifting activity of the Spirit through the mission of Christ's disciples prepares for the final act of separation in the messianic judgment. Cf. Menzies, *Development*, 143-44.

17. The present middle participle in the plural *(diamerizomenai,* 'dividing up') implies multiple tongues of flame spreading out across the room. The second verb *(ekathisen,* 'sat, rested') is singular in most MSS, probably to emphasize that 'one tongue-like flame rested upon each person' (Barrett 1994, 114).

18. The related adjective *plērēs* is mostly used to describe the state or condition of being 'full of the Holy Spirit' or of some particular grace (Lk. 4:1; Acts 6:3, 5, 8; 7:55; 9:36; 11:24; contrast 13:10; 19:28). In such cases it refers to a permanent endowment that becomes part of a person's character. The verb *plēroō* is applied to those who 'were being filled with joy and with the Holy Spirit' in 13:52 (the imperfect tense here suggesting a continuing process; cf. Eph. 5:18). Cf. Peterson, 'Fulfillment', 85-87, on the language of fulfillment in Luke-Acts.

ment of a person with the Spirit (Lk. 1:15 [John the Baptist]; Acts 9:17 [Paul]). It can also refer to the special inspiration of a person for prophetic utterance, for preaching, or for testimony to Christ in some other way (Lk. 1:41, 67; Acts 4:8, 31; 13:9; cf. Lk. 12:11-12). Someone who is already filled with or full of the Spirit can receive a further filling or enabling for a particular ministry (cf. Acts 4:31). So 'our western logical concept that something which is full cannot be filled any further is misleading if applied to the Spirit. One filling is not incompatible with another'.[19] Acts 2:4 speaks of a filling specifically for inspired utterance: *All of them were filled with the Holy Spirit and began to speak in other tongues as the Spirit enabled them.* The wider context, however, suggests that this was also the reception of a permanent endowment. It was the promise of the Father of which Jesus had spoken — the baptism with the Holy Spirit predicted by John (cf. 1:4-5 note) — the unprecedented outpouring of God's Spirit 'in the last days' predicted by Joel (Acts 2:16-21). The apostles received this permanent, eschatological gift of the Spirit at Pentecost, which they then offered in Christ's name to all who repented and received water baptism (2:38-39). At a later stage, Peter speaks of Cornelius having received the Spirit 'just as we have' (10:47), and this is regarded as a fulfillment of John's prophecy about being baptised with the Holy Spirit (11:15-17).[20]

Luke describes the Spirit-baptism of the disciples as a 'filling' because of the particular point and purpose of the Spirit's coming. They were filled with the Spirit so that they could *speak in other tongues*. In OT times, the regular consequence of a person's possession by the Spirit of God was prophecy (e.g., Nu. 11:26-29; 1 Sa. 10:9-10; 2 Sa. 23:2; Is. 61:1-3), and this was the specific outcome of the Spirit's advent on this occasion too. Inspired and equipped for what would be essentially a verbal ministry, they were empowered to bear testimony to the exalted Christ (cf. 1:8). The *other tongues* (*heterais glōssais*) on this occasion were intelligible languages different from their own, not the sort of tongues mentioned in 1 Corinthians 12–14, which could only be understood if someone interpreted. Suddenly delivered from the limitations of their Galilean speech, the disciples praised God and rehearsed his mighty works in such a way that each hearer recognized with surprise his or her own language (vv. 6, 8). But it was not simply a miracle of hearing: it was a miracle of speech.[21] This is indicated by the expression

19. Marshall, 'Significance', 355. Cf. G. Delling, *TDNT* 6:128-31, 283-98; Turner, *Power*, 165-69. The verb 'to baptise' is not used by Luke for subsequent experiences of the Spirit, only for the initial endowment.

20. So Peter's reaction to the experience of Cornelius offers something of a commentary on the experience of the first disciples at Pentecost. Dunn, *Baptism*, 70-72, notes seven parallel expressions used by Luke to describe the coming of the Spirit in Acts.

21. Cf. Dunn, *Jesus and the Spirit*, 148-52; M. M. B. Turner, 'Spiritual Gifts Then and Now', *VE* 15 (1985), 17-24, 38-46; D. A. Carson, *Showing the Spirit: A Theological Exposition of 1 Corinthians 12–14* (Homebush West, Sydney: Lancer; Grand Rapids: Baker, 1988), 138-43; Stott 1990, 65-68, for assessments of various theories about the nature of this particular manifestation of glossolalia.

as the Spirit enabled them, which could be rendered more literally 'as the Spirit gave them utterance' (KJV, NKJV, ESV *kathōs to pneuma edidou apophthengesthai autois*). The verb 'to utter' *(apophthengesthai)* was used in Greek literature of ecstatic speech, but ordinarily it meant 'to speak one's opinion plainly', or 'to speak with emphasis'.[22] That is how it is employed in 2:14, where Peter *addressed* the crowd, and in 26:25, where Paul insisted that what he was 'saying' in his defence speech was true and reasonable. The disciples were not preaching in 2:4, but they were certainly declaring the wonders of God (v. 11) in languages that could be understood without interpretation. Perhaps it is best to describe these initial utterances as ejaculations of praise (cf. 10:46 note) and to view the prophetic outbursts of praise in Luke 1:46-55, 67-79; 2:28-32 as the closest parallels.

5-6 *When they heard this sound (genomenēs tēs phōnēs tautēs*, 'when this sound was heard') — the speaking in v. 4, in view of v. 6b — *a crowd came together in bewilderment (synēlthen to plēthos kai synechythē*, 'the multitude came together and were confused'). Those involved are described as *God-fearing Jews from every nation under heaven*, who were *staying in Jerusalem*. The adjective *eulabeis (God-fearing)* here 'can hardly be taken to denote a specific class of "God-fearers"',[23] but it is a way of denoting pious or faithful Jews. Their *staying (katoikountes)* in Jerusalem could have been temporary, to enable them to participate in the festival of the Passover and then Pentecost (cf. *visitors from Rome*, v. 10). But it is likely that many were Jews from the Dispersion who had settled permanently in Jerusalem at some earlier stage.[24] Proselytes are also mentioned *(converts to Judaism*, v. 11, *prosēlytoi)*, meaning Gentiles who dedicated themselves to live as Jews. So the apostolic testimony to Christ was unquestionably for *Jews* first, and the geographic origin of those mentioned suggests the universality of the Jewish foundation of the church.[25] Marshall rightly observes that, 'if the description of Pentecost is meant to foreshadow the world-wide expansion of the church, it is an expansion among *Jews* scattered throughout the world

---

22. It is used in connection with the giving and interpretation of oracles in the examples noted by J. Behm, *TDNT* 1:447. In the LXX it is used of prophesying (1 Chr. 25:1) and soothsaying (Mi. 5:12).

23. Barrett 1994, 118. He notes that the adjective occurs in the NT only in Lk. 2:25; Acts 2:5; 8:2; 22:12, where it is consistently applied to Jews. Distinctive terminology is employed elsewhere with reference to God-fearing Gentiles. Cf. 10:2 note; Barrett, 499-501.

24. Johnson 1992, 43, cites Josephus, *War* 1.397, 437, 672, as evidence for the mixed population in the city. Witherington 1998, 135, points to archaeological evidence for this.

25. The word 'Jews' *(Ioudaioi)* does not occur in Codex ℵ of v. 5 and is variously placed in some other uncial manuscripts. Since 'God-fearing men' *(andres eulabeis)* in Luke-Acts is used only of Jews, and not proselytes or devout Gentiles, the word 'Jews' is really unnecessary and could be secondary. However, since it is witnessed by the overwhelming mass of MSS, it is best to conclude that *Ioudaioi* was 'either dropped as seemingly contradictory to *apo pantos ethnous* ('from every nation'), or moved to a position considered less objectionable from a stylistic point of view' (Metzger, *Textual Commentary*, 251). Cf. Barrett 1994, 117-18.

that is used to provide the picture'.[26] What bewildered the gathering crowd was the fact that *each one heard their own language being spoken (ēkouon heis hekastos tē idia dialektō lalountōn autōn,* 'each one of them heard them speaking in his own language'). Jews from the east would have known Aramaic and Jews from the west would have known Greek, but what they heard was in their native language or local dialect (*dialektos* can have either meaning). For one brief moment of time, the divisions in humanity expressed through language difference (cf. Gn. 11:1-9) were overcome. These divisions are presented in Genesis as the judgment of God. What happened on the day of Pentecost suggests that God's curse had been removed. But the confusion of tongues was not undone by providing a common Spirit language. Communication actually took place through the diversity of languages represented there.[27] God was expressing his ultimate intention to unite people 'from every tribe and language and people and nation' (Rev. 5:9-10; 7:9) under the rule of his Son (Eph. 1:9-10), providing reconciliation through him and 'access to the Father by one Spirit' (Eph. 2:14-18).

7-8 The expression *'each in his own language' (tē idia dialektō)* is repeated from v. 6 to emphasize the nature of the miracle from the viewpoint of the witnesses. But 'in which we were born' *(en hē egennēthēmen)* is added this time (TNIV *native*) to make it quite clear that regional languages are meant. The narrator's description of their confusion in v. 6 is replaced in v. 7 by the words 'amazed and astonished' *(existanto de kai ethaumazon;* TNIV *utterly amazed*). The questions which come from the crowd (vv. 7-8) outline their perception of what was going on and encourage readers to share in this amazement. God did something at Pentecost that defied rational explanation, and the appropriate response was praise and adoration. The questions of the crowd appear in a choral form, as a literary device to highlight what was being articulated by many individually. People were marvelling that *'Galileans'* were not inhibited by their own distinctive manner of speech from communicating in other languages.[28]

9-11 The wonder of the occasion is further stressed by the listing of places from which the audience was drawn. Only fifteen countries are

26. Marshall, 'Significance', 357. Cf. S. G. Wilson, *The Gentiles and the Gentile Mission in Luke-Acts,* SNTSMS 23 (Cambridge: Cambridge University, 1973), 122-24; Spencer 1997, 34. R. Bauckham, 'James and the Jerusalem Church', in R. Bauckham (ed.), *The Book of Acts in Its First-Century Setting,* Vol. 4: *Palestinian Setting* (Grand Rapids: Eerdmans; Carlisle: Paternoster, 1995), 422, observes that at the beginning of his story of how the gospel was taken out into the world from Jerusalem, Luke provides his readers with 'the Jewish Jerusalem-centred geographical perspective appropriate to that story'.

27. Cf. Spencer 1997, 32-33. Spencer also notes how the experience of Zechariah in Lk. 1:64-79 anticipates Pentecost.

28. B. J. Malina and J. H. Neyrey, 'Conflict in Luke-Acts: Labelling and Deviance Theory', in J. H. Neyrey (ed.), *The Social World of Luke-Acts: Models for Interpretation* (Peabody: Hendrickson, 1991), 104, also argue that the designation 'Galileans' may be a way of dismissing them as backward 'boorish dolts in the eyes of sophisticated Jerusalemites'. Cf. Spencer 1997, 33-34; Witherington 1998, 136.

mentioned to support Luke's claim that they were *Jews from every nation under heaven* (v. 5), but these broadly represent the extent of the Jewish Dispersion at that time.[29] Three nationalities are mentioned first — *'Parthians, Medes and Elamites'* — corresponding to that area in the east of the Roman Empire that we know as Iran. With a change of construction in the Greek, Luke moves westward to include *'residents of Mesopotamia'* (modern Iraq) and *'Judea'*. Next come the regions that figure so prominently in Acts 13–20 — *'Cappadocia, Pontus and Asia, Phrygia and Pamphilia'*. Moving south to North Africa, Luke mentions *'Egypt and the parts of Libya near Cyrene'*. *'Visitors from Rome'* receive special mention, and these are further defined as *'both Jews and converts to Judaism'* (*prosēlytoi*; cf. 6:5; 13).[30] Many Jews lived in the imperial capital at that time, and perhaps some of the visitors present in Jerusalem on the Day of Pentecost returned with the gospel and formed the nucleus of the church there (cf. 28:14-15).[31] No mention is made of Greece or Macedonia or Syria, where there were also sizeable Jewish communities. The list concludes with *'Cretans and Arabs'*. How far Luke may have been influenced in his choice of countries by similar catalogues in other ancient documents we cannot say.[32] The whole point of the list is to stress again the miracle they were witnessing: *'we hear them declaring the wonders of God in our own tongues!'* What the disciples were actually celebrating in these other languages *(tais hēmeterais glōssais)* with their Spirit-inspired praise was 'the mighty things of God' *(ta megaleia tou theou*; cf. Dt. 11:2; Pss. 71:19 [LXX 70:19]; 106:21 [LXX 105:21]). From Peter's sermon in vv. 16-36 we may judge that this included affirmations about Jesus and his exaltation, as well as thanksgiving for the gift of his Spirit, but such speech cannot simply be identified as missiological proclamation.[33] Clearly there was a missio-

29. Bruce 1988, 55-59, gives details of the Jewish Dispersion as it was manifested in the countries mentioned here. Gaventa 2003, 75, observes that the locations are grouped around the four compass points, 'viewed through the assumption that Jerusalem is the center of the earth (cf. Ezek. 5:5; *Jub.* 8:19; *1 En.* 26:1)'. This explains the inclusion of Judea in the list.

30. In later Jewish literature, proselytes are Gentiles who have been admitted to membership of the chosen people by circumcision and, in some sources, a purificatory self-baptism in the presence of witnesses. Witherington 1998, 344, holds that the term 'proselyte' may on occasion be used by Luke in this technical sense, but concludes that 'we cannot be sure, especially in light of the LXX use of the term and the influence of the Greek OT on Luke'. In the LXX the term is used for resident aliens (e.g., Ex. 20:10; 23:12; Nu. 15:13-16). Cf. S. McKnight, 'Proselytism and Godfearers', *DNTB*, 835-47.

31. Ambrosiaster, a fourth-century Latin writer, speaks of the church at Rome having been founded 'according to the Jewish rite, without seeing any sign of mighty works or any of the apostles'.

32. Cf. B. M. Metzger, 'Ancient Astrological Geography and Acts 2:9-11', in *New Testament Studies: Philological, Versional and Patristic*, NTTS 10 (Leiden: Brill, 1980), 46-56; Johnson 1992, 43; Bauckham, 'James and the Jerusalem Church', 417-27.

33. Contra Menzies, *Development*, 211 note 3, Turner, *Power*, 271-72, describes this as 'invasive charismatic praise' directed to God, as in 10:46; 19:6. Cf. Hur, *Dynamic Reading*, 223-25.

logical implication of their praise, but this was not its primary function and purpose.

12-13 TNIV fails to translate the word *pantes* ('all'), but the Greek text makes it clear that 'all' who heard the praises of God in their own languages were *amazed and perplexed* (*existanto de pantes kai diēporounto*; cf. v. 7). They could not grasp what was going on, and so they kept asking one another, *'What does this mean?'* Some, hearing their own language spoken by one disciple and various other languages being spoken by the rest, *made fun of them* (*diachleuazontes*, 'mocking' or 'sneering'). They dismissed the disciples as having had *'too much wine'* (*gleukos*, meaning 'new [sweet] wine'). This is a reminder that 'the miraculous is not self-authenticating, nor does it inevitably and uniformly convince. There must also be the preparation of the heart and the proclamation of the message if miracles are to accomplish their full purpose. This was true even for the miracle of the Spirit's coming at Pentecost.'[34] Such puzzlement and misunderstanding cried out for explanation, pointing to the need for Peter's sermon.

2. Peter's Interpretation of the Event (2:14-40)

Peter's speech fulfills several functions in Luke's narrative. First, it offers an interpretation of the events described in vv. 1-11, responding to the genuine question of the bystanders in v. 12 and the mocking in v. 13. Joel's prophecy is used to explain that this is a fulfillment of what was promised by God long ago and confirmed in recent time by John the Baptist and Jesus (cf. 1:4-5). In his time, Moses had wished that the Lord would put his Spirit on all his people, so that every Israelite might prophesy (Nu. 11:29), and Joel predicted that this would happen as an eschatological event, before the coming of 'the great and glorious day of the Lord'. This scriptural citation 'provides important clues concerning the mission that is beginning, and the subsequent narrative provides reminders that the mission is fulfilling the prophecies of Scripture'.[35] Secondly, the real cause of this event is shown to be the resurrection and ascension of Jesus (vv. 22-35). In other words, the sermon is an opportunity to explain the significance of Jesus in the plan of God for his people. Instead of focussing on the Spirit, the preacher directs the attention of his audience to the glorified Messiah.[36] Here Peter demonstrates the way

---

34. Longenecker 1981, 273.

35. Tannehill 1990, 29. Tannehill, 29-33, notes various ways in which the terminology of the Joel citation reappears in consequent chapters of Acts.

36. This testimony to the glorified Messiah fulfills the promises of Jesus himself about the Spirit's role in and through the disciples (cf. Jn. 15:26-27; 16:8-11). Barrett 1994, 129, thinks that there is an abrupt change in the sermon at v. 22 'marked by a fresh address to the listeners'. But this is a failure to recognize the logic of the message as a whole: Christ is proclaimed (vv. 22-36) in order to bring the audience to repentance and faith and then offer the Spirit as part of the experience of salvation through Jesus (vv. 37-41). Cf. Gaventa 2003, 73.

in which his understanding of Jesus and his mission has developed in the period of instruction described in 1:3, 6-8 (cf. Lk. 24:36-49). God is shown to be the hidden actor behind Jesus' mighty works (v. 22), his death (v. 23), his resurrection (vv. 24, 32), his exaltation and giving of the Spirit (vv. 33-34), and his enthronement as Lord and Christ (v. 36). Thirdly, the sermon illustrates the kind of preaching from Scripture that moved many Jews to repent and be baptized in the name of Jesus, forming the messianic community in Jerusalem (2:42–5:41). 'The speech not only interprets what has happened; it causes something to happen. The audience makes a shattering discovery and is moved to repentance in large numbers.'[37] Luke wants to establish a theology of the gospel as 'the word of God', and part of his concern is to explain how the gospel was preached to bring conviction to various audiences. At the same time, however, we see how the speeches in these early chapters provoke opposition and conflict in Jerusalem.[38]

a. The Gift of the Spirit Is a Sign That the Day of the Lord Is at Hand (2:14-21)

14-15 Although a larger group than the Twelve appears to have received the gift of the Spirit at Pentecost, it was *Peter* who soon *stood up with the Eleven, raised his voice and addressed the crowd.* In line with Jesus' commission (1:8), the apostles now presented themselves as his witnesses in Jerusalem. Empowered by the Spirit, they showed a new boldness in confronting their contemporaries (cf. 4:13-20). But Peter acted as spokesman to the perplexed crowd on this first occasion, just as he had earlier taken the lead in ministering to the community of disciples (1:15-24). The word translated *addressed (apephthenxato)* is also used in v. 4, in a statement about the Spirit giving them 'utterance' (TNIV *as the Spirit enabled them*). Peter's extensive and carefully argued speech has a prophetic character and is as much a Spirit-inspired utterance as the speaking in other languages. His opening words acknowledge the presence of a wider group of *'Fellow Jews'* (*Andres Ioudaioi,* 'Men Jews'),[39] in addition to those living in the city (*hoi katoikountes Ierousalēm pantes,* 'and all who live in Jerusalem'). Peter intends to *'explain'* (*touto hymin gnōston estō,* 'let this be known to you', NKJV, NRSV, ESV) what has happened in their midst and calls for them to *'listen carefully'* (*enōtisasthe,* 'give ear') to his words. Given that the final

---

37. Tannehill 1990, 26. It is interesting to note that the final part of the message comes in response to another question from the crowd (v. 37; cf. vv. 12-13).

38. On the authenticity, character, and purpose of the speeches, cf. INTRODUCTION TO ACTS: III.C. Historical Reliability (pp. 23-25) and IV.A.2. Narrative Dominated by Speeches (pp. 27-29); Barrett 1994, 130-33; Johnson 1992, 53-55; Witherington 1998, 116-20, 137-39.

39. Here and in vv. 22, 29, we may assume that women were included in the address (cf. 1:16 note). For an assessment of Western variations in the text of v. 14, cf. Barrett 1994, 133-34.

challenge of his message would be a call to repent and be baptized in the name of Jesus (vv. 36-39), he may have expected some solid resistance. In response to the charge that the disciples were drunk (v. 13), Peter suggests with good humour that it is too early in the morning for anyone to be inebriated (*'nine in the morning'*, *hōra tritē tēs hēmeras* ['the third hour of the day'])!

16-18   In response to the question 'What does it mean?' (v. 12), Peter begins with the claim that *'this is what was spoken by the prophet Joel'*.[40] The Greek could actually be translated 'through the prophet' (*dia tou prophētou*), making it quite clear that God spoke through a human mouthpiece (cf. 1:16 note). What God revealed in Joel 2:28-32 (LXX 3:1-5a) concerning the 'pouring out' of his Spirit *'"on all people"'* (*epi pasan sarka*, 'on all flesh') was now being fulfilled, in the presence of Jews from 'every nation under heaven' (cf. 2:5). Although a universal note is sounded with the expression *'"all people"'*, a series of defining phrases indicate that the gift of the Spirit is for Israel in the first instance. Thus, the promise about prophesying is for *'"your sons and daughters"'*. The pronoun *'"my"'* is then added to 'male slaves' (*tous doulous mou*) and 'female slaves' (*tas doulas mou*) in v. 18 (TNIV *'"my servants, both men and women"'*), indicating that the people in question are specifically servants of God.[41] The Greek particle *ge* (*'"even"'*) suggests that these terms are meant to give further definition to the groups previously mentioned. So the gift of the Spirit is for all who are truly God's servants, *'"both men and women"'* (cf. 1 Cor. 12:13; Gal. 3:28).[42] Whereas the Spirit especially designated and empowered the prophets and other leaders of Israel under the Old Covenant, God promises that *'"all"'* his people will be

---

40. This expression has been taken to mean that 'a pesher interpretation of Scripture' is being introduced. Peter is identifying a portion of the OT as pertinent to the Messianic Age and explicating it 'in accordance with the tradition and principles of Christ' (R. N. Longenecker, *Biblical Exegesis in the Apostolic Period* [Grand Rapids: Eerdmans, 1975], 99-100). The 'pesher' technique is particularly associated with the DSS, where Scripture was interpreted as having its imminent, eschatological fulfillment in the life and personalities of the sect (Longenecker, 38-45). NT preachers and writers certainly shared a sense of eschatological completion and the desire to apply Scripture to contemporary history. But they differed significantly from the Qumran sectarians in their understanding and use of the OT. Although midrashic and pesher-type techniques can be identified in certain NT contexts, 'the characterization of these instances by the term midrash or pesher would be to describe, illegitimately, the whole according to one of its parts' (D. J. Moo, *The Old Testament in the Gospel Passion Narratives* [Sheffield: Almond, 1983], 392).

41. The terms in the Hebrew original and LXX could be taken to mean literal slaves, thus highlighting an additional group in Jewish society who would receive the Spirit. But the modifications in Acts 2:18 give the terms religious significance ('slaves of God'), making explicit what is implicit in the message of Joel: 'the gift of the Spirit is given only to those who are members of the eschatological community of salvation' (Menzies, *Development*, 218-19). Turner, *Power*, 270, lists all the modifications to the Joel text in Acts 2.

42. Although women gradually emerge as having significant roles in Acts (e.g., 12:12-15; 16:13-15, 40; 17:34; 18:24-26; 21:9), the focus in earlier chapters is on the leadership of men in the new communities of the Spirit.

possessed by the Spirit in the last days. The verb ' *"pour out"* ' *(ekcheō)* suggests an unprecedented deluge of God's Spirit (cf. Is. 32:15; 44:3). In due course, Luke shows how believing Samaritans and Gentiles came to share in the blessing as well.

This lengthy citation includes several variations from the LXX and the Hebrew original. Most of these modifications serve to demonstrate the relevance of the text to the situation being addressed. Instead of Joel's introductory 'afterwards' (LXX *meta tauta*), which points quite generally to future events, Acts has ' *"in the last days"* ' *(en tais eschatais hēmerais)*, signifying that this is part of God's final act of redemption.[43] There is no doubt that Joel's oracle concerns events leading up to ' *"the coming of the great and glorious day of the Lord"* ' (v. 20), and so Peter's interpretive phrase (possibly influenced by Is. 2:2 or Mi. 4:1) makes that obvious from the beginning. This sharper eschatological note 'injects a strong sense of urgency into the disciples' ministry'.[44] The coming of the Spirit means that God's purpose for humanity is about to be consummated (Acts 2:19-21). However, it is overstating the case to say that 'the "last days" did not begin for the disciples till Pentecost',[45] since in Luke's perspective the time of fulfillment began with Jesus' miraculous birth (Luke 1-2). Peter also adds the words ' *"God says"* ' (v. 17), a variation of the more common prophetic claim to divine inspiration, 'thus says the Lord'. This merely clarifies what is evident from the broader context of Joel's oracle.

Although the words ' *"and they will prophesy"* ' occur only in the first verse of the original oracle (Jl. 2:28; Acts 2:17), they are used again in Acts 2:18. This addition makes it abundantly clear that the Spirit has been poured out to enable all God's people to *prophesy* (cf. Nu. 11:29) — young and old, male and female.[46] Seeing ' *"visions"* ' *(horaseis)* and dreaming ' *"dreams"* ' *(enypnia)* were prophetic activities in the OT. In the parallelism of Joel's oracle, with the words *will prophesy* before and after, they are presented as a subset of prophesying. Visions and dreams such as OT prophets enjoyed gave insight into the heavenly world, so that God's character and

43. Although some MSS of Acts 2:17 bring the quotation into line with the LXX, the best-attested reading is *en tais eschatais hēmerais*. The Western text reads *legei kyrios* ('the Lord says') instead of *legei ho theos* ('God says') and twice substitutes *autōn* ('their') for *hymōn* ('your'), suggesting that the oracle applies to Gentiles as well as to the Jews being addressed by Peter. Cf. Metzger, *Textual Commentary*, 255-58, for textual variations in the citation of Joel's prophecy.

44. Spencer 1997, 35.

45. Dunn, *Baptism*, 47. The Pentecostal bestowal of the Spirit is proof that 'the last days' have arrived, but 'it is one in a series of such events and does not mark the beginning of "the last days"' (Menzies, *Development*, 216). Cf. Turner, *Power*, 352-53.

46. The Western text does not include these words in v. 18. This is best explained as an accidental omission rather than as an attempt to conform to the LXX. Cf. Metzger, *Textual Commentary*, 257-58. Turner, *Power*, 82-138, discusses the Jewish notion of 'the Spirit of prophecy', as it was understood in NT times, suggesting how Luke may have understood the fulfillment of Joel's prophecy.

will could be proclaimed.[47] However, in Acts, the knowledge of God which the Spirit kindles in believers comes from the glorified Christ through the preaching of the gospel. This knowledge of God then becomes the basis of ministry to others through the gospel and the operation of the Spirit. There are certain occasions on which visions are used by God to guide and sustain key figures in the narrative (e.g., Acts 9:10, 12; 10:3, 17, 19; 11:5; 12:9; 16:9, 10; 18:9, using the related word *horama*; cf. 27:23), but these are rare. Dreams are not specifically mentioned, though some visions occur at night (16:9; 18:9) or in a trance (10:10; 11:5). Furthermore, only a few people are specifically designated as prophets (11:27; 13:1; 15:32; 21:10), though others are described as 'prophesying' (19:6; 21:9). Readers of Acts must therefore consider ways in which Joel's prophecy is fulfilled for Christians in general. 'Prophesying' appears to be a particular way of describing Spirit-directed ministry, both to believers and unbelievers. However, Turner helpfully considers the quotation from Joel in the light of the promises in Acts 1, the rest of Peter's sermon in Acts 2, and its consequences in the formation of the first Christian community. He suggests that

> the "Spirit of prophecy" to be given will be the effective power, not merely of Israel's witness, but also the power by which the messiah continues and deepens the New Exodus liberation and purging restoration of Israel, and so continues to fulfill to her the promises of her salvation.[48]

Although the Spirit was explicitly given to empower particular individuals for witness to the resurrected Jesus and for prophetic leadership (cf. Lk. 24:46-49; Acts 1:8; 4:8; 6:5, 10; 13:1-4; 16:6-7), Luke presents a more comprehensive view of the Spirit's work in terms of a fulfillment of the promise in Acts 1:5. The Spirit created and verified new communities of believers in Jesus, enabling them to enjoy the messianic salvation and minister its benefits, both inside and outside their fellowship (cf. 2:41-47; 4:31-37; 8:14-17; 10:44-48; 11:14-18; 15:8; 19:1-7). The delayed experience of the original disciples — following Jesus in his earthly ministry and then receiving his Spirit — is not a simple paradigm that can be applied to others.[49]

---

47. Visions and dreams were regular means of receiving prophetic revelation in the OT. For visions, see Nu. 24:4; 1 Sa. 3:1; 2 Sa. 7:17; Ps. 89:19; Is. 1:1; Je. 14:14; Ezk. 1:1; 8:2-4. For dreams, see Gn. 37:5; 41:8; Dt. 13:1-5; 1 Sa. 28:15; Dn. 1:17; Zc. 10:2. Visions play an important role in Acts 7:55-56; 9:3-12; 10:3, 9-19; 11:5-10; 16:9-10; 18:9-10; 27:23-24. Witherington 1998, 142, notes that in the Greco-Roman world dreams and visions were also 'widely recognized as a means of divine guidance'.

48. Turner, *Power*, 356 (original emphasis removed). Turner 352-400, argues at length that Acts 2:38-39 is programmatic for understanding how the Spirit is offered and received by individuals after the initial endowment of the disciples on the Day of Pentecost.

49. Cf. THE THEOLOGY OF ACTS: III. THE HOLY SPIRIT (pp. 60-65). Turner, *Power*, 344, points out that 'the ending of Luke and the Prologue of Acts undoubtedly focus "the promise" of the Spirit to the disciples especially as prophetic endowment empowering for

19-20 In association with the gift of the Spirit for prophesying, the Lord promises to ' *"show (dōsō*, 'give') *wonders in the heaven above and signs on the earth below"* '. Joel 2:30 (LXX 3:3) has only 'wonders in heaven and upon earth' *(terata en tō ouranō kai epi tēs gēs)*, but the citation in Acts adds the noun *signs (sēmeia)* and the prepositions *above (anō)* and *below (katō). Signs* are often paired with *wonders (terata)* in Acts (2:22, 43; 4:30; 5:12; 6:8; 7:36; 14:3; 15:12) and in the OT (e.g., Ex. 7:3; Dt. 4:34; 6:22).[50] Some commentators have limited the signs and wonders of Acts 2:19 to the miracles of Jesus (as in 2:22), or to the miracles of the apostles (as in 2:43). But it is more likely that the *wonders in the heaven above* are the cosmic portents of ' *"the day of the Lord"* ' mentioned in Joel 2:30-31 (cf. Mk. 13:24-25; Rev. 6:12-14) and that *signs on the earth below* are singled out as a separate but related category. These could include all the events anticipating the arrival of the end — everything from Jesus' supernatural birth and miraculous activity to his resurrection and ascension, the outpouring of the Spirit at Pentecost, and the miraculous events recorded in Acts.[51] ' *"The great and glorious day of the Lord"* ' refers to that terrible occasion when God judges the nations, as portrayed in Joel 3:1-15 (cf. Am. 5:18-20). Elsewhere in the NT, this is described as 'the day of our Lord Jesus Christ' (1 Cor. 1:8), 'the day of the Lord Jesus' (2 Cor. 1:14), 'the day of Christ Jesus' (Phil. 1:6), or 'the day of Christ' (Phil. 1:10; 2:16). The prophet Joel does not indicate the length of time between the outpouring of God's Spirit and the outpouring of his wrath, but the former is a sign that the latter will most definitely take place. It is perhaps surprising, in view of the angelic words in 1:11, that there is no specific mention of the return of Jesus to judge in the rest of Peter's sermon (cf. 10:42; 17:31). However, his quote from Joel's prophecy makes it clear that final

---

witness, rather than, for example, as the gift of inward transformation by the Spirit (as in Ezek. 36)'. Menzies, *Development*, 198-204, and other Pentecostal scholars view this as normative, describing the gift of the Spirit as a *donum superadditum* — an additional gift for mission proclamation — not as the essential means of ethical and spiritual renewal under the New Covenant. Turner 344-400, goes on to argue against the Pentecostal position, demonstrating from the Joel citation and teaching about the Spirit elsewhere in Acts that 'the gift of the "Spirit of prophecy" is necessary for the ongoing experience of "salvation" among the people of God'.

50. Cf. THE THEOLOGY OF ACTS: VIII. MIRACLES (pp. 83-87). K. H. Rengstorf, *TDNT* 7:216-17 note 65, gives all the instances of the expression 'signs and wonders' in the MT. The reference is almost always to the extraordinary acts of God associated with the exodus redemption. But note Is. 8:18; 20:3; Je. 32:20-21. Additional instances of the expression in the LXX are noted by Rengstorf (221), and these too are almost always connected with recollection of the exodus.

51. Cf. Menzies, *Development*, 222-23. He rightly insists that the miracles in Luke-Acts, including Pentecost, are 'precursors of those cosmic signs which shall signal the Day of the Lord'. Bruce 1988, 62, includes the cosmic signs associated with the death of Jesus in the Gospels among the signs and wonders that anticipate the end. Cf. Metzger, *Textual Commentary*, 258, on the omission of the words *blood and fire and billows of smoke* from the Western text of v. 19.

judgment must be close at hand and that it is necessary to seek salvation from the Lord before it is too late. But who is that Lord?

21 If signs of the nearness of the end are so clearly around them, it is time for Peter's audience to take careful note of the climax of Joel's oracle. The prophet promised deliverance from the judgment of God for ' *"everyone who calls on the name of the Lord"'*. No one may presume to be automatically among the saved. The positive dimensions of that salvation are portrayed in Joel 3:16-21 as pardon and peace for all who live in the presence of God, enjoying the blessings of a transformed creation or new Jerusalem. The rest of Peter's sermon is then designed to show that Jesus is the Lord on whom they are to call in the messianic era (vv. 22-36; cf. Rom. 10:9-13). Furthermore, the explanation is given that calling on his name means submitting in repentance and faith to baptism in his name (vv. 37-39; cf. 22:16). Indeed, there are repeated references both to the name of Jesus and to the salvation available through him in Acts 3:6, 16; 4:7, 10, 12, 17, 18, 30; 5:28, 40. Joel 2:32 appears to have had a profound influence on early Christian preaching to Jews and the related ministry of healing 'in the name of Jesus Christ'.

b. Jesus Is the Lord on Whom to Call for Salvation (2:22-36)

22 Peter addresses his audience again directly (*Andres Israēlitai,* 'Men Israelites'; cf. v. 14 note) and challenges them to listen to his words. He begins by announcing the name of his subject (*'Jesus of Nazareth'*),[52] and goes on to make various claims about Jesus that will be repeated, with variation, in a series of speeches in Acts (cf. 3:13-26; 4:10-12; 5:30-32; 10:36-43; 13:23-41), each one adapted to its context.[53] These samples of apostolic preaching have an important function in Luke's narrative, illustrating how opportunities were taken to testify to the person and work of Christ in a variety of situations. As such, they are part of the unique revelation of God that forms our NT and must be foundational for our own faith and understanding of the gospel. Their method of proclamation, point for point, may not be applicable in every situation, but reflection on the theological issues they affirm will be a stimulus to effective evangelism in every age and culture. The first concern of Peter here is the divine attestation of Jesus. As the *'man'* from Nazareth, he was *'accredited by God to you by miracles, wonders*

52. Jesus is here called 'the Nazorean' (*ho Nazarēnos;* cf. Lk. 18:37; Acts 3:6; 4:10; 6:14; 22:8; 26:9). Luke's reference to the 'sect of the Nazoreans' (24:5) may suggest that 'the Nazorean' is a title for Jesus, but the expression elsewhere appears to be an alternative for 'Nazarene' (cf. Lk. 4:34; 24:19) and to mean no more than 'from Nazareth' (cf. 10:38, *ton apo Nazareth*). Cf. H. H. Schaeder, *TDNT* 4:874-79; Barrett 1994, 140.

53. Note the six themes in Peter's sermons identified by C. H. Dodd, *The Apostolic Preaching and Its Developments* (London: Hodder, 1936), 37-45. Longenecker 1981, 278, observes that the preaching in Acts is functional in nature — proclaiming certain facts about Jesus and identifying God as the true author of what happened — rather than philosophical. Barrett 1994, 129-33, fails to perceive the link between 2:22-32 and the first part of the sermon.

and signs'. The Greek syntax in vv. 22-23 suggests that God had already *accredited (apodedeigmenon)* Jesus as Messiah when he was crucified.[54] Three terms are used to describe the way in which this took place in the course of his ministry. There were *miracles (dynameis,* 'powers') or mighty works, signifying the operation of God's power or kingly rule through him (cf. Lk. 11:20). But these could also be called *wonders (terata)*, because of the amazement they effected in the witnesses, and *signs (sēmeia)*, because they pointed beyond themselves to the character of Jesus and the significance of his coming.[55] Such things *'God did through him'*, among the very people listening to Peter's sermon *('among you')*. Even Jews from other places could not escape the compelling evidence of Jesus' life and ministry that was available to them *('as you yourselves know')*. This theme surfaces only once more in the apostolic preaching (cf. 10:37-38), but a detailed recording of the mighty works of Jesus was clearly important for the writers of the Gospels. Such evidence might simply lead to the conclusion that he was 'a prophet, powerful in word and deed before God and all the people' (Lk. 24:19). However, Peter proceeds to identify him specifically as the promised Messiah.

23 If Jesus was so powerfully accredited by God, why was he rejected and crucified? The apostle goes on to speak of Jesus actually being *'handed over' (ekdotos)* by God. The words *'to you'* are added in the TNIV, implying that he was handed over to Israel.[56] But the Greek could just as easily mean that Jesus was handed over or delivered up to death or to the Romans who actually crucified him (cf. 3:13, *paredōkate*). Without doubt, the emphasis is on God's sovereignty in everything that happened: he was handed over *'by God's deliberate plan and foreknowledge' (tē hōrismenē boulē kai prognōsei tou theou)*. Here we find the first reference in Acts to God's 'purpose' or *plan (boulē,* cf. Lk. 7:30; Acts 4:28; 5:38-39; 13:36; 20:27), which was 'predetermined' or 'set' by him. This plan, which had particular reference to the suffering of the Messiah, was revealed in advance in Scripture (cf. Lk. 22:22, 37; 24:26, 46; Acts 3:18; 4:25-28; 17:2-3; 26:22-23). Little attempt

54. Barrett 1994, 140-41, notes that *apodedeigmenon* (a perfect passive participle) would normally be translated 'appointed' when it has a personal object. In such cases a complement such as 'Christ' would be expected (as in 1 Cor. 4:9). However, the verb basically means 'show forth' or 'display', and hence could be translated 'attested' (BDAG; cf. KJV, NRSV, ESV), with the following words revealing in what sense he was accredited.

55. The Greek word for miracles (*terata,* 'wonders') is never used in the NT except in conjunction with *sēmeia* ('signs'). Cf. 2 Cor. 12:12; 2 Thes. 2:9; Heb. 2:4. Since the phrase 'signs and wonders' in the OT almost always refers to extraordinary acts of God associated with the exodus (cf. note 50 above), the use of this expression in connection with the mighty works of Jesus (Acts 2:22) and of his apostles (Acts 2:43) suggests the advent of a similarly significant divine act of redemption in association with Jesus. Cf. THE THEOLOGY OF ACTS: VIII. MIRACLES (pp. 83-87).

56. KJV ('ye have taken') reflects the addition of *labontes* in some MSS followed by the Received Text. But this is 'a typical scribal expansion, introduced in order to fill out the construction' (Metzger, *Textual Commentary,* 258).

is made in the apostolic sermons to explain how the death of Jesus actually achieves our salvation. Philip's use of Isaiah 53 in 8:32-35 to tell 'the good news about Jesus' and various references to Jesus as God's servant may reflect a wider use of that particular passage to interpret Jesus' suffering (cf. 3:13; 20:28). However, the focus in Acts is mostly on the offer of forgiveness, not on the process by which atonement for sins was accomplished.[57]

God's *foreknowledge (prognōsis)* means more than his ability to anticipate the future. It is another way of talking about his determination of events in advance, according to his own plan (cf. Rom. 8:29; 11:2; 1 Pet. 1:2, 20).[58] Jesus came into the world to fulfill certain God-given roles, and those associated with him had their own roles to play in the drama of redemption. Despite this emphasis on God's sovereignty, there is no diminution of human responsibility here (cf. 1:17 note).[59] Peter acknowledges that the betrayal and death of Jesus took place *'with the help of wicked men' (dia cheiros anomōn*, 'by the hand of lawless ones'), apparently identifying the Roman authorities as those who 'lacked the privilege of the law'.[60] Judas Iscariot, together with the Jewish and Romans leaders, all had a part to play (cf. 4:27). But Peter lays a particular responsibility for the suffering of Jesus at the feet of the Jews in Jerusalem with the expression *prospēxantes aneilate*, which literally means 'you fixed him (to the cross) and (thereby) slew him.' (TNIV *'put him to death by nailing him to the cross').*[61] They disowned Jesus and handed him over to the secular authorities who actually crucified him (cf. 3:13-14; 5:30). Preaching to a later synagogue audience in Pisidian Antioch, Paul also blamed the Jews in Jerusalem for the way Jesus died

---

57. Cf. THE THEOLOGY OF ACTS: VI. THE ATONING WORK OF JESUS (pp. 75-79).

58. Cf. P. Jacobs and H. Krienke, *NIDNTT* 1:692-93. 'Perhaps no NT author is more concerned than Luke to testify to the accomplishment of the will of God in history or so caught up in the language of the divine plan and predetermined intention, purpose and necessity' (D. L. Tiede, *Prophecy and History in Luke-Acts* [Philadelphia: Fortress, 1980], 33). Cf. D. B. Wallace, *Greek Grammar beyond the Basics: An Exegetical Syntax of the New Testament* (Grand Rapids: Zondervan, 1996), 288, on the way *boulē* ('plan') and *prognōsis* ('foreknowledge') relate together.

59. J. T. Squires, *The Plan of God in Luke-Acts*, SNTSMS 76 (Cambridge: Cambridge University, 1993), 181-82, rightly observes that the apostles continue to preach to those held responsible for the death of Jesus, in the hope that they might repent. This is another indication that Luke-Acts presents something more than a simple determinism. D. A. Carson, *Divine Sovereignty and Human Responsibility: Biblical Perspectives in Tension* (London: Marshall, 1981), 201-22, reviews different ways in which the tension between divine sovereignty and human responsibility has been handled by theologians.

60. Barrett 1994, 142. KJV ('by wicked hands') and NKJV ('by lawless hands') provide an odd rendering of the Greek here. The adjective *anomōn* is plural but *cheiros* is singular, suggesting that the adjective is used as a substantive for the people concerned and not in any attributive way.

61. This is not a blanket condemnation of the Jews in general but an accusation against those who were dwelling in Jerusalem at the time (cf. 2:5; 13:27). Peter's rhetoric is designed to bring that particular audience to repentance and faith in Jesus. Cf. F. J. Matera, 'Responsibility for the Death of Jesus according to the Acts of the Apostles', *JSNT* 39 (1990), 77-93.

(13:27-28). He went on to warn his hearers about the danger of rejecting the evidence about Jesus presented to them (13:40-41), but he did not accuse them of complicity in his betrayal. Any attempt to blame subsequent generations of Jews for the death of Jesus is unwarranted and unjust.

24 The crucifixion of Jesus, of course, was far from the end of the matter. Continuing the emphasis on God's sovereignty, the third point in Peter's message is that *'God raised him from the dead'*. The contrast between God's exaltation of Jesus and the attitude of those who opposed him is a central aspect of the apostolic preaching (cf. 2:36; 3:14-15; 4:10; 5:30; 10:39-40; 13:28-30). Jesus' resurrection was his ultimate accreditation and vindication as God's servant and Messiah. The latter point comes out emphatically as Peter begins to demonstrate the fulfillment of David's words (vv. 25-36). When it is claimed that God freed Jesus *'from the agony of death, because it was impossible for death to keep its hold on him'*, a word that normally applies to the 'agony' of childbirth is used (*tas ōdinas*, 'the birth pangs'). The whole expression (*lysas tas ōdinas tou thanatou*, 'loosed the pangs of death'), part of which is borrowed from Psalm 18:4 (LXX 17:5), provides a mixed metaphor in which *death* is regarded as being 'in labour' and unable to hold back its child. God 'brought the pangs to an end' so that 'the "birth" which is to bring Christ to light, may attain its goal'.[62] It was *impossible* for the Son of David to be prevented by death from exercising his eternal, kingly rule. The expression from Psalm 18:4 is used as a way of explaining the meaning of Psalm 16:10 (LXX 15:10), which is about to be cited. The implication is that Jesus was resurrected because he already was the Messiah, not that he 'became' Messiah through resurrection (cf. v. 36 note).

25-28 As the prophecy of Joel was used to interpret and explain the gift of the Spirit in vv. 16-21, so now a second OT citation is drawn into Peter's argument, to prepare for the claim that Jesus is the Christ (v. 36). Psalm 16 (LXX 15):8-11 is not quoted to 'prove' the resurrection as a historical event — the apostles present themselves as witnesses in that particular respect (v. 32) — but to show how the resurrection testifies to Jesus' messiahship. The link with v. 24 is unfortunately obscured in the TNIV by omission of the word 'for' (*gar*) in v. 25.[63] It was impossible for death to keep its hold on Jesus because of what *'David'* said about him. Davidic authorship is affirmed by both the Hebrew and Greek versions of this psalm and is clearly foundational to the argument here (cf. 1:20; 2:34-35 notes).

---

62. BDAG (*lyō*). Cf. G. Bertram, *TDNT* 9:673. The expression *ōdines thanatou* ('pangs of death') is found in Ps. 18:4 (LXX 17:5); 116:3 (LXX 114:3), and the parallel expression *ōdines hadou* ('pangs of Hades') in Ps. 18:5 (LXX 17:6). Cf. B. Lindars, *New Testament Apologetic: The Doctrinal Significance of the Old Testament Quotes* (London: SCM, 1961), 39-40; Barrett 1994, 143-44. The Western texts of Acts 2:24 substitute *hadou* for *thanatou*, presumably as an assimilation to vv. 27 and 31.

63. Cf. KJV, NRSV, ESV. The words from the psalm that are repeated in 2:31 confirm that the main point of the quotation is David's claim that the Christ would not be abandoned to the grave or see decay.

The same passage is employed in connection with Paul's preaching about
the resurrection of Jesus in 13:34-37.

Psalm 16 celebrates the benefits of a life lived under the rule of God.
These include the protection that is mentioned in v. 8 (Acts 2:25): '*"Because
he is at my right hand, I will not be shaken."*'[64] But David's joy reaches beyond
his present circumstances to include the hope that he will always be with
God (vv. 9-10; Acts 2:26-27). Death no longer terrifies him, and he affirms:
'*"you will not abandon me to the realm of the dead"*' (*eis hadēn*, 'to Hades'),
'*"you will not let your holy one see decay"*'. The impotence of death to destroy
his relationship with God is David's confidence.[65] Since God has already
made known to him '*"the paths of life"*', he anticipates that God will continue to fill him with joy in his '*"presence"*' (v. 11; Acts 2:28). The last clause
of Psalm 16:11 ('with eternal pleasures at your right hand') is not quoted in
Peter's sermon. But the implications of Jesus' presence at God's 'right
hand' are soon discussed in relation to the citation of Psalm 110:1 (cf. Acts
2:33-34). What elements in Psalm 16 lead to the understanding that it is
about the bodily resurrection of Jesus? In what sense could David have
spoken *'about him'* (*eis auton*, 'with reference to him')? Such questions are
answered in vv. 29-31.

29-30 As Peter comes to apply the psalm citation to Jesus, he addresses his audience again quite directly (*Andres adelphoi*, 'Men brothers',
TNIV '*brothers and sisters*'; cf. vv. 14, 22 notes). They are 'brothers' in this
context because they are fellow Jews. The fact that *'the patriarch David died
and was buried, and his tomb is here to this day'*, is sufficient proof for Peter
that Psalm 16 speaks about something beyond David's personal experience.[66] Bodily resurrection is the key issue because of the expression 'you
will not let your holy one see decay.' If David's own body had been raised,
his grave would have been disturbed or would no longer be present. Peter's second assumption is that David was *'a prophet'*. This is implicit in
what is said in 1:16 and 4:25 and was a common theme in Palestinian Juda-

---

64. The text quoted in 2:25-28 follows the LXX where it differs from the Hebrew in
minor details. The first verb, 'I saw', is substituted for the Hebrew 'I have set'; 'my tongue'
for the Hebrew 'my glory'; the expression 'in hope' for the Hebrew 'securely'; and 'decay'
for the Hebrew 'the Pit'. None of these changes is decisive for a new understanding of the
text. Cf. D. L. Bock, *Proclamation from Prophecy and Pattern: Lucan Old Testament Christology*,
JSNTSS 12 (Sheffield: JSOT, 1987), 174-77.

65. W. Eichrodt, *Theology of the Old Testament*, 2 vols. (ET, London: SCM, 1961, 1967),
2:524-25, concludes that 'here we stand before *a conquest of death which proceeds from a profoundly inward knowledge of what life really is*'. Anyone who finds in Psalm 16 reference to
nothing more than preservation from the evil of an early death 'externalizes the joy of the
psalmist, which has its roots in the depths of the inner life, in a most intolerable way, and
degrades the three concluding verses into a remarkably empty piece of phrase-making'. Cf.
Bock, *Proclamation*, 173-74.

66. David's tomb was situated on the slope of Ophel near the Pool of Siloam (cf. Neh.
3:16). It was entered and robbed during the siege of Jerusalem in 135/134 BC. Over a century
later Herod the Great built a monument of white marble at its entrance (cf. Josephus, *War*
1.61; *Ant.* 7.393; 13.249; 16.179-83). Cf. Barrett 1994, 146-47; Witherington 1998, 146.

ism.[67] Jesus himself suggested the prophetic status of David when he gave a messianic interpretation of Psalm 110:1 (cf. Lk. 20:41-44 par.). Since that passage is paired with Psalm 16:8-11 in Acts 2:24-36, it is possible that Jesus' interpretation of Psalm 110 was the basis for the messianic reading of Psalm 16. In the present context, allusion is also made to another important Davidic psalm. David *'knew that God had promised him on oath that he would place one of his descendants on his throne'*.[68] The wording of Psalm 132:11 is recalled, reflecting the promise of God to establish the throne of David's offspring forever (cf. 2 Sa. 7:12-16; Ps. 89:3-4, 35-37). But how would this happen? Would it be by one descendant of David after another occupying the throne in Jerusalem? After the Babylonian Exile of the sixth century BC there were no more Davidic kings. How would God's covenant with David be maintained?

31 Peter describes David as *'seeing what was to come' (proïdōn)* and speaking of *'the resurrection of the Messiah'*. The title *Messiah (ho Christos)* is used here in the technical sense of 'the anointed One', who was the Son of David expected by pious groups in Israel.[69] Peter's point is that only through *resurrection* from the dead could a son of David rule forever over God's people. David's confidence about this was an oracular statement, inspired by the Spirit of God. It enabled him to indicate many centuries beforehand how God's covenant with him would ultimately be fulfilled. When Psalm 16:10 is cited again in v. 31, two significant changes are made. The past tense is employed to emphasize fulfillment *('he was not abandoned to the realm of the dead, nor did his body see decay')* and *his body (hē sarx autou,* 'his flesh) is substituted for *'"your holy one"'* (cf. v. 27). This last change 'guarantees that the point of the passage is not merely spiritual translation, bodily preservation, or terminal illness, but bodily resurrection'.[70] The holy one is saved from death in *his body*. But who is this *holy one*? Most likely, the title *your holy one (ton hosion sou,* Heb. *ḥasîḏekā)* was taken by the earliest Christians to be another way of referring to the messianic Son of David and is a key for understanding Peter's use of this text. In Psalm 16:10, David is

67. Cf. J. A. Fitzmyer, 'David, Being Therefore a Prophet . . . (Acts 2:30)', *CBQ* 34 (1972), 332-39. It is surprising that Fitzmyer makes little of 2 Sa. 23:1-2 as an OT precedent.

68. Following the Received Text, KJV has 'that of the fruit of his loins, *according to the flesh, he would raise up Christ*, to sit on the throne'. This is based on later MSS and the similar wording of Codex D. The older and better-attested reading is represented in TNIV. Modifications appear to have taken place in the course of time because of the harshness of the Greek syntax in earlier manuscripts of v. 30. Cf. Metzger, *Textual Commentary,* 259-60, for other minor textual variations in vv. 30-31.

69. Cf. R. N. Longenecker, *The Christology of Early Jewish Christianity* (London: SCM, 1970), 63-119; A. Motyer, *IBD* 2:987-94; K. H. Rengstorf, *NIDNTT* 2:334-43. According to 1 Pet. 1:10-12, the prophets were nevertheless limited in their foreknowledge with respect to the time and circumstances in which their oracles would be fulfilled.

70. Bock, *Proclamation,* 178. This change reflects the explanatory parallelism of the psalm as recorded in Acts 2:26b, 27, where 'the last two elements of the line define how *the flesh* shall dwell in security with hope' (v. 26; TNIV *my body*).

God's 'holy one', 'yet not David as a mere person but David as the recipient and conveyor of God's ancient but ever-renewed promise'.[71]

32 Peter specifically links the hope of the psalmist with *Jesus* and his resurrection. *'God has raised this Jesus [to life]'* (*touton ton Iēsoun anestēsan ho theos*; cf. v. 24), and the apostles are *'all witnesses of the fact'* (*hou pantes hēmeis esmen martyres*; cf. 1:8, 21-22). They had seen the empty tomb and many convincing proofs that he was alive (1:3). They were convinced that Jesus, unlike David, had been raised immediately from death, never to experience decay. By implication, he is the Messiah. But that declaration is held over until the dramatic climax of the message in v. 36. A mark of authentic gospel proclamation in every age will be a similar emphasis on the fact of the resurrection and its biblical significance. The resurrection demonstrates that Jesus is the Messiah, who fulfills a complex of Jewish hopes (cf. 3:15, 26; 4:10-12; 5:30-32; 10:40-43; 13:30-39). He is the saviour-king of David's line, who reigns forever over God's people, bringing the blessings of forgiveness and peace with God. As the one appointed to be the judge of the living and the dead, he offers salvation and a share in his resurrection life to all nations (cf. 13:46-48; 16:30-31; 17:30-31).

33 The fourth point that Peter makes about Jesus concerns his ascension and the pouring out of the Holy Spirit. TNIV does not translate the Greek connective *oun* ('then', 'therefore'), obscuring the point that conclusions are about to be drawn (contrast KJV, NRSV, ESV). In fact, the two themes of the sermon so far — an explanation of the gift of the Spirit (vv. 16-21) and a proclamation of Jesus as Lord and Messiah (vv. 22-32) — are tied together here. As a sequel to his resurrection, Jesus was *'exalted to the right hand of God'*.[72] In the ancient world, *the right hand* was often identified with greatness, strength, goodness, and divinity. From Psalm 110:1 it will shortly be demonstrated that *the right hand of God* is the proper place for the Messiah (vv. 34-35). Meanwhile, Peter makes the startling claim that Jesus *'has received from the Father the promised Holy Spirit'* and, as anticipated in Luke 24:49, *'has poured out what you now see and hear'*.[73] In Joel's prophecy, God

---

71. W. C. Kaiser Jr., *The Uses of the Old Testament in the New* (Chicago: Moody, 1985), 34. He argues that Heb. *ḥāsîd*, which occurs thirty-two times in the MT, should be rendered in a passive form ('favored one') rather than in an active form ('one who is loyal to God'). However, cf. D. A. Baer and R. P. Gordon, *NIDOTTE* 2:211-18 (213). A messianic interpretation of Ps. 16:9 is found in the much later *Midrash Tehillim* ('my glory rejoices over the Lord Messiah, who will rise from me', i.e., from David). As the Messiah, Jesus was God's Holy One *par excellence* (cf. Acts 3:14; 4:27, 30, where the adjective *hagios* ['holy'] is used).

72. Bruce 1988, 66, translates *tē dexia tou theou* instrumentally ('by the right hand of God'), as does KJV, following the wording of Ps. 118 (LXX 117):16. Cf. Barrett 1994, 149-50. But the statement in v. 33 is supported by the argument from Ps. 110:1 in vv. 34-35, which shows that Jesus' exaltation was to a status *at* God's 'right hand'. Cf. NKJV, NRSV, ESV; D. M. Hay, *Glory at the Right Hand: Psalm 110 in Early Christianity*, SBLMS 18 (Nashville/New York: Abingdon, 1973), 71 note 82; Bock, *Proclamation*, 352 note 88.

73. Lindars, *Apologetic*, 51-59; J. Dupont, 'Ascension du Christ et don de l'Ésprit d'après Actes 2:35', in B. Lindars and S. S. Smalley (eds.), *Christ and Spirit in the New Testa-*

said, 'I will pour out my Spirit' (v. 17, *ekcheō*), but in Peter's proclamation the exalted Jesus *has poured out (execheen) what you now see and hear* (v. 33). What the crowd at Pentecost could *see and hear* were signs of Jesus' exaltation to the situation of absolute glory, power, and authority in the universe. As the dispenser of the Spirit, he was now acting with *'the Father'*, sharing fully in his heavenly rule. Given the relationship between God and his Spirit in the OT, the foundation was thus provided for later formulations of the doctrine of God as Trinity. The risen Jesus is 'Lord of the Spirit' (cf. 16:7; 8:39).[74] Turner has suggested a fusion of Davidic and Mosaic Christologies here, as part of a New Exodus soteriology in Luke-Acts. David did not ascend to God to receive a gift for God's people, but Moses did (cf. Exodus 19, 24, 34). Moreover, Moses was involved (at least passively) in the distribution of the Spirit to other Israelites, and it was his wish that the Spirit might be given to all Israel (Nu. 11:26-30), which Joel's promise 'fulfills'.[75]

34-35 David's authorship of Psalm 110 (LXX 109):1, which is cited here, is critical for its messianic application. Moreover, the fact that David himself *'did not ascend to heaven'* compels us to look for the interpretation of this oracle beyond his own experience (cf. the argument used in connection with Psalm 16 in Acts 2:29). Fundamentally, this psalm speaks about the enthronement of a son of David as king of Israel. God's invitation (*'"'Sit at my right hand until I make your enemies a footstool for your feet'"'*) suggests that a king who rules in Jerusalem is the Lord's earthly vicegerent. God rules his people through his chosen representative (his 'anointed') and promises to put down all his enemies (a theme that is developed in Ps. 110:5-6). Jesus' discussion of Psalm 110:1 indicates that a messianic interpretation was already known to the teachers of the law in his day (Lk. 20:39-44 par.).[76] Nevertheless, he uses the text to challenge accepted views and question the

---

ment: In Honour of C. F. D. Moule (Cambridge: Cambridge University, 1973), 219-28; Barrett 1994, 149-50, have argued that Ps. 68:18 (MT 68:19; LXX 67:19) has influenced this verse and was the origin of the view that the Spirit was given by the ascended Jesus. Bock, *Proclamation*, 181-83, thinks that Jesus' own promise in Lk. 24:49 is Luke's primary explanation of the apostolic claim and that Peter's interpretation of Jl. 2:28-32 in the light of Ps. 110:1 explains the link. Turner, *Power*, 287, insists that Acts 2:33-34 affirms 'a New Moses fulfilment of Ps. 68:18, re-contextualized in the light of Joel and the Pentecost events'.

74. Hur, *Dynamic Reading*, 233-34. Turner, *Power*, 277, argues that the fulfillment of the promise envisaged in 2:17-18, 33, 'takes the reader beyond anything Judaism conceived of the messiah, for it relates the Spirit to Jesus in the same way as to God, the Father, himself'. Cf. THE THEOLOGY OF ACTS: II. JESUS AS MESSIAH AND LORD (pp. 56-60).

75. Turner, *Power*, 279-89, follows three lines of argument to establish his case: Jewish associations of Pentecost with the giving of the law at Sinai, parallels with Sinai in the narrative of Acts 2:1-13, and Moses/Sinai parallels in Peter's speech. Bock, *Proclamation*, 182-83, on the other hand, holds that a Mosaic background is 'not significant at all for the Pentecost event.'

76. Cf. Hay, *Glory*, 22-33, for interpretations of this text in Jewish tradition. Influenced by Jesus' teaching, early Christian preachers and writers quoted from and alluded to this psalm extensively (Hay, 34-51). But only Acts 2:33-36 uses it in a plainly apologetic setting to argue that Jesus is the Christ.

sense in which David can address his son as '"*my Lord*"'. David's son is his superior, and the messianic kingdom is not simply a renewal of David's earthly dominion. For Jesus, the enthronement of the Messiah at God's right hand is clearly a transcendental event (cf. Lk. 22:67-69 par.).[77] The apostles of Jesus proclaim his resurrection-ascension as that event. By this means his heavenly rule as the saviour-king of his people was inaugurated. Teaching about the resurrection of Jesus is inadequate if it does not incorporate the notions of heavenly exaltation and eternal rule. In other words, resurrection and ascension belong together in Christian theology (cf. 1:9 note).

36 An indication that the sermon has reached its climax is given by Peter's address to '*all Israel*' again (*pas oikos Israēl*, 'all the house of Israel', KJV, ESV), recalling v. 14. The link word '*therefore*' (*oun*, as in v. 33) also shows that he intends to summarize and conclude the argument of the preceding section. Peter's audience and subsequent readers of Acts are to '*be assured*' about who Jesus is and how God has vindicated him:[78] '*God has made this Jesus, whom you crucified, both Lord and Messiah.*' The two titles given to Jesus relate back to the psalm citations in vv. 25-34 and the prior claim of Joel 2:32 that whoever calls on the name of 'the Lord' will be saved (v. 21). Jesus is the *Lord* on whom to call since he is the *Messiah*, resurrected by God in fulfillment of Psalm 16:8-11 and now exalted to his right hand in fulfillment of Psalm 110:1. It is important to note that the first occurrence of *kyrios* ('Lord') in Psalm 110:1 represents the sacred name of God in Hebrew, whereas the second is qualified by 'my' and represents the ordinary Hebrew expression 'my lord'. The one whom David addresses as 'my lord' is distinguished from God ('the Lord'). However, since Jesus has been uniquely exalted to the Father's side through his heavenly ascension and has poured out the promised Spirit, he can be called *Lord* in the full sense that God is. The fulfillment of the psalm takes us beyond the literal meaning of the original text. God now calls people to himself though Jesus and offers them forgiveness and the Holy Spirit 'in the name of Jesus Christ' (2:38-39).[79]

---

77. Cf. Hay, *Glory*, 110-16; Bock, *Proclamation*, 128-32. In the final analysis, Luke shows that 'the Messiah Jesus is not merely the Son of David or the messianic Son of God. He is Son in a fuller sense that entails complete authority and direct access to God' (Bock, 143).

78. 'Be assured' (*asphalōs ginōsketō*) in 2:36 recalls Luke's promise at the beginning of his work to provide 'assurance' (*asphaleian*) to Theophilus and others of the things they have learned (Lk. 1:4). TNIV translates *asphalēs* in various ways in Acts 21:34; 22:30; 25:26.

79. Bock, *Proclamation*, 184-87, insists that the flow of the argument in Peter's sermon compels us to understand 'Lord' in v. 36 as 'God's name' and nothing less. L. W. Hurtado, *One God, One Lord: Early Christian Devotion and Ancient Jewish Monotheism* (Minneapolis: Fortress; London: SCM, 1988), 94-95, 100, argues that we have here a mutation of Jewish 'divine agency' thinking, involving 'an unprecedented reshaping of monotheistic piety to include a second object of devotion alongside God'. Cf. Longenecker, *Christology*, 120-47; C. F. D. Moule, 'The Christology of Acts', in L. E. Keck and J. L. Martyn, *Studies in Luke-Acts* (Nashville: Abingdon, 1966; London: SPCK, 1976), 160-61; Barrett 1994, 152.

When Peter says *God has made (epoiēsan)* Jesus Lord and Messiah, we may not conclude that this is evidence of 'adoptionism', the view that Jesus was merely adopted as God's heavenly co-regent at this point in time. In Luke's Gospel, Jesus is proclaimed as Saviour, Messiah, and Lord from his birth (2:11; cf. 1:31-35, 43; 3:22). Peter's sermon highlights the way in which this became known, as Jesus was progressively attested by God through 'miracles, wonders and signs' (v. 23), and then climactically through the resurrection (v. 24). Since he *is* Messiah, Jesus is raised from death and exalted to God's right hand! However, just as there are several important stages in the life of a king, from birth as heir to the throne, to anointing, to actual assumption of his throne, so it is with Jesus in Luke-Acts. 'Although Jesus was called Lord and Messiah previously, the full authority of these titles is granted only through death, resurrection, and exaltation. Peter's proclamation in 2:36 makes it clear that something new and important has happened through these events. Jesus has been enthroned as Lord and Messiah for Israel, to fulfill all the divine promises. This newly enthroned ruler will also offer salvation to the world, having been granted universal power to rule and judge.'[80] The final words in the Greek text *(hon hymeis estaurōsate, whom you crucified)* prepare for the call to repentance that follows, indicating where the audience stands in relation to the message about Jesus.[81] This suggests that, in one way or another, demonstrating the need for repentance is part of the evangelistic task (cf. 3:17-21; 5:30-31; 10:42-43; 11:18; 14:15; 17:30-31).

c. Calling upon Jesus Involves Repentance and Baptism in His Name (2:37-40)

37 'The Pentecost speech is part of a recognition scene, where, in the manner of tragedy, persons who have acted blindly against their own best interests suddenly recognize their error.'[82] The speech is actually designed to produce the response indicated here. When the people discovered how

---

80. Tannehill 1990, 39. The power that Jesus exercised during his earthly ministry for the benefit of a limited number of people is now to be offered to all. Only the exalted Lord is able to extend the blessing of his ministry to all Israel and the world. So the Spirit that rested on him is poured out on others for this work. Longenecker 1981, 281, similarly argues that Peter is proclaiming 'not an adoptionist Christology but a functional one with ontological overtones'. Cf. Turner, *Power*, 294-97. Contrast Barrett 1994, 140-41, 151-52.

81. Barrett 1994, 152, rightly makes the latter point, noting that 'the crucifixion of one who shares the throne of God is a sin against God'. However, he also seeks to establish the time reference as the basis for arguing an adoptionist Christology in this verse. Contrast Witherington 1998, 147-53.

82. Tannehill 1990, 35. Cf. Barrett 1994, 153; Metzger, *Textual Commentary*, 260, for Western expansions of this verse. The word 'others' *(loipous)* is missing from some ancient MSS but is otherwise well attested. Its omission seems to have been accidental, due to homoeoteleuton.

stubborn and foolish they had been (v. 36), they were *cut to the heart*, meaning that they were conscience-stricken or remorseful,[83] *and said to Peter and
the other apostles, 'Brothers, what shall we do?'* Their address to the apostles as
brothers is an appeal to their common heritage as Israelites.[84]

38 Peter's call to *'repent' (metanoēsate)* echoes the preaching of John
the Baptist (Lk. 3:3, 8; cf. Mt. 3:2) and Jesus (Lk. 5:32; cf. Mt. 4:17), who
linked repentance with the proclamation that 'the kingdom of heaven is at
hand'. But repentance in Acts is normally demanded on the specific basis
of what is proclaimed about *Jesus Christ* (e.g., 2:26-36; 3:17-21; 17:30-31;
20:21; 26:20; cf. 8:22). So many things promised in connection with God's
eschatological rule have already been fulfilled through him, and he is the
only saviour from the coming judgment. Jesus' death, resurrection, and ascension bring the realization of OT kingdom expectations for Israel and the
nations. Repentance involves a change of mind about Jesus and his role in
God's kingdom purposes, as the Greek terminology suggests. But *metanoein* in the LXX almost always translates the Hebrew *niḥām* (niph.), meaning 'to be sorry' about something. Moreover, the OT regularly shows that
genuine sorrow for sin involves an alteration of attitude towards God that
brings about a 'conversion' or reorientation of life.[85] NT use of the terminology must be interpreted within this biblical-theological framework. In Acts
2:38, repentance means a radical reorientation of life with respect to Jesus,
expressing sorrow for having rejected the one accredited by God as Lord
and Christ (cf. 2:22-36). Repentance is a human responsibility — something
we are commanded to do. But it is also the gift of God — repentance is possible only by God's enabling (cf. 3:26; 5:31; 11:18).[86]

The command to *'be baptised, every one of you, in the name of Jesus Christ'*
expresses the positive side of repentance, involving a calling upon him for
salvation and allegiance to him as Lord and Messiah.[87] Water baptism was
offered by John the Baptist as a sign of repentance, 'for the forgiveness of
sins' (Lk. 3:3; cf. Mt. 3:1-6; Mk. 1:4). John was preparing Israel for the com-

---

83. Witherington 1998, 153 note 89, outlines the use of such terminology in the LXX.

84. R. C. Tannehill, *The Shape of Luke's Story: Essays on Luke-Acts* (Eugene: Cascade,
2005), 169, observes that the readers of Acts are not directly addressed in the mission
speeches in Acts: 'rather, readers are allowed to overhear skilled interpreters of the gospel
addressing a particular audience in a particular situation of the past.'

85. Cf. J. Behm, *TDNT* 4:989-99. The NT, like the Jewish Hellenistic writings, really
expresses the Hebrew notion of 'turning' or 'returning' to the Lord (*šûḇ*) by *metanoein* ('to repent') and *metanoia* ('repentance'). It is totally inadequate to represent Peter's call to repentance as 'feel sorry' or 'change your mind' or 'do penance'. Nothing less than 'convert' or
'be converted' will do (Behm, 999-1000). Cf. J. Goetzmann, *NIDNTT* 1:357-59. Note how
'turning' to God *(epistrephein)* is closely associated with repentance in 3:19 and 26:20, making it quite clear that a radical reorientation of life towards God is intended.

86. Cf. Tannehill, *Shape*, 84-101.

87. Barrett 1994, 153-54, observes that the call to repent is in the plural and 'is presumably addressed to the whole house of Israel (v. 35)', but the call to be baptized is in the
singular *(baptisthētō)* and 'is specifically directed to the individual members of the crowd'.

ing of the Messiah and his baptism with the Holy Spirit (Lk. 3:16; cf. Mt. 3:11; Mk. 1:7-8). He also clearly associated the Messiah's coming with the fulfillment of scriptural promises about a definitive forgiveness of sins in the end time (e.g., Je. 31:34; Ezk. 36:25). When Jesus was raised from death, he declared that forgiveness could be preached in his name to all nations (Lk. 24:47; cf. Jn. 20:23), and subsequently poured out the promised Holy Spirit on his disciples. So Peter proclaimed that what John had been preparing for was now available for all to enjoy. There are similarities and differences between the baptism of John and baptism *in the name of Jesus*. Like the Baptist, Peter calls upon his fellow Israelites to be baptized *'for the forgiveness of your sins'* (*eis aphesin tōn hamartiōn hymōn*; cf. Lk. 3:3; Acts 22:16). But he does this with the certainty that such forgiveness is a present possibility because of the Messiah's death, resurrection, and ascension. In the apostolic preaching, the offer of forgiveness is directly linked with repentance towards God and faith in Jesus as the Christ (cf. 3:19-20; 5:31; 10:43; 13:38-39). Baptism is not always explicitly mentioned in this connection. It is regularly associated with commitment to Christ, but it is not a rite that can secure the blessings of salvation apart from genuine repentance and faith. Christian baptism is virtually defined as being *in the name of Jesus Christ* (cf. 10:48). This expression may suggest that the person being baptized actually called upon Jesus as Lord and Christ, as a way of confessing faith in him (cf. 22:16).[88] The *name* of Jesus represents his divine authority and power to grant the blessing of the Spirit and to save people from the coming judgment through the forgiveness of sins (cf. Jl. 2:32; Acts 4:12; 5:31; 10:43; 13:38). At the human level, calling upon Jesus as Lord and Messiah is essentially what makes a person a Christian (cf. Rom. 10:9-10).

Water baptism is closely connected with the bestowal of the Spirit in 2:38 (*'And you will receive the gift of the Holy Spirit'*). But the link cannot be pressed too strongly since the gift of the Spirit sometimes precedes and sometimes follows water baptism in other contexts (cf. 8:12, 14-17; 9:17-18; 10:44-48; 19:5-6).[89] The expression *gift of the Holy Spirit* recalls Jesus' promise to those who pray (Lk. 11:13; cf. Acts 8:20; 10:45; 11:17). Christian baptism can be regarded as a means of prayer to God for the gift of his Spirit. But note that the *gift* consists of the Spirit himself and that this gift is to be distinguished from the gifts which the Spirit imparts (cf. 1 Cor. 12:7-11). In

---

88. Cf. Bruce 1990, 129. *epi* ('in') is the reading of some MSS and is the more unusual preposition in such a context. *en* ('in') is found in other MSS and in 10:48, where there is no variant. *epi* is the harder reading, and *en* is more likely to be a scribal change. The more common expression is *eis to onoma* ('into the name'; cf. 8:16; 19:5; Mt. 28:19; 1 Cor 1:13, 15), where *eis* may have a final or a causal sense. L. Hartman, 'Into the Name of Jesus', *NTS* 20 (1973-74), 432-40, argues from Semitic usage that *eis to onoma tou Iēsou* means 'with reference to Jesus'. Cf. J. A. Ziesler, 'The Name of Jesus in the Acts of the Apostles', *JSNT* 4 (1979), 28-32.

89. Peter's preaching at Pentecost should be understood as being 'theologically normative for the relation in Acts between conversion, water baptism and the baptism of the Holy Spirit', whereas later incidents are more historically conditioned and should be 'circumstantially understood' (Longenecker 1981, 285).

Acts 2:38-39 this gift is closely associated with the idea of calling upon Christ for salvation. In other words, the Spirit is not simply given to equip believers for service but to make possible the sort of transformed relationship with God promised in passages such as Isaiah 32:15-17; 44:2-5; Ezekiel 11:19-20; 36:26-27 (cf. Je. 31:31-34). The Spirit is given to minister the benefits of Jesus' saving work to believers, individually and corporately, and to make possible the conversion of others.[90] We see the practical effect of all this in the life of the early church, as illustrated in 2:42-47.

39 *'The promise'* is most obviously the promise of the Spirit about which Jesus spoke during his earthly ministry (cf. Lk. 24:49; Acts 1:4). More generally, however, God's promise in Acts means his covenant commitment to Abraham and the patriarchs of Israel (7:17; 26:6; cf. 3:25). This finds its consummation in the sending of the Messiah (13:23, 32), who pours out the promised Holy Spirit on his disciples (2:33). Luke seems to share Paul's equation of 'the blessing given to Abraham' with the gift of the Spirit (Gal. 3:14). 'Implicit here, therefore, is the thought of the Spirit as the new covenant fulfillment of the ancient covenant promise.'[91] The expression *'for you and your children and for all who are far off'* develops Joel's promise of the Spirit being poured out 'on all people' (Jl. 2:28-29). God's covenant mercies were for Peter's Jewish audience and for their descendants (*for you and your children;* cf. Gn. 13:15; 17:7-9; Acts 13:32-33).[92] They were also for Jews scattered throughout the whole world (*for all who are far off*). This allusion to Isaiah 57:19 could be taken to include the Gentiles, since they were soon to share the benefits of the New Covenant (cf. Acts 22:21; Eph. 2:13, 17 applying Is. 57:19 to Gentiles). However, given Luke's 'geographical approach to history writing and the telling of the story of the early church', the most probable reference in this early context is to 'Jews in distant lands'.[93] The final description of the people for whom the promise is made recalls the last clause of Joel 2:32 (not quoted in Acts 2:21). The blessings of salvation will be *'for all whom the Lord our God will call'.* People everywhere must call on the name of the Lord for deliverance, but he must first *call* them and enable them to respond to his gracious initiative.

40 When Luke says, *With many other words he warned them,* it is a reminder that the sermon as we have it is an abbreviated version of what was

90. Turner, *Power*, 352-60, argues against the view that the Spirit is simply a *donum superadditum* — an additional gift for mission proclamation — and contends that the Spirit is given as an element of the salvation promised. Cf. THE THEOLOGY OF ACTS: III. THE HOLY SPIRIT (pp. 60-65).

91. Dunn, *Baptism*, 47. Cf. Barrett 1994, 155.

92. The possibility of children being included in later household baptisms is discussed in connection with 16:15, 31-34; 18:8.

93. Witherington 1998, 155-56. Acts 10 shows that Peter needed some persuading before he could go to the house of a Gentile and preach the gospel to him. However, his statement in 3:26 that God sent his servant to bless Israel *first* implies some awareness that the Gentiles will somehow benefit from the messianic salvation. The issues for Peter must have been 'how' and 'under what conditions'.

said. Indeed, if about three thousand were added to their number that day
(v. 41), it is possible that preaching of this kind continued in various contexts throughout the day. *Warned (diemartyrato)* is literally 'testified', indicating that proclamation of the facts about Jesus was accompanied by persuasive argument and exhortation (*and he pleaded with them*; cf. 8:25; 10:42;
18:5; 20:21, 23, 24; 23:11; 28:23). Peter's appeal (*'Save yourselves'*) picks up
the language of v. 21, where salvation from the coming judgment of God is
meant (v. 20).[94] NKJV more accurately renders the Greek passive (*sōthēte*),
'be saved', which implies that salvation is the action of God in the lives of
those who repent and believe. But salvation *'from this corrupt generation'*
points to the need for rescue from something more immediate. In order to
escape from the judgment of God, Peter's audience needed to be rescued
from the corrupting and damning influence of their society. This recalls the
charge of Jesus that his *generation* was unbelieving, perverse (Lk. 7:31-35;
9:41), and wicked (11:29-32). They followed the trend of previous generations, who rejected God's messengers (11:50-52; 17:25) and effectively
killed the one sent to them by God (Acts 2:22-23; cf. 3:13-15; 7:51-53). But
the need for salvation from *this corrupt generation* (*tēs geneas tēs skolias tautēs*;
cf. Phil. 2:15; 1 Pet. 2:18) should not simply be linked with the recent events
in Jerusalem.[95] The wider use of this terminology suggests that people in
general need to be saved 'because they are part of one of the many generations that have failed or is presently failing before God and thus constitute
corrupt humanity'.[96] Those who want to be saved from the judgment of
God need to distance themselves from their generation and identify with
Jesus and his cause. As in v. 39, there are echoes of Joel 2:32, with its promise that a remnant would be delivered from the catastrophe about to over-
take the mass of the people. Even though Peter's message was to Israel, it
was effectively a call to come out from among them and be separate (cf. Is.
52:11). The implication is that the disciples were the believing remnant of
Israel or, more precisely, the nucleus of a renewed Israel. Later generations

94. Cf. THE THEOLOGY OF ACTS: IV. SALVATION (pp. 65-70). Note the inclusion
formed between v. 40 and v. 47 by the use of the expression 'those who were being saved' in
the latter.

95. *genea* ('generation') can refer to 'those exhibiting common characteristics or interests, *race, kind*', or 'the sum total of those born at the same time, expanded to include all
those living at a given time and freq. defined in terms of specific characteristics, *generation,
contemporaries*', or more generally 'the time of a generation, *age*' (BDAG). In the LXX, *skolios*
('corrupt') expresses 'the nature of the man who does not walk in the straightness and up-
rightness which God has ordained for him but who in a way which is guilty and worthy of
punishment is crooked, cramped, distorted and hence corrupt' (G. Bertram, *TDNT* 7:406).

96. C. Stenschke, 'The Need for Salvation', in I. H. Marshall and D. Peterson (eds.),
Witness to the Gospel: The Theology of Acts (Grand Rapids/Cambridge: Eerdmans, 1998), 140.
Stenschke, 135-40, reviews the use of 'generation' language in Luke-Acts and discusses OT
parallels. Bruce 1990, 130-31, notes the specific use of such language in connection with the
generation of Israelites that came out of Egypt in Dt. 1:35; 32:5; Ps. 78 (LXX 77):8, and in later
Jewish literature. Sin is treated as a universal problem in Acts, requiring salvation for Jews
and Gentiles alike.

have not had the same opportunity to see and hear Christ directly. But it remains true that people in every age need to take a stand against their generation in its rejection of Jesus and his message. They need to know about the consequence of persisting in unbelief and rebellion against God. Authentic gospel proclamation will communicate the challenge to take this step and 'be saved' from the approaching judgment of God by calling upon the name of Jesus for deliverance (cf. 1 Thes. 1:9-10; 2 Thes. 1:5-10). The following verse explains how that salvation was appropriated by a very large number of Jews in Jerusalem and how the Spirit united them in a new fellowship of commitment and care.

C. The Community Created by the Spirit (2:41-47)

Acts 2 finishes with a portrait of the first Christian church, suggesting that 'the gift of the Spirit brought about a community which realized the highest aspirations of human longing: unity, peace, joy and the praise of God'.[97] The narrative shifts from description of particular events on a particular day to a general description of the inner life of the Jerusalem church. Many of the same details are recorded in a different order and in an expanded form in 4:32-37 and 5:12-16. These summary passages have several functions in the narrative. First, they indicate how growth and development progressively took place through the preaching of the gospel and the work of the Holy Spirit. Secondly, they highlight the fact that God was building a new community and not simply dealing with individuals in isolation. Thirdly, they suggest that Luke was presenting something of an 'apology' for this group, shaping the response of his readers from the beginning of Acts. While disarming any criticism that might rise from subsequent episodes, Luke was also commending the positive example of the earliest community of Christians to his readers.[98] This was not a breakaway movement from Judaism, but the true Israel, where his Spirit was powerfully at

97. Johnson 1992, 62. Johnson notes parallels with the sort of 'foundation story' that was rather widespread in Hellenistic literature and suggests that Luke was commending Christianity to Hellenistic readers by the way he worded the summary in 2:41-47. However, Johnson, 61, also notes that in this work of the Spirit we are shown 'the realization of the restored people of God within historic Judaism'. Cf. B. Capper, 'Reciprocity and the Ethic of Acts', in Marshall and Peterson, *Witness to the Gospel*, 499-518.

98. Cf. M. C. Parsons, 'Christian Origins and Narrative Openings: The Sense of a Beginning in Acts 1–5', *Review and Expositor* 87, no. 3 (1990), 404-22; M. A. Co, 'The Major Summaries in Acts: Acts 2.42-47; 4.32-35; 5.12-16: Linguistic and Literary Relationship', *EphThLov* 68 (1992), 49-85; Barrett 1994, 160-61. To suggest that Luke is simply generalizing from his own time, rather than using historical sources, is to miss the primitive nature of the community life portrayed in Acts 2–5. Witherington 1998, 157-60, makes an important distinction between summary passages and summary statements in Acts, with the latter explaining the growth of Christian communities more generally and the former dealing with the interior life of the church in Jerusalem in the earliest chapters.

work, fulfilling God's end-time promises. With its unity and joyful sharing, it also fulfilled certain ideals of the Hellenistic world, which would have been appealing to Gentile readers.[99] Luke does not hide its weaknesses (cf. 5:1-10; 6:1), but he implies that the church in Jerusalem was a model of what could happen when people were bound together by a belief in the gospel, an understanding of its implications, and an enjoyment of its blessings. Elsewhere, he touches only on aspects of what believers did when they met together, or emphasizes historical events to which the activities of a gathering were something of a backdrop (e.g., 13:2; 20:7-11).

41 A new section of the narrative is indicated in the Greek — but not adequately by TNIV — describing the response to Peter's preaching: 'Those then (*hoi men oun;* cf. 1:6 note) who accepted his message were baptised.'[100] Luke further indicates that *about three thousand were added to their number that day* (numerical increase is noted again in 2:47; 4:4; 5:14; 6:1, 7). The population of Jerusalem at the time is estimated to have been between 180,000 and 200,000. Even 3,000 converts in the temple precincts would have been 'a distinct minority of the crowd'.[101] Nevertheless, it is extraordinary evidence of the convicting work of the Spirit, through the testimony of Christ's witnesses (cf. Jn. 16:8-11), that so many should have been brought to repentance and faith at one time. Presumably, mass baptisms took place over a period of days. There was an ample supply of water in Jerusalem, especially at the pools of Bethesda and Siloam, though some of these baptisms may have taken place elsewhere. The 120 disciples were the nucleus of a new community within Judaism, the first recipients of the eschatological blessings promised by God to all Israel.[102] What they had to offer was rightly the inheritance of every Jew: the fulfillment of God's ancient promises. When others *'accepted'* their message and were *'baptised'*, they could experience the same blessings in the fellowship of the messianic community (cf. v. 47). The flow of the narrative suggests that every aspect of their new life was then brought about by the Holy Spirit.

42 Some commentators regard the four elements specified here as a

---

99. Cf. D. Seccombe, *Possessions and the Poor in Luke-Acts,* SNTSU (Linz: Fuchs, 1983), 200-218; Johnson 1992, 61-63. Seccombe, 207, argues from the use of *koinōnia* in Hellenistic literature that Luke's description of the common life, meals, and material sharing of the Jerusalem church was designed 'to commend Christianity, or perhaps the church itself, to people for whom *koinōnia* was a supreme virtue'.

100. Cf. Barrett 1994, 159. The connective *oun* is represented in other EVV by 'then' or 'so'.

101. Witherington 1998, 156. Cf. J. Jeremias, *Jerusalem in the Time of Jesus: An Investigation into Economic and Social Conditions during the New Testament Period* (ET, London: SCM, 1969), 83.

102. In 24:5, 14; 28:22 they are called a 'sect' *(hairesis)* by others, comparable with the Pharisees or Sadducees (cf. 5:17; 15:5; 26:5). But that is not the way Christians speak about themselves in Acts. Cf. Seccombe, *Possessions,* 215-18. In most MSS, the word *ekklēsia* ('church') is first used to describe this community in 5:11. However, Western texts introduce *ekklēsia* into the text of v. 47, and for this reason 'church' is found in the KJV translation of that verse.

primitive liturgical sequence, implying that their meetings regularly involved instruction, (table) fellowship, then the Lord's Supper and
prayers.[103] However, vv. 44-47 appear to be an expansion on this initial
summary, and some of the things mentioned there clearly took place at different times and in different places. Luke is giving a description of the ministry of these disciples to one another in a variety of contexts, not simply
telling us what happened when they gathered for what we might call
'church'. They first of all *devoted themselves (ēsan proskarterountes) to the apostles' teaching*.[104] Meeting together in the temple courts (v. 46) appears to
have been for the express purpose of hearing the apostolic preaching (cf.
3:11-26; 5:21), though doubtless there were also opportunities for teaching
in the home context.[105] We may surmise that these earliest converts desired
to be encouraged in their faith but also to identify with the public preaching of the gospel to their fellow Israelites as an act of testimony to its truthfulness. Apostolic instruction continued to be at the centre of church life
later in Gentile contexts (e.g., 11:25-26; 18:11; 19:9-10; 20:7-12, 20-21, 28-32;
28:30-31).

Secondly, they devoted themselves *to the fellowship (tē koinōnia)*. The
koinōn- words in Greek normally mean 'to share with someone in something' above and beyond the relationship itself, or 'to give someone a share
in something'.[106] The sharing in this case could simply refer to material
blessings, as described in vv. 44-45, where we are told that the believers had
everything in *common (koina)*. Yet this sharing was clearly a practical expression of the new relationship experienced together through a common
faith in Christ (cf. vv. 38-41). This is affirmed in 4:32, where a similar state-

103. So J. Jeremias, *The Eucharistic Words of Jesus* (ET, London: SCM; Philadelphia:
Trinity, 1966), 118-22, followed by I. H. Marshall, *Luke: Historian and Theologian* (Exeter: Paternoster, 1970), 204-6; 1980, 83. Haenchen 1971, 191, argues strongly against this position,
asserting that 'the activities paired with *kai* probably represent detached and self-contained
units'. Cf. C. F. D. Moule, *Worship in the New Testament*, Ecumenical Studies in Worship 9
(London: Lutterworth, 1961), 18-19.

104. *proskarterountes* normally means 'to occupy oneself diligently with something',
'to pay persistent attention to', 'to hold fast to something', or 'continually to be in' (it is used
in the last sense in 2:46). Cf. W. Grundmann, *TDNT* 3:618. Luke uses the same verb to describe the devotion of the 120 to prayer (1:14) and the resolve of the apostles to occupy
themselves with prayer and the ministry of the word (6:4). The periphrastic construction in
2:42 (with the imperfect indicative *ēsan* and the present participle *proskarterountes*) stresses
the ongoing nature of this activity. Johnson 1992, 58, translates 'constant in their attention'.
The verb applies to the four nouns in the dative case that follow, though the Greek connectives put them in pairs: 'to the apostles' teaching and to fellowship, to the breaking of bread
and to the prayers.'

105. Barrett 1994, 163, rightly argues that the teaching of the apostles 'cannot be
sharply or consistently distinguished from their preaching'.

106. Cf. F. Hauck, *TDNT* 3:804-9. Originally a commercial term, *koinōnia* is used in a
number of NT contexts to refer to the joint participation of believers in Christ (e.g., 1 Cor.
1:9) or the Holy Spirit (e.g., 2 Cor. 13:13) or their share in the demands and blessings of the
gospel (e.g., Phil. 1:5). Common participation in Christ necessarily leads to a mutual fellowship among members of the Christian community (e.g., 1 Jn. 1:3).

ment about having 'all things common' *(hapanta koina)* is prefaced by the words 'All the believers were one in heart and mind'. That relationship brought a certain sense of responsibility to one another. The sharing of goods came to include the distribution of food to the needy in their midst (cf. 6:1-2) and was certainly not restricted to formal gatherings of the believers. It may be best, therefore, to give *koinōnia* its widest interpretation in 2:42, including within its scope 'contributions, table fellowship, and the general friendship and unity which characterized the community'.[107]

They also devoted themselves *to the breaking of bread*, which most obviously refers to the common meals shared by the earliest disciples in their homes (v. 46). Some scholars have argued that the expression in v. 42 is a technical term for the Lord's Supper and that this was already separated from their ordinary meals.[108] However, the term describes the initiation of an ordinary meal in the Jewish fashion of breaking a loaf with the hands and giving thanks to God (e.g., Lk. 9:16; 22:19; 24:30, 35; Acts 27:35 note). To 'break bread' was to eat together.[109] The adoption of this term as a title for the Lord's Supper is not formally attested until the second century AD (cf. *Did.* 14.1; Ignatius, *Eph.* 20.2). When Luke mentions in v. 46 that they were 'breaking bread in their homes', he goes right on to say (literally), 'they were partaking of food' *(metelambanon trophēs)*. What is the ground for giving the expression a different meaning in v. 42? The reality of Christian fellowship was expressed from the earliest times in the ordinary activity of eating together. But these meals were doubtless given a special character by the fact that they were associated with teaching, prayer, and praise. They ate together *with glad and sincere hearts* (v. 46), and this gladness issued in *praising God* (v. 47). Perhaps as they gave thanks for their food they focussed also on the person and work of the Lord Jesus, reminding one another of the basis of their fellowship in him. In this way, a meal could be given the same sort of significance that Paul ascribed to the community suppers at Corinth (1 Cor. 10:16-17; 11:17-34).[110]

107. Seccombe, *Possessions*, 204. Cf. D. G. Peterson, *Engaging with God: A Biblical Theology of Worship* (Leicester: Apollos; Grand Rapids: Eerdmans, 1992), 153-55; Co, 'Major Summaries', 70-71; Barrett 1994, 163-64.

108. Jeremias, *Eucharistic Words*, 120-21, takes 'the fellowship' of 2:42 to refer to the fellowship meal (called the Agape) and 'the breaking of bread' to refer to 'the Eucharist', which had become separated from the meal proper. However, this is an illegitimate narrowing of the meaning of *koinōnia* in the context. Cf. Peterson, *Engaging*, 155-57, 215-18.

109. Cf. J. Behm, *TDNT* 3:728-30. He argues that 2:42, 46 'has nothing to do with the liturgical celebration of the Lord's Supper' (731), but says that the meal in 20:11 'within the context of the Pauline mission' must be the cultic meal described by Paul as the Lord's Supper in 1 Cor. 11:20. It is not likely, however, that Luke would use the same expression in two different ways like this.

110. Cf. Moule, *Worship*, 20-21; Spencer 1997, 39-40. Moule rightly argues that 'it is not in the words "the breaking of the loaf", but in their context that one must look if one is to detect any further significance in what the Christians did together at their meals'.

Finally, they devoted themselves 'to the prayers' *(tais proseuchais)*. The plural form with the article in Greek suggests that the reference is to specific 'prayers' (KJV, NRSV, ESV) rather than to prayer in general (TNIV *to prayer*). In the context, this most obviously points to their continuing participation in the set times of prayer at the temple (cf. 3:1 note). However, since their eating together in households involved *praising God* (v. 47), they doubtless also prayed together in these groups, petitioning God about their own needs and the needs of others. Prayer was certainly an important part of their community life (e.g., 4:31) and of apostolic leadership (e.g., 6:4).

43 The apostolic preaching and the response it generated (vv. 41-42) had an ongoing effect in Jerusalem: *Everyone was filled with awe (egineto de pasē psychē phobos*, 'and fear came upon every soul'; cf. 5:5, 11). This clause, with its use of the imperfect tense *(egineto)*, suggests 'an enduring sense of awe inspired by the consciousness that God was at work in their midst, so that they were witnesses of the final drama, and indeed participants in it'.[111] Moreover, *many wonders and miraculous signs (polla de terata kai sēmeia) were done (egineto) by the apostles*. By such means, God confirmed the teaching and the special status of the apostles in his plan and purpose (cf. 4:30; 5:12; 14:3; 15:12). Apart from Jesus, the only other persons who are said to do 'signs and wonders' in Acts are Stephen and Philip (6:8; 8:13). Such mighty works were signs of the approaching 'day of the Lord' (cf. vv. 19-20) and were an indication of the close connection between these individuals and Jesus (cf. v. 22). Signs and wonders were particularly performed *by the apostles,* as Christ's agents.[112] A notable example follows in 3:1-10, where it is made clear that the healing was achieved 'in the name of Jesus Christ of Nazareth' (3:6; cf. 3:12-16).[113]

44-45 The unity of *the believers* is stressed in two ways here. Firstly, we are told that they were *together (epi to auto;* cf. 2:1 note). They met together regularly in the ways defined by Luke, without actually living together (cf. vv. 46-47). Secondly, we are told that they *had everything in common (eichon hapanta koina).*[114] The explanation of this clause is found in v. 45. The imperfect tense is used with both verbs *(epipraskon . . . diemerizon)*, indicating the regular practice of the community (reinforced by the particle *an)*: they were 'selling' *property and possessions (ta ktēmata kai tas hyparxeis)* and

---

Witherington 1998, 161 note 115, considers the social significance of this portrait of the Jerusalem church.

111. Bruce 1990, 132. 'Everyone' *(pasē psychē)* is a hyperbolic way of referring to nonbelievers in Jerusalem (contrast 'all the believers', v. 44). On the variation in the MS tradition in v. 43, which does not change the sense of the verse, cf. Metzger, *Textual Commentary*, 262.

112. Cf. THE THEOLOGY OF ACTS: VIII. MIRACLES (pp. 83-87).

113. Co, 'Major Summaries', 62-63, 69-70, argues that 2:43 and 5:1-11 form an inclusion, framing 3:1–5:10.

114. The Greek expression *hapanta koina* (cf. 4:32) recalls the proverb widely quoted in Hellenistic literature that 'friends hold all things in common'. Against Johnson 1992, 59, who argues that it was 'a feature of utopian visions of society', Seccombe, *Possessions*, 202, claims that the proverb had 'broken free of its Platonic connection to express in a general and imaginative way the openness and sharing of friends'.

they were 'distributing' the proceeds *to anyone who had need (pasin kathoti an tis chreian eichen,* 'as any had need'). Their behaviour appears to have been a response to the teaching of Jesus in passages such as Luke 12:33-34; 18:22. The word *ktēmata* often means property in the sense of land (5:1; cf. 5:3, 8). Another general term for possessions *(hyparxeis)* is also used, literally meaning 'the things that belong (to someone)'.[115] It is important to note that this sharing of possessions was voluntary and occasional. Their needs were related to the physical and social environment in which they found themselves. Their progressive isolation from unbelieving Israel must have made the economic situation of many quite precarious. Here was no primitive form of 'communism', but a generous response to particular problems in their midst (cf. 4:34-5). The examples given in 4:37; 5:4 show that people did not necessarily dispose of their whole estate but only certain portions of it. Believers continued to maintain their own homes and used them for the benefit of others in the church (cf. 12:12). There was no rule about the common ownership of property such as was found among the men of the council of the Qumran Community. What appeared to motivate such generosity was a sense of God's grace towards them, as indicated in the following verses.

46-47 The expression *every day (kath' hēmeran)* is in the emphatic position, at the beginning of the first sentence (vv. 46-47a). The same Greek expression is also found in the second sentence (v. 47b), where it is translated *daily.* In this way Luke stresses the regularity of all the events he records here. When he says that *they continued to meet together (proskarterountes homothymadon),* he uses the verb found in v. 42 ('devoted') and the adverb employed in 1:14; 4:24; 5:12 ('together') to stress the degree to which they were committed to practical expressions of their common life. One of their venues was *the temple courts,* where large groups could gather.[116] Solomon's Colonnade, which ran along the east side of the outer court, is twice mentioned as the place where they actually met (3:11; 5:12). The purpose of such gatherings was considered in the comments on v. 42. They also *broke bread in their homes (kat' oikon,* 'by households', cf. 20:20), which is then explained in terms of eating together (cf. v. 42 note) *with glad and sincere hearts.* Their *gladness* was doubtless motivated by more than the provision of daily needs. They were aware that God was at work in their midst in a new way and that they were enjoying the benefits of the messianic salvation (the

---

115. Cf. F. Selter, *NIDNTT* 2:845-47. The word *hosoi* is introduced into v. 45 by Western MSS, giving the reading *'as many as* had possessions or goods sold them'. This was apparently to give the impression that not all were property owners. Codex D also removes *kath' hēmeran* ('daily') from v. 46 and attaches it to *diemerizon* ('to give to, distribute'), to suggest that there was a daily distribution. For other variations in the Western text of vv. 45-47, cf. Metzger, *Textual Commentary,* 263-65.

116. *en tō hierō* refers to the whole temple complex rather than to the sanctuary itself. Cf. W. von Meding, *NIDNTT* 3:781-85. *naos* ('sanctuary') is used in Lk. 1:9, 21-22; 23:45; Acts 7:48; 17:24; 19:24.

same noun *agalliasis* and the related verb are used in Lk. 1:14, 44, 47; 10:21; Acts 2:26; 16:34). The phrase translated *sincere hearts (aphelotēti kardias)* occurs only here in the Greek Bible. But there is a related expression in Ephesians 6:5 and Colossians 3:22 ('with sincerity of heart'; cf. 1 Chr. 29:17; Wis. 1:1).[117] God's kindness to these believers bound them wholeheartedly to himself and to one another in a fellowship of generous self-giving. They expressed their gladness and devotion to God by constantly *praising* him and caring for one another.

The TNIV translation of the next clause is similar to that of other EVV: *enjoying the favour of all the people (echontes charin pros holon ton laon)*. This fits in with other passages describing the positive reception the earliest Christians received from the people of Jerusalem (cf. 4:21; 5:13-16, 26), as distinct from the attitude of the authorities. It also ties in with the following clause in v. 47, since those who were well disposed to the apostolic community are more likely to have believed their message and joined them. However, it is possible to translate the Greek 'having goodwill towards all the people',[118] which would be appropriate to the context. The believers continued to express gratitude to God and were favourably disposed towards everyone else in Jerusalem (as regularly in the LXX, *laos* is used of the people of Israel). Their gracious attitude was a significant factor in the turning of many more to Jesus as Lord and Christ. In the process of what is often called 'church growth', Luke highlights both the behaviour of believers and the sovereign determination of God. As the message of salvation was proclaimed and disciples testified to its truth in every facet of their lives, *the Lord added to their number daily those who were being saved*. Identifying new converts as *those who were being saved*,[119] Luke recalls Joel's promise (v. 21) and Peter's plea (v. 40). An increasing number of people in Jerusalem were saved because they turned to the Lord Jesus in repentance and faith. In that God-ordained response to the gospel, *the Lord* himself (the ascended Lord of v. 36) was continuing to draw people into the fellowship of his church *(added to their number)*.[120]

---

117. Barrett 1994, 158, renders the expression in Acts 2:46 *'simplicity* of heart', but Bruce 1990, 133, thinks that the context points more specifically to the meaning 'generosity'. Johnson 1992, 59, observes that the adjective is apparently related to *haplotēs*, 'which has the sense of simplicity and generosity, as opposed to double-mindedness and grudging envy (see Luke 11:34; Rom. 12:8; 2 Cor. 8:2; 9:11, 13; Eph. 6:5; Col. 3:22 and Jas. 1:5)'.

118. Cf. T. D. Andersen, 'The Meaning of ECHONTES CHARIN PROS in Acts 2:47', *NTS* 34 (1988), 604-10, shows how *charin pros* occurs six times in Josephus and three times in Philo with the accusative and in every case the object of *pros* is the person towards whom *charin* is directed. He also argues that the lexicons give virtually no support for *pros* with the accusative having the meaning 'from' or 'with' (TNIV *of all the people*).

119. The force of the present participle *tous sōzomenous* is probably iterative, suggesting that they were added to the church *as* they were being saved. Nothing in the context suggests that salvation is viewed as a process.

120. The expression *to their number* translates the phrase *epi to auto* ('together'; cf. 1:15; 2:1, 44; 4:26). Codex D adds *en tē ekklēsia* ('to the church') as an explanatory phrase, and

Believers in every age have much to learn from Luke's account of the coming of the Spirit at Pentecost, the preaching of Peter about the Lord Jesus, and the fellowship and ministry of the first Christians in Jerusalem. However, it is not legitimate to argue that these experiences should be simply replicated in the life of every believer or contemporary church. Acts 2 is a narrative about the historic fulfillment of God's covenant promises to Israel by the renewal of his people in Jerusalem. Luke is highlighting the faithfulness of God and outlining the way salvation was provided for believing Israelites by Messiah Jesus. That theme continues in Acts 3–7, until the persecution following Stephen's death leads to the proclamation of the gospel in Samaria and beyond. As the story unfolds, we see how the gospel has its effect in different cultures. The Spirit progressively brings diverse groups to share in the New Covenant blessings first experienced by repentant and believing Israelites in Jerusalem. Although the pattern of fulfillment is never the same again, there is no suggestion in Acts of a decline from an idealised primitive community.

D. A Particular Sign of the Messianic Restoration (3:1-26)

Luke begins to illustrate one of the points made in his preceding summary (2:42-47) by recording a notable miracle and its sequel.[1] On one of their daily visits to the temple (2:46), Peter and John brought healing to a man crippled from birth. Although a later passage repeats that 'the apostles performed many miraculous signs and wonders among the people' (5:12; cf. 2:43; 4:30; 5:15-16), the healing in 3:1-10 is the only detailed account of such activity in Jerusalem. The narrative stresses the suddenness and completeness of the cure, together with the wonder and amazement of the bystanders (cf. 2:43). In the speech that follows, this miracle is attributed to the glorified Lord Jesus (3:11-26; cf. 2:14-40), whose identity is then proclaimed in terms of the fulfillment of various Scriptures. The audience is challenged to repent and turn to God for forgiveness, especially acknowledging their part in the death of Jesus. As Peter speaks of the Christ bringing about the promised restoration of all things, it becomes clear that the physical healing of the lame man is a sign of the messianic salvation in all its dimensions (3:11-26; cf. 4:9-12). With the offer of this salvation comes also a warning about continuing to reject Jesus and thus being cut off from 'the people' (3:22-23). The positive result of this proclamation is that many more in Jeru-

---

other MSS employ it as a substitute (hence the KJV translation). Cf. Metzger, *Textual Commentary*, 264-65. Whatever the understanding of the early copyists, *epi to auto* appears to be used by Luke in a semitechnical way for the community of disciples formed by Jesus in the course of his earthly ministry and subsequently expanded through the preaching of the gospel. Pentecost was not 'the birthday of the church'!

1. Witherington 1998, 165-73, has an excellent note on Luke's use of sources according to his own intentions in the composition of Acts.

salem are added to the number of the disciples (4:4; cf. 2:47). But the incident also introduces a narrative of opposition, stretching to 5:42.

Peter and John are arrested by the authorities and are brought before the Sanhedrin (4:1-22), where they are charged not to speak any longer in the name of Jesus. This subsection ends as it began, with a reference to the healing and its effect on the people of Jerusalem (4:21-22; cf. 4:1-3). The prayer that follows is a response to the threats of the Sanhedrin (4:23-31). The apostles are later re-arrested and tried concerning their right to teach in the name of Jesus (5:17-42). All this takes place with constant reference to the name of Jesus and its authority (cf. 3:6, 16; 4:7, 10, 12, 17, 18, 30; 5:28, 40, 41).[2] Spencer notes that there is a 'private house interlude' in 4:23–5:11, before another temple narrative occurs (5:12-41). As opposition from the temple authorities develops, 'the apostles find succour and fresh empowerment in a private, prayerful gathering with "their own (friends)" (4:23)'.[3]

Also prominent in these chapters is the proclamation of salvation through Jesus, suggesting that Acts 2–5 provides 'an exposition, in narrative and characters' commentary, of the promise that "everyone who calls on the name of the Lord will be saved"'.[4] As in Acts 2, the preaching about Jesus that brings mass conversions is shown to be the means by which God's end-time restoration of Israel takes place, even though it brings serious division among the people. Tannehill makes an interesting observation about the significance of this development for understanding Acts as a whole: 'although Jesus' witnesses face other conflicts, the central conflict of the plot, repeatedly emphasized and still present in the last major scene of Acts, is a conflict within Judaism provoked by Jewish Christian preachers (including Paul). Acts 2:1–8:3 traces the development of this conflict in Jerusalem.'[5]

1. Healing in the Name of Jesus (3:1-10)

This miracle story is similar in style and structure to many in the Gospels, particularly Jesus' healing of the paralytic in Luke 5:17-26. A dire need is identified and met by Jesus, in this case the risen Lord working through the agency of Peter and John. Wonder and amazement are then expressed by all who perceive what has happened. Something of the theological significance of the healing is revealed in Acts 3:8-9 by the use of language recalling Isaiah

---

2. Tannehill 1990, 40, observes that 'the "name" of Jesus represents his royal power and authority, which is invoked by his subjects'.

3. Spencer 1997, 42. Spencer observes that the dynamic centre of messianic worship becomes the house-church situation. In Acts 3–5 a *spatial* antithesis between public temple and private house accompanies a *social* conflict between temple authorities and church leaders.

4. Tannehill 1990, 31, with reference to Jl. 2:32a, as cited in Acts 2:21.

5. Tannehill 1990, 34.

35:6. It is a sign that the promised messianic salvation is available to be enjoyed in the present, in anticipation of the universal restoration that Jesus
will accomplish on his return (3:20-21). A particular feature of this incident
is the offer of healing to the man before he requests it, illustrating the way
God's provision of forgiveness and the Holy Spirit comes to those in need of
salvation (2:27-29; 10:43-46). The promise of healing is the basis on which
the challenge to believe is given and restoration is experienced (3:6-7).[6]

1 TNIV begins this narrative in a decisive way *(One day)*, whereas
the best Greek MSS simply link it with the preceding summary passage by
means of a loose connective *(de,* 'and').[7] *Peter and John* now become the focus of Luke's attention for two chapters, with Peter generally appearing as
spokesman for the two. John the son of Zebedee (Lk. 5:10), who was one of
the Twelve chosen by Jesus (Lk. 6:14), is most obviously Peter's companion
here.[8] The purpose of their *going up to the temple (eis to hieron,* as in 2:46) is
indicated by the expression *at the time of prayer (epi tēn hōran tēs proseuchēs).*
They wanted to be present for the service of public prayer that accompanied the evening sacrifice each day *at three in the afternoon (tēn enatēn,* '[at]
the ninth [hour]').[9] Even though Jesus had implied that he would replace
the temple in the plan and purpose of God (cf. Mt. 12:6; Jn. 2:19-22; 4:21-24),
his disciples did not immediately disengage themselves from the temple
and separate themselves from the traditional practices of their religion.[10]
As a group of pious Jews, aware that Israel's hopes were being fulfilled in
Jesus, they knew that their fundamental task was to bear testimony to him
before fellow Israelites (1:8) and so become the means by which other Jews
might be spared in the coming judgment and share in the blessings of the
messianic era (cf. 3:17-26). The temple area remained an important context
for that witness until they were excluded from it by mounting opposition
to the gospel.

2-3 Their attention was taken by a man who was *lame from birth*

6. Cf. THE THEOLOGY OF ACTS: IV. SALVATION (pp. 65-70).

7. The Western text introduces the expression 'and in those days', apparently to mark
the beginning of a new section of the text more obviously. For other textual variations of the
link between 2:47 and 3:1, see Metzger, *Textual Commentary,* 264-65.

8. Barrett 1994, 175, suggests that Luke included John to clarify that 'from the beginning the church, represented by the Twelve, acted as a fellowship'. But there is no need to
conclude with Barrett that the name of John was added to a narrative that originally did not
contain it.

9. Ex. 29:38-41 prescribes a pattern of sacrifice for each morning and evening. The
stated times for public prayer in Judaism thus became (1) early in the morning, at the time
of the morning sacrifice; (2) at the ninth hour, when the evening sacrifice was offered; and
(3) at sunset. Cf. SBK 2:696-98; Josephus, *Ant.* 14.65.

10. Cf. D. P. Seccombe, *Possessions and the Poor in Luke-Acts,* SNTSU (Linz: Fuchs,
1983), 217. On the probable continuance and ultimate adaptation of the great festivals of Judaism by early Jewish Christians, cf. C. F. D. Moule, *Worship in the New Testament,* Ecumenical Studies in Worship 9 (London: Lutterworth, 1961), 15-17. Theological reflection on the
sayings of Jesus about the temple must have become more pressing as the antagonism of the
Jewish leadership to the gospel increased.

(*chōlos ek koilias mētros autou*, 'lame from his mother's womb'; cf. 8:7; 14:8). Luke's description highlights his desperate need and the wonder of the healing that follows. First, he had a long-standing congenital condition (from 4:22 we learn that he was 'over forty years of age'). Secondly, he could not move himself and was in the process of *being carried to the temple gate called Beautiful* (cf. 3:10).[11] Since the fifth century AD, this gate has been identified as the Shushan Gate in the eastern wall of the temple, leading from outside into the Court of the Gentiles. This solution makes good sense of v. 11, if it is understood that Peter and John moved immediately with the beggar into *Solomon's Colonnade.* However, many modern commentators argue that *the temple gate called Beautiful* was the Nicanor Gate, leading from the eastern part of the outer Court of the Gentiles into the first of the inner courts of the temple (the Court of the Women).[12] The title *Beautiful* suggests that it was out of the ordinary, which would agree with the tradition in Josephus (*War* 5.201) that the Nicanor Gate was made of Corinthian bronze and 'far exceeded in value those plated with silver and set in gold'. But this interpretation requires us to understand *eis to hieron* to mean 'into the inner precincts of the temple', which is a narrower application of this terminology than is usual in Luke's writings (cf. 2:46 note). Thirdly, the lame man had no means of subsistence and had to *beg from those going into the temple courts.*[13] There is no ground for suggesting that he was prevented from entering the temple because of his condition, though it is true that the lame are included among social and religious outcasts in passages such as Luke 7:22; 14:13, 21.[14] When he saw Peter and John about to enter, he naturally asked them for what he thought was his greatest need *(money).* On the basis

11. The Greek imperfects could also be taken to mean that he was habitually carried and placed there.

12. The weight of evidence from Josephus, *Ant.* 14.410-25; *War* 5.190-221, and *m. Mid.* 1:3-4; 3:3 (SBK 2:260-65), seems to favour this identification, even though the name 'Beautiful' is not used in these sources. The Nicanor Gate is sometimes identified as the gate leading from the Court of the Women into the Court of Israel. But this conclusion is based on rabbinic sources, which may not be as reliable as Josephus in this matter. Cf. J. Jeremias, *TDNT* 3:173; G. Schrenk, *TDNT* 3:236. The scholarly debate on the issue is summarized by M. Hengel, *Between Jesus and Paul: Studies in the Earliest History of Christianity* (ET, London: SCM, 1983), 102-4.

13. J. Jeremias, *Jerusalem in the Time of Jesus: An Investigation into Economic and Social Conditions during the New Testament Period* (ET, London: SCM, 1969), 116-17, observes that, according to rabbinic tradition, 'almsgiving was regarded as particularly meritorious when done in the Holy City'. Cf. SBK 1:387-88. If the Beautiful Gate was the Nicanor Gate, *eis to hieron* in vv. 2 and 8 would mean 'into the inner precincts of the temple'.

14. Cf. Spencer 1997, 45. Witherington 1998, 173-74, argues from Lv. 21:17-20, which is about priests not being blind or lame (2 Sa. 5:8) and the Mishnah tractate *Shabbath* 6:8, that the lame man could not fully participate in the temple worship. However, the Mishnah refers to a cripple with an artificial limb and is concerned about impurity from possible bleeding associated with the wearing of such a device. Cf. P. Blackman (ed.), *Mishnayoth II: Order Mo'ed* (2nd ed.; Gateshead: Judaica, 1990), 42. This text cannot be applied to someone born lame. Cf. Johnson 1992, 65, who illegitimately applies 1QSa 2:5-6 to the situation in Jerusalem.

of past experience, he may not have expected to receive much,[15] but God was about to give him far more than he had hoped for.

4-5 Peter and John first *looked straight at him* (*atenisas eis auton*, 'fixed their gaze on him'; cf. 1:10; 3:12; 6:15; 7:55; 10:4; 11:6; 13:9; 14:9; 23:1), preparing him to respond to their challenge (v. 6). When Peter said, '*Look at us!*' it was an indication that the man was about to get more than the usual response to his begging. The apostles had made up their mind to offer him healing, without waiting for a specific request.[16] In this respect the miracle is unusual. Their initiative would demonstrate the sovereign grace of God, acting through Jesus Christ to rescue and restore those powerless to save themselves (cf. vv. 17-26; 4:8-12). They wanted him to listen carefully to what they would say. *So the man gave them his attention, expecting to get something from them.* What he received was beyond his wildest imagining!

6 Peter's first words — '*Silver or gold I do not have*' — offered little hope. Whether by choice or by circumstance, the apostles had no money with them on this occasion.[17] But the sentence is deliberately structured to make an important point: what the man thought he needed (*silver or gold*) is contrasted with what he really needed (*what I have*). The apostles had something far better to offer him, which they expressed in terms of a command ('*In the name of Jesus Christ of Nazareth, walk*'). The *name of Jesus Christ* represents his divine authority and continuing power to grant the blessings of salvation (cf. 2:38; 3:16 note). The name in question is not 'Jesus' but 'the name which belongs to Jesus by virtue of his resurrection and glorification, i.e. Lord and Christ (Acts 2:36)'.[18] Peter does not beg the exalted Lord for healing, but 'releases the very power of healing through utterance of the name of Jesus Christ (whose identity is further defined by *ho Nazōraios* [the Nazarene])'.[19] Healing does not take place because the right formula is pronounced but because Jesus is openly acknowledged as the only source of help and salvation. The deeper significance of that *name* is explored in Pe-

15. Spencer 1997, 46-47, argues on the basis of Jesus' teaching in Luke 18–21 that the lame man probably gained little from his regular begging, either from the temple economy or its worshippers. Contrast Barrett 1994, 180; Gaventa 2003, 84-5.

16. Against Williams 1985, 49, it is neither valid nor necessary to argue that the beggar already had faith in Jesus at this stage of the narrative (contrast 14:9). Cf. Metzger, *Textual Commentary*, 266-67, for variations in the Western text of Acts 3:3-5.

17. There is no need to conclude that the sharing described in 2:44-45 left the apostles without money of their own (cf. Tannehill 1990, 48). The apostles are later represented as the custodians of community funds for the needy (cf. 4:35, 37), but they were clearly in no position to share these resources with anyone as they made their way to the temple for prayer.

18. L. L. O'Reilly, *Word and Sign in the Acts of the Apostles: A Study in Lucan Theology*, Analecta Gregoriana 243 (Rome: EPUG, 1987), 100. It is overstating the case to say that the name is 'a kind of sacramental representation of the Jesus who is in heaven' (O'Reilly, 95). Barrett 1994, 176-77, 182-883, helpfully summarizes the 'name' theology of Acts 2–5, contrasting it with the use of names in magic practices.

19. Haenchen 1971, 200. There is no significant difference in the terminology used in Acts to identify Jesus as coming from Nazareth (2:22, *ton Nazōraion*; 3:3, *tou Nazōraiou*). Cf. Barrett 1994, 183.

ter's sermon (vv. 12-26). Although Peter proceeded to help him up, the crippled man had to respond to the challenge given to him in the name of Jesus and *walk*.[20] At this point, rather than in vv. 4-5, the apostle seeks to elicit faith. It may have been rudimentary, but faith in Jesus was required in response to his command (cf. v. 16 note). The authority of the apostles to heal was intimately connected with their role as the primary witnesses of the Messiah to Israel. Johnson observes that, in this paradigmatic narrative, by means of a literary parallelism with Luke 5:17-26, 'Luke communicates the simple point that the apostles are prophetic successors of Jesus'.[21] Elsewhere in Acts, such extraordinary miracles of restoration are limited to the Twelve (5:12-16; 9:32-43) and to prophetic figures such as Stephen (6:8), Philip (8:6-7, 13), Ananias (9:17-18), and Saul and Barnabas (13:9-12; 14:8-10; 15:12; 16:18; 19:11-16). Christians today cannot simply command healing in the name of Jesus. However, we may confidently point the needy to the risen Lord and pray confidently for them in his name, knowing that he remains gracious and powerful to heal. In so doing, it is important to remember the perspective that Peter gives in his sermon on this occasion, that God will not restore everything until Jesus returns and his saving purposes are consummated in a new creation (3:21; cf. Rev. 21:1-5).

7-8 Healing occurred as Peter took the lame man *by the right hand* and *helped him up* (cf. Mk. 1:31). Luke's language is not distinctively medical, but he indicates a detailed interest in the way life was given to this man's disabled limbs: *instantly* (*parachrēma*, as in Lk. 5:25; 8:47, 55; 13:13; 18:43) *the man's feet and ankles became strong* (*estereōthēsan*) and *he jumped to his feet and began to walk*.[22] The next step was to go with the apostles *into the temple courts* (cf. v. 11 note), expressing joy and gratitude by *walking and jumping, and praising God*. This description recalls Isaiah 35:6 ('Then will the lame leap like a deer'), where the lame man leaping is a sign of the salvation of God's people, in the context of a renewed creation. So Luke's healing account suggests that the end-time restoration of all things is underway (cf. v. 21 note). *Praising God* does not mean that he has yet identified Jesus as the one who has healed him, but Peter's address is clearly designed to

---

20. The longer form of the command that is found in KJV, NKJV, and ESV ('rise up and walk') is the reading of many Greek MSS and other ancient versions. But the shorter form in the TNIV and other modern translations is more likely to have been the original. The shorter reading is generally preferable because the tendency of copyists is to add words from other sources (cf. Mt. 9:5; Mk. 2:9; Lk. 5:23; Jn. 5:8). In Acts 3:6, the combination of Alexandrian witnesses with some versions and Athanasius in favour of the shorter reading is very compelling. Cf. Metzger, *Textual Commentary*, 267.

21. Johnson 1992, 71. As such, they emerge as 'the leaders over this restored people'. Cf. V. C. Pfitzner, '"Pneumatic" Apostleship? Apostle and Spirit in the Acts of the Apostles', in *Wort in der Zeit: Neutestamentliche Studien*, Festgabe für H. Rengstorf, ed. W. Haubeck and M. Bachmann (Leiden: Brill, 1980), 221-22; THEOLOGY OF ACTS: VIII. MIRACLES (pp. 83-87).

22. Barrett 1994, 183-84, outlines the ordinary use of such language in Greek literature.

help him and all those standing by to make that connection and to acknowledge Jesus as Messiah and Lord (cf. 2:36).

9-10 *When all the people saw him walking and praising God,* they recognized who he was — *the same man who used to sit begging at the temple gate called Beautiful.* As in 2:47, the expression *all the people (pas ho laos)* indicates a widespread reaction, perhaps including those who were not initially present for the healing.[23] For the third time, the man is described as *walking!* The crowd perceived at once that a remarkable cure had taken place, and people were *filled with wonder and amazement at what had happened to him.* Such a response is often noted by Luke at the end of miracle stories (e.g., Lk. 4:36; 5:9, 26; 7:16), without suggesting that the observers believed in Jesus. Marshall rightly observes that 'one can be impressed by the spectacular without responding to what it signifies, the power and the grace of God'.[24] Peter's sermon would now seek to persuade them of the implications of this event.

2. Peter's Interpretation of the Sign (3:11-26)

Peter's speech builds on some of the key ideas in his Pentecost sermon, but adds important new perspectives on the person and work of Christ. The deeper significance of the 'name' of Jesus is specifically explored. On this basis, Luke provides his readers with a second example of how the gospel was preached to Jews.[25] This sermon first seeks to explain how the healing of the man who was lame from birth was effected 'by faith in the name of Jesus' (vv. 12, 16). It then indicates that this healing by the heavenly Lord Jesus is an anticipation of the restoration of all things promised in Scripture, now linked with the return of Jesus as Messiah (vv. 19-21). Peter illustrates the need to teach those who have been healed how to identify and explain what has happened, giving glory to the exalted Lord and Saviour. However, more profoundly, the sermon begins and ends with a reference to God's promises to the patriarchs of Israel (vv. 13, 25-26). The first aim with this biblical-theological foundation is to show how God's intention to bless Israel and all the nations through Abraham's offspring is fulfilled through the glorification of Jesus as the Servant of the Lord (vv. 13-15). The benefits

---

23. Cf. Gaventa 2003, 85.

24. Marshall 1980, 89. With related terminology, the note of wonder in 3:10 *(thambous)* is sounded again in 3:11 *(ekthamboi)* and 3:12 *(thaumazete).*

25. Barrett 1994, 187-191, discusses the special features of this speech and enters the debate about its authenticity. He feels that most of the speech is 'not characteristically Lucan', thus proposing that Luke has only moderately adapted the tradition that was available to him. Witherington 1998, 176, argues that 'in regard to both technique and rhetorical strategy the speech material in this section varies little from the speech found in Acts 2'. However, as Bock 2007, 165-66, observes, there is much new theological material here. The first part of the speech is defensive or judicial (vv. 12-18), and the second part is deliberative (vv. 19-26), making the application to the audience.

available to those who repent and turn to God are both immediate and future (vv. 19-21), amounting to full participation in all the eschatological blessings intended by God for his people. The rejection of Jesus as God's Servant is coupled with the proclamation of his resurrection (vv. 13-15, 18) as a foundation for offering a definitive cleansing from sin and 'times of refreshing from the Lord' (v. 19). An atonement theology is suggested by this sequence. Peter's final aim with this presentation of the gospel is to warn his hearers about the danger of rejecting the Lord's prophet and being 'cut off from the people' (vv. 22-26). In other words, the sermon reiterates the idea that the promised restoration of Israel has begun and promises that this will lead to the blessing of the nations and the restoration of the whole created order. But not everyone who claims to be an Israelite will automatically enjoy the promised blessings. Only those who acknowledge Jesus as the key to their future will prove to be 'heirs of the prophets and of the covenant God made'.

a. The Author of Life (3:11-16)[26]

11 *Solomon's Colonnade* was a covered portico that ran the entire length of the eastern portion of the outer court of the temple known as the Court of the Gentiles.[27] Jesus had taught there (Jn. 10:23), and it soon became a favoured place for all the Jerusalem Christians to meet together (Acts 5:12). The most natural way to read Luke's narrative is to suppose that the crippled man was seated at the Shushan Gate in the eastern wall of the temple, opening into the outer court (cf. v. 2 note). When he was healed, he went immediately with the apostles into that court (v. 8, taking *eis to hieron* to mean 'into the temple complex'), where the crowd *came running to them in the place called Solomon's Colonnade*.[28] If, however, the Beautiful Gate was the Nicanor Gate, the beggar may have gone with Peter and John into the inner courts for the time of prayer (v. 8, taking *eis to hieron* to mean 'into the inner precincts of the temple') before returning to Solomon's Colonnade (v. 11). Luke emphasizes that *the man held on to Peter and John*, attaching himself enthusiastically to the men who had brought such a dramatic

26. The headings for the three sections of this sermon, highlighting the Christological claims of the message, are those of Gaventa 2003, 86-89.

27. According to Josephus, *Ant.* 20.220-22; *War* 5.185, this portico remained from Solomon's temple. But this tradition is contradicted 'not only by the structure itself but also by Josephus's own testimony concerning the Herodian expansion of the temple platform' (W. LaSor, *ISBE* 2:1028).

28. J. Finegan, *The Archaeology of the New Testament: The Life of Jesus and the Beginning of the Early Church* (Princeton: Princeton University, 1969), 129-30. Codex Bezae records that they went into the inner precincts and then, 'as Peter and John were going out, he went out with them, holding on to them; and they stood wondering in the portico that is called Solomon's, astounded'. This version of the text, which contains several grammatical errors, is a later attempt to sort out some of the ambiguity of the original. Cf. Metzger, *Textual Commentary*, 267-69; Barrett 1994, 191-92.

change into his life. Meanwhile, *all the people* (cf. 3:9-10 note) ran to them, *astonished* at what had happened (KJV 'greatly wondering' [*ekthamboi*], echoing v. 10 [*thambous*, 'wonder']).

12 When Peter saw this reaction, he knew it was time to deflect attention from himself and John and to identify the risen Lord as the one responsible for the healing. Later, in pagan contexts, the response to miraculous healing is more obviously blasphemous (14:8-18; 28:1-6). But even in Jerusalem, an undue focus on the human agents of divine healing could detract from the glory of God. Peter's opening words to the crowd (*'People of Israel'*) are the same as those in 2:22 (*Andres, Israēlitai*; cf. 1:16; 2:14 note), acknowledging their common faith and identity as Israelites. Peter first questions their *surprise* or wonder (*thaumazete* recalls related terms in vv. 10 and 11) *at this* (*epi toutō* could refer to 'this man' or 'this healing'). He then questions the fact that they cannot take their eyes off the apostles (*'Why do you stare at us?'* [*atenizete*; cf. *atenisas* in v. 4]), suspecting that their understanding of the event is misguided. Such a mighty work was not a demonstration of the *'power'* of the apostles. Neither can it be imagined that God has shown his power because of their *'godliness'*.[29] The real explanation is delayed until v. 16, after Peter has proclaimed Jesus as God's servant.

13 Peter introduces a theme familiar to us from 2:22-36, declaring that God has accomplished his purposes through Jesus, despite the opposition of his people. This paradox is repeated and developed more fully in 3:14-15. Moreover, God is described in familiar terms as *'the God of Abraham, Isaac and Jacob, the God of our fathers'*, using a phrase from Exodus 3:6, 15.[30] The quotation varies from the original mainly by changing the pronoun 'your' to 'our', allowing the apostles to identify themselves with their audience as children of the patriarchs. The quotation also varies from the original by placing the expression *the God of our fathers* at the end rather than at the beginning of the phrase. Highlighting God's relationship with *Abraham, Isaac and Jacob* in this way, Peter recalls God's covenant with them and his faithfulness in fulfilling his promises to them. This perspective returns at the conclusion of the speech (vv. 25-26), establishing a broad theological framework in which to understand the person and work of Jesus. So Peter's second sermon takes us back behind the eschatological and messianic prophecies that were the basis of his Pentecost address, linking these with the foundational covenant promises of Scripture (e.g., Gn. 12:1-3; 13:14-17; 15:1-21; 17:1-22; 22:15-18; 26:1-6; 28:10-15). In this way he affirms

29. Barrett 1994, 193, suggests that Jews would not have ascribed such a healing to men, but they may have thought that God had acted because of the piety of the apostles. Witherington 1998, 179, notes the significance of Peter's disclaimer for Gentile readers.

30. Some of the best Greek MSS repeat the word 'God' before 'Isaac' and 'Jacob', as in the LXX of Ex. 3:6, 15 and as in Mt. 22:32; Mk. 12:26; Lk. 20:37. TNIV follows the shorter text. This is preferable since any form of OT quotation differing from the LXX is likely to have been modified in the course of time by copyists to conform to the LXX. Cf. the similar textual variation in Acts 7:32.

that he is proclaiming no new religion but the fulfillment of God's ultimate intentions for Israel and the nations of the world.

It was the God of Israel's forefathers who *'glorified his servant Jesus'* (*edoxasen ton paida autou Iēsoun*). This is apparently an allusion to Isaiah 52:13 (LXX *ho pais mou . . . doxasthēsetai sphodra*, 'my servant will be highly exalted'), a verse which introduces the so-called 'Fourth Servant Song' in Isaiah 52:13–53:12. The glorification of the servant refers to his exaltation (Heb. *gābah*) over the nations and their kings, after terrible humiliation and suffering. An identification of Jesus as God's *servant* is also found in Acts 3:26 (cf. 4:27, 30 notes; 1 Pet. 2:22, 24-25). The title is more than a formal, honorific way of describing Jesus as a faithful follower or child of God.[31] Peter's sermon goes on to describe Jesus' rejection, death, and exaltation by God (vv. 13-15) in a way that mirrors the portrait of the Servant in Isaiah 53. When Peter insists that God has fulfilled what the prophets said about the suffering of *'his Christ'* (v. 18), it is logical to conclude that Isaiah 53 is a key text in his thinking. Jesus is the messianic servant who accomplished God's saving purposes for Israel and the nations by fulfilling the pattern set out in that prophecy. The link between Isaiah 53 and the experience of Jesus is further established by the argument in Acts 8:32-35 (cf. Lk. 22:37).[32]

The explanatory sentence that follows suggests that Jesus was *glorified* as God's servant after he was dishonoured by those who *'handed him over to be killed'* and who *'disowned him before Pilate'* (cf. 2:23; 4:10; 5:30).[33] The Roman governor wanted to release Jesus because he could find no fault in him and *'had decided to let him go'* (cf. Lk. 23:4, 14-16, 20, 22). But the chief priests, the rulers, and the people insisted on his death. Peter develops the theme of Israel's rejection of Jesus in vv. 14-15 before declaring that *'God raised him from the dead'*. Without doubt, Jesus was glorified by his resurrec-

---

31. Haenchen 1971, 205, takes 'servant' as a term adopted from Jewish prayers, 'in which great men of God, especially David, were called God's *pais*' (cf. Acts 4:25). D. L. Jones, 'The Title "Servant" in Luke-Acts', in C. H. Talbert (ed.), *Luke-Acts: New Perspectives from the Society of Biblical Literature Seminar* (New York: Crossroad, 1984), 148-65, develops this argument, concluding that Luke used the title 'servant' interchangeably with 'Son of God' and 'Christ', without any identification of Jesus as the Suffering Servant. It is true that two of the references to Jesus as God's servant in Acts are in the context of prayer (4:27, 30) and that the title mainly lived on as a fixed liturgical formula in some later Christian works, without necessarily connoting his vicarious suffering. But the usage in Acts 3:13, 26 is in an explanatory and apologetic context, with Isaianic associations clearly established in the intervening argument. Cf. O. Cullmann, *The Christology of the New Testament* (ET, London: SCM, 1959), 73-75; C. F. D. Moule, 'The Christology of Acts', in L. E. Keck and J. L. Martyn, *Studies in Luke-Acts* (Nashville: Abingdon 1966; London: SPCK, 1976), 169-70; Barrett 1994, 194; Bock 2007, 168-69.

32. Cf. THE THEOLOGY OF ACTS: VI. THE ATONING WORK OF JESUS (pp. 75-79).

33. Compare my comment on Peter's condemnation of the Jerusalemites in 2:23-24, 36. A number of new elements are added in 3:13-15 to make the contrast between their actions and the action of God more dramatic. In particular, the role of Pilate is outlined in a way that highlights the guilt of the Jews. For an assessment of the character and career of Pontius Pilate, prefect of Judea, AD 26-37, cf. Bruce 1990, 140.

tion and subsequent exaltation into heaven. However, it should not be forgotten that Peter's sermon began as an explanation of the healing of the lame man (v. 12) and that the apostle soon identifies Jesus as the power behind this miracle (v. 16). It is possible, therefore, that Jesus' glorification may have a double meaning in this context. Jesus was glorified by his heavenly exaltation and continues to be glorified by the exercise of his heavenly authority in a healing like this.[34]

14 As in 2:23, 36, the Jerusalemites are directly charged with repudiating Jesus (cf. 4:10; 5:30; 7:52; 13:28), but the theme of rejection is much more prominent in 3:13-15 than in Peter's first sermon. The plural pronoun *'you' (hymeis)* is used for emphasis (as in 3:13), and the verb *'disowned' (ērnēsasthe)* is repeated to highlight the note of denial and refusal. Peter stresses the enormity of this rejection by describing Jesus as *'the Holy and Righteous One'*. From 7:52 and 22:14 it seems that 'the Righteous One' *(ho dikaios)* was a messianic designation, derived from prophetic expectations (e.g., Is. 32:1; 53:11; Je. 23:5; Zc. 9:9; cf. *1 Enoch* 38:2; 53:6; *Ps. Sol.* 17:35). 'The Holy One' *(ho hagios)* is probably a synonym here (cf. Lk. 4:34 par.; Jn. 6:69; 1 Jn. 2:20; Rev. 3:7), even though it is not used in exactly the same way elsewhere in Acts (cf. 4:27, 30).[35] Refusing to accept the saviour-king provided by God, the Jews asked that *'a murderer be released'* to them (cf. Lk. 23:18-19, 25).[36]

15 The accusation of v. 14 is repeated in more startling terms, charging them with killing *'the author of life' (ton archēgon tēs zōēs)*. The term *archēgos* in Greek literature and the papyri hovers between the two senses of 'leader, prince' and 'author, originator'.[37] In 5:31 this noun is used in conjunction with the title *sōtēr* in an expression which English versions render 'Prince and Saviour' or 'Leader and Saviour'. In 3:15 the translation 'Prince of life' (KJV, NKJV) is similarly possible, since Jesus by his resurrection has become the one who has 'led the way to life' (NEB).[38] However, the full im-

---

34. Cf. D. L. Bock, *Proclamation from Prophecy and Pattern: Lucan Old Testament Christology*, JSNTSS 12 (Sheffield: JSOT, 1987), 189-90; Tannehill 1990, 53; Barrett 1994, 195. Jesus' exaltation is testified to by this healing just as it is testified to by the pouring out of the Holy Spirit (2:33-36).

35. Barrett 1994, 195, rightly notes that 'the use of only one article binds together the two substantival adjectives, and makes it less likely that we should look for two distinct lines of Christological thought'. However, he goes on to argue against either title being taken as specifically messianic, viewing them as 'simply descriptive' of one who was holy and righteous. Contrast Witherington 1998, 181.

36. The verb *charisthēnai* in a legal context means 'to be given over (as a favour)' (for life, 3:14 [cf. 27:24]; or for death, 25:11, 16). Cf. H. Conzelmann, *TDNT* 9:393.

37. Cf. P. G. Müller, CHRISTOS ARCHĒGOS: *Der religionsgeschichtliche und theologische Hintergrund einer neutestamentlichen Christusprädikation*, Europäische Hochschulschriften Reihe 23, Vol. 28 (Frankfurt/Bern: Lang, 1973), 1-247. For a discussion of the use of *archēgos* in Heb. 2:10; 12:2, cf. D. G. Peterson, *Hebrews and Perfection: An Examination of the Concept of Perfection in the 'Epistle to the Hebrews'*, SNTSMS 47 (Cambridge: Cambridge University, 1982), 57-58, 171-72.

38. Cf. Barrett 1994, 197-98, who notes that in this case 'a genitive of direction, not of ob-

port of the construction is better conveyed by the translation *author of life* (NRSV, ESV, TNIV). By virtue of his death and resurrection, Jesus is the originator of new life for others, as the argument in vv. 16-21 goes on to suggest. His life-giving power has just been powerfully illustrated in the restoration of life to the lame man's limbs.[39] Although Peter accuses his audience of putting to death the one sent to bring them new life, he proclaims that *'God raised him from the dead'. God* stands in strong contrast to *you* in v. 14 (cf. 2:23-24; 4:10). God's saving purposes were not frustrated by Israel's rebellion but were fully established! By a mighty reversal, he brought his servant Jesus, the Holy and Righteous One, from death to life. The distinctive role of the apostles was to be *'witnesses of this'* (*hou hēmeis martyres esmen* could also mean 'we are witnesses of him'). Their charge was to bear witness to the person of Jesus and to the fact and significance of his resurrection (1:8, 21-26).

16 Peter has restated in a simplified form the central argument of his sermon on the Day of Pentecost (vv. 13-15; cf. 2:22-36). But the introductory sentence in v. 13 has also suggested another way of looking at these foundational claims. As Messiah, Jesus fulfilled the role of the Suffering Servant and became the means by which God consummated his covenant promises to the patriarchs of Israel. Moreover, he is the Author of Life, who has made resurrection life possible for all who trust in him. Before Peter goes on to develop these perspectives (vv. 17-26), he stresses the link between this gospel proclamation and the healing that has just taken place.

The Greek of v. 16 is awkward, reading literally: 'By faith in his name has his name made strong this man whom you see and know, and the faith which is through him has given him [the lame man] this complete healing in the presence of you all.' Such awkwardness is uncharacteristic of Luke's style and may reflect an unwillingness to smoothe over difficulties in a written source where critical issues are at stake.[40] It may also simply be the result of trying to link two seemingly contradictory notions together. First of all, there is the focus on *'the name of Jesus'*, by which this healing had been effected (there is a chiastic pattern — faith-name/name-faith — which puts *name* at the centre). Healing was not accomplished by the power or character of the apostles (v. 12), but *the name* of the one whom God raised from death *made strong* (*estereōsen*, as in v. 7) the man who was lame from birth (cf. v. 6). The name of Jesus is not a magical formula or an absolute power that operates apart from the person it represents. 'It is, in fact, a dynamic, personal symbol of Jesus' continuing presence and power on earth. Al-

---

ject' must be understood. If *archēgos* is the equivalent of *nāsî* ('prince') here, it represents one of the strands in the primitive Christology that saw Jesus as the fulfillment of the Davidic hope.

39. Cf. Witherington 1998, 181-82; Bock 2007, 171-72.

40. Various attempts to relieve the difficulties in the text are discussed by Bruce 1990, 142, and Metzger, *Textual Commentary*, 270-72. None of these alternatives is convincing. Cf. C. K. Barrett, 'Faith and Eschatology in Acts 3', in E. Grässer and O. Merk (eds.), *Glaube und Eschatologie: Festschrift für W. G. Kümmel zum 80. Geburtstag* (Tübingen: Mohr, 1985), 4-9.

though ascended to heaven awaiting (we now learn) a return to earth at "the time of universal restoration" (3:21), Jesus is not trapped within a fixed spatio-temporal system. Far from being an absentee landlord until his return, he remains in the interim an active friend and savior of God's people, channelling God's life-giving energy (cf. 3:15) to the poor and the lame just as he did before his departure.'[41] It was the exalted Lord Jesus who healed him, but the *name* of Jesus continues to be the focus of Peter's thinking because he wants to reinforce his claim that the salvation promised by Joel and other prophets (cf. Jl. 2:32 in Acts 2:21) is only for those who call upon that name (cf. Acts 2:38). The healing of this crippled man is a pointer to the saving power of Jesus in the widest sense (cf. 4:10-12). Since 'calling upon the name of the LORD' was a distinguishing mark of Israel in the ancient world, it was extremely provocative for the apostles to claim that Jesus was the one on whom to call for salvation. It was an implicit claim to divinity, which could not be ignored by pious, monotheistic Jews.[42]

The second point which v. 16 makes is the need for *'faith in the name of Jesus'*. Jesus does not heal or save apart from the trust of those who seek his help. Faith is essential because the mission of Christ is to restore people to a right relationship with God. Faith on the part of the apostles was a necessary factor in this healing, but did the crippled man share that faith?[43] The second part of v. 16 speaks about *'the faith that comes through him'*, indicating that Jesus himself is the source and inspiration for the faith that secures God's blessing. This phrase appears to confirm that Peter's use of the name of Jesus in v. 6 aroused at least a rudimentary faith on the part of the beggar. What has been given by the name of Jesus in response to genuine faith is 'this complete healing' (*tēn holoklērian tautēn*, TNIV *'has completely healed him'*).[44] Such a miracle calls for faith in Jesus on the part of Peter's audience. They are addressed as those who *'see and know'* the man who was lame from birth and who have witnessed his transformation (*apenanti pantōn hymōn*, 'in the presence of you all'; TNIV *'as you can all see'*).

41. Spencer 1997, 48. Spencer, 47, observes that 'the power of the divine name to deliver and protect God's people is a prominent theme in Israelite worship (Ps. 20:1-7; 44:4-8; 54:1-7), linked to the localization of this name in the Solomonic temple ("a house for the name of the Lord, the God of Israel", 1 Kgs 8:17; cf. 8:14-30)'. The name of the exalted Jesus now conveys God's glory and strength in the temple context.

42. Cf. THE THEOLOGY OF ACTS: II. JESUS AS MESSIAH AND LORD (pp. 56-60).

43. Barrett 1994, 200, and Witherington 1998, 182, argue that the apostles' faith is meant. But Bock 2007, 172, rightly notes that the lame man responded to the challenge of the apostles and concludes that his faith is more likely to be in view.

44. This is the only NT occurrence of the noun *holoklēria* ('completeness, wholeness'), but the adjective *holoklēros* is used in 1 Thes. 5:23; Jas. 1:4. In Greek papyri and inscriptions this noun is an equivalent for *sōtēria*, 'physical health and safety', without any of the spiritual dimensions sometimes conveyed by *sōtēria* (*ND* 4 [1987], 161-62); cf. 4:10 (*hygiēs*), 'completely healed'. Witherington 1998, 182, suggests that the noun is used 'because formerly the lame man was "blemished" and could not enter the sanctuary'. However, see note 14 above. TNIV has translated the expression in 3:16 verbally (*has completely healed*).

b. The Appointed Messiah (3:17-21)

17 A new phase of the sermon's appeal begins with the words 'and now' *(kai nyn)*. As Peter begins to call for a response to his claims, he addresses the people of Jerusalem as 'brothers' *(adelphoi;* TNIV *'brothers and sisters')*, meaning 'fellow Israelites' (cf. vv. 12-13). He acknowledges that they *'acted in ignorance' (kata agnoian epraxate)*,[45] as also their leaders did *(hōsper kai hoi archontes hymōn)*. They did not realize who Jesus was, despite his plain words and powerful deeds (cf. Lk. 23:34; 1 Cor. 2:8; 1 Tim. 1:13). Yet the apostle is not excusing his contemporaries on the basis of this ignorance. He has just made a series of powerful accusations against them (vv. 13-15) and goes straight on to challenge them to repentance, so that their sins may be wiped out (v. 19). There may be an echo here of the OT distinction between sinning unintentionally or 'in ignorance' and sinning defiantly (cf. Nu. 15:27-31; Lv. 4:2, 27; 5:17). Even for those who participated in the death of the Messiah cleansing is now available, though not through the traditional avenue of the sacrificial system.

18 Peter goes on to proclaim the sovereign outworking of God's saving plan 'in this way' *(houtōs;* TNIV *'this is how')*, that is, through their ignorance (cf. 13:27).[46] In the rejection of Jesus and all the events associated with his death, *'God fulfilled what he had foretold through all the prophets, saying that his Messiah would suffer'* (cf. Lk. 24:45-46; Acts 17:3; 26:22-23). What God *foretold (prokatēngeilen)* or 'announced in advance' came *through all the prophets (dia stomatos pantōn tōn prophētōn,* 'through the mouth of all the prophets'). The emphasis here and in v. 24 is on the prophets as living agents through whom God spoke at different times in Israel's history. Since many of their oracles were written down for the benefit of subsequent generations, 'all the prophets' could become a generalization covering the rest of the OT apart from the law of Moses (Lk. 24:27; cf. 24:44; Acts 10:43). But in what sense did the prophets testify to the suffering of the Christ? Messianic predictions are not to be found in every prophetic book, though many prophets reveal different dimensions of God's end-time salvation. The earliest Christian preachers saw these expectations fulfilled in the person and work of the Messiah. They linked specifically messianic passages with

---

45. The Western text adds 'evil' after the verb 'you did' in v. 17, to emphasize the culpability of the people of Jerusalem and their leaders. It also inserts Gk. *men* ('on the one hand') to contrast more emphatically the rebellion of the Jews with the purpose of God (v. 18). For the anti-Judaic tendencies of the Western text of Acts, cf. E. J. Epp, *The Theological Tendency of Codex Bezae Cantabrigiensis in Acts,* SNTSMS 3 (Cambridge: Cambridge University, 1966), 41-171.

46. There really is no ground for arguing that Peter mitigates the guilt of his audience by saying that 'God himself had willed it in order to fulfil the words of the prophets' (Longenecker 1981, 297). See my comments on 1:17; 2:23. Bock 2007, 173, observes that rulers and people acted ignorantly in the sense that 'they did not understand what it was they were truly doing (Acts 13:27)'. The healing and Peter's message gave them another opportunity to understand the identity of the one whom they had rejected and the seriousness of their situation before God.

other strands of prophecy, as Jesus had taught them. Most obviously, prophecies of the Suffering Servant in Isaiah and passages reflecting the experience of David or some other righteous sufferer in the Psalms were applied to the passion of Jesus (e.g., Pss. 22, 31, 34, 69).[47] Once it was acknowledged that passages about the suffering of prophets and kings, or even Israel itself, could be applied typologically to the Messiah, anticipations of the rejection and death of Jesus could be found in many other contexts (e.g., Je. 11:19; Dn. 9:26; Zc. 12:10; 13:7). In short, *God fulfilled* (*eplērōsen*; cf. Lk. 1:20; 4:21; 24:44; Acts 1:16; 13:27), or brought to full and final expression in Jesus, many predictions and patterns of experience found in the prophetic literature of the OT. Note how the expression *his Messiah* links Jesus and his mission very intimately to God (cf. Lk. 9:20; Acts 4:26; Rev. 11:15; 12:10). Jesus was the one personally anointed by God to fulfill his saving purposes for Israel and the nations (cf. Lk. 3:21-2 par.).

19-20 The word *'then'* (*oun*) shows that the challenge to *'repent'* (*metanoēsate*) in this next part of Peter's address is firmly based on the preceding argument. The foolishness and wickedness of rejecting Jesus had been dramatically demonstrated by God's glorification of him as the Servant-Messiah. Peter's audience had alienated themselves from God and destroyed any hope of enjoying the blessings of the messianic era by turning away from their saviour. As in 2:38, repentance is demanded on the basis of what is proclaimed about Jesus. The related verb *epistrephein* ('to turn, return') is extensively used by Luke (cf. Lk. 1:16-17; 2:39; 8:55; 17:4, 31; 22:32; Acts 9:35, 40; 11:21; 14:15; 15:19, 36; 16:18; 26:18, 20; 28:27). It is added here (*kai epistrepsate*) and in 26:20 to indicate that genuine repentance involves a radical reorientation of life, turning back to God to seek reconciliation and to express a new obedience (cf. 2:38 note).[48] Informed belief is an essential aspect of repentance: there can be now no genuine turning to God without acknowledging the centrality of Jesus to God's purpose, as proclaimed in Peter's message.

Three positive encouragements to repent and turn to God are now given in a series of purpose clauses.[49] The first is *'so that your sins may be*

47. C. H. Dodd, *According to the Scriptures: The Sub-Structure of the New Testament* (London: Nisbet, 1952), 88-103, gives a convenient list of such quotations and allusions in the NT. On the diverse strands of OT expectation that find their fulfillment in the messiahship of Jesus, cf. A. Motyer, *IBD* 2:987-94. For the originality and influence of Jesus' use of the OT, cf. R. T. France, *Jesus and the Old Testament* (London: Tyndale, 1971), 172-226.

48. The words *to God* have been added by TNIV and NRSV to bring out the point so clearly expressed in 20:21, that the gospel demands a turning back to God ('repentance towards God') and 'faith in our Lord Jesus'. Cf. 17:30-31; 26:20. ESV more literally has 'and turn again'; KJV, NKJV 'and be converted'. The idea that salvation is for those who have faith 'in the name of Jesus' is made clear in the immediate context by 3:16 and 4:10-12. Barrett 1994, 203, thinks that *epistrepsate* is added to *metanoēsate* simply as a means of emphasis. Cf. R. C. Tannehill, *The Shape of Luke's Story: Essays on Luke-Acts* (Eugene: Cascade, 2005), 84-101, on repentance in the context of Lukan soteriology.

49. The first purpose clause is expressed by an articular infinitive with *eis* in most

wiped out'. Elsewhere in the NT, the verb *exaleiphein* ('to cause to disappear by wiping', BDAG) is used for erasing names from the book of life (Rev. 3:5), wiping away tears (Rev. 2:14; 7:17), and canceling the bond that the law creates (Col. 2:14). In Acts 3:19 the meaning is similar to that in Psalm 51 (LXX 50):9 ('blot out all my iniquity'; cf. Ps. 109 [LXX 108]:14) and Isaiah 43:25 ('I am he who blots out your transgressions'; cf. Je. 18:23).[50] When God forgives, he wipes the slate clean! But Peter's strong language must be related to the promise of 2:38 that forgiveness is available only for those who are baptized 'in the name of Jesus Christ' (cf. Lk. 24:47). In other words, those who have rejected the Messiah can experience God's forgiveness only if they approach him with repentance in the name of Jesus, acknowledging that he is the Messiah. Notice further that Peter's promise in 3:19 is closely connected with the claim that the Messiah had to suffer (v. 18). It is possible that the atonement teaching of Isaiah 53 is in mind here and that Jesus' suffering is being viewed as the means by which sins have been dealt with definitively and may no longer remembered by God (cf. Je. 31:34; Acts 5:30-31 note).[51]

The idea that this offer of forgiveness is new and decisive, having eschatological significance, is brought out by the second purpose clause: *'that times of refreshing may come from the Lord'* (*apo prosōpou tou kyriou*, 'from the face of the Lord'). No verbal parallels to the expression *times of refreshing* (*kairoi anapsyxeōs*) have been found in Scripture, though the noun *anapsyxis* is used in Exodus 8:15 (LXX) to describe the 'relief' from God's judgment experienced by the Egyptians. Some have argued that *times of refreshing* refers to the messianic salvation in all its fullness, which God will send speedily if Israel repents.[52] This involves taking the next clause (*'and that he may send the Messiah'*) as a complementary statement about the same event. However, the argument in vv. 19-21 is cumulative, implying that these seasons of refreshment occur in an intervening period, before Christ's return and the consummation of God's plan in a renewed creation (cf. v. 21 note). Even now, those who turn to him for forgiveness may enjoy in advance some of the blessings associated with the coming era. Perhaps these times

---

MSS but with *pros* in two key Alexandrian witnesses. Since the construction *pros* ('to') with the infinitive is not found elsewhere in Luke-Acts, it should perhaps be accepted as the original, being the harder reading (contra Metzger, *Textual Commentary*, 272-73). But the meaning is not affected either way. The second and third purpose clauses are formed by the subjunctives *ethōsin* ('come') and *aposteilē* ('send') after *hopōs an* ('so that').

50. In the LXX, as in classical Greek, *exaleiphein* (a derivative of *alaiphein*, 'to anoint, rub with oil, polish by rubbing smooth') is also used literally in the sense of 'plaster' (cf. Lv. 14:42, 43, 48), and metaphorically for God's judicial work of wiping out life (Gn. 7:23) and the names and memory of offenders (Ex. 17:14; Dt. 9:14), and of erasing names from the book of life (Ex. 32:32-33). Cf. J. I. Packer, *NIDNTT* 1:471.

51. Cf. Witherington 1998, 180, and note 32 above.

52. E.g., Haenchen 1971, 208 note 8; E. Schweizer, *TDNT* 9:663-65. The verb *anapsychein* basically means 'to cool, refresh' (e.g., Jgs. 15:19; 2 Sa. 16:14; 2 Macc. 4:46, LXX; 2 Tim. 1:16). The sense of relief from suffering is prominent in Ps. 38:14 (LXX).

of refreshment are more specifically 'moments of relief during the time men spend in waiting for that blessed day'.[53] A comparison with Peter's promises in 2:38 suggests that the Holy Spirit may be the one who brings this refreshment. Peter may be describing the subjective effect of the gift of the Spirit for believers, whose presence anticipates and guarantees the full inheritance God promises his children (cf. 2 Cor. 1:22; Eph. 1:14).

The apostle finally urges the Jerusalem Jews to repent so that God may *'send the Messiah, who has been appointed for you — even Jesus'*.[54] There is no specific mention of Jesus' second coming elsewhere in the sermons in Acts, though Jesus' role as 'judge of the living and the dead' is highlighted (10:42; cf. 7:55-56; 17:31). Jesus himself had spoken cryptically about a future revelation of the Son of Man (Lk. 17:22-37; 18:8; 21:27), and Acts 1:11 speaks clearly of his personal return from heaven. Acts 3:19-21 offers further comment on the significance of Jesus' ascension and sets the work of evangelism and its present effects within the wider context of God's ultimate purposes. Peter's description of Jesus as *the Messiah, who has been appointed for you* makes the point that he is the one chosen by God (implied by the perfect passive participle *prokecheirismenon*) for Israel *(for you)* — even for those who disowned him! The verb *procheirizomai* ('select, appoint') is later used in 22:14; 26:16 with reference to the divine choice of Paul for his apostolic ministry. But Peter does not mean that Jesus is merely 'the Messiah-designate', whose investiture is still awaited.[55] Jesus was the one 'accredited' (2:22) by God to Israel in the course of his earthly ministry. He suffered as 'the Christ' (3:18), but by means of his resurrection and ascension he became the heavenly, enthroned ruler envisaged in Psalm 110 (cf. 2:36 note). Peter's point in vv. 19-20 is that the previously rejected Messiah will return only if Israel repents.

53. Barrett, 'Faith and Eschatology', 12. His comments on the syntax of 3:19-21 are very helpful (9-10). He suggests that we have here 'an example of Luke's personalizing, or individualizing, of eschatology' (12-13). Note the use of the plural *kairoi* in the expression 'times of the Gentiles' (Lk. 21:24), in a context suggesting the delay of the Son of Man for a period established by God and in Acts 1:7. Cf. Gaventa 2003, 88. Bock 2007, 176, suggests that *anapsyxis* in Acts 3:20 alludes to 'the Spirit's washing work in the messianic age that points to spiritual refreshment'.

54. Although some MSS have the sequence 'Jesus Christ' (so KJV, NKJV), a good combination of Alexandrian and Western witnesses have 'the Christ . . . Jesus' (so NRSV, ESV, TNIV). The first reading appears to have arisen because copyists failed to perceive that 'the Christ' was being used as a formal title here.

55. J. A. T. Robinson, *Twelve New Testament Studies*, SBT 34 (London: SCM, 1962), 139-53, expounded such a view, claiming that in Acts 3:19-21 we find 'the most primitive Christology of all'. His view is ably critiqued by Longenecker 1981, 297-98, who argues that Robinson's theory makes Luke appear incredibly naive in placing two distinct and differing Christologies side by side (v. 18 [Jesus suffered as the Christ] and vv. 19-21 [Jesus is yet to be appointed as the Christ]). Cf. Barrett 1994, 204. Bruce 1990, 144, notes that 'nothing in the verb *procheirizomai* suggests designation as distinct from full appointment. The prefix *pro-* probably means "forth" rather than "before" in the temporal sense'. However, cf. 22:14 note.

21 The second coming of Jesus is not represented as an occasion for judgment here. Rather, *'Heaven must receive him (hon dei ouranon men dexasthai,* 'whom heaven must receive') *until the time comes for God to restore everything'.* The word *must (dei)* indicates that Jesus' present withdrawal from the earthly scene is an important stage in the divine plan of salvation. His withdrawal will continue (lit.) 'until the times of restoration of all things' *(achri chronōn apokatastaseōs pantōn).* Some have argued that the translation 'establishment of all things' is more appropriate here (RSV 'establishing'). But 'restoration' is quite suitable (NRSV, ESV, TNIV; KJV, NKJV, 'restitution'), reflecting the conviction that the end will be as the beginning: 'God, through Christ, will restore his fallen world to the purity and integrity of its initial creation.'[56] TNIV implies that this will take place when Christ returns. But the Greek could just as easily mean that a process of restoration is already underway and that Jesus' return will mark its climax and dramatic conclusion. The restoration of 'the kingdom' to Israel is probably meant to be understood as part of this process (cf. 1:6 note, where the cognate verb *apokathistēmi* is used). Acts 2 suggests that the restoration of Israel began with the preaching of the gospel and the pouring out of God's Spirit. Acts 3 illustrates that restoration with the healing of the crippled man. However, this miracle also anticipates the ultimate renewal of the whole created order, *'as he promised long ago through his holy prophets'* (e.g., Is. 35:1-10; 65:17-25; Ezk. 47:1-12; cf. Rom. 8:18-23; 2 Pet. 3:10-13; Rev. 21:1-7; 22:1-5).[57] Furthermore, Peter goes on to teach that the blessing of all the peoples on earth through the messianic restoration of Israel must first take place (Acts 3:25-26; cf. 1:7-8). In other words, the restoration of all things has begun and will continue until it is consummated at Christ's return. But 'times of restoration of all things' and 'times of refreshing' (v. 19) are not simply synonymous or interchangeable terms.[58] 'Consistent with his eschatological scenario sketched in Luke 21:5-36, Luke separates the time of witness from the end-time.'[59] Yet there is also a sense in which he

56. Barrett, 'Faith and Eschatology', 16. Barrett, 14-15, rightly critiques the argument of Bruce 1974, 67. Cf. Mt. 19:28; 2 Pet. 3:13.

57. As in 3:18, the Greek indicates that God spoke (lit.) 'through the mouth of his holy prophets'. But v. 21 adds the expression *ap' aiōnos* ('from of old', or 'since ages past'), pointing to the antiquity of this revelation. Cf. Lk. 1:70. For the variation of word order in some MSS, cf. Metzger, *Textual Commentary,* 273. The Western text omits 'from of old'.

58. A. Oepke, *TDNT* 1:391, suggests that *anapsyxeōs* ('refreshment, relief') denotes the subjective side of what God is doing in the present and that *apokatastaseōs* ('restoration, reconstitution') denotes the objective side of the matter (the restoration of right relationships and the reconstitution of the creation). However, I am not convinced by his distinction between the two different words for 'times', *kairoi* (marking 'the beginning of the transformation') and *chronōn* (conveying 'the thought of the lasting nature of the renewed world'). Cf. Barrett, 'Faith and Eschatology', 10-11.

59. Johnson 1992, 74. Cf. J. Nolland, 'Salvation-History and Eschatology', in I. H. Marshall and D. Peterson (eds.), *Witness to the Gospel: The Theology of Acts* (Grand Rapids/ Cambridge: Eerdmans, 1998), 63-81.

proclaims the realization of end-time blessings in the present through the preaching of the gospel.

So the blessings offered in vv. 19-21 are the definitive forgiveness of sins, spiritual refreshment through the Holy Spirit, and ultimately a share in the restoration of all things. These blessings are made possible by the suffering, heavenly exaltation, and return of Messiah Jesus.

c. *The Prophet like Moses (3:22-26)*

22-23 Peter has given positive reasons for repenting, but now he provides a negative or threatening counterpart. His scriptural quotation combines words from Deuteronomy 18:15, 19 and Leviticus 23:29. The plural *'"for you"' (hymin)* is inserted early in the citation, and another plural is inserted at the end of v. 22 *(pros hymas,* 'to you'), to emphasize the need for the audience to respond collectively to Jesus as the prophet like Moses. When Moses said, *'"The Lord your God will raise up for you a prophet like me from among your own people"'*,[60] it was in the context of warning Israel not to be like the nations. Instead of practicing sorcery or divination, God's people were to *'"listen to everything he tells you"'*. The warning is then individualized in v. 23 with the addition of words from Leviticus 23:29: *'"anyone"' (pasa psychē)* who does not listen to that prophet as God's mouthpiece *'"will be completely cut off"' (exolethreuthēsetai)* from the people *(ek tou laou).*[61] The verb here describes utter destruction (BDAG). TNIV's *from their people* is a more generalized rendering of the final phrase, which does not adequately indicate that Israel is specifically in view. A succession of prophets was raised up to follow Moses, but none was recognized as a prophet specifically like Moses himself (cf. Dt. 34:10). In time, Moses' words were interpreted as referring to one particular prophet who was yet to come and who would function as prophet-king and prophet-lawgiver in the end time.[62] Moses' prophecy came to be regarded as messianic in its scope. Peter envis-

---

60. Some Greek MSS of Acts 3:22 add 'to the fathers', or some variation of that expression, to the word 'said' (so KJV, NKJV). But this appears to be a later addition to the original, influenced by the wording of v. 13 ('the God of our fathers'). 'Your God' is better attested than 'our God'. But a number of MSS in the Alexandrian family have no pronoun after 'God' at all, which Metzger, *Textual Commentary,* 274, explains as an example of the usual tendency towards parsimoniousness in this textual tradition.

61. The words from Lv. 23:29 are added to the quotation to bring out the implications of God's warning in Dt. 18:19 ('I myself will call him to account'). Those who were unwilling to heed God's prophet would show themselves unworthy to be counted among his people. Acts 3:22-23 produces 'a warning to obey that evokes conceptual parallels of the blessing and cursing pattern of the Law' (Bock, *Proclamation,* 194). Cf. Barrett 1994, 209-10.

62. For Jewish, Samaritan, and Christian interpretations of this hope, see H. M. Teeple, *The Mosaic Eschatological Prophet,* JBLMS 10 (Philadelphia: JBL, 1957), 63-68, 100-121, and Bock, *Proclamation,* 191-4. Jesus is hailed as 'the Prophet' in Jn. 6:14; 7:40, and the divine command at his transfiguration ('listen to him', Mk. 9:7 par.) echoes Dt. 18:15, suggesting that Jesus is the expected prophet.

ages Jesus as the eschatological prophet because he brings the ultimate revelation of God's will and leads God's people to final salvation (cf. 7:35-38
note). Jesus functions for Israel now as Moses did at the time of the exodus.
By their response to the resurrected Jesus, Peter's audience will show
whether they belong to the true Israel or not!

24 As in v. 18, *'all the prophets who have spoken have foretold'* (*katēn-*
geilan, 'announced') *these days.* Peter moves on from Moses as a prophet of
the end time to the succession of prophets *'beginning with Samuel'.* The focus of their revelations was not simply the suffering of the Messiah (as in
v. 18), but the events and blessings of the messianic era in general (as in vv.
19-21). But in what sense could a prophet like Samuel, who spoke so decisively to his own time, have been announcing eschatological matters? Inas-
much as Samuel anointed David and spoke of the establishment of his
kingdom (e.g., 1 Sa. 13:14; 15:28; 16:13; 28:17), he was declaring God's intention to save and bless his people through the house of David. Samuel
superintended the process by which David was appointed, having earlier
declared the pattern of kingship that would fulfill God's purpose for Israel
(1 Sa. 12:13-15). The early Christian preachers regarded the promises made
to David and the whole pattern of God's dealing with Israel through him as
finding ultimate fulfillment in the Messiah and his kingdom (cf. comments
on 1:15-17, 20; 2:25-36; 13:32-37).

25-26 Emphatic second-person plural pronouns return at the end of
the speech to stress the potential involvement of Peter's audience in the
messianic salvation (contrast the use of such pronouns in vv. 13-15, in his
accusations against them).[63] *'You are heirs of the prophets'* (*hoi huioi tōn*
prophētōn, 'sons of the prophets'), he declares, meaning that they ought to
be the beneficiaries of everything promised by the prophets concerning the
messianic era. He also claims that they are heirs of *'the covenant God made*
with your fathers', meaning that they are in line to experience the ultimate
blessing of the covenant made with Abraham, Isaac, and Jacob (cf. v. 13
note). This last point is so foundational to Peter's understanding of Scripture and its revelation of God's purposes that he develops and expands it
as the climax of his appeal. In so doing, he conflates the promise of Genesis
12:3 LXX ('and all peoples on earth will be blessed through you') with the
promise of Genesis 22:18 LXX ('and through your offspring all nations on
earth will be blessed'). It is clear, however, 'that they do not have a right to
the covenant itself irrespective of their reaction to Jesus'.[64]

Does the expression ' "raised up his servant" ' (*anastēsas*) refer to Jesus'
first appearance on the stage of history, as the prophet from Nazareth, or to
his resurrection from the dead? The verbal link with v. 22 and the quotation

---

63. From beginning to end, this speech is 'shaped to fit its narrative setting and to
move its narrative audience to respond' (Tannehill 1990, 55). Some MSS read 'the God of our
fathers' in v. 25 (*hēmōn,* instead of *hymōn*). But this appears to be a change by copyists, to
conform to the general usage of Acts.

64. Barrett 1994, 212.

from Deuteronomy 18:15 might suggest the former. The preceding context could suggest that the reference is to the ministry of the risen Christ through his apostles.[65] Peter declares that, through the apostolic preaching, God has sent his exalted servant first to Israel, *'to bless you by turning each of you from your wicked ways'*. The use of the word *'first' (prōton)* implies the sort of sequence portrayed in Isaiah 49:5-6, where the Servant of the Lord is used to 'restore the tribes of Jacob' so that they can be 'a light for the Gentiles' and bring God's salvation 'to the ends of the earth' (cf. Acts 1:6; 13:46-48; 26:16-18). In other words, that significant 'Servant Song', which reveals the way in which God will ultimately fulfill his promise to Abraham, appears to lie behind the final challenge of Peter's sermon. In this sequence of thought, the raising up of Jesus more naturally refers to God sending him as his Servant, to fulfill the divine plan for Israel and the nations.[66] The messianic blessing includes all the benefits of Jesus' saving work outlined in vv. 19-21, together with the gift of repentance *('by turning each of you from your wicked ways')*. Turning to God or to the Lord Jesus is the positive side of this reorientation of life (cf. 9:35; 11:21; 14:15; 15:19; 26:18, 20). In the present context, God (or the Lord Jesus as his Servant) is the implied subject of the verbal expression *turning from (en tō apostrephein)*. This highlights the Lord's role in making repentance possible. Repentance or turning to God 'is a human action which, theologically discerned, is also a divine action in individuals and societies'.[67] It is a blessing of the New Covenant for the Jews first, but also for the Gentiles (cf. 5:31; 11:18; 14:15; 26:17-18). At this point in the narrative, Peter clearly anticipates that the messianic salvation will somehow be extended to the nations. In Acts 10–11, he is faced with more precise questions: How might Gentiles actually receive the gospel from believing Jews and be united with them in the community of the Messiah?

E. The Leadership of the New Israel (4:1-22)

Two issues in this first half of the chapter are signalled in 4:2 and then dealt with in reverse order.[1] The authority of the apostles to teach 'the people' in the name of Jesus is mentioned, but not explicitly challenged until 4:13-22. More immediately, their 'proclaiming in Jesus the resurrection of the dead'

---

65. This interpretation is consistent with the fact that the sermon in Acts 3 is perceived by the leaders of the Sanhedrin as essentially 'proclaiming in Jesus the resurrection of the dead' (4:2). Cf. O'Reilly, *Word and Sign*, 112-19.

66. Cf. Barrett 1994, 213.

67. Tannehill, *Shape*, 89. Tannehill, 84-101, examines the terminology of repentance (*metanoia — metanoeō*) and turning (*epistrophē — epistrephō*) in Luke-Acts and considers this usage in the context of Lukan soteriology. Cf. Bock 2007, 181-82.

1. Barrett 1994, 216-17, misses this point and argues that Luke is demonstrating inconsistency in the use of his sources.

is confronted in connection with questions about the healing of the lame man (4:5-12). Acts 2–3 implies that the restoration of Israel had begun in Jerusalem, as many responded in faith to the preaching about Jesus. Acts 4 shows how the leaders of the old Israel, associated with the temple and the Sanhedrin, were being 'cut off from the people' (3:23) because they would not listen to Jesus (3:22). The apostles as his 'prophetic successors',[2] in healing and convicting proclamation, emerge as the leaders of a renewed Israel, whose ministry is profoundly threatening to the old order. Through them, the significance of Jesus continues to be proclaimed and many more believe (4:4). Jesus' prediction that they would rule over 'the twelve tribes of Israel' (Lk. 22:30) is shown to be already in the process of fulfillment. A conflict of leadership over the people of God emerges again in 5:12-42. In both passages, however, the ultimate focus is on Jesus rather than on the apostles. He is the one in whom the resurrection from the dead (4:2) and all the blessings of salvation (4:11-12) are to be found. God has exalted Jesus to his own right hand as 'Prince and Saviour' for Israel (5:31). Allegiance to the glorified Christ is what determines membership in the true people of God. The authority and power of the apostles is derived from him, and their essential task is to point others to him, telling 'the people' the full message of 'this new life' (5:20). In Acts 4 we have the first of three persecution episodes in this early stage of Luke's narrative (cf. 5:17-42; 6:8–8:4).

1. Proclaiming in Jesus the Resurrection from the Dead (4:1-12)

Peter expands on the Christology of the preceding chapters, using Psalm 118:22 in his defence speech (4:8-12). Psalm 2:1-2 then forms the basis of a community prayer for deliverance from oppression and for continuing boldness in proclamation (4:23-30). Both quotations explain something of the significance of Jesus in the divine plan and warn about the consequences of rejecting him. The first is used to justify the claim that 'salvation is found in no one else' (v. 12), and the second to highlight the futility of banding together '"against the Lord and against his anointed one"'. It is interesting to recall that Psalms 16:8-11 and 110:1 were foundational to the Christological teaching in 2:24-36. Two of these four passages were used by Jesus in his own teaching (Ps. 118:22-23 in Mt. 21:42-43; Mk. 12:10; Lk. 20:17 and Ps. 110:1 in Mt. 22:41-45; Mk. 12:35-37; Lk. 20:41-44). The other two psalms may well have been chosen because of the postresurrection teaching of Jesus, which included learning from 'the Law of Moses, the Prophets and the Psalms' (Lk. 24:44-46) about the necessity of his suffering and resurrection.

---

2. Johnson 1992, 80. The word *laos* as a specific designation for the 'people' of Israel is used more frequently in Acts 4 and 5 than in any other chapter (4:1, 2, 8, 10, 17, 21, 25 ['the peoples'], 27; 5:12, 13, 20, 25, 26, 34, 37 ['a band of people']), signalling that the relationship of the apostles and the nascent church to the people of Israel is a critical issue in this section.

1-2   Considering the accusations and warnings in Peter's address to the crowd (3:12-26), it is not surprising that the temple officials were *greatly disturbed* (*diaponoumenoi*, 'worn out', 'unable to put up with any more', 'vexed'),[3] and *came up to* (*epestēsan*, 'confronted') Peter and John, even *while they were speaking to the people (lalountōn de autōn pros ton laon)*.[4] The authorities in question were *the priests and the captain of the temple guard and the Sadducees*. The *captain of the temple guard* (*stratēgos tou hierou*, 'captain of the temple') was the highest ranking priest after the high priest. He assisted the high priest in the performance of his ceremonial duties and was the chief of police in the temple area, with power to arrest (cf. 5:24, 26).[5] *The Sadducees* as a party had no specific authority in the temple, but many of the priests came from their ranks. All were offended because the apostles were usurping the role of *teaching the people* in the temple precincts. This is mentioned twice in 4:1-2, but not specifically confronted until 4:13-22 (cf. 5:25, 42). 'The people' *(ho laos)* is a distinctive term for Israel, deeply rooted in the covenant theology of the OT. Although the priests had a responsibility to protect God's people from the corrupting effect of false teaching, they are later described as being driven by jealousy in opposing the apostles and their ministry (5:17). What disturbed them most about the apostolic message was their *proclaiming in Jesus the resurrection of the dead*. The Saducean party, which was made up of chief priests and elders, the priestly and the lay nobility, denied that on the last day there would be a general resurrection from the dead (cf. Lk. 20:27; Acts 23:7-8).[6] Apart from their theological concerns, they perhaps also thought that the apostles' teaching could be 'politically, socially, and religiously destabilizing to their relatively good relationship with Rome'.[7] The Pharisees had made this hope popular among the common people, but the apostles were going a step further than the

3. Cf. Barrett 1994, 215, 219.

4. Cf. note 2 above on 'the people' in Acts 4–5. A clear link to the preceding scene is made by the use of a genitive absolute construction in 4:1, with the participle *lalountōn* ('speaking') in the present tense. Barrett 1994, 218, observes that it is 'a characteristic Lucan device to represent a speech as unfinished' (cf. 7:54; 10:44; 17:32; 22:22; 26:24). However, it is possible that the plural pronoun *autōn* ('they') indicates that Peter and John were together in a more informal mode of speaking to the people — after the speech had ended — when they were arrested. Cf. Witherington 1998, 188-89. Johnson 1992, 76, notes Luke's use of the verb 'came upon' *(epestēsan)* for sudden appearances.

5. Cf. J. Jeremias, *Jerusalem in the Time of Jesus: An Investigation into Economic and Social Conditions during the New Testament Period* (ET, London: SCM, 1969), 160-61, 163. Some MSS of v. 1 have *archiereis* ('chief priests'). This reading, which is not well attested, may have arisen because two chief priests are mentioned together in v. 6. Metzger, *Textual Commentary*, 274-75, discusses variations in the Codex D text of 4:1-4.

6. 'The patrician families stood in the same relationship to the priestly nobility as the Pharisees to the scribes. In both cases, the laity formed the mass of supporters; the "men of religion" — Sadducean clergy, Pharisaic theologians — were the leaders' (Jeremias, *Jerusalem*, 230). On the Sadducean beliefs, see Josephus, *Ant.* 13.297-98; 18.16-17; *War* 2.164-65; G. G. Porton, 'Sadducees', *DNTB* 1050-52.

7. Bock 2007, 186.

Pharisees and claiming its fulfillment *in Jesus* (*en tō Iēsou* may mean 'in the case of Jesus' or 'by means of Jesus').[8] This expression could refer to the resurrection of Jesus alone or to his resurrection as proof of a coming general resurrection. The flow of the argument in Acts 3–4 suggests the latter. Jesus' resurrection guarantees that God's promise to 'restore everything' (3:21) will most surely be fulfilled and that those who trust in Jesus will enjoy all the benefits of the salvation that his resurrection makes possible in the new creation.[9]

3-4   The reaction of the people and their leaders is dramatically contrasted. The authorities *seized Peter and John,* hoping to silence them. Since it was evening, *they put them in jail until the next day,*[10] when an investigation could take place (vv. 5-7). However, *many who heard the message* about Jesus *believed* (cf. 2:37). Indeed, Luke records a further advance in numbers from the three thousand who believed on the Day of Pentecost (2:41): *the number of men who believed grew to about five thousand* (*egenēthē [ho] arithmos tōn andrōn [hōs] chiliades pente;* NRSV, ESV, 'the number of men came to be about five thousand'). This number probably included the three thousand baptised at Pentecost. If *men (andres)* means only males, the total number of believers, including women and children, will have been much larger. However, as noted in connection with 1:16, females are included with males in some NT uses of this Greek word.[11] The perspective of these chapters is that people in Jerusalem continued to be generally favourable to the new movement (2:47; 4:21; 5:13, 26), until they were swayed by the false charges levelled against Stephen (6:11-14) and became part of the opposition.[12]

8. Cf. Barrett 1994, 220, for possible renderings and understandings of this expression. On Pharisaic beliefs, see Josephus, *Ant.* 13.297-98; 18.12-17; S. Mason, 'Pharisees', *DNTB* 782-87.

9. K. L. Anderson, *'But God Raised Him from the Dead': The Theology of Jesus' Resurrection in Luke-Acts* (Milton Keynes: Paternoster, 2006), shows how Jesus' resurrection plays a pivotal role in four aspects of Lukan soteriology: theology (as part of God's purpose for the whole world); ecclesiology (as the inaugural action of God in the restoration of Israel); Christology (as an act of God that establishes Jesus as the definitive leader of the people of God); and eschatology (as the first installment of the full realization of the kingdom of God among humankind).

10. Barrett 1994, 215, 221, suggests that *ethento eis tērēsin* could be rendered 'put them under guard' or 'took them into custody'. Witherington 1998, 190, picks up this point and argues with B. Rapske, *The Book of Acts in Its First-Century Setting,* Vol. 3: *The Book of Acts and Paul in Roman Custody* (Grand Rapids: Eerdmans; Carlisle: Paternoster, 1994), 9-35, that Jews did not punish by custody but held suspects until a trial could be arranged. The expression *ēn gar hespera ēdē* ('for it was already evening') implies that some time had elapsed since Peter and John first went to the temple (3:1).

11. Barrett 1994, 221-22, defends the number 5,000 as credible, arguing that the word 'men' *(andres)* in Acts regularly refers only to adult males and that the overall number of believers could have been much greater. Cf. Bock 2007, 188-89. Metzger, *Textual Commentary,* 275, discusses the textual uncertainty about the word *hōs* ('about'), but notes that it is a favourite of Luke when referring to numbers.

12. Cf. Tannehill 1990, 59-60, for a fuller discussion of the role played by 'the people' in Luke's narrative and my note 2 above.

5-6 Those who *met in Jerusalem* the next day to question the apostles were literally 'their rulers and elders and scribes' *(autōn tous archontas kai tous presbyterous kai tous grammateis)*. *Jerusalem* is probably mentioned again at this point to highlight the significance of the context in which opposition to the gospel was coming. In Roman times, this group constituted the Jewish council called the Sanhedrin.[13] It is a pity that the TNIV does not translate 'their' *(autōn)*, since the word is used here to distinguish the leadership of the old Israel from the leadership of the new. *Rulers (archontes)* is a general term, which would certainly have included the chief priests mentioned in v. 6. *Elders (presbyteroi)* is another general term, applicable to both priests and laymen.[14] The *teachers of the law (grammateis,* 'scribes') were the lay, Pharisaic scholars, who were gradually increasing their influence in what had been a predominantly Sadducean assembly. Among the chief priests, *Annas the high priest* is mentioned first, even though he had held office much earlier, from AD 6 to 15. His influence in national affairs apparently continued beyond the period of his official rule (cf. Lk. 3:2).[15] *Caiaphas*, his son-in-law, was actually high priest at the time, officiating from AD 18 to 36 (cf. Josephus, *Ant.* 18.26-35; Jn. 18:13, 24). *John* and *Alexander* are otherwise unknown members of *the high priest's family (hosoi ēsan ek genous archieratikou,* 'those who belonged to the high-priestly clan').[16] Luke thus indicates that the apostles were arraigned before the same court that tried and condemned Jesus. Indeed, here and in 5:17-42, the trial of Jesus is effectively reopened and the evidence about him is presented once more to the leaders of Israel and to Luke's readers.

7 *They had Peter and John brought before them,* or, more literally (as in most EVV), 'set them in the midst' *(stēsantes en tō mesō)*. Given that the Sanhedrin was arranged 'like the half of a round threshing-floor so that they might see one another' *(m. Sanh.* 4:3), Luke is probably making a deliberate reference to this formidable setting (cf. Josephus, *Ant.* 14.168-76). As *they began to question them (epynthanonto)*, they asked, *'By what power or what*

13. The Sanhedrin is mentioned by name in Lk. 19:47; 22:66; Acts 4:15; 5:21, 27, 34, 41; 6:12, 15; 22:30; 23:1, 6, 15, 20, 28. On the composition and operation of this council, see Bruce 1990, 153-54; E. Lohse, *TDNT* 7:861-71; G. H. Twelftree, 'Sanhedrin', *DNTB* 1061-65. Witherington 1998, 191-92, responds to recent scholarly challenges about the existence of the Sanhedrin as a legislative and judicial body in the apostolic period.

14. Cf. Twelftree, 'Sanhedrin', 1063. Note that 'rulers of the people and elders' is a convenient way of summarising the membership of the Sanhedrin in v. 8.

15. Cf. Witherington 1998, 190-91. Barrett 1994, 224, suggests that Luke may have placed Annas before Caiaphas to suggest that 'Annas, though deposed by the Romans, was still the rightful High Priest. Caiaphas might carry out the functions but could not (in strict Jewish opinion) replace his father-in-law.'

16. Cf. Barrett 1994, 215. The Western reading 'Jonathan', instead of 'John', may be a reference to the son of Annas, who succeeded Caiaphas as high priest (Josephus, *Ant.* 18.95). Jeremias, *Jerusalem,* 175-81, argues that the term *archiereis* ('chief priests' or 'high priests') can refer to a group of leading priests, who 'by virtue of their office had seats and votes in the Sanhedrin, where they formed a well-defined group' (179).

name did you do this?' This form of questioning recalls the challenge to Jesus in Luke 20:2 ('Tell us by what authority you are doing these things' and 'Who gave you this authority?'). At one level, the Sanhedrin knew the answer already, since the accused had been proclaiming the resurrection of Jesus in connection with the healing miracle (3:12-21). However, the challenge was presumably made here to expose their theology before the court and provide grounds for accusing them of blasphemy. *By what power* implies 'By what supernatural power?' and *by what name* 'Who is the source of that power?' These questions are specifically answered by Peter in v. 10. While being concerned about the great religious issues of the day, these Jewish leaders were like many others in similar positions throughout history, 'preoccupied with issues of power and reputation'.[17]

8   With reference to the healing of the man crippled from birth (3:1-10), Peter had already stated publicly that the power was not their own (3:12) and that the restoration took place 'by faith in the name of Jesus' (3:16). The *name* of Jesus, which is given some prominence in 2:38; 3:6, 16, continues to be a dominant theme in Acts 4:7, 10, 12, 17, 18, and 30. Now, *filled with the Spirit (plēstheis pneumatos hagiou)*, Peter boldly restates his claim in a much more threatening situation, before the *rulers and elders of the people,* and effectively puts them on the spot.[18] The verb used here (*plēstheis,* 'filled') is the one employed to describe the coming of the Spirit at Pentecost in 2:4. In 4:8, the aorist passive participle may signify that Peter was already full of the Spirit (as a result of Pentecost) and spoke accordingly (cf. 13:9, with reference to Paul, and the use of the adjective *plērēs* ['full'] in 6:3, 5, 8; 7:55; 11:24).[19] However, it must be acknowledged that the same verb is used in 4:31 in a way that suggests a further endowment of the Spirit for boldness in proclamation (cf. the parallel term *eplērounto* ['they were being filled'] in 13:52). Either way, Jesus' promise of 'words and wisdom that none of your adversaries will be able to resist or contradict' (Lk. 21:15) was being fulfilled for Peter in this critical context by the Spirit's enabling (cf. Lk. 12:12).

9-10   At one level, this trial was simply about *'an act of kindness shown to a man who was lame' (anthrōpou asthenous,* 'sick person') and about *'how he was healed' (sesōstai).* Peter begins his defence by appealing to the *kindness* of their action (*euergesia,* 'a good deed').[20] At the same time, the perfect pas-

17. Spencer 1997, 50. However, Gaventa 2003, 92-93, says that the questions were not disingenuous because the Gospels show the populace accepting the reality of miracles but knowing that they can originate either with Satan (e.g., Lk. 11:15) or with God (e.g., Mt. 13:54; Lk. 5:17; Jn. 3:1).

18. KJV and NKJV follow the longer, largely Western reading ('rulers of the people and elders of Israel'), which Metzger, *Textual Commentary,* 276, argues was a later addition 'made in the interest of symmetry and balance'.

19. Bruce 1990, 151, suggests that *plēstheis pneumatos hagiou* implies 'a specially inspired utterance for the occasion, in fulfilment of Jesus' promise in Mk. 13:11 par. Mt. 10:19f. and Lk. 12:11 (also Lk. 21:15)'. He believes that the adjective *plērēs* is used with reference to 'the Spirit's abiding presence in a believer's life'. Cf. Barrett 1994, 226.

20. Cf. Witherington 1998, 193-94, on the character and style of this speech.

sive of the verb *sōzō* is used to confirm the man's restored condition and possibly to hint at the deeper significance of the event. This verb can refer to healing in the physical sense (cf. the parallel term *tetherapeumenon* ['had been healed'] in v. 14), but it mostly refers to salvation in the sense of rescue from the coming judgment of God and enjoyment of life under God's rule in the Messianic Age (cf. 2:21, 40, 47).[21] Although Peter wants to introduce that eschatological dimension of salvation into his defence, he first reaffirms that *'this man stands before you healed'* (using the adjective *hygiēs*, 'healthy, sound', BDAG). He then takes the opportunity to make public (*gnōston estō pasin hymin*; NRSV, ESV, 'let it be known to all of you') the true source of this healing. In so doing, he appeals to the leaders and, through them, to *'all the people of Israel'* (*panti tō laō Israēl*; cf. 4:1-2 note). Ignorance can no longer be an excuse when the facts are proclaimed like this. The short speeches here and in 5:30-32 restate in various ways elements of the argument in 3:11-19, dramatically demonstrating the need for *'persistent speaking in the face of opposition'*.[22] Peter insists that the healing took place *'by the name of Jesus Christ of Nazareth'*,[23] reminding them that it was the same Jesus whom they *'crucified but whom God raised from the dead'*. As in 2:22-36 and 3:13-18, Peter is arguing that God has accomplished his purposes through Jesus, despite the opposition of his own people (cf. Jn. 1:11-13). In raising him from the dead, God began the great process of renewal and restoration that will culminate in a transformed creation and the general resurrection of all believers to eternal life (cf. 3:19-21 note). What happened to the crippled man was an anticipation of the glory to come, but also a sign of the present, heavenly authority of the exalted Christ to save in the ultimate sense.

11 The text that Jesus used at the end of his parable of the vineyard (Mt. 21:42; Mk. 12:10; Lk. 20:17) is modified here to highlight even more directly the tragic error of his opponents (cf. 1 Pet. 2:7). The verb *'"rejected"'* in the Greek version of Psalm 118:22 (LXX 117:22, *apedokimasan*) is replaced with another which more literally means 'scorned' *(exouthenētheis)* and the words 'by you' *(hyph' hymōn)* are inserted before *'"the builders"'* to make the application to Peter's audience abundantly clear.[24] The pattern of v. 10 is re-

---

21. Cf. THE THEOLOGY OF ACTS: IV. SALVATION (pp. 65-70).

22. Tannehill 1990, 62. Tannehill says, 'It is dramatically important that the apostles repeat what they have said in spite of threats from the powerful.' However, it is also practically important to challenge opposition with a consistent message and not to modify it to avoid persecution (cf. Gal. 1:6-10).

23. *en tō onomati* could also be rendered 'in the name'. The Greek of this verse is actually more complex than TNIV shows, with a further expression *en toutō* ('in this [name]' or 'by him') used to emphasize that the man has been healed by the same Jesus whom they crucified (the living person behind the name). Cf. Barrett 1994, 215, 228-29. *tou Nazōraiou* ('the Nazorean') is also used as a title in Lk. 18:37; Acts 2:22; 3:6; 6:14; 22:8; 26:9.

24. Barrett 1994, 230, observes that the modifications in the quotation imply 'a preaching context', and does not think that Luke himself reworded the psalm. The change of verb suggests 'the identification of the *stone* with a person'.

flected in the two lines of the quotation. Jesus is the despised '*"stone"*', scorned by the leaders of Israel but exalted by God to the place of highest honour and significance. He is now '*"the cornerstone"*' (lit. 'head of a corner', *kephalē gōnias*), which plays an essential part in the building which God is constructing.[25] In other words, he is the key figure in God's plan for the restoration of Israel and the whole of his creation. In the original context of the psalm, the stone is either Israel or Israel's king, rejected by the nations but chosen by God for the accomplishment of his purpose. As elsewhere in the NT, however, 'God's purpose for Israel finds its fulfilment in the single-handed work of the Christ'.[26]

12 Following his use of Psalm 118:22 as a warning to the leaders of Israel (Lk. 20:17-18), Jesus predicted that 'not one stone' would be left on another in Jerusalem and its temple (Lk. 21:6), because his contemporaries did not recognise the time of God's coming to them (Lk. 19:41-44). Although the prospect of judgment is implicit in what he says, Peter goes on to offer hope, even to those who put Jesus to death, with the assertion that '*Salvation is found in no one else*'. This is so because '*there is no other name given under heaven by which we must be saved*'.[27] *Under heaven* means in all of God's creation (cf. Eccl. 1:13). Once more, the point is made that Jesus' *name* is 'the inescapable decision point concerning salvation'.[28] Members of the Sanhedrin would have agreed that the God of Israel is humanity's only true saviour (cf. Ex. 15:1-11; Is. 43:11-12; 45:22; Ps. 96:1-5). But Peter now insists that the name of Jesus is the exclusive means by which God's saving power can be invoked and experienced. God's ultimate act of salvation, in preparation for 'the coming of the great and glorious day of the Lord', has been accomplished through Jesus, so that he is now the exalted Lord upon

25. Longenecker 1981, 304-5, notes that in the first-century-AD *Test. Sol.* 22:7–23:4 'the stone at the head of the corner' unambiguously refers to 'the final copestone or capstone placed on the summit of the Jerusalem temple to complete the whole edifice'. Cf. J. Jeremias, *TDNT* 1:792-93. The cornerstone envisaged is not merely ceremonial, as in modern buildings, but 'a stone that bears weight for the entire construction' (Gaventa 2003, 93). This imagery is picked up by Eph. 2:19-20; 1 Pet. 2:4-7 with reference ot the 'building' of the church.

26. Bruce 1988, 93. Gaventa 2003, 93, plays down the full Christological implication of this psalm citation by arguing that it serves 'less to identify Jesus in some specific way than to indict the audience for its rejection of him'. The enormity of the rejection is highlighted by identifying the significance of Jesus in the plan of God.

27. The Greek includes the expression *en anthrōpois* (KJV, NKJV, ESV 'among men'), perhaps to indicate that behind the name stands a person, who lived among us as the agent of God's salvation. Cf. Barrett 1994, 232. Metzger, *Textual Commentary*, 276-77, discusses Western variations in the text of 4:12.

28. Tannehill 1990, 61. Cf. 2:38; 3:16. Contra Gaventa 2003, 94, who states that 'the emphasis falls on God's gift of salvation rather than on a negation of other religious practices', the primary challenge in the context is for the Jewish leaders to see their need to call upon Jesus as Saviour and Lord. This implies the inadequacy of remaining where they are in relation to God. If such a challenge is presented to the leaders of Judaism, it must surely mean that there is a negation of all religious systems and practices that do not lead people to Christ.

whom to call for that salvation (2:20-21, 33-36). Even the leaders of Israel must acknowledge their utter dependence on him. Using different terms, Paul makes a similar challenge to a Gentile audience in 17:30-31, and later he states his divine commission to present Jesus as the only saviour for Jews and Gentiles alike (26:15-23). History has revealed many self-appointed saviour figures and humanity has devised many ways of 'salvation', but there is a divine necessity (*dei, must*) that should be communicated to everyone about calling upon the name that God has provided.[29] This is so because of Jesus' unique place in the divine plan (v. 11). People in a relativistic, multi-faith society find such an exclusive claim very difficult to accept. Alternatives have been proposed to weaken its impact, including the notion that Jesus somehow benefits sincere adherents of other religions, even though they do not acknowledge him as Saviour and Lord.[30] But such approaches are not consistent with the teaching of Acts 2–3, that it is actually necessary to call upon the name of Jesus with repentance and faith to benefit from the salvation he offers. Furthermore, the claim of Acts 4:12 is consistent with the testimony that Jesus bears to himself in passages such as Matthew 11:27-30; John 5:19-27; 14:6. Bruce rightly observes that 'the founders of the great world-religions are not to be disparaged by followers of the Christian way. But of none of them can it be said that there is no saving health in anyone else; to one alone belongs the title: the Savior of the world'.[31] As the lame man experienced healing when he was encouraged to trust in the name of Jesus Christ (3:7), so salvation in the sense of forgiveness, reception of the Holy Spirit, and enjoyment of life in the age to come is available for everyone who repents and is baptised 'in the name of Jesus Christ' (2:38-40).[32]

2. Teaching the People in the Name of Jesus (4:13-22)

There is distinct irony in this section. The authorities have the power to punish the apostles, but they are afraid to use it because public opinion is

29. Bock 2007, 194, lists a number of saviour-figures in the Greco-Roman world that could be seen as rivals to Jesus.

30. D. Strange, *The Possibility of Salvation among the Unevangelised: An Analysis of Inclusivism in Recent Evangelical Theology* (Carlisle: Paternoster, 2001), 191-94, argues convincingly against those who propose that Acts 4:12 and Paul's use of Joel 2:32 in Rom. 10:12-15 allow for the salvation of those who do not actually call upon the name of Christ. Cf. Bock 2007, 200, on the exclusivism of Acts 4:12.

31. Bruce 1988, 94.

32. Barrett 1994, 231, argues that the primary meaning of salvation in Acts is detachment from 'this perverse generation' and punishment for that perversity (2:40), and attachment to the people who are 'being saved' (2:47), as they experience the new life of the Spirit. However, Barrett does not think Luke explains how the work of Jesus achieves this salvation. Cf. I. H. Marshall, *Luke: Historian and Theologian* (Exeter: Paternoster, 1970), 94-102, and note 21 above.

against them (vv. 15-17, 21). Peter and John have no political power, but demonstrate a God-given courage that is compelling in conjunction with the evidence of the healing miracle (vv. 13-14). They appear as true leaders of the people, bearing witness to what they have seen and heard, despite the consequences for them personally. 'Although they are outside the religious power structure, they are the ones who seek to obey God (vv. 19-20) and through whom God is praised (v. 21).'[33] The Jewish leaders demonstrate stubborn unbelief in the face of what they acknowledge to be 'a notable sign' (v. 16), and place an impossible demand on the apostles 'not to speak or teach at all in the name of Jesus' (v. 18). This moves the apostles to affirm their primary loyalty to God and intention to keep speaking about what they have seen and heard (vv. 19-20).

13 What particularly struck the leaders of the Jewish community about this response was *the courage of Peter and John*. The word translated *courage (parrēsia)* and the related verb are regularly used by Luke to highlight the 'freedom of speech' of those empowered by the Spirit to speak the word of God (2:29; 4:13, 29, 31; 9:27-28; 13:46; 14:3; 18:26; 19:8; 26:26; 28:31). Most often it is employed in connection with the proclamation of the gospel to Jews. In ordinary Greek usage, this terminology described the right of citizens to say anything in the public assembly, openness to truth, and the courage of openness or candour.[34] For Luke, however, the underlying notion is that of a prophetic compulsion (v. 20) and a divine enabling (vv. 29, 31) to speak the truth about God. Such courage was remarkable in the case of Peter and John because they were regarded as *unschooled, ordinary men (anthrōpoi agrammatoi kai idiōtai)*. The terms used here mean that they were 'unlettered' *(agrammatoi)* and unskilled 'laymen' *(idiōtai)*, in the sense that they were not trained as interpreters of Scripture and rabbinic tradition.[35] Their interrogators were *astonished*, but they also *took note (epeginōskon te autous,* 'they recognized them') that they *had been with Jesus (hoti syn tō Iēsou ēsan)*. They realized who their master had been and the influence he had had upon them. Jesus himself had not been professionally trained (cf. Jn. 7:15), but he was widely acknowledged as 'Rabbi' or 'Teacher'. Peter and John had obviously been taught by Jesus and shared something of his wisdom, insight into the Scriptures, and prophetic authority!

14-15 The Jewish leaders were also unable to escape the fact that

---

33. Gaventa 2003, 94.

34. Cf. H. Schlier, *TDNT* 5:872-73; W. C. van Unnik, 'The Christian's Freedom of Speech in the New Testament', *BJRL* 44 (1961-62), 477. Johnson 1992, 78, notes that the quality of *parrēsia* was particularly associated with philosophers of the Cynic strain and argues that Luke's use of both noun and verb forms to identify his prophetic characters is 'a nice example of his blending of prophetic and philosophical images'.

35. For the use of such terms in Greek literature and for possible Hebrew parallels cf. Barrett 1994, 233-34; Witherington 1998, 195-96. In Greek usage, *idiōtēs* is first the private person over against the state, and then the unskilled person over against the expert. The term *idiōtai* is not included in the Codex D version of Acts 4:13. Cf. Metzger, *Textual Commentary*, 277-78.

they could see the man who had been healed standing there with them. The evidence for his cure could not be avoided, and *there was nothing they could say* (NRSV, ESV more helpfully translate *anteipein*, 'nothing to say in opposition'; KJV, NKJV 'say nothing against it'). The use of this particular verb suggests a fulfillment of the specific promise of Jesus in Luke 21:15. Although the speech of the apostles was Spirit-inspired, the authorities were not convinced about the need to acknowledge Jesus as the one responsible for this healing, nor ready to call upon his name for salvation themselves. Neither logic nor prophetic power necessarily undermines prejudice and moves hard-hearted people to faith! The apostles and the man who had been lame from birth were ordered to *withdraw from the Sanhedrin* so that the members could confer together in private.[36]

16-17 It could not be denied that *'a notable sign' (gnōston sēmeion)* had been done by the apostles and that this was 'manifest' *(phaneron)* to *'everyone living in Jerusalem'*. Two key terms are used ironically here: *gnōston* recalls Peter's challenge to recognise Jesus as the one responsible for the healing (v. 10), and *sēmeion* is Luke's term for what the apostles were doing (2:43; 4:22, 30), following the pattern of Jesus in his ministry (2:22). At one level, this particular sign was inescapable. But the interpretation given by Peter was rejected because of the status it gave to Jesus as the risen Christ and because it challenged the Sadducean position on resurrection (4:2), threatening their leadership of the people. So Luke makes it clear that signs and wonders are not necessarily persuasive, even if their supernatural significance is made known by faithful explanation. The main concern of the authorities was to *'stop this thing from spreading any further among the people'*. It was not only the message, but also the growing number of believers in the name of Jesus that troubled them (4:4). Their own prejudice and desire for self-protection prevented them from evaluating the evidence properly. They therefore determined to *'warn'* the apostles *'to speak no longer to anyone in this name'*.[37] But this was an impossible demand, as Peter was quick to point out.

18-20 When they were commanded *not to speak or teach at all in the name of Jesus,* the apostles could not comply.[38] To do so would have been to deny their experience of Jesus, his teaching, his death and resurrection, the ascension, and his gift of the Holy Spirit. It would also have been a denial

36. We have no way of knowing how Luke obtained information about the private deliberation of the Sanhedrin, though Witherington 1998, 196, suggests that Saul/Paul could have been involved in this meeting, as a member of the council (cf. 22:4-5; 26:9-10). Cf. Bock 2007, 197.

37. The word translated 'warn' *(apeilēsōmetha)* in 4:17 could have the more serious meaning 'threaten' (BDAG). TNIV renders the compound *prosapeilēsamenoi* 'after further threats' in 4:21.

38. Barrett 1994, 236-37, suggests a difference between the two verbs used here: *phthengesthai* may imply public proclamation (noting the use of the compound *apoph-thengesthai* in 2:4, 14; 26:25) and *didaskein* more the private teaching of individuals or small groups. Metzger, *Textual Commentary*, 278, discusses textual variations in 4:18-19.

of their commission to be witnesses of the risen Christ (Lk. 24:48; Acts 1:8). The members of the Sanhedrin were therefore challenged to judge for themselves whether their command could actually be obeyed: '*Which is right in God's eyes (enōpion tou theou,* 'before God'): *to listen to you, or to him?*' (*hymōn akouein mallon ē tou theou;* NRSV, ESV 'to listen to you rather than to God'; NKJV 'to listen to you more than to God'; cf. 5:29, 38-39). The Sanhedrin could well have replied that God's authority was vested in them, as the religious and civic rulers of Israel! But many prophets in Jewish history had resisted kings and other leaders when they believed that their directions were contrary to the revealed will of God. Such a confrontation could not simply be dismissed as rebellion against the authorities established by God (cf. Rom. 13:1-2), when those leaders refused to heed the word of God and even sought to suppress it. The question of truth had to be faced and not simply dismissed for the sake of political expediency (cf. 5:29 note). Peter and John could not abandon their responsibility to witness to the risen Lord ('*we cannot help speaking about what we have seen and heard*'), no matter what the cost (*hēmeis,* 'we', is an emphatic pronoun in v. 20). Thus, Luke's narrative indicates 'approval of those who, in proclaiming the name of Jesus, obey God rather than humans and suggests their boldness as a model for others'.[39] Faithful gospel ministry demands such courage and willingness to suffer the consequences.

21-22 The members of the Sanhedrin could not accept that their view was out of line with the will of God. 'When they had further threatened them' (*prosapeilēsamenoi;* cf. v. 17 note), they released them, 'finding no way to punish them' (*heuriskontes to pōs kolasōntai autous),* because all the people were praising God for what had happened. The crowd appeared to affirm Peter and John's claim to be God's messengers, and so the authorities were unable to go as far as they wished in stamping out this new movement. Luke concludes this part of his narrative by restating that the healing was a true 'sign' (*to sēmeion touto tēs iaseōs;* ESV 'this sign of healing'), which in terms of vv. 8-12 pointed to the saving power of the exalted Lord Jesus. Luke also gives a final piece of information which makes it clear why the authorities found the evidence for miraculous healing so hard to deny, *for the man who was miraculously healed was over forty years old.*[40]

---

39. Tannehill 1990, 62. Witherington 1998, 197, compares and contrasts the precedent of Socrates, who told the court which condemned him, 'I shall obey God rather than you' (Plato, *Apol.* 29D). Witherington argues that Luke was trying to portray early Christians as 'like the most noble philosopher'. But note also the Jewish models in 2 Macc. 7:2; 4 Macc. 5-12; Josephus, *Ant.* 17.158-59.

40. Spencer 1997, 52, suggests that the lame man's restoration after forty years establishes a temporal link to Israel in the wilderness, so that 'the healed man represents an image of restoration for the entire nation'. While it is clear from the context that the lame man is a symbol of hope for Israel as a whole, it seems fanciful and unnecessary to establish this argument with reference to the use of the term 'forty years'.

F. The Boldness and Generosity of the New Israel (4:23-37)

Once more Luke focuses attention on the corporate life of the new community (4:23–5:11), before resuming his portrait of the wider ministry of the apostles in Jerusalem (5:12-16) and returning to the theme of opposition from the authorities (5:17-42). The fellowship of believers in prayer and their care for one another is first highlighted (4:23-37; cf. 2:42-47), suggesting that they are 'the true household of God'.[41] The powerful presence of the Holy Spirit in their midst is reaffirmed in 4:31; 5:3, 9. A surprising contrast is introduced with the narrative about Ananias and Sapphira, but the supernatural character of genuine Christian fellowship is further expressed by that narrative (5:1-11). The apostles are still in the foreground, exercising leadership in the messianic community, but 4:23-37 begins to demonstrate how others became partners with them in their calling to bear witness to the exalted Christ (1:8).[42] A comparison of this whole section with the first summary passage in 2:42-47 indicates that we have here a 'parallel composition with motif-rearrangement'.[43]

1. Their Prayer for Boldness (4:23-31)

The prayer life of the earliest Christians is mentioned a number of times in Acts (e.g., 1:14, 24-25; 2:42, 46-47; 12:5; 13:2-3), and here for the second time we are we given an example of how they actually prayed (cf. 1:24-25).[44] Their confidence and unity in prayer are obvious marks of the Spirit's presence in their midst. The prayer itself bears some similarity to the appeal of Hezekiah for the deliverance of God's people from the hand of their enemies (cf. Is. 37:16-20; 2 Ki. 19:15-19). The request in Acts 4:29-30, however, is not for the removal of enemies but for boldness to speak the word of God in the face of opposition. It begins with an extended address to God (vv. 24-

---

41. Spencer 1997, 52. They pray 'together' (*homothymadon*, 4:24; cf. 1:14; 2:1, 46) and are 'one in heart and soul' (*kardia kai psychē mia*) as they share 'everything they had' (*hapanta koina*, 4:32; cf. 2:44-45).

42. Johnson 1992, 90-91, overstates his case when he argues that, in contrast to the first summary in 2:42-47, 'the entire point of this one is to show the authority of the apostles'.

43. M. A. Co, 'The Major Summaries in Acts: Acts 2,42-47; 4,32-35; 5,12-16. Linguistic and Literary Relationship', *EphThLov* 68 (1992), 81.

44. Cf. P. T. O'Brien, 'Prayer in Luke-Acts', *TynB* 24 (1973), 111-27; A. A. Trites, 'The Prayer-Motif in Luke-Acts', in C. H. Talbert (ed.), *Perspectives on Luke-Acts* (Edinburgh: Clark, 1978), 168-86; M. M. B. Turner, 'Prayer in the Gospels and Acts', in D. A. Carson (ed.), *Teach Us to Pray: Prayer in the Bible and the World* (Grand Rapids: Baker; Exeter: Paternoster, 1990), 58-83; S. F. Plymale, *The Prayer Texts of Luke-Acts* (New York: Lang, 1991); J. B. Green, 'Persevering Together in Prayer: The Significance of Prayer in the Acts of the Apostles', in R. N. Longenecker (ed.), *Into God's Presence: Prayer in the New Testament* (Grand Rapids: Eerdmans, 2001), 183-202.

28) which is really a form of praise, acknowledging his sovereignty in all things, even in the events associated with the death of Jesus. The apostles imply that what they have just experienced is a continuation of the opposition experienced by Jesus himself. The petitions that follow ask God to allow the work of testifying to Jesus to continue, unimpeded by the threats of the authorities (vv. 29-30).[45] A further filling of the Spirit to enable such boldness is the stunning response (v. 31). 'Thus Luke makes it clear, not for the last time, that attacks upon the church and its message result only in further Christian expansion.'[46]

23 *On their release* (picking up the story from v. 21, where the same Greek verb *apolyein* is used), Peter and John went back to *their own people (tous idious).* Some commentators have taken this last expression to refer only to the remaining apostles. The prayer in vv. 29-30, viewed in the light of 4:33 and 5:12, certainly suggests that 'the apostles, as leaders in speech and action, are primarily in mind'.[47] But Luke's expression in v. 23 more naturally applies to a wider fellowship of friends and supporters. In the context of numerous references to 'the people' in the earlier part of this chapter (4:1, 2, 8, 10, 17, 21), this suggests an awareness of the church as an entity emerging from Israel but clearly distinct from it. The word 'church' (*ekklēsia*) is finally used by Luke in 5:11 to describe this body.[48] Those who presumably prayed for the apostles during their ordeal needed to be informed of *all that the chief priests and elders had said to them* (cf. 12:12-17). The term *chief priests* in the plural apparently includes the current high priest and other members of the high priest's family mentioned in v. 6.[49]

24 Those who heard the report of Peter and John *raised their voices together in prayer to God.* Luke once more uses the word *homothymadon* to highlight their togetherness (cf. 1:14 note; 2:46). It is most likely that one person prayed in the name of the whole company, expressing the convictions and concerns of all.[50] With this first taste of persecution, they immediately acknowledged God's rule over nature and history, especially his good providence in revealing beforehand the pattern of opposition that would be experienced by the Messiah and those associated with him (vv. 25-28).[51]

45. Witherington 1998, 200, suggests that the structure of the prayer is invocation, quotation, explanation/narration, petition. He goes on to note the apologetic thrust of this prayer in Luke's work.
46. Barrett 1994, 241.
47. Barrett 1994, 243. Barrett, 241, observes that 'Peter and John may have seemed to be acting on their own; in truth however they are acting in relation to and on behalf of their own people'. Bruce 1990, 156, notes other examples of Gk. *hoi idioi* being used in the sense of 'one's own folk', 'one's true friends'. Contra Johnson 1992, 83, 90.
48. Cf. THE THEOLOGY OF ACTS: X. THE CHURCH (pp. 92-97).
49. Cf. Barrett 1994, 223. 'The chief priests and elders' is a convenient way of summarising the membership of the Sanhedrin here (cf. v. 8).
50. Bock 2007, 203-4, notes the use of the singular *phonēn* ('voice'), together with *homothymadon* ('together'), to stress that they prayed 'with one voice'.
51. Barrett 1994, 241-42, holds that Luke adapted a form of prayer current in his own

In other words, they did not simply regard their opponents as attacking them personally, but assessed the situation theologically and historically. The title *'Sovereign Lord'* or 'Master' (*Despota*, as in Lk. 2:29; cf. Je. 4:10; Dn. 9:8 [LXX]; 2 Tim. 2:21; 2 Pet. 2:1; Jude 4; Rev. 6:10) is appropriately linked here with the belief that God is the creator and sustainer of all things: *'you made the heaven and the earth and the sea, and everything in them'* (cf. Acts 14:15; 17:24).[52] These last words are almost a direct quote from Psalm 146 (LXX 145):6, where they are the basis for confidence in God's ability to help his people when they are oppressed (cf. Is. 37:16-20). The one who has control over nature is also sovereign in human affairs, even in the lives of those who rebel against him, as the following verses show. Such belief in the sovereignty of God is an incentive for bold petition (vv. 29-30).

25-26 The divine inspiration of Psalm 2 is asserted before the first two verses are quoted and then applied. God is addressed as the one who *'spoke by the Holy Spirit through the mouth of your servant, our father David'* (KJV adopts the shorter reading, 'who by the mouth of thy servant David hast said', as does NKJV).[53] David is identified as the human author of the psalm, but what he uttered is regarded as the word of God because God's Spirit was speaking through him (cf. 1:16; 2:25, 34; Heb. 3:7; 4:7; 2 Pet. 1:21). David is also described as God's *servant* (*pais*, as in Lk. 1:69; cf. 2 Sa. 3:18; 1 Ki. 11:34; Ps. 89:3, 20), just as Jesus is in Acts 3:13, 26; 4:27, 30.[54] But there is clearly a profound difference between David and Jesus (cf. 3:13 note), expressed here by the identification of Jesus as the promised *'"Anointed One"'* (v. 26, *tou Christou*). Jesus fulfills the Davidic ideal in suffering and exaltation, being made 'both Lord and Christ', at the right hand of God (cf. 2:34-36, using Ps. 110:1). David is finally identified as *'our father'*, meaning that

---

time to suit this occasion. Some MSS add the words 'and recognized the working of God' after 'those who heard', but this is unlikely to be original since Luke nowhere else uses the word *energeia* ('working'). Other additions after 'you', such as 'O God' or 'O Lord God', in some MSS are also unlikely to be original. Cf. Metzger, *Textual Commentary*, 279.

52. Spencer 1997, 54, comments on the use of the title *despotēs* in Jewish literature, with reference to the God of Israel. He then notes that there are four 'brokers' of God's control over world events mentioned in Acts 4:25-30, namely David as the prophetic psalmist (v. 25), Jesus as Israel's ideal servant-king (vv. 26-27), rulers and mobs who oppose his will (vv. 25-28), and praying disciples, who want to continue their bold proclamation of God's word to an unbelieving world (vv. 29-31).

53. A number of textual variations of this clause occur in the MSS. This is presumably because the reading of the oldest witnesses is grammatically awkward and perhaps also because the idea that God speaks 'through the Holy Spirit' (*dia pneumatos hagiou*) is unusual (though cf. 1:16 for David and the Spirit). NRSV, ESV, and TNIV represent the longer reading, which in this case, as the harder reading, is probably 'closer to what the author wrote originally than any of the other extant forms of text' (Metzger, *Textual Commentary*, 281). Cf. Barrett 1994, 244-45; D. L. Bock, *Proclamation from Prophecy and Pattern: Lucan Old Testament Christology*, JSNTSS 12 (Sheffield: JSOT, 1987), 202-3.

54. The term *pais* ('child' or 'servant') is used in the Greek version of Is. 42:1; 49:3, 6; 52:13; 53:11 with reference to 'the Servant of the Lord'. A different Greek term (*doulos*) is used to describe apostles and Christians more generally as 'servants' of God in Acts 4:29.

'the early Christians saw themselves as the true Israel, true messianic Jews, and the heirs of the OT promises'.[55]

Psalm 2:1-2 is quoted exactly as it is in the LXX. The psalm reflects the certainty of Israel's king that he is the Lord's anointed, installed by God on Zion, his holy hill, destined to rule as his representative on earth. At the same time, there is a recognition that the nations of the world are in a fruit-less rebellion against God: '*"Why do the nations rage and the peoples plot in vain?"*' They express that rebellion by gathering together to plot against God's anointed: '*"The kings of the earth rise up and the rulers band together against the Lord and against his anointed one"*'. In this prophetic view of his-tory, the destiny of the nations is determined by their response to the God of Israel and his 'Son', the one appointed to possess and rule them all (cf. Ps. 2:7-9, not cited here). Elsewhere in the NT, Psalm 2:7 is used to proclaim Jesus as the Son of God who ultimately fulfills this ideal (Acts 13:33; Heb. 1:5; 5:5). Exalted to God's right hand by resurrection and ascension, he will bring the nations to 'serve the LORD with fear' (Ps. 2:11). Only here in Acts 4 are the opening verses of the psalm quoted. Once Jesus was confessed as the *Anointed One* of Psalm 2, it was easy enough to relate his opponents to the other characters in the psalm and for his disciples to see themselves sharing in the suffering of the Messiah. These verses express their confi-dence that 'the problems which they face are an extension of the opposition to Christ Jesus and as such are part of the will of God'.[56]

27   The psalm text is applied to their situation by matching up its words with the events of recent history (TNIV does not translate *gar* ['for'], which makes it clear that interpretation of the text follows). The emphatic expression '*indeed*' (*ep' alētheias*, 'in truth'; cf. 10:34) introduces this applica-tion. '*Herod and Pontius Pilate*' are identified as 'the kings of the earth' and 'the rulers' who met together '*with the Gentiles and the people of Israel (syn ethnesin kai laois Israēl) in this city (en tē polei tautē)*' to conspire against Jesus. The surprising fulfillment of the psalm is that *Herod* and *the people of Israel* aligned themselves with foreign nations and their rulers in opposing *the Lord* and *his Anointed One*, here identified as '*your holy servant Jesus*'. As the Gospel narrative shows, Pilate was the reluctant partner in a conspiracy that was initiated by the Sanhedrin and furthered by their incitement of the crowds in Jerusalem and the cooperation of Herod (cf. Lk. 23:1-25). 'The in-clusion of Israel among the foes of the Messiah marks the beginning of the Christian understanding that insofar as the people of Israel reject the Mes-siah they cease to be the Lord's people and can be ranked with unbelieving Gentiles.'[57] Jesus is identified as God's *holy servant* (*ton hagion paida sou*; cf.

---

55. Witherington 1998, 202.

56. Bock, *Proclamation*, 206. A Jewish messianic application of Psalm 2 is found in the first-century-BC document *Ps. Sol.* 17:26, where the Lord's Anointed will 'dash the sinner's pride in pieces like a potter's vessels, break all their substance with a rod of iron'. For a simi-lar use of Ps. 2:9, cf. Rev. 2:27; 12:5; 19:15.

57. Marshall 1980, 106. Spencer 1997, 53, observes that, 'with its back against the wall,

v. 25) in the specific sense that he is the one whom God *'anointed'* (*echrisas*) to fulfill the role of ruling the nations, as set forth in the psalm (cf. Acts 10:36-42).[58]

28 Acknowledging that the opponents of Jesus were doing what Scripture predicted, the apostles and those gathered to pray with them were able to confess, *'They did what your power and will had decided beforehand should happen'*. The word *boulē* ('purpose, plan, will') appears again (cf. 2:23 note), together with the verb *proōrisen* ('decided beforehand', a compound of the verb used in 2:23; 10:42; 11:29; 17:26, 31), now with the expression *'your power'* (*cheir*, 'hand'; cf. 4:30; 11:21; 13:11) added to stress God's sovereignty in all these events. Once in each chapter of Acts so far, Peter has expressed the confidence that God is able to carry out his purpose even through rebellious human beings who do not accept his revealed will (1:16-20; 2:23-36; 3:13-15). With this understanding, the earliest Christians were able to accept that their decision to follow Jesus and proclaim him as the Christ committed them to experience something of the persecution he endured (cf. Lk. 9:22-24, 57-62; 12:49-53; 21:12-19; Jn. 15:18-20). This last point is suggested by the fact that they go on to pray, not for deliverance from suffering nor for the judgment of their enemies, but for the continuing ability to proclaim the gospel in the face of such opposition. 'In a time of threat, prayer can be a rediscovery of the sovereign God who wins by letting our opponents win and then transforming the expected result. This rediscovery can keep God's witnesses faithful in spite of threats.'[59]

29-30 With the bridging formula *'Now, Lord'* (cf. *kai ta nyn* in 5:38; 17:30; 20:32; 27:22), two petitions are offered, based on what has been said about God's sovereignty in nature and human affairs.[60] *'Consider their threats'* (*epide epi tas apeilas autōn*) means 'take note of their threats and act accordingly' (cf. vv. 17, 21). The same people who opposed Jesus have now 'gathered together' (*synēchthēsan* in v. 27, *synachthēnai* in v. 5) to threaten his apostles.[61] Psalm 2 makes it plain that the judgment of God must inevitably fall on those who reject his Son. However, while there is still a chance to preach sal-

---

the persecuted community currently shows little concern with making fine distinctions among those who resist God's purpose in Christ'.

58. Bruce 1988, 99, talks about Jesus being 'anointed or made Messiah — at his baptism'. However, Bock 2007, 208, warns about reading an adoptionist Christology here in view of Lk. 1:31-35. Cf. THE THEOLOGY OF ACTS: II. JESUS AS MESSIAH AND LORD (pp. 56-60).

59. Tannehill 1990, 73.

60. Two aorist imperatives are used in Greek, namely *epide* ('consider, look upon') and *dos* ('give, grant'). A present active infinitive with a preposition (*en tō ekteinein se*, 'while you stretch out') then describes an action contemporaneous with the preceding ones. This clause and the following one also express to God what his people want him to keep doing as the word is preached.

61. 'The opponents of Jesus and the opponents of the church are viewed as one continuous group, a simplification facilitated by the Sanhedrin's leading role in both situations' (Tannehill 1990, 71). Cf. Spencer 1997, 53.

vation in Jesus' name, the prayer of his people is, '*Enable your servants to speak your word with great boldness*' (*dos tois doulois sou meta parrēsias pasēs lalein ton logon sou;* ESV 'grant to your servants to continue to speak your word with all boldness'; cf. v. 31 note). If it is true that a wider group shared with the apostles in this petition, it follows that such prayer is a means of furthering the apostolic work and sharing in the task of bearing witness to Christ (cf. Eph. 6:19-20; Col. 4:2-4; 2 Thes. 3:1-2). Those who had spoken with such courage and freedom in v. 13 *(parrēsia)* needed to have their courage renewed (v. 29, 'with all courage', *meta parrēsias pasēs*) to proclaim the gospel in the face of recent threats (v. 21).[62] Such boldness is a divine gift, not a moral virtue to be acquired by repeated exercise. Christians who have been bold in one context can easily be intimidated in another, unless they seek God's enabling. Associated with this prayer was the request that God would continue to stretch out his hand '*to heal and perform miraculous signs and wonders through the name of your holy servant Jesus*'. The Greek suggests that, as God acted to heal, signs and wonders would occur.[63] The image of God stretching out his '*hand*' (*cheir,* as in v. 28), to perform *signs and wonders* through Moses, is common in the book of Exodus (e.g., 3:20; 6:6; 7:3, 5). Such activity in Acts is normally associated with the apostles (cf. 2:43; 3:6-8; 5:12-16), although it is also noted in relation to the ministry of other key agents of the word such as Stephen and Philip (6:8; 8:6-7). The function of these signs and wonders was to authenticate the messengers rather than the message. However, healings illustrated the power of the risen Lord to restore and save in the full sense outlined by Peter in 3:16-21 and 4:8-12 and, as such, were also a confirmation of the eschatological realities proclaimed in the gospel.[64] The task of the messengers in the process was to offer healing *through the name* of Jesus, not using that name as a magic formula but as a way of directing attention to his authority and calling upon him to act with power in the present.

31 Three remarkable results of this prayer are recorded. First, *the place where they were meeting was shaken,* meaning that a special manifestation of God's power was imminent (cf. Ex. 19:18; Is. 2:19, 21; 6:4). Second, *they were all filled with the Holy Spirit,* and third, as a consequence, they *spoke the word of God boldly.* 'The faithful community "gathered together" in the dynamic presence of the Holy Spirit, on the one side, proves to be much more than the political and religious rulers "gathered together" against

---

62. Witherington 1998, 203, rather too narrowly says, 'The prayer is for Spirit-inspired rhetoric that will persuade'.

63. A clause with an infinitive in the present tense (*en tō tēn cheira [sou] ekteinen se eis iasin*) indicates a continuing activity ('while you stretch out your hand for healings') concurrent with the enabling of the apostles to speak with great boldness. The next clause (*kai sēmeia kai terata ginesthai*) indicates what follows from this divine initiative ('and signs and wonders happen'), though the human factor in calling upon the name of Jesus is signalled by highlighting the name as the agency of healing (*dia tou onomatos tou hagios paidos sou Iēsou,* 'through the name of your holy servant Jesus'). Cf. Barrett 1994, 249. See my comments on 'signs and wonders' in connection with 2:19, 22, 43, and Stott 1990, 100-104.

64. Cf. THE THEOLOGY OF ACTS: VIII. MIRACLES (pp. 83-87).

them, on the other side, can constrain.'[65] This was not a second Pentecost, but the experience must have assured them of the ongoing significance of that unique event for their lives and ministries. The apostles received a fresh filling of the Spirit so that 'with great power' they were able to continue their work of testifying to the resurrection of the Lord Jesus (v. 33). But if others were praying with them on this occasion, the word *all* implies that they too were empowered by the Spirit to speak the word of God boldly. Perhaps this first involved sharing the word of God with one another, in outbursts of praise and thanksgiving, as on the Day of Pentecost (cf. 2:4 note). In due course, the outcome was that ordinary believers took opportunities to share the gospel with unbelievers 'wherever they went' (8:4; 11:19). Praying for God to bless the ministry of others can be a dangerous way of getting caught up in it yourself!

2. Their Impressive Generosity (4:32-37)

Luke again highlights the generosity of the earliest Christians to one another (cf. 2:44-45). Greater vividness is introduced into this account by including the specific example of Barnabas, which is then followed by the contrasting story of Ananias and Sapphira. The latter reveals that Christian fellowship is not just a community of friends but 'an enterprise of divine character'.[66] However, already in 4:32-35, the sharing of material blessings among believers is portrayed as a particular sign of the grace of God at work in this community. Reading backwards, we may also discern how the grace of God has been at work enabling believers to share in the suffering of Christ (4:24-30). Luke progressively reveals what it means to be the new people of God. Although he may be commending the example of the earliest Jerusalem believers to his readers, it cannot be argued that the particular way in which they expressed their generosity is prescriptive. Later passages illustrate other practices (e.g., 6:1-4; 11:27-30; 16:15, 34; 20:33-35), but the common factor is a generous spirit providing appropriate care for the needs of others in the church.

32 NRSV more adequately conveys the dramatic transition suggested by the opening words of this verse ('Now the whole group of those who believed were of one heart and soul, and no one claimed private ownership of any possessions, but everything they owned was held in common'; cf. ESV, NKJV). The noun *plēthos* (NRSV 'whole group'; NKJV 'multi-

---

65. Spencer 1997, 55. Metzger, *Textual Commentary*, 282-83, discusses Western additions to the text of 4:31. The imperfect *elaloun* could be inceptive here ('began to speak'). However, in view of the present infinitive in the prayer of v. 29 (*lalein*, 'to go on speaking'), ESV reads an iterative or customary imperfect in v. 31 ('continued to speak').

66. S. J. Noorda, 'Scene and Summary', in *Les Actes des Apôtres: Traditions, Rédaction, Théologie*, ed. J. Kremer, BETL 48 (Leuven: Leuven University, 1979), 481. Noorda makes helpful observations about the differences between 2:42-47 and 4:32-37 in style and content.

tude'; ESV 'full number'; TNIV *all*) draws attention to the considerable size of the community by now (cf. 4:4 note).[67] Another expression in 5:11 (*holēn tēn ekklēsian*, 'the whole church') further defines this group and marks the end of a section in which there has been a focus on describing its character and life (cf. 2:42-47). Their unity and care for one another are highlighted in 4:32, which is remarkable since a rapid expansion of any group can lead to division and the neglect of individual needs.

When Luke writes that they were *one in heart and mind* (*kardia kai psychē mia*, 'one in heart and soul'), he implies both friendship and unity of purpose. He goes on to explain the practical outworking of this in their corporate experience. *No one claimed that any of their possessions was their own, but they shared everything they had* (*ēn autois hapanta koina*, 'they held all things in common'). Such language was employed in Hellenistic treatises on friendship (cf. 2:42-47 notes). Witherington observes that friendship in the Greco-Roman mould often involved 'reciprocity between those who were social equals', but Luke portrays a community where funds are provided for those who are needy without any thought of return, 'and thus he is suggesting something more akin to family duties'.[68] It should also be remembered that the OT looks forward to the time when God will give his people 'singleness of heart and action' (Je. 32:39) and 'a new heart' and 'a new spirit' (Ezk. 36:26; cf. vv. 34-35 below on the fulfillment of Dt. 15:4). Acts 2:42-47 suggests that such a renewal began to take place when the gospel was preached and the Spirit was poured out at Pentecost, enabling a new love for God and for others. Perhaps Luke's manner of expression in both passages is designed to indicate how the primitive community in Jerusalem realized 'the best ideals both of Hellenism and Judaism concerning life together'.[69] But he does not mean that they automatically sold everything and put the proceeds in a common purse (cf. 4:36-37). They formed a closely knit community, but lived in their own homes and used them for the benefit of the church (cf. 2:46; 12:12).[70] There was a readiness to share what they had, because *no one claimed that any of their possessions was their own*. They did not regard possessions as being exclusively for their own benefit and were consequently not captivated by the need to hold on to them. As need arose, *they shared everything they had* in order to help others (vv. 34-35). Sharing was not a matter of compulsion, and only some prop-

---

67. Bruce 1990, 159, argues that *plēthos* here and in 6:2, 5; 15:12, 30 refers to the Christian community in a technical way and is the equivalent of *ekklēsia* ('church') in 5:11. In my view, this is likely only when *plēthos* is used in an unqualified way, as in 6:5; 15:12, 30.

68. Witherington 1998, 205. Witherington, 206, actually argues that the phrase 'heart and mind' is not found in pagan Greek literature and is more likely to have been influenced by a text such as Dt. 6:5 (LXX). Witherington 210-13, has an important extended note on the social status and level of the earliest Christians.

69. Johnson 1992, 91. Cf. Barrett 1994, 253-54; Seccombe, *Possessions*, 200-209. Je. 32:39 in Hebrew says, 'I will give them one heart and one way' (*lēb 'eḥād wᵉderek 'eḥād*).

70. Longenecker 1981, 311-12, contrasts the activities of the Essenes and the community at Qumran. Cf. Witherington 1998, 207-8.

erty was sold (v. 37). Possessions and money were disposed of at will, as individuals saw fit (5:4).[71]

33 A significant link is now drawn between the specific ministry of the apostles and the general effect on the church. *With great power (dynamei megalē) the apostles continued to testify to the resurrection of the Lord Jesus,*[72] meaning that God enabled them to proclaim the gospel with all boldness in the face of increasing opposition (v. 31). It was this Spirit-empowered ministry of the word of God that then brought 'great grace upon them all' (*charis te megalē ēn epi pantas autous*; TNIV *God's grace was so powerfully at work in them all*). In this way the prayer of 4:24-30 was answered. The *grace* that is mentioned here is 'the divine favour and presence which rests upon the community and which is somehow tangibly manifest'.[73] The sharing described in vv. 34-37 is a particular sign of this grace at work among them. But the remarkable point about this verse is the implication that it was the powerful preaching of the gospel that motivated the earliest Christians to such generosity, not specifically preaching about money or impassioned exhortations from leaders to share possessions! The gospel message about God's grace in Christ inspired a culture of self-giving in love (cf. 2 Corinthians 8–9).

34-35 The biblical ideal that there should be no *needy persons* among God's people was realized in the Jerusalem church (cf. Dt. 15:4 LXX, where the same word for 'poor' or 'needy' [*endeēs*] is used).[74] This happened because the grace of God was at work (v. 33), moving *those who owned land or houses (hosoi ktētores chōriōn ē oikiōn hypērchon,* 'as many as were owners of land or houses') to sell them and bring *the money from the sales and put it at the apostles' feet.*[75] This last expression suggests some formal transfer to a common fund, administered by the apostles for the benefit of the needy (cf.

---

71. 'The point is not one of *ownership* but of common use and mutual support as an expression of *koinōnia*' (Noorda, 'Scene and Summary', 482).

72. EVV follow the most likely of several possible readings here, as indicated by Metzger, *Textual Commentary*, 283-84. The imperfect *apedidoun* is used with the noun *to martyrion* in an iterative or customary way ('continued to give testimony').

73. D. P. Seccombe, *Possessions and the Poor in Luke-Acts,* SNTSU (Linz: Fuchs, 1982), 221. Seccombe, 218, says that the character of the church's fellowship in Acts 4 is 'congruent with God's work in it. It has a reality and a beauty which marks it out, even to Gentiles, as the sphere of God's activity.' The grace of God is a key concept in Acts 2:47; 4:33; 6:8; 7:10, 46; 11:23; 13:43; 14:3, 26; 15:11, 40; 18:27; 20:24, 32. Gk. *charis* is used differently in 24:27; 25:3, 9.

74. Seccombe, *Possessions,* 222 note 126, observes that the absence of poverty in Dt. 15:4 is 'a characteristic of the faithful people enjoying the blessing of God in the land; i.e. it is consonant with salvation.' Consequently, such a passage might be regarded as having eschatological significance.

75. TNIV has expressed the link between vv. 33 and 34 by translating *and God's grace was so powerfully at work in them all that there was no needy person among them.* More literally, the Greek has a simple statement at the end of v. 33 ('and great grace was upon them all'). The next verse has a connective (*gar,* 'for'), implying that justification for this claim is that 'there was no needy person among them'. This is further explained by another clause with the same connective (TNIV *for from time to time . . .*).

4:37; 5:2; and comments on 6:1-4). The Greek does not actually say *from time to time*, though the imperfect tense of the verb 'bring' *(epheron)* could mean that their giving was an intermittent or regular activity ('would bring'). Despite the use of the relative adjective *hosoi* ('as many as') in the expression above, only commentators who want to isolate these verses from what follows will insist that all property owners sold everything they had and contributed the proceeds to the common fund. There is no doubt that the distribution was *to anyone as he had need,* and this suggests that the rate of contribution was also determined by the need. Moreover, Barnabas is represented as selling only a single field. For all that, it can scarcely be doubted that Luke wanted such extraordinary examples of Christian generosity and social concern to act as 'an ideal and an incentive to those within and those entering the later church'.[76]

36-37   The generosity of *Barnabas* is highlighted as a prime example of the common practice of the Jerusalem church. He is first identified as *Joseph, a Levite from Cyprus.* Several first-century Levites are known to have been outstanding in wealth and education.[77] Since he came from Cyprus, he may have been one of those Levites who never served at the temple in Jerusalem. But as a prominent Jew from the Dispersion, he was uniquely placed to become a mediator between Jewish and Gentile Christians and an encourager of the Gentile mission (e.g., 11:22-4; 14:22). One reason why the apostles named him *Barnabas* may have been to distinguish him from Joseph called Barsabbas (also known as Justus, 1:23). But there can be little doubt that the interpretation *'son of encouragement'* identifies him as one generally known for his kindness and support of others (cf. 9:26-27; 11:22-26; 15:37).[78] Luke similarly introduces Philip (6:5) and Saul (7:58; 8:1, 3) in a brief way, before returning at a later stage to reveal their characters more fully. Luke could have learned about Barnabas from Saul or Philip through his later contacts with them (cf. 21:8).

Although only *a field* was sold, ownership of land was the principal source of wealth and social standing in the Greco-Roman world. Barnabas

76. Seccombe, *Possessions,* 222. 'Luke sees the church's sharing fellowship as part of its present experience of salvation, and thus as a pattern of societal activity which is congruent with, and in some ways anticipates, the life of the age to come' (221-22).

77. Cf. Jeremias, *Jerusalem,* 105, 207-13. On the Levites and their responsibilities according to the OT, cf. McCready, *ISBE* 3:965-70. Although Levites were to have no land according to Jos. 21:1-41, by NT times they clearly did (cf. Josephus, *Life* 68–83). Witherington 1998, 205, suggests that 'Barnabas is being held up as an example for Theophilus himself as a person of some social status to follow'.

78. The significance of the name lies 'less in the etymology of the Aramaic, as it does in the role Barnabas will play later in this story' (M. C. Parsons, 'Christian Origins and Narrative Openings: The Sense of a Beginning in Acts 1–5', *Review and Expositor* 87, no. 3 [1990], 416). Barrett 1994, 258-59, argues from the use of *paraklēsis* and the cognate verb in Acts that *huios paraklēseōs* 'must mean *son of exhortation, that is, preacher,* and it corresponds with this that Barnabas is represented in Acts as an outstanding evangelist and (until their separation) partner of Paul's'.

thus embodies the ideal of the 'servant-benefactor', well known in that culture, but to Luke 'pre-eminently exemplified by Jesus of Nazareth (Luke 22:26-30)'.[79] When he humbly places the proceeds *at the apostles' feet*, he forgoes the usual social benefit of praise and public honour. In effect, his donation is a private contribution to the common purse. With this narrative, Luke encourages others with wealth and status in the church to cross social barriers and benefit those in need.[80] It is also possible that the narrative has a deeper significance. One of the future leaders of the Gentile mission expresses his submission to the Twelve by receiving from them a new name and laying his goods at their feet. Luke is presenting an early expression of the unity between the leaders of the Jewish and Gentile missions.[81]

Genuine Christian community is presented in this chapter as involving both mission and mutual support or fellowship. 'These occur because people care about one another and the cause they share.'[82] Such community is experienced when the grace of God is powerfully at work through the preaching of the gospel and the ministry of the Holy Spirit. Barnabas is progressively revealed as a model disciple because he unites in himself such a concern for mission and the welfare of other believers.

G. The Awesome Presence of God (5:1-16)

Luke's second summary of life in the Jerusalem church really extends from 4:32 to 5:16. There is a different order in this section, but the high degree of correlation in subject matter suggests that 4:32–5:16 is an expanded version of 2:42-47. A comparison of the two summaries suggests that the particular purpose of the Ananias and Sapphira story is to explain more fully why 'everyone was filled with awe' (2:43).[1] Within the passage itself, this interpretation is suggested by two references to the great fear that seized those who heard about the death of Ananias (5:5) and then Sapphira (5:11).

79. D. J. Lull, 'The Servant-Benefactor as a Model of Greatness (Luke 22.24-30)', *NovT* 28 (1986), 305.

80. Cf. A. C. Mitchell, 'The Social Function of Friendship in Acts 2:44-47 and 4:32-37', *JBL* 111 (1992), 255-72. Although the community of goods is not mentioned in subsequent chapters of Acts, the crossing of social barriers and Christian generosity are highlighted in other ways.

81. Cf. L. T. Johnson, *The Literary Function of Possessions in Luke-Acts*, SBLDS 39 (Missoula: Scholars, 1977), 204. It is, however, an overstatement to conclude with Johnson that Luke 'is subtly but effectively creating an image in the reader's mind: the image of the Gentile mission under the authority of the Twelve'. There is no suggestion in Acts that the mission of Paul and Barnabas is subject to the direction of the Twelve.

82. Bock 2007, 218.

1. Cf. Seccombe, *Possessions*, 210-14. D. Marguerat, 'La Mort d'Ananias et Saphira (Ac 5.1-11) dans la Stratégie Narrative de Luc', *NTS* 39 (1993), 209-26, notes five different ways in which this passage has been interpreted, each employing 'an external hermeneutical canon'. Noting the structure of the narrative in Acts 2–5, he proposes the view that I have taken.

Allied to this, three references to the presence of the Holy Spirit and God in that community of believers (vv. 3, 4, 9) highlight the supernatural character of their fellowship. Of course, it is also true that the narrative in 5:1-11 illustrates the destructive power of greed and deceit. Ananias and Sapphira behave in a way that directly contrasts the example of Barnabas (4:36-37) and the generosity of the Jerusalem Christians more generally (4:32-35). This is made clear by the repetition in 5:1-11 of key words and phrases from 4:32-37. Although Luke does not expect that the greedy will always meet with instantaneous judgment, he has no doubt about their ultimate accountability to God (cf. Lk. 12:13-21). More generally, however, this narrative warns against anything that hinders the expression of unity, love, and holiness in the fellowship created by the Spirit. Two themes link the story of Ananias and Sapphira with the concluding verses of this section (vv. 12-16). First, the miraculous divine judgment produces a widespread reaction of fear, and secondly, Peter, in conjunction with the other apostles, continues to demonstrate the presence of God's Spirit within the Christian community.[2]

1. Judgment in the Church (5:1-11)

For the first time since the defection of Judas, the community of believers in Jerusalem experiences a serious internal conflict, 'which jeopardizes its unity and relationship with the Spirit'.[3] Faced with mounting opposition from unbelievers, they prayed for boldness to continue proclaiming the word of God and were filled afresh with the Spirit for that purpose (4:31). But *Satan* filled the heart of Ananias and Sapphira, moving them to lie to the Spirit by practising deceit in the church (5:3). As the narrative comes to its climax, Peter reaffirms that the fundamental problem is their conspiring 'to test the Spirit of the Lord', who is uniquely at work in this fellowship (v. 9). 'The powerful opposition of Satan in Luke's Gospel here re-emerges, as even those within the community of believers fall prey to Satan's influence. Without understanding that feature of the story, it is impossible to make sense of the fierce retribution that takes place here.'[4] Jesus had warned his disciples about Satan's desire to sift them all 'like wheat', but had promised to pray that Peter's faith might not fail and that he might be able to strengthen those who were under attack (Lk. 22:31-32). Luke illustrates a fulfillment of those predictions in this narrative.

2. Cf. S. J. Noorda, 'Scene and Summary', in *Les Actes des Apôtres: Traditions, Rédaction, Théologie*, ed. J. Kremer, BETL 48 (Leuven: Leuven University, 1979), 482.
3. Spencer 1997, 52-53. Spencer rightly notes that the church is thus embroiled in 'a spiritual battle with cosmic forces as well as a political struggle with earthly rulers'.
4. Gaventa 2003, 105. Spencer 1997, 56-57, notes 'a pattern of diabolical efforts to infiltrate and sabotage the Jesus movement by appealing to human greed'. Cf. Lk. 4:5-8; 22:3-6; Acts 1:18-19.

1-2   Flowing straight on from the narrative about Barnabas (4:36-37), Ananias (Heb. *ḥānanyāh(u)*, 'Yahweh is gracious') and Sapphira (Aram. *šappîrā*, 'beautiful') are introduced as two more disciples who *sold a piece of property (epōlēsan ktēma).*[5] However, the expression *with his wife's full knowledge (syneiduiēs kai tēs gynaikos*, 'his wife also being aware of it') highlights the complicity of husband and wife in a blatant act of rebellion against God. Here is one of several details in the story suggesting a parallel with the sin of Adam and Eve in Genesis 3. The 'original sin' of the church is portrayed in terms of the misuse of money and possessions! Ananias and Sapphira disregarded the presence of God in the Christian community, the sacredness of that fellowship in God's eyes, and the relational aspect of their sin. They failed to discern that a deliberate act of deceit against the church was a sin against the Lord of the church. Ananias *kept back (enosphisato)* or 'misappropriated'[6] *part of the money for himself (apo tēs timēs;* cf. 4:34, *tas timas* ['the money']), *but brought the rest and put it at the apostles' feet.* Although they presented 'only a part' (*meros ti*, 'a certain portion'; TNIV *the rest*) to the apostles, in view of the regular community practice (4:35, 37), they appeared to be dedicating all the proceeds to the church. This verb *kept back* may have been chosen by Luke to make a link with Joshua 7:1 *(enosphisanto)*, where it describes the sin of Achan, who retained for private use property that had been 'devoted to the Lord'. But the sin of Ananias was different, as Luke goes on to show. The land and its proceeds were his (v. 4), and he was not under any obligation to give it to the apostles. His error was to pretend that he had given everything when he had given only a part, thus making himself out to be more generous and self-sacrificing than he really was.[7]

3   With prophetic insight, Peter accuses Ananias in a series of questions. The first exposes the heart of the problem: *'How is it that Satan has so filled your heart that you have lied to the Holy Spirit and have kept for yourself some of the money you received for the land?'* The language of 'filling' is normally associated with the presence of the Holy Spirit or with the graces and gifts supplied by the Spirit (e.g., 2:4; 4:8, 31; 6:3, 5, 8; 7:55; 9:17; 11:24; 13:9),

---

5. The term *ktēma* generally means 'that which is acquired or possessed' (BDAG; cf. Mt. 19:22; Mk. 10:22; Acts 2:45). In Pr. 23:10 the LXX's *ktēma* represents Heb. *śāḏeh*, 'open field'. It is clearly used in the more restricted sense of 'property, field, piece of ground' in Acts 5:1, in parallel with *chōrion* ('field') in 5:3, 8. Barrett 1994, 264, discusses the possible etymology of the names of Ananias and Sapphira.

6. Gaventa 2003, 102, notes that this verb frequently refers to the misappropriation of funds belonging to others (e.g., Josephus, *Ant.* 4.274; 14.164; Epictetus, *Disc.* 2.20.35; Plutarch, *Pompey* 4.1). BDAG 'to put aside for oneself, *keep back*'. The verb is used again in v. 3.

7. Bock 2007, 220, lists further differences between this story and Joshua 7. Barrett 1994, 262, thinks that the story of Ananias and Sapphira 'does not fit neatly into the context in which Luke has placed it'. He contends that the assertions in 5:4 contradict 4:34b, 'the plain meaning of which is that all who owned land sold it and brought the proceeds — the whole proceeds — to the apostles'. However, his argument is circular. He interprets 4:34 in a way that isolates this verse from what follows.

though the specific verb employed here *(eplērōsen)* is only so used in 13:52. Rather than being filled with the fruit of the Spirit, the heart of Ananias was filled by *Satan* with deceit and hypocrisy (cf. 8:23; 13:10).[8] Satan is mentioned in Luke 10:18; 11:18; 13:16; 22:3, 31; Acts 26:18, and the devil in Luke 4:2, 3, 6, 13; 8:12; Acts 10:38; 13:10. 'If the devil's first tactic was to destroy the church by force from without, his second was to destroy it by falsehood from within'.[9] The Evil One is regarded as the ultimate cause of this attack on the unity and holiness of the church, but Ananias is clearly responsible for his actions. The way in which the question is phrased in Greek suggests that the heart of Ananias was filled by Satan so as to move him 'to lie to the Holy Spirit' *(pseusasthai to pneuma to hagion)*. When Ananias lied to Peter and the church, it was a sin against the Spirit who creates, fills, and sustains the church. The parallel with v. 4 *('You have not lied just to human beings but to God'* [*ouk epseusō anthrōpois alla tō theō*]*)* emphasizes the deity of the Spirit. That deceit is then explained in terms of the accusation that follows *(kai nosphisasthai apo tēs timēs tou chōriou,* 'and to keep back part of the proceeds of the land', NRSV, ESV).[10]

4 It is clear that there was no obligation to sell the land *('Didn't it belong to you before it was sold?')*, and there was no obligation to share all the proceeds of a sale with others *('And after it was sold, wasn't the money at your disposal?')*. The sharing of goods was voluntary in the Jerusalem church, and there was no rule about the common ownership of property such as was found among the members of the Qumran community.[11] But Ananias had pretended to give all the money he received to the apostles, while holding back a portion for himself. He was seeking human praise rather than the praise of God (cf. Jn. 12:43). Despite the reference to Satan's inspi-

---

8. Papyrus 74 and some ancient versions read 'tempted' *(epeirasen)* instead of the much-better-attested 'filled' *(eplērōsen)*. The original of Codex ℵ and some later manuscripts read 'disabled' *(epērōsen)*, which probably arose through accidental omission of a letter from *eplērōsen*. This reading could then have produced the more natural 'tempted' *(epeirasen)*. There are good reasons, therefore, for taking 'filled' as the most ancient reading. Cf. Metzger, *Textual Commentary*, 285-86. Barrett 1994, 266, disputes the view that 'fill the heart' is a Semitic idiom which means to 'dare (to do something)' (cf. Est. 7:5; Eccl. 8:11).

9. Stott 1990, 112. The link between Satan and greed in Luke-Acts is noted by Spencer 1997, 56-57. Evil supernatural influences which oppose the work of the gospel are highlighted in 8:9-11, 18-23; 16:16-18; 19:13-20. Cf. H. Bietenhard and C. Brown, *NIDNTT* 3:468-73, on Satan and the devil in biblical teaching.

10. Thus, two Greek infinitives identify what it meant for Satan to have filled the heart of Ananias: to lie to the Holy Spirit by deceiving the church and to keep back part of the proceeds of the land. The indicative form of *nosphisasthai* ('to keep back') is used in v. 2.

11. Comparing the requirements of the Qumran community, B. J. Capper, 'The Interpretation of Acts 5.4', *JSNT* 19 (1983), 117-31, has argued that Ananias was expected to transfer all of his property to the apostles provisionally, while he was a candidate for membership in the church. But there is no evidence for any preliminary 'catechumenate' at this early stage. Cf. J. D. M. Derrett, 'Ananias and Sapphira and the Right of Property', in *Studies in the New Testament* (Leiden: Brill, 1977), 193-201, on the voluntary nature of the sharing of goods in Acts.

ration in v. 3, the culpability of Ananias is stressed again at the end of v. 4 (*'What made you think of doing such a thing?'*). His deceit was an act of rebellion against God (*'You have not lied just to human beings but to God'*). A similar identification of the risen Jesus with the church under attack is found in 9:4-5; 22:7-8; 26:14-15.

5 *When Ananias heard this* (*akouōn tous logous toutous,* 'hearing these words'), *he fell down and died* (*exepsyxen,* 'expired').[12] Peter's Spirit-inspired words laid bare the attitude and action of Ananias and condemned him before God and his people (cf. 1 Cor. 14:24-25). What is surprising in this situation is that the sentence of God fell immediately upon Ananias, without any chance for repentance.[13] Although it may be possible to explain such a sudden death in naturalistic terms, given the shock of a public exposure of guilt, Luke is clearly presenting this as a divine visitation, anticipating the final judgment of God. Such an outcome shows how seriously God regards anything that mars the holiness of the church (cf. 1 Cor. 3:16-17; 2 Cor. 6:14-18). Parallels are sometimes drawn with the story of Achan's sin and the summary judgment that fell upon him and his family in Joshua 7.[14] The most that can be said is that a serious act of deceit marked the early days of the life of God's people under both covenants and that a remarkable expression of God's wrath followed. In both cases, the event was a manifestation of God's distinctive presence with his people and a warning about his intention to preserve their holy identity and character. Following the death of Ananias, *great fear seized all who heard what had happened,* presumably including people outside the church as well as those within. The *great fear* (*phobos megas*) involved here is a healthy sense of awe at the supernatural and reverence for God, rather than terror or panic.[15] Since Luke mentions this again in v. 11, it seems clear that he wished to commend such fear as a worthy response to such events. Such a response to the actions and words of God is recorded at significant points in Luke's Gospel (1:12, 65; 2:9; 5:26; 7:16; 8:25, 35, 37; 9:34, 45; 21:26), as well as in Acts (2:43; 9:31; 19:17).

6-7 Immediate removal of the body of Ananias by *some young men* (*hoi neōteroi,* 'the young men', in most EVV; *hoi neaniskoi* in v. 10) suggests an action by certain members of the church rather than professional undertakers. In a hot climate, burial is desirable as soon as possible after death,

12. The verb *exepsyxen* ('expired') is used only in 5:5, 10 and 12:23 (of Herod) in the NT, always with reference to the wicked who die a sudden or unpleasant death (cf. Jgs. 4:21, LXX). The word itself, however, is simply a parallel to *ekpnein,* which is used of Jesus in Mk. 15:37, 39; Lk. 23:46. Cf. Barrett 1994, 267-68.

13. Bruce 1988, 103-4, argues against those who question the morality of this story and especially Peter's part in it. Peter is portrayed by Luke as 'the prophet who exposes and rebukes the deceptive heart' (Tannehill 1990, 79). Cf. 8:18-23; 13:6-12; 16:16-18.

14. Johnson 1992, 91-93, helpfully outlines the similarity and differences between the stories. Marguerat, 'La Mort', 222-25, argues that the deceit of Ananias and Sapphira is rather presented as a reduplication of the original sin of Adam and Eve.

15. 'Fear' of God and his actions can certainly involve terror (e.g., Lk. 2:9; 21:26), though that is not always the case. Cf. W. Mundle, *NIDNTT* 1:621-24.

but this one proceeded with great haste, without Sapphira being informed or involved. The terminology suggests that the body was appropriately *wrapped up (synesteilan auton)*,[16] then carried out for burial *(kai exenenkantes ethapsan)*. Such a death, signalling God's condemnation of Ananias, may have caused the believers to fear that, if the body was left in their midst, further acts of divine judgment might follow (cf. Dt. 21:22-3 for a possible parallel). The return of Sapphira *about three hours later* put her in the same position as her husband, with an opportunity to be straightforward and honest about the deceit, *not knowing what had happened* to her husband.[17]

8-9   Peter's first question to Sapphira *('Tell me, is this the price you and Ananias got for the land?')* exposed the true situation immediately, since the apostle already knew what had been donated from the sale. His next question charged her with being a willing partner with her husband in a serious provocation of God's anger: *'How could you conspire (ti hoti synephōnēthē hymin*, 'How is it that you have agreed together?' in most EVV)[18] *to test the Spirit of the Lord (peirasai to pneuma kyriou*; cf. 15:10)?' Their deception of the community was actually a challenge to the Spirit of the Lord, who is the source of the church's life and holiness (cf. 1 Cor. 3:16-17; 1 Thes. 4:7-8). It was 'an act of arrogance, not just avarice'.[19] The idea of putting God to the test is prominent in the stories of Israel's wandering in the desert (e.g., Ex. 17:2, 7; Nu. 14:22; Dt. 6:16; 33:8). In practice it meant provoking God to judge, by misrepresenting him, disobeying his commands, or refusing to believe his promises. Peter goes further in the case of Sapphira than he did with Ananias in pronouncing a sentence of death. In the manner of a prophet, he reveals the solemn truth about the death of her husband *('Listen! The feet of those who buried your husband are at the door')* before declaring that she will share his fate *('and they will carry you out also')*.[20] The young men who had buried Ananias were about to return to bury her as well (v. 10).

10   The sudden death of Sapphira *(parachrēma*, 'immediately', *at that moment)*, like the death of her husband before her (v. 5), cannot simply be

16. Barrett 1994, 261, 268-69, takes *synesteilan auton* to mean 'prepared his body for burial'. Bruce 1990, 164, notes the use of this verb in the sense of 'wrapped up' (in a winding sheet).

17. It is inappropriate to argue that 'at this stage Peter had not much experience in pastoral ministry; otherwise he would probably have broken the news of Ananias's death to her before he questioned her, and the result might have been happier' (Bruce 1988, 107). Luke presents Peter in a prophetic role here, with the task of exposing error and pronouncing God's judgment (cf. Paul in 13:8-11). Bock 2007, 225, discusses the delay of Sapphira in coming before Peter.

18. The verb translated *conspire (synephōnēthē)* is ironic in the context. Johnson 1992, 89, observes that 'their "harmony" in collusion was a mockery of the "one soul" that led the community to share its possessions in common'. Metzger, *Textual Commentary*, 286, discusses minor textual variations in vv. 8-10.

19. Bock 2007, 226.

20. It is, however, going beyond the evidence to say that 'Peter *kills* her by announcing her husband's demise and her own imminent death' (Haenchen 1971, 239). Contra Barrett 1994, 269, he gives her the chance to confess and repent by the form of his questions in v. 8.

explained in psychological terms. Luke represents these events as unique acts of divine judgment, manifesting the awesome presence of God at this critical stage in the life of the early church. Ironically, *she fell down at his feet and died.* Falling down at someone's feet was normally a gesture of respect in that culture. Previously, Ananias and Sapphira had refused to honour Peter by being open and honest about their contribution, but now they appeared to express submission to his leadership in dying.

11 Luke first employs the term *church* in this context, with reference to the community of believers in Jerusalem.[21] When he says that *great fear seized the whole church (holēn tēn ekklēsian),* the adjective *whole* doubtless includes those not present when the judgment was visited upon Ananias and Sapphira. The noun *ekklēsia* was commonly used in the Greek-speaking world with reference to a public gathering or assembly of the citizens of a city (cf. 19:32, 39, 41; Josephus, *War* 1.550, 666; 4.159). But the LXX employed this word especially to describe Israel as the congregation or assembly gathered by God to himself through the great exodus redemption from Egypt (e.g., Dt. 9:10; 18:16; 23:1-2; 31:30; Jos. 8:35; Jgs. 20:2; cf. Acts 7:38).[22] By reserving the use of such a significant term for this climactic moment in his narrative, Luke was characterizing the group that God had been gathering to himself through the preaching of the gospel as the community saved by Jesus for entrance into his end-time kingdom. By the positive work of his Spirit in their midst (illustrated in Acts 2–4) and by this summary act of judgment, excluding from among them those who were not 'one in heart and mind' (4:32), God was unmistakably designating them as his own, the new Israel in the midst of the old. The additional expression, *and all who heard about these events,* will refer to people outside the Christian community who were seized by fear but were reluctant to join the church, as the following section makes clear.

2. Signs and Wonders among the People (5:12-16)

Having focussed on the inner life of the church in 4:23–5:11, Luke once more highlights the public ministry of the apostles. As they continued to perform signs and wonders among the people in the temple courts, many more believed and became disciples of the Lord Jesus (vv. 12, 14). Between these positive statements, however, there is an acknowledgment that some

---

21. Cf. THE THEOLOGY OF ACTS: X. THE CHURCH (pp. 92-97). The noun *ekklēsia* is also found as a gloss to 2:47 in some texts and versions, hence the reading of KJV and NKJV ('the Lord added to the church daily'). This is not as well attested as the shorter reading and is unlikely to have been the original.

22. Cf. K. L. Schmidt, *TDNT* 3:513-29; L. Coenen, *NIDNTT* 1:291-307. *Ekklēsia* is the regular LXX rendering of Heb. *qāhāl* ('assembly'), though the latter is also represented by *synagōgē*. *Ekklēsia* was a more suitable term than *synagōgē* for the earliest Christians to adopt to distinguish themselves from contemporary Jewish gatherings.

were reluctant to join the apostolic community (v. 13), doubtless because of
the fear recorded earlier (vv. 5, 11). In the final analysis, however, a confidence in Peter's power to heal developed in Jerusalem (v. 15). This in turn
led to a growing enthusiasm on the part of people in surrounding towns to
bring their sick and demon-possessed to benefit from the blessings (v. 16).
Thus Luke records how the apostolic witness extended beyond the limits of
the city, without the apostles themselves moving out into that region.

12 *Signs and wonders* are once more in view (cf. 2:19, 22, 43; 4:16, 22,
30), showing how the prayer in 4:30 was answered. Luke emphasizes the
role of the apostles in this activity by recording that it was 'by the hands of
the apostles' (*dia tōn cheirōn tōn apostolōn*; cf. 14:3) that 'many signs and
wonders were done among the people'. This could be a specific reference to
the fact that they healed the sick with the laying on of their hands. But it is
more likely to be a general reference to their part in the process by which
God stretched out his 'hand' to heal and perform miraculous signs (cf.
4:30).[23] And they did so in an open way, *among the people*, that is, before the
Jerusalem public. Most EVV then render the expression *kai ēsan homothymadon* 'and they were all together', leaving open the possibility that Luke is
still dealing with the work of the apostles. TNIV, however, has assumed
that others were with the apostles, translating *and all the believers used to
meet together*.[24] Once again we are told that they were *in Solomon's Colonnade*
(cf. 3:11 note), a prominent place in the outer court of the temple, where a
large number could gather together.

13-14 Many in Jerusalem were caught in a dilemma. Even though
the apostles were *highly regarded by the people* — because of the awesome
deeds which they performed — *no one else* (*tōn loipōn oudeis*, 'none of the
rest') *dared join them*. The verb *join (kollasthai)* could be used here in the particular sense of 'join the community of believers' (cf. 9:26; 17:34), but the
more general sense of 'approach' suits the context best (cf. 8:29; 10:28).[25]
Luke's point is that fear engendered by the activity of the apostles actually
kept others from drawing near to them. Yet it is clear from what follows
that *more and more men and women believed in the Lord* (cf. 2:41, 47; 4:4).[26] Luke

---

23. The image of God stretching out his hand to work signs and wonders among the
people is common in references to the exodus (e.g., Ex. 3:20; 7:5; Dt. 4:34; 5:15; 6:21-22). It is
interesting to note that, within this context, Moses is called to stretch out his hand as a
means of furthering God's saving purpose (e.g., Ex. 7:19).

24. In favour of the TNIV translation, *homothymadon* ('together') is often used to describe the unity of believers as a whole (cf. 1:14 note).

25. D. R. Schwartz, 'Non-joining Sympathizers (Acts 5, 13-14)', *Biblica* 64 (1983), 550-
53, insists that Luke is referring to 'non-joining sympathizers'. Witherington 1998, 225-26,
thinks that the reference is to 'the rest of the Christians who were afraid to join the apostles
in the temple in view of what happened the first time — namely, the arousal of the anger of
the Jewish authorities and the trial of the Christian leaders'. This is a possible, though less
likely reading. Cf. Barrett 1994, 274-75; Bock 2007, 230-31.

26. Barrett 1994, 275 observes that *mallon* at the beginning of v. 14 retains its comparative sense and *de* marks simple continuation (as in vv. 13, 16). This would give the sense

emphatically declares that there were 'crowds both of men and of women' (*plēthē andrōn te kai gynaikōn*). TNIV has concluded that the expression (*prosetithento pisteuontes tō kyriō*) means that these believers were *added to their number*, but the Greek could just as easily be translated, 'believers were added to the Lord in increasing numbers'.[27] The link between v. 13 and v. 14 is awkward grammatically and in terms of the flow of the argument, but the overall meaning must be that, whatever restraints there were, many eventually came forward to join the community: 'on the one hand an awe-struck reserve, on the other great missionary successes'.[28] In other words, Luke's statement in v. 14 qualifies the apparently absolute claim in v. 13 that *no one else dared join them*. The brevity of the account here should not be taken to mean that people believed simply because of signs and wonders. Throughout Acts, signs and wonders 'authenticate the word of missionary preaching as the word of God'.[29] It is the word that saves, as people come to believe and put their trust in God as its source and Christ as its content.

15-16 The clause at the beginning of v. 15 (*hōste, as a result*) could mean that those who had come to believe in the Lord *brought those who were ill into the streets and laid them on beds and mats*. But Luke is probably speaking again about the reaction of the population of Jerusalem more generally, with the result clause relating to the whole preceding paragraph. The healing ministry of the apostles paralleled that of Jesus in many respects, including such popular enthusiasm for what was taking place (cf. Mk. 6:55-56). Even if people would not approach the apostles directly in Solomon's Colonnade, they still hoped to benefit from their healing power in *the streets* (cf. 19:12). They hoped that *at least Peter's shadow might fall on some of them as he passed by*. Luke does not say that Peter's shadow actually had any healing effect, but that this was the expectation of the crowds (cf. 19:11-12 note).[30] The words *at least* (*kan*) suggest a desire for closer contact with Peter, despite the apprehension noted in v. 13. Luke concludes this section by recording the healing of *their sick and those tormented by evil spirits*. These

'and believers were the more added' (KJV, NKJV). But a strong adversative (NRSV 'yet more than ever believers were added'; TNIV *nevertheless*) seems necessary to the flow of the argument.

27. Barrett 1994, 272, 275, and most EVV.

28. Haenchen 1971, 244.

29. L. O'Reilly, *Word and Sign in the Acts of the Apostles: A Study in Lucan Theology*, Analecta Gregoriana 243 (Rome: EPUG, 1987), 194. Cf. THE THEOLOGY OF ACTS: VIII. MIRACLES (pp. 83-87).

30. Johnson 1992, 96, unnecessarily concludes that 'the divine *dynamis* is so powerfully present in Peter that it radiates automatically'. P. W. Van der Horst, 'Peter's Shadow: The Religio-Historical Background of Acts 5:15', *NTS* 23 (1976-77), 207, argues that in the Hellenistic world, as in other cultures, 'to be touched by a man's shadow means to be in contact with his soul or his essence and to be influenced by that, whether it be for the better or the worse'. But there is no evidence for such a belief in first-century Judaism. Witherington 1998, 220-24, has an interesting excursus on Luke's attitude to the miraculous and his manner of recording such events. Some Western MSS imply that Peter's shadow actually had a healing effect (cf. Metzger, *Textual Commentary*, 287-88).

were brought from *the towns around Jerusalem,* indicating that the message about what God was doing through the apostles was spreading now into the Judean countryside.

H. Conflict with the Authorities Again (5:17-42)

In the preceding summary section, Luke has shown how the ministry of the apostles made such an impression on the people of Jerusalem and its region that more and more 'believed in the Lord and were added to their number' (v. 14). This increased activity on the part of the apostles and their winning of many more disciples aroused the jealousy of the Sadducees in the Sanhedrin (v. 17) and led to another arrest (v. 18). Three markers in the Greek text point to a development in the narrative and suggest a simple structure for the passage.[31] The first section is introduced by noting that the high priest 'stood up' (*anastas,* not translated by TNIV), together with all his associates, to take official action against the apostles. The same verb is used in v. 34 to introduce the Pharisee Gamaliel and his speech to the Sanhedrin, urging caution about the possibility of 'fighting against God'. A different construction in v. 41 (*hoi men oun;* literally, 'they then') introduces a concluding statement about the rejoicing of the apostles after their release and their subsequent ministry. This last section also serves as a summary-conclusion to the whole division of Luke's work that began with the description of life in the Jerusalem church in 2:42-47 (an inclusion is formed by the use of similar words in both passages).

1. *The Apostles Are Re-Arrested (5:17-33)*

There are obvious parallels between 5:17-40 and 4:1-31, but Luke makes it clear that a fresh stage in the controversy has been reached. This second episode builds on the first, 'but the differences increase the tension of the narrative'.[32] The repetitive patterns in these chapters actually serve to 'emphasize and enrich a vision of God as one who works by irony, subverting and overruling the human powers who appear to be in control. Because of this

31. Longenecker 1981, 318, notes these markers. Although *anastas* may be little more than a copula in some contexts, it certainly implies a new development in the narrative at 5:17, 34.

32. S. Cunningham, *'Through many tribulations': The Theology of Persecution in Luke-Acts,* JSNTSS 142 (Sheffield: Sheffield Academic, 1997), 193. This escalation builds towards a climax in the arrest and death of Stephen, leading to widespread persecution against the believers in Jerusalem (6:8–8:4). Witherington 1998, 197, argues that 5:17-42 should not be seen as a doublet or second version of 4:5-22 because the usual Jewish practice was to warn the accused first and prosecute only if the action occurred again. Barrett 1994, 281, outlines seven differences between this narrative and the account in Acts 4.

God, there can be a mission in which courageous people speak boldly of realities denied and rejected by these human powers.'[33] There are also correspondences between these passages and the predictions of Jesus in Luke 12:4-12; 21:12-19, and parallels with Luke's passion narrative, strengthening 'the persecutional interlock between Jesus and his followers.'[34] Cunningham argues that disciples under persecution in Acts are in continuity with their Lord; the context of persecution is mission; persecution is the occasion of divine triumph; persecution is firmly placed within divine providence; persecution is a manifestation of divided Israel.[35]

17-18 TNIV obscures the somewhat dramatic introduction to this new section. The Greek *(anastas de ho archiereus)* implies a new initiative (KJV, NKJV, ESV 'then the high priest rose up'; NRSV 'then the high priest took action').[36] As in 4:1-8, official opposition to the apostles came from the high priest *and all his associates (kai hoi syn autō)*. Luke once more indicates that they were *members of the party of the Sadducees (hē ousa hairesis tōn Saddoukaiōn)*. The Pharisees, who are later represented in the narrative by Gamaliel (vv. 34-40), appear to have had fewer numbers in the Sanhedrin at this stage. They too are later described as a *party (hairesis)* within Judaism (cf. 15:5; 26:5).[37] Although they were concerned about issues of theology and social order (cf. 4:1-2), the high priest and his associates are said to have been *filled with jealousy (eplēsthēsan zēlou)*.[38] They were gripped by the ordinary human reaction of envy at the success of others. Since Peter and John were the focus of attention in Acts 4, it is possible that they are *the apostles* mentioned here. However, it is likely that the reference is to the apostles more generally and that this is a sign of the escalation of opposi-

---

33. Tannehill 1990, 77. Tannehill, 64-79, shows how Acts 4–7 must be read as a whole, as it moves from preliminary hearing, to trial, to an act of passion by a mob, as the bold preaching of the gospel and performance of mighty works precipitate a crisis of authority at the heart of Judaism. Cf. B. Rapske, 'Opposition to the Plan of God and Persecution', in I. H. Marshall and D. Peterson (eds.), *Witness to the Gospel: The Theology of Acts* (Grand Rapids/Cambridge: Eerdmans, 1998), 235-56.

34. Cunningham, *Persecution*, 197. Cunningham, 194-97, details the correspondences.

35. Cunningham, *Persecution*, 197-203.

36. Some MSS accentuate the link with the preceding section and the sense of a dramatic initiative in 5:17 *(kai tauta blepōn anastas*, 'and seeing these things he stood up'). A few MSS ascribe the priesthood to Annas here. However, the shortest text is the best attested and most likely to be the original. Cf. Metzger, *Textual Commentary*, 288. Note 31 above comments on the use of *anastas* in vv. 17 and 34.

37. Josephus *(War* 2.118-19) uses the Greek term in a similar way. Christians are similarly identified as a 'party' in Acts 24:5, 14; 28:22, though the TNIV implies a more negative application of the same word in these verses, translating it each time as 'sect'. Gk. *hairesis*, from which we get 'heresy', can have a quite negative meaning with respect to divisions in the church (1 Cor. 11:19; Gal. 5:20) and false teachings that create such divisions (2 Pet. 2:1). But it does not have a negative connotation here.

38. It is possible that *eplēsthēsan zēlou* (a genitive of content) means 'full of (religious) zeal'. However, the same expression in the context of 13:45 most obviously means 'full of jealousy'. The cognate verb is similarly used in 17:5 to suggest that jealousy was the motive for Jewish antagonism to Christians. Cf. Johnson 1992, 96; Bock 2007, 238.

tion in comparison with 4:1-31.[39] When it is said that the high priest and his associates arrested the apostles and *put them in the public jail (ethento autous en tērēsei dēmosia)* the meaning may be that they 'put them in prison publicly', that is, they acted in a way that publicly demonstrated their authority over the apostles.[40]

19 If the Jewish leaders acted publicly to assert their influence, *an angel of the Lord* acted secretly *(during the night)* to rescue and re-commission the apostles. In Scripture, Gk. *angelos* and Heb. *mal'āk* can refer to a supernatural being or a human messenger of God. The expression *an angel of the Lord* may even be a way of speaking about God himself, manifesting his power and presence in his dealings with his people.[41] Lack of information in the present context prevents us from being sure about the means used by God, but Luke wishes to make it clear that the apostles were released by divine intervention. The angel first *opened the doors of the jail* and then *brought them out.* Here we have the first of three stories in Acts about the miraculous opening of prison doors (cf. 12:6-11 [by an angel of the Lord]; 16:26-30 [by an earthquake]). It has been argued that these narratives are at least to some extent legendary, following the form of popular stories in the ancient world about prison doors that open themselves under divine instigation. Some interpreters have also suggested that 5:19 is 'an inferior variant of the liberation episode in 12:3ff.'[42] There are, however, significant differences of detail in each of the stories told by Luke. Furthermore, similarity in the way stories are told does not necessarily mean that the events described are unhistorical. Although there are three such accounts of miraculous deliverance in Acts, Luke is clear that others were not delivered and had to endure death (7:57-60 [Stephen]; 12:1-2 [James]) or suffered an extensive period of imprisonment (21:30-36 [Paul]). Miraculous deliverance is not the normal expectation of Luke or the characters in his narrative.

20-21a Most importantly, the divine agent of their release commanded them to *'Go, stand in the temple courts and tell the people all about this new life'* (*panta to rhēmata tēs zōēs tautēs*, 'all the words of this life', KJV,

---

39. Cf. Cunningham, *Persecution*, 190-93. Barrett 1994, 281, suggests that Luke wished to show that 'the apostles, as representative Christians, *all* the apostles as representative of *all* Christians, are exposed to public disgrace and suffering, yet are nevertheless under divine protection'.

40. Most EVV read *dēmosia* as an adjective agreeing with *tērēsei* ('the public prison'). But Gaventa 2003, 106, rightly notes Luke's adverbial use of *dēmosia* ('publicly') in 16:37; 18:28; 20:20. Cf. Barrett 1994, 279, 283.

41. Strictly speaking, *'the* angel of the Lord' is distinguished in the OT from other angels, as the one who is 'the personified help of God for Israel' (H. Bietenhard, *NIDNTT* 1:101; S. F. Noll, *NIDOTTE* 2:941-43). Cf. Ex. 3:2-7; 14:19; Nu. 22:22-23; Jgs. 6:11-24; 2 Ki. 1:3f. Luke speaks here only of *'an* angel of the Lord'. Angelic figures play an important role in Luke-Acts (e.g., Lk. 1:11, 26; 2:9, 13; 22:43; 24:23; Acts 7:30, 35, 38, 53; 8:26; 10:3, 7, 22; 11:13; 12:7-15, 23; 23:8-9; 27:23).

42. Haenchen 1971, 256. Against the view that 5:17-40 is a doublet of 4:1-31, see Barrett 1994, 281.

NKJV, ESV; 'the whole message about this life', NRSV; cf. 13:26, *ho logos tēs sōtērias tautēs*, 'the word of this salvation'). TNIV has rightly added the word *new* to make it clear that *this life* refers to the life made possible by the saving work of Jesus, who is 'the author of life' (3:15). The gospel is later described as the source of eternal life for Gentiles (11:18; 13:46, 48), but here the apostles are re-commissioned to be steadfast in proclaiming that hope to Israel first *(the people)*. They were to take their stand at the very centre of Israel's national and religious life *(in the temple courts)*, indicating the fulfillment of their hope in the Messiah Jesus. Moreover, they were to do this in the face of mounting opposition (cf. Paul in Corinth, 18:9-10). Their obedience to this divine imperative is indicated by the fact that they went into the temple *at daybreak*, as they had been told, and began to teach.[43]

21b-24 *When the high priest and his associates arrived*, expecting to be able to summon the prisoners before them, *they called together the Sanhedrin — the full assembly of the elders of Israel (kai pasan tēn gerousian tōn huiōn Israēl*, 'even all the senate of the sons of Israel').[44] With some irony, Luke then reports that they *sent to the jail for the apostles*, only to discover what readers already know, that the jail was empty! Human attempts to restrain the messengers of 'this new life' (v. 20) and curtail their influence among the people had been divinely frustrated. The report of the officers highlights the wonder of the miracle: *'We found the jail securely locked, with the guards standing at the doors; but when we opened them, we found no one inside'*. When the captain of the temple guard and the chief priests heard these words, they were rightly *puzzled (dieporoun*, 'perplexed', as in Lk. 9:7; Acts 2:12; 10:17) by them, *wondering what this might lead to*.[45]

25-26 The report of an unnamed witness soon clarified the situation: the men who had been put in jail were *'standing in the temple courts teaching the people'*. The wording here recalls the angelic commission of v. 20 and reinforces the impression given in v. 21 that the apostles did exactly as they were told. They remained true to their commitment to listen to God rather than to human authorities, and to go on speaking about what they had seen and heard, whatever the cost (4:18-20). When the captain of the guard and his officers went to apprehend the apostles, they took account of the contin-

43. As noted previously, the word for 'temple' *(to hieron)*, which is used in vv. 20 and 21, encompasses the whole temple complex and so is rightly translated 'temple courts' by TNIV. The reference will be to 'Solomon's Colonnade', as in v. 12. The gates of the temple would have been opened at daybreak in time for the morning sacrifice (cf. Ex. 29:39; Nu. 28:4).

44. Most EVV imply that a body of elders in addition to the Sanhedrin is indicated by this expression, but Barrett 1994, 285, argues that the *kai* is explicative ('that is'): the Sanhedrin was the Council of Elders. Cf. Bruce 1990, 170-71. A similar expression *(pasan gerousian huiōn Israēl)* is used in Ex. 12:21 LXX for the body of elders (cf. L. Coenen, *NIDNTT* 1:194-96). Gk. *gerousia* was used of various boards or councils, especially the Sanhedrin in Jerusalem (BAGD). Metzger, *Textual Commentary*, 289, discusses Western variant readings of vv. 21-22.

45. Barrett 1994, 279, translates *ti an genoito touto* 'what this might mean', but says the corresponding direct question would be, 'What will be the end, or result, of this?' (286).

uing popularity of the prisoners with the Jerusalem crowd (cf. 2:47; 4:4; 5:12-16). Fearing *that the people would stone them*, they refrained from using force. 'The people respect the apostles and do not see them as religious criminals, even if they do not believe them.'[46] For their part, the apostles reacted as Jesus did, without violence or resistance (cf. Lk. 22:47-53).

27-28 Arraigned before the Sanhedrin, the apostles were once again *questioned by the high priest.* No reference is made in this brief account to their amazing disappearance from prison. Even though the report given in v. 23 suggests divine intervention, the authorities were not willing to consider that God might have been behind their deliverance. The high priest's charge was first of all one of disobedience: *'We gave you strict orders not to teach in this name' (parangelia parēngeilamen* is a Hebraism meaning 'we strictly ordered'; cf. 4:17-18).[47] Instead of obeying this instruction, the apostles had *filled Jerusalem* with their teaching. In strict terms, they were guilty of contempt of court. The second charge was that of making the Jewish authorities *guilty of this man's blood* (cf. 2:23; 3:13-15, 17-18; 4:10). 'You intend to bring this man's blood upon us' (KJV, NKJV, ESV) is a more literal rendering of *boulesthe epagagein eph' hēmas to haima tou anthrōpou toutou.* 'Bringing blood' on others means blaming them for another's death (cf. 2 Sa. 1:16; Ezk. 18:13; Hos. 12:14). Perhaps they feared that the apostles were 'invoking divine vengeance' (cf. Jgs. 9:24).[48] More immediately, they may have feared a popular uprising against them (cf. the fear of stoning in v. 26). The truthfulness of apostolic claims about Jesus was not even considered at this point, since the Sadducees were more concerned about maintaining their reputation and leadership among the people.

29 Once again, *Peter* speaks, and the impression is given that he does so on behalf of *the other apostles.*[49] He answers the first charge as before (4:19-20): *'We must obey God rather than human beings (anthrōpois)'.* Although the apostles did not resist arrest and acknowledged the right of the Sanhedrin to try them, they could not deny God's overriding commission — now reaffirmed by the angel — to 'tell the people all about this new life' (v. 20). Christians should generally submit themselves to governing authorities, showing proper respect and cooperation, recognizing that political leaders

---

46. Bock 2007, 242. Barrett 1994, 287, notes that such stoning could not be a formal legal penalty, since only the Council could authorise that. It could either be a non-specific form of protest against the authorities or a way of accusing them of blasphemy because of their treatment of the apostles.

47. Some Greek MSS read a question implying a positive answer here (including the particle *ou*): 'Did we not strictly order you?' (so KJV, NKJV). The reading represented by the TNIV, however, is better attested and is more likely to have been the original. Cf. Metzger, *Textual Commentary,* 289.

48. Barrett 1994, 288.

49. Most MSS have the awkward construction *apokritheis de Petros kai hoi apostoloi eipan* ('but Peter answered and the apostles said'), but the Western MSS simplify this and enhance the role of Peter by making him the only speaker. Cf. Metzger, *Textual Commentary,* 289-90.

and institutions have been established by God for the good order of society (cf. Rom. 13:1-7; 1 Pet. 2:13-17). At the same time, they cannot deny their fundamental calling as 'a chosen people, a royal priesthood, a holy nation, God's special possession', to declare the praises of the one who called them 'out of darkness into his wonderful light' (1 Pet. 2:9). When that opportunity is denied or thwarted by governments, a terrible clash of loyalties arises. Imprisonment and death are sometimes the lot of those who, in imitation of the apostles, cannot keep silent about God and the gospel.

30 Peter answers the second charge by proclaiming again the resurrection of Jesus *('The God of our ancestors raised Jesus from the dead')* and by reasserting the responsibility of the high priest and his associates for that death *('whom you had killed by hanging him on a cross').*[50] When the apostle claims that Jesus was raised by *the God of our ancestors* (cf. 3:13), he implies that those who condemned him to death were in rebellion against the God who had made a covenant with their ancestors and revealed his will to them. Jesus had been vindicated by Israel's God, so that those who stood against him were in a desperate plight. 'The Christian faith is the fulfillment, not the contradiction, of Judaism, if Judaism is rightly understood.'[51] Gk. *xylon* (TNIV *cross*) is normally used for a piece of wood, a stake, or 'a tree' (so most EVV here). It is also found in Acts 10:39; 13:29; Gal. 3:13; 1 Pet. 2:24. It appears to have been chosen because of its use in the execution of a death penalty in various contexts.[52] To Jewish ears, especially in the light of Deuteronomy 21:23 ('anyone who is hung on a pole is under God's curse'), it would have highlighted the shameful nature of Jesus' death, and suggested its penal character (cf. Gal. 3:13-14). Scholars debate whether there is any atonement theology in the sermons in Acts. However, the use of this term, in conjunction with the claim that Jesus is the eschatological *'Saviour'* who makes possible a definitive *'repentance'* and *'forgiveness of sins'* (v. 31), suggests that an atonement theology is definitely indicated here.[53] 'Surely no Christian preacher would have chosen to describe the death of Jesus in terms which drew attention to the curse of God resting upon the executed criminal, unless he had faced the scandal of the cross

---

50. Gaventa 2003, 107, observes that the apostolic response to the high priest 'in effect concedes his charges, since they have every intention of filling Jerusalem with Christian teaching and they do regard the leaders as culpable in Jesus' death'.

51. Barrett 1994, 289. Gk. *ēgeiren* ('raised') could mean 'brought on the human scene' (cf. *anistanai* in 3:22, 26; 7:37; 13:33), but the sequence suggested in 5:30-31 is crucifixion, resurrection, exaltation to God's right hand, and *ēgeiren* is normally used for *raised from the dead* (with or without *ek nekrōn*; cf. 3:15; 10:40; 13:30, 37; 28:8).

52. The word is regularly used in Greek literature for instruments of punishment. Cf. J. Schneider, *TDNT* 5:37-41.

53. Cf. D. G. Peterson, 'Atonement Theology in Luke-Acts: Some Methodological Reflections', in P. J. Williams, A. D. Clarke, P. M. Head, and D. Instone-Brewer (eds.), *The New Testament in Its First-Century Setting: Essays on Context and Background in Honour of B. W. Winter on His 65th Birthday* (Grand Rapids/Cambridge: Eerdmans, 2004), 56-71; THE THEOLOGY OF ACTS: VI. THE ATONING WORK OF JESUS (pp. 75-79).

and had come to believe that Jesus had borne the curse on behalf of others.'[54]

31 The apostle develops the theme of vindication by claiming that
'*God exalted him to his own right hand as Prince and Saviour*'. Similar language
is used here to 2:33 (*hypsōsen tē dexia autou*, 'exalted to his right hand'),
where the ascension and heavenly session of Jesus are the ground for
claiming that he fulfills Psalm 110:1 as 'Lord and Christ' (Acts 2:34-36). A
different term is used to describe the exaltation of Jesus in 3:13. The titles
Prince and Saviour (archēgon kai sōtēra)[55] now explain more fully the implications of his ascension in terms of his destiny to lead and rescue Israel in the
face of impending judgment. Indeed, he was exalted to God's right hand as
Prince and Saviour '*so that he might bring Israel to repentance and forgive their
sins*' (*[tou] dounai metanoian tō Israēl kai aphesin hamartiōn*, 'to give repentance to Israel and forgiveness of sins', as in most EVV).[56] Even as Peter uttered these words, the offer of salvation was once more extended to those
who condemned Jesus to death (cf. 2:23, 38; 3:13-15, 17-19; 4:10-12). The offer of forgiveness makes genuine repentance possible (cf. Rom. 2:4). Jesus,
the rejected and crucified Messiah, had died and been raised so as 'to give'
(dounai) repentance and forgiveness to Israel (cf. 3:26 note).[57] This remarkable paradox expresses the incredible grace of God towards all who set
themselves against him and his anointed one (cf. 4:25-28). The authorities
in the Sanhedrin, like everyone else in Israel who had rejected Jesus,
needed to acknowledge his true identity and their need of the salvation being offered to them. Repentance and forgiveness were even available to
such as these! Later in Acts, it is made clear that the nations more generally
can benefit from these gifts, through faith in Jesus as Lord and Saviour (cf.
repentance in 8:22; 11:18; 17:30; 20:21; 26:20; forgiveness of sins in 10:43;
13:38; 26:18).

32 Repentance for the high priest and his associates specifically
meant confessing their role in the denial of the Messiah and accepting the
testimony of those who were '*witnesses*' of his resurrection and ascension. It
also meant acknowledging the testimony of '*the Holy Spirit, whom God has
given to those who obey him*' (cf. 2:38-39). In other words, they needed to heed

54. G. B. Caird, *The Apostolic Age* (London: Duckworth, 1995), 40.

55. In 3:15 Jesus is proclaimed 'author of life' *(ton archēgon tēs zōēs)*, though the expression could also mean 'prince' or 'leader' of life. 'Prince' or 'leader' is certainly the most
natural rendering of the unqualified *archēgon* in 5:31, linked as it is with *sōtēra*. 'Saviour' is
the title given to Jesus in Lk. 1:47; 2:11; Acts 13:23. But the 'salvation' achieved by Jesus is
mentioned many times throughout Luke-Acts (cf. Acts 4:12 note).

56. The Western text has two variations in 5:31. The first appears to be an ancient
transcriptional error *(tē doxē autou*, God exalted him 'for his glory') and the second appears
to be a typically Western expansion *(en autō* after *aphesin hamartiōn*, 'forgiveness of sins *in
him*'). Cf. Metzger, *Textual Commentary*, 290, for textual variations in 5:31-32.

57. R. C. Tannehill, *The Shape of Luke's Story: Essays on Luke-Acts* (Eugene: Cascade,
2005), 84-101, discusses the way repentance is God's gift but also a human responsibility in
Luke-Acts.

the witness of the apostolic preaching about Jesus and respond to the witness of the Holy Spirit in the community of faith created by that preaching. In Acts 2–5, Luke has been illustrating the practical effect of the Spirit's presence in the Jerusalem church. Peter implies that the work of the Spirit in individuals and in the community of the Messiah is a divine endorsement of the sort of claims made in vv. 30-31. The Spirit is *given (edōken)* by God, just as repentance and the forgiveness of sins is given (*dounai*, v. 31) by the exalted Lord Jesus. Implicit in these verses is the view of God as Trinity: three 'persons' but one God.[58]

33 Just as they were too blinded to evaluate the true significance of the healing in 4:8-22, so now those who heard Peter's claims were unable to weigh up the evidence and make a proper response. In fact, *they were furious (dieprionto,* 'torn through', 'cut to the quick', 'infuriated', BDAG; cf. 7:54) *and wanted to put them to death.* 'The enraged response of those present goes well beyond the amazement of 4:13',[59] indicating an escalation of antagonism and opposition to the gospel. This escalation comes to a climax with the death of Stephen and persecution of the church in Jerusalem (7:54–8:3). 'Luke has nothing to say about the vexed question of the Jewish senate's right to inflict the death penalty. But he *assumes* throughout his narratives that the council can both condemn and execute offenders against Jewish law.'[60] Of course, a suitable accusation could have been made before a Roman court to secure the execution of Christian leaders.

2. *The Moderating Influence of Gamaliel (5:34-40)*

When it is noted that a leading Pharisee stood up to address the Sanhedrin, a contrast with the initiative of the Sadducees (v. 17) is signalled.[61] For the first time in Acts, an unbeliever speaks to others about the early Christians and offers some defence of their position. Gamaliel's advice seems tolerant and appealing because it hinders further aggressive action against the apostles. There is truth in his assertions that 'if the movement is God's, it cannot be overpowered' and that 'attempts to silence the movement are the equivalent of resisting God'.[62] These assertions are confirmed in the events

58. There are further reflections on the witness of the Spirit in THE THEOLOGY OF ACTS: VII. WITNESS AND MISSION (pp. 79-83).

59. Gaventa 2003, 108. Barrett 1994, 292, notes that there is little to choose between the variants *eboulonto (they wanted)* and *ebouleuonto* ('they planned').

60. S. Mason, 'Chief Priests, Sadducees, Pharisees and Sanhedrin in Acts', in R. Bauckham (ed.), *The Book of Acts in Its First-Century Setting*, Vol. 4: *Palestinian Setting* (Grand Rapids: Eerdmans; Carlisle: Paternoster, 1995), 157. G. H. Twelftree, 'Sanhedrin', *DNTB*, 1064, discusses the conflicting evidence regarding the right of the Sanhedrin to execute a capital sentence.

61. TNIV does not show that v. 17 begins with the same verb *anastas* (v. 34, *stood up*), signalling the initiative of the high priest and other members of the party of the Sadducees.

62. Gaventa 2003, 111.

that follow, with the death of Stephen and the persecution of the Jerusalem church leading to an amazing spread of Christianity in Samaria and beyond (8:4–9:31). But Gamaliel does not call for an examination of the truthfulness of apostolic claims. In the final analysis, his advice is fatalistic and flawed, because it does not take seriously the challenges presented by Peter (4:8-12, 19-20; 5:29-32).

34 Gamaliel is portrayed as *a teacher of the law* (*nomodidaskalos*, as in Lk. 5:17; 1 Tim. 1:7), *who was honoured by all the people* (cf. Josephus, *War* 5.527), and the only councillor who appears to have had any interest in discussing the Christians' claims. 'This alone sets him apart from the chief-priestly councillors, just as the Pharisees of the Gospel, who loved to debate issues, were different from the chief priests there.'[63] The name 'Pharisee' probably derives from the Aramaic verb 'divide, separate' (*p^eraš*). The Pharisees saw themselves as 'the separated' or 'the holy ones', who kept aloof from those who were casual about keeping God's law. They were a continuation of the ancient Hasidim ('pious ones'), who joined the Hasmonean rulers in their struggle for religious freedom in the second century BC, when the Seleucids controlled Palestine. They withdrew their support, however, when the Hasmoneans went on to establish political as well as military supremacy for themselves and assumed the high priesthood.[64] The Pharisees came from diverse backgrounds to devote themselves to the study of the law in its written and oral forms. They applied the law to every aspect of life and sought to prepare God's people for the coming of the Messianic Age by summoning them to live a holy life. In later rabbinic tradition, Gamaliel appears as Hillel's successor in the headship of his school.[65] He was so highly esteemed that the Mishnah declares: 'Since Rabban Gamaliel the elder died there has been no more reverence for the law; and purity and abstinence died out at the same time' (*m. Soṭah* 9:15). Assuming leadership of the debate at this critical moment (cf. v. 33), Gamaliel *ordered that the men be put outside for a little while*. A closed session was perhaps a better context in which to consider the fate of the apostles more objectively. It certainly avoided giving them the impression that they were right. Possibly, the essential thrust of Gamaliel's argument soon became public, or Luke learned the details from Saul/Paul, who was a student of Gamaliel (22:3) and on close terms with the priestly authorities at this time (9:1-2).

35-37 Gamaliel urged the furious and vindictive assembly, '*consider*

63. Mason, 'Chief Priests', 150. Some Pharisees in the Gospel are favourable towards Jesus (cf. Luke 7:36; 11:37; 14:1) and in Acts some become Christians (15:5). Some of the Pharisees in the Sanhedrin side with Paul against the Sadducees in Acts 23:9. Cf. R. L. Brawley, *Luke-Acts and the Jews: Conflict, Apology and Conciliation*, SBLMS 33 (Atlanta: Scholars, 1987), 84-106; Cunningham, *Persecution*, 202-3.

64. Cf. Bruce 1988, 114 note 51; Bruce 1990, 174-75; Barrett 1994, 292.

65. Cf. J. Neusner, *The Rabbinic Tradition about the Pharisees before 70*, Vols. 1-3 (Leiden: Brill, 1971), 1:341-76.

carefully what you intend to do to these men', giving two examples of recent uprisings which *'came to nothing'*. This prepares for the argument that the court should wait and see whether the new movement was of human origin or from God (vv. 38-39). Much debate has taken place about the reference to *'Theudas'* and then *'Judas the Galilean'*. Some commentators propose that Luke was ill informed about these characters, that he composed the speech himself, and that he put historical errors into the mouth of Gamaliel. According to Josephus, the Jewish historian, a certain Theudas appeared between AD 44 and 46, claiming to be a prophet and leading many to follow him into the wilderness (*Ant.* 20.97-98). This sounds like Gamaliel's description of the Theudas who *'appeared, claiming to be somebody, and about four hundred men rallied to him'*. Josephus records that Theudas was killed by the Romans and many of his followers were either killed or captured. Luke similarly records that Theudas *'was killed, all his followers were dispersed, and it all came to nothing'*. The problem with this apparent parallel, however, is that Gamaliel is supposed to be speaking well before AD 44, the year in which Herod Agrippa I died (cf. Acts 12:20-23). A further problem is the mention of *Judas the Galilean*, who is said to have appeared *'after'* Theudas, but *'in the days of the census'*. That uprising, which is also described by Josephus (*Ant.* 18.4-10), occurred in AD 6, well before the Theudas incident. It is unlikely that Luke has confused the evidence of Josephus, since the latter's work was not published until about AD 93. It is also unnecessary to accuse Josephus of error in this connection. Much more probable is the suggestion that Gamaliel refers to another Theudas, who was one of many insurgent leaders who arose in Palestine at the time of Herod the Great's death in 4 BC and thus preceded the appearance of Judas the Galilean in AD 6.[66]

38-39 To some extent, Gamaliel serves as a spokesman for Luke here, since the form of his advice 'gives a higher degree of probability to the possibility that the activity of the apostles may be from God than to the possibility that it may have a human origin.'[67] From the perspective of Luke and his readers, the success of Christianity indicated that it was truly *'from God'*. Gamaliel advised the Sanhedrin, *'Leave these men alone!'*

---

66. Cf. Marshall 1980, 122-23; Longenecker 1981, 323; Bruce 1990, 176; Barrett 1994, 294-96; Witherington 1998, 235-39. Josephus describes four men bearing the name of Simon within forty years and three called Judas within ten years, all of whom were instigators of rebellion. There could certainly have been more than one Theudas in such a role in a forty- or fifty-year period. However, Johnson 1992, 100, suggests that Luke and Josephus may have been using independent traditions about the same characters. Metzger, *Textual Commentary*, 291-92, discusses Western variants of vv. 35-37.

67. Brawley, *Conflict*, 89. Two different forms of conditional clauses are found in the Greek of 5:38-39. The first, with *ean* and the subjunctive, has the force of 'if it should be'. The second, with *ei* and the indicative, expresses what is more likely ('if it is a fact that'). However, such a distinction must be attributed to Luke rather than to Gamaliel's Aramaic. Cf. Bruce 1990, 178. Metzger, *Textual Commentary*, 292-94, discusses the much-expanded version of 5:38-39 in the Western text.

(*apostētate apo tōn anthrōpōn toutōn*, 'Keep away from these people'), and '*Let them go!*' presuming that God would reward or punish them as they deserved. His first option is that 'this purpose' *(hē boulē hautē)* or 'this activity' *(to ergon touto)* might be '*of human origin*' *(ex anthrōpōn)*. Five times in Acts, the Greek word *boulē* is used with reference to the plan or purpose of God (2:23; 4:28; 5:39; 13:36; 20:27; cf. Lk. 7:29) and three times with reference to human plans (5:38; 27:12, 42; cf. Lk. 23:51). If the apostolic plan and method of achieving it is '*of human origin, it will fail*', just as the movements mentioned in vv. 36-37 failed. But if it is '*from God*', it will succeed, and '*you will not be able to stop these men*'. Those who oppose it will find themselves '*fighting against God*'.

Gamaliel's point about not being able to stop the apostles has been described as 'sound Pharisaic teaching; God is over all and needs no help from men for the fulfillment of his purposes; all men must do is to obey, and leave the issue to him.'[68] But such teaching is closer to fatalism than a truly biblical view of the way God works in his world and expects people to respond to the unfolding of events. Gamaliel's temporizing approach does not highlight the importance of considering the truthfulness of the apostolic claims, with their challenge about the fulfillment of Scripture and signs of God's Spirit at work in the Christian movement (4:8-12; 5:29-32). Waiting to see how things turn out is not an adequate form of guidance for difficult situations.[69] Gamaliel's pupil, Saul of Tarsus (22:3), saw the issue more clearly. If a movement is wrong, it should be vigorously opposed (22:4-5). Nevertheless, Gamaliel may have been more open to the preaching of Jesus and the resurrection than the majority in the Sanhedrin (4:1-2), cautiously sharing some of the admiration of the common people for the apostles. In such a context, he rightly warns opponents of Christianity about *fighting against God*.[70]

40 It comes as something of a surprise to read that *his speech persuaded them*. Was it the rhetorical skill of Gamaliel or the force of his argu-

---

68. J. A. Findlay, *The Acts of the Apostles* (London: SCM, 1934), 85. Bruce 1988, 115, compares the teaching of the second-century Rabbi Yohanan the sandlemaker: 'Every assembly which is in the name of heaven will finally be established, but that which is not in the name of heaven will finally not be established' (*Pirke 'Abot* 4:11). Longenecker 1981, 323, concludes that 'such sentiments of tolerance and moderation, with history being viewed as the final judge of whether something is of God, characterized the better Pharisee of the day'. Witherington 1998, 233-35, is similarly positive about Gamaliel's argument.

69. Johnson 1992, 103, argues that Gamaliel's prudent advice is actually an example of bad faith. 'He is (in the sense that Luke uses the term of the Pharisees and teachers of the law), a "hypocrite", for he wants to appear to be righteous, and he has all the right convictions, but he will not respond to the prophetic call before him. Like the Pharisees and teachers of the law described in Luke 7:29, he "rejects God's plan *(boulē)*."'

70. The term *theomachai* ('fighters against God') and its cognates are common in Hellenistic literature (J. T. Squires, *The Plan of God in Luke-Acts*, SNTSMS 76 [Cambridge: Cambridge University, 1993], 175-76). On the lips of Gamaliel, this would have had a special appeal to readers from the Hellenistic world.

ment? Both of these factors may have been significant, but Luke makes another point. Gamaliel was honoured by all the people (v. 34), and the people were still well disposed towards the apostles (v. 26). Gamaliel therefore carried disproportionate weight in the Sanhedrin because he represented the popular will. But he is no more a partisan of the Christians than he is of the other groups mentioned in vv. 36-37. 'Gamaliel appears as a shrewd popular politician, weighing popular piety against administrative needs. Like the Pharisees of the Gospel, he adopts a cautious wait-and-see approach, which does not preclude a sound flogging.'[71] Flogging by the Sanhedrin or synagogue officials was a serious punishment for those who broke the law (*m. Mak.* 3:10-15a prescribes thirty-nine stripes; cf. 22:19; 2 Cor. 11:24). In this case, it was accompanied once again by the order *not to speak in the name of Jesus* (cf. 4:17, 18; 5:28).

3. The Ministry of the Apostles Continues (5:41-42)

These verses form a climax to the whole section that began with a description of life in the Jerusalem church in 2:42-47. Luke presents a final summary of the first main section of his book. The preaching of Jesus and the resurrection was at the heart of apostolic ministry and the daily life of the first Christians. In chapters 3–5, this preaching was characterized as proclaiming *the name* of Jesus Christ. Healing in the name of Christ, such as the healing of the man who was lame from birth, illustrated the power of Christ to 'heal' or save in the ultimate sense (3:19-21; 4:8-12). But preaching and healing in the name of Christ aroused opposition from the priestly Sadducean leaders of Israel. This provoked the arrest, trial, and imprisonment of Peter and John in the first case (4:1-22) and possibly also other apostles in the second case (5:17-40). Both times their remarkable deliverance is related to the popular support of the ordinary people of Jerusalem and the continuing boldness of the apostles in testifying to the truth. In the second case, their deliverance is also attributed to angelic intervention and the advocacy of Gamaliel. In all this, however, the sovereign hand of God is discerned (4:23-31; 5:38-39), protecting his servants and advancing 'the word'.

41-42 After the flogging and warning not to speak in the name of Jesus (*hoi men oun*, 'they then', implies a definite consequence of the preceding verse; cf. 1:6; 2:41), the apostles actually left the Sanhedrin *rejoicing because they had been counted worthy of suffering disgrace for the Name.* 'Here we have a concrete example of that "rejoicing in suffering" which should be the hallmark of the Christian under persecution (1 Pet. 4:13; cf. Mt. 5:11f.; Rom. 5:3f.; 2 Cor. 6:10; 1 Pet. 1:6f.).'[72] Indeed, 14:22 makes clear that Chris-

71. Mason, 'Chief Priests', 151. There is not enough evidence to conclude that he is 'the genuine Jew on the verge of affirming Christianity' (Brawley, *Conflict*, 98).
72. Marshall 1980, 124. Metzger, *Textual Commentary*, 294, notes various additions af-

tians in general 'must go through many hardships to enter the kingdom of God'. Here in 5:41-42, Luke affirms that the daily ministry of the apostles continued undeterred, despite the opposition, *in the temple courts and from house to house* (cf. 2:26). An interesting innovation at this point, however, is the introduction of the word 'evangelising' *(euangelizomenoi)* to describe more fully the nature of the teaching in which they engaged *(teaching and proclaiming the good news that Jesus is the Messiah)*. This verb becomes a key term in subsequent chapters (8:4, 12, 25, 35, 40; 10:36; 11:20; 13:32; 14:7, 15, 21; 15:35; 16:10; 17:18), where it is sometimes combined with the notion of proclaiming the kingdom of God, as in the ministry of Jesus himself (cf. Lk. 4:43; 8:1; 16:16). The apostles are still the main characters involved in *teaching and proclaiming the good news*, but Luke is about to show how the task came to be shared by other Spirit-filled leaders and the members of the Jerusalem church more generally (6:6-10; 8:1-40).

I. Resolution of a Significant Conflict in the Jerusalem Church (6:1-7)

This brief but important passage brings to a climax Luke's narrative about the growth of the church in Jerusalem. Dissension among the believers is resolved by the appointment of a new group of leaders to meet the particular needs of 'Hellenists' in the community. The Seven (cf. 21:8) are set apart for a ministry of 'serving tables', but they are not called 'deacons' and Luke's intention cannot simply have been to describe how the order of deacons originated (cf. 1 Tim. 3:8-13).[1] Their appointment liberates the Twelve to devote themselves to prayer and 'the ministry of the word' (6:4). At the same time, it provides for the pastoral care of an important group within the church and propels Stephen and Philip into positions of greater responsibility and prominence. They are soon shown to be engaged in a ministry of the word like the apostles, inaugurating the next stage in the fulfillment of Jesus' commission (1:8). As Luke introduces these two key figures, he establishes their authority and link with the Twelve. With a 'marked *ministerial* increase' of personnel outside the circle of the apostles, Luke records 'the church's *territorial* progress beyond Jerusalem'.[2] However, 'whereas

---

ter *tou onomatos (the Name)* in different textual traditions, but the simplest form is most likely to be the original. Bock 2007, 252, comments on the difficulty of adopting this apostolic attitude to suffering and disgrace in the strongly shame-honour society of the Greco-Roman world.

1. So Barrett 1994, 304, who nevertheless believes that 'the story embodies the method of appointing ministers that was familiar to Luke himself: popular choice, approval by those already ministers, and the laying on of hands'. But Barrett, 306, argues from 21:8 that the original designation of Philip and his colleagues may have been 'the seven evangelists'! Philip could have been Luke's source for much of the material in Acts 6–8 because of the meeting recorded in 21:8-10.

2. Spencer 1997, 62. Against Barrett 1994, 305, Luke does not imply that the difference

the inner life of the community continually resolves the critical issues that threaten its survival, the strife between the establishment and the community increasingly escalates as the narrative progresses'.[3]

The passage begins and ends with a record of the remarkable growth in the number of believers in Jerusalem, and the point is clearly made that this happened because the ministry of the word continued unhindered (cf. 5:42; 6:7). This is a critical paragraph for Luke's development of a theology of 'the word of God' (cf. 6:2, 4, 7). At three points in the narrative, he writes about the word of God growing and multiplying (6:7; 12:24; 19:20). Each reference climaxes a section recording the resolution of some conflict or the cessation of opposition and persecution. The gospel is shown to prosper in spite of, and even because of, struggle and suffering.[4] Most importantly, however, the present context suggests that, if decisive action had not been taken to deal with the social issue disturbing the church, 'growth' of the word may not have continued.

1 The expression *in those days* does not simply begin a new section of the narrative but makes a clear link between the increase in the number of disciples in 6:1 and the activity described in 5:42. Church growth continued because the apostles persisted in their daily ministry of public proclamation and teaching about Jesus. For the first time in Acts, those who believed are described as *disciples*.[5] The term *mathētēs* was used in the Greco-Roman world to describe a 'learner' or 'apprentice', who was attached to and followed a respected teacher, usually in a school or fellowship of disciples. In Luke's Gospel, the term refers to the followers of John the Baptist (5:33), to those who attached themselves to Jesus with varying degrees of commitment (6:17) and, more narrowly, to those whom Jesus drew into an intimate relationship of trust and obedience with himself (9:18-27).[6] Acts uses 'disciples' with reference to all Christian believers. Disciples are no longer simply those who followed Jesus in the course of his earthly ministry, but those

---

between the Seven and the Twelve was simply that the former were 'Hellenists' and the latter 'Hebrews'.

3. T. Penner, *In Praise of Christian Origins: Stephen and the Hellenists in Lukan Apologetic Historiography*, Emory Studies in Early Christianity 10 (New York/London: Clark International, 2004), 263.

4. Cf. P. R. House, 'Suffering and the Purpose of Acts', *JETS* 33 (1990), 317-30.

5. According to Barrett 1994, 305, this is an indication that Luke is following a fresh tradition or source. However, the term continues to be used extensively from this point, across what may be considered different possible sources. Cf. 6:2, 7; 9:1, 10, 19, 25, 26 (twice), 38; 11:26, 29; 13:52; 14:20, 22, 28; 15:10; 16:1; 18:23, 27; 19:1, 9, 30; 20:1, 30; 21:4, 16 (twice). Use of the word *mathētēs* ('disciple') is unusual in 9:25; 19:1. Before 6:1, Christians are 'believers' (2:44; 4:32) or 'brothers' (1:15-16, though in 2:29, 37; 3:17, 22 this term is also used for Israelites more generally).

6. K. H. Rengstorf, *TDNT* 4:415-61, discusses the way the NT differs from Greco-Roman and rabbinic views of discipleship. Rengstorf, 458, argues that the distinctive use of *mathētēs* in Acts reflects 'the common name by which Palestinian Christians called themselves'. The term was not taken up by Paul or by the Greek churches because 'this might give rise to the idea that Christianity was simply a philosophical movement' (459).

who become 'obedient to the faith' (6:7), signifying obedience to the apostolic pattern of belief and lifestyle. This paragraph begins and ends with a statement about the number of disciples *increasing* (*plēthynontōn*, v. 1; *eplēthyneto*, v. 7; cf. 9:31; 12:24). But even as this exciting increase in numbers was taking place, a problem was emerging.

The Hellenistic Jews among them complained against the Hebraic Jews because their widows were being overlooked in the daily distribution of food. Luke does not gloss over the conflicts and difficulties of the earliest churches (e.g., 5:1-11; 8:18-24; 9:26-28; 11:1-18; 15:1-35; 21:20-36), but, in reporting problems, he regularly focuses on the way they were resolved. The issue here was more than 'natural stress created by rapid community growth, with needs outstripping administration'.[7] One group in the church sensed discrimination in the impressive ministry of love and generosity provided in *the daily distribution of food* (*tē diakonia tē kathēmerinē*, 'the daily ministry').[8] The claim that *their widows were being overlooked* (*paretheōrounto*) implies neglect in this context (BDAG). Gaventa points out that 'because most women spent their lives in households that belonged to their fathers and then their husbands, they controlled little property and had little economic opportunity'.[9] When widowed, they were particularly vulnerable economically and socially. The OT has much to say about the care of widows (e.g., Ex. 22:22-24; Dt. 14:28-29; 24:17-22), and Luke seems to have a particular interest in their welfare (e.g., Lk. 2:36-38; 4:24-26; 7:12; 18:1-8; 21:2-3; Acts 9:39, 41). Neglect of any group in a community where it was claimed that 'there was no needy person among them' would have been a problem, but this was potentially a very divisive matter.[10]

The word translated *Hellenistic Jews* (*Hellēnistai*) is not found in any literature prior to Acts and is used by Luke on only two other occasions (cf. 9:29; 11:20 [though some MSS of both texts read *Hellēnas*, 'Greeks']). The contrasting group in 6:1 is defined as *Hebraioi* (TNIV *Hebraic Jews*, but in most EVV 'the Hebrews'), which fundamentally means 'those who speak

---

7. Johnson 1992, 105. Witherington 1998, 248, may be nearer the mark in suggesting that 'the Greek-speaking Jewish Christians were just fewer in number and so the widows of this group had less of a natural constituency to rely on'.

8. Bruce 1990, 182, points out that the 'daily ministry' or 'daily distribution' could have been in the form of money (NRSV, TNIV add 'of food' in v. 1, though this is not required by the Greek) and that *trapeza* ('table') could be used in a financial sense (Mk. 11:15; Jn. 2:15; cf. Mt. 25:27; Lk. 9:23). More broadly, Johnson 1992, 106, relates this terminology to what we know from rabbinic sources about organized Jewish charity: 'Each community would offer a daily "soup kitchen" for transients and the destitute, and a "chest" for meeting long-term needs.' Cf. J. Jeremias, *Jerusalem in the Time of Jesus: An Investigation into Economic and Social Conditions during the New Testament Period* (ET, London: SCM, 1969), 126-34; Barrett 1994, 310.

9. Gaventa 2003, 112.

10. Cf. Spencer 1997, 65. Penner, *Christian Origins*, 265-66, notes the OT parallels, but goes on to argue that Luke demonstrates 'continuity between the Deuteronomic emphasis on care for the widows and the Greek stress on maintaining *koinōnia, philanthrōpia* and charity' (Penner, 275). Luke presents the Christian community as fulfilling the best ideals of both Hebrew and Greek traditions, using the form of 'epideictic historiography', written in praise of Christian origins.

Hebrew (or Aramaic)'.[11] A narrowly 'linguistic' definition of *Hellēnistai* allows us to make the best sense of its different application in Luke's three contexts. In 6:1 it refers to Jewish Christians who spoke only Greek, as opposed to Jewish Christians whose everyday spoken language was Aramaic (or less likely Hebrew), but who may also have spoken Greek.[12] In 9:29 it refers to Greek-speaking Jews who were hostile to Christianity, but in 11:20 it refers to Greek-speaking persons in Antioch who were not Jews at all. The context defines more precisely in each case what sort of Greek-speaking person Luke has in mind, 'ranging from Jewish Christians, to Jews, to pagans'.[13] *The Hellenistic Jews* in 6:1 would have been Greek-speaking Jews from the Dispersion or their descendants, who lived in or around Jerusalem and attended synagogues where Greek was spoken (cf. 6:9). Those who had come to believe in Jesus as the Messiah had joined the church, where they were in close fellowship with Christian *Hebraic Jews*. It cannot be assumed that there was a doctrinal rift between the Hellenists and the Hebrews, but language and culture are closely linked, and it is likely that these two groups brought differences of outlook and attitude with them into the community of Christian disciples. Old prejudices and resentments may have reasserted themselves — or appeared to have been an issue — when practical problems relating to the care of widows became obvious.[14] Christians in every age and social context need to be aware of the threat that cultural and racial differences can pose to their unity in Christ.

A perception of neglect brought about the situation in which the Hellenistic Jewish Christians *complained* (*egeneto gongysmos*, 'there arose a complaint') against the Hebraic Jewish Christians. This probably also involved a challenge to the leadership of the apostles. Not long after the Israelites were redeemed from Egypt, complaints about their situation and the leadership of Moses and Aaron arose (e.g., Ex. 16:2-12; Nu. 11:1; 17:5, 10). As in

11. Etymologically, the noun *Hellēnistai* appears to have been derived from the verb *hellēnizein*. In 2 Cor. 11:22; Phil. 3:5 Paul uses the term *Hebraios* more broadly to describe his racial and religious identity. Luke employs the noun *Hebraios* only in Acts 6:1, though elsewhere he uses the adjectival equivalent *hebrais* to mean 'the Hebrew (or Aramaic) dialect' (e.g., Acts 21:40; 26:14). A helpful assessment of the debate that has taken place about the meaning of these terms in Acts is provided by Longenecker 1981, 327-29; Barrett 1994, 307-9; Witherington 1998, 240-47.

12. It is clear that some Hebrew/Aramaic-speaking Jews such as Peter and Paul were also fluent in Greek. The point about the use of *Hellēnistai* is that there were some Jews who spoke Greek exclusively.

13. Witherington 1998, 242.

14. Longenecker 1981, 329-40, notes the possible implications for Hellenist and Hebraic Jews who became Christians. P. F. Esler, *Community and Gospel in Luke-Acts: The Social and Political Motivations of Lucan Theology*, SNTSMS 57 (Cambridge: Cambridge University, 1987), 139-45, reads too much into the evidence when he proposes that the two groups in Acts 6 were characterised by different attitudes to the temple and different liturgies. Bock 2007, 258, rightly argues that 'the way the problem is eventually solved indicates that it may well have surfaced not because of ethnic malice but because of a lack of administrative organization caused by the new community's growth across diverse ethnic lines'.

Acts 6, there was concern in Exodus 16 about the adequate provision of food. Since the apostles appear to have administered the community resources at this stage (cf. 4:34-37; 5:2), complaints about *the daily distribution of food* were thus also a challenge to their leadership. At the deepest level, however, such grumbling is condemned in Scripture because it is seen as a complaint against God's gracious and providential care for his people (cf. 1 Cor. 10:10-11; Phil. 2:14-15; 1 Pet. 4:9). The antidote to such grumbling is prayer and a humble sharing of concerns with others.

2 Here only in Acts the apostles are called *the Twelve* (cf. Lk. 6:13; 8:1; 9:1, 12; 18:31; 22:3, 47), the reconstituted group being designated differently in 1:26; 2:14. Their leadership in the situation was expressed when they *gathered all the disciples together* (*to plēthos tōn mathētōn*, 'the multitude of the disciples') and made a proposal about providing practical care and preserving good relationships in the community (compare the relationship between apostles and community in 1:23). Rabbinic literature reveals more or less contemporary Jewish customs of relieving the poor.[15] The earliest Christians were concerned to maintain their own pattern of care and thus fulfill the injunctions of Scripture, especially as they related to widows and others in need (e.g., Ex. 22:22-24; Dt. 14:28-29; Ps. 146:9; cf. 1 Tim. 5:3-16). This was an important indication of their faithfulness to the God of Israel and of his Spirit's work in their midst. At the same time, the apostles recognised a particular, God-given responsibility for them to preach and teach about Jesus and the kingdom (cf. Lk. 24:47-48; Acts 1:1-8; 4:20; 5:19-20). So they argued that it would not be *'right'* (*areston* could be rendered 'acceptable' or 'appropriate'; cf. v. 5 note) for them *'to neglect (the ministry of) the word of God'* (*kataleipsantas ton logon tou theou*, 'forsake the word of God'). With such growth in the church and the need for more practical care of the widows, they could not be available *'to wait on tables'* (*diakonein trapezais*, 'to serve at tables') if they were to devote themselves *'to prayer and the ministry of the word'* (*tē proseuchē kai tē diakonia tou logou*, v. 4).[16] *The word* is mentioned three times within the space of a few verses (6:2, 4, 7). Previously it was identified as the message about Jesus which the apostles preached (2:41, 'his message'; 4:4, 'the word'), which was God-given (4:29, 'your word'; 4:31, 'the word of God'). Luke goes on to use either 'the word' or 'the word of God' many times to describe the apostolic gospel, which soon came to be central to the ministry of others as well (e.g., 8:4, 14; 11:19).[17] While maintaining the priority of gospel ministry, which was given to them by Jesus, the apostles wanted a ministry of care for the needy to flourish in Jerusalem.[18] With the latter as

15. Cf. note 8 above.

16. The word *diakonia* is used in 1:17, 25 to describe the 'ministry' received by Judas, and then by Matthias, and in 20:24; 21:19 with reference to a ministry of the word, as in 6:4. However, in 11:29; 12:25 the word is used of material service to those in need, as in 6:1.

17. I discuss the content of this 'word' in THE THEOLOGY OF ACTS: V. THE GOSPEL (pp. 70-75).

18. Spencer 1997, 66-67, misreads the situation when he concludes that the apostles

their responsibility, at least two of the Seven could still develop as preachers, as the narrative goes on to demonstrate. Many churches today could learn from the creative way in which this issue was handled. 'The early church seems to have been prepared to adjust its procedures, alter its organizational structure, and develop new posts of responsibility in response to existing needs and for the sake of the ongoing proclamation of the Word of God.'[19]

3 The whole church (TNIV *'Brothers and sisters'*, for *adelphoi*, 'brothers') was to *'choose'* (*episkepsasthe*, 'look out for') seven men from among them who would be suitable for this task.[20] They were to be 'of good repute' (*martyroumenous*, 'attested' [TNIV *known*]; cf. 16:2; 22:12, where the same verb is used of a character 'witnessed to' by others, and 1 Tim. 3:7, where the cognate noun *martyria* is used). Specifically, it was to be testified that they were *'full of the Spirit and wisdom'* (*plēreis pneumatos kai sophias*), implying that wisdom would be a particular manifestation of the Spirit's presence in their lives.[21] Wisdom may have been especially necessary in dealing with the complexity of relationships hinted at in the passage (but see below on 6:10). These requirements highlight the importance of a properly managed ministry of practical care in the life of the church. Outstanding candidates were required for this work. Gospel preaching may have been the apostolic priority (v. 2), but this in no way lessened the importance of good leadership in the care of widows. The role of the apostles in the process was to *'turn this responsibility over to them'* (*hous katastēsomen epi tēs chreias tautēs*, 'whom we will appoint over this business').[22]

4 The outcome for the apostles would be the freedom to 'devote' themselves (*proskarterēsomen*; TNIV *'we will give our attention'*) *'to prayer and the ministry of the word'* (*tē proseuchē kai tē diakonia tou logou*).[23] If the Jerusa-

---

were retreating from 'Jesus' holistic model of ministry'. It is precisely because they were seeking to maintain appropriate pastoral care that they appointed the Seven to take charge of the important ministry of caring for the widows. But, following the example of Jesus, the apostles would not abandon his priority of teaching and preaching (cf. Mk. 1:35-39; 6:32-34). Stott 1990, 122-23, considers how to maintain a proper balance between the two different types of ministry highlighted in this passage.

19. Longenecker 1981, 331. Johnson 1992, 110-11, is unnecessarily sceptical about the benefit to the Twelve in giving this care of the widows to the Seven.

20. Metzger, *Textual Commentary*, 294-95, discusses textual variations in the opening words of 6:3. Codex B uniquely alters the verb to include the apostles in the selection of the Seven (*episkepsōmetha*, 'let us choose, look out for').

21. Against Barrett 1994, 313, it does not seem right to describe wisdom here as a natural gift (cf. Jas. 3:17). The parallel expression in v. 5 ('full of faith and of the Holy Spirit') surely means that the Holy Spirit is the source of the faith that is mentioned as the outstanding characteristic in Stephen's life. In v. 3, despite the different word order, wisdom will be the outstanding characteristic produced by the Spirit in each of the Seven. Cf. Is. 11:2, where the Spirit of the Lord is further defined as 'the spirit of wisdom'; also Ex. 28:3; Dt. 34:9.

22. Cf. Barrett 1994, 313.

23. The pronoun *hēmeis* ('we') at the beginning of v. 4 emphasizes the role of the apostles, in contrast with the role of the community in v. 3.

lem church is presented as a model because 'they devoted themselves (2:42, *proskarterountes*) to the apostles' teaching' and to prayer, the apostles are presented as a model for those who would lead and inspire such communities. *The ministry of the word* doubtless included the whole pattern of preaching the gospel and teaching about its implications illustrated in the apostolic sermons and in the later account of Paul's ministry in Ephesus (20:18-35). Even though the word of God is represented in Acts as the powerful means of winning converts and growing churches (especially in 6:7; 12:24; 19:20), *prayer* was a necessary accompaniment because it expresses dependence on the Lord, to give boldness in speaking the word, to protect its agents, and to provide opportunities for the word to be heard and believed (cf. 4:24-31; 12:5-17; 13:1-3; 20:28-36; Col. 4:2-4; 2 Thes. 3:1-2).[24]

5 *This proposal pleased the whole group* (*pantos tou plēthous*, 'the whole multitude'; cf. 4:32 note).[25] Since the verb *pleased* (*ēreson*) is an echo of the word translated 'right' in v. 2 (*areston*), the implication may be that the people were pleased because they recognised that the proposal was in agreement with God's will.[26] Those chosen for the role all have Greek names. This does not prove that they were all Hellenists (Greek names such as Andrew, Philip, and Bartholomew are found among the apostles), though, given the situation, it is likely that they were. *Stephen* is mentioned first, presumably because his story is about to be told next. He is described as *a man full of faith and the Holy Spirit* (*plērēs pisteōs kai pneumatos hagiou*), with the syntax highlighting *faith* as a particular manifestation of the Spirit's presence in his life (cf. v. 3, *plēreis pneumatos kai sophias*, 'full of the Spirit and wisdom'). *Philip* follows, again presumably because of his position in the unfolding narrative of Acts. He is distinguished from Philip the apostle (1:13) by his calling and function in this context. Nothing more is known of *Procorus, Nicanor, Timon*, or *Parmenas. Nicolas*, however, is identified as being *from Antioch, a convert to Judaism*.[27] Since he is literally a 'proselyte' (*prosēlytos*; cf. 2:10; 13:43),[28] the

24. Cf. M. M. B. Turner, 'Prayer in the Gospels and Acts', in D. A. Carson (ed.), *Teach Us to Pray: Prayer in the Bible and the World* (Grand Rapids: Baker; Exeter: Paternoster, 1990), 72-75. There is no need to distinguish between private and public prayer in applying what is said in Acts 6:4.

25. Western texts add *tōn mathētōn* ('of the disciples') to make it clear that *pantos tou plēthous* refers to the church and not to the non-Christian multitude.

26. Cf. Barrett 1994, 311, 314. Johnson 1992, 106, notes that the issue in v. 2 is not a moral one but 'rather of what is "fitting" or "appropriate"'. Cf. *arestos* in LXX Dt. 6:18; 12:8, 25; Pr. 21:3; Tob. 3:6.

27. For the later association of Nicolas with the Nicolaitans mentioned in Rev. 2:6, 15, cf. Witherington 1998, 250 note 224; Bruce 1990, 184; Bock 2007, 262.

28. Later Jewish literature identifies proselytes as circumcised Gentiles. In some sources they are also said to have experienced water lustrations like baptism. However, in the LXX the term is used more generally to refer to resident aliens (e.g., Ex. 20:10; 23:12; Nu. 15:13-16). Witherington 1998, 344, holds that the term 'may on occasion be used by Luke in a more technical sense of circumcised Gentile converts to Judaism, but we cannot be sure, especially in light of the LXX use of the term and the influence of the Greek OT on Luke'. Cf. S. McKnight, 'Proselytism and Godfearers', *DNTB* 835-47.

implication is that the other six were born Jews, either in Palestine or the Dispersion.

6 The account concludes by indicating that the whole church *presented them to the apostles* (*hous estēsan enōpion*, 'whom they set before'), *who prayed and laid their hands on them*.[29] This should not be understood in terms of postbiblical ideas of ordination. These seven were not ordained to an office, but were commissioned to fulfill a specific administrative task.[30] In due course, the roles of Stephen and Philip changed, so that they became preachers like the apostles. In different ways — as those 'full of the Spirit and wisdom' (v. 3) — they were led into new patterns of ministry, becoming initiators of the next stage of gospel outreach beyond Jerusalem. Doubtless, the experience of humble service to widows in the church tested and prepared them for more prominent roles as ministers of the word. The text does not suggest that the apostles authorised the seven to be their successors, as Moses commissioned Joshua (Nu. 27:15-23; Dt. 34:9). A stronger biblical analogy would be the appointment by Moses of God-fearing and trusty men as 'officers' or 'judges' over the people (Ex. 18:13-26; Dt. 1:9-18, though there is no laying on of hands mentioned in these passages). A later parallel might be the practice of Jewish inhabitants of a Palestinian city choosing seven men to look after their common affairs. Such administrators had full power of representation, 'as if they were the city itself'.[31] Later in Acts we read of a group of elders in the Jerusalem church receiving money for the relief of the poor (11:30). This group may have taken over some of the 'diaconal' responsibilities given to the seven in 6:1-6.

7 *So the word of God spread.*[32] TNIV here and in 12:24; 19:20 does not adequately convey the meaning of the verb *ēuxanen* ('grew', 'increased'). The word of God 'grew' in the sense that its influence extended and the

29. A more literal reading of the Greek would suggest that 'the whole company of believers, not the apostles alone, laid their hands on the seven men' (Barrett 1994, 315; cf. D. Daube, *The New Testament and Rabbinic Judaism* [London: Athlone, 1956], 237-38). However, the impracticality of the whole church laying hands on the Seven and the sequence implied in vv. 2-3 would suggest that Luke's intention in v. 6 is not clearly expressed in Greek and that TNIV and NRSV have rightly represented the true sense.

30. The laying on of hands is associated with the giving of the Spirit in 8:17-19; 19:6, and with healing in Lk. 13:13; Acts 9:12, 17 (together with the filling of the Spirit); 28:8. Note the commissioning in 13:2-3 with the laying on of hands, at the instigation of the Spirit. I disagree with Bock 2007, 256, who says that the Seven were chosen because they could both preach and serve the widows. The former does not come into view in 6:1-6.

31. Daube, *Rabbinic Judaism*, 237. But 'the Seven of a City' were installed without the imposition of hands. The apostles were doing something original in adapting the Jewish practice of the 'laying on of hands' in this way. Cf. A. Harman, *NIDOTTE* 3:270-71.

32. Some MSS have *ho logos tou kyriou* here ('the word of the Lord'), as in 8:25; 13:49; 15:35, 36; 19:10, 20. But *ho logos tou theou* ('the word of God') is better attested and parallels the expression in 6:2. Cf. Metzger, *Textual Commentary*, 296, for other references where this reading is similarly in doubt. Metzger also comments on the alternatives to *tōn hiereōn* ('of the priests') in some MSS.

number who believed it grew. In Scripture, 'the word of God' is viewed as a vital force, reaching into people's lives and transforming situations according to God's will (e.g., Is. 2:3; 55:10-13; Je. 23:28-29; Rom. 1:16; 10:17-18; 1 Thes. 2:13; Heb. 4:12-13; 1 Pet. 1:23-25). Jesus' parable of the soils (Lk. 8:4-15) was probably particularly in Luke's mind, with its encouragement that the seed of the gospel which fell on good ground 'came up and yielded a crop, a hundred times more than was sown' (Lk. 8:8). Thus, Luke coined an expression which means that the church which is the creature of the word grew.[33] This is made clear by the following clause — *the number of disciples in Jerusalem increased rapidly (eplēthyneto ho arithmos tōn mathētōn en Ierousalēm sphodra)* — which is linked with the first clause by the word *kai* ('and', which is not translated by TNIV).[34] An inclusion is thus formed with 6:1, where we are told that 'the number of disciples was increasing' *(plēthynontōn)* because the daily teaching and evangelism of the apostles continued unabated (5:42). The satisfactory resolution of the conflict in the Jerusalem church made it possible for this ministry of the gospel to flourish and for church growth to take place even more *rapidly (sphodra)*. Church growth continued because the word of God had free course among the believers, and outsiders were able to witness its practical effect in a loving, united community, as well as hear its challenge from the lips of the apostles. But why is there special mention of the fact that *a large number of priests became obedient to the faith?* Many of the priests were Sadducees, who took the lead in opposing the apostles (4:1, 6; 5:17). Their obedience to 'the faith' *(pistis* here refers to the content of Christian belief and the lifestyle it demands) must have been a remarkable demonstration of God's intention to change lives through the ministry of his word.[35] It must have been a cause of alarm for the Jewish leaders more generally. But did the coming of so many priests 'strengthen the ties which bound a large proportion of the believers to the temple order'?[36] If so, it must have made Stephen's position more difficult, as he sought to explore the implications of the gospel for Christian attitudes towards the law and the temple (6:11-14).

---

33. Cf. J. Kodell, '"The Word of God Grew" — The Ecclesial Tendency of *Logos* in Acts 6:7; 12:24; 19:20', *Biblica* 55 (1974), 505-19, and note 17 above.

34. The verbs 'grew' *(ēuxēthēsan)* and 'multiplied' *(eplēthynthēsan)* are used together with the adverb *sphodra* in Ex. 1:7 to describe the rapid growth of the people of Israel in Egypt, and a parallel may be intended in Acts 6:7 (cf. 7:17-18). In 12:24 Luke uses an abbreviated formula that incorporates the same two verbs. These verses, and the slightly different 19:20, are deliberate editorial markers in the flow of Luke's narrative, with the later references alluding to the clear meaning of the first in its context. Luke significantly uses the imperfect tense with these verbs, to express the idea of continuing growth and multiplication.

35. Note the emphasis on 'the obedience of faith' in Rom. 1:5; 16:26, the need for everyone to 'obey the gospel' in Rom. 10:16 (TNIV ['accepted the good news'] obscures this), and Paul's intention to lead the Gentiles 'to obey God' (Rom. 15:18). Obedience to 'the faith' in Acts 6:7 signifies genuine discipleship.

36. Bruce 1990, 185.

III. THE WORD GOES OUT FROM JERUSALEM (6:8–9:31)

With the summary verse in 6:7, a major 'panel' of Luke's narrative about the growth of the word in Jerusalem concludes.[37] The next panel (6:8–9:31) concentrates on the Hellenists Stephen and Philip, and the early period of Saul's ministry, showing how the gospel spread throughout Judea, Galilee, Samaria, and even to Syria. There is a summary-conclusion in 9:31 that marks this development. It reflects the same theology of church growth through proclamation of the word expressed in 6:7, but uses different terminology to make the point. Stephen's death is mentioned three times in Acts as a particular turning point in the story of the gospel's progress (8:1-4; 11:19; 22:20). Stephen's speech (7:1-56), which is the longest in the book, is highly critical of the way that Israel has consistently resisted Moses and the prophets, culminating in the betrayal and murder of the Messiah. It is provocative enough to bring about his stoning and a great persecution against the church (7:57–8:3). Nevertheless, those who are scattered from Jerusalem because of this attack preach the gospel wherever they go (8:4). Philip emerges as the first key player in this new outreach of the word. Then Saul is introduced, and his significance in the unfolding plan of God is indicated. His commission to proclaim the risen Lord 'to the Gentiles and their kings and to the people of Israel' (9:15) begins to be fulfilled in Damascus and Jerusalem. In certain respects, Saul the persecutor replaces Stephen in bold witness to Hellenistic Jews (9:28-29). At the same time, Saul begins to experience suffering for Jesus and the gospel, as predicted at his commissioning (9:15). Thus, Luke continues to demonstrate how 'expansion and persecution ironically work together'.[38]

A. The Prophetic Ministry of Stephen (6:8-15)

In this section, there is a shift in Stephen's role for which we are not prepared by the preceding verses. 'Stephen, chosen because he was "full of Spirit and wisdom" (6:3), uses that Spirit and wisdom not just to organize charity but in speaking (6:10), and he performs wonders and signs as the apostles have been doing (2:43; 5:12; 6:8).'[39] Stephen speaks and acts with prophetic authority and ends up being arrested as the apostles were. Like them, he experiences a sequence of public witness, arrest, and interrogation before the Sanhedrin, though there is an intensification of the opposition in

---

37. Longenecker 1981, 233-34; 2007, 695-96, makes Acts 1:1–2:41 the Introduction and divides the rest of the book into six 'panels', based on the summary statements or 'progress reports' in 6:7; 9:31; 12:24; 16:5; 19:20; 28:30-31. In my INTRODUCTION TO ACTS: IV.B. Structure (pp. 32-36), I have modified this approach.

38. Spencer 1997, 63.

39. Tannehill 1990, 82. But Tannehill speaks of 'the division of labour' breaking down in the face of Stephen's demonstrated power in mission to Hellenistic Jews.

Acts 4–7, from warning (4:17, 21), to flogging (5:40), to death (7:57-59).[40] Instead of listening to the advice of Gamaliel, the Sanhedrin now vigorously opposes the new movement. The accusers are Diaspora Jews, who share Stephen's background but who maintain a conservative approach to Judaism and who succeed in turning the people of Jerusalem and the authorities against him. So Stephen is presented as being in prophetic succession to the apostles. This is not succession in terms of ordination to carry on their role, but rather 'the succession of apostolic power and authority emanating outward from Jerusalem through the power of the Spirit'.[41] At the same time, however, with the wording in 6:10 recalling Luke 21:14-15 (cf. 12:11-12), Stephen is an implied example to disciples more generally, to be faithful under trial and trust the Spirit for a convincing testimony to Jesus.[42]

8 The first indication that Stephen became involved in a wider ministry than waiting on tables comes with the claim that he *performed great wonders and signs among the people.* Luke attributes this to the fact that he was *a man full of God's grace and power* (*plērēs charitos kai dynameōs,* 'full of grace and power'; cf. vv. 3, 5).[43] There is an important link here with Luke's description of Jesus (Luke 2:40, 52), and Stephen's later reference to Joseph (Acts 7:10 note) and Moses (7:22). If the parallel syntax in vv. 3, 5 is taken as a guide, *grace* here refers to the divine favour shown in the empowerment of his ministry. *Full of God's grace and power,* as other key figures in biblical history were, Stephen *did great wonders and signs,* like Jesus (2:22), the apostles (2:43; 4:16, 33; 5:12), and Moses (7:36).[44] Stephen is presented as a prophetic figure, fulfilling a pattern of prophetic destiny which involves rejection and suffering, but ultimately vindication by God. As such, he shares something of the authority and significance of the apostles for the people of the New Covenant. Furthermore, we will see how Stephen is a forerunner of Paul in several respects (cf. 9:20-30). But it is important not to overstate this argument, since Peter's use of Joel 2:28-29 in Acts 2 indicates that the

---

40. S. Cunningham, *'Through many tribulations': The Theology of Persecution in Luke-Acts,* JSNTSS 142 (Sheffield: Sheffield Academic, 1997), 204, lists the parallels between the Stephen narrative and the experience of the apostles in Acts 3–5, but goes on to illustrate the intensification of the persecution in Acts 6–7.

41. Penner, *Christian Origins,* 270.

42. Cunningham, *Persecution,* 205-6, observes how the brief association of Saul with Stephen in 7:58; 8:1 prepares the reader for a number of points of correspondence that are developed between them. So there is also, as it were, a succession of suffering, from the apostles, to Stephen, to Saul/Paul in later narratives (cf. 9:16 note). Cf. Bock 2007, 268.

43. KJV and NKJV have 'full of faith and power', following the reading of H, P, S, most minuscules, and the Received Text. However, the more ancient and more widely attested reading is *plērēs charitos kai dynameōs* ('full of grace and power'; so NRSV, ESV, TNIV). Cf. Metzger, *Textual Commentary,* 296, who argues that the reading 'full of faith' is an assimilation to v. 5.

44. Tannehill 1990, 83. Tannehill agrees with E. Richard, *Acts 6:1–8:4: The Author's Method of Composition,* SBLDS 41 (Missoula: Scholars, 1978), 238, that 'the important relationships between Stephen and various personalities in Jewish history are clearly intentional'.

Spirit of prophecy is given to all believers. The Spirit's powerful presence is experienced in a range of gifts and ministries in Acts (cf. 1 Cor. 12:7-11). Stephen's special role and enabling by the Spirit are to be viewed within that general framework.[45] It was not, however, the working of miracles that provoked opposition, but Stephen's teaching.

9 *Opposition arose,*[46] *however, from members of the Synagogue of the Freedmen (as it was called) — Jews of Cyrene and Alexandria as well as the provinces of Cilicia and Asia.* The opponents of the gospel here are Jews from the Dispersion, who share Stephen's identity as a Hellenist. But they are radically opposed to his preaching, which they take to be a blasphemous assault on the central tenets of their religion (vv. 11, 13-14). Perhaps the intensity of their opposition was due to the fact that they themselves were constantly exposed to similar charges and wanted to affirm their orthodoxy before the Sanhedrin.[47] The structure of the Greek in v. 9 *(tōn ek tēs synagōgēs tēs legomenēs Libertinōn kai Kyrēnaiōn kai Alexandreōn kai tōn apo Kilikias kai Asias)* is complex and has caused some to propose that five synagogues were intended, one for each of the groups mentioned. Others have proposed two synagogues (understanding a second *synagogēs* after the repetition of the article *tōn*), so that there was one for *Jews of Cyrene and Alexandria* and another for those from *the provinces of Cilicia and Asia.* More probably one synagogue only is intended: 'the Synagogue of the Freedmen, comprising both Cyreneans and Alexandrians and those from Cilicia and Asia'.[48] The title *the Synagogue of the Freedmen (as it was called)* suggests that members of the congregation were characteristically Jews who had either been enslaved for one reason or another and then been emancipated, or were the sons of such persons (the Greek word *Libertinos* is a loanword from the Latin *Libertinus*, 'freedman').[49] It may seem strange to modern readers to learn that there were synagogues in Jerusalem, where the temple was clearly the focus of attention and theologically at the centre of Jewish religion (cf. 1 Kings 8; Pss. 26:8; 27:4; 43:3-4; 48:1-3; 132:6-9, 13-14). But there is evidence from archaeology and from rabbinic writings that at least one

45. Johnson 1992, 110-13, overstates the uniqueness of Stephen's prophetic role, ignoring the programmatic importance of Joel 2:28-29 in the theology of Acts. This is not to deny Stephen's significance as an insightful and bold preacher or as a transitional figure in the progress of the gospel from Jerusalem to the Dispersion.

46. Gk. *anestēsan* ('there arose') is used to signify a new development in the narrative (as in 5:17, 34), and so TNIV rightly renders this *opposition arose*. Metzger, *Textual Commentary*, 296-97, discusses variants of 6:9 in the MSS.

47. Disparaging talk about the law and the temple would mean agreeing to anti-Jewish polemics and assimilating to paganism, which was a particular temptation for Diaspora Jews. Cf. Josephus, *Against Apion* 1.145; Longenecker 1981, 336. Note the opposition to Paul in 9:29; 21:27-28 from Hellenistic Diaspora-Jews, the circle to which he also belonged.

48. Bruce 1990, 187. Cf. C. J. Hemer, *The Book of Acts in the Setting of Hellenistic History*, ed. C. Gempf, WUNT 49 (Tübingen: Mohr, 1989; repr. Winona Lake: Eisenbrauns, 1990), 176.

49. Cf. Barrett 1994, 323-24; Bruce 1990, 187. Metzger, *Textual Commentary*, 296-97, argues that there is no compelling reason to emend *Libertinōn* to 'Libyans'.

synagogue building existed in the city before its destruction in AD 70.[50] Furthermore, synagogues had a different, though related function in Judaism. There was no sacrificial ritual, but the primary object was instruction in the law of God, which meant the study of Scripture, together with the oral law, which, in Talmud and Midrash, finally was written down. An endeavour was made to educate the whole community in its faith, applying the words of God to every area of life, working out the implications of covenant obedience. This was done, not merely through Sabbath gatherings, but through the use of synagogues more generally as places for elementary education and more advanced studies.[51] Hellenistic Jews in this context *began to argue* with Stephen (*syzētountes*, 'disputing').

10   Nevertheless, *they could not stand up against the wisdom the Spirit gave him as he spoke* (*ouk ischyon antistēnai tē sophia kai tō pneumati hō elalei*, 'they could not withstand the wisdom and the Spirit with which he was speaking', ESV).[52] It was a requirement that those chosen to care for the widows in a potentially divisive situation should be 'full of the Spirit and wisdom' (*plēreis pneumatos kai sophias*, v. 3). Here we are assured that Stephen's God-given wisdom manifested itself in the way he *spoke*, particularly, as we shall see, in his interpretation of Scripture and its application to the situation of the early church. The only other references to *wisdom* in Acts are in Stephen's own description of Joseph (7:10) and Moses (7:22). These biblical figures also shared with Stephen the qualities of 'grace' and 'power' (6:8; 7:10, 22), suggesting Stephen's prophetic authority and significance. Nevertheless, when it is said that his opponents *could not stand up against the wisdom the Spirit gave him as he spoke*, Stephen is specifically portrayed as experiencing the fulfillment of Luke 21:14-15 (cf. 12:11-12). In this respect, he is not so much a special prophetic figure as an example for all who are on trial for their faith in Jesus and who trust in his promises. But

---

50. Cf. Jeremias, *Jerusalem*, 60, 66; R. Riesner, 'Synagogues in Jerusalem', in R. Bauckham (ed.), *The Book of Acts in Its First-Century Setting*, Vol. 4: *Palestinian Setting* (Grand Rapids: Eerdmans; Carlisle: Paternoster, 1995), 204-6. This is sometimes called the synagogue of the Alexandrians and sometimes the synagogue of the Tarsians or Cilicians. The Theodotus inscription, which is recorded by Riesner, 193-94, notes that there were rooms and a water supply 'as an inn for those who have need when they come from abroad'. Against those who would give this inscription a late date, Riesner, 194-200, argues that there is no reason to date it later than AD 70.

51. Cf. B. Chilton and E. Yamauchi, 'Synagogues', *DNTB* 1145-53; S. Cato, 'A Critical Analysis of the Present State of Synagogue Research and Its Implications for the Study of Luke-Acts', *TynB* 57, no. 2 (2006), 313-15. So long as temple and synagogue existed together, the latter remained a supplement to the other. However, the synagogue readings and prayers were linked with all the great festivals at the temple, and in the Dispersion provided a substitute for these services for the very large number of Jews who could rarely, if ever, travel from distant places to Jerusalem.

52. Western expansions of 6:10-11 in different forms are noted by Metzger, *Textual Commentary*, 297-98. These include the additional words 'because they were confuted by him with all boldness' at the end of v. 10 and 'being unable therefore to confront the truth' at the beginning of v. 11.

Stephen's effectiveness in debate against people from his own particular cultural and religious background sparked an outpouring of aggression and defamation that brought his life to an end.

11 The word *then (tote)* marks a significant development in the conflict. Since Stephen's opponents could not better him in theological debate, *they secretly persuaded (hypebalon;* KJV 'suborned'; NRSV 'secretly instigated')[53] *some men to say, 'We have heard Stephen speak blasphemous words against Moses and against God.'* The charge is made more specific and more clear in vv. 13-14. To speak *blasphemous words against Moses* is to speak against the law and the customs handed down from Moses. To speak *blasphemous words against God* is to speak against the temple ('this holy place'; v. 13).[54] Blasphemy here means more than a wrong use of God's name (cf. Ex. 20:7). To the Diaspora Jews, Stephen appeared to have violated the majesty of God by casting doubt on the sacredness and eternal significance of the law and the temple for his people.[55] From a sociological perspective, he was distancing himself from the particular religious community from which he came and renouncing the values which they considered most important. But Stephen's speech gives no direct evidence of such blasphemy, even though he says provocative things about the place of Jesus in God's plan (7:51-58). How far did he explore the implications of his Christology for the law and the temple? Some scholars have argued for the existence of a radical, Hellenistic Christian theology in the early church that goes back to Stephen and is later developed by Paul. However, this involves 'a significant distortion by overmagnification of what little evidence there is'.[56] Stephen's 'defence' in Acts 7 is more of a challenge to his contemporaries about their own unfaithfulness to the law and their wrong attitude to the temple. Furthermore, we have already noted certain sociological and psychological reasons for the conflict with Stephen. Finally, we must observe that the men who were *secretly persuaded* to make these charges against Stephen are later described as *false witnesses* (vv. 13-14). Comparison with the false charges against Jesus and Paul (cf. Lk. 23:2; Acts 21:28) suggests that the witnesses against Stephen distorted or deliberately misrepresented what they had heard. Their charges may have contained elements of truth, but they were polemically exaggerated.[57] Caution is needed in using these

53. Cf. Barrett 1994, 325-26, on the meaning of this verb in other sources.

54. Against Barrett 1994, 319, it is not necessary to suppose that Luke is putting together two sources, 'each of which contained its own formulation of the complaint brought formally or informally against Stephen'. Barrett, 321, develops his theory about two sources to include two accounts of the martyrdom in 7:54–8:1.

55. Cf. H. W. Beyer, *TDNT* 1:621-25.

56. Witherington 1998, 259. Barrett 1994, 320, rightly says that 'it was not Stephen's Hellenism but Stephen's Christianity that (in Luke's view) provoked opposition'.

57. Cf. G. N. Stanton, 'Stephen in Lucan Perspective', *Studia Biblica 1978 III: Papers on Paul and Other New Testament Authors*, JSNTSS 3 (Sheffield: Sheffield Academic, 1980), 347-48; Bock 2007, 271-72.

charges as a basis for determining what Stephen actually believed and taught.

12 *So they stirred up* (synekinēsan, 'aroused') *the people and the elders and the teachers of the law.* The disaffected Diaspora Jews persuaded the Jerusalem populace to oppose Stephen on the basis of the false testimony they instigated against him (v. 11). This change in public opinion doubtless had implications for their relationship with Christians more generally. From previous references it would appear that *the elders and the teachers of the law* needed little encouragement to oppose Stephen and the Christian movement (cf. 4:5, 8, 23). *They seized Stephen and brought him before the Sanhedrin* for examination.[58] The parallel with the experience of the apostles in Acts 4–5 is obvious, although mention of *the people* among Stephen's opponents signifies a dramatic change. The people favoured the apostles in 4:21 and 5:26, making it difficult for the high priests to punish them. But Stephen's enemies were able to change public opinion to the extent that he was left unprotected, making the parallel with Jesus' experience more obvious (compare Lk. 21:38; 22:2 with 23:13-25). Note also the parallel between Stephen's manner of dying and Jesus' (Lk. 23:34, 46; Acts 7:59-60).[59]

13-14 Since Stephen was now in a more formal court context, *they produced* (estēsan, 'set up') *false witnesses* (martyras pseudeis), *who testified, 'This fellow never stops speaking against this holy place and against the law.'*[60] Bearing false witness is prohibited in Scripture (Ex. 20:16; Dt. 19:16-18), and so their testimony is portrayed as unreliable and offensive to God. The charge is really the same as that in v. 11, using parallel terminology, and clarified with the explanation that follows: *'for we have heard him say that this Jesus of Nazareth will destroy this place and change the customs Moses handed down to us'.* Both written and oral traditions are probably intended by *the customs Moses handed down to us.* The claim that *this Jesus of Nazareth will destroy this place* is reminiscent of Jesus' own predictions about Jerusalem and the temple being destroyed as an act of divine judgment (cf. Lk. 21:5-6, 24; Mt. 24:1-2; Mk. 13:1-2). Jesus' words were then distorted by false witnesses at his trial to signify that he himself would destroy the temple (cf. Mt. 26:61; 27:40; Mk. 14:57-58). But the provocative saying in John 2:19 goes further

58. On the composition and operation of this council, see Bruce 1990, 153-54; E. Lohse, *TDNT* 7:861-71; G. H. Twelftree, 'Sanhedrin', *DNTB* 1061-65. Witherington 1998, 191-92, responds to recent scholarly challenges about the existence of the Sanhedrin as a legislative and judicial body in the apostolic period.

59. Witherington 1998, 253, lists the parallels between the passion of Jesus and of Stephen and comments on the significance of Luke's editing in this respect. Johnson 1992, 112, argues that Luke's intention is 'to insure the reader's perception of Stephen as an authentic witness in continuity with the prophet Jesus'.

60. KJV and NKJV read 'blasphemous words', following some ancient MSS and the Received Text. However, the better-attested reading is simply rhēmata ('words'), with blasphēma being most likely an addition assimilated from v. 11. The word toutou ('this') occurs only after tou topou tou hagiou ('holy place') in some MSS and may have 'crept into the text from the next verse' (Metzger, *Textual Commentary*, 298). Cf. Barrett 1994, 327.

('Destroy this temple, and I will raise it again in three days'). At surface level, this appears to suggest that, if the authorities destroy the Jerusalem temple, he will build a new one. However, as the following context indicates (2:21-22), Jesus was referring to his death at the hands of the authorities and his resurrection as the new temple of prophetic expectation.[61] Stephen may have understood this line of thought and may have been developing it, showing how the exalted Christ replaces the temple in God's plan for Israel and the nations (cf. Is. 2:1-4; 56:6-7; Ezekiel 40–48). Stephen may also have been drawing out the implications of Jesus' coming for the law of Moses, which was so integral to the covenant relationship between God and Israel. Although Jesus clearly affirmed that he had not come to abolish the Law or the Prophets but to fulfill them (Mt. 5:17), his teaching and practice called for radical reflection on the meaning and application of the law (e.g., Mt. 5:21-48; 12:1-14; 15:16-20; Mk. 2:23–3:5; 7:14-23; Lk. 6:1-5; 13:10-17; 14:1-6; Jn. 5:1-47).[62] In due course, it would become clear that the inauguration of the New Covenant by Jesus (cf. Lk. 22:14-20) would involve a total reassessment of the role of the law in the life of God's people (e.g., Acts 10:1–11:18; 15:1-29; Rom. 7:1–8:17; Hebrews 7–10). Stephen may have been an early pioneer in this task. However, if this is so, it is paradoxically only out of the mouths of his accusers that we have 'a tribute to his farsighted comprehension of what the gospel involved'.[63]

15 *All who were sitting in the Sanhedrin looked intently* (atenisantes; cf. 1:10; 3:4, 12; 7:55; 10:4; 11:6; 13:9; 14:9; 23:1) *at Stephen, and they saw that his face was like the face of an angel.*[64] In view of the implied comparison with Moses in vv. 8 and 10 (full of grace, wisdom, and power), it is possible that there is a link here with Moses' shining face in Exodus 34:29-35. Stephen spoke calmly as one who saw the glory of Christ (cf. 7:55), who was filled with his Spirit, and who appeared to be his authorised witness and messenger. Other biblical references suggest that an encounter with a genuine representative of God can be interpreted as seeing the face of God (Gn. 33:10), or meeting his angel (1 Sa. 29:9; 2 Sa. 14:17). This description of Stephen paves the way for his speech, implying that it is an inspired utterance, which is to be received as an expression of the mind of God.[65]

61. Cf. D. G. Peterson, *Engaging with God: A Biblical Theology of Worship* (Leicester: Apollos; Grand Rapids: Eerdmans, 1992), 80-102; R. J. McKelvey, *The New Temple: The Church in the New Testament* (London/New York: Oxford University, 1969), especially 75-84.

62. Cf. Peterson, *Engaging*, 113-16; C. L. Blomberg, 'The Christian and the Law of Moses', in I. H. Marshall and D. Peterson (eds.), *Witness to the Gospel: The Theology of Acts* (Grand Rapids/Cambridge: Eerdmans, 1998), 397-416; Bock 2007, 273-74.

63. Bruce 1990, 189. Cf. Longenecker 1981, 335-36; Marshall 1980, 130-31; McKelvey, *New Temple*, 86-87.

64. Some Western MSS add the words 'standing in their midst' after 'like the face of an angel', but this is a poorly attested reading. Cf. Metzger, *Textual Commentary*, 298-99.

65. Barrett 1994, 330. Cf. Est. 15:13 LXX, where the king's face is said to be like that of an angel (cf. Dn. 3:92 LXX), and the second-century-AD *Acts of Paul and Thecla* 3, where Paul is described as at times appearing like a man and at times having 'the face of an angel'.

In this narrative and the chapter that follows, Stephen is 'both contrasted with his opponents and compared to Moses'.[66] He is viewed as praiseworthy because of his association with Moses, and the implication is that he could not have violated the laws and customs of Moses (6:11, 13-14) because of his Spirit-filled character and empowerment. Moreover, the witnesses against him are false. His Christ-likeness in the face of their charges and unjust treatment further highlights his divine authorisation. Stephen is thus portrayed as a reliable witness, in contrast with those who stand against him. At the same time, he functions as a model of faithful witness and godly response for readers who may be in the midst of opposition and suffering.

B. Stephen's 'Defence' (7:1-56)

Stephen's speech, which is the longest in Acts, is not a defence in the sense of a straightforward explanation or reasoned argument designed to win an acquittal. Only incidentally does it engage with the charges against him (6:11, 13-14). The main intention of this prophetic-type utterance is to 'turn the tables' on his opponents by presenting an extensive indictment against them. Stephen develops a scriptural argument which charges Israel with consistently rejecting God and those sent to fulfill his purpose for his people (7:9-10, 23-29, 33-43). A terrible pattern of resisting God's prophets and disobeying his law (7:44-50) has culminated in the betrayal and murder of the Righteous One (7:51-53). In the stunning revelation that climaxes the speech, Jesus as 'the Son of Man' is 'standing at the right hand of God' (7:55-56), ready to vindicate his faithful messenger and to judge those who deny him. Stephen's ultimate aim is to glorify the exalted Lord Jesus and to convict those who have denied him. He offers them no hope of salvation at this point, though he prays for their forgiveness as he dies (7:60).

From a narrative perspective, this address brings to a climax the story of the conflict between the Christian mission and the temple authorities, a conflict that first appeared in 4:1-3.[1] Furthermore, it 'places the new people of God in its true salvation-historical context' and paves the way

---

Barrett rightly points out that surprisingly 'no reaction on the part of the beholders is described'.

66. Penner, *Christian Origins*, 289. Penner 291, gives a table contrasting the characteristics of Stephen and his opponents.

1. H.-W. Neudorfer, 'The Speech of Stephen', in I. H. Marshall and D. G. Peterson, *Witness to the Gospel: The Theology of Acts* (Grand Rapids/Cambridge: Eerdmans, 1998), 280-81, also notes how Luke programmatically places Stephen's speech at the beginning of the next section in which the mission to Gentiles begins. Stephen's ministry is certainly part of the process that moves Jewish Christians out into the Gentile world with the gospel, but a challenge to 'Jewish salvific exclusivity' is only implicit in the speech. Cf. Penner, *Christian Origins*, 276-303.

for Paul's theology and mission.[2] Gaventa observes how the speech addresses both Diaspora Jews (Stephen's accusers) and the Jerusalem leaders (those responsible for the death of Jesus) as the narrative audience. It also addresses the authorial audience (those who are hearing or reading Luke's account). Gaventa holds that the effect on the latter is to teach 'Israel's story to a group that may have known very little about this history, and especially connecting Moses to Jesus, Stephen, and soon to Paul'.[3] However, the authorial audience must also have needed to be informed about how to answer Jewish charges against Christianity such as Stephen received (6:11, 13-14).

What kind of address is it? Some have argued that Stephen's speech is an example of judicial or forensic rhetoric.[4] There is much common ground established with the audience in the *narration* at the beginning of the speech (vv. 2-34) to prepare for the *argument* (vv. 35-50) and the emotional *appeal* or peroration at the end (vv. 51-53). Stephen thus demonstrates that 'he shares a common history with his auditors, and that they both are part of a tragic history of partial acceptance and partial rejection of God's message and the messengers sent to God's people'.[5] 'The mystery of why the early part of the speech is neutral or positive and the latter part is more polemical is solved when the speech is broken down into its normal rhetorical parts.'[6] Parallels with passages from the OT and later Jewish literature have also been drawn, where reviews of biblical history are used to critique and challenge present behaviour.[7] In particular, it should be noted that Stephen addresses in turn 'the three great pillars of popular Jewish piety', the land (vv. 2-36), the law (vv. 37-43), and the temple (vv. 44-50). Nevertheless, the content of Stephen's speech 'runs counter to much of the popular piety of the day'.[8]

---

2. D. P. Seccombe, 'The New People of God', in Marshall and Peterson, *Witness to the Gospel*, 356. Cf. Neudorfer, 'Speech', 294.

3. Gaventa 2003, 120-21.

4. Cf. Witherington 1998, 260-61, following G. A. Kennedy, *New Testament Interpretation through Rhetorical Criticism* (Chapel Hill: University of North Carolina, 1984), 121-22; M. Soards, *The Speeches in Acts: Their Content, Context and Concerns* (Louisville: John Knox/ Westminster, 1994), 57-70; J. Dupont, 'La Structure Oratoire du Discours d'Étienne (Actes 7)', *Biblica* 66 (1985), 153-67.

5. Witherington 1998, 260. He argues that Luke could have structured and edited the material to fit a rhetorical outline (261), though he does not rule out that Stephen was 'rhetorically adept'.

6. Witherington 1998, 261.

7. E.g., Jos. 24:1-18; Neh. 9:6-31; Psalms 78, 106; Ezekiel 20; Jgs. 5:5-21; *1 Enoch* 84–90; Josephus, *War* 5.376-419. Ezekiel 20 is closest to Acts 7 in representing the generation addressed by the prophet as repeating and exceeding the sins of their ancestors, but even Ezekiel 20 gives more hope of renewal for Israel than Stephen does. Cf. Barrett 1994, 336; Neudorfer, 'Speech', 281-83.

8. Longenecker 1981, 337-39. The closest parallel to Stephen's speech in the NT is Paul's sermon in Acts 13:16b-41. Penner, *Christian Origins*, 303-27, argues that Stephen's speech is 'epideictic', praising Christian origins by way of comparison with Israel's past and Stephen's opponents.

Observations about the rhetorical character and structure of Acts 7 are helpful as far as they go. But a detailed analysis of the argument, with its highly selective use of Scripture, repetition of key words, and progressive development of important themes, suggests the following literary and theological structure. *The foundational promises to Abraham* are first highlighted (7:2-8), with special attention to the land (vv. 2-4), offspring (vv. 5-7a), worship (v. 7b), and the covenant of circumcision (v. 8). All of these are 'basic elements in Jewish self-understanding'.[9] The rest of the speech concerns the fulfillment of these promises and Israel's failure to respond appropriately. There is a particular link between the first and the fourth section, which emphasizes the tragic reversal of Israel's situation (7:39-53). Many of the same terms are used again here, by way of contrast and challenge.[10] So, for example, Stephen highlights Israel's history of false worship, to which the prophets responded by predicting that they would be exiled from the promised land (7:39-43). Despite the covenant of circumcision, they showed themselves to be a 'stiff-necked people', with hearts and ears that are 'still uncircumcised' (7:51). Here the Christological implications of Stephen's argument are made clear, as the rejection of Jesus is shown to be *part of a continuing pattern of disobedience to God* (7:51-53).

The intervening sections of the speech focus on Joseph and Moses, showing the particular function of each leader in the fulfillment of God's promises. In the second main division, *Joseph is blessed with grace and wisdom for the salvation of God's people* (7:9-16). The terminology of grace and wisdom has already been used to describe Stephen (6:8, 10), suggesting that a certain parallel with Joseph is being drawn (7:10, 'grace and wisdom before Pharaoh'). However, the Joseph story also displays a pattern that will be developed more fully in the description of Moses, presenting both Joseph and Moses as types of Christ. In the third main division, *Moses is blessed with wisdom and power in words and deeds for the salvation of God's people* (7:17-38). Here the comparison is more obviously with Jesus, who is the one ultimately appointed to be ruler, judge, and saviour of Israel. In particular, Jesus is the prophet like Moses, predicted in Deuteronomy 18:15 (cf. Acts 3:22-23; 7:37). So even as Stephen continues to tell the story of Israel, he is preparing for his denunciation at the end of the fourth section (7:39-53) and his climactic proclamation of *Jesus as the glorified Son of Man* in the fifth section (7:54-56).

1 *Then the high priest asked Stephen, 'Are these charges true?'* As president of the Sanhedrin *ex officio*, the high priest (who was Caiaphas until AD 36) asked Stephen to respond to the accusations against him (cf. 6:13-14). Doubt has been expressed about whether this was a formal trial, since the high priest should not have asked a question that invited the accused to convict himself.[11] Some commentators are also unwilling to attribute the

9. Tannehill 1990, 88.
10. Cf. Tannehill 1990, 89-91; Penner, *Christian Origins*, 307-8.
11. So Barrett 1994, 340. Barrett, 380-81, later argues that Luke has joined together a

speech to Stephen in any way.[12] They rule out the possibility that Luke had even indirect access to the proceedings of the Sanhedrin and insist that much of the speech is irrelevant to the charges of being against the law and against the temple.[13] However, since Saul is identified as a witness to the stoning of Stephen (7:58), he could well have been present at the trial, later becoming a reliable source for Luke.[14] The strangeness of this speech, and yet its appropriateness to its context, is an argument for its authenticity. It has an unusual style and method of argumentation that shows little similarity to the other speeches that Luke records.[15]

1. The Foundational Promises to Abraham (7:2-8)

In this first part of his defence, Stephen begins to lay important theological foundations for the argument to come: divine revelation and calling, covenant promises and pilgrimage, redemption and worship. These are matters with which his accusers should have been in agreement. However, 'Stephen's appeal to the great heroes of Israel's past — Abraham, Joseph, and especially Moses — seems to function more precisely as a means of aligning his case with superior judges and witnesses than those represented by the current Jerusalem council'.[16] These cameos present a progressive challenge to his audience about their own unfaithfulness to God, ultimately expressed in crucifying their Messiah (7:51-53).

2-3 Stephen first focuses on God's encounter with Abraham in Genesis 11:31–12:5). Addressing his judges as *'brothers and fathers'*, he assumes

---

'lynching' source (6:9-11; 7:54-8a) with a 'trial' source (6:12-14; 7:58b-60), which seems to be an unnecessarily speculative way of explaining different elements in the narrative.

12. Johnson 1992, 119-21, for example, argues that the discourse represents 'the special vision of Luke himself', and that it is used to legitimate Christians as 'the authentic realization of the people of God'. However, he does not explain why the speech seems to be so out of character with the more optimistic approach to Israel presented by Luke elsewhere in Acts. This speech is very different in style from the rest of Acts, suggesting a written source that was used by Luke.

13. Cf. Haenchen 1971, 286-90; Barrett 1994, 334-40. Barrett concludes that the speech 'can hardly have been spoken by Stephen in the circumstances described' but that it 'recovers great historical value as a document of that sector of Judaism from which Stephen and his colleagues are said to have come' (339). Barrett assumes that the direct question in 7:1 is inviting the accused to convict himself and proposes that Luke is 'rewriting the story of a lynching'.

14. Barrett 1994, 338.

15. Neudorfer, 'Speech', 294, argues that Stephen's speech reveals Luke as a writer who uses speeches in a literary manner, similar to Thucydides, the Greek historian: 'in doing so he uses reliable information and traditions and displays great skill in incorporating this speech also into the context of his work'. But see note 12 above.

16. Spencer 1997, 77. Stephen seeks to answer the charges against him, but more profoundly he points his opponents to the true character and calling of Jesus, and exposes their culpability before God.

that they share a common faith and spiritual heritage. This relationship is further emphasized by describing Abraham as *'our father'*.[17] Stephen recalls that *'the God of glory appeared to our father Abraham while he was still in Mesopotamia, before he lived in Harran'*. The God of glory (cf. Ps. 29:3; Eph. 1:17) revealed himself to Abraham in a pagan land. Since the concept of God's glory was particularly linked with the tabernacle and temple in OT theology (e.g., Ex. 29:43; 40:34-35; 1 Ki. 8:10-11; Ezk. 43:1-5),[18] Stephen was beginning to challenge a narrow interpretation of that tradition. God's self-revelation was not confined either to the promised land or to the temple. Stephen's speech is framed by references to God's glory, with his vision of the ascended Christ and *the glory of God* (7:55-56), placing him in the line of those, like Abraham and Moses (7:30-34), who received such definitive revelations. Slightly adapting Genesis 12:1, Stephen reminds them that God's call to leave the familiar and secure, to become the pilgrim people of God (*'Leave your country and your people'*), was matched by the promise of an inheritance (*'"and go to the land I will show you"'*). The focus in Acts 7:2-8 is very much on the gracious activity of God (he *appeared* [v. 2], *spoke* [v. 3], *said* [v. 4], *promised* [v. 5], *spoke* [v. 6], and *gave the covenant of circumcision* [v. 8]). Abraham's faith is not mentioned, though it was certainly the reason for his obedience (cf. Romans 4; Heb. 11:8-20). Christians are similarly called to a pilgrim lifestyle, with the promise of a heavenly inheritance as their God-given motivation for persistence and faithfulness (cf. Heb. 3:1–4:11; 1 Pet. 1:3-9).

According to Stephen, the call and promise of God were given to Abraham *while he was still in Mesopotamia, before he lived in Harran*. This is consistent with the testimony of Genesis 15:7, that God brought Abraham out of 'Ur of the Chaldeans' to give him possession of the land of Canaan (cf. Jos. 24:2-3; Neh. 9:7).[19] Stephen's reading of Genesis 11:31–12:3 is that God had already appeared to Abraham and had initiated the process of redemption there, before his father Terah led the expedition to *Harran*. Further discussion of this issue can be found in the Additional Note at the end of this chapter, entitled THE USE OF SCRIPTURE IN STEPHEN'S SPEECH (pp. 270-75).

4-5 *'So he left the land of the Chaldeans and settled in Harran.'* Abra-

17. Cf. 'our fathers' (7:11 [TNIV *people*]; 7:12, 19, 38, 39, 44, 45 [TNIV *ancestors*]), which becomes 'your fathers' (TNIV *your ancestors*) only in the indictment of 7:51-52. 'The debate, therefore, is within the family as to what constitutes authentic family membership' (Johnson 1992, 121).

18. Cf. C. J. Collins, *NIDOTTE* 2:581-87. The idea of God appearing to key figures occurs again in vv. 30, 35, and 44, climaxing with his appearance to Stephen in vv. 55-56.

19. Cf. Philo, *On the Migration of Abraham* 62–67, 71; Josephus, *Ant.* 1.154. Harran is in modern Turkey, about 12 miles north of the Syrian frontier. Ancient Mesopotamia did not normally include Ur, which is located by most scholars today in southern Iraq. But Mesopotamia in Stephen's speech (7:3) cannot be distinguished from 'the land of the Chaldeans' (7:4). In Hellenistic usage, Mesopotamia included Babylonia in the south. Cf. Marshall 1980, 135; Bruce 1990, 192; G. J. Wenham, *Genesis 1–15*, Word Biblical Commentary 1 (Waco: Word, 1987), 272.

ham's obedience to God is implied, despite the unexplained pause in *Harran*. God's initiative in the next stage of the journey is then stressed: '*After the death of his father, God sent him to* (*metōkisen auton eis*, 'settled him in', 'transferred him into') *this land where you are now living*.'[20] Stephen makes a direct connection between God's promise and the situation of his audience. He 'hooks the council's attention by shifting from the third person narration about the past to second person direct address in the present: "this land in which *you now* (*hymeis nyn*) are living"'.[21] They are the inheritors of the promise, whereas God gave Abraham '*no inheritance here, not even enough ground to set his foot on*'. Words from Deuteronomy 2:5 (*bēma podos*, 'a foot's length') are drawn in to stress that, at every stage of the experience of God's people, they only inherited precisely what God gave them (cf. Additional Note). Nevertheless, throughout these chapters, the divine promise is reiterated and confirmed, '*that he and his descendants after him would possess the land, even though at that time Abraham had no child*' (Gn. 12:7; 13:14-17; 15:1-21; 17:1-19; cf. 48:4; Rom. 4:16-22). Offspring and land are linked together in the covenant which God made with Abraham. Offspring or *descendants* (*sperma*, 'seed') is the key concept in vv. 5-6.

6-7 The pilgrim character of the people of God is stressed again in the first part of a quotation from Genesis 15:13-14. '*God spoke to him in this way: "For four hundred years your descendants will be strangers in a country not their own"*' (more literally, the Greek follows Ex. 2:22 and should be translated 'in a country belonging to others'). The prediction about being *strangers in a country not their own* could apply to the period when they were wandering around Canaan as much as to the period when they were in Egypt. The first part of the quotation stresses the suffering they would have to endure ('*"and they will be enslaved and mistreated"*'). Enslavement in Egypt is a theme that Stephen develops in connection with the call of Moses (7:18-34). Here he takes the round figure of *four hundred years* as the time span of that bondage (as in Gn. 15:13), though Exodus 12:40 records the more precise figure of 430 years. The third part of the quotation highlights God's intention to '*"punish the nation they serve as slaves"*', and then predicts the exodus and its outcome ('*"and afterwards they will come out of that country and worship me in this place"*'). The verb *come out* (*exerchomai*) is matched by others in the speech (*apostellō* ['send'] in vv. 12, 14, 34, 35; *exagō* ['lead out'] in vv. 36, 40; as well as the noun *eleusis* ['coming'] in v. 52), implying movement away from a given point. It is possible that these words were chosen in or-

---

20. The claim that it was *after the death of his father* that God sent Abraham into the promised land is a natural reading of the sequence of events in Gn. 11:31–12:5, but it raises problems about chronology when calculations are made about the age of Terah and Abraham at the time of Abraham's departure from Harran. Cf. ADDITIONAL NOTE: THE USE OF SCRIPTURE IN STEPHEN'S SPEECH (pp. 270-75).

21. Spencer 1997, 71. Spencer understands the council to be 'firmly entrenched in "this land" where it seeks to delimit and protect God's interests'. However, as Stephen sees it, 'God's interests range farther and wider'.

der to communicate to Stephen's Jewish audience that they should become more flexible, 'ready to leave some of the traditional positions inherited from their forefathers'.[22]

Stephen's modification of Genesis 15:14 with words from Exodus 3:12 highlights the fact that the purpose of the exodus was to liberate God's people to *worship* God (*latreuein*; cf. Acts 7:42; 24:14; 26:7; 27:23). Employment of a fragment from one text to interpret another was common Jewish practice, enabling Stephen to make a link between two related passages in the Pentateuch (cf. 7:5). He uses this technique to make a theological point, based on his understanding of the unfolding plan of God for Israel. At the same time, he begins to answer the charge that he speaks against 'the holy place' in Jerusalem (*tou topou tou hagiou [toutou]*, 6:13; *en tō topō toutō*, 7:7, *in this place*). Stephen means that the worship of God in the land of Israel and, more particularly, in the temple at Jerusalem can be viewed as the divinely appointed outcome of the exodus redemption. Although Exodus 3:12 actually refers to worship 'on this mountain' (Horeb), Exodus 15:13-17 shows how the idea of meeting God on his holy mountain soon merged into that of engaging with God in the promised land and at Jerusalem on the temple mount.[23]

8 *'Then he gave Abraham the covenant of circumcision.'* Stephen identifies the promises made by God to Abraham as expressions of a *covenant*, with *circumcision* the outward sign of that covenant. The covenantal dimension to the relationship between God and Abraham is first made clear in Genesis 15:17-19, where a dramatic ritual confirms the relationship already established in 12:1-3.[24] *Circumcision* for subsequent generations of males then became a claim to 'inclusion within the Abrahamic relationship' (cf. Gn. 17:9-14).[25] The rest of the verse outlines how the covenant promises of God began to be fulfilled with respect to Abraham's offspring. *'And Abraham became the father of Isaac and circumcised him eight days after his birth'* (cf. Gn. 21:1-5). *'Later Isaac became the father of Jacob'* (cf. Gn. 25:21-26), *'and Jacob became the father of the twelve patriarchs'* (cf. Gn. 29:31–30:24; 35:16-18). So the first section of Stephen's speech concludes by affirming the establishment of Israel and its worship on the basis of divine revelation and divine providence. 'Long before there was a holy place, there was a holy people, to whom God had pledged himself.'[26]

22. Neudorfer, 'Speech', 279. Penner, *Christian Origins*, 307, notes that 'the scheme of slavery-deliverance-worship is fulfilled respectively in 7:9-29; 7:30-43; and 7:44-46'.

23. Stephen gives his hearers 'a paraphrase of what God said to Abraham, using scriptural language based on Exodus 3:12' (Marshall 1980, 136). He thus compresses redemptive history in a way that would have been understood and appreciated by his audience. Cf. D. G. Peterson, *Engaging with God: A Biblical Theology of Worship* (Leicester: Apollos; Grand Rapids: Eerdmans, 1992), 24-26.

24. Cf. W. J. Dumbrell, *Covenant and Creation: An Old Testament Covenantal Theology* (Exeter: Paternoster, 1984), 54-55.

25. Dumbrell, *Covenant*, 74. 'A refusal to accept it is the equivalent of covenant rejection and thus merits excommunication (v. 14).'

26. Stott 1990, 132.

2. Joseph Blessed with Grace and Wisdom
for the Salvation of God's People (7:9-16)

Stephen continues his brief survey of the patriarchal period with a focus on the narratives about Joseph. Jewish literature showed much interest in the experiences of this character,[27] but Stephen concentrates on only a few aspects of the biblical record. Joseph's rejection by his brothers is presented as the context for his rescue and transfer to power in Egypt. God's vindication of Joseph is then shown to be the divine means of rescuing and preserving Israel. Although Stephen may have viewed this biblical story as something of a parallel to his own situation, he uses it more obviously to prepare for the portrayal of Moses in the next section. As leaders rejected by the sons of Israel, Joseph and Moses were nevertheless used by God for the salvation of his people (7:11-16, 27-28, 35). This in turn prepares for the major challenge of Stephen's speech concerning the rejection of Jesus by his contemporaries (7:39-53).

9-10 In view of the charge that is coming about the spiritual condition of his audience (7:51-53), it seems pointed that Stephen should identify the betrayers of Joseph as *'the patriarchs'*, whereas Genesis simply calls them 'his brothers'. Because these forefathers of the nation were *'jealous of Joseph, they sold him as a slave into Egypt'* (cf. Gn. 37:12-36). Jealousy has already been identified as a factor in the opposition of Jewish leaders to Christian preachers (5:17; cf. 13:45; 17:5), and Stephen is pointing to the destructive effect of jealousy in the early life of God's people. Nevertheless, echoing the perspective of Genesis 39:21, Stephen proclaims that *'God was with him and rescued him from all his troubles'*. The God who had revealed himself to Abraham in Mesopotamia now revealed himself to Joseph in *Egypt*,[28] suggesting that 'in making himself known to his people he shows no preference for one place or another'.[29] Cutting short the extensive narrative in Genesis 39–41, Stephen notes that God gave Joseph *'wisdom'* (demonstrated at this stage of the story in his dealings with Potiphar's wife and in his interpretation of dreams) *'and enabled him to gain the goodwill of Pharaoh king of Egypt'* (leaving out the account of how Joseph first gained favour with the chief jailer). 'At this point Stephen's biblical report shades over into personal defense. He, too, is an outsider full of divine *charis* ("grace", 6:8) and *sophia* ("wisdom", 6:10) in a hostile environment.'[30] How-

27. Cf. Johnson 1992, 117-19.
28. Stephen repeats the word *Egypt* six times in seven verses, 'as if to make sure that his hearers have grasped its significance' (Stott 1990, 133).
29. Bruce 1990, 195. The idea that the Lord was with Joseph in his distress is highlighted in Gn. 39:2, 21, 23. Presence theology came to be associated with the tabernacle and the temple. So once again Stephen offers an implied challenge to any narrowness of thinking about God's presence at the temple. Note also what is said about God being with Jesus in Acts 10:38.
30. Spencer 1997, 72. TNIV does not adequately represent the Greek of 7:10 *(charin kai*

ever, the Christological implications of the Joseph narrative are more obviously drawn when Stephen recalls how God made Joseph *'ruler over Egypt and all his palace'* (cf. Gn. 41:40-52; 45:8; Ps. 105:21-22).

11 *'Then a famine struck all Egypt and Canaan, bringing great suffering, and our people (*pateres,* "fathers") could not find food.'* Stephen summarizes the narrative in the rest of Genesis, beginning with a reference to the predicted famine and its effect (cf. Gn. 41:53-57; 42:5). But God had prepared for the survival of his people (and thus the fulfillment of his covenant) by elevating Joseph to power in Pharaoh's service. He had directed his persecuted representative through Pharaoh's dream to store up grain for the years of famine (Gn. 41:17-49). The Greek has a significant play on words: God rescued Joseph *'from all his troubles'* (7:10, *ek pasōn tōn thlipseōn*), so that he might rescue the chosen people from *'the great suffering'* (7:11, *thlipsis megalē*) that came upon them. A typological link with the Lord Jesus Christ may also be implied here. Joseph was rejected by his own people but empowered by God to save those who rejected him. Jesus was raised from suffering and death to bring eternal salvation even to those who rejected him (cf. 4:10-12).

12-16 *'When Jacob heard that there was grain in Egypt, he sent our ancestors (*pateras,* "fathers") on their first visit.'* Once again Stephen identifies with his opponents, speaking of the patriarchs as *our ancestors* and implying that their visit to Egypt for help was a defining moment for the descendants of Israel in every generation. Stephen draws attention to the fact that there was a *first visit* (Gn. 42:8) and that it was only *'on their second visit'* that *'Joseph told his brothers who he was, and Pharaoh learned about Joseph's family'* (Gn. 45:1-3). A typological motif could also be suggested here. Stephen's subsequent argument suggests that 'the theme of "ignorance" in the time of the first visitation applies equally to Joseph, Moses and Jesus'.[31] Recognition of God's appointed saviour leads to deliverance and life. Refusal to acknowledge Jesus in his 'second visitation' through the ministry of figures like Peter and Stephen can only lead to judgment and death.

*'After this, Joseph sent for his father Jacob and his whole family, seventy-five in all. Then Jacob went down to Egypt, where he and our ancestors (*pateres,* "fathers") died.'* It was in a foreign land that God met them in the person of his chosen representative Joseph, and it was there that he sustained and blessed the first generation of the sons of Israel and their families, now grown to be *'seventy-five in all'*.[32] Thus, the purpose of God for his people

---

sophian enantion Pharaō), which literally means that God gave Joseph 'grace and wisdom before Pharaoh'. Ironically, of course, Stephen faces opposition from the leaders of his own people in the promised land.

31. Johnson 1992, 118. Gaventa 2003, 123-24, argues against a typological reading of these first and second visits, but is happy to see parallels between the situations of Joseph and Stephen.

32. The Hebrew text of Gn. 46:27; Ex. 1:5, and Dt. 10:22 says 'seventy in all'. Acts 7:14 follows the LXX in giving the number 'seventy-five'. 'The larger total is arrived at by omit-

continued outside the borders of the promised land, even though the bodies of the patriarchs were *'brought back to Shechem and placed in the tomb that Abraham had bought from the sons of Hamor at Shechem for a certain sum of money'*. Luke appears to have telescoped into one various biblical traditions about the burial sites of the patriarchs (cf. Gn. 23:10-19; 33:18-20; 49:29-32; 50:13; Jos. 24:32).[33] The burial in Canaan expressed faith in God's promise that this whole land would eventually belong to the family of Jacob, though by Stephen's time Shechem was in Samaritan territory! This reinforces Stephen's polemic 'against those who attempt to restrict God's activity to selected sacred zones', and presents a challenge to stay on the move with God — 'to journey with him beyond standard social and cultural boundaries to bless all the families of the earth'.[34]

3. Moses Blessed with Wisdom and Power, in Words and Deeds, for the Salvation of God's People (7:17-38)

The career of Moses is presented in terms of three forty-year phases (7:23, 30, 36), with the first section of the narrative giving the theological and historical context for Moses' life and ministry (7:17-22). 'Rhetorically, this drawn out, clearly ordered Moses-section functions as the centerpiece of Stephen's discourse, inviting careful deliberation on the part of his hearers.'[35] It enables Stephen to declare his positive views about Moses and the 'living words' he received from God to pass on to his people (7:38). This begins to answer the charge that he has spoken blasphemous words against Moses and the law (6:11, 13-14). At the same time, this section again portrays the rejection of God's appointed leaders by his people, but their vindication by God and use by him to further his purposes (7:9-10, 27-28, 35). Such a presentation prepares for the major challenge of Stephen's speech concerning Israel's rejection of Jesus (7:39-53).

17-19 *'As the time drew near for God to fulfill his promise to Abraham, the number of our people in Egypt had greatly increased'* (*ēuxēsen ho laos kai eplēthynthē*, 'the people grew and multiplied'; cf. 6:7 note). The next section of Stephen's narrative begins in an impressive way, picking up the sense of Exodus 1:1-7. There was a specific *time (chronos)* appointed by God for the fulfillment of his promise to Abraham (though the words *to fulfill* are not

---

ting Jacob and Joseph and including the remaining seven of Joseph's nine sons' (Marshall 1980, 138).

33. Cf. ADDITIONAL NOTE: USE OF SCRIPTURE (pp. 270-75); Marshall 1980, 138-39; Johnson 1992, 118-19. In Gn. 33:19 and Jos. 24:32, Shechem is a person, and this is reflected in a variant reading of Acts 7:16 which makes Shechem the father, instead of the son, of Hamor. However, TNIV reads the more likely *en Sychem (at Shechem)*, following the normal OT understanding of Shechem as a place. Cf. Metzger, *Textual Commentary*, 301-2.

34. Spencer 1997, 73-74.

35. Spencer 1997, 74.

actually in the Greek).[36] With the multiplication of descendants came also the predicted captivity of the people of Abraham (cf. 7:5-6). Exodus 1:8-22 is summarized, with mention of *'a new king, to whom Joseph meant nothing'* (*hos ouk ēdei ton Iōsēph*, 'who did not know Joseph', most EVV). 'The meaning is either that he was ignorant of Joseph and his good deeds for Egypt or (perhaps more likely) that he preferred to forget about him in the face of the menace which he saw in the growing might of the Israelites.'[37] This king *'"came to power in Egypt"'* (*anestē basileus heteros [ep' Aigypton]*, 'there arose a different king over Egypt') and *'dealt treacherously with our people'* (*to genos hēmōn*, 'our race') *'and oppressed our ancestors'* (*tous pateras [hēmōn]*, 'our fathers') *'by forcing them to throw out their newborn babies so that they would die'*.

20-22 At that critical point in *'time'* (*en tō kairō*),[38] *'Moses was born'*. And Moses was *'no ordinary child'* (*asteios tō theō*; ESV 'beautiful in God's sight'; NKJV 'well pleasing to God'; NRSV 'beautiful before God'; cf. Ex. 2:2 LXX; Heb. 11:23). There is a special concern for dating in this part of Stephen's speech (vv. 20, 23, 26, 30, 36, 41, 45), giving a sense of the passage of time and of God's care and control in the whole process. The role of Moses' own family is mentioned first (*'for three months he was cared for in his parents' home'* [*en tō oikō tou patros*, 'in his father's house']), before the part played by *'Pharaoh's daughter'* is highlighted. *'When he was placed outside'* refers to the placing of Moses in a papyrus basket, along the bank of the Nile (Ex. 2:3-4).[39] We are then told how *'Pharaoh's daughter took him and brought him up as her own son'* (cf. Ex. 2:5-10). Most importantly, from the perspective of Stephen's entire portrait of Moses, we are told that *'Moses was educated in all the wisdom of the Egyptians and was powerful in speech and action'*.[40] Once again the gift of *wisdom* is noted (*sophia*, as in 7:10). But Moses' distinctive role as a prophet is suggested by the words *powerful in speech and action* (*dynatos en logois kai ergois autou*, 'powerful in his words and deeds'). This last expression is not found in the text of Exodus, but perfectly reflects the presentation of Moses found there (despite Moses' protestations about his lack of eloquence in Ex. 4:10-17!). Moses is a unique figure in salvation history (cf. Ex. 19:3-9; 33:1–34:35; Nu. 12:6-8; Dt. 34:10-12), even though a succession of

---

36. Literally, the text reads, 'As the time of the promise drew near, which God declared to Abraham' (*kathōs de ēngizen ho chronos tēs epangelias hēs hōmologēsen ho theos tō Abraam*). Although the verb 'promised' (*epēngeilato*) is found in some MSS, the better-attested and more likely reading is 'declared' (*hōmologēsen*). Even less well attested is the reading *hōmosen*, which was probably used by some scribes because it is the more common verb in the LXX in such contexts. Cf. Metzger, *Textual Commentary*, 302.

37. Marshall 1980, 139.

38. *kairos* is used in 7:20 with reference to the whole clause *ho chronos tēs epangelias* ('the time of the promise') in v. 17.

39. Some MSS of Acts 7:21 in the Western textual tradition add the words 'into/beside the river', to make this abundantly clear. Cf. Metzger, *Textual Commentary*, 303.

40. Although the OT does not say as much, Marshall 1980, 139, notes that 'Stephen follows the tradition, attested in Philo, that Moses would naturally be given a thoroughly Egyptian education.' Cf. Philo, *On the Life of Moses* 1.21-24.

prophets would later be provided to speak further words from God. He foundationally revealed the law to Israel and, by God's empowering, became the deliverer of the chosen people from slavery in Egypt. In both respects — as revealer and deliverer — he is a type of Christ.[41] This typology is most obvious when we note how Jesus is described in Luke 24:19 as 'a prophet powerful in word and deed *(dynatos en ergō kai logō)* before God and all the people' (cf. Acts 2:22).

23-25 With a specific time reference *('when Moses was forty years old')*,[42] Stephen marks the moment when Moses *'decided to visit'* *(anebē epi tēn kardian autou episkepsasthai*, 'it came into his heart to visit', most EVV) *'his own people'* *(tous adelphous autou tous huious Israēl*, 'his brothers the sons of Israel'). More than the conventional sense of *visit* is implied by the verb here: 'Moses intends to come out of his royal environment not only to see but to assist his fellow Israelites.'[43] Summarising Exodus 2:11-12, Stephen says, Moses *'saw one of them being mistreated by an Egyptian, so he went to his defense and avenged him by killing the Egyptian'.*[44] This was clearly a bold and risky move, alienating Moses from the Egyptian culture that had nurtured him (cf. Heb. 11:24-26). Stephen's comment on the situation *('Moses thought that his own people would realise that God was using him to rescue them, but they did not')* finds no parallel in Exodus. However, it is a reasonable assumption from the text and highlights the theme of ignorance noted earlier in connection with the Joseph story (7:12-13). It also suggests that Moses had some sense of God's purpose for his life before the calling mentioned in 7:30-34. Such a failure to recognise that *'God was using him to rescue them'* *(ho theos dia cheiros autou didōsin sōtērian autois*, 'God was giving them salvation by his hand' [ESV]) anticipates the reaction of many in Israel to Jesus (cf. 3:17-18; 7:51-52).

26-29 Moses next appears as a mediator between *'two Israelites who were fighting'* (cf. Ex. 2:13-14). He tries to *'reconcile them'* and make peace *(synēllassen autous eis eirēnēn)* by saying, '"Men, you are brothers; why do you want to hurt each other?"'' But his concern for the welfare of his own people is not appreciated: *'the man who was mistreating the other pushed Moses aside and said, "Who made you ruler and judge over us?"'* The rejection is both verbal and physical. It is so significant in Stephen's argument that he mentions it again in 7:35. But in the Exodus narrative it is the threat of exposure for the

41. Johnson 1992, 136-37, suggests a more detailed comparison between the story of Moses and the story of Jesus from the argument of Acts 7.

42. According to Dt. 34:7, Moses was 120 years old when he died. Stephen's speech divides Moses life into three equal sections of forty years (7:23, 30, 36). The text of Exodus is not so specific (forty in Acts 7:23 corresponds to 'after Moses had grown up' in Ex. 2:11).

43. Barrett 1994, 357. The verb *episkeptomai* is used of God 'visiting' his people in Lk. 1:68, 78; 7:16; Acts 15:14, and of believers 'watching out for' in Acts 6:3, or 'visiting' one another in 15:36.

44. The Western text of Acts 7:24 adds further details from the account in Ex. 2:11-12, LXX. Cf. Metzger, *Textual Commentary*, 303-4.

crime committed on the day before (*'"Are you thinking of killing me as you killed the Egyptian yesterday?"'*) that causes Moses to flee to *'Midian, where he settled as a foreigner and had two sons'* (cf. Ex. 2:15-22).

30-32 A significant time lapse is once again noted (*'after forty years had passed'*) before the critical encounter with God recorded in Exodus 3 is recalled. The text says literally that forty years were 'fulfilled' (*plerōthentōn*), suggesting that God was acting to advance his purposes in a significant way. True to the biblical narrative, Stephen observes first that *'an angel appeared to Moses in the flames of a burning bush in the desert near Mount Sinai'*. This angel is mentioned three more times (7:35, 38, 53), as a way of reinforcing the significance of the event.[45] Moses was *'amazed at the sight'*, and *'he went over to get a closer look'*. There at the burning bush, *'he heard the Lord say'* (*egeneto phōnē kyriou*, 'there came the voice of the Lord', NRSV, ESV), *'"I am the God of your fathers, the God of Abraham, Isaac and Jacob."'*[46] So what Moses saw was an angel in the flames of a burning bush, but what he heard was 'the voice of the Lord', identifying himself as the God of the patriarchs and, by implication, the God of the covenant. Stephen's words of interpretation (*'Moses trembled with fear and did not dare to look'*) reflect the conclusion of Exodus 3:6.

33-34 God's command (*'"Take off your sandals, for the place where you are standing is holy ground"'*) expresses the belief that the place where God makes his presence known is holy. God's encounter with Abraham and Joseph, outside the borders of the promised land, has already been noted. Stephen progressively shows that he is not against the idea that the temple in Jerusalem could be such a holy place. But he certainly challenges the notion that the temple is the only place, or indeed the ultimate place, where God is met (cf. 7:44-53 notes). 'By this method Stephen was attempting to clear the way for the proclamation of the centrality of Jesus in the nation's worship, life and thought.'[47] Stephen rightly interprets the narrative of Exodus 3 to mean that God was about to deliver his people from bondage (*'"I have indeed seen the oppression of my people in Egypt. I have heard their groaning and have come down to set them free"'*), in accordance with the promise made to Abraham (cf. 7:7). Associated with that revelation was the commissioning of Moses as the human agent of God's deliverance (*'"Now come, I will send you back to Egypt"'*).[48]

---

45. In Ex. 3:2 it is specifically 'the angel of the Lord' who appeared, a detail supplied by Western and Antiochene texts of Acts 7:30. The angel of the Lord is a significant figure in the Exodus narratives, being the agent used by God to deliver and defend the Israelites from their enemies (cf. 14:19; 23:20, 23; 32:34; 33:2). Cf. Metzger, *Textual Commentary*, 304.

46. The plural 'God of your fathers' comes from Ex. 3:15 and replaces the singular 'God of your father' of Ex. 3:6. Manuscript variations in the texts of Acts 7:31-34, reflecting further details from the LXX of Exodus, are noted by Metzger, *Textual Commentary*, 304-5.

47. Longenecker 1981, 342. The exalted Jesus is proclaimed in 7:55-56 as being in the presence of God and sharing in his glory and authority. By implication, he should be honoured by the worship of all.

48. The verb to 'send' here is significantly *apostellein*, used in Lk. 1:19; 4:18; 7:27; 9:2;

35-36 Stephen's speech now takes 'a dramatic rhetorical turn from narrative to a series of declarative statements'.[49] The challenge to his hearers is about to begin in earnest! The very same Moses *'they had rejected with the words, "Who made you ruler and judge?" He was sent to be their ruler and deliverer by God himself, through the angel who appeared to him in the bush.'* The denial of Moses' authority in 7:27 (cf. 3:13-14 [Jesus]) is repeated here for dramatic effect and contrasted with God's undeniable commissioning of Moses to be *their ruler and deliverer.*[50] The word *deliverer* or 'redeemer' *(lytrōtēs)* is applied to God in Psalms 19:14 (LXX 18:15); 78:35 (LXX 77:35), and, in a context recalling the exodus events, Psalm 111:9 declares that God 'provided redemption for his people' (LXX 110:9, *lytrōsis*). Stephen makes it clear that God accomplished that definitive redemption through the leadership of Moses (cf. Ex. 6:6). The terminology implies ransom or release from captivity in order to serve God. In the NT it is applied to the great work of Christ, which the exodus prefigured.[51] Stephen appears to be drawing a link between Moses and Christ by the use of such terminology (cf. also *sōtērian*, 'salvation', in v. 25). The way in which the exodus redemption was achieved is then summarized. Moses *'led them out of Egypt and performed wonders and signs in Egypt, at the Red Sea and for forty years in the wilderness'* (cf. Dt. 34:10-12; Acts 7:22, and compare 2:22 [Jesus]).

37 Suggesting an even more deliberate link between Moses and Christ, Stephen recalls, *'This is the Moses who told the Israelites, "God will send you a prophet like me from your own people"'*. Deuteronomy 18:15 pointed beyond Moses to a prophetic successor whom God would raise up, whom Israel must heed. Peter applied that text specifically to Jesus in Acts 3:22-23. Stephen's speech and vision similarly suggest that Jesus is the promised prophet like Moses, because he brings the ultimate revelation of God's will and leads God's people to final salvation.[52] But whereas Peter addresses his

---

10:1; 11:49; Acts 3:20, 26, for the commissioning of divine messengers. Gaventa 2003, 126, considers why other features of the Exodus narrative are not recalled by Stephen at this point.

49. Johnson 1992, 128-29. Johnson notes that the sentences are hinged by the fivefold repetition of the demonstrative pronoun 'this/this one' (*touton* twice in v. 35 and *houtos* once each in vv. 36, 37, 38), and three relative clauses in vv. 37-38, all pointing to Moses. The form of the first declaration in v. 35 somewhat matches the kerygmatic statement of Jesus' rejection and vindication in 3:13-15. However, Johnson makes too much of this and argues that 'the rhetorical shaping is entirely Luke's'.

50. The words *eph' hēmōn* ('over us'), which are found in Ex. 2:14 and Acts 7:27, are added by some MSS of Acts 7:35. But the shorter reading of this last text is more likely to be original. Cf. Metzger, *Textual Commentary*, 306.

51. Various words from the same root are used in Lk. 1:68; 2:38; 24:21; Rom. 3:24; 8:23; 1 Cor. 1:30; Eph. 1:7, 14; 4:30; Col. 1:14; Tit. 2:14; Heb. 9:12, 15; 1 Pet. 1:18. Cf. Mt. 20:28; Mk. 10:45.

52. Cf. H. M. Teeple, *The Mosaic Eschatological Prophet*, JBLMS 10 (Philadelphia: JBL, 1957), 63-68, 100-121, and the critique by D. L. Bock, *Proclamation from Prophecy and Pattern: Lucan Old Testament Christology*, JSNTSS 12 (Sheffield: JSOT, 1987), 357 note 123. Jesus is hailed as 'the Prophet' in Jn. 6:14; 7:40, and the divine command at his transfiguration ('lis-

audience as heirs of the prophets who should hear the new Moses, Stephen addresses his audience as sons of those who rejected Moses and killed the prophets, finally putting the Messiah to death (7:35-40, 51-53)!

38 Further developing the link between Moses and Christ, Stephen observes that Moses was *'in the assembly in the wilderness, with the angel who spoke to him on Mount Sinai, and with our ancestors' (paterōn,* 'fathers'); *'and he received living words to pass on to us'.* Use of the word *assembly* or 'church' *(ekklēsia)* is the first point of interest here. In the LXX, this terminology translates Heb. *qāhāl,* in passages referring to 'the day of assembly' (e.g., Dt. 9:10; 18:16) or 'the assembly of the Lord' (e.g., Dt. 23:1-2) or 'the assembly of the people of God' (e.g., Jgs. 20:2). Those whom God redeemed from Egypt and gathered together to hear his words at Sinai were constituted as a holy nation, whose role was to express their distinctive relationship with the Lord by continuing to obey his word (cf. Ex. 19:5-6). Gathered by God to himself, they were to regard themselves as the Lord's 'assembly' or 'church'. The use of the term *ekklēsia* in Acts 5:11 for the community of Christians in Jerusalem prepares us to consider a link between the people of Jesus and *the assembly in the wilderness* with Moses.[53] Jesus is a Moses-like figure, forming and sustaining the new people of God around himself. However, his assembly has its locus in heaven, where the Messiah is enthroned, not at some earthly mountain or building (Acts 2:32-36; cf. Heb. 12:22-24; Revelation 5, 7).

The second point of interest in Acts 7:38 is the statement that Moses *'received living words to pass on to us'.* Stephen identifies the law of Moses as *living words* of God *(logia zōnta;* cf. Rom. 3:2) and thus begins to answer the charge that he speaks words of blasphemy against that law (cf. 6:11, 13-14). At the same time, he implies that the true people of God would obey the law of God and prepares for the challenge that Israel has characteristically not done so (7:51-53). Luke may also intend us to recall that Jesus 'received from the Father the promised Holy Spirit' and has poured out this eschatological gift on his church (2:33). Acts indicates from the beginning that the true Israel now consists of those who acknowledge Jesus as Messiah and Lord and come to him to receive salvation and the gift of the Holy Spirit. So there is a new or renewed Israel, whose identity, character, and function are determined, not by Moses and the law, but by Jesus, the Spirit, and the proclamation of the word which the Spirit makes possible. If Stephen's

---

ten to him'; Mk. 9:7 par.) echoes Dt. 18:15, suggesting that Jesus is the expected prophet. J. P. Sweeney, 'Stephen's Speech (Acts 7:2-53): Is It as "Anti-temple" as Is Frequently Alleged?', *TrinJ* 23 n.s. (2002), 196, observes that, even though Stephen does not make a specific link with Jesus at this point, the narrator (Luke) 'surely intends his reader to draw a connection with the earlier reference to Dt 18:15 in Peter's speech (Acts 3:22-23)'.

53. Seccombe, 'People of God', 358, argues that Luke only uses the word *ekklēsia* without restraint in Acts once he has established through Stephen's speech how the new people of God is formed from within the old people. 'There is ever only one people, because there is but one God.'

teaching sought to convey something of this salvation-historical development, it would explain why false witnesses misrepresented him as they did
and brought about his trial. However, his defence does not make this teaching about the people of God explicit.

4. Jesus Rejected as Part of a Continuing Pattern of Disobedience to God (7:39-53)

This section of Stephen's speech continues to highlight Israel's rejection of
Moses and his leadership (7:39-41; cf. 7:27-28, 35). However, instead of
noting the way God vindicated his messenger and blessed his people
through his chosen leader, Stephen now observes how God turned away
from his people in judgment (7:42-43). In telling this story, Stephen makes
use of Amos 5:25-27 as a biting critique of Israel's ongoing pattern of idolatry. He then briefly recounts God's purpose for the tabernacle and the
temple (7:44-47), climaxing this with the challenge of Isaiah 66:1-2a. Israel's pattern of rejecting the prophets and disobeying the law of Moses is
then said to have culminated in the betrayal and murder of Jesus (7:51-53).
The implication is that only divine judgment can follow such covenant unfaithfulness.

39-40 *'But our ancestors (*pateres,* "fathers") refused to obey him. Instead,
they rejected him and in their hearts turned back to Egypt.'*[54] The pattern of rejection noted earlier (7:27, 35) was repeated at a critical point in Israel's history, soon after the people had been led out of Egypt and had passed
through the Red Sea. The OT records many examples of disobedience to
Moses and his teaching, but the one which Stephen highlights is the idolatry committed while they were still at Mount Sinai (Ex. 32:1-6). Acts 7:39-40
shows that rejection of God and rejection of his prophet are the same thing.
The root cause of their apostasy is expressed in words reflecting Numbers
14:3 LXX ('Wouldn't it be better for us to go back to Egypt?'). This later dis-
satisfaction with their situation is taken by Stephen to indicate a problem
manifested in their journey from Sinai to the borders of the promised land.
In their hearts, they were not grateful for their salvation and were unwilling
to be the holy people of God, trusting him and obeying him in every circumstance. Rather, they were still attracted to the relative ease and comfort
of Egypt (cf. Nu. 11:4-6), and continued to be captivated by the idolatry
they had known there. So they told Aaron (the high priest!), *'"Make us gods
who will go before us. As for this fellow Moses who led us out of Egypt — we don't
know what has happened to him!"'* (cf. Ex. 32:1, 23). Moses' absence is taken as

---

54. Some MSS read 'your fathers' in 7:39, though this is not well attested. There is
also textual evidence for reading 'to you' *(hymin)* rather than 'to us' *(hēmin)* in 7:38. This textual uncertainty appears to have arisen because copyists thought Stephen was now distancing himself from unbelieving Israel. However, this distancing does not happen formally until 7:51. Cf. Metzger, *Textual Commentary,* 307.

a sign that they are free to make their own gods, worship as they see fit, and effectively determine their own future.[55]

41 *'That was the time they made an idol in the form of a calf'* (*emoscho-poiēsan en tais hēmerais ekeinais*, 'they made a calf in those days' [most EVV]). A strange verb is used here (*emoschopoiēsan*, 'made a calf') to convey the sense of Exodus 32:4. The following expression — *'what their hands had made'* (*en tois ergois tōn cheirōn autōn*, 'in the works of their hands') — recalls the LXX terminology for idols.[56] Stephen explicitly identifies this calf as an idol when he says 'they brought a sacrifice to the idol' (*anēgagon thysian tō eidōlō*; cf. Ex. 32:6). The verb *revelled* or 'rejoiced' (*euphrainonto*), which is ironically applied to the idolatrous feast at the foot of Mount Sinai, is normally used in connection with the feasts ordained by God (e.g., Lv. 23:40; Dt. 12:7, 12, 18). Sacrifice and celebration before such an idol indicated that Israel was no different from the nations (cf. Pss. 115:4-8; 135:15-18; Is. 44:6-20; Hos. 8:4-6), and that as a people they had abandoned God's holy calling (Ex. 19:5-6). Note the warning given to Christians by the apostle Paul on the basis of this same incident (1 Cor. 10:7-14).

42-43 *'But God turned away from them and gave them over to the worship of the sun, moon and stars'* (*tē stratia tou ouranou*, 'the host of heaven' [most EVV]). This 'handing over' (*paredōken*) of the people to further expressions of idolatrous worship suggests an act of judgment, whereby 'God allowed the people to become captive to the consequences of their own evil choices' (cf. Rom. 1:24, 26, 28).[57] *The sun, moon and stars* were regarded by pagans as deities or the dwelling place of deities. The Israelites were seduced into worshipping such false gods at various points in their history (cf. Dt. 4:19; 2 Chr. 33:1-5; Je. 8:1-2; Zp. 1:5). When Stephen says that *'this agrees with what is written in the book of the prophets'*, he refers to the collection of the Twelve (so-called 'minor') Prophets, which included the quotation from Amos 5:25-27 which follows: ' *"Did you bring me sacrifices and offerings for forty years in the wilderness, house of Israel? You have taken up the tabernacle of Molek and the star of your god Rephan, the idols you made to worship. Therefore I will send you into exile beyond Babylon."'* The form of the question in Amos 5:25 LXX (*mē*) expects the answer 'No', implying that all through their wilderness wanderings they continued the practice of Exodus 32 and offered sacrifices to other gods than the God who had rescued them. In effect, the question is, 'Did you bring sacrifices and offerings *to me*?' The oracle of Amos is used to establish the fact that Israel had been consistently idolatrous from the time of the exodus and had been judged by God accordingly.[58] There are two significant

---

55. At one level, 'the people's request is for a substitute to take Moses' place in leading them'. At another level, they are demanding 'a substitute for Yahweh himself' (B. S. Childs, *Exodus: A Commentary* [London: SCM, 1974], 564). Cf. Ps. 106:20.

56. *Cheiropoiēta* ('things made with hands') is the expression used in passages such as Lv. 26:1, 30; Is. 2:18; 16:12; 46:6; Dn. 5:4, 23.

57. Johnson 1992, 131.

58. See ADDITIONAL NOTE: USE OF SCRIPTURE (pp. 270-75) on the way in which Ste-

variations from the LXX text in Acts 7:42-43. First, the words 'to worship them' *(proskynein autois)* are added. Since worship of the true God was at the heart of his saving purpose for Israel (7:7), their compromise with idolatry was a failure to fulfill their destiny as the covenant people of God. Secondly, *beyond Babylon (Babylōnos)* is substituted for 'beyond Damascus'. Amos addressed the northern tribes, who went into exile beyond Damascus as God's punishment for their unfaithfulness (cf. 2 Kings 17). Stephen addresses a Judean audience, for whom the Babylonian exile was a more recent experience of divine judgment for the very same reason (cf. 2 Kings 24–25).[59] The LXX gives two specific examples of the worship of 'the heavenly host' beyond the incident of the golden calf. Lifting up *the tabernacle of Molek* is one, referring to worship of the Canaanite-Phoenician sun god Molek. *The star of your god Rephan* apparently then refers to worship of the Egyptian god Repa.[60]

44 Instead of bringing sacrifices and offerings at *the tabernacle of Molek* (vv. 42-43), Israel's worship should have been associated with *'the tabernacle of the covenant law'* (*hē skēnē tou martyriou*, 'the tent of testimony'), which their forefathers had *'with them in the wilderness'*. This tabernacle had been made *'as God directed Moses, according to the pattern he had seen'* (cf. Ex. 25:8-9, 40; Heb. 8:5). *The tabernacle of Molek* was a purely human invention, designed to honour a false god. Paradoxically, Moses was on the mountain being shown the image or *pattern (typos)* of the Lord's sanctuary — which contained no idol — at the very time when the people were making their idol below! 'The tabernacle of the testimony' was so called because it contained 'the ark of the testimony' (Ex. 26:33-34, 27:21), in which the tablets of the law were kept (Ex. 25:16, 21), bearing witness to the exclusive covenant relationship between God and Israel.

45-46 *'Having received the tabernacle, our ancestors (pateres, "fathers") under Joshua brought it with them when they took the land from the nations God drove out before them.'* This brief record of the conquest highlights the fulfill-

---

phen understands and uses the text of Amos 5. Stephen means that 'the worship of the planetary powers, for which the nation lost its liberty and suffered deportation, was the climax of that idolatrous process which began in the wilderness' (Bruce 1988, 145).

59. 'An allusion to the Babylonian captivity moreover carries with it a reminder of the fate of the First Temple' (C. A. Evans, 'Prophecy and Polemic: Jews in Luke's Scriptural Apologetic', in C. A. Evans and J. A. Sanders, *Luke and Scripture: The Function of Sacred Tradition in Luke-Acts* [Minneapolis: Fortress, 1993], 196). Spencer 1997, 77, notes that 'Stephen's appropriation of Amos demonstrates not only a basic agreement with the prophet's radical view of Israel's history, but also an extension of this view reflected in a key geographical modification of the Amos text'. Most EVV have followed LXX and transliterated 'Moloch'. However, TNIV's *Molek* reverts to a form more closely representing Heb. *Molech* or *Milcom*. Cf. Bruce 1990, 204; J. M. Hadley, *NIDOTTE* 2:965-66.

60. Cf. Marshall 1980, 145; Witherington 1998, 272 note 309. The Hebrew of Amos 5 speaks of Sakkuth and Kaiwan, which are probably Assyrian deities. There is a striking parallel use of Am. 5:25-27 in the *Damascus Rule* from Qumran to prove that the exile happened because of Israel's disobedience.

ment of the promise to Abraham about possessing the land and worshipping God 'in this place' (7:7). Stephen notes the central importance of the tabernacle, which they brought with them and set up at Shiloh (Jos. 18:1). It continued to be used until the temple was built by Solomon. Consistent with the record of 1 Samuel 1–7, Acts 7:45-46 says literally that God drove out the nations before them 'until the days of David *(heōs tōn hēmerōn Dauid)'*, who found favour with God and asked 'to find a dwelling place for the God of Jacob *(heurein skēnōma theō Iakōb)'*. A difficult textual problem occurs here. The reading 'house of Jacob' *(oikō Iakōb)* is found in some of the best and earliest manuscripts. This is regarded as the more difficult reading by some scholars, and therefore more likely to be the original.[61] They argue that copyists changed such a reading to *'the God of Jacob'*, to conform more closely to the wording of Psalm 132:5 (LXX 131:5), which Stephen was apparently recalling. However, 'house of Jacob' is a strange way of speaking about the tabernacle or temple and the Greek pronoun *autō* in the next verse makes better sense if the reading here is *the God of Jacob* (Solomon built a house *'for him'*).[62] Gaventa rightly notes that the reference to *God's favour* in connection with David's request to build a temple 'surely negates any attempt to view David's request as an act of bad faith or flawed judgment'.[63]

47-50   Stephen moves immediately to the record of 1 Kings 5–9 and notes that *'it was Solomon who built a house for him'*. Solomon brought the ark of the Lord and 'the tent of meeting' into the temple (1 Ki. 8:4), signifying that the exodus traditions would now be centred there. When the glory of the Lord filled the temple, it was taken by Solomon as a sign that the Lord had placed his 'name' or 'presence' there, so that his people could pray to him there (cf. 1 Ki. 8:10-13, 17-21, 27-30; 9:3). However, Solomon's prayer of dedication acknowledges that heaven is God's dwelling place and that the temple cannot contain him (1 Ki. 8:27-30).[64] Stephen echoes this point when he declares that *'the Most High does not live in houses made by human hands'* (*en cheiropoiētois katoikei*, 'does not dwell in things made by human hands'; cf. 17:24 [Paul]). The issue in Acts 7 is not 'tent' versus 'house' but rather 'true and false thinking about God's presence'.[65] The expression *en*

61. Cf. Metzger, *Textual Commentary*, 308-9.

62. Cf. Longenecker 1981, 347. Johnson 1992, 133, gives three reasons for 'overturning the rule of textual criticism here' and reading *the God of Jacob*, as in KJV, NKJV, ESV, TNIV. But Witherington 1998, 272-73, argues that 'house of Jacob' (NRSV) makes sense because 'the temple was thought to be a place where God's people could come and be with God, and so in a real sense it was a dwelling place for the house of Jacob'.

63. Gaventa 2003, 129.

64. Cf. Peterson, *Engaging*, 43-45. The temple was a means of directing the prayers of the faithful to the throne of God in heaven. Sweeney, 'Stephen's Speech', 200-201, suggests that Stephen quotes Is. 66:1-2a in Acts 7:49-50, rather than 1 Ki. 8:27, because Is. 66:1-4 stresses more the disobedience of Israel, 'despite the prerogative of the temple'.

65. Witherington 1998, 263. The strong adversative particle *alla (however)* at the beginning of v. 48 does not imply that Solomon made a mistake in building the temple. The cita-

cheiropoiētois ('in things made by human hands') is often interpreted in the light of 7:41 and the use of such terminology in the LXX with reference to idolatry. This leads some scholars to argue that Stephen is attacking the building of the temple as a declension from God and effectively an idolatrous activity.[66] It has also been suggested that 'the brevity with which Solomon's building is introduced and dismissed, and the contrast implied with David's intention, which was not to be realized until the advent of a greater than Solomon, expresses plain disapproval'.[67] However, the focus of the verse is rather on the temple as 'a man-made institution which, by seeking to express some claim upon God, limits the divine freedom and so impairs the divine transcendence'.[68] Stephen makes this clear by quoting from Isaiah 66:1-2a: '*"Heaven is my throne, and the earth is my footstool. What kind of house will you build for me? says the Lord. Or where will my resting place be? Has not my hand made all these things?"'* Stephen contrasts *things made by human hands (cheiropoiētois)* with the creation of all things by God's *hand (ouchi hē cheir mou epoiēsen tauta panta).* Isaiah insists that no earthly building can contain the maker of all things, who rules in sovereign freedom from heaven. An earthly dwelling, where he chooses to manifest his presence and reveal his will, cannot be taken to be his permanent *resting place (topos tēs katapauseōs).* Moreover, 'this declaration of God's independence of the Jerusalem temple is also a declaration of God's availability to all with or without the temple'.[69] Stott's concluding comment on this section is worth quoting in full: 'It is evident then from Scripture itself that God's presence cannot be localized, and that no building can confine him or inhibit his activity. If he has a home on earth, it is with his people that he lives. He has

---

tion from Is. 66:1-2a echoes theology such as Solomon expressed in 1 Ki. 8:27-30. The implication is that this theology is to be taken into account when evaluating the significance of the earthly temple.

66. Cf. M. Simon, *St. Stephen and the Hellenists in the Primitive Church* (London: Longmans, 1958), 24-26; Spencer 1997, 78-79; Penner, *Christian Origins*, 310-18. *Cheiropoiētos* in every passage in which it is used in the NT 'sets forth the antithesis of what is made with men's hands to the work of God' (E. Lohse, *TDNT* 9:436). Cf. Mk. 14:58; Acts 17:24; 2 Cor. 5:1; Eph. 2:11; Col. 2:11; Heb. 9:11, 24.

67. Bruce 1988, 149. However, there is insufficient evidence in the speech to argue that Stephen believed that the promise of 2 Sa. 7:11b-16 is truly fulfilled only in Christ. For a full critique of such views, cf. Sweeney, 'Stephen's Speech', 185-210.

68. E. R. Franklin, *Christ the Lord: A Study in the Purpose and Theology of Luke-Acts* (London: SPCK, 1975), 105. Stephen's speech is an attack on an attitude that assigned permanence and finality to the temple. Franklin rightly says, 'it is a discussion of the Jews' attitude to it in the light of their rejection of the Christ'. Cf. Johnson 1992, 133. Evans, 'Prophecy and Polemic', 198, also sees the implication that, 'allegiance to a temple built with human hands could place Israel in danger of repeating its earlier wilderness sin, for the golden calf had also been made by "their hands" (v. 41)'.

69. Tannehill 1990, 93. Stephen's teaching thus paves the way for the taking of the gospel to the Gentiles, as well as pointing Jews away from the temple to the presence of God in the person of Jesus and in the Spirit-filled community created through faith in him. Sweeney, 'Stephen's Speech', 205-6, takes the expression 'made by men' in a salvation-historical sense, contrasting the old order with the new, and compares Mk. 14:58; Mt. 26:61.

pledged himself by a solemn covenant to be their God. Therefore, according to his covenant promise, wherever they are, there he is also.'[70] However, it is also possible that Stephen's reference to a house for God 'not made with hands' was meant to point more specifically to the way God's purpose is fulfilled in Christ and the church.[71] We do not know whether Stephen was explicitly teaching such things, but it is a reasonable assumption, even from the false charges levelled against him (6:13-14).

51-53 Stephen now turns to direct denunciation. '*You stiff-necked people*' echoes the accusation of God immediately after the incident of the golden calf (Ex. 33:3, 5). Moses later indicates that this was an ongoing characteristic of Israel (Dt. 9:6, 27). The charge that they have hearts and ears that are '*still uncircumcised*' (*aperitmētoi kardiais kai tois ōsin*, 'uncircumcised of heart and ears') implies that 'the covenant of circumcision' (7:8) has not affected their inner disposition (their '*hearts*'; cf. Dt. 10:16) or their ability to heed God's word (their '*ears*'; cf. Je. 6:10). They are no more responsive to God than uncircumcised pagans! Stephen has been willing to speak about 'our ancestors' up to this point, even when recounting their rebellion against Moses and God (7:39). Now he distances himself from them, accusing his audience of being '*just like your ancestors*' (*hōs hoi pateres hymōn kai hymeis*, 'as your fathers, so also you') in resisting God. A separation is taking place in Israel, and, by implication, Stephen speaks as one of the renewed people of God.[72]

'*You always resist the Holy Spirit!*' indicates a continuity of behaviour stretching back to the time of the exodus, when God 'set his Holy Spirit among them' (Is. 63:9-14). God's Spirit continued to confront his people whenever he sent a prophet into their midst. In the light of many OT examples, Stephen asks, '*Was there ever a prophet your ancestors* (*pateres*, "fathers") *did not persecute?*' (cf. 1 Ki. 19:10; 2 Chr. 36:15; Neh. 9:26; Je. 26:20-24; Lk. 11:47-51; 13:34).[73] Indeed, '*they even killed those who predicted the coming of the Righteous One*'. The title *Righteous One (ho dikaios)* implies the innocence of Jesus and the guilt of those who opposed him. However, it also appears to have been a recognised designation for the Messiah (cf. 3:14 note; 22:14). By silencing those who predicted the messianic salvation, their ancestors gave themselves no hope. The Spirit confronted them in a new way in the person and work of Jesus (Lk. 4:1-21), but their hearts remained hardened and

---

70. Stott 1990, 139. Cf. Mt. 18:20; 28:20.

71. Cf. Peterson, *Engaging*, 80-107, 200-205. Note particularly Mk. 14:58; Mt. 26:61; Jn. 2:19-22; 1 Cor. 3:16-17; 2 Cor. 6:16-18; Eph. 2:19-22. Stephen could well have been echoing the teaching of Jesus on the future of the temple in God's plan.

72. Neudorfer, 'Speech', 289, concludes that Stephen identifies himself here 'with the Jews of the Diaspora, the "Hellenists"'. His later argument suggests that he means by this 'early Christian Hellenists', but I think it is more appropriate to conclude that Stephen speaks quite generally on behalf of the early church at this point.

73. Longenecker 1981, 343, notes various writings from the period of Late Judaism that elaborated on this theme.

their ears closed. The outcome of this pattern of resistance and persecution was that they *'betrayed and murdered him'*. 'The responsibility for Jesus' death is now placed squarely on the leadership (compare Lk. 24:20; Acts 4:10; 5:30) without any mitigation by "ignorance".'[74] The final irony that Stephen manages to express is that those who killed the Messiah *'received the law that was given through angels (eis diatagas angelōn;* NKJV 'by the direction of angels'; NRSV 'as ordained by angels') *but have not obeyed it'*. Far from speaking against the law (6:13), he affirms its divine authority, by stressing that it was delivered by angels.[75] His accusers are actually the ones who have dishonoured and disobeyed God's law, particularly by putting to death the Righteous One.

So Stephen does not 'speak words of blasphemy against Moses and against God' (6:11), but argues that his own people have regularly been guilty of rebellion against Moses and the law and implies that they have limited God's power and presence to the temple in Jerusalem. 'Stephen's speech is *not* Law or temple critical, it is people critical on the basis of the Law and the Prophets, and of a proper theology of God's presence and transcendence and so a proper theology of God's dwelling place.'[76]

5. Jesus as the Glorified Son of Man (7:54-56)

A bitter reaction to Stephen is expressed only when he accuses the Sanhedrin of being as obtuse and rebellious as their ancestors. In this context, Stephen's prophetic status is dramatically confirmed by his extraordinary vision of the glorified Lord Jesus. As a recipient of divine revelations he resembles Abraham and Moses (7:2, 30-31). His vision of Jesus as 'the Son of Man standing at the right hand of God' recalls Daniel 7:13-14; Psalm 110:1 and Jesus' own prediction before the Sanhedrin (Mt. 26:64; Mk. 14:62; Lk. 22:69). His declaration of this vision confirms the resurrection and glorification of Jesus to those who were responsible for his death. It proclaims his centrality to the purposes of God, and implies that the risen Christ is about to judge those who oppose him. Only the vision given to Paul in 22:17-21 parallels this one in terms of Christological significance in Acts.[77]

---

74. Johnson 1992, 134. Johnson argues that even the leaders could be forgiven for ignorance in Acts 3:17, but they then rejected the apostles in full knowledge of the signs and wonders done by them (4:1–5:42). 'Now another prophet ordained by the apostles, full of the Holy Spirit and wisdom, who has worked signs and wonders among the people, stands before the Jewish leadership' (138). Hence, the unmitigated condemnation at the end of Stephen's speech.

75. This Jewish tradition (cf. Dt. 33:2 LXX; *Jub.* 1:29; Philo, *On Dreams* 1.141-43; Josephus, *Ant.* 15.136) is acknowledged also by Gal. 3:19; Heb. 2:2.

76. Witherington 1998, 275.

77. 7:56 is the climax and conclusion of the speech, with the editorial note about the audience reaction to the preceding argument (v. 54) providing the motivation for Stephen's

54-56 *'When the members of the Sanhedrin heard this, they were furious* (*dieprionto tais kardiais autōn,* 'sawn through their hearts'; cf. 5:33) *and gnashed their teeth at him.'* In the OT, gnashing the teeth is a sign of hostility and rage, often by the wicked against the righteous (e.g., Ps. 35:16 [LXX 34:16]; 37:12 [LXX 36:12]; 112:10 [LXX 111:10]; Lam. 2:16). In the Gospels it is the response of those excluded from the kingdom of God (e.g., Mt. 8:12; 13:42, 50; 22:13; 24:51; 25:30; Lk. 13:28). Here the implication is that the members of the Sanhedrin felt exposed and condemned by Stephen's argument. As one *'full of the Holy Spirit'* (*plērēs pneumatos hagiou;* cf. 6:5, 10), Stephen remains calm in the face of such anger and is granted a special vision. He *'looked up to heaven and saw the glory of God, and Jesus standing at the right hand of God'.* His defence began with a reference to the God of glory appearing to Abraham (7:2; cf. Moses in 7:30, 35, 44). Now he claims to have his own vision of God's glory and to see Jesus in that context. Stephen thus bears witness to the resurrection and heavenly exaltation of the crucified Messiah (cf. 3:13). His actual testimony was, '"*I see heaven open and the Son of Man standing at the right hand of God"'.* The perfect passive participle *diēnoigmenous* expresses a present phenomenon *(open)* and indicates that God himself has taken the initiative and drawn back the veil, so that heavenly realities can be seen (cf. Is. 64:1 [LXX 63:19]; Jn. 1:51; Acts 10:11; Rev. 4:1; 19:11). The description of Jesus as *the Son of Man standing at the right hand of God* recalls Daniel 7:13 and Psalm 110:1, two texts that were linked by Jesus in his prophecy before the same Sanhedrin (Mt. 26:64; Mk. 14:62; Lk. 22:69).[78] In effect, Stephen is proclaiming the fulfillment of Jesus' prediction about his exaltation as *the Son of Man,* though his *standing at the right hand of God* is unexpected and calls for comment.

It is remarkable that Stephen is given such a vision (cf. Rev. 1:12-18; 14:14) and that he is the only person in the NT apart from Jesus who specifically uses the title *the Son of Man.* The appropriateness of this to Stephen's situation is obvious. Jesus has effectively been on trial again before the leaders of Israel through the testimony of his witness. The vision granted to Stephen proclaims the fulfillment of Jesus' own prediction. As the Messiah at God's right hand, Jesus is the one who will judge and rule the nations (Dn. 7:14; Ps. 110:2-7). Whether or not Stephen perceived the full implications of his vision, 'the presence of the Son of Man at God's right hand meant that for his people a way of access to God had been opened up more immediate and heart-satisfying than the temple ritual could provide'.[79] Jesus fulfills and replaces the temple and the sacrificial

Spirit-filled proclamation of the true identity of the ascended Lord Jesus. Cf. 2:37 as an editorial bridge to the final declarations of Peter's Pentecost speech in 2:38-40.

78. The Western text characteristically adds 'the Lord' to 'Jesus' in 7:55, and a few witnesses read 'Son of God' instead of 'Son of Man' in 7:56. However, neither of these readings has any real claim to being original. Cf. Metzger, *Textual Commentary,* 310.

79. Bruce 1988, 157. Bruce continues with an observation about the end of the age of particularism. 'The sovereignty of the Son of Man was to embrace all nations and races

system and provides a way of approach to God for people from every nation. But why is the Son of Man revealed to Stephen as *standing* rather than sitting? This posture has been variously interpreted. It could symbolize Jesus' readiness to welcome Stephen as a persecuted prophet, soon to enter his presence.[80] Perhaps the vision serves as 'assurance of Jesus' supportive witness in the heavenly court' (cf. Lk. 12:8).[81] Perhaps it implies a personal coming to the martyr at the time of his death, as at the end he will come to all.[82] At this particular point in the narrative, however, it is more likely to be a way of asserting the readiness of the Son of Man to act in judgment against those who deny him (cf. Is. 3:13, where standing is the posture for judgment). Such an apocalyptic vision does not mean that the opportunity for the Jews has finally and decisively ended. It is rather a specific warning to those who have rejected Jesus and his witnesses in the past and who are about to reject him again by killing Stephen.

C. Stephen's Martyrdom (7:57-60)

For his courageous testimony Stephen is stoned to death, imitating Jesus himself in the way he dies. In a remarkable shift, 'while Stephen's opponents accuse him of violating the law (6:11, 13-14), Stephen's own death in line with the rejected prophets demonstrates the law-breaking character of his narrative adversaries'.[83] Rejection of Stephen and his message by the Jerusalem authorities leads to a terrible outburst of persecution against the church (8:1-3). This initiates a pattern of dispersion which enables the preaching of the gospel by many others, progressively beyond Judea (8:4-40; 11:19-26). However, at no point does Luke suggest that God has definitively turned his back on Israel as a whole.[84] Perspectives on persecution which emerged in Acts 4–5 are reexpressed and developed in the story of Stephen. The persecution of Jesus and his witnesses is shown to stand in continuity with Israel's persecuted prophets. The persecuted witness stands in particu-

---

without distinction: under his sway there is no place for an institution which gives religious privileges to one group in preference to others.' Cf. Longenecker 1981, 350.

80. Cf. Johnson 1992, 139.

81. Tannehill 1990, 99. Cf. Bruce 1988, 156; Longenecker 1981, 350; Witherington 1998, 275.

82. Barrett 1964, 32-38. Barrett 1994, 384-85, outlines eleven alternative interpretations in all, but prefers this one.

83. Penner, *Christian Origins,* 300. Penner argues that Luke uses Stephen representatively, and in contrast with his opponents, 'to enhance the praiseworthy features of the nascent Christian movement attested to in 6:1-7'.

84. Cf. Seccombe, 'People of God', 349-72. J. T. Sanders, 'The Prophetic Use of the Scriptures in Luke-Acts', in C. A. Evans and W. F. Stinespring (eds.), *Early Jewish and Christian Exegesis* (Atlanta: Scholars, 1987), 191-98, argues that we must see within Luke-Acts an 'intramural polemic' within Judaism, 'to define the people of God, the heirs of the biblical promises'. Cf. Tannehill 2005, 105-65, on the story of Israel in Luke-Acts.

lar continuity with Jesus, and persecution once more arises from the unbelief of Israel. But persecution now serves as a catalyst of mission (as well as
being aroused by mission).[85] Spencer observes how this segment of Acts
'dramatically propels the early church up and out from Jerusalem: up into
the heights of heaven and out toward the ends of the earth'.[86]

57-58 *'At this they covered their ears and, yelling at the top of their voices,
they all rushed at him, dragged him out of the city and began to stone him.'* Covering their ears and yelling at the top of their voices was an attempt to stifle
Stephen's testimony to the exalted Christ. Unless they were prepared to admit that their judgment on Jesus was tragically mistaken, they had no logical option but to find Stephen guilty of blasphemy as well. Rushing 'all together' (*homothymadon*; cf. 2:46; 4:24; 5:12) expressed their concerted anger
at him in an even more frightening way. Luke does not record any formal
verdict or sentence from the high priest, giving the impression that this was
a mob lynching. They *'dragged him out of the city and began to stone him'*, like
Jesus' townspeople when they tried to silence him (Lk. 4:28-29; cf. Acts
14:19). However, 'the possibility of a legal execution cannot be ruled out,
especially since we have also to account for the way in which Saul could
undertake persecuting missions immediately afterwards'.[87] Stoning 'outside the camp' was the punishment for blasphemy under the law of Moses,
which required the witnesses 'to lay their hands on his head, and the entire
assembly is to stone him' (Lv. 24:14; cf. *m. Sanh.* 6:1, 4; 7:4). The Mishnah
also required the victim to be stripped of his clothing, but here *the witnesses*
remove their outer garments to engage in their task as executioners. When
Luke records that they *'laid their coats at the feet of a young man named Saul'*, it
is the first mention of Saul in the narrative of Acts (cf. Paul's recollection of
the event in 22:20). *Young man (neanias)* could mean someone between the
age of twenty-four and forty, not a youth in our modern sense.[88] He is first
introduced as a minor character, before his full significance is revealed (cf.
Barnabas in 4:36-37). The fact that the witnesses laid their clothes at Saul's
feet suggests that he was already the acknowledged leader in the opposition to the early church (cf. 8:1, 3).[89] In preparation for Acts 9, 'Luke is hint-
ing at the remarkable character of Saul's subsequent transformation'.[90]

85. So S. Cunningham, *'Through many tribulations': The Theology of Persecution in Luke-
Acts,* JSNTSS 142 (Sheffield: Sheffield Academic, 1997), 206-14.

86. Spencer 1997, 64.

87. Marshall 1980, 148. Marshall 149, notes that 'there were formal procedures for
stoning laid down in the Mishnah, but it seems unlikely that they were followed in the first
century, especially on such an occasion as this'. Cf. Bruce 1988, 157-59. Gaventa 2003, 131,
suggests that, whatever the legal situation about stoning at the time, resistance to the Christian proclamation in this narrative has 'not only reached the level of violence, but it has now
burst out of the council and into mob action'.

88. BDAG. Cf. Acts 20:9; 23:17-18, 22.

89. In 4:35, 37; 5:2, laying something at someone's feet implies a recognition of that
person's authority.

90. Marshall 1980, 150.

59-60 *'While they were stoning him, Stephen prayed, "Lord Jesus, receive my spirit".'* Stephen follows the pattern of Jesus in facing death and thereby shows himself to be a model disciple. In 7:56 he makes a bold confession before the Sanhedrin as Jesus did (Lk. 22:69). Here he also commends his spirit to God's care as Jesus did (Lk. 23:46; cf. Ps. 31:5). But he pointedly 'calls upon' (*epikaloumenon*, as in 2:21) the Lord Jesus in prayer instead of the Father, trusting him for salvation through death and beyond. Thus, he articulates his belief in the divinity of Christ. Then *'he fell on his knees and cried out, "Lord, do not hold this sin against them"'*. Jesus prayed to the Father that those who crucified him might be forgiven (Lk. 23:34),[91] and Stephen prays for the forgiveness of those stoning him, once again addressing Jesus as *Lord*. True to his vision (7:55-56), Stephen believes that Jesus is the judge who can either condemn or forgive even those who unjustly brought about his death. This prayer serves as a substitute for the offer of forgiveness normally found in the speeches in Acts (cf. 2:38; 3:19; 10:43; 13:38). 'Stephen cannot speak of forgiveness to an audience that has stopped its ears (7:57), but as his last act he prays for their forgiveness, thus expressing his desire for their good and testifying to God's saving possibility.'[92] Both Jesus and Stephen shout their final prayer 'in a great voice' (*phōnē megalē*; Lk. 23:46; Acts 7:60), then both expire (*ekoimēthē*, 'he fell asleep'; cf. Lk. 23:46, *exepneusen*, 'he breathed his last').[93] Thus, the leaders of Israel fulfill Stephen's accusation against them (7:51-52), resisting the Holy Spirit speaking through Stephen and showing themselves again to be children of those who rejected and killed the prophets.

Luke does not present this story of the first Christian martyr to encourage his readers to seek martyrdom. Stephen's death is shown to be the inevitable outcome of his courageous testimony to Christ and his indictment of those who wrongly accused both Jesus and himself. Luke draws particular attention to the Christ-like way in which Stephen offers a form of nonviolent resistance to sin and corruption in high places and faces his own death as a consequence.[94] He dies expressing faith in Christ and love for his enemies, 'a rare example of a man dying in a godly and holy way'.[95] It has sometimes been argued that his Hellenistic background and theology made him more insightful and outspoken than the apostles about the inevi-

---

91. Lk. 23:34 is absent from some of the best early MSS. Marshall 1978, 867-68, concludes that the balance of the evidence favours acceptance of the saying as Lukan, 'although the weight of the textual evidence against the saying precludes any assurance in opting for this verdict'.

92. Tannehill 1990, 86.

93. Further parallels between Jesus and Stephen are noted by Johnson 1992, 142-43. He emphasizes that Luke's concern is 'not to emphasize the personality of his characters but rather their prophetic power that is effected by the Holy Spirit'. There is continuity from Moses through Jesus to Stephen.

94. Cf. C. H. Talbert, 'Martyrdom and the Lukan Social Ethic', in R. J. Cassidy and P. J. Scharper (eds.), *Political Issues in Luke-Acts* (Maryknoll: Orbis, 1983), 99-110.

95. Calvin 1965, 221.

table break between Judaism and Christianity.[96] In my judgment, there is not enough evidence in Acts 6–7 to be certain about this. Indeed, there is a sense in which Stephen dies because of mounting resistance to the witness of many others, including the apostles, as recorded in Acts 4–6. He suffers because of their faithful and courageous testimony, as well as his own. Martyrs arise from such a context and experience in the most violent way the hatred and rejection directed to the whole church. The challenge for readers of Acts is to mirror the authentic witness of those early Christians in whatever context they find themselves, knowing that the outcome for some could even be martyrdom (cf. Lk. 9:23-26).

ADDITIONAL NOTE: THE USE OF SCRIPTURE IN STEPHEN'S SPEECH

Stephen's speech is highly selective in its approach to Scripture, but not arbitrary. The survey from Abraham through Joseph to Moses (7:2-44) highlights the significance of key events and important personalities in the biblical narrative by the use of careful citation (usually involving disclosures about God's purpose for his people), repetition of important words (such as 'land'), and the blending of ideas from different texts (such as a fragment of Ex. 3:12 being used with Gn. 15:14 in Acts 7:7). Amos 5:25-27 is used as a climax to Stephen's accusation about Israel's failure to obey Moses and worship God as he required (7:39-43). Isaiah 66:1-2a is used to challenge the views of Stephen's audience concerning the holy place in Jerusalem (7:48-50). So a substantial citation from the Prophets is used in both cases to critique and challenge Israel's response to the provisions of the Law.

Stephen's focus is on theological issues, such as the means by which God made known his character and purpose for his people, the land as the promised sphere in which Israel was called to worship God, and the law as the means by which he would express his ongoing rule over them and enable them to serve him appropriately. Through all this, however, he sounds the note of failure, culminating in the condemnation of 7:51-53, in which he portrays the rejection of the Messiah as the climax of a long history of rejecting God and his will. Israel's history is presented as 'a tale of God's visitations that were turned away by a faithless people, a vision very close to that attributed to Jesus himself in the parable of the vineyard (Lk. 20:9-18)'.[97]

Stephen's speech is somewhat reminiscent of 'biblical retellings' within Judaism, where biblical material is selected and shaped in order to justify or support a specific understanding of it.[98] Compared with such ap-

---

96. Cf. Longenecker 1981, 351.

97. Johnson 1992, 137. Penner, *Christian Origins*, 304-6, notes that a pattern of praise and blame is common in epideictic literature generally in the ancient world and in Jewish apologetic particularly.

98. Cf. Johnson 1992, 120. Johnson cites Josephus, *War* 5.376-419, the Qumran use of

proaches, it is first interesting to note the degree of compression in Acts 7: 'although long by the measure of other speeches in Acts, this discourse is truly extensive only in the amount of material it manages to cover'.[99] Secondly, it is important to note the way the text of the LXX is used in direct quotations but also in snippets, as part of the construction of the discourse and as an interpretative key to the unfolding story. Thirdly, it emerges from comparison with other 'biblical retellings' that Acts 7 has a tight focus on certain biblical characters (Abraham, Joseph, and Moses) and establishes certain patterns in recounting biblical stories (e.g., God's surprising way of fulfilling his promises; God's revealing himself and being with his people to bless them outside the borders of the promised land; the ignorance of those associated with the saving figures of Joseph, Moses, and Jesus). Finally, it is important to recognise that Stephen speaks from the perspective of a personal commitment to Jesus as Lord and Christ and that he has a belief that the messianic community is the true Israel.

With regard to specific problems created by Stephen's use of the OT, Longenecker's advice is not to try to harmonise the difficulties but to see them in relation to 'the conflations and inexactitude of popular Judaism'.[100] At various points, Stephen seems to be following patterns of biblical interpretation found in roughly contemporary Jewish writings, which we as modern readers find unfamiliar and uncomfortable. It is also right to observe that he is speaking in an emotionally charged situation, with prophetic insight and God-given eloquence. Stephen is not engaged in a scholarly review of God's dealings with Israel. At the same time, his method of handling Scripture requires some explanation, and the problems it raises must be faced. Several important examples will now be examined, to obtain a better understanding of Stephen's hermeneutical method.

There are two issues of chronology. The first relates to Stephen's claim that God appeared to Abraham and called him 'while he was still in Mesopotamia, before he lived in Harran' (7:2). This is problematic if Genesis 12:1-3 is read as following chronologically after the events described in 11:31-32. However, if Genesis 11:31-32 gives background information about Abram's family and homeland and 12:1-3 sets out 'the divine word that prompted his journey',[101] there is no conflict. Even though the LXX of Genesis 12:1 (*kai eipen kyrios*, 'and the Lord said') implies a simple sequence from the events described in chapter 11, Stephen could have been influ-

---

The Book of Jubilees, as well as their own *Genesis Apocryphon* and *Damascus Rule*, and the works of various Jewish apologists to support his argument.

99. Johnson 1992, 121.

100. Longenecker 1981, 340. For an overview of Jewish hermeneutics in the first century AD, see R. N. Longenecker, *Biblical Exegesis in the Apostolic Period* (Grand Rapids: Eerdmans, 1975), 19-50. Cf. G. K. Beale and D. A. Carson (eds.), *Commentary on the New Testament Use of the Old Testament* (Grand Rapids: Baker Academic; Nottingham: Apollos, 2007), 556-72.

101. Wenham, *Genesis 1–15*, 269. TNIV translates Gn. 12:1, 'The LORD had said'.

enced by a tradition of interpretation that allowed for a harmonisation with Genesis 15:7; Joshua 24:2-3, and Nehemiah 9:7. His understanding is that God first spoke to Abraham in Ur and that God was thus the initiator and director of the whole process of salvation from the very beginning.[102]

The second chronological issue concerns Stephen's claim that it was 'after the death of his father' that God sent Abraham into the promised land (7:4). According to Genesis 11:26, 32, Terah was 70 when Abraham was born and 205 when he died in Harran. But Abraham was 75 when he left Harran (Gn. 12:4), which would make Terah 145 at this point in the narrative, with sixty years left to live. On that time scale, Terah would still have been alive when the events of the following chapters took place. Some commentators have concluded that Stephen's speech follows a variant tradition of the text of Genesis, since the Samaritan version of the Pentateuch gives Terah the age of 145 when he died and the version that Philo used allowed him to conclude that Abraham left Harran after the death of his father.[103] Another solution has been to take Abraham not as Terah's eldest but as his youngest son, assuming that he is mentioned first in Genesis 11:26 because of his subsequent prominence in the narrative. This theory allows for the possibility that Abraham was born sixty years after Terah was 70 and makes it possible to conclude that Abraham left Haran after his father's death at the age of 205.[104] The problem with this solution is that there is no evidence that people in the first century adopted it. Theologically, the point Stephen seems to be making is that God was directing and using Abraham, whatever the role of Terah in the movement of the family from Mesopotamia to Harran.

There are several examples of Stephen's modifying biblical texts, using a fragment from another context to amplify and explain the significance of what he is alluding to or quoting. Acts 7:5 uses a portion of Deuteronomy 2:5 (*'not even enough ground to set his foot on'*) to describe Abraham's situation in Canaan, whereas the original context relates to God's prohibition to Israel not to dwell in Mount Seir because it had been given to Esau. This adaptation of the words of God from another context is used to stress that Israel only inherited precisely what God gave them. Stephen's modification of Genesis 15:14 with words from Exodus 3:12 in Acts 7:7 is another example of the interpretative use of a textual fragment. It is drawn in to highlight the fact that the purpose of the exodus was to liberate God's people to worship God. It is further modified with the words *'in this place'*, meaning

---

102. Terah was notionally head of the family throughout most of the period of the Abraham cycle (Abraham was 135 when Terah died and only 137 when Sarah died). Terah's death is recorded prematurely in 11:32 because he plays no subsequent part in the story after the family reaches Harran.

103. Cf. Philo, *On the Migration of Abraham* 177; Marshall 1980, 135; Bruce 1988, 134 note 21; Barrett 1994, 342-43.

104. Cf. G. L. Archer, *Encyclopedia of Bible Difficulties* (Grand Rapids: Zondervan, 1982), 378, endorsed by Larkin 1995, 106-7; Beale and Carson, *Commentary*, 557.

either the promised land or more probably the temple, to suggest that the worship of God in the temple at Jerusalem could be viewed as the divinely intended outcome of the exodus redemption.[105] Stephen thus conveys a simplified overview of redemptive history and affirms the place of the temple in God's plan with this adaptation of Genesis 15:14. A third example of a link between related events is found in 7:39, where a portion of Numbers 14:3 is used to illuminate the Exodus narrative of an earlier incident. A continuity of behaviour from Sinai to the borders of the promised land is suggested by this means.

The compressing of biblical material about the burial place of the patriarchs in Acts 7:16 is similar to the telescoping of traditions about Abraham in 7:2 and the linking of two divine messages from Genesis 15:13 and Exodus 3:12 in Acts 7:7. According to Genesis, Jacob was buried in the cave of Machpelah near Hebron (49:29-32; 50:13), which Abraham had bought from Ephron the Hittite (23:1-20). Joseph was buried at Shechem (Jos. 24:32), in land which Jacob had bought from the sons of Hamor (Gn. 33:18-20). At first glance, Stephen appears to have Jacob and his offspring buried together at Shechem, in the tomb that he strangely describes as having been bought by Abraham 'from the sons of Hamor at Shechem for a certain sum of money'. Given the careful retelling of the biblical story elsewhere in this speech, it is valid to assume that there is a deliberate conflation of the evidence here, rather than a mistaken recollection of the details. Stephen's focus is on the burial place at Shechem, perhaps because it was a challenge to his audience to recognise that this sacred site was now in Samaritan territory. With Shechem in focus, he omits any reference to Jacob's burial near Hebron and may mean in v. 16 only that 'our ancestors' were buried at Shechem (the patriarchs other than Jacob).[106] The statement of Joshua 24:32 was probably generalized to cover all the brothers.[107] It is possible that Jacob is understood to have purchased the Shechem burial ground in Abraham's name, since Abraham was still alive at the time.[108] This incorporation of Abraham into the picture links his original purchase with the later one and shows a continuity of thought and practice among the patriarchs with regard to burial in the promised land.

Stephen includes various details that are not in the text of the Pentateuch. Some, such as the reference to Moses' education 'in all the wisdom of the Egyptians' (7:22), follow a tradition of exegesis found in certain Jewish

105. As noted in the comment on Acts 7:7, although Ex. 3:12 actually refers to worship 'on this mountain' (Horeb), Ex. 15:13-17 shows how the idea of meeting God on his holy mountain soon merged into that of engaging with God in the promised land, particularly at Jerusalem on the temple mount, at the place chosen by God

106. So Barrett 1994, 351. Cf. Beale and Carson, *Commentary*, 559-60.

107. So Barrett 1994, 351. Some Jewish sources maintain that Jacob's other sons (and by implication Jacob himself) were buried together at Hebron (*Jub.* 46:9; *Test. Reub.* 7:2; Josephus, *War* 4.532; *Ant.* 2.199). However, this tradition is not unanimous.

108. So Stott 1990, 134.

sources. Others, such as the division of Moses' life into equal spans of forty years (7:23, 30, 36), or the claim that 'Moses thought that his own people would realise that God was using him to rescue them, but they did not' (7:25), are reasonable assumptions from the text. In short, then, Stephen compresses historical narratives to achieve his rhetorical and theological purposes. He also uses fragments from other places to draw links between contexts and to show either continuity or development within the unfolding of redemptive history. Finally, he adds interpretive detail to illuminate the meaning of the text and to prepare for the challenge to his audience that comes at the climax of the speech.

In conclusion, I will comment further on the use of Amos 5 in Acts 7:42-43 as a bridge between Stephen's recollection of the incident of the golden calf and the paragraph about the tabernacle and the temple. Amos 5:25-27 was directed to the northern tribes of Israel in the middle decades of the eighth century BC. The passage points back to the wilderness period and thus forms a commentary on that era and the subsequent worship of the people of God. The opening question ('Did you bring me sacrifices and offerings forty years in the wilderness, house of Israel?') has been taken to mean that sacrifice and offerings were not offered to God in that period, but rather an obedience producing justice and righteousness.[109] The wilderness is pictured as a time of faithfulness, whereas Amos sees his generation being sent into exile for their unfaithfulness! However, Stephen follows the LXX, which can be taken to mean that when the Israelites engaged in sacrifice they were in fact worshipping false gods from the beginning. Molek and Rephan are cited as examples of 'the host of heaven' the Israelites were guilty of pursuing (v. 42; TNIV *the sun, the moon and stars*). These names were used by the LXX to replace Heb. 'Sakkuth your king' and 'Kaiwan'. The latter names appear to be Assyrian deities, whereas the former names are older Canaanite-Phoenician or Egyptian gods. 'It was particularly under the influence of Assyria in the eighth century B.C. that the worship of the planetary divinities became so popular in Israel, but the evidence of Canaanite place names shows that they were worshiped as early as the period of the Tell el-Amarna correspondence (*c.* 1370 B.C.).'[110] The LXX thus gives a greater sense of historical continuity, implying that the idolatry which the prophets later condemned had its origins in the wilderness and early conquest period of Israel's life. Stephen then modifies the LXX version of Amos 5:27, substituting 'Babylon' for 'Damascus', to give the full sweep of Israelite apostasy, up to and including the exile of the southern kingdom. The prophecy of Amos is thus used to draw links between generations of Israelites from the incident of the golden calf to the time of the Babylonian exile and beyond. It is interesting

---

109. So J. L. Mays, *Amos: A Commentary* (London: SCM, 1969), 111. Bruce 1988, 144, offers a modification of this view.

110. Bruce 1988, 146 note 71. Cf. Beale and Carson, *Commentary*, 565-66.

to note that Amos 9:11-12 is used at the climax of another important speech, in Acts 15:15-18.

D. Persecution Leads to Expansion (8:1-3)

The story of the gospel's impact on Jerusalem comes to a terrible climax with the death of Stephen and the scattering of 'all except the apostles'. However, in God's good providence, this leads to the next stage in the fulfillment of Jesus' prediction about the apostolic witness spreading beyond Jerusalem into Samaria and Judea (8:1, recalling 1:8).[1] Persecution leads to gospel growth, not because a mission plan is approved and put into action by the leaders of the church, but because ordinary believers take the opportunities given to them to preach the apostolic message wherever they go (8:4, expanded with specific examples in 11:19-21). Luke does not suggest that this took place because of any specific guidance from the Holy Spirit, though believers were doubtless moved by the Spirit to be faithful and bold in proclaiming Christ (cf. 8:29, 39). The apostles functioned as witnesses to Christ in ever-increasing circles beyond Jerusalem because others who were convinced by their unique and authoritative testimony to Christ shared it with those they met.[2] Luke introduces a pattern of events that will be repeated in other contexts: rejection in one place becomes the opportunity for people elsewhere to receive the gospel and become part of the messianic community. God and the gospel are not defeated by human opposition, however evil and intense. The efforts of the Sanhedrin and Saul to halt the preaching of the gospel and wipe out the early church only resulted in expansion and wider impact.

    1 *And Saul approved of their killing him.* This sentence really concludes the narrative in 7:60. The fact that the witnesses laid their clothes at Saul's feet (7:58 note) suggests that he was the acknowledged leader in the opposition to Stephen. Saul was from Cilicia (22:3), as were some of those who attacked Stephen (6:9). He could even have been one of those disputing with Stephen in the synagogue (cf. 6:10-14).[3] There is no doubt that he was a key figure in the persecution that followed (8:3). The same emphasis on giving approval to Stephen's death is found in Paul's report of the event in 22:20 (where *martys* ['witness'] seems to have the sense 'one who gives his life for his testimony' [TNIV *martyr*]). A new narrative begins with a

    1. It was noted in connection with 6:7 that a second large 'panel' of the narrative is signalled by the report of church growth in 9:31. It is also true that a minor inclusion is formed between 8:1 and 9:31, with common words ('church', 'Judea', 'Samaria'), and an indication that those who had endured persecution now enjoyed a time of peace.

    2. Tannehill 1990, 102, observes that the apostles become 'the stabilizing, verifying, and unifying element in a mission that moves to new areas and groups without their planning or control'.

    3. Cf. Johnson 1992, 141; Witherington 1998, 278.

dramatic time reference (*egeneto de en ekeinē tē hēmera diōgmos megas*; ESV 'and there arose on that day a great persecution'; TNIV *on that day a great persecution broke out*).[4] The persecution was *against the church in Jerusalem*, and the consequence was that *all except the apostles were scattered throughout Judea and Samaria*. Bruce argues that 'it was the Hellenists in the church (the group in which Stephen had been a leader) who formed the main target of this attack, and that it was they for the most part who were compelled to leave Jerusalem'.[5] This enables Bruce to conclude that the twelve apostles remained in Jerusalem, 'partly no doubt because they conceived it to be their duty to stay at their post, and partly, one may gather, because the possible resentment was directed not so much at them as at the leaders of the Hellenists in the church'. This is a possible reconstruction of the events, which takes Luke's expression *all except the apostles* to be hyperbole. However, Witherington rightly questions whether there is enough evidence to conclude that the persecution was particularly directed against the Hellenists. He also helpfully suggests that the apostles were exempted from the general attack on the Christians in Jerusalem 'since Acts 1–6 has stressed the great respect for these early Jewish Christian leaders among the populace of Jerusalem and the fear of them by the authorities'.[6] According to Bauckham, Luke does not mean that the apostles escaped persecution but that, 'whereas many prominent members of the Jerusalem church were *permanently* dispersed to other parts of the country (cf. 8:40; 11:19-20), the apostles remained the leaders of the Jerusalem church'.[7]

2   *Godly men buried Stephen and mourned deeply for him.* If we take literally the record that the church was scattered and only the apostles remained in Jerusalem, these *godly men (andres eulabeis)* are likely to have been non-Christian Jews.[8] This would mean that the opponents of Stephen do not represent the views of all the Jews in Jerusalem: some sympathy for Stephen and his cause is implied. Indeed, if the Mishnah rule which forbade lamentation for one who had been executed (*m. Sanh.* 6:6) was recognized at this time, their action is quite remarkable. It represented either a belief that Stephen was not legally executed or a public protest against the Sanhedrin's action.[9]

3   *But Saul began to destroy the church.* The verb *destroy (lymainomai)* is

4. Western MSS expand the text of 8:1 by adding 'afflictions' to 'great persecution', and by adding that the apostles 'remained in Jerusalem'. Cf. Metzger, *Textual Commentary*, 310-11.

5. Bruce 1988, 162. Cf. Marshall 1980, 15; Longenecker 1981, 353; Barrett 1994, 390.

6. Witherington 1998, 278. Cf. S. G. Wilson, *The Gentiles and the Gentile Mission in Luke-Acts*, SNTSMS 23 (Cambridge: Cambridge University, 1973), 137, 142-43.

7. R. Bauckham, 'James and the Jerusalem Church', in R. Bauckham (ed.), *The Book of Acts in Its First-Century Setting*, Vol. 4: *Palestinian Setting* (Grand Rapids: Eerdmans; Carlisle: Paternoster, 1995), 429.

8. Cf. Longenecker 1981, 354. However, Bruce 1988, 162 note 7, argues that they were 'probably Jewish followers of Jesus'.

9. Cf. Witherington 1998, 277 note 328; Tannehill 1990, 101 note 63.

used of physical injury as well as oppression or indignity (e.g., 2 Chr. 16:10; Ps. 80:13 [LXX 79:13]; Is. 65:25; Am. 1:11). In view of Stephen's reference to 'the assembly in the wilderness' (*ekklēsia*; 7:38 note), it is interesting that Luke makes *the church* the object of Saul's attack. At this critical point in the narrative, that significant title for the people of God in the OT is applied again to Jewish believers in Jesus (cf. 5:11; 11:22; 12:1, 5), though the term will soon embrace many others as well (9:31; 11:26; 13:1; 14:23, 27; 15:3, 4, 22, 41; 16:5; 18:22; 20:17, 28). Luke implies that Saul is opposing the true Israel, those who have responded to Jesus as Messiah (cf. 9:1 note, 'the Lord's disciples').[10] Saul's strategy is then described: *going from house to house, he dragged off both men and women and put them in prison.* The community life, which found its strength in house meetings and spread its influence from that joyful and caring context (2:46-47), was now systematically dismantled. Saul is portrayed as one who 'breaks and enters',[11] violently dragging the believers off to prison and securing the death of some (cf. 22:4; 26:10). 'These people, he thought, were not merely misguided enthusiasts whose sincere embracing of error called for patient enlightenment; they were deliberate impostors, proclaiming that God had raised from the tomb to be Lord and Messiah a man whose manner of death was sufficient to show that the divine curse rested on him.'[12]

E. The Word Goes to Samaria (8:4-25)

The focus is now on the founding of Christian communities outside Jerusalem, in active fellowship with that first community of believers.[13] Special attention is drawn to the gift of the Spirit to the Samaritans (8:14-17). As in later narratives about Cornelius and his household (10:44-46; 11:15-17), this gift verifies God's true people, 'regardless of their past ethnic or cultural hostility to Jews'.[14] The Spirit specifically directs Philip's ministry (8:29, 39), and causes him to preach effectively and to perform 'great signs and miracles' (8:6-7, 12-13), just like 'the Spirit-inspired Jesus, the apostles and Stephen in Galilee and Jerusalem'.[15] But once again in Luke's narrative the primary focus is on the word and its effect (8:4, 14, 25; cf. 8:21 note). 'The

---

10. Cf. THE THEOLOGY OF ACTS: X. THE CHURCH (pp. 72-77).

11. Johnson 1992, 142.

12. Bruce 1988, 163. Cf. Acts 5:30; Gal. 3:13.

13. Cf. J. T. Squires, 'The Function of Acts 8:4–12:25', *NTS* 44 (1998), 613-14. He views Acts 8:4–12:25 as a unit, and argues that Luke here makes careful preparations for the "turn to the gentiles" which takes place from chapter 13 onwards' (616).

14. J. Hur, *A Dynamic Reading of the Holy Spirit in Luke-Acts*, JSNTSS 211 (Sheffield: Sheffield Academic, 2001), 241.

15. Hur, *Dynamic Reading*, 239. Hur 238, speaks about the Holy Spirit being dynamically characterized in Acts 8 as 'mission director' in relation to Philip's work and notes how this 'foreshadows the role of the Spirit in the future mission carried out by Peter, and Barnabas and Paul.'

word' and related terms are used extensively in this chapter to describe the
content of the message and explain how it is communicated. In effect, Luke
unfolds a theology of evangelism here.

Philip's role as 'the evangelist' (cf. 21:8) in this expanding work is indicated first in Samaria (8:5-25) and then on a wider circuit (8:26-40). He
proclaims the Messiah (8:5), preaches the good news of the kingdom of
God and the name of Jesus Christ (8:12), makes it possible for people to receive the word of God (8:14), uses the Scriptures to proclaim the good news
about Jesus (8:35), and preaches the good news in all the towns he visits
(8:40). Each of these terms gives a slightly different perspective on the task
of evangelism. The gospel is 'the word of God' (8:14) or 'the word of the
Lord' (8:25), indicating that it is not a humanly devised message but a revelation from God himself, to be communicated on his terms (cf. Lk. 5:1; 8:11,
21; Acts 4:29, 31; 6:2, 4). Fundamentally, it involves proclaiming Jesus as the
Christ, with all the implications of salvation and judgment associated with
that name in biblical theology (cf. 2:22-40; 3:12-26; 4:8-12). Evangelism can
proceed directly from an explanation of specific OT texts (8:30-35) or from
an outline of kingdom of God theology (8:12), showing how Jesus fulfills
every biblical expectation in his person and work. Luke will continue to
give us many further examples of people engaged in evangelism and show
us different ways in which the message was preached in a variety of contexts. However, Philip is identified as one especially gifted in this ministry.
His dramatic exorcisms and healings demonstrated Satan's subjugation
and the certainty of the kingdom of God with Christ as Lord. 'Philip's
deeds were visible and audible enactments of his proclamation; consequently, the deeds were regarded by Luke as fostering belief in the things
that Philip spoke.'[16]

Philip's work in Samaria created two problems, which are addressed
in 8:5-25. The first is that many Samaritans believed the gospel and were
baptized, but did not immediately receive the promised Holy Spirit. The
second is the manipulative behaviour of Simon, which had the potential to
lead the Samaritans back into false religion, but now with a Christian ve-
neer. This is the first encounter between Christianity and magic in Luke's
narrative. In later passages (13:4-12; 19:11-20), the conflict is further illustrated and the power of 'the word' is demonstrated. Simon is portrayed
here as a satanic figure, whose power is manifested in magic and idolatry.
In connection with these problems, Luke outlines the critical role of the
apostles Peter and John and shows how links with Jewish Christianity were
maintained as the gospel moved further and further away from Jerusalem.
Through his portrayal of Simon, Luke is demonstrating that 'Christians in
the post-resurrection period have authority over Satan'.[17]

---

16. S. Garrett, *The Demise of the Devil: Magic and the Demonic in Luke's Writings* (Minneapolis: Fortress, 1989), 65.

17. Garrett, *Demise*, 75. Garrett shows how this narrative contributes to the over-

4 Before he launches into a description of Philip's distinctive ministry, Luke observes the extent to which *those who had been scattered (hoi diasparentes;* cf. 8:1) were involved in the task of evangelism (cf. 11:19).[18] The cognate noun of the verb used here *(diaspora)* was a technical term for the worldwide dispersion of the Jews among the Gentiles (cf. Jn. 7:35). Here another sort of dispersion begins, involving the Jewish disciples of Christ but soon to include believing Samaritans and Gentiles (cf. Jas. 1:1; 1 Pet. 1:1).[19] Ordinary believers *preached the word wherever they went (diēlthon euangelizomenoi ton logon;* ESV 'went about preaching the word').[20] In 8:25 we are told that Peter and John also 'spoke the word of the Lord' *(lalēsantes ton logon tou kyriou)* and 'were preaching the gospel' *(euēngelizonto)* in many Samaritan villages.[21] *Preached* may be an unfortunate translation if it is always taken to mean 'giving a sermon'. Speaking the word of the Lord can take many forms, though it has the element of proclamation because it is a declaration of what God has said and done. With various combinations of such terms, Luke continues to highlight the centrality of the word or gospel to his narrative and to the outworking of God's saving plan for Israel and the nations. The inclusion formed by the use of this terminology in v. 4 and v. 25 indicates that the apostles and all who were scattered because of the persecution proclaimed the same message and were engaged in the same activity of winning people for Christ. In a book that concentrates on the evangelistic efforts of apostles and prophetic figures such as Stephen, Philip, and Paul, this is a significant point. Here and in 11:19-21 Luke implicitly challenges his readers about their own involvement in this great work of God.

---

arching story in Luke-Acts about the cosmic struggle that results in Satan's fall from authority at the time of Jesus' death and resurrection. Cf. THE THEOLOGY OF ACTS: IX. MAGIC AND THE DEMONIC (pp. 87-92).

18. Luke includes the words *men oun* ('so', 'then') — not translated by TNIV — to mark the beginning of a new stage in the account. The same expression is found in 8:25, introducing the wider ministry of the apostles Peter and John. Squires, 'Function', 608-9, uses this observation, in conjunction with several others, to argue with Johnson 1992, 143, that this marks 'the first major transition in the Acts narrative'.

19. Cf. K. L. Schmidt, *TDNT* 2:98-104.

20. Several Western MSS add *tou theou* ('of God') after *ton logon* ('the word'). Cf. Metzger, *Textual Commentary*, 311.

21. The verb *euangelizomai* ('preach good news') is used almost exclusively by Luke among the Gospel writers to describe the proclamations of angels (Lk. 1:19; 2:10), and the preaching of John the Baptist (3:18) and Jesus (4:18, 43; 7:22; 8:1; 16:16; 20:1). Cf. Mt. 11:5. Jesus authorizes his disciples to engage in the same work (Lk. 9:6), and we read of the apostles evangelizing in Jerusalem after Pentecost (Acts 5:42). From Acts 8 onwards the verb is used with reference to apostles and disciples more generally (Acts 8:4, 12, 25, 35, 40; 10:36; 11:20; 13:32; 14:7, 15, 21; 15:35; 16:10; 17:18). A parallel term is *kēryssō* ('proclaim'), which is used in Lk. 3:3; 4:18, 19, 44; 8:1, 39; 9:2; 12:3; 24:47; Acts 8:5; 9:20; 10:37, 42; 15:21; 19:13; 20:25; 28:31.

1. Some Samaritans Find Their True Deliverer (8:5-13)

Philip's initial impact on a group of Samaritans is remarkable (vv. 5-8), especially since it is made clear that they were previously enthralled by Simon's sorcery and false religion (vv. 9-11). His proclamation of Jesus and the kingdom of God brings many to faith, including Simon himself (vv. 12-13). Although the signs and miracles performed by Philip are a significant factor in capturing the attention of the Samaritans (v. 6) — previously focussed on Simon (v. 10) — it is clearly his proclamation of the gospel that converts them and brings them to baptism.

5 *Philip went down to a city in Samaria and proclaimed the Messiah there.* In Acts, *Samaria* generally denotes the territory, not the city of that name (cf. 1:8; 8:1, 9, 14; 9:31; 15:3). The TNIV reading without the article *(to a city in Samaria)* makes excellent sense in the context. Although it is vague about the precise location, it highlights the extraordinary fact that Philip's ministry took place in the region marked out in 1:8 as the next context for apostolic witness. However, there is better manuscript evidence for including the definite article and translating, 'to the city of Samaria'.[22] It may be that 'Samaria' was regarded by Luke as the only city in the district or that the expression is a circumlocution for 'the main city of Samaria'.[23] Herod the Great renamed the capital Sebaste in 27 BC, in honour of the Roman emperor (Gk. *Sebastos* was used as the equivalent of Lat. *Augustus*). Luke possibly uses the traditional title because of its historic associations, which were fundamental to the hostility between Jews and Samaritans. The first century was a time of very strained relations between these two neighbours. 'The old antithesis of North and South, of Israel and Judah, was revived in all its sharpness.'[24] Mt. Gerizim rather than Jerusalem was the centre of worship for the Samaritans (cf. Jn. 4:20), and they recognized only the Pentateuch as Scripture (in a form that differed significantly from the Masoretic text). In practice, the Jews put the Samaritans on a level with Gentiles and had restricted dealings with them (cf. Jn. 4:9), even though the Samaritans claimed to worship the same God and follow the law of Moses.[25] So Philip's offer of the gospel to this despised people was a radical step forward, signifying the newness of the situ-

---

22. Cf. Metzger, *Textual Commentary*, 311, who notes the strong support for the reading with the article *(eis tēn polin tēs Samareias)* in Alexandrian MSS.

23. Cf. Barrett 1994, 402-3. 'Other conjectures, such as that Luke had Shechem in mind (cf. Acts 7:16, but it had been basically destroyed in 128 B.C. along with the temple on Mount Gerizim) or even Gitta, the hometown of Simon Magus, can neither be proved nor refuted' (Witherington 1998, 282).

24. J. Jeremias, *TDNT* 7:90. Jeremias gives a neat summary of the history of relations between Jews and Samaritans and outlines the distinctive features of Samaritan religion (7:88-94). Cf. Longenecker 1981, 356-57; Gaventa 2003, 135-36.

25. Cf. J. Jeremias, *TDNT* 7:91. J. Jervell, *Luke and the People of God* (Minneapolis: Augsburg, 1972), 113-32, insists that the Jews regarded the Samaritans not as Gentiles but as schismatics, part of the 'lost sheep of the house of Israel'. Luke shows great interest in the Samaritans (Lk. 9:51-6; 10:30-37; 17:11-19; Acts 1:8; 8:1-25; 9:31; 15:3), as does John (4:4-42).

ation brought about by Jesus and the gospel. The essential message proclaimed by Philip, even among the Samaritans, was that Jesus is *the Messiah*. The Samaritans looked for the prophet like Moses promised in Deuteronomy 18:15-19, calling him Taheb ('restorer')[26] rather than an eschatological saviour and ruler from the line of David (cf. 2 Sa. 7:12-16; Is. 11:1-9 and related prophecies; Acts 2:31, 36 notes). But if the Samaritan woman whom Jesus met could easily relate her expectation of an eschatological prophet to the Jewish hope (Jn. 4:25), it is not surprising to find Philip preaching *the Messiah* so directly to his Samaritan audience. The fulfillment of Deuteronomy 18:15-19 in the coming of Jesus was an aspect of Peter's preaching in 3:22-26 (cf. 7:37).

6-8 Literally, v. 6 begins, 'The crowds together paid close attention to the things said by Philip' *(proseichon de hoi ochloi tois legomenois hypo tou Philippou homothymadon)*. The same Greek verb *(proseichon)* is used again with reference to the response of the Samaritans to Simon in 8:10, 11, suggesting that the close attention they had previously paid to Simon was now transferred to Philip. Such close attention to the claims of the gospel is the prelude to genuine faith. It was the gospel about Jesus that interested them most, and they applied themselves to understand it together *(homothymadon* is translated *all* by TNIV, but elsewhere 'together', e.g., in 1:14; 2:46; 4:24; 5:12). Luke then indicates that they paid close attention to the things said by Philip 'as they listened and saw the signs that he performed' *(en tō akouein autous kai blepein ta sēmeia ha epoiei)*. Philip's preaching was accompanied by *signs (sēmeia)*, as was the preaching of Jesus and the apostles.[27] Luke then details what happened, illustrating the comparison in terms of exorcisms and healings (v. 7): *with shrieks, evil spirits came out of many* (cf. Lk. 4:33; Acts 5:16), and *many who were paralysed* (cf. Lk. 5:18; Acts 9:33) *or lame* (cf. Lk. 7:22; Acts 3:2) *were healed.*[28] In Acts, signs and wonders establish the credentials of a prophet before all the people and authenticate or verify the prophet's message by actually conveying a partial realization of the salvation proclaimed.[29] Encounter with demonic forces is specifically high-

---

26. Cf. J. Macdonald, *The Theology of the Samaritans* (London: SCM, 1964), 362-71. A. Oepke, *TDNT* 1:388, argues that the basic meaning of *Taheb* is 'he who returns', rather than the causative 'restorer'. He thinks that the Samaritan belief is 'possibly a relic of the Messianology which was not systematically connected with the house of David and which found an echo in Jewish expectation of Messiah ben Joseph'.

27. 'What they did he is now doing, but he does it in a new area and with a new ethnic group' (Tannehill 1990, 104). However, John 4 indicates that Jesus himself initiated the work of the gospel in Samaria.

28. Metzger, *Textual Commentary*, 312-13, discusses the awkward syntax in the better witnesses to 8:7, illustrating why this was changed in later MSS. KJV ('For unclean spirits, crying with loud voice, came out of many that were possessed with them') reflects the modification found in the Received Text.

29. Garrett, *Demise*, 63, observes that 'Philip's "signs" *(sēmeia)* were not regarded by Luke as random displays of power (as were, presumably, Simon's unspecified magic tricks, *mageiai*), but, rather, as virtual enactments of the word that Philip preached. Sign and proc-

lighted by mention of the exorcism of *evil spirits* (*pneumata akatharta*, 'unclean spirits', in most EVV). This prepares for the detailed account of the conflict with Simon the sorcerer. So the preaching and the signs worked together, and *there was great joy in that city* (cf. 8:39; 13:48; 15:31).

9-11 *Now for some time a man named Simon had practised sorcery in the city and amazed all the people of Samaria.* Luke pauses to introduce Simon before continuing the story of how the Samaritans believed and were baptised (8:12). Simon had been there before Philip *(prohypērchen)* and was already influential in the situation. Luke outlines the spiritual oppression from which the Samaritans needed to be delivered and prepares for the encounter between Simon and the apostles (8:18-24). Simon is not mentioned elsewhere in the NT, though the second-century Christian writer Justin Martyr, who was himself a Samaritan, represents Simon as empowered by demons to perform magic and as later honoured in Rome as a god (*Apol.* 1:26; cf. 56; *Trypho* 120.6). Irenaeus (*Against Heresies* 1.23) describes him as the founder of the sect of the Simonians and as one 'from whom all sorts of (Gnostic) heresies derived their origin'.[30] However, there is nothing in Acts to suggest that Simon was the initiator of Gnostic doctrine, even though this became a widely accepted tradition in early church writings.[31] Luke portrays Simon as 'practicing sorcery' (*mageuōn*; cf. v. 11, *mageia*) and 'amazing the Samaritan nation' (*existanōn to ethnos tēs Samareias)*, suggesting a widespread and powerful influence. The cognate word *magys* was borrowed from Persian, where it denoted a member of the priestly Median tribe. It came to be used of anyone possessing supernatural knowledge or ability (cf. the 'wise men' in Matt. 2:1), anyone practicing magic (cf. Elymas in Acts 13:6, 8), or anyone who was a deceiver or seducer.[32] The term is clearly used in a negative way by Luke, who is keen to highlight the differences between Christianity and contemporary magical beliefs and practices. Jews were strictly forbidden from any involvement in magical practices (Dt. 18:9-14) because of their association with idolatry and the demonic, and the earliest Christians adopted the same stance.[33]

There was certainly a religious dimension to the hold that Simon had on the Samaritans. *He boasted that he was someone great, and all the people, both high and low, gave him their attention and exclaimed, 'This man is rightly called the Great Power of God' (Houtos estin hē dynamis tou theou hē kaloumenē Megalē;*

---

lamation were coherent, and therefore mutually reinforcing.' Cf. THE THEOLOGY OF ACTS: VIII. MIRACLES (pp. 83-87).

30. Further details about the references to Simon in early Christian literature are given by Bruce 1988, 166-67. Cf. Johnson 1992, 146-67.

31. Cf. Barrett 1994, 405-6; Garrett, *Demise*, 61-62. Witherington 1998, 284, also argues that there is nothing in Acts to suggest that Simon was really a Gnostic, 'but that Luke has polemically downgraded him into a mere magician'.

32. Cf. G. Delling, *TDNT* 4:356-59; Barrett 1994, 405-6. Hence Simon becomes known in early Christian literature as Simon Magus.

33. Cf. Garrett, *Demise*, 13-17, 65-69; THE THEOLOGY OF ACTS: IX. MAGIC AND THE DEMONIC.

NRSV, ESV 'This man is the power of God that is called Great').[34] Popular opinion accepted what Simon apparently claimed for himself. He did not presume to be the supreme God but 'inculcated the belief that of all the Powers of God he was the great one'.[35] The Samaritans were gripped by his magic and by his idolatrous claim to be in some sense 'a divine man'. They were therefore caught up with a strange syncretism of Hellenistic-pagan and Samaritan-Jewish beliefs. More specifically, Garrett has shown that magic in Luke's narrative is presented as 'satanic power actualised'.[36] The verb translated *gave him their attention (proseichon)* in v. 10 is also rendered *they followed him* in v. 11. We have already noted the use of the same verb in v. 6 to describe the reaction of the crowds to the preaching of Philip. So 'the story involves competition for conversion'.[37] The Samaritans, who had previously been captivated by Simon *because he had amazed them for a long time with his sorcery (mageiais,* 'magic practices'), were now captivated by Philip's message and by the Christ he proclaimed.

12 *But when they believed Philip as he proclaimed the good news of the kingdom of God and the name of Jesus Christ, they were baptized, both men and women.* Proclaiming the good news is a key idea in this chapter, with the verb *euangelizomai* being used five times (8:4, 12, 25, 35, 40). Stephen was literally 'gospelling about the kingdom of God and the name of the Lord Jesus Christ'. The kingdom of God was the focus of Jesus' teaching (e.g., Lk. 4:43; 6:20; 7:28; 8:1, 10; 11:1), and, in the course of his public ministry, he sent his disciples to preach the same message (Lk. 9:2; 10:9-11). After Pentecost, the apostolic preaching became more explicitly Christological, as the role of the crucified and resurrected Christ in the fulfillment of God's kingdom plans was more clearly understood. However, the kingdom remains the theological context in which to understand and proclaim Christ in Acts (1:3 note, 6; 8:12; 14:22; 19:8; 20:25; 28:23, 31). To use another term from Paul's address to the Ephesian elders, it is a way of preaching 'the whole will of God' (20:27 note). Interestingly, in 8:12 we find *the kingdom of God* coupled with *the name of Jesus Christ.* So Philip proclaimed that God's

34. The awkward *kaloumenē* ('called') is omitted by the later Byzantine text — hence KJV and NKJV ('this man is the great power of God') — but is well attested in earlier MSS. Cf. Metzger, *Textual Commentary,* 313-14.

35. Barrett 1994, 407. Barrett notes that a distinction between the supreme Being and a 'great power' *(megalē dynamis)* is supported by inscriptions. Similarly, Witherington 1998, 284, argues that 'the designation seems close to the inscriptional evidence about a god who is less than the supreme god but nonetheless very powerful'. Cf. *ND* 1 (1981), 107; 3 (1983), 32. Johnson 1992, 147, observes that Justin, *Apol.* 1.26; *Trypho* 120.6, record that the Samaritans confessed Simon 'as their first God' on the basis of his own claim. However, *Acts of Peter* 4 and Pseudo-Clementine *Homilies* 2.22.2-3 have Simon claiming to be the power of God rather than God himself.

36. Garrett, *Demise,* 60. Her treatment of Acts 8:4-25 is on pp. 61-78.

37. Johnson 1992, 146. Garrett, *Demise,* 67-68, 76-77, argues that Luke deliberately portrayed the magician as a false prophet, in line with the approach of roughly contemporaneous Jewish and Christian writings.

kingly rule had been established in fulfillment of prophecy through the person and work of the Lord Jesus. He used the 'name' theology of the earliest preachers, who were presumably influenced by the prophecy of Joel (Acts 2:21, 38; 3:6, 16; 4:10, 12), to make clear who Jesus is and how they should respond to him. Jesus is the saviour upon whom everyone must call to be delivered from the coming judgment, since God has made him 'both Lord and Christ' (2:36). Also of interest in this verse is the statement that *they believed Philip.* This does not mean that their trust was in Philip rather than in Christ, or that their belief in the gospel was somehow deficient.[38] The meaning is rather that they were convinced by the truth of Philip's message: *they believed Philip as he preached the good news of the kingdom of God and the name of Jesus Christ.* It was out of genuine conviction, then, that *they were baptized, both men and women.* Here again Luke makes the point that women shared equally with men in this new community, with respect to its blessings (1:14; 5:14) and its suffering (8:3; 9:2).

13 *Simon himself believed and was baptized.* The word 'also' *(kai)* is included in the Greek, suggesting that Simon was a special and unexpected case. He seemed to be like the rest of the Samaritan converts in making a public commitment to Christ. However, Luke highlights two worrying aspects of his behaviour. First, we are told that *he followed Philip everywhere (ēn proskarterōn tō Philippō,* 'he was attaching himself to Philip', BDAG). The verb used here has previously been applied to the devotion of believers to prayer and various forms of mutual ministry (1:14; 2:42, 46; 6:4), and so Simon's personal attachment to Philip seems out of place or unusual. Secondly, we learn that he was *astonished by the great signs and miracles he saw (theōrōn te sēmeia kai dynameis megalas ginomenas existato;* ESV 'and seeing signs and great miracles performed, he was amazed'). In vv. 9, 11 the Samaritans' astonishment with Simon's magic is noted, and so it seems that Simon was 'at the same point where the Samaritans were *initially* when they heard Philip (cf. vv. 6-7)'.[39] Obsession with the spiritual power of the apostles would soon prove to be the dominant issue for him (vv. 18-19). Simon's magical worldview had not changed, and a more thorough renunciation of his former beliefs and practices was still necessary (cf. 19:18-20). Longenecker suggests that 'Simon's belief in Jesus seems to have been like that spoken of in John 2:23-25 — i.e., based on miraculous signs and thus inferior to true commitment to Jesus'.[40]

---

38. J. D. G. Dunn, *Baptism in the Holy Spirit: A Re-examination of the New Testament Teaching on the Gift of the Spirit in Relation to Pentecostalism Today,* SBT (Second Series) 15 (London: SCM, 1970), 65, claims that *pisteuein* with the dative here indicates intellectual assent rather than commitment of heart. However, the same construction in 16:34; 18:8 is used for genuine belief. M. M. B. Turner, *Power from on High: The Spirit in Israel's Restoration and Witness in Luke-Acts,* JPTSS 9 (Sheffield: Sheffield Academic, 1996), 362-67, carefully responds to Dunn's argument that the Spirit was not given in baptism because of the inadequate faith of the Samaritans.

39. Witherington 1998, 285. Cf. Garrett, *Demise,* 69.

40. Longenecker 1981, 358.

2. *Jerusalem Witnesses Samaria's Reception of the Holy Spirit (8:14-17)*

The visit of Peter and John is not a problem-solving expedition on behalf of the apostles in Jerusalem, but rather a response to the news that 'Samaria had accepted the word of God' (v. 14). Even so, when they arrive they perceive that the Spirit 'had not yet come on any of them' (vv. 15-16). The impartation of the Spirit through prayer (v. 15) and the laying on of hands (v. 17) are presented by Luke as unusual events, related to the uniting of Jews and Samaritans in one community through baptism into Christ (v. 16b, 'baptized into the name of the Lord Jesus'). The importance of having apostolic witnesses present for this outpouring of the Spirit is better understood when the narrative is compared with what is later said about the incorporation of the Gentiles into the church (10:44-48; 11:15-18).[41]

14 *When the apostles in Jerusalem heard that Samaria had accepted the word of God, they sent Peter and John to Samaria.* The fact that *the apostles in Jerusalem* sent representatives to check on these developments shows that evangelism took place in Samaria without their authorization or supervision. However, Peter and John were sent for positive reasons, to verify the surprising news that *Samaria had accepted the word of God.*[42] Tannehill suggests that the visit can be considered from two perspectives. First, Philip's mission is incomplete until Peter and John pray for the Samaritans to receive the Holy Spirit. 'The result is a cooperative mission in which an established church affirms and contributes to the establishment of new churches.'[43] Second, the effect on Peter and John is that they become convinced that the Samaritans are truly included in the messianic salvation. This event is comparable to 10:44-48, where the coming of the Holy Spirit is a sign that God wants to include believing Gentiles on the same basis as believing Jews in the benefits of the New Covenant (cf. 11:15-18).[44] On both occasions, there is a stunning break with traditional cultural and religious barriers, as the Spirit draws Samaritans, and then Gentiles, together with Jews into the fellowship of Christ.

41. Hur, *Dynamic Reading*, 241, observes that in 8:14-17 Luke as narrator 'confirms Philip's mission through the reliable characters' co-work (i.e. praying and laying on of hands) of the apostles (sent from Jerusalem) and God's sending the Spirit'. Hur, 245-49, comments on the significance of the coming of the Spirit upon Gentiles in Acts 10–11.

42. The sweeping reference to Samaria here is interesting because Luke knows that there are many more Samaritan villages that need to hear the gospel (8:25). He is drawing attention to the fact that the Samaritans as a race or culture have embraced the gospel in this first city visited by Philip.

43. Tannehill 1990, 104. 'The point is not that the Spirit can be received only when apostles lay on their hands, for in later scenes it comes in other ways (cf. 10:44) or through other persons (cf. 19:6).' Cf. Longenecker 1981, 359-60.

44. Tannehill 1990, 105, also compares the sending of Barnabas from Jerusalem to verify the new work begun in Antioch by those scattered following Stephen's death (11:19-26). Cf. THE THEOLOGY OF ACTS: III. THE HOLY SPIRIT (pp. 60-65).

15-17 *When they arrived, they prayed for the new believers there that they might receive the Holy Spirit.* The apostles' willingness to pray for the gift of the Spirit suggests an awareness that a work of God had actually taken place among the Samaritans *(they had simply been baptized into the name of the Lord Jesus)*, but that something was missing. Instead of preaching the gospel or correcting misunderstandings, *Peter and John placed their hands on them, and they received the Holy Spirit.* Prayer is mentioned in connection with the laying on of hands in 6:6; 8:15-17; 13:3; 28:8 and may be assumed in other places where it is not mentioned. This gesture appears to represent identification with and concern for the person who is prayed for.[45]

But why had the Holy Spirit *not yet come upon any of them* (*epipetōkos,* 'fallen upon'; cf. 10:44; 11:15)? Given the promise that those who repent and are baptized in the name of Jesus Christ will have their sins forgiven and receive the gift of the Holy Spirit (2:38-39), are we to conclude that there was something deficient in the faith of the Samaritans?[46] Luke seems to be at pains to stress the orthodoxy of Philip's preaching, the close attention paid by the Samaritans to what they heard, and the genuineness of their response (8:5-6, 12; contrast the 'disciples' in 19:1-5). Was it because there were no apostles present? Luke later makes it clear that the Spirit can be given when the person baptizing is not an apostle (9:17-18). Was it because they needed to receive the Spirit in a fuller sense, for inspiration,[47] or for the reception of charismatic gifts?[48] Was it because they specifically needed the Spirit to be given to them in this way to empower them for mission?[49] The idea that they needed more of the Spirit is ruled out by Luke's insistence that *the Holy Spirit had not yet come upon any of them.* With the

45. The laying on of hands is mentioned in connection with the authorization and commissioning of the seven in 6:6 (note) and the setting apart of Barnabas and Saul for their mission by the leaders of the church at Antioch (13:3 note). It is loosely connected with baptism in 8:17, 19; 9:12, 17 (notes) and more directly in 19:5-6. In 9:12, 17: 28:8, the laying on of hands is for healing (in 9:17 this is associated with the gift of the Spirit). Cf. Turner, *Power,* 372-73.

46. Cf. Dunn, *Baptism,* 55-68, and the response of Turner, *Power,* 362-67.

47. Cf. Barrett 1994, 398, 412.

48. Calvin 1965, 236, cannot believe that Philip's baptism failed to confer the Spirit and argues that 'Luke is not speaking here about the general grace of the Spirit, by which God regenerates us to be His own sons, but about those special gifts, with which the Lord wished some to be endowed in the first days of the Gospel'. Likewise, G. R. Beasley-Murray, *Baptism in the New Testament* (Exeter: Paternoster, 1962), 118-19, argues from 2:38-39 that the Samaritans must have received the definitive gift of the Spirit in baptism and that the gift in 8:17 was for charismatic endowment. Cf. Turner, *Power,* 368-9, for a response to such arguments.

49. This is the approach advocated by writers such as J. Shelton, *Mighty in Word and Deed: The Role of the Holy Spirit in Luke-Acts* (Peabody: Hendrickson, 1991), and R. P. Menzies, *The Development of Early Christian Pneumatology with Special Reference to Luke-Acts,* JSNTSS 54 (Sheffield: JSOT, 1991); *Empowered for Witness: The Spirit in Luke-Acts* (Sheffield: JSOT, 1994; repr. London: Clark International, 2004), but critiqued significantly by Turner, *Power,* 371-73.

words *not yet (oudepō)*, Luke indicates that the Samaritan incident provides 'a clear break with the "norm" we might expect from Acts 2:38-39'.[50] The best explanation is that God himself withheld the Spirit until the coming of Peter and John, 'in order that the Samaritans might be seen to be fully incorporated into the community of Jerusalem Christians who had received the Spirit at Pentecost'.[51] God withheld the gift for his own revelatory and salvific purpose, not because of an inadequate response on the part of the Samaritans. The apostles needed to be there as reliable witnesses on behalf of the Jerusalem church, not to impart the Spirit because of their office. Significantly, in 8:25 they return to Jerusalem to report what God has been doing. The delay in the sending of the Spirit put the Samaritans somewhat in the position of the Jewish disciples before Pentecost. They had a genuine faith in the risen Lord, but had not yet received the promised Holy Spirit. Neither the experience of those first disciples nor the experience of the Samaritans can be made the basis for a two-stage view of Christian initiation, either in a Catholic or Pentecostal sense.[52] These were unique events in salvation history, not the normal pattern of initiation known to Luke.

3. A Pretender Is Exposed (8:18-25)

Simon's preoccupation with spiritual power (v. 13) leads him to make a monetary offer to the apostles for the authority to impart the Spirit through the laying on of his hands (vv. 18-19). Peter's response is first of all in the form of a curse, since Simon does not understand the grace of God and thinks he can 'buy the gift of God with money' (v. 20). Secondly, Peter declares that Simon cannot be part of this ministry because his heart is not right before God (v. 21). Despite the curse, Peter offers Simon the chance to repent and seek the Lord's forgiveness, warning him that he is in a bondage to wickedness from which he can be delivered only by God (vv. 22-23). Simon recognizes his spiritual impotence when he asks Peter to pray for him (v. 24), though Luke gives no explicit indication of the outcome. The concluding note about the freedom of the apostles to continue their evangelistic ministry (v. 25) may, however, suggest that the battle with demonic forces in the encounter with Simon was satisfactorily ended.

---

50. Turner, *Power*, 360.

51. Marshall 1980, 157, following G. W. H. Lampe, *The Seal of the Spirit* (London: SPCK, 1967), 70-72. Cf. Turner, *Power*, 374. Bruce 1988, 170, and Witherington 1998, 289, expound the view that the ancient schism between Jews and Samaritans was the particular reason for this delayed gift of the Spirit.

52. Stott 1990, 151-59, provides an extended discussion of this issue. Turner, *Power*, 374, makes the interesting point that the disciples themselves experienced 'salvation' before Pentecost, 'through Jesus' Spirit-empowered ministry'. Philip became the Spirit-empowered agent of salvation for the Samaritans, before the completion of their whole conversion-initiation experience in 8:17.

18-19   There is no mention of outward signs to confirm the coming of the Spirit, though these may be implied by the reference to what Simon *saw*. In some way, Simon *saw that the Spirit was given at the laying on of the apostles' hands*, and this appeared to him to be a new type of magic. His offer of *money* to obtain this power became notorious in church history and gave rise to the name 'simony' for the purchase of spiritual positions. What he really wanted is expressed with the request, *'Give me also this ability (tēn exousian tautēn,* 'this power') *so that everyone on whom I lay my hands may receive the Holy Spirit'.* 'The magician's characteristic interest appears in Simon's desire to connect the possession of the Spirit to a specific ritual without reference to dispositions such as faith.'[53] Doubtless he also saw this power as a way of regaining his hold over the Samaritans, even 'a way of gaining a "share" in the leadership of the movement'.[54] Garrett observes that Simon mistakenly regarded the Christian leaders as magicians like himself. 'Luke then exploits Simon's apparent misconception, using it as a foil to display the apostles' utterly opposed view: they, unlike Simon, would never take money for what they had to offer (cf. Acts 3:6). Thereby Luke illustrates that the Christians do not share one of the most widely recognized traits of practitioners of magic.'[55] Tannehill also notes a concern to expose corrupt religion in the way Luke tells this story. 'Whenever religion is used to make its leaders seem great and powerful, and whenever religion becomes a commodity by serving the interests of those who have or want money, it has become corrupt.'[56]

20-21   *Peter answered: 'May your money perish with you, because you thought you could buy the gift of God with money!'* Use of the Greek optative mood to express a wish (*to argyrion sou syn soi eiē eis apōleian,* 'May your money go with you to destruction') implies a curse against Simon, 'consigning him and his money with him to destruction'.[57] Money cannot buy *the gift of God* (cf. 2:38; 10:45; 11:17). 'Magic seeks a craft that can rationally control the divine powers; it has no real place for 'gift' as the free disposition of the divine apart from human manipulation.'[58] Such a pagan worldview can only undermine the gospel and hinder its progress. Peter further declares, *'You have no part or share in this ministry, because your heart is*

---

53. Johnson 1992, 148. The longer reading 'Holy Spirit' is attested by a good range of early MSS, but the shorter reading 'Spirit' is more likely to be original since scribes tended to add rather than subtract such familiar words. Cf. Metzger, *Textual Commentary*, 314.

54. Johnson 1992, 152.

55. Garrett, *Demise*, 70.

56. Tannehill 1990, 107. He notes how different is the portrait of the apostles painted in Acts.

57. Marshall 1980, 159. Gk. *apōleia* ('destruction') is used with hades and death in the LXX to convey the idea of final destruction (e.g., Pr. 15:11; 27:20; Ezk. 26:19-21). The term is used for eternal destruction in the NT (e.g., Mt. 7:13; Jn. 17:12; Rom. 9:22; Phil. 3:19; 2 Thes. 2:3; 1 Tim. 6:9; 2 Pet. 2:1, 3; 3:7, 16; Rev. 17:8, 11), meaning 'an everlasting state of torment and death' (A. Oepke, *TDNT* 1:397).

58. Johnson 1992, 149.

not right before God'. TNIV translates *en tō logō toutō* as *in this ministry* (lit. 'in this thing'), which is certainly possible in the context. It is also possible that Peter means 'in this message', taking *logos* to refer to the gospel. Simon is showing himself to have no part or share in the gospel and its blessings. He appears to be unconverted, a pretender. The reason for this is that his *heart is not right before God* (cf. Ps. 78:37 [LXX 77:37], where *eutheia*, 'straightforward, frank, honest', is also used). 'Simon is attempting to cheat God, to infringe the divine prerogative of bestowing the Spirit in accordance with his own will.'[59] He does not understand the grace of God and has not yielded his heart to God's rule.

22-23   The only way for Simon to escape the judgment of God is to *'repent of this wickedness and pray to the Lord in the hope that he may forgive you for having such a thought in your heart'* (cf. Ps. 78:38). Here the call to repentance, which is normally associated with initial gospel proclamation (2:38; 3:19; 17:30; 26:20), is applied to one who has already made a profession of faith. The indefinite construction used in the Greek (*ei ara aphethēsetai soi hē epinoia tēs kardias sou*; NRSV, ESV 'if possible, the intent of your heart may be forgiven you') highlights the seriousness of the situation.[60] Simon cannot take the mercy of God for granted. Although he needs forgiveness for a specific sin *(for having such a thought in your heart)*, Peter discerns that this reveals a deep-seated, underlying problem that needs to be resolved. Simon is still *'full of bitterness and captive to sin'* (*eis cholēn pikrias kai syndesmon adikias*; KJV, ESV 'in the gall of bitterness and in the bond of iniquity').[61] This terminology recalls Deuteronomy 29:18 (LXX 29:17, *en cholē kai pikria*), where the image of a root producing 'bitter poison' describes a person going after false gods and leading others to do the same (cf. Heb. 12:15). The Lord's punishment for such people is severe (Dt. 29:20-21; Heb. 10:26-31). There was a bitter poison in Simon that needed to be extracted. The expression *captive to sin* appears to be an allusion to Isaiah 58:6 (*syndesmon adikias*, 'the bond of unrighteousness'). Clearly Simon had not experienced the release from captivity to sin which Jesus came to provide (cf. Lk. 4:18-19; Rom. 6:11-18). His inadequate understanding of the gospel made him an idolater, in danger of corrupting the new Samaritan converts with his beliefs. Longenecker rightly observes that, 'Simon's response to the presence of God's Spirit and the evidence of God's power is one of those tragic sto-

---

59. Barrett 1994, 415. Compare the way Peter exposes the corrupt hearts of Ananias and Sapphira in 5:3-9.

60. The use of *ei* plus the future indicative passive indicates a possible but uncertain condition. The use of *ara* strengthens the measure of doubt. C. F. D. Moule, *An Idiom Book of New Testament Greek* (Cambridge: Cambridge University, 1953), 158, suggests the translation 'in the hope that perhaps'.

61. Barrett 1994, 416-17, renders this expression '[full of] bitter poison and bound by unrighteousness', arguing that the *eis* is best understood in the sense of 'in' (hence 'full of'), describing the condition which Peter perceives rather than 'destined for, reserved for'. *Cholē* is used for 'gall, bile' (LXX Jb. 16:13; Pr. 5:4; Lam. 3:15; Mt. 27:34 [cf. Ps. 69:21]) or for 'poison, venom' (LXX Dt. 29:17; Jb. 20:14), translating different Hebrew words (BDAG).

ries that accompany every advance of the gospel. Whenever and wherever God is at work among people, there are not only genuine responses but also counterfeit ones.'[62]

24 *Then Simon answered, 'Pray to the Lord for me so that nothing you have said may happen to me'.* Simon perceives that he is in such bondage and that others must pray for his deliverance, but his desire seems to be 'to escape the consequences of his sin rather than to amend his life'.[63] Since Luke does not record the outcome for Simon, it is possible that he viewed his penitence as insincere. This lack of closure is often explained in terms of the original readers knowing something of the later developments recorded by the early church fathers and understanding that Simon remained unconverted. However, Garrett is rightly cautious about any supposition that Luke knew more than he was telling. We should rather consider how Simon's response contributes to the author's ongoing plot and character development. 'Satan in the person of his servant Simon has been trampled down. Satan does still have some power, but he is handily subjugated when confronted by the vastly greater divine authority that Christians wield.'[64] Attention is thus directed to the apostles again, who begin to share in Philip's ministry to the Samaritans even more extensively, unhindered by the devil.

25 *When they had further proclaimed the word of the Lord (lalēsantes ton logon) and testified (diamartyramenoi;* TNIV adds *about Jesus) in that place, Peter and John then returned to Jerusalem, preaching the gospel (euēngelizonto) in many Samaritan villages.* Luke combines familiar terms here, forming an inclusion with 8:4 *(euangelizomenoi ton logon)*, and making it clear that the apostles preached the same message as all the believers who had been scattered from Jerusalem.[65] Peter disappears from the narrative until 9:32, and John is mentioned again only in connection with his brother James (12:2). Luke is highly selective in the way he records the progress of the word and the ministry of the apostles.

62. Longenecker 1981, 360. Bruce 1988, 171-72, is more generous towards Simon than the text will allow!

63. Barrett 1994, 418. The Western text differs from other witnesses in adding words that express greater remorse and perhaps repentance: 'And Simon answered and said *to them, "I beseech you, pray for me to God, that none of these evils of which you have spoken to me* may come upon me" — *who did not stop weeping copiously'.* Cf. Metzger, *Textual Commentary,* 314. Garrett, *Demise,* 72, says that Simon resembles 'a cornered criminal, frightened at the prospect of punishment although not obviously remorseful over his crimes'.

64. Garrett, *Demise,* 73-74. Garrett 74, continues: 'Peter's righteous rebuke reduces Simon from a famous magician, impiously proclaimed by all the people of Samaria as "the great power of God", to a meek man who fears his own destruction and so asks the servant of the Lord to intercede for him (just as Pharaoh had requested of Moses)'.

65. As in 8:4, *hoi men oun* ('they then') marks the beginning of a new stage in the narrative.

F. The Word Goes to Ethiopia (8:26-40)

The Lord now leads Philip through the territory of Judea, with a sudden detour south to Gaza (8:26; directed by an angel of the Lord), and then a journey back up the coast to Caesarea (8:39-40; directed by the Spirit of the Lord). The encounter with the Ethiopian eunuch is clearly the centrepiece of this section, representing another remarkable step forward for the gospel. Tannehill observes that the Ethiopian is 'a very strong representative of foreignness within a Jewish context. He comes from the edge of the known world, of the black race, is a castrated male, and probably a Gentile.'[66] The prohibition against admitting eunuchs into the assembly of the Lord (Dt. 23:1) makes it unlikely that he was a Jewish proselyte in the full sense. However, he was certainly devout and God-fearing, having journeyed to Jerusalem to worship the God of Israel. He was a keen student of the Jewish Scriptures and was apparently fascinated with prophecies about God's plans for the future of his people. Philip explained the passage from Isaiah 53 to him in Christological terms and the Ethiopian was baptized. Tannehill argues that Philip initiated the mission to the Gentiles at this point and that in Acts 10 Luke shows how Peter and the Jerusalem church were 'brought to recognize that Gentiles can now be accepted through the conversion of Cornelius'.[67] However, this approach plays down the Cornelius incident and the initiative of Peter, which is clearly of great significance for Luke (10:1–11:18). More accurately, Johnson argues that 'the conversion of the Ethiopian does not yet represent a formal opening to the Gentiles, but rather to those who were marginalized within the people of God'.[68] The eunuch is portrayed as someone on the fringes of Judaism, who is drawn into the fellowship of Jewish Christianity through Philip's teaching about Jesus. Perhaps the promise of Isaiah 56:3-5, about eunuchs finding an honoured place among the renewed people of God, is particularly in Luke's mind as he records this story. At the same time, it is true that Philip makes contact with a representative of peoples at 'the ends of the earth' (1:8). Ethiopia had a much better claim than Rome to be described in that way (cf. Herodotus, *Hist.* 3.25.114; Strabo, *Geog.* 1.1.6; 1.2.24; Philostratus, *Apoll.* 6.1). 'A reasonable case can be made for seeing this narrative as being about the reaching of those from the parts of Africa that were at or beyond the borders of the empire, those that were at the ends of the earth.'[69] Luke tells us nothing of

66. Tannehill 1990, 108. Ethiopia (Cush) is represented in the OT as economically and militarily powerful, destined from a prophetic perspective to submit her people and resources to the service of the God of Israel (e.g., Jb. 28:19; Ps. 68:31; Is. 45:14; Zp. 3:9-10).

67. Tannehill 1990, 110. Barrett 1994, 421, argues that the difference between the incidents is that 'after his baptism the eunuch saw Philip no more but continued on his journey to his native Ethiopia, whereas Cornelius was baptized as one of a group who formed the kernel of a church which continued in existence and in relation with the church of Jerusalem'.

68. Johnson 1992, 160. Cf. Wilson, *Gentiles,* 171-72; Witherington 1998, 293.

69. Witherington 1998, 293.

the impact of the Ethiopian's conversion on his own people but, from a narrative point of view, the story 'forms part of the gradual progress of the church towards the Gentiles'.[70]

1. A Divinely Arranged Encounter (8:26-31)

The focus is first on the process by which the Lord achieved a meeting between Philip and an unnamed Ethiopian court official. In Acts 8–11 Luke progressively exposes the way God made it possible for the gospel to move out from Jerusalem, thus fulfilling the promise in 1:8. The strangeness of this particular encounter is highlighted by a brief characterization of the Ethiopian (vv. 27-28, 31), explaining his readiness to be taught by Philip from the Jewish Scriptures. Thus begins the first of three significant 'conversion' accounts, each illustrating the kind of transformation appropriate to different individuals from different religious and cultural backgrounds (cf. Saul in 9:1-19 and Cornelius in 10:1-48). The Ethiopian is apparently a would-be proselyte, prevented by his condition as a eunuch from entering fully into Jewish life, but ready to receive the gospel proclaimed by Philip.

26 *Now an angel of the Lord said to Philip, 'Go south to the road — the desert road — that goes down from Jerusalem to Gaza'.* The word *now* brings out the contrast between this verse and the preceding one implied by the Greek: Peter and John went on their way to Jerusalem (v. 25, *men*), but an angel of the Lord directed Philip further south (v. 26, *de*). Alerted to the way in which Philip had been identified as a prophet (being filled with the Spirit, working signs and wonders, proclaiming the word of God), we may discern in this narrative certain parallels with the prophet Elijah.[71] Philip is addressed by *an angel of the Lord* (cf. 2 Ki. 1:15), moved from place to place by the Spirit (8:29, 39; cf. 1 Ki. 18:12), and runs down the road with the chariot of an important person (8:30; cf. 1 Ki. 18:46). References to an angel and the Spirit highlight the fact that the initiative in this mission is entirely with God. It is unclear whether Philip and the Ethiopian were approaching Gaza on the direct route to Jerusalem or on the coast road.[72] It is also unclear whether *Gaza* here means the old deserted city, which was destroyed by Alexander Jannaeus in 96 BC, or the newer city which replaced it in 56 BC

---

70. Marshall 1980, 160. There is no record of an Ethiopian church earlier than the fourth century, but this does not mean that the eunuch was unsuccessful in planting a church in his own country. Cf. Irenaeus, *Against Heresies* 3.12.10; B. M. Metzger, 'The Christianization of Nubia and the Old Nubian Version of the New Testament', *Historical and Literary Studies: Pagan, Jewish and Christian*, NTTS 8 (Leiden: Brill, 1968), 111-22.

71. So Johnson 1992, 158. Witherington 1998, 292, argues that Luke has 'written up his own source material so that it has the sound and the "echoes" of certain aspects of the narratives of the LXX (more a matter of style than substance), in this case the Elijah-Elisha cycle'. Witherington also notes echoes of the Emmaus-road story in Luke 24.

72. Cf. Barrett 1994, 423. It is thus unclear whether Philip begins this journey from Samaria or from Jerusalem.

(*hautē estin erēmos*, 'this is desert', might apply either to Gaza or to the road). Since the action takes place on the road, the city itself plays no part in the story, and TNIV is probably right to translate *the desert road*. More significantly, the angelic command took Philip away from 'the scene of successful evangelism and led him to a place which must have seemed entirely inappropriate for further Christian work'.[73] It is possible that the expression translated *south (kata mesēmbrian)* should be rendered 'at midday', which would make the divine command to meet a traveler on a hot desert road at that time all the more unusual.[74]

27-28 *So he started out, and on his way he met an Ethiopian eunuch, an important official in charge of all the treasury of Kandake (which means 'queen of the Ethiopians').* Ethopia is known in the Bible as the land of Cush (e.g., Gn. 2:13; Ezk. 29:10). This does not correspond to modern Ethiopia (Abyssinia), but to the Nubian kingdom whose capital was Meroe, south of Egypt, which is today part of Sudan. In Isaiah 11:11, Cush is specified as one of the lands from which the Lord will 'reclaim the remnant that is left of his people', when the Messiah stands 'as a banner for the peoples' and the nations 'rally to him' (cf. Ps. 68:3; Zp. 3:9-10). Luke draws particular attention to the Ethiopian's high social status.[75] His function as chief finance officer in the Ethiopian court made him directly responsible to *Kandake* (Gk. *Kandakēs*, rendered Candace in most EVV), who was *queen of the Ethiopians. Kandake* was a dynastic rather than a personal name, applied to a succession of queens over several generations.[76] Castrated males held positions of honour and trust in oriental courts (cf. Herodotus, *Persian Wars* 8.105; Philostratus, *Apoll.* 1.33-36). Such people were excluded from becoming full proselytes of Judaism (cf. Dt. 23:1). It is possible that *eunuch* simply refers to a man impotent from birth (cf. Is. 56:3-5), but his 'station as treasurer and servant to a queen suggest that he was both a man of position and a physical eunuch'.[77] The genuineness of his devotion to the God of Israel is revealed in the statement that he had made a considerable journey to Jerusa-

73. Marshall 1980, 161; Gaventa 2003, 141.

74. Cf. Barrett 1994, 422-23. There are twenty-five uses of *mesēmbria* in the LXX and all except Dn. 8:4, 9 appear to mean 'midday'. Cf. Acts 22:6 for Saul's conversion 'at noon' *(peri mesēmbrian).* Spencer 1997, 94, argues that travel at such an extraordinary time and under such unusual circumstances has the literary effect of suggesting an opportunity for 'world-shattering knowledge and experience'.

75. Witherington 1998, 295, suggests that Luke's interest in the conversion of people of relatively high social status may have been partly related to the standing of Theophilus and others addressed by Luke-Acts. Johnson 1992, 158, notes that 'it is no small part of apologetic literature to emphasize how one's special claims have met with approval from respectable people (see, e.g., Josephus, *Against Apion* 1.176-212)'.

76. Hence TNIV *(which means 'queen of the Ethiopians').* Cf. Johnson 1992, 155; Barrett 1994, 425; Bruce 1990, 175 note 61.

77. P. H. Kern, 'Paul's Conversion and Luke's Portrayal of Character in Acts 8–10', *TynB* 54 (2003), 65. Kern 67, observes that the eunuch represents 'the ultimate outsider, not even capable of circumcision should he desire it, and inadmissible to the temple'. Cf. Spencer 1997, 93.

lem *to worship* (the future participle *proskynēsōn*, indicating purpose). This probably took place in the Court of the Gentiles at the temple, though his involvement must have been limited.[78] The genuineness of his faith is further illustrated by the fact that, *on his way home*, he was *sitting in his chariot reading the Book of Isaiah the prophet*. It is a measure of his enthusiasm and wealth that he possessed his own copy of a biblical book. His journey to Jerusalem left him with a hunger to know the Scriptures better, but with no one to guide him.

29-31   *The Spirit told Philip, 'Go to that chariot and stay near it'.* Luke carefully outlines the different stages by which Philip was enabled to speak to the Ethiopian. The angel sent him on his way without mentioning the possibility of such an encounter (8:26). *The Spirit* then gave Philip the inward assurance that he should approach this high-ranking man, from such a distant culture. This assurance came before Philip *ran up to the chariot and heard the man reading Isaiah the prophet*. The chariot might have been an ox-drawn wagon, moving at not much more than a walking pace. Its occupant clearly followed the ancient custom of reading aloud. Realizing the opportunity he had to proclaim Christ, Philip then took the initiative and asked, *'Do you understand what you are reading?'* Acknowledging his need for someone to interpret, the Ethiopian took the next step and *invited Philip to come up and sit with him.* Jesus is the key to unlock the meaning of the OT (Lk. 24:25-27; 44-47) and passages such as the one being read by the Ethiopian cannot be satisfactorily understood apart from their fulfillment in him.

2. Finding Christ in the Scriptures (8:32-38)

Luke continues to show how God was sovereign in this situation, providing Philip with Isaiah 53:7-8 as a basis for proclaiming Christ! Given Jesus' application of this prophecy to his impending suffering (specifically Is. 53:12 in Lk. 22:37), it is not surprising to read that Philip used it to proclaim the gospel to the Ethiopian. The Christological significance of the passage 'could very well have been fixed quite early in Christian thought'.[79] The

---

78. D. R. Schwartz, 'On Sacrifice by Gentiles in the Temple of Jerusalem', in *Studies in the Jewish Background of Christianity*, WUNT 60 (Tübingen: Mohr, 1992), 102-16, argues from rabbinic evidence and the writings of Josephus that Gentiles could make voluntary offerings, such as gifts and sacrifices resultant from vows, but not offer the sacrifices required of Israel in the law. Gentile sacrifices could have been regarded as gifts brought to the temple authorities for the upkeep of the building or for the use of others in the temple ritual, but not strictly for the benefit of the offerer. The 'worship' of Cornelius may simply have involved prostrating himself in prayer. Cf. D. G. Peterson, *Engaging with God: A Biblical Theology of Worship* (Leicester: Apollos; Grand Rapids: Eerdmans, 1992), 57-63.

79. R. N. Longenecker, *Biblical Exegesis in the Apostolic Period* (Grand Rapids: Eerdmans, 1975), 102. Bruce 1990, 227-29, discusses Jewish interpretations of Is. 52:13–53:12. It was suggested in connection with Acts 3:13 and the application of the term *pais* ('servant')

portion that is cited speaks only of the Servant's humble submission to an unjust death, though Philip may have explained the atoning significance of Christ's death and the consequences of his resurrection from the oracle as a whole (Is. 52:13–53:12).[80] When the Ethiopian suggests his own baptism and this takes place immediately (vv. 36-38), the implication is that some period of instruction intervened, allowing Philip to explain the meaning of baptism and the nature of commitment to the risen Lord Jesus. 'Luke offers a story suffused with the unexpected, and in so doing he presents the Ethiopian as the ideal convert, one who is already seeking God, who hears and responds, and who rejoices in the gift of the gospel.'[81]

32-33 *This is the passage of Scripture the eunuch was reading: 'He was led like a sheep to the slaughter, and as a lamb before its shearer is silent, so he did not open his mouth. In his humiliation he was deprived of justice. Who can speak of his descendants? For his life was taken from the earth.'* The point has sometimes been made that the quotation contains no specific reference to the Servant of the Lord or to his vicarious suffering. Indeed, the final words of Isaiah 53:8 ('for the transgression of my people he was punished') are not cited. However, 'a common-sense view of the verses suggests that on a long slow journey the Ethiopian would be likely to cover more than six lines, and that these are quoted as a summary of a longer passage'.[82] The quotation takes us to the whole so-called Servant Song (Is. 52:13–53:12) and is to be understood in that literary and theological context.[83] Elsewhere in the NT, we find verses from this passage quoted at Luke 22:37; John 12:38; Romans 10:16; and 1 Peter 2:21-25. However, the Song appears to have had greater influence on early Christian thinking about the death of Christ than even these quotations would suggest. The LXX version of the passage is quoted here with small variations.[84] The Servant is submissive and silent before those who would oppress and afflict him. He is humiliated to the extent that he is *deprived of justice* (*hē krisis autou ērthē*; KJV 'his judgment was taken away'). He appears to have no descendants (*tēn genean autou tis diēgēsetai*; NRSV, ESV *Who can describe his generation?*) because *his life was taken from the earth.*[85] But the wider context reveals that his punishment was

---

to Jesus there that Peter proclaimed the fulfillment of the Fourth Servant Song in the death and exaltation of Jesus. Cf. 3:26; 4:27, 30.

80. Cf. THE THEOLOGY OF ACTS: VI. THE ATONING WORK OF JESUS (pp. 75-79).

81. Gaventa 2003, 145.

82. Barrett 1994, 429.

83. Often in the NT verses from the OT are quoted as a way of referring to the whole context from which they are taken. Cf. C. H. Dodd, *According to the Scriptures: The Sub-Structure of the New Testament* (London: Nisbet, 1952), 88-94.

84. Cf. Barrett 1994, 430; Johnson 1992, 156.

85. Against Barrett 1994, 431-32; Johnson 1992, 156, it seems unnatural in this context to take 'his descendants' as a reference to disciples, who are so numerous because of the Servant's sacrifice. This is more the sense of Is. 53:10-11. Rather, the text suggests that he had no physical offspring because of his untimely death. Again, Barrett's suggestion that *his life was taken from the earth* refers to Christ's ascension seems an unnatural way to apply the text.

for the sins of others and that he brings them peace and healing because of his suffering (Is. 53:4-6, 11-12). Moreover, he is 'raised and lifted up and highly exalted' (52:13), and 'will see his offspring and prolong his days' (53:10).

34-35 The eunuch does not ask Philip for a general explanation of the passage but specifically inquires, '*Who is the prophet talking about, himself or someone else?*' Various views about the interpretation of the Suffering Servant were held by Jews in NT times.[86] But Philip, already convinced about its Christological application, *began with that very passage of Scripture and told him the good news about Jesus* (*euēngelisato autō ton Iēsoun;* NKJV 'preached Jesus to him'). Jesus saw himself as fulfilling the role of the Servant and must have passed on that interpretation to his earliest disciples.[87] The passage continues to be a powerful testimony to the person and work of Jesus and an effective means of evangelism. It begins with the claim that the Servant's suffering and exaltation will benefit many nations (52:13-15). It continues with the amazing story of his rejection and suffering, claiming that this punishment by God was 'for our transgressions' (53:1-6). Then comes the portion that the Ethiopian was reading, with its focus on the Servant's willingness to suffer and experience injustice (53:7-9). The passage concludes with a further statement of God's intention to make his life 'an offering for sin', to 'justify many', and to 'bear their iniquities' (53:10-12). The thoughtful reader may indeed ask, *who is the prophet talking about, himself or someone else?* There is no one else in history, apart from Jesus of Nazareth, to whom these words can truly be applied.

36-38 *As they travelled along the road, they came to some water and the eunuch said, 'Look, here is water. What can stand in the way of my being baptized?'* (*ti kōlyei me baptithēnai;* ESV 'what prevents me from being baptized?') This question presumes the passage of time and some instruction from Philip about the way to turn to Christ and receive the benefits of his death and resurrection through baptism. Of course, it is also possible that the Ethiopian had learned something about the process of Christian initiation during his stay in Jerusalem. What is remarkable, however, is that he takes the initiative at this point, signifying a real work of God in his heart. The provision of water for baptism in that place is another indication of God's sovereignty over the whole affair. Verse 37 is found in only a few Western MSS and in some texts of other ancient versions of the NT. Although it does not occur in the early and highly regarded Alexandrian textual tradition, it found its way into the so-called Received Text, which was influenced by the editions of the Greek NT edited by Erasmus, 'who

---

86. Cf. J. Jeremias, *TDNT* 5:682-700. Barrett 1994, 430-31, takes issue with the view of Jeremias that there was at this time a strand of interpretation that identified the Servant with the Messiah.

87. Cf. R. T. France, *Jesus and the Old Testament* (London: Tyndale, 1971), 26-52; J. Jeremias, *TDNT* 5:700-717.

thought it had been omitted through scribal carelessness'.[88] It is read by KJV and NKJV because of the reliance of those translations on the Received Text. On the ground of poor attestation, it is unlikely to have been part of the original text of Acts, but was presumably added because copyists felt that the Ethiopian would not have been baptized without such a confession of faith. It responds to the question in v. 36 and reads: 'Philip said to him, "If you believe with all your heart, you may". And he replied, "I believe that Jesus Christ is the Son of God".' Having made the conditions for baptism clear in an earlier passage (cf. 2:38-39), Luke had no need to spell them out again in this context. So the Ethiopian *gave orders to stop the chariot. Then both Philip and the eunuch went down into the water and Philip baptized him.* Once again the text is brief and mentions little about the way this baptism was conducted. The words *went down into the water* (*katebēsen eis to hydōr*) mean 'went down from the chariot into the water' here and do not necessarily mean that the Ethiopian was fully immersed in whatever water was available.

3. Philip's Continuing Ministry (8:39-40)

Luke brings a simple closure to the narrative by indicating the immediate outcome of this encounter for Philip and the Ethiopian. But we hear nothing more of Philip until much later in the narrative (21:8-9), and we are given no hint of the consequences for the Ethiopian and the country to which he was returning. This reinforces the view taken above, that Luke is progressively exposing the way God made it possible for the gospel to move out from Jerusalem by recording a series of conversion accounts.[89]

39-40 *When they came up out of the water, the Spirit of the Lord suddenly took Philip away, and the eunuch did not see him again, but went on his way rejoicing.* Once more the focus is on the sovereign action of the Spirit in directing Philip to another evangelistic opportunity. When Luke says that the Spirit *suddenly took Philip away* (*hērpasen ton Philippon*), the meaning is that the Spirit 'seized' or 'took hold of' Philip and moved him on to a new place (cf. Mt. 11:12; 12:29; 13:19; Jn. 6:15; Acts 23:10). There is no need to conclude that 'the Spirit brings Philip by supernatural means to Azotus',[90] though the emphasis is clearly on the Spirit's forceful direction of Philip.

---

88. Bruce 1990, 229. Cf. Metzger, *Textual Commentary*, 315-16; Barrett 1994, 433; INTRODUCTION TO ACTS: VI. TEXTUAL MATTERS (pp. 49-52).

89. Gaventa 1986, 107, describes the Ethiopian's experience as an 'alteration' rather than a 'conversion', meaning that his Christian commitment grew out of his prior understanding of Scripture and faith in the God of Israel. However, see my discussion about conversion in the introduction to Acts 9.

90. Barrett 1994, 435. This verb can be used with reference to the rapture of persons to heaven or to God (2 Cor. 12:2, 4; 1 Thes. 4:17; Rev. 12:5), but that is obviously not the meaning in this context.

He *appeared* (*heurethē,* 'was found') *at Azotus,* which is the Ashdod of the OT (modern Esdud), just over 20 miles (32 km.) up the coast from Gaza. From there, he *travelled about, preaching the gospel in all the towns until he reached Caesarea,* which is 55 miles or so (more than 88 km.) further up the coast and was the capital of Roman Judea.[91] Several textual witnesses read 'the Holy Spirit fell on the eunuch and an angel of the Lord caught up Philip'.[92] This longer reading is another testimony to the concern of copyists to fill out the story, indicating that the Ethiopian actually received the Spirit when he was baptized. Such additions suggest that the passage may have been used with reference to the practice of baptism in the early church. But the shorter reading is the best attested and is consistent with the brevity of Luke's account at this point in the narrative. Philip next appears in Acts, at a much later date, as settled in Caesarea with his four unmarried daughters (21:8-9).

G. Saul's Conversion and Commissioning (9:1-19a)

Saul of Tarsus (9:11; 22:3), later called Paul (13:9), was previously introduced in connection with the death of Stephen (7:58; 8:1), and was then identified as the leader in a campaign of devastating persecution against the early church (8:3; cf. 1 Cor. 15:9; Gal. 1:13; Phil. 3:6; 1 Tim. 1:13). As the testimony to the risen Christ moved out from Jerusalem (8:4-40), so did the persecution. But on the road to Damascus, the arch-persecutor met the glorified Lord Jesus and was transformed (cf. 1 Cor. 9:1; 15:8; Gal. 1:15-16). This brought a period of peace for the church and led to a whole new phase of growth (9:31). So important is the event that Luke gives three versions of it (cf. 22:3-21; 26:9-18). The second and third are autobiographical in style, forming part of Paul's defence before a hostile Jewish crowd in one case, and before a bemused King Agrippa in the other. The turning of a Pharisaic persecutor into a Christian apologist and missionary is 'a paradox so profound that it requires multiple retellings, with each version bringing out some further nuances of significance'.[1] Luke, however, is not interested in exploring the psychological dimensions of Saul's transformation. The emphasis in this first account is on the sovereign, merciful intervention of God

91. Barrett 1994, 436, notes that Caesarea was named in honour of the Emperor Augustus, when Herod the Great rebuilt it with great magnificence. The population was chiefly Gentile (Josephus, *War* 3.409), and there were many conflicts between Jews and Greeks, until the Jewish population was massacred in AD 66.

92. Cf. Metzger, *Textual Commentary,* 316. Marshall 1980, 165, argues that 'although the MS evidence for the longer text is weak, it could be original'.

1. Johnson 1992, 166. Barrett 1994, 439-41, 444-45, provides a helpful comparison of the three accounts and argues that 'the agreements are much more important than the disagreements'. Cf. D. M. Stanley, 'Why Three Accounts?', *CBQ* 15 (1953), 315-18; C. W. Hedrick, 'Paul's Conversion/Call: A Comparative Analysis of the Three Reports in Acts', *JBL* 100 (1981), 415-32; Witherington 1998, 305-14.

in Saul's life. This brings him to Christ and makes him 'a chosen instrument', destined to carry Christ's name 'before the Gentiles and their kings and before the people of Israel' and to suffer for the sake of that name (9:15-16). A distinctive feature of each version of this story is the identification of the risen Lord with the church. The declaration 'I am Jesus, whom you are persecuting' (9:5; 22:8; 26:15) suggests that the exalted Christ is present through his Spirit with his people on earth (cf. 2:33). They, for their part, are united with him through faith and baptism and in their willingness to suffer with him and for his sake. So for Saul, 'if the living and powerful Lord identifies himself with this community, then joining this community is the sign of obedience to his presence'.[2] In Acts 9, Luke continues to reveal more of what it means to be part of the Messiah's people.

Some have argued that what follows should not be called a conversion account, since Saul did not change his religion or abandon his loyalty to the God of Israel, but came to experience the fulfillment of Jewish hopes in Jesus as Messiah. Furthermore, parallels with certain OT narratives suggest to these scholars that it is rather a commissioning, story.[3] However, what is meant by conversion in this debate? Luke's approach can be discerned by examining his notion of 'turning' to the Lord and 'repenting',[4] and by observing certain features of his narrative method. Peter's paradigmatic address on the Day of Pentecost (2:36-40) suggests a way of defining conversion that is applicable to the various individuals and groups that are progressively introduced in subsequent chapters. In positive terms, the challenge is to turn to Jesus as Lord and Messiah, to receive the salvation proclaimed in his name. In negative terms, Jews in Jerusalem are called to repent of their rejection of Jesus (2:36-38; 3:17-20; 5:30-31), whereas pagans in Lystra (14:15-17) and Athens (17:22-31) are later called to turn from idolatry. In some narratives, a negative challenge is not articulated, though Luke ultimately makes it clear that repentance towards God and faith in the Lord Jesus are demanded of 'both Jews and Greeks' (20:21; cf. 26:17-18, 20). Observing that there are three 'conversion' stories in Acts 8–10 (the Ethiopian, Saul, and Cornelius), we may note that Saul lacks the virtues of

2. Johnson 1992, 168. Saul's calling includes the specific promise, 'I will show him how much he must suffer for my name' (9:16; cf. the apostles in 5:41).

3. K. Stendahl, 'The Apostle Paul and the Introspective Conscience of the West', *HTR* 56 (1963), 199-215, and *Paul among Jews and Gentiles — and Other Essays* (Philadelphia: Fortress, 1976), 7-23, is the most articulate exponent of this view. Barrett 1994, 441-42, notes the parallels with theophany stories in Jewish literature (e.g., 2 Macc. 3; *Joseph and Aseneth* 10:15; 14:6-8), arguing that the resemblances are 'unmistakable, but superficial'.

4. The verb 'turn' *(epistrephein)* is used extensively (3:19; 9:35; 11:21; 14:15; 15:19; 26:18, 20; 28:27) to describe the response required of people from various religious and cultural backgrounds to the gospel. The verb 'repent' *(metanoein)* and the cognate noun *(metanoia)* are similarly used to describe the reorientation of life towards God and the exalted Lord Jesus that mark the beginning of Christian discipleship (2:38; 3:19; 5:31; 11:18; 17:30; 20:21; 26:20). The challenge to Simon in 8:22 is to make real the commitment to Christ ostensibly expressed in his baptism (8:13).

either the Ethiopian eunuch or Cornelius. 'He is not presented as searching the Scriptures to understand the Suffering Servant — he has already formed his assessment of Jesus and his followers. Nor is he presented as a pious follower of God.'[5] Rather, through various means, Luke characterizes Saul as God's enemy, 'stiff-necked' and resisting the Holy Spirit like all the other opponents of Stephen (7:51-52). He has murderous intentions against 'the Lord's disciples' (8:3; 9:1) and is set like Herod and Pontius Pilate 'against the Lord and his anointed one' (4:26-27; cf. 9:4-5). He experiences a blinding like that of Elymas, who is later described as 'an enemy of everything that is right', who perverts the ways of the Lord (13:10-11; cf. 9:8-9). Finally, Luke demonstrates Saul's changed relationship with God by showing how he becomes 'totally immersed in, and advances the cause of, the community which he formerly sought to destroy'.[6] In the flow of Luke's narrative, then, the story in 9:1-19 appears as both a conversion and a commissioning of Saul.

1. Meeting the Ascended Lord (9:1-9)

Saul experiences a Christophany in broad daylight, in which 'a light from heaven' surrounds him and he is addressed by the voice of Jesus. This encounter has a physical as well as a spiritual effect on him (vv. 3-9). As well as being temporally blinded, he is humbled by the encounter and is moved to fast for three days, before being visited by Ananias and being told what he must do. Even in this brief passage, the change in Saul — from the opening description (vv. 1-2) to the concluding one (vv. 8-9) — is dramatic. At first glance, this seems to be a resurrection appearance like those recorded in Luke 24:13-49. Like no one else in Acts apart from the apostles, Saul is latter described as having 'seen the Lord' and being addressed by him (9:27). However, in the post-ascension situation, it is likely that this encounter lacked the physicality emphasized in Luke 24 or in Acts 1:3-4.[7]

---

5. P. H. Kern, 'Paul's Conversion and Luke's Portrayal of Character in Acts 8–10', *TynB* 54 (2003), 73. B. R. Gaventa, *From Darkness to Light: Aspects of Conversion in the New Testament*, Overtures to Biblical Theology 20 (Philadelphia: Fortress, 1986), 107, 122, labels the experience of both the Ethiopian and Cornelius as an 'alteration', since their new position in Christ grew out of previous commitments to the God of Israel and there is no challenge in Luke's narrative for them to reject past commitments. However, turning to Jesus in both cases involved a transformed view of the world and God's purpose, with the crucified and resurrected Saviour at the centre. In that sense, each was a life-changing conversion.

6. Kern, 'Conversion', 73. Cf. S. Cunningham, *'Through many tribulations': The Theology of Persecution in Luke-Acts*, JSNTSS 142 (Sheffield: Sheffield Academic, 1997), 204-6; Gaventa 2003, 155-56.

7. Marshall 1980, 169, argues that 'the account is of a revelation of Jesus from heaven rather than an appearance of Jesus before his ascension, and therefore we are not to think of Jesus appearing in such a form that he might (for example) be confused with an ordinary traveller (Lk. 24:15)'. S. Kim, *The Origin of Paul's Gospel* (Grand Rapids: Eerdmans, 1982; first

1-2 Luke makes a link with 8:3 by reminding us that *Saul was still (eti) breathing out murderous threats against the Lord's disciples* (TNIV and NRSV clarify that link by adding the word 'meanwhile'). Saul is described in language that recalls 7:51-52, suggesting that he was now 'the major representative of the attitude condemned by Stephen'.[8] He was so opposed to this new movement that he threatened to slaughter the Christians and in some cases actually carried out his threats (22:4; 26:10).[9] Moreover, his indiscriminate anger was directed against Christians of both sexes (*whether men or women;* cf. 8:3). Saul doubtless believed that he was following godly precedents in rooting out these dangerous schismatics and apostates from the law of Moses.[10] But his behaviour demonstrated that he was stiff-necked, resisting the Holy Spirit, and in no mood to consider the claims of Christ. 'Saul is a Jew, but his behavior as enemy has removed him from those who may legitimately be called "brother".'[11] Luke's narrative therefore stresses the sovereign grace of God in transforming one so utterly opposed to his will. In this frame of mind, Saul *went to the high priest* (Caiaphas from AD 18 to 36; cf. 4:6 note) *and asked him for letters to the synagogues in Damascus* (22:5 implies that 'all the council' were involved with the high priest in giving him letters). Such letters presuppose some authority on the part of the high priest over Jewish communities outside Palestine. How such authority was exercised cannot be determined with certainty. The idea that he might take members of the synagogues *as prisoners to Jerusalem,* rather than punish them locally, could imply a formal right of extradition. But Saul's authority in this case may have depended on the goodwill of the local synagogues as much as on the letters of the high priest.[12]

---

published as WUNT 4 [Tübingen: Mohr Siebeck], 1981), 56, argues that Paul's use of the terminology of *apokalypsis* ('revelation') for this Christophany (cf. Gal. 1:12, 16) suggests that it was 'a proleptic realization or an anticipation of the parousia and that Christ was revealed to Paul in the form in which he will come at the end-time'.

8. Tannehill 1990, 114, following Gaventa, *Darkness,* 55. S. Légasse, 'Paul's Pre-Christian Career according to Acts', in R. Bauckham (ed.), *The Book of Acts in Its First-Century Setting,* Vol. 4: *Palestinian Setting* (Grand Rapids: Eerdmans; Carlisle: Paternoster, 1995), 365-90, provides a helpful summary of the evidence regarding Paul's pre-Christian career and activity. Cf. Kim, *Origin,* 32-50.

9. Literally, the Greek says that Saul was 'breathing threatening and slaughter' (*empneōn apeilēs kai phonou*). Barrett 1994, 445, rejects the reading of a hendiadys here (TNIV 'murderous threats'), arguing that a progression from threat to killing is intended by Luke (most EVV have 'breathing threats and murder').

10. Cf. Nu. 25:1-15; 1 Macc. 2:23-28, 42-48; Longenecker 1981, 368-69. Kim, *Origin,* 32-50, argues that Paul persecuted the Christians for two particular reasons: because of their attack on the law of Moses and because of their proclamation of the crucified Jesus as Messiah.

11. Gaventa, *Darkness,* 123.

12. Barrett 1994, 446-47, evaluates the available historical evidence and concludes that 'the extent to which Jews outside Judaea were willing to obey the orders of the Sanhedrin always depended on how far they were favourably disposed to it'. Cf. B. Rapske, *The*

Damascus, which is about 135 miles (217 km.) from Jerusalem, was one of ten self-governing cities in the Decapolis League. It was a prosperous commercial centre in the Roman province of Syria, with a large Jewish population and several *synagogues*.[13] Luke has not told us about a church being planted there, but disciples such as Ananias are mentioned (9:10, 14, 19). This is an indication that Luke is selective in telling us about the way the gospel spread and the church grew (cf. 9:31 note). Since Ananias had only 'heard many reports' about Saul (9:13), he can hardly have been a recent refugee from Jerusalem. He was probably one of several Christians already living in Damascus and perhaps still a member of a synagogue. When Luke stresses that Saul was opposing *the Lord's disciples (tous mathētas tou kyriou)*,[14] this is clearly a parallel way of describing *the church* (8:3). *The Lord* is doubtless a reference to the Lord Jesus in this context, especially in view of vv. 4-6, 10-17. For the first time in Acts, disciples of Jesus are then further distinguished from other Jews by being designated as those who *belonged to the Way (tinas tēs hodou*, 'any of the way'; cf. 19:9, 23; 22:4; 24:14, 22). Luke alone in the NT uses this terminology to describe Christians. Other terms, such as 'the way of salvation' (16:17), 'the way of the Lord' (18:25), and 'the way of God' (18:26), are related and may explain the origin of the abbreviated term *the Way*. What presumably began as a reference to the messianic salvation and the call to follow Jesus was adapted to describe those who responded and became disciples.[15] As this chapter progresses, Luke records other terms that help identify the character of the church ('saints' [v. 13], 'all who call on your name' [v. 14], 'brother[s]' [vv. 17, 30]). The words of the risen Christ to Saul (vv. 4, 5) throw further light on this. Luke's concluding summary (v. 31) indicates how 'the whole church throughout Judea, Galilee and Samaria' survived and was strengthened through the period of Saul's persecuting activity and its sequel. So there is a particular focus in this section on how the church emerged from its Jewish roots and came to identify itself as a distinct entity.[16] Paul paradoxically

---

Book of Acts in Its First-Century Setting, Vol. 3: *The Book of Acts and Paul in Roman Custody* (Grand Rapids: Eerdmans; Carlisle: Paternoster, 1994), 100-102; Bruce 1998, 180-81; Witherington 1998, 315-16; Josephus, *Ant.* 14.192-95.

13. Cf. Witherington 1998, 316. For background information on Syria in the first century, see R. Tracey, 'Syria', in D. W. J. Gill and C. Gempf (eds.), *The Book of Acts in Its First-Century Setting*, Vol. 2: *Graeco-Roman Setting* (Grand Rapids: Eerdmans; Carlisle: Paternoster, 1994), 223-78.

14. This is the only time in Acts when the expression *the Lord's disciples* is used, though *mathētēs* ('disciple') is employed frequently to describe Christians, notably six times in this chapter (9:1, 10, 19, 26 [twice], 38). The reference in 9:25 is probably to Paul's disciples.

15. Barrett 1994, 448, discusses possible parallels in the Qumran texts. The language is reminiscent of biblical teaching about the 'two ways' (e.g., Pss. 1:1-6; 119:26-30; Mt. 7:13-27; Mk. 12:14). However, the soteriological overtones in the usage of Acts suggest that it goes beyond the 'two ways' discussion of Jewish and early Christian literature, which has 'more of a parenetic focus' (Witherington 1998, 316). Cf. *1 Enoch* 91:18; *2 Enoch* 30:15; *Test. Asher* 3:1-6:5; *Sib. Or.* 8:399; *Did.* 1-6; *Barn.* 18-21; G. Ebel, *NIDNTT* 3:935-43.

16. The term 'Christian' was first used at Antioch in Syria (11:26) and is mentioned

joins *the Way* because of what happens to him when he is 'on the way' (vv. 17, 27, *en tē hodō*) to persecute Christians in Damascus.[17]

3 *As he neared Damascus on his journey, suddenly a light from heaven flashed around him.* The appearance of lightning or of a brilliance like lightning is a feature of theophanies in the Bible (e.g., Ex. 19:16; 2 Sa. 22:13, 15; Pss. 77:18; 97:4; 144:5-6; Ezk. 1:4, 13, 14; Dn. 10:6; Lk. 9:29; 17:24; 24:4). This supernatural light outshone the noonday sun (cf. 22:6). Subsequent references in Acts make it clear that Saul saw the exalted Messiah, not just *a light from heaven* (*phōs ek tou ouranou*; cf. 22:14-15; 26:16).[18] Yet in all three accounts the brilliant light is emphasized, and in the first two Saul is blinded and has to have his sight restored. The light in this context appears to be a manifestation of Christ's heavenly glory (cf. 2 Cor. 4:6). The supernatural impacts on the natural as Saul is blinded. But there is also a symbolic aspect to this light. Saul is 'forced by the Messiah's light to recognize his own blindness and to receive his sight through him'.[19] Having seen the light of Christ himself, Saul was then required to bear witness to what he had seen and heard (22:14-15; 26:16). The risen Lord Jesus appointed him to fulfill the Servant's role outlined in Isaiah 49:6 and become 'a light for the Gentiles' (Acts 13:47; cf. 26:17-18, 23).

As noted above, parallels with certain OT narratives (e.g., Ex. 3:2-4; Is. 6:1-13; Je. 1:4-10) have suggested to some commentators that this event should be described as a call rather than as a conversion.[20] The call element is clear from what follows, but the conversion element cannot be ignored. Saul did not find a new God to worship, but he discovered that he had been in rebellion against the God of Abraham, Isaac, and Jacob by refusing to acknowledge Jesus as the Son of God (cf. 9:20 note) and Messiah (cf. 9:22). His persecution of the Lord's disciples (9:1), by which he sought to destroy the church (8:3), meant that he was actively opposing God's saving purpose for Israel and the nations. Acts 9:1-30 marks a radical change of religious direction accompanied by a radical change of action. The active persecutor became an even more active preacher and evangelist, and he who made others suffer for calling upon the name of Jesus came to suffer himself for the

---

only once again in Acts (26:28; cf. 1 Pet. 4:16). Jewish opponents spoke of Christians as members of 'the Nazarene sect' (24:5, *tēs tōn Nazōraiōn haireseōs*; cf. 24:14; 28:22, *hairesis*, 'sect').

17. Spencer 1997, 96-100, discusses the significance of three distinctive locations in this story: the road to Damascus (9:1-9), the house on Straight Street (9:10-19), and the synagogue in Damascus (9:20-22).

18. Note also that Barnabas reports how Saul had 'seen the Lord' (9:27). In 1 Cor. 9:1 Paul claims that he is an apostle because he has 'seen Jesus our Lord', and in 1 Cor. 15:5-8 he lists this as the last in a series of resurrection appearances to the apostles and others. Barrett 1994, 449, says it is pointless to ask whether Luke meant by *ek tou ouranou* 'from heaven' or 'from the sky', since 'these were not distinguishable.'

19. Tannehill 1990, 121. Gaventa, *Darkness*, 85, notes that 'imagery about blindness and the giving of sight appears frequently in Luke-Acts'. Cf. Lk. 2:30; 4:18; 24:16, 31; Acts 9:8, 18, 40; 13:11; 28:27.

20. Cf. note 3 above.

sake of that name. Barrett rightly observes that 'if such radical changes do not amount to conversion it is hard to know what would do so'.[21]

4-6 In common with other biblical theophanies, Saul *fell to the ground and heard a voice* (cf. Ezk. 1:28; Dn. 8:17; Rev. 1:17). The divine voice addressed him personally, using his Hebrew name twice *('Saul, Saul')*, and asking a revealing question *('why do you persecute me?')*.[22] Properly understood, this question would challenge his whole belief system and pattern of life. So many of his later insights can be traced back to the Damascus-road event or the outworking of that event in his experience.[23] Momentarily, however, he was perplexed about the identity of the one who confronted him and asked, *'Who are you, Lord?'* The word *Lord (kyrie)* appears to be a recognition that he is dealing with a divine representative, though he is not sure *who* (*Lord* continues to be the way Jesus is identified in 9:10-17). So the ascended Christ identifies himself and repeats the charge of persecution with the unmistakable declaration, *'I am Jesus, whom you are persecuting'*. Saul's presuppositions about Jesus and the claims of his disciples, about Judaism and the church, were at once challenged. Saul had been persecuting *the Lord's disciples* (9:1), on the understanding that Jesus was a dangerous imposter and a blasphemer. The risen Lord viewed the persecution of his disciples as an attack on himself, clearly identifying himself with the church (cf. Lk. 10:16; Mt. 25:40). Those who are united to Christ by faith suffer as he did, and he identifies with them in their struggle.[24] The only re-

---

21. Barrett 1994, 442. Conversion and calling to gospel ministry are both implied in Paul's account in Gal. 1:13-24. Barrett also draws attention to Paul's testimony in Phil. 3:7-11 and concludes that what happened to Paul was 'the appearance of Christ to a self-satisfied and self-righteous man, an appearance that had the immediate effect both of providing a new basis for his personal life and of initiating the Gentile mission' (443). Cf. Witherington 1998, 304.

22. The clause 'It is hard for you to kick against the goads' (26:14) is also found in some MSS of 9:4 and in the Received Text of 9:5-6 (with additional words from 22:10, KJV 'And he, trembling and astonished, said, Lord, what wilt thou have me to do? And the Lord said unto him'). However, these are poorly attested readings and appear to be assimilations from the later passages. Metzger, *Textual Commentary*, 317, makes the point that 'it is always suspicious when a variant reading, which agrees with a parallel passage, has no fixed location but vacillates between two points of attachment in Western witnesses'. Even more suspicious is the fact that the additional words came into the Received Text when Erasmus translated them from the Latin Vulgate into Greek (Metzger, 318).

23. Longenecker 1981, 371, comments: 'in this supreme revelational encounter, Saul received a new perspective on divine redemption, a new agenda for his life, and the embryonic elements of his new Christian theology'. Cf. Kim, *Origin*, 67-329.

24. Given the fact that the persecution broke out against *'the church* at Jerusalem' (8:1) and that the identity and character of the true people of God are an issue in Acts 9, it is inadequate to conclude with Tannehill 1990, 114, that the words of the risen Christ simply 'identify Saul with those previously accused of Jesus' rejection and death in the speeches of Peter and Stephen'. Barrett 1994, 449, similarly does not think that Luke's thought at this point is 'profoundly theological'. But Longenecker 1981, 371, rightly suggests that Christ's question provoked Saul to realize 'something of the organic and indissoluble unity that exists between Christ and his own'.

maining instruction from the Lord at this point in time was, '*Now (alla,* 'but') *get up and go into the city, and you will be told what you must do'*. This last clause *(ho ti se dei poiein)* implies a divine necessity (cf. 1:16, 21; 17:3; 19:21; 23:11). Saul must now begin walking by faith in the Son of God, obedient to the heavenly vision and the revelation to follow (cf. 26:19; Gal. 2:20).

7-9 Saul's nameless fellow travellers *stood there speechless; they heard the sound but did not see anyone.* This description highlights the fact that something objective happened. By implication, Saul saw what his companions did not see (cf. 9:17, 27). They saw 'the light' *(to men phōs etheasanto,* 22:9), but they *did not see anyone (mēdena de theōrountes, 9:7).*[25] They also *heard the sound (akouontes men tēs phōnēs, 9:7),*[26] but 'did not understand the voice of him who was speaking' *(tēn de phōnēn ouk ēkousan tou lalountos, 22:9).*[27] Both accounts stress that the revelatory element of the encounter was for Saul alone. But when he got up from the ground and opened his eyes, *he could see nothing.*[28] In view of what happens to Elymas in 13:11, this appears to be an act of divine judgment for Saul's opposition to the Lord and his people (9:5). Saul is humbled until he realizes his need to be delivered from physical and spiritual darkness by the Lord's gracious intervention. Blinded by the brilliance of this Christophany (22:11), he is led like a child into Damascus, where *for three days he was blind, and did not eat or drink anything.* Saul may have been overcome by penitence as well as by the shock of his experience.[29] Fasting in Scripture can be an expression of repentance (cf. Neh. 1:4; Je. 14:12; Jl. 1:14; Jon. 3:7-8), but also a way of preparing to receive further revelation from the Lord (cf. Ex. 34:28; Dt. 9:9; Dn. 9:1-3).

25. Gaventa 2003, 150, points out that the verb *theōreō* is frequently employed for 'seeing some manifestation of God's activity' (e.g., Lk. 10:18; 24:37, 39; Acts 3:16; 7:56) or 'for understanding the import of an event' (Acts 4:13; 17:22; 21:20; 27:10).

26. *phōnē* can mean 'an auditory effect, *sound, tone, noise*', or 'the faculty of utterance, *voice*', or 'a verbal code shared by a community to express ideas and feelings, *language*' (BDAG).

27. Witherington 1998, 312, argues that in classical Greek the verb *akouō* ('hear') with the genitive normally means 'that someone has heard the sound of something or someone, while this same verb with the accusative refers to both hearing and understanding something'. Bruce 1990, 236, proposes that this distinction 'does not accord with Lukan usage.' So also Barrett 1998, 1038-39. However, Witherington, 313, finally follows Polhill 1992, 235 note 15, in noting that the distinction between the verses is primarily by means of an added qualifying participial phrase in 22:7 ('the voice of him who was speaking'), not on the basis of the mere case of the object of the verb 'to hear'. Cf. 22:9 note.

28. Instead of the words 'Saul got up from the ground', several Western MSS heighten the pathos of the account by reading, 'He said to them, "Raise me up from the ground"', followed in some MSS by 'and they raised him'. These poorly attested readings are secondary. Instead of the better-attested *ouden* ('nothing'), some manuscripts read *oudena* (KJV 'no man'; NKJV 'no one'). Cf. Metzger, *Textual Commentary,* 318.

29. Marshall 1980, 170. Gaventa 2003, 150, argues that the evidence of Luke-Acts does not support this interpretation (cf. Lk. 4:2; 7:33; Acts 23:12).

2. Accepted into the Fellowship
of the Persecuted Church (9:10-19a)

A particular feature of this account is the role given to Ananias (he is briefly mentioned again in 22:12-16, but not in 26:12-18). The risen Lord Jesus encounters both Saul and Ananias, but in different ways, bringing them together and changing both of them in the process. Ananias is addressed by the Lord 'in a vision' (v. 10), through which the divine will for Saul's life is revealed and the genuineness of his conversion and calling is established.[30] 'Not only must Saul's aggression toward the disciples be curbed but Ananias' fear of the persecutor must be overcome.'[31] Ananias thus becomes the means by which God's intentions for Saul are first articulated. He also becomes the means by which Saul's sight is restored, he is filled with the Holy Spirit, baptized, and introduced to the fellowship of believers in Damascus (vv. 17-19). 'The rhetorical effect of delineating Saul's future through Ananias's vision stresses Saul's limited knowledge (blindness) at this stage and dependency on the assistance of other believers.'[32]

10-12 Ananias is simply introduced as *a disciple* — *(mathētēs)* here meaning Christian (cf. 6:1, 2, 7; 9:1) — though in 22:12 he is also described as 'a devout observer of the law *(eulabēs kata ton nomon)* and highly respected by all the Jews living there'. As noted with reference to 9:2, he appears to have been a long-term resident of *Damascus*, and he was perhaps still a member of a synagogue there. Ananias had an understandable fear of Saul (9:13-14) that needed to be overcome before he could fulfill his task. So *the Lord called to him in a vision* (note the significance of visions in 10:3, 11-17, 19; 11:5; 16:9-10; 18:9). *The Lord* here is clearly again the Lord Jesus, who has just encountered Saul.[33] This is confirmed by the fact that Ananias speaks to the Lord about Saul's having arrested *'all who call on your name'* (9:14). Addressed by name, the simple response *'Yes, Lord' (Idou egō, kyrie,* 'Here I am, Lord') indicates 'both his presence and his readiness to carry out the Lord's will'.[34] By means of a double vision, with very specific directions, the Lord then brings Saul and Ananias together. This reassures both parties of God's will in the situation. A double vision in Acts 10 similarly indicates God's intention that Peter and Cornelius should meet. Ananias is

---

30. Tannehill 1990, 114, observes that, in Acts 8–10, the church is led by divine direction to include within its number 'two foreigners (the Ethiopian and the Roman centurion) and its bitter enemy Saul'. Note also that Saul has a vision (v. 12), which presumably took place in the three days mentioned in v. 9. This was to prepare him for the role that Ananias would play in his life.

31. Tannehill 1990, 116.

32. Spencer 1997, 99.

33. Luke has the disciples address Jesus as 'Lord' from the beginning of Acts (1:6, 24) and uses the title 'the Lord' of Jesus explicitly from 1:21.

34. Barrett 1994, 453. Contrast the confusion and uncertainty of Saul in response to the Lord's initiative (9:5). Ananias responds in the way OT characters do to a revelation from God (e.g., Gn. 22:1; 1 Sa. 3:6, 8; Is. 6:8).

given specific instructions about where to find Saul (*'Go to the house of Judas on Straight Street and ask for a man from Tarsus named Saul, for he is praying'*). The street called *Straight* is commonly identified with Darb el-Mostakim, which still runs east-west in a somewhat modified form through Damascus. *Judas* was probably a Jewish acquaintance of Saul or one of his companions. The last clause about Saul *praying* suggests that he has been humbled and is seeking God's help. It is introduced by the words *idou gar* ('for, behold'), which are not translated by TNIV, but which suggest something worthy of special attention (cf. Lk. 1:44, 48; 2:10; 17:21). This is accompanied by the assurance that *'in a vision he has seen a man named Ananias come and place his hands on him to restore his sight'*.[35] With this vision, Saul has been assured in advance that he is to be healed by the disciple of Christ whom God will send (cf. 9:17-18). He has even been told to expect a named individual!

13-14 Ananias serves as 'the community's (and reader's) spokesperson in voicing reluctance and fear at so rapidly accepting into fellowship this murderous fellow'.[36] His hesitancy is legitimate. He knows Saul's reputation (*'I have heard many reports about this man and all the harm he has done to your people in Jerusalem'*), and he knows his reason for coming to Damascus (*'he has come here with authority from the chief priests to arrest all who call on your name'*).[37] Voicing his concerns in this way, Ananias uses two further terms to describe the Lord's disciples (9:1). They have already been identified as those who belong to the Way (9:2) and as those who are united by faith and suffering with the glorified Christ (9:4-5). Now they are identified as the true 'saints' or 'holy ones' of the Lord (*tois hagiois sou*; TNIV *to your people*; 9:13; cf. 9:32, 41; 26:10; Rom. 1:7; Eph. 1:1) and as those *who call on your name* (9:14; cf. 2:21; 9:21; 22:16; 1 Cor. 1:2; Rom. 10:12-13). In the OT, Israel became the holy people of the Lord by his redemptive act in bringing them to himself and revealing his law to them (Ex. 19:1-6; 20:1-17; 31:13). They were to express their separation from the nations and their consecration to God and his service by obeying his commands (cf. Lv. 11:44-45; 19:2; 20:7, 26; Dt. 14:2).[38] Under the New Covenant, the 'saints' (*hagioi*) are specifically those who have been 'sanctified' (*hēgiasmenois*, 20:32; 26:18) or set apart to belong to Christ and inherit his eternal kingdom (cf. 1 Cor. 1:2; 6:11; 1 Pet. 1:2). In Acts 9, the saints are specifically Jew-

---

35. The words 'in a vision' are omitted by several key MSS and a number of versions, and stand in several positions in other MSS. Metzger, *Textual Commentary*, 319, suggests that the phrase may be an explanatory gloss introduced to complete the sense of *eiden* ('he has seen'). There is no doubt that a vision is intended by the words 'he has seen a man'.

36. Johnson 1992, 169.

37. The plural 'chief priests' seems to mean 'the High Priest together with his entourage, with whom he acts in concert' (Barrett 1994, 455). Cf. 4:1, 6, 23; 5:17, 21, 24, 27.

38. See D. G. Peterson, *Possessed by God: A New Testament Theology of Sanctification and Holiness* (Leicester: Apollos; Grand Rapids: Eerdmans, 1995), 19-22. For a brief survey of the development of the concept of 'the saints' from the Intertestamental period through to the New Testament era, see H. Seebass and C. Brown, *NIDNTT* 2:227-32.

ish believers in Jesus,[39] but the implication of 9:15 is that Gentiles will be able to call upon the name of Christ and be included in his community. The gospel conveys the benefits of Christ's saving work, and those who respond appropriately receive the forgiveness of sins and 'a place among those who are sanctified by faith' (26:18). Calling upon the name of Christ is another way of describing the human side to the essentially divine work of conversion.[40]

15-16   The Lord speaks to Ananias alone here. Luke does not indicate when the message was conveyed to Saul. In 22:14-15, however, Paul recalls that it was after his sight was restored (22:13), but before he was baptized (22:16). Ananias is not mentioned at all in the third, abbreviated account of this event, where Paul has the Lord speaking to him directly about what he has in store for him (26:16-18). In each version, there are different emphases and aims, but 'Luke agrees with Paul in seeing that at the Damascus Christophany Paul received his message and call for missionary work among the Gentiles (even if not exclusively among them as far as Luke is concerned)'.[41] In Acts 9, Ananias needs to be told about the Lord's plan for Saul before he has the courage to go and meet him. In other words, this revelation is God's way of overcoming his fear and mistrust before he can fulfill his ministry to Saul. Ananias has protested that Saul has been persecuting those who call on Christ's name (9:14). Now the Lord says he will use Saul to 'carry my name (*tou bastasai to onoma mou*) before the Gentiles and their kings and before the people of Israel', meaning that he will bear witness to what he has seen and heard of the risen Jesus and preach in his name (cf. 9:27; 22:15 note). The element of character witness to Christ through Saul's lifestyle appears to be included in the concept of carrying the name, and so TNIV's translation (*'proclaim my name'*) is not an adequate rendering. This is suggested by the fact that Saul himself will have to *'suffer'* for the sake of that name (*hyper tou onomatos mou*; TNIV *'for my name'*).[42] Such a calling implies a Christ-likeness in life and ministry (cf.

39. Barrett 1994, 455, notes that the term 'the saints' is occasionally applied by Paul quite narrowly to the Christians of Jerusalem (Rom. 15:26; 1 Cor. 16:1; 2 Cor. 8:4) and suggests that it may also have that narrow sense here and in 26:10. The saints in 9:32, 41, are then Jewish Christians more generally (cf. Eph. 2:19) or, even perhaps, 'country members' of the Jerusalem church.

40. Cf. Peterson, *Possessed*, 55-58.

41. Kim, *Origin*, 65. Cf. Cunningham, *Persecution*, 222-28, on the missiological thrust of the passage. The prophecy of Jesus to disciples about being persecuted because of his name (Lk. 21:12, 17) is applied to Paul in particular. Pauline suffering is logically and causally linked to Pauline mission.

42. TNIV has not translated the connective 'for' in the sequence *egō gar hypodeixō* (9:16). The meaning is that Ananias can go to Saul not only because of what is revealed about his calling in 9:15 but also because of what God will show to Saul about the suffering entailed in this calling. If Saul is ready to receive such a message and serve in this way, he must be a changed man! Against R. Maddox, *The Purpose of Luke-Acts* (Edinburgh: Clark, 1982), 79, it is not right to conclude that 'God has declared from the very beginning that Paul is to bear his witness for Jesus even more through persecution and suffering than

20:18-35). The great antagonist of the gospel will become its outstanding protagonist. The persecutor will become the persecuted and suffer like Jesus himself.[43] He will join the fellowship of those who are afflicted because of their identification with the Lord Jesus (cf. Lk. 21:12). These verses particularly anticipate the defense and trial scenes in Acts 22–26. However, the suffering that Paul must experience will come more generally as a result of his preaching, as is immediately illustrated in 9:20-30.

The designation of Saul as *'my chosen instrument'* (*skeuos eklogēs moi*, 'a vessel of choice for me') is significant.[44] The terminology of election is used in Luke 18:7; Acts 13:17 for God's gracious choice of people for salvation. In Luke 6:13; Acts 1:2, 24; 6:5; 15:7, 22, 25, however, the choice is for a special role or mission that not all disciples share.[45] The 'election' of Saul in 9:15 refers to his ministry, not to his conversion. His role as 'apostle to the Gentiles' (Rom. 11:13; cf. Rom. 1:5; Gal. 2:7-9) is highlighted first (*'[to carry] my name to the Gentiles and their kings'*). This is summed up in terms of bringing the message about 'the name' of Christ (8:12 note) to nations and their rulers. But, climactically in this prophecy, he is also called to bear witness to Israel (*'and to the people of Israel'*). Since Paul often preaches first to Jews and any Gentiles attached to the synagogue, then to Gentiles more generally (e.g., 13:4-12, 13-48), this verse is not so clearly programmatic as is 1:8.[46] However, it does set forth in broad terms the character of the ministry given to him. Tannehill helpfully summarizes the phrases used in Acts to describe Saul's distinctive commission in the following way. He is chosen by the Lord (9:15; 13:47; 20:24; 22:14; 26:16) and sent as witness to both Jews and Gentiles (9:15; 13:46-47; 20:21; 22:15; 22:18-21; 26:16-17). His mission will encounter rejection and require suffering (9:16; 13:46; 20:19; 20:23; 22:18; 26:17), but will bring light (13:47; 26:17-18; 26:23). He will preach repentance (20:21; 26:18; 26:20), and his witness to Jesus will be based on what he has seen and heard (22:14-15; 26:16).[47]

17-19a The obedience of Ananias to the divine command (vv. 11-12) is simply recorded (*Then Ananias went to the house and entered it*). He immediately 'placed his hands on him' (*epitheis ep' auton tas cheiras*) and ad-

---

through his famous mission'. However, persecution and suffering form a dominant part of that witness in Acts 21–28. Cf. M. L. Skinner, *Locating Paul: Places of Custody as Narrative Settings in Acts 21–28*, SBLAB 13 (Atlanta: SBL, 2003), 96-97.

43. 'In view of the frequently perceived "triumphalism" of Luke's portrayal of Paul, this note of suffering struck from the very beginning is impressive' (Johnson 1992, 165).

44. Note the metaphorical use of *skeuos* at Rom. 9:22, 23; 2 Cor. 4:7; 2 Tim. 2:21.

45. This is likely to be the meaning here because the genitive articular infinitive *tou bastasai* conveys a purposive sense. Saul's election is for the purpose of bearing witness to Christ in the way specified. On the use of election terminology more generally in the NT, see G. Schrenk, *TDNT* 4:172-92. Luke has other ways of expressing the idea of election to salvation or eternal life (cf. 13:48 note).

46. Cf. Gaventa 2003, 152. She notes the use of *dei* (*must*) in vv. 6 and 16, and observes that suffering is part of the divine necessity for Saul's ministry.

47. Tannehill 1990, 119-20.

dressed him as *'brother Saul'*. Then he expressed the reason for his coming (*'the Lord — Jesus, who appeared to you on the road as you were coming here — has sent me'*). This simple declaration by Ananias must have confirmed for Saul the authenticity of his encounter with the glorified Christ. His welcome as *brother Saul* signified his acceptance into the fellowship of Christians.[48] Ananias explains that the laying on of hands is for healing (*'so that you may see again'*; cf. Lk. 5:13; 13:13; Acts 4:30; 5:12) and for the bestowal of the Spirit (*'and be filled with the Holy Spirit'*; cf. Acts 8:17-19; 19:6). Prayer is mentioned in connection with this action in 6:6; 8:17; 13:3; 28:8 and may be assumed in other places where it is not mentioned.[49] Baptism is not mentioned until after the healing of his blindness, when *something like scales fell from Saul's eyes, and he could see again.*[50] The process of physical healing presumably took place as he was filled with the Holy Spirit. In Saul's case, as with Cornelius and his household, the Spirit brought understanding and conviction about Jesus before water baptism was experienced (cf. 10:44-48). 'By the gift of the Spirit Paul is made to stand on the same level as the original apostles (2:4); but indeed this means no more than that he is a Christian (2:33, 38; etc.).'[51] Paul later recalls that Ananias transmitted to him the revelation about his future at this time, before challenging him to 'get up, be baptized and wash your sins away, calling on his name' (22:14-16). So the conversion and initiation of Saul as a Christian was a process, involving several stages, over a period of at least *three days* (9:9).[52] *After taking some food, he regained his strength,* signifying the end of the fast that was forced upon him by his life-changing encounter with the Lord Jesus.

There are many ways in which Saul's conversion was unique. Indeed, neither the Ethiopian, nor Saul, nor Cornelius, is presented as an ideal ex-

---

48. The word *brother* in a context like this certainly points to the particular fellowship of Jewish Christians (cf. 1:15-16; 6:3; 9:30; 10:23; 11:1, 12, 29; 12:17, etc.). However, it should also be noted that the term is used in addresses to wider Jewish audiences, as an appeal to their common heritage and common hope (e.g., 2:29, 37; 3:17, 22; 7:2, 23, 25, 26, 37; 13:26, 38). So the 'brotherhood' of Christians emerges from this context, as another way of defining what it means to be the church of Christ.

49. A command like 'Brother Saul, receive your sight', could be understood as a form of 'wish-prayer' (cf. 22:13 note). The laying on of hands appears to represent identification with and concern for the person who is prayed for (cf. 8:17 note).

50. The term *lepis* ('scale', 'scaly substance') is used in Tob. 3:17; 11:13, for that which covered Tobit's eyes and blinded him. But Luke's expression is deliberately vague (*hōs lepides*, 'like scales').

51. Barrett 1994, 457.

52. M. M. B. Turner, *Power from on High: The Spirit in Israel's Restoration and Witness in Luke-Acts*, JPTSS 9 (Sheffield: Sheffield Academic, 1996), 375, agrees that 'Paul only *completes* his conversion-initiation when he submits to Ananias's direction (narrated in Acts 22:16)'. Cf. J. D. G. Dunn, *Baptism in the Holy Spirit: A Re-examination of the Teaching of the New Testament on the Gift of the Spirit in Relation to Pentecostalism Today*, SBT 15 (London: SCM, 1970), 73-78. So Turner, 376-78, argues against R. P. Menzies, *The Development of Early Christian Pneumatology with Special Reference to Luke-Acts*, JSNTSS 54 (Sheffield: JSOT, 1991), 260-63, that we do not find here an instance of the reception of the Spirit clearly subsequent to conversion-initiation.

ample of how people became Christians. 'Each individual whose conversion appears in Acts represents some larger group or some thread in Luke's narrative. No conversion, not even that of the crowd at Pentecost, establishes a pattern that is to be followed by later believers or is appealed to in preaching.'[53] Luke illustrates the sovereign freedom of God to bring about faith in Christ in a way that is suitable to the situation of each individual. In the case of Saul, the narrative shows how he was transformed by the Lord's sudden intervention in his life and how he was accepted by the church and encouraged forward in his ministry through the Lord's use of Ananias. Saul's conversion and his commissioning took place simultaneously. This complex event serves to explain his apostolic-type authority (though he is called an apostle only by Luke in 14:4, 14) and the extraordinary attention given to his ministry in the rest of Acts.[54] More generally, however, Luke shows his readers that even the hardest heart can be softened by God and the most formidable opponent can become a servant of Christ and a vigorous agent of his gospel.

H. Saul Preaches in Damascus and Jerusalem (9:19b-31)

Like Philip in Samaria, Saul begins a preaching mission in Damascus without the prior approval of the apostles in Jerusalem. They have a role in verifying individuals and missions (8:14-17; 9:27-28; 11:1-18, 22-24), but 'they are not their initiators or directors'.[55] Moreover, Saul begins preaching immediately after his conversion, without apparently being instructed by those who were Christians before him (cf. Gal. 1:11-24). When he returns to Jerusalem, he is accepted because of the testimony of Barnabas. He assumes the role of Stephen in debating with Hellenistic Jews, who then plot to kill him (9:29; cf. 6:9-11). In Damascus and Jerusalem, the same pattern of preaching, plot, and escape is highlighted (9:20-25, 28-30). This whole section shows how quickly the Lord's words about Saul in 9:15-16 are fulfilled. The persecutor soon becomes the persecuted! Luke's editorial summary in 9:31, with its focus on peace and church growth following the conversion of Saul, brings a further 'panel' of the narrative of Acts to an end.[56] The Holy Spirit is specifically the agent of growth here, and the Spirit's work in Paul's particular ministry is suggested by the terminology in 9:22.

53. Gaventa, *Darkness*, 124. However, in narrative terms Acts 2:36-40 presents something of a paradigm of conversion. Later contexts emphasize various aspects of what is outlined here as the way to acknowledge Jesus and receive the benefits of the salvation proclaimed in his name.

54. Cf. A. C. Clark, 'The Role of the Apostles', in I. H. Marshall and D. Peterson (eds.), *Witness to the Gospel: The Theology of Acts* (Grand Rapids/Cambridge: Eerdmans, 1998), 169-90, on the role of the apostles in Acts.

55. Tannehill 1990, 113.

56. Cf. INTRODUCTION TO ACTS: IV.B. Structure (pp. 32-36).

1. Proclaiming the Son of God in Damascus (9:19b-25)

Saul preaches fearlessly 'in the name of Jesus' (9:27-28), suggesting continuity with the ministry of the apostles (4:17-18; 5:28, 40).[57] Moreover, he
proclaims Jesus as the Son of God (9:20) and proves that Jesus is the Messiah (9:22), suggesting also a parallel with Philip, who 'proclaimed the
Messiah' in Samaria (8:5) and preached 'the name of Jesus Christ' (8:12).
'Shifts in the central character of the narrative (from Peter to Stephen to
Philip to Saul) could fragment the narrative, but the narrator stresses the
similarity of the mission that central characters share, calling this similarity
to our attention through similar descriptive phrases. This procedure unifies
the narrative and gives this mission central thematic significance.'[58] However, since Jesus is specifically identified as 'the Son of God' only here in
Acts (though cf. Lk. 1:32, 35; 3:22; 4:3, 9, 41; 22:70), and given that Son-
Christology is so significant in Paul's letters, it is likely that Luke is drawing attention to a distinctive of Paul's teaching in this first account of his
public ministry as a Christian (cf. Gal. 1:15-17). If that is so, 'Son of God' expresses more about the significance of Jesus than 'Messiah' here.

19b-20 *Saul spent several days with the disciples in Damascus,* enjoying
the company of those he had set out to destroy. They doubtless shared with
him insights from Scripture and their own experience as Christians, to encourage the new convert. However, whatever help or instruction he received at this time, Paul himself later insisted that he did not receive the
gospel 'from any human source, nor was I taught it; rather, I received it by
revelation from Jesus Christ' (Gal. 1:12). Indeed, Luke stresses that it was *at
once (eutheōs,* 'immediately') that he *began to preach in the synagogues that Jesus is the Son of God.* According to Galatians 1:17, Saul 'went immediately
into Arabia and later returned to Damascus', but Luke says nothing about
this period in Arabia. 'After three years' in Galatians 1:18 could allow for
an initial period of preaching in Damascus (Acts 9:19b-22), followed by a
stay in Arabia (the Nabatean kingdom on the eastern frontier of Syria), and
further ministry in Damascus (Acts 9:23-25), before going up to Jerusalem.[59] But how was he able to preach so soon after his conversion with clarity and conviction?

Doubtless Saul had 'gone to some trouble to inform himself concerning the erroneous teaching which he took it upon himself to stamp out. The
appearances of Jesus proved at once that Jesus was alive and (since God
had vindicated him) that he had been right and his opponents wrong, and

---

57. References to 'the name of Jesus' tend to cluster in Acts 2–5 and 8–9.
58. Tannehill 1990, 115.
59. Cf. Marshall 1980, 173-76; Longenecker 1981, 375-76; Witherington 1998, 320-25,
on the differences between Acts and Galatians here. Barrett 1994, 460-62, too readily accepts
that Luke is wrong in detail in 9:19b-30, since he is 'not following closely a clearly defined
source but making his own composition on the basis of a rather sketchy general acquaintance, not so much with the events themselves as with their outcome' (462).

that the new faith which was focused on him was true. The rest followed, not indeed in detail and immediately but as the result of theological reflection.'[60] Although references to Jesus as the Son of God are common in Paul's letters, this is the only occurrence of such terminology in Acts (though cf. Ps. 2:7 in 13:33, the poorly attested 8:37, and Lk. 1:32, 35; 3:22; 4:3, 9, 41; 22:70). Luke highlights the fact that, from the time of his conversion, this was a distinctively Pauline way of preaching the gospel (e.g., Rom. 1:1-4, 9; 5:10; 1 Cor. 1:9; 2 Cor. 1:19; 4:3-6; Gal. 1:16; 2:20; 1 Thes. 1:10). In Acts, the term suggests what is meant by both 'Lord' and 'Messiah' in Peter's programmatic sermon on the Day of Pentecost (2:36 note). There is a certain parallel in *proving that Jesus is the Messiah* (9:22; cf. 13:33-39).[61] The exalted status of the resurrected Christ demonstrates that he shares in the rule of God as saviour and judge. He is 'the Lord' mentioned in Joel 2:32, on whose name we must call for deliverance on the day of wrath (2:21-39), and 'the Messiah' through whom God will finally restore all things (3:19-21). References to Jesus as God's Son in Paul's writings particularly communicate 'Jesus' unique status and intimate relationship with God'.[62] The pre-existence of the Son of God, before his birth as Jesus of Nazareth, which is an important element in the Son-Christology of Paul's letters (e.g., Rom. 8:3; Gal. 4:4; Col. 1:13-20), is not specifically articulated in Acts.[63]

21-22 *All those who heard him were astonished* (*existanto*, as in 2:7, 12; 10:45; 12:16) at the sudden transformation of the notorious persecutor. What they *heard* was so contrary to his reputation as *'the man who raised havoc in Jerusalem among those who call on this name'*. Moreover, they knew that he had come to their city to take the followers of Jesus *'as prisoners to the chief priests'*. Despite the priority given to his role among the Gentiles in the prophecy of Ananias (9:15), Saul turned immediately to evangelise *'the Jews living in Damascus'*. This was a logical first step, given his own background, experience, and status as a rabbinic scholar (22:3; 26:4-6). A theological justification for this is given later (13:46-47; cf. Rom. 1:16, 'first to the Jew, then to the Gentile'). Acts 22:17-21 records that there was a further direct challenge from the Lord about ministry to Gentiles, while Saul was praying at the temple in Jerusalem, before he took that radical step. When Luke says that Saul *grew more and more powerful*, the term he uses (*enedynamouto*) suggests the empowerment of the Spirit (cf. Jgs. 6:34; 1 Chr. 12:18; Eph. 6:10; Phil. 4:13; 2 Tim. 4:17). The way in which that empower-

60. Barrett 1994, 443. Cf. Kim, *Origin,* 100-136, regarding the development of Paul's Christology in the light of the Damascus-road revelation and Paul's subsequent reflection on Christian confessions about Jesus.
61. Cf. Longenecker 1981, 376; Bruce 1988, 190, on the links between 'Messiah' and 'Son of God' in the NT and Jewish literature.
62. L. W. Hurtado, 'Son of God', in *DPL* 900. Hurtado, 900-906, summarizes and discusses the Son-Christology of Paul's letters. Witherington 1993, 95-100, summarizes and discusses Paul's use of the title 'Christ'.
63. Cf. THE THEOLOGY OF ACTS: II. JESUS AS MESSIAH AND LORD (pp. 56-60).

ment was experienced is indicated by what follows. Saul *baffled* (*synechyn-nen*, 'confounded' in most EVV) the Jews,[64] throwing them into confusion as Stephen did with his God-given wisdom (6:10). He did this by *proving* (*symbibazōn*),[65] no doubt from the Scriptures, *that Jesus is the Messiah* (cf. 13:16-41). Faced with such arguments, his hearers were neither able to respond positively to his message nor to contradict it effectively.

23-24 Luke's time reference is vague but impressive (*hōs de eplērounto hēmerai hikanai*, 'when many days were fulfilled'; TNIV *after many days had gone by*). This signifies the completion of a significant period in the narrative (cf. Lk. 9:51) and is consistent with Paul's mention of a three-year gap between his conversion and his first journey to Jerusalem as a Christian in Galatians 1:17-18.[66] Luke then indicates that *there was a conspiracy among the Jews to kill him* (*synebouleusanto hoi Ioudaioi anelein auton*, 'the Jews plotted to kill him' in most EVV). *The Jews* are here designated for the first time as a hostile group, plotting to overthrow Saul and his ministry.[67] The intensity of their desire is expressed by the fact that *day and night they kept close watch on the city gates in order to kill him* (the verb *anaireō* is used in 9:23, 24, 29, for Jewish plots to kill Saul).

25 When Saul *learned of their plan*, he and *his followers* were able to arrange his escape.[68] They *took him by night and lowered him in a basket through an opening in the wall*. At this point, Luke's narrative must be squared with the account in 2 Corinthians 11:32-33, where we are told that 'the governor under King Aretas had the city of the Damascenes guarded in order to arrest me' and that Paul was 'lowered in a basket from a window in the wall and slipped through his hands'. Aretas IV ruled the Nabateans (Arabians)

64. The verb here literally means 'pour together', and figuratively 'cause dismay, confuse, confound, trouble, stir up' (BDAG; cf. 2:6; 19:32; 21:27, 31). Spencer 1997, 99-100, compares the response of the crowd at Pentecost which 'split into two juries' in response to what they heard and saw.

65. This verb means 'bring together, unite' (Eph. 4:16; Col. 2:2, 19), 'conclude, infer' (Acts 16:10), and 'instruct, teach, advise' (1 Cor. 2:16; Acts 19:33). The idea of teaching by bringing together arguments to 'demonstrate, prove' is indicated by the context of Acts 9:22. Cf. BDAG; Barrett 1994, 465.

66. Cf. 9:19b-20 note on the evidence of Acts in the light of Paul's chronology in Galatians 1.

67. Gaventa 2003, 154, observes that the phrase 'the Jews' in Acts 'frequently signals those who actively oppose the gospel (e.g., 13:45, 50; 14:2, 5; 17:5, 13; 18:12; 20:3, 19)'. However, Luke also makes it clear that many Jews became disciples of Christ. Opposition from Jews in one place also did not hinder the earliest Christians from continuing to preach the gospel to Jews elsewhere.

68. The oldest and best-attested reading here is *hoi mathētai autou* ('his disciples', as in NRSV, ESV, TNIV). This unusual reading is clearly more difficult and is therefore preferable to the later alternatives that remove the pronoun or change it to *auton* ('the disciples took him', as in KJV and NKJV). Metzger, *Textual Commentary*, 321-22, argues that 'the oldest extant text arose through scribal inadvertence', when an original *auton* was taken as *autou*. But we must surely allow Luke some flexibility in the use of *mathētai* (cf. 19:1 note) and view these as Paul's converts in the context (an indication of the success of his ministry in Damascus). Cf. Barrett 1994, 466-67.

from 9 BC to AD 40, but we do not know whether he was ever in control of Damascus.[69] The 'governor' *(ethnarchēs)* may have been his appointed leader to the Nabatean community in Damascus. The governor's attempt to seize Paul may have been because of 'misdemeanors committed inside Damascus or in "Arabia", that is, within the Nabatean kingdom'.[70] But Luke's focus is on *the Jews* who *conspired to kill him* and who *kept close watch on the city gates in order to kill him*. Given the evidence of later chapters (e.g., 14:1-7; 17:1-9; 18:12-17), it is possible that the Jews in Damascus 'sided with the enthnarch or even listed his support in their hostility to Paul'.[71] There is no need to favour one account against another, because they put the focus on different opponents and depict the same event from different perspectives.

2. Disputing with Hellenists in Jerusalem (9:26-31)

We see here another example of the theme introduced in 8:1-4, that opposition to the gospel in one context leads to fearless proclamation and church growth elsewhere. In Jerusalem, the pattern of preaching, plot, and escape seen previously in 9:20-25 is illustrated again (9:27-30). Barnabas secures Saul's acceptance among believers in Jerusalem as Ananias did in Damascus. But Barnabas receives no vision as Ananias did, simply asserting the evidence of Saul's transformation for all to consider. Debating with Hellenistic Jews paradoxically places Saul in the same position as Stephen (6:9-14), and the opposition is life-threatening until the believers secure his escape. Luke's summary-conclusion highlights the significance of Saul's conversion for 'the church throughout Judea, Galilee and Samaria' (9:31). Incidentally, this confirms the force of his previous opposition to the gospel and the wonder of his transformation.

26-27 *When he came to Jerusalem, he tried to join the disciples, but they were all afraid of him, not believing that he [really] was a disciple (mē pisteuontes hoti estin mathētēs).* Resistance to Saul was first expressed by Ananias (9:13-14), but now by *the disciples* in Jerusalem. This is remarkable if the visit

---

69. It is possible that Aretas IV may have died in AD 38 or 39 and that Paul's flight from Damascus was in AD 36 or 37.

70. P. Barnett, *The Second Epistle to the Corinthians,* NICNT (Grand Rapids/Cambridge: Eerdmans, 1997), 554-55. Saul possibly aroused the wrath of Aretas during his time in Arabia (Gal. 1:17), where it is likely that he was engaged in evangelism (not simply meditating, as some commentators would have it!). Cf. Bruce 1988, 191-92; Witherington 1998, 323-24.

71. Marshall 1980, 174. This is a more probable solution than the suggestion of Barrett 1994, 460, that Luke 'blames the Jews because he had no exact information and had come to think that whenever trouble arose it must have been caused by them'. Barrett, 466, concedes that there may have been 'collusion between Jews and Arabs, the former watching the gates within, the latter guarding the city without', but then dismisses this as unlikely. Cf. M. Hengel, *Acts and the History of Earliest Christianity* (Philadelphia: Fortress, 1979), 85.

was three years after Saul's conversion (cf. Gal. 1:18). However, such unbelief and fear would be natural if there was no personal contact, and such
an amazing transformation was beyond their experience and expectation.
Even believers who have seen the power of God at work in their own lives
can doubt God's ability to change others. It is also true that 'this shows a
misdirected fear of the persecutor rather than God (cf. Luke 12:4-5)'.[72] *But
Barnabas took him and brought him to the apostles.*[73] Presumably the logic was
that if the apostles were convinced about Saul, the rest of the church in Jerusalem would follow. Barnabas has already been introduced as 'Son of
Encouragement' (4:36-37), and he now demonstrates that quality in a most
significant way (cf. 11:23-26; 15:36-41). Barnabas told the apostles about
the genuineness of Saul's experience *(how Saul on his journey had seen the
Lord and that the Lord had spoken to him),* anticipating to some extent the
manner of Peter's report to the Jerusalem church about the conversion of
Cornelius and his household (11:1-18). The change in Saul is attributed to
the Lord Jesus. Barnabas also reported Saul's subsequent behaviour,
which confirmed the reality of his conversion *(how in Damascus he had
preached fearlessly in the name of Jesus).*[74] So Barnabas helped the apostles to
accept Saul as a Christian and to welcome him as a fellow believer and
partner in the gospel. Thus also began a relationship between Saul and
Barnabas that would soon bear fruit in their shared missionary work
(11:25-26; 13:1-4).

28-30 *So Saul stayed with them and moved about freely in Jerusalem*
(*eisporeuomenos kai ekporeuomenos eis Ierousalēm,* 'going in and going out, at
Jerusalem' in most EVV). He continued what he had done in Damascus,
speaking boldly (*parrēsiazomenos,* translated *preached fearlessly* in v. 27) *in the
name of the Lord.* Luke then draws attention to what this specifically involved. *He talked* (*elalei*) *and debated* (*synezētei*) *with the Hellenistic Jews* (*tous
Hellēnistas*), which resulted in another threat to his life *(they tried to kill him).*
These *Hellēnistai* were apparently Jews whose roots were in the Greek-
speaking world (cf. 6:1 note), being the group with whom Stephen came
into conflict (6:9, *syzētountes,* 'debating').[75] They radically opposed Ste-

72. Tannehill 1990, 117.

73. According to Gal. 1:18-20, Paul saw only Peter and James the Lord's brother
among the apostles. Paul has reason in writing to the Galatians to be precise in this matter,
whereas Luke speaks more generally about the encounter. Barnabas's introduction of Paul
'to the apostles' could have been by way of a specific meeting with the leaders Peter and
James. Longenecker 1981, 378, suggests that Luke's use of the term 'apostles' in Acts 9:27
must be considered 'a generalizing plural to be taken more broadly than "the Twelve"', but
I doubt that this is really necessary.

74. The verb translated 'preached fearlessly' (*eparrēsiasato*) occurs also at 9:28; 13:46;
14:3; 18:26; 19:8; 26:26; Eph. 6:20; 1 Thes. 2:2. It denotes speech with openness or boldness
(*parrēsia;* cf. 28:31), not glossolalia. It is followed in 9:29 by verbs indicating that this involved talking (*elalei*) and debating (*synezētei;* cf. 6:9).

75. Cf. Longenecker 1981, 327-29; Barrett 1994, 307-9; Witherington 1998, 240-47. The
Hellēnistai in 6:1 were Greek-speaking Jewish *Christians* in Jerusalem.

phen's preaching as a blasphemous assault on the central tenets of their religion (6:11, 13-14) and saw Saul as a similar threat. They must have been particularly angry that the one who had led them in suppression of this new movement was now its vigorous advocate. So Saul the persecutor came under persecution again himself. *When the believers (hoi adelphoi, 'the brothers') learned of this, they took him down to Caesarea and sent him off to Tarsus.* Paul later reports a vision in the temple at this time, warning him to flee the city (22:17-21). This doubtless encouraged him to accept the believers' help and escape. The Lord's will was not for him to die in Jerusalem but to move out with the gospel into the Gentile world. The journey to *Caesarea* appears to have been the first step towards a sea trip to his home town (v. 11). Tarsus was in Cilicia (cf. Gal. 1:21), on the southern coast of what is now called Turkey. When Saul next appears in the narrative (11:25), Barnabas has gone to Tarsus to find him and bring him to Antioch in Syria, to share in the ministry there. 'One section of the story of Saul ends by placing him in the location where the next section of the story will find him.'[76] Although Luke is silent about Saul's activity in Tarsus, given what we know of him from 9:20-29, it is likely that he continued to be occupied with evangelism there.

31 A whole 'panel' of Luke's narrative (6:8–9:31) concludes with an impressive summary statement. A formula is used which often begins a new section (*men oun*, emphatic 'then', as in 8:4), or introduces the conclusion to a section (as in 8:25). This particular summary statement functions retrospectively, but also to introduce the stories of healing and conversion that follow in 9:32-43.[77] The verse recalls 6:7 by emphasizing numerical growth: the church *increased in numbers* (*eplēthyneto*; cf. 6:1, 7; 7:17; 12:24). It also recalls the fact that Saul was persecuting *the church* at Jerusalem (8:1, 3) and seeking to destroy the disciples of the Lord, wherever they could be found (9:1). A minor inclusion is thus formed between 8:1 and 9:31, indicating that the theme of the church under attack is the controlling motif. However, a major inclusion between 6:8 and 9:31 highlights Stephen and Saul as the main characters in this conflict. Paradoxically, Saul changes from being Stephen's opponent to being a vigorous advocate of the same message.

The entity in view now is *the church throughout Judea, Galilee and Samaria.* Luke, who normally uses the word *church* in the singular to refer to a congregation in a given place, here refers to the sum of Jewish believers over a large area, corresponding to the boundaries of ancient Israel.[78] Many

---

76. Tannehill 1990, 124.

77. Gaventa 2003, 156, notes the *men* ('on the one hand') and *de* ('on the other hand') construction (as in 8:4-5, 25-26), which is not translated by EVV, but which clearly links vv. 31 and 32. This suggests that 9:31 is also transitional.

78. The singular *ekklēsia* ('church') is read by a wide range and various ages of MSS, but the plural *ekklēsiai* ('churches') is found in some Western and Byzantine MSS (some adding *pasai*, 'all'), and is read by KJV and NKJV. There is no doubt that the plural form is used

were doubtless refugees from Jerusalem, while others were persuaded by their testimony to Jesus. Despite persecution, *the church* grew in size and maturity, not least because of the conversion of Saul, which brought *a time of peace*. Most EVV form two sentences out of one complex Greek sentence in v. 31. TNIV concludes the first with *and was strengthened* (*oikodomoumenē*, 'and was being built up'). It begins a new sentence with *living in the fear of the Lord* (*poreuomenē tō phobō tou kyriou*), creates another participial clause with *encouraged by the Holy Spirit* (*kai tē paraklēsei tou hagiou pneumatos*, 'and in the comfort of the Holy Spirit'), and concludes with the affirmation that *it increased in numbers* (*eplēthyneto*). There is some logic in attaching the first Greek participle to the preceding indicative ('had peace and was built up') and beginning a new sentence by linking the second participle to the second indicative ('Living in the fear of the Lord and in the comfort of the Holy Spirit, it increased in numbers'). However, the text reads literally, 'Then the church throughout Judea and Galilee and Samaria had peace, being strengthened and going in the fear of the Lord, and in the comfort of the Holy Spirit it multiplied'. Most importantly, Luke tells us how the end of persecution brought church growth. The church *was strengthened* (*oikodomoumenē*, cf. 20:32; 1 Cor. 8:1; 10:23; 14:4, 17; 1 Thes. 5:11; 1 Pet. 2:5) extensively and intensively, meaning that it was 'being built up' in terms of size and maturity.[79] The passive voice implies that God was the agent, and the present tense implies that this was an ongoing divine activity. Then an active participle is used (*poreuomenē*, 'going', 'walking') to stress that believers, for their part, were *living* or continuing in *the fear of the Lord* (cf. 10:2, 22, 35; 13:16, 26).[80] The concluding clause summarizes all this by saying that 'in the encouragement of the Holy Spirit, (the church) was being multiplied'. Growth in numbers and in the godliness of believers resulted from the work of the Holy Spirit, enabling leaders and people to minister to each other and to live in a way that expressed fear of God rather than fear of their persecutors (cf. Phil. 1:27-30; 1 Pet. 3:13-17).

---

in 15:41; 16:5, and it is probable that the singular form in 9:31 was changed by some copyists to conform to the two later passages and the usage of the Pauline letters. Cf. Bruce 1990, 245-46; Metzger, *Textual Commentary*, 322-23; K. N. Giles, 'Luke's Use of the Term *ekklēsia* with Special Reference to Acts 20.28 and 9.31', *NTS* 3 (1985), 135-42; THE THEOLOGY OF ACTS: X. THE CHURCH (pp. 92-97).

79. I have explored the use and meaning of the terminology of edification in the NT in D. G. Peterson, *Engaging with God: A Biblical Theology of Worship* (Leicester: Apollos; Grand Rapids: Eerdmans, 1992), 206-21, 247-50. Cf. Barrett 1994, 474.

80. Since 'the Lord' is most obviously the risen Lord Jesus in 9:5, 10-17, 27, 35, 42, the reference is arguably the same in 9:31. Thus the fear of the Lord, which is such an important aspect of OT piety in relation to the God of Israel, is here applied to the relationship between the glorified Jesus and his disciples. Cf. W. Mundle, *NIDNTT* 1:621-24.

IV. THE WORD ADVANCES
IN JUDEA AND SYRIA (9:32–12:25)

A new panel of Luke's work begins as he proceeds to illustrate the sort of church growth described in 9:31. First, he focuses on Peter's itinerant ministry in the coastal region of Judea (9:32-42), where Christians are strengthened in their walk with the Lord and encouraged by the Holy Spirit through the ministry of the apostle. At the same time, Luke notes how many others 'turned to the Lord' (v. 35), and 'many people believed in the Lord' (v. 42). Then Peter receives the summons to go to Caesarea, to share the gospel with Cornelius and his household. The importance of this incident for Luke is demonstrated by the length and detail of the account (10:1-48), which is coupled with a review and interpretation of the event (11:1-18). An outpouring of the Holy Spirit (10:44-46), reminiscent of the experience of Jewish Christians on the Day of Pentecost (10:47; 11:17; cf. 15:8-9), persuaded Peter and many of the 'circumcised believers' that believing, uncircumcised Gentiles could be as much the recipients of the blessings of the New Covenant as they were. Although Luke goes on to record other initiatives in preaching the gospel to Gentiles (11:19-26), the incident involving Peter and Cornelius is critical because of the divine guidance given to both, and because Peter was able to persuade the church in Jerusalem to acknowledge God's hand in this. 'Here Luke narrates both the revelation of the light to a Gentile household and the church's resistance to that development.'[81] This next step in the fulfillment of the mission agenda in 1:8 required a revelation of how Jewish and Gentile believers could be spiritually and practically united in Christ. When the church in Antioch provides help for the believers living in Judea (11:27-30), something of the outworking of that relationship is illustrated. Closure to this panel of the narrative is provided by focusing again on the situation of the church in Jerusalem (12:1-25). James is put to death, but Peter is rescued from prison for the second time (cf. 5:18-20). The death of Herod Agrippa I apparently alleviated the persecution in Jerusalem, just as Saul's conversion did on an even wider scale (9:31), since Luke marks the event with another editorial note about the word of God growing and multiplying (12:24; cf. 6:7).

A. Peter's Pastoral and Evangelistic Ministry
in Western Judea (9:32-43)

This last section of Acts 9 reintroduces Peter in preparation for the great events of Acts 10–11. Peter travels to Lydda and then to Joppa, moving further and further away from Jerusalem into Gentile territory. As he responds to various needs, God blesses his pastoral and evangelistic endeavours. Aeneas is healed, Tabbitha (Dorcas) is raised from death, and many people

---

81. Gaventa 2003, 162.

turn to Christ. So Peter is led by God to the house of Simon the tanner, where he receives the vision that will impel him to preach the gospel to a Roman household in Caesarea. The healing of the paralytic and the resuscitation of the widow parallel the ministry of Jesus (cf. Lk. 5:17-26; 7:11-17) and the earlier ministries of Elijah and Elisha (cf. 1 Ki. 17:17-24; 2 Ki. 4:18-37). Thus, 'Peter is validated once more as an authentic representative of the line of prophets who "work signs and wonders among the people." '[82] His Christ-likeness is highlighted 'at a moment when his authority is decisive to Luke's argument'.[83] These two narratives form a pair, with a number of common elements, but with the second account more detailed. The first focuses on a man and the second on a woman, highlighting her good works and the respect she commanded among the believers in Joppa.[84]

1. Healing Aeneas in Lydda (9:32-35)

32-35 *As Peter travelled about the country* (*dierchomenon dia pantōn*, 'passing through the whole [region]'), *he went to visit the Lord's people who lived in Lydda* (*katelthein kai pros tous hagious tous katoikountas Lydda*, 'he came down also to the saints who lived at Lydda').[85] As in 9:13, these 'saints' are Jewish Christians who either came from Jerusalem because of the persecution (8:1), or turned to Christ because of the preaching of Philip, when he journeyed from Azotus to Caesarea (8:40). *Lydda* (the Greek form of Lod; cf. 1 Chr. 8:12; Ezr. 2:33; Neh. 11:35) was about a day's journey (25 miles or 40 km.) on the road from Jerusalem towards the coastal town of Joppa (another 12 miles on). It was situated in the plain of Sharon and was capital of one of the ten local government areas in Judea.[86] In Lydda, Peter

---

82. Johnson 1992, 180. Tannehill 1990, 126-27, draws the parallels between these narratives in great detail.

83. D. P. Seccombe, 'The New People of God', in Marshall and Peterson, *Witness to the Gospel*, 361 note 17. Witherington 1998, 327, suggests that Peter is dwelling here 'on the rhetorically important matter of *pathos*, the deeper emotions. He seeks to arouse strong feelings in his listener not just for winsome characters like Tabitha but also for Peter himself.'

84. Witherington 1998, 328, argues that this deliberate literary pattern is 'Luke's way of suggesting that the good news and all the aspects of salvation, including healing, are intended equally for men and women'. Cf. H. Flender, *St. Luke — Theologian of Redemptive History* (London: SPCK, 1967), 10. Witherington 1998, 334-39, discusses 'Luke, Women, and Ministry', assessing the views of those who have written on this subject since the publication of his 1988 work on this topic.

85. The expression 'through the whole' (*dia pantōn*) is strangely plural, without a noun to define it. It is also unusual that Luke should say that Peter came down '*also* to the saints' (*kai*). In 8:4, 40 the verb 'to pass through' (*dierchesthai*) is associated with evangelism, and so it is possible that Peter was on an evangelistic tour in which he also made a pastoral visit to the saints in Lydda. As an evangelist, he 'gradually extended his range of operation till he covered the whole racial and religious scale, though not the whole geographical area, available' (Barrett 1994, 479).

86. Pliny, *Nat. Hist.* 5.70; Josephus, *War* 3.55. In size it was not inferior to a city.

found a man named Aeneas, *who was paralysed and had been bedridden for eight years* (*ex etōn oktō katakeimenon epi krabattou*, 'who for eight years had lain on his bed').[87] As in the following miracle story, the detail of the condition evokes pathos in the reader and highlights the wonder of the cure. Aeneas (a Greek name) is not specifically identified as a disciple, as Dorcas is, but mention of his name in the context of visiting the saints suggests that he was one of them. Peter took the initiative (cf. 3:1-7; Lk. 7:13-15; 13:12) with a declaration (*'Jesus Christ heals you'*),[88] and a command (*'Get up and roll up your mat'*).[89] The narrative is brief, without reference to any supportive action (cf. 3:7), putting the focus on the sudden outcome (*immediately Aeneas got up*) and the effect on those outside the church (*All those who lived in Lydda and Sharon saw him and turned to the Lord*). Many unbelievers — in Lydda and the surrounding coastal plain of Sharon — turned to Jesus as Lord (here and in v. 42), acknowledging his divine authority and saving power through the actions and words of his apostle.[90] The risen Jesus continues to heal through Peter.

2. Raising Tabitha/Dorcas in Joppa (9:36-43)

36 Despite its close association with Judea, Joppa seems to have been a distinctly Greek city.[91] So when Peter reached this point, he was definitely in Gentile territory. Joppa (Arabic, Jaffa) is mentioned in the OT (Jos. 19:46; 2 Chr. 2:16; Ezr. 3:7; Jon. 1:3). In that city there lived *a disciple* (the feminine form *mathētria* is used only here in the NT, but cf. 6:1; 9:25, 38 for the more general form). Her Aramaic name was *Tabitha* (the feminine form for 'deer, gazelle', LSJ), and her Greek name *Dorcas* similarly meant 'an animal of the deer kind'.[92] She had a reputation for *always doing good and helping the poor*. Further details of her good works are given when mention is made of *the robes and other clothing that Dorcas had made while she was still with them*

---

87. Barrett 1994, 480, points out that *ex etōn oktō* could mean 'from the age of eight', though 'for eight years' is more probably intended.

88. NKJV's 'Jesus the Christ' is based on a reading found in some reliable ancient MSS and 'seems to have a certain primitiveness' (Metzger, *Textual Commentary*, 323). However, the majority of early witnesses omit the definite article.

89. The expression *strōson seautō* (lit. 'spread for yourself') could mean 'tidy up your mat' (most EVV, 'make your bed') or 'set the table for yourself/prepare a meal for yourself'. Either action would demonstrate the reality of the cure. Cf. Bruce 1990, 247; Johnson 1992, 177; Lk. 5:24.

90. 'Here the use of *pas* (all), as elsewhere in Acts, should not be taken literally but is an example of rhetorical hyperbole, intended to indicate a large response and to impress the hearer' (Witherington 1998, 330). Barrett 1994, 482, notes several textual variants regarding the spelling of Sharon.

91. Josephus, *War* 3.56; Bruce 1990, 248.

92. Barrett 1994, 483, says that it is probable that 'in the mixed society of Joppa, both names, the Aramaic and the Greek, would be in use'.

(v. 39). It is reading too much into the example of this one faithful disciple to suggest that there was in Joppa 'a fairly developed charitable organization'.[93] But there is no doubt that Luke wishes to highlight the importance of Dorcas and her ministry to the needy. She was probably a woman of means, 'with leisure and freedom to do good deeds for others'.[94] Once again, generosity surfaces in the narrative of Acts as a sign of the Spirit's work in those who turn to Christ (cf. 2:44-45; 4:32-37).

37-38 *About that time (en tais hēmerais ekeinais, 'in those days'), when* Peter was in the region, *she became ill and died, and her body was washed and placed in an upstairs room.* Perhaps the church met in her house, in that same *upstairs room* (cf. *hyperōn* in 1:13; 9:39; 20:8). The washing of her body in preparation for burial suggests 'something of her significance for this community of believers'.[95] *When the disciples heard that Peter was in Lydda, they sent two men to him and urged him, 'Please come at once!'* Did they simply want him to pay his respects to this outstanding Christian lady at her impending burial, or did they hope that he might raise her from death?[96]

39-40 Whatever their intentions, Peter moved swiftly to the place of mourning, and was *taken upstairs to the room.* Luke then paints a very sad picture. *All the widows stood round him,* encouraging him to share in their grief by *crying and showing him the robes and other clothing that Dorcas had made while she was still with them.* Somewhat like Jesus in Luke 8:51-56, Peter *sent them all out of the room,* though this miracle occurs even more privately. Furthermore, whereas Jesus took the little girl by the hand and commanded here to get up, Peter *got down on his knees and prayed.* Like Elijah, he expressed in prayer his total dependence on God for the resuscitation of the dead (2 Ki. 4:33). Then, *turning towards the dead woman, he said, 'Tabitha, get up',* recalling Jesus' address to the daughter of Jairus (Mk. 5:41; Lk. 8:54). The same word *get up (anastēthi)* is used in v. 34 and v. 40, though here with reference to an even more remarkable event than the healing of a man who was paralysed.[97] It is the verb frequently associated with the resurrection of Jesus. In dependence upon the risen Lord, Peter called upon a dead person

93. Barrett 1994, 478. Tabitha is not in charge of an order of widows (cf. 1 Tim. 5:3-16), and we are not told that she is a widow herself. Barrett makes the suggestion that there was such an order and that the church in Joppa was therefore 'not of recent origin'. Spencer 1997, 107-8, is more restrained in speaking about the significance of her ministry.

94. Witherington 1998, 331. Spencer 1997, 103, compares 6:2-4 and speaks of Peter now becoming 'more personally involved in helping needy widows by restoring — through prayer (9:40) — their beloved benefactress (9:39, 41)'.

95. Gaventa 2003, 160.

96. Marshall 1980, 179, suggests that laying the body in the upper room instead of burial and sending for Peter may indicate some hope of resurrection. Longenecker 1981, 382, believes that they were perhaps encouraged by news of the healing of Aeneas. There is no previous evidence of the apostles being involved in raising the dead.

97. Several Western MSS add in slightly varying forms the words *en tō onomati tou kyriou hēmōn Iēsou Christou* ('in the name of our Lord Jesus Christ') after 'get up' in 9:40. Cf. Metzger, *Textual Commentary*, 324.

to rise. The reality of the miracle is stressed in simple terms: *she opened her eyes, and seeing Peter she sat up.*

41-43 Peter's continuing care for her is stressed (*he took her by the hand and helped her to her feet*). He then confronted *the believers* in general and *the widows* in particular with this mighty act of God and *presented her to them alive* (the language here is reminiscent of 1:3). Such a miracle could not be kept secret, so that *this became known all over Joppa, and many people believed in the Lord* (Jesus, as in v. 35). Luke ends this story on a strange note: *Peter stayed in Joppa for some time with a tanner named Simon.* Indeed, this Simon the tanner is mentioned again several times in the following narrative (10:6, 17-18, 32). Tanners were considered unclean by more scrupulous Jews because of their contact with the hides of dead animals.[98] Peter was apparently not troubled by such concerns, but he would soon have difficulty taking the more radical step of visiting a Gentile household (cf. 10:6 note).[99] He would need a series of revelations from God to move him in that direction.

2. Peter's Role in the Evangelisation of the Gentiles (10:1-48)

Jesus' programmatic prophecy (1:8) continues to be fulfilled, as the apostolic witness moves decisively to the Gentile world. Like the story of the Ethiopian eunuch in 8:27-38, Acts 10 records the baptism of a person of some social status, who is a Gentile at the fringe of Judaism. However, the Cornelius event is even more significant for Luke. The apostle Peter is involved and has to give some explanation of his actions to 'the circumcised believers' in Jerusalem (11:2-3) and then again later to the council in Jerusalem (15:7-9).[1] The Ethiopian returns to his own country, but Cornelius and his household form the nucleus of a new group of Gentile Christians in Caesarea, the capital of Judea and official seat of the Roman procurator. A heavenly vision and other divine initiatives authorize Peter's actions and eventually lead the Jerusalem church to endorse the reception of Gentiles into the messianic community (11:18, 22).[2] As a 'God-fearer', Cornelius appears to be a synagogue adherent, but not yet a full convert to Judaism. He is a bridge figure, 'standing at the boundary between Judaism and paganism, and living in a very Hellenized city full of Gentiles, yet in the Holy

98. Cf. Barrett 1994, 486; Witherington 1998, 333. Metzger, *Textual Commentary*, 325, discusses MSS variants of the expression *hēmeras hikanas meinai* ('to stay for some time').

99. Spencer 1997, 113, suggests 'a complex developmental *process* in Peter's socio-religious orientation, pushing certain radical boundaries here while toeing the party line there'.

1. For a discussion of problems raised by Acts 10–11 and an assessment of various scholarly views as to their composition and intention, see Barrett 1994, 491-98.

2. Witherington 1998, 340, argues that the 'conversion' of Saul in Acts 9 and the 'conversion' of Cornelius in Acts 10 together form the catalyst 'to change the character and general direction the early church would take thereafter'. Compare n. 54 below.

Land'.[3] Despite his prayers and gifts to the poor, in orthodox Jewish terms he is still technically 'unclean', and Peter is unwilling to come to his house and eat with him. A threefold vision, the visit of the men sent by Cornelius, and the clear leading of the Spirit enable Peter to overcome his prejudice and take the gospel to a Gentile home. Geographical factors make concrete the divine will to bring Jews and Gentiles together in the renewed people of God. 'Acts 10–11 begins from two poles (Caesarea and Joppa) and ends up with one (Jerusalem). The text is full of movements, sometimes ascending and sometimes descending. The horizontal shifts are often noted in the form of some kind of entrance. Looking more closely, we see that every divine irruption (angel, vision, Holy Spirit) originates a human movement and that this movement corresponds to someone's welcome.'[4]

Some scholars have questioned whether the issue of clean and unclean food was originally part of the story received by Luke.[5] However, this matter is not incidental to the structure and flow of the narrative. What needed to be resolved for Peter was not whether the gospel was for Gentiles (cf. Lk. 24:47; Acts 1:8; 2:39; 3:25-26), but how they could receive it in view of their 'uncleanness' in Jewish eyes and be one with Jewish believers in the fellowship of the church. In practical terms, Jews and Gentiles could not share food and shelter. 'By means of the issue of *hospitality*, Luke demonstrates that the conversion of the first Gentile required the conversion of the church as well. Indeed, in Luke's account, Peter and company undergo a change that is more wrenching by far than the change experienced by Cornelius.'[6] Reading the narrative as a continuous whole, Gaventa observes a series of parallel scenes which, for the purpose of exposition, I have combined into three divisions for this chapter.[7]

3. Witherington 1998, 340 note 46. Witherington rightly observes that Acts 10:1–11:18 represents 'another step along the way toward a more universal religion, universal both in its geographical and social scope'. See his discussion of the terms 'God-fearer' and 'proselyte' (341-44), and I. Levinskaya, *The Book of Acts in Its First-Century Setting*, Vol. 5: *Diaspora Setting* (Grand Rapids: Eerdmans/Carlisle: Paternoster, 1996), 19-126.

4. D. Marguerat and Y. Bourquin, *How to Read Bible Stories: An Introduction to Narrative Criticism* (London: SCM, 1999; trans. J. Bowden from *Pour Lire les Récits Bibliques* [Paris: Les Éditions du Cerf, 1998]), 81.

5. So M. Dibelius, *Studies in the Acts of the Apostles*, ed. H. Greeven, trans. M. Ling (London: SCM, 1956), 109-22, and others cited by Witherington 1998, 344-5. Witherington counters with the arguments that 'the specifics of the story anchor it in Caesarea, a place where Luke seems to have spent a considerable amount of time' and that Luke found the vision and the story of Peter's encounter with Cornelius together in his Petrine or Caesarean source. Cf. Marshall 1980, 181-83; M. M. B. Turner, *Power from on High: The Spirit in Israel's Restoration and Witness in Luke-Acts*, JPTSS 9 (Sheffield: Sheffield Academic, 1996), 378-80.

6. B. R. Gaventa, *From Darkness to Light: Aspects of Conversion in the New Testament*, Overtures to Biblical Theology 20 (Philadelphia: Fortress, 1986), 109. The question of hospitality and shared meals plays an important role in the text (cf. 10:23, 27, 48; 11:3). A mission to Gentiles simply could not have proceeded on any significant basis apart from the resolution of this matter.

7. Gaventa, *Darkness*, 111.

Vision Scene	1	Cornelius	10:1-8
	2	Peter	10:9-16
Journey and Welcome	3	Cornelius	10:17-23a
	4	Peter	10:23b-29
Proclamation	5	Cornelius	10:30-33
	6	Peter	10:34-43
Confirmation	7	Holy Spirit	10:44-48
	8	Community	11:1-18

This structure highlights the way in which God's guidance was experienced. Cornelius and Peter both received visions which prepared them to meet together. Two journeys were required to bring about this encounter, with the Spirit directing Peter's understanding and enabling him to respond appropriately to his Gentile visitors (10:1-29). The preaching of the gospel to Cornelius and his household was followed by an unmistakable outpouring of the Spirit (10:30-43). This persuaded the Jewish Christians that believing Gentiles were as much the recipients of the blessings of the New Covenant as they were and so they baptized them with water (10:44-48). As already noted, two further stages in discerning God's will come later: 'the new insight and relationship must be justified publicly before the church (11:1-18), and its implications must be worked out in public debate with contrary understandings of God's will (15:1-29)'.[8]

Sociologically, the visions in this chapter have the purpose of 'opening a relationship between persons of different cultures'.[9] Theologically, however, the threefold vision given to Peter offers a new perspective on the way in which Scripture is to be interpreted and the gospel is to be preached. The provisions of the Mosaic law for cleansing and sanctification are fulfilled in Christ and thus the cultic restrictions excluding Gentiles from the community of God's people are no longer applicable (cf. Eph. 2:11-22).

1. Two Significant Visions (10:1-16)

The godly character of the Gentile Cornelius is outlined by Luke and confirmed by an angel in a vision (vv. 1-4). However, the angelic challenge is to send for Peter, since Cornelius needs to hear the gospel in order to experience the salvation promised to all who trust in Israel's Messiah. Cornelius responds immediately, as directed (vv. 5-8). Meanwhile, Peter also receives a vision that challenges his understanding about the continuing relevance

---

8. Tannehill 1990, 132. Tannehill offers a detailed reflection on the process by which God's will was discerned in this context, to which I am indebted. Cf. L. T. Johnson, *Decision Making in the Church: A Biblical Model* (Philadelphia: Fortress, 1983).

9. Tannehill 1990, 131.

of the 'clean' and 'unclean' distinctions in the levitical law (vv. 9-16). The meaning of this vision is further revealed to Peter as the Spirit directs his attitude and actions in the following scene (vv. 17-23).

1-2 The city of *Caesarea*, which had been the centre of Roman administration in the province of Judea since AD 6, was where the Roman governors lived (cf. 23:23-24).[10] Its population was mainly Gentile. Philip had previously gone as far as Caesarea in his evangelistic ministry (8:40), and at some stage settled there with his family (21:8-9). Paul had also stopped there on his way to Tarsus (9:30). As *a centurion*, Cornelius would have commanded an auxiliary force of approximately one hundred men (one sixth of a *regiment* [*speira*] or cohort). Although he was a noncommissioned officer, 'his responsibilities were more like those of a modern army captain'.[11] The so-called *Italian Regiment* would have been made up of freedmen, who were enrolled only in periods of great need.[12] By name and occupation, Cornelius was a Roman citizen, and yet *he and all his family were devout and God-fearing.* The description of Cornelius as *devout (eusebēs)* and *God-fearing (phoboumenos ton theon)* has been much discussed. Similar terminology is found in 10:22, 35; 13:16, 26. Parallel expressions using another verb (*sebesthai*, a cognate of *eusebēs*) are found in 13:43, 50; 16:14; 17:4, 17; 18:7, 13; 19:27. Fundamentally, fearing God means respecting, honouring, and hence worshipping him (e.g., Mt. 15:9; Mk. 7:7 [both citing Is. 29:13]; Acts 10:35; 18:13; contrast 19:27, the worship of Artemis). In some contexts, the Greek participles are used attributively in the sense of 'devout' (e.g., 10:2, 22; 13:43, 50; 17:4). When these participles are used substantivally, they have been taken to refer to a specific class of persons who were not Jews and not full proselytes, but Gentiles who were attached to the synagogues and were sympathetic to Jewish theology and ethics (e.g., 13:16, 26; 17:17; cf. 16:14; 18:7). Scholars continue to debate whether 'God-fearers' is a technical term for Luke and whether he used the term 'proselyte' for the same group.[13] Proselytes embraced Judaism and all its rituals fully, including circumcision (cf. 2:10; 6:5; 13:43). However, inscriptions and other evidence show that there were many Gentiles in the first century who did not become proselytes in the full and technical sense, but who frequented syna-

---

10. Caesarea is mentioned fifteen times in Acts. Herod the Great established it in the second decade BC, with a splendid harbour, and named it in honour of Caesar Augustus. Cf. M. Hengel, 'The Geography of Palestine in Acts', in R. Bauckham (ed.), *The Book of Acts in Its First-Century Setting*, Vol. 4: *Palestinian Setting* (Grand Rapids: Eerdmans; Carlisle: Paternoster, 1995), 55-58.

11. Bruce 1990, 202.

12. So Barrett 1994, 499. There were no legionary troops in Judea AD 6-66, but the Roman governors commanded auxiliary forces. The 'Italian Regiment' would presumably have been so called because it was originally raised in Italy. Inscriptional evidence indicates the presence of an Italian cohort in Syria in AD 69, and possibly earlier. Cf. Witherington 1998, 346.

13. Cf. Barrett 1994, 499-501; Witherington 1998, 341-44; Levinskaya, *Diaspora Setting*, 19-126.

gogues and sought to live as much as they could by Jewish law. Such people provided 'the key socially stabilizing link between Jews and Greco-Roman society',[14] and were ripe for conversion to Christianity. Cornelius was just such a person, as indicated by all that is said about him in this verse, rather than by identification with the title 'God-fearer'. He was actually an exemplary believer in the God of Israel, who influenced his whole *family* (*oikos*, 'house, household') to follow him.[15] His piety was demonstrated by the fact that he made many charitable gifts to the Jewish people (*tō laō*, 'to the people'). TNIV, *he gave generously to those in need*, obscures this specific reference. He also *prayed to God regularly*, presumably following the Jewish 'hours' of prayer.[16] Jewish Christians would have recognized in him a truly biblical piety.[17]

3-4 The process by which Cornelius became a Christian is described in great detail, with many narrative indications of God's initiative and direction. The pattern of divine guidance here is unique and complex, though it combines elements found elsewhere in Acts. Long-standing barriers between Jews and Gentiles were being removed, and Jewish believers like Peter had to learn to welcome Gentiles into the church on the basis of their faith in Christ alone. God's guidance came first in the form of *a vision* which Cornelius received (*eiden en horamati phanerōs*, 'he saw in a vision clearly'), not when he was asleep but *at about three in the afternoon*. This was the time of prayer at the temple in Jerusalem associated with the evening sacrifice (cf. 3:1 note). Following the practice of devout Jews throughout the Dispersion, Cornelius was praying at this time (cf. 10:30), though at home rather than at a synagogue.[18] In his vision, *he distinctly saw an angel of God, who came to him* and addressed him personally. Angels play an important part in furthering God's purposes in 5:19; 8:26; 10:3; 12:7; 27:23. They appear only at significant points in the narrative, to provide guidance and help to key figures. In this case, the angel is one of several means by which God progressively makes his will known. Cornelius *stared at him in fear* (*ho de atenisas autō kai emphobos genomenos*, 'and when he looked at him, he was afraid'). This was not so much terror as reverent fear or awe in the presence of the supernatural. His question (*'What is it, Lord?'*) acknowledges the presence of a divine messenger and enquires about the purpose of his visit. The angel's reply confirms that God is pleased with him (*'Your prayers and*

---

14. Witherington 1998, 344, summarizing the argument of Levinskaya.

15. His household could have included slaves (*oiketai*, as in 10:7), as well as his own relatives. Cf. Josephus, *Against Apion* 2.210, 258, 282; Juvenal, *Sat.* 14.96-99; Acts 16:15, 31, 34; 18:8.

16. Cf. D. K. Falk, 'Jewish Prayer Literature and the Jerusalem Church in Acts', in Bauckham, *Palestinian Setting*, 267-301.

17. Cf. Mt. 6:1-6; Tob. 12:8; and the piety of Peter and John, who come to the temple to pray and heal a man who is begging for alms (Acts 3:1-7). Spencer 1997, 109-10, comments on the significance of the three centurions in Luke's two-volume work (cf. Lk. 7:1-10; 23:47).

18. Cf. Falk, 'Jewish Prayer Literature', 274.

gifts to the poor have come up as a memorial offering before God').[19] God
has taken note of the genuineness of his faith, expressed in prayers and
charitable gifts, and is about to lead him to enjoy the benefits of the messianic salvation promised in Scripture to believing Jews and Gentiles (e.g., Is.
49:5-6). God does not act in this way because Cornelius 'deserves it',[20] but
because he graciously blesses those who trust him and seek to do his will
(cf. 10:34-35 note). Putting it another way, Luke records 'the transition of a
godly believer (dependent upon OT revelation) into the new age of the
Spirit, rather than the conversion of an unbeliever'.[21]

5-8 Cornelius is instructed to *'send men to Joppa to bring back a man
named Simon who is called Peter'*. Practically, this initiates the process by
which he receives the gospel. *Joppa* (cf. 9:36) was about 30 miles (50 km.)
from Caesarea. The information given in 9:43 about Peter's location is repeated *('He is staying with Simon the tanner')*, with additional detail *('whose
house is by the sea'*; cf. 10:32). Such knowledge confirms the divine origin of
the revelation. But perhaps the threefold mention of Simon's location is
also meant to suggest that he would be open to an invitation from a Gentile
like Cornelius. Rabbinic literature reveals 'a consistent disdain for tanners
and tanneries as unclean people and places'.[22] Peter does not seem to have
been bothered about close contact with such a person, but had come part of
the way towards meeting with people regarded as ritually unclean and eating with them. *When the angel who spoke to him had gone, Cornelius called two
of his servants* (*tōn oiketōn*, 'household servants') *and a devout soldier*
(*stratiōtēn eusebē*, 'devout' like Cornelius himself in 10:2), *who was one of his*

---

19. Description of his prayers ascending as *a memorial offering before God (eis
mnēmosynon emprosthen tou theou)* is reminiscent of what is said about the burnt offerings in
LXX Lv. 2:2, 9, 16; 5:12. Cf. Bruce 1990, 204; Johnson 1992, 183. P. F. Esler, *Community and Gospel in Luke-Acts: The Social and Political Motivations of Lucan Theology*, SNTSMS 57 (Cambridge: Cambridge University, 1987), 162, argues that the language suggests that his prayers
and alms were accepted by God 'in lieu of the sacrifices which he was not allowed to enter
the Temple to offer himself'.

20. As Barrett 1994, 503, proposes.

21. G. N. Davies, 'When Was Cornelius Saved?', *RTR* 46 (1987), 44. Davies rightly argues against the view that the works that Cornelius performed were without grace. Rather,
they were 'the result of his faith in God and in response to the promises of God which included the Gentiles' (45). Gaventa, *Darkness*, 122, suggests a difference between the experience of Saul and that of Cornelius. Like the Ethiopian eunuch, Cornelius experienced an 'alteration' rather than a 'conversion', meaning a new position proceeding naturally from
prior commitments. Cf. P. H. Kern, 'Paul's Conversion and Luke's Portrayal of Character in
Acts 8–10', *TynB* 54 (2003), 63-80. However, in my introduction to Acts 9, I argue that there is
a sense in which both the Ethiopian and Cornelius are positively converted by turning to
the Lord Jesus for salvation.

22. Spencer 1997, 113. Cf. H. L. Strack and P. Billerbeck, *Kommentar zum Neuen Testament aus Talmud und Midrasch*, 6 vols. (München: Beck, 1922-61), 2:695. After some discussion of the possible significance of this evidence, Barrett 1994, 486-87, concludes that Simon's residence with the tanner was not important. But Spencer rightly suggests that the
text is indicating 'a complex developmental *process* in Peter's socio-religious orientation,
pushing certain radical boundaries here while toeing the party line there'.

attendants. These were clearly men to whom he could give an account of the revelation he had received and whom he could trust to carry out the angelic command *(He told them everything that had happened and sent them to Joppa).*

9-10 Luke now tells us about the parallel vision given to Peter. It happened on *the following day (tē epaurion)*, at *about noon (peri hōran hektēn)*, just as the emissaries from Cornelius *were on their journey and approaching the city.* Like Cornelius, Peter received a vision while praying *(Peter went up on the roof to pray).* However, this was not normally a time to pray, but a time to eat, and so Peter was hungry. As he prayed and waited for the meal to be prepared, *he fell into a trance (egeneto ep' auton ekstasis,* 'there came upon him a trance'; cf. 11:5; 22:17). Luke implies that his physical condition and his prayerfulness made him receptive to the vision that is now described.

11-14 Instead of an angel, Peter saw *heaven opened and something like a large sheet being let down to earth by its four corners.* The expression *heaven opened* signifies the beginning of a divine revelation (cf. Lk. 3:21; Acts 7:56). Here the heavens open 'to stimulate the church to move out toward the ends of the earth (cf. 1:8-11; 7:55–8:4; 9:3-16)'.[23] The vision is literally of 'a sort of vessel coming down' *(katabainon skeuos ti),* 'like a large piece of cloth, by its four corners being lowered upon the earth' *(hōs othonēn megalēn tessarsin archais kathiemenon epi tēs gēs).*[24] This cloth *contained all kinds of four-footed animals, as well as reptiles of the earth and birds of the air.*[25] Creatures of every variety mentioned in Genesis 1:24 *(tetrapoda kai herpeta,* 'four-footed animals and reptiles'), and 1:20 *(peteina,* 'birds'), are included in this vision (cf. Gn. 6:20; Rom. 1:23). Peter is then challenged to satisfy his hunger with any one of these creatures — clean or unclean in terms of the Mosaic law — by a voice telling him, *'Get up, Peter. Kill and eat.'* The verb translated *kill (thyson)* is regularly used with reference to sacrifice and may imply a ritual killing before eating.[26] Peter's stay in Gentile territory may already have made him wonder about the continuing relevance of Jewish food regulations. However, faithful to texts such as Leviticus 11:1-47; 20:25-26, he replies, *'Surely not, Lord!' (mēdamōs, kyrie,* 'not so Lord'). *'I have never eaten anything impure or unclean' (oudepote ephagon pan koinon kai akatharton).* He

23. Spencer 1997, 108.
24. The word *katabainon* ('coming down') is omitted by some Western texts, and the vessel is described as 'tied *(dedemenon)*' at the four corners'. A good range of more ancient texts record that the vessel was 'coming down' and being 'lowered *(kathiemenon)*' by (the) four corners'. This is most likely the original reading (so NRSV, ESV, TNIV). Later texts then conflate the options to include the three participles 'coming down', 'tied', and 'being lowered' (so KJV, NKJV). Cf. Metzger, *Textual Commentary,* 326.
25. There is a fuller account of this vision in 11:6, which seems to have influenced various readings of 10:12 (cf. KJV, NKJV). However, the reading that best explains the origin of the others and is the best attested is the one translated by NRSV, ESV, and TNIV. Cf. Metzger, *Textual Commentary,* 326-27.
26. Cf. J. Behm, *TDNT* 3:180-81.

recognizes that the voice is divine but refuses to eat indiscriminately, perhaps viewing this as a test of his loyalty. 'Peter staunchly affirms his kosher
commitment in the grand tradition of Daniel (Dan. 1:8), Tobit (Tob. 1:10-11),
Judith (Jdt. 10:5; 12:1-2), Judas Maccabeus (2 Macc. 5:27), Eleazar (2 Macc.
6:18-31) and other faithful Israelites who refused to defile themselves with
foreign food (cf. 1 Macc. 1:62-63).'[27] He certainly fails to evaluate the challenge in the light of Jesus' practice and teaching (cf. Mk. 7:1-23; Mt. 15:1-
20).[28]

15-16   A second divine command then explains the significance of
the first: *'Do not call anything impure that God has made clean'* (*ha ho theos
ekatharisen, sy mē koinou*, 'what God has cleansed do not you defile'). This
command contains 'a concise and pointed antithesis that helps to make
these words challenging'.[29] Peter must acknowledge God's right to determine what is clean and to redefine boundaries for the gospel era. The message was so important that it was given *three times*, before *the sheet was taken
back to heaven.* Peter must not treat any of the creatures in the vision as profane, since God has declared them to be clean (*ekatharisen*, 'cleansed' them).
Some have taken this as a reference back to the pronouncement of Jesus in
Mark 7:18-23, where the editorial comment indicates that Jesus was effectively 'cleansing all foods' (*katharizōn;* cf. Mt. 15:16-20). However, since
Luke does not record that incident in his Gospel, the implication may be
that God has cleansed all foods with this revelation to Peter, coinciding
with a new stage in the progress of the gospel.[30] What was implicit in the
teaching of Jesus is now made explicit. The clean and unclean provisions of
the law were temporary, designed to keep Israel a holy and distinct people,
until the time when Jews and Gentiles could receive the forgiveness of sins
and sanctification on the same basis, through faith in Christ (Acts 20:32;
26:17-18; cf. 15:9, 'having cleansed their hearts by faith'). By the time he explains the vision to Cornelius and his household, Peter recognises that he
should no longer allow the levitical laws to keep him from associating with

27. Spencer 1997, 111. Johnson 1992, 185, observes that 'Peter resists God's initiative,
then the leaders in Jerusalem (11:1-18), then the members of the Pharisaic party in Antioch
(15:1-2)'.
28. Barrett 1994, 507, first suggests a test of loyalty, but then argues that this is improbable. He doubts that Peter could have honestly said that he had never eaten anything
unclean. He rightly points out that Peter's response indicates a failure to see the logical implications of Jesus' practice and teaching. Witherington 1998, 350, thinks that Peter may
have considered that 'because of the considerable presence of unclean animals and the possible problem of contamination, there was nothing fit to eat in the sheet'.
29. Tannehill 1990, 132. The antithesis uses the same terminology as Peter's disclaimer (v. 14). Tannehill continues, 'The command gains its force by presenting a sharp
warning of the potential conflict between divine and human action'.
30. So Marshall 1980, 186. Against Barrett 1994, 509, who takes *ekatharisen* to refer to
'what is eternally in the mind of God', the aorist is more likely to be perfective than timeless
in this context. The list of creatures in the vision recalls Genesis 1 and suggests to Barrett
that 10:15 confirms God's original purpose to create all things 'clean'.

Gentiles (v. 28). The events that follow (vv. 30-48) make it clear that Gentiles do not have to become Jewish proselytes in order to benefit from the messianic salvation.

2. *Two Significant Journeys (10:17-29)*

Two journeys play an important role in the narrative. Both are expressions of obedience to specific divine commands (vv. 5-6, 19-20), and both contribute to the understanding of God's will in the situation. The trusted servants of Cornelius must bring the Jewish apostle to their master's house, so that they can hear what he has to say (v. 22), and understand the significance of what they already know about Jesus and his ministry (v. 37, 'you know'). Peter must not hesitate to go with them because he is assured by the Spirit that God has sent them (vv. 19-20). As he invites the visitors to be his guests, then travels with them to Caesarea and reflects on the meaning of the two visions (vv. 23-29), Peter becomes aware that he 'should not call anyone impure or unclean' (v. 28). It is thus in obeying God that Peter is prepared to preach to the Gentiles and offer them salvation on the same basis as Jews, namely through faith in the crucified and risen Lord Jesus (vv. 34-43).

17-20 *While Peter was wondering about the meaning of the vision (en heautō diēporei ti an eiē to horama ho eiden,* 'doubted in himself what the vision he had seen might mean'),[31] *the men sent by Cornelius found out where Simon's house was and stopped at the gate.* Their cautious approach is highlighted *(They called out, asking if Simon who was known as Peter was staying there)*, along with Peter's continuing confusion about the vision *(while Peter was still thinking about the vision).* But God's control over the situation is made clear again *(the Spirit said to him).* As in 8:26-29, the pattern of divine guidance includes an angelic message or divine voice associated with a vision, providential circumstances, and the direction of the Holy Spirit. In both passages, the last form of guidance apparently refers to an inner conviction or word from God by which the meaning of the circumstances is made clear.[32] The Spirit speaks to Peter while he is *still thinking about the vision,* suggesting that he is actively seeking the meaning of what has been revealed so far. He will discover what it is all about only if he follows the Spirit's prompting. Peter is told that *'three men'* are looking for him,[33] and so

---

31. Some Western MSS read *egeneto* after *heautō*, giving the sense that 'as Peter came to himself' he pondered the meaning of the vision. However, the best-attested reading is the shorter one reflected in the TNIV translation. Cf. Barrett 1994, 510.

32. So also Marshall 1980, 187. It should be noted that the Spirit addresses him in the first person (*egō apestalka autous,* 'for I have sent them'), and so we are not to think of Peter's conviction as merely a feeling or inclination that is somehow self-generated.

33. MSS evidence is confused at this point, with some omitting the number 'three' and one mentioning two men. The reading supported by the broadest spectrum of exter-

to *'get up and go downstairs'*. When he meets them, he must not *hesitate to go with them*, since they are sent by God himself *('for I have sent them')*. The verb translated *'hesitate' (diakrinomenos)* has 'a double nuance that is important for the development of the story',[34] suggesting that Peter should 'make no distinction' that would cause him to doubt and to delay.

21-23   Peter announces that he is the man they are looking for and asks why they have come. The visitors identify their master in terms recalling Luke's opening description of him as *'a righteous and God-fearing man, who is respected by all the Jewish people'* (cf. vv. 1-2). As they summarize the angel's message *('to ask you to come to his house so that he could hear what you have to say'*; cf. vv. 3-6), Peter's apprehension of God's will in the situation becomes clearer. It is also new information for us as readers that the angel wanted Cornelius to hear what Peter had to say. Luke presumably held back this information until now for dramatic effect. When Peter invites the men *into the house to be his guests,* he is not yet going beyond what a law-abiding Jew might do in entertaining Gentiles.[35] He would be able to keep the levitical rules in showing hospitality to Gentiles, even though he was himself a guest in the house of another. But he would have no control over the situation in visiting the house of a Gentile like Cornelius. Even so, the next day he starts out with them, and some of the brothers from Joppa accompany him. According to 11:12, there were 'six brothers' who witnessed what happened to Cornelius and his household (cf. 10:45, *the circumcised believers who had come with Peter).*

24-27   On the fourth day of the story, Peter *arrived in Caesarea.* Luke now puts the focus on the personal encounter between Peter and Cornelius, mentioning Peter's companions again only in vv. 45-46.[36] *Cornelius was expecting them and had called together his relatives and close friends.* This shows that Cornelius anticipated hearing a message of great importance for himself and for those he loved. Perhaps, as one familiar with the Jewish Scriptures, he was genuinely looking for the coming of the Messiah and already

---

nal evidence is 'three', which corresponds with 10:7; 11:11. Cf. Metzger, *Textual Commentary,* 328.

34. Johnson 1992, 185. Barrett 1994, 511, considers the possibility that it means 'making no distinctions', but then opts for 'with no hesitation'. The same verb is used in the active form in 15:9, where it clearly means 'he made no distinction'. The verb is used in the middle or passive in 10:20, but in the active form in the best MSS of 11:12. In the middle or passive it can mean 'dispute, take issue with someone' or 'be at odds with oneself, doubt, waver' (BDAG). It is possible that the middle is used in 10:20 with the same sense as the active or to intensify that meaning ('make no distinction for yourself').

35. Cf. Marshall 1980, 187.

36. The MSS evidence for 10:24 is fairly evenly divided between the singular *eisēlthen* ('he entered') and the plural *eisēlthon* ('they entered'). Since there is a plural verb at the end of v. 23 and we know there was a group of brothers with Peter, it is likely that early copyists were surprised by the singular and changed it to the plural. Cf. Metzger, *Textual Commentary,* 329. Some Western MSS indicate that one of Peter's servants 'ran ahead and announced that he had arrived', but this reading is not well attested and seems to have been added to explain how Cornelius knew when to call his relatives and friends together.

knew something of Peter's claims about Jesus. Treating Peter as an angelic messenger, Cornelius *fell at his feet in reverence (pesōn epi tous podas prosekynēsan;* cf. Rev. 19:10; 22:8-9, where even an angel resists such homage).[37] Even though he brings the word of the living God, Peter insists that he is only human *(egō autos anthrōpos eimi, 'I am only human myself'),* and will not accept the deference due to God in the situation. After conversing with Cornelius, Peter went inside and *found a large gathering of people.*

28-29 Peter's audience is well enough informed about the strictures of Judaism to recognise the strangeness of the occasion *('You are well aware that it is against our law for a Jew to associate with Gentiles or visit them').* Association with Gentiles was a cause of defilement in Jewish tradition (cf. *Jub.* 22:16; *Test. Jos.* 7:1), rather than being strictly defined as such by the law of Moses. It was 'unlawful' *(athemitos)* in the more general sense of being against their custom. This was especially so because Gentiles did not observe the biblical rules about food. Such defilement would have to be removed by following the provisions of the law for cleansing. Even Gentile possessions needed to be purified before they were used by Jews.[38] *'But God has shown me that I should not call any anyone impure or unclean.'* The vision in vv. 11-16 was about not calling anything impure that God has made clean. Peter now applies this to human beings,[39] which explains why he has come *'without raising any objection'.* His question *('May I ask why you sent for me?')* then provides Cornelius with the opportunity to declare how God had been encountering him and preparing him to receive the gospel.

3. Salvation for Gentiles in the Fellowship of the Spirit (10:30-48)

Peter has been prepared to visit the house of a Gentile by all that has happened so far, but he still needs to hear from Cornelius personally about the vision he has received (vv. 30-3). God's acceptance of Cornelius and provision for him to meet Peter encourages the apostle to begin his address with an important affirmation about God's impartiality (vv. 34-35). The centurion's humble seeking after God and his desire to hear everything the Lord

---

37. The verb *proskynein* is normally translated 'to worship', though here it is used in the more general sense 'pay homage, reverence'. Bending over or bowing down was a respectful gesture made to some human authorities in Scripture (e.g., Gn. 18:2; 23:7; Ex. 11:8; 18:7). The same gesture directed towards God expressed awe and surrender to the divine king (e.g., Ex. 4:31; Jgs. 7:15; Ps. 95:6). Cf. D. G. Peterson, *Engaging with God: A Biblical Theology of Worship* (Leicester: Apollos; Grand Rapids: Eerdmans, 1992), 57-63.

38. Cf. Barrett 1994, 515.

39. Barrett 1994, 493-94, 497, 516, considers the possibility that the vision and the interpretation here do not belong together, but he acknowledges that one major cause of the uncleanness of the Gentiles for Jews was the unclean food they ate. As noted in connection with vv. 17-23, the visit of the men from Cornelius, so soon after the vision given to Peter, is used by the Holy Spirit to enable Peter to make the connection between unclean food and unclean people.

has commanded Peter to say (v. 33) move the apostle to offer those present the message of 'peace through Jesus Christ', who is appropriately identified as 'Lord of all' (v. 36). The gospel presentation in vv. 37-43 recalls previous messages delivered to Jewish audiences in various respects (2:22-39; 3:13-26), with some important additional features relevant to the situation. These include the clear testimony that Jesus has been appointed as 'judge of the living and the dead', and that the prophets speak of the messianic forgiveness being available for 'everyone who believes in him' (vv. 42-43). Even as Peter speaks these words of grace, the Holy Spirit is poured out on all who are listening to the message, and the Jewish believers are persuaded that nothing should prevent these Gentiles from being baptised (vv. 44-48). This divinely determined sequence of events not only opens the door for Gentiles to experience the benefits of the messianic salvation, but also to share with Jewish believers on exactly the same basis in the life of the church, which is clearly identified here as the community created and sustained by the Spirit of God.

30-33 Cornelius affirms that it was 'four days ago' (*apo tetartēs hēmeras*),[40] when he was in his house *'praying at this hour, at three in the afternoon'* (*tē enatēn proseuchomenos*, 'praying the ninth hour [prayers]'), that God confronted him.[41] The Lord's angelic representative is here described as *'a man in shining clothes'* standing before him (a detail not found in 10:3, but cf. 1:10; Lk. 24:4). Cornelius then summarizes the encounter recorded in vv. 4-6. As he thanks Peter for coming, Cornelius acknowledges that *'we are all here in the presence of God (enōpion tou theou) to listen to everything the Lord has commanded you to tell us'*.[42] This is a remarkable confession. Hearing the message God gave Peter was as much an experience of being in the divine presence as being addressed by an angel. As readers, we are implicitly challenged to receive what follows as the word of the Lord. God continues to make his presence and his purpose known every time the apostolic word is proclaimed and taught (cf. Col. 3:16; 1 Thes. 2:13).

34-35 Peter begins the fourth of his messages in Acts (cf. 2:14-39;

---

40. TNIV has *three days ago,* which is presumably 'inclusive reckoning' (Bruce 1990, 259). However, all EVV, including the NIV, translate 'four days ago'.

41. Barrett 1994, 516-17, discusses the complexities of the Greek in this verse and translates 'four days ago, at this very hour, I was saying the ninth hour of prayer in my house'. Some MSS add that Cornelius was fasting, which is the reading of the Received Text, and which KJV translates, 'Four days ago I was fasting until this hour; and at the ninth hour I prayed in my house' (cf. NKJV). Apart from poor MS attestation, the awkwardness of this rendering suggests that the reference to fasting is not original. Cf. Metzger, *Textual Commentary*, 330-31.

42. Several variants to 10:32-33 are examined by Metzger, *Textual Commentary*, 332-33. At the end of v. 32, Western and Byzantine texts add *hos paragenomenos lalēsei soi* (KJV 'when he cometh, shall speak unto thee'). In v. 33, the Western text makes several modifications, including *enōpion sou* 'in your presence' (instead of 'in the presence of God'). Some MSS refer to the things commanded 'by God' (*hypo tou theou*) rather than 'by the Lord'. However, the TNIV has translated the best-attested readings in each case.

3:12-26; 4:8-12) with another remarkable confession: '*I now realize how true it is* (*ep' alētheia katalambanomai,* 'truly I am coming to realize') *that God does not show favouritism* (*ouk estin prosōpolēmptēs ho theos,* 'God is not one to show partiality')'.[43] The vision given to Peter (vv. 10-16), together with the realisation that God had been communicating directly with Cornelius (vv. 30-33), has led him to this conclusion. Peter now sees this biblical teaching 'more sharply and more clearly, for it is being demonstrated in a new way'.[44] A key text on this theme is Deuteronomy 10:17-19. Although God gave a special status and role to Israel (e.g., Ex. 19:5-6), he declared his intention to bless the nations through his chosen people (e.g., Gn. 12:3). We see that happening in various ways, as some were brought into the sphere of Israelite life (e.g., Ex. 12:38; Dt. 10:18-19; Jos. 6:25; Ru. 4:11-15), and others were blessed by God without joining that community (e.g., 1 Ki. 10:1-13; 2 Ki. 5:1-15; Jonah 3). Job is a foreigner who is described in terms very similar to those used of Cornelius: he was 'blameless and upright' because 'he feared God and shunned evil' (Job 1:1, 8; 2:3). Cornelius was acceptable to God because of a God-given faith which found practical expression in godly living. This was his response to the revelation of God conveyed to him by believing Israelites, not simply the result of his reflections on God from the created order (cf. Rom. 1:18-21). Nevertheless, as a believer in the God of special revelation, he still needed to hear the gospel and trust in Jesus as the Messiah to experience the blessings of the New Covenant.[45] He was not converted from idolatry or a dissolute life, but when he came to understand the significance of Jesus and his ministry it changed his life dramatically. Peter's further assertion that God '*accepts those from every nation who fear him and do what is right*' is not a claim that all religions lead to God, but another way of affirming God's impartiality in judgment and salvation. What counts with God is not outward appearance, race, nationality, or class, since 'in every nation whoever fears God and works righteousness is acceptable to him' (*en panti ethnei ho phoboumenos auton kai ergazomenos dikaiosynēn dektos autō estin*).[46] This does not mean that Cornelius was already saved before he met Peter, but that non-Jews are 'acceptable' or welcome to come to Christ on the same basis as Jews. Anyone like Cornelius, who genuinely fears God and expresses that fear by doing what is right in

43. The Greek adjective *prosōpolēmptēs* ('one who raises up the face') occurs only here in the NT. However, the cognate noun *prosōpolēmpsia* ('partiality') is found in Rom. 2:11; Eph. 6:9; Col. 3:25, with reference to God showing no favouritism in judgment. In Jas. 2:1, it refers to a partiality in congregational life that is displeasing to God.

44. Tannehill 1990, 138.

45. Marshall 1980, 190, rightly points out that Cornelius was not expecting his good deeds to win him favour with God. Rather, his godly life led him to see his need for the gospel, to find out how he might share in the promised messianic salvation.

46. TNIV's 'accepts' may be misleading. The adjective *dektos* ('acceptable') is used in the LXX for the reception of sacrifices by God (e.g., Lv. 1:3-4; 19:5; Mal. 2:13) and more generally with reference to a life that is pleasing to God (e.g., Pr. 11:1; 15:8). Cf. Johnson 1992, 191. In Lk. 4:24 *dektos* is used in the sense of 'welcome'.

God's eyes, must still come to Christ for salvation. There is no ground here for arguing that God will save people apart from an articulate faith in Christ (cf. 4:11-12 note).[47] Indeed, Peter underscores the universal scope of God's favour in 10:43 by insisting that *'everyone who believes in him receives forgiveness of sins through his name'*. Forgiveness is available for *everyone who believes in him*, but forgiveness *through his name* implies calling upon the name of Christ for that blessing (cf. 10:43 note).

36   Peter reminds his Gentile audience that God sent the message of the gospel *'to the people of Israel, telling the good news of peace through Jesus Christ, who is Lord of all'*.[48] TNIV adds the words *'you know'*, which are found in v. 37 in Greek, where they are also translated. There is an echo of Psalm 107:20 (LXX 106:20) in the way Peter speaks about God sending his word to Israel (*ton logon apesteilen tois huiois Israēl*, 'the word sent to the sons of Israel').[49] There is also an echo of Isaiah 52:7, with its promise that someone would come 'proclaiming peace' (*euangelizomenos eirēnēn*) to God's people. In its fulfillment, that long-expected *peace* has now been proclaimed *'through Jesus Christ'* (cf. Lk. 1:67-79 [Zechariah's prophecy]; 2:14 [the heavenly host]; 4:16-21 [Jesus' preaching]). Peace in Luke-Acts is a synonym for salvation, as it is in Isaiah 52:7 (cf. Lk. 2:14, 29-32; 19:42), involving release from the judgment of God through the forgiveness of sins and freedom to serve God in holiness and righteousness (cf. Lk. 1:67-79).[50] However, since Jesus is *Lord of all* (cf. 2:36 and Rom. 10:12-13, which both apply Jl. 2:32 to Jesus), his message of peace is for all who fear him (10:34-35). Jews and Gentiles who are reconciled to God through Christ can therefore experience a new peace with one another in Christ (cf. Eph. 2:14-18). The overall perspective of Luke-Acts is that 'the messianic lordship of Jesus, which brings peace to the Jewish people in fulfillment of scriptural promises, applies to all peoples, for they are invited to share with Israel in this messianic peace'.[51]

37-38   Peter's message now follows the pattern presented in 2:22-24; 3:13-15, but in a more expanded form. It has sometimes been argued that

---

47. See D. Strange, *The Possibility of Salvation among the Unevangelised: An Analysis of Inclusivism in Recent Evangelical Theology* (Carlisle: Paternoster, 2001), 194-97, arguing against the inclusivism of C. H. Pinnock, *A Wideness in God's Mercy: The Finality of Jesus Christ in a World of Religions* (Grand Rapids: Eerdmans, 1992), and others.

48. EVV vary in translating the opening words of 10:36, because the syntax is awkward and there is a variant reading in the Greek, with only some MSS including the relative pronoun 'which' (*hon*) in the first line ('the message which'). Cf. Metzger, *Textual Commentary*, 333-34. The meaning of the verse is nevertheless clear, despite these difficulties (cf. Barrett 1994, 521-24; Marshall 1980, 190-91 note 1).

49. See G. N. Stanton, *Jesus of Nazareth in New Testament Preaching* (Cambridge: Cambridge University, 1974), 70-85, for an analysis of the allusions to the OT woven into the text of Peter's sermon.

50. Cf. H. Beck and C. Brown, *NIDNTT* 2:776-83; THE THEOLOGY OF ACTS: IV. SALVATION (pp. 65-70).

51. Tannehill 1990, 140. Johnson 1992, 192, draws attention to intimations of such inclusivity in Jewish writings such as 3 Macc. 5:28; 6:39; Wis. 6:7; 8:3; Sir. 36:1.

this broadly reflects the structure of Mark's Gospel.[52] However, if 10:36 specifically recalls the themes of Luke's birth narratives, it may be better to view 10:36-43 as highlighting some of the main emphases of Luke's own Gospel, from the birth of Jesus to the commissioning of the apostolic witnesses in Luke 24.[53] Given their geographical proximity to the events of Jesus' ministry, Peter expects Cornelius and his household to '*know what has happened throughout the province of Judea*' (*kath' holēs tēs Ioudaias*, 'throughout the whole of Judea'). It is also possible that Philip was in some way directly responsible for this knowledge (cf. 8:40; 21:8-9), perhaps founding a Jewish Christian community in Caesarea which provided the stimulus for Gentiles like Cornelius to learn more.[54]

The story of Jesus' preaching ministry begins '*in Galilee after the baptism that John preached*' (cf. Lk. 3:1-20). At his baptism, '*God anointed Jesus of Nazareth with the Holy Spirit and power*' (cf. Lk. 3:21-2). Subsequently, '*he went around doing good and healing all who were under the power of the devil, because God was with him*' (cf. Lk. 4:1–9:17). Although the statement that *God was with him* 'represents in itself a minimal Christology',[55] we should read this in the light of the claim that he is *Lord of all* (v. 36). The anointing *with the Holy Spirit and power* testified to his messianic status and role (cf. Is. 11:1-3; 42:1; 61:1; Lk. 4:17-21). However, the full implications of his messiahship were seen only in his death, resurrection, and heavenly exaltation, which revealed his divine kingship (cf. 10:42-43; 2:36 notes).[56]

39-40 Peter affirms his own distinctive role in the story, as one of the '*witnesses of everything he did in the country of the Jews and in Jerusalem*' (cf. 10:41; 1:8, 22; 2:32; 3:15; 5:32; 13:31). The final part of the story, in which Jesus was betrayed, tried, crucified, and raised from death (cf. Lk. 9:18–24:53), is summarized in simple terms: '*They killed him by hanging him on a cross* (*xylou*, 'tree'), *but God raised him from the dead on the third day and caused him to be seen*'. The Gospel narratives make it clear that the Romans actually crucified Jesus, but Peter ascribes moral responsibility for this to the Jews who rejected him as their Messiah (cf. 2:22-23; 3:13-15; 4:10-11; 5:30; 13:27-29). As in 5:30, the unusual expression '*by hanging him on a tree*' (*kremasantes epi xylou*) is apparently used to stress both the shameful nature of Je-

52. Cf. C. H. Dodd, *New Testament Studies* (Manchester: Manchester University, 1953), 1-11; Bruce 1990, 212-13.

53. Tannehill 1990, 140. Witherington 1998, 355, sees Peter's speech as 'an example of apologetic and therefore forensic or judicial rhetoric, which God interrupts'.

54. Cf. Stanton, *Jesus of Nazareth*, 20-21, on ways in which knowledge of Jesus may have reached Cornelius. However, Stanton rightly stresses the evangelistic nature of Peter's address and argues that the life and character of Jesus were an important part of early evangelistic preaching (30). Such matters were not obscured by the resurrection faith of the church (191).

55. Barrett 1994, 524 ('that Jesus was a man whom God accompanied and aided as he might have been said, and was said, to have accompanied and aided e.g. Abraham, Moses or David').

56. Cf. THE THEOLOGY OF ACTS: II. JESUS AS MESSIAH AND LORD (pp. 56-60).

sus' death and its penal character (cf. Dt. 21:22-23; Acts 13:29; Gal. 3:13-14; 1 Pet. 2:24). This is linked with the forgiveness of sins in v. 43, suggesting that Jesus' death was the vicarious atonement which made possible the inauguration of the New Covenant (cf. Je. 31:31-34; Lk. 22:20; Acts 20:28; Heb. 10:15-18).[57] The Father's sovereign hand in these events is noted with reference to the resurrection itself *(God raised him from the dead on the third day)* and in causing him to be seen by witnesses *(edōken auton emphanē genesthai,* 'gave him to become manifest'). Apart from the Gospels, only Acts 10:40 and 1 Corinthians 15:3 explicitly mention resurrection *on the third day.*[58]

41-42   Peter now dwells on the character of the resurrection appearances and their significance in the plan of God, reflecting the tradition recorded in Luke 24 and Acts 1. The risen Christ was not seen *'by all the people, but by witnesses whom God had already chosen — by us who ate and drank with him after he rose from the dead'.* The witnesses were literally 'appointed beforehand' *(prokecheirotonēmenois)* by God. It was important for them to be witnesses of Jesus' ministry from the beginning (v. 39; cf. 1:21-22), so that they could understand the climactic events in terms of everything Jesus had said and done previously. It was thus only a limited group who *'ate and drank with him after he rose from the dead'* (cf. Lk. 24:36-43), and who were then specifically commanded *'to preach to the people and to testify that he is the one whom God appointed as judge of the living and the dead'* (cf. Lk. 24:44-49; Acts 1:1-8).[59] This preaching was to be first *to the people,* meaning to Israel, because of God's promises to his covenant people in Scripture. The witnesses proclaimed the same Jesus whom they knew in his earthly ministry as the resurrected saviour (2:32; 3:15; 5:32), but also as the one designated by God to be *'judge of the living and the dead'.* Apart from 17:31, this is the most explicit statement in Acts about Jesus' role as universal judge, though it is implied in 2:34; 3:23; 7:56 (cf. Jn. 5:27, alluding to Dn. 7:13-14). He will fulfill the divine role of judging humanity on the 'day of the Lord', as predicted in many OT prophecies. That coming judgment is truly the context in which to understand and receive the gospel offer of salvation (e.g., Jl. 2:30-32, cited in Acts 2:19-21). Our need for the forgiveness of Christ in the present is accentuated by the fact that he is to be our judge on the last day (cf. 1 Thes. 1:9-10; 5:9-10).

43   Peter offers no scriptural citation in his gospel presentation on this occasion, though there are scriptural allusions throughout.[60] In conclusion, he makes the general claim that *'all the prophets testify about him that everyone who believes in him receives forgiveness of sins through his name'.* Specific passages promising a definitive forgiveness of sins in the last days include

---

57. Cf. THE THEOLOGY OF ACTS: VI. THE ATONING WORK OF JESUS (pp. 75-79).

58. Luke's Gospel records the expression 'on the third day' in 9:22; 18:33; 24:7, 46 (cf. 13:32; 24:21). Cf. Bruce 1990, 215 note 61. Metzger, *Textual Commentary,* 334-35, discusses variants of this expression in the MSS of 10:40.

59. Metzger, *Textual Commentary,* 335, discusses minor textual variations in 10:41-42.

60. Cf. Stanton, *Jesus of Nazareth,* 70-85.

Isaiah 33:24; 55:6-7, Jeremiah 31:34, and Ezekiel 36:25. Since Israel's Messiah is the one through whom the divine promises of redemption are accomplished, forgiveness of sins is only *through his name* (cf. Lk. 24:47). As in Acts 2:38; 4:11-12, calling upon Christ as the only saviour is suggested by this reference to his *name* (cf. 2:21). However, as we have seen, the Messiah is also *'the one whom God appointed as judge of the living and the dead'* (v. 42). His *name* or character is to be both judge and saviour. All people need to recognize and respond to him in this dual function, so as to receive the forgiveness he offers. As noted in connection with vv. 39-40, this offer of forgiveness is linked with the nature and outcome of his death (cf. Lk. 22:20; Acts 20:28 note).

44 In the normal course of events, Peter would probably have mentioned the gift of the Holy Spirit in connection with the offer of forgiveness in Christ. This was the pattern of his preaching to Jews.[61] However, while Peter was still speaking these words, *the Holy Spirit came on* (*epepesen to pneuma to hagion epi*, 'the Holy Spirit fell upon'; cf. 8:16; 11:15) *all who heard the message* (*pantas tous akouontas ton logon*, 'all who were hearing the word'). With this coming of the Spirit, 'those previously regarded as unclean have been granted a share in the holy'.[62] Luke highlights the initiative of God here in a way that is reminiscent of Pentecost, though it is important also to note the differences in the two situations.[63] By this means, Luke indicates that 'the gift of the Spirit to Cornelius's household is the "Spirit of prophecy" promised by Joel and fulfilled through the Christ-event at Pentecost'.[64] Cornelius and his household had not yet openly professed faith in Jesus as Lord and Christ, but the Spirit enabled them to respond appropriately to the gospel. They experienced the benefits of Jesus' saving work and articulated their response to him in 'tongues' with praise (v. 46), and then in baptism (vv. 47-48; contrast the pattern in 2:37-41). In this way, it is shown that Gentiles belong to the renewed people of God, on the same basis as believing Israelites. For further reflection on the significance of this initiation experience, see my comments on 11:15-18.

45-46 *The circumcised believers who had come with Peter were astonished that the gift of the Holy Spirit had been poured out even on the Gentiles.* This is the first time that Peter's companions are identified as *the circumcised believers (hoi ek peritomēs pistoi).* As those marked out by that physical badge of

61. Barrett 1994, 528-29, argues that Peter had completed the outline of preaching common to many occasions in Acts with the offer of forgiveness. However, it seems to me that the programmatic pattern that is found in 2:38 and implied also in 3:19-20 (see my comment) includes the promise of the Spirit.

62. Tannehill 1990, 136.

63. The verb in 2:4 is 'filled' (*eplēsthēsan*), but the verb 'fell upon' (*epepesen*) is used in 10:44 (cf. 8:16; 11:15). The sounds 'like the blowing of a violent wind' and the 'tongues of fire' are unique to Acts 2, as is the ability to speak in other languages without the need for an interpreter ('xenolalia').

64. Turner, *Power*, 381. Turner highlights the similarities between the accounts in Acts 2 and 10–11. Cf. THE THEOLOGY OF ACTS: III. THE HOLY SPIRIT (pp. 60-65).

membership in Israel's covenant community, they were not prepared for this divine demonstration of the full and equal status of uncircumcised Gentiles in the church, despite Peter's visions and his growing awareness of their significance. Later in Jerusalem, Peter acknowledges that the coming of the Spirit in this way signified the genuine belief of these Gentiles in the Lord Jesus and that God had granted them 'repentance that leads to life' (11:17-18). The outward sign of the Spirit's coming was that they were *speaking in tongues and praising God*. The first expression *(lalountōn glōssais)* is similar to 2:4, though the latter speaks of 'other tongues' *(lalein heterais glōssais)*. A distinctive feature of the apostolic experience at Pentecost was the ability to speak in languages which could be understood by those present from different parts of the world (called 'xenolalia'). There is no indication in the NT that this ever happened again. The glossalalia in 10:46 and 19:6 is more likely to have been the phenomenon described in 1 Corinthians 12–14, which required interpretation.[65] Paul indicates that this was a special endowment, not bestowed on all members of the church (1 Cor. 12:10, 30), and in Acts it appears that *tongues* did not always accompany the gift of the Spirit. *Praising God (megalynontōn ton theon,* 'magnifying God'; cf. 19:17) describes the content of their speaking in tongues (cf. 2:11, *lalountōn . . . ta megaleia tou theou,* 'declaring the mighty works of God'). They were presumably praising God for the fact that, as Gentiles, they too could enjoy the benefits of Christ's saving work.

47-48 Then Peter said, *'Surely no one can stand in the way of their being baptized with water'* (*mēti to hydōr dynatai kōlysai tis tou mē baptisthēnai toutous;* NRSV 'can anyone withhold the water for baptizing these people?'). Since God had brought the Gentiles into the same experience of salvation as Jewish believers (*'They have received the Holy Spirit just as we have'*), there could be no justification in delaying water baptism.[66] As noted in connection with 2:38, water baptism is closely connected in Acts with the bestowal of the Spirit, though the gift sometimes precedes and sometimes follows baptism (cf. 8:12, 14-17; 9:17-18; 10:44-48; 19:5-6). Even after the gift of the Spirit, baptism remains an important means of calling upon the name of Jesus with repentance and faith and identifying with the community of believers. The initiation sequence is not complete without water baptism, because of its character as a public act of commitment and reception of the gospel promises. Peter did not carry out the baptism himself but *ordered*

---

65. So also J. Hur, *A Dynamic Reading of the Holy Spirit in Luke-Acts,* JSNTSS 211 (Sheffield: Sheffield Academic, 2001), 247 note 211. Hur, 247-48, argues that 'the coming of the Spirit upon Gentiles alongside notable manifestations is apologetically designed to verify *Gentiles,* like the Samaritan believers, as members of God's community. Hence, the Spirit here is presented as the decisive and legitimate verifying cause of Cornelius and his household's (i.e. Gentiles') acceptance by God.'

66. Note that a similar Greek expression is used in 11:17 (*dynatos kōlysai,* 'able to forbid') with reference to opposing God's purpose (10:47, *dynatai kōlysai*). The sign of God's purpose in that context is once again the giving of the Spirit to the Gentiles.

that they be baptized in the name of Jesus Christ. When he agreed *to stay with them for a few days,* this was a further indication that he recognized them as fellow Christians, in the same relationship with the Lord Jesus, now truly 'made clean' by faith (cf. 15:9). Staying with these Gentiles involved eating with them. Thus, the reality of their common participation in Christ and the benefits of his saving work were expressed in the novelty of table fellowship.[67]

This narrative marks a significant turning point in Luke's story of the gospel's progress. It shows how God provided a way for Jewish believers like Peter to preach to Gentiles and welcome them into the messianic community on the same basis of faith in the Lord Jesus. It also reveals something about the interpretation of Scripture in the light of this development. Readers from every cultural and religious background can be grateful for the way in which God prepared from the beginning for believers to be 'all one in Christ Jesus' (Gal. 3:28). He did this by 'making peace' through the blood of Christ, removing ancient barriers, and creating 'one new humanity' in Christ (Eph. 2:14-16). However, the challenge remains in every local context to express the reality of that fellowship by abandoning every form of prejudice, and adopting habits such as sharing food and hospitality, which practically demonstrate the unity which the NT proclaims.

C. Peter's Report to the Church in Jerusalem (11:1-18)

Luke's repetition of the story about Peter and Cornelius in this context shows how important the incident is for his developing narrative and for his understanding of what God was doing at this time. When Peter returned to Jerusalem, he was called to account for his meeting with Gentiles (vv. 1-3). He responded to the charge by explaining how God had led him to preach the gospel to Cornelius and his household and then to enjoy their hospitality (vv. 4-17). In the final analysis, the process of discerning God's will, which is an important theme in Acts 10, is shown to necessitate a confirmation by the church of new insights and consequent actions.[1] The conclusion to this encounter is the acknowledgement that 'even to Gentiles God has granted repentance that leads to life' (v. 18). By implication, a wider mission by Jews to Gentiles can begin because, as Peter's experience shows, 'God has removed the social barrier between Jews and Gentiles'.[2] Witherington compares the editorial introduction in 11:1 with 8:14, making it clear that 'a whole new ethnic group, involving the multitude of pagan nations, has

67. Cf. 1 Cor 10:16-17; 11:17-34, and Peterson, *Engaging,* 215-18, for the theological significance of the community meals at Corinth.
1. Johnson 1992, 199, also observes that 'this encounter enables Luke's readers to assimilate and more deeply appreciate the events being related by Peter'.
2. Tannehill 1990, 136. The objection in v. 3 receives an appropriate answer by retelling the story of God's actions in the situation.

come into the picture'.[3] 11:1-18 is an abbreviated retelling of the events of chapter 10, with certain differences arising from the fact that the narrative is presented from Peter's point of view. 'Not only the order of the narrative but also the references to Pentecost (11:15), Jesus' promise of the Spirit (11:16), and Peter's Pentecost preaching (11:14) show Peter interpreting his experience as a unified story with a divine purpose.'[4] Indeed, the three accounts of the Cornelius episode (cf. 15:7-9) demonstrate 'narrative development and modulation', successively clarifying for readers the significance of what took place.[5] None of the accounts is sufficient on its own to explain the implications of this extraordinary event.

1. Peter Is Called to Account (11:1-3)

Luke's introduction highlights the extent to which news of events in Caesarea had spread among believers in Judea. While there may have been some rejoicing in the news that 'the Gentiles also had received the word of God', there was disquiet about the fact that this initiative involved Peter lodging and eating with 'the uncircumcised'. So the issue with which Peter had had to struggle individually (10:28-29) was raised in a public way, requiring a passionate defence from the apostle. With the use of circumcised-uncircumcised terminology, Luke signals the inevitability of a debate that will soon surface about the initiation of Gentiles into the church (15:1-29).

1-3 The whole church *throughout Judea* — leaders and people together (*hoi apostoloi kai hoi adelphoi hoi ontes kata tēn Ioudaian*, 'the apostles and the brothers who were throughout Judea') — soon heard the news that *the Gentiles also had received the word of God* (cf. 8:14; 11:22; 15:24). But sometime later, *when Peter went up to Jerusalem,* he faced the sort of criticism that Jesus did when challenged by the Pharisees and the teachers of the law about eating with sinners (Lk. 5:30; 15:2; 19:7).[6] The difference now was that the objections came from *the circumcised believers* (*hoi ek peritomēs*, 'those of the circumcision') and the problem was specifically Peter's going into the

---

3. Witherington 1998, 361. The story of Cornelius is thus shown to be 'not just an exceptional situation (as with the eunuch)', but the acceptance by the Gentiles of 'God's word about Jesus'. The comparison of 11:1 with 8:14 shows that Luke is arranging his historical data in terms of the movement through nations and races from Jerusalem to Rome outlined in 1:8.

4. Tannehill 1990, 145. Tannehill further observes that Peter is speaking to people who share key aspects of his experience and so his interpretation is effective for them.

5. Cf. M. M. B. Turner, *Power from on High: The Spirit in Israel's Restoration and Witness in Luke-Acts*, JPTSS 9 (Sheffield: Sheffield Academic, 1996), 385, especially note 111; R. D. Witherup, 'Cornelius Over and Over Again: "Functional Redundancy" in the Acts of the Apostles', *JSNT* 49 (1993), 45-66.

6. NRSV, ESV, and TNIV translate *hote de* 'so when', assuming that criticism of this event is the logical consequence. However, an adversative reading ('but when') seems more appropriate to the context (KJV, NKJV 'and when').

house of *'the uncircumcised'* and eating with them (cf. 10:48, where his stay with them for a few days clearly involved eating with them). They *criticized him* for an action that seemed to have more significance for them than the salvation of these Gentiles. But it must be remembered that Peter's action challenged their understanding of Scripture and what it meant to be the holy people of God. Such criticism by members of the Jerusalem church shows that Peter's authority was 'not such as to carry automatic approval of his activities'.[7] Although it is true that the whole church in Judea at that time could be described as *the circumcised believers*, it is possible that Luke is using the term *hoi ek peritomēs* to describe a particular group within the church.[8] If so, he is making a link with 15:1-5, where 'some of the believers who belonged to the party of the Pharisees' required Gentiles to be circumcised and to keep the law of Moses. It is certainly true that, 'once introduced, circumcision joins table-fellowship as the major points of contention surrounding the Cornelius incident'.[9] No one makes any further objection when Peter has defended his actions (v. 18), but there were probably some who remained uneasy about the situation. Peter's argument may have silenced them only temporarily. Jewish believers soon expressed different views on the incorporation of Gentiles into the church.

2. Peter Recalls God's Direction and Control (11:4-17)

Peter does not respond directly to the criticism of v. 3, but recounts how God brought him to preach to Cornelius and his household and to stay with them. He does this to persuade Jewish believers in Jerusalem of the rightness of this way of encountering Gentiles. Presumably, with Jerusalem convinced, the rest of the believers throughout Judea would also be in agreement. Peter speaks as one who needed to have his own attitude in this regard changed by God. This happened first through a series of divine revelations (vv. 4-14). Then, the coming of the Holy Spirit upon the Gentiles recalled for him both the experience of the first Jewish believers at Pentecost and the promise of the Lord about its significance (vv. 15-17). This demon-

7. Barrett 1994, 535. The Western text expands v. 2 considerably to avoid the impression that Peter was compelled to break off his missionary work and go to Jerusalem to defend himself. However, this tendency to avoid putting Peter in a bad light leads most textual critics to dismiss this as a later addition to Luke's text. Cf. Metzger, *Textual Commentary*, 337-38.

8. Cf. S. G. Wilson, *Luke and the Law*, SNTSMS 50 (Cambridge: Cambridge University, 1983), 73; Bruce 1990, 267; Johnson 1992, 197; Witherington 1998, 362. Marshall 1980, 195, and Barrett 1994, 536-37, oppose the argument that there was a definite circumcision party in the church at this stage. Luke uses the full expression 'the circumcised believers' *(hoi ek peritomēs pistoi)* in 10:45 to described those who accompanied Peter and who presumably stayed on with Cornelius and his household after their baptism. He does not use such a term anywhere else, but note Paul's reference in Gal. 2:12.

9. Spencer 1997, 117.

strated God's acceptance and blessing of all who believe in the Lord Jesus Christ on the same basis (cf. 15:8-9). Finally, Peter's own conviction about not standing in God's way (v. 17; cf. 10:47) becomes an implied challenge to his audience about the attitude towards Gentiles which at least some of them have expressed (v. 3).

4-8 TNIV translates v. 4, *starting from the beginning, Peter told them the whole story*. A more literal rendering of the Greek would be, 'but Peter began and explained it to them in order' (NRSV, ESV *arxamenos de Petros exetitheto autois kathexēs*). However, the 'order' (*kathexēs*, as in Lk. 1:3) is not exactly the same as in Acts 10. Peter begins with the vision given to him, not with the vision given to Cornelius, telling the story from his own perspective. The audience is being led through the sequence of events that changed Peter from rejecting intimate social contact with Gentiles to accepting it as God's will. Stott notes that 'it took four successive hammer-blows of divine revelation before his racial and religious prejudice was overcome'.[10] Some see this as technically a defense speech, 'a piece of forensic rhetoric',[11] though the context is not a formal trial. Peter omits some of the detail recorded in 10:9-11 and declares simply, *I was in the city of Joppa praying, and in a trance I saw a vision*. When he recounts the contents of the vessel *like a large sheet being let down from heaven by its four corners*, he includes *wild beasts* (*thēria*, 'beasts of prey') — not mentioned in 10:12 — along with *four-footed animals of the earth, reptiles, and birds of the air*. Perhaps this addition is designed to emphasize the note of uncleanness (cf. Lv. 11:13-40; Dt. 14:1-21). He also indicates how close the sheet came to him (*it came down to where I was*) and how closely he examined it (*I looked into it and saw*).[12] In response to the voice telling him, ' *"Get up, Peter. Kill and eat,"* ' Peter says, ' *"Surely not, Lord!"* ' He then uses a different expression from the one used in 10:14, when he claims, ' *"Nothing impure or unclean has ever entered my mouth"* ' (*koinon ē akatharton oudepote eisēlthen eis to stoma mou*).[13]

9-10 Peter recalls how *the voice spoke from heaven a second time*, and repeats exactly the words found in 10:15 (*"Do not call anything impure that God has made clean"*). The fact that this happened *three times* before the vessel and its contents were *pulled up to heaven again*, recalls 10:16 in slightly different terms. The divine words that interpret the vision have profound implications for mission, for the doctrine of the church, and for a Christian perspective on the law of Moses. Holiness in terms of ritual

---

10. Stott 1990, 194. The 'hammer-blows' were the divine vision (vv. 4-10), the divine command (vv. 11-12), the divine preparation (vv. 13-14), and the divine action (vv. 15-17).

11. Johnson 1992, 200, and Witherington 1998, 363. M. Soards, *The Speeches in Acts: Their Content, Context and Concerns* (Louisville: John Knox/Westminster, 1994), 77, argues that the form of defence is basically a transference of responsibility for what happened to God.

12. So Spencer 1997, 118.

13. The expression in 11:8 is a Hebraism, reflecting the sort of language found in the Hebrew of a verse like Ezk. 4:14 (cf. Mt. 15:11, 17).

cleanness is now replaced by cleansing and sanctification through faith in Christ (cf. 10:15-16 note; 15:9; 20:32; 26:17-18). Consequently, Jewish evangelists can offer salvation to Gentiles on the same basis that they themselves received it. Moreover, Jewish and Gentile believers can have table fellowship together, as an expression of their shared holiness in the new community of God's people. Finally, the law of Moses can be seen to have been fulfilled and replaced by Christ's saving work. The reality that it anticipated has come, and so the laws which formerly functioned as a way of identifying the people of God can no longer be allowed to separate Jew and Gentile (cf. Gal. 2:11-18; Eph. 2:11-22).[14]

11-14 The next part of the story is told briefly, summarizing 10:17-23a. Peter stresses that it was *'right then'* (*exautēs*, 'immediately') that he was visited by three men who had been sent to him from Caesarea.[15] Cornelius is not even named, and the manner of God's intervention in his life is only briefly outlined in vv. 13-14. Nevertheless, God's control over the whole situation is implied by the direction of these visitors to the right place at the right moment, with the further recollection that *'the Spirit told me to have no hesitation* (*mēden diakrinanta*, 'making no distinction') *about going with them'*.[16] Peter also mentions the Jewish Christian witnesses who went with him to Caesarea (*'six brothers'*) and who *'entered the man's house'* with him. Their authentication of the whole experience was clearly important for 'the circumcised believers' in Jerusalem to receive. The unnamed Gentile begins to tell his story through Peter, describing *'how he had seen an angel appear in his house and say, "Send to Joppa for Simon who is called Peter"'*. The most important part of that angelic revelation, as far as Peter was concerned, was the prediction that Peter would bring to Cornelius a message through which he and all his household *'"will be saved"'* (an expansion on 10:22, 33, by which the outcome of such preaching is indicated). So both the appearance of the angel to Cornelius and the precise nature of his message confirmed for Peter that God wanted him to offer this Gentile salvation through faith in Christ. His own extraordinary vision had prepared him to receive such an invitation and to preach the gospel

14. Cf. C. L. Blomberg, 'The Christian and the Law of Moses', in I. H. Marshall and D. Peterson (eds.), *Witness to the Gospel: The Theology of Acts* (Grand Rapids/Cambridge: Eerdmans, 1998), 397-416.

15. Some Greek MSS refer to the house where *'I was'* (*ēmēn*), and this is followed by KJV, NKJV, and TNIV. But the better-attested reading is *ēmen* ('we were'), and this is also the harder one in this case (so NRSV, ESV). It is not clear from the context exactly who might be included, and so the tendency would have been to read the text exclusively with reference to Peter. Cf. Barrett 1994, 540.

16. In 10:20, the middle voice of the participle *diakrinomena* is read by TNIV, NRSV, and ESV to mean 'not hesitating'. The best MSS of 11:12 have the active participle *diakrinanta*, which ought to be translated 'making no distinction' (so NRSV, ESV; Barrett 1994, 540). This is the way Peter uses the same verb in 15:9. I suggest that this nuance can also be discerned in 10:20. Some MSS of 11:12 have the middle form of the participle (hence presumably TNIV *have no hesitation*; KJV 'nothing doubting'), and some omit the participle completely, but the best-attested reading is the active form.

without discriminating against Gentiles in any way. 'The first explicit use of "save"-language *(sōzō)* in Acts 10–11 closely links the Cornelius incident to Peter's preaching at Pentecost ('everyone who calls on the name of the Lord will be saved', 2:21; cf. 2:40, 47), which was so foundational for the Jerusalem church.'[17] Such terminology is used again in 15:1, 11, when the way of salvation for Gentiles comes to be disputed.

15 Recalling the critical events of 10:34-48, Peter says it was as he *'began to speak' (en de tō arxasthai me lalein)* that *'the Holy Spirit came on them as he had come on us at the beginning' (epepesen to pneuma to hagion ep' autous hōsper kai eph' hēmas en archē)*. The first implication of this verse is that Peter had something more to say before the Spirit came upon his hearers.[18] As noted in connection with 10:44, the apostle would normally have mentioned the gift of the Holy Spirit in connection with the offer of forgiveness in Christ. But God had already prepared these Gentiles to receive the gospel and all its benefits. The Spirit came upon Cornelius and his household even before they were invited to trust in Christ and be baptized in his name. In terms of their outward behaviour, the coming of the Holy Spirit enabled them to speak in tongues and praise God (10:46). However, an inward work of the Spirit is also implied, by which he moved them to believe that Jesus was Saviour and Lord and gave them the assurance that all the blessings of the messianic era were theirs, thus enabling them to praise God. The second implication of 11:15 is that the Spirit's coming on the Gentiles in Caesarea was reminiscent of his coming upon the apostles in Jerusalem *('as he had come on us at the beginning')*. Using language which recalls that incident *(epepesen to pneuma to hagion ep' autous,* 'the Holy Spirit fell upon them'; cf. 10:44-46), Peter implies that this was effectively the Pentecost outpouring for the Gentiles (cf. 2:4, *eplēsthēsan pantes pneumatos hagiou,* 'they were all filled with the Holy Spirit').

16 The theological significance of the Spirit's coming in this way is confirmed by Peter's reference to the prediction of John the Baptist (Lk. 3:16), which the risen Jesus endorsed in Acts 1:5 (' *"John baptized with water, but you will be baptized with the Holy Spirit"'*), applying it to the approaching event of Pentecost with the words *'in a few days'*. It does not appear from the evidence of Acts that 'baptism with the Holy Spirit' was a common way of describing Christian initiation, but, by implication, the expression is used in that way here.[19] In 1:4-5 it refers to the gift promised by the Father in passages such as Joel 2:28-29, applied by John the Baptist to the Messiah's ministry. Peter's 'remembrance' of this saying points to the fact that

17. Spencer 1997, 118. However, note the language of 'peace through Jesus Christ' in 10:36, which is virtually synonymous with salvation in some biblical contexts (e.g., Is. 52:7; Lk. 1:77-79; 2:29-30).

18. So Marshall 1980, 197.

19. Marshall 1980, 197-98, discusses the application of Jesus' prediction in 1:5 to the narrative in Acts 11, especially considering the relationship between faith, the gift of the Spirit, and water baptism.

the Spirit received by Cornelius and his household was that gift which the exalted Messiah had poured out on his Jewish disciples at Pentecost (2:4, 33).[20] Acts 10:44-48 was an extension, or further expression of Pentecost, in the sense that it was a coming of the Spirit upon a select group of Gentiles, when they responded to the preaching of the gospel with God-given faith and repentance (11:17-18). This signalled the beginning of a great new work of God among the nations (cf. 15:12-18).

Turner observes that 'in the account of Cornelius's conversion in 10:34-48 events follow too rapidly for us to be able to tease out the respective operations of the Spirit, but 11:14 and 15:7 might naturally be taken to imply that such faith was kindled by Peter's words, and 15:8 would then mean that God *attested* this operation of the Spirit in the hearers by granting them the Christian gift of the Spirit of prophecy'.[21] Turner insists that 'the Spirit of prophecy' involves more than the assurance of forgiveness, but makes a close connection between the Spirit's work in kindling faith through Peter's words and the Spirit's work in enabling a joyful articulation of such faith. With 11:15-18, he rightly affirms that we have 'returned to the "norm" of the gift of the Spirit being immediately associated with conversional repentance and baptism, even if the order within the complex differs from the one presupposed in Acts 2:38'.[22] What seems more obvious here, however, is the Spirit's role as the facilitator of faith and repentance. Turner makes two further helpful observations about the application to this context of Jesus' promise in 1:5. First, the implicit argument is that 'Gentiles who believe and receive the Spirit may most assuredly be considered "clean", because the Spirit manifest in them is the very power by which the Messiah purges "Israel"'. The Spirit sanctifies all who trust in the gospel of God's grace (20:32; 26:18). Second, the charismata manifest through Cornelius's believing household and friends show that these Gentiles too have a place in the 'transformation of Israel being performed through the Spirit poured out by the ascended and glorified Christ'.[23]

---

20. It is unnecessary to ascribe to Peter a defective memory, as does Barrett 1994, 542, because Peter attributes this saying to Jesus rather than to John the Baptist. For the way in which the prophecy of the Baptist relates to Jesus' ministry in a broader sense, incorporating the notion of judgment and division in Israel, as well as predicting the eschatological outpouring of the Spirit in a salvific sense, see Turner, *Power*, 170-87. The application of Jesus' prophecy in Acts 1:5 to 11:16-18 is discussed by Turner, 386-87.

21. Turner, *Power*, 382, critiquing J. D. G. Dunn, *Baptism in the Holy Spirit: A Reexamination of the New Testament Teaching on the Gift of the Spirit in Relation to Pentecostalism Today*, SBT (Second Series) 15 (London: SCM, 1970), 80. Dunn argues that the Spirit was not something additional to God's acceptance and forgiveness, but constituted that acceptance and forgiveness which Cornelius sought. Cf. J. D. G. Dunn, 'Baptism in the Spirit: A Response to Pentecostal Scholarship on Luke-Acts', *JPT* 3 (1993), 3-27.

22. Turner, *Power*, 384 (author's emphasis removed), arguing that Luke attributes greater significance to the Spirit in salvation than R. P. Menzies, *The Development of Early Christian Pneumatology with Special Reference to Luke-Acts*, JSNTSS 54 (Sheffield: JSOT, 1991), 267, allows. Turner is closer to Dunn than Menzies in this respect.

23. Turner, *Power*, 387. Cf. THE THEOLOGY OF ACTS: III. THE HOLY SPIRIT (pp. 60-65).

The Spirit now defines the boundaries and character of the people of God, not the law of Moses.

17 The link with Pentecost is further reinforced with a rhetorical question: *'So if God gave them the same gift as he gave us who believed in the Lord Jesus Christ, who was I to think that I could stand in God's way?'*[24] TNIV (following KJV) has taken the participle in the expression *hōs kai hēmin pisteusasin* to be adjectival and attributive *(who believed)*, agreeing with the pronoun *hēmin* ('us') which immediately precedes it. This is logical and makes the point that the same Spirit was given to Gentiles as to Peter and his Jewish audience, who shared a common faith in Jesus as Lord and Christ (cf. 2:36). However, NRSV, ESV, and NKJV take the participle as adverbial, modifying *edōken (gave)*, and translate 'when we believed'. This is the most natural way to read the syntax, but it could give the impression that the apostles only truly believed in Jesus at Pentecost. In fact, the 120 disciples mentioned in 1:15 were already believers in Jesus before the events of Acts 2 took place. The delay in their experience of the Spirit resulted from their unique position in salvation history. It is possible, however, that the participle *pisteusasin* could be taken with the pronoun *autois* ('them'), giving the sense, 'God gave to them when they believed in the Lord Jesus Christ the same gift as he gave to us'.[25] This would remove the confusion that could arise from the NRSV, ESV, and NKJV rendering. Peter's rhetorical question *('who was I to think that I could stand in God's way?')* then warns his hearers about the possibility of resisting God's will and hindering his purpose. He does this by using the same verb employed in 10:47 with reference to the baptism of these converts (*kōlysai ton theon*, 'to hinder God'; cf. Lk. 9:49; 11:52; 18:16; Acts 8:36; 27:43).[26] Peter makes his own example a challenge to his audience. Anyone who stands in the way of the full incorporation of others into the church, when they genuinely trust in the Lord Jesus Christ for their salvation, stands in opposition to God himself! So there is a positive reason for accepting Gentiles who believe — God has given them the same gift of the Spirit — and a negative reason — beware of opposing God's revealed will.[27]

---

24. The omission of *ho theos* ('God') in some Western MSS appears to infer that the Holy Spirit was the gift of Christ. Various words, in part or whole saying 'that he should not give them the Holy Spirit after they had believed on him', occur after the concluding *ton theon* in Western MSS. These additions appear to involve a misreading of 10:47. Cf. Metzger, *Textual Commentary*, 339-40.

25. Barrett 1994, 542. Barrett also considers that in grammar and sense the participle could properly be taken with both pronouns.

26. Noting that a similar Greek expression occurs in 10:47 (*dynatai kōlysai*, 'able to forbid'), in connection with the baptism of the Gentiles, Stott 1990, 196, comments: 'Water-baptism could not be forbidden to these Gentile converts, because God could not be forbidden to do what he had done, namely give them Spirit-baptism'.

27. God's intention for solidarity between believing Jews and Gentiles was clearly evidenced in 'the common dynamic "gift of the Spirit" and prophetic "word of the Lord"' (Spencer 1997, 118).

3. The Church Acknowledges God's Leading (11:18)

The response to Peter's speech is not specifically an acknowledgement that he was right to stay with a Gentile and eat with him (v. 3). But this is effectively conceded by the more fundamental confession that if God gave the Gentiles 'the same prestigious gift of the Spirit of prophecy as Jewish Christians received at Pentecost, then he must have allowed these Gentiles the same "repentance" previously only known to the Israel of fulfilment (cf. 5:31-32), and set them on the same path leading to "life" (cf. 13:48; Lk. 18:30)'.[28] This is one of several key statements in Acts about God's sovereignty in the process of conversion (cf. 2:47; 5:14; 10:33, 44; 11:21; 13:48; 15:4, 8-9, 14; 16:14; 18:27). However, the particular significance here is that God intends salvation to be enjoyed by Gentiles in precisely the same way as by Jews.

18 When they heard Peter's argument, the believers in Jerusalem *had no further objections* (*hēsychasan*; ESV 'they fell silent'). However, Acts 15 reveals that the underlying issue raised in v. 3 was not settled for some. Could Gentiles really become the beneficiaries of the New Covenant without conforming in some way to the demands of the Mosaic law? The impression is given in Acts 11 that the majority were persuaded of the rightness of Peter's actions in preaching to Cornelius and his household and then baptising them into Christ. They praised God (*edoxasen ton theon*, 'glorified God') for his gracious initiative and his miraculous confirmation of the conversion of these Gentiles. Indeed, they affirmed more broadly that *'God has granted even the Gentiles repentance that leads to life'*. The narrative does not record a repentance from idolatry or from an immoral life on the part of Cornelius and his household (cf. 14:15; 17:30-31; 1 Thes. 1:9-10). Yet even for those described as devout and God-fearing (10:2), turning to Christ involved a radical reorientation of allegiance and devotion, which is what is meant in this case by *repentance that leads to life (tēn metanoian eis zōēn)*. Not simply repentance of particular sins, but a rejection of everything that hinders the reception of salvation through faith in Christ is meant. The claim that God has *granted* repentance (*edōken*; cf. 5:31 with reference to Israel) implies that 'God gives the Gentiles not simply the possibility of repentance, but repentance itself'.[29] Reference to *the Gentiles*, rather

---

28. Turner, *Power*, 382. Turner rightly resists equating the gift of the Spirit (v. 17) with the gift of repentance (v. 18), noting that elsewhere repentance is clearly 'the *condition* for receiving the gift of the Spirit (2:38-39), not the gift itself'. However, expanding my comment on v. 17, Turner may be unnecessarily divorcing the Spirit's work in kindling repentance and faith through the preaching of the gospel from the gift of the Spirit offered in response to repentance and faith. In Acts 11:16-17, baptism with the Holy Spirit appears to involve a complex of events: 'repentance that leads to life', faith in Jesus for forgiveness and salvation, and the articulation of that new relationship with God in Christ through tongues and praise (cf. 10:46).

29. Gaventa 2003, 173. Cf. C. Stenschke, *Luke's Portrait of Gentiles Prior to Their Coming*

than simply to Cornelius and his household, indicates that the wider implications of this event have been clearly understood. However, since the next section of Acts shows that the initiative in the Gentile mission passed to Antioch, 'it is not clear how far the church at Jerusalem was prepared to follow Peter's lead'.[30]

In practical terms, this narrative challenges Christians to be wary of allowing any cultural, social, or inherited religious barriers to hinder the acceptance of new converts into the church. At the same time, it is an encouragement to recognize when a work of God's Spirit is taking place — perhaps in unexpected ways, in unexpected quarters — and a warning not to be found opposing that work. Sadly, history shows that some of the greatest opposition to gospel initiatives has come from church officials.

D. The Word Goes to Antioch in Syria (11:19-30)

The opening verse of this section recalls 8:1, 4, allowing Luke to resume his account of how the gospel went out from Jerusalem, when persecution irrupted in connection with the death of Stephen. Unnamed, ordinary believers took the gospel to Phoenicia, Cyprus, and Antioch in Syria (11:19), so that a church was founded in the third largest city in the Roman Empire. This became a base for even more extensive advances into Gentile territory (13:1-4; 14:26-28; 15:22-23, 30-35). Gaventa notes the parallels with the narrative of the gospel's arrival in Samaria (8:5-17): 'both Philip and the unnamed proclaimers meet with a generous reception; in both cases the report about a favorable response causes the Jerusalem church to send representatives; in both cases there is joy (among the Samaritans in chapter 8, and on the part of Barnabas in chapter 11)'.[31] However, parallels with the growth of the church in Jerusalem are suggested by some of the language in 11:21-26. Witherington further observes that 'Luke's ordering principle is only secondarily chronology; it is primarily by region and ethnic or sociological group'.[32] Despite the focus on regional factors and human agents, here as elsewhere, the word is a central 'character' in Acts, which Luke presents as 'the powerful force that is able to conquer the world'.[33] The 'growth' of the word leads to the creation and growth of

---

to Faith, WUNT 2, no. 108 (Tübingen: Mohr Siebeck, 1999), 156-64; R. C. Tannehill, *The Shape of Luke's Story: Essays on Luke-Acts* (Eugene: Cascade, 2005), 84-101. This claim is especially significant in the light of the promise in 3:26 that God would first bless Israel by turning Jews from their 'wicked ways'. It shows that Gentiles are saved in the same way as Jews under the New Covenant.

30. Marshall 1980, 198.

31. Gaventa 2003, 177.

32. Witherington 1998, 368. He argues that 'Luke is presenting a historical narrative in a fashion that would seem orderly, familiar, and reasonable to his first-century audience'.

33. D. W. Pao, *Acts and the Isaianic New Exodus*, WUNT 2, no. 130 (Tübingen: Mohr

churches (6:7 note). This next stage in the progress of the word is neither organized by the church in Jerusalem nor directly inspired by Peter's preaching to Cornelius.[34] Nevertheless, the flow of Luke's narrative suggests that 'the theological outcome of the Cornelius account is the formation of an *ekklēsia* outside of Jerusalem and among non-Jews'.[35] In Antioch we meet the first church that is made up of Jewish and Gentile believers together.

1. The Planting of a New Church (11:19-21)

Hellenistic Jewish Christians ('men from Cyprus and Cyrene'), who were doubtless influenced by the ministry of Stephen and Philip before being thrust from Jerusalem, made their way further and further into Gentile lands. Their preaching was initially to Jews, but they soon took the initiative in speaking to non-Jews (v. 20). This is the first detailed account of evangelism by ordinary believers (cf. 8:4). Previous accounts involved apostles or prophetic leaders such as Stephen and Philip. However, just as the account of Peter's ministry to Cornelius and his household finished with affirmations about God's sovereignty in the situation (vv. 17-18), so here the founding of the church in Antioch is ultimately attributed to 'the Lord's hand' (v. 21).

19 New churches were planted in significant parts of the Gentile world by *those who had been scattered by the persecution that broke out when Stephen was killed*. Luke's terminology (*hoi diasparentes*, 'those who had been scattered'; cf. 8:1, 4) draws attention to the existence of a dispersion of Christian Jews from Jerusalem, paralleling in some respects the 'diaspora' of Jews more generally, though sadly caused by *persecution* in Jerusalem. It is likely that these were Hellenistic Jews who emerged from the same circle as Stephen and Philip (6:1-6). Some were possibly drawn to minister in

---

[Siebeck], 2000; repr. Grand Rapids: Baker Academic, 2002), 150. Pao, 147-79, notes that the phrase 'the word of God' appears eleven times in Acts, while 'the word of the Lord' appears ten times. 'The word of salvation' (13:26), 'the word of his grace' (14:3; 20:32), and 'the word of the gospel' (15:7) are parallel phrases. The absolute use of the term *logos* ('word') can be found throughout the first twenty chapters of Acts (cf. note 35). Pao traces the 'itinerary' of the word in Acts and considers the theological significance of Luke's use of this terminology in terms of the fulfillment of Isaiah's New Exodus predictions.

34. Tannehill 1990, 146, rightly observes that 'the Cornelius episode justifies a gentile mission for those who have problems with gentile uncleanness, but the narrator reaches back behind it when indicating the human factor that brought the gospel to Antioch'. We also have no way of knowing the time relation between the events in 10:1–11:18 and 11:19-21. Barrett 1994, 546, similarly argues that Luke justifies this mission on the basis of its links with the Jerusalem church, not because of the Cornelius incident.

35. Gaventa 2003, 177. In 11:22 we find the first use of *ekklēsia* applied to an entity that is not either the church in Jerusalem (5:11; 8:1, 3) or part of the 'church throughout Judea, Galilee and Samaria' (9:31).

such places because they had family or business connections there (v. 20 note). By the power and grace of God (v. 21), and by simply 'speaking the word' (*lalountes ton logon*, v. 19; TNIV *spreading the word*),[36] they founded churches where they had not existed before. *Phoenicia* describes the narrow coastal plain between the Lebanon and the Mediterranean, containing the ancient cities of Sidon, Tyre, and Biblos (cf. 12:20). Luke later mentions believers in Tyre (21:2-7) and Sidon (27:3). *Cyprus* is an island off the coast of Syria which passed under Roman rule in 58 BC, becoming an imperial province in AD 23.[37] Barnabas came from its substantial Jewish community (4:36) and later led a mission there with Paul (13:4-12). The island is mentioned by Luke in several other journey contexts (15:39; 21:3, 16; 27:4). *Antioch* in Syria was situated about 18 miles (29 km.) inland from the Mediterranean, on the bank of the Orontes River. According to Josephus (*War* 3.29), it was 'third among the cities of the Roman world', after Rome and Alexandria. By the middle of the first century AD, its population is estimated to have been about 500,000 people. Founded in 300 BC by Seleucus Nicator, the city was named after his father, Antiochus. Many Jews lived there and enjoyed privileges received from its founder (Josephus, *Ant.* 12.119-20; *Against Apion* 2.39). The Roman governor normally resided at Antioch and administered the province of Syria from there.[38] In this pagan city, which was of great strategic importance for the spread of Christianity, the gospel was first shared *only among Jews*.

20 In due course, *men from Cyprus and Cyrene went to Antioch and began to speak to Greeks also, telling them the good news about the Lord Jesus*. Luke makes it clear that some of those scattered from Jerusalem by the persecution originated from other countries. Since *Cyprus* contained a substantial Jewish community (v. 19 note), there is likely to have been a steady stream of pilgrims and traders venturing from there to Jerusalem. Jews from *Cyrene* were present in Jerusalem on the Day of Pentecost (2:10; cf. Lk. 23:26, 'Simon of Cyrene'; Acts 13:1, 'Lucius of Cyrene'), and there was a 'synagogue of the Freedmen' in that city for Jews from Cyrene and other parts of the Jewish Dispersion (6:9). The reference in each case is probably to Jews from the country of Cyrenaica, rather than from the city of Cyrene exclusively.[39] That part of North Africa was settled by the Greeks in the seventh century BC and remained Greek-speaking through-

36. The absolute term *logos* ('word') is apparently used with reference to the gospel in 4:4, 29; 6:4; 8:4, 21; 10:36, 44; 11:19; 14:25; 16:6; 17:11; 18:5. Cf. note 33 for other ways in which *logos* is used in expressions describing the gospel.

37. Cf. A. Nobbs, 'Cyprus', in D. W. J. Gill and C. Gempf (eds.), *The Book of Acts in Its First Century Setting*, Vol. 2: *Graeco-Roman Setting* (Grand Rapids: Eerdmans; Carlisle: Paternoster, 1994), 279-89.

38. Bruce 1990, 271, notes that it was a commercial centre as well as a political capital and argues that, 'since it was near the frontier between the Graeco-Roman area and the eastern states, it was even more cosmopolitan than most Hellenistic cities.' Cf. R. Tracey, 'Syria', in Gill and Gempf, *Graeco-Roman Setting*, 236-39; Witherington 1998, 366-67.

39. Cf. Barrett 1994, 550; Witherington 1998, 369 note 12.

out the period of the Roman Empire. It is clear from the syntax of these verses that a contrast is being made between speaking to Jews *only* (v. 19, *ei mē monon*) and speaking to non-Jews *also* (v. 20, *kai pros*). However, there is debate about whether to read 'Hellenists' (*Hellēnistas*, NRSV, ESV, NKJV) or 'Greeks' (*Hellēnas*, TNIV) in v. 20. The textual and transcriptional evidence points strongly towards the former as the original text and the latter as an easier reading introduced by copyists to clarify that these were truly Gentiles.[40] Part of the confusion is Luke's use of the term 'Hellenists' in 6:1 to describe Greek-speaking Jewish Christians, but in 9:29 with reference to Greek-speaking Jews who were not Christians. I agree with Witherington that the context defines more precisely in each case what sort of Greek-speaking person Luke has in mind, 'ranging from Jewish Christians, to Jews, to pagans'.[41] 'Greeks' would be more naturally natives of Greece, but 'Hellenists' in this context would be Greek-speaking Gentiles more generally.

21 The Lord's role in the process of conversion is stressed (*the Lord's hand was with them*),[42] together with a clear statement of the human response involved (*and a great number of people believed and turned to the Lord*).[43] Here, as in 4:30-31, the context suggests that *the Lord's hand* is manifested in the work of the Holy Spirit (cf. 11:17-18). Repentance and faith are the essential requirements for salvation, baptism being the outward expression of a turning to Christ as Saviour and Lord (cf. 2:38; 3:19-21; 11:17-18). As Luke begins to describe the growth of the church in Antioch, he speaks of *a great number (polys arithmos)*, recalling the initial growth of the church in Jerusalem (cf. 2:41, 7; 4:4; 5:14; 6:7). In v. 24 he also speaks of many people being 'added to the Lord' (*prosetethē tō kyriō*; TNIV *brought to the Lord*), just as in 2:41, 47; 5:14. Further parallels are noted below in connection with 11:26-30, suggesting a deliberate attempt to show how God worked in Antioch as he did initially in Jerusalem.

40. Cf. Metzger, *Textual Commentary*, 340-42; Barrett 1994, 550-51. The Alexandrian witnesses are divided, with Papyrus 74, the second corrector of ℵ, and A reading *Hellēnas*, in conjunction with the original of D, and this reading is reflected in some early versions. The original of ℵ has the peculiar reading *euangelistas* ('evangelists'). However, transcriptional probability is in favour of *Hellēnistas*, because of the temptation for copyists to substitute a more familiar word for a less familiar one.

41. Witherington 1998, 242. Metzger, *Textual Commentary*, 340-42, comes to a similar conclusion, noting that the noun *Hellēnistēs* is derived from the verb *hellēnizein*, which strictly means 'one who uses Greek [language or customs]'.

42. 'The Lord' in v. 21 could be 'the Lord Jesus', who is mentioned at the end of v. 20. If it is a more general reference to God's power and control (cf. Ex. 9:3; 1 Sa. 5:3; Is. 59:1; Lk. 1:66; Acts 4:28, 30; 13:11), Gaventa 2003 179, rightly notes that 'the proximity of this phrase to the phrases "turned to the Lord" and "to the Lord Jesus" in v. 20 exemplifies Luke's close association of Jesus and God'.

43. Literally, 'a great number who believed turned to the Lord' (*polys te arithmos ho pisteusas epestrepsen epi ton kyrion*).

2. The Encouraging Ministry of Barnabas and Saul (11:22-26)

This passage says more about the growth of the church in Antioch and highlights the extent to which that was due to Barnabas and Saul. Barnabas was sent by the church in Jerusalem (v. 22; cf. 8:14) to observe what was happening and to strengthen these new believers in their commitment to Christ (vv. 23-24).[44] As the church grew in size, Barnabas encouraged Saul to join him for an extensive teaching ministry (vv. 25-26). Thus the scene was set for their future partnership with that church in planting other congregations (cf. 13:1-3; 14:26-28). This new community made such an impact on the city of Antioch that there was a need to identify them as a distinct group. The title 'Christians' recognizes the fact that they are a new phenomenon, comprising Jewish and Gentile believers in the Christ (v. 26).

22 *News of this reached the ears of the church in Jerusalem, and they sent Barnabas to Antioch.*[45] Luke has not used the word *church (ekklēsia)* since 9:31, and he will use it again in 11:26 to describe the community of Christians in Antioch (cf. 13:1; 14:27). Reference to *the church in Jerusalem*, immediately followed by an application of the term *church* to the gathering of believers in Antioch, suggests an equality of status and significance. It also shows how *church* could be defined geographically, in terms of those who belonged to Christ and assembled in his name in a given city or region (cf. 9:31 note). Luke does not tell us why the church in Jerusalem sent a key figure like Barnabas to investigate the new work in Antioch.[46] A parallel with the situation in Samaria may be implied (cf. 8:14), though in this case the investigation was by one man alone. To some extent, Barnabas functioned in Antioch as Peter and John did in Samaria, though there was apparently no need for him to pray that they might receive the Holy Spirit.

23-24 When Barnabas arrived and *saw what the grace of God had done* (*idōn tēn charin [tēn] tou theou*, 'saw the grace of God'),[47] *he was glad (echarē, 'he rejoiced') and encouraged them all to remain true to the Lord with all their*

---

44. Tannehill 1990, 147, suggests that through Barnabas 'the Jerusalem church is being led in to the gentile mission, not because it planned this course of action but because it recognizes that what it values most highly is present also in the lives of others'.

45. KJV 'they sent forth Barnabas, *that he should go as far as* Antioch' (so also NKJV) reads the additional verb *dielthein* with *heōs*, which is found in Western and Byzantine MSS and is reflected in some early versions. This is in accord with Luke's style (Lk. 2:15; Acts 9:38; 11:19), but the shorter version followed by NRSV, ESV, and TNIV is read by Alexandrian MSS and is reflected in several earlier versions. Cf. Metzger, *Textual Commentary*, 343.

46. Barrett 1994, 552, notes that the word 'church' is 'a noun of multitude' here because it is followed by a plural verb *(exapesteilen)*. So the meaning is effectively that 'the Christians in Jerusalem' sent Barnabas: he was their 'apostle' in the situation, not carrying out an official inspection ordered by the Twelve.

47. Metzger, *Textual Commentary*, 343, notes that the extra *tēn* that is read by some MSS suggests that 'Barnabas rejoiced because he recognized that grace was obviously that of God' *(tēn tou theou)*. However, this seems to be a pedantic and unnecessary addition by some early copyists. The point that Luke is making is simply that he saw the grace of God demonstrated in the developments in Antioch.

hearts (tē prothesei tēs kardias prosmenein tō kyriō, 'with steadfastness of heart to continue with [cf. 13:43] the Lord'). This is consistent with the picture of Barnabas presented elsewhere (cf. 4:36-37, 'son of encouragement'). His ability to discern the grace of God at work in others gave him a generous and encouraging spirit. This enabled him to facilitate the ministry of Saul in Jerusalem when others were suspicious of his intentions (9:26-29), and of John Mark when he had previously abandoned his missionary partners (15:36-39). The ministry of encouragement exercised by Barnabas in Antioch is further explained in terms of the fact that he was *a good man, full of the Holy Spirit and faith* (v. 24 is linked to the preceding verse by *hoti* ['because'], which TNIV obscures). Note how Stephen is similarly described in 6:5. It was the work of the Spirit, enabling Barnabas to recognize and trust in the grace of God that made him *a good man*.[48] The result of his strengthening of the believers was continuing success in evangelism: *a great number of people were brought to the Lord (prosetethē ochlos hikanos tō kyriō)*.[49] The passive verb here implies divine action, continuing the emphasis of v. 21 that church growth took place because 'the Lord's hand was with them'. When we see that the Lord is 'both subject and object, source and goal, of evangelism, we have to repent of all self-centred, self-confident concepts of the Christian mission'.[50] Furthermore, growth in the size of a church is closely linked here with its growth in maturity, not simply with its outreach programme.

25-26 The goodness and generosity of Barnabas were expressed in further pastoral wisdom: he *went to Tarsus to look for Saul, and when he found him, he brought him to Antioch*.[51] We last heard of Saul in 9:30, when he went back to Tarsus, his hometown (cf. 22:3). Once again, Barnabas grasped an opportunity for introducing Saul to a place of significant public ministry, (cf. 9:26-29), travelling a considerable distance to Tarsus and back to obtain his help. Barnabas apparently recognized his own inadequacy to cope with the demands of a growing church and the need to bring another gifted apologist, evangelist, and teacher into the situation (cf. 13:1). They teamed up *for a whole year* in Antioch, where they *met with the church and taught great numbers of people*.[52] This emphasis on teaching in a communal setting recalls

48. The adjective 'good' is applied only to Barnabas in the narrative of Acts, though Tabitha is described as being 'full of good works' (9:36) and Paul is recorded as claiming to have lived 'in all good conscience' (23:1). Cf. Joseph of Arimathea in Lk. 23:50 ('a good and upright man'). Against Witherington 1998, 370, it is unlikely that the expression 'full of the Holy Spirit and faith' simply refers to the inspiration of the Spirit which made Barnabas so effective in exhorting the believers in Antioch.

49. As in v. 21, Luke's use of such terminology deliberately compares the growth of the church in Antioch with the initial growth of the church in Jerusalem (cf. 2:41, 47; 5:14).

50. Stott 1990, 204.

51. The Western text of v. 25 records that Barnabas 'entreated him to come to Antioch. When they had come, for a whole year a large company of people were stirred up . . .'. This seems to be an adaptation of the simpler Alexandrian text (*ēgagen*, 'he brought [him]'). Cf. Metzger, *Textual Commentary*, 343-44.

52. The verb translated 'met' *(synachthēnai)* could mean that they were given board

2:42 and the growth of the church in Jerusalem. Luke regularly shows the importance of teaching as an essential aspect of evangelism (e.g., 2:14-36; 3:12-26; 13:16-41) and as a vital means of growing a church to maturity and keeping believers faithful to the Lord (e.g., 14:21-22; 18:11, 24-28; 19:8-10; 20:17-35). So significant was the growth of the church in size and maturity that *the disciples were called Christians first at Antioch* (cf. 26:28; 1 Pet. 4:16). The name suggests 'belonging to Christ' or the people who 'habitually named the name of Christ' (cf. Mk. 3:6; 12:13, where 'Herodians' are those identified with Herod).[53] They were known as Christ's people because they spoke so often of Christ and were followers of his way. But did they give themselves this title, or was it given by others? It seems best with Barrett to take the active infinitive *chrēmatisai* in this context to mean '*to take and bear a title* or *name, to be called* or *styled* so and so'.[54] He further observes that 'the new designation was probably needed when it first became apparent that the believers, who had left their old Gentile way of life, were no more Jews than heathen — in fact, a third race, Christians'.[55] Luke soon shows us how this church became the base of operation for Paul's missionary journey with Barnabas (13:1-3; 14:26-27), and subsequently for his journey with Silas (15:35-41; 18:22-23). 'Thus two mission bases appear in the narrative, Jerusalem and Antioch, and these are the centers of two missions, those of the apostles and of Paul.'[56] Maintaining harmony between these two missions surfaces as an important challenge in 15:1-35 (cf. Gal. 2:1-10).

3. Generosity in Ministry to Christians in Jerusalem (11:27-30)

Luke's account of the founding of the church in Antioch concludes with mention of the relief aid sent to Christians in Judea, in response to a prophetic challenge. Church growth is shown to be a matter of maturation, not simply numerical increase, and an important sign of maturation is generosity in giving to believers in need. Here Luke shows an extension of the principle of practical care from a purely congregational context (2:44-46; 4:32-37; 6:1-4) to an interchurch one. Partnership between churches involves different levels of giving and receiving in ministry to one another. It is espe-

---

and lodgings by the Christians in Antioch, as well as joining them in their meetings. Hence, it could be translated 'hospitably received'.

53. Cf. Bruce 1990, 274-75.

54. Barrett 1994, 555-56. Bruce 1990, 274, argues that the literal sense is that they 'transacted business' under the name Christians, suggesting that they chose to be publicly known as such. However, Barrett's argument is that the disciples were first called Christians by outsiders: the name did not emerge from the church itself. The earliest clear use of *Christianoi* as a self-designation by Christians is in Ignatius, *Eph.* 11:2; *Rom.* 3:2; *Magn.* 10:3; *Pol.* 7:3. Cf. Witherington 1998, 371 (especially note 23).

55. Barrett 1994, 548. The implication of his statement is that the church was by this stage predominantly made up of Gentiles.

56. Tannehill 1990, 150.

cially significant in the light of 11:1-18 that the interchange is between Jewish and predominantly Gentile churches.

27-28 With a vague time reference (*en tautais de tais hēmerais*, 'in these days'), Luke records how *some prophets came down from Jerusalem to Antioch*. The church at Antioch had been founded by the original missionaries from Jerusalem and strengthened by the ministry of Barnabas and Saul. Now *prophets* from Jerusalem would contribute to the growth of the new church (cf. 13:1; 15:32), and *one of them, named Agabus*, would bring a special challenge. This is the first reference in Acts to *prophets (prophētai)* as a distinct group. The expectation from 2:17-18 is that all believers under the New Covenant would 'prophesy' *(prophēteusousin)*, and so share to some extent in the prophetic role (cf. 19:6). However, it is clear that some of the early Christians were especially gifted in prediction (cf. 21:4, 9, 10-11), and others in exhorting and strengthening believers in their discipleship (cf. 15:30-32). Prophecy in the OT involved these and other ministries, such as warning and rebuking, or comforting and consoling God's people. Agabus appears here and in 21:10-11 in a narrowly predictive role — *through the Spirit [he] predicted (esēmainen*, 'signified') — but he could well have engaged in a wider range of prophetic activities as well. When it says that he *stood up (anastas)*, the reference is probably to his contribution in a gathering of the church (cf. 1:15).[57] In 5:17, 34, the same term indicates the intention of someone to speak in the Sanhedrin. Debate has taken place about the identity and timing of the *severe famine that would spread over the entire Roman world (limon megalēn mellein esesthai eph' holēn tēn oikoumenēn)*. Luke relates this to events apparently known to the readers by noting that *this happened during the reign of Claudius*. Claudius was emperor from AD 41 to 54, and there are several records of famines in his time (e.g., Josephus, *Ant.* 3.320; 20.51-53; 20.101). TNIV rightly translates *over the entire Roman world*, since the word *oikoumenē* ('inhabited world') could be used in that narrow sense (cf. Lk. 2:1; Acts 17:6; 24:5; Lucian, *The Octogenerians* 7; Josephus, *War* 3.29). A great famine occurred specifically in Judea when Tiberius Alexander was procurator (AD 46-48), probably in AD 47.[58] A poor harvest in AD 45 in Egypt was followed by a severe grain shortage and high prices in the re-

---

57. Western MSS provide a longer reading that includes the words *synestrammenōn de hēmōn* ('when we were gathered together'). If authentic, this would be the first 'we' passage in Acts, signifying that Luke came from the church at Antioch. However, textual critics are generally sceptical of readings that are found in only one textual tradition, and that without early Greek attestation. Cf. Metzger, *Textual Commentary*, 344-45.

58. Cf. J. Jeremias, *Jerusalem in the Time of Jesus: An Investigation into Economic and Social Conditions during the New Testament Period* (ET, London: SCM, 1969), 141-43; C. J. Hemer, *The Book of Acts in the Setting of Hellenistic History*, ed. C. Gempf, WUNT 49 (Tübingen: Mohr Siebeck, 1989; repr. Winona Lake: Eisenbrauns, 1990), 164-65. Barrett 1994, 563-64, asserts that 'it is mistaken to claim that Luke dates the famine wrongly because 11:27-30 precedes the death of Herod Agrippa I (12.23); what happens in 11.27 is not the famine but a prophecy that there will be a famine. It is possible that this is why Luke completes the story in 12.24, 25'.

gion, and this state of affairs could well have extended to AD 47. Since Egypt was the 'breadbasket' for the whole region, a drought or famine there meant trouble for the poor in Judea.[59]

29 Whether or not Agabus made a specific appeal for help, the disciples, *as each one was able* (kathōs euporeito tis, 'as anyone prospered'), *decided to provide help for the believers living in Judea.* In this practical way, they expressed their gratitude for receiving the gospel from Christians in Judea (cf. Rom. 15:25-27, for a later argument along this line). Perhaps Barnabas, who appears as a model of generosity in 4:36-37, played a key role in this response. Once again, Luke suggests a parallel with the earliest Christian community in Jerusalem. The language recalls the loving care and generosity mentioned in 2:44; 4:32-37; 6:1. However, this ministry (diakonia; TNIV *help*)[60] was to believers living at some distance, belonging to other congregations. It was not a pooling of capital for use whenever needed, but a giving 'in proportion as any prospered'.[61] There is an emphasis on the free decision of individuals to use their profit to serve the needs of 'brothers' in Christ (adelphois; TNIV *believers*). In short, Acts does not commend any one method of giving, but sets before readers several different examples of generosity and practical care for one another. When Paul later urged individuals to make a convinced and cheerful decision to do likewise (2 Cor. 9:7), he stressed that such giving is a 'ministry' (9:1) which brings glory to God (9:12-13) and demonstrates the extent to which God's grace has impacted them (9:14).

30 Even though Luke highlights the significant role played by Paul in this relief effort (*this they did, sending their gift to the elders by Barnabas and Saul*), this collection is not to be confused with the later one mentioned in 1 Corinthians 16:1-4, 2 Corinthians 8–9, and Romans 15:25-32.[62] It is likely that their trip to Jerusalem on this occasion took place in AD 48 and was the one described somewhat differently in Galatians 2:1-10, when the opportunity for a serious theological engagement with the apostles in Jerusalem was taken.[63] Chronologically, it appears that 11:30 foreshadows the visit, which actually took place after the death of Herod Agrippa I in AD 44 (cf. 12:25 note). There are good reasons for suggesting that the famine 'really

---

59. Cf. K. S. Gapp, 'Notes: The Universal Famine under Claudius', *HTR* 28 (1935), 258-65; B. W. Winter, 'Acts and Food Shortages', in Gill and Gempf, *Graeco-Roman Setting,* 59-78; Witherington 1998, 372-73.

60. Gk. *diakonia* is used in Acts 1:17, 25; 6:1, 4; 12:25; 20:24; 21:29, with reference to word 'ministry' but also to the practical care of Christians in need.

61. Barrett 1994, 565, commenting on the use of the verb *euporeito* ('had plenty'). TNIV ('as each one was able') and most EVV translate this verb rather weakly.

62. Tannehill 1990, 148, follows J. Koening, *New Testament Hospitality: Partnership with Strangers as Promise and Mission,* Overtures to Biblical Theology (Philadelphia: Fortress, 1985), 110, in noting how Luke presents Christian leaders as similarly preacher-teachers and 'stewards of material goods' (cf. the apostles in 4:35, 37, and Stephen and Philip in 6:1-6).

63. See Witherington 1998, 375, for a summary of arguments in favour of equating the famine relief visit of Acts 11:29-30 with the visit described in Gal. 2:1-10.

began to affect Jerusalem and Judea in 46, and its effects were exacerbated in Judea by the sabbatical year 47-48'.[64] The *gift* from Antioch was delivered *to the elders,* who are mentioned for the first time as those responsible for these and other matters in the early churches (cf. 14:23; 15:2, 4, 6, 22, 23; 16:4; 20:17; 21:18). Acts also mentions Jewish elders (2:17; 4:5, 8, 23; 6:12; 23:14; 24:1; 25:15). It is likely that the pattern of eldership found in Jewish synagogues served as the basis for the Christian institution.[65] The sending of a gift from the mixed Jewish-Gentile church in Antioch to the more established Jewish Christian communities in Judea is an important expression of solidarity across social and cultural boundaries. 'Although the two groups do not physically sit down to eat together, the sharing of food symbolically betokens an experience of table-fellowship in line with the recent breakthrough in Cornelius' house.'[66]

E. Peter's Deliverance in Jerusalem (12:1-25)

This section provides a 'retrospective' on the Jerusalem church, which 'reaffirms some important themes already set forth in the first depiction of the Jerusalem community (1.1-5.42) before concluding with a trademark Lukan summary (12:24)'.[1] Closure is provided to a major section of the narrative which began in 9:32, before an entirely new section begins in 13:1. As the gospel has moved out from Jerusalem, Luke has been keen to highlight the links with that church and its leadership, particularly with the apostle Peter. Thus, in Acts 12, as Luke prepares to show how the gospel spread among Gentiles, 'he reinforces the continuing role of Jewish individuals and especially of the messianic Jewish community in this process'.[2] Luke presents his readers with a significant challenge at this point, as he brings together the themes of persecution, prayer, divine deliverance, and gospel advance. This

64. Witherington 1998, 80. Witherington believes that the prophecy of Agabus may have been given in AD 44, though he notes that 'Luke's data for the period AD 37-46 are clearly sketchy' (p. 82). The famine visit to Jerusalem he estimates took place in AD 48 (Witherington, 83, 368, 373). Cf. Gapp, 'Notes', 258-65.

65. Cf. J. A. Fitzmyer, *Essays on the Semitic Background of the New Testament* (London: Chapman, 1971), 295. R. Bauckham, 'James and the Jerusalem Church', in R. Bauckham (ed.), *The Book of Acts in Its First-Century Setting,* Vol. 4: *Palestinian Setting* (Grand Rapids: Eerdmans; Carlisle: Paternoster, 1995), 429-30, holds that the elders may have been a body of leaders alongside the apostles at this time.

66. Spencer 1997, 122. Even if money alone was sent, it was, as Spencer suggests, 'an important expression of solidarity defying conventional sociocultural boundaries'.

1. J. T. Squires, 'The Function of Acts 8:4–12:25', *NTS* 44 (1998), 610. Squires highlights the threat of persecution (12:1-5; cf. 4:15; 5:17-18; 8:1); the assurance of ongoing divine guidance through the intervention of angelic figures (12:6-7, 23; cf. 8:26; 10:3, 22, 30; 11:13); and the nature of community life in Jerusalem (12:5, 12; cf. 2:42-47; 4:32-35).

2. Squires, 'Function', 614. However, it is an exaggeration for Squires to conclude that 'nothing takes place in this section of Acts without being initiated or authorised by the community in Jerusalem'. Cf. 8:4; 11:19-21.

challenge is set within the context of a deteriorating situation for the church in Jerusalem. Prior to the ministry of Stephen, despite the opposition of their leaders, the people of Jerusalem continued to be sympathetic to the apostles and their message (2:47; 4:21; 5:13, 26). However, Stephen's enemies aroused the people against him (6:12; cf. 12:4 note), and the great persecution against 'all except the apostles' followed (8:1). Before Luke focuses on the mission to the Gentiles and the suffering endured by gospel messengers in that context, he brings us up to date on the struggle experienced by Christians in Jerusalem.[3] Readers can assume that hostility to Christians in Jerusalem continued, even as converts in distant places began to experience opposition from 'the Jews' as well (e.g., 13:45, 50; 14:1-5, 19; 17:4-5, 13).

1. Persecution and Arrest (12:1-5)

Here we have a record of the second martyrdom of a Christian leader (cf. 7:57-60). The chief threat to James, Peter, and the Jerusalem church was now Herod Agrippa I rather than the high priest and temple authorities, though their continuing involvement is suggested by Herod's seeking approval for his actions 'among the Jews' (v. 3).[4] Additionally, several details in 12:1-5 recall previous occasions of opposition from evil rulers, 'helping the skilled imagination to construct the layers of background that give this episode its deeper meaning'.[5]

1-3 *It was about this time that King Herod arrested* (epebalen tas cheiras, 'laid hands upon') *some who belonged to the church, intending to persecute them* (kakōsai tinas, 'to harm some').[6] The time reference is vague (kat' ekeinon de ton kairon, about this time; cf. 19:23). Luke's expression 'does not itself mean the period during which Barnabas and Saul were in Jerusalem, though this may be implied by the resumption of 11:27-30 in 12:25'.[7] *King Herod* in this

---

3. Spencer 1997, 123-24, observes that two 'snippets' featuring King Herod (12:1-4, 20-23) surround the story of Peter's imprisonment. 'But the unfolding plot of these incidents ironically shatters their restrictive frame in dramatic fashion, as Peter miraculously breaks out of Herod's maximum security prison and then, at the end, Herod himself meets a violent death.'

4. A wider group than these authorities may be intended by the expression 'the Jews' (cf. 9:23).

5. Tannehill 1990, 152. Tannehill notes verbal links between Luke's description of Peter's arrest (syllabein, Acts 12:3) and Jesus' arrest (Lk. 22:54; Acts 1:16) at Passover time ('during the Feast of Unleavened Bread', Acts 12:3; 'after the Passover', 12:4; cf. Lk. 22:1-7). Other verbal links with the arrest of Jesus and threats to apostles and others in Acts are noted in my comments on the relevant verses.

6. The Western text adds the information that it was the church in Judea that Herod was persecuting, which ties in with the reference to 'believers living in Judea' in 11:29. However, the shorter reading that is found in a good range of MSS is to be preferred. Cf. Metzger, *Textual Commentary*, 345.

7. Barrett 1994, 573. However, cf. my notes on 12:22, 25 for further comments about dating.

context means Herod Agrippa I (reigned AD 41-44), who was son of Aristobulus and grandson of Herod the Great (reigned 37 BC-4 BC). The emperor Caligula gave him the tetrarchies formerly held by Philip and Lysanias (cf. Lk. 3:1) and allowed him to be called king. Claudius, the next emperor, then added Judea and Samaria to his kingdom, allowing him to rule over the area formerly governed by his grandfather. 'Herod did his best to win the favour of the Jews and especially cultivated the Pharisees.'[8] The threat to Peter and the church is highlighted by Luke's description of him as Herod rather than as Agrippa.[9] This, together with mention of his use of the sword against James, particularly associates him with Herod the Tetrarch of Galilee (reigned 4 BC-AD 39), who arrested John the Baptist (Lk. 3:19-20) and had him beheaded (Lk. 9:7-9). That same Herod was one of those who conspired to have Jesus killed (Lk. 13:31; 23:6-12; Acts 4:27-28). As in previous persecution episodes, Luke establishes an interlock between Jesus and his disciples.[10] This Herod's first move against the Christians in Jerusalem was to have *James, the brother of John, put to death with the sword,* thus fulfilling the prophecy of Jesus in Mark 10:39. James the son of Zebedee (Mk. 1:19-20) was one of the twelve apostles (Mk. 3:17; Acts 1:13). He is to be distinguished from the James mentioned in 12:17; 15:13-21; 21:18-25, who was 'the Lord's brother' (Gal. 1:19) and one of the 'pillars' of the Jerusalem church (Gal. 1:9). Despite his Roman and Greek interests, Herod sought to live as a faithful Jew (cf. *m. Soṭah* 7.7; Josephus, *Ant.* 19.292-94, 331), and so he might naturally be concerned to put down a heretical sect. However, use of *the sword,* rather than any other means of execution, suggests that Herod may have seen the Christian movement as being also a political threat to his regime.[11] Executing one of the twelve apostles was a deliberate attempt to destroy the church by systematically removing its leadership. When Herod saw that *this met with approval among the Jews, he proceeded to seize Peter also.*[12] *The Jews* who approved of the arrest and execution of James appear to be a wider group than the leadership, since Luke tells us that Herod intended to bring Peter out of prison before 'the people' (v. 4, *tō laō*; TNIV *for public trial*). Just as rulers and people conspired together to destroy Jesus (cf. 4:27), so there was collusion to eliminate his apostle. Luke suggests a further parallel with the arrest and trial of Jesus, noting that *this happened during the Feast of Unleavened Bread.* Cunningham rightly observes that the death of James is not glossed over

8. Marshall 1980, 207.

9. Contrast later references to his son Agrippa II in Acts 25:13–26:32. Agrippa I also had two daughters, Drusilla, who is mentioned in 24:24, and Bernice, who is mentioned in 25:13.

10. Cf. note 5 above.

11. Barrett 1994, 574-75.

12. Western MSS once more expand what is found in the majority of texts and versions, to define more specifically what Herod did to please the Jews. Cf. Metzger, *Textual Commentary,* 345-46.

with any embarrassment here. It rather prepares the reader for the deliverance of Peter 'by showing how desperate his situation really is and thereby the enormity of the miracle'.[13] Without explanation, one apostle is executed but another is rescued, teaching the church to live with the mystery of God's providence and to rely afresh in each situation on the mercy and continuing care of God (cf. 4:24-31). Note also that the death of one of the Twelve does not necessitate the election of another apostle (cf. 1:21-22 note). James the apostle is replaced by James the Lord's brother, who works with a group of elders in the leadership of the Jerusalem church (cf. 11:30; 12:17; 15:2, 4, 6, 22, 23; 21:18).

4-5 *After arresting him, he put him in prison, handing him over to be guarded by four squads of four soldiers each.* The narrative detail shows how securely Peter was imprisoned, thus heightening the wonder of the deliverance soon to be recorded (*two chains* are also mentioned in v. 6). Such detail could also reflect Peter's eyewitness account, now presented in a third-person narrative form. *Four squads of four soldiers each* were probably meant to guard the prisoner in turn, throughout the four watches of the night. 'Peter's notoriety for nocturnal jail-breaks has obviously preceded him.'[14] TNIV indicates that Herod's intention was *to bring him out for public trial after the Passover.* NRSV and ESV more literally render *anagagein auton tō laō,* 'to bring him out to the people'. Given the fate of James, it is more likely that Herod intended to bring Peter up from the prison for a public execution, rather than for a trial. Once again, the time reference links Peter's situation with that of Jesus (cf. Lk. 22:1). However, since *the Passover,* with the associated *Feast of Unleavened Bread,* was the annual celebration of Israel's deliverance from captivity in Egypt (cf. Ex. 12:1–13:16), the symbolic parallelism may be 'positive rather than negative'.[15] There are hints of a Passover-type deliverance for Peter in vv. 6, 7, 8, and 11. Meanwhile, as the feast was in progress, he was *kept in prison,* and *the church was earnestly praying to God for him.* 'On the one side, the king exercises his own political authority to bind and humiliate Peter in a public prison. On the other side, the church, still based in a private home (cf. 12:12), appeals — through prayer — to superior divine authority for Peter's release and vindication.'[16] Peter's deliverance is presented as an answer to this prayer, even though those who interceded for him were actually surprised by the outcome (vv. 15-17). Luke has a particular interest in prayer throughout his two-volume work.[17] In a context such as this, intercession is closely linked to the progress of the gospel and the protection of gospel messengers (cf. 4:23-31; 10:2,

---

13. S. Cunningham, *'Through many tribulations': The Theology of Persecution in Luke-Acts,* JSNTSS 142 (Sheffield: Sheffield Academic, 1997), 236.

14. Spencer 1997, 125. Cf. Metzger, *Textual Commentary,* 346, for Western expansions of the text of v. 5.

15. Barrett 1994, 577. Cf. Cunningham, *Persecution,* 237-40.

16. Spencer 1997, 125.

17. Note the references given in connection with 4:23-31.

9; 13:2-3; 21:4-5). When Luke records that they were praying *earnestly* (*ektenōs*, 'at full stretch'), he uses an adverb applied to the praying of Jesus in Gethsemane (Lk. 22:44; cf. 1 Pet. 1:22, with reference to love).[18]

2. Unexpected Deliverance (12:6-19)

Here we find the second of three narratives in which Christian leaders are rescued from prison (cf. 5:18-20; 16:23-29). 'These three scenes, plus the sea rescue in Acts 27, show the narrator's interest in stories of divine rescue.'[19] At key points in Luke's account, supernatural deliverance proves to be necessary for the advancement of the gospel. This is clearly signalled in Acts 12 by the editorial note about the word of God growing and spreading (v. 24; cf. 6:7). Links with the language of Exodus in particular suggest that the God who brought out Israel from bondage in Egypt is 'still the God of rescue and exodus for oppressed people who bear faithful witness to Jesus'.[20] In the previous prison rescue account (5:17-26), the irony of the situation is that opponents of the gospel prove futile in the face of God's intervening power. In 12:18-19, a similar confusion of the arresting officials is presented, but the surprising twist in the narrative this time is the confusion of the church in the face of God's amazing answer to prayer (12:12-16). 'The church, too, experiences God ironically. New discoveries of the wonder of God are also discoveries of its own myopia.'[21] God acts in response to the prayers of his people, even though they are shown to be doubters at the very moment when Peter is returned to them, safe and sound.

6-7 The night before Herod was to *bring him to trial* (*proagagein auton*, 'to bring him forward'),[22] *Peter was sleeping between two soldiers, bound with two chains, and sentries stood guard at the entrance.* The time reference suggests that Peter's imprisonment had lasted for several days. Luke further stresses the security with which Peter was held, giving precise eyewitness details that were presumably from Peter himself. At the same time, he highlights the fact that Peter *was sleeping* (*koimōmenos* as a present participle emphasising a continuing state of sleep). This suggests that he had some confidence about his future. Peter and those who were praying for him are

18. The adjective *ektenēs* ('earnest', 'constant') is used in the Received Text, whereas the adverb *ektenōs* ('earnestly', 'constantly') is found in most Alexandrian witnesses. There is no difference in sense, but the latter appears to be the original. Cf. Metzger, *Textual Commentary*, 346.

19. Tannehill 1990, 151. Note also Paul's reference to divine rescue in his trial before King Agrippa (26:17, 22).

20. Tannehill 1990, 154-55.

21. Tannehill 1990, 156. Luke reinforces this message by repeating it. Twice the narrative leads up to a 'moment of recognition', by Peter first (vv. 6-11), and then by the Christians gathered in Mary's house (vv. 12-17).

22. Metzger, *Textual Commentary*, 346, discusses three variants of the verb used here, but argues that *proagagein* is most likely to be the original.

presented as faithful disciples, who were nevertheless surprised by God's response to their prayers. As in 5:19, *an angel of the Lord appeared* (not specifically 'the angel of the Lord', as in Gn. 16:7), but the extra feature in this narrative is that *a light shone in the cell* (cf. Lk. 2:9; Acts 9:3; 22:6; 26:13).[23] Indeed, there is much more detail in this narrative than in 5:18-19, highlighting the amazing nature of the intervention. The angel then *struck Peter on the side and woke him up* (contrast the angel's striking of Herod in judgement, v. 23). The command to get up quickly and leave by night is the first hint of a parallel with the escape of the Israelites from Egypt on that first Passover night (cf. Ex. 12:11). Obedience is made possible because *the chains fell off Peter's wrists.* Barrett rightly observes that 'everything turns upon God's gracious initiative, exercised through an angel. Peter is fast asleep, and contributes nothing more than sheer incomprehension and incredulity.'[24]

8-11 The angel's specific instructions to Peter, *'Put on your clothes and sandals'* and *'Wrap your cloak round you and follow me'*, demonstrate God's care and control in the situation. Once again, his leaving in haste, in obedience to God's instructions, recalls the exodus flight from Egypt. But the most extraordinary aspect of this event is that, as Peter *followed him out of the prison*, the guards were not alerted to what was happening and did not try to prevent him *(They passed the first and second guards)*. Moreover, Peter's trusting obedience is emphasised, since Luke tells us how mystified he was *(he had no idea that what the angel was doing was really happening)*. Indeed, *he thought he was seeing a vision.* When they came to *the iron gate leading to the city, it opened for them by itself, and they went through it.* This detail suggests that Peter was imprisoned in the Antonia tower, one side of which opened to the city and the other to the temple.[25] Then the angel went with him *the length of one street* before suddenly leaving him. Peter could now look after himself, but as he *came to himself (en heautō genomenos)*, he realised what had actually been happening. The affirmation *'Now I know without a doubt'* (*alēthōs*, 'truly'; cf. Lk. 9:27; 12:44; 21:3) is a solemn acknowledgment of what God has been doing. Peter declares that *'the Lord has sent his angel and rescued me'*, recalling Nebuchadnezzar's words about the deliverance of the three Hebrews from the fiery furnace (Dn. 3:28). Only in Peter's case, the rescue had been from the clutches of a Jewish king and, paradoxically also,

---

23. Metzger, *Textual Commentary*, 347, again notes Western additions and modifications to this statement.

24. Barrett 1994, 570. Marshall 1980, 209, rightly observes that 'the person who believes in the reality of the supernatural will not find it difficult to accept this story as it stands, along with other, similar stories in the Bible and Christian history'. Acts contains a limited number of such stories, indicating that such divine intervention was experienced only on certain critical occasions in the early church.

25. Barrett 1994, 581. Codex D adds that they 'walked down the seven steps' (and there are traces of this in some ancient versions). This is unlikely to have been part of the original text and may reflect the sort of information found in Acts 21:35, 40, or more specific local knowledge of the Antonia tower. Cf. Metzger, *Textual Commentary*, 347-48.

from Peter's own people (*'from everything the Jewish people were hoping would happen'*).

12 A further expression stresses that it was only after the event that Peter came to understand what had really happened (*when this had dawned on him*). Sensing the need to make contact with those who were concerned about him, *he went to the house of Mary the mother of John, also called Mark, where many people had gathered and were praying.*[26] John Mark's association with Barnabas and Saul is mentioned in 12:25; 13:5, 13; 15:37, 39; Col. 4:10; 2 Tim. 4:11; Phlm. 24. But in 1 Peter 5:12-13 he is mentioned along with Silas as a companion of Peter. Later Christian writings identify Mark as Peter's 'interpreter' in the writing of the Gospel of Mark.[27] In the next stage of Luke's narrative, John Mark provides a personal link between the Jerusalem Christians and the mission to the Gentiles. We know nothing of Mark's father, though his mother was clearly a Christian and their house was large enough to accommodate *many people* for prayer. There were probably other such houses in Jerusalem where large numbers of Christians could also meet, since growing opposition from unbelieving Jews would have made it impossible for them to meet in the temple courts (cf. 2:46).

13-15 Peter knocked first at *the outer entrance*, and was met by *a servant named Rhoda* ('Rose'), who probably belonged to the household of John Mark and may also have been a member of the church. The fact that she *recognized Peter's voice* suggests that he was a regular visitor to the house. She was *so overjoyed she ran back without opening [the door]*, showing how ready she was to believe that the prayers of the church had been answered. In stark contrast, the disbelief and incredulity of the others is expressed quite vigorously (*'You're out of your mind,' they told her*).[28] Moreover, *when she kept insisting that it was so, they said, 'It must be his angel'.*[29] It is possible that the Greek word *angelos* is used of a human messenger here (cf. Mt. 11:10; Jas. 2:25), implying that someone had come with a message from Peter. If a supernatural visitor is implied, the reference may be to his 'guardian angel' (cf. Dn. 3:28; 6:22; Mt. 18:10). In connection with the Jewish belief in protect-

---

26. It is not necessary to assume with Spencer 1997, 127, that Mary must have been a recent immigrant to the city. Those scattered in 8:1 could well have returned by now. Indeed, the intensity of opposition to Peter and James suggests that the number of Christians in Jerusalem had once more become a significant problem for the authorities.

27. Papias in Eusebius, *Hist. Eccl.* 3.39.15, is the earliest such testimony. C. P. Thiede, *Simon Peter: From Galilee to Rome* (Exeter: Paternoster, 1986), 153-58, argues unconvincingly that Peter went to Rome immediately after the events recorded in Acts 12 and assisted Mark with the writing of his Gospel between AD 44 and 46. This theory reads too much into the expression *for another place* (12:17 note) and relies rather uncritically on certain pieces of early Christian literature.

28. Spencer 1997, 127, overplays the significance of the event, describing Rhoda's function as prophetic and accusing the disciples who rejected her message as being 'not yet ready to adopt the Pentecost agenda fully' (cf. 2:18).

29. The Western text enhances the naïvete of the account by adding *tychon* ('perhaps') before 'it is his angel'. Cf. Metzger, *Textual Commentary*, 349.

ing and guiding angels, Barrett notes that 'these were sometimes thought to resemble the human beings they protected'.[30] However, the evidence for this is much later, and Rhoda is said to have *recognized Peter's voice* rather than to have seen his physical likeness. Luke's honesty in recording these reactions raises questions about the nature and sincerity of the prayer being offered for Peter. Were the disciples genuinely asking for his release, or were they simply praying for Peter to be faithful in the face of death? Were they praying for his release but doubting in their hearts that it would happen this time because of the seriousness of the circumstances? Since Luke has already stated that 'the church was earnestly praying to God for him' (v. 5), we must conclude that they were surprised by the nature and timing of God's response (Peter's release was just before he was due to be executed). They were discovering that God 'is able to do immeasurably more than all we ask or imagine' (Eph. 3:20).

16-17   Peter's persistence in knocking was finally rewarded. When they opened the door and saw him, *they were astonished (exestēsan;* cf. 2:7, 12; 8:13; 9:21; 10:45). Then Peter *motioned with his hand,* using an orator's gesture and calling for them *to be quiet.*[31] This was his opportunity to describe *how the Lord had brought him out of prison,* encouraging them to recognise the grace and power of God which had been manifested in his deliverance.[32] God is glorified when his people acknowledge and make known his answers to prayer. Peter's instruction, *'Tell James and the other brothers and sisters about this',* reveals something of the importance of James in the leadership of the church at this time. Paul informs us that this James was the brother of Jesus (Gal. 1:19; cf. Mk. 6:3; 1 Cor. 15:7). Along with Peter (Cephas) and John, James is identified as one of the 'pillars' of the Jerusalem church in Galatians 2:9. James plays a key role in the Jerusalem Council (Acts 15:13-21), maintaining the freedom of the Gentiles with respect to the law of Moses, but proposing a solution with respect to their recognition of Jewish Christian sensitivities. He finally reappears in the narrative of Acts with the elders, giving advice to Paul when he visits Jerusalem for the last time (21:17-25). Some have argued that Peter effectively ceded the headship of the church to James at this point, in order to be a missionary.[33] Bauckham

---

30. Barrett 1994, 585, with references.

31. Barrett 1994, 586, with references. The Western text modifies v. 17 to include *eisēlthen kai* ('he came in and'), to make it clear that Peter did not remain at the entrance. Cf. Metzger, *Textual Commentary,* 349.

32. Luke uses *diēgeisthai* ('to relate, describe') in 12:17, which he also employs in Lk. 8:39; 9:10; Acts 8:33 (= Is. 53:8); 9:27. Cf. Lk. 1:1, *diēgēsin* ('narrative').

33. Cf. O. Cullmann, *Peter: Disciple-Apostle-Martyr: A Historical and Theological Study* (ET, London: SCM, 1953), 40-41. Cullmann argues that James originally played a somewhat leading role *beside* Peter, but acted as a *substitute* in Peter's absence. The 'final transfer of the leadership to James is connected with the imprisonment and liberation of Peter, as a result of which the latter has to leave Jerusalem'. Thiede, *Simon Peter,* 153, supposes that Peter had appointed James as his successor at the time of his arrest, 'when he must have been expecting certain death'. R. E. Brown, K. P. Donfried, and J. Reumann, *Peter in the New Testament: A*

argues that Acts 12 is 'so placed as to indicate that Peter's leading role — which has hitherto been seen both in his leadership in Jerusalem (chapters 1-5) and in his pioneering role in the mission out from Jerusalem, including the first breakthrough to the Gentiles (8:14-25; 9:32–11:18) — passes not merely to one successor but to two: James (12:17) in Jerusalem, and Paul (13:2) in the mission to the Gentiles'.[34] However, such approaches may be reading too much into the evidence, and 'it is probably anachronistic to think in terms of such regional delimitations of authority, or indeed of the kind of authority that could be so delimited'.[35] When Luke tells us that Peter then left *for another place (eis heteron topon)*, the most natural presumption is that he was seeking to avoid re-arrest by Herod and his officials. Some have wanted to argue that *another place* might mean Rome, but the Greek expression is vague and could apply to anywhere. In simple terms, 'from this point on Peter gives up his fixed residence in Jerusalem, and so also his position in the church there'.[36] However, he certainly continued to engage in apostolic ministry, in Jerusalem (15:6-11 note) and elsewhere (cf. Gal. 2:11-14; 1 Cor. 1:12; 3:22; 9:5; 1-2 Peter), not as 'the archetype of the church official but of the missionary'.[37]

18-19 *In the morning, there was no small commotion among the soldiers as to what had become of Peter.* The implication is that the soldiers had been in a supernaturally induced sleep and were totally unaware of what had happened to Peter. With good reason, their mental agitation or confusion *(tarachos ouk oligos, no small commotion)*[38] was far more intense than the puzzlement of the officials reported in 5:22-24. Herod's close personal concern about this escape is immediately stressed. He *had a thorough search made for him*, because he was intent on removing Peter and his influence from the scene. When he did not find him, *he cross-examined the guards and ordered that they be executed.* The death penalty for allowing prisoners to escape was the norm in the Roman Empire, and Herod applied this rule to his own kingdom.[39]

Collaborative Assessment by Protestant and Roman Catholic Scholars (London: Geoffrey Chapman, 1973), 48-49, note three different views about the relationship between Peter and James and the early church leadership, as it involved Jerusalem.

34. R. Bauckham, 'James and the Jerusalem Church', in R. Bauckham (ed.), *The Book of Acts in Its First-Century Setting*, Vol. 4: *Palestinian Setting* (Grand Rapids: Eerdmans; Carlisle: Paternoster, 1995), 435. Spencer 1997, 128, makes an elaborate case for a parallel between Peter and Jesus in commissioning others to carry out his work.

35. Barrett 1994, 587.

36. Cullmann, *Peter*, 38-39. Thiede, *Simon Peter*, 153-58, is one of those who identify *another place* with Rome. However, this creates difficulties for constructing a chronology of Peter's movements with respect to Acts 15 and Gal. 2:11-14.

37. Cullmann, *Peter*, 41.

38. The Greek here is a form of 'litotes' that is used again in 14:28; 15:2; 17:4, 12; 19:23-24; 27:20. It is an understatement used to emphasize the opposite: there was actually a great commotion! Some MSS actually replace *ouk oligos* with *megas* ('great') or leave out the expression. Cf. Barrett 1994, 588.

39. Cf. Barrett 1994, 588.

Luke prepares for the next stage of the narrative by recording that Herod then *went from Judea to Caesarea and stayed there*. Since Caesarea was actually the Roman capital of Judea, Luke must be using the expression *went from Judea* to refer to Herod's departure from Jerusalem (*katerchesthai*, 'come down', is so used in 8:5; 9:32; 11:27). At this point, Luke's account finds an important parallel in Josephus (*Ant.* 19.343-53; *War* 2.219), who records that Herod visited Caesarea to celebrate certain spectacles in honour of Caesar. If these games were held on March 5, AD 44, which was the foundation day of that city, Peter's arrest must have been at Passover time in the preceding year (March 5 was before Passover in 44). However, if the games were held on August 1, AD 44, which was the birthday of Claudius, the arrest of Peter will have been at Passover of that year.[40] See 11:28-30 (note) and 12:25 (note) on the dating of the famine relief visit to Jerusalem by Barnabas and Saul. This appears to have been after the imprisonment of Peter and the death of Herod. Consequently, the material in 12:1-24 is out of sequence chronologically and is located here for thematic reasons. As suggested previously, before Luke focuses on the mission to the Gentiles and the suffering endured by gospel messengers in that context, he brings us up to date on the struggle experienced by Christians in Jerusalem.

3. Divine Judgment on Herod Agrippa I (12:20-23)

Luke's intention in this section is to link Herod's end with his arrogance towards God and his fellow human beings. Herod's treatment of James and Peter (12:1-5) is an earlier expression of that same attitude and behaviour. Divine retribution does not come upon him until he finally manifests his idolatrous self-glorification in a very public way (12:21-3). Meanwhile, God has shown that he is still sovereign over those who conspire against him and his people (12:6-19; cf. 4:25-31; 9:1-19). In various ways throughout Acts, readers are assured that God will judge those who oppose his work (cf. 1:15-20) or provoke him to anger by self-promoting deceit and idolatry (cf. 5:1-11; 8:18-24; 13:8-11; 17:30-31; 24:25), either in this life or the next.

20 *Tyre and Sidon* were free, self-governing cities on the coast of Phoenicia, within the province of Syria. Herod had been *quarreling* with these neighbours for unspecified reasons. So serious was the situation that their leaders *joined together and sought an audience with him* (*homothymadon de parēsan pros auton*, 'together they presented themselves before him').[41] In their approach to Herod, they wisely *secured the support of Blastus, a trusted personal servant of the king*. Josephus (*Ant.* 19.343-53; *War* 2.219) records the

40. Cf. Barrett 1994, 592; Bruce 1990, 288.

41. The Western text differs in a number of details in vv. 20-22, suggesting that Herod came to Caesarea specifically to hold an audience with representatives from Tyre and Sidon, and adding that it was 'on the occasion of his reconciliation with the Tyrians (and the Sidonians)' that he was acclaimed as a god. Cf. Metzger, *Textual Commentary*, 349.

visit of Herod Agrippa I to Caesarea for celebrations in honour of the emperor, but does not mention Blastus and this audience with representatives from Tyre. Writing independently, Luke uses his own source to describe something extra that happened on this occasion. The people of Tyre and Sidon were concerned to bring an immediate end to hostilities because Herod had economic power over them *(they asked for peace, because they depended on the king's country for their food supply)*. If Judea was able to supply food to its neighbours in any quantity, this was clearly not the time of the famine mentioned in 11:28-30 (cf. 12:19, 25 notes on the dating of these events).

21-22 On the day appointed for this audience with representatives from Tyre and Sidon, Herod put on *his royal robes, sat on his throne and delivered a public address to the people*. Other important people were clearly present, while Herod was arrogantly asserting his majesty and importance in the city where Caesar was the real political power. Josephus similarly records that on the second day of the festival Agrippa entered the theatre at daybreak, 'clad in a robe made altogether of silver, of quite wonderful weaving' (*Ant.* 19.344). Luke says that the crowd shouted, *'This is the voice of a god, not of a mere mortal'*. Josephus notes that the king's flatterers were astonished at the radiance of his silver robe when it was touched by the first rays of the rising sun and addressed him as a god, crying out, 'Be gracious to us! Hitherto we have reverenced you as a human being, but henceforth we confess you to be of more than mortal nature.'[42]

23 Luke then records God's response to this whole situation. *Immediately, because Herod did not give praise to God, an angel of the Lord struck him down*.[43] Adulation of kings was common in the ancient world, but no faithful Jew could accept divine honours in this way. Herod refused to give God the *praise* (*doxa*, 'glory, praise'; cf. Rom. 1:21) which was due to him and had improperly allowed it to be ascribed to himself (cf. the charge against the Prince of Tyre in Ezk. 28:1-10 and contrast Paul and Barnabas in Acts 14:14-18). Josephus similarly notes that Agrippa would not repudiate the adoration of the crowd and its flattery. In his account, the king was seized with violent internal pains, was carried home, and died five days later. In Luke's account, an angel of the Lord is responsible for having *struck him down*.[44] We are not necessarily meant to think of an angelic appearance, as in vv. 7-11, but rather that the affliction was sent by God as a

---

42. Bruce 1990, 289, notes also the Jewish tradition that recalls this event. 'In the name of Rabbi Nathan it is taught: In that hour the enemies of Israel earned destruction, for they flattered Agrippa' (*t. Soṭah* 7:16; cf. *b. Soṭah* 41b).

43. Codex D, supported in part by two other MSS, adds that *he came down from the platform* [and] *while he was still living* he was eaten by worms and *thus* died. Cf. Metzger, *Textual Commentary*, 350. This enhances the drama and horror of the situation.

44. The same verb (*epataxen*) is used in Ex. 12:12, 23, 29 LXX with reference to the Lord's judgment on Pharaoh, and in Acts 12:7 for a gentler strike by which Peter is rescued from a tyrant king.

punishment. The particular manner of his death *(he was eaten by worms and died)* is frequently mentioned by ancient writers, 'especially as having been endured by people who were considered to have richly deserved it'.[45] Luke gives no indication of the length of time the illness was experienced but simply records that it led to his death. For the date of Herod's death see 12:19 note. From this time on, Judea reverted to government by Roman procurators.

4. The Word Continues to Grow (12:24-25)

Luke's editorial conclusion marks a significant, transitional step in the narrative. Once again, gospel growth means church growth (cf. 6:7). As in 9:31, the context for growth appears to be the relaxation of persecution — in this case through the death of Herod. God's sustaining of the church under persecution (12:5-17) has meant that, with the removal of hindrances, the word has been able to burst out and spread again in Jerusalem. With a reference to the return of Barnabas and Saul to Antioch, Luke turns the attention of his readers to the great outreach that is about to begin from that city. Nevertheless, until we hear further news in 21:20, we are left with the impression that gospel growth continued in Jerusalem, whatever the opposition encountered.

24-25 A familiar note is first sounded: *But the word of God continued to increase and spread* (cf. 6:7; 19:20).[46] The enemies of the gospel had attempted to hinder its progress in Jerusalem, but God enabled his word to 'grow' and 'multiply' (*ēuxanen kai eplēthyneto*). The same two verbs are used in 6:7, where the second clearly relates to the growth in the number of disciples. Putting the two verbs together with 'the word of God' as subject in 12:24, Luke makes it absolutely clear that gospel growth means church growth in terms of conversions. Secondly, there is a bridge between the famine relief story in 11:27-30 and a new section of the narrative in which Antioch becomes the base for missionary outreach on a wide scale. TNIV translates 12:25, *When Barnabas and Saul had finished their mission, they returned from Jerusalem, taking with them John, also called Mark* (so also KJV, ESV). However, the best-attested reading is *eis Ierousalēm,*

---

45. Bruce 1990, 289 (compare Acts 1:18, where different terms are used). Bruce mentions various medical explanations that have been given for the death of Herod Agrippa I. These have included peritonitis resulting from a perforated appendix, arsenical poisoning, and acute intestinal obstruction. Cf. Barrett 1994, 591; O. W. Allen Jr., *The Death of Herod: The Narrative and Theological Function of Retribution in Luke-Acts,* SBLDS 158 (Atlanta: Scholars, 1997). Note 43 above mentions Western textual additions to the account in v. 23.

46. Instead of 'the word of God', Codex B and the Latin Vulgate read 'the word of the Lord'. Although it could be argued that this reading is the original because it is not Luke's usual phrase, it is poorly attested and is probably influenced by the immediately preceding expression 'the angel of the Lord' (v. 23). Cf. Metzger, *Textual Commentary,* 350.

which, when taken with the preceding verb *hypestrepsan,* means 'they returned to Jerusalem' (so NRSV). This does not make sense in the context, and so it has been argued that it was a primitive error that infected a variety of normally reliable manuscripts. However, the alternative readings which make more sense are divided, using two different Greek words for 'from' (*apo* and *ex*). This has led to various conjectures about how to read *eis Ierousalēm* appropriately. It seems best to relate the phrase to the following clause (*plērōsantes tēn diakonian*), giving the sense 'having fulfilled their service in Jerusalem.' The verse should thus be translated, 'Barnabas and Saul returned, having fulfilled their service in Jerusalem, and having picked up as companion John who was called Mark'.[47] Their mission to provide famine relief stands in marked contrast with Herod's apparent restriction of food supply to Tyre and Sidon.[48] This implies that Barnabas and Saul were in Jerusalem when Peter was arrested and that they returned to Antioch, from where they had come on their famine-relief mission. However, we have already argued from external evidence that the date of Herod's death was probably AD 44 and that the most likely date for the famine was at least three years later. Chronologically, therefore, the famine relief visit would belong at the end of Acts 14. Luke appears to have rearranged his material for thematic reasons and inserted the editorial comment in 12:24-25 to make an easy transition to the next main section of his story. The famine relief visit is recorded out of order at the end of the section about the foundation of the church in Antioch (11:27-30) because it represents a grateful response from that church for the ministry received from Jerusalem. The story of Peter's imprisonment and the death of Herod is then recorded to mark the end of a major section of the narrative in which Jerusalem and Peter are central. Luke arranged his material in this way to convey the message that the church in Antioch had developed in such a way that it was 'now ready to move out into new fields and establish new churches dependent on itself'.[49] The next main division of Acts will focus on Paul and his ministry among the Gentiles. Jerusalem is left behind until it emerges again in the narrative concerning the council in Acts 15. We are meant to conclude that gospel growth continued there, despite opposition of various kinds (cf. 21:20 for the next estimate of the number of disciples in Jerusalem). 'Luke's belief in the victory of the gospel is thoroughly realistic and recognizes that though the word of God is not fettered, its servants may well have to suffer and be bound (2 Tim. 2:9).'[50]

---

47. Barrett 1994, 593, 595-96. Cf. Bruce 1990, 290. This is a logical and defensible solution, though Metzger, *Textual Commentary,* 350-52, discusses other proposals.

48. Cf. Spencer 1997, 129.

49. Barrett 1994, 594. Thus, 12:24-25 functions as a conclusion to both 11:27-30 and 12:1-23, as well as providing an introduction to chapter 13.

50. Marshall 1980, 207.

V. THE WORD GOES TO CYPRUS
AND ASIA MINOR (13:1–16:5)[1]

In broad terms, Acts now changes from a focus on Jerusalem and Peter (1–12) to a concentration on the Gentile churches and Saul (13–28), called 'Paul' from 13:9. Step by step, the immediately preceding section (9:32–12:25) has shown how the gospel moved out into the Gentile world. Explicit statements at key points interpret these events as guided by God,[2] though Paul's particular commission to proclaim Christ 'to the Gentiles and their kings and to the people of Israel' was first revealed in 9:15. Three times in the remainder of Acts Paul announces a specific turning to the Gentiles, but this never signals a final and definitive abandonment of his ministry to Jews (13:46; 18:6; 28:28). Jewish opposition and rejection of the gospel in each particular context gives rise to a concentration on ministry to Gentiles, yet Paul's pattern in each new situation is to minister to Jews first, wherever possible. Furthermore, as he moves from Antioch (13:1-3) to Rome (28:14-31), he returns to Jerusalem for several important visits (15:1-35; 18:22; 20:16), showing a continuing desire to maintain links with that church and its leadership. In general, it is true to say that 'turning to the gentiles does not mean creating communities of gentiles which replace the Jewish messianic communities; rather, it means including gentiles within such Jewish communities, which thus become broader, inclusive kinds of communities'.[3] However, this often eventually means setting up a new base of operation for the church outside the synagogue, where Gentiles soon outnumber Jewish believers. The first dramatic turning to the Gentiles in 13:46-48 is significant because it is given a theological rationale by Paul. Clearly, Luke intends this to provide an explanation of Paul's strategy in later contexts as well. Opposition to Paul and his ministry regularly comes from Jewish and Gentile sources in the narrative of Acts 13–28. This fulfills another aspect of the Lord's prediction in 9:15-16, where it is indicated that Paul must suffer many things 'for my name'. More than any other character in Acts, Paul fulfills the earlier prophecy of Jesus in Luke 21:12-19 regarding the persecution disciples will face.[4]

Geographically, the movement is to Cyprus first (13:4-12), where pre-

---

1. Spencer 1997, 131, designates this as the Mediterranean Expedition and calls the second missionary journey the Aegean Expedition (16:6–21:36). He draws a parallel between the main features of each expedition, arguing that the so-called third missionary journey is really an extension of the Aegean Expedition.

2. J. T. Squires, 'The Function of Acts 8:4–12:25', *NTS* 44 (1998), 612-13, takes 8:4 as the starting point of the section.

3. Squires, 'Function', 617.

4. S. Cunningham, *'Through many tribulations': The Theology of Persecution in Luke-Acts*, JSNTSS 142 (Sheffield: Sheffield Academic, 1997), 243, observes that 'the pattern of rejection of the gospel and persecution of its witnesses that was earlier established in Acts is extended in the first journey of Paul, who is thus shown to share in the sufferings and persecution first experienced by the Jerusalem disciples'.

vious believers had already spread the word among Jews (11:19). Luke notes that Barnabas and Saul continued that ministry in the synagogues, and illustrates the evangelisation of Gentiles in terms of the encounter with the Roman proconsul. The next movement is to Antioch in Pisidia (13:13-52), where the synagogue ministry is given great prominence and a Christ-centred sermon is recorded. However, opposition from unbelieving Jews necessitates a turning away from synagogue ministry and a more direct engagement with Gentiles. The same pattern is repeated in Iconium (14:1-7). In Lystra, however, there appears to be no synagogue and there is an immediate encounter with paganism, as Paul challenges the inhabitants to turn from idolatry to the living God (14:8-18). Jewish opposition to this ministry comes from Antioch and Iconium, forcing the missionaries to move on to Derbe (14:19-20). The return to Syrian Antioch enables them to strengthen and encourage the churches (14:21-28), before they have to leave for Jerusalem, to represent the interests of Gentile believers at the Jerusalem Council (15:1-29). This important gathering deals with matters relating to the salvation of Gentiles and their fellowship with Jewish believers in Christian communities. With the resolution of these issues, at least to the satisfaction of the church in Antioch (15:30-35), Paul and Barnabas feel free to move out on another campaign in the Gentile world. However, differences over the reliability of John Mark mean that two teams are formed (15:36-41), and Luke records only the journey of Paul and Silas. With an overland return to Derbe and Lystra, it is as if Paul takes up where he left off before (16:1-5). Accompanied now by Timothy as well, Paul delivers the decisions of the Jerusalem Council, and Luke marks the end of another panel by noting that 'the churches were strengthened in the faith and grew daily in numbers'.

A. The Release of Barnabas and Saul from Antioch in Syria (13:1-3)

As well as introducing the larger division (Acts 13–28) in which Paul is the central character, this chapter also begins a smaller division (Acts 13–14) which is marked off by an inclusion between the release of Barnabas and Saul from their ministry in Antioch (13:1-3) and their return to report to that church about their missionary campaign (14:26-27).[5] This mission took place roughly from AD 46 to 49. Readers already know from 9:15 that Saul has been chosen for a special task, but this must be revealed by the Holy Spirit to the prophets and teachers of Antioch, to secure their support and a willing release of the missionaries from their leadership role in Antioch. The nature of their task is progressively exposed as chapters 13 and 14 unfold. Refer-

5. Barrett 1994, 599-600, observes that 13:1-13 'stands in the midst of a considerable sequence in which the church at Antioch looks back to its origins and also relates to its own contribution to Christian missionary expansion'. Luke adapted and edited this Antiochene material, 'which may run back to a fairly early date', and which must surely have involved more than a list of the names of places visited (Barrett, 608).

ence to Paul as a prophet provides specific background for the next scene, 'in which Paul speaks as a prophet, filled with the Holy Spirit (13:9-11)'.[6]

1 *Now in the church at Antioch there were prophets and teachers.* Luke resumes the story of Christianity at Antioch from 11:27-30 (though brief mention of the visit of Barnabas and Saul to Jerusalem in 12:25 forms the first narrative link with the previous section).[7] Luke uses a participial construction to describe the church (*tēn ousan ekklēsian*), which suggests the meaning 'the church in that place' or 'the local church'.[8] It is clear from 11:27 that 'prophets came down from Jerusalem to Antioch', though we cannot be sure whether any of them were included in the present list. Certainly Agabus, who features so prominently in 11:28, is not mentioned. *Barnabas* and *Saul* have already been identified as *teachers* in 11:26 (the noun *didaskaloi*, 'teachers', is found only at 13:1, though the verb *didaskein*, 'to teach', is used in 11:26 and elsewhere in Acts).[9] Saul also appears in the following narrative as a prophetic figure, 'filled with the Holy Spirit' (13:9-11). So Luke is unlikely to be making a hard-and-fast distinction between these ministries here: some, like Saul, were gifted as both prophets and teachers.[10] Indeed, the distinction between these ministries may have been 'a matter of manner rather than of content'.[11] Since *Barnabas* and *Saul* do not appear together in this list of names, it is unlikely that Luke is identifying any particular pairs or groups. Perhaps Barnabas comes first because he was an early contributor to the life of the church in Antioch, and Saul comes last because he was a late arrival. What is most obvious is the ethnic diversity of the leadership of this church. *Barnabas* was from Cyprus, *Simeon called Niger* may have been from Africa (*Niger* is a Latinism, meaning 'black'),[12] and *Lucius of Cyrene* certainly came from North Africa (cf. 11:20

---

6. Tannehill 1990, 160.

7. The simple Greek connective *de* in 13:1 suggests a continuation from, rather than a disjunction with, 12:25. Luke normally uses a construction like *men oun* to begin a new subject or stage in the narrative, while asserting continuity with what precedes it (e.g., 1:6; 8:4; 11:19; 13:4). So 13:4 is rather more obviously the beginning of a new section.

8. Cf. Barrett 1994, 601; Johnson 1992, 220; THE THEOLOGY OF ACTS: X. THE CHURCH (pp. 92-97).

9. The ministry of teachers in local churches is mentioned in Rom. 12:7; 1 Cor. 12:28-29; Eph. 4:11; Jas. 3:1, and extensively in the Pastoral Epistles.

10. Longenecker 1981, 416, notes the double *te* construction in Greek and argues that this probably means that Barnabas, Simeon, and Lucius were prophets, and Manaen and Saul were teachers. However, the stylistic variation of connectives in this verse should not be made the basis for a hard-and-fast distinction between prophets and teachers.

11. Barrett 1994, 602. Barrett notes that Luke's own preferred word for ministers or church leaders is elders (*presbyteroi*; cf. 11:30; 14:23; 15:2, 4, 6, 22, 23; 16:4; 20:17, 18). He argues from what follows that in the church at Antioch prophets and teachers, 'in addition to giving inspired exhortation and instruction, took the lead in planning and administering the church's work'. However, this may be reading too much into the role exercised by the prophets and teachers with respect to the missionary calling of Barnabas and Saul (cf. 13:3 note).

12. Witherington 1998, 392, rightly argues against the view that this may have been the Simon of Cyrene mentioned in Lk. 23:26.

note). *Manaen* is described as having been *brought up with Herod the tetrarch*, the ruler of Galilee when Jesus was born (Lk. 3:1),[13] and *Saul* was from Tarsus. The remarkable diversity of the backgrounds and origins of these leaders was 'appropriate to the cosmopolitan context of Antioch'.[14]

   2 *While they were worshipping the Lord and fasting, the Holy Spirit said, 'Set apart for me Barnabas and Saul for the work to which I have called them'.* The context here is probably a meeting of the leaders mentioned in the previous verse (*autōn* most naturally refers back to the list of names in v. 1), though it seems that the whole church was eventually involved in commissioning the missionaries (cf. 14:26-27 note).[15] The participle *leitourgountōn*, which is loosely translated *worshipping* by TNIV, was generally used of a public service rendered by someone to benefit others (e.g., Isocrates, *Against Callimachus*, 58, 64; Aristotle, *Pol.* 3.5, p. 1278a, 12; Rom. 15:27; 2 Cor. 9:12), though the verb and related terms were also employed in the LXX in a technical sense to describe priestly service to the God of Israel (e.g., 2 Chr. 11:14; Jl. 2:17; Ezk. 45:4; cf. Lk. 1:23; Heb. 10:11).[16] Since *the Lord* is the object of service or ministry here, Luke may be suggesting that corporate prayer is the 'cultic' activity which replaces the sacrificial approach to God which was at the heart of Judaism. Coupled with *fasting*, the reference is most likely to prayer, though it is also possible that the meaning is 'serving the Lord' with their gifts, as they engaged in prophecy and teaching.[17] *Fasting* is mentioned again in Acts only at 14:23, where the appointment of elders is in view, and at 27:9, where 'the fast' refers to the Jewish Day of Atonement. Christians are not commanded to fast in the NT, though Jesus gives guidance about how to fast in a way that is pleasing to God (Mt. 6:16-18). Some apparently took over the practice from Judaism, 'partly as self-discipline, partly as a reinforcement to prayer'.[18] In the present context there was probably a commitment to fast as an aid to prayer. Perhaps these leaders were actively seeking

---

13. Gk. *syntrophos*, translated 'brought up with' by TNIV, was used for someone adopted by a family as a childhood playmate (Herodotus, *Persian Wars* 1.99) or as a court title, meaning 'intimate friend' (Lucian of Samosata, *Nigrinus* 12; 15). See 1 Macc. 1:6; 2 Macc. 9:29; J. Jeremias, *Jerusalem in the Time of Jesus: An Investigation into Economic and Social Conditions during the New Testament Period* (ET, London: SCM, 1969), 88; Barrett 1994, 604. Witherington 1998, 165ff., 392, proposes that Manaen may have been a source for Luke's information about the Herods.

14. Spencer 1997, 137.

15. See Barrett 1994, 604, and compare Marshall 1980, 215; Stott 1990, 216-17; Spencer 1997, 137-38.

16. Cf. H. Strathmann, *TDNT* 4:215-19; D. G. Peterson, *Engaging with God: A Biblical Theology of Worship* (Leicester: Apollos; Grand Rapids: Eerdmans, 1992), 66-68, 150-51.

17. Bruce 1988, 245, suggests the meaning 'carrying out their appointed ministry in the church'. Cf. *1 Clem.* 44:3; *Did.* 15:1. However, most commentators take the meaning to be praying to the Lord.

18. Barrett 1994, 605. Barrett notes that fasting did not form part of 'official' Greek and Roman religions. Spencer 1997, 138, observes that fasting 'both expresses and produces a humble attitude conducive to receiving special revelations'. Cf. Hermas, *Vis.* 3.10.6; *Sim.* 5.1.2.

the Lord's will for the progress of the gospel in the Gentile world. 'The mission journey of Paul and Barnabas, like the missions of Jesus and the apostles, is born out of the searching and alertness of prayer and is empowered by the Spirit.'[19] References to prayer in Luke 3:21 and Acts 1:14 are followed by actions of the Holy Spirit (Lk. 3:22; Acts 2:1-4), leading to mission (Lk. 4:14, 18; Acts 2:5-41). In the present context, the Spirit does not so much anoint or empower Barnabas and Saul for their mission as direct their colleagues to set them apart for the work to which they have been called. Paul himself makes the point in 20:28 that the Holy Spirit appoints leaders in the church. The Greek particle *dē* indicates the need for immediate action and could be translated 'now' (cf. 15:36). When Luke writes that *the Holy Spirit said,* he may mean that the Spirit spoke publicly through one or more of the prophets in the church. However, it is also possible that a conviction about God's will in the situation was given to each one present (cf. 8:29; 10:19; 11:2, where the Spirit's guidance of individuals is noted). The Spirit's charge (*'Set apart for me Barnabas and Saul for the work to which I have called them'*) is for the leaders of the church to acknowledge by their actions what God has already decided and revealed (Gk. perfect *proskeklēmai* suggests that they have already been called to this work). Paul uses the same verb 'set apart' *(aphorizein)* to describe God's action in his life in Romans 1:1; Galatians 1:15 (cf. Nu. 16:9; 1 Chr. 23:13, where the divine initiative in 'setting apart' for a ministry is highlighted). The Spirit here speaks for the risen Christ, who first separated Paul to himself for a special work (9:5-6, 15-16). Barnabas apparently now shares in this calling by association with Saul. So here we have 'the first piece of planned "overseas mission" carried out by representatives of a particular church, rather than by solitary individuals, and begun by a deliberate church decision, inspired by the Spirit, rather than somewhat more casually as a result of persecution'.[20] Effective Christian leaders will likewise see the need to discern God's gifting for ministry in others, to support (and where necessary train) those whom God is leading to local ministry or mission elsewhere, and to affirm them by acts of ordination or commissioning (cf. 14:23; 1 Tim. 4:14; 5:22; 2 Tim 2:2; Tit. 1:5-9).

3 *So after they had fasted and prayed, they placed their hands on them and sent them off.* Luke's language here parallels the Pastoral Epistles in their description of ordination to congregational leadership (with prophecy [1 Tim. 1:18; 4:14] and the laying on of hands [1 Tim. 4:14; 2 Tim. 1:6]). However, the context indicates that this was a separation from existing ministerial responsibilities and a prayerful commissioning for a different task, not ordination as in 14:23 or in the Pastorals. Barrett suggests that this could have been an appointment of Barnabas and Saul as 'apostles of the church' of Antioch (cf. 2 Cor. 8:23), though he rightly insists that 'in Paul's own con-

---

19. Tannehill 1990, 161.
20. Marshall 1980, 214. Cf. THE THEOLOGY OF ACTS: III. THE HOLY SPIRIT (pp. 60-65).

viction, he became an apostle at the time of his conversion'.[21] However, the verb translated *sent them off (apelysan)* has the sense of 'release', 'dismiss', or 'send away' (e.g., 3:13; 4:21; 5:40; 15:30, 33), not 'appoint'. Moreover, from a narrative perspective, readers know that Paul has already been commissioned as an apostle of Christ (9:5-6, 15-16), even if the specific designation 'apostle' has not so far been used. The revelation of the Holy Spirit in 13:2 was God's way of showing the leaders of the church something of his plan for Barnabas and Saul, so that they might willingly release them from their responsibilities at Antioch and prayerfully support them in their God-given mission (cf. 14:26, *committed to the grace of God* for the work to which they had been called). Like fasting, the laying on of hands in this context was an aid to prayer, as well as an act of commissioning (cf. 6:6 note). The action could express both blessing and identification with others in their task or calling. It was neither an authorization for ministry nor a means of imparting some spiritual gift. Barrett rightly observes that the Christians in Antioch were 'acting in a new situation, without precedents, and simply committed their brothers to the grace of God for the task ahead'.[22]

B. The Word in Cyprus (13:4-12)

The mission to Cyprus provides a cameo of much that will occur in subsequent narratives. There is a summary account of ministry to Jews in various synagogues, followed by a memorable engagement with an interested Gentile (in this case the Roman proconsul), in the context of opposition from Jewish quarters (in this case a sorcerer and false prophet). Here the theme of magic and the gospel is introduced again (cf. 8:9-24). Paul's prophetic insight and authority result in the temporary blinding of his opponent — as an expression of divine judgment for his deceitful ways — but the conversion of the proconsul. This is the first occasion in Acts on which Paul encounters a sympathetic Roman official. His coming to believe in 'the teaching about the Lord' is remarkable enough, but especially so because of the negative influence of the Jewish sorcerer and false prophet who was his attendant.

It is not necessary to conclude that Luke's sources were meagre and that he 'filled out with inference and added information'.[23] We have al-

---

21. Barrett 1994, 601. Barrett, 666-67, 671-72, discusses the fact that Paul and Barnabas are called apostles in 14:4, 14, but nowhere else in Acts. Barrett, 610, notes the absence of *apostellein* from 13:4, 'which would unmistakably have called to mind the noun *apostolos*'. Cf. A. C. Clark, 'The Role of the Apostles', in I. H. Marshall and D. G. Peterson (eds.), *Witness to the Gospel: The Theology of Acts* (Grand Rapids/Cambridge: Eerdmans, 1998), 181-85; C. Brown, *NIDNTT* 1:135-36.

22. Barrett 1994, 607. Marshall 1980, 216, Bruce 1990, 294, and Witherington 1998, 393-4, agree that this was not an ordination but a recognition and endorsement by these church leaders of the call of God in this situation.

23. Barrett 1994, 608-9.

ready noted Luke's selectivity in previous chapters, where he seems to
have been driven by two interlocking concerns. First, he tells the story of
the gospel's progress in different geographical regions, with narratives involving an increasing diversity of persons and situations, to convey the developing breadth and impact of this work of God. Secondly, he records the
struggles encountered with unbelievers, and sometimes also with those inside the believing community, to show how the earliest Christians learned
to cope with such situations. Luke's selectivity is thematically driven, but
that does not mean that he creates stories to teach theology and inspire his
readers. With this qualification, we may agree with Haenchen when he describes Luke's interests in the present passage as apologetic (showing Paul
to be on the best of terms with a Roman proconsul), as ecclesial (showing
how Paul emerged as leader over his colleagues), and as theological (showing a rooted objection to magic and its influence and the power of the gospel to overcome it).[24]

4-5 Although the preceding verse stresses the role of the prophets
and teachers at Antioch in sending off Barnabas and Saul, here they are
clearly *sent on their way by the Holy Spirit* (using another verb, *ekpempein*).
The divine initiative in this missionary campaign is thus stressed on either
side of v. 3, which highlights the obedient response of the church to God's
call. The missionaries went first to the port town of *Seleucia*, which was
near the mouth of the Orontes, about 16 miles (26 km.) west of Antioch.
From there they sailed to *Cyprus*, which was about 60 miles (96 km.) away.
Luke now becomes quite selective in telling the story of this first missionary campaign. We learn little about what happened at *Salamis* and much
more about events in *Paphos*. We hear nothing about what was proclaimed
in those towns, though we have a singular example of Paul's synagogue
preaching given in Pisidian Antioch (13:16-41).

Cyprus was a natural place to begin this missionary campaign,
though others had previously spread the word among Jews there (11:19).[25]
It was the homeland of Barnabas (4:36), an important mining and trading
centre, and a convenient stopover point for a sea journey to what is now
called southern Turkey. *Salamis*, which was at the eastern end of Cyprus,
had previously been the capital, but the Romans transferred that honour to
Paphos (Cyprus had been a senatorial province of the Roman Empire since

24. Haenchen 1971, 389. Johnson 1992, 226, identifies a further goal of this passage as
showing that Paul is a genuine prophet in continuity with Jesus and Peter.

25. Cf. A. Nobbs, 'Cyprus', in D. W. J. Gill and C. Gempf (eds.), *The Book of Acts in Its
First-Century Setting*, Vol. 2: *Graeco-Roman Setting* (Grand Rapids: Eerdmans; Carlisle: Paternoster, 1994), 279-89. Cyprus had been annexed from Egypt by the Romans in 57 BC. It became a separate province in 27 BC, governed on behalf of the emperor by a legate. In 22 BC it
became a senatorial province, governed by a proconsul. There was a large Jewish population when Barnabas and Saul visited (1 Macc. 15:23; Philo, *On the Embassy to Gaius* 282;
Josephus, *Ant.* 13.284-87). Mention of a plurality of *synagogues* in Salamis (13:5) is further
evidence of this.

22 BC). In Luke's account, Salamis was important because it was where the missionaries first *proclaimed the word of God in the Jewish synagogues.* Luke nowhere states the Pauline principle 'first to the Jew, then to the Gentile' (Rom. 1:16), though he regularly records Paul's practice of preaching in synagogues before engaging with Gentiles in a region (cf. 13:14; 14:1; 17:1, 10, 17; 18:4, 19; 19:8). However, in 13:46-47 a theological rationale is suggested. Understood in its context, the citation from Isaiah 49:6 implies that Paul shared the gospel with Jews first because he believed that he was fulfilling the role of the Servant of the Lord in restoring 'the tribes of Jacob' and gathering a renewed Israel to God, before being a light for the Gentiles.[26] In short, Luke indicates that Paul was acting for more than pragmatic reasons in preaching to Jews first. Moreover, Luke's own presentation in Acts 1–7 shows that the gospel was for the Jews first, since Jesus is regularly presented as the fulfillment of God's promises to Israel about the messianic salvation. Acts 3:25-26 *(he sent him first to you)* indicates a covenantal priority for this, which has its roots in Genesis 12:1-3. Somewhat surprisingly, *John* is introduced as being *with them as their helper.* This is presumably the John mentioned in 12:12, 25. What is said about the Holy Spirit in verses 2 and 4 is not directly applied to him, suggesting that he had only a supporting role in the mission team.[27] As *helper (hypēretēs),* he may simply have been looking after the material needs of the leaders (the word is used quite broadly for a servant or functionary in 5:22, 26; cf. Lk. 4:20). However, the more specialised use of the same term in Luke 1:2 ('servants of the word') and Acts 26:16 (a 'servant' of the gospel) allows for the possibility that John was involved in preaching and teaching.

6-8 *They traveled through the whole island,* presumably preaching as they went, until they came to the capital, which was actually new *Paphos,* at the western end of Cyprus.[28] Luke does not record an active seeking after Gentiles by the missionaries at this point in the narrative, though this could well have taken place. Rather, he introduces one highly prestigious Gentile, who *sent for Barnabas and Saul because he wanted to hear the word of God.* As *proconsul,* Sergius Paulus was the Roman consular governor of the island.[29]

---

26. Spencer 1997, 141-43, draws attention to the importance of islands in Greco-Roman thinking and notes how fitting it is that Paul begins to fulfill the mission of the Isaianic Servant on an *island,* in view of Is. 49:1.

27. It is reading too much into the situation to say that Luke expresses himself this way so that Mark's defection in 13:13 may not appear as a sin against the Holy Spirit. Cf. Haenchen 1971, 387; Barrett 1994, 612. Bruce 1990, 296, suggests that Mark may have provided eyewitness reminiscences of Jesus that neither Paul nor Barnabas could supply.

28. Salamis and Paphos can be taken to represent the whole island (*Sib. Or.* 4:128-29; 5:450-2), even though they are both on the southern coast. Luke implies that the island was evangelised, because the gospel was planted in key towns and the message could then be taken by converts in those places to other regions (cf. 19:10 note). Cyprus is about 140 miles (223 km.) long.

29. Barrett 1994, 613-14, and Witherington 1998, 399-400, discuss the inscriptional evidence that scholars have investigated in an attempt to identify this Sergius Paulus.

Witherington observes that 'Luke is thoroughly familiar with the govern-
mental arrangements of the Roman Empire, and in particular the difference
between an imperial and a senatorial province, and time and again we find
him giving the proper designations for the Roman officials he mentions'.[30] As
an intelligent man, who had heard something of what was being proclaimed,
the proconsul wished to find out more. However, before revealing the impact
of the gospel on this man's life, Luke mentions the malevolent influence of *a
Jewish sorcerer and false prophet named Bar-Jesus, who was an attendant of the proconsul.* The words *Jewish* and *sorcerer* (*magos,* 'magician', 'astrologer') do not
really belong together, because of scriptural condemnation of those involved
with magic and the occult (e.g., Dt. 18:10; 2 Ki. 17:17; Je. 27 (LXX 34):9; Ezk.
12:24).[31] As a *false prophet,* he was also one of a long line of pretenders who
opposed God's revealed truth and its messengers (e.g., 1 Kings 22; Je. 23:9-
32). With the Aramaic name *Bar-Jesus* ('son of Jesus [Joshua]') he appears to
be a devilish alternative to the true saviour (cf. v. 10, 'child of the devil'). This
man was an apostate Jew, who had succumbed to the attractions of heathenism, using his power and influence as *an attendant of the proconsul.* Perhaps he
functioned as a court astrologer or magician.[32] It is interesting to compare Peter's conflict with the Samaritan *magos* (8:9-13, 18-24) and Paul's later encounter with divination in Philippi (16:16-21) and magic and sorcery in
Ephesus (19:13-20). The early Christians saw their main rivals as being 'other
Near Eastern religions, especially other forms of Judaism; magic in various
forms, especially in some combination with Jewish ideas; and traditional
Greek deities and philosophies'.[33] Luke's narratives highlight the distance
between Christianity and the magic of popular Greco-Roman religion. In Cyprus, the sorcerer, who is now identified as *Elymas,*[34] actively opposed Barna-

---

Witherington is more confident that 'the inscriptional evidence clearly places the Sergii
Pauli on the island of Cyprus and the Latin inscription about Lucius of that family may
point us to the man in question'. The Latin inscription is datable to the 40s, during the reign
of Claudius, which is an appropriate time in the chronology of Acts for the visit of Paul to
Cyprus. Witherington, 403-4, supports the view that Sergius Paulus directed Paul and Barnabas to go next to Pisidian Antioch, where his family had land, power, and influence.

30. Witherington 1998, 395. Johnson 1992, 222, also notes that the title used here
(*anthypatos*) properly designates the administrator of a senatorial province. *Hēgēmōn* is the
title used for military prefects who administered imperial provinces (cf. Lk. 2:2; 3:1; Acts
23:24, 26; 24:27).

31. Cf. T. Klutz, *The Exorcism Stories in Luke-Acts: A Sociostylistic Reading,* SNTSMS 129
(Cambridge/New York: Cambridge University, 2004), 215-17. Witherington 1998, 396, notes
that 'A *magys* was a diviner who through various rituals claimed to be able to evoke the
dead, including the shades or spirits of one's ancestors; and coupled with the word
"prophet" our text suggests that he claimed to be able to tell the future, perhaps through
necromancy, perhaps through astrology or magical spells and rituals involving both'.

32. Cf. S. Garrett, *The Demise of the Devil: Magic and the Demonic in Luke's Writings* (Minneapolis: Fortress, 1989), 81; THEOLOGY OF ACTS: IX. MAGIC AND THE DEMONIC (pp.
87-92).

33. Witherington 1998, 394. Cf. 14:8-18; 17:16-33; 19:23-41.

34. *Elymas* is not a known Greek word or title. It is not a literal translation of the Se-

bas and Saul as they shared the gospel with Sergius Paulus. He *tried to turn the proconsul from the faith,* presumably realising the implications for his own position if the proconsul became a Christian.[35] In the next paragraph, Saul is presented as the Lord's true prophet, who supernaturally overcomes the influence of this opponent of God's truth.[36]

9-11 Until this point in the narrative, Luke has used the Hebrew name *Saul,* to stress his Jewish roots and perhaps also because it was in the sources he used for writing the preceding chapters. Now, however, the name *Paul* is introduced and identification with the previously mentioned Saul is made clear. It is nothing more than a coincidence that *Paulus* was also the name of the proconsul. The Greek (*ho kai Paulos,* 'who is also [called] Paul') signifies a name by which he had been known for some time. As a Roman citizen, Paul would have had three names, the third of which would have been the Latin *Paulus.* It is possible that *Saul* was a fourth name, given at birth and used in Jewish environments.[37] Luke consistently uses the more familiar name *Paul* now that the setting for the rest of the narrative is predominantly the Gentile world (the transliterated Hebrew *Saoul* is found again in the accounts of his conversion in 22:7; 26:14). The description of Paul as *filled with the Holy Spirit* indicates a special enabling of the Spirit for the ministry he is about to exercise (cf. 2:4; 4:8). That ministry is clearly prophetic (cf. Peter in 5:1-11; 8:20-24), with Paul exposing the character of Elymas as a satanically inspired deceiver and opponent of God's truth (*'You are a child of the devil and an enemy of everything that is right! You are full of all kinds of deceit and trickery. Will you never stop perverting the right ways of the Lord?'*).[38] In prophetic mode, he also pronounces a curse on him (*'Now the hand of the Lord is against you. You are going to be blind for a time, not even able to see the light of the sun'*). The expression *the hand of the Lord* represents God's power at work in the world (e.g., Jgs. 2:15; 1 Sa. 12:15; Acts 4:28, 30; 11:21). Paul's limitation of this judgment *for a time* suggests that the period of blindness is meant to give the sorcerer a chance to repent (cf. 8:20-

mitic name *Bar-Jesus* (any more than the Latin *Paul* is a translation of the Semitic *Saul*). So Luke's expression *this is what his name means* (lit. 'so his name is translated') will mean 'this is what his name was taken to mean'. Bruce 1990, 297, Barrett 1994, 615-16, and Witherington 1998, 401, consider various explanations for the link between the two names. Metzger, *Textual Commentary,* 355-56, notes an alternative spelling of the name in some MSS and the possible implications.

35. Some MSS in the Western tradition add the words 'because he (the proconsul) was listening with the greatest pleasure to them'. Cf. Metzger, *Textual Commentary,* 356.

36. Cf. Spencer 1997, 139.

37. Cf. Marshall 1980, 220; Bruce 1990, 298.

38. *Son of the devil* is probably used as a counter to his name *Bar-Jesus* ('son of Jesus'). Paul is filled with the Holy Spirit, but Elymas is 'full of (*plērēs*) all kinds of deceit and trickery'. He is 'an enemy of all righteousness', who continually makes crooked the straight paths that the Lord reveals for his people. This has been illustrated in his opposition to the gospel. Cf. Je. 5:27; Pr. 10:9. Garrett, *Demise,* 81-85, examines Paul's accusations and subsequent curse in some detail, setting these within a wider biblical context.

24), though we have no way of knowing whether he did. The authenticity of Paul's authority to speak in this way on God's behalf is demonstrated by what follows: *Immediately mist and darkness came over him, and he groped about, seeking someone to lead him by the hand.*[39] To the modern reader, Paul's curse may look as magic-like as anything Elymas might have done. However, although Luke shared with ancient magicians the view that words backed up with sufficient authority could achieve terrible things, his aim was to show how Paul, filled with the Holy Spirit, actually conquered magical-satanic powers. Biblical words and actions were needed to counteract the words and actions of an influential false prophet. Moreover, 'in the Bar Jesus incident one can discern a pattern of conflict between good and evil, between the purposes of God and the purposes of Satan, and between the repentant and the uncircumcised in heart which characterizes much of Christian existence as portrayed in Luke-Acts'.[40]

12 The conclusion to the narrative is a simple but convincing description of the governor's conversion.[41] Despite the opposition of Elymas to the gospel and its messengers, *when the proconsul saw what had happened, he believed, for he was amazed at the teaching about the Lord.* What the proconsul *saw* was an amazing supernatural event, which enabled him to believe. But what truly *amazed* him was *the teaching about the Lord*, and it was clearly this teaching that he believed.[42] The exposure and blinding of Elymas was used by God to remove an obstacle to belief (the influence and power of the sorcerer) and to authenticate Paul and his message. Luke shows with this narrative that Paul could actually do the work to which he had been called by God 'because he possessed authority over all the power of the Enemy (cf. Luke 10:19)'.[43] However, it was not this display of the supernatural that converted the proconsul. He became a believer in the gospel as the Lord en-

39. Paradoxically, this parallels the experience of Paul, who opposed the work of the gospel until he was converted and then was struck blind for a time, needing to be led by the hand (9:1-9). Tannehill 1990, 162, notes also the parallel between Lk. 4:32 (the initial impact of Jesus' teaching) and Acts 13:12 (the initial impact of Paul's teaching). Paul used to be like Elymas, but now he is like his master! Cf. Garrett, *Demise*, 84-85.

40. Garrett, *Demise*, 87. Cf. Spencer 1997, 139, on the difference between Paul's response to Elymas and the magician's own technique.

41. Garrett, *Demise*, 85, overstates her case when she says that the governor's conversion is of secondary importance in the narrative. Witherington 1998, 402-3, expresses unnecessary caution about Luke's claim that the proconsul believed. There is no ground in the text for saying that his belief was as questionable as that of Simon in 8:13. Furthermore, it is unreasonable to expect Luke to give every detail of a conversion experience, such as the coming of the Spirit or baptism, in every context (cf. 14:1; 17:34; 19:18). Barrett 1994, 619, argues that, if Sergius Paulus was not truly converted because he was not baptized, this would mean that 'there were no conversions on this missionary journey: there is no reference to baptism'.

42. MSS in the Western tradition seek to clarify the narrative by adding extra words, giving the reading, 'The proconsul, when he saw what had occurred, *marvelled and* believed *in God*, being astonished at the teaching of the Lord'. Cf. Metzger, *Textual Commentary*, 357.

43. Garrett, *Demise*, 84.

abled him to acknowledge the truth of the message he had received. Contemporary Christians may wish for such demonstrations of divine power to remove obstacles to faith and enable conversions today. But it should be remembered that even in Acts they are rare and are usually related to the movement of the gospel into some new area, the overcoming of some form of spiritual opposition, or the winning of some particularly significant figure for Christ. Luke portrays a prophetic succession from Jesus to the twelve apostles and then to other specially selected individuals such as Stephen, Philip, and Paul. He does not suggest that signs and wonders were done by all the earliest preachers of the gospel. He does not even suggest that signs and wonders were a necessary aspect of the progress of the word in every context. The overall message of Acts is that the work of God is advanced in the world by Spirit-filled messengers who proclaim the gospel faithfully and boldly. A sustained and concentrated ministry of prayer is a key to effective evangelism and will be essential if the influence of false prophets, astrology, and the occult are to be overcome. From time to time, God in his sovereign grace may grant special, supernatural answers to such prayer, in the form of accompanying signs.[44]

C. The Word in Pisidian Antioch (13:13-52)

The mission to Antioch in Pisidia provides Luke with the opportunity to record a sample of Paul's synagogue preaching and a more detailed account of the opposition experienced when he had some success preaching to Gentiles. So, in many ways, Acts 13 is programmatic for the second half of the book, just as Acts 2 is programmatic for the first half. Tannehill notes that, 'like Jesus (Luke 4:18-21) and Peter (Acts 2:14-40), Paul makes a major statement near the beginning of his new mission. His speech resembles that of Jesus in setting (a synagogue service with reading of Scripture) and resembles Peter's in points of content'.[45] This sermon functions as a model of Paul's synagogue preaching, paralleling the preaching of Peter in some respects, but with its own distinctive emphases. As well as being evangelistic, it demonstrates how Christians engaged in a defence of their gospel from the Jewish Scriptures.

13 *From Paphos, Paul and his companions sailed to Perga in Pamphylia,* which is on the south coast of present-day Turkey. Perga was actually a river port, a short distance up the river Cestrus.[46] With this geographical note, Luke indicates that Paul was now the leader of the group *(Paul and his*

44. Cf. THEOLOGY OF ACTS: VIII. MIRACLES (pp. 83-87).
45. Tannehill 1990, 160. He further observes that 'the three speeches either contain or lead to a Scripture quotation that interprets the mission that is beginning (Luke 4:18-19; Acts 2:17-21; 13:47). They lead immediately (Luke 4:24-30) or in due course (Acts 4:1-3; 13:45-52) to an outbreak of opposition.'
46. Bruce 1990, 300, provides details of Perga and Pamphylia.

companions). It would appear that Paul emerged as leader after the demon-stration of his prophetic authority in Cyprus. Surprisingly, there is no indi-cation of any ministry in this important town at this time (though cf. 14:25). Without further comment, Luke adds that this was *where John left them to re-turn to Jerusalem.* The seriousness of this departure is not signalled until 15:37-39, where Paul refuses to take John with Barnabas and himself on a return visit to the towns previously evangelised. The reason given there is that John had 'deserted them in Pamphylia and had not continued with them in the work'. The participle *apochōrēsas* (13:13) can have the milder sense of *left* or the more negative sense of 'betrayed' or 'abandoned' (cf. 3 Macc. 2:33). The latter sense is clearly brought out in 15:38 with the use of another participle *(ton apostanta),* describing John as one who deliberately deserted them. Luke waits for the appropriate point in the narrative to make this clear, though he does not explain why John left the work so sud-denly.[47]

1. Ministry in the Synagogue (13:14-43)

The message that follows is the only extensive example we have of Paul's synagogue preaching, though there are later, brief summaries which match this model in certain respects.[48] Even this message appears to have been much abbreviated, as the exposition will suggest. Other speeches in Acts show how he addressed a group of cultured Gentiles (17:22-31) and a group of Christian leaders (20:18-35). With unjustified scepticism, some commentators doubt that what we read here is a genuine account of what Paul said. So, for example, Johnson says, 'We do not expect by this time a *précis* of Pauline theology, but recognize that in his speeches Luke stretches over the discourses of several speakers a single midrashic argument con-cerning the messianic movement and its crucified and raised founder'.[49] Although we must allow for Luke's own influence in the editorial process, there are sufficient differences between the sermons with respect to style and content to warrant the conclusion that they substantially reflect the standpoint of the preachers to whom they are attributed. These are not arti-ficial constructions, designed to address imagined situations in the prog-ress of the gospel from one context to another. Where there are common ap-proaches to Scripture, or to the events of Jesus' life, death, and resurrection,

47. Stott 1990, 221, and Barrett 1994, 627, note a number of suggestions that have been made, but there is no evidence to support any of these speculations.

48. Cf. Tannehill 1990, 164, for some examples. Barrett 1994, 624, following J. W. Bowker, 'Speeches in Acts: A Study in Proem and Yelammedenu Form', *NTS* 14 (1967), 96-111, observes that there is a degree of correspondence between Paul's sermon and a recognized form of synagogue homily, particularly with reference to the way scriptural texts are used.

49. Johnson 1992, 237. Barrett 1994, 622-24, is similarly sceptical. Contrast Withering-ton 1998, 406-8.

these cannot simply be attributed to Luke's own theology or interests. Just as Jesus' announcement in the synagogue at Nazareth (Lk. 4:16-27) and Peter's Pentecost speech (Acts 2:14-39) are vital for understanding the missions of Jesus and Peter, so this speech and the following events are essential for understanding Paul's ministry. Moreover, there are aspects of this speech which have certain parallels in the Pauline letters.

The argument begins with shared premises about God's election of Israel to be his people and David to be their king (vv. 17-23).[50] The new and challenging aspect of the message is the claim that Jesus is the fulfiller of God's promises to David and therefore the key to Israel's future (vv. 24-37). Indeed, 'the present episode underscores the conviction that Jesus' death and resurrection mark the "necessary" (13:46) fulfillment of Israel's *entire* scriptural canon — "the law and the prophets" (13:15, 27, 39-40) together with the psalms (13:33, 35)'.[51] The final section is an appeal not to miss out on the salvation being offered through Jesus (vv. 38-41).

14-15 *From Perga they went on to Pisidian Antioch,* which necessitated crossing the Taurus mountains. There were many towns in the ancient world called Antioch, often founded by members of the family of Antiochus. This one was strictly in Phrygia, near the Pisidian border, which was a region in the Roman province of Galatia (cf. 16:6). Antioch had been made a Roman colony by Caesar Augustus in 25 BC and was 'the governing and military centre of the southern half of the vast province of Galatia'.[52] Politically, it belonged to Galatia, but ethnically and culturally it was Phrygian. Josephus records that there was a substantial Jewish population in the city (*Ant.* 12.147-53), which helps to explain why Paul and Barnabas went there immediately after landing at Perga, a journey of about a hundred miles (160 km.). However, if the Sergius Paulus who was proconsul in Cyprus had family connections in Pisidian Antioch, which some scholars propose, then it is possible that he influenced Paul and Barnabas to go there first.[53] *On the Sabbath they entered the synagogue and sat down,* taking their place with others who had met to hear the Scriptures read, to reflect on their meaning, and to pray together.[54] *After the reading from the Law and the*

---

50. Tannehill 1990, 166, notes that this section intends to affirm 'the community relationship that connects speaker and audience' (see the reference to 'our ancestors', v. 17) and 'to make present some shared presuppositions that will be important for the following argument'. Cf. Longenecker 1981, 425, proposes a four-point confessional summary in 13:17-22.

51. Spencer 1997, 143. Cf. Lk. 24:44-45. Bruce 1990, 303, mentions various possible OT models or bases for Paul's sermon as we have it.

52. W. M. Ramsay, *The Church in the Roman Empire before AD 170* (London: Hodder & Stoughton, 1893), 25. Cf. Bruce 1990, 300-301. Ramsay, *Church*, 62-64, and *St Paul the Traveller and the Roman Citizen* (London: Hodder & Stoughton, 1895), 92-7, argued that Paul travelled straight to Antioch because he was suffering from a debilitating illness. Cf. G. W. Hansen, 'Galatia', in Gill and Gempf, *Graeco-Roman Setting*, 377-95.

53. Cf. Witherington 1998, 403-4, and my note 29 above.

54. A typical Sabbath synagogue service would have included a recital of the *Shema'*

Prophets, the leaders of the synagogue sent word to them, saying, 'Brothers, if you have a word of exhortation for the people, please speak'. It was a responsibility of the *leaders of the synagogue* to arrange for suitable people to read the lessons, to pray, and, where appropriate, to preach.[55] Paul and Barnabas were addressed as fellow Jews *(brothers)*, but also as those qualified to give *a word of exhortation* to the congregation *(logos parakleseos;* cf. 2:40; 1 Tim. 4:13; Heb. 13:22).[56] Presumably, their reputation as preachers and teachers had in some way gone ahead of them.

16 Synagogue preachers normally sat (cf. Lk. 4:20), though Philo of Alexandria records that in the synagogues of his acquaintance 'one of special experience rises and sets forth' *(On the Special Laws* 2.62). Paul's *standing up* may simply have been necessary so that he could be seen and heard in a large group.[57] The message is addressed to Jews *('people of Israel')* and those who have attached themselves to the synagogue *('Gentiles who worship God', hoi phoboumenoi ton theon* ['those who fear God']). There is continuing debate about whether there was a group technically known as 'God-fearers' in first-century synagogues, but there is widespread agreement about the presence of Gentiles who were not yet proselytes.[58] Paul's double address is repeated in a modified way at a key point in the sermon (v. 26).

(Dt. 6:4-9; 11:13-21; Nu. 15:37-41), the praying of the Benedictions with responses, readings from the Law (so ordered that the whole of it was read in a three-yearly cycle) and the Prophets (following no continuous pattern), translation of the readings into Aramaic, an exposition related to the lessons if someone competent was present, and the priestly blessing (Nu. 6:24-26). Cf. B. Chilton and E. Yamauchi, 'Synagogues', *DNTB* 1145-53.

55. Since there was normally only one such officer in each synagogue, the plural number here may suggest that the congregation in Pisidian Antioch was a particularly large one. *ND* 4:213-20, reviews the epigraphical evidence for the use of *archisynagōgos* in the imperial period, showing that the title was variously used and the role and responsibilities varied from place to place.

56. Witherington 1998, 406-8, notes that this is 'a piece of deliberative, not epideictic, rhetoric meant to urge a change not just in belief but also in behavior, as vv. 40-42 makes clear'. Three direct addresses to the congregation in vv. 16, 26, and 38, signal new divisions in the speech, which correspond to some extent with the divisions recognised from formal rhetorical analysis. Paul appears to be 'an orator of some skill and flexibility, something his letters also suggest'.

57. Longenecker 1981, 424, suggests that the difference of posture may have been because Paul's word of exhortation did not strictly arise from the Scripture readings for that day. However, Bowker, 'Speeches', 96-111, argues that Paul is actually following readings for that Sabbath from Dt. 4:25-46 and 2 Sa. 7:6-16, using 1 Sa. 13:14 as a bridge text.

58. See my discussion of God-fearers in connection with 10:2; Barrett 1994, 629-31; S. McKnight, 'Proselytes and Godfearers', *DNTB* 846-47. In v. 43 Paul specifically identifies 'the devout converts' *(tōn sebomenōn prosēlytōn).* Are these proselytes included in Paul's earlier designations of 'those who fear God' (vv. 16, 26), or are they co-terminus with these designations? Barrett argues that it is natural to think that in v. 26 Paul is addressing Jews and proselytes. My own judgment is that proselytes are mentioned with Jews in v. 43 because Luke is stressing that the most orthodox members of the congregation were persuaded by Paul's argument at this stage. It is possible that proselytes were encompassed by the designation 'those who fear God', but more likely that they were included in the first designation in vv. 16 and 26 because of their full incorporation into the people of Israel in the appropriate manner.

He also stresses his own position in the family of God by calling his audience 'brothers' (vv. 26, 38; TNIV's *'brothers and sisters'* rightly captures the inclusive intention of the original *adelphoi*).

a. The Election of Israel and the Election of David (13:17-23)

17-20 The narrative approach in the first part of this sermon is designed to affirm the truth and significance of the assertion with which it begins: *'The God of the people of Israel chose our ancestors'*. The relation between God and his people 'results from an act of election on God's part. This is put into effect in an act of salvation.'[59] Paul links his brief allusion to the choice of the patriarchs and his promises to them (Genesis 12–50) with a summary of the exodus events, by which he began to fulfill his purpose for them: *'he made the people prosper during their stay in Egypt; with mighty power he led them out of that country'* (Exodus 1–15).[60] The wilderness period, which is covered in the rest of Exodus and in Numbers, is then briefly summarized (*'for about forty years he endured their conduct in the wilderness'*), with language indicating his patience in the face of their unfaithfulness (so most EVV).[61] Paul signals a further fulfillment of God's promises to the patriarchs when he encapsulates the message of the book of Joshua with the words, *'and he overthrew seven nations in Canaan, giving their land to his people as their inheritance'*.[62] TNIV has made the next clause a separate sentence (*'All this took about 450 years'*), even though it appears as a conclusion to verse 19 in the best manuscripts of the Greek text (NRSV 'for about four hundred and fifty years'). The TNIV rendering is helpful because it shows that the reference is to the whole time spent in Egypt, in the wilderness, and in the initial period of the conquest of Canaan (so also NASB). The reference is not simply to the time that passed between the division of the

59. Barrett 1994, 631. The election of Israel is mentioned in Dt. 4:37; 7:7; 10:15. Johnson 1992, 230-31, notes that this part of the sermon treats the early history of Israel much more briefly than Stephen's speech, pointing to the different purposes of the preachers in their handling of this material.

60. *hypsōsen* in v. 17 (TNIV *he made [the people] prosper*) could also be translated, 'he made [the people] great' (NRSV). Either way, this appears to allude to the promise in Gn. 12:2, which is seen to be fulfilled by the multiplication of the Israelites and God's care for them (Ex. 1:7, 9). God's deliverance with mighty power is mentioned in Ex. 6:1, 6.

61. The reading 'he put up with (them)' *(etropophorēsan)* is slightly better attested than the alternative 'he cared for (them)' *(etrophophorēsan)*. Dt. 1:31 LXX presents the same two variants. Metzger, *Textual Commentary,* 357, argues for the former, which differs from the prevailing LXX text, 'on the ground that scribes would have been more likely to accommodate the two than to make them diverge'. However, Marshall 1980, 223, Johnson 1992, 231, Barrett 1994, 632, and Witherington 1998, 408-10 all argue that the latter reading suits the context of Paul's sermon better.

62. Cf. Dt. 7:1-2. TNIV's *to his people* is a rendering of *autois* ('to them'), which is found in some MSS of v. 19, but is not the best-attested reading. Metzger, *Textual Commentary,* 358, views this either as an assimilation to Dt. 3:28 or as an expansion made in the interests of clarification ('he gave *them* their land as an inheritance').

land by Joshua and the institution of the judges.[63] It was *'after this'*, the long
period of care for Israel in captivity and then redeemed and established in
the land, that *'God gave them judges until the time of Samuel the prophet'*.

21-23 Samuel is presumably mentioned at the end of v. 20 because
he was the one *'the people asked for a king'* (*ētēsanto* [middle voice], 'asked for
themselves'; cf. 1 Sa. 8:6). However, Paul passes over the fact that Samuel
was unwilling to meet this request and recalls that God overruled and *'gave
them Saul son of Kish, of the tribe of Benjamin, who ruled forty years'*.[64] With no
further explanation, Paul moves directly to the fact that God removed Saul
from office, and *'made David their king'*. This concludes his brief overview of
Israel's history and allows him to move straight to Jesus and the gospel.
Paul concludes this first section of the sermon with a conflation of words
from 1 Samuel 13:14 ('the LORD has sought out a man after his own heart
and appointed him ruler of his people') and Psalm 89:20 (LXX 88:21, 'I have
found David my servant'). God's testimony about David in these combined
scriptures is thus: *'"I have found David son of Jesse, a man after my own heart;
he will do everything I want him to do"'*.[65] Once David is mentioned, the rest
of the message focuses on him and the promises made to him. However,
Paul presents an immediate challenge to his audience with the words, *'from
this man's descendants God has brought to Israel the Saviour Jesus, as he promised'* (*kat' epangelian*, 'according to promise'; cf. 2 Sa. 7:12-16; Ps. 89:29; Is.
11:1-16; 4QFlor).[66] Paul speaks of the promised Son of David as having already come, and identifies him with Jesus. God's faithfulness *to Israel* is
mentioned again in v. 32, as Paul begins to explain how the promise has
been fulfilled through the resurrection of Jesus and cites various Scriptures
to prove his case (cf. 5:31). 'Thus the fulfillment of the promise to Israel of
an heir to David's throne is the leading idea of the speech.'[67] The sense in
which Jesus is *Saviour* will now be unfolded.

63. KJV and NKJV follow the Received Text, which transposes the temporal clause to
the following sentence and makes it appear that the period of the judges was about 450
years. However, the Alexandrian text is to be preferred because of its age and because the
chronology suggested fits better with other biblical indications of the time involved. Cf.
Bruce 1990, 304-5; Metzger, *Textual Commentary*, 358-59.

64. 1 Sa. 13:1 (Heb.) only has Saul reigning for two years. However, this text appears
to be corrupt. Josephus, *Ant.* 6.378, records a Jewish tradition that Paul may be echoing,
which claims that Saul reigned for eighteen years during Samuel's life and twenty-two
years after his death (though cf. twenty years in *Ant.* 10.143).

65. The words *he will do everything I want him to do* reflect the Jewish Targum on the
words 'after his own heart' in 1 Sa. 13:14. Cf. Barrett 1994, 636. These words offer an implied
contrast with Saul, whose disobedience is not mentioned by Paul, but which would have
been well known to his synagogue audience. It is less likely that the words are taken from
the prophecy about Cyrus in Is. 44:28, as proposed by Witherington 1998, 410, and others.

66. The best MSS of v. 23 read *ēgagen* (brought), though some MSS have *ēgeire* ('raised
up'), which seems to have been influenced by the presence of the same verb in v. 22. Instead of
sōtēra Iēsoun (*a saviour Jesus*), some MSS (including Papyrus 74, H, and L) have *sōtērian* ('salvation'). Metzger, *Textual Commentary*, 359, explains the latter as 'a palaeographical oversight'.

67. Tannehill, 1990, 167.

b. Jesus the Fulfiller of the Promise to David (13:24-37)

24-25 The key proposition about Jesus being the promised Davidic saviour (v. 23) is defended with a narrative about his ministry, death, and resurrection (vv. 24-31), and a series of scriptural citations (vv. 32-37). Narrative and citations are used to convey theology and to challenge the congregation to respond with faith. The outline of the *kerygma* here is comparable to the one ascribed to Peter in 10:36-43.[68] Just as the Gospel writers do, Paul begins his account with reference to the coming of John the Baptist (cf. also Acts 1:5; 10:37). '*Before the coming of Jesus (pro prosōpou tēs eisodou,* 'before the face of his entrance' [cf. Mal. 3:1; Lk. 1:76]), *John preached repentance and baptism to all the people of Israel.*' John's ministry is first described in terms of the need for *all the people of Israel* to repent and be baptized, thus becoming ready to meet their Messiah (cf. Lk. 3:1-20, citing Is. 40:3-5). John made it clear that Israel was estranged from God, which implicitly challenged Paul's audience to see their need for the forgiveness that would be offered to them through Christ (vv. 38-39). Paul's second recollection of John's ministry relates to the period when he '*was completing his work*' (*eplērou Iōannēs ton dromon* 'as John was finishing his race'; cf. 20:24; 2 Tim. 4:7). The text here reflects the substance of Luke 3:15-16 (cf. also Jn. 1:19-23). John's rhetorical question ('*Who do you suppose I am?*') and his answer ('*I am not the one you are looking for*') contradicted the belief of many that he might have been the Messiah.[69] With this denial, John pointed to the absolute supremacy of the one coming after him: '"*But there is someone coming after me, whose sandals I am not worthy to untie*"'. John did not consider himself worthy to perform a slave's task and untie the shoes of such a master!

26-27 A renewed, more intense address to the congregation (cf. v. 16b) signifies the importance of what is about to be proclaimed. His fellow Jews are '*brothers and sisters from the children of Abraham*' (TNIV rightly representing the inclusive sense of 'brothers' in the original), and the rest of those present are '*God-fearing Gentiles*'.[70] Paul stresses that, '*it is to us that this message of salvation has been sent*'.[71] 'Application to the audience and ap-

---

68. Cf. THE THEOLOGY OF ACTS: V. THE GOSPEL (pp. 70-75).

69. Cf. Metzger, *Textual Commentary,* 360; Barrett 1994, 638, on the textual variants in the form of the question here. Both textual traditions have John making the same disavowal. Bruce 1990, 307, highlights affinities with the wording of the Synoptics and the Fourth Gospel.

70. Against Barrett 1994, 639, it is unnecessary to take the expression *hoi en hymin phoboumenoi ton theon* to mean 'proselytes' rather than 'uncircumcised God-fearers'. Barrett lets his reading of v. 43 determine the meaning of the expressions in vv. 16 and 26 and argues that the expression *en hymin* ('among you') strengthens his case. The word *kai* ('and') is missing from v. 26 in two key MSS, leading Barrett also to propose that the original could have been '. . . children of Abraham — those at least among the audience who truly fear God'. See my comments in note 58.

71. There is a variant reading 'to you' (*hymin*), which is not as well attested as 'to us' (*hēmin*), though both readings have early support in papyrus MSS. Metzger, *Textual Commentary,* 360, concludes that 'the context as well as a combination of Alexandrian and Western witnesses strongly support the first person pronoun'.

peal for their response is not reserved for the end of the speech but is inter-
spersed with the narration and scriptural argument.'[72] Paul and Barnabas
include themselves in the group to whom this message has been sent. *This
message of salvation* refers back to v. 23, where Jesus is described as the God-
appointed *'Saviour'* for Israel. Unfortunately, TNIV does not translate the
Greek connective *gar* ('for', v. 27), which indicates that what follows is the
beginning of the explanation of that *salvation*. As he tells the story of what
happened in Jerusalem, Paul prepares for the warning against unbelief that
will climax his sermon (vv. 40-41). The congregation in Pisidian Antioch
should beware of being like *'the people of Jerusalem and their rulers'*, who *'did
not recognise Jesus'* and condemned him to die. Their unbelief was culpable
because, unwittingly, *'they fulfilled the words of the prophets that are read every
Sabbath'* (cf. 4:25-28). This note of prophetic fulfillment is struck three times
in this sermon (vv. 27, 29, 32-33).[73] The people of Jerusalem should have
known from the Scriptures that the Messiah would be betrayed, and they
should have recoiled from involvement in such wickedness. As in 2:23;
3:17-18; 4:27-28, the paradox is that, 'acting in ignorance and intending to
get rid of Jesus, the people of Jerusalem actually played a destined role contributing to the exaltation of Jesus as Messiah'.[74]

28-31   Although the people of Jerusalem and their rulers *'found no
proper ground for a death sentence, they asked Pilate to have him executed'*.[75]
Three times Luke records that Pilate was also unable to find grounds for
the death penalty (Lk. 23:4, 14, 22). With such references to the innocence of
Jesus, we are challenged to ask why God allowed this to happen. Paul gives
two hints that begin to answer the question, offering the basis for a theology of atonement (cf. Rom. 3:25; 2 Cor. 5:21; Gal. 3:13-14; and Col. 2:13-15
for Paul's more articulated view). First, he indicates that they *'carried out all
that was written about him'*, implying that there is a scriptural explanation
for this travesty of justice (cf. v. 27, where the condemnation of Jesus fulfills
Scripture). Isaiah 53 particularly comes to mind, because of the Servant's
unjust suffering and death, followed by his burial and then divine vindication (cf. 3:13 note). Secondly, there is literally reference to the cross as a tree
(*xylon*, TNIV *'the cross'*). As in 5:30 and 10:39, this word is apparently used

72. Tannehill, 1990, 167. He notes a development in the sermon from the reference to
Jesus as the saviour for Israel (v. 23), to the announcement of 'this message of salvation'
(v. 26), to the proclamation of the fulfillment of the promise (vv. 32-33), ending with the emphasis on the resulting opportunity and danger for the audience (vv. 38-41).

73. Johnson 1992, 238, observes how the Jews at Antioch repeat the pattern: they fail
to recognise their Messiah in the preaching of Paul and ironically fulfill the prophecies of rejection (vv. 44-52).

74. Tannehill, 1990, 169. Several forms of the Western text of vv. 27-29 supply various
additions to provide a smoother text and a more complete account of Jesus' trial and death.
Cf. Metzger, *Textual Commentary*, 360-61; Barrett 1994, 642-43.

75. TNIV rightly translates the participle *heurontes* in a concessive sense, setting the
call for execution against the discovery of 'no cause of death' (*mēdemian aitian thanatou*). Cf.
Bruce 1990, 308.

to stress both the shameful nature of Jesus' death and its penal character (cf. Dt. 21:22-23; Gal. 3:13-14; 1 Pet. 2:24). Linked with the offer of the forgiveness of sins through Jesus (vv. 38-39), this suggests that his death was the vicarious atonement which made possible the inauguration of the New Covenant (cf. Je. 31:31-34; Lk. 22:20; Acts 20:28; Heb. 10:15-18).[76] With Pilate's permission, it was Joseph of Arimathea who actually *'laid him in a tomb'* (Lk. 23:50-54), but the story is simplified here by attributing the burial to those who carried out all that was written about him (cf. Is. 53:9). After the finality of burial came the supernatural vindication of Jesus by way of physical resurrection *('God raised him from the dead')* and a series of appearances *('for many days he was seen by those who had travelled with him from Galilee to Jerusalem'*; cf. 1:1-8). The action of God is set against the action of the people of Jerusalem and their rulers. The particular importance of the apostolic group as *witnesses* to the people of Israel (*pros ton laon*, 'to the people') is then highlighted (cf. 1:21-22; 10:39-42). *'Those who had travelled with him from Galilee to Jerusalem'* knew Jesus and his teaching in a way which enabled them to understand the significance of what they experienced and to interpret this appropriately. Paul was not one of the Twelve and confirms their special status and calling. Yet the very next verse calls attention to his own role in the process of testifying to the risen Christ.[77]

32-33 The emphatic pronoun at the beginning of v. 32 (*kai hēmeis,* 'and *we* tell you the good news') links what Paul was doing in Pisidian Antioch with the witness of the Twelve mentioned in v. 31. The content of that good news is essentially the same as Peter's proclamation in 2:24-36, but Paul and Barnabas function as witnesses to those in the Diaspora, both Jews and devout Gentiles. At one level it can be described as *'what God promised our ancestors'*, which *'he has fulfilled for us, their children'*.[78] The gospel for Israel is fundamentally about the fulfillment of God's promises (cf. Mk. 1:14-15; Lk. 4:16-21). At another level it is about historical events by which God has achieved this fulfillment, specifically here *'by raising up Jesus'*. Paul then cites one of the promises he has in mind. *'As it is written in the second Psalm:*[79] *"You are my son; today I have become your father"'* (*egō*

76. Cf. THE THEOLOGY OF ACTS: VI. THE ATONING WORK OF JESUS (pp. 75-79). The contrast with the era of the law of Moses is particularly strong in 13:38-39.

77. Cf. 22:14-15; 26:16; THE THEOLOGY OF ACTS: VII. WITNESS AND MISSION (pp. 79-83). Paul's encounter with Christ on the Damascus road qualified him to be a witness to the risen Lord and an apostle to the Gentiles (cf. 1 Cor. 9:1-2; 15:8; Gal. 1:1, 15-16), even though he did not have the privilege of sharing in his earthly ministry and experiencing the resurrection events in Jerusalem.

78. The best-attested reading is *hēmōn* ('for *our* [children]'). Since this is also the harder reading, it has a strong claim to be regarded as original, even though *autōn hēmin* (*'for us their* [children]') makes more sense in the context. Cf. Metzger, *Textual Commentary*, 362; Barrett 1994, 645, for alternative views.

79. Although the reading *in the second Psalm* is well attested, the Western text has 'in the first psalm' and the earliest papyrus has 'in the psalms'. This confusion may be related to some patristic and rabbinic evidence that 'in the early Christian period what is now reck-

sēmeron gegennēka se, 'today I have begotten you'). This 'begetting' and the enthronement the psalm implies have been fulfilled in Jesus' resurrection from the dead (cf. 2:33-36, where resurrection and exaltation to the right hand of God are viewed as linked events).[80] *Son* in the context of Psalm 2 is to be understood as a royal and messianic title: when the Davidic king is installed on Zion, God's holy mountain (v. 6), the Lord in heaven recognises him as his own son (v. 7; the 'begetting' is metaphorical), promising to put down his enemies and make the nations his inheritance (vv. 8-9). Applied to Jesus and his resurrection, this psalm suggests that his resurrection-ascension brings him to the full experience of his messianic destiny in a heavenly enthronement and rule (cf. Rom. 1:3-4; Heb. 1:3-5).[81] In this context, Paul says nothing about the preexistence of the Son of God (cf. Rom. 8:3; Gal. 4:4-5; Col. 1:15-20), though such teaching needs to be taken into account when seeking to give a full account of what it means to call Jesus the Son of God (cf. Lk. 1:31-33, 35; Jn. 1:1-18; Acts 9:20). In other words, it would be wrong to take this text in isolation and suggest that the exalted Jesus was merely adopted as Son at this point in time.[82]

34-37   The messianic significance of Jesus' resurrection is further explained by means of two scriptural quotations. The paragraph begins and ends with a reference to *'decay'* (vv. 34, 35, *diaphthoran*), picking up a key word from the citation of Psalm 16:10 (LXX 15:10), which lies at the centre of the argument here. A more extensive quotation and application of this psalm is found in Peter's address in 2:25-31. God raised Jesus from the dead so that he might *'never be subject to decay'*. This is another way of explaining the fulfillment of Psalm 2:7. To reign forever at the Father's side, the Son had to be delivered from death and decay (cf. Lk. 1:32-33). Before citing portion of Psalm 16:10 and saying something more about it, Paul quotes from Isaiah 55:3 *(' "I will give you the holy and sure blessings promised to David" ')*. The plural *you (hymin)* makes it clear that the promise of God in this context is for Israel and so for Paul's listeners. But the key text is a promise for the Messiah himself *(' "you will not let your holy one see decay" ')*. *Holy one (hosios)* is understood as a Christological title (cf. 2:27-31; *hagios* in 3:14).[83] The messianic significance of this promise is argued by noting that *'when David had served*

---

oned as the second Psalm was regarded as a continuation of the first Psalm' (Metzger, *Textual Commentary,* 363). Cf. Barrett 1994, 646.

80. Bruce 1990, 310, relates this 'begetting' to the baptism of Jesus, when he was anointed 'with the Holy Spirit and power' (10:38). But the parallels with Psalm 110 are strong, and the enthronement in this psalm is applied to Jesus' resurrection-ascension in Acts 2:33-36.

81. Longenecker 1981, 428, misreads the flow of the argument when he suggests that *anastēsas* in v. 33 refers to Jesus' being 'brought forth' for his people Israel, corresponding with v. 23 (*ēgagen,* 'brought'), while *anastēsen auton ek nekrōn* in v. 34 refers to the resurrection.

82. Cf. THE THEOLOGY OF ACTS: II. JESUS AS MESSIAH AND LORD (pp. 56-60).

83. The adjective *hosios* is actually a linking factor between these two scriptural texts. Cf. Bruce 1990, 310.

God's purpose in his own generation, he fell asleep; he was buried with his ancestors and his body decayed'.[84] The words spoken by David in Psalm 16 find their true fulfillment in the bodily resurrection of Jesus Christ *('But the one whom God raised from the dead did not see decay')*. Linking together the promises from Psalm 16:10 and Isaiah 55:3, we see that the Messiah's deliverance from death and decay is one of *'"the holy and sure blessings promised to David"'* and that this means salvation for Israel too.[85] Israel's future is intimately connected with what happens to her Messiah, though there is no explicit mention of the return of Christ or eternal life here (the expression *'worthy of eternal life'* in v. 46 indicates that the possibility of sharing eternal life with Christ must have been part of the teaching given).

c. The Challenge Not to Miss Out on the Salvation Available through Jesus (13:38-43)

38-39 The application of the teaching given so far begins with these arresting words: *'Therefore, my brothers and sisters, I want you to know'* (cf. *gnōston estō*, 'let it be known', in 2:14; 4:10; 28:28). Like Peter in 10:43, Paul proclaims *'through Jesus the forgiveness of sins'*, but there is no offer of the gift of the Holy Spirit, nor a challenge about baptism in the name of Jesus (cf. Lk. 24:47). We must assume that Luke has given us an abbreviated version of what was said and remember that there was further teaching about the gospel and its implications throughout the week and on the next Sabbath (vv. 42-44). Two things are particularly striking about this offer of forgiveness: first, its comprehensive and definitive nature and, second, its provision *through Jesus*. A Jewish audience may well have wondered why they needed such forgiveness, but John the Baptist's preaching had made it clear that *'all the people of Israel'* needed to express a radical repentance, to be ready to meet their God (cf. v. 25 note). Furthermore, the prophets had promised definitive forgiveness and cleansing as an essential part of the renewal of Israel in the end time (e.g., Je. 31:34; Ezk. 36:25). The provision of such forgiveness *through Jesus* is a consequence of his exalted, eschatological status (cf. Dn. 7:9-10, 13-14; Lk. 5:20-24; 24:46-47). However, the narrative theology expressed in 13:26-30 has indicated that salvation is not simply a function of his resurrection-ascension but the outcome of his unjust death, burial, and vindication by God, in fulfillment of Scripture.

---

84. Barrett 1994, 648-49, discusses the various ways in which this verse can be translated, opting for a version that takes the two datives with *hyperētēsas* ('served'): 'for David, having served his own generation by the will of God, fell asleep and was added to his fathers and saw corruption'. Cf. 1 Ki. 2:10.

85. Tannehill, 1990, 171, notes verbal correspondence between the two citations, understanding them as 'the positive and negative expression of the same promise'. The quotation from Is. 55:3 is modified so that 'I will make an everlasting covenant with you' becomes 'I will give you' (*dōsō hymin*). However, Acts 13:23 makes it clear that Israel is to be blessed with the fulfillment of what God covenanted with David.

The significance of this forgiveness is elaborated by means of the language of justification by faith, bringing the conclusion of this sermon close to the argument of some of Paul's letters. TNIV begins a new sentence and renders the complex Greek construction thus: '*Through him everyone who believes is set free from every sin, a justification you were not able to obtain under the law of Moses*' (*apo pantōn hōn ouk ēdynēthēte en nomō Mōyseōs dikaiōthēnai en toutō pas ho pisteuōn dikaioutai*, 'from all the things from which you could not be justified by the law of Moses, by this man everyone who believes is justified').[86] In his letters, Paul mostly uses the language of justification in a forensic sense, making it clear from Romans 4:5-7 that this involves a non-imputation of sin and a positive reckoning of righteousness to the ungodly because of Christ's atoning work (cf. Rom. 3:21-26). In the same passage, Paul shows the close relation between forgiveness and justification by citing Psalm 32:1. Justification is no legal fiction but 'an act of forgiveness on God's part, described in terms of the proceedings of a law court'.[87] The simple expression in Acts 13:39, 'everyone who believes is justified' *(pas ho pisteuōn dikaioutai)*, could certainly be understood in the normal Pauline sense (cf. Gal. 2:16; 3:11, 24). Gentiles are included in this offer in Romans 1:16; 3:22-30; 4:11; 10:4, 11-13. However, in 13:38, the Greek expression *dikaiōthēnai apo* is rightly translated by TNIV, *set free from*. This unusual application of the verb finds a parallel in Romans 6:7. Justification sets people free from the service of sin, so that they can offer themselves to God as 'instruments of righteousness' (Rom. 6:11-14). In Acts 13:38-39, Paul proclaims that faith in Jesus Christ sets people free from the penalty and control of all those things from which it was impossible to find release in or by the law of Moses.[88] This suggests the ineffectiveness of the law to achieve a satisfactory atonement for sins and a way of moral transformation, so that believers might truly serve God (cf. Heb. 9:1-14). Such justification and renewal are now available for *everyone who believes*, who trusts in the promises of the gospel and relies on the work of Christ that makes them possible.

86. The Western text makes several insertions in vv. 38-39: *metanoia* ('repentance') before *apo pantōn, oun* ('therefore') before *pas ho pisteuōn,* and *para theō* ('before God') after *dikaioutai.* Cf. Metzger, *Textual Commentary,* 366.

87. Barrett 1994, 651, citing words from his own commentary on Romans. Barrett expresses the scepticism of many scholars when he writes that we cannot ascribe Acts 13:38-39 to Paul, and yet he acknowledges a possible parallel with Rom. 6:7. C. L. Blomberg, 'The Christian and the Law of Moses', in Marshall and Peterson, *Witness to the Gospel,* 406, rightly describes 13:38-39 as 'actually one of the most Pauline statements in the entire book'.

88. The preposition *en* can be taken here in a locative sense, meaning 'in (the area marked out by the law)', or instrumentally, meaning 'by (obedience to the law)'. Paul expounds the weakness of the law to achieve justification and transformation of life in passages such as Rom. 3:19-20, 27-31; 7:1-6; 8:1-4. Witherington 1998, 413-14, argues that Acts 13:38 could mean 'that the Law of Moses was capable of setting things right in some matters, but that Jesus could provide justification in all cases'. However, this misses the epoch-changing implications of the sermon and the definitive and comprehensive nature of the forgiveness offered through Christ. Cf. Longenecker 1981, 426-27; Haenchen 1971, 412 note 4; Bruce 1990, 311-12; Blomberg, 'Law', 406.

40-41 Following the challenge to believe and receive forgiveness and justification through Christ, there comes a warning based on Habakkuk 1:5. The prophet's words are taken as representative of a whole series of warnings to Israel in Scripture (*'Take care that what the prophets have said does not happen to you').*[89] The Lord addresses the contemporaries of Habakkuk through the prophet, accusing them of being *scoffers* who are about to *perish ('"look, you scoffers, wonder and perish"').* They will perish in the approaching attack of the Chaldeans because they are unbelievers at heart, who remain unconvinced about God and his purposes. They will remain obdurate in the face of God's mighty actions in history and the report of these events received from his messengers (*'"for I am going to do something in your days that you would never believe, even if someone told you"').* The immediate relevance of these words to Paul's audience in Pisidian Antioch is clear. What God has done in their days is to fulfill the messianic promises by raising Jesus from death.[90] Paul has proclaimed this to them and offered them the forgiveness and justification achieved by Christ in his death and resurrection. They must choose 'which side of the prophetic cause they will embrace, that of the scornful opponents of Jesus, like those of Jerusalem, or that of the believing disciples, like Paul and associates'.[91] If they do not believe, they will perish in the coming judgment of God (cf. 3:22-23; 4:11-12; 10:42; 17:30-31).

42-43 *As Paul and Barnabas were leaving the synagogue, the people invited them to speak further about these things on the next Sabbath.*[92] Their initial desire to learn more is impressive (*parekaloun* means 'urged' here, rather than *invited*), especially in view of what happens in verses 44-45, 49-50. Although the congregation as a whole could not be addressed until *the next Sabbath,* Luke indicates that, *when the congregation was dismissed (lytheisēs* could mean 'broke up' rather than *was dismissed), many of the Jews and devout converts to Judaism followed Paul and Barnabas.* It is strange that Luke talks about *many of the Jews and devout converts to Judaism,* when previously he has Paul address-

89. The words *eph' hymas* ('upon you') are not in most of the best MSS. They seem to have been added by copyists to make the application of Hab. 1:5 to the audience absolutely clear. Metzger, *Textual Commentary,* 366, argues that the second *ergon* ('work') was omitted by some MSS, 'either because it was felt to be redundant, or in order to assimilate the text to the Septuagint text of Hab. 1:5'.

90. Tannehill, 1990, 172, thinks that, in the context of what follows, God's surprising work may also involve 'the inclusion of the Gentiles in the eternal life of the messianic reign'. It is certainly true that in 13:44-45 'the discovery of Gentiles as fellow citizens in Jesus' messianic state is the major stumbling block for the Jews of Antioch, turning them into "scoffers" who refuse to believe God's "work"'. However, this will surely have been true only for those who had already decided against believing in Jesus as Messiah. Cf. Barrett 1994, 652-53.

91. Spencer 1997, 146.

92. Some later MSS have 'the synagogue of the Jews' and add that 'the Gentiles' urged them to speak further about these things, presuming that Paul and Barnabas left before the synagogue was dismissed (v. 43). Cf. Metzger, *Textual Commentary,* 367-68, on the multiple variant readings associated with 13:42-43 in later textual traditions.

ing Jews and God-fearing Gentiles (vv. 16, 26). It appears that *devout converts (tōn sebomenōn prosēlytōn)* are specifically mentioned with *the Jews* in v. 43 because Luke is stressing that many of the most orthodox members of the congregation were persuaded by Paul's argument at this stage. As *converts* to Judaism (cf. 2:10; 6:5), the males may have been circumcised and their families may have undergone a ceremonial cleansing similar to baptism. However, we cannot be sure that the later more technical meaning of the term 'proselyte' is intended by Luke, especially since the LXX uses the term quite generally to refer to resident aliens (e.g., Ex. 20:10; 23:12; Nu. 15:13-16).[93] The description of them as *devout* (using the present participle *sebomenōn*) probably means 'worshipping' in this context. Given the enthusiastic response of Gentiles to the gospel signalled in vv. 44-48, we are expected to conclude that God-fearers in the synagogue were also keen to learn more about the message they had just heard. Paul's ministry to the Gentiles subsequently had to include God-fearers in a context outside the synagogue, together with those who had no previous contact with Judaism. Another point of interest is Luke's statement that Paul and Barnabas *talked with them and urged them to continue in the grace of God*. The verb *to continue (prosmenein)* implies that they had arrived at an apprehension of *the grace of God* through Paul's preaching and were to remain faithful to what they had heard (cf. 11:23, *prosmenein tō kyriō*, 'continue with the Lord'; 14:22, *emmenein tē pistei*, 'continue in the faith'). *The grace of God* could refer to the action of God in sending preachers of the gospel and converting people,[94] but it is more likely in this context to refer to the message of salvation preached by Paul (as in 14:3; 20:24, 32). Nevertheless, we cannot assume from the context that all of those so addressed were yet committed to Christ.

2. Turning to the Gentiles: Fulfilling the Servant's Role (13:44-52)

This first dramatic turning of Paul and Barnabas to the Gentiles is given a theological rationale by Paul in terms of the fulfillment of the Servant's role in Isaiah 49:6. Given their previous ministry in Syrian Antioch (11:22-26), their preaching to Gentiles in Pisidian Antioch was no new thing. However, abandonment of the synagogue, in order to minister to Gentiles in their own context, required some explanation. Even so, the report of their ministry in Iconium (14:1-7) shows an engagement with Jews in the synagogue once more. The pattern observed in 13:44-52 is repeated there, with Jewish unbelief and opposition forcing them out of the synagogue and

---

93. Cf. Witherington 1998, 342-44; McKnight, 'Proselytes and Godfearers', *DNTB* 844-46.

94. So Barrett 1994, 654, drawing a strict parallel with 11:23. Witherington 1998, 414, says, 'It is not impossible that Luke means to suggest that God's prevenient grace is already working in Paul's audience, though they have not yet been fully converted'. Cf. Marshall 1980, 229.

eventually out of the city. So this passage is designed to explain the pattern of Paul's ministry more generally, in terms of the social and theological issues involved.

44-45 *On the next Sabbath almost the whole city gathered to hear the word of the Lord.* The message had been spread by those who attended the synagogue and doubtless also by Paul and Barnabas, taking every opportunity during the week to teach the gospel. Presumably this gathering was in and around the synagogue. However, despite such enthusiasm, there were Jews who *began to contradict what Paul was saying and heaped abuse on him.* At this point, Luke appears to use the expression *the Jews* quite narrowly, referring to those who were not convinced and who were *filled with jealousy* (cf. 5:17) when they *saw the crowds.* TNIV translates *hoi Ioudaioi* as *the Jewish leaders* in verse 50, and perhaps the same expression should be similarly rendered here. It seems unlikely that all the Jews who were enthusiastic about the new teaching (vv. 42-43) turned against it so suddenly. Jealousy at the success of others is sadly a common human failing, and religious leaders are especially vulnerable to such behaviour. Jealousy is expressed here by contradicting the message and blaspheming against God (so NRSV). TNIV's *heaped abuse on him* (ESV 'reviling him') interprets the Greek *blasphēmountes* in way that is possible, but unlikely. Acts consistently uses the verb with a God-ward connotation appropriate to each context (cf. 18:6; 19:37; 26:11).[95] The final expression of jealousy is organised persecution, resulting in expulsion from the region (v. 50). 'Resistance is openly expressed and involves personal attacks that would make preaching in the synagogue difficult or impossible.'[96]

46-47 In the face of this opposition, *Paul and Barnabas answered them boldly* (*parrēsizesthai*, 'speak boldly', is also found at 9:27, 28; 14:3; 18:26; 19:8; 26:26), analysing from a theological perspective what was going on. In effect, they switch to a judicial role, '"boldly" pronouncing the divine verdict on the present contest'.[97] Their foundational claim (*'We had to speak the word of God to you first'*) was justified in the opening section of Paul's sermon (vv. 16-23), but finds further substantiation from considering Isaiah 49:6 in its original context (v. 47).[98] Since the Christian gospel is the fulfillment of God's promises to Israel, Jews everywhere have a prior right to hear what God has done for them. However, the Greek conjunction *epeidē* ('since') indicates a clear causal relationship between the rejection of the

---

95. H. W. Beyer, *TDNT* 1:621-25; Johnson 1992, 240-41; Barrett 1994, 655. Beyer, 624, observes that the opposition of the Jews to the preaching of Paul is necessarily blasphemy, 'because it attacks its basic content, the proclamation of the Messiah.' Luke is thus making a contrast with the Gentiles who 'honoured the word of the Lord' (v. 48).

96. Tannehill 1990, 175.

97. Spencer 1997, 147.

98. *anankaion* ('necessary') is used here instead of the customary *dei*, but the meaning is the same: 'the necessity is one dictated by the divine plan that is being worked out in the story' (Johnson 1992, 241).

gospel by these Jews and the deliberate turning of Paul and Barnabas to ministry among Gentiles in that city. Their rejection of the gospel (*apōtheisthe*, 'push aside, reject'; cf. 7:27, 39) is interpreted ironically as a judgment that they are not *'worthy of eternal life'*. The concept of eternal life is mentioned only here and in verse 48 (though cf. 5:20; 11:18). Although it may be taken as a broad equivalent for salvation or the kingdom of God, the idea that resurrection to eternal life (Heb. *hayyê ha'ôlam habba'*, 'the life of the age to come'; Gk. *hē aiōnios zōē*, 'eternal life') is specifically the outcome of Christ's resurrection is suggested by 3:21; 4:2, 10-12; 17:18, and is implied by 13:32-37. Resurrection from the dead is later described by Paul as the hope of Israel for which he is on trial because of his preaching about Jesus (23:6; 24:21; 26:6-8, 22-23). Such intense and sustained opposition from Jews was the signal to Paul and Barnabas to *'turn to the Gentiles'* (cf. 18:6-7; 28:28). This did not mean that the missionaries would now evangelise Gentiles for the first time (cf. 11:25-26; 13:6-12). Neither did it mean that they would never again preach to Jews, since they immediately go to the synagogue in Iconium (14:1), and Paul continues to preach to Jews first, wherever he can find them (e.g., 16:13; 17:1-3, 10). The citation from Isaiah 49:6 also makes it clear that turning to the Gentiles is not an afterthought or second best solution, following Jewish rejection of the gospel (cf. Lk. 2:30-32; 3:6; 24:45-47). *'We had to speak the word of God to you first'* echoes the portion of that text not quoted: 'it is too small a thing for you to be my servant to restore the tribes of Jacob and bring back those of Israel I have kept'. 'The mission is universal, but it must follow prescribed order. The Jews must be addressed first. If they reject the gospel, the missionaries are free to begin the second phase of their mission.'[99] This phase would concentrate on Gentiles who had no connection with the synagogue. Such a move would have profound implications for the character of the church in that place.

Paul regarded the portion of the text quoted as *'what the Lord has commanded us'* (*entetaltai*; cf. 1:2) in this particular matter: '*"I have made you a light for the Gentiles, that you may bring salvation to the ends of the earth"*' (cf. 9:15; 22:21; 26:17-18). Jesus himself was first identified as 'a light for revelation to the Gentiles' (Lk. 2:32), and thus, foundationally, he is the one in whom Isaiah's prediction is fulfilled.[100] The risen Christ then commis-

---

99. Tannehill 1990, 173. It was certainly Jesus' intention that his Jewish disciples should be 'the light of the world' (Mt. 5:14-16), thus fulfilling the servant role given to the faithful within Israel in Is. 49:5-6. However, Acts makes it clear that this could happen only because Jesus himself fulfilled the role of the Servant in Is. 52:13–53:12, bringing to believing Israelites all the promised benefits on the New Covenant (2:36-39; 3:13-26; cf. Lk. 2:32). The servant community is now comprised of Jews and Gentiles who trust in Christ and share the responsibility of fulfilling the mandate of Is. 49:6.

100. So Barrett 1994, 658, rightly comments that 'Paul is a light of the Gentiles only in virtue of the Christ whom he preaches; Christ is a light to the Gentiles as he is preached to them by his servants'. Cf. Bruce 1990, 314-15.

sioned the apostles to be his witnesses *to the ends of the earth* (1:8, alluding to Is. 49:6). We have seen ways in which that witness was carried by others to different places and ethnic groups (8:4-40; 11:19-26), and we have noted the important step taken by Peter in sharing the gospel with Gentiles and the endorsement of this initiative by the apostles and believers in Judea (10:1–11:18). What we find now is not so much 'a shift in strategy' as a focus on Paul as 'the chief instrument by which the gospel reaches out to the Gentiles and the end of the earth'.[101] In this connection, the agreement reached in Galatians 2:7-9 should not be taken to mean that Peter, James, and John would never preach to Gentiles, and Paul would no longer preach to Jews. Spheres of missionary responsibility were delineated without prescribing exclusive rights to evangelise one group or the other. In Pisidian Antioch, Paul's work among Gentiles would now take precedence and his base of operation would no longer be the synagogue.

48-52 *When the Gentiles heard this, they were glad and honoured the word of the Lord* (*edoxazon;* NRSV 'praised', or ESV 'glorified').[102] We might expect Luke to write that they praised God for the gospel, but he makes it quite clear that they were actually praising or honouring the message (cf. 2 Thes. 3:1). A way of salvation had been opened to them though the gospel, and, as a consequence, *all who were appointed for (tetagmenoi eis) eternal life believed.* 'The Jews "rejected the word of God" and judged themselves "unfit for eternal life"; in contrast, the Gentiles show that they are destined for eternal life by "glorifying" this same "word of the Lord".'[103] Luke draws attention to the way in which God uses the gospel to call out his elect and to save them. 'The present verse is as unqualified a statement of absolute predestination — "the eternal purpose of God" (Calvin) — as is found anywhere in the NT.'[104] Not everyone is affected in the same way by the preaching of the gospel. God must open hearts, to enable people to listen and respond with faith (cf. 16:14; 18:10). Those who seek the Lord from

---

101. Tannehill, 1990, 170. The suggestion that there is a shift in strategy at this point in the narrative does not sufficiently account for the evidence of preceding chapters. The mission of the Twelve was limited and specialized from the beginning. They seem to have been content with the fact that others took their witness in widening circles from Jerusalem and acted as their representatives in taking the gospel to the nations. It is a narrowly literalistic reading of 1:8 to suppose that Jesus wanted each one of the apostles personally to go to the ends of the earth (though Tannehill does not suggest this).

102. The present participle *akouonta*, followed by two indicatives in the imperfect tense *(echairon kai edoxazon)* could be translated, 'as the Gentiles were hearing (this), they began to rejoice and praise (the word of the Lord)'. Some MSS have the more common expression 'the word of God' here and in v. 44, but the more unusual 'the word of the Lord' is more likely to have been the original. Cf. Metzger, *Textual Commentary,* 369-70.

103. Johnson 1992, 242.

104. Barrett 1994, 658, who rightly infers that the perfect passive participle *tetagmenoi* means 'appointed by God'. He also rightly affirms that the rest, who did not believe, 'did not receive eternal life, and were thus appointed to death. The positive statement implies the negative.' It is therefore strange that Barrett says Luke was 'a narrator rather than a theologian', because he failed to mention the work of the Holy Spirit here.

among the nations are those whom he has already claimed as his own (15:17 note). Yet this happens as God enables some to believe through the proclamation of the gospel (14:1 note).

Even though *the word of the Lord spread through the whole region,* and many no doubt believed, unbelief and hardness of heart were everywhere present and led to organised persecution. *The Jewish leaders* moved to the next level of opposition (cf. v. 45) and *incited the God-fearing women of high standing and the leading men of the city.* The former were presumably adherents of the synagogue because they are described as *God-fearing (sebomenas).* The latter may have been Roman magistrates.[105] With the aid of these influential citizens, the Jewish leaders *stirred up persecution against Paul and Barnabas, and expelled them from their region (exebalon,* 'cast out, expel', is also used in Lk. 4:29, with reference to Jesus). So the missionaries followed the practice commended by Jesus in Luke 9:5; 10:11: *they shook the dust from their feet as a warning to them and went to Iconium.* It is likely that this was a particular warning to their Jewish opponents, who would understand the significance of this prophetic-type action, rather than a wholesale condemnation of the city. Those who reject the message of eternal life will themselves not receive eternal life. God's judgment against scoffers (v. 41) will surely come. By shaking the dust from their feet, the missionaries indicated that they did not want to be associated with such unbelief and its consequences. Even in the context of so much persecution, *the disciples were filled with joy and with the Holy Spirit.* The Spirit enabled joy and perseverance in the face of intense opposition (cf. Gal. 5:22; 1 Thes. 1:6). Paul and Barnabas soon returned to strengthen these believers in their faith and to establish them as the new people of God in that city (14:21-23).

ADDITIONAL NOTE: A GOSPEL FOR THE JEW FIRST

As a conclusion to this chapter, it is worth noting again that Luke presents further scenes in which Jews reject the gospel and that there is a definite shift to ministry among Gentiles (e.g., 18:5-7; 19:8-9; 28:23-28). However, he also records some success among Jews (e.g., 17:5, 10-12; 21:20) and repeated attempts to win Jews for Christ in new situations. Luke and the characters in his narrative seem to be driven by the theology expressed in Paul's sermon here. The election of Israel and God's provision of the Saviour Jesus for Israel remain first as foundational truths, despite the rejection of the gospel by many. Here is the impetus for continuing evangelism among Jews, while continuing to share the gospel with ever-widening circles of Gentiles. Paul's

---

105. Cf. Barrett 1994, 660, follows *ND* 3:30-31, which suggests that the expulsion may have taken place because of the perceived threat to the cult of the god Men. It is possible that these women were married to the magistrates and were used to influence their husbands against the missionaries. Longenecker 1981, 430, argues that the expulsion 'probably took the form of a charge that Christianity, being disowned by the local Jewish community, was not a *religio licita*' (legal religion), and therefore was a disturbance to the peace.

approach to the problem in Romans 9–11 makes it clear that 'not all who are descended from Israel are Israel' (9:6) and that it is only because of God's mercy that some believe (9:14-29). God has not rejected his people, but 'at the present time there is a remnant chosen by grace' (11:5). Paul continues to preach the gospel to Gentiles 'to make Israel envious' (11:11). Although he acknowledges that 'Israel has experienced a hardening in part', he anticipates the salvation of all who are truly elect in Israel, when 'the full number of the Gentiles has come in' (11:25-27). Paul's argument in Romans 9–11 offers a further explanation of the mission strategy he pursues in the narrative of Acts and confronts every generation of Christians with the theological importance of bearing witness to unbelieving Jews.[106]

The gospel outline presented in Acts 13 is clearly focussed on persuading those who know the Scriptures and expect an imminent messianic kingdom to recognise in Jesus the fulfillment of their hope. Christians who seek to engage people in the contemporary world with the gospel will not find it easy to use this approach in exactly the same way — even with some Jews. Nevertheless, there are important themes here that need to be explained to everyone at some stage in the process of evangelism, to ground the gospel for them historically and theologically. First, there is the idea that the Christian message is no novelty. The ministry of Jesus was the outworking of God's long-standing plan — first announced to Abraham and progressively made more explicit in the Scriptures — to save and bless Israel and the nations on exactly the same basis. Second, there is the idea that God has chosen to fulfill his saving plan through the leader he has appointed. Given the reputation of Jesus and his character, it is remarkable that he was put to death by some of the very people he came to help and to rescue. However, the resurrection is God's vindication of Jesus as the one who would bring life from the dead. Third, there is the idea that forgiveness of sins and a new freedom to serve God are made possible by the death and resurrection of Jesus. Nevertheless, this is possible only for those who believe in him and turn to him, since God warns of the judgment coming against those who scoff and reject his saving plan.

INTRODUCTION TO ACTS 14

Every chapter in Acts appears to have a particular focus or theme. As Luke tells the story of the gospel's progress from one situation to another, he draws parallels and makes connections with previous narratives, but he

---

106. Cf. R. Wall, 'Israel and the Gentile Mission in Acts and Paul: A Canonical Approach', in Marshall and Peterson (eds.), *Witness to the Word*, 437-57. S. Sizer, *Christian Zionism: Road-map to Armaggedon?* (Leicester: Inter-Varsity, 2004), 106-205, offers a theological critique of Christian Zionism in relation to the view of Israel and the church expounded in this commentary.

also highlights distinctive features relevant to each new context. In Acts 14 there are parallels with the ministry in Pisidian Antioch (14:1-7; cf. 13:13-52) and with the earlier ministry of Peter in Jerusalem (14:8-10; cf. 3:1-10).[1] However, the speech which is recorded here is very different because it is addressed to pagans who have no knowledge of the God of Israel (14:11-18). Apart from this important new example of Paul's preaching, the theme of persecution and suffering is particularly highlighted in the chapter. Indeed, there appears to be an escalation of persecution compared with the previous chapter, just as was noted in Acts 4–7. Paul and Barnabas experience persecution themselves at the end of their ministry in Iconium (14:5) and again in Lystra (14:19). The third mention of this theme occurs when the missionaries return to exhort the churches they had founded to remain faithful in the face of hardship and opposition (14:21-5).[2] Although there have been several accounts of persecution so far in Luke's narrative, the pastoral application in these verses functions to challenge readers more directly about this issue than ever before. Faith is also an important theme in the chapter (14:1, 9, 22, 23), illustrating the claim that God had 'opened a door of faith to the Gentiles' (14:27; cf. 13:48), and preparing for the argument about salvation for Jews and Gentiles alike through faith in Christ (15:9-11). When Paul and Barnabas report back to the church at Antioch in Syria (14:26-28), this completes the journey which began with their commissioning in 13:1-3. Acts 14 begins and ends with bridging narratives in summary form (vv. 1-7, 21-28), and has at its centre a more detailed focus on events in Lystra and their outcome (vv. 8-20).

D. The Word in Iconium, Lystra, and Derbe (14:1-20)

Although Luke continues to illustrate the priority of ministry to Jews wherever possible, the focus of this section is on ministry to Gentiles. As in 13:49-50, unbelieving Jews incite unbelieving Gentiles to join them in opposing the missionaries and their gospel (14:1-7, 19-20). This is a remarkable coalition, considering Jewish antipathy to idolatry and the Gentile way of life. With a miracle of restoration recalling 3:1-10, and a brief message delivered to pagans in Lystra (vv. 8-18), Luke illustrates the sort of direct engagement with Gentiles envisaged in his summary statements. Given the narrative significance of the sermon to Jews and God-fearers in 13:16-41, the address in 14:15-17 stands out as the first specific example of how the beliefs and practices of Greco-Roman religion were encountered. The message here is not about God fulfilling his promises to Israel and sending the Saviour, but good news about the possibility of escaping from

---

1. Cf. Spencer 1997, 149.
2. Tannehill 1990, 180, rightly opposes the view of Haenchen 1971, 434, that Luke intends to play down Paul's sufferings.

the futility of idolatry and coming to know the true and living God. Despite the opposition experienced in these three cities, Luke indicates with respect to the return journey that there was a number of new disciples needing to be strengthened and encouraged there (14:21-22; cf. v. 1).

1. *Concerted Opposition in Iconium (14:1-7)*

The experience of the missionaries in the synagogue at Pisidian Antioch 'had been a lively one, but it did not lead to a change of policy or tactics'.[3] In Iconium they followed the same pattern of preaching first to those in the synagogue, but soon experienced considerable opposition. Once again, Luke shows how unbelieving Jews were able to divide a city by creating antagonism to the gospel and bringing ill-treatment upon its messengers (cf. 13:49-50). A novel feature of this account is the note about the Lord enabling Paul and Barnabas to continue their ministry in Iconium for some considerable time, despite such opposition (v. 3).

1-2 Despite the dramatic turning to the Gentiles mentioned in 13:46-49, *at Iconium, Paul and Barnabas went as usual into the Jewish synagogue (kata to auto,* 'after the same manner'; cf. 17:2). *Iconium* (modern Konya) was 90 miles (145 km.) east-southeast of Antioch, in the same Phrygian area of the province of Galatia. 'While Rome chose Antioch and Lystra as bastions of its authority in the area, Iconium remained largely Greek in temper and somewhat resistant to Roman influence.'[4] Luke records a pattern of response here that parallels the more extensive account in 13:42-50 and is repeated in other places. First, the missionaries *spoke so effectively (lalēsai houtōs,* 'so spoke') *that a great number of Jews and Greeks believed* (cf. 17:4). Following on from the strong statement about God's sovereignty in the process of enabling belief in 13:48, Luke affirms once more that God uses as his instrument the faithful preaching of the gospel. Reference to *Greeks* in this context may reflect the fact that the city was particularly Greek in its character. It is likely that these were God-fearers who were attached to the synagogue (cf. 13:16, 26) rather than full proselytes. But then, *the Jews who refused to believe (apeithēsantes,* 'disobeyed') *stirred up the other Gentiles and poisoned their minds against the brothers.*[5] The word 'other' does not occur in the original text, but it is a reasonable assumption that *the Gentiles* here (v. 2) were not the Greeks who believed (v. 1), but other citizens who were outside the synagogue. 'So Iconium is a divided city, but not on an ethnic

3. Barrett 1994, 667.

4. Longenecker 1981, 431. Emperor Hadrian (AD 117-38) later made it a Roman colony. Longenecker comments on the ethos and situation of Iconium. Bruce 1990, 316, offers a brief history of the city.

5. The Western text of 14:2-7 adds various details to smooth away difficulties and improve the narrative, but these changes all appear to be secondary. Cf. Metzger, *Textual Commentary,* 370-71; Longenecker 1981, 432-34.

basis. There are Jews and Gentiles on both sides of the division, and there are Gentiles among the active persecutors.'[6] By this stage, *the brothers* must have included the new believers as well as the evangelists (cf. 1 Thes. 1:6; 2:14-16).

3-4 *So Paul and Barnabas spent considerable time there, speaking boldly for the Lord* (parrēsiazesthai, as in 9:27; 13:46). The link with verse 2 is strange (*men oun*, 'so then') unless it is understood that Paul and Barnabas stayed because the new believers needed their support: 'the greater the opposition the bolder they became'.[7] Reference to the *considerable time* (hikanon chronon, cf. 8:11; 27:9) they spent there is also paradoxical, viewed in the light of the opposition they experienced. But the theological explanation for their endurance is given in what follows. The Lord supported and encouraged them, 'testifying to' *(martyrounti) the message of his grace by enabling them to do miraculous signs and wonders* (cf. the 'testimony' God provides to himself in the natural order, v. 17). Luke first reminds us that Paul's gospel was essentially about God's grace (cf. 13:43; 20:24, 32), particularly as expressed in the person and work of Christ. Secondly, he reminds us that *signs and wonders* were given by God to testify to the gospel's authenticity and power (cf. 5:12; 13:12; 15:12; Gal. 3:4-5). Nevertheless, despite the teaching of the missionaries and the Lord's own testimony in the working of miracles, *the people of the city were divided; some sided with the Jews, others with the apostles.*[8] Luke has previously asserted in the face of unbelief and opposition that 'all who were appointed for eternal life believed' (13:48). He will soon make it clear that God must work in the heart to enable a saving response to the gospel (16:14). Although the theme is only occasionally expressed (cf. 15:17 note; 18:10 note), we may assume that wherever resistance to the message is recorded, Luke believed the Lord had not yet acted in grace and power to enable belief. Neither miracles nor persuasive argument can effect conversion without that secret work of God's Spirit which is called regeneration (Jn. 3:3-8; Tit. 3:5-6).

Only here and in verse 14 are Paul and Barnabas called *apostles* by Luke. He normally uses the term for the Twelve, who were foundational witnesses of the risen Christ and accompanied him during his ministry (cf.

6. Tannehill 1990, 176. Spencer 1997, 148, also observes that 'the Acts narrative continues to resist sweeping stereotypes'.

7. Barrett 1994, 669. Similarly, Marshall 1980, 232-33, observes that 'the difficulty of the text seems to arise from Luke's desire to emphasize that it was precisely because of the rise of opposition that the missionaries felt they must stay as long as possible to consolidate the infant Christian community, and departed only when they were absolutely forced to do so'. Bruce 1990, 318, argues that 'until the Gentile opposition broke out (v. 5), the missionaries ignored the Jewish hostility and carried on the work of evangelization for a considerable time'.

8. to plēthos tēs poleōs could refer to the general populace or to the assembly of prominent citizens met to conduct the business of a Greek city-state. Cf. Plato, *Apol.* 31C; Longenecker 1981, 433. Luke could be telling us that the official response of the civic assembly to Paul and Barnabas was mixed.

1:21-22 note). It is unlikely that the reference is to the Twelve in this context, meaning that those who believed the gospel were effectively on the side of the apostles, who received it from Christ (this reading would not be applicable at v. 14). Many scholars take the view that Paul and Barnabas were regarded as apostles in a different sense in the source that Luke used for this narrative.[9] But we must still ask why he allowed the term to be included and how he understood it. It is possible that they were regarded as apostles of the church at Antioch in Syria (cf. 2 Cor. 8:23, *apostoloi ekklēsiōn*, 'apostles of churches'; Phil. 2:25; *Did.* 11:3-6),[10] though this raises a further significant question. Does Luke show any awareness of Paul's insistent claim to be the apostle to the Gentiles (e.g., Rom. 1:1, 5; 1 Cor. 9:1-6; Gal. 1:1)? We should recall the application of Isaiah 49:6 to Paul and Barnabas in 13:47, which claims a significant role in salvation history for them. Given the echo of that text in 1:8, it would not be surprising if Luke expected his readers to understand by the use of *apostles* in 14:4 and 14 that Paul and Barnabas were 'fulfilling with respect to the nations the commission originally given to the eleven apostles'.[11] Although Barnabas does not appear to have had the same direct encounter with and commissioning by the risen Christ, he 'shares with Paul in the status as well as the function of apostleship',[12] presumably by association with Paul as his partner and companion (cf. 1 Cor. 9:6).

5-7 The opponents of the gospel *(both Gentiles and Jews, together with their leaders)* united in a *plot (hormē)* or determined effort *to mistreat them and stone them.* No doubt there were different reasons for wanting to get rid of the missionaries and their message. Luke's brief note merely serves to indicate that such concerted opposition made it impossible to continue to min-

9. Cf. Barrett 1994, 666-67, 671-72.

10. Bruce 1990, 319. S. G. Wilson, *Luke and the Law*, SNTSMS 50 (Cambridge: Cambridge University, 1983), 115-18, argues that Luke was content to allow two contradictory ways of using the word *apostolos* to stand side by side in his book, allowing Paul to be viewed as an apostle of Christ in his own right, alongside the Twelve. Barrett 1994, 667, modifies this by noting that Paul and Barnabas were appointed and sent not by men, but by God, 'as truly as were the prophets (see, e.g., Gal. 1:15 and cf. Je. 1:5; Is. 49:1)'. So Barrett concludes that 'Luke therefore was prepared to call them apostles, and did so; but he did so seldom, perhaps because he knew that there were those who would not so describe them'.

11. A. C. Clark, 'The Role of the Apostles', in I. H. Marshall and D. G. Peterson (eds.), *Witness to the Gospel: The Theology of Acts* (Grand Rapids/Cambridge: Eerdmans, 1998), 184. Clark also draws attention to the parallel between 14:3 and 5:12 with respect to signs and wonders and goes on to explore other parallels between Peter and Paul in Acts. See more fully A. C. Clark, *Parallel Lives: The Relation of Paul to the Apostles in the Lucan Perspective* (Carlisle: Paternoster, 2001), 136-49. Marshall 1980, 234, argues that Luke recognises 'a group of apostles, commissioned by Jesus, wider than the Twelve, and he does not deny that Paul and Barnabas belong to this group'. Marshall draws attention to the use of the cognate verb 'to send' *(apostellein)* in 22:21; 26:16-17. Witherington 1998, 420, agrees that Marshall's approach is possible.

12. Clark, 'Apostles', 185 note 73. Stott 1990, 229, suggests that 'Paul and Barnabas were both apostles of the church of Syrian Antioch, sent out by them, whereas only Paul was also an apostle of Christ'. Cf. C. Brown, *NIDNTT* 1:135-36.

ister there (cf. 13:50-51). When Paul and Barnabas found out about the plot, they *fled to the Lycaonian cities of Lystra and Derbe and to the surrounding country*.[13] *Lystra* was about 18 miles (29 km.) south-southwest from Iconium, and *Derbe* was a further journey of some 55 miles (89 km.). Both cities were in the Lycaonian region of the province of Galatia. Lystra had been made a colony by Caesar Augustus in 6 BC. It lay on the imperial road which connected Antioch and Laranda, another important Lycaonian city.[14] In Lystra and the surrounding region *they continued to preach the gospel,* until Jews from Antioch and Iconium found them and forced them to move on to Derbe (14:19-20).

2. Encountering Paganism in Lystra (14:8-20)

Luke moves from a brief summary of the ministry in Iconium, where the pattern of events was similar to what happened in Antioch, and offers a more detailed account of events in Lystra. This narrative begins with the restoration of a man who was lame from birth, paralleling 3:1-10 in several respects (vv. 8-10). In both contexts, the miracle illustrates the signs and wonders that the Lord enabled his servants to perform, first among Jews in Jerusalem, and then among the Gentiles (cf. 2:43; 14:3). Both miracles are followed by potential (3:12, 16) or real misunderstanding about the event (14:11-13), and provoke addresses which challenge those misunderstandings. But Paul urges his audience to turn from their idolatrous worldview and its practices to serve the living God (vv. 11-18), whereas Peter proclaims to his Jewish audience the ultimate 'healing' of all things through Jesus (3:11-26). No mention is made of a synagogue in Lystra, but Luke shows the intensity of opposition from Jewish quarters by noting that some travelled from Antioch and Iconium to win the crowd over and force Paul and Barnabas to leave for Derbe (vv. 19-20). Gaventa observes that the cultural identity of Lystra plays a part in the story. 'As residents of a cultural backwater, Lystrans were frequently characterized as largely rustic and uncivilized. Their gullibility in this story plays on the stereotype, just as the disdainful sophistication of the philosophers in Acts 17 plays on the stereotype of the Athenians.'[15]

13. Iconium was not in Lycaonia. As a frontier town between Phrygia and Lycaonia, it was frequently called a Lycaonian city by ancient writers, though strictly it lay in Phrygia. Bruce 1990, 319, observes that 'the missionaries would have known that they were leaving one region for another by hearing another local language spoken'.

14. Cf. Bruce 1990, 319-20; Barrett 1994, 672-73, for further details about the region and these two cities.

15. Gaventa 2003, 206, citing D. P. Bechard, *Paul outside the Walls: A Study of Luke's Socio-Geographical Universalism in Acts 14:8-20,* AnBib 143 (Rome: Pontifical Biblical Institute, 2000), as a source. This cultural difference explains the difference between the two speeches to pagan audiences in Acts 14 and 17, despite certain similarities.

8-10 The healing of *a man who was lame* parallels the ministry of Peter and John in the temple forecourt (3:1-10; cf. Jesus in Lk. 5:18-26), though subsequent events show a different outcome. This is part of a larger sequence of parallels between Peter and Paul, by which Luke demonstrates the authority and significance of Paul and seeks to convince his readers that 'God works out the divine plan in regular and orderly patterns'.[16] For the first time in Acts, Paul and Barnabas encounter outright heathenism and adapt their preaching accordingly. With elaborate detail, Luke presents the seriousness of the man's situation (*tis anēr adynatos en Lystrois tois posin ekathēto, chōlos ek koilias mētros autou hos oudepote periepatēsan*, 'a certain man used to sit in Lystra, powerless in his feet, lame from his mother's womb, who had never walked'; cf. 3:2).[17] This poor man *listened to Paul as he was speaking* — presumably in Greek — in some public place. Like Peter and John, *Paul looked directly at him* (*atenisas*, as in 3:4), intending to help him. However, the novel element in this narrative is the statement that Paul saw that he had *faith to be healed* (*pistin tou sōthēnai*). The Greek verb is rightly translated 'healed' rather than 'saved' (as in 4:12). Such faith had possibly been aroused by the preaching of the gospel (vv. 6-7), but it was not yet a seeking for salvation in the sense of forgiveness, eternal life, and entrance into the kingdom of God (cf. 13:48; 14:22).[18] The command (*anastēthi epi tous podous sou orthos*, 'stand upright on your feet', TNIV '*Stand up on your feet!*') challenged the lame man to express his faith by doing what seemed impossible for him. Complete healing followed immediately (though there is nothing in the Greek corresponding to TNIV's *at that*): *the man jumped up and began to walk.* The description of the man as jumping *(hēlato)* provides another verbal link with 3:8 *(exallomenos).* The healing in both contexts results in a similar problem, although one setting is Jewish and the other pagan: 'there is a tendency to confuse the power that heals with the healer himself, and the healer acts immediately to set the record straight'.[19]

11-13 *When the crowd saw what Paul had done, they shouted in the Lycaonian language, 'The gods have come down to us in human form!'* In Athens, Paul observed popular idolatry and encountered the varied responses of the philosophers (17:16-34), but here 'a spontaneous outpouring of Helle-

16. Witherington 1998, 423. Clark, *Parallel Lives,* 325, concludes that the main purpose of the Peter-Paul parallels is 'to highlight the themes of continuity in salvation history, and the unity of the Jewish and Gentile missions'.

17. Metzger, *Textual Commentary,* 372-73, discusses the rearrangement of these words in some MSS, and notes that in several Western witnesses there are attempts to explain how the man had faith to be healed.

18. Compare the preaching of salvation by the missionaries in Philippi, which caused unbelievers to use such terminology in their presence, without necessarily understanding the full import of their message (cf. 16:17, 30). Cf. THE THEOLOGY OF ACTS: IV. SALVATION (pp. 65-70).

19. Tannehill 1990, 178. Metzger, *Textual Commentary,* 373-74, notes various additions to vv. 8-10 which are not in the best and earliest manuscripts.

nistic religiosity'.[20] A significant miracle, associated with the preaching of the gospel, was the immediate reason for identifying Barnabas with *Zeus,* the supreme god of the Greek pantheon, and Paul with *Hermes because he was the chief speaker.* Since the people were shouting *in the Lycaonian language,* the missionaries were at first unaware of the honour that was being paid to them. Two inscriptions discovered near Lystra, dating from the third century AD, indicate that Zeus and Hermes were worshipped in the region at that later time. However, the Latin poet Ovid (c. 43 BC–AD 17) had earlier recorded the legend of a visit by the supreme god Jupiter (Zeus to the Greeks) and his son Mercury (Hermes) to 'the Phrygian hill country', disguised as mortals seeking lodging.[21] According to the legend, an elderly couple welcomed the gods, with the result that their house was transformed into a temple and they were made priests. The gods then destroyed the houses of those who did not receive them. The crowd, apparently moved by this legend, assumed that the gods had returned in human form and needed to be honoured appropriately this time![22] The situation became more serious for Paul and Barnabas when *the priest of Zeus,*[23] *whose temple was just outside the city, brought bulls and wreaths to the city gates because he and the crowd wanted to offer sacrifices to them.* Animals were often adorned with garlands *(wreaths)* as they were led to the place of sacrifice — here literally 'to the gates' *(epi tous pylōnas)* — which could refer either to *the city gates* or the gates of the temple of Zeus, *just outside the city (pro tēs poleōs).*[24]

14-15 Although the word *apostles* is missing from some manuscripts, it is well attested and should be read, despite the difficulties of interpretation discussed in connection with v. 4.[25] In both contexts, the title draws attention to the authority of Barnabas and Paul as messengers from God in situations that were challenging for the progress of the gospel. Unusually, *Barnabas* comes before *Paul* here, which may simply reflect the order in which Luke records their names in v. 12, or it may indicate that Luke

20. Johnson 1992, 247. Johnson, 251, rather too optimistically concludes that 'Luke portrays these rustics as having precisely the conditions for genuine faith'. The idea that the gods might visit this world is ancient (cf. Homer, *Odyssey* 17.485-87; Diodorus Siculus 1.86.3; Aesop, *Fabulae* 89P = 140H).

21. Ovid, *Metamorphoses* 8.626-724. Witherington 1998, 421-22, gives a translation of the Ovid text and details of the inscriptions.

22. Barrett 1994, 677, discusses the relationship between these gods in Greek sources and evaluates some of the reasons given by commentators for the identification of the missionaries with Zeus and Hermes. The Lycaonians may well have syncretized their local gods with the Greek gods at some earlier stage in their history.

23. Codex Bezae has 'priests', which could be a correction based on exact knowledge of the probable situation. Cf. Metzger, *Textual Commentary,* 374.

24. Bruce 1990, 322, argues that while *pro tēs poleōs* locates the temple in front of the city, 'it may also mark out Zeus as the protector of the city'.

25. Barrett 1994, 678, argues that there is a possibility that the shorter text should be preferred. But Metzger, *Textual Commentary,* 374, suggests that this omission in Codex D and some MSS of the Old Latin and Syriac 'may have been deliberate because offense was taken at the extension of the title to Barnabas, who, moreover, is here mentioned before Paul'.

is using a different source for the narratives in this chapter. When they heard about the intention to offer them sacrifices, *they tore their clothes and rushed out into the crowd, shouting.* Tearing one's clothes was a gesture suggesting that blasphemy was about to be committed (cf. Jdt. 14:16-17; Mt. 26:65; Acts 22:23). As faithful Jews, they were distressed about receiving such homage and detracting from the glory of the one true God (cf. 10:26; Rev. 19:10; 22:9). Unlike Herod in 12:21-23, they aggressively resisted any implication of divine status and significance! So their opening question — *'Friends (Andres, 'Men'), why are you doing this?'* — was answered with an absolute denial of divinity: *'We too are only human, like you'* (*hēmeis homoiopatheis esmen hymin anthrōpoi,* 'we also are people with the same passions as you'; cf. Jas. 5:17). Instead of beginning with the gospel about the saving work of Jesus, they recognised the need to start further back in their presentation of biblical revelation to this audience. Even the outline address that we have is rich in biblical allusions. 'Both this brief speech and the longer speech in Athens (17:22-31) show careful reflection on the problem of approaching Gentiles who do not share the biblical story nor Judaism's belief in one God, major premises for other speeches in Acts.'[26]

They begin their appeal with the familiar claim to be *'bringing you good news'* (*euangelizomenoi hymas,* as in 13:32). However, the message here is not about God fulfilling his promises to Israel and sending the messianic Saviour, but good news about the possibility of escaping from the futility of idolatry (*'these worthless things'*),[27] and coming to know *'the living God, who made heaven and earth and sea and everything in them'* (cf. Ex. 20:11; Ps. 146:6; Acts 4:24; 17:24). Forgiveness and reconciliation are not mentioned, though the call to *'turn'* (*epistrephein,* as in 3:19; 1 Thes. 1:9; cf. 17:30, *metanoein,* 'to repent') from idols to the living God implies seeking a relationship with him (cf. turning to the Lord [9:35; 11:21]; turning to God [15:19; 26:18]). Conversion involves turning away from every alternative object of devotion and turning *'to the living God'* (*epi theon zōnta*), who created everything.[28] Idolatry is condemned in Scripture because it 'diminishes the divine to human size (as in the mistaken identification of Barnabas and Paul with divinities) and makes God dependent on human actions and subject to human control'.[29]

---

26. Tannehill 1990, 179.

27. The expression *these worthless things (toutōn tōn mataiōn)* refers to idols and the gods they represent as dangerous vanities. The *mataios* word group denotes 'the world of appearance as distinct from that of being' (O. Bauernfeind, *TDNT* 4:519). The terminology is used in the LXX to convey the sense that idolatry is 'worthless' because it is deceptive and ineffectual (e.g., Lv. 7:17 [TNIV 'the goat idols']; 1 Ki. 16:13; Je. 2:5; 10:1-5; Hos. 5:11), provoking God's anger. In the NT, 'everything which resists the first commandment comes under the judgment of *mataios*' (Bauernfeind, 522). Cf. Rom. 1:21; 1 Cor. 3:20 (citing Ps. 94:11); Tit. 3:9; 1 Pet. 1:18.

28. Such language was a challenge to the belief that Zeus was the god who gave life (his name derives from the word *zōē,* 'life'). Cf. Witherington 1998, 426 note 290.

29. Tannehill 1990, 179. Tannehill's excellent commentary on this passage is spoiled

16-17   When Paul asserts that *'in the past (en tais parōchēmenais geneais,* 'in generations gone by'), *he let all nations go their own way',* he is not claiming that their ignorance and rebellion were ignored by God and without consequence (cf. 17:30-31 note). Since, in biblical teaching, his involvement in the life of Israel was for blessing and salvation, his abandonment of the nations 'to go their own ways' (the plural *tais hodois* suggests a diversity of options) was a curse and an anticipation of final judgment (cf. Rom. 1:18-32; 2:1-11). God did not provide the nations with special revelation, such as he gave to Israel, and did not directly offer them a way of salvation, though Israel was always meant to be a source of blessing for the nations (cf. Gn. 12:3). The expression *in the past* hints at a new situation in which Jesus Christ brings redemption for Jews and Gentiles alike, but Paul does not get the chance to develop that idea because of the reaction of the audience (v. 18). Rather, he claims that, even in the face of ignorance and rebellion, God has not left himself *'without testimony' (amartyron),* meaning that 'in the bounty of nature there was testimony to both the being and the nature of God'.[30] God has continued to show *'kindness (agathourgōn,* 'doing good'), *by giving you rain from heaven and crops in their seasons'.* Something of God's character is demonstrated in the regular provision of life's necessities. The result of this care is that *'he provides you with plenty of food and fills your hearts with joy' (empiplōn trophēs kai euphrosynēs tas kardias hymōn,* 'filling your hearts with food and gladness'; cf. Pss. 145:15-16; 147:7-9; Je. 5:24). God's goodness is experienced by everyone who enjoys the benefits of living in his creation. The pleasures of life are an encouragement to believe in a beneficent Creator To worship and serve created things rather than the Creator is the essence of sin, and in Romans 1:18-25 it is the reason why God abandoned the nations to the consequences of their rebellion.

Despite the parallels with the speech in 17:22-31 and Paul's report in 1 Thessalonians 1:9, Barrett concludes that 'it must be considered doubtful whether the Paul who is known to us from the epistles was accustomed to make, even to Gentiles, an approach that owed so much to natural theology'.[31] However, such an argument minimises the significance of Paul's

---

by the observation that Paul 'does not harshly condemn their religious histories'. Marshall 1980, 239, similarly argues that God 'did not regard their ignorance of himself as culpable'. This is hardly consistent with the theme of imminent judgment in 17:30-31 and the scriptural condemnation of idolatry which Tannehill rightly perceives to be the background to Paul's challenge in 14:15.

30. Barrett 1994, 682. M. Soards, *The Speeches in Acts: Their Content, Context and Concerns* (Louisville: John Knox/Westminster, 1994), 90, notes a similarity to the argument in 17:25-27 about the potential to discern God because of his 'witnesses'.

31. Barrett 1994, 665, following Haenchen 1971, 89, proposes that the speech reflects use made by some Christians of Hellenistic Jewish apologetic material. Barrett, 680, claims that the speech uses the language of Scripture to 'express thoughts which some at least among the more thoughtful of their Gentiles hearers would recognize as accepted by Greek philosophical monotheists'. But this fails to acknowledge the parallels with Paul's way of arguing in passages such as Rom. 1:18-25; 1 Cor. 8:4-6; 1 Thes. 1:9-10, and the fact that these

biblical allusions and subtle links with his gospel presentations elsewhere. Starting where the Bible does, with God as creator of all, Paul implies that human beings were created to be in a relationship with God (Genesis 1–2). Idolatry is condemned as a wilful distortion of the truth about God and as a futile way of life (cf. Is. 41:21-29; 44:9-20; Rom. 1:18-25). The daily experience of God's *kindness* in the created order should teach us to thank him and honour him as God (e.g., Psalms 104, 145). The challenge to turn from worthless things to serve the living and true God offers hope of reconciliation before the final judgment of God falls on human rebellion. If Paul had been able to continue, he would doubtless have related this teaching to the coming of Christ and the possibility of forgiveness, as well as to the prospect of his return to judge (cf. 1 Thes. 1:9-10). What we have here is not evangelism in the normal NT sense of proclaiming Christ and his saving work. However, it is a biblical foundation for evangelism in a culture where fundamental presuppositions about God and nature and the meaning of human existence need to be challenged. This is not simply an argument from creation for a pre-gospel era.[32] Evangelists and preachers in many contexts today have much to learn from this approach, using the evidence of God's common grace in the sustaining fruitfulness of nature and the pleasures of everyday life as a basis for communication. For people who are far removed from the Bible and its way of looking at things, this may be the only starting point for an appeal to acknowledge *'the living God, who made heaven and earth and sea and everything in them'*.[33]

18-20 The people of Lystra were so awestruck by the miracle that, even with a disclaimer of divinity and a clear challenge to turn to the living and true God, Paul and Barnabas *had difficulty keeping the crowd from sacrificing to them.* Pagan superstition moved the Lycaonians to offer misdirected homage to the visitors until *some Jews came from Antioch and Iconium and won the crowd over.* The antagonism of these Jews can be measured by the fact that they travelled more than a hundred miles (160 km.) to oppose the missionaries and were unimpressed by any attempt to turn the pagans of Lystra to the worship of the God of Scripture.[34] Once again, Jewish opponents were able to persuade Gentiles to join them in hindering the progress of the gospel (cf. 13:50; 14:2, 5-6). In a quick reversal of their appraisal of the visitors, the Lycaonians *stoned Paul and dragged him outside the city, thinking*

---

simple biblical arguments are being used as a proclamation of special revelation ('bringing you good news'), to bring about conversion ('to turn').

32. Cf. Marshall 1980, 239. Witherington 1998, 426, describes it as 'a speech summary that includes only the introductory matter of a deliberative speech and a brief *narratio*, explaining what God has done for the pagans in the past (vv. 15c-17)', and seeking a change of behaviour 'in the near future'.

33. Cf. Stott 1990, 232.

34. Metzger, *Textual Commentary*, 374-75, discusses the additions to 14:19-20 in the Western text, which are clearly secondary attempts to smooth out the narrative and make it more plausible. Witherington 1998, 427 note 295, deals with objections to the report that Jewish objectors travelled so far to oppose Paul and Barnabas.

he was dead (cf. 2 Cor. 11:25; 2 Tim. 3:11; and possibly Gal. 6:17). This physical attack was presumably directed at Paul alone, because he was the one who had healed the lame man and had called for an abandonment of their traditional gods. Luke is careful to point out that the crowd left *thinking he was dead*, when he was actually only unconscious or semi-conscious.[35] *But after the disciples had gathered round him, he got up and went back into the city.* It is likely that Luke has not told us the whole story of Paul's ministry in Lystra and that there were converts who cared for him in their homes (14:21-22; 16:1-2 suggest that there were *disciples* in Lystra). Otherwise, *the disciples* who helped Paul were members of his team, perhaps joined by converts from other places who had followed him. One way or the other, his return to the city was a sign of God's care and deliverance and an expression of Paul's own trust and confidence.[36] *The next day he and Barnabas left for Derbe,* a journey of about 60 miles (97 km.) southeast of Lystra.[37] No mention is made of others here because Paul and Barnabas are consistently regarded as the key figures in the mission team.

E. Revisiting the Churches (14:21-28)

This passage gives a brief insight into the way Paul strengthened new converts and established a pattern of leadership for the congregations he had founded. The warning about enduring hardships is particularly powerful in the light of the suffering endured by Paul and Barnabas in the preceding narratives. Example and exhortation are brought together in this way. Their return to Antioch in Syria marks the end of the first missionary journey and provides the opportunity for encouraging that church with news of what God had done through them. Whatever their success in winning Jews, the whole campaign is evaluated in terms of opening 'a door of faith to the Gentiles' (v. 27). This indicates a new and more extensive impact of the gospel on the Gentile world than was witnessed previously (11:19-26).

21-22 Paul and Barnabas preached the good news in Derbe *and won a large number of disciples (mathēteusantes hikanous,* 'discipled many'; NRSV, ESV, 'made many disciples'). The Greek verb *mathēteusantes* ('discipled') occurs only here and in Matthew 13:52; 27:57; 28:19. In the present context it implies a process of teaching and training beyond evangelising *(euangelizomenoi),* an example of which is given in v. 22. The ministry in Derbe appears to have been unhindered by Jews from Antioch and Iconium. Presumably, the state in which they left Paul (14:19) convinced his opponents

---

35. Spencer 1997, 150, notes how the persecutor of Stephen is stoned, dragged out of a city, and left for dead, though his ultimate destiny is different from Stephen's.

36. Johnson 1992, 256, describes Paul's return as a sign of his 'indefatigable faith and loyalty'.

37. Bruce 1990, 325; Marshall 1980, 240. Witherington 1998, 418 note 250, details the dispute about the precise location of Derbe.

that he was no longer a threat, and they left Lystra to return to their own cities. Derbe lay on the eastern border of Galatia (cf. v. 20 note). Instead of continuing further east and reaching Syria through Cilicia, Paul and Barnabas *returned to Lystra, Iconium and Antioch, strengthening the disciples and encouraging them to remain true to the faith* (emmenein tē pistei, 'to continue in the faith'; cf. 11:23, 'to continue with the Lord'; 13:43; 'to continue in the grace of God'). This journey was necessary because continuing persecution made it difficult for new converts to survive and flourish. 'Luke makes no comment on their courage in revisiting so soon cities in which they had received such shameful treatment; his matter-of-fact statement that they stopped at each of them is eloquent enough.'[38] Confining their ministry to believers in these places of conflict, Paul and Barnabas did not stir up any further opposition. Two further visits to these South Galatian churches are recorded in 16:1-6; 18:23. It is also likely that Paul's letter to the Galatians was written to them in the period before the Jerusalem Council, when Paul was back in Syrian Antioch (14:28).[39]

Here we have a brief record of the sort of pastoral care offered to newly formed congregations.[40] Paul's role as pastor is more fully presented in 20:18-35. We know from his letters that Paul believed God would keep those who were genuinely converted *true to the faith* (cf. 1 Cor. 1:4-9; Phil. 1:6; 1 Thes. 1:2-10). However, he knew that his own prayers and teaching were part of the process by which God would sustain them (cf. Phil. 1:9-11, 27-30; 1 Thes. 2:17–3:13). *Strengthening (epistērizontes)* is mentioned again in 15:32, together with *encouraging (parakalountes)*, as a ministry of prophets to believers. Strengthening the churches was also the aim of Paul and Silas on their journey through Syria and Cilicia in 15:41 (cf. 16:4-5; 18:23). In 14:22 it is specifically 'the souls of the disciples' *(tas psychas tōn mathētōn)* that need strengthening, meaning the disciples in their inner lives or individual selves before God.[41] There is an individual and a corporate strengthening which can be accomplished by a ministry of exhortation.[42] We find this em-

38. Bruce 1990, 326.

39. Cf. Bruce 1982, 43-56; Witherington 1998, 86-97.

40. Stott 1990, 235-39, discusses the implications of this passage for contemporary missiological strategy and practice.

41. Luke uses *psychē* quite extensively, as a term for whole persons (e.g., Acts 2:41, 47; 3:23; 7:14; 27:37), as a reference to the life bound up with flesh and blood (e.g., Lk. 14:26; 17:33; Acts 15:26; 20:10, 24; 27:10, 22), and as a way of identifying the inner life or self (e.g., Lk. 1:46; 2:35; 10:27; Acts 4:32; 14:2; 15:24 [TNIV *minds*]). Like the 'heart' in biblical teaching, the soul is 'equally the locus of faith as it is of confusion or stimulation, of joy or sorrow' (E. Schweizer, *TDNT* 9:637-56 [640]), since it can praise God (Lk. 1:46), love God (Lk. 10:27), and be exhorted to continue in the faith, despite hardship and opposition.

42. Cf. 9:31, where different terminology is used. The Greek verb *parakalein* has a wide range of meanings, including 'comfort', 'encourage', 'exhort', and even 'admonish'. Cf. O. Schmitz, *TDNT* 5:793-99; D. G. Peterson, 'The Ministry of Encouragement', in P. T. O'Brien and D. G. Peterson (eds.), *God Who Is Rich in Mercy: Essays Presented to Dr. D. B. Knox* (Sydney: ANZEA, 1986), 235-53. Clearly the context in case must determine the appropriate

phasis in some of Paul's letters, as well as here in Luke's brief report of what the missionaries said by way of warning: *'We must go through many hardships to enter the kingdom of God'* (cf. Lk. 9:23-27; Rom. 8:17; Phil. 1:28-30; 1 Thes. 3:3; 2 Thes. 1:5). As in other contexts, the *must* (*dei*, as in Lk. 24:46-47; Acts 17:3; cf. 9:15-16) refers to the divine plan. 'The implication seems to be that the persecution of believers is to be understood as consistent with God's plan, not that it is an entrance requirement that believers must meet by virtue of their own conscious choice.'[43] There is a clear reminder here of the theological context in which the Christian life is to be pursued: the gospel provides a certainty about entering *the kingdom of God*. Even though it is only occasionally mentioned in Acts (1:3; 8:12; 14:22; 19:8; 20:25; 28:23, 31), the kingdom remains the theological framework in which to understand and proclaim Christ (cf. 1:3 note). In the present context it specifically refers to the restoration of all things associated with the return of Christ (3:21; cf. 1:11) and functions as an equivalent for eternal life (13:46, 48).[44] Final entrance into that kingdom will be *through many hardships (dia pollōn thlipseōn)* for those who continue to believe in the face of hostility and opposition. 'The tribulations through which Christians must pass recall the Jewish apocalyptic theme of the Messianic affliction, the travail pains of the Messiah, which must precede the good time to come, a theme which formed an important starting point for the Christian understanding of the suffering and death of Jesus as well as of the sufferings of Christians themselves.'[45] Thus, genuine Christian encouragement is properly a blend of theology and exhortation, gospel and challenge (cf. 20:18-32; Heb. 3:12-14; 10:19-25; 13:22). As noted previously, this report of Paul's ministry in the churches of Lystra, Iconium, and Antioch has an important literary function in Luke's narrative. Persecution has been reported as a regular feature of the ministry of Paul and Barnabas and now the warning about enduring such hardship is implicitly given to Christian readers (cf. 2 Tim. 3:11-12).[46]

23 When Paul and Barnabas *appointed elders for them in each church*, in the context of the preceding exhortation, it was clearly to strengthen the

---

rendering. The more specific sense of 'exhort' is appropriate in 14:22 because of the nature of the ministry that follows. Cf. 13:15; 16:40; 20:1, 2.

43. Gaventa 2003, 209.

44. Barrett 1994, 686, describes it as 'the final state of blessedness into which believers may hope to enter if they continue in faith and in the grace of God'. Cf. Lk. 18:24-25. Witherington 1998, 428-29, observes that Luke faithfully presents this aspect of Paul's preaching and teaching (cf. 1 Cor. 6:9-10; 15:10), even though entering the kingdom is not the way Luke himself normally talks about the future.

45. Barrett 1994, 686. Tannehill 1990, 181, similarly notes the use of the Greek *dei* ('must') in the teaching of Jesus about his own suffering (e.g., Lk. 9:22; 17:25; 24:7) and in the words spoken about Paul in Acts 9:16. Jesus suffered in accordance with a pattern of prophetic destiny that applied also to Paul and Barnabas. In 14:22 they warn that this must also apply to other Christians.

46. Cf. S. Cunningham, *'Through many tribulations': The Theology of Persecution in Luke-Acts,* JSNTSS 142 (Sheffield: Sheffield Academic, 1997), 245-47.

believers in their stand for Christ. The verb *cheirotonēsantes (appointed)* means 'stretch out the hand' and came to be used of voting, choosing, and so appointment to office.[47] The laying on of hands is conveyed by another expression (cf. 13:3 note). However, the addition of the words *with prayer and fasting, committed them to the Lord, in whom they had put their trust* implies some form of ordination to special responsibility and service (cf. 20:17, 28). Some doubt the authenticity of this verse because they dispute the Pauline authorship of the Pastorals and argue that 'the genuine Pauline epistles' never speak of elders.[48] Barrett takes this position and adds that no elders are mentioned in the description of the church in 13:1-3.[49] This argument from silence is weak because Luke so often delays mention of such details until they are particularly relevant. Furthermore, it is possible that Paul and Barnabas were establishing new patterns of leadership in these churches because their foundation was so different from that of the sending church (11:19-26). Luke constantly mentions the elders of the Jewish people (4:5, 8, 23; 6:12; 23:14; 24:1; 25:15), and records a pattern of eldership in the church at Jerusalem (11:30; 15:2, 4, 6, 22, 23; 16:4; 21:18). The latter must have provided something of a model for the Gentiles churches (cf. 11:30 note).[50] It is also noteworthy that 'elders' in 20:17 *(presbyteroi)* are also called 'overseers' *(episkopoi,* 20:28), which is the more common Pauline word for congregational leaders (cf. Phil. 1:1; 1 Tim. 3:2; Tit. 1:7). Luke reveals an overlap of terminology such as we find in the Pastoral Epistles (compare Tit. 1:5 with 1:7 and 1 Tim. 3:2 with 5:17, 19).[51]

24-28 *After going through Pisidia* — 'a wild area where there was probably little opportunity for evangelism'[52] — *they came into Pamphylia,* which was south of Pisidia. There they *preached the word in Perga,* apparently for the first time (cf. 13:13 note). Finally, *they went down to Attalia*

---

47. Bruce 1990, 326. Cf. Plutarch, *Phocion* 34 (758); Xenophon, *Hellenica* 6.2.11; Lucian, *De Morte Peregrini* 41; Acts 10:41; 2 Cor. 8:19; Ignatius, *Phil.* 10:1, *Smyrn.* 11:2, *Pol.* 7:2; *Did.* 15:1; Philo, *On the Life of Joseph* 248; *On the Life of Moses* 1.198.

48. Haenchen 1971, 436, assuming a late date for the Pastorals, says that 'Luke has simply taken for granted that the ecclesiastical constitution of his own day already existed in the time of Paul'.

49. Barrett 1994, 666. He notes from 1 Thes. 5:12-13 that Paul made leadership arrangements for the churches he founded but argues that Luke supplied the term 'elders', which had become current in the church of his day. Cf. Marshall 1980, 241.

50. Spencer 1997, 152, takes Luke to mean that 'even in the Diaspora among developing, mixed communities of Jews and Gentiles, the Pauline mission maintains certain structural associations, if not official ties, with the Jewish capital in Jerusalem'.

51. Cf. L. Coenen, *NIDNTT* 1:188-201. Confidence about Pauline authorship of the Pastorals provides confidence that Luke is not far from the same perspective on congregational leadership. Witherington 1998, 430-38, offers an extended discussion of the relationship between the Paul of Acts and the Paul of the Letters.

52. Cf. Marshall 1980, 242. The Western text also adds that they preached the gospel in Attalia (cf. Metzger, *Textual Commentary,* 376), but because of limited attestation this must be regarded as not part of the original. Note also the additions to 14:27 discussed by Barrett 1994, 691-92.

(modern Antalya), which was the adjacent port on the Mediterranean coast. From there they sailed back to Antioch in Syria, *where they had been committed to the grace of God for the work they had now completed.* Luke's language here helps us to understand more of the significance of the commissioning in 13:3. First, he records that they had been 'handed over to the grace of God' *(paradedomenoi tē chariti tou theou)* for the work which was now completed. This suggests a very specific plan for the first missionary journey. Here *the grace of God* refers to God's protective care (cf. 15:40; 20:32) and his enabling for ministry (4:33; 6:8) Secondly, *they gathered the church together and reported all that God had done through them,* suggesting that the whole church had been involved in sending them out, in response to God's call.[53] Reporting back was a way of encouraging those believers to see how God in his grace had been answering their prayers. Reviewing their experiences, Paul and Barnabas were able to see the hand of God in everything that had happened. In particular, what God had *done through them (met᾿autōn,* 'with them') was to bring many to faith, so that churches were planted and patterns of leadership established over a wide area (cf. 15:4, 12). A key aspect of this is described in terms of God opening *a door to faith to the Gentiles* (cf. 15:9, 11). Although Luke has highlighted some success in ministry to Jews on this campaign, it is the amazing gift of faith to so many Gentiles that is the focus of this report (cf. 11:18 note).[54] Since the implied audience is a predominantly Gentile church in Antioch, where 'a great number of people believed and turned to the Lord' (11:21), the 'door of faith' image must refer to something new: a deep and extensive impact of the gospel on the Gentile world. With the two expressions *all that God had done through them* and *a door to faith to the Gentiles,* Luke prepares us for the debate to follow in the Jerusalem Council regarding the status of Gentiles in the church. 'The emphasis on "faith" *(pistis)* not only picks up a major theme of the entire section (see 13:8, 12, 39, 41, 48; 14:1, 9, 22, 23), but prepares for the formal statement concerning faith as the principle of salvation in 15:9, 11.'[55] Finally, the importance placed on the pastoral care of churches by Paul and Barnabas is once again indicated by mention of their long stay with the disciples at Antioch *(chronon ouk oligon,* 'no little time').[56] They settled back

53. Barrett 1994, 691, rightly suggests that the word *ekklēsia* ('church') here 'may have the special sense of the *assembled* body of Christians'. He also notes that the disciples (v. 28) are the church 'resolved into its individual components' (693).

54. Barrett 1994, 692, notes that the genitive *pisteōs* could be objective *(leading to faith;* so TNIV), subjective *(where faith enters),* or appositional *(a door [into salvation] consisting of faith;* so NRSV, ESV). However, he rightly insists that it would be a mistake to be too precise. Here Luke means that 'Gentiles may believe, and thereby receive all the blessings to which faith leads'. Paul uses 'door' metaphorically in 1 Cor. 16:9; 2 Cor. 2:12; Col. 4:3, in each case signifying an opportunity or opening provided by God.

55. Johnson 1992, 255.

56. Luke once again uses a figure of speech called litotes, by which an affirmative is expressed by the negative of the contrary. Cf. 12:18 note.

into the task of nurturing the church until the advent of false teachers made it necessary for them to journey to Jerusalem (15:1-4).

F. The Jerusalem Council (15:1-35)

The Jerusalem Council has been described as 'the turning-point, "centre-piece" and "watershed" of the book, the episode which rounds off and justifies the past developments, and makes those to come intrinsically possible'.[1] Contextually, the narrative (15:1-35) is framed by Paul's first missionary journey (13:1–14:28) and his second campaign (15:36–18:22).[2] More broadly, the Gentile mission set in motion by Peter's preaching to Cornelius, the growth of the church at Antioch in Syria, and Paul's first missionary journey had created problems about the status of Gentile converts and their relationship with Jewish Christians. These issues had to be resolved before the work of Paul could continue and new initiatives could be taken with the gospel. Various rhetorical and spatial elements have been identified which help to determine the structure of 15:1-35. The narrative begins and ends in Antioch (vv. 1-2, 30-35).

A dispute arises in the church about whether Gentiles need to be circumcised, and thus become Jewish proselytes, in order to be saved. The issue emanates from Judea and is so serious that Paul and Barnabas are appointed along with other believers to go up to Jerusalem to see the apostles and elders about this question (vv. 1-2). 'Theologically and spatially, Jerusalem is critical for an understanding of Acts 15.'[3] Jerusalem is both the source of the problem and the place where it is resolved. The debate about the question occurs twice, following a similar pattern. There is

1. Haenchen 1971, 461. Haenchen overstates the subordination to Jerusalem of the various missions and churches mentioned in Acts 8–14, but he rightly points to the changes after Acts 15: 'not only does Peter make his last appearance here, the Apostles also are mentioned for the last time in reference to the decree at 16.4. Both are henceforth replaced by James and the elders.' Marshall 1980, 242, says the account of the assembly at Jerusalem 'forms the centre of Acts both structurally and theologically'.

2. A. T. M. Cheung, 'A Narrative Analysis of Acts 14:27–15:35: Literary Shaping in Luke's Account of the Jerusalem Council', *WTJ* 55 (1993), 139-44, argues that the narrative of the first missionary journey ends at 14:26 and that the first episode of the next section is 14:27–15:2. However, this leads him to make an unwarranted assumption about the silence of the church at Antioch concerning the mission report (14:27-28), in contrast with the joy of the churches in Phoenicia and Samaria about the same news (15:3). 14:27-28 is a bridge between narratives and nothing is to be read into the fact that Luke concludes the section without mentioning any celebration at Antioch. Cheung, 142, proposes a somewhat artificial structure based on the idea that four mission reports (14:27; 15:3; 15:4; 15:12) introduce four episodes leading to disputes and resolutions.

3. E. Richard, 'The Divine Purpose: The Jews and the Gentile Mission (Acts 15)', in C. H. Talbert (ed.), *Luke-Acts: New Perspectives from the Society of Biblical Literature Seminar* (New York: Crossroad, 1984), 190. I am indebted to Richard's structural observations, though I disagree with his conclusion about the application of the law to Gentile Christians.

first a statement of the problem (vv. 1, 5),[4] followed by a dispute (vv. 2a, 7a), and then a report about the conversion of the Gentiles (vv. 2b-3, 7b-11), concluding with a recognition of what God has done among the Gentiles (vv. 4, 12). In the first round of the debate the concerns are pastoral (vv. 1-4), but in the second round the discussion is more theological (vv. 5-12). The speech of James (vv. 13-21) is a sequel to the second round of the debate and the centre-piece of the chapter, directing attention to the more fundamental matter of God's purpose for Jews and Gentiles, as revealed in Scripture.[5] Luke demonstrates the unanimity of the Christian community as the debates proceed, leading to a resolution in vv. 22-29.[6] James submits two proposals, arising from his use of Amos 9:11-12. The first is a formal rejection of the demand of the Judaizers (v. 19) and the second is a way for Gentiles to take account of Jewish concerns without compromising their freedom from the Mosaic law (vv. 20-21). The resolution of the problem involves a decision to send representatives back to Antioch with Paul and Barnabas (vv. 22-23a), with a letter conveying the proposals of James (vv. 23b-29). Conciliation, encouragement and the strengthening of believers in Antioch is the outcome (vv. 30-35). So the attempt to assimilate Gentile Christianity into Judaism is opposed and a way by which Jewish and Gentile believers can live together is agreed. At the same time, the council succeeds in examining 'the fundamental role that Judaism plays within the world-wide mission'.[7] Acts 15 concludes with a frank acknowledgement of the sharp disagreement between Paul and Barnabas over John Mark, resulting in the formation of two new mission teams (vv. 36-41). Paul begins his second missionary journey in partnership with Silas.

There are a number of issues that need to be addressed as the exposition proceeds. First, there are questions regarding the historicity of Luke's account and the significance of the so-called Apostolic Decree. For example, there are three versions (15:20; 15:29; 21:25), which do not agree precisely in

4. Each statement of the problem is made by a Jewish group, making fundamental demands on Jewish converts (vv. 1, 5). The Pharisees in v. 5 go a step further in terms of the demand for Gentile converts to keep the law of Moses.

5. Richard, 'Divine Purpose', 192-95, shows how various elements in the chapter, such as statements about the actions of God and temporal references in relation to the unfolding of God's will, continue to elaborate the divine purpose as it relates to Jews and the Gentile mission. Spencer 1997, 153-54, sees this four-act structure in the passage: Dissension (Antioch and Jerusalem, 15:1-5); Discussion (Jerusalem, 15:6-18); Decision (Jerusalem, 15:19-29); Dissemination (Antioch and Southern Asia Minor, 15:30–16:5).

6. R. E. Brown, K. P. Donfried, and J. Reumann, *Peter in the New Testament: A Collaborative Assessment by Protestant and Roman Catholic Scholars* (London: Geoffrey Chapman, 1973), 50, argue that 'the overriding theme in this chapter, as elsewhere in Acts, is found in the term *homothymadon*, "one-mindedness" (15:25)'. *homothymadon* is found in 1:14; 2:1 (some MSS); 2:46; 4:24; 5:12; 7:57; 8:6; 12:20; 15:25; 18:12; 19:29, sometimes also with the sense of physical assembly.

7. Richard, 'Divine Purpose', 201.

content and word order, and there are significant textual variants for each of these versions. Secondly, there is the problem of relating this account to the evidence in Galatians 2:1-14 and the fact that Paul apparently makes no reference to the decree in his writings, suggesting to some scholars that Paul either did not know about it or did not agree with it.[8] Thirdly, there is the issue of overall meaning and application. At a narrative level, Luke shows us 'the early Church reaching decision by means of an articulation of its faith, as a process of *discernment* of God's activity'.[9] Some would argue that the most significant, ongoing relevance of Acts 15 is as a model for theological argument and ecclesial decision making. But the chapter also raises questions about the role of the Mosaic law in the Christian community, the nature of the church, and the role of the Holy Spirit in revealing new truths. These and other hermeneutical matters will be discussed in an additional note (pp. 442-46).

1. The Need for the Council (15:1-5)

The previous pattern of blessing coming from Judea to Antioch and being reciprocated (11:19-30) is overtaken by another. Disturbing teaching about the need for Gentiles to be circumcised if they are to be saved arrives in Antioch (v. 1). When Paul and Barnabas make their second journey to Jerusalem, it is for the purpose of questioning the apostles and elders about this challenge and establishing the freedom of Gentiles from the demands of the Mosaic law (v. 2). The positive reception they get in Phoenicia, Samaria, and Jerusalem to news about the conversion of the Gentiles (vv. 3-4) highlights the seriousness of the challenge from certain 'believers who belonged to the party of the Pharisees' (v. 5).

1 *Certain individuals came down from Judea to Antioch and were teaching the believers: 'Unless you are circumcised, according to the custom taught by Moses, you cannot be saved'.*[10] From its earliest days, the church at Antioch

8. Barrett 1998, xxxvi-xli, provides a summary of the sort of problems perceived by many scholars and offers an account that has Luke writing 'honest history but writing in an atmosphere different from that of the period that he described' (xli). Johnson 1992, 269-70, makes a brief attempt to deal with some of the historical questions that need to be answered, but concludes that we are able to 'engage the author's narrative perspective and thereby engage a quality of narrative "truth" which is not confined to referential accuracy'. However, evangelical writers have not been content to leave the question of historicity so unresolved. Cf. Bruce 1990, 329-32; Witherington 1998, 77-97, 439-70.

9. Johnson 1992, 271. Cf. L. T. Johnson, *Decision Making in the Church: A Biblical Model* (Philadelphia: Fortress, 1983), 46-58, 67-87.

10. Barrett 1998, 698, suggests that Judea may be intended 'in an ethnic rather than a strictly geographical sense; they came from Jewish territory and may therefore be expected to represent a Jewish point of view'. The Western text of v. 1 identifies them as travelling members of the Pharisaic party introduced in v. 5. The language of 'going up' (*anerchesthai*, or *anabainein*, as in v. 2) and 'coming down' (*katerchesthai*, as in vv. 1, 30) to and from Jerusalem was used for pilgrimages. These teachers doubtless saw themselves as coming from the holy city to set things straight in the provinces!

contained uncircumcised Gentiles as well as Jewish believers (11:19-20; cf. Gal. 2:11-14). The church in Jerusalem soon sent Barnabas to investigate developments at Antioch and to encourage the ministry there (11:22-24). Prophets later came down from Jerusalem to Antioch, to contribute to the life of the church (11:27; 13:1). One of them predicted a severe famine in Judea, provoking the Christians to send Paul and Barnabas with practical aid (11:28-30). This was probably the visit to Jerusalem mentioned by Paul in Galatians 2:1-10,[11] where he set before James, Peter, and John the gospel he preached among the Gentiles and they 'added nothing' to his message. They acknowledged a common gospel and a God-given partnership in the work, with the Jerusalem leaders broadly accepting responsibility for ministry to Jews, and Paul and Barnabas ministry to Gentiles. On this occasion, even Titus, who was with the team from Antioch, was not compelled to be circumcised, though pressure was applied by some 'false believers' who had infiltrated the situation. We cannot be certain when the next incident mentioned by Paul in Galatians 2:11-14 took place, though it is most likely to have been before the resolutions of the Jerusalem Council brought public agreement between Peter, James, Paul, and Barnabas on such matters. Paul accused Peter, Barnabas, and the other Jewish Christians of 'not acting in line with the truth of the gospel' (Gal. 2:14), because they withdrew from eating with Gentile believers after 'certain people came from James' (2:12).[12] We have no way of knowing how satisfactorily

11. This identification is much disputed, many scholars arguing that Gal. 2:1-10 parallels Acts 15. Thus, for example, Barrett 1998, 711, insists that there are such close parallels between the two passages that 'it is hard to doubt that somewhere behind both lies a single event'. However, this requires him to say that Luke has reversed the order of events found in Galatians: a council involving Paul and Barnabas with James, Peter, and John (Gal. 2:1-10) and then a visit to Antioch by certain people from Judea, who caused a separation between Jewish and Gentile Christians (2:11-14). Cf. J. D. G. Dunn, *The Theology of Paul's Letter to the Galatians* (Cambridge: Cambridge University, 1993), 69-80. The identification of Gal. 2:1-10 with Acts 15 means that Paul provided no parallel to the visit mentioned in Acts 11:29-30, which is hard to believe since he claims to be providing a record of all his contacts with Jerusalem in his appeal to the Galatians. Those who argue persuasively for the identification of Acts 11:29-30 with the Council visit include Longenecker 1981, 440-42; D. Wenham, 'Acts and the Pauline Corpus, II. The Evidence of the Parallels', in B. W. Winter and A. D. Clarke (ed.), *The Book of Acts in Its First-Century Setting*, Vol. 1: *Ancient Literary Setting* (Grand Rapids: Eerdmans; Carlisle: Paternoster, 1993), 226-43; R. Bauckham, 'James and the Jerusalem Church', in R. Bauckham (ed.), *The Book of Acts in Its First-Century Setting*, Vol. 4: *Palestinian Setting* (Grand Rapids: Eerdmans; Carlisle: Paternoster, 1995), 469-70; Witherington 1998, 440-43 (with a chart on pp. 445-49 showing correspondences between the letters of Paul and the evidence in Acts). Witherington shows that there are good reasons for dating Galatians just before the Jerusalem Council in AD 49.

12. These emissaries cannot be identified with the false teachers mentioned in Acts 15:1, since James and the other leaders of the Jerusalem church disassociated themselves from any Judaizing stance (15:24). Whatever the brief from James, the consequence of their visit was uncertainty and division. Those who then troubled the Galatians about the need for circumcision and 'works of the law' (1:6-7; 3:1-3; 5:2-12; 6:12-16) appear to have been a

that issue was resolved before the next serious challenge came from Jerusalem to Antioch through the visit of those mentioned by Luke. Their message was: *'Unless you are circumcised, according to the custom taught by Moses, you cannot be saved'*. Although it is embodied in the Mosaic law (e.g., Lv. 12:3), the command to circumcise 'every male among you' goes back to God's covenant with Abraham (Gn. 17:10-14). The implications of the demand in v. 1 are brought out in v. 5, where it is made clear that circumcision would be the beginning of a life devoted to keeping the law of Moses.[13]

It was widely accepted that Gentiles could become proselytes of Judaism and so share in the blessings promised to Israel. The biblical foundation for this can be seen in passages such as Genesis 17:10-14, 23-27 and Exodus 12:43-45, 48. Male converts would be circumcised, and the whole family would undertake to live in obedience to the law. But these Judaizers had failed to grasp the radical change in God's dealings with the nations brought about by the coming of Christ and the gift of the Holy Spirit (cf. vv. 8-11). The idea that God had granted Gentiles 'repentance that leads to life', without becoming Jewish proselytes, seemed to have been settled by Peter's reflection on the Cornelius incident (11:18). But clearly some Jewish Christians were not persuaded and were insistent that circumcision and all that it entailed was necessary for eternal salvation. 'The issue in chapter 15 is thus not merely post-conversion behaviour but what constitutes true conversion in the first place.'[14] Paul soon wrote to the Christians in Galatia about the same problem, because the false teachers spread their influence through Syria and Cilicia into the towns where Paul and Barnabas had conducted their first missionary campaign (cf. Acts 15:23; 16:1-4).

2-4 The aggressive approach of the Judaizers *brought Paul and Barnabas into sharp dispute and debate with them* (staseōs kai zētēseōs ouk oligēs, 'no small dissension and debate').[15] As well as being concerned about the local

later group, whose agenda was more in line with that of the false teachers mentioned in Acts 15:1, 5. Cf. Bruce 1990, 329-32.

13. The Western text makes a number of additions to Acts 15:1-5, including an extension of the demand being made in v. 1 ('unless you are circumcised *and walk* according to the custom of Moses'). This version also has the visitors from Jerusalem *order* Paul and Barnabas to go up to Jerusalem (v. 2) to give account of themselves before the apostles and elders. Once again, this attempt to smooth out the text and fill in the gaps must be rejected as secondary. Cf. Metzger, *Textual Commentary*, 376-78.

14. S. G. Wilson, *Luke and the Law*, SNTSMS 50 (Cambridge: Cambridge University, 1983), 72.

15. Luke once again uses the figure of speech called litotes, by which an affirmative is expressed by the negative of the contrary. Cf. 12:18 note. The first Greek word used in v. 2 (*stasis*) has the sense of 'dissent', 'conflict', or 'disorder' (cf. Lk. 23:19, 25; Acts 19:40; 23:7, 10), and the second (*zētēsis*) has the sense of 'inquiry' or 'discussion' (cf. 15:7; 1 Tim. 6:4; 2 Tim. 2:23; Tit. 3:9). Related to this last term is the word translated 'question' at the end of v. 2 (*zētēma*). Cf. Johnson 1992, 259; Barrett 1998, 700.

situation, Paul and Barnabas presumably had an eye to the possible impact of the teaching on the churches they had founded elsewhere. Although it is not clear from v. 2 who *appointed* them *to go up to Jerusalem to
see the apostles and elders about this question,* v. 3 says that *the church,* and not
simply its leaders, *sent them on their way.*[16] Those who had united in commissioning Paul and Barnabas for their first missionary campaign, and
had been privileged to hear the report of what God had done through
them (14:26-27), were concerned about a right resolution of this gospel issue. They were also presumably concerned about the deteriorating relationship between their church and the church in Jerusalem. As Paul and
Barnabas travelled through Phoenicia and Samaria,[17] *they told how the
Gentiles had been converted (ekdiēgoumenoi tēn epistrophēn tōn ethnōn,* 'recounting the turning of the Gentiles'). Here we find an anticipation of the
argument in vv. 7-12. Fundamentally, the problem would be solved by recognising that God had been saving Gentiles on the same basis as Jews,
namely though faith in Jesus as the crucified and resurrected Messiah. The
Gentile mission is shown to have had wide support outside Judea *(This
news made all the believers very glad),* and then Luke records that *they were
welcomed by the church and the apostles and elders* in Jerusalem. Only the apostles and elders are mentioned in v. 6, but the whole church participated in
the final decision to send representatives with a letter to the Gentile believers in Antioch, Syria, and Cilicia (v. 22). This suggests that the council
was 'open to all disciples',[18] and that the church in Jerusalem was as much
concerned to resolve the issue as the church in Antioch was. Witherington
notes that the way to resolve conflict in antiquity was to call a meeting of
the assembly of the people (cf. vv. 12, 22), 'and listen to and consider
speeches, following the conventions of deliberative rhetoric', the aim of
which was to overcome *stasis* ('conflict', as in v. 2) and 'produce concord or
unity'.[19] The cumulative effect of vv. 3-4 is to show the positive response of
many Jewish believers to Paul and Barnabas and their work among the

16. Witherington 1998, 452, notes that the verb *propempein (sent them on their way)* can
be used to refer to the giving of provisions and financial aid, to enable people to reach their
intended destination in good order (cf. Rom. 15:24; 1 Cor. 16:6). The journey was about 250
miles long. Barrett 1998, 701, seeks to argue for an identification of Gal. 2:1-10 with the visit
mentioned in Acts 15. But Gal. 2:2 says that Paul and Barnabas went up to Jerusalem on that
visit 'in response to a revelation', which is hard to reconcile with the evidence of Acts 15:2
that they were 'appointed' to go as representatives on the church. Cf. note 11 above.

17. Phoenicia denoted the coastal area of Palestine stretching northwards from Car-
mel and including Tyre and Sidon (cf. 11:19; 21:2). Samaria was on its southern border. Both
areas had been evangelized by Hellenists.

18. Tannehill 1990, 183, noting also that 15:12 refers to 'the multitude' *(to plēthos)* and
that this same expression refers to the church in 15:30. S. G. Wilson, *The Gentiles and the Gentile Mission in Luke-Acts,* SNTSMS 23 (Cambridge: Cambridge University, 1973), 182, suggests that a preliminary meeting of the whole church is envisaged in v. 4 and that the meeting that follows in v. 6 involved only the apostles and elders. However, this could be
countered by noting particularly vv. 12 and 22.

19. Witherington 1998, 450.

Gentiles, as *they reported everything God had done through them* (*met' autōn*, 'with them', as in 14:27; cf. 15:12).

5 In contrast with this widespread support, *some of the believers who belonged to the party* (*hairesis*, as in 5:17) *of the Pharisees stood up and said, 'The Gentiles must be circumcised and required to obey the law of Moses'*. These particular Pharisees had apparently come to believe that Jesus was the Messiah, but had not abandoned their allegiance to Moses and the law.[20] They used the language of necessity *(dei, must)*, implying that this was God's will. Although they appear to extend the demand being made on Gentiles, by including the requirement *to obey the law of Moses*, submission to a totally law-directed life was probably already implied by the initial challenge (15:1; cf. Gal. 5:2-3). In other words, the demand for Gentile Christians to become proselytes of Judaism, which was first made by the visitors to Antioch, was reaffirmed by Pharisees who were members of this general assembly of the church in Jerusalem. At this point Luke appears to reveal that they were the source of the disruptive teaching that had been spreading from Jerusalem to Syria and beyond.

2. The Proceedings of the Council (15:6-29)

This first general council of the church focussed on vital theological issues (vv. 6-18) before providing practical guidance for 'the Gentiles who are turning to God' (vv. 19-21) and expressing this in a pastoral letter from the apostles and elders in Jerusalem to Gentile believers in Antioch, Syria, and Cilicia (vv. 22-29). The challenge about circumcision and keeping the law of Moses (vv. 1, 5) raised important prior questions about God's guidance and the way he saves Jews and Gentiles on the same basis, 'through the grace of our Lord Jesus' and by faith in him (vv. 6-11). Signs and wonders were brought into the discussion to indicate God's validation of preaching the same message to Gentiles as to Jews (v. 12). The climax of this time of theological analysis was the recognition that God had 'intervened to choose a people for his name from the Gentiles', using Amos 9:11-12 as a scriptural explanation and justification (vv. 13-15). This text relates God's purpose for the Gentiles to his plan to restore the line of David and save Israel. Following on from these arguments, James proposes a formal rejection of the demand of the Judaizers and a fourfold challenge to Gentiles not to offend Jews by their behaviour in certain critical ways (vv. 19-21, 28-29). Here is an attempt to allow the gospel free course among Jews and Gentiles, maintain-

---

20. Josephus, *Life* 113, tells of an incident when Jews attempted forced circumcision on Gentiles 'as a condition of residence among them' (cf. *Ant.* 13.258, where a group of Gentiles willingly underwent this procedure). But the Pharisees in Acts 15:5 were presumably relating the necessity for circumcision to the enjoyment of eternal salvation, as were the false teachers mentioned in v. 1. They were probably foremost among those 'zealous for the law' in the Jerusalem church (21:20).

ing a spiritual and practical unity among believers while showing a particular concern for the sensitivities and scruples of Jews.

a. Debate (15:6-21)

6 *The apostles and elders met to consider this question.* As noted above in connection with v. 4, it seems likely that the whole body of believers in Jerusalem was involved at some level in the debate and its outcome (cf. vv. 12, 22). If the council was called and led by *the apostles and elders,* others were present to hear the arguments and be persuaded. Bauckham argues that 'the Jerusalem council presupposes the authority of Jerusalem to decide the issue of Gentile Christians' obedience to the law (Acts 15). Its decision binds not only Antioch and its daughter churches (15:22-31) but also the churches founded by Paul and Barnabas (16:4).'[21] However, such an authority structure is not really evident in the relationship between Jerusalem and the Gentile churches in the preceding narratives, and the letter which is sent to the churches (15:23-9) has a hortatory rather than a legislative tone. With regard to the council itself, Tannehill rightly comments that 'Peter and James play important roles in the decision, but the scene gives the impression that their authority is informal — resting on the respect they have gained and lasting as long as they can persuade their fellow apostles and elders, and the assembly as a whole to follow'.[22] As already noted, Jerusalem is the place where this issue must be decided because the problem emerged from that context. Three speeches together present a single perspective on God's purpose, though the contribution of Paul and Barnabas is given only briefly in narrative form (v. 12).

7-9 Peter made his contribution *after much discussion* (*zētēsis*, 'inquiry'; as in v. 2, where the same word is translated *debate*) had taken place. He first reminded the assembly that *'some time ago God made a choice among you that the Gentiles might hear from my lips the message of the gospel and believe'.*[23] The apostle appealed to common knowledge (*'you know'*) and re-

---

21. Bauckham, 'James and the Jerusalem Church', 450.

22. Tannehill 1990, 184. Barrett 1998, 709, follows B. Gerhardsson, *Memory and Manuscript: Oral Tradition and Written Transmission in Rabbinic Judaism and Early Christianity,* ASNU 22 (Lund: Gleerup, 1964), 249-61, in arguing that the apostles and elders gathered together like a group of rabbis to make an authoritative decision, which was then put to the church for agreement (v. 22). In so doing, the apostles were engaged in 'the ministry of the word' to which they devoted themselves in 6:4. But this view makes the apostles 'the only real decision makers' (Barrett, 713).

23. To enhance the solemnity of the occasion and the authority of Peter, several Western MSS add the words 'in the Holy Spirit'. The scribe of Papyrus 45 has amplified the text by repeating information from 15:2. However, none of these additions can be defended as being part of the original text of 15:7. Cf. Metzger, *Textual Commentary,* 378. Witherington 1998, 453, shows how Peter's speech is an example of deliberative rhetoric, designed to silence those who objected to the Gentile mission. Witherington, 455-56, argues against the proposal that Luke may have been freely composing this speech without the benefit of sources.

garded the issue as having been decided *'some time ago' (aph' hēmerōn archaiōn*, 'from former days'). God demonstrated his will by deliberately choosing that the Gentiles would hear the gospel and believe through Peter's preaching and thus be saved (10:34-43).[24] Peter claims to have a special right to be heard in this debate, and Luke's narrative has shown us why. Even though others were pioneers in evangelising Gentiles (cf. 8:26-40; 11:19-20), Peter had a unique role in receiving the vision about God's will and witnessing the outpouring of God's Spirit in a way that paralleled Pentecost. When he was called to account for entering the house of the uncircumcised and eating with them (11:2-3), he offered a personal recollection of the Cornelius incident (11:4-16), with a brief theological conclusion (11:17). Now he interprets the main events in a distinctly theological way, explaining what God was doing.

God was sovereign in the whole process by which Cornelius and his household were brought to faith in Christ. Most importantly, he 'testified to them' *(emartyrēsan autois) 'by giving the Holy Spirit to them, just as he did to us'* (10:44-47; 11:15-17). The gift of the Spirit was a witness to the Gentiles themselves that they were accepted by God. Indirectly, it was also a testimony to Jews who had received the same Spirit through believing in Jesus that Gentiles were united with them in the New Covenant community.[25] This last point is specifically related to a scriptural truth that would have been acknowledged by everyone present, that God *'knows the heart'* (*kardiognōstēs*, 'knower of the heart'; cf. 1:24; 1 Sa. 16:7; Ps. 139:1-12). God knew what was in the hearts of Cornelius and his household, and he bore witness to their genuine faith in Christ by giving them the Spirit. However, even that faith was the gift of God. Peter's final observation is that God *'did not discriminate between us and them, for he purified their hearts by faith'*. The verb 'to purify' *(katharizein)* was used quite generally in 10:15, 28, with reference to God's cleansing of the Gentiles. Now it is made clear that Gentiles, who were previously unclean because they lacked the purifying benefits of the law, have been cleansed because God enabled them to believe the gospel.[26] God worked in the hearts of Gentiles to provide the

---

24. The verb *exelexato* ('chose') has no direct object, though Johnson 1992, 261, reads *ta ethnē* ('the Gentiles'). It is best to understand the object as the whole accusative and infinitive construction that follows *(akousai ta ethnē . . . kai pisteusai)*, which leads to the sort of translation given by TNIV. Barrett 1998, 714, notes also the way some copyists dealt with the difficulty of the text. Bruce 1990, 335, suggests that the events of Acts 10 could have taken place 'anything up to ten years earlier'.

25. Barrett 1998, 716, rightly comments on the logical outcome: 'since evidently God did not see fit to require circumcision before bestowing his gifts it was not for men to demand it'. The aorist participle *dous* is rightly understood in an instrumental sense by TNIV *(by giving)*. Cf. THE THEOLOGY OF ACTS: III. THE HOLY SPIRIT (pp. 60-65).

26. 'By faith' (v. 9, *tē pistei*) must relate specifically to 'believe' (v. 7, *pisteusai*) and describe the response of Cornelius and his household to the preaching of the gospel. Even though Cornelius had a genuine faith in God before he heard Peter's message (e.g., 10:2-4, 22, 31), his faith became explicitly focussed on Jesus as the promised saviour so that he and

cleansing or purification of life that comes from faith in Christ. Foundationally, this involves believing in the definitive forgiveness of sins, which the crucified and exalted Jesus makes possible (cf. 13:38-39). Unity among Christians at the experiential level is located in the *faith* which God makes possible, and not simply in the gift of the Spirit, which is represented here as a testimony to saving faith. We are 'all one in Christ Jesus' through trust in the same Saviour (Gal. 3:26-29).

10-11 Applying these theological observations to the present situation *(nyn oun, 'now then')*, Peter's rhetorical question implies that the demand for Gentiles to be circumcised and obey the law will provoke God's anger *('why do you try to test God?')*. Putting God to the test *(peirazete ton theon;* cf. Ex. 17:2; Dt. 6:16; Ps. 95:9; Acts 5:9 [Ananias and Sapphira]) is another way of talking about hindering his purpose (cf. 5:39 [Gamaliel's warning]; 11:17 [Peter's previous warning]). Insisting on something which is against his will stretches his patience and invites his judgment. The Greek infinitive *epitheinai* explains how they are testing God *'by putting'* this demand on Gentile believers. Peter implies that the divine command for foreigners to be circumcised, and thus become members of the covenant community (Gn. 17:12-14), has now been superseded by God's action in bringing Gentiles to faith through the preaching of the gospel and giving them his Holy Spirit. God has moved on in his dealings with humanity, and it is sinful to demand obedience to the old way (cf. Gal. 2:18). Peter also insists that the old way was unbearable *('a yoke that neither we nor our fathers have been able to bear').*[27] A yoke was used as a restraint, enabling animals to pull heavy loads. Figuratively, the yoke was used as a metaphor for political or social control (e.g., 2 Chr. 10:10; Ps. 2:3; 1 Tim. 6:1). 'It was therefore already paradoxical for rabbinic Judaism to adopt the image (perhaps as early as Sir. 51:26) as a symbol for the acceptance of responsibility to keep the commandments of Torah (see *Sifra* 57b; *Sifre on Deuteronomy* Re'eh 117; *m. Ber.* 2:2; *Pirke 'Aboth* 3.5).'[28] Jesus used the image differently, challenging the weary and burdened to take his yoke upon them and learn from him, claiming that his yoke was easy and his burden light (Mt. 11:28-30). As the one who came to fulfill the Law and the Prophets (Mt. 5:17), he offered the way that leads to eternal life ('rest for your souls', 11:29). Jesus also criticised the teachers of the law and the Pharisees for placing heavy burdens on the

---

his companions were baptised 'in the name of Jesus Christ' (10:48). The aorist participle *katharisas* is rightly understood by TNIV in a causal sense *(for he purified)*.

27. J. Nolland, 'A Fresh Look at Acts 15.10', *NTS* 27 (1980-81), 105-15, observes that this is the only place in Luke-Acts where *bastazein* means 'endure, put up with'. Peter's point is not the burdensomeness of the law but rather the inability of the Jews to gain salvation through it. However, Witherington 1998, 454, gives reasons why the actual keeping of the law may have been regarded by a Galilean fisherman as being a burden.

28. Johnson 1992, 263. However, Nolland, 'Fresh Look', 111 note 21, insists that the word 'yoke' is used in Jewish sources to denote 'constraining religious obligation without any negative colouring at all'. Cf. Je. 5:5; Sir. 51:26-27.

shoulders of others — in the form of their teaching — and not being willing to lift a finger to help them (cf. Mt. 23:4; Lk. 11:46). Viewing the way of salvation through faith in Christ as the ultimate expression of God's will for his people, Peter spoke quite frankly about the yoke of the law as an obligation his fellow Jews had never really managed to fulfill — 'a yoke which they had not had the strength to carry'.[29] Since God did not require Gentiles who trusted in Jesus to live that way, Peter found it objectionable that some of his fellow Jews wanted to place such a burden on Gentile converts.

Peter concludes his address to the Jerusalem Council with an affirmation that Jews and Gentiles are saved on exactly the same basis: *dia tēs charitos tou kyriou Iēsou pisteuomen sōthēnai kath' hon tropon kakeinoi;* 'through the grace of the Lord Jesus we believe in order to be saved, just as they do'.[30] This echoes the perspective of previous chapters, that the gospel is fundamentally about the grace of God displayed in the person and work of the Lord Jesus (13:43; 14:3; cf. 11:23; 20:24, 32). While this most obviously refers to the historic expression of God's grace in the cross and resurrection of Jesus, the immediate context also suggests that *'the grace of our Lord Jesus'* extends into the present. Whenever and wherever the gospel of God's grace is preached, God himself enables belief and sends his Spirit upon those whom he chooses (cf. 13:48 note). 'Faith itself is of the Lord's gracious appointment.'[31] This applies to Jews as well as to Gentiles, uniting all in a common dependence on God's grace for salvation. Any other demand, such as the Judaizers were making (vv. 1, 5), is a hindrance to God's saving purpose, since it requires something other than trust in *the grace of our Lord Jesus* for salvation (cf. Rom. 3:21–5:11; Gal. 2:15–3:14). Peter's final statement in 15:11 is similar to Paul's assertion in 13:38-39, that God now offers a justification through faith in Christ which was not available through the law of Moses. From Luke's perspective, Peter and Paul were united on this central gospel claim (cf. Gal. 2:15-16), even though Paul is not heard articulating this position in the record that follows. 'What Peter disputed was thus the need to obey the law in order to *be saved;* whether Jews kept it for other reasons was a secondary matter.'[32] This legitimation of the mission to the Gentiles is effectively Peter's last contribution to the narrative of Acts.

---

29. Nolland, 'Fresh Look', 112.

30. Tannehill 1990, 185, follows Nolland, 'Fresh Look', 112-13, in arguing that the standard translation of 15:11 in EVV weakens the sense of *pisteuomen* to 'we think' or 'we are convinced', whereas Peter has already emphasized faith in the preceding speech as the key to salvation. The infinitive *sōthēnai* in this context is best read as a purpose clause ('in order to be saved, just as they do'). Johnson 1992, 263, offers a more awkward translation but agrees that the basic sense is, 'we are believing in order to be saved'.

31. Barrett 1998, 720. Cf. THE THEOLOGY OF ACTS: IV. SALVATION (pp. 65-70).

32. Marshall 1980, 250. Acts 21:20 indicates that many Jewish Christians in Jerusalem were 'zealous for the law', without explaining why. Marshall suggests that 'the force of habit and custom in a strictly Jewish Palestinian environment remained very strong'. We may add that there must have been a concern to keep open the possibilities for evangelising fellow Jews.

12 Whereas previously there had been much dispute (v. 7), Peter's speech produced a significant change in the situation: *the whole assembly became silent* (*pan to plēthos*, 'the whole multitude' is equivalent to 'the church' in vv. 4, 22). 'Luke could mean simply that the company were silenced, but probably intends to suggest that they were convinced and agreed.'[33] TNIV gives the impression that the silence was induced *as they listened to Barnabas and Paul telling about the miraculous signs and wonders God had done among the Gentiles through them.* However, the connective *kai* is obscured by this translation, but captured by NRSV and ESV ('the whole assembly kept silence *and* listened to Barnabas and Paul'). Peter's argument had a profound impact and prepared them all to listen attentively to the confirming evidence of Barnabas and Paul. Their contribution to the council was limited, probably because they were regarded by the Judaizers as the main reason for the inclusion of Gentiles in the church without circumcision. In Luke's account they bring no theological argument, because Peter has already persuasively done so.[34] Paul is named after Barnabas, perhaps reflecting the order in which they spoke, giving a brief report of what *God had done among the Gentiles through them.*[35] This summary statement (cf. v. 4) supports Peter's argument about God working powerfully among the Gentiles (vv. 7-9). Note what Paul says in Romans 15:19; 2 Corinthians 12:12; and Galatians 3:5 about the verifying impact of *signs and wonders.* Specific mention of signs and wonders *among the Gentiles* is significant in view of the association of such events with the establishment of Israel as God's people at the time of the exodus (e.g., Dt. 4:34; 26:8) and the renewal of Israel through the preaching of the gospel and the pouring out of the Spirit at Pentecost.[36] The argument of Peter and the testimony of Barnabas and Paul ultimately led James to claim that God had chosen 'a people for his name from the Gentiles' (v. 14).

33. Barrett 1998, 721. Several Western witnesses seek to enhance the prestige of Peter by adding the words 'and when the elders assented to what had been spoken by Peter' before 'the whole multitude became silent'. Cf. Metzger, *Textual Commentary,* 379.

34. Some have regarded this brief reference to Barnabas and Paul as a Lukan invention, arguing that Barnabas and Paul did not actually take part in such a debate or were not responsible for the decree in 15:29. This solution is partly driven by the presupposition that Paul could never have agreed to placing such restrictions on Gentile Christians. Cf. Barrett 1998, 710, 722.

35. Bruce 1990, 338, suggests that the naming of Paul after Barnabas is 'the order to be expected in a Jerusalem setting; so also in the apostolic letter (v. 25). After 13:2 the only other occurrence of this order is in 14:14, where it may have been influenced by the sequence Zeus-Hermes in 14:12.' Witherington 1998, 449-50, 456, argues that the placing of the name of Barnabas before that of Paul and the brevity of the account in 15:12 are evidence of a non-Pauline source that Luke was using to write up his account.

36. Signs and wonders in Acts are first associated with the earthly ministry of Jesus (2:22) and then with the coming of the Spirit at Pentecost (2:19, 43; 4:16, 22). They are mentioned in connection with the ministry of the gospel to Jews (4:30; 5:12; 6:8), Samaritans (8:6, 13), and Gentiles (14:3), testifying to its authenticity and the powerful presence of the Spirit in each new situation. Cf. THE THEOLOGY OF ACTS: VIII. MIRACLES (pp. 83-87).

13-14 *When they finished, James spoke up.*[37] James was first introduced as a leader of the Jerusalem church in 12:17. The fact that he spoke last and had such a decisive role in the council suggests a seniority or primacy in the leadership (cf. 21:18). James endorsed Peter's speech, using his Semitic name *'Simon'* (Gk. *Symeōn*).[38] However, he draws out more explicitly the ecclesiological significance of the events recalled by Peter. Every word of his brief statement is important. He first acknowledges that Peter has *'described'* or reported (v. 14, *exēgēsato*; cf. v. 12, *exēgoumenōn*) a significant work of God. The issue being considered by the council was effectively resolved when God took action *'at first'* (v. 14, *prōton*; cf. v. 7, 'some time ago'). Using a term previously employed to describe God's saving action in sending the Messiah to Israel (Lk. 1:68, 78; 7:16; cf. 19:44), James proclaims that God *'intervened' (epeskepsato)* or 'visited' the nations.[39] God first did this when Peter visited Cornelius with the message of salvation, but every gospel initiative after that can also be classified as a divine visitation: God encounters people personally through the preaching of the gospel. The purpose of this visitation was not simply to save individuals but *'to choose a people for his name from the Gentiles' (labein ex ethnōn laon tō onomati autou,* 'to take from the nations a people for his name'; cf. Ex. 6:7 LXX; Dt. 4:20, 34). Certain Gentiles can now be called *a people for his name* (*laos* is used for Israel in 2:47; 3:23; 4:10; 5:12; 7:17, 34; 13:17, but cf. 18:10), even though they lack what had previously been the necessary qualification for this. *For his name* means for his possession. In Exodus 19:5, which provides the foundational declaration of Israel's calling and identity, the Lord says, 'out of all nations you will be my treasured possession' (cf. Dt. 7:6; 14:2). There the Lord singles out from all nations *(apo pantōn tōn ethnōn)* one particular nation to be his 'treasured possession'. Here he creates a new people for himself, consisting of representatives out of all nations *(ex ethnōn).* 'The events directing Peter and

37. *meta de to sigēsai autous* ('when they became silent') refers to Barnabas and Paul, whereas in v. 12 the same verb is used of the whole assembly. Bruce 1990, 339, unnecessarily concludes from the use of this verb in v. 13 that 'no one appears to have taken any notice of what they said'. But Luke is simply suggesting that Barnabas and Paul added to the persuasive argument of Peter and then James followed, addressing an audience in which the opposition had been significantly countered.

38. The fact that James does not refer at all to the testimony of Barnabas and Paul (v. 12) is taken by some as evidence that they were not present at the Council (cf. note 34). It is Peter's theological assessment that James specifically takes up, and readers know from 13:38-47 that this is also Paul's position, which does not need to be re-expressed here. Witherington 1998, 456-57, shows how the speech of James is another clear example of deliberative rhetoric. However, James is more than just a rhetor: 'he is portrayed as a judge or authority figure who can give a ruling that settles a matter'. Bruce 1990, 339, observes that 'James takes his cue from Peter's argument, and reverts to it in v. 19' (*mē parenochlein,* 'not make it difficult').

39. The LXX also uses this verb to speak of God's visitation of Israel at the time of the exodus from Egypt (e.g., Ex. 3:16 [*episkopē epeskemmai*], 'I have surely visited' or 'I have surely taken action'). The terminology is used to denote God's saving initiative through Jesus in Lk. 1:68, 78; 7:16; 19:44. Cf. Acts 7:23 (Moses).

Cornelius to each other and the subsequent coming of the Spirit have the same meaning for Gentiles as the election of Israel has for the Jewish people.'[40] This does not imply the abandonment of Israel as his people. However, Peter has already made it clear that faith in the Lord Jesus will be the mark of Israelites who inherit the promised salvation (v. 11). James goes on to explore the relationship between these two peoples, theologically and pastorally.

15-18   James now claims, *'The words of the prophets are in agreement (symphōnousin) with this'*, namely the interpretation of events just given. He could have cited Zechariah 2:11, where the prediction is given that 'many nations will be joined with the LORD on that day, and will become my people'. However, Amos 9:11-12 is chosen because of the salvation-historical perspective it gives.[41] The text is cited with the introductory formula, *'as it is written'* (perfect passive *gegraptai*), suggesting that the words now quoted have the continuing authority of divinely inspired Scripture. Note, however, that James says *the words of the prophets are in agreement with this*, rather than 'this agrees with the prophets'. 'God's action dictates how we should understand the text of Scripture.'[42] The first verse retains the basic sense of the LXX translation but differs significantly in wording, simplifying and abbreviating the Greek text. This version is chosen and modified, according to the pattern of contemporary Jewish midrashic practice, because of its exegetical potential 'as a legitimate way of reading the Hebrew text'.[43] Some would argue that 'it is not James but Luke who is speaking here',[44] because the LXX is being used as scriptural proof in such a context. How-

40. Tannehill 1990, 186. Tannehill, 187, rightly observes that 'a series of election texts in the Septuagint provides patterns for the formulations in Acts 15:14 and 18:10. The resulting biblical style is important to the message. The Gentiles now turning to God are God's people in the full sense that Israel is, for the God who long ago chose a people for communion and mission is doing the same now among the other peoples of the world.' This is more accurate than the proposal of Johnson 1992, 264, that the word 'people' here gives 'an extension in the meaning of "Israel" defined in terms of faith rather than in terms of ethnic or ritual allegiance'. Cf. C. L. Blomberg, 'The Christian and the Law of Moses', in I. H. Marshall and D. G. Peterson (eds.), *Witness to the Gospel: The Theology of Acts* (Grand Rapids/Cambridge: Eerdmans, 1998), 407-8.

41. The plural 'the prophets' may refer to the collection of books known as 'The Twelve Prophets'. Cf. 7:42; 13:40.

42. Johnson 1992, 271. The interpretive translation of the LXX can be used because it fits with the action of God proclaimed in the testimonies of Peter, Paul, and Barnabas.

43. R. Bauckham, 'James and the Gentiles (Acts 15:13-21)', in B. Witherington III (ed.), *History, Literature and Society in the Book of Acts* (Cambridge: Cambridge University, 1996), 161. Bauckham, 165, further notes that 'all the variations of the text of Acts 15:16-18 from that of Amos 9:11-12 LXX belong to a consistent interpretation of the text with the help of related texts which refer to the building of the eschatological Temple (Hos. 3.4-5; Je. 12.15-16) and the conversion of the nations (Je. 12.15-16; Zech. 8.22; Isa. 45.20-23) in the messianic age'. This is a midrashic or interpretive rendering of the original text. Cf. G. K. Beale and D. A. Carson (eds.), *Commentary on the New Testament Use of the Old Testament* (Grand Rapids: Baker Academic; Nottingham: Apollos, 2007), 589-93.

44. Haenchen 1971, 448.

ever, we should not quickly rule out the possibility the James knew and used Greek. The form of the text here is similar to that applied to the Qumran community in CD 7:16; 4QFlor, and could have been recognised as a legitimate variant.[45] Tannehill notes a neat chiasm in v. 16, built around four first-person singular future verbs beginning with the Greek prefix *an-*:[46]

> After these things *I will return (anastrephō)* (cf. Je. 12:15 LXX, *epistrepsō*)
> And *I will rebuild (anoikodomēsō)* the tent of David that has fallen
> And its demolished ruins *I will rebuild (anoikodomēsō)*
> And *I will restore (anorthōsō)* it.

The focus of this interpretive translation is the predicted rebuilding of 'the tent of David that has fallen' (TNIV *'David's fallen tent'*). This refers to the restoration of the 'house' or family of David and thus to the promised Davidic kingdom. Amos 9:11 LXX has *skēnē* ('tent'), instead of *oikos* ('house,' as in 2 Sa. 7:11-16), because the Hebrew *sukkâ* means 'tabernacle, tent, hut', conveying the sense of shelter rather than permanent abode. 'The promise looks back to the remembered security of national life under the umbrella of David's rule and announces that freedom from fear of foes will be established again by the revival of the Davidic kingdom.'[47] With this promise of restoring the rule of David's line, James highlights a theme that has featured in Luke's birth narratives (Lk. 1:32-33, 69; 2:10-11), in Peter's preaching (Acts 2:30-36), and in Paul's preaching as well (Acts 13:22-23, 32-34). 'The seating of Jesus on David's throne and installation as royal Son of God have already taken place through Jesus' resurrection and exaltation to the right hand of God.'[48] Scripture has been fulfilled because the heavenly and universal reign of the crucified Messiah or Son of David has begun. The restoration of Israel follows from the reestablishment of David's kingdom in Jesus' resurrection (cf. Lk. 1:68-69), though James does not develop this theme.

45. Cf. J. A. de Waard, *A Comparative Study of the Old Testament Texts in the Dead Sea Scrolls and in the New Testament* (Leiden: Brill, 1965), 24-26, 47, 78-79; Barrett 1998, 726. However, note the caution of Bruce 1990, 340.

46. Tannehill 1990, 188.

47. J. L. Mays, *Amos: A Commentary* (London: SCM, 1969), 164. Bauckham, 'James and the Jerusalem Church', 453-56, takes the rebuilding of 'the tent of David that has fallen' to refer to the construction of the eschatological temple. This, however, can hardly have been the original intention of Amos, since the temple in Jerusalem was still standing when he delivered his prophecy and he does not predict its fall.

48. Tannehill 1990, 189. Tannehill notes that the absence of the verb *anastēsō* from the citation in Acts 15:16 (even though it is twice used in the LXX version) weakens the case of those who interpret the rebuilding of the tent of David as primarily a reference to Jesus' resurrection (this verb is used for the resurrection of Jesus in 2:24, 32; 3:26; 13:33, 34; 17:31). Against Wilson, *Gentiles*, 224-5, it is unlikely that Amos 9:11 was taken to mean that the admission of Gentiles must not hinder the mission to Jews.

The citation from Amos 9:12 follows the LXX fairly closely, though this version differs from the Massoretic (Hebrew) text in significant ways.[49] 'Precisely the divergence of the LXX from the Hebrew enables the text to be used midrashically.'[50] The purpose of this restoration of the Davidic rule is not simply to bless Israel but also ' *"that the rest of humanity may seek the Lord, even all the Gentiles who bear my name, says the Lord, who does these things"'*. James adds words possibly taken from Isaiah 45:21 (*'"things known from long ago"'*) as a gloss on the concluding words from Amos 9:12 (*'"these things"'*).[51] This addition strengthens the claim that God's plan to save Gentiles along with Jews is no novelty, since it was part of his eternal purpose (cf. Rom. 15:8-12). Of course, it was always possible for Gentiles to become proselytes of Judaism, but Amos envisaged a massive number of Gentiles *(the rest of humanity)* seeking the Lord when the house of David had been restored. This group is further defined as all the Gentiles *who bear my name* (*eph' hous epikeklētai to onoma mou ep' autous,* 'upon whom my name has been named'), exposing the scriptural basis for the claim that God has taken from the Gentiles 'a people for his name' (v. 14, *laon tō onomati autou*). Those who seek the Lord from among the nations are those whom he has already claimed as his own (*epikeklētai* [perfect passive implying divine agency], 'has been named'; cf. 13:48, 'all who were appointed for eternal life'). They constitute a new people of God and not simply a large addition to the existing people known as Israel. The critical question is therefore how these two peoples relate to each other. Theologically, the point has already been made that they have a profound unity through a common faith in Jesus the exalted Messiah. Practically, James now makes two proposals regarding the way that Jewish and Gentile Christians can coexist and support one another.

19-21   James has agreed with Peter's interpretation of what God was doing and added his own ecclesiological and salvation-historical perspective, basing his argument on an interpretive translation of Amos 9:11-12. He

---

49. The MT has 'so that they may possess the remnant of Edom and all the nations that bear my name', signifying Israel's dominion over all other nations, including what is left of Edom. Gerhardsson, *Memory and Manuscript*, 260, holds that James might have followed the rabbinic practice of citing any known textual variant that would serve the purpose of the argument, but Barrett 1998, 728, doubts that James would have used a form of the text that differed so markedly from the Hebrew in such a context. Cf. Marshall 1980, 252-53.

50. Johnson 1992, 265. Cf. Bruce 1990, 340-41; Bauckham, 'James and the Gentiles', 160-61. The LXX apparently reads the Hebrew for 'possess/inherit' (*yirshu*) as 'they will seek' (*yidreshu*), and the Hebrew for 'Edom' (*'edom*) as 'mankind' (*'adam*). The citation in Acts 15:17 adds that they will seek 'the Lord' (*ton Kyrion*), which is implied by the LXX. This version is regarded as authoritative 'midrash' because it interprets the original in the light of its fulfillment in Christ and reflects also the perspective of other eschatological prophecies (v. 15).

51. Since the ending is so elliptical (*tauta gnōsta ap' aiōnos* being the most likely original), various copyists made attempts to round it out as an independent sentence. Cf. Metzger, *Textual Commentary*, 379.

now proposes a formal rejection of the demand of the Judaizers (v. 19): '*It is my judgment, therefore, that we should not make it difficult for the Gentiles who are turning to God*'.[52] Submission to the law through the act of circumcision cannot be demanded of *Gentiles who are turning to God* by believing in Jesus. Jewish Christians should recognise the freedom of Gentile Christians to live a life that is determined by Christ and his Spirit, not by the demands of the law. The main issue for which the council was called has been resolved. James then proposes what at first glance appears to be a qualification of the freedom of Gentile Christians (vv. 20-21): '*instead we should write to them, telling them to abstain from food polluted by idols, from sexual immorality, from the meat of strangled animals and from blood*'.[53] The first prohibition is literally to abstain from 'the pollution of idols' or 'the defilements caused by idols' *(tōn alisgēmatōn tōn eidōlōn)*.[54] TNIV *(to abstain from food polluted by idols)* unfortunately obscures this more general reference, making the language of v. 20 sound more like the term used in 15:29; 21:25 (*eidōlothytōn*, 'things sacrificed to idols'). What James is demanding in the first instance is a complete abandonment of the spiritual defilement that comes from idolatry. When this is later expressed in terms of avoiding 'things sacrificed to idols', the reference is most likely to participation in pagan temple feasts, not simply to the uncleanness incurred from eating meat bought in the marketplace.[55] *Sexual immorality* in the broadest sense is most probably intended by the use of the

52. The Greek is solemn and emphatic *(dio egō krinō)*, giving the sense, 'Therefore I give my judgment'. 'James is at least acting as chairman and expressing in his own words the sense of the meeting' (Barrett 1998, 729). The present infinitive *parenochlein* with *mē* could be taken to mean 'to stop annoying', since the Gentiles have already been troubled with regard to the necessity of circumcision. Johnson 1992, 266, argues from the use of this verb in Aristotle, *Rhetoric* 1381B; Jgs. 14:17; 1 Sa. 28:15; and 1 Macc. 10:35 that it characterizes the Pharisees' demands as 'a form of *harassment* of the Gentiles'.

53. There are a number of textual variants in 15:20, 29 and 21:25 with respect to the word order and content of the so-called Apostolic Decree, showing some confusion among copyists as to whether the prohibitions were entirely ceremonial, or entirely ethical, or a combination of the two. Metzger, *Textual Commentary*, 379-83, argues that 'the least unsatisfactory solution of the complicated textual and exegetical problems of the Apostolic Decree is to regard the fourfold decree as original (foods offered to idols, strangled meat, eating blood, and unchastity — whether ritual or moral)', and to explain the two forms of the threefold decree as later attempts to simplify and justify the requirements. Barrett 1998, 735-36, points out that later textual traditions tend to transform the requirements in a more ethical direction, whereas the earliest and best MSS tend to combine both ceremonial and ethical demands.

54. The noun *alisgēma* ('pollution') occurs only here. Its meaning must be derived from the use of the related verb *alisgein* in the LXX of Mal. 1:7; Dn. 1:8; Sir. 40:29. These texts make it 'fairly certain that "the things polluted by idolatry" refers specifically to the food offered at the shrines of idols' (Johnson 1992, 266). Cf. Bruce 1990, 342.

55. Witherington 1998, 461-64. Witherington rightly proposes that the four elements mentioned by James and included in the decree in v. 29 must be viewed together and applied to a particular social context. The most natural way to read the text would be to see it as a prohibition of attending temple feasts and all that they entailed in the Greco-Roman world. Cf. 2 Macc. 6:4-5.

Greek word *porneia,* rather than simply spiritual adultery in the practice of idolatry.[56] *The meat of strangled animals* refers to meat from which the blood has not been drained because of the way it was killed (e.g., Ex. 22:31; Lv. 17:13-16).[57] *Blood* most naturally refers to the consumption of blood in any form (cf. Gn. 9:4; Lv. 7:26-27; 17:10-14; Dt. 12:16, 23).[58]

One interpretation of the requirements here is that they simply arose out of the practicalities of life in the Gentile world. Barrett suggests that 'Jews had long known that the temptation to idolatry came most often through the butcher's shop and the brothel'.[59] But Witherington more persuasively relates the prohibitions to participation in temple feasts, where sexual immorality was regularly found in association with meat offerings that were an abomination to Jews. The issue of food and fellowship between Jewish and Gentile Christians was discussed in Acts 10–11, and another social matter is under discussion here, namely, 'what to do about Gentiles' associations with pagan temples, both before and even after their conversion to Christianity'.[60] A more elaborate interpretation explains the restrictions in terms of the so-called Noachian precepts, which at least one strand of Jewish tradition believed were applicable to all nations. However, 'the parallel is not close, and there is nothing in the text of Acts to call Noah to mind'.[61] More widely accepted is the view that the rules in Leviticus 17:8–18:18 relating to Jews and resident aliens in the land of Israel were being applied to Christian Gentiles in the Jewish Dispersion. Gentile converts were not required to become Jewish proselytes and keep the whole law, but

56. Cf. Johnson 1992, 266-67.

57. H. L. Strack and P. Billerbeck, *Kommentar zum Neuen Testamentum aus Talmud und Midrasch,* 6 vols. (München: Beck, 1922-61), 2:730-34, claim that rabbinic teaching excluded the meat of any beast not slaughtered in the ritually correct manner and the meat of any beast which, dead or alive, had a disqualifying blemish. Cf. Josephus, *Ant.* 3.260.

58. Since this appears somewhat redundant after the last prohibition, bloodshed, in particular murder, has been taken as the possible meaning. Cf. Barrett 1998, 733. Johnson 1992, 267, surveys the use of the terms (*pniktos* as a substantive formed from *pnigein,* 'to strangle or choke', and *haima,* 'blood') and concludes that they can be connected 'into a single ritual prohibition: to abstain from "strangled things" and "from blood" is equivalent, since when something is strangled and then eaten, the blood remains within it'. Witherington 1998, 464, argues that 'each term in the decree should be taken separately and all be seen as referring to four different activities that were known or believed to transpire in pagan temples.'

59. Barrett 1998, 733.

60. Witherington 1998, 470. Witherington, 461-64, provides detailed argument for this conclusion. Compare the particular evidence of 2 Macc. 6:4-5. Marshall 1980, 243, sees this as a further provision in the matter of table fellowship and does not recognise the more precise context identified by Witherington.

61. Barrett 1998, 734. *Jubilees* 7:20 gives the earliest form of these precepts. Strack and Billerbeck, *Kommentar,* 3:37-38, outline their subsequent development into seven prohibitions: idolatry, blasphemy, murder, incest, stealing, perverting justice, and eating flesh containing blood. What James suggests possibly parallels the first, third, fourth, and seventh prohibitions. But why were these singled out and others ignored if this tradition was the inspiration for the Apostolic Decree?

only those parts of it that were required by Moses of resident aliens.[62] But this implies that Gentile Christians were living with Jewish believers in the Dispersion in a way that was comparable to living with Jews in the Holy Land, ignoring the argument that God has taken for himself a new and distinctive people from among the nations (15:14).[63] Moreover, 'there is, in fact, no known Jewish parallel to the selection of precisely these four commandments from the Law of Moses as those which are binding on Gentiles or a category of Gentiles'.[64] It is difficult to align the command to avoid 'the defilements caused by idols' with Leviticus 17:8-9 and hard to explain why other laws binding on resident aliens are not included in Acts 15:20 (e.g., Lv. 16:29; 17:15-16; 20:2; 22:18; 24:22; 25:47). Finally, 15:21 is a call to recognise the importance of the law for Jews, not a justification for imposing some of its requirements on Gentiles. Another possible background is provided by a group of rabbinic texts which indicate three matters on which compromise by Jews was impossible: idolatry, the shedding of blood, and incest.[65]

Any specific background proposed must be squared with the rationale given in v. 21: *'For the law of Moses has been preached in every city from the earliest times and is read in the synagogues on every Sabbath'*. The long-standing and widespread practice of reading the law and teaching about the law in every synagogue of the Jewish Dispersion should have alerted Gentile Christians to the concerns of faithful Jews.[66] Although some have argued that this verse looks back to v. 19, or relates to everything that is proposed

62. Cf. Wilson, *Luke and the Law*, 85-102. Richard, 'Divine Purpose', 196, argues that these regulations are invoked as 'a way of more correctly applying the law to Gentiles'. Johnson 1992, 268, similarly proposes that 'the inclusion of the Gentiles does not mean the elimination of the Torah, but rather the fulfillment of its prophetic intention, "made known from long ago" (15:18), as well as the continuation of those aspects of Torah that have always applied to the proselyte and sojourner'. Cf. Bauckham, 'James and the Jerusalem Church', 459-60; M. Bockmuehl, *Jewish Law in Gentile Churches: Halakah and the Beginning of Christian Public Ethics* (Edinburgh: Clark, 2000), 49-83, 145-73.

63. Bauckham, 'James and the Jerusalem Church', 459-60, proposes an exegetical link with Lv. 17:8–18:18 via Je. 12:16 LXX. This text suggests that Gentiles who join the eschatological community will live 'in the midst' of God's people and provides the basis for James's highlighting four commands from Leviticus that apply to Israelites and 'any foreigner residing among them'. However, this is a highly speculative reconstruction of the reasoning behind Acts 15:16-20, for which there is no evidence in the text of Acts itself. Witherington 1998, 464, comments on the inappropriateness of applying regulations for 'the stranger within the gates', that is, Gentiles living in the land of Israel, to Gentile Christians in the Jewish Dispersion.

64. Bauckham, 'James and the Gentiles', 174. Witherington 1998, 464-65, points to a number of difficulties in making Leviticus 17–18 the background to the Apostolic Decree.

65. Cf. Barrett 1998, 734-35. Johnson 1992, 273, combines this view with the proposal that the rules in Lv. 17:8–18:18 were being applied to Gentile Christians.

66. For the synagogue service see on 13:15. The verb to preach *(kēryssein)* in 15:21 is normally used for the proclamation of Christ (e.g., 8:5; 9:20). The sense here may be that the law is both read and urged upon the Jews through exhortation and discussion in the synagogues of the Dispersion.

in vv. 19-20, the most obvious link is with v. 20 alone.[67] James implies that
there are observant Jews everywhere and that Gentile Christians will know
why the requirements of v. 20 are being suggested. The rationale is specifically scriptural, and not simply practical or even rabbinic in its expression.
It also seems that James expected synagogue worship to go on in every city
and that the issue of obedience to the law would not quickly be resolved for
Jewish Christians. As Christians wrestled with the question of the law's ongoing relevance and application, reflecting on Christ's own teaching and
the events by which he inaugurated the New Covenant, there was need for
sensitivity and generosity on all sides. Luke goes on to record that Paul was
later willing to circumcise Timothy 'because of the Jews who lived in that
area' (16:1-3). This narrative is linked to the report that Paul and Silas travelled from town to town, delivering the decisions reached by the apostles
and elders in Jerusalem for the people to obey (16:4). Both activities seem to
reflect a common concern not to offend Jews unnecessarily, so that the gospel may have free course in their midst (cf. 1 Cor. 9:19-23).[68] The only other
mention of the so-called Apostolic Decree is in 21:25. There it is recalled as
part of a response to the accusation that Paul is teaching Jews who live
among Gentiles to abandon Moses and the law (21:21-25). The decree is
used as evidence that the church has already taken steps to avoid putting
pressure on Jews in this way. At this later stage in the narrative we see that
'the problem is no longer the demands being made on Gentiles to become
Jews but the pressure being felt by Jews to conform to a Gentile way of
life.'[69] This pressure must have been considerable wherever Gentile believers came to outnumber Jewish believers. Further reflection on the meaning
and application of the advice of James in v. 20 and the decree of v. 29 will be
given in the ADDITIONAL NOTE: THE MEANING AND APPLICATION OF THE
COUNCIL NARRATIVE below (pp. 442-46).

b. Resolution (15:22-29)

22 The resolution of the problem involved a decision (*edoxe, decided,*
cf. vv. 25, 28) by the whole assembly *(the apostles and elders, with the whole
church)* to send representatives back to Antioch with Paul and Barnabas (vv.
22-23a), conveying a letter with the proposals of James (vv. 23b-29). We do

67. Cf. Barrett 1998, 737.
68. R. L. Brawley, *Luke-Acts and the Jews: Conflict, Apology and Conciliation,* SBLMS 33
(Atlanta: Scholars, 1987), 151-52, views the decision of the Jerusalem Council and the circumcision of Timothy as examples of a 'pattern of conciliatory action', specifically for the
sake of unity with Jewish Christians. A third example is found in 21:23-26.
69. Tannehill 1990, 191. Tannehill further observes that 'the Jerusalem meeting that
guarantees the Gentiles' freedom from the law also anticipates the problem that will arise as
the gentile portion of the church grows, for James is proposing that Gentiles be asked to abstain from certain things especially offensive to a Jewish sense of cultic purity so that Jewish
Christians may remain in the fellowship of the church without being forced to give up their
way of life'.

not have enough evidence to say precisely how agreement was reached and need to be careful about reading into the situation specific patterns of decision making. Choosing *some of their own men* to accompany Paul and Barnabas, they hoped for a clear explanation of their intentions in writing the letter (v. 27) and a healing of any strained relationship between the churches. *Judas (called Barsabbas) and Silas* were chosen because they were *leaders among the brothers* (and presumably also because they were *prophets*, v. 32 note). Nothing more is known about this Judas, but Silas became the companion of Paul, in succession to Barnabas (v. 40; cf. the latinized form 'Silvanus' in 2 Cor. 1:19; 1 Thes. 1:1; 2 Thes. 1:1; 1 Pet. 5:12).

23-29 The decision was made by the whole assembly, but the letter was actually sent in the name of *the apostles and elders, your brothers*.[70] It was addressed specifically to 'the brothers in Antioch, Syria and Cilicia, who come from among the nations' (Antioch was the administrative capital of the united province of Syria and Cilicia; cf. v. 41; Gal. 1:21). Paul later also delivered it to the churches founded on his first missionary journey (16:1-4), indicating his desire to apply its message to the South Galatian churches as well. There is no geographical restriction implied in 21:25, where James says the letter was intended for 'the Gentile believers'. Here and in 23:26-30 we may have 'the direct citation of transcripts' available to Luke.[71] After the formal introduction, identifying the senders and the addressees, and stressing their relationship as brothers in Christ, comes the common Greek greeting *chairein*, which literally means '(We wish you) to rejoice' (TNIV *Greetings*; cf. 23:26; Jas. 1:1). There is then an acknowledgement that the problem created by the Judaizers originated in Jerusalem, without any official backing *(We have heard that some went out from us without our authorisation and disturbed you)*.[72] The fact that they came from Jerusalem probably gave them authority enough in the eyes of some.[73] Their harass-

---

70. F. W. Danker, 'Reciprocity in the Ancient World and in Acts 15:23-29', in R. J. Cassidy and P. J. Sharper (eds.), *Political Issues in Luke-Acts* (Maryknoll: Orbis, 1983), 54, argues that the apostles and elders functioned like the council and the rest of the church like the popular assembly in provincial cities of the Roman Empire. The council made proposals, but the assembly voted on them and made amendments. Cf. Witherington 1998, 450-51. Barrett 1998, 739-40, discusses the textual confusion in the opening words of v. 23. Some MSS read *kai hoi adelphoi* ('and the brothers'), but others omit *adelphoi* because it is somewhat harsh in apposition to *hoi apostoloi kai hoi presbyteroi* ('the apostles and elders'). The hardest reading is also the best attested and is to be preferred. It is translated by TNIV *the apostles and elders, your brothers*. Cf. Metzger, *Textual Commentary*, 384-85.

71. E. A. Judge, *ND* 1:26 (p. 78). Ancient historians included such documents in their narratives. Since this document is said to have circulated widely, there were probably several places where Luke could have seen a copy.

72. Barrett 1998, 741, asks 'if the circumcisers of 15.1, 5 had had no backing, would they have caused so much trouble and precipitated a high-level conference?' However, he rightly suggests that those genuinely commissioned with some particular task may go beyond their brief. Cf. Witherington 1998, 468 note 448. The verb *tarassein* (15:24, *disturbed*) is also used in Gal. 1:7; 5:10 of those who were troubling the Galatians with the same teaching.

73. The word *exelthontes* ('went out') is missing from some ancient MSS. This shorter

ment of Gentile believers is further defined as *troubling your minds by what they said* (*etaraxan hymas logois anaskeuazontes tas psychas hymōn*, 'disturbed you by what they said, unsettling your souls'). Any teaching that compromises the simple message of the gospel will rob Christians of their assurance and leave them feeling confused. Then comes the notification of two formal decisions, the first of which emerged 'when we came together [in unity]' or 'when we met together' (*hēmin genomenois homothymadon*).[74]

The first decision (marked by the use of *edoxen* in v. 25, as in v. 22),[75] was *to choose some men and send them to you with our dear friends Barnabas and Paul — men who have risked their lives for the name of our Lord Jesus Christ.* This elaborate commendation of Barnabas and Paul (with names reversed, as in v. 12) involves a recognition of them as 'beloved' (*agapētois*; TNIV *good friends*) to the Jerusalem leaders, and faithful to the Lord Jesus (*anthrōpois paradedōkosi tas psychas autōn*, 'men who have devoted their lives' to the name of our Lord Jesus Christ).[76] Nevertheless, it was considered appropriate to send *Judas and Silas to confirm* (*apangellontas*, 'proclaiming' or 'reporting') *by word of mouth what we are writing.* With the help of such representatives from the church in Jerusalem, the message of the letter would come to the recipients in a more personal and convincing way (cf. Eph. 6:21-22; Col. 4:7-8).

The second decision (marked again by the use of *edoxen*, v. 28) is attributed *to the Holy Spirit and to us.* Luke has not claimed anywhere in the account so far that any of the speakers was particularly directed by or filled with the Holy Spirit. At one level, the claim could be that the unanimity of the gathering in acknowledging the will of God was a sign of the Spirit's presence and guidance.[77] There is a parallel between v. 25 and v. 28, con-

---

and harder reading has a claim to be the original, giving the sense, 'some of us had disturbed you'. Cf. Barrett 1998, 741-42. However, Metzger, *Textual Commentary*, 385, argues for the inclusion of *exelthontes* because of the weight of external evidence supporting this reading.

74. The word *homothymadon* ('together') is often used by Luke with the sense of unanimity, but also sometimes with the sense of physical togetherness (cf. note 6). Brown, Donfried, and Reumann, *Peter*, 50, argue that this is demonstrated in the fact that 'Peter provides the decisive witness; James provides the decisive judgment or decision; the apostles and elders provide the sentence or the enforcement of the decision'.

75. The impersonal verb *edoxen* (vv. 25, 28) was frequently used of public resolutions, 'especially in decrees and the like' (LS 242, s.v. II.4b). Cf. Herodotus, *Persian Wars* 1:3; Josephus, *Ant.* 6.321; 16.163.

76. For the translation of *psychē* here *(lives)*, in v. 24 *(minds)*, and elsewhere in Luke-Acts, see 14:22 note. The Western text of 15:26 adds that they risked their lives for the Lord Jesus Christ 'in every trial', perhaps because the expression *paradedōkosi tas psychas autōn* was not normally applied to someone who was still alive. Cf. Metzger, *Textual Commentary*, 386. The Greek makes it clear that this is a description of Barnabas and Paul, not of the men sent with them.

77. 'The invocation of the Holy Spirit as a partner to the decision has an odd sound to contemporary ears, but it nicely captures the dynamics of the process as portrayed by Luke' (Johnson 1992, 277).

veyed by two similar expressions in Greek, saying the same thing in different ways ('it was decided by us, when we came together [in unity]' = 'it was decided by the Holy Spirit and us'). At another level, it is clear that the council came to affirm what the Spirit had already shown them to be true. There was an objective testimony of the Spirit to which the various speakers had drawn attention.[78] Peter's speech highlighted the critical role of the Spirit in testifying to the salvation of Gentiles apart from obedience to the law (vv. 8-9). Barnabas and Paul confirmed this by referring to what God had done among the Gentiles through them (v. 12). James then argued that the Spirit-inspired 'words of the prophets' are in agreement with the conclusion that God 'intervened to choose a people for his name from the Gentiles' (vv. 13-18). So the Spirit's work in the Council was to enable the participants to acknowledge these historical and scriptural evidences and to come *together* to the right conclusions about the practical implications. This text, therefore, cannot simply be applied to any meeting of Christians claiming the Spirit's guidance for their decisions.[79] Only when Christians are united in interpreting the acts of God in the light of Scripture can it be said that the Spirit has been leading like this. The Spirit's work in leading the Jerusalem Council was to provide a solution consistent with the truth of the gospel, enabling Jewish and Gentile Christians to live together in love.

This decision conveyed the recommendation of James in slightly different terms and with a variation in word order. The first expression (*not to burden you with anything beyond the following requirements*, v. 28) recalls the warning of v. 10 and the recommendation of v. 19, and prepares for the list of 'necessary things' (*epanankes*; TNIV *requirements*) in v. 29, but based on v. 20.[80] Barrett is right to say that Luke regarded these as matters 'not of courtesy but of compulsion', but it is hard to see how this might mean that they were 'a condition of salvation'.[81] The order here is different from v. 20 (where the prohibition is against idolatry, fornication, what is strangled, and blood), though the variation does not appear to be significant: *You are to abstain from food sacrificed to idols, from blood, from the meat of strangled ani-*

78. J. McIntosh, '"For it seemed good to the Holy Spirit" (Acts 15:28): How Far Did the Members of the Jerusalem Council *Know* This?', *RTR* 61 (2002), 133, affirms 'a *threefold*, collectively incontrovertible, objective testimony of the Holy Spirit' in the evidence placed before the council. Cf. G. W. H. Lampe, *St. Luke and the Church of Jerusalem* (London: Athlone, 1969), 25.

79. Marshall 1980, 255, claims that 'the decision reached by the church was regarded as being *inspired by the Spirit*, who is throughout Acts the guide of the church in its decision and actions' (my emphasis). Cf. McIntosh, 'Jerusalem Council', 131-33, for alternative ways of viewing this expression.

80. The difficult *toutōn tōn epanankes* ('these necessary things') prompted several alterations in the MS traditions. Cf. Barrett 1998, 745, who notes that 'however the text is taken and construed, it includes the notion of necessity, compulsion'.

81. Barrett 1998, 745. There are many commands in the NT that are not conditions of salvation. Johnson 1992, 277, suggests that these necessary things were 'the minimal requirements for communion between Jew and Gentile believers'.

mals and from sexual immorality. The more general expression 'the pollution of idols' (v. 19) is replaced by the specific term *food sacrificed to idols* (*eidōlothytōn*, as in 21:25), and the plural *pniktōn* ('strangled things') is used instead of the singular *pniktou* for *the meat of strangled animals.*[82] An exhortation precedes the final greeting *(You will do well to avoid these things. Farewell)*, suggesting that the compulsion indicated by the word *requirements* in v. 28 should not be read as a legal obligation, but as a moral appeal.[83]

The Jerusalem Council acknowledged that Gentile Christians were not obligated to live under the yoke of the law. At the same time, it challenged them to exercise their liberty with wisdom, restraint, and love, recognising the concerns of some Jewish Christians about contamination through any association with idolatrous practices. The requirements commended to Gentile believers by letter and urged upon them by prophets and teachers in the local church context (15:30-32; 16:4) were designed to keep the lines of fellowship open with Jewish believers by giving warning to Gentiles about any compromise with the idolatry and immorality that was so much a part of their world. Luke's record of the Council, with its repetition of these recommendations (15:20, 28-29) and his subsequent account of the joyful acceptance of the message at Antioch (15:31), suggests that he viewed this whole process and its outcome enthusiastically (cf. 21:21 note).

3. The Result of the Council (15:30-35)

When Paul and Barnabas return to Antioch with the letter from the apostles and elders in Jerusalem, the process of resolving the issue for the Gentiles continues. The church rejoices in the letter's confirmation of their freedom from the law and accepts the regulations commended to them for the sake of harmony between believers (vv. 30-31). The prophets sent from Jerusalem to 'confirm by word of mouth' what has been written (v. 27) are successful in encouraging and strengthening the believers, so that they are released 'with the blessing of peace to return to those who had sent them' (vv. 32-34). Paul and Barnabas continue with many others in Antioch to preach the word of the Lord, apparently unhindered by any further Judaizing challenge (v. 35).

30-32 *So they were sent off and went down to Antioch, where they gathered the church together and delivered the letter.* Luke begins a new stage of the nar-

---

82. There are textual variants in v. 29 similar to and, in some cases, related to those noted in v. 20. Cf. Metzger, *Textual Commentary*, 386-87. Witherington 1998, 460-61, argues that *eidōlothyton* is a Christian and not an early Jewish term, which refers to 'something given, dedicated, even sacrificed to idols'.

83. Johnson 1992, 277, notes the use of similar terminology elsewhere and suggests that *you will do well (eu praxate)* can be read as 'signifying both moral rectitude and fittingness'.

rative with a significant marker in the Greek text (*men oun;* cf. 1:6 note), at the same time making the link with the preceding section clear. Having been *sent off* by the Jerusalem Council with a specific responsibility, or perhaps 'released' (*apolythentes;* cf. v. 33 note) for this ministry, they went straight to Antioch and fulfilled it.[84] The people read the letter and *were glad for its encouraging message*. Since Paul was one of the party who conveyed and commended the letter, Luke is indicating that Paul was happy with the decision (cf. also 16:4). This is an important starting point for any consideration of the view of Paul on this subject and for an evaluation of any proposed difference between Luke and Paul. *Judas and Silas, who themselves were prophets, said much to encourage and strengthen the brothers*. Like Barnabas, when he first came from Jerusalem to Antioch, they engaged in a ministry of exhortation (*parakalein* in 11:23; 15:32). Like Paul and Barnabas in the South Galatian churches, they strengthened the believers by their exhortation (14:22). The verbal nature of their encouragement is brought out by the expression *said much* (*dia logou pollou*). Since they were sent by the apostles and elders in Jerusalem to confirm and explain the letter (v. 27), their specific brief was to persuade the Gentiles of the necessity for keeping the 'requirements' in the letter (vv. 28-29). The emphatic description of Judas and Silas as *themselves prophets* (*kai autoi prophētai*) is significant in the context. It suggests that prophetic ministry involved explanation and application of apostolic teaching, such as was found in the letter, and not simply prediction, as in the case of Agabus (13:28; 21:10-11), or special guidance, as with the commissioning of Barnabas and Saul for their missionary campaign (cf. 13:1-2).

33-35 *After spending some time there, they were sent off by the brothers with the blessing of peace to return to those who had sent them*. Judas and Silas did not simply deliver the message and return immediately to Jerusalem. They stayed for some time (*poiēsantes chronon;* cf. 18:23; 20:3), and engaged in the ministry just described (v. 32), before the Antiochene brothers 'let them go' (*apelythēsan;* cf. 15:30; 13:3 note). The phrase *with the blessing of peace* (*met' eirēnēs,* 'with peace') indicates reconciliation between the churches after the disruption caused by those who came down from Judea to Antioch in the first place (v. 1). The KJV includes v. 34 ('Notwithstanding it pleased Silas to abide there still'), though this is not found in modern translations (except NKJV). It is the reading of some later Greek texts, followed by the Received Text, on which the KJV and NKJV were based. A still more expanded reading is found in Codex D ('But it seemed good to Silas that they remain, and Judas journeyed alone'). The earliest and best manuscripts do not contain these additions, which were probably made by copyists to account for the fact that Silas is present at Antioch in v. 40.[85] Of course, Silas

---

84. The language of 'going down' (*katerchomai*) from Jerusalem is used again (cf. 15:1 note). There is no doubt that *plēthos* ('multitude') here refers to the church (cf. v. 12) or the whole company of Christians in Antioch.

85. Cf. Metzger, *Textual Commentary,* 388; Barrett 1998, 750.

could have returned to Antioch in time to set out with Paul on his next missionary journey. Luke does not trouble to explain this! *But Paul and Barnabas remained in Antioch, where they and many others taught and preached the word of the Lord.* After the satisfactory resolution of the important doctrinal and practical issues raised by the Judaizers, there was a notable advance in gospel work (cf. 6:1-7, where there is the same pattern of conflict, resolution, and gospel growth). Those engaged in teaching and preaching were *many*, signalling an advance on the situation portrayed in 13:1-2.

ADDITIONAL NOTE: THE MEANING AND APPLICATION OF THE COUNCIL NARRATIVE

At one level, Luke wrote to record the amazing way in which God brought unanimity and agreement to a potentially disastrous situation in the early church. God guided the debate and the decision-making process, protecting the church from error and division, and allowing the respective missions to Jews and Gentiles to flourish separately, but in harmony together. The various contributions of Peter, Barnabas and Paul, and then James, directed attention to the action of God in recent history and its significance for understanding the way of salvation and the fulfillment of Scripture, highlighting the need for a practical resolution of the problem presented by the Judaizers.

In this historical framework, Luke presented conflict and debate as legitimate and necessary elements in the process of discerning God's will. He showed how such disagreement 'serves to reveal the true bases for fellowship, and elicit the fundamental principles of community identity'.[86] His presentation of events suggests that the task of the church is 'not to dictate God's action but discern it, not to close the Scriptures to further interpretation but to open them'.[87] However, the aim of the Council was not unity at any cost. In the process of discerning God's will, there was complete agreement in *disapproval* of the Pharisaic alternative. The final component in the decision-making process was the agreement of the church in Jerusalem with the apostles and elders (v. 22) and the joyful acceptance of the affected communities (vv. 31-32). Luke provides here another 'foundation story', as in Acts 2 and 4, expressing the ideals of life together and providing 'a model for making decisions within this people constituted by faith'.[88]

However, Acts 15 is not simply commending a particular process of decision making and the ideal of a community united in discovering and applying the will of God. Subtly and surely, Luke 'uses the apostles' state-

---

86. Johnson 1992, 271. Cf. Johnson *Decision Making*, 46-58, 67-87.

87. Johnson 1992, 280.

88. Johnson 1992, 279. He notes how Eusebius of Caesarea seems to reflect the same perspectives in his account of the second-century debate over the observation of Easter (*Hist. Eccl.* 5.23-25).

ments to shape a new definition of "the people of God" as one based on messianic faith rather than on ethnic origin or ritual observance'.[89] Here we find an important manifestation of the church as an entity involving local congregations in partnership, working together to maintain the truth of God's word and promote the work of the gospel. The Jerusalem Council makes the gospel of salvation by faith alone the key to defining the true nature of this church, which involves Jewish and Gentile believers together. At the same time, there is further reflection on the role of the law in the new community created through faith in Christ.

In recent times, the Jerusalem Council has served as a paradigm for a number of proposals concerning the theologian's task and the way in which Christians might resolve their theological differences. These proposals raise serious questions about the way the narrative in Acts 15 can be interpreted and applied. Timothy Wiarda helpfully surveys and critiques five of these.

The first suggests the Council as a model for contextualization, but does so on the assumption that circumcision and the law of Moses were primarily matters of Jewish culture.[90] Wiarda questions whether any of the participants in the original debate held that these matters were essentially cultural and argues that their decisions were conceived of as having universal rather than local application (restricted to one cultural community). The second approach views the Council as a model for Spirit-led community interpretation of Scripture, but does so on the assumption that the James was led to focus on one particular type of text, while bypassing others which potentially supported an opposition theology. 'The implication for today's churches is that, when faced with issues concerning which there seems to be a diverse range of biblical data, each community should look first to its own Spirit-given experience and its own sense of the Spirit's leading, then on that basis choose those particular strands of the Bible's witness that seem most fitting. This limited selection of texts becomes the community's source of authoritative teaching.'[91] Wiarda says that this view

89. Johnson 1992, 280. T. Wiarda, 'The Jerusalem Council and the Theological Task', *JETS* 46, no. 2 (2003), 245, rightly argues that the narrative of Acts 15 'forcefully highlights a theological message, that God's purpose for the Gentiles is salvation without circumcision'. The issue of decision making is only 'a secondary paradigmatic point'.

90. Wiarda, 'Jerusalem Council', 233-6, reporting the perspective of J. Davis, 'Biblical Precedents for Contextualisation', *Asia Theological Association Journal* 2 (1994), 21; D. Hesselgrave and E. Rommen, *Contextualisation, Meanings, Methods and Models* (Grand Rapids: Baker, 1989), 10-11; C. Kraft, *Christianity in Culture: A Study in Dynamic Biblical Theologizing in Cross-Cultural Perspective* (Maryknoll: Orbis, 1979), 340-41. I am greatly indebted to Wiarda's analysis, as the following paragraph shows.

91. Wiarda, 'Jerusalem Council', 237, reporting the perspective of J. C. Thomas, 'Women, Pentecostals and the Bible: An Experiment in Pentecostal Hermeneutics', *JPT* 5 (1994), 41-56; J. C. Thomas, 'Reading the Bible from within Our Traditions: A Pentecostal Hermeneutic as a Test Case', in J. Green and M. Turner (eds.), *Between Two Horizons: Spanning New Testament Studies and Systematic Theology* (Grand Rapids: Eerdmans, 2000), 108-22.

is undermined by Luke's presentation of the churches at Antioch and Jerusalem as united in their response to the challenge of the Judaizers. He rightly critiques the view that the Spirit sometimes guides churches into differing and even mutually incompatible theologies. He does this by drawing attention to the *timing* of the Jerusalem Council (the Spirit's hermeneutical guidance 'may have been decisively tied to the eschatological change brought about by the once-for-all [all times and all communities] work of Christ') and by noting *who participated* in the debate ('the leading figures depicted in Acts 15 are something other than typical Christians, or even typical church teachers').[92] The third hermeneutical approach views the Jerusalem Council as a pattern for a bimodal authority structure: the Spirit's guidance is seen as 'a second source of authority alongside of Scripture rather than simply assistance in interpreting Scripture', and this guidance is given 'specifically through the church's leadership structure (the apostles and elders) rather than through the community at large'.[93] Wiarda denies that apostolic authority can be viewed as a source of authority independent from Scripture. He observes that Acts sometimes displays 'a duality of OT authority plus apostolic "new covenant" witness (closely allied to what we now have in written form in the NT), not a duality of Scripture plus extra-scriptural apostolic tradition'.[94] He also again critiques the view that the apostolic figures in Acts 15 are presented as typical church leaders. The fourth approach to the chapter has viewed the council as an example of 'canonical conversations'. The disagreements among the apostles 'exemplify or set a pattern for the widespread NT phenomenon of theological diversity', and 'this kind of unresolved conversation then provides a pattern for today's churches as they work together through theological issues'.[95] However, Wiarda notes that Acts 15 emphasizes resolution and unity rather than unresolved debate, and says that this chapter (together with Galatians 2) makes an ironic choice as a basis for legitimating intercanonical and interecclesial disagreement. The fifth hermeneutical approach takes the council as a precedent for theological decision making

92. Wiarda, 'Jerusalem Council', 238.

93. Wiarda, 'Jerusalem Council', 239, reporting the perspective of J. Shelton, 'Epistemology and Authority in the Acts of the Apostles: An Analysis and Test Case Study of Acts 15:1-29', *The Spirit and Church* 2, no. 2 (2000), 231-47.

94. Wiarda, 'Jerusalem Council', 239. Like the second view, the third approach fails to take seriously enough the fact that the apostles were making once-for-all decisions about gospel and law, Jew and Gentile, and the fulfillment of Scripture in the light of Christ's epoch-changing work. To put it another way, they were involved in writing the ground rules for teaching that would later be expressed in the documents of the NT. So their authority is linked with the formation of the NT and is not an additional source of teaching separate from Scripture.

95. Wiarda, 'Jerusalem Council', 240, reporting the perspective of R. Wall, 'Canonical Context and Canonical Conversations', in J. Green and M. Turner (eds.), *Between Two Horizons: Spanning New Testament Studies and Systematic Theology* (Grand Rapids: Eerdmans, 2000), 165-82.

based on a concept of progressive revelation. God's past revelation concerning the law was replaced by new revelation at the time of the council. In the same way, for example, 'an old revelation that uses almost exclusively male language for God must now give way to new insights concerning feminine aspects of God'.[96] Although God's new revelation in Christ is regarded as final, the Holy Spirit is said to reveal progressively the implications of that definitive revelation. Wiarda challenges this paradigm by noting that it focuses on just one element of Acts 15 (something old was replaced by something new and better) and by opposing the view that the Spirit leads away from the revelation already given in the Bible, including the NT.

Some very important matters are raised by these debates, and much more could be said on each topic. Here it is sufficient to stress again that the whole structure and flow of the narrative in Acts 15 must govern our thinking, not an atomistic approach to aspects of the text. The historical and theological context of the debate must be taken seriously, acknowledging a distinctive and unrepeatable role for the Jerusalem Council in working out the implications of Christ's saving work. Nevertheless, Luke's narrative is rhetorically shaped and is designed to show readers the significance of the events for their lives and for their church context. 'The narrative forcefully highlights a theological message, that God's purpose for the Gentiles is salvation without circumcision.'[97] Christians in every age are bound to consider as of first importance the application of this theological principle in their own context. A second paradigmatic point about the narrative might be a pattern for resolving church problems in a harmonious way, but only when due regard is paid to the unique and unrepeatable aspects of the Jerusalem Council, as presented to us by Luke.

Another significant issue, however, remains to be investigated. Are the 'necessary things' of Acts 15:29 still binding in any way on Gentile Christians? Related to this is the question of any parallel NT teaching that might assist in the application of the Apostolic Decree. Witherington observes first the teaching in 1 Thessalonians 1:9 about the demand for Gentiles to turn from idolatry to serve the living and true God, coupled with instructions about avoiding all forms of sexual immorality in 4:1-8. More extensively, Paul deals with *porneia* in 1 Corinthians 5–6 and then the issue of eating food sacrificed to idols in 1 Corinthians 8–10, where the word *eidōlothyton* is used several times (8:1, 4, 7, 10; 10:19; cf. Acts 15:29). A specific connection between sexual sin and dining at a pagan temple feast is made in 1 Corinthians 10:7-22. 'For Paul, the issue is clearly one of venue rather than menu, as the advice in 1 Cor. 10:23-28 shows. . . . In short, Paul,

---

96. Wiarda, 'Jerusalem Council', 242, reporting the perspective of P. Smith, *Is It Okay to Call God 'Mother'? Considering the Feminine Face of God* (Peabody: Hendrickson, 1993), 215-26.

97. Wiarda, 'Jerusalem Council', 245.

like James, insists that pagans flee idolatry and immorality and the temple context where such things are thought to be prevalent.'[98]

Witherington's approach is generally more helpful than attempts to explain the Apostolic Decree specifically in terms of the Noachian precepts, or the rules in Leviticus 17:8–18:18, or rabbinic texts indicating matters on which compromise by Jews was impossible. Witherington suggests a particular social context in which the four prohibited activities were believed to occur together. His solution fits with Jewish evidence that during the NT era Jews believed that 'the chief source of Gentile impurity was their contact with "the defilement of idols," not their contact with nonkosher food'.[99] It avoids the implication that Gentiles were somehow placed under some modified obligation to keep parts of the Mosaic law (without circumcision and Sabbath observance!).[100] It shows how Paul could have happily consented to such a solution and commended the decision to his Gentile converts (Acts 16:4). The decree was expressly formulated in a way that would be understood by those who knew something about the law of Moses and Jewish concerns about Gentiles (15:21). It was a warning to abstain from acts that would offend Jewish scruples and hinder social intercourse between Jewish and Gentile believers. But its deeper significance is the implied challenge to break completely with every pagan association and practice (cf. 2 Cor. 6:14–7:1) and to do all things, even eating and drinking, to the glory of God, causing no one to stumble, 'whether Jews, Greeks or the church of God' (1 Cor. 10:31-32). John Stott helpfully concludes his discussion of the Jerusalem Council by observing that it 'secured a double victory — a victory of truth in confirming the gospel of grace, and a victory of love in preserving the fellowship by sensitive concessions to conscientious Jewish scruples'.[101]

G. Disagreement between Paul and Barnabas (15:36-41)

Some scholars would describe this as the beginning of Paul's second missionary journey. More precisely, however, it forms the first part of a bridge

---

98. Witherington 1998, 466. Paul indicates that it was acceptable to eat food sacrificed in a pagan temple at home under certain conditions. He even chooses a different term to refer to food that comes from the temple and is eaten elsewhere (*hierothyton*; 1 Cor. 10:28). Witherington notes that there may be verbal allusions to the apostolic decree in Rev. 2:14, 20, where prohibitions against idolatrous foods and sexual immorality are mentioned together. He also notes *Did.* 6:2 ('in matters of food do what you can; but abstain at any cost from *eidōlothyton*, which is the worship of dead gods'). Bruce 1990, 347, details further references to the Apostolic Decree in Christian literature.

99. Witherington 1998, 462, citing particularly the research of G. Alon, *Jews, Judaism, and the Classical World: Studies in Jewish History in the Times of the Second Temple and the Talmud* (Jerusalem: Magnes, 1977), 146-89.

100. Cf. Blomberg, 'The Christian and the Law', 397-416.

101. Stott 1990, 257.

(15:36–16:5) between events following the Jerusalem Council (15:30-35) and Paul's entrance into fresh territories (16:6ff.). At this stage, he simply revisits churches planted on the first journey, to strengthen them by delivering 'the decisions reached by the apostles and elders in Jerusalem for the people to obey' (16:4-5). Luke also has another purpose for this bridge passage. He shows how Paul and Barnabas were agreed on the strategy to revisit and strengthen the churches, but divided in their attitude to a potential colleague. Luke does not hide their sharp disagreement or the sadness of their parting company. At the same time, however, he shows that good actually came out of this situation, with two mission teams being formed, and both teams being 'commended by the believers to the grace of the Lord' (vv. 39-40). In other words, although Paul took the harder line, he did not lose the support of the church in Antioch.

36-38 Time references such as *some time later (meta de tinas hēmeras)* are regularly used in the second half of Acts to begin a new section (cf. 18:1; 21:15; 24:1, 24; 25:1; 28:11, 17). This is the beginning of a bridge passage which leads into the account of Paul's missionary campaign (16:6–18:22). The possibility of moving into fresh territory is not raised at this point, 'although the rest of the story (16:6) suggests that the idea was probably present right from the beginning'.[102] Barnabas appears to have agreed with Paul's proposal to go back and visit all the towns where they had preached the gospel and *'see how they are doing'.* However, when Barnabas *wanted to take John, also called Mark, with them,* a serious division emerged. Perhaps it was his family connection (Mark is called the cousin of Barnabas in Col. 4:10), but more likely it was the character of Barnabas to give those who failed a second chance. Luke gives more space to explaining why Paul was opposed to this proposal, suggesting the need to justify Paul's harder line. *Paul did not think it wise to take him, because he had deserted them in Pamphylia* (indicating the blameworthiness of Mark's departure in 13:13) *and had not continued with them in the work* (indicating that Mark could not be trusted to finish what he started).[103] Paul considered that the work of the gospel would be at risk if John Mark accompanied them again.

39-40 *They had such a sharp disagreement (paroxysmos) that they parted company.* We cannot know if the disagreement was expressed in anger,[104]

---

102. Marshall 1980, 256. Cf. Witherington 1998, 471-72, on the function of this transitional passage in Luke's narrative.

103. For different views about the personal factors involved in this dispute, compare Bruce 1990, 349-50, and Spencer 1997, 158. Codex D has expanded the sentence in 15:38 with additional clauses, which are not part of the earliest and best-attested MS traditions, seeking to enhance Mark's blameworthiness. Cf. Metzger, *Textual Commentary*, 388.

104. *paroxysmos (sharp disagreement)* is used in Dt. 29:28 (LXX 29:27); Je. 32:37 (LXX 39:37) to convey the sense of 'indignation', in association with words for 'anger' and 'wrath' (cf. the related verb in LXX Nu. 14:11; 15:30; Dt. 1:34; 9:19; Ps. 9:34). The noun is used in a positive sense in Heb. 10:24, but the cognate verb is used quite negatively in Acts 17:16, where it is said that Paul's spirit was 'provoked' within him *(parōxyneto)* when he saw the idolatry in Athens. Cf. 1 Cor. 13:5.

but it certainly led to the separation of friends. Sometimes disagreements among Christians seem to be intractable because they arise from differences of experience, insight, or character. In this case the partners disagreed about the wisdom of taking a colleague on a long and arduous journey, with a small team requiring unanimity, trust, and mutual support, when the person himself had previously proved to be unreliable in the course of a similar undertaking.[105] Marshall describes it as 'a classic example of the perpetual problem of whether to place the interests of the individual or of the work as a whole first, and there is no rule of thumb for dealing with it'.[106] Luke does not hide the seriousness of the situation, showing that they finally *parted company (apochōristhēnai)*, because John Mark had previously left them (13:13, *apochōrēsis*). Barnabas is not mentioned again in Acts (though in 1 Cor. 9:6 he is mentioned as a colleague of Paul again). The validity of his confidence in Mark is later shown by Paul's later acceptance of Mark as a colleague (Col. 4:10; Philemon 24; 2 Tim. 4:11). Luke does not pass judgement on either party, but indicates that good came out of the separation, because two mission teams were formed. *Barnabas took Mark and sailed for Cyprus*, covering the first stage of the proposed revisitation of the churches. Paul's choice of *Silas* as his partner is particularly significant in the context. He represents 'the unity of purpose between Jerusalem and the mission launched from Antioch, a unity achieved through the Jerusalem agreement'.[107] Silas was one of the emissaries from Jerusalem chosen to accompany Paul and Barnabas on their return to Antioch with the letter from the council (vv. 22-32). His way of encouraging and strengthening the believers (v. 32) clearly commended him to Paul as a suitable mission partner. Luke makes no mention of the way either Mark or Silas made their way from Jerusalem to Antioch to take part in these new ventures (cf. vv. 33-35 note). The second journey began from Antioch as the first one did, with the leaders *commended by the believers to the grace of the Lord* (cf. 14:26).[108] Per-

---

105. Haenchen 1971, 476-77, considers various theories about the link between this disagreement and the one between Paul and Barnabas mentioned in Gal. 2:13. Cf. Barrett 1998, 756. If the incident described in Galatians 2 occurred before the Jerusalem Council, as seems most likely (cf. notes 11-12 above), these disagreements were separated by some time and were over very different matters. According to Marshall 1980, 257, 'it could be that the memory of it still lingered, and that Paul felt uncertain of Barnabas's attitude in the tricky situation in the Galatian churches'. Cf. R. Bauckham, 'Barnabas in Galatians', *JSNT* 2 (1979), 61-70. However, Witherington 1998, 472, rightly observes that the very fact that Paul suggested the revisitation of the churches with Barnabas (15:36) 'intimates that he had no qualms about working with Barnabas again'.

106. Marshall 1980, 258.

107. Tannehill 1990, 196. Their partnership demonstrates 'the full meaning of the Jerusalem agreement by showing the unified mission that it makes possible'. Witherington 1998, 473, gives several reasons why Silas was a wise choice as a travelling companion for Paul. Haenchen 1971, 474, notes that, 'similarly, the companionship of John Mark symbolizes — albeit in less illustrious fashion — the recognition of Jerusalem for the mission of Barnabas'.

108. Some ancient witnesses read 'the grace of *God*', but this seems to be a scribal assimilation to 14:26. Cf. Metzger, *Textual Commentary*, 388-89.

haps there is a special point here in mentioning such commendation, since Paul had taken such a hard line on John Mark and split from Barnabas. This probably caused a division of opinion in the church, but both teams were commended to *the grace of the Lord* in prayer. Paul revisited Antioch when this campaign was over (18:22-23), demonstrating a continuing relationship of mutual care and support between them.

41 Travelling overland this time, Paul and Silas went *through Syria and Cilicia, strengthening the churches* (cf. 14:21-22), initially covering the area specifically addressed in the letter from Jerusalem (15:23).[109] They were possibly following the route of the false teachers as they made their way towards South Galatia. This meant walking through the narrow pass in the Taurus mountains known as the 'Cilician Gates' and traversing some rugged territory before reaching Derbe (16:1). Luke gives us no details about the founding of churches in Syria and Cilicia, but Galatians 1:21, 23 indicates that some of Paul's earliest evangelistic endeavours were in the region.

H. Revisiting the South Galatian Churches (16:1-5)

This is the second part of a bridge passage (15:36–16:5) showing how Paul's second missionary journey began with a visit to strengthen existing congregations in Syria and Cilicia (15:41), and then Derbe, Lystra, and Iconium (16:1-5). Both sections 'underscore the place of continuing pastoral oversight in Luke's understanding of evangelism'.[1] Two features of this particular narrative are of special importance. First, there is the introduction of Timothy, who figures significantly in subsequent narratives as a member of Paul's new team. His circumcision by Paul is explained in terms of his family situation and Paul's concern to facilitate the team's acceptance in Jewish contexts (16:1-3). Once more, Luke demonstrates Paul's desire to keep the way open for the evangelisation of Jews. Second, there is the note about delivering the decisions reached by the Jerusalem Council, thus strengthening the churches (16:4-5). The impression is given that these predominantly Gentile congregations were sufficiently satisfied with the decisions for Paul and his team to move on and minister elsewhere. Luke illustrates again Paul's concern to further the mission among the Gentiles while keeping the door open for further evangelisation among Jews. With a summary verse in 16:5 reminiscent of 9:31, Luke signals the end of one panel of his work and the beginning of another.

1-3 *Paul came to Derbe and then to Lystra,* where congregations had been established on the first missionary journey with Barnabas (14:6-23).

---

109. Codex D adds 'delivering the commands of the elders', and this is expanded with further detail in several versions. These additions express what is stated in 16:4 and are not part of the earliest and best evidence for 15:41.

1. Gaventa 2003, 234.

Coming with Silas from the east on this occasion, he travelled from Syria to Cilicia (15:41),[2] and then crossed the Taurus range by the Cilician gates, to visit Derbe before Lystra. There Paul met *Timothy*,[3] who was to play such an important role in his subsequent life and ministry (17:14-15; 18:5; 19:22; 20:4; cf. Rom. 16:21; 1 Cor. 4:17; 16:10; 2 Cor. 1:1, 19; Phil. 1:1; 2:19; Col. 1:1; 1 Thes. 1:1; 3:2, 6; 2 Thes. 1:1; 1 Tim. 1:2, 18; 6:20; 2 Tim. 1:2). Timothy is described as *a disciple (mathētēs)*, meaning a Christian in this context (cf. 6:1; 9:36, 38), with a good reputation in the churches of the region *(The believers at Lystra and Iconium spoke well of him)*.[4] He was, however, of mixed parentage. His mother, who had the Greek name Eunice (2 Tim. 1:5), was *Jewish and a believer (huios gynaikos Ioudaias pistēs;* NRSV, ESV, 'the son of a Jewish woman who was a believer'). But his father is simply described as *a Greek*, the form of the sentence implying that he was neither a Jew nor a believer. Timothy's father had possibly objected to his son's circumcision on the eighth day after birth.[5] Paul's motivation for having Timothy circumcised as an adult is first described in positive terms: he *wanted to take him along on the journey*, suggesting a practical need in relation to the mission. In negative terms, he circumcised him *because of the Jews who lived in that area, for they all knew that his father was a Greek* (the imperfect tense of the verb *hypērchen* probably implies that his father was now dead).[6] As an uncircumcised son of a mixed marriage, Timothy would have been regarded by Jews in the region as 'technically an apostate Jew'.[7] Hengel argues that Paul was bound to circumcise Timothy if he wanted to have him as a colleague, otherwise 'he would have supported apostasy and would no longer have been allowed to appear in any synagogue'.[8] Luke's record at this point has been regarded with scepti-

---

2. The Western text continues its expansion of 15:41, making it clear that Lystra and Derbe were not in Syria and Cilicia. Cf. Metzger, *Textual Commentary*, 389.

3. Some commentators take 1 Cor. 4:17 to mean that Paul was responsible for Timothy's conversion on his first journey. Cf. Haenchen 1971, 478; Marshall 1980, 259; Witherington 1998, 474.

4. From 2 Tim. 3:14-15 we learn that Timothy was taught the Scriptures from infancy, making him 'wise for salvation through faith in Christ Jesus.' His mother and grandmother appear to have been responsible for this (2 Tim. 1:5). Timothy was thus prepared to receive the gospel and believe in the Lord Jesus with them, when Paul first visited their town.

5. Johnson 1992, 284, argues that this explanation is supported by the wording of v. 3. The Jews of the area would have taken Timothy's circumcision seriously 'because they knew that his Gentile father (who had authority in such matters) had prevented the circumcision before this'. Bruce 1990, 351, observes, 'That a Jewess should marry a Gentile reflects a less rigid degree of social separation than was customary in Jewish Palestine'.

6. Cf. Barrett 1998, 761-62. The present tense would have been used if his father was still alive.

7. Bruce 1990, 352. Barrett 1998, 759-60, argues that the principle of matrilineal descent was not in operation in the first century AD in Jewish circles. S. J. D. Cohen, 'Was Timothy Jewish? Patristic Exegesis, Rabbinic Law, and Matrilineal Descent,' *JBL* 105 (1986), 251-68, uses this argument to propose that Timothy would have been viewed by Paul and Luke as a Gentile. However, see the response to Cohen by Bruce 1990, 352; Witherington 1998, 475-76.

8. M. Hengel, *Acts and the History of Earliest Christianity* (Philadelphia: Fortress, 1979), 64.

cism by some commentators. Acts 15 proves that circumcision was not required of Gentile believers, and we know from Galatians 2:3-5 that Paul resisted attempts to have his Greek colleague Titus circumcised. Moreover, Paul made several appeals in his letters for Gentiles not to submit to circumcision (e.g., Gal. 5:1-12; 1 Cor. 7:18-20). So Barrett asks whether it is likely that Paul would, 'apparently without pressure, circumcise his intended companion?'[9] Part of the answer to this question lies in the words 'without pressure'. Paul resisted the circumcision of Titus because it was being urged upon him by certain false believers who had 'infiltrated our ranks to spy on the freedom we have in Christ Jesus and to make us slaves' (Gal. 2:4). But there was no such pressure in the case of Timothy. Furthermore, the issue here was the voluntary circumcision of a *Jewish* believer, to 'make an honest Jew of him'.[10] If Paul himself became like a Jew to the Jews in order to win Jews (1 Cor. 9:20), why should not Timothy also be circumcised to win the circumcised, although as a Christian Jew he was free from the law like Paul himself?[11] Both Luke and Paul give evidence of a flexibility in such matters that should not be dismissed as inconsistent or unhistorical.

From a narrative perspective, this story has three functions. First, it clarifies what was decided at the Jerusalem Council: 'by opening a door of freedom to Gentile Christians, the Church did not close the door to Jewish Christians; everything appropriate to that tradition could still be practiced, so long as it was understood to have cultural rather than soteriological significance'.[12] Second, Luke is concerned to show that Paul's mission to the Gentiles is 'not in any way an abandonment of his commitment to Judaism'.[13] Third, Luke prepares for 21:21, making it clear in advance that 'there was no basis for the complaint that Paul was insisting that *Jews* forsake Moses, in particular that they not circumcise their children'.[14]

9. Barrett 1998, 761. Barrett (753) thinks that 'it is just credible that Paul did this, but only just'. Cf. Haenchen 1971, 480-82, for a more sceptical assessment.

10. Barrett 1998, 762. This is the only explanation of the situation that Barrett will allow. Johnson 1992, 289, argues that 'Luke regards circumcision as a legitimate expression of national *ethos* for Jews'. Longenecker 1981, 455, argues that it was 'both proper and expedient for Paul to circumcise him. As Paul saw it, being a good Christian did not mean being a bad Jew. Rather, it meant being a fulfilled Jew. Paul had no desire to flout Jewish scruples in his endeavour to bring both Jews and Gentiles to salvation in Christ.'

11. Haenchen 1971, 481, puts this question in order to oppose its argument. However, his response is speculative, presuming that the Paul who wrote 1 Cor. 7:17-20 would have nothing to do with 'the supplementary circumcision of a Christian'. Haenchen makes much of the argument that Paul could not disregard the religious significance of circumcision and simply act pragmatically. This point can be accepted without implying that Paul was being inconsistent and abandoning his argument about circumcision being irrelevant to the question of eternal salvation (cf. Gal. 5:15-16; 1 Cor. 7:19-20).

12. Johnson 1992, 289.

13. Johnson 1992, 289. At the very beginning of his turn to Europe, Paul 'asserts that commitment through this action, and he will continue to the end trying to bring "the hope of Israel" to his own people'.

14. Witherington 1998, 475. Cf. Johnson 1992, 290.

4-5 *As they traveled from town to town, they delivered the decisions reached by the apostles and elders in Jerusalem for the people to obey.*[15] The letter containing those decisions was addressed only to 'the Gentile believers in Antioch, Syria and Cilicia' (15:23), but Paul and Silas saw the need to make it more widely known. One reason for this must have been the disturbance caused by those who were preaching the necessity of circumcision for Gentile believers in the South Galatian churches (cf. Gal. 5:1-12; 6:12-16). 'Since the decisions explicitly relieved the Gentile Christians from taking the step of circumcision, the mention of them here underlines the fact that Timothy was being treated *as a Jew*, and that his experience was no precedent for what Gentiles should do.'[16] *So the churches were strengthened in the faith and grew daily in numbers.* Once again, Luke makes the important point that resolution of doctrinal and practical issues in the churches promoted the work of the gospel and led to rapid growth (cf. 6:7; 9:31). The construction *hai men oun ekklēsiai* ('the churches then') clearly links the strengthening and growth of the churches to the ministry descibed in 16:4. There is a singular form of the same construction in 9:31. Both summary verses signify the progress of the word of God in terms of church growth. As such, they indicate the end of one panel of Luke's work and the beginning of the next.[17]

VI. THE WORD GOES TO EUROPE (16:6–18:22)

Sir William Ramsay argued that it is anachronistic to make much of Paul crossing over to Europe at this point in the narrative. 'A broad distinction between the opposite sides of the Hellespont as belonging to two different Continents had no existence in the thought of those who lived in the Aegean lands . . . and the distinction had no more existence in a political point of view, for Macedonia and Asia were merely two provinces of the Roman Empire, closely united by a common language and character, and divided from the Latin-speaking provinces further west.'[18] However, Witherington insists that the crossing of ethnic and geographical boundaries is important to Luke, and that this is another significant step in his

15. The Western text adds that they boldly preached the Lord Jesus Christ, perhaps to provide an explanation for the growth of the churches in numbers. Cf. Metzger, *Textual Commentary*, 389-90.

16. Marshall 1980, 260-61. Paul is silent in his letters about the decisions of the Jerusalem Council, where he argues the case for Gentile freedom from the law from basic principles. On occasions, however, he insists on acting in accord with the general practice of the churches (1 Cor. 11:16; 14:33-34), and this suggests that he would not have been averse to using the Jerusalem Decree to support his argument.

17. Cf. INTRODUCTION TO ACTS: IV.B. Structure (pp. 32-36).

18. W. M. Ramsay, *St Paul the Traveller and the Roman Citizen* (London: Hodder & Stoughton, 1895), 199.

'one geographical region at a time' approach.[19] There are certainly narrative clues to suggest that this was Luke's view. The second missionary journey involved an initiating work of the Holy Spirit, as the first one did (13:1-4). However, the issue here is not commissioning and release by the church, but unexpected guidance for missionaries already journeying beyond boundaries previously reached (16:6-10). As in the previous campaign, Paul and his team continue to preach to Jews first, wherever possible (16:13; 17:1-4, 10-12, 17; 18:4, 19). However, encounters with Gentiles outside the synagogue are more in evidence in this section of Acts and are more varied in character. These include meetings with a fortune-teller (16:16-18), a jailer (16:23-37), ordinary citizens in a marketplace (17:17), and philosophers in the Council of the Areopagus (17:18-31). The last scene involves a major speech from Paul to a pagan audience, corresponding to, but more extensive than, the one in Lystra (14:15-17). There is no speech to a synagogue audience recorded for this journey, Luke having given a good example of this in 13:16-41. The second missionary journey expands on the theme of unbelieving Jews stirring up opposition to the gospel among Gentiles (13:45, 50; 14:2-5, 19; 17:5-9, 13), climaxing in the scene at Corinth (18:12-17). However, this section also shows how the direct impact of the gospel on Greco-Roman culture was such as to arouse economic, social, and religious opposition (16:19-24; 17:18-21, 32). There are increasing encounters with Roman officials, as accusations are brought against Christians (16:19-24, 35-39; 17:6-9; 18:12-17). But Luke continues to illustrate the growth of different types of churches, as the gospel penetrates into various levels of society. The second missionary journey finishes with an account of Paul's eighteen-month ministry in Corinth (18:1-17) — the longest since his time in Syrian Antioch — and a brief period of ministry in Ephesus on the way back to Jerusalem and Antioch (18:18-22).

A. Remarkable Guidance (16:6-10)

Paul and his companions only broke new ground when they travelled through the Phrygian-Galactic region and Mysia to Troas, where a vision was used by God to call the missionaries to preach the gospel in Macedonia (16:6-10). The issue of special divine guidance surfaces again here (cf. 8:26-40; 9:1-16; 10:1-33; 11:1-18; 13:1-4; 15:1-29). The Holy Spirit — also identified as the Spirit of Jesus — keeps them from preaching in certain regions, which may have been considered the next places to visit on a journey north through Asia Minor. A vision is then given to Paul to direct them to the place of God's choice. 'Once again the narrator shows keen interest in the

19. Witherington 1998, 486. Cf. Johnson 1992, 290. Spencer 1997, 131, describes 16:6–21:36 as the Aegean Expedition and argues that what is often called the third missionary journey is only an extension of work begun on the second.

dialogue between human purpose and divine purpose, indicating that Jesus' witnesses, too, must patiently endure the frustration of their own plans in order to discover the opportunity that God holds open. This opportunity may not be the next logical step by human calculation.'[20] At this point, Luke apparently joined the team, since he tells the story from 16:10 for the first time in the first person plural. The narrator becomes more intimately involved in the story at the very moment when the characters must decide how to respond to the visionary call of God.

6-8 References to the Spirit and a vision in vv. 6-10 recall the guidance given to Peter in 10:10-20 and the initiating role of the Spirit in Paul's first missionary journey (13:2). In effect, the divine commissioning for the second campaign comes at this point. The visit to the believers in Syria, Cilicia, and South Galatia was a wisely considered human initiative which God blessed by strengthening and growing the churches (15:41; 16:5). Remarkably, however, the Spirit then acted as a frustrating force on two successive occasions, before the positive direction of the vision was given. First, *Paul and his companions traveled throughout the region of Phrygia and Galatia, having been kept by the Holy Spirit from preaching the word in the province of Asia.* Phrygia and Galatia were both ancient kingdoms in Asia Minor. In 116 BC the greater part of Phrygia was absorbed into the Roman province of Asia, and in 25 BC the remaining eastern portion was absorbed into the Roman province of Galatia. The province of Galatia thus included parts of Phrygia, as well as parts of Lycaonia (where Derbe, Lystra, and Iconium were situated) and Pisidia.[21] Paul and his companions travelled northwest through the Phrygian-Galatian region, because they were prevented from turning west into Asia by the Holy Spirit.[22] It is quite extraordinary that the Spirit would prevent the preaching of the gospel in this way, suggesting that the ministry in Macedonia and Greece was God's priority at this point in time.[23] Such guidance was possibly given through a prophetic word (cf.

20. Tannehill 1990, 195.

21. Cf. Bruce 1990, 353-54; Barrett 1998, 767. Barrett (766-67) discusses the various possibilities for translating the phrase *tēn Phrygian kai Galatikēn chōran* and concludes that this most naturally refers to one region defined by two adjectives (so also NRSV, ESV, TNIV). So also Witherington 1998, 477-78. KJV and NKJV ('Phrygia and the region of Galatia') follow the Received Text, which adds another article to the Greek (*tēn Phrygian kai tēn Galatikēn chōran*) and implies two regions, the second being ethnic Galatia in the north of the province. This is not a well-attested reading (cf. Metzger, *Textual Commentary*, 390). Nevertheless, the question remains whether *Phrygia* is used adjectivally or as a substantive proper name. It is used as a noun in 18:23, but this does not prove the case for 16:6. C. J. Hemer, *The Book of Acts in the Setting of Hellenistic History*, ed. C. Gempf, WUNT 49 (Tübingen: Mohr Siebeck, 1989; repr. Winona Lake: Eisenbrauns, 1990), 280-99, gives clear evidence for 'Phrygia' being used as an adjective or ethnic designation.

22. The aorist participle *kōlythentes* ('prevented, kept') in its position after the aorist indicative *diēthon* ('travelled through') should be read in a circumstantial or causal fashion, describing the reason for taking the path they did. Cf. Johnson 1992, 285; Barrett 1998, 768-69.

23. Paul's desire to preach in Asia is highlighted again in 18:18-21. He finally re-

13:1-3), perhaps through Silas (15:32), or perhaps 'on the occasion when Timothy joined the missionary company (1 Tim. 1:18; 4:14; cf. 2 Tim. 1:6)'.[24] The province of Asia was a wealthy and highly civilized region, bounded by Bithynia in the north, Lycia in the south, and Galatia in the east. As the missionaries travelled further north, *they came to the border of Mysia (kata tēn Mysian,* 'opposite, over against Mysia'), which was part of the Roman province of Asia (Asia and Mysia had been historically separate regions). At this point, *they tried to enter Bithynia,* which was a senatorial province to the east of Mysian Asia. But once more *the Spirit of Jesus would not allow them to.* The Holy Spirit is more narrowly defined here as *the Spirit of Jesus,* suggesting that the exalted Christ continued to direct the progress of the gospel through the Spirit which he 'received from the Father' and 'poured out' on his disciples at Pentecost (2:33; cf. Rom. 8:9-10 ['the Spirit of Christ']; Phil. 1:19 ['the Spirit of Jesus Christ']). In other words, Luke's change of expression here is not simply for stylistic variation but to recall an important theological perspective about the Spirit's relation to the ascended and enthroned Messiah. 'Jesus continues to take an active role in the story (7:56; 9:5).'[25] TNIV *(so they passed by Mysia and went down to Troas)* is slightly misleading (so also most EVV). *Troas* was actually situated in Mysia and could be approached only by passing west through Mysia.[26] So they 'traversed' Mysia, without preaching there, and went down to the ancient Greek city known as Alexandria Troas, which had been made a Roman colony by Augustus. It was an important commercial centre and a key spot in the Roman network of communications, being a pivotal port between the land masses of Europe and Asia Minor and the great waterways of the Aegean and Black seas. It was the sort of centre where Paul was likely to preach and found a church. However, he did not get that opportunity until he visited again at a later date (2 Cor. 2:12-13; cf. Acts 20:7-12; 2 Tim. 4:13).

9-10 The Spirit had blocked every direction sought by human initiative since the missionaries left Lystra and Iconium. Now it was time to understand why. *During the night Paul had a vision of a man of Macedonia standing and begging him, 'Come over to Macedonia and help us'.* Luke records several visions that were given to guide key individuals at significant points in their

---

turned to Ephesus to begin an extensive ministry there, 'so that all the Jews and Greeks who lived in the province of Asia heard the word of the Lord' (19:10).

24. Bruce 1990, 354.

25. Johnson 1992, 285. The expression 'the Spirit of Jesus' is so unusual that various MSS substituted 'the Spirit of the Lord' or 'the Holy Spirit' or reduced the expression to 'the Spirit' (so the Received Text and KJV, NKJV), but the evidence for 'the Spirit of Jesus' is overwhelming. Cf. Metzger, *Textual Commentary,* 390-91. Bruce 1990, 355, considers the possibility that the prophecy may have been uttered expressly in the name of Jesus.

26. Barrett 1998, 770-71, notes some examples of the verb *parerchesthai* being used in the sense of 'pass through' ('pass by' or 'pass alongside' is its normal sense). However, Barrett also suggests that the verb could be used in the sense of 'arrive at'. The Western text substitutes *dielthontes* ('passed through'), which is an easier reading, but clearly not the original.

lives (7:31 [Stephen]; 9:10 [Ananias]; 9:12 [Saul]; 10:3 [Cornelius]; 10:9-17, 19; 11:5 [Peter]; 16:10; 18:9; 22:17 [Paul]). However, in the total record of Acts, such visions are rare and unexpected by the characters concerned. We should therefore conclude that this is an unusual form of divine guidance. The man who identified himself as coming from Macedonia was *standing and begging* Paul to cross the Thracian Sea (the northern part of the Aegean), to *help* the people he represented. Paul shared this vision with his companions, including Luke. Most commentators uphold the view that Luke introduces his own eyewitness material at this point — using the first-person plural form *(we got ready)* — because it was at Troas that he first became an active participant in the Pauline mission.[27] The 'we' portion of this chapter extends to v. 17, covering the sea journey to Philippi and the first stage of the mission there. 'At every place where the narrator refers to the people with Paul (and often, apparently, Paul with the group), he uses the first-person plural, until the narrative clearly takes up a consistently maintained third-person stance.'[28] This same style, which gives a sense of eyewitness involvement and authenticity, then reappears in the accounts of sea voyages in 20:5-15; 21:1-18; 27:1–28:16. When Paul shared the details of the vision with his companions, some form of reflection and discussion took place about its meaning. This is suggested by the terminology employed *(concluding [symbibazontes] that God had called us to preach the gospel to them)*. They reasoned together that the *help* required in Macedonia would come from preaching Christ to them.[29] All were persuaded *at once (eutheōs) to leave for Macedonia,* indicating unhesitating obedience to God's direction (cf. 18:11; 20:22-24; 26:19).

In conclusion, it ought to be said that the narrative stretching from 15:36 to 16:10 shows both the importance and the limitation of human initiative in Christian work. The plan to revisit the South Galatian churches was clearly appropriate and was blessed by God. But the plan to move on

27. Cf. Marshall 1980, 263-64; 1992, 84-91. Barrett 1998, 772-73, 776-77, argues that it is not necessary to assume that this was where Luke joined the team of missionaries (Luke may have switched from third-person to first-person narrative 'for some reason of his own'), or he could be using a source in which someone else such as Timothy or Silas was recording events as an eyewitness. But this seems to be an unnecessarily complicated solution. The Western text once more makes additions, presumably to ensure that readers understood what was in the vision. Cf. Metzger, *Textual Commentary*, 392.

28. S. E. Porter, *Paul in Acts* (Peabody: Hendrickson, 2001, a reprint of *The Paul of Acts: Essays in Literary Criticism, Rhetoric, and Theology,* WUNT 115 [Tübingen: Mohr, 1999]), 30. Witherington 1998, 480-86, and Hemer, *Book of Acts,* 308-34, discuss at some length the authenticity and function of the 'we' passages. W. S. Campbell, *The 'We' Passages in the Acts of the Apostles: The Narrator as Narrative Character,* SBLSBL 14 (Atlanta: SBL; Leiden: Brill, 2007), argues that the 'we' narrator replaces Barnabas in the story as Paul's trustworthy companion, to help establish Paul's credibility as a reliable witness.

29. Marshall 1980, 263, rightly observes that 'psychological explanations, such as that the dream was occasioned by a visit by Macedonians (possibly including Luke) to Paul in Troas are speculative'. Witherington 1998, 479-80, assesses various views about who the man in the vision might have been and concludes that such speculation misses the point of Luke's narrative, which is to stress the divine commissioning for what is to follow.

into Asia and Bithynia with the gospel, though logical and practical, was resisted by God because he had another priority. In due time, God allowed the gospel to be planted in those regions (cf. 18:23; 19:1-10; 1 Pet. 1:1). Similarly, Paul's decision not to take John Mark appears to have been wise, for, though the consequences were painful in terms of the separation from Barnabas, they were fruitful in terms of the establishment of two mission teams. The wider evidence of the NT indicates a reconciliation between the parties in due course. We cannot expect the regular guidance of visions and prophecies in our everyday decision making, but we are encouraged by Luke's narrative to believe in God's sovereign overruling and intervention to direct the progress of his word and his people, where necessary. Meanwhile, the norm that is suggested by Acts is the taking of initiatives for the gospel, with wise planning (cf. Jas. 1:5-8) and a loving concern for those we seek to reach, trusting God to open or close the way as he sees best. Whether God's direction comes through circumstances, through prophetic insight, or through a vision, God's people will need to reflect together on the guidance they receive. They will need to relate what is perceived to be the specific will of God in a given situation to the general will of God revealed in the pages of Scripture.[30]

B. Salvation Comes to Philippi (16:11-34)

Luke's account of the ministry in Philippi covers the rest of Acts 16. It is the longest record of Paul's activity in any European city or town, though we have no way of calculating how long he actually stayed there. In previous chapters the focus has been on Paul's public preaching in synagogues and town centres, but here the pattern is individual encounter or evangelism with households. Salvation, rather than the kingdom of God or eternal life, is highlighted as the message proclaimed in this city (16:17, 30-31; cf. 13:46-48; 14:22; 15:1, 11). Greco-Roman religion was familiar with the language of salvation, but used it in a variety of ways which Paul's gospel would have challenged. Three cameos of the kind of people encountered by the missionaries in this city are presented, illustrating the consequences of preaching the gospel across the spectrum of Greco-Roman culture and life. Other people were no doubt converted, but Luke gives us only these examples, together with the households of Lydia and the jailer. It is particularly important to Luke that Philippi was a Roman colony (v. 12), where the people considered themselves to be Romans rather than Philippians or Macedonians (vv. 20-21). Paul and Silas were flogged and jailed on the charge of

---

30. Longenecker 1981, 456, observes that 'the missionary journeys of Paul reveal an extraordinary combination of strategic planning and sensitivity to the guidance of the Holy Spirit in working out the details of the main goals'. Stott 1990, 261, suggests further specific principles of divine guidance arising from Acts 16:6-10.

throwing the city into an uproar 'by advocating customs unlawful for us Romans to accept or practice'. Their vindication as Roman citizens forms an important climax to the chapter (vv. 37-39). This is the first of four examples in Acts 16–19 which show Luke's strong concern with 'the way that the outside world perceives the Christian mission and the effect those perceptions may have on Christians'.[31] Later references to the edict of Claudius (18:2) and Gallio's proconsulate (18:12) enable us to date the journey to Macedonia and Achaia in the period AD 50-52.[32]

1. Lydia and Her Household (16:11-15)

Paul went first to a 'place of prayer' on the Sabbath, where he shared the gospel with the Jewish women and others who gathered there (16:13). In Paul's vision, it was a man of Macedonia who begged the missionaries to come and help (16:9), but it was Lydia, a God-fearing Gentile woman, who was the first to believe the message and be baptized, together with all her household (16:14-15). References to Lydia and her household frame the rest of the material in this chapter (cf. v. 40), drawing attention to her significance as a patroness of the community and hostess for the missionaries.[33] As a dealer in purple cloth, she had some degree of wealth and independence. However, it is difficult to be certain about her social status.[34] Mention of Philippi as a Roman colony (16:12) prepares for what follows concerning the impact of Christian ministry on Greco-Roman culture and some of the consequences for believers (cf. vv. 34, 37-39).

11-12 From Troas, the missionaries *put out to sea and sailed straight for Samothrace*, an island at the northern extremity of the Aegean Sea, where they presumably spent the night. The total distance from Troas to Neapolis was about 156 miles (250 km.). With a favourable wind, this could easily be accomplished in a couple of days, although the return journey took five (20:6). *The next day* they went on to *Neapolis* (modern Kavalla), the port of Philippi, which was about 10 miles or 16 km. further inland. Here, for the first time, we encounter Luke's fascination with the details of sea travel (16:11-12; 20:5, 13-15; 21:1-8; 27:1–28:16). In each of the 'we' passages on this theme, 'we have a specific port-to-port description of the voyage complete with specific mention of the time it took and usually a description of the

31. Tannehill 1990, 202. Cf. 16:19-24; 17:5-9; 18:12-16; 19:25-29. Jews are the accusers in Thessalonica and Corinth, but Gentiles in Philippi and Ephesus.

32. Witherington 1998, 77-84.

33. Spencer 1997, 165, rightly notes that the narrative in Acts leaves her ministerial status somewhat in doubt. 'Lydia appears more as a *passive hearer and helper* of Paul than a dynamic co-worker.'

34. Spencer 1997, 165, stresses her marginal status in Greco-Roman society, but see notes 45 and 47 below. Gaventa 2003, 242, also describes her as 'somewhat outside acceptable society'.

weather conditions and the like'.[35] No evangelistic work is mentioned in Samothrace or Neapolis, perhaps because there was not a synagogue or Jewish place of prayer in either context, or perhaps because Paul was deliberately heading for the larger and more influential centre of *Philippi*. Situated on the Via Egnatia, the main east-west route across Macedonia connecting Rome with its eastern provinces, Philippi was a prosperous city, which 'outstripped other cities in this district of Macedonia, including the city that had been named in 167 BC the capital of the district, Amphipolis'.[36] Philippi is the only city in Acts specifically described as *a Roman colony* (*kolōnia*, a Latin loanword), though Paul clearly visited other such colonies, such as Pisidian Antioch and Troas.[37] This is an important preparation for the narrative to follow (cf. v. 34 note, vv. 37-39). Roman colonies were originally settlements of Roman citizens in conquered territory, with legal rights the same as their fellow citizens in Italy. They then became places to which surplus Italian population could be assigned or where soldiers could be pensioned off with land.[38] They had a Roman form of local government, were free from tribute and taxation, and used Roman law in local as well as external matters. They were effectively a piece of Rome transplanted abroad. 'This situation is reflected in the Philippi narrative, not just to add local color but because the narrative is centrally concerned with the mission's encounter with the Roman world.'[39] TNIV also describes Philippi as *the leading city of that district of Macedonia*. There are a number of variants in the manuscripts at this point, apparently because of confusion over the status of Philippi in the political structure of the region. Philippi was neither the capital of Macedonia (Thessalonica was) nor the capital of the region in which it was situated (Amphipolis was). Macedonia was divided into four districts, and some have conjectured that Luke identifies Philippi as 'a city of the first district of Macedonia' (*prōtēs meridos tēs Makedonias polis*).[40] However, despite the difficulties involved in the commonly received text (*prōtē tēs meridos tēs Makedonias polis*), it appears ill advised to abandon this reading, especially since it can be taken to mean 'a leading city of the [or

35. Witherington 1998, 486.

36. Witherington 1998, 488. Longenecker 1981, 459-60, gives further historical and geographical information about Philippi.

37. Philippi was an ancient town, which had been renamed by Philip of Macedon in about 360 BC. The Roman colony of Philippi was founded by M. Antonius in 42 BC and was augmented by Octavian (Augustus), who defeated him at Actium in 31 BC.

38. Cf. Barrett 1998, 780.

39. Tannehill 1990, 201. Note the description of the chief officials in v. 20 and their subordinates in vv. 35 and 38. The accusers speak of themselves as Romans, not Philippians or Macedonians, in vv. 20-21. Although Paul had encountered a Roman official at 13:7, there is no doubt that the issue of Paul and his gospel confronting Roman government and culture is an important theme in Acts 16.

40. Cf. Metzger, *Textual Commentary*, 394-95, though Metzger himself, together with Kurt Aland, presented a minority report arguing against this. Marshall 1980, 266, supports this option.

"that"] district of Macedonia' (so NASB, ESV).[41] 'This is not a statement about Philippi's political role in the province, but rather Luke's view of its honor rating in that portion of Macedonia.'[42] The missionaries stayed there *several days (hēmeras tinas)*, the Greek suggesting a continuous, though not protracted stay.

13-14 *On the Sabbath we went outside the city gate to the river, where we expected to find a place of prayer.* A synagogue could be established only where there were ten Jewish men (cf. *m. Sanh.* 1:6; *Pirke 'Aboth* 3:6), and so it may be significant that no men are mentioned. What the visitors found was a meeting where women gathered for prayer *(We sat down and began to speak to the women who had gathered there).*[43] 'In terms of its focus on Sabbath-day prayer and worship, this assembly functions as a synagogue; however, its physical location — twice removed from the city limits by architectural (gate) and natural (river) boundaries — and socioreligious composition — women devoted to the Jewish faith — betray its restricted, marginal status within the Roman colony.'[44] *One of those listening was a woman from the city of Thyatira* in the region of Lydia in Asia Minor (cf. Rev. 2:18-29). This woman had been named after the area from which she came. It was famous for its purple dye and textiles, and Lydia was *a dealer in purple cloth.* Purple clothes were for the wealthy (Lk. 16:19) and the royal (1 Macc. 10:62; Dio Chrysostom, *Or.* 4.71). 'It is not clear whether Lydia was a sort of commercial traveller in purple cloth, who visited Philippi frequently enough to know her way to the place of prayer, or had opened a retail establishment there.'[45] Luke's interest is in the fact that she was a successful businesswoman, who was attached to the Jewish community as a God-fearer *(sebomenē ton theon, a worshiper of God).*[46] The fact that she is named could

41. So Metzger and Aland in Metzger, *Textual Commentary*, 395. Cf. Barrett 1998, 778-80.

42. Witherington 1998, 489. Witherington, 489-90, supports the conjecture of Ramsay, *Paul the Traveller*, 206-9, that it was Luke's hometown, about which he wrote with some pride. Cf. A. N. Sherwin-White, *Roman Society and Roman Law in the New Testament* (Oxford: Clarendon, 1963), 94-95, on the attitude of Roman colonies to other provincial Greek cities.

43. Cf. Marshall 1980, 266-67; Barrett 1998, 780-82. The textual variants on this verse are discussed by Metzger, *Textual Commentary*, 395-96. While there is some debate about the original form of v. 13, there is little doubt about the sense that the travellers were looking for the place where Jews gathered for prayer. T. Klutz, *The Exorcism Stories in Luke-Acts: A Sociostylistic Reading*, SNTSMS 129 (Cambridge/New York: Cambridge University, 2004), 213-14, argues that *proseuchē* means 'house of prayer' (cf. Philo, *Against Flaccus* 41.7; 45:2; *Against Allegorical Interpretation* 132.6; 134.3; Josephus, *Life* 277.2; 280.5) and that Paul's team did not find exactly what they were looking for. However, this interpretation does not work for v. 16. Witherington 1998, 491, follows Longenecker 1981, 460, in supposing that there was a more formal synagogue-type service.

44. Spencer 1997, 164. The river Gangites flowed west of the city, outside the walls. Spencer continues, 'A Macedonian male may have been the first to call for Paul's gospel (16.9), but Macedonian women are the first to hear and receive it'.

45. Barrett 1998, 782.

46. Cf. 10:2 note. For Luke's interest in the conversion of women to Christianity, cf.

mean that she was a person of some status, 'since it was normal in such a Greco-Roman setting *not* to mention women by personal name in public unless they were either notable or notorious'.[47] However, by the time Luke wrote, she may have become well known as a Christian rather than because of her social status. Perhaps she first became acquainted with Judaism in Thyatira. Luke tells us that she was *listening* (imperfect tense *ēkouen*) to the message proclaimed to her, but that it was *the Lord* who *opened her heart* (*diēnoixen tēn kardian*; cf. Lk. 24:45; 2 Macc. 1:4) *to respond to Paul's message* (*prosechein*, as in 8:6, 10, 11; 1 Tim. 4:13; Heb. 2:1; 2 Pet. 1:19, meaning 'to pay close attention, follow, adhere to'). Lydia's engagement with what Paul was saying and God's sovereignty in the process of conversion are highlighted together (cf. 13:48 note; 2 Cor. 4:5-6; 1 Thes. 1:4-5; 2 Thes. 2:13-14). Stott observes that, 'although the message was Paul's, the saving initiative was God's. Paul's preaching was not effective in itself; the Lord worked through it. And the Lord's work was not in itself direct; he chose to work through Paul's preaching. It is always the same.'[48]

15 Some period of instruction involving her household presumably took place before *she and the members of her household were baptized* (cf. v. 32, *pasin tois en tē oikia autou*, 'all who were in his house'; v. 33, *hoi autou pantes*, 'all who were with him'). The term used here and in v. 31 (*oikos*, 'house, household') might have included small children and other family members, as well as slaves. This does not prove the possibility of infant baptism, but it would be remarkable if no babies were included in any of the four household baptisms mentioned by Luke (11:14 [the God-fearing centurion]; 16:15 [the God-fearing Gentile woman], 33 [the pagan jailer]; 18:8 [the synagogue leader]; cf. 1 Cor. 1:16 [Stephanas]).[49] Household baptisms were practised across the spectrum of people turning to Christ, mirroring the Jewish practice of incorporating families as proselytes through baptism. A woman such as Lydia might have been head of a household in Greco-Roman culture because her husband had died or she was divorced, and less probably because she was a single woman of means.[50] The invitation to come and stay in her house (or

1:14; 8:3, 12; 9:2; 16:1; 17:4, 12, 34; 18:2, 26; 21:5; 22:4. P. R. Trebilco, *Jewish Communities in Asia Minor*, SNTSMS 69 (Cambridge: Cambridge University, 1991), 104-26, discusses the prominence of women in Jewish communities of Asia Minor.

47. Witherington 1998, 492. *ND* 2:26 indicates that dealing in purple was an imperial monopoly, though the evidence may date from later than this period. *ND* 2:28 shows that those involved in this trade were regarded as members of 'Caesar's household', the elite who were in imperial service. Witherington, 492-93, takes up the roles of Roman women in the provinces more generally. Spencer 1997, 165, presents Lydia as a more socially marginalised person than Witherington does.

48. Stott 1990, 263.

49. J. Jeremias, *Infant Baptism in the First Four Centuries* (ET, London: SCM, 1960), 19-24, puts the case for infant baptism, and G. R. Beasley-Murray, *Baptism in the New Testament* (Exeter: Paternoster, 1972), 312-20, puts the case against. Cf. Witherington 1998, 339

50. Cf. Witherington 1998, 493; *ND* 4:93; 5:108. Witherington 338, argues that Luke presents five cameos of important Christian women and the variety of roles they fulfilled. 'In

with her household) reflected the possibility that the missionaries might not yet consider her *'a believer in the Lord' (ei kekrikate me, 'if you consider me')*. She was quite insistent *(parebiasato hēmas, she persuaded us)*, and so they accepted her hospitality and put her at ease. As well as acknowledging her conversion, this visit marked the beginning of a distinctly Christian fellowship in Philippi.[51] Luke highlights the importance of this by concluding the narrative about Philippi with another reference to a meeting of the believers in Lydia's house (v. 40). The importance of practising hospitality, especially to encourage Christian ministry and fellowship, is stressed in Romans 12:13; 1 Timothy 3:2; Hebrews 13:2; 1 Peter 4:9; and 3 John 5-8. In her open-hearted generosity, Lydia demonstrated the reality of her conversion.

2. A Fortune-Teller and Her Masters (16:16-24)

An unnamed female slave, with a 'spirit' by which she told fortunes, recognized the preachers as 'servants of the Most High God'. Moreover, she perceived that they were offering 'a way of salvation'. 'Unlike Lydia, this woman is in control of nothing. She is a slave. Like Lydia, she earns money, but it belongs to someone else.'[52] There is no indication that she became a Christian, only that she was exorcised by Paul. Release from such spiritual bondage must have been a blessing for her, but Luke recounts the outcome for Paul and Silas rather than completing the story of the slave girl.[53] Her owners were clearly annoyed by the consequent loss of income. They brought Paul and Silas before the magistrates, who ordered them to be flogged and thrown into prison (16:16-24). The charge ignores the economic reason for their opposition, focussing on religious and sociopolitical issues. This is Paul's second encounter with demonic forces and their impact on popular religion (cf. 13:6-12). In both cases, the encounter leads to a significant demonstration of the power of Christ, though here with negative consequences for the missionaries.[54]

---

the mother of John Mark (Acts 12:12-17) and in Lydia (Acts 16:12-40) we see women assuming the role of "mother" or patroness and benefactor to the then fledgling Christian communities in Jerusalem and Philippi respectively.' Witherington also comments on Tabitha (Acts 21:9), Philip's daughters (Acts 21:9), and Priscilla (Acts 18:18-26).

51. Witherington 1998, 493, observes that the proof of her conversion is shown in her imploring Paul and his colleagues to come and stay at her house. Johnson 1992, 297, observes that, here as elsewhere, 'Luke connects spiritual dispositions to the disposition of possessions'. Spencer 1997, 165, considers Lydia's role as leader of the church in her home. In 16:14-15 she appears 'more as a *passive hearer and helper* of Paul than a dynamic co-worker.'

52. Gaventa 2003, 238.

53. Spencer 1997, 166, suggests that she may have been received by the small community of believers. But then, noting the way the narrative becomes preoccupied with the troubles of Paul and Silas, Spencer unnecessarily concludes that Luke treats this woman poorly.

54. Cf. THE THEOLOGY OF ACTS: IX. MAGIC AND THE DEMONIC (pp. 87-92).

16-17 The link between this event and the preceding one is the fact that the missionaries had their next significant encounter while *going to the place of prayer*. They were intent on winning someone else from the gathering of Jews and God-fearers by the river when they met a Gentile *slave girl* (*paidiskē*, as in 12:13), described as having *a spirit by which she predicted the future* (*pneuma pythōna*, 'a pythonic spirit' or 'a pythian spirit' [KJV, NRSV, ESV, 'a spirit of divination']).[55] Luke assumes that his readers will be familiar with such terminology and pagan modes of divination. Unlike the demonic beings in Luke's Gospel, who made their victims impure and ill (Lk. 4:31-37; 8:26-39; 9:37-43), 'the spirit in the present story is characterised chiefly by its routine inspiration of oracular pronouncements'.[56] With this gift, she *earned a great deal of money for her owners by fortune-telling*. Most of the girl's contemporaries would have considered this spirit beneficial or neutral, but Luke indicates its evil nature in two ways. First, the term he uses (*manteuomenē*, 'by giving oracles') points to something prohibited in Scripture (e.g., Dt. 18:10; 1 Sa. 28:8; 2 Ki. 17:17; Je. 27 (LXX 34):9; Ezk. 12:24).[57] Second, as in 8:4-24; 19:11-41, Luke shows a close connection between 'magic, pagan or false religion, and the profit motive of humans'.[58] The girl followed Paul and the rest of his team, shouting, *'These men are servants of the Most High God, who are telling you the way to be saved'*. Such insight recalls the recognition of Jesus by the demon-possessed in the course of his ministry (e.g., Lk. 4:33-34; 8:27-28). Indeed, the parallels with Luke 8:26-39 suggest that Paul is being portrayed as 'a legitimate and very loyal follower' of Jesus.[59] Paul is later identified, together with Jesus, by another 'spirit' in Ephesus (19:15). The evil spirit within the slave girl enabled her to

55. Luke means that the girl was possessed by an underworld spirit, who spoke through her. Python was originally the name of the snake or dragon that inhabited Delphi (originally Pythia) and in Greek mythology was killed by Apollo. This snake became a symbol or representative of the underworld. Apollo was thought to be embodied in the snake and to inspire 'pythonesses' as his female mouthpieces. Plutarch, *De Defectu Oraculorum* 9.414E, called such soothsayers 'ventriloquists' because they uttered words beyond their own control. Cf. Johnson 1992, 293-94; Barrett 1998, 784-85.

56. Klutz, *Exorcism Stories*, 215. Spencer 1997, 166-67, makes an unwarranted equation between the suppression of this girl's prophetic activity and the suppression of female Christian prophets (cf. my following note).

57. Cf. Klutz, *Exorcism Stories*, 215-17, on the use of this verb in the LXX. The practice of divination is associated with falsehood and deceit in Scripture. If Luke had wanted to present the girl's activity in a more positive fashion, he could easily have labelled it 'prophesying'.

58. Witherington 1998, 494. Johnson 1992, 294, draws attention to Lk. 12:21; 16:1-9, 16, 19-26; Acts 1:18-20; 5:1-11. Klutz, *Exorcism Stories*, 210, observes that Paul and his companions are portrayed in 16:16-21 as 'Torah-observant Jews, who not only stand firm against the forces of paganism but also subvert the most acquisitive and immoral elements of the same system'.

59. Klutz, *Exorcism Stories*, 229. Klutz, 217-19, explores the parallels with Lk. 8:26-39, but shows how Paul is dependent on the name of Jesus for exorcism and submissive to the Spirit sent by Jesus. Klutz, 229-42, argues that one of the aims of Luke-Acts is a legitimation of Paul and his ministry.

acknowledge the true identity of the travellers (*these men are servants of the Most High God*) and the true nature of their mission (*who are telling you the way to be saved* [*hodon sōtērias*, 'a way of salvation']). Although the designation *the Most High God (ho hypsistos)* was common in the LXX (e.g., Nu. 24:16; Ps. 78:35; Is. 14:14; Dn. 3:26; 4:32; 5:18, 21; 1 Esdr. 2:3), it was also used in pagan literature, so that 'a resident in Philippi, with no first-hand knowledge of Judaism, might well identify the one Jewish God with the highest god in his own pantheon'.[60] Salvation in material and spiritual ways was the object of vows and prayers to many gods in the Greco-Roman world, and it was 'the desired object set before initiates in various mystery cults'.[61] Salvation in Luke's understanding involved the forgiveness of sins and the gift of the Holy Spirit through trusting in Israel's Messiah, with the ultimate blessing of sharing in God's eternal kingdom through resurrection. What the slave girl was saying was true at one level, but it doubtless lacked these gospel perspectives. Her message was false because it was being proclaimed by someone who did not really know what she was talking about. On her lips, even the assertion that there was 'a way of salvation' could so easily have been interpreted in a polytheisitic and pagan fashion.

18 *She kept this up for many days,* implying regular daily contact with her as the missionaries sought opportunities for teaching and preaching. There is no suggestion that she was hostile to them and her cries may not have seemed offensive at first. Finally, however, after displaying much patience with her, *Paul became so annoyed* (*diaponētheis,* 'deeply disturbed' [lit. 'worked over'], as in 4:2) *that he turned around and said to the spirit, 'In the name of Jesus Christ I command you to come out of her!'* Paul's concern was that she was saying these things under the influence of an evil spirit and was thus confusing his pagan audience. On her lips, this claim could have been easily misunderstood. Moreover, bystanders could have imagined that Paul and Silas were possessed by similar spirits from the underworld. So Paul acted as an exorcist, with authority to command demonic spirits *in the name of Jesus Christ* (cf. Lk. 9:1; 10:17; Acts 19:12). His effectiveness, without elaborate ritual or repetition of the command, is simply recorded *(At that moment the spirit left her).* Whether or not the slave girl turned to Christ and received the salvation proclaimed in his name remains an open question.[62] Luke does not give us enough information to be sure. But she clearly experienced the benefits that came from being in the presence of a prophetic fig-

60. Barrett 1998, 786. Cf. Bruce 1990, 360. Witherington 1998, 494-95, rightly insists that the utterances of the slave girl should be seen in their 'proper polytheistic and pluralistic context'.

61. Bruce 1990, 361. Cf. Witherington 1998b, 145-66; THE THEOLOGY OF ACTS: IV. SALVATION (pp. 65-70).

62. Stott 1990, 265, suggests that 'the fact that her deliverance took place between the conversions of Lydia and the gaoler leads readers to infer that she too became a member of the Philippian church'. The name of Jesus is powerful to heal and to save in 3:6, 16; 4:10, 30, and so it could be implied here that she was 'saved' as well as 'healed'.

ure like Paul and being liberated from the powers of evil by his authoritative command. The kingdom of God drew near to her in this way, and she
had the opportunity to turn to the one in whose name she was released
from the power of darkness. Abandoned by her owners, she was perhaps
cared for by the little community of believers.

19-21   As with the healing stories in 3:1-10; 14:8-9, 'the intervention
by God's servants causes a public reaction with consequences for the mission'.[63] In this context, the economic and social implications of the girl's liberation from the powers of evil come immediately into focus. *When her owners realized that their hope of making money was gone, they seized Paul and Silas
and dragged them into the marketplace to face the authorities.*[64] From this point
in the narrative about Philippi, the 'we' disappears until 20:5. It is likely
that Paul and Silas alone were arrested and imprisoned, perhaps because
they were more clearly Jewish than their companions. Did Luke not accompany them on the next stage of the journey? Witherington suggests that
'Luke lived in Troas or perhaps Philippi and travelled back and forth between these locations. This would account for the brief "we" passages during the second missionary journey and why they occur just where they do.
We would then have to assume that by the time of the third missionary
journey Luke had agreed to travel with the group for a more extended period of time.'[65] There is a humorous play on words in vv. 18-19, revealing
the economic reason for the attack on Paul and Silas. It was when the spirit
left the slave girl *(exēlthen)* that her owners' hope of making money from
her *was gone (exēlthen)*. However, *before the magistrates (tois stratēgois)*,[66] they
stated their case in religious and political terms: *'These men are Jews, and are
throwing our city into an uproar by advocating customs unlawful for us Romans
to accept or practice'.* These businessmen sought to '"broaden the respect-
ability" of their claim by enlisting the support of other "agents of censure",
both legal (magistrates) and popular (crowds)'.[67] They used labelling to

---

63. Tannehill 1990, 197. Cf. Spencer 1997, 159-61.

64. Barrett 1998, 788, observes that the marketplace of a Greek city was much more
than a place for buying and selling (cf. 17:17): 'it was used for all kinds of public purposes,
including judicial purposes'. Here 'the authorities' *(tous archontas,* v. 19) were found.
Witherington 1998, 496, suggests that the girl's owners 'should probably be seen as persons
of considerable social status in the community, for it was normally only people of considerable financial wherewithal who would take the risk of going to court with the expectation of
winning'. Cf. B. Rapske, *The Book of Acts in Its First-Century Setting,* Vol. 3: *The Book of Acts
and Paul in Roman Custody* (Grand Rapids: Eerdmans; Carlisle: Paternoster, 1994), 119-20.

65. Witherington 1998, 485.

66. Barrett 1998, 789, thinks that the magistrates ought to be differentiated from 'the
authorities' in v. 19, arguing that the authorities sent the captives on to the magistrates.
However, it is possible that the authorities are described by a term more clearly defining
their judicial function in v. 20. Inscriptions attest that the proper title for the magistrates was
Lat. *duoviri* (since there were two of them who acted in this capacity). The Greek word
stratēgos is the standard Greek equivalent for Lat. *praetor,* which was no longer the term normally used for the magistrates of colonies. Cf. Sherwin-White, *Roman Society,* 92-93.

67. Spencer 1997, 167.

'heighten social boundaries',[68] appealing to the xenophobia and anti-Semitism of the people, and justifying their opposition to this new religious teaching by an apparent concern to maintain peace and social cohesion in the city (cf. 17:6; 24:5). The Philippians were proud of their Roman citizenship and customs (*ethē;* cf. v. 12 note), and it was easy to present this new teaching as a threat to the existing social order. Judaism, however, was a 'legal religion' in the Roman Empire at this time, and no objection was made in Rome itself to religions that did not offend against public order and morality. Anti-Jewish feeling on the part of some Roman officials is suggested elsewhere (18:2, 12-17), but 'it is perhaps characteristic that it is in an isolated Roman community in the Greek half of the Roman Empire that the basic principle of Roman "otherness" should be affirmed, whereas in Italy the usual custom prevailed of treating alien cults on their merits'.[69] Paul and Silas did not have an explicit social agenda, yet Luke shows that the preaching of salvation and the practice of healing in the name of Jesus had profound economic and political implications (cf. 17:6-7; 19:25-26). There must be similar effects in any culture where the gospel begins to make its impact on individuals, transforming their relationships, ambitions, and values.

22-24 *The crowd joined in the attack against Paul and Silas,* no doubt moved by the rabble-rousing accusations of the slave girl's owners and the implications for their own lifestyle.[70] Responding to the charges and concerned about escalating public antagonism, *the magistrates ordered them to be stripped and beaten with rods.* Being *beaten with rods* was a Roman form of punishment, which differed from the lashing Paul received in Jewish contexts (cf. 2 Cor. 11:24-25).[71] However, it was not a form of punishment that should

68. Tannehill 1990, 198. Tannehill notes the way some characters in Acts manouevre 'without scruple for their own advantage', and this is shown by the discrepancy between characters' statements and the narrator's statements. Cf. Witherington 1998, 496, on the polemical forensic rhetoric used to mask the real cause of the action here.

69. Sherwin-White, *Roman Society,* 82. Barrett 1998, 790, adds that the reference to Paul and Silas as Jews may be significant: 'Roman policy was to be tolerant towards Jews in the practice of their religion, but there is some ground for thinking that there was at this time a reaction against any kind of proselytization'. It is interesting to contemplate whether Paul and Silas were presenting the Christian message as the fulfillment of Judaism. Johnson 1992, 302, simply speaks of Judaism's susceptibility to sudden surges of anti-Semitic fury at the local level.

70. Rapske, *Roman Custody,* 121-23, argues that it is misleading to assert that the scene was one of chaos and near riot. 'The Philippian magistrates, being Romans chosen from among their fellow citizens to discharge the duties of governance, would formally have had an eye on those assembled and their general demeanour, attending particularly to Romans who could corroborate the truth (or falsehood) of the charges.' In other words, crowds played an important role in some Roman judicial processes.

71. Witherington 1998, 497 note 119, proposes that this is not an example of *coercitio,* 'which was a flogging which preceded a trial, as a means of exacting the truth'. It is much more likely to have been a public beating 'meant to humiliate those involved and perhaps also to discourage their followers'.

have been inflicted on Roman citizens such as Paul and Silas (v. 37 note). 'In a Roman colony it appears that arrest, beating, and imprisonment were normal for aliens, but that it was potentially dangerous to give citizens the same treatment.'[72] They were *severely flogged* (*pollas de epithentes autois plēgas*, 'they laid many stripes on them'), and were *thrown into prison*, apparently without a genuine trial. The jailer was commanded to *guard them carefully*, perhaps because the magistrates feared that 'such prisoners, who had displayed supernatural powers, needed to be guarded especially carefully'.[73] When he received these orders, *he put them in the inner cell and fastened their feet in the stocks* (*xylos*, 'stock', could be used as a means of extra security or as an instrument of torture).[74] This summary justice assumed their guilt and was an attempt to restore order in the city. The accused were apparently considered wrongdoers 'entirely lacking legal and social merit'.[75]

3. A Jailer and His Household (16:25-34)

As in Acts 5 and 12, imprisonment is an attempt by the authorities to control the proclamation of the gospel, but in this narrative an earthquake transforms the situation. 'Compared to the apostles' rather passive role in their prison breaks, particularly exemplified in Peter's slumber until awakened by the angel (12:6-7), Paul and Silas are busy praying and singing to God at the midnight hour (16:25).'[76] Instead of escaping, they remain to rescue the jailer from killing himself and to share the gospel with him (16:26-31). Whatever the jailer meant by his question about being saved (cf. v. 17 note), Paul took the opportunity to point him to the Lord Jesus. The prisoners then instructed the jailer and his family, while their wounds were washed and they received his hospitality. Once again, Luke records the baptism of the chief character and his household (16:32-34; cf. v. 15), and portrays the emergence of Christian community as the gospel is proclaimed and received (cf. 2:40-47). 'These events vividly illustrate Paul's own claim in his Philippian letter that imprisonment, far from being an obstacle to his mission, poses a unique opportunity to spread the gospel boldly to Roman guards and others who come his way (Phil. 1:12-14).'[77]

72. P. Garnsey, *Social Status and Legal Privilege in the Roman Empire* (Oxford: Oxford University, 1970), 268; cf. Rapske, *Roman Custody*, 124-25.

73. Marshall 1980, 271.

74. Cf. Barrett 1998, 792.

75. Rapske, *Roman Custody*, 127. Rapske 126-27, argues that the inner cell was 'for those who had committed the most serious crimes and who occupied the lowest levels of society'. The use of stocks as a security measure was a further indignity and a form of punishment. However, not yet knowing that Paul and Silas were Roman citizens, 'the Philippian magistrates did not consciously pervert the law' (p. 129).

76. Spencer 1997, 168.

77. Spencer 1997, 168. Of course the letter is speaking about a later imprisonment experience.

25 *About midnight Paul and Silas were praying and singing hymns to
God, and the other prisoners were listening to them* (cf. 12:4-5; Jas. 5:13). Their
praying may have included a cry for justice, release from prison, and the
freedom to continue their ministry in an unhindered way. At the same
time, *singing hymns to God*, they acknowledged God's character and expressed their trust in him as their deliverer. They could have been using
any one of a number of the Psalms, which combine such prayer and praise
(e.g., Psalms 140–143). This is 'a concrete depiction of the Christian ideal of
"joy amid suffering" (Rom. 5:3; Jas. 1:2; 1 Pet. 5:6)'.[78] As they engaged with
God in this fashion, *the other prisoners were listening to them*, implying that
their prayers and praises were having an impact on everyone around
them.[79] Here, and in Acts 27, Paul in captivity takes the opportunity to testify to the character of God in the presence of unbelievers and to demonstrate before them his own confidence in the God he proclaimed. Put another way, he was doubtless conscious of the evangelistic potential of his
difficult circumstances (cf. Phil. 1:12-14).

26-28 *Suddenly there was such a violent earthquake that the foundations
of the prison were shaken.* As in 5:19-21; 12:6-11, divine deliverance came in
answer to prayer, though in this case, *all the prison doors flew open, and everyone's chains came loose.* The prison was not destroyed, but the earthquake
brought potential release to all the prisoners. Earthquakes were not uncommon in Greece and Macedonia and were often seen as the work of a god.[80]
Apparently there was no time for escape, since *the jailer woke up, and when
he saw the prison doors open, he drew his sword and was about to kill himself because he thought the prisoners had escaped.* Paul and Silas may also have anticipated the opportunity they would have for further ministry in the situation if they remained and encouraged the others to remain as well.[81] Paul
certainly seems to have taken charge of events, seeking to prevent the jailer
from committing suicide by shouting, *'Don't harm yourself! We are all here!'*
Indeed, he stays to save the jailer's life in more than one sense. 'Paul's at-

---

78. Marshall 1980, 271.

79. Rapske, *Roman Custody*, 203-4, suggests that all the prisoners were put together in
the inner cell at night (v. 24), and hence they could hear more easily what was being said
and sung.

80. Johnson 1992, 300; Witherington 1998, 497. Haenchen 1971, 500-504, expresses the
cynicism of scholars who cannot take the evidence for divine deliverance by means of an
earthquake seriously. Haenchen himself adopts a form-critical line, arguing that the miracle
story was developed to explain the conversion of the gaoler and his house and justify for
the reader the suffering of the missionaries. Cf. Longenecker 1981, 464-65; Marshall 1980,
265.

81. Tannehill 1990, 198-99, notes that Paul twice refuses opportunities for freedom in
this chapter (vv. 26, 35-36). 'These developments focus attention not on the fact of miraculous release but on Paul's reasons for rejecting these opportunities, which involve his relation to the jailer, on the one hand, and to the city officials, on the other.' Tannehill (204) also
suggests that the earthquake gives Paul the opportunity to show the jailer the love of enemies Jesus taught (Lk. 6:27).

tention to the welfare of another in the midst of his own suffering — somewhat like Jesus' concern for the criminal crucified beside him — brings to the jailer a share in the salvation that God offers through Jesus'.[82] Noting some of the critical questions that have been asked about this sequence of events, Marshall rightly concludes that we are dealing here with 'a condensed story in which the narrative is limited to the points significant for the author's purpose, and he does not bother to furnish the details which attract the interest of the historian anxious to reconstruct the scene in every particular detail'.[83]

29-31 *The jailer called for lights, rushed in and fell trembling before Paul and Silas.*[84] He was clearly disturbed by the events that had taken place and connected them with the men who had been praying to their god for deliverance. Perhaps also he was grateful to Paul and Silas for saving him from shame 'by not escaping themselves and restraining the other prisoners from escaping'.[85] When he brought them out of the inner cell, his one concern was to find deliverance for himself, and so he asked, *'Sirs, what must I do to be saved?'* As in 27:20, 31, the verb 'to save' (*sōzein*) could have been simply used with reference to rescue from physical danger. Yet, it is likely that the jailer was specifically looking for deliverance from the God whom Paul and Silas proclaimed, wishing to know more of the teaching for which they had been imprisoned (cf. vv. 17, 20). As in 4:9, 12, there is probably movement from a purely physical notion of salvation or healing to the concept of salvation made possible through the death and resurrection of Jesus Christ.[86] They replied, *'Believe in the Lord Jesus, and you will be saved — you and your household'*. Eternal salvation is offered in the simplest possible way to those who *believe in the Lord Jesus* (cf. 5:14; 9:42; 11:17; 15:11). Such belief involves confession or acknowledgement of Jesus as the exalted *Lord* (*kyrios*, as in 2:21, 36; Rom. 10:9; 1 Cor. 12:3; Phil. 2:11) — trust and committal, not merely intellectual assent. As with Peter's preaching to Jews in 2:39,

82. Tannehill 1990, 204. 'Paul and the narrator do not despair that God will open hearts to their message even among persecutors.' Paul's concern for the jailer recalls also Stephen's prayer for those who were stoning him (7:60).

83. Marshall 1980, 272. Cf. Barrett 1998, 776-77, raises several questions that the historian might ask.

84. The Western text adds that the jailer fell down 'at the feet' of Paul and Silas (v. 29), indicating special deference to them (cf. 10:25; 14:11-13). It also adds that the jailer 'secured the rest' of the prisoners before bringing Paul and Silas out to question them. These additions detract from the urgency and simplicity of the narrative, with its focus on the climactic question and answer in vv. 30-31. Cf. Metzger, *Textual Commentary*, 397-98.

85. Johnson 1992, 303, drawing attention to the importance of honour and shame in the Greco-Roman world.

86. Marshall 1980, 273, does not think there was anything of the ordinary sense of 'rescue from danger' in the jailer's question. 'Rather the jailer is forced by the supernatural confirmation of the message to realize that he must come to terms with the God proclaimed by Paul and Silas.' Compare C. Stenschke, 'The Need for Salvation', in I. H. Marshall and D. Peterson (eds.), *Witness to the Gospel: The Theology of Acts* (Grand Rapids/Cambridge: Eerdmans, 1998), 129-30, and contrast Witherington 1998, 498.

the offer of salvation to Gentile is for families as well as for the individuals addressed *(you and your household)*. God blesses family units under the New Covenant, just as he did in Israel (e.g., Gn. 12:2-3; 17:7-14; 18:17-19), when the heads of houses (Lydia in v. 15 and the jailer in v. 34; cf. 18:8) turn to Christ and acknowledge him as Lord.[87]

32-34 Such a brief answer to the jailer's question clearly needed filling out with more information and teaching, and so Paul and Silas *spoke the word of the Lord to him and to all the others in his house*.[88] Luke implies that there was sufficient instruction for all who were baptized, and yet the emphasis in v. 34 is on the fact that the jailer had come to believe in God. Salvation came to this house because of the conversion of the head. The issue of infant baptism is not really addressed by this text, though it is possible that infants were included in the initiation process (v. 15 note). Luke's focus is on the belief of this household. *At that hour of the night the jailer took them and washed their wounds; then immediately he and all his household were baptized.* The conversion of the jailer is not just one more in a sequence of similar stories, but 'the conversion of a member of the oppressive system that is punishing Paul and Silas'.[89] His care for the prisoners, his willingness for his household to be instructed about the way of salvation, and his desire to be baptised *immediately* show a profound change in this man's values and beliefs. *The jailer brought them into his house and set a meal before them; he was filled with joy (ēgalliasato; cf. 2:46, agalliasei ['glad'])* *because he had come to believe in God — he and his whole household*. Strictly speaking, the expression *and his household (panoikei)* belongs with the verb *filled with joy* rather than with the following causal participle *because he had come to believe (pepisteukōs)*. This gives the sense that 'he rejoiced along with his entire household that he had believed in God' (NRSV, ESV). Belief in the Lord Jesus Christ (v. 31) is equated with belief in the one true God (v. 34). Although it is quite clear from v. 32 that his entire household was instructed before being baptised, the stress in v. 34 is on the fact that the head of the house had been brought to faith and that salvation had come to the house by that means. Such a joyful meal together with the missionaries was a celebration

---

87. 1 Cor. 7:14-16 speaks about the sanctifying of an unbelieving husband by the faith of his wife and the sanctifying of children by the faith of one parent. But Paul does not use the terminology of sanctification here as he does in 1 Cor. 1:2; 6:11, to describe the salvation of such family members. Indeed, the exhortation of 7:15-16 is to live in peace with the unbeliever so that he or she might be saved. Unbelieving partners or children are there understood to be in a relationship with God of special privilege and opportunity, without yet being personally saved through faith in Christ.

88. The Alexandrian witnesses to the text of 16:32 are divided, some reading 'the word of God'. But the most widely attested is 'the word of the Lord', with 'the word of God' apparently being a scribal refinement in this context. Cf. Metzger, *Textual Commentary*, 398. It is strange that Barrett 1998, 799, writes of the jailer and his household being baptized 'without instruction, upon conversion and profession of faith', when Luke stresses that instruction was given (v. 32).

89. Tannehill 1990, 204.

of salvation, reminiscent of the household meetings mentioned in 2:46. 'The joyful experience of God's saving work that marked the earliest church appears now in a Roman environment.'[90]

C. Leaving Philippi Peacefully (16:35-40)

The final section of this chapter covers the release of Paul and Silas by the magistrates, who effectively give them a public apology because they reveal themselves to be Roman citizens, unjustly treated (16:35-39).[91] Paul's insistence upon such vindication shows a concern with the public standing of the mission. Agents of the gospel who are Roman citizens and their converts deserve to be protected from harassment and mistreatment. However, despite the focus of the chapter on the social, economic, and political implications of the Christian mission, Luke concludes with a simple picture of Paul and Silas meeting with the believers in Lydia's house, encouraging the nascent church (16:40). As already noted, references to Lydia and her household 'form a frame around the rest of the episode (cf. 16:14-15, 40) and show an interest in the key role of a patroness of the community and hostess for the missionaries in the founding of a church'.[92]

35-36 *When it was daylight, the magistrates sent their officers to the jailer with the order: 'Release those men'.* The presumption here is that the prisoners had been returned to the jail and secured once more with the others. *The officers* (*rhabdouchoi*; also in v. 38) were those who carried a rod or staff (*rhabdos*), symbolizing their task of carrying out arrests and punishments. No reason is given for this apparent about-face on the part of the magistrates. They can hardly have been ignorant of the earthquake and its aftermath, and may have been afraid of divine retribution if they continued to keep Paul and Silas captive.[93] However, Tannehill suggests that such

90. Tannehill 1990, 200. The Roman context is stressed in 16:12, with reference to Philippi as a Roman colony, and in vv. 37-38, by the insistence of Paul and Silas that they be treated as Roman citizens. Barrett 1998, 799, rightly argues against the view that this was a Eucharistic meal in any formal sense. Contrast Marshall 1980, 274.

91. M. L. Skinner, *Locating Paul: Places of Custody as Narrative Settings in Acts 21–28*, SBLAB 13 (Atlanta: SBL, 2003), 92-93, shows how Paul uses this transformed situation 'as a platform for his and Silas's vindication by those representatives of the public who were responsible for their degradation'.

92. Tannehill 1990, 196. Previous hosts and hostesses have been mentioned in connection with the ministry of Peter (9:43; 10:48; 12:12), but this is the first such reference in connection with Paul's work. Later sponsors of Paul's mission are mentioned in 17:5-9; 18:2-3, 7; 21:8, 16. 'In this way the narrator acknowledges the important role that local sponsors played in the establishment of the church and demonstrates the necessary partnership between travelling missionaries and local supporters' (Tannehill, 197). Cf. J. Koenig, *New Testament Hospitality: Partnership with Strangers as Promise and Mission*, Overtures to Biblical Theology (Philadelphia: Fortress, 1985), chapter 4.

93. This is the implication of the Western text, which adds to v. 35, 'recollecting the earthquake that had taken place, they were afraid'. Leaving nothing to the imagination of

'blanks' in Luke's narrative should not surprise us: 'they should be taken as guides to what does and does not interest the narrator. They are not a major disturbance to the integrity of the narrative.'[94] Repetition of the magistrates' order for the release of the prisoners highlights the strangeness of Paul's response. The jailer declares: *'The magistrates have ordered that you and Silas be released. Now you can leave. Go in peace.'*

37 Paul refuses another opportunity for freedom (cf. v. 26) because, in this case, he wants to make the point that they are *Roman citizens (anthrōpous Hrōmaious)*, who ought to have been treated accordingly.[95] They had been *publicly* beaten without a trial (*akatakritous* means 'uncondemned, without due process', BDAG; cf. 22:25), and had been thrown into prison, which was against Roman law and custom.[96] Paul later claims that he was 'born a citizen' (cf. 22:28), and much discussion has taken place about how and when this privilege was extended to his Jewish family.[97] Uncertainty also exists about the way in which Paul and Silas might have been able to prove their claim. A false claim to Roman citizenship might be punishable with death (Suetonius, *Claudius* 25; cf. Epictetus, *Discourses* 3.24.41). It is unlikely that Paul was wearing the toga which only Roman citizens might wear, 'but he may have been carrying his *diploma,* a small wooden diptych which would attest his registration (and birth) as a citizen'.[98] However, since the prisoners had previously been stripped of their clothing (v. 22), 'it may be that the bare claim would be enough to frighten the magistrates on the ground that though it might be false it could possibly be true and that if it were they could be involved in expensive legal proceedings with an unfortunate outcome'.[99]

---

the reader, the Western text makes several further additions to vv. 36-38. Cf. Metzger, *Textual Commentary,* 398-99. Marshall 1980, 274, suggests that the magistrates simply regarded the beating and the night's imprisonment as 'sufficient exercise of their authority over the trouble-makers'.

94. Tannehill 1990, 199. Following M. Sternberg, *The Poetics of Biblical Narrative: Ideological Literature and the Drama of Reading,* Indiana Literary Biblical Series (Bloomington: Indiana University, 1985), 236, he distinguishes between 'blanks' (material judged by the narrator to be unimportant) and 'gaps' (material that is important to the narrator, but which is withheld until the appropriate moment in the narrative).

95. As Roman citizens they had the power to seek legal redress for any wrongs committed against them. Cf. Sherwin-White, *Roman Society,* 58-59; Barrett 1998, 801; Witherington 1998, 499.

96. Cf. Barrett 1998, 801, 805; H. H. Tajra, *The Trial of St. Paul: A Juridical Exegesis of the Second Half of Acts,* WUNT 2, no. 35 (Tübingen: Mohr [Siebeck], 1989), 29; Rapske, *Roman Custody,* 303-4. Johnson 1992, 303, draws attention to the importance of honour and shame in the Greco-Roman world and says that 'Paul will not be content with freedom if his honor as a citizen still stands publicly impugned'.

97. Cf. Rapske, *Roman Custody,* 86. Witherington 1998, 681-83, concludes that the most likely reason was that one of Paul's parents or grandparents had distinguished themselves by some sort of service or loyalty to Rome.

98. Barrett 1998, 1048, commenting on 22:28. Cf. Suetonius, *Nero* 12; Sherwin-White, *Roman Society,* 55-72, 144-54; Rapske, *Roman Custody,* 130-33.

99. Barrett 1998, 802. Barrett points out that Paul makes no reference to Roman citizenship in his letters and that he received a Roman flogging three times and was often im-

Paul derides their attempt to sweep this injustice under the carpet (*'And now do they want to get rid of us quietly?'*) and demands some form of public recognition of the evil done to them (*'No! Let them come themselves and escort us out'*).

Paul was not in the habit of insisting on his own rights (cf. 1 Cor. 9:12), so why did he do so here? 'The refusal to settle without a public act of vindication shows a concern with the public standing of the mission. Acts of ignorance and injustice must not be allowed to masquerade as truth and justice in the public eye.'[100] Paul and Silas were not simply demanding satisfaction for the abuse of their personal rights. The context suggests a wider concern, 'specifically with the fate of the mission before Roman magistrates, reacting to their proud and suspicious citizens'.[101] Tannehill notes four scenes in Acts 16–19 that feature accusations against Christians in similar sequences of events (16:19-24; 17:5-9; 18:12-16; 19:25-29). These four examples show 'the narrator's strong concern with the way that the outside world perceives the Christian mission and the effect those perceptions may have on Christians'.[102] Although Paul has frequent disputes in synagogues, in these four cases the dispute does not begin or does not remain in the synagogue, but 'spills over into the public sphere and is brought to city officials, the provincial governor, or the public assembly'. Paul is caught between 'two suspicious communities'. 'Both Jews and Gentiles view the mission as a threat to the customs that provide social cohesion, to the religious basis of their cultures, and to political stability through Caesar's rule.'[103] Witherington adds that they were right to do so — 'Paul and his co-workers are those who turn the religious world upside down, offering one God and saviour instead of many (and also instead of the emperor), one way of salvation instead of many, one people of God that is not ethnically defined'.[104] But why did Paul delay the claim of Roman citizenship until this late stage? Rapske suggests that an earlier introduction of this form of self-defence 'would probably have been construed by the magistrates and populace as an assertion of commitment to the primacy of Roman, over against Jewish (i.e. Christian) customs. The signals sent would also have put the church at risk of dissolution if the new Philippian converts did not possess the Roman franchise. At least there would have been uncertainty surrounding Paul's commitment to his message.'[105] Paul had an attitude of

---

prisoned (2 Cor. 11:23, 25). However, he argues that this does not prove that Paul did not possess Roman citizenship.

100. Tannehill 1990, 205. Cf. Marshall 1980, 274.

101. Tannehill 1990, 201. Tannehill notes that the role of stirring up opposition attributed to Jews in 13:50; 14:2, 19 is here taken by the Gentile owners of the slave girl, 'who speak as Romans opposed to subversive Jewish preachers'. Cf. 19:23-40.

102. Tannehill 1990, 202. Jews are the accusers in Thessalonica and Corinth, but Gentiles in Philippi and Ephesus. Cf. Spencer 1997, 159-61.

103. Tannehill 1990, 203. Thus the narrative shows awareness of 'the culture-shaking power of the mission'.

104. Witherington 1998, 500.

105. Rapske, *Roman Custody*, 134, endorsed by Witherington 1998, 500-502.

detachment to his Roman citizenship (cf. his detachment about his Jewish-ness in 1 Cor. 9:20) and believed he should take advantage of this only inso-far as it furthered the cause of Christ.

38-39 *The officers reported this to the magistrates, and when they heard that Paul and Silas were Roman citizens, they were alarmed.* As noted in connec-tion with v. 37, the magistrates may have been *alarmed* because they consid-ered the possibility of becoming involved in expensive legal proceedings with an unfortunate outcome. So they came in person to the jailer's house, *to appease them and escorted them from the prison, requesting them to leave the city.* There was a public acknowledgement of wrongful treatment by the magistrates and an attempt to *appease (parekalesan)* these *Roman citizens,*[106] to avoid any recrimination. Thus, in terms of Luke's overall narrative, the imprisonment and release of Paul and Silas in this manner hold out the hope that 'the forces of opposition are either open to conversion (as with the jailer) or correction (as with the magistrates)'.[107]

40 The final picture we are given of Philippi is of Paul and Silas in Lydia's house, *where they met with the brothers and encouraged them (parekalesan,* used differently than in v. 39). Having been asked to *leave* the city (v. 39, *apelthein*), they went into Lydia's house (v. 40, *eiselthon*), and only after ministry to the believers *left* the city *(exelthan).* The missionaries were not only responsible for founding this house-church but also for encourag-ing its growth and stability by their teaching and actions, not least by de-fending the mission in the public sphere. 'It was vital for Paul to find a venue where Christians could meet in this Roman colony, for he was pro-mulgating a foreign religion, and one not clearly licit, especially if it was distinguished from Judaism. Lydia's providing of a meeting place was thus crucial to the existence and growth of Christianity in this place.'[108] Paul

106. The verb *parekalein* is used with a wide range of meanings in Acts (e.g. 11:23; 14:22; 15:22; 16:40). Here the word means 'urged, begged' (NKJV 'pleaded with them'), im-plying perhaps that they 'apologized' to them (NRSV, ESV) or placated them in some way. Cf. Barrett 1998, 803. Tajra, *Trial,* 29, referring to Dio Cassius, *Hist.* 60.24.4, observes that the magistrates 'left themselves open to severe punishment, for they could be deprived of office and disqualified from any further government service for having violated the rights of Ro-man citizens in a Roman colony'.

107. Tannehill 1990, 204. The narrative suggests 'a resilient optimism in spite of oppo-sition from society'. The Western text provides further additions to vv. 39-40: the magis-trates arrive 'with many friends' (presumably hoping to add weight to their request) and say, 'We did not know the truth about you, that you are righteous men'; they urge the mis-sionaries to depart, lest the people of the city 'again assemble against us, crying out against you' (they are concerned about their own safety as well as that of the prisoners); and when Paul and Silas go to Lydia's house, 'they reported the things which the Lord had done for them'. Cf. Metzger, *Textual Commentary,* 399-400; Barrett 1998, 804-5. This is a classic exam-ple of the expansionist tendency of this textual tradition, with the aim of justifying the Christian faith and its advocates, and showing the justice and sympathy of Roman officials when properly informed.

108. Witherington 1998, 487. Cf. Witherington 338, on Lydia as 'mother' or patroness and benefactor to the fledgling Christian community in Philippi.

later returned to the region, without apparent hindrance (20:1-2, 6), and then wrote to the Philippians a warmly affirming and encouraging letter. It was a church that had a 'partnership in the gospel from the first day' with Paul (Phil. 1:5) and which supported him financially (Phil. 4:15-18; 2 Cor. 11:9). 1 Thessalonians 2:2 is independent evidence of Paul's suffering and shameful treatment in Philippi before he journeyed to Thessalonica.

Stott observes that 'it would be hard to imagine a more disparate group than the business woman, the slave girl and the gaoler. Racially, socially and psychologically they were worlds apart. Yet all three were changed by the same gospel and were welcomed into the same church.'[109] Luke's Philippian narrative highlights 'both the universal appeal of the gospel (that it could reach such a wide diversity of people) and its universal effect (that it could bind them together in God's family)'.[110] But the gospel also brings challenge and change, even for those who reject it, and thus division in the community and persecution for believers.

INTRODUCTION TO ACTS 17

Acts 16–19 progressively shows the way the gospel impacted the Greco-Roman world, as Paul and his associates preached in Macedonia, Achaia, and then Asia. Luke illustrates in successive narratives how the outside world reacted to the Christian mission and the effect those reactions had on Christians and their evangelistic task. Nevertheless, despite his interest in the engagement of the missionaries with Gentile beliefs and practices, Luke does not allow us to forget that Paul's custom, wherever possible, was to preach to Jews first. In Acts 17:1-15 he focuses again on Paul's synagogue ministry, highlighting the contrasting responses to the gospel in Thessalonica and Berea. Even as Paul goes to Athens and is provoked by the idolatry of that city, Luke tells us that 'he reasoned in the synagogue with both Jews and God-fearing Greeks', as well as talking to people more generally in the marketplace (17:17). Paul's synagogue ministry was similarly the starting point for mission in Corinth (18:4-5) and Ephesus (18:19-21; 19:8-10). The juxtaposition of jealous, persecuting Jews in Thessalonica with eager, reflective Jews in Berea shows that 'the narrator has not completely stereotyped Diaspora Jews'.[1]

Having restated the Jewish foundation for his mission, Luke provides Paul's Areopagus speech as a model of the way Jesus and his resurrection might be proclaimed to Gentiles with no relation to Judaism. Indeed,

---

109. Stott 1990, 268. Although Luke does not say that the slave girl was converted and joined the embryonic church in Philippi, he possibly intended his readers to infer this.

110. Stott 1990, 270.

1. Tannehill 1990, 207. Spencer 1997, 169, gives these episodes the heading 'Hunted in Thessalonica; Welcomed in Beroea'.

Tannehill suggests that the order of the narrative in Acts invites us to understand Paul's work in Corinth and Ephesus in the light of this programmatic speech. 'This speech is the charter of the mission that can reach all because it no longer depends on the instruction of Gentiles by the synagogue, which has prepared some to accept the God of Israel revealed in Scripture.'[2] Without quoting Scripture, it confronts people with the God of the Bible and his claim on their lives, and points them to the resurrected Jesus as the one in whom they can find a true and lasting relationship with God.

D. The Word in Thessalonica and Berea (17:1-15)

Luke presents a pair of contrasting narratives highlighting the different responses of Jews in Thessalonica and Berea to the gospel (cf. the pairing of narratives for rhetorical purposes in 4:32–5:11; 18:18–19:7). The response of the Bereans as a community of Jews stands out because they 'examined the Scriptures every day to see if what Paul said was true' (17:11). Although some Jews and God-fearers in Thessalonica were persuaded and joined Paul and Silas (v. 4), others from the synagogue became jealous. They sought the help of bad characters from the marketplace, as well as city officials, to oppose the preachers (vv. 5-9). Paul's proclamation of Jesus' messianic kingship was used by his Jewish opponents as a basis for claiming that the newcomers and their followers were socially and politically dangerous. So intense was the opposition of these Thessalonian Jews to the gospel that they followed the missionaries to Berea and sought to stir up the crowds against them there as well (v. 13).

1. The Gospel Provokes Jealousy and Turmoil (17:1-9)

This narrative begins with a reminder that Paul's synagogue ministry essentially involved arguing from the Scriptures that the Messiah had to suffer and rise from the dead (vv. 2-3; cf. 13:16-41). However, such teaching — and the identification of Jesus as the promised Messiah — provoked considerable opposition from certain Jews in Thessalonica (v. 4), whose resistance took the form of 'attack instead of argument'.[3] Their use of a marketplace mob to seek out the missionaries and bring them before the popular

---

2. Tannehill 1990, 213. Tannehill quotes P. Schubert, 'The Place of the Areopagus Speech in the Composition of Acts', in J. C. Rylaarsdam (ed.), *Transitions in Biblical Scholarship* (Chicago: University of Chicago, 1968), 260-61, with approval, who argues that the Areopagus speech is 'a hellenized but also a universalized version of Luke's *boulē*-theology' ('plan of God' theology). Moreover, 'Luke regarded the Areopagus speech as the final, climactic part of his exposition of the whole plan of God'. Cf. Witherington 1998, 511-12; THE THEOLOGY OF ACTS: V. THE GOSPEL (pp. 70-75).

3. Gaventa 2003, 244.

assembly was unsuccessful (v. 5). But they managed to drag some of the believers before the city officials and discredit the message by presenting it as politically and socially inflammatory (vv. 6-9). 'While the charges are false, they are in another, ironic and more profound, sense also true.'[4] Luke has already shown how Paul's proclamation of the kingship of Jesus had begun to have a world-changing effect.

1-3 Paul and his companions travelled west along the Via Egnatia, the main route from Rome to the east, and *passed through Amphipolis and Apollonia.*[5] *Amphipolis* was the capital of the first district of Macedonia in which Philippi was situated, about 30 miles (48 km.) west-southwest. *Apollonia* was further inland, a day's journey beyond *Amphipolis.* It is likely that these were the places 'where the travellers spent successive nights, dividing the journey into three stages of about 30, 27 and 35 miles'.[6] Finally, they came to *Thessalonica* (Saloniki), the most populated city in the region, capital of the second district of Macedonia and seat of the Roman provincial government from 146 BC. It was made a free city by the Romans in 42 BC, with the rights of self-government on a Greek, rather than a Roman, pattern.[7] Luke's observation that *there was a Jewish synagogue* in Thessalonica suggests that there may not have been one in the other two cities visited. Paul's *custom* of first visiting the synagogue for ministry (v. 2, *kata to eiōthos*; cf. 13:5, 14; 14:1), and continuing there as long as he could, is further illustrated in vv. 10 and 17 (cf. 18:4-5, 19-21; 19:8-9). Although the expression *epi sabbata tria* could mean 'for three weeks', TNIV has rightly translated *on three Sabbath days.* Philippians 4:16 and 1 Thessalonians more generally suggest that Paul stayed in Thessalonica 'a good deal longer than three weeks'.[8] So it was three Sabbaths in the synagogue and then a longer period ministering elsewhere in the city. The interpretation of Scripture played a key role in the synagogue ministry, as Paul *reasoned with them from the Scriptures (dielexato autois apo tōn graphōn;* cf. 17:17; 18:4, 19; 19:8, 9; 20:7, 9; 24:12, 25; cf. 20:1-3 note). The focus of such biblical argumentation was *explaining (dianoigōn,* 'opening up' [the Scriptures]) *and proving (paratithemenos)*[9] *that the Messiah had to suffer and rise from the dead* (cf. 1:3; 3:18).

---

4. Gaventa 2003, 245.

5. Bruce 1990, 368, observes that the verb *diodeusantes (passed through)* emphasizes the fact that they took the journey by road *(hodos),* and says, 'The highways of the empire became for Paul the highways of the kingdom of God'.

6. C. J. Hemer, *The Book of Acts in the Setting of Hellenistic History,* ed. C. Gempf, WUNT 49 (Tübingen: Mohr Siebeck, 1989; repr. Winona Lake: Eisenbrauns, 1990), 115. Horses or some other form of transport would be needed to cover such distances in a day. Codex D implies that Paul and Silas stopped off at Apollonia. Cf. Metzger, *Textual Criticism,* 400-401.

7. Cf. A. N. Sherwin-White, *Roman Society and Roman Law in the New Testament* (Oxford: Clarendon, 1963), 95-98.

8. Bruce 1990, 369; Barrett 1998, 809. Cf. Witherington 1998, 504, on the length of stay and the way in which Paul supported himself in Thessalonica.

9. Bruce 1990, 369, observes that the participle *paratithemenos* ('setting before, demon-

This recalls, not only the style of preaching set out in 13:26-39, but also the teaching of the risen Christ, as recorded in Luke 24:25-27, 45-47, when he 'opened' the Scriptures for his disciples (cf. 24:32, 45, *diēnoigen*).[10] Jesus argued that everything written about him in what we call the Old Testament must be fulfilled (Lk. 24:44). In particular, the prophets had spoken about the need for the Messiah to suffer and rise from the dead, making it possible for 'repentance for the forgiveness of sins' to be preached in his name to all nations, beginning at Jerusalem (24:45-47). Foundationally, Jesus taught that God's saving plan for humanity necessitated his death and resurrection. Paul similarly sought to explain and prove from the Scriptures *that the Messiah had to* (*edei*, 'it was necessary', implies a divine necessity) *suffer and rise from the dead*. His first concern was doubtless apologetic, to explain how the crucified Jesus could possibly be the Messiah (*'This Jesus I am proclaiming to you is the Messiah'*).[11] But he must also have wanted to explain and offer to his audience the benefits of that death and resurrection. We are not told how those benefits were outlined at Thessalonica, though we know from elsewhere that Paul could have talked in terms of the forgiveness of sins (13:38-39), eternal life (13:46, 48), entrance into the kingdom of God (14:22), or salvation (15:11). The reason for Luke's brief account seems clear when we compare his record of the ministry in Berea. Luke is making the particular point that the Jews were divided in their response to the Christian way of interpreting the Scriptures and in their personal response to the claims about Jesus. These two issues are intimately connected. There is a plan or purpose of God (20:27, *boulē*, 'will') that Paul discerned in the Scriptures and expounded in his teaching. Peter's sermons in Acts 2-3 show a similar understanding and focus. This way of looking at Scripture, which stems from the teaching of Jesus himself, explains why it was necessary for the Messiah to suffer and then enter his glory and justifies the claim that Jesus of Nazareth is the only one who fulfills the divine plan. The issue of how to interpret the messianic prophecies of the OT and see them in the light of God's total plan for Israel and the nations continues to be critical for Christian dialogue with Jews.

4 The effectiveness of Paul's ministry is outlined before the opposition is described. *Some of the Jews were persuaded and joined Paul and Silas.* The verb translated *joined* by TNIV (*proseklērōthēsan*) occurs only here in the

---

strating') suggests 'setting (the Scriptures) side by side' with the events which had fulfilled them, or 'bringing (the Scriptures) forward as evidence'. Cf. Plato, *Pol.* 275B; Dio Chrysostom, *Or.* 17:10; Johnson 1992, 305.

10. 'In opening the Scriptures to the Jews of Thessalonica, Paul is playing the same revelatory role as the risen Lord played on Easter, and the core of his message is the same' (Tannehill 1990, 207). Witherington 1998, 505-6, examines the rhetorical significance of such language.

11. A wide variety of readings seems to have arisen from the unusual reading preserved only in Codex B (*ho Christos ho Iēsous*), but the meaning in any case is: 'this is the Messiah, this Jesus whom I am proclaiming to you.' Cf. Bruce 1990, 369; Metzger, *Textual Criticism*, 401.

NT. In the passive it would normally mean 'were assigned to (possibly by lot)' (cf. Josephus, *War* 2.567; Philo, *On the Embassy to Gaius* 68). In the light of 13:14; 16:14, this appears to be a reference to God's action in their lives, so that the passive voice should be rendered 'were joined'.[12] God uses belief in the gospel to bring new converts into immediate fellowship with those who introduce them to Christ. Paul and his team were the nucleus of a new community which Paul later called 'the church of the Thessalonians in God the Father and the Lord Jesus Christ' (1 Thes. 1:1). Others became members of this church by believing the gospel and being 'joined' to them (cf. 2:41-47; 1 Cor. 12:13; Eph. 2:19-22). Luke also mentions the persuasion of *a large number of God-fearing Greeks and not a few prominent women*. The general category of *God-fearing Greeks (sebomenōn Hellēnōn)* recalls earlier references to 'God-fearers' (cf. *phobeomai* in 10:2; 13:16, 26; *sebomai* in 13:43, 50; 16:14; 18:7), meaning Gentile believers who were attached to the synagogue in some way.[13] Luke once more specifically highlights the fact that *not a few prominent women* became Christians (cf. v. 12 note).[14] Although Luke's interest in the conversion of women and their role in the church is obvious from the beginning of Acts (1:14; 5:14; 8:3, 12; 9:2), this theme is more prominent in chapters 16–18 (16:15, 40; 17:4, 12, 34; 18:2, 18, 26). Several of these later references acknowledge that 'women of economic means and social influence played an important role in the growth of the church in certain localities'.[15] Luke tells us nothing of Paul's ministry beyond the synagogue, though by the time he wrote 1 Thessalonians 1:9-10 he could describe the majority of the believers in that city as having been idol worshippers. Whatever the success among Jews and God-fearers, many more were apparently converted from paganism. No doubt Paul engaged with such people in the marketplace between Sabbaths and after he was excluded from the synagogue, but Luke is exclusively interested in his ministry to Jews at this point in his narrative.

5 *But other Jews were jealous (zēlōsantes) of their success.*[16] The jeal-

12. Barrett 1998, 811, suggests that, in the light of Luke's 'predestinarian view of conversion', he may have thought that 'those who attached themselves to Paul and Silas did so because God had allocated them to this end'. Cf. Johnson 1992, 306. Luke uses a different verb (*kollēthentes*, 'joined, became followers of') in v. 34.

13. The actual expression *sebomenōn Hellēnōn* does not occur anywhere else, prompting some ancient copyists to add *kai* ('and') between the words to indicate two classes of people instead of one ('God-fearers and Greeks'). However, Barrett 1998, 812, observes that the present verse distinguishes these God-fearers from proselytes, and indicates that notwithstanding their piety they count as Greeks, not as Jews.

14. Gk. *gynaikōn te tōn prōtōn* could be a title or a descriptive way of referring to 'leading women' in the city. Alternatively, it could refer to 'wives of the leading men' (which is the translation required by the Western text [*kai gynaikes tōn prōtōn*]). Cf. Barrett 1998, 812; Metzger, *Textual Criticism*, 401-2.

15. Tannehill 1990, 208.

16. KJV 'the Jews which believed not' and NKJV 'the Jews who were not persuaded' reflect the reading of Codex D and some later Byzantine texts rather than the best earliest

ousy motif previously surfaced in 13:45 (*zēlos*), where Paul's ability to gather crowds of Gentiles to hear him preach appears to have been the cause. It is likely that most of the opposition came from synagogue leaders. 'The Jewish authorities probably looked on the God-fearing Gentiles as potential proselytes, so that in preaching to them Paul was poaching on their preserves.'[17] In this replay of the public accusation–type scene presented in 16:19-24, where the personal motive for the attack is jealousy rather than anger over economic loss, the accusation is once again framed in social and political terms (vv. 6-7). The Thessalonian opponents are distinguished from the previous antagonists by the way in which they handled the attack. A sense of desperation on their part is suggested by the fact that they found it necessary to seek the help of *some bad characters from the marketplace* (cf. 13:50; 14:2). The designation of these bad men (*andras ponērous*) as 'marketfolk' (*agoraiōn*) is interesting (NRSV 'some ruffians in the market-places'; ESV 'some wicked men of the rabble').[18] In the ancient world, the term *agoraioi* designated common labourers, artisans, and people who traded in the town centres. In terms of social status, they were regarded as 'people of low birth . . . contrasted with the nobility or upper classes'.[19] They may have been unemployed day labourers, who had been 'marginalized by the highly stratified society of the ancient world and reduced to catch-as-catch-can work, when someone needed temporary help'.[20] It is ironic that the Jewish leaders *formed a mob and started a riot in the city*, but then accused the missionaries of being trouble makers (v. 6)! They were trying to create the impression that Paul and Silas were responsible for this social disorder. *Jason* is introduced into the narrative as a supporter of the missionaries, in whose house Paul and Silas might be found. This could be the same Jason mentioned in Romans 16:21 as a fellow Jew and co-worker with Paul.[21] Perhaps Jason was converted because he first opened his home

---

MSS. Cf. Metzger, *Textual Criticism*, 402. However, the sense conveyed by this later reading is obviously correct: those who were jealous were the unbelieving Jews.

17. Bruce 190, 370. Jealousy was also the impulse that turned Joseph's brothers against him (7:9) and the temple leaders against Peter and John in Jerusalem (5:17). Spencer 1997, 170, suggests that the issue in 17:5 is 'not so much a doctrinal dispute over Paul's handling of Scripture as it is a social conflict arising from Paul's popularity in the community'. However, the context suggests that the issue was both doctrinal and social.

18. Barrett 1998, 806, translates the expression 'evil men from among the marketplace louts'.

19. A. J. Malherbe, *Paul and the Popular Philosophers* (Minneapolis: Fortress, 1987), 16. Spencer 1997, 171, notes that in 1 Thes. 2:5-9; 2 Thes. 3:7-10 Paul draws attention to his own example as one who worked as a manual labourer in Thessalonica. However, he then improperly concludes that Acts 17 'seems more concerned with building a prestigious rather than a proletarian image of Paul'. The fact that Luke highlights the conversion of people from the upper classes (17:4, 12) does not mean that he is identifying Paul and Silas with such people, over against those of lower status. The point of the narrative is the use of *agorairoi* by Jewish leaders to achieve their own ends.

20. Witherington 1998, 507.

21. Bruce 1990, 370, notes that 'it was customary for Jews in the Hellenistic world to

to these traveling preachers and then came to accept the gospel they proclaimed. Presumably, the embryonic church in Thessalonica was meeting in his home and people were being drawn from the synagogue to gather with other believers there. Hence the jealousy of those who remained with the synagogue. The aim of the mob was *to bring them* (Paul and Silas) *out to the crowd (eis ton dēmon)* to the popular assembly, which in a free city had juridical functions.

6-7 *But when they did not find them, they dragged Jason and some other brothers before the city officials (epi tous politarchas).* Luke uses the term 'politarch', which was a mainly Macedonian title for the non-Roman magistrates of a city. It is found in inscriptions ranging from the second century BC to the third century AD.[22] This change of action possibly took place because 'it seemed more appropriate to arraign the Thessalonian citizens themselves before the magistrates, or they may have feared that the town assembly would have been more sympathetic to the townsfolk'.[23] The frustration of their opponents at not being able to find Paul and Silas is expressed by the fact that they presented their case *shouting (boōntes).* No explanation is given for the absence of the missionaries, and to offer one without any clues from the context would be foolish. The focus of the narrative is now on the way the nascent church was implicated in the charges (cf. 1 Thes. 1:6; 2:14-16). From a literary perspective, the accusers extend and sharpen the accusation of 16:20-21 in two ways. First of all, they claim that the missionaries *'have caused trouble all over the world' (hoi tēn oikoumenēn anastatōsantes),* which probably means throughout the Roman Empire.[24] There were outbreaks of Jewish unrest around this time not only in Judea but more widely, and 'the authorities could not be expected to distinguish the militant messianism of the Jewish nationalists from the messianism proclaimed by Paul and Silas'.[25] As well as being a general threat to Roman society, the charge is that the perpetrators have *'now come here' (houtoi kai enthade pareisin),* and local supporters who have offered them refuge are contributing to this social and political upheaval (*'Jason has welcomed them into his house').* Secondly, they accuse Paul and Silas of sedition, claiming that *'they are all defying Caesar's decrees' (houtoi pantes apenanti tōn dogmatōn Kaisaros).* Normally, *Caesar's decrees* were not binding on the

adopt Greek names with some resemblance to their Hebrew ones; thus Jason corresponds to Joshua'.

22. Cf. Sherwin-White, *Roman Law,* 96; Hemer, *Book of Acts,* 115; ND 2:34-35.

23. Marshall 1980, 278-79.

24. 'Turned [the world] upside down' is the usual rendering of *anastatōsantes* in EVV. However, Barrett 1998, 806, 815, who notes the use of the same verb in 21:38, suggests that the meaning is much more like 'led [the world] into revolt'. Cf. Johnson 1992, 307 ('subverting the Empire'). Barrett asserts that *oikoumenē* (used eight times in Luke-Acts and seven times elsewhere in the NT) means 'the whole civilized world'. However, within the present context it clearly refers to the realm in which Caesar is supposed to be supreme.

25. Bruce 1990, 371.

magistrates of a free city like Thessalonica.[26] However, in this case the reference may have been to a special edict, such as the decree of Claudius (about AD 49), banishing Jews from Rome because of their rioting 'at the instigation of Chrestus'.[27] Alternatively, the reference may have been to 'edicts against predictions, especially of the death or change of rulers, first promulgated by the aged Augustus in AD 11 (Dio Chrysostom, *Or.* 56.25.5-6) and enforced through the local administration of oaths of loyalty'.[28]

In one sense, of course, they were right. Paul was advancing 'a truly world-changing mission',[29] with the proclamation of Jesus as the promised messianic ruler at its heart (v. 3). His Jewish opponents knew what he meant when they accused him of saying that *'there is another king (basilea heteron), one called Jesus'*. But they also knew that the Roman emperor was called *basileus* ('king') by his Greek-speaking subjects. It would not have been hard to present the teaching about Jesus' kingship as politically offensive 'predictions of a change of ruler'.[30] However, at another level, these accusations missed the mark, as Paul had 'never aligned his messianic mission with plots to overthrow Roman rule or incite public disturbances'.[31] Accepting the lordship of Christ would mean new priorities and loyalties for those who became disciples. It would lead to the transformation of personal relationships, business and personal ethics, social structures and ambitions, new attitudes towards other religions, and changed ways of relating to Caesar and his representatives. The Holy Spirit would progressively bring about these changes as Christians reflected together on the implications of their new life in Christ and received guidance from leaders such as Paul (e.g., Romans 12–14) and Peter (e.g., 1 Peter 2). But even the preaching of the gospel itself is disturbing to the social and political status quo, wherever it is taken seriously.

8-9 *When they heard this, the crowd and the city officials were thrown into turmoil.* It is important to notice that Acts 16–19 gives a varied picture of the opponents of the Christian mission and the officials who administered Ro-

26. Sherwin-White, *Roman Law*, 96.
27. A. Ehrhardt, *The Acts of the Apostles* (Manchester: Manchester University, 1969), 96, argues this case, based on the evidence of Suetonius, *Claud.* 25.4. Cf. Acts 18:2. If the riots in Rome were caused by the preaching of Christ ('Chrestus' in the Latin source) among Jews, the implications in a place like Thessalonica might have been that the Jewish leaders stirred the mob 'to side with that party which was loyal to the Emperor'.
28. Hemer, *Book of Acts*, 167, summarizing E. A. Judge, 'The Decrees of Caesar at Thessalonica', *RTR* 30 (1971), 1-7. Cf. Bruce 1990, 371-72.
29. Spencer 1997, 171. Witherington 1998, 508, highlights the politically charged language in the Thessalonian letters as further proof of the political impact of Paul's teaching in the city.
30. Judge, 'Decrees', 3. As in Lk. 23:2, with the use of the word *basileus*, the confession of Jesus as Messiah is put in 'the most politically inflammatory form' (Johnson 1992, 307).
31. Spencer 1997, 171. Nevertheless, Spencer, 133-36, provides an interesting survey of the way in which Paul's missions disrupt conventional social-symbolic systems, but not always in the same way among the same people.

man society. The missionaries are twice accused by Jews (17:5-7; 18:12-13), and twice by Gentiles (16:19-21; 19:24-27). Twice the charge is given some credence by public officials (16:22-4; 17:8-9), and twice it is dismissed (18:14-17; 19:35-40).[32] In this case, Jason and other members of the new Christian community were *forced to post bond* by the magistrates (*lambanein to hikanon*, 'to take that which is sufficient/necessary'). This was a good behaviour bond. They were cautioned and 'required to give security for their own behaviour as well as that of Paul and Silas before being dismissed'.[33] Perhaps Jason was required to guarantee that Paul and Silas left the city quietly and did not return. If Paul chafed under any such exclusion order, he 'could not take action which would seriously embarrass his Thessalonian hosts.'[34]

2. The Gospel Provokes an Eager Searching of the Scriptures (17:10-15)

This synagogue community is contrasted with the one in Thessalonica. Although not everyone believed, their initial reception of the message was such as to provoke careful, daily study of the Scriptures, 'to see if what Paul said was true' (vv. 10-12). Luke's careful description suggests that he saw this pattern of response as the ideal for Jews confronted with the gospel. Perhaps more would have believed in Jesus, had not Jews from Thessalonica appeared and stirred up opposition, forcing the believers to send Paul away (vv. 13-15). Silas and Timothy were able to stay behind for a time to continue the work, but Paul was a marked man!

10 *As soon as it was night, the believers sent Paul and Silas away to Berea.* It is unwarranted to assume that Paul and Silas were hiding from their opponents in Thessalonica, but they were doubtless anxious to avoid arrest and punishment so as to continue their mission elsewhere. *The believers (hoi adelphoi*, 'the brothers') were either bound by an exclusion order to send Paul and Silas away or realised that it was time for them to leave anyway. The situation had become intolerable for the visitors, and now it would be left to their converts to be the means by which the gospel was proclaimed in the region (cf. 1 Thes. 1:6-8; 2:13-16).[35] *Berea* was off the Via Egnatia,

32. I am indebted to Tannehill 1990, 209, for these observations.

33. Barrett 1998, 816-17.

34. Bruce 1990, 372.

35. Spencer 1997, 171-72, observes a 'sudden shielding of Paul from physical suffering, unlike his treatment at Philippi and even before that at Lystra (14.5, 19)', arguing that this coordinates with 'his developing profile as a Roman citizen of some standing'. However, as suggested previously, the focus of the narrative is on the way the nascent church comes to share in the suffering of the missionaries (cf. 1 Thes. 1:6; 2:14-16). Furthermore, it is inconsistent with the picture of Paul we have elsewhere in Acts to say that he would allow himself to be spirited away from suffering, unless open evangelism was no longer pos-

which the missionaries had been following from Philippi, some 45 miles (72 km.) west-southwest of Thessalonica. When they arrived there, *they went to the Jewish synagogue* and received a very positive response to their teaching.

11-12   The Berean Jews are described as being *of more noble character (eugenesteroi) than those in Thessalonica.* The term used here referred originally to noble birth, but came to be applied more generally to high-minded behaviour (cf. Cicero, *Ad Att.* 13, 21a.4; Josephus, *Ant.* 12.255). 'Luke means that the Beroean Jews allowed no prejudice to prevent them from giving Paul a fair hearing.'[36] Their nobility of character was demonstrated in two practical ways. First, *they received the message with great eagerness,* responding enthusiastically because they realised its relevance to their own lives (cf. 2:41). Second, they *examined the Scriptures every day* (kath' hēmeran, 'day by day') *to see if what Paul said was true.* They were not gullible or unthinking in their approach. Paul had offered them a new way of understanding the Scriptures, proclaiming the fulfillment of Israel's messianic hope in the death and resurrection of Jesus (cf. v. 3). They needed to 'test' or 'cross examine' (*anakrinontes* is used in a legal sense, as in 4:9; 12:19; 24:8; 28:18) the Scriptures to see if Paul's case proved true. The result of Paul's preaching and the open-minded study of Scripture by the Bereans was that *many of them believed, as did also a number of prominent Greek women and many Greek men.* These *Greek* converts were probably attached to the synagogue, though Luke does not use the term *God-fearing* here (cf. v. 4). As in Thessalonica, there were *prominent* Greek women (*euschēmonōn,* as in 13:50, rather than *prōtōn,* as in 17:4) and *many Greek men* (*andrōn ouk oligoi,* 'not a few men', a figure of speech called litotes, by which an affirmative is expressed by the negative of the contrary, as in 17:4).[37] Thus, the conversions in Berea were similar in character to those in Thessalonica. The real difference between the situations was that the unconverted in Berea did not persecute the missionaries and seek to silence them. Perhaps they realised that there was still a case to answer from the Scriptures. Luke contrasts the jealousy and emotive defiance of the Thessalonians with the rational and reflective approach of the Berean Jews. By implication, he commends the latter as the way to respond to the challenge of the gospel and its approach to the Scriptures. Initial expressions of belief, however enthusiastic, need to be reinforced and strengthened by examining the scriptural basis for the gospel more holistically.

---

sible. Sherwin-White, *Roman Law,* 95-96, simply argues that Paul and Silas were dispatched 'out of the way to Beroea, where the jurisdiction of the magistrates of Thessalonica was not valid.'

36. Barrett 1998, 817.

37. Metzger, *Textual Criticism,* 402-3, discusses the way Codex D smooths the grammar of 17:12 and lessens the importance given to women. The 'anti-feminist' tendency of this MS is also particularly noted by some scholars in connection with 17:34 and 18:26. Contrast Barrett 1998, 818-19.

13-15 The extraordinary antagonism of *the Jews in Thessalonica* is illustrated by the fact that they *learned that Paul was preaching the word of God at Berea* and took the trouble to travel some forty-five miles to continue their opposition there. This pattern of Jews from one place following Paul to another in order to hinder his ministry was previously noted in 14:19. The Thessalonian Jews used the same method as before (v. 5), *agitating the crowds and stirring them up,*[38] making it necessary for *the believers* (*hoi adelphoi*, 'the brothers') *immediately* to send Paul in the direction of the sea. TNIV *(to the coast)* follows NRSV, NKJV, and ESV ('on his way to the sea') in preferring the largely Alexandrian reading *heōs epi tēn thalassan*. This indicates that Paul went to Athens by ship, avoiding the land journey through Thessalonica. However, since no port of embarkation is mentioned, which is unusual for Luke, some have argued in favour of the KJV reading ('as it were to the sea'), which is a rendering of the variant found in Byzantine manuscripts (*ōs epi tēn thalassan*).[39] This could mean that Paul's companions acted as if to conduct Paul to the sea to put his opponents off the trail, but then accompanied him overland to Athens via Thessalonica. The hardest reading from a grammatical point of view is *heōs epi tēn thalassan*. Since this is found in more ancient manuscripts, it is most likely to be the original text, which was then modified by copyists for reasons of clarity and simplicity. *But Silas and Timothy stayed at Berea,* presumably to nurture and encourage their new converts. Timothy has not been mentioned since 16:1-3. However, since Luke tends not to mention secondary figures unless they are central to a particular narrative, it is a reasonable to presume that Timothy accompanied Paul and Silas from Lystra to Berea.[40] So *those who escorted Paul brought him to Athens,* which was a considerable journey by land or sea (approximately 222 miles [357 km.] by land). They returned *with instructions for Silas and Timothy to join him as soon as possible.* 1 Thessalonians 3:1-2 suggests that Timothy at least joined Paul in Athens and was sent off from there to Thessalonica again. In Acts 18:5 Silas and Timothy come from Macedonia to meet Paul in Corinth. Luke makes no mention of any meeting

38. Many witnesses lack the words *kai tarassontes tous ochlous* ('and stirring up the crowds'). This shorter reading is found in the Received Text that was followed by the translators of KJV and NKJV. The shorter text appears to be the result of transcriptional oversight or deliberate correction, occasioned by the fact that the expression seems to double what is conveyed by the word *saleuontes* ('agitating'). Cf. Metzger, *Textual Criticism,* 403; Barrett 1998, 819.

39. Cf. Bruce 1990, 374. Barrett 1998, 819-20, allows for this possibility, but argues that *heōs* may be original and mean '(in English as awkward as the Greek would be) that Paul was accompanied *as far as to the sea;* that is, his companions saw him on board (cf. 20.38)'. Metzger, *Textual Criticism,* 404, similarly argues for the Alexandrian reading, noting that *heōs* with a following preposition occurs elsewhere in Acts. The Western text simplifies the issue by reading *epi tēn thalassan*.

40. Cf. Bruce 1990, 373. Commenting on the interpretation of 1 Thes. 3:2 in the light of Acts 17:14, Barrett 1998, 820, suggests that the former should perhaps be understood 'as an assurance that this hitherto slightly regarded assistant was in fact a trusted lieutenant'.

with Paul in Athens prior to this, but there would certainly have been time for Paul's assistants to visit him in Athens, return to Macedonia, and then meet him in Corinth.[41]

E. The Word in Athens (17:16-34)

The heart of this section is Paul's Areopagus address (vv. 22-31). This is preceded by the expression of his anger at the idolatry of the city and the culture it represented. Paul's consequent evangelistic efforts aroused the interest of the philosophers who heard his marketplace preaching and brought him before the Areopagus (vv. 16-21). A summary of Paul's speech is then followed by a brief reference to the responses from Dionysius, Damaris, and others (vv. 32-34). It is important to interpret the speech with reference to the narrative framework in which Luke has placed it.[42] In broad terms, Luke is concerned to outline the way Paul argued in this unusual context and to show the variety of reactions to his teaching. While there are certain parallels with Paul's speech in Lystra (14:11-18), 'in this more sophisticated setting, Paul confronts intellectual speculation concerning his own ideas about God rather than superstitious deification'.[43] However, many scholars have doubted that this speech is a record of what Paul actually said. Indeed, the passage seems to have attracted more scholarly debate than any other in Acts. Barrett, for example, argues that it was a Lukan construction: 'Luke was not in a position to recount something that he had himself heard but used what had come to be the accepted Christian approach to Gentiles. It is very doubtful whether he was correct in ascribing this approach to Paul.'[44] While there are certain parallels with Romans 1:18-32, it has been argued that the differences between the passages are sufficient to conclude that Paul could not have preached as Luke imagined. For example, Acts 17:22-31 looks hopefully at the possibility that Gentiles will seek after God and come to repentance, whereas Romans 1:18-32 seems to view human society as being without hope because of its stubborn and culpable ignorance

41. Cf. Bruce 1990, 374-75; Witherington 1998, 510-11.
42. Cf. B. Gärtner, *The Areopagus Speech and Natural Revelation* (Lund: Gleerup, 1955), 45-65.
43. Spencer 1997, 172.
44. Barrett 1998, 825. Cf. M. Dibelius, *Studies in the Acts of the Apostles*, ed. H. Greeven, trans. M. Ling (London: SCM, 1956), 26-77. Barrett acknowledges many features in the narrative that 'may constitute a case for believing that the writer was personally familiar with the city, whether or not he had been there in company with Paul'. However, he argues that Luke was not present with Paul (this is not one of the 'we' passages) and that the style of argument is different from anything found in Paul's letters. Haenchen 1971, 527-31, proposes that Luke used Jewish-Hellenistic traditions for engaging with paganism, with the doctrine of the resurrection being 'tagged on in a sudden transition in verse 31'. Johnson 1992, 318, describes the speech as 'Luke's idealized version of what ought to have happened', but goes on to say 'how cunningly Luke has got everything right'!

of God. Acts 17:28b-29a regards kinship with God 'as an innate characteristic of humanity, whereas in Romans human beings are by nature children of Adam (5:12) and divine sonship is the gift of election realized through faith in Christ (8:14)'.[45] Finally, the motives for repentance suggested in Acts 17:24-31 are failure to respond appropriately to God in view of the witness of creation and the certainty of God's coming judgment. These themes can also be discerned in Romans 1:18–2:11, though the message of salvation through Christ is much more clearly the motive for repentance and faith in the wider presentation of Romans (cf. 1:16-17; 2:1-4; 3:21-31). Some of these differences can be accounted for by the fact that Acts 17 represents an abbreviated missionary speech in a specific situation, whereas Romans 1 is part of an extensive argument to Christians about the way the gospel meets the needs of the human condition more generally. Wilson expresses the contrast between these texts quite starkly: 'the one view emphasises the Gentiles' culpability, while the other interprets their basic response as correct but misguided. Paul's is a passionate condemnation, while Luke's is a combination of magnanimity and admonition.'[46] Witherington rightly takes issue with this approach and argues convincingly that the differences of emphasis in the two texts are far from being irreconcilable.[47] Some of the details raised in this debate will be addressed as the interpretation of the passage proceeds. Much depends on the way the argument of the speech is understood and how it is thought to relate to the literary context and the historical setting established by Luke.

1. Responding to Idolatry (17:16-21)

The external impulse for Paul's speech was the specific context in Athens and the challenge of Greek thought and practice more generally. Luke makes it clear that Paul's response to idolatry and the ignorance of pagan worship was to proclaim Jesus and the resurrection in the marketplace to anyone who happened to be there (17:16-18). For this he was called to account by representatives of two of the major schools of philosophy present

45. R. Maddox, *The Purpose of Luke-Acts* (Edinburgh: Clark, 1982), 83. Maddox also suggests that human sin seems to be treated rather lightly in Acts 17:30, being identified with the ignorance shown in worshipping cult-objects of human manufacture (v. 29; cf. vv. 16, 22b-23), 'but in Rom. 1:23f., 25f., 28, idolatry is interpreted as a deep-seated perversion of the honour due to God, which leads to moral depravity'. Cf. S. G. Wilson, *The Gentiles and the Gentile Mission in Luke-Acts*, SNTSMS 23 (Cambridge: Cambridge University, 1973), 196-218.

46. Wilson, *Gentiles*, 214.

47. Witherington 1998, 533-35. Bruce 1990, 379, also observes that, if the tone of the speech in Acts 17 is different from that of Romans 1–3 (as it is), 'Paul's ability to adapt his tone and his approach to his audience must not be underestimated'. Cf. Gärtner, *Areopagus*, 133-69, for an extensive comparison of the passages. Gärtner, 248-52, summarizes his reasons for affirming the Pauline character of the speech in Acts 17.

in the city at that time, the Epicureans and the Stoics. They brought him before a meeting of the Areopagus to discover the precise content and meaning of the new teaching he was presenting (17:19-21). In responding to this request, Paul had to deal with an audience that was more educated and cultured than the one addressed in Lystra, and yet some of the issues were the same. Knowledge and ignorance are distinctive themes here (vv. 19, 20, 23, 30), but false views about God and the way to worship him are common to both contexts.

16 'Athens, the cradle of democracy, attained the foremost place among the Greek city-states early in the fifth century BC by reason of the lead she took in resisting the Persians.'[48] She took the lead again in the fourth-century resistance to Philip of Macedon. After his victory in 338 BC, Athens was treated generously and allowed to retain much of her ancient freedom. The Romans conquered Greece in 146 BC but again allowed Athens to carry on her own institutions as a free and allied city within the empire. The cultural and intellectual significance of Athens in the ancient world is aptly summarised by Bruce:

> The sculpture, literature and oratory of Athens in the fifth and fourth centuries BC remain unsurpassed. In philosophy, too, she took the leading place, being the native city of Socrates and Plato and the adopted home of Aristotle, Epicurus, and Zeno. Her cultural influence in the Greek world is also seen in the fact that it was the Attic dialect of Greek, spoken at first over a very restricted area as compared with Ionic and Doric, that formed the base of the later Hellenistic speech (Koine). It was at this time a leading center of learning; in modern idiom we might describe it as a great university city.[49]

Three things about first-century Athens are identified in vv. 16-21 to set the scene for Paul's speech: the idolatry of the masses (v. 16), the high value placed on knowledge by the philosophical schools (vv. 19-20), and the preoccupation of all the Athenians and the foreigners who lived there with the latest ideas (v. 21). It was while Paul was waiting for Silas and Timothy in Athens that *he was greatly distressed* (*parōxsyneto to pneuma autou en autō*, 'his spirit was aroused within him') *to see that the city was full of idols* (*theōrountos kateidōlon ousan tēn polin*). Stott suggests that the unusual expression *kateidōlon* means 'a city submerged in its idols'.[50] Paul initially occupied himself with observation of Athenian religious practices rather than

---

48. Bruce 1990, 375.

49. Bruce 1990, 375-76. Bruce cautions that the university analogy has been overdone by some writers.

50. Stott 1990, 278; BDAG 'full of cult-images/idols'. Barrett 1998, 827-28, considers the possibility of translating *kateidōlon* 'a veritable forest of idols', but prefers 'overgrown with idols'. Barrett concludes that, 'what is important is that Paul was impressed by Athens not as a city of art but as a city of false religion.' Witherington 1998, 512-13, describes the kind of idols Paul would have seen.

launching straight into evangelism. Luke implies that it was uncertainty about how long he would have to wait for Silas and Timothy that caused him to enter slowly into his normal pattern of ministry. The visit to Athens was not planned, but was the result of Paul's sudden exclusion from Macedonia (vv. 14-15). However, as one who was passionate about giving glory to the God of the Scriptures, Paul could not remain silent for long. The verb *paroxynō* in the passive means 'become irritated, angry' (BDAG; cf. 15:39, *paroxysmos*, 'irritation, sharp disagreement'). In the imperfect tense, the verb expresses 'not a sudden loss of temper but rather a continuous settled reaction to what Paul saw'.[51] This terminology is regularly used in the LXX to describe God's reaction to idolatry (e.g., Dt. 9:7, 18, 22; Ps. 106 [LXX 105]:28-29; Is. 65:2-3; Hos. 8:5). Paul shared something of the jealousy of God for his own name or character (e.g., Ex. 20:4; 34:14; Is. 42:8). The pain or anger which Paul felt in Athens was due to 'his abhorrence of idolatry, which aroused within him deep stirrings of jealousy for the Name of God, as he saw human beings so depraved as to be giving idols the honour and glory which were due to the one, living and true God alone'.[52]

17 *So he reasoned in the synagogue with both Jews and God-fearing Greeks*,[53] as he had done elsewhere (e.g., 14:1; 17:2, 10-12), though the flow of the argument suggests that Paul's primary topic was the idolatry of the city. 'And it was a material point with Luke that Paul should demonstrate how he came to terms with Greek belief and pagan idolatry in this particular setting, for Athens had a reputation for great religiosity.'[54] In the synagogue he met with those who shared his distress about false religion. But Paul also knew that the gospel would empower believing Jews to have a greater impact on the idolatry of the pagan world because it was a message of grace and salvation for everyone on the same basis (cf. 13:46-48; 15:11). Ancient barriers between Jews and Gentiles were removed in Christ. Luke says little about Paul's synagogue ministry in Athens since he is more interested in the engagement with passersby *in the marketplace* (*agora*, as in 16:19). In Greco-Roman times, the marketplace was the hub of urban life — a centre for commerce and trade, but also for the sharing of ideas. For the first time we are told that Paul directed his mission to the marketplace on a daily basis (*day by day with those who happened to be there*). This was not

51. Stott 1990, 278.

52. Stott 1990, 279. Stott considers the implications of this for contemporary thinking about mission and evangelism.

53. The use of *men oun* in 17:17, as elsewhere in Acts (cf. 1:6 note), signals a new development in the narrative, in this case the beginning of Paul's public ministry in Athens. The verb *dielegeto* ('reasoned', as in 17:2; 18:4, 19; 19:8-9; 20:7, 9) applies to Paul's ministry in the synagogue and in the marketplace in 17:17. It suggests discussion and argument rather than simply proclamation.

54. Gärtner, *Areopagus*, 46. Stott 1990, 280-81, considers the contemporary implications of Paul's ministry 'to religious people in the synagogue, to casual passersby in the city square, and to highly sophisticated philosophers both in the *agora* and when they met in Council'.

because he was excluded from the synagogue, but because he wished to engage directly with as many Gentiles as possible, in the place where discussion and debate might easily take place. Socrates, the archetypal philosopher of Athens, was always available for discussion with anyone willing to converse with him in the marketplace, and some have suggested that Luke intended an analogy with Socrates in his presentation of Paul's ministry here.[55]

18 Two different groups of philosophers *began to debate with him* in the marketplace. The Epicureans were known for 'their pursuit of happiness and contentment through detachment from social competition and denial of divine interference in human affairs, especially the threat of retribution'.[56] They believed in the existence of many gods, but argued in deistic fashion that the gods took no interest in the events of everyday life. Consequently, Epicureans were critical of popular religion with its localising of gods in many temples and its concern to supply their needs (cf. vv. 24-25). The Stoics believed that the human race was one, proceeding from a single point of origin. Through logic and discipline, they sought 'to live in harmony with the natural order, which they believed was permeated by a rational divine principle or *Logos*'.[57] They were essentially pantheistic and thought of the divine being as 'the World-soul' (cf. vv. 26-29). Epicureanism and Stoicism were 'the popular Greek alternatives for dealing with the plight of humanity and for coming to terms with life apart from the biblical revelation and God's working in Jesus Christ'.[58] From one point of view, Paul's speech appears to be 'an attempt to see how far a Christian preacher can go in company with Greek philosophy'.[59] However, the speech is clearly determined by biblical theology, and develops in biblical order certain themes found in the early chapters of Genesis.

Some of those who argued with Paul were far from polite, asking one another, *'What is this babbler trying to say?'* The word translated *babbler* (*spermalogos*) was originally used of seed-eating or scavenging birds and meant 'picking up seeds' (BDAG). Metaphorically, it was applied to people who obtained scraps of information from others and retailed them as their own. So they were accusing Paul of being an ignorant plagiarist and a religious charlatan. In contemporary terms, Barrett suggests the translation

55. Cf. Barrett 1998, 824, 828-29, 830.

56. Spencer 1997, 172. Cf. Marshall 1980, 283-84; Johnson 1992, 313; Barrett 1998, 829. The Epicureans were named after their founder, Epicurus (342-270 BC). Gärtner, *Areopagus*, 47-48, argues that representatives of other philosophical schools are not mentioned because Luke was aware that the Epicureans and Stoics had most influence at this time.

57. Spencer 1997, 173. The Stoics took their name from the 'painted Stoa' or portico in the Athenian marketplace, where their founder, Zeno (340-265 BC), expounded his philosophy. Witherington 1998, 514, provides a helpful summary of the beliefs of Epicureans and Stoics and shows how Paul's sermon interacts with these at various points. Cf. N. C. Croy, 'Epicureanism', *DNTB* 324-27; J. C. Thom, 'Stoicism', *DNTB* 1139-42.

58. Longenecker 1981, 474.

59. Barrett 1998, 829.

'this third-rate journalist'![60] Others *remarked, 'He seems to be advocating for-eign gods'.* The plural *xenōn daimoniōn* ('foreign divinities'), followed by the explanatory clause *because Paul was preaching the good news about Jesus and the resurrection,* suggests that they understood Paul to be preaching in poly-theistic fashion about a god named Jesus (a masculine name in Greek) and his consort 'Resurrection' (*anastasis* is feminine in Greek).[61] It is important to note that Paul returns to the subject of Jesus and the resurrection at the climax of his speech (v. 31), after he has established some common ground with his audience. This he does by first advancing 'views that would not appear ridiculous in the eyes of respected Greco-Roman thinkers',[62] while at the same time setting forth biblical views about God and his purpose for humanity. *Jesus and the resurrection* was Paul's ultimate response, both to popular paganism and to the more refined views of the philosophers (cf. Rom. 10:9). With this focus, Luke tells us Paul was evangelising *(euēnge-lizeto).* Although the argument which follows resorts to forensic rhetoric, presenting elements of 'defense and attack for his vision of God, human-kind, salvation, resurrection and judgment',[63] Paul's aim continues to be evangelistic.

19-21 In these verses there is a twofold use of the verb 'to know' *(gnōnai)* with reference to the new teaching and its significance *('May we know what this new teaching is that you are presenting? You are bringing some strange ideas to our ears, and we want to know what they mean').*[64] Paul picks up this theme in his speech, identifying what they worship 'without knowing' (v. 23, *agnoountes*) and describing the past as 'the times of ignorance' (v. 30, *agnoias*) from which they must repent in order to know the true God.

---

60. Barrett 1998, 830. The objection to introducing new deities may have been partly political (cf. Dio Cassius, *Hist.* 52.36.1-2). However, the main sense in 17:18 is that Paul is an inferior speaker, with an unimpressive philosophy assembled from insights gained from others. Philostratus, *Apoll.* 5.20, uses the term with reference to the peddler of second-rate religious opinions.

61. Cf. Gärtner, *Areopagus,* 48; Longenecker 1981, 474; Spencer 1997, 173. Barrett 1998, 830-31, is sceptical about this interpretation, arguing that the comment is 'cast in a form in-tended to recall the story of Socrates, and means no more than, This is a strange new reli-gion, with all this talk about a man called Jesus and a resurrection'. Socrates was charged with bringing in 'strange new gods' (*hetera de kaina daimonia;* Xenophon, *Memorabilia* 1.1.1; cf. Plato, *Apol.* 24 B-C). The word *daimonia* is used in both contexts of deities, not of 'demons' as in the Gospels (e.g., Mk. 1:34). The explanatory clause is omitted by Codex D and one Old Latin MS (cf. Metzger, *Textual Criticism,* 404).

62. Tannehill 1990, 217, drawing attention to the parallels in the writings of Greek philosophers and poets noted by Dibelius, *Studies,* 42-43, 47, 53-54.

63. Witherington 1998, 517-18. Witherington, 524, agrees that the ultimate aim is evangelism.

64. B. W. Winter, 'On Introducing Gods to Athens: An Alternative Reading of Acts 17:18-20', *TynB* 47 (1996), 80-83, argues that Paul was not being asked to provide an explana-tion in v. 19. Rather, reading the words within the semantic field of Greek *politeia,* Paul was being told by these representatives of the Council that 'we possess the legal right to judge what this new teaching is that is being spoken by you'.

'Starting from a cultural value acknowledged by the audience enables Paul to engage them in the discourse. Denying that this value has been realized within the present culture and calling for repentance turns this into a critical engagement.'[65] That engagement took place when *they took him (epilabomenoi) and brought (ēgagon) him to a meeting of the Areopagus*. The terminology here matches 16:19-20, where Paul's opponents 'seized' *(epilabomenoi)* both him and Silas and 'brought' *(prosagagontes)* them before the magistrates. However, 'the Athenian scene has more the appearance of an open inquiry than a hostile inquisition; there is no flogging or sentencing, only asking and hearing'.[66] A closer parallel is suggested by the use of the same terms in 9:27, when Barnabas took the newly converted Saul and brought him to the apostles in Jerusalem. Opinions vary about whether the expression *epi ton Areion Pagon* refers literally to the Hill of Ares (the Greek god identified by the Romans as Mars, hence KJV 'Mars' hill'), which was west of the Acropolis, or to the administrative body that took its name from this place. NRSV, ESV, and NKJV leave the issue open, translating the expression 'to the Areopagus'. TNIV more specifically identifies the venue as *a meeting of the Areopagus*. This is a reasonable assumption since Paul appears to be addressing not only the philosophers but also 'an official body that has responsibility for the city'.[67] In the first century, the Council of the Areopagos seems to have been 'the effective government of Roman Athens and its chief court. As such, like the imperial Senate in Rome, it could interfere in any aspect of corporate life — education, philosophical lectures, public morality, foreign cults.'[68] Luke concludes the section with a note that *all the Athenians and the foreigners who lived there spent their time doing nothing but talking about and listening to the latest ideas*. This Athenian curiosity was

65. Tannehill 1990, 215. Tannehill explores the implications of this model, arguing that 'a mission that does not engage the presuppositions and dominant concerns of those being approached leaves those presuppositions and concerns untouched, with the result that the message, even if accepted, does not transform its hearers'.

66. Spencer 1997, 173. The Western text embroiders the sentence in 17:19, adding 'some days' to the period before Paul is taken to the Areopagus and the word 'inquiring', suggesting something more informal than a trial. Cf. Metzger, *Textual Criticism*, 404; Barrett 1998, 832-33. Winter, 'Introducing', 80-83, argues that it was an informal meeting of council members after it had been reported that Paul was possibly the herald of new divinities: 'they would know that, if he gained popular support in Athens, he might secure a rightful place for his deities in the Athenian pantheon' (83).

67. Tannehill 1990, 216. Paul addresses the people of Athens through this body (v. 22), not just the philosophers who question him, and the concluding reference to the conversion of an Areopagite (member of the Areopagus council) confirms this view (v. 34). Cf. Gärtner, *Areopagus*, 52-65; Marshall 1980, 284-85; Winter, 'Introducing', 84-87.

68. T. D. Barnes, 'An Apostle on Trial', *JTS* n.s. 20 (1969), 413. Bruce 1990, 378, observes that 'its jurisdiction in religious matters made it the appropriate body to examine one who was charged with proclaiming "strange divinities"'. The court traditionally met on the Hill of Ares, but in Paul's time, at least on occasion, it met in the Royal Portico in the northwest corner of the marketplace (cf. C. J. Hemer, 'Paul at Athens: A Topographical Note', *NTS* 20 [1973-74], 341-50).

well known (cf. Demosthenes, *Philippic* 1.10; Thucydides, *Hist.* 3.38.5), and many people visited Athens, either as students or tourists, to share in the preoccupation of its citizens with *talking about and listening to the latest ideas.*[69] This verse adds to the impression, created by vv. 19-20, that the main concern of those who took Paul to the Areopagus was to gain information and enlightenment. However, the sharper edge that we have seen to the comments in v. 18 should not be forgotten. Some derided him, and, if the parallel with Socrates is to be taken seriously, some were concerned about the implications of his teaching for the city.

2. Establishing God's Claim on All People (17:22-31)

This is the second of three major speeches by Paul in Acts (17:22-31; cf. 13:16-41; 20:18-35). It is closest in style and content to the brief message delivered to Gentiles at Lystra (14:15-17). Tannehill suggests that 'there is an internal as well as an external impulse toward the viewpoint expressed by Paul in Athens'.[70] The external impulse is outlined in 17:16-21. Internally, in a variety of ways, Luke-Acts has been highlighting the universal scope of God's saving work. 'Effective mission, however, requires reflection on theological foundations in order to discover a message that can address the whole world. More than instruction in the Jewish gospel is needed.'[71] I would modify the last sentence by saying that the biblical roots of the gospel which make it a message with universal appeal needed to be explored and articulated. Paul's speech in Athens is ultimately messianic and evangelistic because it concludes with a proclamation of the resurrected man by whom God will judge the world and calls upon all people everywhere to repent in response to this (17:30-31). But the earlier part of the speech sounds more like a reflection on the opening chapters of Genesis (even though no text is actually cited), moving from a proclamation of the one true Creator, to an assertion of his purpose for humanity, and concluding with a declaration of universal accountability before God as judge (cf. Genesis 1–11).

22-23 *Paul then stood up in the meeting of the Areopagus.* As noted in connection with v. 19, it seems most likely that Paul was brought to an informal meeting of the Areopagus court, with possibly a wider group of people present.[72] What took place was more of an open inquiry than a hos-

---

69. Barrett 1998, 833-84, comments on minor variations in the Western text of 17:21.

70. Tannehill 1990, 210.

71. Tannehill 1990, 211. However, Tannehill, 211-12, rightly goes on to show that 'a good share of the Athens speech repeats themes already presented in Luke-Acts'. In other words, there are closer links with gospel presentations elsewhere in Acts than first meets the eye.

72. Cf. Winter, 'Introducing', 86-87. Barrett 1998, 834, notes that *en mesō* ('in the midst') in 17:22 (cf. 1:15; 2:22; 4:7; 27:21) suggests 'in the middle of a group of people rather

tile inquisition. Furthermore, Paul took the opportunity to address the city and its culture (*'People of Athens'*), not simply to engage with the philosophers. Debate has raged about whether his opening words (*'I see that in every way you are very religious'*) are an accusation or a mild compliment. The piety of the Athenians was proverbial (cf. Pausanias, *Description of Greece* 1.17.1; Sophocles, *Oedipus Coloneus* 260), and the word translated *very religious (deisidaimonesterous)* could be understood positively.[73] According to Lucian (*De Gymnastica* 19), however, attempts to secure the goodwill of the Areopagus court with compliments were discouraged. Furthermore, Paul's reaction to the idolatry of the city in v. 16 suggests that the whole expression *ōs deisidaimonesterous* (v. 22) should be understood negatively, but given an ironic sense ('I see that you make a great display of piety').[74]

The basis of Paul's accusation was his careful observation of their *'objects of worship'* (*sebasmata*; cf. Wis. 14:20; 15:17; Josephus, *Ant.* 18.344; 2 Thes. 2:4 [*sebasma*]). He had seen an abundance of statues and altars devoted to the worship of many gods, even coming across *'an altar with this inscription: TO AN UNKNOWN GOD'*. 'Altars of unknown gods' are firmly attested in the literature (e.g., Pausanias 1.1.4; Philostratus, *Apoll.* 6.3), though no inscription specifically 'to an unknown god' has been found in Athens.[75] Any such altar could have perished, or its inscription could have become indecipherable through the ravages of time. Even in the singular, such a dedication implied polytheism — the need to acknowledge any god that might exist — but Paul used it to affirm monotheism.[76] In their anxiety to honour any gods inadvertently ignored, the Athenians had displayed

---

than at the mid-point of an area'. So also Bruce 1990, 379. Barrett, 854, also argues that the use of *ek mesou* in 17:33 'confirms the view that the Areopagus is a company of people, not a locality'.

73. Cf. Johnson 1992, 314; Barrett 1998, 835. Festus appears to use the word *deisidaimonia* positively when speaking of Judaism to Agrippa (25:19), though Witherington 1998, 520, interprets this in a negative sense. Discussing the use of this term in Greek literature more widely, Barrett concludes that the context must determine in what sense 'religious' is to be understood: 'to the sceptic, this means superstitious; to the religious, judgment depends on whether the religion is one he shares, or at least approves, or is one that he rejects'.

74. The translation of Barrett 1998, 822. Discussion has also taken place about the comparative form of the adjective and the use of the particle *hōs*. The sense of the expression could be comparative ('more religious [than ordinary or than I had supposed]'), elative ('extremely religious'), or superlative ('very religious'). Barrett, 836, suggests also that *hōs* could have something of the sense 'as if' (cf. Rom. 9:32): 'Athens presents a show of (idolatrous) piety, but it is an unreal, uninformed piety directed towards a deity who must remain unknown (v. 23)'. KJV ('too superstitious') is too negative.

75. Cf. Bruce 1990, 380-81. Witherington 1998, 521-23, discusses the issue in some detail.

76. Barrett 1998, 838. The masculine *theos* ('God') is followed by the neuter pronoun *ho* ('that which') in the best MSS, but this is modified to the masculine pronoun *hon* in some MSS, doubtless because copyists wanted to make it clear that Paul was proclaiming a personal God. Bruce 1990, 381, suggests that 'Paul starts with his hearers' belief in an impersonal divine essence, pantheistically conceived, and leads them to the living God revealed as creator and judge'. Compare *to theion* (*the divine being,* v. 29).

their ignorance of the one true God. Paul makes this claim in a sentence that says something about the Athenians and something about himself (*'you are ignorant of the very thing you — and this what I am going to proclaim to you'*). 'The Athenians reverence a certain object, Paul proclaims it.'[77] What in the practice of their religion they admitted not to know was, in fact, the God who had revealed himself to Israel as creator, judge and saviour (cf. Is. 45:15-25; Je. 10:25; Gal. 4:8; Eph. 4:18; 1 Thes. 4:5). 'This altar both testifies to the Athenians' rudimentary awareness of the God proclaimed by Paul (who is, then, not a "foreign" divinity) and confesses that this God is unknown in Athens.'[78]

a. The Truth about God (17:24-25)

24-25 Paul begins to develop his argument with three negative statements which expose misunderstandings about God. The first is that *'the God who made the world and everything in it is the Lord of heaven and earth and does not live in temples built by hands'*. The second misunderstanding about God is that *'he is not served by human hands, as if he needed anything. Rather, he himself gives everyone life and breath and everything else.'* The third misunderstanding about God is that he cannot be represented by *'an image made by human design and skill'* (v. 29). 'In all three cases there is confusion between God and a location or an image that humans create, or with the mutual meeting of needs that characterizes human life.'[79] God is not to be understood in anthropomorphic terms — as being essentially like us! The first assertion, that *the God who made the world and everything in it is the Lord of heaven and earth,* recalls not only the creation narrative in Genesis 1 but also texts such as Exodus 20:11; Isaiah 42:5 (cf. Wis. 9:1, 9; Acts 4:24). Marshall notes that 'Paul employs the language that we would expect a Greek-speaking Jew to use, especially when addressing pagans'.[80] As universal creator and lord, God cannot be confined to any particular sacred space (*does not live in temples built by hands*), a claim that again reflects biblical teaching (e.g., 1 Ki. 8:27-30; Is. 66:1-2; cf. Acts 7:48-50). Paul is critical of Athenian religion as expressed in its temples, its views about serving God, and its attempts to represent and honour God through idols. The one true

77. Barrett 1998, 838. The sentence is complex in Greek because the subjects are different, and the verbs are different, but the objects are the same (*ho . . . touto*).

78. Tannehill 1990, 217-18. Marshall 1980, 286, observes that 'Paul hardly meant that his audience were unconscious worshippers of the true God. Rather, he is drawing their attention to the true God who was ultimately responsible for the phenomena which they attributed to an unknown god.' Cf. Winter, 'Introducing', 84-86.

79. Tannehill 1990, 215. Tannehill further observes that, 'the speech upholds God's transcendence not by implying God's distance from humans (cf. vv. 27-28) but by understanding God's role in creating and giving as irreversible. God gives and creates for humanity; humanity may give and create but not for God.'

80. Marshall 1980, 286. He says this particularly with reference to the word 'world' (Gk. *kosmos*), for which there is no corresponding term in Hebrew.

God cannot be confined and controlled by those whom he has created, and he cannot be manipulated by human religion. Parallel assertions by Greek writers are often noted by commentators. Paul's critique 'seems to go out of its way to find common ground with philosophers and poets',[81] but his presuppositions are 'not drawn from Platonism or Stoicism but unambiguously from the OT'.[82] In v. 25 he attacks one of the basic tenets of humanly devised religion, that God must be *served by human hands, as if he needed anything.* This is illogical and totally dishonouring to God as creator, since *he himself gives everyone life and breath and everything else.* God not only created all things in the beginning but continues to give (*didous*, present participle) his creatures all they need for their existence. As the sustainer of all life, he does not need to be sustained by us. 'We depend on God; he does not depend on us.'[83] Once again there are biblical parallels to Paul's assertions (e.g., Gn. 2:7; Ps. 50:9-13; Is. 42:5), which are echoed in extrabiblical Jewish writings, and there are also certain parallels in non-Jewish sources.[84] Repeated use of the Greek adjective *pas* in one form or another supports the claim that there is one God who is the all-encompassing *Lord of heaven and earth:* he made the world and *everything (panta)* in it, he himself gives *everyone (pasi)* life and breath and *everything else (panta)*, and he made *all (pan)* nations to inhabit the *whole (pantos)* earth.

b. The Truth about Humanity (17:26-29)

26 Following, as it were, the argument of Genesis, Paul moves from the creation of the world and everything in it (v. 24, *poiēsas*, 'made'; cf. Gn. 1:1 LXX) to the specific creation of human beings within this environment: *'from one man he made all the nations'* (v. 26, *epoiēsen*, 'made'). TNIV's *from one man* translates the Greek expression *ex henos* (NRSV 'from one ancestor').[85] This is a distinctly biblical perspective, based on Genesis 2–5, where God formed Adam first and then Eve, and caused their offspring to multiply (cf. Lk. 3:38; Rom. 5:12). The Greeks did not have such a view, but largely considered themselves superior to other races, whom they called barbarians. 'Against such claims to racial superiority Paul asserts the

---

81. Tannehill 1990, 216. Cf. Dibelius, *Studies*, 42-43, 47, 53-54; Barrett 1998, 839-40.
82. Bruce 1990, 382.
83. Stott 1990, 285.
84. Cf. Bruce 1990, 382; Barrett 1998, 840-41.
85. The Western text, with the support of a wide range of early versions and patristic witnesses, adds *haimatos* ('blood') after *henos*. This reading became part of the Received Text and explains KJV and NKJ's 'of one blood'. This longer reading has been defended on the ground that *haimatos* may have been accidentally omitted in other MSS, or even deliberately deleted since it appears to contradict Gn. 2:7. However, the MSS supporting the shorter reading ('of one') are diverse and ancient. The addition could have been made because there was no parallel in Greek thought to the biblical idea that one man was the father of all and 'blood was added as a different way of expressing the unity of all races' (Barrett 1998, 842). Cf. Metzger, *Textual Criticism*, 404-5.

unity of all mankind, a unity derived *ex henos,* i.e., from Adam.'[86] God's intention for humanity is indicated by two explanatory clauses containing infinitives in Greek: 'to inhabit' (v. 26, *katoikein*) and 'to seek' (v. 27, *zētein*). Humanity as a whole (*pan ethnos anthrōpōn,* 'every race of people' or 'the whole race of people') is meant to *'inhabit the whole earth'* (*katoikein epi pantos prosōpou tēs gēs,* 'to dwell on the whole face of the earth').[87] This echoes the teaching of Genesis 1:28-29, even including the Semitic expression 'the whole face of the earth'.[88] From a biblical perspective, humanity as a whole is to rule over, to care for, and to enjoy God's creation. A sense of racial superiority can only be overcome by recognising the unity of the human race in terms of its origin and God's purpose in creating us. Yet the next clause — *'and he marked out their appointed times in history and the boundaries of their lands'* — indicates that, in the plan of God, there are specific destinies for races and nations. The Greek (*horisas prostetagmenous kairous kai tas horothesias tēs katoikias autōn*) may be more literally translated 'having determined their appointed times and the boundaries of their dwelling places'. A parallel with 14:17 could suggest that *kairous* in 17:26 means 'seasons', but there are not the same clues in 17:26 to take the word in that sense. Moreover, the addition of the participle *prostetagmenous* ('foreordained') favours the translation *their appointed times in history* (NRSV 'the times of their existence'; ESV 'allotted periods'; NKJ 'their preappointed times'; cf. 1:7). If 'seasons' is read, the allusion will be to Genesis 1:14, but if *appointed times in history,* then a text like Daniel 2:36-45 will provide the theological background. *The boundaries of their lands* seems to be a reference to the various areas in which the races live (cf. Dt. 32:8), and so it could be argued that the preceding expression refers to the periods in history when those regions are dominated by particular races.[89] Thus, there is a collective responsibility and privilege shared by humanity as a whole in God's creation. Yet God has also ordained special times and places for nations within that overarching purpose. The two truths must be held in tension when applying biblical teaching to situations in our world today. However, Paul's argument also has religious implications. Different gods were associated with different races and different lands. 'If

86. Bruce 1990, 382. A. D. Nock, *Essays on Religion and the Ancient World I and II* (Harvard: Harvard University, 1972), 2:831, confirms that 'the Greeks did not have the idea of a First Man from whom humanity was sprung'.

87. Cf. Marshall 1980, 287-88, on the issues raised by Dibelius, *Studies,* 27-37, in connection with this verse.

88. Gn. 1:29 LXX has *epanō pasēs tēs gēs* ('over the whole earth'), but Acts 17:26 (*epi pantos prosōpou tēs gēs*) more literally represents the Hebrew expression *'al penê kol ha'aretz* ('on the face of the whole earth'). Cf. Gn. 2:6; 11:8; Je. 25:26 (LXX 32:12).

89. Cf. Gärtner, *Areopagus,* 146-52. Barrett 1998, 842-4, discusses the alternatives in some detail and concludes, 'in any case, the point made is that all the affairs of men and nations are in the hand of God'. Stott 1990, 286, rightly observes that 'although God cannot be held responsible for the tyranny or oppression of individual nations, yet both the history and the geography of each nation are ultimately under his control'.

God is working to unite all peoples in Christ, crossing national boundaries, then God is also working against polytheism.'[90]

27 Physical existence and the enjoyment of the earth's bounty was not the final purpose of God in creating human beings. *'God did this so that they would seek him and perhaps reach out for him and find him.'*[91] Seeking God is a challenge presented to Israel in various ways in the OT (e.g., Dt. 4:29; Is. 45:19; 51:1; 55:6), though the supposition in many contexts is that this means responding to the special revelation mediated through the prophets. Gentiles are classified as being ignorant of the true God and praying to gods that cannot save (e.g., Is. 45:20; cf. Ps. 14:2-3; Je. 10:1-16; Wis. 13:1-10). In the biblical record, some Gentiles were drawn to the God of Israel and expressed their trust in him because of what they heard about his dealings with Israel (e.g., Jos. 2:1-11; 2 Ki. 5:1-18). But there are no exact parallels to Paul's declaration that Gentiles may seek God *and perhaps reach out for him and find him.* It is important to note the qualification in this sentence provided by a conditional clause in the Greek (introduced by *ei ara ge,* translated by most EVV 'in the hope that'). This conditional clause contains two verbs in the optative mood *(psēlaphēseian . . . heuroien),* which expresses some doubt. Bruce describes this as a 'telescoped conditional and final construction',[92] meaning that it expresses a purpose that will not be unconditionally achieved. The verb *psēlaphēseian* ('to look for something in uncertain fashion, *to feel around for, grope for',* BDAG) expresses the idea of 'groping for God in the darkness, when the light of special revelation is not available'.[93] Paul is describing a potential that was not fulfilled in the Athenian situation. There was plenty of reaching out for God in the form of popular religion and philosophical reflection, but the result was a proliferation of idolatry and self-confessed ignorance of the true God (vv. 16, 22-23). Nevertheless, God's purpose for humanity remains, despite the blinding and corrupting effects of sin. The possibility of seeking after God and finding him is based on the fact that God *'is not far from any one of us'.* 'If the con-

---

90. Witherington 1998, 527, suggesting a reversal of the dispersion of the nations in judgment, as portrayed in Genesis 11.

91. Codex E and a few other ancient witnesses read *zētein ton kyrion,* which became part of the Received Text and explains KJV and NKJ's 'seek the Lord'. However, the best-attested reading is *zētein ton theon* ('seek God'), which is acknowledged by almost all modern versions. Codex D reads *malista zētein to theion estin* ('especially to seek if there is divinity'), which modifies the text by introducing the more abstract term *to theion* (cf. v. 29). Cf. Metzger, *Textual Criticism,* 405-6.

92. Bruce 1990, 383, compares 8:22; 27:12, 39. Cf. Barrett 1998, 844-45; D. B. Wallace, *Greek Grammar beyond the Basics: An Exegetical Syntax of the New Testament* (Grand Rapids: Zondervan, 1996), 484.

93. Bruce 1990, 383. Cf. Gärtner, *Areopagus,* 152-61. Witherington 1998, 528-29, considers the use of this verb in biblical and nonbiblical sources and concludes that the image is not an encouraging one. 'Though God is omnipresent, and so not far from any person, ironically human beings are stumbling around in the dark trying to find God. When one is blind, even an object right in front of one's face can be missed.'

struction of the previous clause emphasized mere possibility, this one expresses stronger confidence.'[94] God is immanent or present with us in the created order, in a spiritual and personal sense, though not being found in created things as pantheists teach. The reality finally conveyed by Paul's message is that, because of human failure to find God as he really is, he can be truly known only through repentance and faith in the resurrected Jesus (vv. 30-31). In its total structure and flow, the speech in Acts 17:22-31 is not all that different from the argument in Romans 1-3.

28 Paul offers support for the preceding claim by asserting that '*"in him we live and move and have our being"*'. This triad is used 'to bring out all sides of man's absolute dependence on God for life'.[95] Some have argued that Paul is citing words originally addressed to Zeus in a poem attributed to Epimenides of Crete, who flourished in the sixth century BC. However, we do not have the original poem, and there are similar assertions by other Greek writers (e.g., Dio Chrysostom, *Or.* 12.43).[96] Whatever the source, Paul will have been using these words to convey the biblical truth that God, not merely the creation, is the environment in which we exist (cf. 14:17). As a personal being he can be known, understood, and trusted. In the syntax of the sentence, the words '*as some of your own poets have said*' most naturally relate to what follows.[97] Paul goes on to quote Aratus of Cilicia (*Phaenomena* 5), a philosopher-poet from the third century BC, who said of Zeus, '*"we are his offspring"*' *(tou gar kai genos esmen)*. The poet will have understood these

94. Johnson 1992, 316. Ps. 145 (LXX 144):18 expresses God's nearness 'to all who call on him, to all who call on him in truth'. This is set against the background of God's goodness to all and his compassion 'on all he has made' (v. 9). However, the universalism of this psalm is tempered by the acknowledgement that only his faithful people extol him, tell of the glory of his kingdom, and speak of his might (vv. 10-11), 'so that all people may know of your mighty acts and the glorious splendour of your kingdom (v. 12). The role of God's people in mediating his truth to unbelievers is thus highlighted. Witherington 1998, 529, contrasts the Stoic-type argument of Dio Chrysostom, *Or.* 12.28, that all persons have innate conceptions of God by nature, since God indwells all things and persons. Cf. Gärtner, *Areopagus*, 162-64.

95. Gärtner, *Areopagus*, 195. Codex D adds *to kath' hēmeran* ('daily') as a gloss. Cf. Metzger, *Textual Criticism*, 406; Barrett 1998, 848-49.

96. Bruce 1990, 384-85, argues the case for the quote coming from Epimenides, though he acknowledges that the evidence for this comes from early Christian writers. Gärtner, *Areopagus*, 195, argues that this is 'not a veiled poetic quotation, but a combination that must be ascribed to Paul or Luke'. Barrett 1998, 847, more cautiously suggests that 'Paul (Luke) was responsible for the use of the triad in the speech, but may have heard it used and borrowed it'. Cf. Marshall 1980, 288-89.

97. Barrett 1998, 848, suggests that the plural 'may be a device for concealing ignorance of the actual author, or for suggesting that the words were used (as in fact they were) by more than one'. The rhetorical effect is not to draw attention to the authority of Aratus as the source of this belief, but rather to present his words as a confirmation of the argument already given. Some MSS read, 'as some of *our* own poets have said'. This may be due to scribal confusion between *hymas* ('you') and *hēmas* ('us'), as Metzger, *Textual Criticism*, 406, argues, or the change to *hymas* may have been made by copyists judging it appropriate in the mouth of Paul, who was a Cilician like Aratus, as Bruce 1990, 385, argues.

words in a pantheistic sense, but Paul appears to have viewed them in the light of the image of God theology in Genesis 1:26-27 (see further below). He recognized that a search for God had been taking place in the Greco-Roman world,[98] but condemned the result — the idolatry which was everywhere present and the ignorance of the true God which it betrayed (vv. 22-25). In short, he indicated that the search had been ineffective because of human blindness and stubbornness (cf. Rom. 1:18-32). Paul goes on to encourage a new seeking after God on the basis of his gospel about Jesus and the resurrection (vv. 30-31). The words of Aratus are used to affirm that, in a sense, all human beings are God's 'family' *(genos, offspring)*. This is an important starting point for his appeal to those who stand outside the influence of special revelation. It is remarkable in view of the fact that Israel's distinctive relationship with God is represented in Scripture in familial terms, arising from his covenant with them and his redemptive activity on their behalf (e.g., Ex. 4:22-23; Hos. 11:1; Am. 3:1-2; Rom. 9:4; Gal. 4:1-5). However, God's commitment to bless 'all peoples on earth' through Abraham's offspring (Gn. 12:3, lit. 'all the families of the earth') shows the Creator's continuing care and concern for everyone made in his image and likeness (Gn. 1:26-27). In other words, there is a biblical truth echoed in the pagan poet's reflection on the relationship between Creator and human beings. It is natural for people to seek after God, since he made us to have a relationship with himself. Consequently, 'as God's relation to Israel carries with it a promise, so all humanity as God's family is promised that God is available to those who seek. Human ignorance of God has hampered this search, but now God is available in a new way, and those who respond with repentance will be able to find their Creator.'[99]

29 *'Therefore since we are God's offspring, we should not think that the divine being is like gold or silver or stone — an image made by human design and skill.'* It was noted above that in biblical teaching we are not free to think anthropomorphically, imagining God to be like ourselves. His character and ability cannot be limited to what we may imagine and accomplish as human beings. But this verse reminds us that the image theology of Genesis 1:26-27 allows us to say what God is not. 'Since we are the thinking and feeling persons that we are, we ought not to suppose that the divine being . . . is made of metal, even precious metal, or of wood.'[100] If we are personal

---

98. Tannehill 1990, 219, observes that Paul grounds the possibility of this search 'in human existence as such and in the universally shared relation of Creator and creature'. Tannehill, 219 note 22, understands v. 27 to mean that 'the real possibility that every person may seek and find God is being affirmed'.

99. Tannehill 1990, 219. Gärtner, *Areopagus*, 164-67, 177-202, offers an extensive comparison of Stoic and biblical thinking on the subject of human kinship with God.

100. Barrett 1998, 849. Barrett, 850, notes that the use of the impersonal *to theion (the divine being)* refers to the property of being divine — divinity contrasted with humanity. Since the verse majors on the relation between God and man, there is no question of the personality of God raised by the use of this word.

beings, able to relate to one another with love and trust, God our creator cannot be anything less. How can the impersonal give birth to the personal?[101] It is absurd and totally dishonouring to God to represent him in any form conceived and constructed by human beings (cf. Ex. 20:4-6). The prophetic attack on image worship (e.g., Is. 40:18-20; 41:5-7, 29; 44:9-20; Je. 1:16; 2:26-28; 10:2-5; cf. Ps. 115:4-8; 135:15) was echoed in many Jewish writings (e.g., Wis. 13:10-19; 15:4-17; Philo, *On the Contemplative Life* 7; *On the Decalogue* 66). Even pagan philosophers condemned the practice, though 'the polemic is not often levied direct at the images, since the general opinion obviously was that an identification of the image and the god was too absurd to require treatment'.[102] Paul's argument is a challenge to all forms of religion which seek to make a god to suit the needs of the worshippers. Moreover, idolatry can take many forms, both intellectually (with false ideas about God) and practically (with the worship of created things rather than the Creator).[103]

c. The Truth about Divine Judgment (17:30-31)

30 *'In the past God overlooked such ignorance.'* A new section of the argument is signalled by the Greek *men oun* ('so', as in v. 17, not translated by TNIV in v. 30), though there are links with what has gone before. The ignorance involved in representing the divine being with humanly devised images has just been highlighted (v. 29). A call for repentance in this context provides 'a vivid rebuttal of the position that a "natural revelation" is itself without need of correction and supplement'.[104] Indeed, Paul identifies the era in which they have been living as 'the times of ignorance' *(tous chronous tēs agnoias)*, recalling further the charge of ignorance in v. 23. He goes on to speak of what God *now* requires in the light of Christ's coming. The two-age perspective of Jewish eschatology is thus adapted and applied to the Gentile situation. The present evil age is overtaken by the new age in Christ, in which salvation is made possible for Jew and Gentile alike. Although the speech has suggested possible areas of agreement between Paul and cultured Greeks, it has been full of challenge from a biblical perspective. No one is exempt from the call to repent, neither idolaters nor those who critique them. 'The philosophers' teaching has not solved the problem of religions that restrict God to human space and shape, and some of the wise, perhaps, are not even concerned to reform religious

---

101. This argument is relevant to contemporary debates about human origins, as well as to the evaluation of false religion.

102. Gärtner, *Areopagus*, 224. Cf. Barrett 1998, 850.

103. Cf. Stott 1990, 287.

104. Johnson 1992, 317. Cf. Gärtner, *Areopagus*, 229-41. Johnson, 319, argues that 'Luke does not construct or canonize a "natural theology"; he simply shows Paul picking up the inchoate longings of this "exceptionally religious" people and directing them to their proper object. . . . The groping search is not itself the finding.'

practices that treat God in this way.'[105] Paul's critique of Greco-Roman religion and culture applies to leaders and people alike: individually and corporately, they belonged to the times of ignorance. God did not approve
this ignorance, nor did he suppress it or bring retribution, as he might
have. He *'overlooked'* it (*hyperidōn*, 'disregarded'; cf. 14:16 note).[106] We
might compare Romans 3:25, where Paul says that in his forbearance, before the coming of Christ, God had 'left the sins committed beforehand
unpunished'. The new situation *now* relates to the coming of Christ (*ta
nyn*; cf. *nyni de* in Rom. 3:21; *tō nyn kairō*, 'at the present time', in Rom.
3:26). Paul says little about the epoch-changing significance of Jesus' ministry other than to mention his resurrection as an assurance of the coming
judgment (v. 31). He does not even explain that forgiveness is available
through Jesus (cf. 2:38; 3:19; 5:31; 10:43; 13:38; 26:18), though the offer is
implicit when God *'commands all people everywhere to repent'* (cf. 2:38; 3:19;
8:22; 20:21; 26:20). The divine challenge to turn back and seek a new start
would make little sense and would carry little power if it did not include
the possibility of reconciliation with God and cleansing from sin. Repentance for the Athenians would have meant turning to God from idols 'to
serve the living and true God' (1 Thes. 1:9). With instruction such as the
Thessalonians received, this would also have involved waiting 'for his Son
from heaven, whom he raised from the dead — Jesus, who rescues us from
the wrath to come' (1 Thes. 1:10).

31 Positively, Paul has argued that human beings were created to
seek God and have a genuine relationship with him as their creator (vv. 27-
28). Negatively, he has shown that their beliefs and practices have kept them
from a true knowledge of God. Now he makes it clear that they must be
judged for this. *'For he has set a day when he will judge the world with justice by
the man he has appointed.'* To *judge the world with justice* (*krinein tēn oikoumenēn
en dikaiosynē*) is a biblical phrase, (e.g., Pss. 9:8 [LXX 9:9]; 96:13 [LXX 95:13];
98:9 [LXX 97:9]), describing the activity of God which finds ultimate expression on the last 'day' of human history. But the gospel proclaims that God
will accomplish this *by the man he has appointed* (*en andri hō hōrisen*). Even
though he is not named, this gives an extraordinary role to Jesus of Nazareth. God has *set* (*estēsan*) the day (cf. Am. 5:18; Is. 2:12; Rom. 2:5, 16; 1 Cor.
1:8; Phil. 1:6, 10; 1 Thes. 5:2, 4; 2 Thes. 1:10; 2:2), and *appointed* (*hōrisen*) the
judge (cf. 10:42, 'the one whom God appointed as judge of the living and the
dead'; Phil. 1:6, 'the day of Christ Jesus'). Barrett suggests that the absence of
the name of Jesus in 17:31 simply means that, 'at this stage, the speaker is
more interested in the theme of judgment than in the details of the pro-

---

105. Tannehill 1990, 218. Paul sees the need and opportunity for a radical transformation of the religious culture of the Greco-Roman world' as 'a necessary preparation for the
coming world judgment'.

106. This verb can be used literally, in the sense of 'look over', or metaphorically, in
the sense of 'look down, despise' or 'overlook, disregard'. Cf. Barrett 1998, 851; BDAG. Wis.
11:23 says that God overlooks (*paroras*) human sins 'so that they may repent.' Cf. Rom. 2:4.

cess'.[107] However, the focus is also on the fact that this judgment will take place by a particular man (cf. Dn. 7:13-14; Mk. 13:26; 14:62; Mt. 25:31; Jn. 5:27). In view of Paul's exposure of the Athenian failure to find God and know him, this is an extraordinary claim. What kind of man could be appointed to *judge the world with justice?* Who could be capable of fulfilling such a role? Paul does not provide an answer here, but provokes his audience to inquire further about this and other important issues (cf. v. 32). Even though we have only a brief summary of what Paul said on this occasion, Luke is surely conveying to us something of Paul's rhetorical technique, as well as the content of his argument.[108] His concluding assertion was that God *'has given proof of this to everyone by raising him from the dead'* (cf. v. 18; Rom. 1:4; 1 Thes. 1:10). Such *proof (pistin)*[109] challenged Greek views about the immortality of the soul and the belief that the dead do not rise (cf. Homer, *Il.* 24.551; Aeschylus, *Eumenides* 647-48; *Agamemnon* 1360-61; Sophocles *Electra* 137-39). The resurrection of the dead was no more believable in that context than it is for many in our so-called scientific age. The very idea made some of his audience sneer (v. 32)! Yet, if the resurrection of Jesus took place, it challenges human scepticism about the possibility of encountering God and being judged by him. It is the best proof we have of a general resurrection and makes Jesus the key figure in God's plans for humanity.

3. Founding a Church (17:32-34)

Luke clarifies that the teaching about resurrection from the dead was what prompted a negative response to Paul's address. Yet, even in the rarefied atmosphere of the Areopagus, 'some became followers of Paul and believed'. The implication is that preaching Jesus and the resurrection to such an audience is the way forward (cf. v. 18), despite the cynicism this arouses. In both Jewish and Gentile contexts, it is 'the word' by which God grows the church (cf. v. 3).

32-34 *When they heard about the resurrection of the dead, some of them sneered* (echleuazon, 'scoffed, sneered'; cf. 2:13, diachleuazontes), *but others said, 'We want to hear you again on this subject'.* The Greek construction *men . . . de (some . . . others)* highlights the fact that there were two different reactions to Paul's speech.[110] The sneering of some continued because of Paul's return to

107. Barrett 1998, 853. After 'man' in v. 31 several Western witnesses add the name 'Jesus'. If this were the original, it would hardly have been so widely omitted.

108. Cf. Witherington 1998, 530-31.

109. The word *pistin* is normally translated 'faith'. It is used in the sense of 'proof' by Aristotle, *Rhetoric* 3.13 [1414AB]; Plato, *Phaedo* 70B; Josephus, *Ant.* 15.260. Barrett 1998, 853, rightly argues that 'the suggestion that the word does have its usual NT meaning, and that the clause means that, in the resurrection, God was offering to all (the opportunity of) faith, is unconvincing'.

110. Cf. Barrett 1998, 854.

the subject of *the resurrection from the dead* (v. 31; cf. v. 18). But others expressed a desire to hear Paul again 'concerning this' *(peri toutou)*, which could refer to the topic of the resurrection or allude to the person mentioned in v. 31 (the unnamed Jesus). Those who *became followers of Paul and believed* must have had a later opportunity to ask their questions and hear more before turning to Christ. Luke's abbreviated version of the speech indicates that Paul said little about the way of salvation and the Saviour who makes it possible. *Among them was Dionysius, a member of the Areopagus, also a woman named Damaris, and a number of others.* The association of *Damaris* with *Dionysius* may imply that Damaris was also 'a distinguished Areopagite'.[111] Her presence at the meeting addressed by Paul certainly implies some status, either in the council or in the philosophical schools represented on that occasion. So Paul's time in Athens was not a complete failure and the implication is that he left behind a small group of believers. 1 Corinthians 16:15 describes the household of Stephanas as 'the first-fruit of Achaia' (cf. 1:16). Corinth was the capital city of the province of Achaia and soon became the centre of Paul's ministry in the region. In the context of his argument to the Corinthians, he means that the household of Stephanas was 'the first of more converts to come in Achaia'.[112] If Paul's focus was on the newness of the situation in Corinth, this does not deny the possibility that there were previous converts in Athens, the other leading city of Achaia.

What, finally, can contemporary Christians learn from Paul's apologetic and evangelistic strategies in Acts 17:16-31? In a detailed review of the passage, against the background of Greco-Roman thought, Winter suggests this model for interaction with unbelievers:[113]

> Connecting with the hearers, correcting their misconceptions, conversing with the theological or ideological framework, convicting them of their compromises with their consciences in the light of their own intel-

111. Spencer 1997, 173-74. Epicureans and Stoics were among the more inclusive philosophical groups who accepted women as both students and teachers in their societies of 'friends'. Cf. I. R. Reimer, *Women in the Acts of the Apostles: A Feminist Liberation Perspective*, trans. L. M. Maloney (Minneapolis: Fortress, 1995), 246-48. Codex D omits 'a woman named Damaris' and substitutes another flattering term *(euschēmōn*, 'high-standing') for Dionysius (which was unnecessary because 'Areopagite' already indicated his high status). The omission could have been accidental, but the addition makes the whole reading seem like a more deliberate attempt to write an influential woman out of the story. Cf. Metzger, *Textual Criticism*, 407-8.

112. A. C. Thiselton, *The First Epistle to the Corinthians: A Commentary on the Greek Text*, NIGTC (Grand Rapids/Cambridge: Eerdmans; Carlisle: Paternoster, 2000), 1338. Witherington 1998, 533, suggests that 1 Cor. 16:15 means that the house of Stephanas, 'through the conversion of his family, became the first Christian household and locus for a house church in Achaia'. This would not be a denial of several previous conversions in Athens.

113. B. W. Winter, 'Introducing the Athenians to God: Paul's Failed Apologetic in Acts 17?' in R. Chia and M. Chan (eds.), *A Graced Horizon: Essays in Gospel, Culture and Church in Honour of the Reverend Dr. Choong Chee Pang* (Singapore: Genesis, 2005), 83.

lectual commitment are critical steps. It is also necessary to confront them with their need of repentance towards God and faith in the Lord Jesus Christ because of the coming day of judgment. These are all the essential features of a dialogue that is distinctly Christian and biblical.

F. The Word in Corinth (18:1-17)

Luke links together four short scenes in this section 'to show Paul having a long and fruitful ministry in Corinth in spite of strong Jewish opposition'.[1] The first scene (vv. 1-4) confirms that, as usual, his ministry began in the synagogue, but that in this city he formed a new partnership with Aquila and Priscilla. We are later told that this couple assisted Paul in establishing the gospel in Ephesus and ministered significantly to Apollos (vv. 18-28). The second scene (vv. 5-8) has Paul devoting himself to the evangelisation of Jews in Corinth until they become resistant and abusive, at which point he warns them of impending judgment and states his intention to turn to Gentiles in the city. The third scene (vv. 9-11) records that Jews and Gentiles continued to believe in the Lord Jesus, but that the opposition was such that Paul needed a special vision from the Lord to encourage him to stay there for a year and a half. In the fourth scene (vv. 12-17), the Jews finally bring Paul before the proconsul and charge him with 'persuading the people to worship God in ways contrary to the law'. The proconsul rightly discerns that this dispute between Jews and Christians is not a matter for him to judge and does not even intervene when the crowd turns on Sosthenes, the synagogue leader. There are parallels between vv. 1-17 and previous narratives, though 'key spatial and temporal variations disrupt the stereotypical plot'.[2]

> Whereas we have come to expect Paul to leave not only the synagogue but also the city as soon as becoming the target of persecution, in Corinth, after being attacked by 'the Jews', he moves only a short distance from the synagogue — right *'next door'* in fact — and ends up staying a long time — a full *'year and six months'* — proclaiming God's message to *'many'* receptive Jews as well as Gentiles who believe the word and are baptized (18.7, 11). All of this occurs before the public accusation scene. But even after Paul appears before the tribunal, he continues to remain 'many days' longer (18.18). The Corinthian mission thus flourishes in spite of Jewish opposition.[3]

1. Tannehill 1990, 221. Tannehill notes how the narrative is structured around three significant pronouncements: by Paul (v. 6), by the Lord (vv. 9-10), and by Gallio (vv. 14-15). Each of these words changes the direction and focus of the narrative.

2. Spencer 1997, 176.

3. Spencer 1997, 176. The Corinthian narrative further enriches the plot of Acts by introducing new characters, whom Spencer groups into pairs associated with different movements in the story: Aquila and Priscilla, Titius Justus and Crispus, Gallio and Sosthenes.

It is also important to note impressive points of agreement between the Acts account and the Corinthian correspondence, though it seems clear that Luke did not use the latter as one of his sources.[4]

1. Jews Together in Corinth (18:1-4)

In one of the most important centres of the Gentile world, Paul meets Aquila and Priscilla, who are Jewish Christians recently come from Italy. They become co-workers with Paul, both with respect to tentmaking (v. 3) and gospel ministry (vv. 18-19; cf. Rom. 16:3; 1 Cor. 16:19; 2 Tim. 4:19). They also 'join the ranks of those who display discipleship by offering hospitality to Christian witnesses (e.g., 10:48; 16:15; 17:7)'.[5] With this support, Paul engages in a synagogue ministry every Sabbath (v. 4; cf. 13:5, 14-15; 14:1; 17:1-4, 10-12, 17).

1 When the Athenian ministry was completed, *Paul left Athens and went to Corinth,* an overland journey of some 37 miles (60 km.). Corinth had been the capital of the Roman province of Achaia since 27 BC. Situated on the isthmus of Corinth, with the Corinthian Gulf to the west and the Saronic Gulf to the east, the city had long been a commercial and naval rival to Athens. There were two seaports, Lechaeum being the gateway to the Adriatic Sea and Cenchreae the gateway to the Aegean (cf. v. 18).[6] Corinth had been built on the north side of the Acrocorinthus, which served as a citadel and source of fresh water. The temple of Aphrodite, the goddess of love, was on the summit of the mountain, and the temple of Melicertes, the patron of seafarers, was at the bottom. The city was devoted to the worship of many 'gods' and many 'lords' (1 Cor. 8:5), and this was linked with sexual immorality in a way that was infamous even in the Greco-Roman world. Corinth had survived many crises in its history, but in 146 BC the ancient city was destroyed by the Romans because of the leading role it had taken in the rebellion of the Achaean League against Roman rule. Its population had been enslaved and its land had been claimed for the Roman state. The city lay derelict until it was refounded by Julius Caesar in 44 BC. What Paul therefore saw was a relatively new and prosperous city. Corinth was the chief sponsor of the Isthmian Games, which brought many travel-

---

4. Cf. Johnson 1992, 324-25. Priscilla and Aquila are likely to have been an important resource for the writing of this part of Acts.

5. Gaventa 2003, 256. Paul's own labour made it possible for him not to become a financial burden for them (cf. 20:34-35).

6. Bruce 1990, 390, points out that various attempts were made in antiquity to dig a canal across the isthmus. But boats were regularly dragged on wooden carriages across a slipway, from one port to the other. More information about ancient Corinth is given by D. W. J. Gill, 'Achaia', in D. W. J. Gill and C. Gempf (eds.), *The Book of Acts in Its First-Century Setting*, Vol. 2: *Graeco-Roman Setting* (Grand Rapids: Eerdmans; Carlisle: Paternoster, 1994), 448-53.

lers on a biennial basis. In many ways, it was well placed to be a centre of influence for the region.

2 *There he met a Jew named Aquila* (*Akylas* is a hellenized form of the Lat. *Aquila*, 'eagle'). It seems probable that Aquila and Priscilla were already Christians when Paul met them (the participle *heurōn* could mean that he *met* them after a search [cf. 9:2] or that he simply came upon them [cf. 9:33]), and that they had encountered the gospel in Rome.[7] When Paul 'found' them, he *went to see* (*prosēlthen*, 'approached') them. The context suggests that Paul sought accommodation and work with fellow Jews and was blessed to meet a couple who were believers in Jesus. Luke mentions that Aquila was *a Jew* partly to stress that Paul's initial ministry in Corinth was with and among his own people (vv. 1-4), and partly to prepare for the explanation about their sudden departure from Rome. As *a native of Pontus*, Aquila came from a region in Asia Minor that had been united with Bithynia to form a Roman province (cf. 2:9; 16:7; 1 Pet. 1:1).[8] However, at some stage he had moved to *Italy*, and he had only recently come from there *with his wife Priscilla*.[9] Luke takes the opportunity to link his narrative about Corinth with a well-known event in Roman history *(because Claudius had ordered all the Jews to leave Rome)*. The imperial edict banning Jews from Rome is recorded by the historian Suetonius (*Claud.* 25.4) in these terms: 'since the Jews constantly made disturbances at the instigation of Chrestus (Lat. *impulsore Chresto*), he expelled them from Rome'.[10] Chrestus may be a corruption of Christus, meaning that the Jewish community in Rome had become seriously divided over Christian claims about Jesus. However, Chrestus was a relatively common name at the time, and the man in question could have been a Jewish activist who had no connection with Christianity.[11] There is no way of being certain about the meaning of this brief allusion. Furthermore, Suetonius supplies no evidence for the date of the expulsion. Anti-Jewish action was taken by Claudius in AD 41 (Dio Cassius, *Hist.* 60.6.6), but this is too early to be identified with the events outlined in

7. This is likely since nothing is mentioned about their conversion or baptism in Corinth. Cf. Marshall 1980, 293; Spencer 1997, 177.

8. Bruce 1990, 390, thinks that this is more likely than the suggestion that Aquila came from the kingdom of Pontus further east. MSS in the Western tradition have expanded and smoothed out the narrative in vv. 2-4, including a statement that Paul 'introduced the name of the Lord Jesus' in his discussions about the OT in the synagogue (v. 4). Cf. Metzger, *Textual Commentary*, 408-9.

9. Paul calls her 'Prisca' (Rom. 16:3; 1 Cor. 16:19; 2 Tim. 4:19), but Luke uses the diminutive and more conversational form 'Priscilla'. Both Luke and Paul regularly name her before her husband (cf. 18:18, 26), from which some have inferred that she was of higher rank. Bruce 1990, 390, suggests that 'she may have been a freedwoman, if not a freeborn member, of the *gens Prisca*, a noble Roman family'.

10. Translation of J. C. Rolfe, *Suetonius* (Loeb Library), 2:53. Witherington 1998, 539-44, has an extended note on 'Claudius, Jews and a Religio Licita'.

11. Cf. A. D. Clarke 1994, 'Rome and Italy', in Gill and Gempf, *Graeco-Roman Setting*, 469-71.

Acts 18:1-17 (cf. vv. 12-13 for the dating of Gallio's proconsulship). It is likely that 'though Claudius did act against the Jews early in his reign, he did not expel them till much later'.[12] The most likely date for that was in his ninth year, namely AD 49. Leaving Rome under such circumstances must have been a great trial for those concerned, but Luke shows how, in God's providence, the coming of this couple to Corinth and then Ephesus advanced the work of the gospel significantly (vv. 18-28).

3 It was *because he was a tentmaker (skēnopoios) as they were,* that Paul *stayed and worked with them.*[13] Some have argued that 'Paul's trade was probably connected with the chief manufacture of his native province, *cilicium,* a cloth of goats' hair from which were made coverings designed to give protection against cold and wet'.[14] However, the same occupation is ascribed to Priscilla and Aquila, though they were from Pontus, and Paul probably did not learn his trade until he began his formal theological education in Jerusalem (22:3). It is more likely that his trade involved working with leather rather than with weaving.[15] Jewish tradition encouraged rabbis to support themselves with some other occupation, while giving religious instruction (cf. *Pirke 'Aboth* 2.2; 4.7). Greek culture, however, tended to despise manual labour, which makes Luke's matter-of-fact record of Paul's practice here unusual. 'By lodging with an artisan couple and, beyond that, actually joining in their trade, Paul suddenly appears no longer as the rising star among noble ladies and gentlemen and lofty academicians.'[16] In his farewell speech to the Ephesian elders, Paul makes much of the fact that he worked with his own hands, to support himself and his companions, while engaging in ministry (20:33-35). Although he urged Christians to share all good things with those who taught them (Gal. 6:6),

---

12. Barrett 1998, 859. Barrett 862, argues that the expulsion took place in the ninth year of Claudius (AD 49), which corresponds with the evidence for Gallio's proconsulship being in AD 51-52 (cf. v. 12 note). Cf. Bruce 1990, 390-91; Witherington 1998, 540-41, 545.

13. TNIV has simplified this sentence (*dia to homotechnon einai . . . ēsan gar skēnopoioi tē technē*), which literally reads 'because (they) were of the same trade . . . for they were tentmakers by trade'.

14. Bruce 1990, 392.

15. Cf. R. F. Hock, *The Social Context of Paul's Ministry: Tentmaking and Apostleship* (Philadelphia: Fortress, 1980), 21; B. Rapske, 'Acts, Travel and Shipwreck', in Gill and Gempf (eds.), *Graeco-Roman Context,* 7; B. Rapske, *The Book of Acts in Its First-Century Setting,* Vol. 3: *The Book of Acts and Paul in Roman Custody* (Grand Rapids: Eerdmans; Carlisle: Paternoster, 1994), 106-8; Barrett 1998, 863. Tents and awnings were widely used in the Roman Empire. Leather was used for coats, curtains, and tents.

16. Spencer 1997, 178. Bruce 1990, 391-92, supports the view that Luke's background is that of the Greek scientific writers, who were more respectful of manual labourers. However, Hock, *Social Context,* 36, argues that tentmakers belonged to a class of humble artisans who were looked down upon by aristocrats and some leisured intellectuals. Hock, 41, discusses the workshop as a social setting for Paul's missionary preaching, but B. Blue, 'Acts and the House Church', in Gill and Gempf, *Graeco-Roman Setting,* 172-77, argues for the household as the standard base for ministry outside the synagogue. Cf. R. F. Hock, 'Paul's Tent-Making and the Problem of His Social Class', *JBL* 97 (1978), 555-64.

Paul did not normally avail himself of such rights (1 Cor. 9:3-18). Two reasons are given in Acts 20:33-35 for what we know to have been his practice in Ephesus, Thessalonica (1 Thes. 2:3-9; 2 Thes. 3:6-8), and Corinth (1 Cor. 4:12; 9:6; 2 Cor. 11:7). Negatively, Paul sought to avoid any hint of covetousness.[17] Positively, he was determined to help 'the weak', inspired by an otherwise unrecorded saying of Jesus about the blessedness of giving instead of receiving. Paul's behaviour thus reflected his trust in God and God's generosity to his people, demonstrating two important aspects of the message he preached.

4 *Every Sabbath he reasoned* (*dielegeto*, 'discussed, reasoned, argued'; cf. 17:2, 17; 18:19; 19:8, 9; 20:7, 9; 24:12, 25) *in the synagogue, trying to persuade Jews and Greeks*. TNIV has rightly translated the imperfect tense of the verb *epeithen* in a conative sense *(trying to persuade)*. As in 14:1; 17:4, 12, these *Greeks* were apparently Gentiles who were attached to the synagogue, sometimes designated as God-fearers. A fragmentary inscription from a Corinthian synagogue has been found, dating between 100 BC and AD 400. Barrett observes that 'it is not surprising that a wealthy and cosmopolitan city such as Corinth should contain a colony of Jews, or that they should be able to provide themselves with a building (contrast the Jews at Philippi, 16.13)'.[18] Acts 18:1-17 makes the point that ministry to Jews in Corinth was productive but extremely challenging, perhaps particularly because of the size and influence of the Jewish community in the city.

2. A New Centre for Ministry (18:5-8)

When Silas and Timothy arrive, Paul devotes himself more fully to the evangelisation of Jews (v. 5). This appears to be possible because financial aid from the Macedonian churches relieves him from having to support himself by tentmaking (v. 3). As in previous contexts, synagogue ministry essentially involves testifying that Jesus is the Messiah (cf. 13:16-41; 17:3). However, opposition from Jews eventually necessitates turning to focus on ministry to Gentiles (v. 6; cf. 13:46-48; 14:1-7). Making the house next door his base of operation for reaching Gentiles is a new strategy (v. 7).[19] Many

17. Witherington 1998, 547-48, adds that Paul 'did not want to give the impression of being a huckster, a travelling philosopher, peddling God's word and then disappearing with people's money or at least having abused privileges of hospitality (see 2 Cor. 2:17)'. He also did not want to get caught up in the social web of patronage that was an aspect of the culture in his time.

18. Barrett 1998, 864. Codex D adds to the text of 18:4 that Paul was 'inserting *(entitheis)* the name of the Lord Jesus'. Johnson 1992, 322-33, argues that the most obvious way to do this would be to read the name of Jesus into those places where the Scriptures used the title 'Lord'. However, we cannot be certain that this was the meaning intended by the copyist. Furthermore, this particular reading is poorly attested.

19. From the beginning, the church in Philippi gathered in Lydia's house, because

conversions, including that of Crispus, the synagogue leader, and his entire household, apparently exacerbate opposition from the Jews.

5 *When Silas and Timothy came from Macedonia, Paul devoted himself exclusively to preaching.* The movements of *Silas and Timothy* after Paul left them in Macedonia were discussed in connection with 17:14-15. 1 Thessalonians 3:1-2 suggests that Timothy at least joined Paul in Athens and was sent off from there to Thessalonica again. Luke makes no mention of this, but there would certainly have been time for one or both of Paul's assistants to visit him in Athens, return to Macedonia, and then meet him in Corinth.[20] TNIV rightly implies that there was a change in Paul's pattern of ministry *when Silas and Timothy came from Macedonia.* Prior to their coming, Paul was engaged in a Sabbath ministry in the synagogue and was working with Aquila and Priscilla during the week. The Greek expression *syneicheto tō logō,* if read as a passive, means 'constrained by the word' (BDAG 'wholly absorbed in preaching').[21] If read as a middle voice, it can be understood reflexively (TNIV *devoted himself exclusively to preaching*).[22] The imperfect tense is often translated as a simple past continuous, suggesting that this is how Silas and Timothy found Paul when they arrived (NRSV 'Paul was occupied with proclaiming the word'; ESV 'Paul was occupied with the word'). However, this rendering gives no narrative significance to the arrival of Paul's co-workers at this stage. If the imperfect is taken inceptively, the meaning is that Paul began to be wholly occupied by preaching when they arrived. A possible reason for this changed pattern of work is that Silas and Timothy were able to support Paul financially or that they had brought money from Macedonia to supply his needs (cf. 2 Cor. 11:8-9; Phil. 4:15-16).[23] The content of Paul's message is simply defined as *testifying to the Jews that Jesus was the Messiah.* This recalls an important aspect of Paul's ministry in the synagogues of Pisidian Antioch (13:23-37) and Thessalonica (17:2-3).

6 A pattern of behaviour previously seen in Pisidian Antioch was repeated at Corinth, but in reverse order. After the second Sabbath in Antioch,

---

there was no synagogue (16:15, 40). But in Corinth, the house of Titius Justus became a mission centre replacing the synagogue.

20. Barrett 1998, 865, observes that *ho te Silas kai ho Timotheos* (18:5) could mean 'both Silas *and* Timothy', 'implying an earlier occasion when only one of the two came down from Macedonia'.

21. KJV ('pressed in the Spirit') and NKJV ('compelled by the Spirit') reflect a variant reading found in later MSS and a few early versions of the text. However, the majority of the earliest Greek MSS have *syneicheto tō logō,* which seems to have been modified to *syneicheto tō pneumati* because the original expression was misunderstood. Cf. Metzger, *Textual Commentary,* 409; Barrett 1998, 866. The verb *synechō* is used in Lk. 4:38; 8:37, 45; 12:50; 19:43; 22:63; Acts 7:57; 18:5; 28:8, mostly in the negative sense of 'constrain or confine'. Cf. 2 Cor. 5:14; Phil. 1:23.

22. Cf. Longenecker 1981, 482-83; Witherington 1998, 548.

23. Cf. Haenchen 1971, 534; Marshall 1980, 294; Longenecker 1981, 482-83; Bruce 1990, 392; Witherington 1998, 548-49. However, Barrett 1998, 866, is not entirely persuaded by this argument, and Gaventa 2003, 257, contends that 'the arrival of Silas and Timothy simply offers another opportunity for reinforcing the nature of Paul's activity'.

Paul and Barnabas found the opposition from Jews so intense that they turned to the Gentiles, abandoning any hope of working in the synagogue (13:44-48). Finally, they were forced out of the city because of Jewish-led persecution and 'shook the dust off their feet as a warning to them' (13:49-52). In Corinth, when the Jews *opposed Paul and became abusive, he shook out his clothes in protest and said to them, 'Your blood be on your own heads! I am innocent of it.'* As in 13:45, the verb *blasphēmeō* could refer to abusive speech directed at Paul (TNIV *became abusive*), or it could mean blasphemy against God in the sense that they denied what Paul said about Jesus (v. 4).[24] The latter is more likely since Paul went on to stress that the Jews were responsible for their own *blood* (death viewed as a punishment for rejecting God's word). When he *shook out his clothes in protest,* it was a symbolic way of breaking off relations with these people. Declaring himself to be *innocent (katharos,* 'clean') of their imminent punishment, Paul indicated that he had acted like the faithful watchman in Ezekiel 33:1-9. God's warning to the person who does not heed the message is that 'his blood will be on his head' (Ezk. 33:4-5 *to haima autou epi tēs kephalēs autou estai*). As a faithful messenger of the Lord, he would not be responsible for the punishment of those who rejected the gospel he proclaimed to them (cf. 20:26). With this gesture and associated warning of God's impending judgment, Paul left the synagogue, declaring, *'From now on I will go to the Gentiles'.* This is not a decisive abandonment of ministry to Jews since he goes straight to the synagogue again when he arrives in Ephesus (v. 19). His pattern of speaking first to Jews and only later turning to Gentiles indicated a sense of prophetic obligation, expressed positively in terms of Isaiah 49:6 (cf. Acts 13:46-47 note). Ezekiel's teaching about the duty of the watchman released Paul from his obligation 'to the Jews first' when he met strong public resistance within the Jewish community. A third allusion to Paul's prophetic role and status is found in 18:9-10. In such a situation he began 'the second phase of his mission within a city, a phase in which the conversion of individual Jews is still possible, although Paul is no longer preaching in the synagogue nor addressing Jews as a community'.[25] The novel element here is this theological justification for leaving the synagogue and finding another base for ministry.

7-8 Going to the Gentiles in this context meant leaving the synagogue and going *next door to the house of Titius Justus, a worshiper of God.*[26]

---

24. The Western text inserts extra words at the beginning of 18:6 (cf. comment on vv. 2-4), indicating that this took place 'after there had been much discussion and interpretations of the Scriptures.' Cf. Barrett 1998, 866.

25. Tannehill 1990, 223. Tannehill notes that the same motif reappears in 20:26-27 with reference to Paul's inclusive mission, which entailed responsibility for both Jews and Gentiles. He also notes that the two-phase pattern was not followed in Athens (17:17), 'where Paul apparently conducted simultaneous missions in the synagogue to Jews and in the marketplace to Gentiles'.

26. The Western text indicates that Paul separated from Aquila, implying that he went to lodge with Titius Justus. But there is no indication of this move in the wider textual

This Gentile God-fearer was presumably converted during Paul's time in the synagogue. His willingness to use his house as a base for Christian ministry displayed great courage and commitment. It must also have been very disturbing for the synagogue to have the rival Christian meeting taking place in the house next door. But worse was still to come for Paul's opponents: *Crispus, the synagogue ruler, and his entire household believed in the Lord.* It is possible that Crispus had also been converted during Paul's synagogue ministry, though the narrative sequence implies that it was after Paul moved to the house of Titius Justus. Crispus is mentioned in 1 Corinthians 1:14-16, along with Gaius and the household of Stephanas ('the first converts in Achaia', 1 Cor 16:15), as having been baptized by Paul himself. Although he was a notable convert, his action was 'evidently not weighty enough to carry with him the Jews as a group, or even his colleagues in office'.[27] Nevertheless, the conversion of the *synagogue ruler (archisynagōgos)* must have intensified the opposition from those who remained behind. The location of this new centre of ministry suggests that Jews and God-fearers continued to have 'access or proximity to the gospel, but not by virtue of their being members of the synagogue'.[28] Such people were doubtless included along with Gentile pagans among *many of the Corinthians who heard Paul believed and were baptized.* The use of continuous tenses in the Greek (*akouontes*, 'hearing'; *episteuon*, 'were believing'; *ebaptizonto*, 'were being baptized') indicates that this was an ongoing pattern of response to the preaching of the gospel.[29] Luke

---

tradition. The meaning seems to be that Paul used the house of Titius Justus as an alternative centre for preaching, and thus a meeting place for the church (cf. 19:9). Cf. Barrett 1998, 867-68, who also discusses the textual variations in the spelling of the name of Titius Justus. Blue, 'House Church', 172-74, argues that the house of Aquila and Priscilla was used from the beginning as a place for instructing those who responded to the gospel and thus as a meeting place for the church. The house of Titius Justus then became the place where the whole church met (assuming that this is the Gaius mentioned in Rom. 16:23). Cf. Marshall 1980, 294-95. Witherington 1998, 550, is not so sure about the proposed identification of Titius Justus with the Gaius of Rom. 16:23.

27. Barrett 1998, 868. Given the opposition of Jewish leaders to Paul's ministry in other contexts, the conversion of this synagogue ruler is extraordinary.

28. P. H. Towner, 'Mission Practice and Theology under Construction' in I. H. Marshall and D. G. Peterson (eds.), *Witness to the Gospel: The Theology of Acts* (Grand Rapids/Cambridge: Eerdmans, 1998), 430. F. Pereira, *Ephesus: Climax of Universalism in Luke-Acts. A Redactional Study of Paul's Ephesian Ministry (Acts 18:23–20:1)*, Jesuit Theological Forum 10, no. 1 (Anand: Gujarat Sahitya Prakash, 1983), 151-52, takes the use of the aorist verb *episteusen* in relation to Crispus to prove that his conversion was the result of the preaching of the gospel in the synagogue. However, it reads too much into the tense of the verb to insist on that meaning.

29. Some MSS supplement the reference to baptism, adding 'through the name of the Lord Jesus Christ' or 'believing God through the name of the Lord Jesus Christ'. However, the simplest reading is better attested and most likely to be the original. Cf. Metzger, *Textual Commentary*, 411; Barrett 1998, 868-69. The participle *akouontes* ('hearing') is taken by TNIV, NRSV and ESV to mean that they heard Paul; however, it could mean 'hearing about the conversion of Crispus'. Cf. Johnson 1992, 324.

does not actually say that the household of Crispus was baptized, though it is a reasonable assumption. This is significantly the third time that the conversion of a whole household is mentioned in Acts (cf. 16:15, 31-33).

3. An Encouraging Vision (18:9-11)

Luke's third scene contains a visionary pronouncement from the Lord encouraging Paul to persist in ministry for a year and a half or more (cf. v. 18 note), despite the opposition from Jewish quarters. The first ground for confidence is a promise of the Lord's presence and protection such as was given to Jeremiah in his calling to bring the word of the Lord to Israel (Je. 1:5-8, 19; 15:19-21). The second ground is a promise that many more will become believers and show themselves — both Jews and Gentiles — to be true people of God. Such promises bring a change to the pattern of events previously witnessed in Paul's mission, enabling him to stay and establish the work quite extensively on his first visit.[30] Paul is not forced out of Corinth, but departs when he is ready (v. 18).

9-11 In 1 Corinthians 2:3, Paul reveals that he first visited the city 'in weakness with great fear and trembling'. According to Luke's account, it was not a sense of inadequacy about his rhetorical skills nor the idolatry of the city that caused Paul to be troubled (cf. 17:16), but the antagonism of fellow Jews to the gospel he preached. In effect, he needed a recommissioning for ministry. Commissioning stories in Luke-Acts follow a pattern that is well illustrated here (cf. 5:19-21; 9:10-17; 16:6-10; 23:11; 27:23-24).[31] There is first the confrontation — the appearance of the divine commissioner — who in this case appears to be the risen Lord Jesus *(one night the Lord spoke to Paul in a vision)*.[32] Here, and in 22:17-21; 23:11, the exalted Jesus behaves towards Paul 'as deity supreme in power and knowledge and as one who is personally present'.[33] Secondly, there is the commission to undertake a God-given task, with the assurance of divine enabling *('Do not be afraid; keep on speaking, do not be silent. For I am with you, and no one is going to attack and harm you, because I have many people in this city')*. Paul's allusion to Ezekiel 33:4 in v. 6 indicates that he had a theological reason for withdraw-

30. Although Paul remained in some places for a considerable time (e.g., 11:26; 14:28; 15:33, 35), the specification of 'a year and a half' (18:11) suggests that this is the longest stay in the narrative so far. This is surpassed only by more than two years in Ephesus (19:8-10).

31. Cf. B. J. Hubbard, 'Commissioning Stories in Luke-Acts: A Study of Their Antecedents, Form and Content', *Semeia* 8 (1977), 103-26; B. J. Hubbard, 'The Role of the Commissioning Accounts in Acts', in C. H. Talbert (ed.), *Perspectives on Luke-Acts*, Perspectives in Religious Studies Special Studies Series 5 (Danville: Association of Baptist Professors of Religion, 1978), 187-98.

32. Direct speech which may be attributed to the risen Lord Jesus occurs at 9:4-6, 10-16; 10:13, 15; 11:7, 9; 18:9-10; 22:18, 21; 23:11. Cf. 16:9-10 note on visions in Acts.

33. H. D. Buckwalter, 'The Divine Saviour', in Marshall and Peterson, *Witness to the Gospel*, 117.

ing from synagogue ministry to focus on Gentiles in a given place (cf. Is. 49:6 in 13:46-47). When that became an impossibility because of mounting opposition, he moved on to another town (13:49-52; 14:4-7, 19-20; 17:5-10, 13-15). However, the clear message in Corinth was not to be afraid of the opposition, but to *keep on speaking and not be silent*.[34] 'The Lord intervenes both to require and (through divine protection) allow a change in the pattern of events that has been common to this point in Paul's mission. There is to be no quick mission and escape.'[35] The encouragement for doing this is twofold. First, there is the assurance of God's presence to protect Paul *(For I am with you, and no one is going to attack and harm you)*, given in words that recall the commissioning and recommissioning of Jeremiah as 'a prophet to the nations' (Je. 1:5-8, 19; 15:19-21; cf. Gal. 1:15).[36] The promise that *no one is going to attack and harm you* was fulfilled when Paul escaped the clutches of his opponents in vv. 12-17 and continued his work in Corinth (v. 18). Second, there is the promise, *because I have many people in this city*. This takes up the theme introduced in 15:14 (God intervened 'to choose a people for his name from the Gentiles'), where the covenant formula of Exodus 19:5 (cf. Ex. 23:22; Dt. 7:6; 14:2) was applied to those who believe in Jesus from among the nations. Luke's narrative has already established the foundation of this 'large people' in Corinth, comprising a God-fearer, a synagogue leader with his entire household, and many of the citizens more generally (vv. 7-8). They were to be regarded as 'part of the one covenant people that began with Israel, not by accepting Israel's circumcision but through being cleansed by faith (15:9).'[37] The Lord's promise is that, as a result of Paul's preaching, more will become believers and show themselves to be part of this elect but inclusive people of God. In other words, those 'appointed for eternal life' will believe (cf. 13:48).[38] The final element of the typical com-

34. TNIV has rightly rendered the present imperative *lalei* as *keep on speaking* and the aorist subjunctive *mē siōpēsēs* as *do not be silent* (meaning 'do not become silent'). The present imperative *phobou* with the negative *mē* in this context will mean 'do not continue to be afraid'. Cf. Witherington 1998, 551.

35. Tannehill 1990, 224. Towner, 'Mission Practice', 425-26, observes that such divine direction typically features in the taking of new steps in Paul's expanding evangelistic mission (cf. 13:2; 16:6-10; 20:22-23). 'A noticeable development in mission practice' is signalled in 18:9-10, which Luke connects with a revelation from the Lord.

36. Similar words of divine assurance can be found in Gn. 26:24; Ex. 3:12; Is. 41:10, 13; 43:5, but the link with Jeremiah's call is more obvious because of the promise of protection from opponents. This is even clearer in 26:16-17, where the word 'rescue' *(exairoumenos)* is used (Je. 1:8; 15:21, *exaireisthai*). With allusions to these and other scriptural passages (Is. 49:6 in 13:46-47; Ezk. 33:4 in 18:6), Paul's special prophetic status with regard to Israel and the nations is affirmed. The fulfillment of the promise of Joel 2:28-29 about all believers 'prophesying' does not exclude the possibility that some will have a unique and distinctive prophetic role.

37. Tannehill 1990, 225. Barrett 1998, 870, points out that *laos esti moi polys*, with the adjective *polys* used in a predicative sense, literally means 'there is to me a people, and a large one.' There is one people of God in Corinth, and it includes both Jews and Gentiles.

38. As Barrett 1998, 870 puts it, 'There are in Corinth many who are potentially and

missioning story is the conclusion, which states how the one commissioned carried out the task *(So Paul stayed for a year and a half, teaching them the word of God)*. This was apparently the period of time before the attack mentioned in vv. 12-17, so that v. 18 indicates a further period of ministry in Corinth 'for some time' after that. Given that this was an unusually long time for Paul to spend in one place, and given that he carried out his extensive ministry to the city in the unusual setting of the house of Titius Justus, we may see here a definite development in mission practice linked to the revelation of God's will in Paul's vision.[39] This same development recurs in Ephesus (19:8-10, without a vision). Indeed, 'there are connections between the Corinth and Ephesus episodes which bind them together and suggest that they should be held together to understand developments in mission practice in relation to a theology of the inclusive people of God'.[40]

4. Jews and Christians in Public Dispute (18:12-17)

In this fourth Corinthian scene, Jews in the city charge Paul before the proconsul with 'persuading the people to worship God in ways contrary to the law' (v. 13). Paul's alienation from the Jewish community here is in sharp contrast with the closeness portrayed in vv. 1-4. Yet, even in the opening scene, a reference to the expulsion of Jews from Rome (v. 2) anticipates the turmoil experienced by Jews and Christian together in Corinth (vv. 12-17). The proconsul refuses to pass judgment on matters which he considers to be 'questions about words and names and your own law' (v. 15). Gallio's decision establishes an important precedent: 'Roman authorities should not treat Christianity as a subversive cult but as a disputed option within one of the approved religions *(religio licita)* of the empire'.[41] However, his lack of concern about the beating of Sosthenes leaves readers with a sense of unease about Roman justice in such a context (v. 17).

12 This public accusation before a Roman official is reminiscent of 16:19-24 and 17:5-9. However, 'rather than being beaten and put in prison

---

by predestination (cf. 13:48), the Lord's people, and it is therefore impossible that Paul's work should be in vain'.

39. Cf. Towner, 'Mission Practice', 424-27. Towner, 426-27, argues that 'mission experience and developments in mission practice are closely bound up with theology; the historical experiences characterized by opposition, dissonance, paradox and divine revelation finally lead to a breakthrough which enables a nascent theology to be implemented in practice'. However, it must be said that the pattern of ministry in Corinth is only an extension of what appears to have taken place in Pisidian Antioch and Thessalonica, where a base for ministry and church growth was established outside the synagogue.

40. Towner, 'Mission Practice', 429. Towner, 427-35, takes issue with the approach of Tannehill 1990, 230-40 and Pereira, *Ephesus*, 150-53.

41. Johnson 1992, 334. Johnson rightly observes that, in the final analysis, Gallio's 'judicial restraint' does nothing to *positively* protect the Christians. The context suggests that deliverance comes only from the hand of God (v. 10).

(as in Philippi) or having to put up a bond (as with Jason in Thessalonica),
Paul is released when the accusation is rejected out of hand, a turn of human events that appears as the Lord's providential care in the light of
18:10'.[42] The Roman official in this case was *Gallio*, who was born Marcus
Annaeus Novatus, oldest son of Seneca the orator and brother of the famous writer and philosopher Seneca. He was adopted by the rhetorician
Lucius Junius Gallio and became Lucius Junius Gallio Annaeanus. Under
Claudius, he became *proconsul of Achaia*. The date of his proconsulship can
be fixed rather precisely by an inscription from Delphi. He appears to have
begun no later than May, AD 51, and had left office by May or June the following year, for health reasons.[43] The emperor had re-established Achaia as
a senatorial province in AD 44, administered by a *proconsul (anthypatos)*.[44] In
Gallio's time, *the Jews made a united attack on Paul and brought him to the place
of judgment.* Although the *place of judgment* has often been identified with
the impressive podium excavated in the marketplace of ancient Corinth,
the Greek term *bēma* 'denotes the place where the judge holds his court,
and is determined by the presence of the judge, not topographically (cf.
25:10, 17)'.[45] So the tribunal may not have taken place in that context. However, the mob reaction to Gallio's judgment (v. 17) gives the impression of
an encounter in such a public place.

13 'The Jews in various cities throughout the empire were allowed
to exercise a considerable degree of jurisdiction over members of their own
community, subject to the overriding authority of the Roman power.'[46] In
this case, they brought the leader of a troublesome new movement into
their midst before the proconsul, charging Paul with *'persuading the people to
worship God in ways contrary to the law'*. Although some have argued that
this meant 'giving religious teaching not countenanced by Roman law and
forming his adherents into a *collegium illicitum'*,[47] it seems more likely that
the Jews were appealing to Gallio for protection of their own religious community 'against a disturbing intruder'.[48] Gallio certainly saw the matter as

42. Tannehill 1990, 226.

43. Cf. Bruce, 1990, 394-95; Barrett 1998, 870-71. J. Murphy-O'Connor, *St. Paul's Corinth: Texts and Archaeology*, Good News Studies 6 (Wilmington: Michael Glazier, 1983), 149-
50, dates Paul's arraignment before Gallio 'between July and October AD 51'. Witherington
1998, 552, estimates 'the fall of AD 51.' B. W. Winter, 'Rehabilitating Gallio and His Judgement in Acts 18:14-15', *TynB* 57 (2006), 296, says '1st July, 51 until 30th June, 52'.

44. Cf. Gill, 'Achaia', 436.

45. Barrett 1998, 871.

46. Bruce 1990, 396. Cf. A. N. Sherwin-White, *Roman Society and Roman Law in the New
Testament* (Oxford: Clarendon, 1963), 99-107, on the legal issues. Once again the Western text
expands the account in ways that are not attested elsewhere ('having talked together among
themselves against Paul, and having laid hands upon him, they brought him to the governor, crying out and saying'). Cf. Metzger, *Textual Commentary*, 411.

47. Bruce 1990, 396. The expression 'against the law' (*para ton nomon*) is actually at the
beginning of the charge, creating the impression that Paul's teaching is a threat to Roman law.

48. Tannehill 1990, 226. Barrett 1998, 872-73, concludes that 'perhaps the Jews wished

a dispute among Jews about words and names and their own law (v. 15). They themselves spoke of worshipping *God* in the singular and were affirming their right under Roman law to worship the one true God according to the dictates of the law of Moses (cf. Josephus, *Ant.* 14.190-95 [probably relating to Judea]).[49] Paul was perceived to be challenging that practice and the theology undergirding it. He was creating a situation in which Jewish identity might be lost and the security of Jews in the Empire might be compromised. Recent events in Rome had confirmed that theological debates between Jews and Christians could have serious social and political consequences (cf. v. 2 note). When Paul arrived in Jerusalem for the last time, he had to respond once more to accusations that he was teaching against the law of Moses and therefore threatening the ethos of Judaism (21:21, 24, 28; cf. 22:3; 24:14; 25:8; 28:17).

14-15 Paul was prepared to make a defence, but Gallio intervened and dismissed the case. If the Jews had been making a complaint about *'some misdemeanor'* (*adikēma*, 'unrighteous deed, wrongdoing'; cf. Aristotle, *Nichomachean Ethics* 1135A; Acts 24:20) or *'serious crime'* (*rhadiourgēma ponēron*, 'wicked deceit, fraud'; cf. Plutarch, *On Exile* 7 [*Mor.* 602A]) against the state, Gallio indicates that it would have been reasonable for him (*kata logon*) to be forbearing with them (*aneschomēn*, 'endure, bear with').[50] But he dismissed the case on the ground that it involved *'questions about words and names and your own law'* (cf. 25:19). Gallio did not want to engage with their theological debates and instructed the Jews to settle these matters themselves, declaring, *'I will not be a judge of such things'*.[51] Haenchen believes that Luke makes Gallio 'occupy that standpoint which he himself considers as the correct one and which he passionately desires that Rome itself should take as her own: that Christianity is an inner-Jewish affair in which Rome does not meddle'.[52] At first glance this appears to be correct, but the beating of Sosthenes in front of the proconsul, about which Gallio showed 'no concern whatever' (v. 17), suggests otherwise. 'Gallio's rejection of the

---

to prove that Christianity was so different from Judaism that it could not be regarded as a *religio licita'*. H. W. Tajra, *The Trial of St. Paul: A Juridical Exegesis of the Second Half of Acts*, WUNT 2, no. 35 (Tübingen: Mohr [Siebeck], 1989), 56, suggests that 'there was a deliberate and conscious ambiguity in the accusation which demonstrates a certain cunning, but also the weakness of the plaintiffs' case against Paul'.

49. Sherwin-White, *Roman Law*, 99-107, suggests that the Jews may have been appealing to an edict of Claudius guaranteeing them the quiet enjoyment of their own customs. Paul was interfering with this right.

50. Cf. Barrett 1998, 873-74, on the terminology used in 18:14. The cognate *rhadiourgia* is used in 13:10. TNIV's 'to listen to you' does not quite capture the sense of the verb *anechesthai*.

51. Sherwin-White, *Roman Law*, 102, points out that this is the way a Roman magistrate would refuse to exercise his right to accept a novel charge, relating to a matter *extra ordinem*. Sherwin-White, 99-107, discusses Paul's experience before Gallio in the light of Roman law.

52. Haenchen 1971, 541. Cf. Barrett 1998, 876, who suggests that Christians on trial might have been able to cite Gallio's response with advantage.

Jews' accusation might simply be the result of good political and legal judgment. The beating at the end, however, suggests that a less noble motive is involved.'[53]

16-17 Gallio *drove them off* (*apēlasen autous apo tou bēmatos*, 'he drove them from the place of judgment') because he believed there was no charge to be answered under Roman law and because he had no time for Jewish theological debates (vv. 14-15). The verb *apēlasen* could indicate the use of physical force (cf. Ezk. 34:12 LXX). Whatever the form of the dismissal, it was a deliberate snub to the Corinthian Jews and their concerns. *Then the crowd there turned on Sosthenes the synagogue leader and beat him in front of the proconsul.* Sosthenes was either the replacement for Crispus, who had converted (v. 8), or for one of several remaining leaders of the synagogue (13:15 is evidence of a plurality of synagogue leaders in one place). The earliest manuscripts read 'all' (*pantes*) as the subject of these actions, whereas the Western text and later manuscripts read 'all the Greeks' (so KJV, NKJV). This expansion of the text could be correct and reflect the sort of anti-Semitism that flourished in the Roman Empire at the time. However, it is also possible that the Jews themselves could have joined in the attack on Sosthenes (so TNIV *the crowd*), perhaps because he mismanaged the case against Paul.[54] Somewhat surprisingly, *Gallio showed no concern whatever* (*ouden toutōn tō Galliōni emelen*, 'none of these things mattered to Gallio'). Presumably, he felt that public order would not be threatened if he allowed a few angry people to vent their rage like this. However, 'by refusing to intervene, Gallio gives implicit approval to gentile hostility towards Jews. In that case, his negative attitude toward Jews may also have been a factor in his legal decision.'[55] This is one of three cases of Gentile hostility to Jews in situations where Christians were also involved (cf. 18:2; 19:33-34). Jews and Christians faced the same hostility from pagans in the Roman Empire.

The end of this story, therefore, offered little comfort to Luke's readers. They could easily have concluded that such prejudice and hostility might soon be directed at them. Gallio was hardly the model to encourage trust in the Roman system of justice (cf. 19:35-41 note)! More broadly, the incident is also a warning about attempting to settle religious debates before unbelieving civic authorities (cf. 1 Cor. 6:1-8 for a specific warning about taking other Christians to court).

---

53. Tannehill 1990, 228. Cf. R. Cassidy, *Society and Politics in the Acts of the Apostles* (Maryknoll: Orbis, 1987), 92-93; Witherington 1998, 554-55; Winter, 'Gallio', 291-308.

54. Barrett 1998, 875, also considers the possibility that this might be the Sosthenes mentioned in 1 Cor. 1:1. If Sosthenes as another synagogue leader had converted to Christianity, it would have been a source of great anger and annoyance for the Jewish opponents of the gospel in Corinth. However, Sosthenes was not an uncommon name, and the identification with 1 Cor. 1:1 cannot be made with any certainty. Cf. Marshall 1980, 299.

55. Tannehill 1990, 228. Tannehill argues that 'the final sentence of the scene does not present Gallio as a clearheaded administrator, guided by a strong tradition of Roman justice, but only as a Roman official who is indifferent to the suffering of a troublesome Jew'.

G. Completion of the Second Missionary Journey (18:18-22)

Paul's return to Syrian Antioch marks the end of another missionary campaign (cf. 14:26-28). The vow he takes at Cenchreae (v. 18) could relate to the preceding context, in which he was challenged to trust God for protection in Corinth, or to the following section, in which he undertakes a long and dangerous sea voyage. Either way, he is portrayed as a pious Jew, apparently preparing to visit the church in Jerusalem (v. 22).[56] Unusually, he visits a place for potential mission as he travels, stopping only to minister in the synagogue at Ephesus for a while, and leaving Priscilla and Aquila to continue the work in his absence (vv. 19-21). In short, this narrative gives the impression that Paul was determined to visit Jerusalem and Antioch before engaging in another missionary venture.

18 *Paul stayed on in Corinth for some time* (*hēmeras hikanas*, 'a number of days'; cf. 9:23, 43; 27:7), implying a short stay in addition to the eighteen months mentioned in v. 11.[57] Paul was not forced out of Corinth, but *he left the believers* when he was ready, *and sailed for Syria, accompanied by Priscilla and Aquila*. Silas and Timothy were perhaps left behind to minister to the Corinthians, since Priscilla and Aquila now appear as Paul's primary travel companions.[58] They sailed from *Cenchreae*, which was the eastern seaport of Corinth (Rom. 16:1 indicates that there was a church there) and a natural place to embark for a journey to *Syria*. Before they sailed, *he had his hair cut off at Cenchreae because of a vow he had taken*.[59] The reason for making the vow is obscure, though it could be related to the Lord's promise of protection from danger and Paul's determination to stay in the city and keep preaching (vv. 9-11). 'Jews made vows to God either in thankfulness for past blessings (such as Paul's safekeeping in Corinth) or as part of a petition for future blessings (such as safekeeping on Paul's intending journey).'[60] Marshall inclines towards the former interpretation, because of the preceding context. Paul appears to have taken a temporary Nazirite vow, which involved abstinence from alcohol and not cutting his hair until the period

56. Jerusalem is not mentioned in the Greek, but TNIV and NRSV have rightly indicated that this is the best way to read the text (cf. v. 22 note).

57. Bruce 1990, 397, suggests six months or more — 'at least until the Aegean was open for sailing after the winter of 51-52'.

58. Spencer 1997, 178, observes that the alternating order of the names of Priscilla and Aquila in Acts can be taken as a reinforcement of the 'mutuality of the couple's relationship'. The reversal of the normal husband-wife sequence may also signal Priscilla's 'rising importance in the Pauline mission'. Cf. note 84 below on the antifeminist tendency of the Western text.

59. Some MSS make Aquila or Aquila and Priscilla the ones who had their hair cut. The best MSS are not so explicit. Aquila could have been meant (Aquila is the nearest noun to the verb in question), but Paul is more likely to be the subject since he is obviously the subject of the first singular verb in v. 19. Cf. Metzger, *Textual Commentary*, 412; Barrett 1998, 877.

60. Marshall 1980, 300. Cf. Barrett 1998, 877.

of the vow was completed at Cenchreae. Paul was later urged to participate in the completion of a Nazirite vow of four others (21:23-26; cf. Nu. 6:1-21; *m. Nazir* 1:1–9:5; Josephus, *War* 15:1). However, Bruce describes the incident in 18:18 as 'a private religious exercise, not conforming to the requirements of a Nazirite vow, which in any case could not be observed outside the land of Israel, because of the constant exposure to defilement in a Gentile environment (*m. Nazir* 7:3; cf. 3:6)'. He then adds, 'even if a Nazirite vow were undertaken in a Gentile environment, it could not be completed without 30 days' residence in the land of Israel; only at the end of that period would the hair be cut and offered at the temple (cf. Num. 6:18)'.[61] With this reading of the situation, the cutting of the hair in Cenchreae could mark the beginning of the period of a vow which would be completed when Paul went to Jerusalem and had his head shaved (18:22).[62] Whatever its specific meaning in Paul's life at this time, the incident portrays him as a pious Jew, living at least in certain respects according to Jewish custom.[63] Yet the taking of vows was not an obligatory act like Sabbath-keeping. Paul voluntarily continued certain Jewish practices because he did not see them to be inconsistent with his new status in Christ. Nevertheless, his lifestyle and his whole focus on salvation through faith in Christ must have raised many questions about the continuing role of the law for Jews in the messianic era. Making a vow and shaving the head when it was completed was a way of demonstrating his trust in God and showing loyalty to the traditions of Israel, without compromising his gospel message. Perhaps such gestures allowed Paul to talk more freely with fellow Jews about the gospel (cf. 1 Cor. 9:20).

19-21 *They arrived at Ephesus* (KJV and NKJV reflect the singular reading found in some manuscripts ['he arrived']),[64] *where Paul left Priscilla and Aquila. Ephesus* is mentioned for the first time, though it appears from 16:6 that Paul had earlier tried to preach in the province of Asia, where Ephesus was the capital (cf. 19:1 note). Most of Paul's third missionary campaign was spent in that important centre (19:1–20:38), where there were Jews in great numbers.[65] *Priscilla and Aquila* played a key role in the work there, ministering to Apollos (18:24-28) and using their house as a meeting

---

61. Bruce 1990, 398.

62. Cf. Johnson 1992, 330, who notes that the verb 'cut' *(keirō)* rather than 'shave' *(xyreō,* as in 21:24) is used, and argues that the imperfect *euchēn* should be translated literally as 'he was making a vow'.

63. Barrett 1998, 860, rightly says, 'Paul was the adversary of Judaizers, but he remained a true Jew'. However, he later notes the evidence for the possibility that this may have been 'a standard Greek cultural reaction to some dream through which came divine guidance' (Barrett, 877, citing *ND* 1:24; 4:114f.).

64. Cf. Metzger, *Textual Commentary,* 412; Barrett 1998, 878. The singular reading is more consistent with the other verbs in the context, but for that reason is most likely not the original. Copyists tended to smooth out anomalies such as a plural among several verbs in the singular.

65. Cf. Bruce 1990, 398-9; *ND* 4:116.

place for at least some of the Ephesian Christians (1 Cor. 16:19). But by the time Paul wrote Romans 16:3-4, they were back in Rome again. *He himself went into the synagogue and reasoned* (dielexato; cf. 17:2, 17; 18:4; 19:8, 9; 20:7, 9; 24:12, 25) *with the Jews*. Luke's emphatic language (autos de eiselthōn, 'he himself entered') does not necessarily mean that Paul went alone to the synagogue in Ephesus. The construction in Greek begins a new stage in the record, where the focus is specifically on Paul and his movements (vv. 19b-23). Luke regularly writes this way when we know from the context that others were with him. *When they asked him to spend more time with them, he declined.* No explanation is given about Paul's desire to leave so soon after arriving. Perhaps he wanted to fulfill his vow with the requisite period of residence in Israel and a thank offering in Jerusalem.[66] Perhaps he was already aware of the sort of criticisms expressed on a later visit (21:20-21) and wished to build bridges of trust with believers in Jerusalem. His return to Antioch in Syria (vv. 22-23) suggests a concern to encourage his home church and secure its support for another missionary campaign (cf. 14:26-28; 15:30-35). The Western text gives a longer reading, which is picked up by some later manuscripts and is represented in KJV and NKJV ('I must by all means keep this feast that cometh in Jerusalem'). Bruce argued that, if the feast was Passover, there was good reason for haste: 'the seas were closed to navigation until March 10, and in AD 52 Passover fell in early April'.[67] However, this reading, which may have been influenced by 20:16, is not found in the best and most ancient manuscripts. *But as he left, he promised, 'I will come back if it is God's will'*. Paul's resolution to return is accompanied by a clear expression of his dependence on God to make it happen (cf. Rom. 1:10; 1 Cor. 4:19; 16:7; Jas. 4:13-15). *Then he set sail from Ephesus.*

22 Luke gives no account of the voyage from Ephesus, which is likely to have involved several stops along the way. When Paul landed at *Caesarea*, the headquarters of the governor of Judea, he 'went up and greeted the church and then went down to Antioch' (anabas kai aspasamenos tēn ekklēsian katebē eis Antiocheian). Caesarea was not in Syria, which was his stated destination (v. 18). Perhaps northerly winds had prevented a more direct approach to Antioch or perhaps a prior visit to Jerusalem was always intended. The text does not specifically say that he visited Jerusalem, though this is a reasonable conclusion from the use of the terms *went up*

---

66. Cf. Witherington 1998, 557. Witherington believes that the vow should be related to Paul's thankfulness for being kept from harm in Corinth, and argues that he took the vow to remain unshorn in response to the vision he had. Completing the vow in Jerusalem would have been an expression to fellow Jews of his piety, but more fundamentally a sign that God had been with him in his missionary endeavours, protecting and blessing him.

67. Bruce 1988, 356. Marshall 1980, 301, cites this as a reason for saying that the scribe who added these words may have 'hit on the truth' about Paul's reason for abruptly leaving Ephesus. However, Metzger, *Textual Commentary*, 412, 415-16, points out that the addition of the Western text to 19:1, which is not translated by KJV and NKJV, suggests that the visit to Jerusalem did not take place. On the ground of external attestation and internal factors such as the style of the argument in 19:1, these are later interpolations into the original text.

and *went down,* coupled with the reference to *the church* (so also NRSV; cf.
8:5; 11:27; 15:1-2).[68] This visit was not an expression of Paul's subordination
to the twelve apostles or to the church in Jerusalem. Rather, it was part of
his strategy to maintain good links between the Gentile churches and the
centre from which the gospel first came (cf. 11:29; 15:1-4; 19:21; 20:16, 22;
Gal. 1:18–2:10).[69] He merely *greeted the church* in Jerusalem, but he spent
some time in Antioch, thus rounding off the second missionary journey that
had begun in Antioch (15:35-41). There he presumably reported back to his
praying friends all that God had been doing through him and his team (cf.
14:26-28).

VII. THE WORD IN EPHESUS: THE CLIMAX OF PAUL'S MISSION AS A FREE MAN (18:23–20:38)[70]

Since the motif of strengthening the churches marks the end and the beginning of previous missionary journeys (cf. 14:21-22; 15:36–16:5), it is argu-
able that the second missionary journey ends when Paul returns to Antioch
(18:22), and the third journey begins when Paul and his team travel overland through the region of Galatia and Phrygia, 'strengthening all the disciples' (18:23) and finally arriving at Ephesus (19:1). However, the churches
visited on this journey are once again those founded on the first missionary
journey. The churches of Macedonia and Greece which were established on
the second missionary campaign are revisited when Paul has finished his
work in Ephesus (19:21; 20:1-3). This final journey to Jerusalem also includes the farewell to the Ephesian elders (20:17-38). 'Thus Paul's work on
the second and third journeys is completed through a single sequence of final visitation, which binds these areas of work closely together. Although
the second and third journeys are distinct, the narrative also encourages us
to consider Paul's work in the Aegean region as a whole.'[71]

---

68. It is possible that the church in Caesarea is meant, though this would be an odd
way of expressing a visit to the church in that city. Barrett 1998, 880-81, observes that the terminology is used for visiting a capital or holy place (cf. 11:2), and it is therefore more likely
that, 'though its name is not mentioned, Jerusalem may be the goal of Paul's journey'. He
surmises that Paul may have decided to find out how far the Jerusalem authorities were behind the Judaizing troublemakers who had come to Galatia, Corinth, and other places, 'and
if possible to stop the trouble at its source'. Cf. Bruce 1990, 400; Witherington 1998, 559.

69. Johnson 1992, 335, similarly states that Paul went up to Jerusalem 'to assert his
continuing fidelity to the original apostolic community'. By the time Luke records Paul's final visit to Jerusalem, where he is charged with teaching the abandonment of the Jewish
ethos (21:20-24), Luke has shown that the accusation is false.

70. Elements of this title are borrowed from Tannehill 1990, 230. On the structure of
Acts and the importance of this subdivision, see my INTRODUCTION TO ACTS: IV.B.
Structure (pp.32-36).

71. Tannehill 1990, 231.

The third journey is different in that Paul has a settled and extensive ministry in only one city. The evangelistic impact of his preaching on the whole province of Asia is noted (19:10), and the pastoral significance of his ministry to the church in the capital is further explicated in his farewell speech to the elders (20:17-38). Tannehill is right to conclude that 'Ephesus is not just another stop in a series. It is Paul's last major place of new mission work; indeed, it is the sole center of mission noted in the last stage of Paul's work as a free man.'[72] Nevertheless, there are similar patterns of ministry in Corinth and Ephesus, which suggest that we should observe the way the preceding narrative prepares for what eventuates in Ephesus. Here we have 'two complemenatry episodes which illustrate a mature stage of development in Pauline mission practice and theology'.[73] The narrative about the ministry of Priscilla and Aquila to Apollos in Ephesus (18:23-28) prepares for the next section in which Paul encounters the twelve disciples (19:1-7). Luke's main outline of the Ephesian ministry is in 19:8-41, after which there is a brief record of the journey to minister to the believers in Macedonia, Greece, and Troas (20:1-12). His charge to the Ephesian elders effectively summarizes and concludes the whole presentation of his missionary work in Acts 13-20.

A. Priscilla, Aquila, and Apollos in Ephesus (18:23-28)

While Paul was away from Ephesus, Priscilla and Aquila presumably continued the ministry in the synagogue (18:19), though Luke's interest is in their engagement with Apollos (18:24-28). When they privately explained to him 'the way of God more adequately', they prepared him for a vigorous and effective ministry in Corinth. In this way Luke illustrates something more of the interconnection and interdependence of churches in the apostolic period. Priscilla and Aquila took time out of their ministry in Ephesus to help someone who would prove to be an enormous benefit to the churches of Achaia. But the narrative also functions to prepare readers for Paul's encounter with a group of anonymous 'disciples' in Ephesus (19:1-7). There are certain similarities in their situation: Apollos 'knew only the baptism of John' (18:25; cf. 19:3) and needed to be better instructed about 'the way of God' (18:26; cf. 19:1-5). But Apollos already knew about Jesus and taught about him accurately and with Spirit-given fervour (18:25), whereas the Ephesian disciples needed to learn about Jesus, to be baptized in his name, and to receive the Holy Spirit (19:4-7). The experience of

---

72. Tannehill 1990, 231.

73. Towner, 'Mission Practice', 433. In particular, Towner notes the setting up of a new base of operation outside the synagogue, affirming in practice 'the inclusive gospel and people of God which embrace both Jew and Greek without distinction'. In both cities, there is mounting opposition to Paul's ministry from Jews and Gentiles, resulting from prolonged evangelism.

Apollos is sufficiently different to demonstrate that the Ephesian disciples were not yet Christians, even though they shared something of the same background as Apollos. So here, as in 4:32–5:11 and 17:1-15, Luke uses a pair of narratives to highlight similarities and differences between individuals or groups of people.[74] It seems likely that some of John the Baptist's disciples retained their distinctive beliefs for a while after his death and continued to urge other Jews to prepare for the coming of the Lord by accepting the baptism offered by John. While many of the Baptist's disciples recognized in Jesus the fulfillment of their expectations, others may have had a mixture of beliefs and practices that fell short of the understanding and experience of mainstream Christianity as portrayed in Acts.[75] Apollos and the Ephesian 'disciples' appear to have emerged from that sort of background. Apollos was clearly Christian when Priscilla and Aquila met him, but the Ephesians had not come so far when Paul encountered them. Luke's account of Apollos provides an important background for understanding the situation portrayed by Paul in 1 Corinthians 1:10-12; 3:1-8, 21-23; 4:6; 16:12.

23 Paul set out on his third campaign from Antioch in Syria and *traveled from place to place throughout (dierchomenos kathexēs, 'passing through in order') the region of Galatia and Phrygia, strengthening all the disciples.* The reference to his *strengthening all the disciples (epistērizōn pantas tous mathētas)* suggests a return to Galatian towns in the south, rather than a new initiative in the north. Both the second and the third missionary journeys began with visits to strengthen churches previously founded by Paul and his companions (cf. 15:36–16:5). In this case, the churches were once again those founded on the first missionary journey. Congregations established in Macedonia and Achaia on the second missionary campaign were not revisited until Paul had finished his work in Ephesus (19:21; 20:1-3). The phrase *the region of Galatia and Phrygia (tēn Galatikēn chōran kai Phrygian)* has been much discussed. Hemer proposes that the *the region of Galatia* is resumptive of 16:6 and recalls Paul's work in South Galatia, but *Phrygia* (here used as a noun, rather than adjectivally as in 16:6) is 'appended loosely in the awareness that Phrygia extended into the province of Asia, beyond Galatia in any sense, and on Paul's present route towards Ephesus'.[76] The term *kathexēs* points to the visit of two distinct districts 'in order'.

---

74. Barrett 1998, 885, notes that the two paragraphs (18:24-28 and 19:1-7) are united by two themes: the work of John the Baptist and the Holy Spirit, 'inadequate and adequate marks respectively of the Christian faith'.

75. Cf. C. K. Barrett, 'Apollos and the Twelve Disciples of Ephesus', in W. C. Weinrich (ed.), *The New Testament Age: Essays in Honor of Bo Reicke*, Vol. 1 (Macon: Mercer, 1984), 29-39.

76. Hemer, *Book of Acts*, 120. Witherington 1998, 559-60, notes that this journey of some fifteen hundred miles through the Cilician gate and on to Ephesus must have taken place during spring and summer, when the passage through the mountains was possible. This strongly suggests to Witherington that 'whatever other calculations we make, it is unlikely Paul *arrived* in Ephesus before the fall of AD 53'.

24-25 Every detail about *Apollos* is significant for understanding the impact of his later ministry, though the final comment in v. 25 introduces a note of uncertainty.[77] As *a Jew, who was a native of Alexandria,*[78] he had apparently encountered Christianity before he *came to Ephesus. Alexandria* was the second largest city in the Roman Empire and was 'the leading intellectual and cultural center of the Hellenistic world (as Athens had been of the classical world), built around a massive museum and 400,000-volume library'.[79] It was in Alexandria that Jewish scholars had produced the Greek version of the Hebrew Scriptures called the Septuagint (LXX). The fact that Apollos was *a learned man (anēr logios* could also mean 'eloquent man') from Alexandria, *with a thorough knowledge of the Scriptures (dynatos en tais graphais,* 'powerful in the Scriptures'), meant that he had the potential to be an influential teacher of the faith. Apollos had been *instructed in* (*katēchēmenos* probably here means 'formally taught') *the way of the Lord.* This term recalls the ministry of John the Baptist (Lk. 1:76; 3:4; 7:27), though in Acts it refers specifically to 'the way of salvation' in Jesus the Messiah (9:2; 16:17; 18:25, 26; 19:9, 23; 22:4; 24:14, 22). Moreover, *he spoke with great fervour (zeōn tō pneumati elalei,* 'was fervent in the Spirit as he spoke'),[80] suggesting the influence of the Holy Spirit (cf. Rom. 12:11) rather than merely a lively human spirit. There is a good deal of attention in Acts to manifestations of the Spirit through speech (1:16; 2:4, 17-18; 4:8, 25, 31; 6:10; 10:44-46; 13:9-10; 19:6; 21:4, 11). The parallel with 6:10 (*tō pneumati hō elalei,* 'the Spirit by which he spoke') is particularly suggestive. Additionally, we are told that he *taught about Jesus accurately (akribōs;* cf. v. 26, *akribesteron,* 'more accurately'). 'The powerful Apollos, refuting the Jews through Scripture, resembles Stephen, whose opponents could not withstand "the wisdom and the Spirit by which he was speaking" (6:10) and who interpreted Scripture to the Sanhedrin.'[81] Given his background and the fact that Apollos had been instructed in the *way of the Lord,* none of this is surprising. But Luke finally qualifies his description by saying, *though he knew only the baptism of John.* This prepares us to compare and contrast the situation of the 'disciples' in

77. Metzger, *Textual Commentary,* 412-13, discusses the different spellings of the name Apollos in some MSS. The name is virtually unattested outside Egypt. Cf. *ND* 1:88; Hemer, *Book of Acts,* 233-34.

78. As in v. 2, the word *genos* is used in v. 24 with reference to a place of origin, rather than race (in both cases the race is clearly Jewish). The Western text modifies v. 25 to read that he was 'instructed in his own country in the word of the Lord', reflecting a reasonable inference from the original text. Cf. Metzger, *Textual Commentary,* 413.

79. Spencer 1997, 183. There is no way of knowing when Christianity was established in Alexandria. There was a large community of Jews there and good communication with Jerusalem, making it probable that the gospel reached Alexandria at an early date. Details about Alexandrian Christianity emerge in the second century, but there is no reason why it should not have been established there by AD 50. Cf. Bruce 1990, 401.

80. Cf. Barrett 1998, 883, 888; Bruce 1990, 402. Tannehill 1990, 232, says that the expression describes 'the effect of the Holy Spirit on his speech'.

81. Tannehill 1990, 233.

19:1-7, who similarly had received only John's baptism. What did it mean for Apollos and his ministry to know only this baptism?[82] Since Priscilla and Aquila did not urge him to receive baptism 'into the name of the Lord Jesus' (contrast 19:5), they clearly thought that he had saving faith in Christ and was not deficient in his own experience of the benefits of the gospel. In whatever context he had come in touch with John's teaching, Apollos had accepted John's testimony and recognized Jesus as the promised Messiah. In this respect he differed markedly from the 'disciples' in 19:1-7. Although he preached Jesus *accurately*, it would have been confusing and misleading if he offered converts only *the baptism of John*. This was only a preparatory rite, looking forward to the messianic era, and not specifically a means of acknowledging Jesus as Messiah and receiving the benefits of his saving work. Perhaps this was the issue about which he needed further instruction. The rite of baptism needed to be reinterpreted in the light of Messiah's advent. Tied up with this was the re-evaluation of traditional Jewish eschatological expectations.

26 Apollos *began to speak boldly* (parrēsiazesthai as in 9:27, 28) *in the synagogue.*[83] But boldness coupled with an inadequate grasp of 'the way of the Lord' is dangerous. A gifted speaker can convince people to follow his own interpretation of things. Christian leaders who fall into this trap need to be challenged and guided, for the sake of the gospel and for the sake of those who may be misled. *When Priscilla and Aquila heard him,*[84] *they invited him to their home* (proselabonto auton, 'they took him aside', BDAG) *and explained to him the way of God more adequately* (akribesteron; cf. v. 25, akribōs, 'accurately'). In view of what was said above in connection with v. 25, it may be that the meaning and significance of baptism were central to their teaching. Apollos was a Christian himself, and fervently tried to persuade other Jews to trust in Jesus as the promised Messiah. If he still offered people baptism as only John had done, there was something deficient about his eschatology and his way of explaining how the benefits of Jesus' saving work could be appropriated in the present. Priscilla and Aquila ministered to him in a timely and discreet fashion when they 'took him aside'. As Bruce observed, 'How much better it is to give such private help to a preacher whose ministry is defective than to correct or denounce him publicly!'[85]

27-28 *When Apollos wanted to go to Achaia, the believers encouraged him*

82. It is possible that Apollos had been baptized by John himself in the Jordan, though it is also possible that disciples of John the Baptist continued his ministry after his death, some moving to distant places such as Alexandria and Ephesus, where large Jewish communities existed.

83. Barrett 1998, 889, rightly suggests that this bold preaching was a manifestation of the fervency in the Spirit with which he spoke (v. 25). The Western text unusually has a shorter reading ('the way') in v. 26, where the majority reading is 'the way of God'.

84. The Western text mentions Aquila before Priscilla here and refers to Aquila without Priscilla in vv. 3, 18, and 21, apparently demonstrating an antifeminist tendency. Cf. Metzger, *Textual Commentary*, 413-14.

85. Bruce 1988, 360.

and wrote to the disciples there to welcome him.[86] The Ephesian believers recognised his potential and felt some responsibility to write a letter of recommendation on his behalf (cf. Rom. 16:1; Col. 4:10). They were concerned to further his ministry, but also to benefit other congregations by commending him to them. Perhaps they were particularly motivated to help because they had heard about the opposition to the gospel from Jews in Achaia and knew what a powerful apologist for Christianity Apollos could be in such a context (cf. v. 26). *When he arrived, he was a great help to those who by grace had believed.* Luke is once more at pains to point out the sovereign *grace* of God by which people became believers (cf. 13:48; 15:11; 16:14).[87] According to Paul, Apollos 'watered' the seed which he had planted in the capital of the province (1 Cor. 3:6), meaning that he nurtured the spiritual life of the church. However, Luke emphasizes the way in which Apollos helped Christians throughout Achaia by engaging with unbelievers as an apologist and evangelist, *for he vigorously refuted the Jews in public debate, proving from the Scriptures that Jesus was the Messiah.* Jews agreed with Christians that there was to be a Messiah, but Apollos had to prove from the Scriptures that *Jesus was the Messiah.* It is clear from previous contexts that the suffering and death of Jesus was a particular problem to be addressed when appealing to Jewish audiences (2:23-36; 3:17-19; 13:26-37; 17:3).

B. Twelve Disciples of John the Baptist Become Christians (19:1-7)

Like the narrative of Paul's ministry in Philippi (16:11-40) and Corinth (18:1-17), Acts 19 presents several scenes portraying ways in which the gospel impacted Ephesus and the surrounding region. The number and length of these scenes indicate the diversity and significance of Paul's encounter with various groups in Ephesus. Overall, the impression is given of an amazing impact on this city, which was profoundly influenced by magic and the cult of the goddess Artemis. A previous reference to Paul's synagogue ministry in Ephesus (18:19-21) is picked up and developed in 19:8-10. However, before that, the ministry of Priscilla and Aquila to Apollos

86. Once more the Western text includes a large addition to the majority text: 'And some Corinthians who were on a visit to Ephesus and had heard him invited him to cross over with them to their native place. When he agreed, the Ephesians wrote to the disciples to receive the man; and when he took up residence in Achaia he was of great help in the churches'. Metzger, *Textual Commentary*, 415, points out that it is hard to see why a letter of recommendation would have been necessary if Apollos had genuinely been invited to Achaia by believers from that region. Barrett 1998, 891, sees this Western reading as evidence of 'the more developed situation in the second century than in the first'.

87. Cf. Barrett 1998, 890. Marshall 1980, 304, is inclined to read *dia tēs charitos* ('by grace') with the verb *synebaleto* ('helped'): 'by his (gift of) grace he helped the believers.' This would be a very unusual way to read *dia tēs charitos* in the light of 15:11, and Barrett rightly argues that 'it seems better to take the adverbial phrase with the nearer verb' (with NRSV, ESV, TNIV).

(18:24-28) is recalled by the account of Paul's ministry to the twelve 'disciples' in 19:1-7. Apollos had received the baptism of John and had come to recognise Jesus as the one to whom John's testimony pointed. He needed only some further instruction to become a truly effective witness to Jesus himself. However, the disciples whom Paul met in Ephesus had received John's baptism but did not understand the purpose of John's mission. They needed to grasp where Jesus fitted into the picture, to be baptized in his name, and to receive the promised Holy Spirit. 'They represent a degenerate form of John's heritage, from the viewpoint of Paul and the narrator. Even so, John's heritage helped lead them to recognize what they had missed.'[1] The pair of narratives in 18:24-28 and 19:1-7 show the continuing influence of the Baptist in places like Alexandria and Ephesus, more than twenty years after his death. They reflect 'different ways of receiving disciples of John the Baptist into the church',[2] and indicate that people came to Christ in ways beyond the pattern generally outlined by Luke. Paul appears to be like Peter and John in 8:17, placing his hands on these newly baptized believers so that they might receive the Holy Spirit. The full incorporation of these disciples into the messianic community is publicly demonstrated, as the Spirit endorses Paul's plan to revisit Ephesus (18:21) and signals the establishment of a mighty gospel work in the province of Asia.[3]

1-2 *While Apollos was at Corinth, Paul took the road through the interior and arrived at Ephesus.* According to 18:27, Apollos went to Achaia, but now we are specifically told that he visited the provincial capital of that region (cf. 1 Cor. 1:10-12; 3:1-8, 21-23; 4:6; 16:12).[4] Meanwhile, Paul *took the road through the interior* (*ta anōterika merē*, 'the upper regions') and arrived back in the administrative centre of the province of Asia (cf. 18:19-21).[5] The proconsul was resident in Ephesus, which was also the commercial centre of the region and the fourth largest city in the Empire.[6] It had come within the

---

1. Tannehill 1990, 234.

2. Barrett 1998, 898. The Baptist movement seems to have continued well into the fourth century AD. Johnson 1992, 338, points out that this is the fifth occasion when John's role as a precursor to Jesus has been mentioned in Acts (1:5; 11:16; 13:25; 18:25), suggesting its importance to Luke.

3. Cf. THE THEOLOGY OF ACTS: III. THE HOLY SPIRIT (pp. 60-65).

4. The Western text, with partial support from some other MSS, omits the first clause of 19:1 and begins, 'Although Paul wished, according to his own plan, to go to Jerusalem, the Spirit told him to return to Asia'. This textual tradition does not recognise the possibility of a visit to Jerusalem in 18:22. It seems to have arisen as another illustration of the way Paul's own plans were overruled by God (cf. 16:6, 7). The majority text makes better sense of the flow of the argument from 18:21. Cf. Barrett 1998, 894-95.

5. Gk. *ta anōterika merē* probably refers to the hill country between Phrygia and Ephesus (cf. 18:23). It is likely that Paul followed the route through the Cayster valley, north of Mt. Messogis. Cf. C. J. Hemer, *The Book of Acts in the Setting of Hellenistic History*, ed. C. Gempf, WUNT 49 (Tübingen: Mohr Siebeck, 1989; repr. Winona Lake: Eisenbrauns, 1990), 120; Barrett 1998, 892-93.

6. After Rome, Alexandria and Antioch were the largest cities. For more information on Ephesus in Paul's time, cf. Bruce 1990, 398-99; P. R. Trebilco, 'Asia', in D. W. J. Gill and

Roman sphere in 133 BC, but was not elevated to the status of provincial capital until the reign of Augustus. At that time, it experienced tremendous growth because of its advantageous situation, being located on a number of important land and sea routes. In inscriptions it called itself 'the first and greatest metropolis of Asia'.[7] The temple of Artemis, which was outside the city wall, was the chief glory of the city and one of the seven wonders of the ancient world. It was about four times the size of the Parthenon in Athens and was richly decorated with the works of the greatest painters and sculptors of the age. Luke's later narratives illustrate the amazing impact of Paul's ministry on the cult of Artemis and the practice of magic in the city (19:11-41). First, however, he informs us about Paul's encounter with an unusual group of Jewish *disciples*.

The term *mathētēs* is extensively used in Luke-Acts for Christian disciples,[8] leading some to insist that these Ephesians must have been Christians.[9] Noting in particular that Paul asked them, *'Did you receive the Holy Spirit when you believed?'* (v. 2), some argue that the aorist participle *pisteusantes (when you believed)* refers to Christian conversion.[10] A parallel is observed with the experience of the Samaritan believers in 8:14-16, who believed the gospel but did not receive the Holy Spirit until Peter and John prayed for them and laid hands on them (cf. 19:6). These passages are taken together to build a case for a post-conversion experience of the Spirit being normative. However, the parallel with Acts 8 is significantly diminished when it is noted that the Samaritans had received Christian baptism, but the Ephesian disciples had received only John's baptism (19:3). Moreover, when asked by Paul, *'Did you receive the Holy Spirit when you believed?'* the Ephesian disciples answered, *'No, we have not even heard that there is a Holy*

C. Gempf (eds.), *The Book of Acts in Its First-Century Setting*, Vol. 2: *Graeco-Roman Setting* (Grand Rapids: Eerdmans; Carlisle: Paternoster, 1994), 302-59. Trebilco, 307, describes Ephesus as the third largest city because its population is estimated to have been 200,000 to 250,000.

7. Trebilco, 'Asia', 306.

8. Lk. 5:30; 6:1, 13, 17, 20, 40; 7:11; 8:9, 22; 9:14, 16, 18, 40, 43, 54; 10:22, 23; 11:1; 12:1, 22; 14:26, 27, 33; 16:1; 17:1, 22; 18:15; 19:29, 37, 39; 20:45; 22:11, 39, 45; Acts 6:1, 2, 7; 9:1, 10, 19, 25, 26 (twice), 38; 11:26, 29; 13:52; 14:20, 22, 28; 15:10; 16:1; 18:23, 27; 19:9, 30; 20:1, 30; 21:4, 16 (twice).

9. See J. D. G. Dunn, *Baptism in the Holy Spirit: A Re-examination of the New Testament Teaching on the Gift of the Spirit in Relation to Pentecostalism Today*, SBT (Second Series) 15 (London: SCM, 1970), 83-84, and M. M. B. Turner, *Power from on High: The Spirit in Israel's Restoration and Witness in Luke-Acts*, JPTSS 9 (Sheffield: Sheffield Academic, 1996), 388-91, for brief reviews of different conclusions about these disciples. Bruce 1990, 406, has a helpful bibliography in this connection.

10. R. P. Menzies, *The Development of Early Christian Pneumatology with Special Reference to Luke-Acts*, JSNTSS 54 (Sheffield: JSOT, 1991), 271, takes 'disciples' to mean Christians, and reads the aorist participle in a sequential sense (*'after* you believed'). However, it is more likely that the participle is used in a coincidental or circumstantial way (cf. Dunn, *Baptism*, 86-87; Bruce 1990, 406; D. B. Wallace, *Greek Grammar beyond the Basics: An Exegetical Syntax of the New Testament* [Grand Rapids: Zondervan, 1996], 622-25).

Spirit'. How could genuine Christians make such a response? The plural noun *mathētas* is used in v. 1 without a definite article, the indefinite adjective *tinas* giving the sense *some disciples*. Perhaps this expression was used because they gave the appearance of being Christians when Paul met them.[11] Whatever the precise designation of this term, Paul soon expressed doubt about their spiritual condition by asking his critical question in v. 2. Their answer showed that they were definitely not Christians. Since Luke employs the term *mathētēs* with reference to the disciples of John the Baptist (Lk. 5:33; 7:18; 11:1), that could possibly be the meaning here.[12] Perhaps they acquired their knowledge of John's teaching in a secondhand way and were baptized by someone else rather than having direct contact with the Baptist himself.[13] They were certainly in something of a time-warp, not having recognised the coming of either the Messiah or the promised outpouring of the Holy Spirit through Jesus. John the Baptist had proclaimed that the Messiah would soon baptize his followers with the Spirit (Lk. 3:16), and Jesus endorsed that prediction, proclaiming its imminent fulfillment and describing the Spirit as 'the gift my Father promised' (Acts 1:4-5). This last expression alludes to the promise of an eschatological outpouring of the Spirit given to Israel in passages such as Isaiah 44:3-5, Ezekiel 36:26-27 and Joel 2:28-29. It is surprising that anyone who knew the Scriptures could say, *we have not even heard that there is a Holy Spirit*. It is particularly puzzling that people who had received John's baptism could be ignorant of his teaching on this subject.[14] When they *believed*, they apparently did not appropriate this vital aspect of his legacy. Luke does not explain the reason for this, but continues his account of the way they came to acknowledge Jesus as Messiah and receive the Spirit promised by John.

3-4 Paul's further question (*'Then what baptism did you receive?'*) indicates some surprise that they had not received baptism 'into' *(eis)* the name

11. Cf. Marshall 1980, 305-6. Marshall rightly argues that 'the NT does not recognize the possibility of being a Christian apart from the possession of the Spirit (Jn. 3:5; Acts 11:17; Rom. 8:9; 1 Cor. 12:3; Gal. 3:2; 1 Thes. 1:5f.; Tit. 3:5; Heb. 6:4; 1 Pet. 1:2; 1 Jn. 3:24; 4:13)'.

12. Cf. K. H. Rengstorf, *TDNT* 4:456-57; Witherington 1998, 569-71. Dunn, *Baptism*, 84-85, insists that the term 'disciples' still requires some connection with Christianity, but acknowledges that they 'do not yet belong to *the* disciples; they are not yet Christians'.

13. Against Spencer 1997, 185, there is really no basis for arguing that Apollos was the teacher of these twelve men. Luke's insistence on the fact that Apollos 'taught about Jesus accurately' (18:25), even before being corrected by Priscilla and Aquila, speaks against this.

14. Page 1886, 203, suggests that the reply meant, 'We did not *at our baptism* hear whether there is a Holy Spirit'; that is, 'Our baptism (John's baptism) was simply a baptism of repentance and conveyed no promise beyond that of the forgiveness of sins'. The reply pointed to defective teaching at the time of their baptism, presumably by a disciple of John, and not to complete ignorance about the person of the Holy Spirit. There is a textual variant that seeks to overcome the difficulty of the majority text by replacing *estin* with *lambanousin tines*, giving the sense, 'We have not even heard whether some are receiving the Holy Spirit'. However, this reading is not widely attested (Papyrus 38 [41], the original of D, and some Old Latin, Syriac, and Coptic MSS).

of Jesus Christ,[15] the outcome of which was normally the reception of the Spirit (cf. 2:38-39). They then disclosed that they had received only *John's baptism*. The Baptist's ministry was a summons to definitive repentance, initially expressed in baptism *('John's baptism was a baptism of repentance')*, and the motivation for this was the imminent coming of the Lord and his salvation (cf. Lk. 3:3-14). There was something defective about the way the Ephesian disciples had understood the significance of their baptism, since John had told the people *'to believe in the one coming after him, that is, in Jesus'* (cf. Lk. 3:15-17).[16] John indicated that the Christ was yet to come, that he would be mightier than John, and that he would baptize with the Holy Spirit. Paul's report of this does not refer to the Holy Spirit but focuses on the name of *Jesus* as the one who fulfilled the Baptist's prediction (cf. 17:3 note).[17] If they came to put their trust in Jesus as Messiah, they would receive the gift of the Spirit and become Christians.

5 *On hearing this, they were baptized into the name of the Lord Jesus.* Once again, Luke's narrative is brief and does not appear to record all that was said. Paul presumably told them that baptism *into the name of the Lord Jesus* was the way to rectify their situation and express their trust in Jesus as the messianic Saviour.[18] This is the only instance of re-baptism recorded in the NT, highlighting the unusual nature of the recipients and their situation. Marshall rightly argues that 'it would be wrong to conclude from this incident that people today who did not receive the Spirit at their baptism (whether as infants or adults) ought to be rebaptised in order to receive the Spirit; the characteristic and essential feature of the ceremony of *Christian* baptism is that it is performed in the name of Jesus, and the chronological relation of the gift of the Spirit to the actual rite is unimportant, as the varied order in Acts demonstrates (before baptism: 10:47; at baptism: 2:38; 8:38f.; after baptism: 8:15f.)'.[19]

6 Somewhat paralleling the Samaritan incident (8:15-17), *when Paul placed his hands on them, the Holy Spirit came on them, and they spoke in tongues*

---

15. *eis ti oun ebaptisthēte* ('into what then were you baptized?) points in this direction. This and the following expression (*eis to Iōannou baptisma*, 'into John's baptism') are variations on a baptismal formula with *eis* and the name of the Lord Jesus which is found in Acts 8:16; 19:5 (elsewhere the prepositions *epi* or *en*, meaning 'in', are used instead of *eis*). Cf. Witherington 1998, 571.

16. Bruce 1990, 407, points out that the word order in Greek throws the expression *eis ton erchomenon met' auton (in the one coming after him)* into prominence, 'thus stressing the preparatory character of John's ministry'.

17. Against D. A. Carson, *Showing the Spirit: A Theological Exposition of 1 Corinthians 12–14* (Homebush West, Sydney: Lancer; Grand Rapids: Baker, 1988), 184-50, it does not seem from this report that Paul was rehearsing what they already knew about Jesus.

18. By way of contrast, Apollos was not called to receive Christian baptism because he had been instructed in 'the way of the Lord', was 'fervent in spirit', and taught accurately about Jesus (18:25 note). Apollos also did not need the laying on of hands in order to receive the Holy Spirit.

19. Marshall 1980, 307.

and prophesied. Like Peter and John in Samaria, Paul had a special prophetic role and status within the general pattern of 'prophesying' made possible for all believers at Pentecost (cf. 2:15-21, 38-39). However, there is no record of tongues and prophecy being expressed in Samaria (though outward signs of the Spirit's coming may be implied), and in Ephesus there was no significant delay between baptism and the laying on of hands. In neither case is Luke indicating that the gift of the Spirit is normally a supplement to baptism. In fact, Paul's question in v. 3 identifies baptism with the reception of the Spirit. Apart from the narrative about the Samaritans, this is the only account in Acts where the laying on of hands is specifically linked with the coming of the Spirit. It is 'the climax of a single ceremony whose most important element is baptism, and whose object is the reception of the Spirit'.[20] In the context, it expresses prayer for the recipients, while welcoming them into the fellowship of Christ.

When Luke says that *the Holy Spirit came on them, and they spoke in tongues and prophesied,* he affirms the fulfillment of Joel 2:28-29 for this particular group of people. It could be argued that 'they experienced a mini-Pentecost. Better, Pentecost caught up on them. Better still, they were caught up into it, as its promised blessings became theirs.'[21] The expression *came on them (ēlthe . . . ep' autous)* recalls the promise of 1:8 *(epelthontos eph' hymas),* and the sign of the Spirit's coming is tongues and prophecy, as in 2:1-13.[22] Turner insists that there is no need here, 'with Lampe, to invoke a special missionary endowment separate from an alleged baptismal gift of the Spirit; nor are there any sure grounds for Menzies' conclusion that "through the laying on of hands, Paul commissions the Ephesians as fellow-workers in the mission of the church and the twelve are thus endowed with the prophetic gift"'.[23] They became Christians and were empowered for Christian life and ministry by a single endowment of the Spirit.

Turner argues that Luke expected the reception of the Spirit to be 'a matter of immediate perception',[24] but that such manifestations as we find in 2:1-13; 8:17-19; 10:46; 19:6, are not to be regarded as normative for ongoing Christian experience. Judaism anticipated only an initial outburst of charismata when 'either the illapse of the Spirit was a dramatic one, or when public attestation to the transfer of the Spirit was necessary to legiti-

20. Dunn, *Baptism,* 87. Dunn makes the further point that 'when Paul learned that they had not received the Spirit he immediately inquired after their baptism, not their faith, and *not* any other ceremony'. There is no evidence for a regular or formal association of the laying on of hands with baptism before AD 200.

21. Stott 1990, 305. Cf. THE THEOLOGY OF ACTS: III. THE HOLY SPIRIT (pp. 60-65).

22. Some MSS embroider the best-attested text, adding 'other tongues, and they themselves knew them, which they also interpreted for themselves and certain also prophesied.' Cf. Metzger, *Textual Commentary,* 416.

23. Turner 1996, 393. Cf. G. W. H. Lampe, *The Seal of the Spirit* (London: SPCK, 1967), 76; Menzies, *Development,* 271.

24. Turner, *Power,* 392 (emphasis removed).

mate the recipients in some way to Israel'.[25] So why did the group in Ephesus collectively experience the phenomena of tongues and prophecy when other converts in Acts apparently did not? At one level, it was the appropriately dramatic inauguration of Paul's ministry in this city, where God's Spirit would be remarkably at work, opposing the power of magic and false religion, and winning many to Christ throughout the region.[26] At another level, it was specifically related to the identity and need of these particular men. As those influenced in some way by the ministry of John the Baptist, they were brought collectively into the community 'established by Jesus and his disciples through the Spirit'.[27] In salvation-historical terms, they were a transitional group, whose full incorporation into the church needed to be openly demonstrated.

7 Luke's interest in numbers surfaces again when he mentions that *there were about twelve men in all.* There is no reason to attribute any special significance to the number 'twelve' on this occasion. However, *twelve men* (*andres,* 'males') probably implies a considerable number of family members with similar beliefs, who also needed to be brought to Christ and receive the Spirit. A sizeable group of new Christians is thus indicated. They presumably remained attached to the synagogue until Paul was forced to leave and take the whole body of Christian disciples with him (vv. 8-9).

C. Teaching and Mighty Works in Asia (19:8-20)

This section provides 'a climactic presentation of Paul as a channel of divine power and servant of the Lord's word'.[28] Putting it another way, he is portrayed as a prophetic figure in word and deed, like Jesus (cf. Lk. 6:18-19; 24:19) and the Twelve (e.g., Acts 2:41, 43; 5:12-16). Like them, he also experiences intense opposition from Jewish quarters, though in 19:23-31 — as in 16:19-24 — Paul is attacked by antagonistic Gentiles. Spencer observes that

25. Turner, *Power,* 393, summarising his argument on pp. 357-58. Thus, Pentecost was of unique salvation-historical importance; the charismata in 8:17-19 mark 'the end of an anomalous delay, and ratify (that) the Spirit has come upon a group whose status with respect to the Israel of fulfillment was uncertain'; in 10:46 the irruption of the Spirit 'assures Peter and the Jewish Christian church that the gift of the Spirit could be bestowed even on Gentiles' (p. 394).

26. So Turner, *Power,* 396, suggests that 'Luke may well have considered the initial outburst of charismata to be a form of attestation and sign of encouragement to Paul that it was now the appropriate time for the important ministry based in Ephesus that was to follow'. Cf. J. Hur, *A Dynamic Reading of the Holy Spirit in Luke-Acts,* JSNTSS 211 (Sheffield: Sheffield Academic, 2001), 260-62.

27. Turner, *Power,* 396. Carson, *Showing the Spirit,* 150, says that the tongues and prophecy 'serve as the attestation to the Ephesian believers themselves of the gift of the Spirit that transfers them as a group from the old era to the one in which they should be living'.

28. Tannehill 1990, 236. Note the strong accusations against Paul in Jerusalem presented by Jews from Asia (21:27-29; cf. 24:19). This is a further indication of the impact of Paul's ministry in Asia.

the scenes in 19:8-41 'become progressively longer as the distance from Paul's position widens; put another way: the greater the conflict with Paul, the greater the attention given to resolving it'.[29] Luke concludes this segment with another reference to the word of the Lord spreading and growing in the face of conflict and opposition (v. 19; cf. 6:7; 12:24), before describing the final experience of conflict in Ephesus.

1. From Synagogue to Lecture Hall (19:8-10)

Paul's ministry in the Ephesian synagogue lasted for three months; then he found it necessary to leave and establish a new centre for teaching in the lecture hall of Tyrannus. There are parallels with his experience in Corinth (18:5-8), though there is no announcement of a decisive move to the Gentiles in Ephesus. Indeed, 'what follows is not an exclusively Gentile mission. Jews cannot be addressed as an assembly, but they can still be addressed as part of the public that Paul encounters in his work.'[30] Opposition from the Jews in Ephesus was intense, but Paul needed no special vision to encourage him to stay. Perhaps it was the pattern of work established in Corinth that guided and empowered him in Ephesus. The lecture hall functioned as a substitute for the synagogue as a place for public teaching and discourse, though presumably Christians also gathered in houses to minister to one another (cf. the pattern in 2:42-47). As a result of his two-year ministry in this central venue, 'all the Jews and Greeks who lived in the province of Asia heard the word of the Lord' (v. 10). Doubtless the message was carried to every part of the province by those who heard Paul, and many were convinced (cf. v. 26).

8 Once more, *Paul entered the synagogue,* taking up where he left off on his first visit to Ephesus (18:19). The members of this synagogue were still receptive to his ministry, and he *spoke boldly there for three months.*[31] Explicit mention of *three months* suggests a longer ministry in this synagogue than in any previous one, which helps to explain his extensive influence on Jews in the province as a whole (v. 10). Three familiar verbs are used to de-

29. Spencer 1997, 183. This helps to explain why the final scene in 19:23-41 is the longest.

30. Tannehill 1990, 235. Tannehill rightly takes issue with F. Pereira, *Ephesus: Climax of Universalism in Luke-Acts. A Redactional Study of Paul's Ephesian Ministry (Acts 18:23–20:1),* Jesuit Theological Forum 10.1 (Anand: Gujarat Sahitya Prakash, 1983), 138-76, who argues that this universal mission in Ephesus means that Paul has a completely new strategy by which he sets aside the priority of preaching to Jews first. There simply is not enough evidence to be so definite about this.

31. For Jews in Ephesus, see P. R. Trebilco, *Jewish Communities in Asia Minor,* SNTSMS 69 (Cambridge: Cambridge University, 1991), 17-18, 24-25, 167. Perhaps this was a particularly tolerant synagogue, having already received the powerful ministry of Apollos (18:24-26) and accommodated the 'disciples' mentioned in 19:1-7. It is also likely that Priscilla and Aquila continued ministering there when Apollos left Ephesus.

scribe Paul's engagement with the synagogue congregation (though TNIV unfortunately combines the last two, translating *arguing persuasively*). Paul *spoke boldly* (*eparrēsiazeto*, as in 9:27, 28; 13:46; 14:3; 18:26 [Apollos]; 26:26), 'reasoning' (*dialegomenos*, as in 17:2, 17; 18:4, 19; 19:9; 20:7, 9; 24:12, 25), and 'persuading' (*peithōn*, as in 13:43; 14:19; 17:4; 18:4; 19:26; 21:14; 23:21; 26:26, 28; 27:11; 28:23, 24). Argument was coupled with persuasion when he told them about *the kingdom of God*. This last term is used at critical points in Acts to make a connection with the preaching of Jesus and show how scriptural expectations about the eschatological rule of God are linked with his person and work (cf. 1:3, 6; 8:12; 14:22; 20:25; 28:23, 31). It is a shorthand way of describing the biblical-theological framework within which the gospel was preached.[32]

9-10 However, the outcome for Paul and his converts was eventually the same as before. *Some of them became obstinate* (*esklērynonto*, 'grew hard'), *refused to believe* (*ēpeithoun*, 'were unbelieving'), *and publicly maligned* (*kakologountes*, 'speaking evil [about]') *the Way*. TNIV translated *enōpion tou plēthous*, which could mean 'in the hearing of the populace',[33] as *publicly*, whereas NRSV and ESV more specifically relate this to the synagogue ('before the congregation'; cf. 4:32; 15:30). Since the synagogue is still the setting, the latter meaning is more natural to the context. The expression *the Way* is once more used to differentiate Christianity from mainline Jewish beliefs and practices (cf. 9:2; 19:23 note). *So Paul left them* and *took the disciples with him,* marking his last contact with a synagogue in Luke's record. Even if Christian believers had also been gathering in homes to minister to each other, they continued to meet in the synagogue until they were forced to leave. At this stage, the majority were apparently converts from the synagogue. However, a dramatic new step was taken when Paul began *discussions daily in the lecture hall of Tyrannus*. If he spent the early morning engaged in manual labour (cf. 20:34; 1 Cor. 4:12), and the middle of the day teaching and debating when most of his clientele could attend, those who heard him must have been 'infected with his keenness and energy.'[34] This *lecture hall* (*scholē*) was possibly owned by *Tyrannus*, who is otherwise unknown,[35] or it could have been the place where Tyrannus as a local philoso-

---

32. Cf. THE THEOLOGY OF ACTS: V. THE GOSPEL (pp. 70-75).

33. So Barrett 1998, 900, 904.

34. Bruce 1990, 408. The Western text adds that Paul argued daily in the hall of Tyrannus 'from the fifth hour to the tenth', which were the siesta hours, when the lecture room would not normally be in use. Metzger, *Textual Commentary*, 417, comments that this may represent 'an accurate piece of information, preserved in oral tradition before being incorporated into the text of certain MSS. Were it present in the original text, there is no good reason why it should have been deleted.' Cf. Marshall 1990, 309-10.

35. The name 'Tyrannus' is not uncommon in inscriptions from Ephesus (cf. Hemer, *Book of Acts*, 120-21). Barrett 1998, 904-5, argues that, although the word *scholē* (from which we get 'school') can mean a 'group of people to whom addresses were given during their leisure hours' (*ND* 1:129f.), in this context it can 'hardly mean anything other than a building'. However, he acknowledges that the meaning 'building' or 'hall' is unusual and late.

pher held classes. This venue, with its *daily discussions* over the course of *two years,* enabled Paul to have the most extensive influence so far recorded in Acts.[36] Presumably the size and location of the building made Paul's work more readily known than his synagogue ministry. More people could come and go, knowing that there was a *daily* opportunity to engage with Paul and his presentation of *the Way.* Moreover, the fact that he identified with the scholarly world by using this instructional centre must have attracted the attention of a wider group of inquirers. The result was *that all the Jews and Greeks who lived in the province of Asia heard the word of the Lord.* TNIV has rightly interpreted *Asia* to mean *the* (Roman) *province of Asia.*[37] *The word of the Lord* was heard throughout the province, as widespread evangelistic activity was encouraged by Paul's ministry in Ephesus (cf. Col. 1:7; 2:1; 4:16; Revelation 2–3, for examples of churches in Asia not personally founded by Paul). Here and in v. 20 it is once again affirmed that the gospel was responsible for this growth and development. Luke's summary description of Paul's Ephesian ministry in vv. 8-10 is further expanded and illustrated in the rest of the chapter. This complex set of narratives, together with the reflection on Paul's experience in 20:18-35, suggests that the narrator viewed this as 'the climax of Paul's missionary work, the place where Paul most fully realizes his calling to be Jesus' "witness to all persons" (22:15)'.[38]

2. Miracles and Their Impact (19:11-20)

The mighty works God accomplished through Paul in Ephesus were 'extraordinary' (vv. 11-12), in certain respects paralleling those attributed to Jesus and Peter. Other events associated with his preaching about the kingdom of God further illustrate the way God's power was at work through his ministry. Certain Jewish exorcists are prompted to use the name of Jesus in imitation of Paul (vv. 13-16), but that name is shown to be no magic formula, and those who use it fraudulently are exposed and embarrassed. The impact of this defeat on Jews and Greeks living in the city is that 'they were all seized with fear, and the name of the Lord Jesus was held in high honour' (v. 17). Moreover, in a public expression of repentance, those who pre-

---

36. The two years must be added to the three months already specified (v. 8) and the 'little longer' mentioned in v. 22, justifying the summary reference to three years in 20:31. The dates are probably Autumn 52 to Spring 55. Cf. Bruce 1990, 409; Barrett 1998, 905. Bruce suggests that one or more of Paul's imprisonments must have been endured during his Ephesian ministry (cf. 2 Cor. 11:23). Apart from a hint in 20:19, the events mentioned in 1 Cor. 15:30-32; 2 Cor. 1:8-10 may not be specifically recorded in Acts.

37. Luke generally uses 'Asia' in that political sense, though in 2:9-11 he refers more narrowly to the western coastal cities of that region and adjacent territory. Cf. Trebilco, 'Asia', 300-302.

38. Tannehill 1990, 236.

viously practised sorcery burn their valuable magic scrolls (vv. 18-19). Luke uses this narrative 'to advance the theme of the ongoing Christian triumph over Satan, and consequently over magic'.[39] The editorial note in v. 20 recalls v. 10, and is a reminder that all this activity is further evidence of the powerful growth and spread of the word.

11-12 *God did extraordinary miracles (dynameis ou tas tychousas,* 'no ordinary powerful deeds')[40] *through Paul, so that even handkerchiefs and aprons that had touched him were taken to those who were ill, and their illnesses were cured (apallassesthai,* 'removed') *and the evil spirits left them.* Although there is some debate about the meaning of the Latin loanwords (originally *sudaria* and *semicinctia*), translated *handkerchiefs and aprons,* it is likely that these were items connected with Paul's work as a tentmaker, which had made contact with his skin.[41] They were sought after because of the widespread ancient belief that the bodies of particular people, or whatever touched them, had healing power.[42] In view of parallels with Jesus' ministry (Lk. 6:18-19) and the ministry of Peter (Acts 5:12, 15-16), Tannehill suggests that 'healing through touching Jesus is extended to indirect contact with the source of the power through Peter's shadow or pieces of cloth taken from Paul to the sick. The power found at Ephesus is comparable to the power found in Peter at Jerusalem.'[43] At first glance, this appears to be a 'magical' activity, but God's sovereign role in the process is highlighted. *God* healed people in this way, graciously accommodating to human beliefs and expectations, to encourage them to draw near and discover what his messenger was proclaiming to them. Paul did not promote himself as a miracle worker, as did Simon Magus (8:9-10) or the itinerant Jewish exorcists soon to be mentioned (19:13-15). This was not a manipulative human process, designed to capture attention and win disciples.[44] As in 8:9-24 and 13:4-12,

39. S. Garrett, *The Demise of the Devil: Magic and the Demonic in Luke's Writings* (Minneapolis: Fortress, 1989), 90. Cf. THE THEOLOGY OF ACTS: IX. MAGIC AND THE DEMONIC (pp. 87-92).

40. Translation of Witherington 1998, 579, who describes this as 'a pleasant redundancy that highlights Luke's rhetorical skills of understatement'. Luke once more uses the figure of speech called litotes (cf. *ouk oligos,* v. 23). Paul himself refers to the signs, wonders, and mighty works that accompanied his preaching (Rom. 15:19; 2 Cor. 12:12; cf. Gal. 3:5).

41. Cf. R. F. Hock, *The Social Context of Paul's Ministry: Tentmaking and Apostleship* (Philadelphia: Fortress, 1980), 26, 42. Barrett 1998, 907, argues that *soudaria* and *simikinthia* could both refer to sweat rags, the former being worn on the head to prevent the sweat from running into the eyes and the latter being carried in the hand for general mopping up. Alternatively, the latter could be an apron or belt (cf. Witherington 1998, 579).

42. Cf. Plutarch, *Pyrrh.* 3.4-5; Eusebius, *Praep. Ev.* 9.27; Trebilco, 'Asia', 313. Witherington 1998, 580, observes that the verb *apallassesthai,* which is only used here in the NT for the removal of sickness, was frequently employed in the medical literature of Luke's day. Though this does not prove Luke was a doctor, along with other evidence, it is consistent with such a view and 'may be a small pointer in that direction'.

43. Tannehill 1990, 237.

44. C. E. Arnold, *Ephesians: Power and Magic: The Concept of Power in Ephesians in the Light of Its Historical Setting,* SNTSMS 63 (Cambridge: Cambridge University, 1989), 19, dis-

Luke distinguishes between Christian miracle-working and the practice of magic in the Greco-Roman world. His purpose is to draw attention to the unique role and status of Peter and Paul in God's purposes, and to help his readers to differentiate their activity from captivating and misleading alternatives.

13-14 Paul's apparent success at healing and exorcism prompted imitation. 'Some also of the Jews who went around' *(tines kai tōn perierchomenōn Ioudaiōn)*[45] *driving out evil spirits tried to invoke the name of the Lord Jesus over those who were demon-possessed.* These itinerant Jewish exorcists, who were fascinated by Paul's power and influence, recognised that his secret was *the name of Jesus.* But theirs was a fraudulent activity, since they were not Christians and used the name of Jesus like a magic formula.[46] Although they sought to emulate Paul by saying, *'In the name of Jesus, whom Paul preaches, I command you to come out'*, they were unsuccessful. The implication is that the *name of Jesus* was effective to deliver and to heal only when used by those who genuinely called upon Jesus as Lord. These pretenders did not have the appropriate moral or spiritual integrity with which to engage the powers of evil. Luke further emphasises the incongruity of the situation by revealing that *seven sons of Sceva, a Jewish chief priest, were doing this.*[47] There is no *Sceva* in the list of Jewish high priests available to us.[48] However, the word *chief priest (archiereus)* is regularly used in the plural in Luke's Gospel (e.g., 9:22; 19:47; 20:1, 19) and in Acts 4:23 (cf. some manuscripts of 4:1), apparently denoting 'members of the Jewish priestly aristocracy, or of the court that determined issues relating to the priests and the Temple'.[49] So Sceva could have

---

tinguishes magic from religion in the ancient world by saying, 'in religion one prays and requests from the gods; in magic one commands and therefore expects guaranteed results'.

45. *kai* is not translated by TNIV, but it is important for the meaning of the text. It suggests that Paul was invoking the name of the Lord Jesus over those who were demon-possessed (cf. 16:18), and so 'also' (or 'even') were these others. The following genitive will be partitive, indicating that not all the Jewish exorcists tried to use the name of Jesus in this way. This is the only place in the NT where the noun *exorkistēs* is used, but Jewish exorcists are presupposed in Mt. 12:27; Lk. 11:19. Cf. Arnold, *Ephesians*, 185; Hemer, *Book of Acts*, 190, 121; Barrett 1998, 908, for further evidence. Mk. 9:38-41/Lk. 9:49-50 records an incident where the name of Jesus was being used outside the circle of his disciples to drive out demons.

46. Cf. Garrett, *Demise*, 92-93.

47. The Western text and, in part, some other MSS and versions rewrite v. 14, with some leaving out the word 'seven'. Metzger, *Textual Commentary*, 417-18, discusses these variants and the various attempts that have been made to explain them, concluding that it is hard to explain how 'seven' came into the majority text and was perpetuated if it were not original.

48. J. Jeremias, *Jerusalem in the Time of Jesus: An Investigation into Economic and Social Conditions during the New Testament Period* (ET, London: SCM, 1969), 377-78, lists the high priests from 200 BC to AD 70. The Western text seems to acknowledge the difficulty, supplying the word *hiereōs* ('priest') instead of *archiereōs* ('high priest'). Cf. Metzger, *Textual Commentary*, 417.

49. Barrett 1998, 909. Cf. Jeremias, *Jerusalem*, 178. However, Bruce 1990, 411, is inclined to think that the word *archiereus* was applied to Sceva by those who wanted to 'authenticate the activity of his sons as *bona fide* exorcists'. Against this, cf. Witherington 1998, 581 (esp. notes 91-92).

been part of this wider high-priestly group. His sons were far from home, both physically and spiritually, being caught up with the magical world-view of this Gentile city. Ephesus was hospitable to magicians, sorcerers, and many forms of religious syncretism. 'Once again the scenario pits *miracle* (Paul) against *magic* (exorcists), authentic transmission of divine power against counterfeit manipulation.'[50] This is the first reference to demonic spirits since the story in 16:16-18, leading Klutz to observe how the Ephesian narratives complement those about Philippi in 16:16-40.

> Once again, interest in the demonic (19:12-16) co-occurs with images of deviant religiosity (19:13-19, 23-27), economic self-interest (19:17-19, 23-27), and political challenge and response (19:28–20:1). Furthermore, just as the possessed girl in chapter 16 is evaluated negatively despite her positive challenge to the missionaries' honour ('servants of the Most High God'), so the sons of Scaeva are portrayed unfavourably even though they acknowledge the high cosmic status of 'the Jesus whom Paul proclaims'. And just as the hostility in Philippi is explained in terms of greed (16:16, 19), misunderstanding (16:35-39), and Judeo-phobia (16:20-21), so in Ephesus, the antipathy of the artisans and their sympathisers is represented as stemming from economic self-interest, public confusion, and anti-Jewish prejudice (19:32-34).[51]

15-16 TNIV inserts *One day* into the text to indicate that Luke now records a specific event in the experience of the sons of Sceva (themselves particular examples of the Jewish exorcists mentioned in v. 13). They entered a house and attempted to exorcise a single spirit from a possessed man. On this occasion, their pretence was revealed by the evil spirit speaking through the man and saying, *'Jesus I know, and I know about Paul, but who are you?'* The forces of evil knew the difference between one who truly ministered in the name of Jesus and pretenders (cf. Lk. 4:34, 41; 8:28; Acts 16:17 for other manifestations of supernatural perception). This spirit was not to be easily overcome, perceiving a profound unity between Paul and Jesus, and thus the authority of Paul as Jesus' representative to exorcise in this way. If the command had been uttered by Paul, the demon would have come out. *Then the man who had the evil spirit jumped on them and overpowered them all.* The language here (*katakyrieusas amphoterōn ischysen kat' autōn*, 'mastered all of them and overpowered them', ESV) recalls the warning of Jesus in Luke 11:21-22, suggesting that 'the seven sons failed to mobilize Je-

50. Spencer 1997, 186.

51. T. Klutz, *The Exorcism Stories in Luke-Acts: A Sociostylistic Reading*, SNTSMS 129 (Cambridge/New York: Cambridge University, 2004), 232-33. Klutz further argues that 'Luke identifies Paul (and indirectly himself) with an idealised Judaism that puts him firmly at odds with the values of paganism, which is portrayed in these and several other sections of Acts in the worst possible light'. Moreover, 'Paul's honour needed defence and his mission needed to be represented as posing no threat to the public good of Roman order'.

sus' power because they lacked the authority to invoke his holy name, and
so the demon remains in control'.[52] The impotence of the imposters was revealed, and they were publicly humiliated. Indeed, the demon-possessed
man *gave them such a beating that they ran out of the house naked and bleeding*.
Several features of this narrative contrast with Jesus' transforming impact
on the Gerasene demoniac in Luke 8:26-39. For example, the latter was delivered from a whole legion of demons, a state of nakedness, and an existence among the tombs. The result was that he could return home 'dressed
and in his right mind' (v. 35). In Acts 19, a group of seven exorcists were
vanquished by a single demon. They ran away naked, injured, and de-
graded.[53]

17 The impact of this event was such that, *when this became known to
the Jews and Greeks living in Ephesus, they were all seized with fear, and the name
of the Lord Jesus was held in high honour*. There was widespread *fear*, as people
began to treat with respect *the name of the Lord Jesus*, which had previously
been profaned by the exorcists (contrast Lk. 8:34-37). This was a way of
magnifying or glorifying *(emegalyneto)* Jesus himself, which presumably
meant that more and more people began calling on him for salvation. The
ignominious defeat of the Jewish exorcists by the demon showed the Ephesians that 'Jesus' is a power that cannot be controlled: 'he will not act as a
lackey for anyone who calls on his name'.[54] Echoes of earlier narratives involving the Jerusalem apostles (2:43; 5:5, 11, 13) suggest that 'the word of
the Lord is equally powerful in Paul's Ephesian ministry and that the
Christian mission can be equally successful in the pluralistic world of
Greeks and Diaspora Jews represented by Ephesus'.[55]

18-19 The remarkable humiliation of the exorcists and the consequent glorification of the name of the Lord Jesus by many led to another
amazing event. *Many of those who believed now came and openly confessed
(exomologoumenoi kai anangellontes, 'confessing and disclosing') what they
had done*. There was a public expression of repentance on the part of *many of
those who believed*,[56] whereby *a number who had practiced sorcery (ta perierga,*

52. Garrett, *Demise*, 94. Barrett 1998, 911, argues that this may be the first example of
the tendency to use *amphoteros* (normally 'both') for 'all' (v. 16), as found in later papyri (cf.
23:8 note). Cf. Bruce 1990, 411, who also considers the possibility that 'the narrative reflects
the vivid description of an eyewitness, implying that, while seven sons attempted the exorcism, only two were attacked by the demoniac'.

53. Cf. Klutz, *Exorcism*, 235. Klutz points to further parallels between the subsequent
narratives in Luke 8:40-56 and Acts 19:17-20

54. Garrett, *Demise*, 94-95.

55. Tannehill 1990, 238.

56. Garrett, *Demise*, 96, argues that the perfect participle *tōn pepisteukotōn (those who
believed)* indicates that 'the confessors' initial act of belief preceded their coming forward
(imperfect *ērchonto*) to confess their "practices", but does not by itself imply that their initial
act of believing had occurred some time ago, or that they had continued their magical practices up until this supposed moment of awakening conscience (cf. John 8:30-31)'. Contrast
Marshall 1980, 312; Witherington 1998, 582.

'superfluous works', a technical term for magic)[57] *brought their scrolls together and burned them publicly.* Apparently they were moved by the exposure and overcoming of the exorcists to realize that their own previous involvement with the magic arts now needed to be acknowledged. Perhaps they had kept scrolls in which spells were written as an insurance policy, in case their newfound faith proved to be inadequate in some situation! Burning the scrolls was a way of repudiating what they contained and represented a greater trust in God to deliver them from trouble and supply their needs.[58] Such repentance before God and his people was costly: *When they calculated the value of the scrolls, the total came to fifty thousand [drachmas]* (*argyriou*, 'of silver', without specifying the units of silver as 'drachmas'). Luke's reference to the price of these scrolls once more suggests 'his strong dislike of the money-making side of magic and his clear rejection of it from the Christian side'.[59] These people recognised that genuine discipleship involved letting go what they treasured in order to enjoy the blessings of God's kingdom (cf. Lk. 9:23-27; 18:18-30). The scrolls that were burned may have contained the famous 'Ephesian letters', with their words of power for warding off demons, and 'the sort of material preserved in the magical papyri such as thaumaturgic formulae, incantations, hymns and prayers'.[60] By depicting the defeat of the magicians in this way, Luke conveyed the message 'that in the name of Jesus, the faithful shall triumph over the forces of darkness: Christians need not fear the devil, for there is no power in him against them'.[61]

20 Luke's conclusion to this part of the Ephesian narrative (*In this way the word of the Lord spread widely and grew in power*) echoes the editorial note in 6:7 and 12:24 (though *ischyen* ['prevailed'] is used instead of *eplēthyneto* ['multiplied'] here and *kata kratos* ['powerfully'] is added).[62] In each case, a similar refrain marks the end of one significant period of ministry and the beginning of another, attributing every spiritual advance to the word of the Lord or the gospel. Perhaps *kata kratos*, 'powerfully', is added here because of the immediately preceding narrative (vv. 17-19): the gospel

57. Bruce 1990, 412.

58. Bruce 1990, 412, observes that, 'as the potency of spells resides largely in their secrecy, their disclosure would be regarded as rendering them powerless'.

59. Barrett 1998, 914. Cf. 8:4-25. The value of these scrolls corresponded to 50,000 days' wages for a day labourer. Cf. Haenchen 1971, 567; Marshall 1980, 312.

60. Trebilco, 'Asia', 314.

61. Garrett, *Demise*, 103. Cf. Lk. 10:17-20; Eph. 6:10-18; Jas. 4:7; 1 Jn. 4:1-4; 5:18-21.

62. The text says literally, 'Thus the word of the Lord grew mightily (taking *kata kratos* with *ēuxanen*) and prevailed' (NRSV). ESV ('So the word of the Lord continued to increase and prevailed mightily') takes *kata kratos* with *ischyen* (as TNIV apparently also does), which seems less likely in view of the word order in Greek. The Alexandrian witnesses are divided, with the majority having the unusual word order *tou kyriou ho logos*. So an alternative translation might be, 'by the power of the Lord the word grew and prevailed'. Cf. Metzger, *Textual Commentary*, 418-19; Barrett 1998, 914, for a discussion of secondary readings in this verse.

brought about that kind of repentance! Each reference to the word 'growing' concludes a narrative about the resolution of some great conflict, either in the church or in relation to unbelievers. From previous contexts we may discern that the church grew because more and more people believed in the gospel.[63] But from this particular context we also learn that the power of the gospel to transform lives was associated with and illustrated by healing, exorcism, and the confounding of false religion and magic. An inclusion with v. 10 ('the word of the Lord') is formed by the conclusion in v. 20, and the intervening material shows how that message had its effect. 'The narrator is not simply glorifying Paul. It is finally the power of the word of the Lord, or the name of the Lord (19:17), that stands behind these events.'[64] Although there is another great conflict story to follow (19:23-41), the summary of Paul's ministry in terms of its overall impact and effect is concluded with v. 20. The next paragraph announces Paul's intention to visit Jerusalem and Rome, which become the goals of his remaining journeys in Acts.

D. Provoking the Idolaters (19:21-41)

Paul does not appear in this scene until vv. 30-31, but the narrative as a whole is Luke's final illustration of the impact that Paul's ministry had in Asia. It records unprecedented opposition and prepares the reader for events to come in Jerusalem (21:27-40). This is the longest narrative in the Ephesian section, showing its importance for the narrator.[65] The disturbance is about 'the Way' (v. 23), but Paul is unquestionably the main source of contention (v. 26). Even though Demetrius does not make his case before the city officials, his role is similar to that of Paul's accusers in Philippi (16:20-21), Thessalonica (17:5-7), and Corinth (18:12-13). Angry protests against Paul and his travel companions follow the claim that his preaching has had a profound economic and religious effect 'on practically the whole province of Asia' (19:23-31). The note about his impending journey to Jerusalem before this disturbance is not incidental (19:21-22). It acts to tie the latter with the scene in Ephesus in several respects. In both cases, the riot is instigated by a small group of people who provoke others (19:23-28; 21:27-29 ['some Jews from the province of Asia']). Each time the accusation refers to the negative effect of Paul's teaching, the great extent of its influence (19:26; 21:28), and its harm to the local temple. 'Members of an established religion are protesting the effect that Paul's mission is having on their religion and its temple.'[66] The speech of Demetrius incites the riot in Ephesus,

63. Cf. J. Kodell, '"The Word of God Grew" — The Ecclesial Tendency of *Logos* in Acts 6:7; 12:24; 19:20', *Biblica* 55 (1974), 505-19.

64. Tannehill 1990, 238.

65. Spencer 1997, 183, observes that 'the greater the conflict with Paul, the greater the attention given to resolving it'.

66. Tannehill 1990, 242. Tannehill goes on to show how the accusations and calls to

and the speech of the city clerk brings it to an end (vv. 35-41). 'The first says Paul is a danger; the second says that these Christians are no real threat to Ephesus' importance as cult center for Artemis.'[67] Although the clerk recognizes the innocence of Gaius and Aristarchus and declares the riot to be unjustified, he naively assumes that the Christian criticism of idolatry has no great significance. This flies in the face of the evidence that Luke has presented. Seeking to calm the situation, this city official plays to the crowd and reinforces the confidence of the Ephesians in their city and its god. Although opposition to Christianity has been momentarily subdued, the impression is given that this kind of treatment from the authorities is no basis of confidence for future security in the face of mounting religious, economic, and social antagonism (cf. 18:14-17).

21-22 *After all this had happened, Paul decided to go to Jerusalem, passing through Macedonia and Achaia.* NRSV and ESV translate *etheto en tō pneumati* 'resolved in the Spirit' (NKJV 'purposed in the Spirit'), but TNIV *(decided)* has apparently taken this to be a resolution in his own spirit (KJV 'purposed in the spirit').[68] A parallel statement in 20:22-23, where Paul speaks about being 'compelled by the Spirit' *(dedemenos en pneumati)* to go to Jerusalem, indicates that he was driven by more than a human resolution. This suggests a parallel with the beginning of Paul's first missionary journey (13:2, 4) and the work of the Spirit in directing him to Troas, where a vision revealed the need to go to Macedonia (16:6-10). There is also an echo of the Gospel narratives in which Jesus is shown to be under a divine necessity to go to Jerusalem to suffer (e.g., Mk. 10:33-34; Lk. 9:51; 13:31-35).[69] Luke mentions nothing of the troubled situation in Corinth which necessitated a further visit from Paul, simply recording that he wanted to travel *through Macedonia and Achaia* (cf. 1 Cor. 16:5-9). Paul later changed his mind, planning to visit Corinth, then Macedonia, and then Corinth again (cf. 2 Cor. 1:15-16), which caused some concern at Corinth (cf. 2 Cor. 1:17-23). The pattern of revisiting churches founded on a previous missionary campaign was already well established (cf. 15:36–16:5; 18:23), but a journey to Rome implied the beginning of a totally new sphere of ministry (cf. Rom. 15:23-33). The last decision is presented in a solemn fashion *('After I have been there,' he said, 'I must visit Rome also'),* suggesting that there was a divine necessity

action cause a similar sequence of events in the two scenes. Protestors shout (using *krazō*, 19:28, 34; 21:28, 36), the crowd is stirred up (using *syncheō*, 19:32; 21:27, 31), and the expression 'some cried one thing, some another' is used to highlight the confusion (19:32; 21:34). The whole city is affected, rushes together, and someone is seized (19:29; 21:30).

67. Tannehill 1990, 243-44.

68. So also Barrett 1998, 919. Bruce 1990, 413, thinks a reference to the Holy Spirit's guidance is more likely, but points to 5:4 as a possible parallel *(ethou en tē kardia sou,* 'resolve in your heart'). Cf. Lk. 1:66; 21:14. Witherington 1998, 588, argues for a reference to the Holy Spirit.

69. Parallels between Jesus' last journey to Jerusalem and Paul's final journeys in Acts are examined by D. P. Moessner, '"The Christ Must Suffer": New Light on the Jesus-Peter, Stephen, Paul Parallels in Luke-Acts', *NovT* 28 (1986), 249-56.

(*dei*) about visiting Rome (further justifying the conclusion that it was the Holy Spirit who enabled him to make this resolution). This visit is the climax of the narrative of Acts, even though Paul arrives in an unexpected way! The purpose of a final visit to Jerusalem is not explained, though we know from Paul's letters that it involved the presentation of financial gifts from the Gentile churches for the relief of poor Christians in Jerusalem (cf. Rom. 15:25-27, 30-31; 1 Cor. 16:1-4; 2 Corinthians 8–9). Acts mentions this collection only in passing (24:17), even though it was personally and theologically so important to Paul himself.[70] However, Luke certainly records an event that was an essential part of the process of gathering the collection: Paul *sent two of his helpers, Timothy and Erastus, to Macedonia, while he stayed in the province of Asia a little longer* (cf. 1 Cor. 4:16-17; 16:8-11, though this may refer to an earlier visit of Timothy to Corinth).[71] Once again we are reminded that the Pauline mission was a team effort. Priscilla and Aquila played a special role in Corinth and Ephesus (18:1-3, 18-28), and Gaius and Aristarchus are soon to be mentioned as travelling companions from Macedonia, who were arrested in Ephesus (v. 29). Timothy and Erastus are described as *two of his helpers* (*duo tōn diakonountōn autō*, 'two of those who served him'). These personal assistants had important pastoral and practical responsibilities (cf. 13:5 note; 16:1-5). Although some would identify *Erastus* with the city treasurer of Corinth (cf. Rom. 16:23, assuming that Romans was written from Corinth; 2 Tim. 4:20), there is no real reason to make such a connection, since the name was common. Paul gathered such associates as he travelled, and used their gifts to enrich the church in other places. These colleagues acted with a measure of independence, standing in for Paul in some contexts, so that, 'for all his heroic stature in Acts, Paul does not stand alone'.[72] Once more, an implicit ecclesiology is indicated by Luke (cf. 18:24-8 notes).

23-24 *About that time* — when Paul was already making plans for the next stage of his missionary work — *there arose a great disturbance* (*tarachos ouk oligos*, 'not a small disturbance' [litotes]) *about the Way*. Christianity itself was the cause, though Paul as the one chiefly responsible for bringing this new teaching to Asia was clearly targeted (v. 26). *The Way* re-emerges here as a term used to describe the distinctive beliefs and practices of Christians (9:2; cf. 18:25-26 ['the way of the Lord/God']). Its appearance twice in

---

70. Marshall 1980, 313, follows Hanson 1967, 194-95, in noting that Luke was writing from a later perspective and recognized that 'Paul's arrest and its sequel were more significant than the delivery of the collection to Jerusalem, although the latter seemed more important to Paul at the time'.

71. Paul himself mentions three messengers, of whom the only one named is Titus (2 Cor. 8:16-24). Barrett 1998, 919, suggests that 'Luke in omitting almost all references to the collection found it expedient to omit Titus too'. In Acts 19:22-26 various witnesses of the Western text incorporate 'a variety of picturesque details' not found in other textual traditions. Cf. Metzger, *Textual Commentary*, 419.

72. Spencer 1997, 182.

this context (19:9, 23) suggests that Christians in Ephesus were being clearly identified as 'constituting a socially cohesive movement, a movement arising out of and grounded in their shared faith in Jesus'.[73] Paul's main opponent is introduced as *a silversmith (argyrokopos) named Demetrius, who made silver shrines (naous argyrous) of Artemis*, and who *brought in no little business (ouk oligēs ergasian) for the skilled workers (tois technitais) there*. It was the making of religious items in Ephesus that enabled the silver trade to flourish. Demetrius had a number of *skilled workers* either in his employ or under contract to produce such things. The term *silversmith (argyrokopos)* is found in a number of inscriptions in Ephesus. 'Shrines which were miniature replicas of the temple, or the part of the temple where the deity stood, were a common part of pagan cults.'[74] Small terra-cotta models of the Ephesian temple have survived, but no *silver shrines (naous argyrous)* have been discovered. Silver being so precious, it is unlikely that any such artifacts would remain, having been melted down and used for other purposes. Although Ephesus was the home of many cults, the most prominent and powerful deity for the Ephesians was *Artemis* (Lat. Diana; cf. KJV). Strabo (*Geog.* 14.1.6) wrote that the goddess received her name because she made people *artemeas*, that is, safe and sound. This mythical daughter of Zeus and Leto was associated with health and help of various kinds and was worshipped because of 'her lordship over supernatural powers'.[75] 'She was a virgin who helped women in childbirth, a huntress armed with a bow, the goddess of death.'[76] Paul's opponents in Thessalonica and Corinth were Jews (17:5-7; 18:12-13), whereas in Philippi and Ephesus they were Gentiles (16:20-21; 19:23-29). Luke progressively illustrates how the gospel was perceived as a threat to religious beliefs and practices throughout the Roman world, and thus also to the social and economic life of the people.

25-27 Seeking wider support for his challenge to Paul, Demetrius called together the skilled workers, who were effectively 'the guild of the sil-

73. R. Cassidy, *Society and Politics in the Acts of the Apostles* (Maryknoll: Orbis, 1987), 95. Since this terminology is mainly used in connection with the church in Jerusalem and its environs (cf. 9:2; 22:4), and then with the church in Ephesus and its environs (cf. 19:9, 23), Luke seems to imply that Christian beliefs and practices were being as firmly established and recognised in the somewhat Romanized Hellenistic culture of Ephesus as in the centre of Jewish culture in Jerusalem.

74. Trebilco, 'Asia', 336-38 (337); Barrett 1998, 922-23. *naos* was either used for a temple or the inner shrine of a temple where the image of the god was placed. Trebilco argues that there would have been a considerable demand for replica shrines as votive offerings dedicated in the temple to the goddess, 'although some may have been taken home by pilgrims, or perhaps placed in graves as an expression of devotion' (338).

75. Trebilco, 'Asia', 316-18 (317). Trebilco, 319-20, argues against the commonly accepted view that Artemis was seen as a fertility goddess. Trebilco, 320-22, outlines the way in which the cult of Artemis was celebrated in Ephesus. The influence of the cult extended beyond the religious sphere to the civic, economic, and cultural life of the city.

76. Barrett 1998, 922. The goddess was usually portrayed as many-breasted, though there have been various explanations of this phenomenon. Cf. Bruce 1990, 415; Witherington 1998, 586-88.

versmiths',[77] *along with the workers in related trades* (NRSV 'workers of the same trade' is also a possible rendering of *tous peri ta toiauta ergatas*). He first addressed the financial implications of the spread of Christianity for this guild, saying, *'You know, my friends, that we receive a good income from this business'*. Anything threatening the cult of Artemis would therefore threaten their pockets. *'And you see and hear how this fellow Paul has convinced and led astray large numbers of people here in Ephesus and in practically the whole province of Asia.'* This claim echoes the editorial note in v. 10 and is not simply hyperbole.[78] By persuasion (*peisas*, 'has convinced'), Paul had moved people all over the province to change (*metestēsan*) from idolatry to Christianity. As noted in connection with v. 10, this was because others had taken his message to places where Paul did not actually visit. Demetrius had rightly perceived that, at least in part, this was because of Paul's teaching *'that gods made by human hands are no gods at all'* (cf. 17:24-25, 29). Jews and a variety of pagan critics in the ancient world were arguing similarly, but the Christian case against idolatry had been clearly heard and widely acted upon.[79] This was presumably because of the framework of judgement and salvation in which it was presented. Demetrius's grievance was then presented as a loss of honour in an ascending hierarchy of values.[80] First he warned that the *trade* (*meros* refers to the 'part' played by the silver workers) of manufacturing miniature shrines of Artemis might *lose its good name* (*eis apelegmon elthein*, 'come into disrepute', NRSV, ESV). Then he highlighted the possibility that the actual *temple of the great goddess Artemis* might be *discredited* (*eis outhen logisthēnai*, 'be counted as nothing', ESV). Finally, he predicted that *the goddess herself, who is worshiped throughout the province of Asia and the world* (*oikoumenē* could refer to the Roman Empire), *will be robbed of her divine majesty* (*kathaireisthai tēs megaleiotētos autēs*, 'will be cast down from her greatness').[81] The temple of Artemis was a great attraction to ancient travellers as well as to the Ephesians themselves, and pilgrims must have contributed greatly to the prosperity of the city. Much was at stake for the silversmiths

77. Trebilco, 'Asia', 341.

78. Trebilco, 'Asia', 348, draws attention to the evidence for the impact of Christianity on pagan cults in other provinces of the Roman Empire, found in the letter of Pliny the younger to the emperor Trajan in AD 112.

79. Cf. Barrett 1998, 925.

80. Witherington 1998, 592, observes that 'in an honor-shame culture such as this one, public humiliation, or being seen as merely mercenary individuals, could ruin reputations and so one's livelihood'.

81. Following Spencer 1997, 187. Spencer claims that 'by positioning himself and his co-workers as clients of the great Asian goddess Artemis and patrons of her holy sanctuary, such that their reputation is wrapped up with hers, Demetrius makes an effective "appeal to higher loyalty", a common tactic in legal argument'. Cf. B. J. Malina and J. H. Neyrey, 'Conflict in Luke-Acts: Labelling and Deviance Theory', in J. H. Neyrey (ed.), *The Social World of Luke-Acts: Models for Interpretation* (Peabody: Hendrickson, 1991), 109, 119-20. Trebilco, 'Asia', 332-36, gives evidence for the worship of Artemis in numerous centres of the Roman Empire and for the special role of Ephesus in promoting this worship.

and for the population of Ephesus as a whole. 'There was no other Graeco-Roman metropolis in the Empire whose "body, soul and spirit" could so belong to a particular deity as did Ephesus to her patron goddess Artemis.'[82] Consequently, any threat to the cult of Artemis and her temple would naturally have provoked a strong response. Christianity had the potential to change the culture of the city, but would it succeed?

28-29 Such a heady combination of issues, climaxing in a call for loyalty to the goddess, provoked a furious reaction (*plēreis thymou*, 'full of anger'; cf. Lk. 4:28). The tradespeople gathered together by Demetrius were moved to cry, *'Great is Artemis of the Ephesians!'* There was a special bond between Artemis and the Ephesians. She was called the founder and guide of the city, and her name and image were found on coins and official documents. Moreover, she was regarded as protector of the city's fortifications and general welfare.[83] The chanting of the slogan *'Great is Artemis of the Ephesians'* soon brought *the whole city* into an *uproar* (*synchyseōs*, 'confusion, tumult' [BDAG]; cf. v. 32). *The people seized Gaius and Aristarchus, Paul's traveling companions* (*synekdēmous*, 'fellow-travellers'; cf. 2 Cor. 8:19; Josephus, *Life* 79) *from Macedonia, and all of them rushed together into the theatre.* Archaeological evidence indicates that the seating capacity of this open-air arena was possibly 25,000.[84] Civic festivals and plays were held in this imposing environment, the tri-monthly meeting of the civic assembly took place there, and it was a natural place for impromptu gatherings.[85] *Aristarchus* is mentioned again as a companion and fellow worker in 20:4; 27:2 (cf. Col. 4:10; Phlm. 24). The *Gaius* mentioned as a companion in 20:4 came from Derbe and appears to be a different colleague.

30-31 *Paul wanted to appear before the crowd* (*eiselthein eis ton dēmon* here may mean 'to enter the assembly').[86] It was not his practice to avoid the dangers to which other Christians were exposed. However, on this occasion, *the disciples would not let him,* counting his life 'too valuable to be risked in this way'.[87] Remarkably, however, *even some of the officials of the province* (*tōn Asiarchōn,* 'Asiarchs'), *friends of Paul, sent him a message begging him not to venture into the theatre.* There has been much debate about the authenticity and significance of this reference to Asiarchs. It was long thought

82. R. E. Oster, 'Ephesus as a Religious Center under the Principate, I. Paganism before Constantine', in *ANRW* 2.18.3 (1990), 1728. Trebilco, 'Asia', 331-32, gives evidence of two other occasions when the city of Ephesus acted as defender of the cult of Artemis.

83. Trebilco, 'Asia', 326-27. R. A. Kearsley in *ND* 6:204, concludes that 'the people of Ephesus appear to have believed that their own lives were deeply affected by the degree of reverence accorded Artemis'.

84. Bruce 1990, 418, says 'nearly 25,000 people', and Barrett 1998, 928, says the lowest estimate is 24,000, but Trebilco, 'Asia', 348, says 'perhaps 20,000.'

85. Cf. Trebilco, 'Asia', 348-50. Trebilco, 338-40, gives evidence of similar disturbances in Ephesus towards the end of the first century, caused by well-organized groups of workers.

86. 'As in 17:5, the *dēmos* is the citizen body of a Greek city' (Bruce 1990, 418).

87. Barrett 1998, 929. This event may be reflected in 1 Cor. 15:32; 16:9; 2 Cor. 1:8.

that there was no evidence for the existence of Asiarchs before the end of the first century AD, but recently discovered inscriptions challenge that view.[88] 'Asiarch' was the title of an office with a fixed term, though some held it more than once because they had performed some public benefaction. 'The duties of an asiarch fell within the sphere of civic administration, not provincial affairs.'[89] They were chosen from among the wealthy and aristocratic inhabitants of the province. Having such *friends (philoi)* in high places further validated 'Paul's rising reputation in the region',[90] revealing another level of society impacted by his ministry. Even if none of the Asiarchs were yet Christians, they were so concerned for his welfare that they *begg[ed] him (parekaloun) not to venture into the theatre.*

32 Returning to his description of the crowd (understanding *men oun* resumptively), Luke notes that *some were shouting one thing, some another.* TNIV makes it clear that the assembly is in view by putting the second Greek sentence first: *the assembly was in confusion (synkechymenē;* cf. v. 29, *synchyseōs).* This further mention of *confusion* suggests that 'these proceedings can hardly be taken seriously'.[91] Indeed, *most of the people did not even know why they were there.* The word *assembly (ekklēsia)* is used informally here and in v. 40, with reference to the gathering of those opposed to Paul and his message (cf. vv. 30, 33, *dēmos*). However, in v. 39 the city clerk speaks of the regular, properly constituted assembly of the city *(en tē ennomō ekklēsia),* which met at least once per month.[92] Elsewhere in Acts, this word is used to describe 'the assembly' of the Israelites in the wilderness (7:38) and 'the church' in a particular place (e.g., 5:11; 8:1; 9:31; 11:22, 26; 12:1, 5). The root meaning of gathering, assembly, or congregation remains fundamental to every application.[93]

33-34 *The Jews in the crowd pushed Alexander to the front, and they shouted instructions (synebibasan) to him.*[94] The word order in Greek suggests that a better overall rendering of the sentence might be: 'some of the crowd gave instructions to Alexander, whom the Jews had put forward' (NRSV).[95]

---

88. Cf. R. A. Kearsley, 'The Asiarchs', in Gill and Gempf, *Graeco-Roman Setting*, 363-76; Barrett 1998, 930. Kearsley goes on to dispute the identification of the titles 'asiarch' and 'high priest' of Asia, which for some time has been the 'consensus view' in Acts studies. Kearsley provides a detailed analysis of five inscriptions to support her case.

89. Kearsley, 'Asiarchs', 366.

90. Spencer 1997, 188.

91. Spencer 1997, 188.

92. Barrett 1998, 931, observes that the informal use of *ekklēsia* in 19:32, 40 is understandable if 'the persons concerned were those who would have been summoned to a lawful assembly even though they were not at the time engaged on lawful business'.

93. Cf. THEOLOGY OF ACTS: X. THE CHURCH (pp. 92-97).

94. A form of the verb *synebibasan* is used elsewhere in Acts with the sense of 'prove' (9:22) or 'conclude' (16:10). Here it means 'to advise by giving instructions, *instruct, teach, advise*' (BDAG). Cf. 1 Cor. 2:16 ('instruct').

95. Cf. Barrett 1998, 932. Bruce 1990, 419, considers the possibility that *synebibasan* means that they 'put [him] up' on a raised place from which he could address the crowd.

There is no real reason for identifying this Alexander with any other mentioned in the NT (cf. Mk. 15:21; Rom. 16:13; 1 Tim. 1:20; 2 Tim. 4:14). Perhaps the Jews intended that their representative should make clear the difference between themselves and the Christians. Jews were known to be opposed to idolatry and were unpopular in the Roman Empire. It is understandable that they would want to avoid being caught up in this mob reaction to Paul and his colleagues. Alexander *motioned for silence in order to make a defense before the people,* implying that the Jews were also under attack, but he was not heeded. *When they realized he was a Jew, they all shouted in unison for about two hours: 'Great is Artemis of the Ephesians!'* At this point, Jews and Christians found themselves facing the same irrational and angry opposition (cf. 18:17 note).

35-36 *The city clerk (grammateus tou dēmou)* was 'one of the highest local officials in Ephesus, who could exercise great influence in the affairs of the city'.[96] He *quieted the crowd* by first suggesting the impossibility of undermining the worship of Artemis. *'People of Ephesus',* he said, *'doesn't all the world know that the city of Ephesus is the guardian of the temple (neōkoron) of the great Artemis and of her image (tou diopetous), which fell from heaven?'* The term *neōkoros* was used by pagan and Jewish writers to refer to those responsible for the administration of a temple and its sacrifices. When Ephesus applied this term to itself, it was 'affirming its divine appointment as the keeper and protector of the religion and cult of the goddess, and as the recipient of the privileges and blessings which go with that office'.[97] The cult's ability to inspire the affection and loyalty of the citizens was clearly important to this city official. TNIV has rightly taken *tou diopetous* to mean *her image which fell from heaven.* The adjective *diopetēs* was used to describe objects such as meteorites, which had 'fallen from heaven' and were honoured in a number of cults because it was thought that they had come from the gods.[98] Ephesus was especially blessed by the presence of a heaven-sent image that was identified with Artemis. Perhaps the term 'fallen from heaven' was deliberately used to answer Paul's charge that 'gods made by human hands are no gods at all' (v. 26). At the centre of Ephesian worship was an object not made by human hands! The city clerk asserted that these claims about the city and its heaven-sent image were *'undeniable'* (*anantirrētōn,* 'not to be contradicted', BDAG), though Paul would doubtless have challenged them

---

96. Trebilco, 'Asia', 351. As well as keeping the records of the city, he drafted documents for the civic assembly, moved decrees, and sometimes took the lead in the assembly, frequently speaking on behalf of the assembly. Cf. A. N. Sherwin-White, *Roman Society and Roman Law in the New Testament* (Oxford: Clarendon 1963), 86-87; Witherington 1998, 597.

97. Oster, 'Ephesus as a Religious Center', 1702. Trebilco, 'Asia', 329-30, gives inscriptional evidence for the use of this title by the Ephesians. Cf. Sherwin-White, *Roman Law,* 88-89; Hemer, *Book of Acts,* 122.

98. Cf. Trebilco, 'Asia', 351-53; BDAG. If it was a meteorite, it presumably had something like a human form. Codex D has *diospetous,* which makes it clear that the object not merely fell from the sky but from the supreme god Zeus. Cf. Barrett 1998, 936.

if he had been given an opportunity. So there was every reason to *'calm down and not do anything rash'*. In effect, the clerk was saying that nothing should disturb the self-confidence of a city dedicated by divine visitation to the worship of Artemis.

37-38 With respect to Gaius, Aristarchus, and possibly also Alexander, the city clerk then argued, *'You have brought these men here, though they have neither robbed temples nor uttered blasphemy against our goddess'*.[99] The word translated *robbed temples* (*hierosylous*, 'temple-robbers', NRSV, NKJV) came to be used in the sense of 'sacrilegious' (ESV), since this was the real crime involved in robbing a temple.[100] No evidence had been presented that these men were guilty of sacrilege or of overt disrespect to the goddess. However, the city clerk was clearly putting the best possible construction on the matter to restrain the crowd, many of whom may have disagreed with his argument. He then proposed that, *'if Demetrius and his associates have a grievance against anybody* (*pros tina logon*, 'a case against anyone', implying a private suit against an individual), *the courts are open and there are proconsuls'*. The word for *courts* here is *agoraioi*, which literally means 'market days', since these were the occasions on which it was most convenient for the proconsul or his deputy to hold court sessions 'in the capitals of the *conventus*, or assize-districts'.[101] Charges could be brought only in the proper legal context, not in the disturbed and unjust environment of a public meeting.

39 The city clerk then indicated to Demetrius and his supporters that there might be 'something further' *(ti periaiterō)* which needed to be brought up, possibly meaning 'something more than a private lawsuit'.[102] Any such matter *'must be settled in a legal assembly' (en tē ennomō ekklēsia)*, the present meeting not being a regular, duly constituted civic assembly, able to transact such business (cf. v. 32 note on *ekklēsia* in this passage). In effect, 'the town clerk simply asks Demetrius to put off the question for a few days'.[103]

---

99. KJV and NKJV, following the Received Text and later MSS, have 'your goddess'. Certain copyists apparently regarded *hymōn* ('your') as suiting better the second person plural *ēgagete* ('you have brought'). Cf. Metzger, *Textual Commentary*, 419.

100. Cf. Trebilco, 'Asia', 354; BDAG. Trebilco refers to two passages in Josephus (*Against Apion* 2.237; *Ant.* 4.207) which show his concern that Jews are neither sacrilegious nor blasphemous with respect to pagan gods.

101. Trebilco, 'Asia', 355; BDAG ('court days/sessions'). Ephesus was the centre of an assize-district. Cf. Hemer, *Book of Acts*, 123. The plural *anthypatoi* ('proconsuls') is surprising, since there was only one proconsul of the province of Asia. Trebilco, 356, argues that the number may be the effect of the previous plural (*agoraioi*, 'courts'), or it may be 'a generalizing plural', meaning "there are such people as proconsuls"'. Cf. Barrett 1998, 937.

102. Sherwin-White, *Roman Law*, 83. The comparative adverb *periaiterō*, from *pera* ('beyond, further', BDAG), appears only here in the NT, in a good number of ancient MSS. However, *peri heterōn* ('about other things') is even more widely attested. Barrett 1998, 937-38, suggests that this may have arisen by accident, but it could also have been a deliberate correction by copyists wishing to broaden the scope of the city clerk's offer.

103. Sherwin-White, *Roman Law*, 88. Trebilco, 'Asia', 356-57, points to inscriptional evidence from Ephesus for a similar phrase, with reference to the sacred and regular meeting of the civic assembly, which took place at least once per month.

40 Revealing something of the complexity of the Greek, TNIV differs from most EVV in translating this verse. NRSV and ESV both provide a simple sentence, similarly structured: 'for we (really) are in danger of being charged with rioting today, since there is no cause that we can give to justify this commotion' (similarly KJV, NKJV). TNIV provides two sentences which do not easily connect or convey the flow of the argument: '*As it is, we are in danger of being charged with rioting because of today's events. In that case we would not be able to account for this commotion, since there is no reason for it*'.[104] The second part of the Greek sentence begins with the genitive absolute construction *mēdenos aitiou hyparchontos* ('there being no cause'). This is then followed by a relative clause beginning with *peri hou* ('concerning which') and containing a verb in the future tense (*[ou] dynēsometha apodounai logon peri tēs systrophēs tautēs*, 'we shall [not] be able to give an account concerning this commotion').[105]

There is a play on words in the opening part of this verse. Demetrius claimed that his business and the worship of Artemis were in danger (v. 27, *kindyneuei*) because of Paul's teaching. The city clerk claimed that the real danger (v. 40, *kindyneuomen*) was the possibility of *being charged with rioting*, based on the events of the day (*peri tēs sēmeron*, 'because of today'). Rioting in support of their religion was provocative and potentially self-destructive. We know of two occasions in the first century AD when the Roman authorities questioned practices connected with the temple of Artemis.[106] Against that background, it is easy to see why the city clerk would not want the cult of Artemis to come again to the notice of the proconsul. As 'the principal liaison officer between the civic administration and the Roman government of the province',[107] he expressed his concern that *we would not be able to account for this commotion, since there is no reason for it*. Barrett suggests that this either means 'there is no rational ground or excuse for what has happened; that is, we shall get what we deserve', or 'even though we have not in fact done anything for which we cannot plead that there was just cause', punishment inflicted by the proconsul will be undeserved and unpleasant.[108] A city charged with riotous behaviour 'could lose the respect of Roman officials, guilds which caused trouble could be disbanded, city officials could be punished, and a city could even lose its freedom'.[109]

104. Barrett 1998, 916, similarly opts for two sentences, giving a quite literal rendering of the Greek, which nevertheless is cumbersome: 'For as for this day, we run the risk of being accused of riot, there being no cause for it. We shall not be able to give a reason for this meeting.'

105. The omission of *ou* ('not') in a range of MSS is an attractive alternative, but as the easier reading it is unlikely to have been the original. Cf. Barrett 1998, 938-40, for a full discussion of the variant readings and complexities of possible meanings in v. 40.

106. Trebilco, 'Asia', 342-44.

107. Bruce 1990, 420.

108. Barrett 1998, 939-40.

109. Trebilco, 'Asia', 344. Trebilco, 345, gives evidence to support this argument and

41 *After he had said this, he dismissed the assembly.* Spencer rightly observes that Demetrius and the silversmiths can hardly have been satisfied with the city clerk's arguments and the outcome of the meeting. 'From their perspective, by diminishing their market of miniature temples of Artemis and denouncing idol worship, Paul *was* a kind of temple robber and blasphemer of the great Asian goddess. Although the narrative comes to an end, it leaves the door open for the affronted artisans to take their case before the proconsuls in the "open courts", as the town scribe suggests (19:38).'[110] At one level, 'the story suggests that the assembly of believers ought to be left alone and allowed to conduct its own affairs. That seemingly small request was an extraordinary privilege in the Roman world, one that had set the Jews apart from other groups'.[111] However, at another level, the narrative leaves the impression that the opposition of Demetrius and his co-workers has not been satisfactorily dealt with and must arise again to trouble Christians and hinder their witness to Christ.

This chapter, then, shows the potential of the gospel to transform the life and culture of a city and its surrounding region. Paul's three-year ministry of teaching the word of the Lord in Ephesus touched people at every level of society and began to transform the religious practices and lifestyle of many. However, Luke shows the need to be realistic about the opposition that will arise when the practical effect of such change is experienced by unbelievers. The self-interest of religious, social, and economic groups may be so intense that the lives of Christians may be threatened. Spiritual opposition may manifest itself in a variety of ways, but the name of Jesus is powerful to overcome even demonic forces and to allow the gospel to prevail. In many cultures today, those who profess to be believers hold on to animistic or magical beliefs and practices. In some situations, this syncretism or folk religion is overlooked or disregarded by church leaders. However, as in ancient Ephesus, there can be no spiritual advance or growth of the church unless such ties are broken and supernatural forces of evil are renounced.

INTRODUCTION TO ACTS 20

In 19:21, Luke indicated that Paul was planning three important journeys: to Macedonia and Achaia, to Jerusalem, and then to Rome. Acts 20 records the completion of the first and the beginning of the second. Paul's pattern was to return to churches that he had previously founded, to en-

---

concludes, 'because of the reality of Roman power, the town clerk seems very aware of the need for good behaviour in the city'.

110. Spencer 1997, 188-89.

111. R. F. Stoops, 'Riot and Assembly: The Social Context of Acts 19:23-41', *JBL* 108 (1989), 88-89.

courage and strengthen the believers (14:21-25; 15:36–16:41; 18:23). Only after his three years in Ephesus did he have opportunity to revisit the churches of Macedonia and Achaia established on his second missionary journey (16:11–18:23). Ephesus was included in that visitation by means of an encounter with the elders of the church in the coastal town of Miletus (20:17-38). Although it marks the beginning of Paul's final journey to Jerusalem and then to Rome, this chapter also represents a conclusion to the narrative about his ministry in Ephesus, which began in 18:19. We are given more details about the nature of that ministry and greater insight into the personal struggle of Paul in that city. This chapter also begins a literary unit (20:1–21:17) in which there are three scenes of Christian community life (the gatherings in Troas [20:7-12], Miletus [20:17-38], and Caesarea [21:8-14]), alternating with four travel reports (20:1-6; 20:13-16; 21:1-7; 21:15-17). Gaventa argues that this literary unit effectively 'draws the scattered Christian communities around the Aegean into a fellowship that resembles Luke's portrait of the early Christian community in Jerusalem'.[1]

Luke emphasizes the thoroughness of Paul's efforts to encourage and warn the churches in 20:1-12. After a brief journey section (20:13-16), he then records a speech in which the precise nature of Paul's encouragement and warning to believers is set out (20:17-38). As Paul begins the long journey to Jerusalem, emotional scenes of parting occur (20:36-38; 21:5-6, 12-15).[2] Paul doubtless said similar things in each situation, but there is a particular poignancy about his speech to the Ephesian elders because of the length of his stay in that city and the closeness of his relationship with that church. This is the third major Pauline speech recorded in Acts (13:16-41; 17:22-31; with a brief outline in 14:15-17) and the only message in the whole book directed to a group of Christians (though note the report of Paul's teaching in 14:22). It clearly addresses those with some theological knowledge, gained from Paul's teaching them 'the whole will of God' (v. 27). The rhetorical function of his exhortation is both to warn about the future of God's flock and to assure leaders and people of the basis on which it will be sustained and preserved. So the main theme in this chapter is pastoral care and leadership, with Paul as the model. As his second volume draws to a close, Luke takes the opportunity to warn and encourage Christian readers about God's will for the churches linked with Paul.

---

1. B. R. Gaventa, 'Theology and Ecclesiology in the Miletus Speech: Reflections on Content and Context', *NTS* 50 (2004), 37. Gaventa 44, rightly emphasizes that the Miletus speech shows how the future of the church rests with God, but overstates her case when she sets this against 'faithfulness to a model established by Paul'. Surely both elements are present in the speech.

2. Stott 1990, 315, draws attention to the parallels with Jesus' last journey to Jerusalem. Cf. S. Walton, *Leadership and Lifestyle: The Portrait of Paul in the Miletus Speech and 1 Thessalonians*, SNTSMS 108 (Cambridge: Cambridge University, 2000), 53-54, 99-117.

E. Encouraging the Churches in Macedonia, Greece, and Troas (20:1-12)

The first two verses of this section introduce the note of encouragement, with the verb *parakalein* being used twice. An inclusion is formed by the repetition of the same Greek word in v. 12, where the context suggests the rendering *comforted*. Between these summary statements, Luke gives us a brief outline of this ministry of encouragement to the churches in Macedonia and Achaia (vv. 2-5), and then more substantially in Troas (vv. 7-11). Paul's activity involved 'speaking many words of encouragement' (v. 2), as illustrated in v. 7 *(until midnight)* and v. 11 *(until daylight)*. It also involved suffering for the sake of the gospel (v. 3) and a mighty work of restoring Eutychus to life (vv. 9-10).

1-3 The first example of Paul's ministry of encouragement in this chapter comes immediately after a reference to the ending of the *uproar* in Ephesus. Although he had been in great danger and suffered considerable distress for the sake of Christ, Paul was so centred on the welfare of others that he *sent for the disciples,* in order to encourage them! The verb *parakalein* is used extensively in Acts, sometimes with the context suggesting more specifically the meaning 'exhort' (e.g., 14:22) and sometimes 'comfort' (e.g., 20:12).[3] The more general rendering *encouraging them* is appropriate here, though a second use of this term in v. 2 *(parakalesas)* is specifically explained in terms of 'much speaking' *(logō pollō).*[4] In Troas this involved an extensive discussion or reasoning with believers (vv. 7, 9, *dielegeto),*[5] and a reassuring 'homily' or exposition of Christian truth to them (v. 11, *homilēsas).*[6] Both dialogue and proclamation were involved in Paul's ministry of encouragement. Luke's emphasis on Paul's thoroughness in executing this task (vv. 2, 7, 12) 'prepares for the speech to the Ephesian elders',[7] which gives us a model of how he provided such encouragement. Paul set out from Ephesus to revisit *Macedonia* (cf. 19:21), probably in the summer of AD 55,[8] and *trav-*

3. Cf. 2:40; 8:31; 9:38; 11:23; 13:42; 14:22; 15:32; 16:9, 15, 39, 40; 18:27; 19:31; 20:1, 2, 12; 21:12; 24:4; 25:2; 27:33, 34; 28:14, 20. The cognate noun *paraklēsis* is used in 4:36; 9:31; 13:15; 15:31.

4. Barrett 1998, 946.

5. *dialegesthai* can mean 'discuss, reason, argue, address' in 17:2, 17; 18:4, 19; 19:8, 9; 20:7, 9; 24:12, 25. D. Fürst, *NIDNTT* 3:821, proposes that the word in Acts has become a technical term for Paul's teaching in the synagogue and 'approaches the meaning of give an address, preach'. However, it should be noted that some of the contexts in which it is used are more informal (e.g., 17:17; 20:7, 9; 24:25), suggesting more of an argument or discussion, with questions from the audience or some interaction.

6. *homiloun* means 'speak, converse' in Lk. 24:14, 15; Acts 24:26 (personal conversation), but in Acts 20:11 the context suggests more of an 'address' or 'homily' by Paul (there is no direct or indirect object). Barrett 1998, 955-56, thinks that the meaning 'converse' probably applies here and says, 'No doubt on such occasions Paul did the lion's share of the talking, but it was not an entirely one-sided engagement'.

7. Tannehill 1990, 246.

8. Bruce 1990, 422, suggests that this was probably so if Paul 'carried out his intention

elled through that area, speaking many words of encouragement to the people. No indication is given about the time spent in the province of Macedonia, though we are told that he stayed *three months* in *Greece* (*Hellas* was the popular name for 'Achaia'; cf. 18:12; 19:21). These three months were probably the winter months of AD 56-57, when he wrote his letter to the Romans from Corinth (cf. Rom. 16:1, 23). He had suffered much opposition from Jews in Macedonia on his first visit (17:5-9, 13-14), but none is recorded on this occasion. It was rather in Greece that *some Jews had plotted against him just as he was about to sail for Syria,* and so *he decided to go back through Macedonia.*[9] It is clear from vv. 16 and 22 that Paul's precise destination was Jerusalem; however, the more general reference to Syria is found in v. 3. On his visit to Macedonia and Achaia, Paul seems to have been successful in gaining the support of the Christians there for the collection he was about to take to Jerusalem (cf. Rom. 15:26-27; 2 Corinthians 8-9). Luke mentions this collection only in passing (24:17), though the identification of representatives from those churches in the following verses may be an indication that this activity was in progress at this time (cf. 1 Cor. 16:3-4).[10]

4-6 Luke names seven companions on this journey from Greece to Jerusalem. *Sopater son of Pyrrhus from Berea,* together with *Aristarchus and Secundus from Thessalonica,* emerged from Paul's second missionary journey.[11] *Gaius from Derbe* and *Timothy* from Lystra were the product of his first journey, though Timothy did not join Paul until the beginning of the second campaign (16:1-2).[12] *Tychicus and Trophimus from the province of Asia* were

---

of staying in Ephesus until Pentecost (1 Cor. 16:8); in that year Pentecost fell on May 25'. This visit to Macedonia was probably the time when he went 'as far as Illyricum' (Rom. 15:19). Cf. Witherington 1998, 77-86, 601. 2 Corinthians 1-7 suggests that Acts 20:2 would cover a considerable amount of time.

9. Barrett 1998, 946, likes the suggestion that the Jews in question may have been on a pilgrimage to Jerusalem for Passover and were travelling on the same ship that Paul was intending to use. This is feasible, but there is no way of being certain about the nature of the plot against Paul or its context. Cf. Bruce 1990, 423. Some Western MSS describe the plots of the Jews as the reason for wanting to travel to Syria and introduce the prompting of the Spirit to account for Paul's going by land route rather than by sea. Cf. Metzger, *Textual Commentary,* 420-21.

10. Johnson 1992, 357, suggests that the reason for Luke's silence about the collection at this point was the failure of the Jerusalem church to rally to Paul's aid when he was arrested, which was 'an embarrassment and a sign that Paul's intended gesture of reconciliation had failed'. Cf. note 15 below and Marshall 1980, 313.

11. Neither Sopater nor Pyrrhus appears elsewhere in the NT, but C. J. Hemer, *The Book of Acts in the Setting of Hellenistic History,* ed. C. Gempf, WUNT 49 (Tübingen: Mohr Siebeck, 1989; repr. Winona Lake: Eisenbrauns, 1990), 124, identifies the Sosipater of Rom. 16:21 with Sopater from Berea, arguing that this is the form of the name in inscriptions from Berea. Aristarchus is mentioned in 19:29; 27:2; Col. 4:10; Phlm. 24, but Secundus is not mentioned elsewhere.

12. Codex D and a few other MSS refer to Doberos, a town in Macedonia, rather than Derbe as the place from which Gaius came. This appears to be an attempt to reconcile this verse with 19:29, where Gaius and Aristarchus are identified as Paul's travelling companions from Macedonia. However, the MS evidence is strongly in favour of reading Derbe in

presumably encountered on his most recent visit to Ephesus.[13] Trophimus is mentioned again in 21:29 as an alleged cause of the disturbance at the temple in Jerusalem. These men represented 'the fruit of his labors in the various areas of his work'.[14] According to 1 Corinthians 16:3-4, Paul intended that local representatives of the churches he had founded should convey the money collected for the poor Christians in Jerusalem, perhaps in his company. It is reasonable to infer that those mentioned in Acts 20:4 (except perhaps Timothy) 'were such local representatives and not assistant missionaries'.[15] Luke mentions that *these men went on ahead*, and then suddenly intrudes himself into the narrative again, noting that they *waited for us at Troas*. This 'we' style first appeared in 16:10, when Paul and his team originally went to Troas. Luke apparently joined them there and went at least as far as Philippi with them (the first person plural ceased at 16:17). There is something to be said for the view that Luke remained in Philippi until this return visit by Paul.[16] Luke's more personal way of telling the story resumes in 20:5-6 and continues until the team arrives in Jerusalem (21:18), though it is absent from the scene in Miletus (20:16-38), where the focus is entirely on Paul and his encounter with the Ephesian elders. A first-person narrator is 'a focalizing channel through whom the story is experienced',[17] though it is possible to exaggerate the importance of this literary device. The journey is more vivid because of Luke's involvement, encouraging us to take particular notice of the details he has recorded. For example, the journey to Jerusalem is dated in relation to Jewish festivals (vv. 6, 16), and once more there is great interest in describing a sea voyage and its outcome.[18] They left Philippi *after the Feast of Unleavened Bread* (v. 6),

---

20:4, which means that two different people with the same name are in view. Cf. Metzger, *Textual Commentary*, 421-22; Barrett 1998, 948.

13. Codex D, with little support from other MSS, has Timothy travelling with Paul only as far as Asia and oddly describes the last two companions as 'the Ephesians Eutychus and Trophimus'. Cf. Metzger, *Textual Commentary*, 420. Trophimus is mentioned in 2 Tim. 4:20 and Tychicus in Eph. 6:21; Col. 4:7; 2 Tim. 4:12; Tit. 3:12 as companions of Paul.

14. Tannehill 1990, 246. Stott 1990, 318, observes that these associates bear witness to the growth, unity, and 'catholicity' of the church in that region, the fruitfulness of Paul's missionary expeditions, and the mission-mindedness of the young Christian communities.

15. Barrett 1998, 947. Barrett, 1001, 1107-8, considers possible reasons why Luke did not mention the collection at this point in his narrative (though cf. 24:17). Marshall 1980, 324, suggests that Luke, who identifies his own involvement in vv. 5-6, was the representative of the church in Philippi who took the collection to Jerusalem.

16. Cf. Barrett 1998, 944-45. The 'we' passages are discussed on pp. 2-3, 17, 456, and 681.

17. Tannehill 1990, 247. Witherington 1998, 604-5, concludes that the most plausible explanation for the 'we' passages is that the author (Luke) was a companion of Paul at those particular points in the narrative. He argues this way on the basis that it was the practice of Greek historians to place themselves in the story only where and when they were actually present, and that the 'we' passages in Acts do not generally involve crucial junctures in the narrative. In other words, these passages do not appear at places where pure redaction or invention might be expected.

18. Longenecker 1981, 508, suggests that 20:5-28:31 contains the kind of details found

presumably sailing from Neapolis (cf. 16:11). The journey in the opposite direction took only two days (16:11), but the journey in an easterly direction took *five days*, presumably because of strong headwinds. *Troas*, where Luke and Paul met up with the others and stayed *seven days*, was clearly an important place in Luke's own experience (16:6-10). It would once again be the context for experiencing the powerful presence of God.

7 Some have suggested that the meeting of the Christians in Troas *on the first day of the week* in order to *break bread (klasai arton)* is a pointer to a formal Sunday gathering for the purpose of the Lord's Supper (cf. 1 Cor. 11:17-34).[19] The evening of *the first day of the week* could be Saturday night, if the Jewish method of reckoning the beginning of the week was being followed. However, since Luke seems to follow the Roman method of reckoning, it must have been Sunday night.[20] This is the first time that 'the breaking of bread' has been mentioned since Acts 2:42, where the context showed that the term refers to the initiating of an ordinary meal (cf. 2:46 note). That appears to be the meaning here also (cf. 27:35-36). Paul's discussion with them occupied their attention until after midnight and again after the meal, suggesting that it was a very unstructured and informal meeting. When Luke mentions in v. 11 that Paul finally broke bread (perhaps on behalf of everyone present), he adds that he *ate (geusamenos;* cf. Lk. 14:24; Acts 10:10; 23:14), meaning that he 'joined his fellow Christians in eating a meal'.[21] Since Christian meetings were largely held in the context of private homes, it is natural that they expressed their fellowship in terms of eating together. Of course it was in such contexts that some formal pattern of celebrating a supper in honour of the Lord emerged. Such meals were doubtless 'full of religious content because of the recollection of the table fellowship which Jesus had with his followers during his earthly ministry'.[22] The

in a travel journal. Witherington 1998, 605, note 189, draws attention to the concern of Greek historians to include in their works appropriate geographical and ethnographical material.

19. Cf. Marshall 1980, 325; W. Foerster, *TDNT* 3:1096. Spencer 1997, 192, points to the Passover reference in 20:6 ('the Feast of Unleavened Bread') and suggests that this, together with the double reference to the breaking of bread (vv. 7, 11), rather evokes a strong memory of Jesus' farewell meal with his disciples in a large upper room (Lk. 22:7-23). 'This meal became the occasion of Jesus' final instructions to his followers before his death, exhorting them to "remember" him in his absence (22:19) and alerting them to trials and temptations they will soon face (22:22-23, 31-8).'

20. Witherington 1998, 606, argues that 'Luke seems to follow the Jewish religious calendar but the Roman means of reckoning time (cf. Lk. 24:1)'. 1 Cor. 16:2 does not refer to a Christian meeting but to individuals setting aside money for Paul's collection on the first day of every week. Rev. 1:10 refers to the Lord's Day as an occasion when John was in the Spirit and heard God speaking to him, but it does not say that this was in the context of a Christian gathering. For meetings on the Lord's Day, see Ignatius, *Magn.* 9:1; *Did.* 14:1; *Barn.* 15:9.

21. Barrett 1998, 955. In view of Luke's use of the verb *geuesthai* in other contexts, Barrett rightly concludes that it would be 'mistaken to infer that the inference was to a sacramental meal, in which a mere fragment of bread was tasted'.

22. J. Behm, *TDNT* 3:730. He argues that Acts 2:42, 46 'has nothing to do with the li-

reality of Christian fellowship was expressed from the earliest times, as Jesus intended it, in the ordinary activity of eating together. These meals were given a special character by the fact that they were associated with teaching, and prayer or praise. So in this case, Paul encouraged the church as he *spoke to the people* (*dielegeto*, 'discussed, reasoned, argued with') *and, because he intended to leave the next day, kept on talking* (*pareteinen te ton logon*, 'prolonged his speech') *until midnight* (cf. 28:23, 'from morning until evening').

8-9   Mention of Paul's lengthy time of interaction with the believers in Troas is coupled with the eyewitness observation that *there were many lamps in the upstairs room where we were meeting*. This prepares for the account that follows. The atmosphere with oil lamps burning was sleep-inducing, with disastrous consequences for Eutychus! This young man (*neanias*, but *pais* in v. 12 may suggest someone younger), whose name means 'Fortunate',[23] was dangerously *seated in a window*, and he was *sinking into a deep sleep as Paul talked on and on* (*dialegomenou epi pleion*, 'was discussing at length'). Members of the Qumran community could be excluded from meetings for thirty days for falling asleep in this way (1QS 7:10), but Luke is not presenting this as a cautionary tale to his readers. There is a serious side to the narrative, but also a 'fortunate' outcome, and a humorous aspect to the way Luke tells the story. The accident provided the occasion for a miracle by Paul and 'serves no other purpose'.[24] *When he was sound asleep, he fell to the ground from the third storey* (in British and American usage 'from the second floor') *and was picked up dead*. Some have argued that the expression *picked up dead* (*ērthē nekros*) should be taken as an example of 'free indirect discourse', not directly attributed to a character yet actually representing 'the limited perspective of a character'.[25] Those who rushed down to find Eutychus took him to be dead, but Paul's prophetic role in the situation was to detect life where others saw only death (cf. v. 10, *'Don't be alarmed', he said. 'He's alive!'*).[26] However, the most

---

turgical celebration of the Lord's Supper' (p. 731), but says that the meal in 20:11 'within the context of the Pauline mission' must be the cultic meal described by Paul as 'the Lord's Supper' in 1 Cor. 11:20. However, it is not likely that Luke would use the same expression in two different ways like this. The celebration of the Lord's Supper, as described by Paul, clearly developed out of these household meals together. Cf. D. G. Peterson, *Engaging with God: A Biblical Theology of Worship* (Leicester: Apollos; Grand Rapids: Eerdmans, 1992), 155-57, 215-18.

23. Hemer, *Book of Acts*, 1990, 237. Witherington 1998, 607, suggests the more colloquial 'Lucky'.

24. Barrett 1998, 954. Barrett rightly opposes all attempts to allegorise or spiritualise the story.

25. Tannehill 1990, 248. However, Barrett 1998, 954, observes that Luke was capable of expressing the thought that observers mistakenly supposed someone to be dead (14:19), and 'probably means that Eutychus was truly dead'. Bruce 1990, 426, takes the expression to mean 'clinically' dead.

26. Tannehill 1990, 249, rather fancifully follows Trémel in suggesting that 'the role of Paul, who does not give up when others despair over the one who has fallen but discovers

natural way to read the text is to presume that Eutychus died and was brought back to life.

10-12 Like the prophets Elijah and Elisha in similar situations, *Paul went down, threw himself on the young man and put his arms around him* (cf. 1 Ki. 17:21-23; 2 Ki. 4:32-34). Then he said, *'Don't be alarmed. He's alive!'* In view of the statement in v. 9 that he was *picked up dead*, the expression *He's alive! (hē psychē autou en autō estin)* must mean, 'his life is now, in virtue of my action, within him'.[27] Similarities between this narrative and the raising of Tabitha in 9:36-42 suggest parallel ministries, whereby 'both Peter and Paul enable the Christian community to discover life in the face of death'.[28] This life is clearly the gift of God, though Peter and Paul are God's instruments in bringing it about. Like the healing in 3:1-16, this miracle points to the new life available through the resurrection of Jesus, in all its dimensions and aspects. *Then he went upstairs again and broke bread and ate* (cf. v. 7 note). After satisying his hunger in the company of his friends, Paul continued *talking (homilēsas;* cf. 20:1-3 note) *until daylight*. He had already spoken to them for a long time (v. 7), but presumably the raising of Eutychus brought many questions and much excitement, motivating Paul to keep talking until dawn. *The people took the young man [home] alive (ēgagon* in this context could mean 'took upstairs' rather than 'took home') *and were greatly comforted (pareklēthēsan ou metriōs,* lit. 'were not a little encouraged').[29] This comfort came from Paul's ministry as a whole to them, which involved his teaching of them in the context of a farewell meal and his raising of Eutychus to life.

F. Saying Farewell to the Ephesian Elders (20:13-38)

This passage begins with a travel narrative, bringing Paul and his companions from Troas to Miletus (vv. 13-17). Paul summons the Ephesian elders to meet him there because he is anxious to avoid spending time in Asia and wants to reach Jerusalem by the Day of Pentecost. His speech to the elders is the only example of a pastoral address to Christians in Acts (though the report of a similar ministry of encouragement is found in 14:21-23). It is the first of several visitation and farewell scenes, in which the focus is on what

---

that there is still life in him, may contribute to the picture of Paul as a dedicated pastor and a model for others, as in 20:31'.

27. Barrett 1998, 955.

28. Tannehill 1990, 247. Tannehill highlights the differences in the accounts, but goes on to argue that Peter and Paul fit a common scriptural type: 'through both, the prophetic power of Elijah and Elisha continues to be available to the church' (p. 248). Peter and Paul both shared to some extent in Jesus' prophetic task, which included raising the dead (Lk. 7:16-17, 22).

29. This is another example of litotes, as in 12:18; 19:11; 21:39; 28:2. Codex D has Paul bring the young man alive as they were saying their farewell. Once again, this is a reading without wider support. Cf. Metzger, *Textual Commentary,* 423.

will happen to Paul when he goes to Jerusalem (20:22-24; 21:4-6; 21:10-14). The Miletus speech gives Paul the opportunity to review his past ministry, to alert the elders to the danger of false teaching, unfaithfulness, and division in the ongoing life of the church, and to commit them to the Lord and to 'the word of his grace'. In various ways, Paul commends to them his own pattern of leadership.[30] The image of the church as the people purchased to belong to God through the shedding of Christ's blood is striking. Christians are precious to God and therefore must persevere as 'the sanctified', faithful to the end. The encouragement of v. 32 is specifically that 'the message of his grace' will be sufficient to sustain leaders in their task of enabling Christ's flock to enter the inheritance secured for them by Christ's sacrifice. Like Jesus' words at the Last Supper (Lk. 22:14-38), this speech offers a significant challenge about the future, linked to a certain understanding of the atoning work of Christ. Paul's legacy to the church was 'not only the manner of his ministry — his devotion to his calling, his acceptance of suffering, his willingness to work with his hands — but also the gospel that he preached and the vision of God's purpose that it contained'.[31] Although there are various 'Lukanisms' present in this speech, the parallels with Paul's letters (especially 1 Thessalonians) are considerable, so that 'the denial of a Pauline basis for this address is unwarranted'.[32] Indeed, Walton concludes that 'Luke's Paul, when he speaks to Christians as a pastor, sounds like Paul writing as a pastor. Further, when Paul himself writes about pastoral ministry in 1 Thessalonians he sounds similar to Luke's portrayal of him teaching pastors about pastoral ministry.'[33]

Scholars have proposed different ways of understanding the structure of the speech. Tannehill argues that it moves forward from an initial statement about Paul's past ministry (vv. 18-21), to announcements about a new situation that is about to arise, with warnings and exhortations (vv. 22-35). 'References to Paul's past ministry mingle with references to the new situation in vv. 22-35, but these past references support statements and ex-

30. Spencer 1997, 192, describes the two functions of this speech as review and preview. Barrett 1977, 107-21, shows how the address contains elements that would be expected in the type of farewell discourse familiar at the time. Gaventa, 'Theology and Ecclesiology', 44-52, rightly argues that Paul is not portrayed as a 'hero' to be followed, but downplays too much the extent to which Paul's ministry is presented as a model for others to follow.

31. Tannehill 1990, 255. This gospel is the message of God's grace (vv. 24, 32), proclaimed in the context of kingdom theology (v. 25), which is otherwise designated as 'the whole will of God' (v. 27) because it involves the fulfillment of the plan of God revealed in all the Scriptures. This message calls for Jews and Greeks to 'turn to God in repentance and have faith in our Lord Jesus Christ'.

32. Marshall 1980, 330. Cf. Johnson 1992, 367; Witherington 1998, 610-11 (where parallels between the speech and Paul's letters are listed); Barrett 1998, 964.

33. Walton, Leadership, 213. Walton, 1-32, reviews different approaches that have been taken to this speech, especially with regard to its relationship with the Pauline corpus. He goes on to make an extended comparison between the speech and 1 Thessalonians, and concludes that 'Luke knows Pauline tradition independently of the epistles' (p. 212).

hortations that bear on the present and future.'[34] Paul's past ministry is thus a resource and inspiration for the continuing work of the elders. Walton suggests four aspects of the passage that need to be taken into account: the Greek sentence structure, the repetitions, the time references, and the shift in the subject of the content from Paul to the elders. This leads him to an outline which observes Tannehill's first division, but effectively subdivides his second as follows: vv. 18-21, retrospect; vv. 22-24, the future of Paul in Jerusalem; vv. 25-27, prospect and retrospect; vv. 28-31, a charge to the elders; vv. 32-35, conclusion.[35] Tannehill's broad approach is combined with Walton's insights in the exposition below.

Bruce observed that 'the speech is hortatory in character, but, like Paul's other speeches in the remaining part of Acts, it has a clear apologetic note. Paul's opponents have evidently been attacking him in his absence; he defends his teaching and general behavior by appealing to the Ephesians' knowledge of him.'[36] Similarities with farewell addresses in Jewish and Greco-Roman literature have often been noted, though Walton's caveats to this description of the literary genre need to be taken seriously.[37] There is great variation among farewell speeches in the literature, and so the particular characteristics and emphases of the Miletus speech need to be highlighted.

1. Gathering (20:13-17)

13-15 The team mentioned in v. 4 — but now including Luke — left Troas and *went on ahead to the ship and sailed for Assos.* 'To get to Assos from Troas, the ship had to round Cape Lectum (Bababurun), thus requiring longer time than the 20-mile land journey, especially since the prevailing wind was the stormy northeaster.'[38] It was there that they planned *to take Paul aboard.* For some unspecified reason (and the speculations of the commentators at this point are largely unhelpful), *he had made this arrangement because he was going there on foot.*[39] When they met him at Assos, they *took him*

---

34. Tannehill 1990, 252-53. Tannehill 253-54, goes on to explore the possibility that a chiastic pattern can be discerned in the whole message.

35. Walton, *Leadership*, 28-32, 66-75.

36. Bruce 1990, 430. Witherington 1998, 613, argues that 'the partial apologetic tone of the speech gives it a forensic cast, even though the overall function or aim of the speech is deliberative'. Deliberative rhetoric was for advice and consent — what might be 'useful and imitable' for a church. So the speech is not so much a personal defence of Paul's ministry as 'advice about the apologetics the elders will need to undertake'.

37. Cf. Walton, *Leadership*, 55-66; Gaventa, 'Theology and Ecclesiology', 44-52.

38. Bruce 1990, 427. Instead of 'Assos' in vv. 13-14, a range of MSS have 'Thasos'. This is an impossible reading in the context, since Thasos is an island east of Amphipolis. Metzger, *Textual Commentary*, 423, writes, 'how it arose in such diverse witnesses is a puzzle'.

39. Hemer, *Book of Acts*, 169, 216, argues for a precise dating of this journey between

aboard and went on to Mitylene, some 44 miles (71 km.) further south. *Mitylene* was the largest town on the island of Lesbos and was an important centre of Greek culture and commerce. After an overnight stay, they *set sail from there and arrived off Chios.* The Greek expression *antikrys Chiou* 'probably means that they sailed between the island of Chios and the mainland ("right through")'.[40] *The day after that,* they crossed over to *Samos,* which was another of the Ionian islands, separated from the mainland by a channel which was just over a mile wide. It was between Chios and Samos that the ship sailed past Ephesus, *and on the following day* they came to *Miletus,* which was on the south coast of the Latmian Gulf.[41]

16 Paul's choice *to sail past Ephesus* was simply *to avoid spending time in the province of Asia.* The pluperfect tense *(kekrikei, had decided)* suggests 'a fixed decision rather than a spur-of-the-moment impulse'.[42] Of course, he was on the edge of the province at *Miletus,* but he did not want to be delayed by involvement with the whole church in Ephesus or ministry in other places. This is extraordinary when we think of Paul's much illustrated commitment to evangelism and the nurture of believers. Luke's explanation for Paul's hurry is his desire *to reach Jerusalem, if possible, by the day of Pentecost.*[43] Paul's loyalty to Jewish tradition and practice may be highlighted by this explanation. However, knowing from Paul's letters his concern to deliver the collection from the Gentile churches, we may surmise that he thought it particularly appropriate to do this on such a significant festive occasion. Pentecost was the time when the Spirit first marked out those who believed in Jesus from other Jews. Although Luke mentions the positive communal implications of their new life in Christ (2:42-47; 4:32-37), there must have been social and economic costs for many who became separated from family and friends to join the church. Famine made the situation worse from time to time (11:27-30). At this Pentecost, Paul hoped to shower Christians in Jerusalem with practical expressions of love and gratitude from Gentile believers for the gospel they had received from the Jews (Rom. 15:25-27).

Passover and Pentecost in AD 57. However, Barrett 1998, 952, offers a number of criticisms of his approach.

40. Barrett 1998, 958. Barrett notes that the town Chios was situated on the east coast of the island, 'and it may be the town rather than the island that is in mind'.

41. Bruce 1990, 428, gives a brief history of Miletus and its significance. There is a longer reading in Western and Byzantine MSS, translated by KJV ('and tarried at Trogyllium' [NKJV 'stayed at Trogyllium']). Trogyllium lay on the mainland, opposite Samos. Although it is entirely possible that this was a port of call on the journey to Miletus, the best and most ancient MSS do not include this detail. Cf. Metzger, *Textual Commentary,* 423-24.

42. Johnson 1992, 356. Cf. B. Rapske, 'Acts, Travel, and Shipwreck', in D. W. J. Gill and C. Gempf (eds.), *The Book of Acts in Its First-Century Setting,* Vol. 2: *Graeco-Roman Setting* (Grand Rapids: Eerdmans; Carlisle: Paternoster, 1994), 15-17, on Paul's reason for spending time in Miletus rather than in Ephesus.

43. Spencer 1997, 190, reads too much into the significance of these references for the narrative in Acts 20–21. There is no need for Barrett 1998, 945, to be sceptical about Paul's desire to reach Jerusalem by Pentecost simply because we are not given an explicit reason.

17 *Miletus* was an ancient, prosperous, coastal town, about 30 miles (48 km.) from Ephesus. TNIV has obscured the forcefulness of the Greek, which indicates that from Miletus Paul 'sent to Ephesus and summoned' *(pempsas eis Epheson metekalesato)* the elders of the church. Such language highlights the solemnity of the occasion. The *elders (presbyteroi)* are called *episkopoi* in v. 28 ('overseers' or 'bishops'; cf. Phil. 1:1; 1 Tim. 3:1), suggesting that this interchange of terminology was familiar to Luke's readers and needed no explanation (cf. Tit. 1:5-9; 1 Tim. 3:1-7; 5:17-19). Perhaps 'elders' described Christian leaders from a sociological point of view and 'overseers' (bishops) described the same people from a functional or theological point of view.[44] It is important to notice that there was a team of presbyter-bishops who shared the responsibility of pastoral leadership in this church (cf. 14:23; Tit. 1:5). As well as avoiding delay in Ephesus, Paul may have asked the elders to come to Miletus because he was carrying a considerable sum of money, 'the product of his collection for the saints in Jerusalem'.[45] Perhaps he felt safer in Miletus than in the great city of Ephesus. Perhaps his time was simply limited by the fact that the ship was due to sail again on a certain date.

2. Recalling the Past (20:18-21)

18-19 The basis for the rest of the speech is given in vv. 18-21, as Paul recalls the extent and manner of his ministry at Ephesus. What the future demanded of both Paul and the elders is then set forth in vv. 22-35, where elements from this first section are repeated and related to the new situation that will arise with his departure.[46] When the elders arrived at Miletus, Paul first reminded them of how he lived the whole time he was with them, *'from the first day'* he came into the province of Asia. Three times in this speech he appeals to their knowledge and remembrance of the past, using different verbs in Greek (vv. 18, 31, 34).[47] His opening words here include an emphatic pronoun *(hymeis,* 'you yourselves'), suggesting that the elders especially knew what he was talking about. A closeness of relation-

---

44. Cf. Stott 1990, 323-24; L. Coenen, *NIDNTT* 1:188-201; Barrett 1998, 975. Elders appear to have been those with some maturity and seniority in the community (cf. 1 Pet. 5:1, 5). In 1 Pet. 2:25 *episkopos* is used of Christ, in parallel with *poimēn* ('shepherd', 'pastor'). As Chief Shepherd, he entrusts the care of his flock to those whom he chooses. J. A. Fitzmyer, *Essays on the Semitic Background of the New Testament* (London: Chapman, 1971), 293-94, argues that the word *episkopos* was picked up by Christians from secular institutions but that they were encouraged to use it by associations which came mainly through the verb in biblical Greek.

45. Barrett 1998, 960. However, Barrett is unnecessarily sceptical about whether the Ephesian elders were actually addressed at Miletus in the way that Luke records.

46. Following Tannehill 1990, 254.

47. This is also the pattern in some of Paul's letters (e.g., 1 Thes. 2:1-2, 5, 10-11; 3:3-4; 4:2; 2 Thes. 2:5; 3:7; Gal. 3:2-5; 4:13).

ship and a shared experience of leadership is suggested by this address to them. The *'whole time'* Paul was with them is later specified as being three years (v. 31 note). The manner of his ministry, rather than the content of his teaching, is then highlighted: *'I served the Lord with great humility and with tears and in the midst of severe testing by the plots of the Jews'* (cf. Rom. 1:1; 12:11, 16; 16:18; 1 Cor. 7:22; 2 Cor. 2:4; Gal. 1:10; 1 Thes. 2:14-15, for echoes of such language in the letters of Paul). Although this speech specifically focuses on Paul's Ephesian ministry, it recalls also certain features of his ministry in other locations, functioning as a summary-conclusion to Acts 13–19. So, for example, *severe testing by the plots of the Jews* was a feature of his experience in 13:50; 14:2-7, 19; 17:5-9, 13; 18:6, 12-17; 19:9; 20:3. In such contexts, he doubtless also *served the Lord (douleuōn tō kyriō) with great humility and with tears.*[48] This pattern of humble service reflected something of the ministry of Jesus himself (cf. Lk. 22:26-27, *ho diakonōn,* 'he who serves'). Paul's 'service' involved the ministry of the gospel (v. 24, *diakonia . . . diamartyrasthai to euangelion*) and working to supply his own practical needs and those of his companions (v. 34, *hypēretēsan* is another verb which could be rendered 'served').

20-21 Here and again in v. 27, Paul insists that he never *'hesitated'* *(hypesteilamēn)* to teach them *'anything that would be helpful'* (*tōn sympheron-tōn,* 'things that were profitable'; cf. 1 Cor. 6:12; 10:23; 12:7).[49] The verb translated *hesitated* could have the sense of 'shrink back' in fear (cf. Heb. 10:38), but the context rather suggests no withholding of the truth (cf. Plato, *Apol.* 24A).[50] Use of the same verb twice in this speech suggests that some of the elders may have faced the temptation to water down the message. Paul's refusal to dilute the truth is highlighted in several of his letters (e.g., 2 Cor. 2:17; 4:2-5; Gal. 4:16). The comprehensive nature of Paul's gospel ministry is then outlined by the use of several word-pairs. His first priority was 'to proclaim and teach' (*anangeilai kai didaxai;* TNIV *'preach'*) anything that would benefit the Ephesians. This was done *'publicly'* — in the synagogue and then in the lecture hall of Tyrannus (19:8-9) — *'and from house to house'* (not specified in Acts 19, though see 18:7-8). His testimony (*dia martyromenos,* as in 2:40; 8:25; 10:42; 20:23, 24; 23:11; 28:23) was addressed *to both Jews and Greeks,* and involved the summons to *'turn to God in repentance and have faith in our Lord Jesus'.*[51] As in 26:20, his message is summarized in

48. Evidence for this in Paul's letters can be found in 1 Cor. 2:3; 2 Cor. 1:8; 2:4; Rom. 9:2; Phil. 3:18.

49. Witherington 1998, 614, argues that the expression *tōn sympherontōn* is a clear indication that Paul's speech is an example of deliberative rhetoric, designed to be useful or helpful to the audience.

50. Cf. Barrett 1998, 968. Perhaps this was designed to answer in advance the charge of not explaining sufficiently the trials and difficulties of Christian discipleship.

51. Spencer 1997, 193, rightly observes from the parallel structure of vv. 20-21 and v. 27 that the purpose of God is the salvific plan of leading Jews and Gentiles to experience repentance towards God and faith in our Lord Jesus. Marshall 1980, 331, notes that the chi-

terms of its final appeal rather than in terms of its historical or theological content. A call for 'repentance towards God' *(tēn eis theon metanoian)* — a turning away from every form of rebellion in order to serve the living and true God on his own terms — was made to Jews and Gentiles alike (2:38; 3:19; 14:15; 17:30-31). *Faith in our Lord Jesus* was the positive aspect of such repentance, since Jesus had to be confessed as the only saviour from God's impending judgment (4:11-12; 10:42-43; 13:38-41; 15:11).[52] Paul's preaching sometimes focussed on the specific need to turn away from idolatry (14:15; 17:30-31), and at other times on the need for faith in our Lord Jesus (13:38-41; 16:31; 17:2-3). But these are really two sides of the same coin. Paul makes it clear in his letters that repentance involves turning to Christ (cf. 2 Cor. 3:14-16 [for Jews]; 1 Thes. 1:9-10 [for Gentiles]), and continual turning away from everything that displeases God (cf. Rom. 2:4; 2 Cor. 7:9-10; 12:21; 2 Tim. 2:25-26). In an age when many are searching for different ways to attract people to church and make an impact on their society for Christ, it is salutary to recall Paul's formula, both for evangelism and the nurture of believers (cf. Col. 1:28-9). His preaching and teaching consistently issued in a call for repentance and faith, in response to God's gracious, saving initiative in Jesus Christ (cf. vv. 24, 28, 31, 32).[53] Genuine faith demands repentance, and sincere repentance will continue to flow from saving faith.

3. Facing the Future (20:22-35)

a. Paul's Future in Jerusalem (20:22-24)

22-23 In 19:21 we were told of Paul's decision 'in the Spirit' *(en tō pneumati)* to go to Jerusalem and then to Rome. With a dramatic turn in his address to the Ephesian elders *(kai nyn idou,* 'and now behold'; cf. vv. 25, 32 *[kai ta nyn]),* Paul expresses the same divine constraint in a more emphatic way *('And now, compelled by the Spirit, I am going to Jerusalem').* The Greek perfect passive participle with a dative of agency *(dedemenos tō pneumati)* suggests that the Holy Spirit was the source of the compulsion ('a captive to the Spirit', NRSV; 'constrained by the Spirit', ESV). Acknowledging some uncertainty about the outcome *('not knowing what will happen to me there'),* he nevertheless reveals for the first time a conviction about imprisonment and hardship awaiting him in Jerusalem *('I only know that in every*

---

asmus often suggested in v. 21 (Paul proclaimed to Jews the need for faith and to Greeks the need for repentance) is really an oversimplification of the evidence presented in Acts and in the Pauline letters.

52. Some reliable MSS have 'faith in our Lord Jesus Christ'. The shorter reading is more likely to have been the original, since there is no reason why 'Christ' should be omitted and scribes tended to expand the names of the Lord. Codex D, supported by only one Old Latin text, has 'through our Lord Jesus Christ'. Cf. Barrett 1998, 969.

53. Cf. THE THEOLOGY OF ACTS: V. THE GOSPEL (pp. 70-75).

city the Holy Spirit warns me that prison and hardships are facing me').[54] Such warnings by *the Holy Spirit* are mentioned again in 21:4 (Tyre) and 21:10-14 (Caesarea), where the last reference shows that the Spirit addressed him through a Christian prophet. The Holy Spirit was both the driving force to undertake this journey and the source of revelation about its dangerous outcome (cf. Rom. 15:31).

24 Paul's willingness to lose his life for the sake of his ministry suggests a close link with the teaching and example of Jesus (cf. 21:13). Jesus' challenge in this regard (e.g., Lk. 9:24; 14:26-27; 17:33) is echoed by Paul's claim, *'I consider my life worth nothing to me'*.[55] A parallel with Jesus' own determination to fulfill his God-given role (Lk. 13:32-33) is then indicated by the words, *'my only aim is to finish the race and complete the task (hōs teleiōsai ton dromon mou kai tēn diakonian,* 'so that I may complete my course and the ministry')[56] *the Lord Jesus has given me'.* Two images are joined here: there is a race to be run and a service or ministry to be accomplished. Paul did not in fact die in Jerusalem, since it was God's plan for him to reach Rome, but he had much to endure on the way. 'His sufferings extend over a long period of imprisonment and stretch from the Jewish to the Gentile capital. Paul follows his master in suffering, but there is a new twist that corresponds to the new dimensions of Paul's universal mission.'[57] The task or ministry *(diakonia)* given to Paul is specifically defined as *'testifying to the gospel of God's grace'* (cf. 14:3; 20:32). Surprisingly, the word *gospel (euangelion)* is used only here and on one other occasion in Acts (15:7), though the verb to evangelise *(euangelizomiai)* is extensively employed. Peter speaks about the gospel in a context which also shows that it is a message about 'the grace of our Lord Jesus Christ', providing salvation for Jews and Gentiles on exactly the same basis (15:11). Luke makes the point that both Peter and Paul shared the same *gospel of God's grace.* The grace of God is regularly the subject of the gospel in Paul's letters (e.g., Rom. 3:24; 5:15-17;

54. M. L. Skinner, *Locating Paul: Places of Custody as Narrative Settings in Acts 21–28,* SBLAB 13 (Atlanta: SBL, 2003), 100, insists that, in view of the use of *thlipsis* in Acts 7:10, 11; 11:19, the word here translated 'hardships' refers to physical suffering. Acts 21–28 shows what is meant by 'prison and hardships' for Paul.

55. Codex D modifies the awkward, yet idiomatic Greek of the largely Alexandrian text *(all' oudenos logou poioumai tēn psychēn timian emautō)* to read, 'But I make no reckoning of anything for myself, nor do I account my life as precious [to me]' *(all' oudenos logon echō moi oude poioumai tēn psychēn mou timian emautou).* The Received Text combines elements of this variant with the Alexandrian *(all' oudenos logon poioumai oude echō tēn psychēn mou timian emautō),* so that KJV has, 'But none of these things move me, neither count I my life dear unto myself'. Cf. Metzger, *Textual Commentary,* 424-25; Barrett 1998, 971.

56. Barrett 1998, 971-72, discusses the textual variants and contends that either *hōs* with the infinitive *teleiōsai* or with the subjunctive *teleiōsō* can be read as final clauses, giving the sense, 'My purpose in discounting the value of my life is that I may . . .'. In Lk. 13:32 Jesus says, 'on the third day I will reach my goal *(teleioumai)'*, and the following verse makes it clear that this means death in Jerusalem. In 2 Tim. 4:7 the expression *ton dromon teteleka* ('I have finished the race') is found.

57. Tannehill 1990, 259.

2 Cor. 6:1; Eph. 1:7-8; 2:7-8; Col. 1:6). Elsewhere in Acts the gospel is mostly called 'the word'.

b. *Paul's Confidence in Saying Farewell (20:25-27)*

25-27 With a second 'and now behold' (*kai nyn idou*; cf. v. 22), Paul clarifies the significance of what he has just said. This would be a final farewell, but not because he believed that his death was imminent. Whatever the danger awaiting him in Jerusalem, Paul planned to use Rome as a base for evangelising the western Mediterranean region (cf. 19:21; Rom. 1:15; 15:23-24, 28-29). In view of his travel plans, he declares, '*I know that none of you among whom I have gone about preaching the kingdom will ever see me again*'. In the flow of the argument, *preaching the kingdom* appears to be synonymous with testifying to the gospel of God's grace (v. 24).[58] As he leaves the province of Asia, he claims to have fulfilled his God-given responsibility among them, echoing again the perspective of Ezekiel 33:4-5 (as in 18:6). Paul speaks emphatically (*martyromai, 'I declare'*), to emphasize the truth of his claim (cf. 26:22; Gal. 5:3; Eph. 4:17; 1 Thes. 2:12).[59] Like the faithful watchman in Ezekiel's prophecy, he declares himself to be '*innocent* (*katharos*; cf. 18:6) *of the blood of everyone*'. This was so because he had not held back or obscured the revelation of God to his people: '*For I have not hesitated* (*hypesteilamēn*, as in v. 20) *to proclaim to you the whole will of God*' (*pasan tēn boulēn tou theou*).[60] This last expression, which can also be rendered 'the whole purpose of God' (NRSV) or 'the whole counsel of God' (KJV, ESV), recognises the 'world-embracing dimensions' of the gospel.[61] However, its use in parallel with 'the kingdom' (v. 25) suggests that it refers more precisely to the whole plan of God for humanity and the created order revealed in the Scriptures and fulfilled in Jesus Christ (cf. Lk. 24:25-27, 44-49). Such an understanding of the term is consistent with the scriptural framework and foundation of Paul's gospel presentation in 13:16-41, which

58. Mention of 'the kingdom' in this context suggests continuity with the teaching of Jesus (cf. Lk. 4:43; Acts 1:3, 6) and the preaching of other disciples such as Philip (8:12). However, in Acts this terminology is mostly used of Paul's preaching (14:22; 19:8; 20:25; 28:23, 31). It is a way of alluding to the fulfillment of God's kingdom purposes in the person and work of Jesus Christ, which is the biblical-theological framework within which the gospel was preached. The Western text adds 'of Jesus' after 'the kingdom', and the Received Text adds 'of God' (so KJV, NKJV). However, the shorter reading is to be preferred, and it is well attested. Cf. Metzger, *Textual Commentary*, 425.

59. The compound form *diamartyresthai* is used in Acts 2:40; 8:25; 10:42; 18:5; 20:21, 23, 24; 23:11; 28:23, with no apparent difference in meaning. The expression translated *today* (*en tē sēmeron hēmeras*) is also emphatic (in effect, 'this very day').

60. *boulē* is used in Lk. 7:30; 23:51; Acts 2:23; 4:28; 5:38; 13:36; 20:27; 27:12, 42, and only in 1 Cor. 4:5; Eph. 1:11; and Heb. 6:17 elsewhere in the NT.

61. Tannehill 1990, 257. Barrett 1998, 973, says, 'it must refer to the saving purpose of God for the human race'. Tannehill notes that 'if he had not announced the *whole* purpose of God, he would bear guilty responsibility for the death of some, for he would be presenting a gospel that excluded some'.

parallels the outlines of Peter's preaching in many respects (2:15-39; 3:13-26). Paul gave them a comprehensive view of the will of God, which included the promise of salvation for people of every race, together with an appeal for individuals to repent and believe the gospel promises. The breadth and depth of Paul's teaching about *the whole will of God* can be discerned from an examination of his letter to the Romans, which he had just written and sent ahead of him at this time.

c. The Elders and the Future of the Ephesian Church (20:28-31)

28 This verse is described by Barrett as both the practical and the theological centre of the speech: the practical centre, 'because Paul's primary intention is to urge the Ephesian elders to do their duty effectively', and the theological centre, 'because here only in Acts is there an attempt to state the significance of the death of Christ and at the same time to bring out the ground of the church's ministry in the work of the Holy Spirit'.[62] This Trinitarian reference makes it clear that the church belongs to God and is fundamentally in his care. Nevertheless, in terms of human responsibility, Paul was concerned about what might happen to the congregation(s) at Ephesus. In view of his imminent departure, anticipating no return, he charged the elders with a solemn responsibility: *'keep watch over yourselves and all the flock of which the Holy Spirit has made you overseers'*. Christian leaders cannot care adequately for others if they neglect the care and nurture of themselves (cf. 1 Tim. 4:16). There are echoes here of OT passages that express the need for the leaders of Israel to pastor God's flock in a way that reflects his own shepherding care (e.g., Je. 23:1-4; Ezk. 34:1-16; Zc. 10:3). The title *overseers (episkopoi)* was chosen to describe their particular function as elders (v. 17, *presbyteroi*).[63] It recalls the use of the related verb *episkeptomai* ('look at, examine, inspect, visit') in the LXX passages just mentioned (cf. Acts 15:14 note). A different verb is used to describe the need for these overseers to *keep watch over (prosechete,* 'be concerned about, care for', BDAG) both themselves and the people in their care. The reasons for watchfulness are set out in vv. 29-31. As those *made* or appointed *(etheto)* overseers by *the Holy Spirit,* they are like the elders chosen by Moses, but empowered by God's Spirit as prophetic leaders of Israel (Nu. 11:24-26). Doubtless, the Ephesian elders were appointed by Paul because of their

---

62. Barrett 1998, 974. Both with respect to the atonement and the work of the Spirit in ministry, I would say that this verse makes explicit what is otherwise implied in various contexts.

63. The terms are used interchangeably here, as in Tit. 1:5-9. The cognate verb *episkopein* ('look at', 'take care of') is used in Heb. 12:15 with reference to the ministry which believers should have to one another, and in some MSS of 1 Pet. 5:2 with reference to the ministry of Christian leaders. Implicitly, the Ephesian elders are also being called pastors, since they are charged to 'pastor the church of God' *(poimainein,* 'to shepherd, pastor'). Cf. note 44 above.

Christian character and gifting (cf. 14:23; 1 Tim. 3:1-7; Tit. 1:5-9), but the focus here is on the Spirit's work in 'choosing and preparing by his gifts those who are to be ministers'.[64] As well as describing the leaders in these terms, Paul also used two important scriptural words to describe the congregation at Ephesus: they are *'the flock'* (*poimēn*; cf. Pss. 77:20; 80:1; 95:7; Is. 40:11; Je. 13:17; 23:2, 3; Ezk. 34:8, 10; cf. Lk. 12:32; 19:10; Jn. 10:1-30; 21:15-17) and *'the church'* or 'assembly' of God (*ekklēsia*; cf. Dt. 23:2-3; Jgs. 20:2; 1 Chr. 28:8; Mi. 2:5; cf. Mt. 16:18; 18:17). In view of the preceding reference to 'the whole will of God' (v. 27), it may be significant that the charge here is to care for *all the flock,* meaning 'the inclusive church of Jews and Gentiles that results from announcing God's saving purpose for all'.[65] Neglect of one group or another will result in the whole congregation being hurt or hindered in its growth and witness (cf. 6:1-7).

TNIV begins a new sentence with the injunction, *'Be shepherds of the church of God, which he bought with his own blood'*. However, in the Greek text, the imperative at the beginning of the verse (*'Keep watch over yourselves and all the flock'*) is explained or amplified by a clause with an infinitive (*poimainein tēn ekklēsian tou theou*, 'to shepherd the church of God'; so NRSV [ESV 'to care for']; cf. Jn. 21:16; 1 Pet. 5:1-2).[66] Their watchfulness was to be for the express purpose of effective pastoral care. The community entrusted to their care is further defined as *'the church of God, which he bought with his own blood'*. Such exalted language suggests that the Ephesian church belonged to God as his personal possession, having been *bought* (*periepoiēsato*) or acquired at a great price (cf. Ex. 19:5 [*laos periousios*]; Is. 31:5; 43:21). Such language can be applied to the church as the whole body of Christ (cf. Eph. 1:14; Tit. 2:14; 1 Pet. 2:9), but there is great significance and rhetorical force in recognising its immediate reference to the Ephesian situation. Each congregation which is brought into existence because of the saving work of Jesus is precious to God and should be so treated by those appointed to be its leaders! The manuscript evidence is fairly evenly divided between 'the church of God' (*tēn ekklēsian tou theou*) and 'the church of the Lord' (*tēn ekklēsian tou kyriou*). The former is probably the original on the basis of being the 'harder' reading.[67] This decision has implications for the translation of the following

64. Barrett 1998, 974-75. Witherington 1998, 623, rightly observes that 'there is nothing in this speech about Paul's passing the torch of leadership to these elders by some sort of ceremony or bequeathal'. The text does not reflect the later post-apostolic concerns of people like Ignatius of Antioch.

65. Tannehill 1990, 257. Tannehill, 259, comments further that 'God's relation to the mixed church of Jews and Gentiles is being understood after the pattern of God's relation to Israel in Scripture. In this respect 20:28 develops and emphasizes the implication of 15:14 and 18:10, where Gentiles are called God's "people (*laos*)", sharing that designation with the ancient people of God.' Cf. THEOLOGY OF ACTS: X. THE CHURCH (pp. 92-97).

66. KJV 'to feed' is too narrow a translation, since the Greek verb means 'to act as a shepherd' and refers to 'all the care that must be exercised in relation to the flock' (Marshall 1980, 334). Cf. E. Beyreuther, *NIDNTT* 3:564-69.

67. Cf. Metzger, *Textual Commentary*, 425-27; Barrett 1998, 976. The reading is 'harder'

expression *(hēn periepoiēsato dia tou haimatos tou idiou).* Most EVV have 'which he purchased with his own blood' (KJV, ESV, TNIV). Since this introduces a notion without parallel in the NT (God shedding his own blood), it may be best to read *tou idiou* as a reference to Jesus Christ as God's 'own' (NRSV 'the blood of his own Son').[68] Although many commentators seek to avoid the implication that Christ's death is presented here as the price paid for redeeming his people, the verb *peripoieomai* in combination with the expression *dia tou haimatos tou idiou* surely means 'acquired by means of the blood'.[69] Paul himself writes about the blood of Christ as the means of divine redemption in Romans 3:24-25; 5:9. The specifically covenantal language employed in 20:28 (*periepoiēsato,* 'bought') and 20:32; 26:18 (*hēgiasmenois,* 'sanctified'; cf. Dt. 33:3) reminds us of Luke's record of Jesus' last meal with his disciples 'wherein he grounds the "new covenant" in his own death (Luke 22:19-20)'.[70] In Acts 20, as in Jesus' discourse in the Upper Room, the shedding of the Messiah's blood is the means by which the New Covenant is inaugurated and Messiah's people are sanctified for their share with him in his eternal inheritance. This is the heart of 'the message of his grace' (v. 32), which is able to sustain the church in the face of persecution and false teaching. In other words, Jesus' atoning work in Luke 22 and Acts 20 is not simply the basis for the proclamation of forgiveness but also for the forming and maintaining of the eschatological people of God.

29-31 The reasons why the elders needed to keep watch over themselves and the flock committed to their care were then made plain. After Paul's departure,[71] there would be threats to the life and growth of the

---

because scribes may have understood the following clause to imply the shedding of God's blood, which is without parallel in the NT, rather than the blood of the Lord Jesus. This difficulty could have been removed by changing the text to 'the church of the Lord'. However, with NRSV, the following clause could still refer to the blood of Jesus ('the blood of his own Son').

68. Cf. Marshall 1980, 334; Bruce 1990, 434; Walton, *Leadership,* 91-98. Barrett 1998, 976-77, weighs the evidence for reading 'his own' as a term of endearment applied to Jesus as the Son of God (cf. Rom. 8:32). However, he argues that it is more natural to read the Greek as a reference to God's own blood, supposing Luke to mean that 'when Jesus Christ shed his blood on the cross he was acting as the representative of God: he was God's way of giving life, blood, for the world'.

69. E. Beyreuther, *NIDNTT* 2:838-40, shows how the verb *peripoieomai* has a range of meanings in different contexts: 'save or preserve for oneself, acquire, get something for oneself, get possession of'. The sense of 'acquired' at a price is conveyed by the unusual combination with *dia tou haimatos tou idiou, dia* with the genitive expressing means, and *haimatos tou idiou* pointing to the unjust death of the Son of God to provide a definitive forgiveness of sins, as previously indicated in 3:13-15, 19; 10:39-43; 13:28-31, 38-39.

70. J. B. Green, '"Salvation to the end of the earth" (Acts 13:47): God as Saviour in the Acts of the Apostles', in I. H. Marshall and D. G. Peterson (eds.), *Witness to the Gospel: The Theology of Acts* (Grand Rapids/Cambridge: Eerdmans, 1998), 99. He argues that, 'although sparsely mentioned, the salvific effect of the cross is not absent from Luke, even if it is not woven fully into the fabric of Luke's theology of the cross'. Cf. THE THEOLOGY OF ACTS: VI. THE ATONING WORK OF JESUS (pp. 75-79).

71. Barrett 1998, 977-78, notes that the word *aphixis* normally means 'arrival', but

church from both outside and inside. Paul first predicted that *'savage wolves'*[72] would come into their fellowship (*eis hymas*, 'among you') and would not *'spare the flock'*. False teachers would pursue their own ends and not care about what happened to Christ's people (cf. 1 Tim. 4:1-3; 6:3-5; 2 Tim. 3:1-9). Even more insidiously, destruction would come from within the church itself, *'even from your own number'*. This last expression suggests that heresy and schism might be caused by one or other of the elders themselves, who would *'distort the truth in order to draw away disciples after them'*. The church at Ephesus certainly had to deal with heretical forces after Paul's departure (cf. 1 Tim. 1:3; 2 Tim. 1:15; Rev. 2:1-7). However, the warning has a wider application. History shows that in every generation it has been all too easy for Christian leaders to attract others to their own way of thinking, to satisfy a deep-seated need for approval or popularity (cf. Gal. 4:17-18). Pastors need to be realistic about the way sin can manifest itself in distortions of the truth and create destructive divisions among Christians. Paul's solution was for the elders to watch out for themselves (*'So be on your guard!'*) In particular, they were to *'remember'* (*mnēmoneuontes*, a present participle, implies continual 'remembering') the pattern of his own ministry (*'for three years I never stopped warning each of you night and day with tears'*).[73] A similar ministry of *warning* with sincerity and compassion would be crucial to the care and support they might provide for one another and for the congregation as a whole. From Paul's letters it is clear that such admonition involved instructing the mind (*nous*), so that Christians might think and act appropriately (*nouthetōn*; cf. Rom. 15:14; 1 Cor. 4:14; Col. 1:28; 3:16; 1 Thes. 5:12, 14; 2 Thes. 3:15; *nouthesia*, 1 Cor. 10:11; Eph. 6:4; Tit. 3:10). 'Admonition as a form of spiritual counselling is also the task of the whole church towards one another (Col. 3:16), provided that it is spiritually fit to do so like the church at Rome (Rom. 15:14).'[74]

d. The Grounds for Confidence (20:32-35)

32 The preceding warning implies that the elders could not even rely on themselves to be faithful and to keep the church undivided in the

gives several examples where the sense of 'departure' could be understood. Cf. also Bruce 1990, 434-35. Witherington 1998, 618-20, argues against the view that Paul's 'departure' means his death.

72. *lykoi bareis* likens arrogant leaders to 'wolves who prey on sheep' (BDAG). A slightly different expression is used in Mt. 7:15 (*lykoi harpages*, 'ferocious wolves') to describe false prophets. Cf. 4 Ezr. 5:18; 1 Enoch 89:13-27.

73. The *three years* can be accounted for by adding together the 'three months' of 19:8, the 'two years' of 19:10, and whatever time Paul spent engaging with the disciples in 19:1-7 and concluding his ministry in Ephesus after the incident in the arena (19:23–20:1). In the final analysis, it must be regarded as a round figure for what was a particularly long period of settled ministry for Paul.

74. F. Selter, *NIDNTT* 1:569.

truth. So Paul committed or entrusted them (*paratithemai*; cf. Lk. 23:46; Acts 14:23) '*to God and to the word of his grace*' (*tō theō kai tō logō tēs charitos autou*). The two parts of this last phrase probably represent one concept: they were entrusted 'to God, who is active in the word of grace'.[75] God and the gospel cannot be divided, since he uses the gospel to save those who believe, both Jews and Gentiles (cf. Rom. 1:16). Once more the gospel is identified as a message of grace from God (cf. v. 24), which not only brings people to Christ in the first place but is also powerful enough to '*build you up*' (cf. 9:31) '*and give you an inheritance*' (cf. 7:5) '*among all those who are sanctified*' (cf. 26:18). Three important Pauline terms are found in this claim. Through the teaching of the gospel, God is 'building' his church (*oikodomēsai*; cf. Rom. 15:20; 1 Cor. 8:1, 10; 10:23; 14:4, 17; Gal. 2:18; 1 Thes. 5:11; *oikodomē*; cf. Rom. 14:19; 15:2; 1 Cor. 3:9; 14:3, 5, 12, 26; 2 Cor. 5:1; 10:8; 12:19; 13:10; Eph. 2:21; 4:12, 16, 29).[76] By means of the gospel, God promises an eternal inheritance to those who trust in Christ and enables them to obtain that inheritance (*klēronomia*, Gal. 3:18; Eph. 1:14, 18; 5:5; Col. 3:24; *klēronomos*, Rom. 4:13, 14; 8:17; Gal. 3:29; 4:1, 7; Tit. 3:7; *klēronomein*, 1 Cor. 6:9, 10; 15:50; Gal. 4:30; 5:21). In the gospel, God declares those who are in Christ to be already 'sanctified' (*hēgiasmenois* [a perfect passive participle indicating that this is a present reality that has been granted to them]; cf. Rom. 15:16; 1 Cor. 1:2; 1:30 [*hagiasmos*]; 6:11; 7:14; Eph. 5:26; 1 Thes. 5:23; 2 Thes. 2:13 [*hagiasmos*]; 1 Tim. 4:5; 2 Tim. 2:21), though believers are called to express their holy status and calling in practical everyday obedience to God (cf. 2 Cor. 7:1; 1 Thes. 3:13; 4:3, 4, 7; 1 Tim. 2:15).[77] So here we have an important contribution to Luke's theology of the gospel. This is the God-given 'word' by which the church grows in size and maturity and is protected from error and division. It is the message which God uses to convert and to sustain believers until they reach the inheritance which the gospel itself promises. When the gospel is faithfully preached and applied to believers, they are assured of their standing with God in Christ and are encouraged to press on in love, unity, and obedience.[78]

33-35 In addition to the danger of false teaching and persecution, Paul recognised the possibility that elders might misuse their position for personal gain. So he returned to his own example as an encouragement to

75. Barrett 1998, 980. This would be an example of 'hendiadys', where the co-ordination of two ideas, one of which is dependent on the other, is expressed in Greek with a simple connective (BDF 442.16). A large majority of witnesses support the reading 'to God', though some have 'to the Lord'.

76. See D. G. Peterson, *Engaging with God: A Biblical Theology of Worship* (Leicester: Apollos; Grand Rapids: Eerdmans, 1992), 206-15.

77. See D. G. Peterson, *Possessed by God: A New Testament Theology of Sanctification and Holiness* (Leicester: Apollos; Grand Rapids: Eerdmans, 1995), 1-92 (esp. 55-58). In Acts 20:32 and 26:18, the terminology of sanctification is used in a covenantal and corporate sense to describe a state or condition of holiness which is made possible for those who believe by the saving work of Christ.

78. Cf. THE THEOLOGY OF ACTS: V. THE GOSPEL (pp. 70-75).

them, introducing an aspect of his ministry not mentioned in preceding verses. Paul's attitude towards money and possessions reflected the influence of Jesus' teaching: *'I have not coveted anyone's silver or gold or clothing'* (cf. Lk. 12:13-34; 16:1-15). With this disclosure we see how 'his humble disinterest in "silver"-based wealth sets him apart from the Ephesian magicians (19:19) and shrinemakers (19:24-27)'.[79] It also set him apart from itinerant philosophers and religious charlatans who made money out of their teaching in the Greco-Roman world (cf. 1 Thes. 2:3-9). Paul even reported an otherwise unknown saying of Jesus in this connection (*'"It is more blessed to give than to receive"'*).[80] This saying does not mean that those who benefit from the generosity of others are less blessed than those who give. The principle is rather, 'It is better for a person who can do so to give to help others rather than to amass further wealth for himself'.[81] Paul's own behaviour is then presented as a practical example of how to put this into practice. Paul did not follow Jesus' teaching by selling his possessions and distributing the proceeds (cf. Lk. 12:33), but he gave to others by working with his own hands (cf. 1 Cor. 4:12) to supply his own needs and the needs of his companions (cf. 18:1-3). In addition, Paul demonstrated that *'by this kind of hard work we must help the weak'*, presumably meaning the economically weak in the church, who might suffer from having to support him, and perhaps also 'those who were sick and unable to earn their own living'.[82] His letters encourage believers to finance gospel ministry (1 Cor. 9:13-14; Gal. 6:6), and he himself accepted gifts from some churches (Phil. 4:10-19), but not others (1 Cor. 9:6-18; 2 Cor. 11:7-11; 12:16-18). However, his aim here is to warn leaders of the dangers inherent in their position and to commend his own solution to the problem of greed. Covetousness spoils relationships and hinders the work of the gospel, since those who are seeking to advance themselves materially will be tempted to evaluate their contacts and ministry opportunities in economic terms. His pattern of working to support himself may not have been continuous (cf. 18:5 note), but he apparently avoided relying on the support of others unless it was voluntarily offered. He does not lay an obligation on other leaders to follow his example but commends it as a way of handling the destructive power of covetousness in ministry. Paul's way of handling this matter is a further ground of confidence for leaders facing the temptations of their position in the church

79. Spencer 1997, 194.

80. Although this saying is not recorded in any of the Gospels, the command to give is found in Lk. 6:30, 38; 11:41; 12:33; 18:22. In the teaching of Jesus generosity to others is an antidote to covetousness and a way to escape the captivating deceit of riches. Witherington 1998, 626, discusses parallels to the saying in Acts 20:35 in extrabiblical writings.

81. Marshall 1980, 336. See also the previous note. Witherington 1998, 626, points out that this saying, together with Paul's example, challenged the principle of reciprocity which was so prevalent in the Greco-Roman world: here was a challenge to serve and help those who could give nothing in return.

82. Bruce 1990, 436.

(God and the gospel being the primary basis for confidence in v. 32). Paul's example shows that there is a way of resisting sin and being a trustworthy model for others.

4. Departing (20:36-38)

36-38 *When Paul had finished speaking, he knelt down with all of them and prayed.* In response, *they all wept as they embraced him and kissed him.* Paul's relationship with the Ephesian elders was one of genuine affection and friendship. Parting from him was distressing enough, but *what grieved them most was his statement that they would never see his face again.* Similar departure scenes in 21:5-6, 12-14, show a surprising depth of relationship with Christians in Tyre and Caesarea, where he had not spent the same length of time as he did in Ephesus. Paul is sometimes misrepresented by his critics as a hard and austere man, lacking compassion and kindness. However, this passage is one of several challenging that distorted view (cf. 2 Cor. 2:4; 1 Thes. 1:7-8). *Then they accompanied him to the ship* for the journey that would take him to imprisonment and many trials before he finally reached Rome.

VIII. PAUL'S FINAL JOURNEY:
TO JERUSALEM AND ROME (21:1–28:31)

'This section contributes nothing to the description of the geographical and cultural spread of Christianity, which has often been taken to (be) the essential theme of Acts, but concentrates on Paul's imprisonment and trial. So, to judge from the structure of Luke's work, it seems that the climax towards which he is bringing his story is "Paul under prosecution".'[1] The pace of the narrative slows considerably in these chapters, drawing attention to the significance of the events, and Paul's speeches include many biographical details: 'his background, his calling as an emissary of the gospel, his fidelity to Jewish traditions, and what he might represent to the interests of the Roman state'.[2] This does not mean that the section was somehow designed to legitimate Paul in the eyes of Roman or Jewish readers. Luke-Acts was not written primarily to persuade outsiders of the truth of Christianity or to defend its main protagonists.[3] Luke wanted his

---

1. R. Maddox, *The Purpose of Luke-Acts* (Edinburgh: Clark, 1982), 12. M. L. Skinner, *Locating Paul: Places of Custody as Narrative Settings in Acts 21–28*, SBLAB 13 (Atlanta: SBL, 2003), 57-58, observes that after his arrest Paul visits no churches (except for his encounter with believers in 27:3; 28:14-15), makes no converts (except perhaps for 28:24), and performs miraculous deeds only when shipwrecked on Malta (28:5-6, 8-9).

2. Skinner, *Locating Paul*, 59.

3. Cf. Maddox, *Purpose*, 19-23, 91-97; P. R. House, 'Suffering and the Purpose of Acts',

patron Theophilus and those he represented to know the certainty of the things they had been taught (Lk. 1:1). Strengthened in that way, Luke's readers would be better able to give a reasoned and persuasive account of the hope that motivated them (cf. 1 Pet. 3:15-16). As a work of edification for Christian believers, Luke's second volume has a number of special interests, one of which is in Paul as 'the greatest of the early Christian leaders and missionaries'.[4] The Twelve Apostles are presented as foundational witnesses of the life, death, resurrection and ascension of the Lord Jesus. After them, great preachers and missionaries, like Philip, Paul, and others, took their testimony to the nations. In Luke's view, Paul particularly functioned as a bridge between the early apostolic period and his readers. The narrative momentum in Acts 21–28 is provided by Paul's trials, in which he defends himself against the accusations of Jewish authorities. After an initial, informal defence in the precincts of the temple (21:37–22:21), there are four detailed accounts of trial or legal inquiries (22:30–23:10; 24:1-23; 25:6-12; 25:23–26:32), together with a private discussion between Festus and Agrippa about the case (25:13-22). However, Maddox rightly argues that Luke's real interest is not in the juridical aspect of Paul's situation: 'the trial-theme serves to emphasize the unjust suffering to which Paul was subjected in his last few years'.[5] Moreover, Paul as a prisoner twice repeats the details of his conversion (22:3-22; 26:4-24), linking his immediate experience back to that original call to proclaim Christ and suffer for the sake of his name (9:15-16). Persecution and suffering form a dominant part of Paul's witness to Christ in Acts 21–28. Given the fact that Paul had a unique calling, he nevertheless functioned to some extent as a model disciple. Luke used these final chapters to illustrate the truth contained in Paul's own exhortation to believers (14:22), showing how he endured persecution and suffering and made the most of every situation for the sake of the gospel.[6] Cunningham observes four particular contributions to the persecution theme in Acts 21–28: persecution continues to stem from Jewish unbelief; the witness is

---

JETS 33 (1990), 317-19; and Skinner, *Locating Paul*, 60, for critiques of various approaches to the purpose of Acts and to these chapters in particular.

4. Maddox, *Purpose*, 70. Skinner, *Locating Paul*, 59-60, rightly takes issue with the sharp distinction made by Maddox between Paul the missionary and Paul the prisoner, arguing that in Acts 21–28 there are new settings and new audiences, but that Paul continues to be an active apologist for the Christian faith.

5. Maddox, *Purpose*, 76. This argument is supported by the fact that Luke says nothing in his final chapter about the outcome of Paul's appeal to Caesar.

6. Cf. Maddox, *Purpose*, 80. However, House, 'Suffering', 320, rightly criticises Maddox, 82, for saying that 'through the Holy Spirit and the Word of God these afflictions are turned into mere annoyances, which a resolute Christian can easily endure'. Luke presents suffering in a more serious and demanding light than that! Indeed, House argues that 'persecution, hardships, troubles, martyrdom, and disputes between Christians and non-Christians (sometimes even between Christians and Christians) provide the theological and literary framework for Acts'.

persecuted because of his belief in the resurrection (cf. 23:6; 24:15; 26:6-7; 28:20); persecution occurs within the context of divine providence; the witness to Jesus is persecuted in continuity with Jesus.[7]

A. Following the Way of Jesus (21:1-16)

Luke's narrative of the Ephesian ministry highlighted Paul's role as a prophet in the line of Jesus and his apostles (18:24–19:20). His likeness to Jesus was further suggested by indications of a divine compulsion to travel to Jerusalem, no matter what the cost, to finish the race and complete the task given to him (19:21; 20:22-24). Acts 21 records the final stages of that journey to the city which rejected the master and sought to dispose of his disciple. 'Within Luke's overall narrative, Paul's journey to Jerusalem works perfectly well within his geographical structure (which centers the entire story on Jerusalem) and his prophetic structure (which has all his heroes follow the pattern of the rejected prophet).'[8] Along the way, Paul meets disciples in Tyre (21:1-6) and Caesarea (21:7-15), who express genuine concern for his welfare. They are moved by revelations from the Holy Spirit about the danger that lies ahead for Paul. Tannehill notes that widespread respect for Paul is indicated by the attention he receives from figures associated with the mission in its early days: Philip the evangelist (21:8), Agabus the prophet (21:10; cf. 11:28), and Mnason, an 'early disciple' (21:16). 'Their attention and support balance the ambiguous reception of Paul in Jerusalem, where Paul is welcomed gladly (21:17) but then is informed of widespread suspicion among Jewish Christians (21:20-21).'[9] However, a struggle takes place between Paul and those who love him. Issues of divine guidance and how to respond to warnings about impending imprisonment are raised and are finally resolved by Paul's determination to face the inevitable suffering (21:13-14). To readers who may be faced with the necessity to suffer for the Lord's sake in a variety of situations, the response of Paul's colleagues and friends is a challenging model: *'The Lord's will be done'*.

---

7. S. Cunningham, *'Through many tribulations': The Theology of Persecution in Luke-Acts*, JSNTSS 142 (Sheffield: Sheffield Academic, 1997), 274-87. In his final analysis, Cunningham 287-94, identifies five prominent theological functions of the persecution theme in Acts: persecution is part of the plan of God; persecution is the rejection of God's agents; the persecuted people of God stand in continuity with God's prophets; persecution is an integral consequence of following Jesus; persecution is the occasion of divine triumph ('not only does persecution not stop the growth of the Word; ironically it functions as its catalyst', p. 293). In a later chapter he adds that persecution is the occasion of the Christian's perseverance (p. 319).

8. Johnson 1992, 351. Witherington 1998, 627-28, evaluates the extent to which we can draw parallels with the final journey of Jesus to Jerusalem in the Gospels.

9. Tannehill 1990, 262.

1. From Miletus to Tyre (21:1-6)

The journey narrative which began in 20:1-16, and which was interrupted by the farewell speech to the Ephesian elders (20:17-38), now continues. Luke's interest in the details of sea travel resurfaces, as does his focus on the joys and sorrows of Christian fellowship. Both here and in the following section, the issue of divine guidance comes to the fore again. The Spirit's warnings about Paul's captivity in Jerusalem (cf. 20:23; 21:11) move the disciples in Tyre to try to hold him back, but Paul presses on towards his God-given goal (cf. 20:22, 24). 'The interspersing of travel and scenes of community life in 20:1–21:17 serves to draw remarkably dispersed groups of believers together in a single narrative, believers who could not gather as did Christians in Jerusalem but who nevertheless are connected by the gospel's activity among them.'[10]

1-3 *After we had torn ourselves away from them,*[11] *we put out to sea and sailed straight to Kos.* This island is in the Aegean Sea, west of Halicarnassus (modern Bodrum). *The next day we went to Rhodes and from there to Patara. Rhodes*, another island off the southwest coast of Asia Minor, also had a capital city with the same name. This journey followed the conventional pattern for small ships in antiquity, which was 'to hug the coastline as much as possible and put into port each night when the winds died down'.[12] *Patara* was on the mainland and in earlier days was the port of Xanthos, the chief city of Lycia. This is where Paul and his party left one ship and joined another, large enough for *crossing over to Phoenicia*, a journey of some 400 miles (644 km.).[13] *Phoenicia* was a narrow coastal strip on the Mediterranean Sea, which was annexed by Rome in 64 BC and incorporated into the province of Syria. *After sighting Cyprus and passing to the south of it, we sailed on to Syria.*[14] Luke now uses the provincial name for their destination and concludes his precise account of the sea journey with the landing at *Tyre*. There the ship was to *unload its cargo*, which explains the more lengthy stay in this port. Tyre was an ancient trade centre, the most notable

10. Gaventa 2003, 296. The communities are strengthened by Paul's visit, as they themselves seek to care for him and his companions.

11. The passive participle *apospasthentas* is used in a middle sense here ('tear oneself away', BDAG), but the active form of the verb is used differently in 20:30 to mean 'draw away' or 'attract'. *Anachthēnai* is used as a nautical technical term for 'set sail' (cf. Lk. 8:22; Acts 27:2; 28:10).

12. Witherington 1998, 629. Witherington, 636-41, considers the perils as well as the opportunities for travel in the Greco-Roman world.

13. A few mainly Western MSS add *kai Myra* ('and Myra'), making Myra on the southern coast of Lycia, some fifty miles farther east than Patara, the port of transshipment. Most commentators view this as an addition influenced by 27:5. Bruce 1990, 439, adds that 'because of the prevalent wind, Patara may have been a more convenient starting point for such a run (to Phoenicia) than Myra'. Cf. Barrett 1998, 988.

14. Bruce 1990, 439, notes here the use of an apparently nautical term for sighting land (*anaphanantes*).

settlement on the Phoenician coast, which was made a free city under the Romans.

4-6 Although Paul was hurrying to reach Jerusalem, 'if possible by the day of Pentecost' (20:16), he and his party had made such good time on their journey that they were able to stay with the Christians in Tyre *(We sought out the disciples there and stayed with them seven days).*[15] The church in that city was probably founded as a result of the outreach to Phoenicia mentioned in 11:19 (cf. 15:3). *Through the Spirit they urged Paul not to go on to Jerusalem.* Most likely, *through the Spirit (dia tou pneumatos)* refers to a revelation by the Holy Spirit of the dangers that lay ahead for Paul. Some have seen this as a Spirit-directed urging not to go, in conflict with the revelation already given to Paul about the need to visit Jerusalem (cf. 19:21 note) and to suffer in the process (20:22-23).[16] However, Luke does not treat this as a different message, requiring discernment by the church. In three successive scenes, the Spirit speaks about the dangers awaiting Paul in Jerusalem, and his resolve is strengthened on each occasion (20:22-24; 21:4, 10-14). In this, the briefest reference, it is best to conclude that the Spirit's revelation was the same. The Lord's will was consistently revealed, and progressively Paul was shown what this might entail. As his friends became aware of the implications, they were moved by a Spirit-given love for Paul to urge him not to go (cf. Gal. 5:22).[17] The Spirit did not to prohibit Paul from going to Jerusalem through their urging but continued to warn him of the dangers. When it was time to leave, *all of them, including wives and children, accompanied us out of the city, and there on the beach we knelt to pray.* Even though there had been only such a short time to get to know one another, a close bond between the travelling believers and the Christians in Tyre had been formed. The presence of whole families at this farewell, gathering to pray for Paul and his companions *on the beach,* highlights the seriousness of the occasion (cf. 20:36-38). Their support and admiration for Paul must have been particularly encouraging for him at this time. Luke concludes this touching scene with the note that, *after saying good-bye to each other, we went aboard the ship, and they returned home.*

2. *From Tyre to Jerusalem (21:7-16)*

The journey to Jerusalem continues, with a further delay to meet Christians along the way. Those in Caesarea, together with Paul's companions, are

---

15. Barrett 1998, 990, suggests that the seven-day stay may have been determined by the need for the ship's crew to unload and reload cargo. He argues that the article is anaphoric in v. 6 *(to ploion),* referring back to the ship in which they had arrived.

16. Cf. Tannehill 1990, 262-27.

17. Cf. Bruce 1990, 439. Tannehill 1990, 263, observes that 'the use of indirect discourse in 21:4 removes the message a step from the Spirit's direct expression'. Barrett 1998, 990, thinks Paul's friends were not acting under the influence of the Spirit but simply out of human concern, but this is not what the text says!

confronted by a specific revelation about Paul's future which causes them to plead with Paul not to continue his journey (vv. 10-12; cf. v. 4). This gives Paul the opportunity to affirm his willingness to die in Jerusalem *for the name of the Lord Jesus* (v. 13; cf. 5:41; 20:22-24), and moves the believers to echo his trust and commitment (v. 14). 'The intense emotional connection that comes to expression in this scene contrasts strikingly with developments that will quickly follow in Jerusalem.'[18] Luke begins and ends this section with references to the practical care and hospitality extended to Paul and his companions by various groups of believers, some of whom are named because of their links with the earliest days of the Christian movement (vv. 7-9, 15-16).

7-9 *We continued our voyage from Tyre and landed at Ptolemais, where we greeted the believers and stayed with them for a day.*[19] *Ptolemais* (otherwise known as Acco; cf. Jgs. 1:31) was a strong fortress and another important trade centre, about 30 miles (48 km.) down the coast from Tyre. It was made a Roman colony in the time of the emperor Claudius. The church there may well have been founded by the same mission that took the gospel to Tyre (cf. 11:19). Hospitality to the travellers is specifically mentioned in vv. 4, 8, and 16, and it is a ministry highlighted elsewhere in Acts, especially in relation to those engaged in gospel work. *Leaving the next day, we reached Caesarea,* journeying either by sea or by road (another 30 miles or 48 km. south).[20] *Caesarea* belonged to the Roman province of Judea and was the seat of its administration (cf. 10:1 note). There the travellers *stayed at the house of Philip the evangelist, one of the Seven.* Philip was last mentioned in 8:40, where we were told of his 'preaching the gospel in all the towns until he reached Caesarea'. He was known as *the evangelist* (cf. Eph. 4:11; 2 Tim. 4:5) because evangelism was his gift (cf. 8:12, 35, 40, where Philip 'evangelizes', *euangelizesthai*), but also presumably to distinguish him from Philip the apostle (1:14). He had apparently ceased his itinerant work and settled in Caesarea to concentrate his work in that important centre and to raise a family. Mention of Philip as an evangelist and his daughters as 'prophesying' conveys something of 'the strength of the community at Caesarea'.[21] Some characters in Acts are specifically designated as prophets (11:27-28; 13:1; 15:32: 21:10). Even so, a wider phenomenon of prophesying is implied by the promise of Joel 2:28-29 (cited in Acts 2:17-18). Indeed, use of the present participle *prophēteuousai* in 21:9 suggests that an ongoing ministry

18. Gaventa 2003, 296.

19. TNIV rightly translates *dianysantes* as 'continued'. Cf. Bruce 1990, 440.

20. Cf. C. J. Hemer, *The Book of Acts in the Setting of Hellenistic History*, ed. C. Gempf, WUNT 49 (Tübingen: Mohr Siebeck, 1989; repr. Winona Lake: Eisenbrauns, 1990), 125-26. The Received Text, following a few MSS, reads *hoi peri ton Paulon ēlthon* ('those who were with Paul went'; KJV 'we that were of Paul's company departed'), but this is not well enough attested to be regarded as the original reading. Cf. Barrett 1998, 992; Metzger, *Textual Commentary*, 427-28.

21. Gaventa 2003, 294.

rather than an office is in view here (cf. 1 Cor. 11:2-6; 14:1-25).[22] Meeting
with Philip provided Luke with a unique opportunity to consult *one of the
Seven* mentioned in 6:3-5, to find out more about the early history of the Jerusalem church and particularly to gain information about the ministries of
Stephen (6:8–8:3) and of Philip himself (8:4-40).[23] Later contact with James
and the elders (21:17-25) could have given him an even wider perspective
on those first years of the gospel's impact, as he prepared to write his two-
volume work.

10-12   It was at Caesarea that Paul had to make a final decision about
going on to Jerusalem. Luke records that *after we had been there a number of
days, a prophet named Agabus came down from Judea.* He speaks of Agabus
coming from Judea (cf. 11:27-28) because, as a predominantly Gentile city,
Caesarea was not considered part of Judea in the ethnic sense.[24] Presumably, Agabus had a greater awareness of the tensions in Jerusalem, which
are soon to be recounted by Luke. *Coming over to us, he took Paul's belt and
tied his own hands and feet with it.* The *belt (zōnē)* is likely to have been a long
piece of cloth wrapped around the waist, possibly used to contain money
and other items (BDAG). This prophetic-type action (cf. 1 Ki. 11:29-31; Is.
20:2-4; Ezk. 4:1-8) illustrated and confirmed the seriousness of the message
he had to deliver: *'The Holy Spirit says, "In this way the Jews of Jerusalem will
bind the owner of this belt and will hand him over to the Gentiles"'*. Echoes of Jesus' predictions about what would happen to him can be heard in these
words (cf. Lk. 9:22, 44; 18:32; 24:7). The implication is that Paul will suffer to
some extent as Jesus suffered, though as a model disciple rather than as one
who sets out to relive the story of Jesus in any literal or quasi-redemptive
sense (cf. Lk. 9:23-26; 12:4-12).[25] A broad prediction is given about what will
happen to him in Jerusalem. In the event, Paul was actually 'delivered *from*
the Jews *by* the Gentiles (vv. 31-36)'.[26] However, in retrospect, he was still
able to say, 'I was arrested in Jerusalem and handed over to the Romans'
(28:17). As a result of their violent reaction to Paul, 'the Jews could be re-

22. Barrett 1998, 994, considers whether the fact that the daughters of Philip were vir-
gins made it easier for them to exercise a public ministry, in view of the sort of restrictions
found in 1 Cor. 11:2-6; 14:34-36. Witherington 1998, 633, rightly argues that there is 'no necessary ascetical connection being made by Luke between women, virginity, and prophecy'.

23. Bruce 1990, 441, discusses the evidence of early Christian sources about Philip
and his daughters. Barrett 1998, 993, also observes that Luke could have discovered much
about the history of the early church from those encountered on this journey. Cf. Mnason,
who was 'one of the early disciples' (21:16).

24. Cf. Bruce 1990, 442. It is strange that Luke introduces Agabus as if he has not appeared in the narrative before. Marshall 1980, 340, suggests that this reference may have
been taken over from the 'we' source in which Agabus had not previously appeared. However, it is still strange that Luke, who had previously recorded the ministry of Agabus in
11:27-28, should reintroduce him into the narrative in this way.

25. Cf. Maddox, *Purpose,* 79-80, for a helpful critique of attempts to draw the parallel
between Jesus and Paul too closely at this point.

26. Bruce 1990, 442. Cf. Barrett 1998, 995-96.

garded as responsible for the fact that Paul fell into the hands of the Romans and remained in custody'.[27] His travel companions and the Christians in Caesarea (*we and the people there*) took the warning of Agabus seriously and *pleaded with Paul not to go up to Jerusalem*. They were moved by a loving concern for Paul's welfare and by the force of the prediction to express themselves in this way (cf. Mk. 8:31-32). Indeed, they implied that the prophecy would come true only if Paul insisted on completing his journey. Luke includes himself among those who did not at this stage share Paul's commitment to the pathway of suffering and captivity.

13-14 It is clear from the forceful and solemn introduction to Paul's response (*tote apekrithē ho Paulos*, 'then Paul answered')[28] that what follows is a notable expression of his devotion to the Lord and his service. His friends were '*weeping*', and this was having the effect of breaking his heart (*synthryptontes mou tēn kardian*).[29] Their emotional appeal made it difficult for Paul to hold to his purpose. All he could do was to give a forthright statement of his resolve: '*I am ready not only to be bound, but also to die in Jerusalem for the name of the Lord Jesus*'. In effect, Paul was saying, 'Stop weeping and trying to dissuade me, for (*gar*, not translated by TNIV) I am ready'. Peter made a similar pledge to Jesus (Lk. 22:33), but was unable to keep it. Paul remained faithful, although he was not, in the end, required to give his life in Jerusalem. When Paul would not be dissuaded, his friends *gave up and said, 'The Lord's will be done*'.[30] His determination to follow in the steps of his master and to honour his *name* was the reason for their acceptance of the will of God (cf. Lk. 22:42; Acts 18:21). Like Jesus, he 'resolutely set out for Jerusalem' (Lk. 9:51), and his submission to the will of God had a powerful impact on those who were with him. Although suffering was an integral part of the ministry to which Paul had been called (9:15-16; 20:24), it is reasonable to ask why he had to suffer precisely as he did in these final chapters. It appears that the completion of his ministry required 'the extensive defense of his work against religious and political accusations that actually follow in the narrative. Paul is facing the cultural consequences of his previous ministry, which has disturbed religion and society, with their guardians, by introducing a new understanding of God's work as reaching

27. Marshall 1980, 340. Luke uses the same verb in v. 30 for the seizing of Paul by the Jews as he does for his arrest by the Romans in v. 33.

28. A number of variants are found in the MSS of this verse, none of which has much support. These appear to have arisen because *tote* ('then') was taken with the preceding verse and some form of connective needed to be inserted. Cf. Barrett 1998, 996; Metzger, *Textual Commentary*, 428.

29. This rare verb means 'to break in pieces, to reduce to powder' (Barrett 1998, 997). Barrett suggests that it might mean 'with sorrow or by weakening my resolve'. Both meanings could be implied: by making Paul sorrowful they were weakening his resolve to go on.

30. Pointing out that the verb *hēsychasamen* is better rendered 'ceased' or 'fell silent' (rather than TNIV's *gave up*), Barrett 1998, 997-98, argues that they were 'prepared at length regretfully to recognize that it is the Lord's will that Paul should suffer; unwelcome as this is, may it nevertheless be done'.

out through Jesus Messiah to both Jew and Gentile, breaking down the barrier between them.'[31] However, even more fundamentally, these chapters represent Paul being persecuted because of his theological claim that the resurrection hope of Israel is fulfilled only through Jesus (cf. 23:6; 24:15; 26:6-7; 28:20).[32] In this respect, he suffered specifically *'for the name of the Lord Jesus'* as Peter and John did (cf. 4:7, 10-12, 17-18, 30). Positively, the following chapters show that Paul's suffering and imprisonment gave him many opportunities to testify about Jesus and his resurrection in unexpected places.

15-16 After the several days mentioned in v. 10 were over, Paul and his team 'got ready and went up to Jerusalem' (ESV).[33] The journey of some 60 miles (100 km.) would have taken three days by foot or 'two with relative ease by horse'.[34] *Some of the disciples from Caesarea accompanied us,* perhaps as a protective escort, *and brought us to the home of Mnason, where we were to stay.* This sounds like a prearranged visit with a well-known Hellenistic Jewish Christian *(he was a man from Cyprus).* Perhaps the Caesarean Christians had organized this for Paul and his party and were leading them to the right spot. Mnason was doubtless sympathetic to Paul and his missionary activities and was not troubled about hosting all the delegates from the Gentile churches travelling with Paul (cf. 20:4-6). Luke reveals a pattern of hospitality offered by Christians, especially to those engaged in itinerant missions (e.g., 9:43; 16:15, 40; 21:4, 8, 16). Given the suspicions expressed about Paul by some in Jerusalem (v. 21), this was a wise and cautious way of seeking accommodation in the city.[35] As *one of the early disciples (archaiō mathētē),*[36] Mnason must have been another source of information for Luke

---

31. Tannehill 1990, 266. Tannehill further argues, 'The world discovers that the challenge is really serious when it learns that the ministers of the new gospel are willing to face the consequences of their own disturbing words. This is a crisis that cannot be avoided without damage to the mission. Paul's decision to go to Jerusalem and to Rome is a decision to face this crisis. Jerusalem and Rome are the centers of the two powers that Paul has disturbed and to whom he must give a reckoning.'

32. Cf. Cunningham, *Persecution,* 277-81.

33. TNIV *(we started on our way up to Jerusalem)* does not capture the sense of *episkeuasamenoi,* which can mean 'having made our preparation' or, more specifically, 'having hired pack animals' (Bruce 1990, 443). Cf. Barrett 1998, 1002.

34. B. Rapske, 'Acts, Travel, and Shipwreck', in D. W. J. Gill and C. Gempf (eds.), *The Book of Acts in Its First-Century Setting,* Vol. 2: *Graeco-Roman Setting* (Grand Rapids: Eerdmans; Carlisle: Paternoster, 1994), 10. Rapske goes on to argue that a journey by foot is more likely from the evidence.

35. The Western text locates Mnason's house in an unnamed village on the way to Jerusalem, where Paul and his friends spent a night. Although the journey from Caesarea probably took two days, 'it is doubtful whether Luke would have named Paul's host on the way and not his host in Jerusalem itself' (Marshall 1980, 341-42).

36. Bruce 1990, 443, notes that this expression could mean 'a disciple from the beginning *(archē)* of the church's existence' or 'a disciple of long standing' (perhaps dating from the time of Paul's mission to Cyprus in 13:4-12 or earlier; cf. 11:19-20). Cf. Barrett 1998, 1003-4. Metzger, *Textual Commentary,* 428, discusses the different account of events in the Western text of vv. 16-17.

about the early days of the Christian movement (cf. v. 8 note). As his narrative draws to a close, Luke seems to be at pains to point out the personal connections he had with 'those who from the first *(ap' archēs)* were eyewitnesses and servants of the word' (Lk. 1:2).

B. Captured in Jerusalem (21:17-40)

Law and temple emerge as two key issues with respect to Paul's teaching and practice, as he engages first with believing Jews in Jerusalem (vv. 17-26), and then is misrepresented by unbelieving Jews from the province of Asia (vv. 27-29). Paul's faithfulness to fundamental Jewish beliefs continues to be a dominant theme in the trial scenes in the rest of Acts. He becomes a captive in Jerusalem because he is willing to put himself at risk for the sake of Jewish Christians who value their Jewish heritage. Later, under house arrest in Rome, he declares that his imprisonment is 'because of the hope of Israel' (28:20). Paradoxically, 'Paul's lengthy imprisonment and the witness that this prisoner bears to Israel's hope are signs of his loyalty to Israel, although he is being attacked as a renegade'.[37] The events of some twelve days are narrated in detail in 21:17–24:23 (cf. 24:11), showing the importance of this story for Luke and his presentation of Paul. The legal proceedings in the following chapters appear to cover a two-year period, 'from about Pentecost AD 57 until sometime in AD 59, including the time when Felix ceased to be and Festus began to be procurator'.[38] A further theme that is introduced in 21:30-40 is the role of Roman authorities in providing protection for Paul against his Jewish opponents and offering him some measure of justice. The commander who is introduced in this chapter becomes increasingly aware of the real issues at stake (cf. 21:37-40; 22:22-30; 23:10) and committed to preserving Paul from the violence and plots of the Jews (cf. 23:12-35). In summary, this whole section is about the misunderstanding Paul had to endure from some fellow believers, the misguided plan to set things straight suggested by James and the elders, the misrepresentation and physical attack he experienced from opponents, and the help he received from the Roman commander who arrested him.

1. A Well-Meaning Proposal (21:17-26)

Paul is received warmly by the Jerusalem Christians. James and the elders openly praise God for what he has done through Paul's ministry among the Gentiles (vv. 17-20a), but affirm that God has also been bringing many Jews in Jerusalem to faith in Christ, whom they describe as being 'zealous for the

37. Tannehill 1990, 271.
38. Witherington 1998, 642.

law' (v. 20b). This moves the Jerusalem leaders to express their concern about Paul's reputation for teaching Jews in the Dispersion to 'turn away from Moses' and to suggest how Paul might prove his orthodoxy as a Jew (vv. 21-24). A brief recollection of the decision of the Jerusalem Council (v. 25; cf. 15:23-29) provides reassurance that the Jerusalem leaders are not reopening the question of Gentiles and the law of Moses. 'The new issue is distinct: is Paul leading Jewish Christians to abandon their Jewish way of life?'[39] Unfortunately, Paul's compliance with their well-meaning suggestion (v. 26) exposes him to misrepresentation and the riot that causes him to be arrested.

17-19 *When we arrived at Jerusalem, the believers received us warmly.* The *believers* mentioned here (*hoi adelphoi*, 'the brothers') could be Mnason and those associated with him, or a wider group of Jerusalem Christians.[40] *The next day Paul and the rest of us went to see James, and all the elders were present.* The rather solemn language used in v. 18 (*eisēei pros*, 'went in to') suggests a more formal scene, with the visitors appearing before the Jerusalem authorities to present their case.[41] Given the importance placed on the collection from the Gentile churches by Paul himself (cf. Rom. 15:25-32; 2 Cor. 9:12-15), it seems strange that Luke makes no mention of it being delivered here (though cf. 24:17). However, as previously suggested, his failure to highlight that aspect of Paul's journey to Jerusalem may be because the collection did not have the effect that Paul intended. Witherington outlines the volatile religious and political situation in Jerusalem in AD 57 and says, 'marching into Jerusalem with Gentiles from various parts of the Empire at this xenophobic moment would hardly have produced a positive result from Jews in general, or from ardent Pharisaic Jewish Christians in Jerusalem'.[42] Moreover, in narrative terms, Luke is preoccupied with showing the harm done to Paul in Jerusalem and its consequences. From here until 27:1, the 'we' form of the narrative disappears, as Paul and his trials become the centre of attention. *Paul greeted them and reported in detail* (*kath' hen hekaston,*

39. Tannehill 1990, 269. Tannehill, 268, points out that this is the third in a series of conflicts focussed on Jerusalem and arising from a mission that includes both Jews and Gentiles (cf. 11:1-18; 15:1-31).

40. Bruce 1990, 444, considers the possibility that v. 17 may anticipate the account of the visitors' reception by James and the elders in vv. 18ff., but rightly concludes that this makes the transition to v. 18 awkward.

41. Cf. Barrett 1998, 1005. James the Lord's brother is evidently the leading man in Jerusalem (cf. 12:17; 15:13), functioning as president of a group of elders. Peter and the rest of the Twelve appear to be absent: no longer is there mention of 'the apostles and elders' (cf. 15:4, 6, 22-23).

42. Witherington 1998, 644. Haenchen 1971, 613-14, has another suggestion. The requirement for Paul to engage in a purification rite and to pay for the expenses of those who had taken a vow could have been to facilitate the acceptance of the gift of the Gentile churches by those in Jerusalem who had accusations against him. Barrett 1998, 1001, notes the use of the word *diakonia* ('ministry') in v. 19, which is employed several times in Paul's letters with reference to the collection (Rom. 15:31; 2 Cor. 8:4; 9:1, 12, 13). But the word can hardly have that specific reference here.

'one by one') *what God had done among the Gentiles through his ministry*. This is reminiscent of Paul's previous visit to Jerusalem for the Council (15:4, 12), where the focus was also on *what God had done among the Gentiles through his ministry*. On that occasion, his law-free offer of the gospel to Gentiles was clearly endorsed.

20-21 *When they heard this, they praised God.* The Jerusalem leaders once more 'gave glory to God' (*edoxazon ton theon*) for the amazing growth of the Gentile churches (cf. 11:18; 15:12-18). However, on this occasion they also took the opportunity to tell Paul: *'You see, brother, how many thousands of Jews have believed, and all of them are zealous for the law'.* They affirmed that God had been working in their midst too, substantially increasing the number of Christians since the last mention of five thousand male believers in the city (4:4; cf. 6:7; 9:31).[43] However, the expression *zealous for the law* implies that many had been influenced by the Pharisaic position (cf. 15:5). This designation suggests 'not only "zeal" for observance, but also "jealousy" for honour paid to Torah, and therefore hostility towards any perceived derogation of that honor'.[44] Since James later confirms the decision of the Jerusalem Council about Gentiles not being obliged to live under the law (v. 25), it would appear that this zeal for the law was with reference to the lifestyle of Jewish Christians. Paul used a similar expression in describing his pre-conversion life (Gal. 1:14; cf. Nu. 25:10-13 [Phinehas]; 1 Ki. 19:10, 14 [Elijah]; 1 Macc. 2:27 [Mattathias]). Despite Luke's evidence of Paul's continuing loyalty to Judaism in many respects, it is unlikely that the Paul we know from his letters would have been happy with such a self-designation by Jewish Christians.[45] Nevertheless, the most disturbing aspect of the report by James was the news that *'they have been informed* (*katēchēthēsan* implies false instruction here, not just hearsay or rumour)[46] *that you teach all the Jews who live among the Gentiles to turn away from Moses, telling them not to circumcise their children or live according to our customs'.* There has been no indication in Acts so far that Paul was explicitly encouraging Jewish converts to abandon their law or their customs. Even in his

43. *myriades* ('tens of thousands') is loosely translated *thousands* here and is taken as hyperbole. J. Jeremias, *Jerusalem in the Time of Jesus: An Investigation into Economic and Social Conditions during the New Testament Period* (ET, London: SCM, 1969), 77-84, estimates that the normal population of Jerusalem at this time was between 25,000 and 55,000. However, the figure in 21:20 may have included many Jewish Christians who were visiting Jerusalem for the festival.

44. Johnson 1992, 374.

45. Bruce 1990, 445, suggests that the Jerusalem Christians were affected by 'the insurgent spirit that was increasing in Judaea during Felix's procuratorship'. We may go further and suppose that they were unaware of the difficulties faced by Jewish Christians in largely Gentile areas and were apparently unmoved by the mighty work that God was doing among Gentiles, without the application of the law to their situation. In the final analysis, these last two factors had serious implications for Jewish believers in Jerusalem and their zeal for the law.

46. The same verb is used in a positive sense in Lk. 1:4; Acts 18:25.

letters he does not do this, though he treats these matters as 'neither necessary for salvation nor binding on the conscience'.[47] However, the strength
of feeling relayed by the Jerusalem leaders on this occasion suggests that
there was some evidence to justify the concern of so many. Tannehill helpfully observes that, with the growth of the Gentile mission, Jewish Christians in the Dispersion must have been included in churches where their
Jewish practices soon became 'a mark of foreignness'.[48] Doubtless, they
soon felt a subtle pressure to conform to the practices of the majority. Even
Paul's arguments about 'strong' believers welcoming and supporting
'weak' believers with scruples about matters of food and drink and ritual
conveyed the impression that his position as a liberated Jew was ultimately
the most desirable (cf. Rom. 14:1–15:13; 1 Corinthians 8–9).[49] For the sake of
the gospel and to win people from every context, Paul felt free to follow
Jewish ways in Jewish, but not in Gentile company (1 Cor. 9:20-23). So the
accusation against Paul reported to him by James was based on a distorted
view of what he said and wrote. Like Jesus and Stephen before him, he had
to contend with false witnesses who misrepresented him.

22-24   The Jerusalem leaders were troubled to know what to do
about protecting Paul's reputation, asking, *'What shall we do? They will certainly hear that you have come' (pantōs akousontai hoti elēlythas)*.[50] They themselves appear to have had confidence in his orthodoxy, but were worried
that Paul's detractors would make life difficult for him.[51] Their advice suggests some division of opinion about Paul in the Jerusalem Christian community, with some being more antagonistic to him than others. James and
the elders advise Paul to take public action by joining in a purification rite
and paying the expenses of four men who were apparently members of the
church and had *'made a vow'*. Reference to having *'their heads shaved'* suggests that these men were completing a temporary Nazirite vow (cf. Nu.
6:1-21; *m. Nazir* 1:1–9:5; Josephus, *War* 15.1). As mentioned in connection

47. Bruce 1990, 446. For example, with respect to circumcision, cf. 1 Cor. 7:18-19; Gal.
5:6; 6:15.

48. Tannehill 1990, 269.

49. Cf. Barrett 1998, 1009, who draws special attention to Paul' position in Gal.
2:12-14.

50. There is a widely supported variant of the last sentence *(pantōs dei plēthos
synelthein akousontai gar elēlythas)*, which is rendered by KJV 'the multitude must needs
come together, for they will hear that thou art come'). However, if the longer form of this
text is original, it is hard to explain why it has been cut down by a range of good MSS. The
only real possibility is an early copying error. In textual criticism, the shorter text is normally judged the original. Cf. Barrett 1998, 1009-10.

51. Bruce 1990, 446, suggests that 'the elders were well-meaning but deeply worried
men who knew that, if they appeared to countenance Paul by accepting the Gentile
churches' gift, it would prejudice their mission to the Jewish people and their influence with
their own flock'. This solution has the merit of taking the Gentile churches' gift as a necessary part of the reconstruction of the event. Cf. Haenchen 1971, 613-14; J. D. G. Dunn, *Unity
and Diversity in the New Testament: An Inquiry into the Character of Earliest Christianity* (London: SCM, 1977), 257.

with 18:18, Jews made such vows of abstinence to God, either in thankfulness for past blessings or as part of a petition for future blessings. The Greek *(hagnistheti syn autois)* literally means 'be purified with them'. In what sense did Paul need to be purified and how could he join with these men in their 'purification'?[52] On his return from Gentile territory, it is likely that Paul would have needed a seven-day period of ritual purification before participating in temple worship (Nu. 19:11-13 gives the pattern of this purification rite; cf. *m. Ohol.* 2:3; 17:5; 18:6). In the process of completing his own period of purification, Paul could have helped four impoverished Nazirites complete their purification or period of separation by paying their expenses (cf. Nu. 6:3, where *hagnisthesetai* means 'he shall abstain'). The completion of two different kinds of purification/separation would thus coincide in time.[53] Paying the cost of the offering these men had to make when discharging their vow would be a pious act of charity on Paul's part. Shaving the hair which had grown during the period of the vow was a critical aspect of the concluding ritual.[54] Thus James and the elders claimed that *'everyone will know there is no truth in these reports about you, but that you yourself are living in obedience to the law'* (stoicheis kai autos phylasson ton nomon, 'you yourself conform by keeping the law'). Although some have doubted that the Paul we know from his letters could have agreed to such a proposal, his co-operation can be understood as 'a sign of his respect for his Jewish heritage and his desire to lay claim to it'.[55] Such a public display of his piety *(everyone will know)* would have been no superficial sop to the complainers, but a risky business, enabling Paul's enemies to plan action against him on a particular day.[56] However, Paul may not have shared the elders' optimism about the effect this action, might have in calming the fears of his opponents.[57] It was certainly a conciliatory action, but, in view

52. Marshall 1980, 345, outlines three possible ways in which the expression 'purified with them' could be understood.

53. Cf. Bruce 1990, 447. The same terminology of purification or separation is used for both rituals (cf. Nu. 6:3; 19:12), but the context in Acts 21 does not imply that Paul took a Nazirite vow at this point or that the four men had to be purified from defilement as Paul did. It seems as though two separate rituals would be brought together by Paul's actions. So also Witherington 1998, 649.

54. Nu. 6:14-15 prescribes the necessary food and drink offerings. According to *m. Nazir* 2:5-6, these offerings, together with 'the hair of his separation' that was cut and then burned at the end of the vow, was called 'a hair offering'. Cf. Barrett 1998, 1011-12.

55. Tannehill 1990, 270. The ritual would be a sort of confessional act, 'a confession of the validity of law and temple for the Jewish people'.

56. Cf. Tannehill 1990, 270. It was also a risky action from the perspective of Paul's teaching about the law and its role in the gospel era.

57. Cf. Bruce 1990, 447. Barrett 1998, 1013, rightly questions whether Paul was prepared to use such an occasion to indicate to Jewish Christians that he was a regular observer of the law, noting that this is different from the policy stated in 1 Cor. 9:19-23, which appears to focus on his behaviour in the presence of unbelieving Jews. Nevertheless, this action was not one that would compromise the truth of the gospel by implying the need for obedience to the law in addition to faith in Christ. Cf. Witherington 1998, 651.

of the outcome, Luke may be suggesting that 'such an action for the sake of peace was the wrong thing for Paul to do, even if it led towards the fulfilment of God's will for him'.[58]

25 The advice to Paul concludes with a reference to the Jerusalem Council decision (15:23-29), which has not been mentioned since 16:4: '*As for the Gentile believers, we have written to them our decision that they should abstain from food sacrificed to idols, from blood, from the meat of strangled animals and from sexual immorality*'. This functions in the present context to reassure those present — and so also the reader — that the Jerusalem leaders are not revisiting the question of the Mosaic law for Gentile believers. Rather, the point at issue is Paul's alleged teaching about the role of the law in the life of Jewish Christians.[59]

26 *The next day Paul took the men and purified himself along with them.* As noted in connection with v. 24, the terminology here *(syn autois hagnistheis)* suggests that Paul began his own weeklong purificatory process in conjunction with the final week of the temporary Nazirite vow taken by these four men. *Then he went to the temple to give notice of the date when the days of purification would end and the offering would be made for each of them.* 'Since Paul's own purification must be complete before he could associate himself with the Nazirites in the discharge of their vow, he probably gave notice at this time both of his undertaking the purification rite required in one returning from a Gentile land and of the impending discharge of their vow.'[60] Into this minefield of ritual requirements and prohibitions Paul willingly stepped, perhaps anticipating the dangerous consequences that followed.

2. Misrepresented and Attacked (21:27-32)

Conflict erupts for Paul when Jews from Asia see him at the temple and accuse him of 'teaching everyone everywhere against our people and our law and this place' (vv. 27-28). This charge is a larger version of the one mentioned in v. 21. Paul is specifically accused of defiling the temple by taking Gentiles into the prohibited area, though Luke makes it clear that this was a distortion of the facts (v. 29). As in Ephesus (19:23-31), Paul's opponents are successful in creating a riot and his life is seriously at risk (vv. 30-31). Men-

---

58. Marshall 1980, 342.

59. Against a variety of critics, Bruce 1990, 448, rightly argues that it is unnecessary to infer from 21:25 that Paul is being told of the Jerusalem decree for the first time. Cf. Barrett 1998, 1013-15. There are a number of textual variants in v. 25 which are discussed by Barrett, including the Western expansion, 'But concerning the Gentiles who have become believers, *they have nothing to say to you, for* we have sent a letter with our judgment that they should *observe nothing of the kind, except to* keep themselves from. . . .' Cf. Witherington 1998, 650-51, and my comments on 15:20, for variations in the way the Jerusalem Decree is recounted.

60. Bruce 1990, 448.

tion of 'the whole city' being aroused and in uproar against him suggests 'rejection of Paul by Israel itself'.[61] Only the intervention of the commander of the Roman troops in Jerusalem saves him from death (vv. 31-32).

27-29 *When the seven days were nearly over* (the period prescribed for ritual defilement; cf. v. 23 note; Nu. 19:12),[62] *some Jews from the province of Asia saw Paul at the temple.* The attack on Paul was not instigated by strict Jewish Christians from Jerusalem but by *Jews from the province of Asia.* If these people had deliberately followed Paul to Jerusalem in order to counteract his influence, they were as determined as the Jewish opponents mentioned in 14:19; 17:13. It is likely that they were among the antagonists Paul met in Ephesus (20:19). Luke further describes them as those who *had previously seen Trophimus the Ephesian in the city with Paul and assumed that Paul had brought him into the temple.* Presumably they knew Trophimus from Ephesus and thought they finally had proof of Paul's treachery. The uproar in Jerusalem is thus directly linked to Paul's recent success in advancing the gospel in Asia. *They stirred up the whole crowd and seized him, shouting, 'People of Israel, help us!'* Their accusation was that Paul had been teaching *'everyone everywhere against our people and our law and this place'.* The expression *everyone everywhere* goes beyond the charge of v. 21, implying that Paul was misleading both Jews and Gentiles. The claim that he had been teaching against *our people and our law and this place* is also broader than the previous one, suggesting that, like Stephen before him (cf. 6:13-14), Paul was attacking the fundamentals of Judaism. But the allegation that *'he has brought Greeks into the temple and defiled this holy place'* was even more serious and, if proven, would have been worthy of a death sentence.[63] Gentiles were allowed into the outer court of the temple but not into the inner precincts where Paul had gone. Paul would hardly have put his own life and that of Trophimus at risk by taking him beyond the wall at the foot of the stairs leading up to the inner courts, with its warning in Greek and Latin about foreigners going no further.[64] Moreover, it is ironical and tragic that

61. Gaventa 2003, 301. Gaventa notes that this is a reversal of what happened on the Day of Pentecost, when Jews from Jerusalem and different parts of the Dispersion came together to listen to Peter's preaching.

62. Bruce 1990, 448-49, notes that the purificatory ritual was performed on the third and the seventh day and argues that Paul was in the temple for the second of these. If the perfect participle in 24:18 is to be given its proper force (*hēgnismenon*), his opponents found him in the temple when he had already been purified. Cf. Marshall 1980, 347.

63. Bruce 1990, 449, cites Josephus, *War* 6.126 as evidence that even Roman citizens could be put to death for defiling the temple in Jerusalem. H. W. Tajra, *The Trial of St. Paul: A Juridical Exegesis of the Second Half of Acts*, WUNT 2, no. 35 (Tübingen: Mohr [Siebeck], 1989), 123, emphasizes that temple profanation was the only basis on which his opponents could secure a death sentence for Paul. *kekoinōken* (v. 28, 'has defiled', perfect tense) implies that the temple is now in a state of defilement, making it impossible for the pious to enter and enjoy its benefits.

64. Cf. Josephus, *War* 5.193-94; 6.124-25; *Ant.* 15.417; Philo, *On the Embassy to Gaius* 212. Two of these notices have been found, one in 1871 and another in 1935. The message

he should have been charged with this offence when he was engaged in an act of purification 'so that he would not defile the temple'![65] Teaching against *our people* doubtless relates to the growth of the Gentile churches and Paul's failure to insist that Gentile converts should become proselytes of Judaism, thus threatening the distinctive position of the Jewish people. Although Luke has not previously alerted us to these concerns about Paul, he shows by means of vv. 21 and 28 that there was a long-standing problem, which had finally been brought to full and open expression. In effect, 'when Paul reaches Jerusalem, he becomes the lightning rod through which the pent-up energy surrounding this issue is discharged'.[66] Paul's attitude towards Judaism dominates the next chapters as he seeks to persuade various people that he is a loyal Jew and that his mission is not anti-Jewish.

30-32 *The whole city was aroused, and the people came running from all directions.* The disturbance created in Jerusalem is reminiscent of the uproar in Ephesus created by Paul's Gentile opponents (19:29-34). *Seizing Paul* (epilabomenoi, 'when they had seized'),[67] *they dragged him from the temple, and immediately the gates were shut.* These would possibly be the gates between the inner and outer courts, which were probably shut by the captain of the temple (cf. 4:1) to prevent further desecration.[68] Normally a person charged with such an offence would have been handed over to the temple authorities for trial and, if found guilty, for execution. But the lynching of someone caught in the act was apparently condoned *(they were trying to kill him).*[69] News soon reached *the commander of the Roman troops that the whole city of Jerusalem was in an uproar.* 'The military tribune in charge of the cohort' *(ho chiliarchos tēs speirēs)* is actually named as Claudius Lysias in 23:26. He plays an important role in the unfolding drama of the next few chapters. The seriousness of the disturbance is indicated by the fact that the commander himself *at once took some officers and soldiers and ran down to the crowd.*[70] Roman troops were stationed in the Antonia Fortress (Josephus, *War* 5.244), which adjoined the western part of the north wall of the temple area. Two flights of stairs led down into the outer court (cf. vv. 35, 40). The

---

reads: 'No foreigner may enter within the barricade which surrounds the temple and enclosure. Anyone who is caught doing so will have himself to blame for what follows — death' (trans. Witherington 1998, 654).

65. Marshall 1980, 347.

66. Tannehill 1990, 270. Tannehill 1985, 69-85, argues that 'the problem of Judaism' is a central theme in Acts and that it becomes more acute as the narrative progresses.

67. A different form of the same verb is translated 'arrested' by TNIV in v. 33.

68. Cf. Jeremias, *Jerusalem*, 210. Johnson 1992, 382, suggests a symbolism in the shutting of the gates to Paul 'that marks Paul as an outsider to the cultic life of Judaism' and is 'the final response of the non-Christian Jerusalem Jews to the apostle'. Witherington 1998, 655, thinks that Luke does not give enough clues that this is his intent here.

69. Bruce 1990, 451.

70. The *officers* are centurions *(hekatontarchas)*, and the plural suggests at least two, 'presumably accompanied by two centuries, with a paper, but not necessarily an actual, strength of 200 men' (Barrett 1998, 1022).

garrison was doubtless well prepared for such events, since riots often took place at festival times, while the city was full of pilgrims.[71] *When the rioters saw the commander and his soldiers, they stopped beating Paul.* The number of troops was sufficient to warn them that the riot could not continue in this way.

3. Arrested and Questioned (21:33-40)

In terms of Luke's narrative, this is the end of Paul's freedom to move about and preach the gospel, though the remaining chapters show him taking every opportunity to testify to Christ while imprisoned. He is rescued from danger, but there is no miraculous release from captivity (cf. 5:17-21; 12:1-17; 16:25-30).[72] Only when he reaches Rome is a measure of freedom restored, so that he is able to preach and teach more openly, while under house arrest (28:16-31). The commander of the Roman cohort in Jerusalem becomes a key player in events from this point until Paul is safely delivered into the hands of the provincial governor in Caesarea (23:31-35). He first suspects that Paul is a returning terrorist, who recently caused havoc in Jerusalem (21:37-38). Hearing Paul's brief self-description and request to speak to the people, he gives Paul the opportunity to defend himself before the crowd (vv. 39-40). In the next two chapters, the commander becomes progressively aware of Paul's true character and the real reasons for the conflict.

33-35 *The commander came up and arrested him* (*epelabato*, 'seized', as in v. 30) *and ordered him to be bound with two chains,* possibly attaching him to a soldier on either side. This commander (*chiliarchos*, 'leader of a thousand'; Lat. *tribunus militum*, 'military tribune'), who was in charge of the troops stationed in Jerusalem, has a further role in Acts 21–23 as 'the first of a small group of Roman officials who go through a process of learning about Paul'.[73] First, he tries to discover Paul's identity and to find out about the charge against him *(Then he asked who he was and what he had done).* However, since *some shouted one thing and some another, and since the commander could not get at the truth because of the uproar,* he ordered that *Paul be taken into the barracks* (the Antonia Fortress; cf. v. 31). *When Paul reached the steps* (cf. v. 31 note), *the violence of the mob was so great he had to be carried by the soldiers.*

71. B. Rapske, *The Book of Acts in Its First-Century Setting*, Vol. 3: *The Book of Acts and Paul in Roman Custody* (Grand Rapids: Eerdmans; Carlisle: Paternoster, 1994), 137-38, provides a description of the fortress and notes its strategic importance for the protection and defence of the city and temple.

72. Tannehill 1990, 271, opposes the view of R. I. Pervo, *Profit with Delight: The Literary Genre of the Acts of the Apostles* (Philadelphia: Fortress, 1987), 24, 27, that Acts presents a 'theology of glory' because imprisonment and danger are regularly occasions for the demonstration of extraordinary power and courage rather than real experiences of weakness and suffering.

73. Tannehill 1990, 273.

36-40 *The crowd that followed kept shouting, 'Get rid of him!' (aire auton;*
cf. 22:22). Use of the same expression by the crowd at the trial of Jesus (Lk.
23:18; Jn. 19:15) suggests a further parallel in Paul's experience. In spite of
this call for his execution, Paul was delivered from death by the intervention of the commander. The latter was surprised when Paul addressed him
in rather formal and polite Greek (*ei exestin moi eipein ti pros se*, 'Is it permitted for me to say something to you?'). This reinforced his suspicion about
who Paul might be, leading him to suggest, *'Aren't you the Egyptian who
started a revolt and led four thousand terrorists out into the desert some time ago?'*
Greek was widely spoken in Egypt and, since Paul appeared to be a foreign
rebel inciting a riot, it was easy to conclude that he was that notorious
Egyptian, renewing his efforts to take Jerusalem.[74] Josephus tells of a false
prophet from Egypt who came to Jerusalem about AD 54 and led a multitude to the Mount of Olives, promising that they could march in and seize
the city when the walls fell down at his command. Felix the Roman governor had sent troops against them, killing four hundred and capturing two
hundred of these *terrorists (andras tōn sikariōn*, 'dagger men').[75] The Egyptian escaped and was never seen again. Since the people of Jerusalem had
assisted the Romans in repulsing him, it was reasonable to suppose that, if
he had reappeared, they might be opposing him again.[76] Such a comparison highlights the degree of public disturbance taking place in response to
the false accusations against Paul. His answer was to declare himself *'a Jew,
from Tarsus in Cilicia, a citizen of no ordinary city'*,[77] indicating that he was
someone who had every right to be heard and to be treated properly. People in antiquity were judged by the importance of the place where they
were born: 'their own personal honor and dignity was in part derived from
the honor rating of the place from which they came'.[78] Tarsus was promi-

---

74. Marshall 1980, 352, renders *ouk ara sy ei ho Aigyptios*, 'Surely, then, you are the
Egyptian?' Barrett 1998, 1024, prefers the less positive, 'So are you not the Egyptian?'

75. *sikarios* is a Latin loanword (from *sica*, 'dagger'). The title *sicarii* ('dagger men',
'assassins') came to be applied to the most fanatical of Jewish nationalists, who began to be
active at this time and, after murdering the former high priest Jonathan, emerged as bitter
enemies of pro-Roman Jews. Bruce 1990, 453, notes that 'they mingled with crowds at festivals and stabbed their victims unawares'. Cf. Josephus, *War* 2.254-57; *Ant.* 20.162-65, 185-87.

76. Cf. Josephus, *War* 2.261-63; *Ant.* 20.169-72. Bruce 1990, 452, suggests that Luke's
record of 4,000 terrorists is more likely than Josephus's 30,000. Josephus tells how many imposters at this time led people into the wilderness, promising to perform miracles (*War*
2.259; *Ant.* 20.167-68). Cf. P. W. Barnett, 'The Jewish Sign Prophets, AD 40-70', *NTS* 27 (1980-
81), 679-97; Barrett 1998, 1025-26.

77. Once again, the use of litotes as a figure of speech (*no ordinary city*) becomes a
means of accentuating the positive: Paul is expressing some pride in his civic status and expects the commander to react accordingly. Witherington 1998, 663-64, notes specific evidence that Jews could be citizens in Hellenistic cities. Cf. Rapske, *Roman Custody*, 72-83, for a
full discussion of the issues relating to Paul's orthodoxy as a Jew and his claim to full citizenship in Tarsus.

78. Witherington 1998, 663. Johnson 1992, 385, observes that, as in 16:35-39, Paul is
'fully conscious of his rights and is willing to take advantage of them; he is by no means shy

nent in the first century because of its political, economic, and intellectual life. An inscription proclaims: 'Tarsus, the first and greatest and most beautiful metropolis'.[79] Paul does not make anything of his Roman citizenship until 22:25, but his claim to be a citizen of an important Hellenistic city impressed the commander enough to allow him to speak to the crowd. The address that follows is designed to explain and defend both his orthodoxy as a Jew and his divine calling to minister to Gentiles (22:1-21). *Paul stood on the steps* (leading up to the barracks) *and motioned to the crowd* (the orator's gesture of waving the hand is mentioned also in 13:16; 19:33; 26:1). When they were all silent, he spoke to them in Aramaic (*tē Hebraïdi dialektō*, 'in the Aramaic speech').[80] In a few minutes, 'Paul has gone from being a passive body, seized by two different groups — almost killed by one, about to be punished by another — to appearing as the central agent in control of the embroilment.'[81] The commander's education about Paul and his situation continues in the following chapters. 'He plans to examine Paul by torture but quickly changes his mind when he learns that Paul is a Roman citizen (22:24-29). He continues his investigation by bringing Paul before the Sanhedrin (22:30), and from the response to Paul's shout before that body he learns that the real issues are disputes of the Jewish law (23:28-29).'[82] By the time he sends him to Felix the governor, his assumptions about Paul have changed considerably (cf. 23:26-30). In the light of erroneous identifications of Paul by his Jewish opponents and the Roman commander, Luke presents Paul carefully defining himself and his God-given mission in the speeches that follow.

INTRODUCTION TO ACTS 22

The predictions relating to Paul's future in Acts 20:23; 21:11 give the expectation of physical hardship, restriction, and humiliation, leading him to express a willingness to die for the sake of the Lord Jesus and the gospel

---

about his heritage or the privileges that accompany it — both from the Greek and from the Jewish side'.

79. Rapske, *Roman Custody*, 73.

80. Except in Rev. 9:11; 16:16, where 'Hebrew' is meant, such expressions in the NT refer to Aramaic, which was the Palestinian vernacular and 'the *lingua franca* of non-Greek speakers in the eastern Roman world and in the Parthian Empire' (Bruce 1990, 453). Cf. Barrett 1998, 1027-28, for a fuller discussion.

81. Skinner, *Locating Paul*, 113. Skinner comments on the way commentators have treated this scene with incredulity. However, Acts 19:30-31 reveals a fearless and courageous Paul, who is keen to seize the opportunity to defend himself and his mission in a similarly dangerous situation. Furthermore, Paul, the hardened traveller, can hardly have been physically overwhelmed by the sort of treatment mention in 21:30-31.

82. Tannehill 1990, 274, who concludes that, in this way, 'the narrator offers a little subplot: the education of a Roman'.

(20:24; 21:13). However, as the narrative unfolds in Acts 21–28, Paul's experience as a prisoner is surprisingly different. Whatever circumstances his detention might impose are 'consistently diminished or overshadowed, while Paul's own confidence, importance, and security are emphasized'.[1] Custody does not truncate his evangelistic and missionary work, but rather offers 'new locations and new audiences for his proclamation to continue'.[2] So the custody settings reflect 'the triumph — although not an unmitigated triumph — of the gospel and of Paul's vocation over the most concentrated attempts of his enemies to squelch and discredit him'.[3] The speeches in Acts 22–26 are forensic in character, more designed for defence and attack than Paul's previous addresses.[4] However, an evangelistic and persuasive aspect to these speeches can also be observed, particularly with reference to Paul's teaching about the resurrection from the dead.

Paul's 'progress' in the closing chapters of Acts may also be charted geographically. 'While not free to move around as he pleases, Paul the prisoner still remains on the move, journeying from one trial venue to another, presenting his case before progressively higher courts of appeal.'[5] The first defensive speech in Jerusalem (22:1-21) is framed by two brief exchanges between Paul and the Roman commander — the first dealing with Paul's request to speak (21:37-40) and the second with the crowd's reaction to his address (22:22-29). Both exchanges involve disclosures about Paul's citizenship status. 'This entire narrative-discourse unit focuses on establishing Paul's Greek, Jewish, and Roman credentials as a model witness and citizen on the basis of his associations with exemplary places and people.'[6] Paul is 'fully a member of the two worlds to which he has been sent',[7] being a devout Jew and a Roman citizen. Acts 22 highlights some of the tensions

---

1. M. L. Skinner, *Locating Paul: Places of Custody as Narrative Settings in Acts 21–28*, SBLAB 13 (Atlanta: SBL, 2003), 109. Paul is not cast as a superhero by Luke, but the narrative highlights the wisdom and protection Jesus promised to disciples in such circumstances.

2. Skinner, *Locating Paul*, 109. Skinner notes that 'the mission of Paul moves from public avenues to the restricted corridors of the highest strata of human authority'.

3. Skinner, *Locating Paul*, 109. What Skinner says about the custody settings is true, but it is not quite the same thing to argue that prisons for Paul are not 'places of physical limitations, suffering, and social ignominy'. Luke plays down the latter while accentuating the former.

4. Witherington 1998, 660-61, describes the speeches prior to Acts 20 as deliberative in character.

5. Spencer 1997, 202. Spencer notes that in Acts 22–23 there is a fairly close correspondence between 'discourse time' (how long it takes to relate the account) and 'story time' (how long the events in the story are presumed to transpire). Later narratives cover much longer spans of time in relatively less space.

6. Spencer 1997, 207. However, 'since two of those with whom Paul aligns himself are executed criminals (Jesus and Stephen), his standard of noble character obviously does not always fit conventional norms'. Witherington 1998, 665, notes that 'the issue of *ethos*, or the character of a person, is paramount in forensic rhetoric'.

7. Tannehill 1990, 284.

involved in this 'dual citizenship' and points to the controlling role of the risen Lord Jesus in shaping Paul's life and ministry.

C. Defending His Mission and His Gospel (22:1-21)

Paul's defence before the Jerusalem crowd is the first of several speeches responding to the apparently intractable problem of Jewish resistance to his mission. For Luke, this is a problem that cannot be ignored, and so it features again and again in the final chapters of his work.[8] An account of Paul's calling is critical to his defence, both here and in 26:9-18. He recalls his former zeal as a Jew and clearly states the reasons why he became a Christian and went to the Gentiles. Paul seeks to explain his actions by setting them within the context of God's calling and the revelation of his will (vv. 14-15, 18, 21). After a brief appeal to listen to his defence, he gives an account of his former life in Judaism (vv. 3-5), his encounter with the risen Jesus on the Damascus road (vv. 6-11), the role played by Ananias in the redirection of his life (vv. 12-16), and the vision of Jesus received later in the Jerusalem temple, confirming his call to preach to the Gentiles (vv. 17-21; cf. 7:55-56 [Stephen]).[9]

1-2 Paul's address *('brothers and fathers')* shows 'proper respect to a gathering which will include his seniors as well as his contemporaries and juniors'.[10] *'Listen now to my defence'* does not introduce a formal trial, responding directly to the charges made in 21:28, but Paul does seek to persuade his audience that his mission is deeply rooted in the world of Judaism and is unquestionably the will of God. The word *defence (apologia)* was a technical term (cf. Plato, *Apol.* 28A; *Phaedr.* 267A; Wis. 6:10; Josephus, *Against Apion* 2:147), used by Christians both formally and informally (cf. Acts 25:16; 1 Cor. 9:3; 2 Cor. 7:11; Phil. 1:7, 16; 2 Tim. 4:16; 1 Pet. 3:15).[11] Witnesses are mentioned who can confirm various aspects of Paul's defence

---

8. See Tannehill 1990, 274-75, against R. I. Pervo, *Profit with Delight: The Literary Genre of the Acts of the Apostles* (Philadelphia: Fortress, 1987), 137-38. On the historicity of Acts 22, see Barrett 1998, 1032-33.

9. Witherington 1998, 666-68, discusses various analyses of the structure of the speech that have been made. He concludes that, from a formal, rhetorical perspective, there is an *exordium* (vv. 1-2), and a *narratio* (vv. 3-21), 'in which Paul will insinuate what the following proofs will involve, but they are never developed'. As in Acts 17, the speech is interrupted at the most contentious point (v. 22).

10. Barrett 1998, 1033.

11. The cognate verb *apologeomai* ('make a defence') is used in Lk. 12:11; 21:14; Acts 19:33; 24:10; 25:8; 26:1, 2, 24. Defence is clearly an important theme in Acts 22–26. Tannehill 1990, 276-77, notes that in some respects Paul's speech follows the pattern recommended for forensic defence speeches in Greco-Roman rhetoric. However, in vv. 17-21, Paul departs from this pattern by speaking of things that arouse further cries for him to be put to death. At this point he 'does not choose words designed to win the hearts of his audience, as the reaction in v. 22 makes clear'. Cf. note 14 below.

(22:5, 9, 12-16), and the Lord's appearance is recorded in a form that would appeal to an audience used to hearing accounts of such divine encounters. Paul's continuing loyalty to Israel is later explained in terms of his commitment to proclaim the hope of Israel fulfilled in Jesus the Messiah (26:6-8; 28:20). A defence of his gospel about the risen Jesus is intimately connected with the defence of his mission. Marshall rightly points out that, in the light of Jesus' words in Luke 12:11-12; 21:12-15, a Christian apology 'includes the concept of witness to him'.[12] Skinner adds that such predictions evoke 'an expectation of and confidence in divine guidance', from the Holy Spirit (Lk. 12:12) and from Jesus himself (Lk. 21:15).[13] Jesus' promises are fulfilled when Paul is enabled to testify in synagogues and prisons, and before governors and kings. Paul secures the attention of the Jerusalem crowd *(they became very quiet)* by addressing them *in Aramaic (en Hebraïdi;* cf. 21:40 note), perhaps suggesting that he was more of a Palestinian Jew than some had imagined.[14]

1. Paul's Former Life in Judaism (22:3-5)

As in 21:39, Paul's fundamental identity is expressed in the confession, 'I am a Jew' (22:3). However, in this context he moves quickly from identifying Tarsus as the place of his birth to establishing his orthodox upbringing and education in Jerusalem. Such training made him as zealous for God as any of his current opponents. A specific proof of this was his former persecution of Christians (v. 4), to which the high priest and 'all the Council' could bear witness. He even obtained their written permission to bring Christians from Damascus to Jerusalem for punishment (v. 5). This description of Paul's former life and character is meant to highlight the transformation he goes on to describe (vv. 6-21).

3   Paul is clearly seeking to persuade a Jerusalem audience here.[15] First, he mentions his birth into a Jewish family *('I am a Jew, born in Tarsus of Cilicia').* Paul's Tarsian citizenship would have commended him to the Roman commander (21:39), given that city's reputation in the ancient world.[16]

---

12. Marshall 1980, 353.

13. Skinner, *Locating Paul,* 113-14. Skinner describes the whole of Acts 22–26 as Paul's defence of himself and his gospel. The speeches Paul gives in custody situations reflect his circumstances and enable him to address various allegations against him.

14. Marshall 1980, 353, notes that many Jews from the Dispersion could not speak the Hebrew or Aramaic languages. Bruce 1990, 454, observes that, 'in spite of the sorry appearance that Paul must have presented after his rough handling, Luke portrays him as an impressive and eloquent speaker'.

15. Cf. Barrett 1998, 1031. Most importantly, Paul's conversion is told as an event 'within and not from Judaism', meaning that he has not abandoned Judaism for some foreign cult.

16. Cf. 21:39 note. Spencer 1997, 208, cites the opinion of the geographer Strabo, *Geog.* 14.5.12-15, about the intellectual life of Tarsus.

However, seeking to prove his orthodoxy to this particular crowd, Paul mentions his place of origin only briefly and moves on to his early life in Jerusalem. There are three participles in the Greek, highlighting successive stages in Paul's experience: he was 'born' in Tarsus *(gegennēmenos)*, 'brought up' in Jerusalem *(anatethrammenos)*, and 'educated' at the feet of Gamaliel *(pepaideumenos)*.[17] So Paul's theological roots were essentially in Palestinian rather than Diaspora Judaism. His rabbinic education took place (lit.) 'at the feet of Gamaliel' *(para tous podas Gamaliēl)*,[18] who was a Pharisaic teacher of the law and member of the Sanhedrin, 'respected by all the people' (5:34). Indeed, Gamaliel I was 'arguably the most significant and influential Pharisaic educator in the early 1st century AD'.[19] This phase of Paul's education probably began some time after he turned thirteen, when he was instructed by Gamaliel 'according to the strictness of our ancestral law' *(kata akribeian tou patrōou nomou;* cf. 21:24; 24:14; 25:8; 26:5; 28:17). The term *akribeia* ('strictness') in this expression refers to the punctilious performance of the law by the Pharisaic school.[20] By implication, Paul excelled in the study and practice of Pharisaic teaching. He compares his zeal for God and for the purity of Judaism with that of the crowd, who had gathered to oppose and attack him: *'I was just as zealous for God as any of you are today' (kathōs pantes hymeis este sēmeron,* 'as all of you are today'; cf. Rom. 10:2; Gal. 1:14; Phil. 3:4-7).[21]

4-5 Paul's zeal for God was particularly demonstrated by the fact that he once *'persecuted the followers of this Way to their death'* (cf. 9:1-2; 22:20; 26:9-11), *'arresting both men and women and throwing them into prison'*.[22] The high priest in the mid-30s AD was Caiaphas. Although the personnel may now have been different, Paul claims that the current high priest and the whole council of elders *(pan to presbyterion)* could *'testify' (martyrei)* about

---

17. Witherington 1998, 668-69, argues that these were stock expressions in Greek literature, with the second covering his early rearing by his parents (cf. Plato, *Crito* 50E, 51C; Philo, *On the Life of Moses* 2:1; *Against Flaccus* 158). The same threefold formula is used with reference to Moses in Acts 7:20-22. Barrett 1998, 1034-36, discusses different ways of punctuating this sentence. Cf. Johnson 1992, 387-88. KJV and NRSV wrongly attach 'at the feet of Gamaliel' to 'brought up in this city', implying only two stages in Paul's experience.

18. The Mishnaic idiom of 'sitting at the feet' expressed the fact that pupils sat on the floor while the teacher was on a raised dais. Johnson 1992, 388, points out that elsewhere in Luke-Acts the expression 'at the feet of' always symbolizes submission (cf. Lk. 7:38; 8:35, 41; 10:39; 17:16; 20:43; Acts 2:35; 4:35, 37; 5:2, 10; 7:58; 10:25).

19. B. Rapske, *The Book of Acts in Its First-Century Setting,* Vol. 3: *The Book of Acts and Paul in Roman Custody* (Grand Rapids: Eerdmans; Carlisle: Paternoster, 1994), 94.

20. Cf. Johnson 1992, 388. In 26:5 Paul says he belonged to 'the strictest sect' *(akribestatēn hairesin)* of Judaism. The Pharisees are described in similar terms by Josephus, *Life* 191; *War* 2.162.

21. Instead of *zēlōtēs hyparchōn tou theou* ('being zealous for God'), Western witnesses offer a variety of secondary readings. Cf. Metzger, *Textual Commentary,* 430.

22. With respect to Paul's personal culpability for the death of Christians, Witherington 1998, 670, rightly takes 22:4 to mean that 'Paul took actions and cooperated with efforts that led to the death of various Christians (cf. 9:1)'. Cf. 26:10 note.

these matters. Paul had *'even obtained letters'* of authorization from their predecessors in those offices, addressed *'to their associates in Damascus'*.[23] Rapske observes that 'this portrayal of Paul the persecutor indicates something of his social standing and office'.[24] He was familiar with, and had access to, the highest levels of Jewish officialdom, probably being a member of the Sanhedrin himself, enjoying their confidence and securing their permission for his activities. With their authority, but on his own intiative, Paul went to Damascus *'to bring these people as prisoners to Jerusalem to be punished'*. His zeal was such that he 'persecuted this Way' (*tautēn tēn hodon ediōxa*) wherever he could! What follows is an attempt to explain to his audience the radical change that he experienced on his way to Damascus, implicitly inviting his opponents 'to reevaluate Paul and Jesus, and thereby be changed themselves'.[25] At this point, at least, Paul has not given up trying to persuade his persecutors to accept the divine initiative behind his calling and the gospel about the glorified Messiah which he preached.

2. Paul's Encounter with the Risen Jesus (22:6-11)

This is the second account of Paul's Damascus road experience (cf. 9:1-18; 26:13-18). Such repetition in the narrative of Acts highlights the importance of the event for understanding the significance of the Pauline mission. The second and third accounts differ in detail and style from the first, especially in that they are told from Paul's own point of view (cf. the retelling of the story of Cornelius from Peter's point of view in 11:5-17) rather than from Luke's perspective as narrator.[26] Luke intends the effect of the three accounts to be cumulative. This account differs from the others by including two questions from Paul to Jesus rather than one. The response to the first ('Who are you, Lord?') is the revelation of the heavenly status of 'the Nazorean' (v. 8). In all three accounts, there is a repetition of the revelation that Paul has been persecuting the glorified Jesus by persecuting his people. The response to Paul's second question ('What shall I do, Lord?') is the command to go into Damascus and wait there for further instruction (v. 10).

---

23. *pros tous adelphous* ('to the brothers'; TNIV *to their associates*) highlights the fact that Paul is speaking as a Jew to Jews.

24. Rapske, *Roman Custody*, 100. However, Rapske 111-12, acknowledges that the overall evidence of Acts should make us wary of proposing 'a single-status Paul'. There are indications of 'status tension' or 'status dissonance' which, 'far from needing resolution, must be appreciated in terms of the extent to which they can account for Paul's treatment, particularly how he fares in crisis situations and resultant custodial evaluations'.

25. Tannehill 1990, 279.

26. Tannehill 1990, 275-76, notes that 'the privileged narrator' in Acts 9 and 10 speaks as though present with both characters in the story (with Saul and Ananias in the first, and Peter and Cornelius in the second). However, in the autobiographical account of 22:6-16, Paul does not tell what the Lord said to Ananias when Paul was not present, only what he heard from Ananias directly.

Between these questions and answers, the wording of v. 9 suggest that, 'although the encounter had a character that all could see, only Paul heard what was said, particularly the words that point forward to his commission'.[27] The beginning of this account stresses the supernatural brightness of the light accompanying the divine voice (vv. 6-7). The conclusion makes it clear that Paul was actually blinded by that light (v. 11).

6-8 Paul first recalls what happened as he *'came near Damascus'*. Two unique features of this account highlight the objective nature of the encounter: it was at the brightest time of day (*'about noon'*) that he saw *'a bright light from heaven'*, which supernaturally flashed more brightly than the sun (cf. 9:3). This was not simply a visionary experience (contrast 10:9-16; 16:9-10; 22:17-21), since he was physically blinded for a time (v. 11). Paul reports, *'I fell to the ground and heard a voice say to me, "Saul! Saul! Why do you persecute me?"'*[28] As noted in connection with 9:4-5, the risen Lord viewed the persecution of his disciples as an attack on himself, clearly identifying himself with the church in its suffering (cf. Lk. 10:16; Mt. 25:40). *'"Who are you, Lord?"'* Paul asked, and the reply came, *'"I am Jesus of Nazareth, whom you are persecuting"'*. Only in this version of the story does Jesus use the title 'the Nazorean' (*ho Nazōraios*), though it is elsewhere employed by Peter (2:22; 3:6; 4:10), Paul (26:9), and those accusing Stephen (6:14) and Paul (24:5). It appears to be an alternative for 'Nazarene' (*ho Nazarēnos*; cf. Lk. 4:34; 24:19) and means no more than 'from Nazareth'.[29] Perhaps 'the Nazorean' was one of the ways Paul himself identified Jesus, before coming to believe in his glorified messianic status.

9-11 Paul then says, *'My companions saw the light,*[30] *but they did not understand the voice of him who was speaking to me'*. At first glance, this appears to contradict 9:7. However, both narratives are stressing that Paul's companions shared to some extent in the experience, while not enjoying the full revelation granted to Paul. They *saw the light*, but did not see the risen Jesus; they heard 'the sound' (9:7, *akouontes men tēs phōnēs*),[31] but *did not understand the voice of him who was speaking* (*tēn de phōnēn ouk ēkousan tou lalountos*). The difference between 9:7 and 22:9 is obvious from the Greek syntax, with the former using *tēs phōnēs* absolutely to mean 'the sound',

---

27. Gaventa 2003, 307, commenting on the significance of v. 9 within the dialogue between Jesus and Paul.

28. Several Western witnesses expand 22:7 by adding elements from 26:14. Cf. Metzger, *Textual Commentary*, 430.

29. Against Johnson 1992, 389, 411; Spencer 1997, 209.

30. The Western text and some other MSS add that Paul's companions 'became afraid' (*kai emphoboi egeneto*). This is the reading of the Received Text, and hence also of KJV and NKJV, but it appears to be an expansion of the earliest and most reliable texts. Cf. Metzger, *Textual Commentary*, 430.

31. *phōnē* can mean 'an auditory effect, *sound, tone, noise*', or 'the faculty of utterance, *voice*', or 'a verbal code shared by a community to express ideas and feelings, *language*' (BDAG). Cf. Gaventa 2003, 307, on the positioning of this comment about Paul's companions here in the midst of the dialogue between Paul and Jesus.

and the latter qualifying *tēn phōnēn* with the substantive participle *tou lalountos* to mean *the voice of him who was speaking*.[32] Paul's companions were not chosen to see or to hear Christ personally as he did (v. 14). Paul then asks, '*"What shall I do, Lord?"*', expressing his readiness to do whatever he is told. This question is not found in 9:7; however, the Lord's words are closely paralleled in both accounts, '*"Get up and go into Damascus. There you will be told all that you have been assigned to do"*'. The Greek perfect tense *(tetaktai)* shows that the task has already been decided and only now needs to be revealed. So Paul records, '*My companions led me by the hand into Damascus, because the brilliance of the light had blinded me*'. Paul here specifies what the account in 9:8-9 only implies, that he was blinded by 'the glory of that light' *(apo tēs doxēs tou phōtos ekeinou)*.[33] Once again it should be noted that Paul's companions were not affected in the same way that he was. All fell to the ground (26:14), but none of them was temporarily blinded by the light they saw.

3. Ananias and the Redirection of Paul's Life (22:12-16)

Ananias is a significant witness to Paul's encounter with the risen Lord and its purpose, here and in 9:10-19. Since he was 'a devout observer of the law' and someone highly respected by all the Jews living in Damascus (v. 12), his testimony is framed in Paul's account so as to have a special appeal to the Jerusalem crowd. In this abbreviated record, he brings physical healing (v. 13) but also the light of God's revelation directly to Paul (vv. 14-15). As God's mouthpiece, he explains God's choice of Paul to know his will, to see the glorified Messiah, to hear words from his mouth, and to be his witness 'to all people' of what he has seen and heard. This prophetic commission clearly included the Gentiles within its scope (cf. 9:15), though Paul does not make that explicit until he recalls the subsequent revelation in the temple (vv. 17-21). Ananias finally becomes the one who challenges Paul to be baptized and have his sins washed away (v. 16). As he calls upon the name of the Lord Jesus for salvation, Paul joins 'the Way' which he previously sought to destroy.

12-13 Telling the story from his own point of view ('*A man named*

---

32. Cf. Polhill 1992, 235 note 15, and my comments on 9:7. Barrett 1998, 1038-39, presents arguments in favour of observing the grammatical distinction between the genitive and accusative case in relation to the verb *akouō* ('hear'). However, he then notes that the accusative is used in 9:4 to explain Paul's experience, whereas the genitive is used in 22:7 to describe the same thing. In short, we cannot say that the difference between 9:7 and 22:9 can be explained simply in terms of the use of the different cases after the verb.

33. Johnson 1992, 389, rightly argues for a literal translation here 'because of the thematic associations throughout the work between light and the "glory of God" by which Luke means God's effective presence in the world (see esp. Luke 2:9, 14, 32; 9:31-32)'. There is also a striking parallel in 2 Cor. 4:6, which appears to have been influenced by Paul's experience on the Damascus road.

Ananias came to see me'), Paul does not include the Lord's separate appearance to Ananias (9:10-16), but simply recounts what Ananias did for him personally. He introduces Ananias, not as a disciple of Jesus (as in 9:10), but as *'a devout observer of the law and highly respected by all the Jews living there'.*[34] This highlights his significance as a reliable witness to Paul's divine encounter, in the context of his appeal to Jews in Jerusalem. In Luke's first telling of the story, the Lord's assurances to Ananias about Paul were designed to convince Ananias and the Christians he represented about the genuineness of Paul's transformation and the importance of the role now given to him. Paul abbreviates the story and has Ananias approach him without fear, in the first instance to restore his sight (*'he stood beside me and said, "Brother Saul, receive your sight!"'*) Addressing him as *brother,* Ananias apparently acknowledges Paul as being already a fellow Christian.[35] Without mentioning the laying on of hands or 'something like scales' falling from his eyes (9:17), Paul then records, *'at that very moment (autē tē hōra,* 'in that very hour') *I was able to see him'.* 'The fact that Paul recovered his sight acted as a divine confirmation that what Ananias had to say to him was indeed a message from the Lord.'[36]

14-15 Ananias now becomes God's mouthpiece to Paul, conveying in his own words the commission previously revealed to him by the Lord (9:15).[37] The term *'"the God of our fathers"'* immediately links Paul with Ananias the 'devout observer of the law' (v. 12) and with the God of Israel. 'He and Saul are servants of the God of the OT; Christianity (it is implied) is the true version of Judaism and Christians are heirs of the OT.'[38] Paul's Damascus road experience is then explained as the means by which *the God of our fathers* indicated that he had *'"chosen"'* Paul *(proecheirisato),*[39] *'"to know his will and to see the Righteous One and to hear words from his mouth"'.* Three infinitives in Greek suggest an equal significance for each item, though a sequence can be discerned. Paul was chosen to know God's will (*gnōnai to thelēma autou)* in a direct and personal way, by being enabled to see the

34. A good spread of the most ancient MSS read *katoikountōn Ioudaiōn* ('the Jews living [there]'). However, the awkwardness of this unqualified use of the verb probably led later scribes to add either *en Damaskō* ('in Damascus') or *ekei* ('there'). Cf. Metzger, *Textual Commentary,* 431.

35. This is clear from the context of 9:17 and, given that the narratives are meant to be read cumulatively, should be taken as the meaning here (rather than simply meaning 'fellow Jew'). Cf. Witherington 1998, 672.

36. Marshall 1980, 356.

37. Bruce 1990, 457, rightly observes that there is no real discrepancy here with Paul's insistence in Gal. 1:1, 12, that he received his message and his apostleship from God and not from any human source.

38. Barrett 1998, 1041.

39. Bruce 1990, 457, following *ND* 3 (1978), § 62, says the meaning of this verb is 'almost "hand-picked"' (cf. 3:20 [Jesus]; 26:16 [Paul]). Barrett 1998, 1041, argues that in a theological context 'this verges on fore-ordination' (Acts 4:28; Rom. 8:29, 30; 1 Cor. 2:7; and Eph. 1:5, 11 use the verb *proorizō* to convey this notion). The appointment in this case is to conversion and to a divinely designated vocation.

risen Christ *(idein ton dikaion)*, and to hear words from his mouth *(akousai phōnēn ek tou stomatos autou*, 'to hear the voice of his mouth'; NRSV 'to hear his own voice').[40] These claims all reappear in the third version of Paul's commissioning in 26:16-17. As before in Jewish contexts, Jesus is described as '*"the Righteous One"*' *(ton dikaion;* cf. 3:14; 7:52). This appears to be a messianic designation, derived from prophetic expectations (cf. 3:14 note), not simply a description of him as a just person. However, it certainly emphasizes his innocence in the face of charges brought against him by his own people.[41] God's new role for Paul is then stated in these terms: '*"You will be his witness to all people of what you have seen and heard"*'. The term *witness (martys)* is most often employed in Acts with respect to the Twelve (1:8, 22; 2:32; 3:15; 10:39, 41; 13:31), who have a foundational and distinctive role. On two occasions, the term is applied to Paul (22:15; 26:16), with clear contextual evidence that he is so called because he has *seen and heard* the risen Christ (cf. 1 Cor. 9:1).[42] His brief was to be Christ's witness *to all people*, which, according to 9:15, meant proclaiming his name 'to the Gentiles and their kings and to the people of Israel' (cf. 1:8). The implication that this includes the Gentiles is made absolutely clear in 22:17-21. Paul quite clearly shared the witness of the Twelve to the risen Christ, but he was not qualified to share their witness to the earthly ministry of Jesus (1:21-22).[43] In the defence scenes in Acts 22–23, he has the opportunity to bear witness to the exalted Jesus before hostile Jewish audiences (23:11; cf. Peter in Acts 4–5), but in Acts 24–26 he has the unique opportunity to bear witness to Jesus also before Gentile rulers. Paul effectively gives testimony to Jesus 'in an ongoing trial that still involves Jesus as well as himself'.[44] In this capacity, he has to suffer in various ways that mirror the suffering of Jesus himself (9:16; cf. 20:23-24; 21:11-14; 22:22).

16 Ananias finally becomes the means by which Paul is baptized

40. Barrett 1998, 1041, considers the possibility that 'to know his will' means that, 'beyond other men, Paul was to understand God's purpose in and his plan for saving mankind, the whole of mankind, including the Gentiles'.

41. Cf. Barrett 1998, 1041.

42. In 22:20 Paul describes Stephen as *martys*, perhaps because he saw and bore witness to the heavenly Son of Man. The term is used in a nontheological sense with respect to the witnesses of Stephen's execution in 7:58. Cf. P. G. Bolt, 'Mission and Witness', in I. H. Marshall and D. G. Peterson (eds.), *Witness to the Gospel: The Theology of Acts* (Grand Rapids/Cambridge: Eerdmans, 1998), 191-214.

43. Tannehill 1990, 280-81, suggests that the scope of Paul's witness is actually wider than that of the Twelve. The narrative of Acts shows that they do not fulfill the command of 1:8 themselves, and Paul speaks of the apostles as Jesus' witnesses 'to the people', meaning Israel (13:31). The scope of Paul's witness is certainly wider in a geographical sense, but Luke is keen to highlight his ministry to Jews in every place where they can be found. Moreover, the commitment of Peter to the Gentile mission is stressed in Acts 10–11, 15. Tannehill's distinction can be upheld only in terms of the wider arena of Paul's work.

44. Tannehill 1990, 281. Tannehill argues that the issues of this trial extend beyond political apologetic and defence of Paul as an individual 'to the claims of the Messiah who, at present, is still accused and persecuted'.

and, by implication, received into the fellowship of the church. His rhetorical question (*'"And now what are you waiting for?"'*) suggests that he completely accepts the genuineness of Paul's conversion. His command (*'"Get up, be baptized and wash your sins away, calling on his name"'*) indicates what Paul must now do in response to God's gracious initiative in his life.[45] There are two imperatives in the Greek middle voice (*baptisai kai apolousai*), suggesting that Paul gets himself baptized and has his sins washed away.[46] A decision has to be made to seek baptism and the cleansing from sin which it represents. The risen Lord had revealed himself and had given a life-changing challenge. Paul's eyes had been opened, both spiritually and physically. Baptism would be an open expression of repentance towards God and faith in the Lord Jesus (cf. 20:21). Although these are unique events in the narrative of Acts, they point to the way in which the Lord continues to encounter people through the preaching of the gospel and to draw them to himself. Baptism expresses repentance and faith because it is a means of *calling on his name (epikaloumenos to onoma autou)*. This expression helps to interpret the meaning of baptism 'in the name of Jesus Christ' (2:38, *epi tō onomati Iēsou Christou*; 10:48, *en tō onomati Iēsou Christou*). 'The name is not a magical instrument effecting supernatural results; the name is invoked, that is, it signifies faith and obedience directed towards Christ.'[47] At the same time, baptism is a means of appropriating the benefits of Christ's saving work (*wash your sins away*) and receiving the promised forgiveness of sins (cf. 2:38 note). The image of washing in 1 Corinthians 6:11; Ephesians 5:26; Titus 3:5; and Hebrews 10:22 is also probably linked to baptism. Outward washing with water expresses the cleansing from sin that is proclaimed in the gospel and received by faith sacramentally in baptism.[48] There is no reference to the gift of the Holy Spirit, as in 2:38; 9:17, since Luke feels no compulsion to mention both elements of the foundational baptismal promise (2:38) in every context.

4. Paul's Subsequent Vision in the Temple (22:17-21)

This narrative is significant both as a sign of Paul's continuing piety as a Jew — visiting the temple to pray — and as a further confirmation of his di-

---

45. Spencer 1997, 209, observes that Paul's implied message to his audience was that his fellowship with Jesus and his followers 'intensified rather than diminished his commitment to purity'.

46. Less probable is a reflexive reading of the middle voice here, indicating that Paul was told to baptize himself. Cf. Bruce 1990, 457-58; Barrett 1998, 1042. The preceding participle *anastas* (meaning 'get up' in this sequence of verbs) seems redundant, though it does suggest the need for Paul to take immediate action.

47. Barrett 1998, 1043.

48. Cf. D. G. Peterson, *Possessed by God: A New Testament Theology of Sanctification and Holiness* (Leicester: Apollos; Grand Rapids: Eerdmans, 1995), 45, 53, 126-27.

vine call to be a witness 'to all people' (v. 15). 'Alongside the Damascus-road Christophany, this second experience creates a "double vision" effect strengthening Paul's testimony.'[49] It clarifies that 'all people' includes Gentiles (v. 21). At the same time, it confirms what Acts has shown in many other contexts, that rejection of the gospel by Jews in one place is the signal to take it to the Gentiles (v. 18). Several other important points are suggested by this narrative. The risen Jesus is Lord of the temple, revealing his will and commissioning his servant in that context. This suggests a certain parallel with the experience of Isaiah (Is. 6:1-13). Paul also acknowledges once more his part in the persecution of the Lord's disciples, particularly in the killing of Stephen (vv. 19-20). The narrative effect of this recollection is to challenge Paul's audience to explain the dramatic transformation of Paul's life and work. In effect, he has taken Stephen's place as the Lord's witness to Israel. Beyond that, he must also bear witness to the nations (v. 21).

17-18   Only in this version of Paul's life is a subsequent vision recorded, which appears to have taken place some three years later, when he *'returned to Jerusalem and was praying at the temple'*.[50] Receiving a vision in the temple marks him out as a prophet of the Lord like Samuel (1 Sam. 3:1-18) or Isaiah (Is. 6:1-9). Moreover, the temple was previously the setting for Simeon (Luke 2:30-32) and Peter (Acts 3:25) to recall God's promises about salvation being available for people from every nation.[51] The vision in 22:17-21 is also significant from a Christological point of view. Paul records how he *'fell into a trance'* (*ekstasis*, as in 10:10; 11:5) and, outside the limits of normal consciousness, *'saw the Lord speaking'*. ' *"Quick!" he said. "Leave Jerusalem immediately, because the people here will not accept your testimony about me."'* Once again it appears to be the risen Lord Jesus who speaks to him. This is implied by the Lord's mention of Paul's *"testimony about me"*, Paul's reference to beating '*"those who believe in you"'*, and his description of Stephen as '*"your martyr"'*. In fact, the parallel with Stephen's vision of the heavenly Son of Man 'standing at the right hand of God' is remarkable (7:55-56). Both visions proclaim the exalted status of Christ, as he shares in the glory and rule of the God of Israel. Moreover, Paul's vision implies that the risen Jesus is Lord of the temple, who reveals his will and commissions

49. Spencer 1997, 210. Note also the 'double vision' effect in Acts 10, as both Cornelius and Peter are guided to come together and divine authorisation is given for Gentiles to receive the gospel and be incorporated in the messianic community through faith in Christ.

50. Luke's only indication of a significant time gap between Paul's initial ministry in Damascus (9:20-25) and his first visit to Jerusalem as a Christian (9:26-30) is in 9:23 ('after many days had gone by'). However, Paul himself is clear in Gal. 1:17-18 that it was 'after three years' that he first visited Jerusalem. Barrett 1998, 1044, is unnecessarily sceptical about the possibility of fitting the story of this temple vision into the framework of either Acts 9 or Gal. 1:17-19.

51. Tannehill 1990, 283, rightly observes that 'the temple setting gives geographical expression to the belief that this promise for the world does not conflict with Israel's calling but, in fact, is rooted in Israel's history and experience of God'.

his servant in that context for his mission to the nations. The parallel with Isaiah's call in Isaiah 6 becomes all the more stunning when it is realised that the risen Lord Jesus takes the role of 'the LORD Almighty' in directing Paul and warning him about the opposition he will receive (cf. the recollection of Is. 6:9-10 in Acts 28:24-28). Although the God of Israel chose him 'to know his will and to see the Righteous One and to hear words from his mouth' (v. 14), he now acknowledges that he was long ago warned about Jewish resistance to his message. According to 9:26-30, Paul was disputing with Hellenists at the time, who then attempted to kill him. The believers rescued him by taking him to Caesarea and sending him off to Tarsus. But now we are told that the Lord's command to *leave Jerusalem immediately* made Paul willing to accept the help of his friends and escape death. Without that command, he may have determined to stay and face the consequences. Once again Luke demonstrates the interplay between divine sovereignty and human responsibility in the process of guidance.

19-21 Continuing the narrative of his visionary encounter in the temple, Paul uses his response to the Lord Jesus to remind the inhabitants of Jerusalem of what their predecessors knew: '*"that I went from one synagogue to another* (*kata tas synagōgas* is best translated distributively, as in TNIV, ESV; contrast KJV, NRSV 'in every synagogue') *to imprison and beat those who believe in you"*'.[52] He further expresses the paradox of his life by insisting that, '*"when the blood of your martyr Stephen was shed, I stood there giving my approval and guarding the clothes of those who were killing him"*' (cf. 7:58; 8:1). Strictly speaking, he acknowledges Stephen's authority as a 'witness' who lost his life because of his testimony to Christ (*martys*; cf. v. 15), and confesses his own role in opposing him. However, it is significant that the text speaks about the blood of Stephen being *shed (exechynneto)*, which suggests the pouring out of blood in sacrifice (cf. Ex. 24:6; Nu. 35:33).[53] For this reason, it is fair to suggest that this particular use of the term 'witness' is 'a step in the direction of the later meaning "martyr" (cf. Rev. 2:13; 17:6)'.[54] Such recollections are designed to remind his audience that Paul himself was once vigorously antagonistic towards Christians and that, in a sense, he took Stephen's place as a witness. His change of direction and subsequent ministry can be explained only in terms of God's unmistakable intervention in his life. So Paul restates the Lord's will for his ministry in the most provocative way possible: '*Then the Lord said to me, "Go; I will send you far away to the Gentiles"*'.[55] Whereas previous announcements in Acts of

---

52. Cf. Marshall 1980, 357; Witherington 1998, 674 note 133.

53. Johnson 1992, 391, notes that this places Stephen in continuity with the prophets who lost their lives because of their testimony (Lk. 11:50), and in particular with Jesus (Lk. 22:20).

54. Bruce 1990, 459. Cf. A. A. Trites, *The New Testament Concept of Witness*, SNTSMS 31 (Cambridge: Cambridge University, 1977), 66-67; Barrett 1998, 1044-45.

55. The future tense 'I will send' (*exapostelō*) probably signifies that 'the fulfilment of the mission belongs to the future' (Barrett 1998, 1045). *eis ethnē makran* could mean 'to far-off

a turning to the Gentiles concerned particular locations (13:46; 18:6), this one involved a 'a significant shift in the cultural context of the mission'.[56] *Far away to the Gentiles* suggests the wider world where Gentiles are in the majority and Jews have little influence. Tannehill suggests that Paul is here expressing the fact that he could not practically resolve the conflict that his life and ministry had created. If he was concerned to win over his audience and escape from captivity, he might have devised a more persuasive conclusion to his speech![57] But Paul was inescapably driven by the conviction that the mission must go forward, despite the cost to him personally. 'When it is blocked among the Jews, it must go forward among the Gentiles, as the Lord commanded.'[58] So the overriding message which Paul conveys to his audience is the sovereign will of God to bring salvation to the nations. God's purpose cannot be denied or ignored, no matter what the implications for the existing structures of religion, culture, and society, or for the individuals who proclaim God's will.

D. Claiming His Right as a Roman Citizen (22:22-30)

Much of Paul's speech was designed to present him as a faithful, law-abiding, and temple-honouring Jew, but 'his commendation of Stephen and legitimisation of his Gentile mission support a more radical image'.[59] As in 21:30-31, mob violence erupts, with another cry for Paul to be put to death (vv. 22-23). The commander is once more concerned to protect Paul (cf. 21:32-36), but he directs that he be scourged and interrogated, since the charge against him is as yet unclear (v. 24). While Paul is being prepared for

---

nations', but the context really demands the more dramatic rendering *far away to the Gentiles.*

56. Tannehill 1990, 282. Tannehill, 283, further notes that Paul and the narrator will not yield on the necessity of turning to the nations when Jews are unreceptive, 'and this necessity will be emphasized again in 28:28'. F. Watson, *Paul, Judaism and the Gentiles,* SNTSMS 56 (Cambridge: Cambridge University, 1986), 31, defends the view that Paul was engaged in preaching only to Jews in his early years as a Christian. However, Bruce 1990, 459, argues that 'this cannot be squared with Paul's own account of his call (Gal. 1:16; 2:7-8), whatever may be said of Luke's account'.

57. Barrett 1998, 1032, points to the fact that Luke uses interruption for effect in 4:1; 7:54, 57; 10:44; 17:32; 19:28; 23:7, but then goes on to consider how Paul might have continued and actually responded to the charges against him in the light of this divine call to go to the Gentiles.

58. Tannehill 1990, 277. Paul will keep trying to remove suspicion against him and his mission in later speeches, but the problem of widespread Jewish opposition will not be solved even by the end of Acts. Tannehill, 278, goes on to suggest that points are being scored in these chapters 'that might persuade some Jews — not an angry mob, perhaps, but those in a more reasonable frame of mind. For Christian readers of Acts these points could serve as suggestions of how Paul's essential position might be maintained without ending the possibility of conversation with Judaism.'

59. Spencer 1997, 211.

this inquisition, he asks whether it is legal to scourge a Roman citizen who has not even been found guilty (v. 25). This leads to a dialogue with the commander about Roman citizenship (vv. 26-28), paralleling the dialogue in 21:37-39 about Paul's identity. The interrogation process ceases (v. 29), and the commander attempts to find out from the Jewish Sanhedrin about the accusation against Paul (v. 30). Thus, Paul's Jewish and Roman credentials are considered in 21:37–22:30, and he is shown to be 'fully a member of the two worlds to which he has been sent'.[60]

22-24 *The crowd listened to Paul until he said this.* Mention of the Gentiles reminded them of their main grievance against him. *Then they raised their voices and shouted, 'Rid the earth of him! He's not fit to live!'* (cf. Lk. 4:24-29; 23:18; Acts 21:36).[61] With this shouting, they were *throwing off their cloaks and flinging dust into the air.* In 13:51, shaking the dust off the feet is a gesture of warning and of disassociation from those who oppose the will of God. Some have taken the participle *rhiptountōn* in 22:23 to mean 'shaking out' and have understood the crowd to be similarly expressing their rejection of blasphemy by shaking out the dust from their clothes.[62] Even if the verb is understood in the sense of 'tearing' or 'throwing off', the crowd appears to be 'repelling the wickedness of Paul's words' with 'the whole repetoire of apotropaic gestures exhibited elsewhere in the narrative: shouting (Acts 7:57; 14:14), tearing the garments (14:14; 18:6), throwing dust (13:51)'.[63] As the situation deteriorated, *the commander ordered that Paul be taken into the barracks* (cf. 21:34) and *directed that he be flogged and interrogated in order to find out why the people were shouting at him like this.* TNIV obscures the full horror of the threat by translating *be flogged.* Luke refers to the Roman practice of examining someone by scourging (*mastixin anetazein tina;* Lat. *flagrum, flagellum*). This involved whipping with leather thongs, to which rough pieces of bone or metal had been attached. The scourge was 'a murderous instrument of torture, much more fearful than the lictors' rods at Philippi. A slave or alien might be scourged in order to make him confess the truth (the theory being that he could not be trusted to confess it without such persuasion).'[64] As in 21:30-40, the commander is concerned to protect Paul from mob violence, but he offers him the only form of justice that seems appropriate in a situation where the charge is as yet unclear.[65]

60. Tannehill 1990, 284.

61. It is possible that *tēs gēs* means 'the land (of Israel)', rather than 'the earth'. Contra Barrett 1998, 1046, Paul's death may have been sought because his zealous opponents believed that he had defiled the temple and thus contaminated the Holy Land.

62. Cf. Witherington 1998, 675-77, following Chrysostom, who is the earliest extant commentator on this verse.

63. Johnson 1992, 391. Cf. Marshall 1980, 358.

64. Bruce 1990, 460. Cf. Rapske, *Roman Custody*, 139; Witherington 1998, 676-77, where there are drawings of these implements of punishment. Bruce further points out that the commander might not have made much of Paul's speech even if it had been delivered in Greek, but, being delivered in Aramaic, 'it was completely unintelligible to him'.

65. Cf. Witherington 1998, 677. Rapske, *Roman Custody*, 135, says that 'Lysias' use of

25-28 However, *as they stretched him out to flog him (proeteinan auton tois himasin),*[66] *Paul said to the centurion standing there, 'Is it legal for you to flog a Roman citizen who hasn't even been found guilty?'* (*akatakriton* means 'uncondemned, without due process', BDAG; cf. 16:37). Paul previously asserted that he was a citizen of Tarsus (21:39, *politēs*), but now he insinuates that he is also 'a Roman person' (*anthrōpon Hrōmaion*; cf. 16:37). 'The practice of possessing full dual citizenship was thoroughly established about the reign of Claudius.'[67] As a Roman citizen, Paul could rightly appeal to be delivered from scourging as a form of inquisition.[68] Cassidy argues that Paul released this information about himself at the appropriate moment, 'as a means of forcing his fellow citizens into altering their plans for treating him improperly'.[69] However, Rapske more accurately observes that in this context, while Paul's self-disclosure indicates that 'he has some confidence that his Roman citizenship may make a difference in his treatment, its manner suggests that Paul is still prepared to suffer or even die without complaint (cf. Acts 21:13) if it is disregarded'.[70] Paul possibly established his citizenship by means of his 'diploma', which was 'a small wooden diptych which would attest his registration (and birth) as a citizen'.[71] *When the centurion heard this, he went to the commander and reported it. 'What are you going to do?' he asked. 'This man is a Roman citizen.'* This moved the commander to approach Paul and ask whether it was true. *'Yes, I am,'* he answered. *Then the commander said, 'I had to pay a lot of money for my citi-*

---

other means of enquiry before resorting to the whip actually shows a high regard for the counsel of Roman law and demonstrates admirable restraint'.

66. TNIV reads the dative in this expression as a dative of purpose ('for flogging'; ESV 'for the whips'), but the dative could be instrumental ('with thongs or straps', KJV, NRSV). Cf. Bruce 1990, 460; Barrett 1998, 1047-48.

67. Rapske, *Roman Custody*, 83. Rapske, 83-90, goes on to discuss how Paul could maintain his Jewish credentials alongside Roman citizenship. Rapske, 141-42, argues that Paul's mention of his Tarsian citizenship before his Roman citizenship is understandable in terms of the ancient Greek tendency to think of identity in terms of mother-city.

68. A. N. Sherwin-White, *Roman Society and Roman Law in the New Testament* (Oxford: Clarendon, 1963), 57-59, 71-76, shows how Paul clearly had the law on his side. Cf. Rapske, *Roman Custody*, 139.

69. R. Cassidy, *Society and Politics in the Acts of the Apostles* (Maryknoll: Orbis, 1987), 102. Witherington 1998, 679-80, makes the point that Paul did not reveal his Roman citizenship earlier in Acts 22 'for the good reason that this would not have helped his cause with the Jewish audience'. Paul's Roman citizenship was clearly less significant to him than his Jewish and Christian identities.

70. Rapske, *Roman Custody*, 143, arguing on the basis of Paul's posing a hypothetical (using Gk. *ei*, v. 25) in the second person (*anthrōpon Hrōmaion*) for clarification on a question of Roman trial procedure.

71. Barrett 1998, 1048. Cf. Suetonius, *Nero* 12; Sherwin-White, *Roman Law*, 148-49. Witherington 1998, 682-83, notes the possibility 'that Paul had a *libellus*, which recorded that the person concerned had this or that sort of citizenship or status, with the original remaining in the municipal registers of the person's hometown'. The penalty for a false claim to citizenship was severe and could involve death (cf. Epictetus, *Diss.* 3.24, 412; Suetonius, *Claud.* 25). Cf. Rapske, *Roman Custody*, 129-34.

zenship.' The expression *pollou kephalaiou* ('at a considerable cost') could refer to money or capital.[72] The price paid for citizenship in the Claudian period was actually 'the bribe given to the intermediaries in the imperial sec-
retariat or the provincial administration who put his name on the list of
candidates for enfranchisement'.[73] *'But I was born a citizen,'* Paul replied.
Luke reveals for the first time that Paul's Roman, as well as his Greek
(Tarsian), citizenship was inherited from birth.[74] As a person who was a
Roman citizen by birth, Paul outranked the commander. Considering
Paul's appearance and condition, the commander was perhaps both
amazed and sarcastic in his response to this revelation. Johnson rightly observes that 'Paul's appeal to his Roman citizenship saves him from a flogging and places him under the protection of the empire, but also makes
him captive to its judicial process, whose various stages the reader will
now follow'.[75]

29-30 *Those who were about to interrogate him withdrew immediately*
(*apestēsan*, 'stood back'), and *the commander himself was alarmed when he realised that he had put Paul, a Roman citizen, in chains* (*auton ēn dedekōs*, 'he had
bound him'). It was possible to arrest a Roman citizen who appeared to be
a threat to public order, but it was illegal to inflict on a citizen 'the disgrace
of being led in public bonds *(in publica vincula)*'.[76] However, the commander was still wanting *to find out exactly why Paul was being accused by the
Jews*, and kept him in prison until he could use the Sanhedrin in an advi-
sory capacity.[77] Claudius Lysias did not seem to have progressed much beyond the state of confusion expressed in 21:33-34, yet he continued to pursue the truth about Paul (22:30, *gnōnai to asphales*, 'to know the truth', as in
21:34). *So the next day he released him and ordered the chief priests and all the
members of the Sanhedrin to assemble.* Although the authority of a Roman mil-

---

72. Cf. Johnson 1992, 392.

73. Sherwin-White, *Roman Law*, 154-55. C. J. Hemer, *The Book of Acts in the Setting of
Hellenistic History*, ed. C. Gempf, WUNT 49 (Tübingen: Mohr Siebeck, 1989; repr. Winona
Lake: Eisenbrauns, 1990), 170, notes that 'the sale of citizenship was certainly a feature of
life under Claudius (Dio Cassius 17.5-7)'. The privilege, first sold at great cost, became
cheapened later under Claudius, which may help to explain the commander's response to
Paul.

74. Witherington 1998, 681-83, discusses the evidence for believing that a Jew like
Paul could have Roman citizenship. He also outlines the various ways in which citizenship
might have been granted to Paul's father and argues that the most likely reason was that he
had distinguished himself by some sort of service or loyalty to Rome. Cf. Barrett 1998, 1050.

75. Johnson 1992, 394.

76. Barrett 1998, 1050. Cf. 16:37-38 note. Rapske, *Roman Custody*, 144-45, suggests also
that the commander would have been further alarmed by the knowledge that Paul was a
citizen by birth, which in such an honour-culture 'threatened great damage to Claudius
Lysias' person and career'.

77. Rapske, *Roman Custody*, 145-49, argues that Paul was now in 'a much lighter and
more dignified military custody without bonds'. Skinner, *Locating Paul*, 116-19, outlines
ways in which the barracks setting influences the reader's perception of Paul's status and
influence on the situation.

itary officer to order a formal trial by the Sanhedrin has been questioned, it is possible that an informal meeting could have been required, 'to serve as a fact-finding (and fact-understanding) commission, allowing it to make inquiries and present a report to him'.[78] He realised that a matter of Jewish law should be examined by the Jewish authorities, and he hoped to determine what he should do with Paul by this means. The Council was doubtless glad to be summoned, giving its members the chance to present their case against Paul. So the commander *brought Paul and had him stand before them.*

As with 16:35-40, we may ask why Paul delayed the disclosure of his Roman citizenship and made use of this particular privilege at all. In both contexts, he appears to have been primarily concerned to identify himself as Jewish and Christian. He used his Roman citizenship only as a means of seeking fair treatment when misrepresentation of his social and political significance had serious implications for the public standing of the mission.[79] In Jerusalem, he was particularly concerned that the real reasons for Jewish opposition should be understood and identified, even by the Romans. It was not right that theological issues should be sidelined because of the pretence that he was a renegade from Judaism, who was deliberately provoking social unrest throughout the Empire.

Persecuted believers today might similarly seek legal and political protection, where mob violence and personal attacks for religious reasons are overlooked by the authorities or are justified for various reasons. Like Paul, they may also seek to obtain a proper exposure of the issues involved in opposition to their pattern of life and testimony to Jesus. But Christians have nothing to fear from systems that seek justice, for 'if a Christian has integrity, then the state has nothing to fear from the believer and the believer can make the case that nothing that has been done is designed to undercut that state's right to both exist and create a society of law, order, and peace'.[80] Whatever the difficulties experienced, it may be suggested that Christians everywhere are bound to seek a public hearing for the gospel in whatever ways are possible in their situation.

---

78. Barrett 1998, 1053-54. Barrett's solution allows him to explain how the commander could thus 'leave a fellow Roman to stand unprotected before an alien body, obviously moved by strong passions', and to observe that the proceedings in Acts 23 begin quite informally, with Paul speaking first.

79. Again in 25:10-11, his Roman citizenship becomes the means of obtaining a fair trial for himself and seeking appropriate recognition for the Gentile churches as legitimate religious entities within the Roman Empire.

80. Bock 2007, 665.

E. Appearing before the Sanhedrin (23:1-11)

Luke now presents us with the second of two defence speeches in Jerusalem, followed by the account of a perilous journey to Caesarea (23:11-35). Three defence speeches then follow in Caesarea — before Felix (24:1-27), Festus (25:1-27), and Agrippa (26:1-32) — after which Paul engages on a second perilous journey from Caesarea to Rome (27:1–28:14).[1] These two travel narratives parallel one another in certain key respects: there is a threat from ambush in one and from natural forces in the other; God reassures Paul of his help in both contexts (23:11; 27:23-5); Paul is supported by anonymous family and friends (23:16-22; 27:3) and named Roman officials superintend the prisoner's transfers (Claudius Lysias in 23:18-35; Julius in 27:1-3, 42-44). So, 'while Paul fulfills God's will and advances Christ's mission as a Roman prisoner in the closing chapters of Acts, this "progress" does not come easily. Roman officials smooth the way a little but scarcely go out of their way to accommodate Paul.'[2] God's care for Paul is highlighted in various ways and contrasts with the antagonism shown by his own people. As Paul moves through a slow progression of legal scenes, 'Luke is able to demonstrate through his defense speeches not only Paul's innocence of the charges brought against him by the Jews, but the reality for which Paul truly stands in witness: that in the resurrection of Jesus the authentic "hope of Israel" was realized (28:20)'.[3]

The Roman commander continues to be a key figure in Luke's narrative. Determined to find out why the Jews were so antagonistic toward Paul, he had given him permission to speak to the Jerusalem crowd (21:39-40). Frustrated by their violent response, and restrained from flogging Paul because of his claim to be a Roman citizen (22:22-29), the commander had ordered the chief priests and all the Jewish Council to assemble to clarify the accusation (22:30). But the Sanhedrin becomes antagonistic when Paul makes explicit what was implied in the preceding speech, that he had consistently fulfilled his duty to God 'in all good conscience' (v. 1). Even as he is unjustly treated by the leaders of his people and condemns them for it, Paul shows remarkable respect towards the high priest (vv. 2-5). The meeting becomes even more violent when Paul claims to be on trial 'because of the hope of the resurrection from the dead' (vv. 6-9). This is no cynical attempt to win the support of the Pharisees against the Sadducees. Through-

---

1. So Spencer 1997, 203. Spencer further observes that 'a number of redundant elements tie the *defense-speeches* together, revolving around an evaluation of the *charges* levelled against Paul and the evidence of his exemplary *character* offered in his defense: in other words — "who he was [*character*] and what he had done [*charges*]" (21.33)'.

2. Spencer, 206, rightly observing a certain ambiguity in the official response to the prisoner. Spencer, 206-7, also identifies ways in which Paul's first defence before the Jerusalem crowd (21:37–22:29) prepares for his defence before the Sanhedrin (22:30–23:10).

3. Johnson 1992, 400.

out the following speeches, Paul regularly comes back to this theme (24:14-16, 21; 26:6-8, 22-23; 28:20), showing that it is central to his apologetic with Jewish audiences. By this means he links the prophetic hope about Israel's future with the resurrection of Jesus from the dead. The commander rescues Paul once more from Jewish attack, taking him away by force and keeping him in the barracks (23:10). But the ascended Lord Jesus is revealed as Paul's true protector. In a vision reminiscent of the one in Corinth (18:9-10), he promises to bring Paul safely to Rome, to testify about him there (v. 11; cf. 27:23-24). 'Every scene in Luke-Acts that takes place in the company of the council has a negative outcome for Jesus and his followers',[4] but the Lord's servants continue to bring his challenge to this centre of influence and authority in the Jewish world.

1-2 The abrupt introduction to the proceedings here suggests that the Sanhedrin had met for a pre-trial hearing rather than for a formal trial. From 22:30 it is clear that 'the tribune is still trying to discern the facts of the case and whether Paul is guilty of an offense that is chargeable under Roman law'.[5] The commander's letter (23:28-29) also does not treat the meeting of the Sanhedrin as a trial. Paul *looked straight* at the Sanhedrin (*atenisas*), seeking to capture and hold their attention by his gaze. He addressed the members of the Council as equals ('*andres adelphoi*', 'men, brothers'; cf. 1:16), as a Jew speaking to fellow Jews, and claimed, '*I have fulfilled my duty to God in all good conscience to this day*'. While it is true that the verb *politeuomai (I have fulfilled my duty)* normally means 'living as a (good) citizen' (cf. *politēs*, 'citizen', 21:39; *politeia*, 'citizenship', 22:28),[6] the expression *to God (tō theō)* indicates that 'his life has been lived in the sight of God, and in obedience to God'.[7] The preceding speech suggests that the reference here is specifically to the way he responded to his divine calling (cf. 23:9 note). As in 26:19, he is claiming to have lived in obedience to the heavenly vision. 'This reading of 23:1 is one of several indications that Paul's statements in the defense scenes are illuminated when understood as part of a progressive narrative development.'[8] When Paul claims that he acted

---

4. M. L. Skinner, *Locating Paul: Places of Custody as Narrative Settings in Acts 21–28*, SBLAB 13 (Atlanta: SBL, 2003), 121. Cf. Lk. 22:66–23:2; Acts 4:5-21; 5:27-41; 6:12, 15. The scene in Acts 23:1-10 signifies Paul's 'rejection by the Jewish leadership, just as the scene in the temple precincts demonstrates his rejection by the Jewish masses' (Skinner, 125).

5. Witherington 1998, 684. Witherington further points out that 'no one from the Sanhedrin actually assumes the legal role of plaintiff before Acts 24'. Barrett 1998, 1053-54, also argues against the possibility that this was a formal trial by the Sanhedrin. Cf. B. Rapske, *The Book of Acts in Its First-Century Setting*, Vol. 3: *The Book of Acts and Paul in Roman Custody* (Grand Rapids: Eerdmans; Carlisle: Paternoster, 1994), 147.

6. Bruce 1990, 463; Johnson 1992, 396; Spencer 1997, 211. Cf. H. Strathmann, *TDNT* 6:516-35.

7. Barrett 1998, 1058. Barrett, 1057, notes that in a theocratic state good citizenship is measured with reference to God as the ruler and lawgiver. Cf. Witherington 1998, 687-88. In Phil. 1:27 Paul uses this verb with reference to gospel-shaped living.

8. Tannehill 1990, 286. Tannehill notes the narrator's assumption that 'Paul's hearers

in all good conscience (pasē syneidēsei agathē), he means that his conscience was clear of any blame with regard to the conduct of his life as a Christian (cf. 24:16).[9] In particular, he was not aware of any fault in responding to God's direction for his ministry. This is not a claim to sinlessness, since Paul elsewhere acknowledges the limitations of his own self-awareness and confesses that the Lord is the ultimate judge (cf. 1 Cor. 4:4-5). In 26:9, he speaks of the conviction that he once thought he was doing God's will when he was 'opposing the name of Jesus of Nazareth', but a dramatic change of perception took place when the risen Jesus confronted him (26:12-23). Conscience can be wrongly informed and needs to be educated by divine revelation to be a reliable check on our behaviour.

The high priest Ananias immediately expressed his rejection of Paul's claim when he *ordered those standing near Paul to strike him on the mouth.* From his perspective, neither the claim to have had a heavenly vision nor the claim that Paul's mission was an expression of faithfulness to God could be entertained. The prisoner was guilty of blasphemy for speaking in this way and could not represent himself as a conscientious Jew. *Ananias, son of Nebedaius,* was appointed high priest by Herod of Chalcis (brother of Herod Agrippa I) and reigned in the period AD 47-59. After that, he continued to wield great authority until he was murdered in AD 66 by revolutionaries, because of his collaboration with Rome.[10]

3-4 Paul responded with a warning of divine judgement, echoing the sort of challenge given by Jesus to the teachers of the law and the Pharisees in Matthew 23:27-28: *'God will strike you, you whitewashed wall! You sit there to judge me according to the law, yet you yourself violate the law by commanding that I be struck!'* Ezekiel 13:10-16 actually uses the image of a 'whitewashed wall' to portray something which looks stable enough but is about to collapse (this is applied to the Jewish leadership in CD 8:12). The issue in Acts 23, however, is more precisely the one addressed by Jesus in Matthew 23, where he uses the image of 'whitewashed tombs' to portray

---

were either present when he spoke to the people or have heard a report of his speech, for members of the Sanhedrin will comment on the story of Paul's call in 23:9'. Thus they would assume that the claim in 23:1 related to the faithful fulfillment of Paul's divine calling. Johnson 1992, 396, 400, wrongly argues that Paul is claiming an equal sincerity for his life before his conversion.

9. Cf. Marshall 1980, 362. C. Maurer, *TDNT* 7:898-919, and Bruce 1990, 463-64, discuss the development and use of the language of conscience in the NT against the background of Greek and Hebrew thinking on the subject. A 'good conscience' is mentioned in 1 Tim. 1:5, 19; Heb. 13:18; 1 Pet. 3:16, 21, and a 'clear conscience' *(kathara syneidēsei)* in 1 Tim. 3:9; 2 Tim. 1:3. Cf. Heb. 9:14; 10:22 for the way in which conscience can be cleansed from guilt.

10. Cf. J. Jeremias, *Jerusalem in the Time of Jesus: An Investigation into Economic and Social Conditions during the New Testament Period* (ET, London: SCM, 1969), 378 (with references); Josephus, *Ant.* 20.103, 131, 205-14; *War* 2.243, 426-29, 441-42. Barrett 1998, 1058, notes the uncertainty among scholars about the popularity of Ananias. The primary sources certainly highlight his wealth and his greed, and speak about his violence with respect to the treatment of his subordinates.

the hypocrisy of the religious leaders with respect to the Mosaic law.[11] Jesus and Paul were united in condemning those who pretended to be righteous, but inwardly were corrupt. At the time of his trial, Jesus was clearly more restrained than Paul in dealing with his accusers (cf. Lk. 22:63-71; Jn. 18:19-23). He submitted to injustice without complaint to accomplish the redemptive work prescribed for the Servant of the Lord (cf. Is. 53:7-8, cited in Acts 8:32-33). Nevertheless, there are occasions when Christians should speak out against hypocrisy and injustice. What Luke wishes us to see in Paul is 'the courage with which he faced official opposition, injustice and violence. When many a man would cringe, Paul answers back, and points out . . . that the Jewish judge is himself not observing the Law that he is appointed to administer.'[12] The form of the sentence (*typtein se mellei ho theos*, 'God will strike you') is not a curse, but a prediction of judgement, coupled with a reproof for the treatment received (*keleueis me typtesthai*, 'you commanded me to be struck'; cf. v. 2).[13] Compared to the Roman officials in 22:22-29, the leaders of Israel had treated Paul badly, dismissing his case without proper investigation and condemning him without proof. In so doing, they were violating the very law they professed to uphold (cf. Stephen's charge in 7:51-53; Lev. 19:15; *m. Sanh.* 3:6-8). The immediate response of *those who were standing near Paul* was to condemn him because he dared to *'insult God's high priest'*. This mocking of God's representative was perceived as a demeaning of God's honour.

5 Somewhat surprisingly, Paul's reply was, *'Brothers, I did not realise that he was the high priest; for it is written: "Do not speak evil about the ruler of your people"'*. How could he not recognise the person he addressed as the current high priest? Some commentators have argued that Paul's response is ironic, meaning 'that it is hard to recognize this priest as God's chosen high priest because of his conduct'.[14] However, Paul's use of Scripture speaks against this interpretation, 'for it turns Paul's outburst into a serious offense that he must correct'.[15] Recalling Exodus 22:28 ('Do not utter blas-

---

11. Bruce 1990, 464, prefers the link with Ezekiel, but concludes that 'there is probably no special biblical allusion here'.

12. Barrett 1998, 1054. Luke's complaint against the Jews in Acts 'is not that they are Jews but that they are not good Jews' (p. 1045). Johnson 1992, 400, draws attention to the difference between Jesus and Paul on trial and unjustly treated.

13. Some interpreters have argued that this is a predictive curse that was fulfilled when Ananias was assassinated in AD 66. Cf. Bruce 1990, 464. However, it is more likely to be a general declaration of God's intention to judge such hypocrisy at the final judgement.

14. R. Cassidy, *Society and Politics in the Acts of the Apostles* (Maryknoll: Orbis, 1987), 65. Cf. Marshall 1980, 364; Johnson 1992, 397; Spencer 1997, 212.

15. Tannehill 1990, 286 note 2. Cf. Barrett 1998, 1055. Every scriptural citation in Acts is significant in the development of the narrative and for revealing the theological convictions of those in the text. The last citation was by James in Acts 15:15-18, at the climax of the Jerusalem Council. There are no explicit quotations in the intervening chapters, but there are biblical allusions in the speeches recorded by Luke in those chapters. This citation is thus important in the flow of the narrative and signals a recognition of the inappropriateness of Paul's response to the high priest.

phemies against God or curse the ruler of your people'), Paul expresses respect for the office of high priest, even if he is critical of the behaviour of the one who currently holds the position. More generally, it is also possible that Paul remembered his own claim to bless when cursed (1 Cor. 4:12, *loidoroumenoi*, 'being cursed, insulted'), and was rebuked about the way he had returned insult with insult (v. 4, *ton archierea tou theou loidoreis*, 'you insult God's high priest').[16] Perhaps the simplest explanation of Paul's confusion about the identity of the high priest is that he had been away from Jerusalem for some time and on this visit had been given no opportunity to meet him or be in his presence.[17] Furthermore, if this was an informal gathering of the Sanhedrin, the high priest may not have been distinctively attired or positioned in such a way that his identity could be immediately discerned.

6 At this point, Paul changes the topic, *knowing that some of them were Sadducees and the others Pharisees.* 'There was always (before AD 70) a potential division in the Sanhedrin, which could be exploited by one who was prepared to align himself with one party and enlist its support.'[18] The chief-priestly families were mostly Sadducean, but the Pharisees were strongly represented in the Council. Given the chaotic outcome (v. 7), 'divide and conquer' may have seemed like a clever ploy to disrupt the proceedings. However, 'the subsequent defense scenes show that Paul's words are more than a tactical move for temporary advantage'.[19] He keeps coming back to the hope of resurrection, even when it no longer provokes disruption (24:15, 21; 28:20), and the theme is central to his climactic defense speech before King Agrippa (26:6-8, 22-23). Definition of the 'main question' was actually an expected part of the statement of facts or *narratio* in a forensic defence speech in ancient rhetoric.[20] Paul seeks to change the focus of his

16. Longenecker 1981, 530-31, acknowledges that Paul's response was less than the ideal established by Jesus himself (cf. 1 Pet. 2:23), but highlights Paul's quickness in acknowledging his wrong. Cf. Marshall 1980, 363.

17. Cf. Witherington 1998, 688. C. J. Hemer, *The Book of Acts in the Setting of Hellenistic History*, ed. C. Gempf, WUNT 49 (Tübingen: Mohr Siebeck, 1989; repr. Winona Lake: Eisenbrauns, 1990), 171, suggests that Paul's previous visit to Jerusalem (18:22 note) was 'ostensibly in summer 52, likely to have been the very time when Ananias had been sent in chains to Rome'.

18. Barrett 1998, 1063. Barrett, 1062-63, takes the aorist form of the participle *gnous* (TNIV *knowing*) as an indication of Lukan composition since 'Paul would not have to *notice* but would know in advance the mixed membership of the court'. However, the participle could be understood in a causal sense ('because he knew').

19. Tannehill 1990, 286-87. Cf. Rapske, *Roman Custody*, 98-99. Spencer 1997, 212, inappropriately argues that Paul takes 'a "divide and conquer" approach, effectively writing off the high priest and the Sadducees and reaching out to the Pharisees'.

20. Cf. J. Neyrey, 'The Forensic Defense Speech and Paul's Trial Speeches in Acts 22–26: Form and Function', in C. H. Talbert (ed.), *Luke-Acts: New Perspectives from the Society of Biblical Literature Seminar* (New York: Crossroad, 1984), 214-15. Neyrey says that the main question introduced by Paul is the resurrection of Jesus. But the general resurrection of the dead is actually the foundational issue, leading Paul in due course to proclaim the fulfillment of this biblical hope in the resurrection of Jesus (26:23; cf. 4:2).

trial from the charges listed in 21:28 to the more fundamental theological issue at stake. This enables him to persuade Roman officials of the religious nature of the antagonism against him (23:28-29). It also enables him to challenge Jews about the true hope of Israel and its fulfillment through Jesus (26:6-8, 22-23; 28:17-20). He is being presented to Christian readers as 'a resourceful witness from whom other missionaries can learn'.[21]

Paul introduces the 'main question' by first insisting, *'My brothers, I am a Pharisee, descended from Pharisees'* (cf. 26:5; Phil. 3:5). This is not necessarily a claim that his father was a Pharisee, but more generally could mean that his upbringing and education were in the Pharisaic tradition.[22] On that basis, he asserts that he stands on trial *'because of the hope of the resurrection of the dead'* (*peri elpidos kai anastaseōs* is a hendiadys [two phrases joining in a single concept]; *nekrōn* is plural, indicating the general resurrection *of the dead*). Without endorsing everything taught by the Pharisees, he willingly identifies with their concern to focus on the eschatological hope of Israel, revealed in Scripture (e.g., Ezk. 37:1-14; Dan. 12:1-3) and developed in the intertestamental period (cf. 2 Macc. 7:9, 11, 14; Josephus, *War* 2.163; *Ant.* 18.14). 'All that Christianity affirmed of his Pharisaism, Paul continues to embrace; all that in Pharisaism threatened the exclusiveness of Christ's salvific provision, he emphatically rejected.'[23] The topic of the general resurrection surfaces again in 24:15, 20-21; 26:6-8 (cf. 28:20 'the hope of Israel'), but this is not explicitly linked with the resurrection of Jesus until 26:23 (Festus also reports that this was Paul's message in 25:19). Luke shows much interest in the outcome of Paul's various trials because of this theological theme. Earlier he showed that this was a fundamental point of contention between the apostles and the Jewish authorities (4:2). Here Paul implies that *the hope of the resurrection of the dead* belongs to all true Israelites. This is an important foundation for arguing that Israel's hope is fulfilled in the resurrection of Jesus, making it possible for all who call on his name to share in the promised resurrection from the dead (cf. 4:10-12; 5:30-32; 13:30-

---

21. Tannehill 1990, 290. This implies that there is a continuing concern in Acts with a mission to Jews, 'even though relations have been poisoned by controversy'. P. F. Esler, *Community and Gospel in Luke-Acts: The Social and Political Motivations of Lucan Theology,* SNTSMS 57 (Cambridge: Cambridge University, 1987), 16-23, 46-70, argues that the emphasis on Paul's Jewish roots in the defence scenes in Acts is designed to legitimate Christians as a sectarian group. However, Tannehill, 289-90, rightly argues that this is not an adequate explanation. Paul seeks to persuade Jewish audiences about a shared hope of resurrection before speaking about Jesus' resurrection. Moreover, there is no attempt to prove the messiahship of Jesus from Scripture (as in Acts 2, 13). In short, the focus is not on legitimating Christians but on winning Jews.

22. Rapske, *Roman Custody*, 95-97, considers the evidence for Pharisaic influence in the Diaspora at the time of Paul's birth. He concludes that Paul's claim can be encompassed within the Jerusalem phase of his life, without regard to the earlier period in Tarsus, as 22:3 indicates. Barrett 1998, 1063, says that Paul's claim in Acts 23:6 is simply that 'it is as a Pharisee, in the interests of Pharisaic doctrine, that he is standing trial'.

23. Rapske, *Roman Custody*, 99, commenting on Phil. 3:7-8 in relation to Acts 23. Cf. R. Maddox, *The Purpose of Luke-Acts* (Edinburgh: Clark, 1982), 40-42.

37). 'Paul's apologetic approach in this entire section, leaving the more specific and objectionable material until last, is very much the same as we find in the Areopagus speech in Acts 17.'[24] Here, however, his aim is to establish a theological foundation upon which to proclaim the significance of the resurrection of Jesus for Jews.[25]

7-8 *When he said this, a dispute broke out between the Pharisees and the Sadducees, and the assembly was divided.* Luke uses the strong word *stasis*, meaning 'strife, discord, disunion' (BDAG) here and in v. 10, to describe what resulted (cf. 15:2; 19:40; 24:5). He then explains this division in terms of fundamental theological differences between the two groups. The evidence that *the Sadducees say that there is no resurrection* is clear (cf. Lk. 20:27-40 par.; Josephus, *War* 2.164-65; *Ant.* 18.16; *m. Sanh.* 10:1). However, what is meant by the claim that they acknowledge *neither angels nor spirits*? As those who acknowledged the authority of the Pentateuch, they can hardly have denied the existence of angelic and spiritual beings. However, in the context of denying the resurrection of the dead they may also have claimed that there was no intermediate or alternate state, 'in which those who had died existed as angels or spirits, these being more or less synonymous terms (see 1 *Enoch* 22:3, 7; 45:4-5; Mt. 22:30; Mk. 12:25; Lk. 20:36)'.[26] Luke rightly goes on to claim that *the Pharisees believe all these things* (*homologousin ta amphotera*, 'confess belief in both').[27] The Pharisaic doctrine (cf. Josephus, *War* 2.163; *Ant.* 18.14) came to be regarded as normative in Judaism, so that the Mishnah decrees, 'he that says there is no resurrection of the dead prescribed in the law' has no share in the life to come (*m. Sanh.* 10:1).

9-10 *There was a great uproar* (*kraugē megalē* implies that the court acted like a rioting mob).[28] At this point, *some of the teachers of the law who*

---

24. Witherington 1998, 685.

25. Tannehill 1990, 287, shows how Paul functions as a model for Luke's readers in these chapters. They are not to engage in endless debates with Jews about the law and the temple but to focus on the scriptural hope of resurrection, which is the true hope of Israel, and from that basis proclaim the messiahship of Jesus. Moreover, they are not to be put off from this engagement with Jews by disinterest, opposition, or persecution. Pharisaism became normative Judaism after the fall of the temple in AD 70, and so the Pharisaic hope is central to Luke's apologetic in the concluding chapters of Acts. Cf. Johnson 1992, 401-2; S. Mason, 'Pharisees', *DNTB* 782-87.

26. Barrett 1998, 1065-66, following D. Daube, 'On Acts 23: Sadducees and Angels', *JBL* 109 (1990), 493-97. Cf. Witherington 1998, 692.

27. B. T. Viviano and J. Taylor, 'Sadducees, Angels, and Resurrection', *JBL* 111 (1992), 496-98, adopt the view of Daube, 'On Acts 23', 493-97, and take the two nouns 'angel' and 'spirit' as standing in apposition to 'resurrection', translating 'the Sadducees say that there is no resurrection either as an angel (i.e. in the form of an angel) or as a spirit (i.e. in the form of a spirit) but the Pharisees acknowledge them both'. This rendering overcomes the difficulty that Luke says the Pharisees 'confess belief in both' (*homologousin ta amphotera*). Barrett 1998, 1066, also considers the possibility that Luke used *ta amphotera* quite loosely (as in 19:16), as understood by TNIV (*all these things*). Cf. Bruce 1990, 466; G. G. Porton, 'Sadducees', *DNTB* 1050-52.

28. Barrett 1998, 1066.

were Pharisees (tines tōn grammateōn tou merous tōn Pharisaiōn, 'some of the scribes of the party of the Pharisees', BDAG) *stood up and argued vigorously.*[29] Their verdict on Paul (*'We find nothing wrong with this man'*) is strangely reminiscent of Pilate's judgement about Jesus (Lk. 23:4, 14, 22), and anticipates the conclusion of the Roman commander (23:29), Governor Festus (25:25), and King Agrippa (26:31-32) about Paul. The beliefs of the Pharisees revealed in v. 8 are clearly the basis for a certain openness to the prisoner and his claims. However, they do not simply endorse him as someone supporting their teaching about the resurrection. Their rhetorical question (*'What if a spirit or an angel has spoken to him?'*) implies that they take seriously the possibility that he received a divine calling and commissioning to carry out his ministry. On theological grounds, they cannot rule out the legitimacy of his testimony, though they clearly cannot yet accept that Paul was addressed by the risen Jesus. In view of what was said about v. 8, it is possible that the Pharisees meant by *a spirit or an angel* that Paul could have encountered someone 'between death and resurrection at the last day'.[30] As with the temple scene (22:22-23), *the dispute (stasis,* as in 23:7) *became so violent that the commander was afraid Paul would be torn to pieces by them.* Once more Paul was rescued by the commander, who *ordered the troops to go down and take him away from them by force and bring him into the barracks.* Once more the Roman barracks function as a place of protection from Jews who seek his life. This verse suggests that the commander may have been either present or within earshot of the proceedings.[31]

11 *The following night the Lord stood near Paul and said, 'Take courage! As you have testified about me in Jerusalem, so you must also testify in Rome.'* As previously noted, this revelation comes at a strategic point in the narrative, just after the irruption of violence in the Sanhedrin and before Paul's life is further threatened by an attempted assassination. The Greek present imperative *(tharsei)* implies the need for continuing courage in the face of ongoing hardship and danger ('Keep up your courage'). This charge is reminiscent of the vision given to encourage Paul to persevere in his Corinthian ministry (18:9-10, *mē phobou,* 'do not be afraid'), in the context of opposition from unbelieving Jews (18:5-6, 12-13). Paul receives a further vision during the dangerous sea voyage to Rome (27:23-24). Once again in 23:11, it appears to be the risen Jesus who addresses Paul, since *the Lord* refers to testifying *about me.*[32] By implication, the Lord commends his witness in Jerusa-

---

29. Cf. Johnson 1992, 398-99, on the scribes in Jewish teaching and in the NT. Johnson suggests that the imperfect tense of *diamachomai* (TNIV *argued vigorously*) should be translated 'took up the battle'.

30. Barrett 1998, 1067.

31. Barrett 1998, 1053-54, suggests that the presence of an 'unclean' Gentile in the Sanhedrin is best explained by arguing that it was an informal meeting of the Jewish Council.

32. Comparing the rescues from prison in 5:17-21; 12:1-11; 16:23-26, Tannehill 1990, 292, observes that 'the Lord's reassurance must take the place of miraculously opening

lem. In the flow of the narrative, this suggests that Paul did not use a clever trick in the Sanhedrin to get out of trouble but that 'he has borne the witness he was intended to bear and that the Lord has protected him and will continue to do so'.[33] A further implication of this text is that Paul will suffer in the process of testifying to Jesus in Rome, just as he has suffered for testifying in Jerusalem. It will be as a prisoner that he gets to bear witness. The divine necessity for this is stressed (*dei*, 'must'), as in 19:21; 27:24. 'The christophany reconfirms Paul's mission; Jesus continues to have Paul as his witness, even in spite of the witness's apparent limitations as a prisoner confined to a place of custody.'[34] By implication, Paul's transfer to Caesarea, which is one step closer to Rome, is also part of the divine plan.

F. Rescued from Death Again (23:12-35)

This section further illustrates the extent to which Paul's Jewish opponents were prepared to go in order to eliminate him. At the same time, it shows the extent to which he was dependent on Roman justice and protection. Faced with another threat to Paul's life, in the form of an ambush by Jewish assassins (23:12-22), the commander makes every effort to bring Paul safely before the governor in Caesarea (23:23-35). 'The use of repetition and detail extend and vivify this story, which shares some features with other ancient narratives of intrigue and conspiracy.'[35] The oath taken by the conspirators is mentioned three times (vv. 12, 14, 21), and the involvement of the Jewish authorities is suggested twice (vv. 15, 20). Conspiracy and accusation are mentioned several times (vv. 12, 13, 28, 29, 30, 35). By such means, 'Luke heightens the sense of danger encompassing Paul'.[36] The commander's letter to Felix significantly insists that the accusation of the Jews involves questions about their law, and that there is no charge against Paul that deserves death or imprisonment (23:29). This verdict is later echoed by Governor Festus (25:25; cf. 25:18-20) and then by King Agrippa (26:30). The commander's conclusion is clearly influenced by the Sanhedrin hearing. However, the letter seeks to present him in the best possible light (23:27), failing to mention his original misunderstanding about Paul (21:37-39) and his later attempt to have him scourged before discovering that he was a Roman citizen (22:23-25). The Lord's promise to Paul (v. 11) is thus fulfilled in the first instance through an unbelieving Roman official, whose self-interest is made quite clear by Luke.

---

doors. The divine power that rescues from prison has become a powerful presence that enables the witness to endure an imprisonment that lasts for years.'

33. Barrett 1998, 1068.

34. Skinner, *Locating Paul*, 127.

35. Gaventa 2003, 318. Cf. R. I. Pervo, *Profit with Delight: The Literary Genre of the Acts of the Apostles* (Philadelphia: Fortress, 1987), 32-34.

36. Gaventa 2003, 318.

1. Hatching the Plot (23:12-15)[37]

A group of Jewish conspirators unite with the religious authorities in a plot
to kill Paul. The danger of the situation is revealed by the fact that more
than forty men make a solemn oath — presumably to God — either to end
Paul's life or their own! Although some Pharisees were more sympathetic
to Paul (v. 9), other members of the Sanhedrin were apparently antagonistic
enough to be drawn into this conspiracy. The plan was to ask the commander to bring Paul before the Council again and to assassinate him on
the way (v. 15). Paradoxically, the very people who accuse Paul of violating
the law of Moses contemplate murdering him. However, 'despite their
numbers and their rage, the mob is powerless because God's plan involves
a witness for Paul in Rome and, more fundamentally, because Paul's life belongs to God'.[38]

12-15 *The next morning the Jews formed a conspiracy and bound themselves with an oath not to eat or drink until they had killed Paul. More than forty
men were involved in this plot.* Conspiracy is a good rendering of *systrophēn*
(v. 12; cf. 19:40, where it is translated 'commotion') because of the context
and use of the parallel term *synōmosian (plot)* in v. 13.[39] Jerusalem was now
an extremely dangerous place for Paul to be. The number of the conspirators and their devout commitment — binding themselves with an oath to
kill him — showed how much hatred he had aroused there.[40] They were
perversely religious in their determination to destroy Paul, dedicating
themselves through fasting to end his life by violent means (cf. Is. 58:4).
Their oath to destroy him is mentioned three times in the narrative, to highlight its significance (vv. 12, 14, 21).[41] The involvement of the religious leaders in the plot was necessary if Paul was to be lured into a place where he
could not be protected by the Romans. So the conspirators approached *the
chief priests and the elders.* 'Since the scribes (who mostly belonged to the
Pharisaic party) are not mentioned, it seems that they approached the
groups in the Sanhedrin most likely to favour their proposal.'[42] They invited them to *petition*[43] the commander to bring him before them *on the pre-*

---

37. I am indebted to Spencer 1997, 215-16, for these three subheadings.

38. Gaventa 2003, 322.

39. BDAG; Witherington 1998, 694.

40. Although a large number of the best MSS read 'the Jews' in v. 12, the variant
'some of the Jews' is also found. This provides better accord with v. 13, where only forty are
involved in the plot. This variant appears to be an attempt by copyists to avoid the impression that all of the Jews were enemies of the new faith. Cf. Barrett 1998, 1072-73.

41. Use of the expression *anethematisan heautous (bound themselves with an oath,* with
the cognate dative *anathemati* added in v. 14; KJV 'bound themselves under a curse') suggests to Barrett 1998, 1072, that those who took this vow undertook to accept the 'ban of the
synagogue' (Heb. *ḥērem*) if they failed to accomplish that which they pledged themselves to
do. Cf. Johnson 1992, 403-4, on this form of oath.

42. Marshall 1980, 367.

43. Barrett 1998, 1073-74, notes that, although the verb *emphanizō* means 'disclose' or

text of wanting more accurate information about his case. The chief priests and the elders would be free from any appearance of complicity if the assassins killed Paul before he reached the Sanhedrin.[44] Spencer detects a touch of satirical irony in the suggestion that they might obtain *more accurate information about his case,* while they were in the process of attempting to lynch him![45] Luke does not tell us whether the chief priests and elders agreed to participate in the plot, though the report in v. 20 suggests that everything proceeded according to plan.

2. *Exposing the Plot (23:16-22)*

The rest of the narrative is about Paul's escape from this life-threatening situation and his safe transfer to Caesarea. The account is detailed and somewhat repetitive because Luke is interested in the characters and their dramatic interaction. This slows the story down and effectively heightens the sense of danger for Paul. As in Acts 27, Luke is also keen to show how God's fulfillment of the promise to bring Paul safely to Rome (v. 11) is effected through various human agents.[46] In both chapters, 'the danger of the situation is vividly depicted, and suspense centers on finding a means of rescue'.[47] Luke's nephew is introduced as a significant figure in Paul's deliverance, perhaps acting as a representative of the Jerusalem church in caring for Paul. He reveals the plot to the centurion, who then gains him access to the commander.

16-19 In this episode, the focus is first on the initiative taken by Paul's nephew: *when the son of Paul's sister heard of this plot, he went into the barracks and told Paul.* This is the first mention of any family connections for Paul, other than indirect references to his parents in the preceding chapter (22:3, 28). Paul and his sister were apparently brought up in Jerusalem, and his sister remained there to marry and have children. Luke often introduces

---

'report' in 23:22, it has a special legal meaning in 24:1; 25:2, 15 ('bring charges against'). In 23:15 the meaning appears to be 'ask' in the sense of making a legal representation to the commander.

44. The position of the words *syn tō synedriō (with the Sanhedrin)* in the text is odd, but the most likely meaning is 'you and the Sanhedrin petition the commander'). The Western Text offers what looks like a free improvement of v. 15 ('Now therefore *we ask you that you do this for us: Gather the Sanhedrin together and give notice* to the tribune . . . *even though we must die too'*). Cf. Metzger, *Textual Commentary,* 432.

45. Spencer 1997, 215. Such hypocrisy with regard to the Jewish law is a continuation of the problem mentioned in 23:2-3. Paul is presented in 23:5 as being 'stricter' about the law than his opponents (cf. 22:3).

46. Krodel 1986, 429, observes, 'Each of the players in the drama retains his freedom and all serve the purpose of God, ignorant though they be of it, except for Paul. Almost nothing is done or spoken by him and yet he remains the center of everyone's intense actions.'

47. Tannehill 1990, 294, noting that rescue from danger is expressed with the verb *diasōzein,* which is used in connection with these two episodes in Acts (23:4; 27:43, 44; 28:1, 4).

new characters with little identification (cf. 12:13; 17:6-7; 19:29; 21:16). Here he gives no information about the way Paul's nephew was informed of the plot or had access to the prisoner. Perhaps his personal link to Paul, combined with his youth, made him less of a security risk within the prison complex.[48] Paul's only role in the process of rescue is to call one of the centurions and say, *'Take this young man to the commander; he has something to tell him'*. Paul's authority and stature in this setting is illustrated by his ability to summon and direct a centurion in this way.[49] The commander's respect for Paul is also once more demonstrated in his response (*[he] took the young man by the hand, drew him aside and asked, 'What is it you want to tell me?'*) 'Despite his youth, anonymity and apparent lack of special social status, Paul's nephew surprisingly enjoys a certain intimacy and assumes a certain authority with the high-ranking Roman tribune.'[50]

20-22   The young man's message to the commander involves a repetition of the details already made known to us, thus heightening the tension in the narrative (*'The Jews have agreed to ask you to bring Paul before the Sanhedrin tomorrow on the pretext of wanting more accurate information about him'*).[51] Paul's nephew adds his urgent plea for help (*'Don't give in to them'*), before giving more detail to emphasize the seriousness of the situation. He informs the commander that *'more than forty of them are waiting in ambush for him'*, that *'they have taken an oath not to eat or drink until they have killed him'*, and that *'they are ready now, waiting for your consent to their request'*. The commander once more appears to be both just and considerate of Paul's welfare. Realising that rumour of the assassination was clearly spreading and that a surprise deliverance of the prisoner would be necessary, he *dismissed the young man with this warning: 'Don't tell anyone that you have reported this to me'*.

3. Preventing the Plot (23:23-35)

The seriousness of the situation is further conveyed by the commander's response. Summoning two centurions to lead a very large military detachment, he arranges for the safe transfer of the prisoner to the governor's headquarters in Caesarea. 'Only a large force traveling secretly at night can

---

48. Cf. Rapske, *Roman Custody*, 149. Marshall 1980, 368, and Witherington 1998, 695, draw attention to evidence for prisoners being accessible to their friends. However, Rapske argues that, given Paul's several brushes with death, it is likely that Paul's nephew needed a special reason for access. Luke's narrative stresses his youth (e.g., the commander took him by the hand, v. 19).

49. Cf. Skinner, *Locating Paul*, 128.

50. Spencer 1997, 216. Spencer argues that this encounter 'enhances the story's popular appeal and heightens dramatic tension'.

51. Barrett 1998, 1076, discusses a complex array of variants on the word *mellon* ('about to') in 23:20, and concludes that this is the best reading because it agrees with the preceding *to synedrion*. The last clause literally reads, 'as though (the Sanhedrin) was about to enquire somewhat more closely about him'.

hope to deliver Paul from what, in Luke's portrait, is a city set upon his destruction.'[52] These provisions, together with the commander's letter (vv. 25-
30), treat Paul as a person of some significance, who is worthy of protection
and just treatment by Roman authorities. However, a discrepancy between
this report and Luke's account of the same events (v. 27) suggests that the
commander is hiding his previous mistakes in dealing with Paul. Luke begins to show how the Lord's promise to Paul (v. 11) is fulfilled by a series of
flawed human agents. 'By rescuing Paul from this plot, Claudius Lysias
puts him one step closer to Rome. He also brings about the final separation
of Paul from Jerusalem.'[53]

23-24   Luke has previously shown the commander to be a man of insight and decisive action (21:31-36; 23:10). Once more, Lysias intervenes to
rescue Paul from mob violence, summoning two of his centurions and ordering them, *'Get ready a detachment of two hundred soldiers, seventy horsemen
and two hundred spearmen to go to Caesarea at nine tonight'* (apo tritēs hōras tēs
nyktos, 'from the third hour of the night'). *Caesarea,* the seat of the Roman
provincial governor, was almost 70 miles (112 km.) by road (cf. Josephus,
War 1.79). If the garrison in Jerusalem had only a single commander and
was a normal Roman cohort, *two hundred soldiers* would have been about
half the force available. The total company of infantry, cavalry, and light-
armed troops was twelve times larger than the band of forty terrorists![54]
The well-known dangers of the route might justify such a large military
presence (cf. Josephus, *War* 2.228, 540-55; *Ant.* 20.113), but the main point
seems to have been the commander's wish to preserve Paul from any further threat from his opponents.[55] The order was also given to *provide horses
for Paul so that he may be taken safely* (diasōsōsi; cf. 27:43, 44; 28:1, 4) *to Governor Felix* (cf. vv. 31-33 note). In literary terms, lavish and secretive provisions for the protection of Paul suggest that he is 'a heroic figure worthy of
the utmost attention'.[56] The commander's letter to Felix (vv. 26-30) also
suggests Paul's importance. It shows that Lysias believed Paul to be innocent of any charge deserving death or imprisonment. He thus saw himself
protecting a Roman citizen from unjust treatment by representatives of his
own race and religion. However, it is also true that 'the Roman army ferries

52. Gaventa 2003, 321.

53. Gaventa 2003, 322.

54. Spencer 1997, 216. The Western text has '100 horsemen', which is an insignificant
variation. Barrett 1998, 1077-78, discusses the meaning of *dixiolaboi* (lit. 'holding with the
right hand'), which is generally rendered 'spearmen', but may refer to someone who 'led
horses' (a change of mount for the cavalry).

55. The Western Text of 23:23-24 provides one of the most extensive variations in
Acts. It contains the explanation that the commander 'was afraid that the Jews would seize
(Paul) and kill him, and afterwards he would incur the accusation of having taken money'.
In other words, the commander wished to avoid giving the impression that he might be
open for a bribe. Cf. Metzger, *Textual Commentary,* 432-33; Barrett 1998, 1079-80.

56. Spencer 1997, 216, following Pervo, *Profit,* 32-33. On the plural *horses,* cf. note 63
below.

him to Caesarea because he is the reason for public unruliness and because Lysias intends to fulfill his charge to keep the peace'.[57]

25-30 The inclusion of this letter in the narrative allows us to observe Lysias giving 'an official report of his own handling of Paul's case to his superior, the governor'.[58] Barrett observes that 'it is hard to imagine how Luke could have obtained access to Roman archives whether in Jerusalem or in Caesarea'.[59] Perhaps so, but Luke occasionally includes apparently private information in his text without disclosing his sources (e.g., 5:34-42; 25:13-22; 26:30-32). If the letter was read aloud by the governor (v. 34), which was the almost universal practice in antiquity, Paul may have been able to recall its message for Luke. However, 'precisely because it was an official report, it was the sort of document that would be preserved for the trial of Paul as an important reference work for Felix (and others?) to use'.[60] If the letter is totally Luke's invention, it is hard to explain a discrepancy between this report and Luke's account of the same events. The letter reveals a Roman official needing to present himself in the best possible light (v. 27), adding a very human touch to the story. In narrative terms, we are told his name for the first time (*Claudius Lysias*).[61] The address to *Governor Felix* gives us a time reference for the event and prepares us to meet an important character and observe his dealings with Paul (*hēgemōn* is a general word for 'governor'; here it is used for 'procurator' [normally *epitropos*]).[62] Lysias abbreviates the account of his first engagement with Paul (*This man was seized by the Jews and they were about to kill him, but I came with my troops and rescued him*) and, in so doing, implies that he knew from the beginning who he was (*for I had learned that he is a Roman citizen*).[63] He conveniently fails to mention his original misunderstanding about Paul (21:37-39) and his later attempt to have him scourged before discovering that he

57. Skinner, *Locating Paul*, 129.

58. Tannehill 1990, 295. Tannehill, 296, notes that, since biblical literature operates with the assumption of a reliable narrator, the narrator's version provides the reference-point against which different accounts should be measured. Cf. Spencer 1997, 21, for a similar evaluation of the commander's report.

59. Barrett 1998, 1071. Barrett, 1081-82, discusses the minor variations in the MSS of 23:25.

60. Witherington 1998, 698. The expression *echousan ton typon touton* (v. 25, not translated by TNIV) is rendered by KJV, 'after this manner' (NRSV, ESV 'to this effect'), which may suggest that Luke's version is a rough copy. However, the expression could mean 'according to (the following) set pattern.' Cf. *ND* 1:77-78, which argues that here and in 15:23-29 Luke means us to understand that he was citing transcripts available to him.

61. Barrett 1998, 1082, observes that it is 'possible, but not certain', that the commander's first name could mean that he received his citizenship from Emperor Claudius (cf. 22:28). Barrett notes several unimportant variants to this verse.

62. Bruce 1990, 470.

63. Barrett 1998, 1083-84, rightly insists that the aorist participle *mathōn* ('learned', 23:27) refers to an action before the main verb *exeilamēn* ('rescued'). A new sentence begins with the present participle *boulomenos* ('wishing'). Against Johnson 1992, 405, it is not possible to repunctuate the sentence to make the commander's report fit the sequence of Acts 21.

was a Roman citizen (22:23-25)! This is doubtless for self-protection. Tannehill observes that 'as we move up the scale of political power to the governors Felix and Festus, the character flaws will become more apparent'.[64] As a result, Roman justice appears to be flawed, even though it offers protection to Paul from the injustice meted out by his own people. Postively, however, Lysias records how he pursued the question of *why they were accusing him*. Bringing Paul before their Sanhedrin, he found that *the accusation had to do with questions about their law* [cf. 18:15], *but there was no charge against him that deserved death or imprisonment*.[65] Violating the temple was certainly deserving of death, but no witnesses had been able to prove the charge. 'Luke is building a set of legal precedents for regarding the Messianists not as revolutionaries threatening to Rome, but as a legitimate variation within Judaism.'[66] Acting to protect this Roman citizen from harm, when he was informed of a plot to be carried out against Paul, the commander records that he sent him to Felix at once. Following due process, he also ordered his accusers to present to the governor their case against him.

31-33 *So the soldiers, carrying out their orders, took Paul with them during the night and brought him as far as Antipatris*. This was approximately 35 miles (56 km.) from Jerusalem, at the foot of the Judean hills.[67] Some commentators have argued that it would be difficult for such a company to reach Antipatris in the course of a night, but Witherington offers evidence to the contrary. He concludes that 'it does not pay to underestimate what Roman troops were capable of when a crisis situation was involved, especially when the only person in the entourage perhaps not capable of such a strenuous effort due to recent abuse was riding on a horse!'[68] Once safely there, it was no longer necessary for Paul to have such a large escort, and so *the next day they let the cavalry go on with him*, while the foot-soldiers *returned to the barracks*. When the cavalry had covered the further distance through the open country to Caesarea, *they delivered the letter to the governor and*

---

64. Tannehill 1990, 295. Cf. Festus reporting to Agrippa in 25:14-21.

65. Rapske, *Roman Custody*, 148, argues that 'chains' would be a better translation of *desmōn* than 'imprisonment' in the context. Paul is in protective custody. The Western text gives more Christian content to the report in 23:29, adding after 'their law' the words 'of Moses and a certain Jesus'. This expansion of the text concludes with the words 'I got him away with difficulty, by force'. Cf. Metzger, *Textual Commentary*, 433; Barrett 1998, 1084-85, for further minor textual variations in 23:30.

66. Johnson 1992, 406. Cf. 25:19; 26:3.

67. Barrett 1998, 1085-86, notes the uncertainty of scholars about the site and their consequent disagreement about the distance from Jerusalem to Antipatris. Josephus, *Ant.* 13.390; *War* 1.99, says that this city was founded by Herod the Great in honour of his father Antipater, in a plain that was well watered and fertile.

68. Witherington 1998, 697. The plural *horses* (*ktēnē*, 'animals for riding') is used in v. 24, suggesting to Witherington, 697-98, that other horses may have been provided to enable Paul to change animals and move rapidly. He also agrees with the possibility that these other mounts could have been for Paul's travelling companions. Cf. Williams 1985, 390.

handed Paul over to him. Caesarea is the context for Paul's custody and trials for the next three chapters (Acts 24–26). According to the Roman historian Tacitus (*Hist.* 5.9), the full name of the governor was Antonius Felix, though Josephus (*Ant.* 20.137) calls him Claudius Felix.[69] His appointment as governor was unusual since he was a former slave, and not part of the Roman aristocracy. His promotion appears to have been due to the influence of his brother Pallas in the imperial court, though Josephus (*Ant.* 20.162) records that Jonathan the High Priest actually suggested his appointment to Emperor Claudius.[70] According to Josephus (*War* 2.247; *Ant.* 20.137-38), Felix succeeded Ventidius Cumanus as procurator of Judea in 52 (cf. 24:27 note for a discussion about the date of his removal from office).[71] Tacitus (*Ann.* 12.54; cf. *Hist.* 5.9) famously describes him as having 'practised every kind of cruelty and lust, wielding the power of a king with all the instincts of a slave'. His term of office was marked by increasing insurgency throughout the province. He put down these uprisings ruthlessly, in a way that alienated more moderate Jews and led to further rebellion.

34-35 *The governor read the letter and asked what province he was from* (cf. Pilate's inquiry in Lk. 23:6-7). Felix acted in the proper legal manner and held a preliminary interrogation. First, he sought to establish Paul's status by discovering *what province he was from.* Perhaps he hoped for 'an answer that would enable him to slip out of the whole affair, but found that he could not do so'.[72] *Learning that he was from Cilicia, he said, 'I will hear your case when your accusers get here.'* The status of Cilicia did not require that natives should be sent to it from Caesarea for trial. Moreover, the Legate of the Roman province of Syria-Cilicia was not to be bothered with minor cases from Judea. Indeed, 'had Felix sent Paul on to Syria he would likely have only created more troubles for himself with both Roman and Jewish officials with whom he had to have ongoing dealings'.[73] So he ordered that Paul be kept under guard *in Herod's palace (en tō praitōriō tou Hērōdou)* until

69. Bruce 1990, 470-71, suggests that the name 'Claudius Felix' could mean that Felix was emancipated by Claudius, but Barrett 1998, 1080, argues that Josephus should be read to mean that 'Claudius sent Felix'.

70. Barrett 1998, 1081, discusses the difficulties of reconciling the accounts of Josephus and Tacitus in connection with the appointment of Felix.

71. Tacitus, *Ann.* 12.54, indicates that Felix had been active in Palestine before his appointment as procurator. Bruce 1990, 471, argues that the confusing evidence of Tacitus should be taken to mean that 'Cumanus was procurator of Judaea (with Samaria) from 48 to 52, while Felix occupied a regional post in Galilee, and that when Cumanus was disgraced in 52, Felix was promoted to procuratorship of the whole province, an unprecedented honor for a freedman'. Cf. Barrett 1998, 1080-81.

72. Barrett 1998, 1087. Barrett also suggests that Felix might have tried to discover whether Paul came from a Roman province or from one of the client kingdoms. In the latter case, 'it would have been unwise not to send Paul back to his place of origin'.

73. Witherington 1998, 702. Cf. A. N. Sherwin-White, *Roman Society and Roman Law in the New Testament* (Oxford: Clarendon, 1963), 55-56; Barrett 1998, 1087. Metzger, *Textual Commentary,* 434, notes how the Western Text transforms the indirect discourse of 23:34 into direct.

his accusers arrived. Archaeological evidence for the 'praetorium' built by Herod the Great in Caesarea, and taken over by the Roman administration, has recently been uncovered.[74] Paul remained in this setting until the journey to Rome began (27:1).

The treatment Paul received from the Romans is in sharp contrast with that meted out by the Jewish leadership, who continued to pursue him by legal harassment (24:1-9). Johnson suggests that the message of the chapter for Luke's first readers is clear. 'If the Christians are to argue what they regard as their legitimate claims to represent the authentic Israel, it will not be possible within the context of direct confrontation with the Jewish leadership, which has shown itself not only unwilling to hear those claims but unwilling to let those making them continue to live. Any debate or defense can take place only within the protection offered by the Roman order.'[75] In contemporary terms, we may observe the difficulty of engaging with those holding any entrenched religious position and the injustice shown to Christians by religious leaders in many countries. At the same time, there may be both protection from secular authorities and a greater willingness on the part of those who have no faith to investigate Christian claims. Acts 23 suggests the need to recognise God's sovereign hand in all such experiences, and to trust that he is working out his saving purpose through the negative, as well as the positive consequences of Christian witness.

G. Appearing before Felix (24:1-27)

'Lysias' decision to send Paul to Caesarea under armed guard rescues him from the assassination plot but not from legal jeopardy. Paul's case is transferred to the highest Roman official of the province, Governor Felix.'[1] He is formally on trial before a significant representative of the Gentile world, but his defence largely follows the lines of previous speeches before fellow Jews, asserting his orthodoxy and piety and making the hope of the resurrection of the dead a central feature of his confession (vv. 11-21). 'Paul is speaking as much to his Jewish accusers as to the Roman governor',[2] thus continuing the apologetic thrust of the preceding chapters. Eventually, Paul has the chance to address the governor directly and chal-

---

74. Cf. B. Burrell, K. Gleason, and E. Netzer, 'Uncovering Herod's Seaside Palace', *BAR* 19 (1993), 50-57, 76; Rapske, *Roman Custody*, 155-58. Bruce 1990, 474, notes that 'the *praetorium* (originally the headquarters of the *praetor* or military commander) was (among other things) the official residence of the Roman governor of an imperial province'. In Mk. 15:16; Jn. 18:28 the word is used of Pilate's headquarters in Jerusalem. In Phil. 1:13 it is probably used of the praetorian guard in Rome.

75. Johnson 1992, 407.

1. Tannehill 1990, 297.

2. Tannehill 1990, 299.

lenge him with the gospel in a personal way (vv. 24-26). So this trial scene has a threefold purpose: Paul has the opportunity to defend himself against false charges before the highest authority in the province, to continue his defence of Christianity before Jewish opponents, and to bear witness to Christ before the governor, thus continuing to fulfill Jesus' prophecy in Luke 21:12-13.

Two theological themes are central to Acts 24: worship and saving faith. Worship terminology has not been widely employed by Luke in his second volume, and so the prominence of two key terms in Paul's defence before Felix is noteworthy. Paul proclaims his continuing piety as a Jew when he speaks about going up 'to worship' in Jerusalem (v. 11, *proskynēsōn*). He later explains that this involved the bringing of alms, the offering of sacrifices, and ritual purification (vv. 17-18). However, using another term that is employed in Scripture for the service of God more widely (v. 14, *latreuō*), he describes his life and ministry as a Christian, 'according to the Way'. This worship involves a belief structure that is wholly biblical but specifically focussed on the hope of a general resurrection from the dead and daily expressed in seeking to have a clear conscience 'before God and all people' (vv. 15-16). Thus Paul defends his way of worship as authentically Jewish, at the same time identifying implicitly with the Pharisaic interpretation of Scripture in terms of fundamental beliefs (cf. 23:6-9). He does not even mention the name of Jesus in this defence, though it is clear from 25:19 that disagreement about the significance of Jesus was a key to his debate with the Jewish leaders. When Paul is finally able to declare his position more fully before King Agrippa, whose acquaintance with Judaism was more precise than that of the Roman governors (26:2-3), Paul returns to the theme of authentic worship and covenantal membership (26:4-7, 16-23). Worship terminology is thus used to proclaim 'the Way' as the fulfillment of biblical hopes and to justify Paul's ministry of incorporating believing Gentiles into the New Covenant community. Putting it another way, the gospel makes it possible for Jews and Gentiles to please and honour God together in the eschatological era. Such worship is no longer focussed on Jerusalem and cultic activity, but on the exalted Christ and the benefits of his death and resurrection.

The message that unites Jews and Gentiles in the worship of the messianic age is then the focus in vv. 24-25. 'Faith in Christ Jesus' is Luke's brief way of describing the first element of Paul's private discourse with Felix and Drusilla (v. 24). It is 'a summary of Paul's Christological preaching comparable to the references to faith in Jesus in Paul's speeches elsewhere (cf. 20:21; 26:18)'.[3] This expression indicates that Paul preached Jesus as the glorified Messiah and called for the response of faith. The following expressions imply also the need for repentance in view of the coming judgment (v. 25). This presentation of the gospel is more explicitly Christological and

---

3. Tannehill 1990, 302.

eschatological than Paul's preaching to Gentiles in 17:22-31, presumably because of Felix's prior knowledge of Christianity (v. 22) and his wife's Jewish connection (v. 24).

Witherington contends that this trial is presented as 'an oratorical duel between two accomplished rhetoricians, Tertullus and Paul, offering us (in précis form) samplings of forensic rhetoric'.[4] The charges are vague and the process unusual because the trial is *extra ordinem*, or outside the usual pattern of Roman justice: 'the accuser simply alleges "facts" against the accused, without necessarily producing any hard evidence, or even eyewitnesses, and then invites the Roman provincial official to evaluate and deal with the matter'.[5] Further outlining the way such cases proceeded, Witherington notes that the burden of proof lay on the accuser, that the judge had flexibility in establishing what the crime was, and that he could either make an immediate decision or postpone rendering a verdict as he saw fit. Paul is shown handling his defence with great skill and refuting the charges against him. Winter observes that he does this 'by prescribing the limits of the evidence based on Roman law proscribing the charges of absent accusers, using forensic terminology, and not least of all, presenting a well-argued defence, even if preserved in summary form'.[6] Johnson concludes that 'the long drawn-out legal process, with all its false starts and delays, serves the literary function of unfolding (slowly and in segments) Paul's true identity and integrity, not for characters in the narrative, but for Luke's readers themselves'.[7]

4. Witherington 1998, 702. Witherington endorses the suggestion of B. W. Winter, 'Official Proceedings and the Forensic Speeches in Acts 24–26', in B. W. Winter and A. D. Clarke (eds.), *The Book of Acts in Its First-Century Setting*, Vol. 1: *Ancient Literary Setting* (Grand Rapids: Eerdmans; Carlisle: Paternoster, 1993), 307-9, that if Luke was not present on this occasion he may have had access to the record of the proceedings, which must have been forwarded to Rome with Paul and Luke on the same ship.

5. Witherington 1998, 703, following A. N. Sherwin-White, *Roman Society and Roman Law in the New Testament* (Oxford: Clarendon, 1963), 49. H. W. Tajra, *The Trial of St. Paul: A Juridical Exegesis of the Second Half of Acts*, WUNT 2, no. 35 (Tübingen: Mohr [Siebeck], 1989), 114, observes that, in this procedure, 'the governor could render justice directly in virtue of his personal *cognitio*'.

6. Winter, 'Official Proceedings', 327. Thus Paul conducted his own defence in an able manner 'against a professional forensic orator'.

7. Johnson 1992, 415. Johnson argues that 'Luke uses these hearings to eliminate once and for all any false apprehension concerning Paul'. However, Acts 24 presents the only real trial in the sequence, with all parties present and able to present their case before the Roman governor.

1. The Accusation of the Jews (24:1-9)

1 Paul was guarded for *five days* in Herod's praetorium (23:35) before *the high priest Ananias went down to Caesarea with some of the elders and a lawyer named Tertullus.* Perhaps these Jewish leaders were hoping that 'their high social status in Israel would help determine the outcome of the case, since this was often the case in Roman trials'.[8] Paul's accusers were clearly anxious to expedite proceedings, using the best possible legal assistance. With the aid of a professional 'barrister' or 'advocate' *(rhētōr),*[9] they then *brought their charges against Paul before the governor* (cf. 23:31-33 for details about Felix). This was the formal process by which a trial was set in motion, with the accused not yet being present to answer the charges.[10] It has been argued that Tertullus was a Greek-speaking Jew because he uses the first person plural in v. 6 *(ekratēsamen, we seized),* speaking as one of those responsible for Paul's arrest.[11] Others have observed that an advocate would naturally associate himself with his clients in this way and have taken the reference to 'all the Jews' in v. 5 to mean that Tertullus was a Gentile.[12] The evidence is insufficient to be convincing either way.

2-4 *When Paul was called in,*[13] *Tertullus presented his case before Felix.* Tertullus began his speech with the customary rhetorical introduction known as *captatio benevolentiae* (cf. Quintilian, *De Institutione Oratoria* 4.1; Cicero, *De Oratore* 2.78, 79 [319-25]). This involved some complimentary exaggeration *('We have enjoyed a long period of peace under you'),* since the governorship of Felix in Palestine was characterized by much social and political disturbance.[14] Nevertheless, this introduction is 'carefully linked to the

---

8. Witherington 1998, 704. However, Witherington points out that 'Felix was no great lover of Jews in general', and so their presence may not have made the impact they had desired. B. Rapske, *The Book of Acts in Its First-Century Setting,* Vol. 3: *The Book of Acts and Paul in Roman Custody* (Grand Rapids: Eerdmans; Carlisle: Paternoster, 1994), 159, suggests that in one key respect Paul's accusers would have been at a disadvantage: Paul was a Roman citizen. 'Roman prejudice would lean towards Paul's innocence and this would need to be adroitly attacked.'

9. Barrett 1998, 1093, gives evidence from the papyri for the use of such professional advocates in certain types of cases. He notes that 'use was not mandatory and probably indicates the importance or complexity of the case'. Dio Chrysostom, *Or.* 76.4; Josephus, *Ant.* 17.226, also show how *rhētōr* can be used in the narrow sense of 'legal advocate'.

10. Cf. Tajra, *Trial,* 119; Rapske, *Roman Custody,* 158-67.

11. So Bruce 1990, 475.

12. Cf. Barrett 1998, 1093.

13. TNIV rightly takes the pronoun in the genitive absolute construction *(klēthentos autou)* to refer to Paul rather than to Tertullus, who is the subject of the main verb in the sentence. Cf. Barrett 1998, 1094.

14. Cf. Josephus, *Ant.* 20.182; *War* 2.252-70. Witherington 1998, 705, comments that Felix 'is usually credited with being most responsible of all the governors leading up to the Jewish War for stirring up ill will and trouble by his brutal suppression of various Jewish and Samaritan groups, some messianic, some more revolutionary'.

charges which follow and is not an example of mere flattery'.[15] For example, since Felix had recently restored law and order by quelling the rebellion of an Egyptian prophet (cf. 21:38), he could be expected to maintain the peace by punishing someone who disturbed the public order in Jerusalem and the Dispersion (cf. vv. 5-6). Tertullus further claimed that it was because of the governor's *'foresight' (pronoia)* or 'providence' that many *'reforms' (diorthōmata)* had happened in the Jewish nation.[16] Speaking on their behalf, Tertullus claimed that this was acknowledged *'everywhere and in every way'* (TNIV has actually reversed the order of the Gk. *pantē te kai pantachou,* 'in every way and in every place'), *'with profound gratitude'.* In other words, he affirmed that Jewish appreciation for the peace and providential reforms brought by Felix was widespread and comprehensive. Luke presents only an outline of the speech, and Tertullus doubtless said more. However, he knew that he could *'weary' (enkoptō)* Felix by continuing in this vein,[17] and so prepared to move to the substance of his speech by saying, *'I would request that you be kind enough to hear us briefly'.* The word translated *kind (epieikeia)* denotes 'reasonableness, fairness, in general and especially perhaps in a judge, who is prepared not to break the laws but to give them an understanding, non-legalist interpretation'.[18]

5-9 The basis of the appeal for a fair hearing (the connective *gar,* 'for', is not translated by TNIV) is the material now disclosed. The essence of the charge is set out in a section of the speech technically known as the *narratio* (vv. 5-6). Speaking on behalf of his clients, Tertullus declares, *'We have found this man to be a troublemaker (loimon,* 'a plague' [ESV], 'a pest' [NRSV 'a pestilent fellow']), *stirring up riots (staseis) among the Jews all over the world'* (*oikoumenē* could refer more narrowly to the Roman Empire).[19]

15. Witherington 1998, 705. This is not noted by many commentators, who simply view the introduction to this speech as a form of flattery. Winter, 'Official Proceedings', 315-22, however, shows how the *captatio benevolentiae* of Tertullus resembles those found in various papyri and plays an important role in presenting the charges against Paul. Spencer 1997, 218, also notes how 'Tertullus counterpoints a litany of the judge's noble attributes and achievements with the defendant's dishonourable traits and deeds'.

16. Winter, 'Official Proceedings', 318-19, observes that the theme of 'providence', employing the word *pronoia,* is found in two forensic papyri, linked with the notion of legal reform. It is not clear what reforms Felix brought to Judea, but Tertullus is simply highlighting 'the judicial competence which Felix brings to this case'.

17. *enkoptō* normally means 'make progress slow or difficult, hinder, thwart' (BDAG; cf. 1 Thes. 2:18). The Syriac and Armenian versions give the meaning 'weary', and this interpretation is supported by the fact that *enkopos* has that sense in *Anthologia Palatina* 6.33 (cf. LXX Job 19; Is. 43:23). Barrett 1998, 1096, also suggests that 'delay' or 'detain' is a possible rendering (so NRSV, ESV).

18. Barrett 1998, 1096. Cf. H. Preisker, *TDNT* 2:588-90; Bruce 1990, 476; Johnson 1992, 410. KJV 'clemency'.

19. Tannehill 1990, 297, takes the accusation to mean that 'like a plague (Paul) has been attacking the health of Roman society; this is the result of his position of leadership in a dangerous movement and is demonstrated in the uprisings that Paul causes among Jews throughout the Roman world'.

The noun *stasis* has a range of meanings in Acts from 'disturbance' to 'riot' (cf. 15:2; 19:40; 23:7, 10). Rebellion and the creation of civil disturbance was 'a capital crime and pre-eminently prisonable as well'.[20] The sociopolitical effect of Paul's ministry was being highlighted to indicate the danger of Christianity for the well-being of the Empire, and the prisoner was being likened to a dangerous disease which must be stopped before it infects everyone. As well as resembling previous accusations against Paul and his co-workers (cf. 16:20; 17:6-7; 18:12-13; 19:26-27), this charge to some extent echoed the one made in Luke 23:2 against Jesus.[21] It was precisely the charge to bring against a Jew during the reign of Claudius or the early years of Nero. 'The accusers of Paul were putting themselves on the side of the government. The procurator would know at once what the prosecution meant.'[22] The seriousness of the charge is further explicated by describing Paul in quasi-military terms as *a ringleader (prōtostatēs, 'chief', 'leader') of the Nazarene sect'*. 'The Jewish leadership assign to Paul the same importance as standard bearer of the messianic movement that Luke himself does.'[23] There were several Jewish sects or parties (*haireseis*, as in 5:17; 15:5) at this time, but Tertullus implies that this new group was dangerously different (cf. 24:14 note). The term 'Nazorean' was normally applied to Jesus (2:22; 3:6; 4:10; 6:14; 22:8; 26:9), but here in the plural to his followers.[24]

According to his accusers, Paul, as leader of this group, *'even tried to desecrate the temple'*. In religious terms, this explained the violent response from the Jews, which, from a Roman point of view, had serious political implications. Such an offence would have incurred the death penalty, had it been proved true.[25] Tertullus climactically asserts that temple desecration was the main reason for Paul's captivity (*'so we seized him'*). Tertullus conveniently omits to say that a riot in Jerusalem prompted the commander to take Paul into custody.[26] Some manuscripts then add words to the end of v. 6 ('and we would have judged him according to our law'), include v. 7 ('but the chief captain Lysias came and with great violence took him out of our hands'), and add words to the beginning of v. 8 ('commanding his accusers to come before you'). This longer Western reading, which passed into the Received Text and hence the KJV, is not found in the earliest and

---

20. Rapske, *Roman Custody*, 160.

21. So Johnson 1992, 411.

22. Sherwin-White, *Roman Law*, 51-52. He observes a similarity to the language used here in a contemporary letter of Claudius to the Alexandrians. Cf. 18:2 note.

23. Johnson 1992, 411.

24. Spencer 1997, 219, observes that the title 'Nazorean' may have been derived from the name of Jesus' native village of Nazareth or with the movement which identified Jesus as the promised Davidic 'shoot' (Heb. *nēṣer*) in Is. 11:1. Cf. Johnson 1992, 284.

25. Bruce 1990, 476. Rapske, *Roman Custody*, 162, notes several factors in the text which blunt the force of this accusation, including the fact that Tertullus speaks only of Paul attempting (*epeirasen*) to desecrate the temple, in some unspecified way.

26. So Bruce 1990, 477.

most reliable manuscripts and is unlikely to be original.[27] It describes the events of 22:22–23:30 in a summary fashion, viewed from the Jewish perspective. A later editor 'no doubt thought that some cross-reference was necessary in order to explain what was taking place'.[28] The best-attested texts then continue, '*By examining him yourself you will be able to learn the truth about all these charges we are bringing against him*'. In what is called the *peroratio* of an address, Tertullus invites the governor himself to cross-examine Paul about the matter.[29] Luke adds that *the Jews joined in the accusation*, using a military term (*synepethento*, 'joined in the attack') to signify the intensity of their opposition to Paul. They joined their lawyer in *asserting that these things were true*. Luke, however, has already made it clear that the accusations against Paul were false from the start (cf. 21:27-29).

2. Paul's Defence (24:10-23)

10 *When the governor motioned for him to speak,* Paul began his response with a brief *captatio benevolentiae*, as Tertullus did (vv. 2-3). In a more restrained fashion, however, he expressed himself glad to make his defence before Felix, knowing that '*for a number of years*' (*ek pollōn etōn*) he had been '*a judge over this nation*'. Although the normal period for a proconsulship in a senatorial province was only two years, there is evidence that Felix had been active in the region, as a junior colleague of Cumanus, before his appointment as procurator.[30] Thus Paul acknowledged him as a judge who was experienced in matters relating to the Jewish people and their disputes.

11-13 Paul now proceeds to establish and interweave several lines of defence, in certain respects 'making use of Tertullus' words to build his own case'.[31] First, he asserts his piety as a Jew in going up to Jerusalem *to*

27. NKJV includes the longer reading (found in the uncial MSS E and Ψ, various minuscules, and some versions), but NRSV and ESV do so only in the margin. TNIV gives no translation of this variant. Metzger, *Textual Commentary*, 434, notes the opinion of some scholars that the longer reading is necessary to the sense of the verses, for the verb *ekratēsamen (we seized)* seems to require some sequel. However, the abruptness of the shorter reading may have prompted the addition, and 'it is difficult to account for the omission of the disputed words if they were original'.

28. Barrett 1998, 1099. Bruce 1990, 477, argues that the longer reading 'bears marks of genuineness'. For example, by presenting the attack on Paul in the temple as an orderly arrest (using *ekratēsamen*) and describing the tribune as taking Paul out of the hands of the Jews 'with great violence', Tertullus appears to score points against Lysias.

29. Barrett 1998, 1100, argues that the verb *anakrinein* ('cross-examine') 'describes a process that would be applied to Paul rather than to the tribune' (cf. 4:9; 12:19). In the longer version of 24:8, the implication is that Lysias should be cross-examined rather than Paul. This change may have been made because the editor of the longer text regarded it as improbable that Paul himself could have been called to bear witness against himself.

30. Cf. Rapske, *Roman Custody*, 162 note 57; Barrett 1998, 1080-1, 1101.

31. Tannehill 1990, 298. Tannehill compares the language in vv. 8 and 11, and then

'worship' (*proskynēsōn,* using the future participle to indicate purpose). The verb here is used by Luke to express homage to God in what might be called a formal act of worship (Lk. 4:8; 24:52; Acts 8:27), or to refer to the practice of idolatry (Lk. 4:7; Acts 7:43, adapting Am. 5:26; cf. Acts 10:25).[32] Further details are given in vv. 17-18, but the main point is his intention to use the temple appropriately as a faithful Jew, not to desecrate it. However, much discussion has taken place about the time reference (*'no more than twelve days ago'*). It is possible that this is reckoned from Paul's arrival in Jerusalem to his transfer to Caesarea and excludes the five days of waiting for his accusers to arrive (v. 1).[33] We know that there was a seven-day purification period in Jerusalem before his arrest (21:27). Paul's trial before the Sanhedrin was on the following day (22:30), and the plot to assassinate him was initiated on the day after that (23:12). At least another day must have been involved in journeying to Caesarea. If the five days of waiting for the trial to begin is included, that makes a total of at least fifteen days since his arrival in Jerusalem. Some have therefore argued that the phrase means, 'I had not been twelve days in Jerusalem when the trouble arose'.[34] Another possibility would be to count twelve days since the temple visit at the end of the seven-day period of purification, when he was seized by the crowd and then arrested by the Romans (21:27-33).[35] Whichever way the expression is taken, the point is that his visit to the temple was very recent, and it should still have been possible to find reliable witnesses concerning the event.

Paul's second line of defence was to question the reliability of his accusers, claiming that they *'did not find me arguing with anyone at the temple, or stirring up a crowd in the synagogues or anywhere else in the city'*. The *synagogues* in this context appear to be those in Jerusalem rather than in the Dispersion. He says nothing about the charge of 'stirring up riots among the

---

notes how Paul picks up Tertullus's reference to Christianity as a 'sect' (vv. 5, 14). Winter, 'Official Proceedings', 322-27, shows how Paul's speech follows the five-part pattern of defence described by Quintilian, and demonstrates the skilful way in which Paul reduced the charges against him to a single theological issue.

32. Although Luke presents a new theology of worship, with the exalted Jesus at its centre, this verb is not employed in Acts to describe either initial acts of homage and devotion to Christ or the content and purpose of regular Christian gatherings. This was presumably because of the particular association of this term with the rites of paganism and with the Jewish cult centred at Jerusalem. Cf. D. G. Peterson, 'The Worship of the New Community', in I. H. Marshall and D. G. Peterson (eds.), *Witness to the Gospel: The Theology of Acts* (Grand Rapids/Cambridge: Eerdmans, 1998), 385-86.

33. Cf. Bruce 1990, 478, who outlines what happened each day in the sequence of events from 21:17 to 23:31-3. So also Witherington 1998, 710, who concludes that Paul's point is that there were only twelve days total that he was in Jerusalem and could make any trouble (and he was in custody for three of these).

34. Barrett 1998, 1102-3.

35. The clause 'since I went up to worship in Jerusalem' need not refer to Paul's primary reason for visiting the city and thus to the beginning of his time there. It could simply refer to the event that triggered the riot and led to his arrest.

Jews all over the world' (v. 5), but confines himself to possible crimes within the area of Felix's responsibility.[36] In this respect, he contests that *'they cannot prove to you the charges they are now making against me'*.

14-16   The third level of Paul's appeal to Felix took the form of a confession (*homologō*, 'admit', 'confess') about his distinctive beliefs and practices. 'In forensic terms, this is a breathtaking turn: after a series of emphatic denials, the accused is about to make a confession!'[37] Yet he was not confessing a crime, but identifying with his fellow Jews by speaking about worshipping (*latreuō*) *'the God of our ancestors'* (cf. 22:3; 28:17). This second worship term (cf. v. 11) can refer to the service of God in everyday life or to particular expressions of devotion in a cultic context (cf. Lk. 1:74; 2:37; 4:8; Acts 7:7, 42; 26:7; 27:23).[38] With the following words, however, Paul differentiates himself from other Jews by identifying himself as *'a follower of the Way, which they call a sect'*. As noted previous, *the Way* appears to have been a self-designation favoured by Christians (cf. 9:2 note; 19:9, 23; 22:4), but *sect* was the term favoured by non-Christian Jews (cf. 24:5 note). Paul served the God of the OT 'according to the way' (*kata tēn hodon*) of Jesus and his followers.[39] Although Luke presents Paul occasionally visiting the temple in Jerusalem and engaging in traditional Jewish practices, his way of worshipping God is largely in the world, in a gospel ministry designed to bring Jews and Gentiles together to acknowledge Jesus as Lord and Saviour.[40] Given the use of the term *sect* (*hairesis*) elsewhere to describe Pharisees and Sadducees, it could have been understood as a tacit admission that followers of the Way were still broadly within the fold of Judaism. But claiming to be *the Way*, the earliest Jewish disciples were insisting that they were the true Israel, experiencing the promised blessings of the messianic era through faith in Jesus rather than being one of several groups within the people of God. Against this background, Jewish opponents of Christianity appear to have used the word *sect* to imply that Christians were a heretical, breakaway group.[41]

Paul further explains how he worships by confessing, *'I believe every-*

36. Tannehill 1990, 299, notes how the narrative of Acts has given sufficient reason to regard Paul's work in the Dispersion with suspicion, if civil calm is the primary value. 'Such disturbances, however, fall outside Felix's area of jurisdiction, and so Paul can take the easier course of limiting his reply to events in Jerusalem.'

37. Johnson 1992, 412.

38. Cf. Peterson, 'Worship', 387-88.

39. Paul happily speaks of *the Way* because it allows him to claim a succession to 'the righteous' in Scripture. Psalm 1, for example, contrasts the way of the righteous with the way of the wicked, and specifies the outcome of the two ways. Paul explicitly refers to the traditional biblical distinction between the righteous and the wicked in Acts 24:15.

40. In Acts 20:19 the verb *douleuein* conveys the same notion of service to the Lord through gospel ministry. Cf. Rom. 1:9-15; 15:15-21 for further descriptions of Paul's ministry using transformed worship terminology.

41. Cf. M. Simon, 'From Greek Hairesis to Christian Heresy', in W. R. Schoedel and R. L. Wilken (eds.), *Théologie Historique* 53 (Paris, 1979), 101-16; Bruce 1990, 476.

thing that is in accordance with the Law and that is written in the Prophets'.
TNIV begins a new sentence here, but the Greek syntax makes it clear that
'believing' (*pisteuōn*, a present participle) the Scriptures as he does is another defining characteristic of his worship.[42] He interprets the Law and
the Prophets as a follower of the Way, but, with respect to biblical eschatology, he implicitly once more identifies his position with that of the Pharisees (cf. 23:6-8). Some Sadducees were doubtless present in the delegation
from Jerusalem, but Paul treats the Pharisaic hope as the authentically biblical one, asserting, *'I have the same hope in God as these people themselves have,
that there will be a resurrection of both the righteous and the wicked'.* There is no
reference to the resurrection of Jesus here (though cf. 25:19), but only to the
hope of a general resurrection from death. Inclusion of *the wicked* in this resurrection implies that they are raised for judgment (cf. 24:25; Jn. 5:28-29;
Rev. 20:12-15).[43] This being so *(en toutō)*,[44] Paul also *(kai autos)*, together with
his accusers, is motivated to please God in every aspect of life, confessing,
'I strive always to keep my conscience clear before God and all people' (cf. 23:1
note for Paul's clear conscience). The verb *askō (strive)*, which is used only
here in the NT, was employed by Greek writers with reference to 'the training of the body for various skills and athletic pursuits but was easily
adapted for intellectual and moral training'.[45] Paul signifies a disciplined
life, practised in obeying God, with a conscience 'void of offence' (KJV
aproskopon; cf. 1 Cor. 10:32; Phil. 1:10), directly *before God* and indirectly in
his dealings with *all people*.[46] Such an appeal to a common hope and desire
to serve God is designed to counter the charge of being a destroyer of Judaism. His attitude and behaviour identifies him as one of *'the righteous'*,
whose life is shaped by the totality of God's revelation in Scripture. Although Paul addresses the governor with these words, he clearly also challenges his Jewish accusers to recognise the genuineness of his relationship
with God.

17-21   The fourth level of Paul's appeal to Felix continues the theme

---

42. Cf. Gaventa 2003, 327-28. Alternatively, as Bruce 1990, 479, suggests, the word
houtōs ('thus') in 24:14 (not translated by TNIV) makes the preceding expression *kata tēn
hodon hēn legousin hairesin* ('according to the Way which they call a sect') the key to understanding how Paul worships *and* how he interprets the Scriptures.

43. Bruce 1990, 480, observes that Paul nowhere makes express mention of the resurrection of the unjust in his letters. He concludes that 'it could not have been for him on the
same footing as the resurrection of "those who belong to Christ"; for them resurrection is
participation (at the parousia) in the resurrection of Christ, the harvest of which his resurrection was the firstfruits (1 Cor. 15:20-23; cf. Phil. 3:20f.)'. However, texts such as Rom. 2:5;
2 Cor. 5:10; 2 Tim. 4:1 could be taken to imply the resurrection of the wicked for judgment.

44. Cf. Barrett 1998, 1105-6.

45. Barrett 1998, 1106. Cf. Bruce 1990, 480. Tannehill 1990, 300, helpfully translates
askō dia pantos 'constantly in training', to bring out the sense of the verb.

46. Marshall 1980, 378, observes that 'Paul's wording reflects the common idea of human duty towards God and man (Pr. 3:4; Lk. 18:2, 4), and ties in with Jesus' summary of the
law in terms of love for God and one's neighbour'.

of his piety, claiming that his most recent behaviour was above reproach. This leads to the accusation that the charges against him are theologically rather than legally driven. Paul asserts that his most recent visit to Jerusalem had been *'after an absence of several years' (di' etōn de pleionōn;* cf. v. 10), indicating that he had not often been in the capital. It is likely that a brief visit is implied in 18:22, which would have been some three to five years earlier. Prior to that, Paul had visited Jerusalem for the Council meeting (15:2-4).[47] His most recent visit had been intended *'to bring my people gifts for the poor (eleēmosynas poiēsōn* is a Hebraism meaning 'to bring alms') *and to present offerings'.* Although Paul's collection for the relief of poor Christians in Jerusalem figures significantly in his own writings (cf. Rom. 15:25-7; 1 Cor. 16:1-4; 2 Cor. 8:4; 9:1-5, 12-13), this is the first allusion to that ministry in Acts. Luke either considered the collection less important than Paul did or he suppressed the details until this point for some reason.[48] Moreover, Luke has Paul declare that the gifts are (lit.) 'for my nation' *(eis to ethnos mou)* rather than being more narrowly for Christian Jews only. 'Paul affirmed his respect for the law in v. 14; here he wishes to demonstrate his respect for the Jewish people and the temple. Thus he touches on all three of the main points in the accusation of 21:28.'[49]

In view of the following expression (*'I was ceremonially clean [hēgnismenon,* a perfect participle, conveying the idea of 'being in a state of purity'] *when they found me in the temple courts doing this'*), it is most likely that the presentation of *'offerings' (prosphoras,* as in 21:26) refers to the ritual activity suggested to Paul by James and the elders in 21:23-24.[50] Whether or not Paul planned to offer any sacrifices before he reached Jerusalem, Luke indicates that he was happy to follow their suggestion and share in purification rites with four Christian brothers.[51] Repeating the claim of v. 12, Paul insisted that *'there was no crowd with me, nor was I involved in any disturbance'.*

47. Barrett 1998, 1107, thinks neither of these previous visits allows for the length of time implied by the use of the comparative *pleionōn,* and suggests that 'what is in mind is the interval since his conversion, when Paul broke off relations with official Judaism in Jerusalem'. But then he considers that this might be taken as a real comparative in relation to *pollōn* in v. 10, giving the meaning, 'My last visit to Jerusalem was before you, Felix, took office'.

48. Bruce 1990, 481, thinks that Luke most probably was reticent about mentioning the collection because 'it failed so disastrously to achieve its purpose'. Bruce also suggests that the collection may have been misrepresented at Paul's trial as 'an attempt to divert from its proper recipients money which should have gone to the Jerusalem temple tax'. Witherington 1998, 712, critiques the view of Tannehill 1990, 300 (shared by Gaventa 2003, 328), that 24:17 refers to the acts of piety of a pilgrim involving the temple treasury, and not to the collection mentioned in Paul's letters.

49. Tannehill 1990, 300.

50. Cf. Marshall 1980, 379; Witherington 1998, 712. Bruce 1990, 480, takes *offerings* to refer to the financial gifts brought by Paul.

51. Marshall 1980, 379, indicates the strength of the argument here: if Paul was engaged in such a pious duty, it is unlikely that he would have been desecrating the temple at the same time.

Denying the charge of being a deliberate troublemaker, Paul indicates that those who accused him of wrong in the first place (*'some Jews from the province of Asia'*; cf. 21:27-29) ought to be present to *'bring charges if they have anything against me'*. Sherwin-White points out that 'Roman law was very strong against accusers who abandoned their charges'.[52] The failure of those witnesses to appear before the governor's court suggested that their charge could not be substantiated. Paul was making a sound technical objection that was sufficient basis for the dismissal of the case. But the broken syntax then indicates the sudden introduction of another line of defence (*'Or these who are here should state what crime they found in me when I stood before the Sanhedrin'*).[53] Paul challenges the representatives of the Sanhedrin to present the conclusions of their examination, knowing full well that the trial ended without a decision and in chaos over a theological issue (23:10).[54] Paul highlights once more the heart of the matter as he sees it: *'unless it was this one thing I shouted as I stood in their presence: "It is concerning the resurrection of the dead that I am on trial before you today"'*. This presents a further challenge to his Jewish accusers (cf. 23:6), as well as being a claim to the governor that there is no legal ground for the charges being made against him. 'In a master stroke, Paul has made his accusers witness on his behalf that he had spoken only of theological matters!'[55]

22 *Then Felix, who was well acquainted with the Way, adjourned the proceedings.* He had 'no intention of being drawn into an internal Jewish dispute, or of doing injustice to a man whose only offence lay in what other Jews regarded as unorthodox theology.'[56] Luke gives no indication of how Felix became *well acquainted with the Way*, but his overall narrative has suggested that Christianity was making significant progress in the eastern part of the Roman Empire, so that its beliefs and practices could be in some measure understood by those in high places.[57] Felix's adjournment of the case is partly explained in terms of his knowledge of the Way and partly in terms of his wanting to hear the evidence of *'Lysias the commander'* (cf.

52. Sherwin-White, *Roman Law*, 52-53. Cf. Witherington 1998, 712-13.

53. The shorter reading *ti heuron adikēma* ('what crime they found') is in the best and most ancient MSS. Later MSS include *en emoi* ('in me'), 'which rounds out the phrase and makes it more explicit' (Metzger, *Textual Commentary*. 435). TNIV assumes the longer reading (so also KJV), but the shorter reading is to be preferred (NRSV 'what crime they had found').

54. Barrett 1998, 1108-10, discusses different ways in which vv. 18-20 can be punctuated and understood syntactically.

55. Witherington 1998, 713.

56. Barrett 1998, 1111. TNIV has read *akribesteron* in v. 22 as an 'elative', meaning *well acquainted*. But Barrett and Witherington 1998, 713, both suggest that it could be taken as a true comparative (meaning 'more accurate') and argue that Felix had a more accurate knowledge of the Way than Paul's accusers and was thus able to discern the weakness of the charges.

57. Since his wife was a Jew (v. 24), she must have had a greater interest in and understanding of events as they developed. Perhaps she influenced Felix to delay reaching a verdict on Paul. Cf. Bruce 1990, 482-83; Rapske, *Roman Custody*, 164.

21:31-40; 22:23-30; 23:10-30). Felix tells Paul's accusers that, when he comes, '*I will decide your case*' (*ta kath' hymas* is plural, indicating that the Jews are being addressed). 'Lysias was, from the Roman perspective, the only independent witness',[58] but we have no way of knowing whether Lysias appeared before the governor to give evidence about Paul or whether his evidence influenced the course of events in any way.

23 Meanwhile, Felix *ordered the centurion to keep Paul under guard but to give him some freedom (anesis) and permit his friends to take care of his needs.* Assignment of Paul to the personal care of *the centurion*, rather than to a lower ranking soldier, 'was probably not so much a token of the higher esteem in which Paul was held by Felix as an indication that Felix wished Paul to be healthily preserved for the longer term from the predictable vagaries of military custody in the hope of exploiting him to his own political and monetary advantage'.[59] The *freedom* (*anesis*, 'relaxation', 'relief') allowed 'probably meant that, while guarded, Paul would not be dependent upon his keeper(s) to sanction his every activity. There would be no oppressively close guarding.'[60] But he remained in chains (26:29), probably in Herod's palace, where he was removed from the possibility of attack from his accusers. This protective custody allowed the access of family or friends (*hoi idioi*, 'his own people'), which may have included his relatives (cf. 23:16), but certainly fellow Christians, to bring food and other practical comforts. Perhaps also they were able to convey letters from Paul to churches and individuals with whom he was connected. Some have suggested that Colossians, Ephesians, Philemon, Philippians, and 2 Timothy could have been written from Caesarea. Such imprisonment was not for punishment but 'a means of keeping people available for trial or for actual punishment'.[61]

3. Challenging Felix and Drusilla Personally (24:24-27)

The knowledge of this more private encounter with the governor and his wife can have come to Luke only from Paul. Although the narrative is brief, it contains significant terms which indicate how Paul presented the gospel to this couple in a way that was relevant to their background and situation.

58. Rapske, *Roman Custody*, 164. Rapske, 164-67, goes on to discuss a variety of reasons why Felix may have adjourned the case against Paul, including the serious possibility that he would lose the support of the Jewish leaders in Jerusalem. On the other hand, if Felix punished Paul, that could spark internecine conflict between Jews and Christians, 'or at least raise the tension to a less comfortable level'.

59. Rapske, *Roman Custody*, 168.

60. Rapske, *Roman Custody*, 169. On the basis that chains are mentioned in 26:29, Rapske, 171-72, argues that Paul was in 'a lightened form of military custody' rather than in strictly open custody. However, this analysis is disputed by M. L. Skinner, *Locating Paul: Places of Custody as Narrative Settings in Acts 21–28*, SBLAB 13 (Atlanta: SBL, 2003), 135-41.

61. Barrett 1998, 1113.

This segment further illustrates how Paul's custody 'operates as the continuance of his missionary work, not the end or suspension of it. The places in which he must remain in custody display themselves as suitable arenas for proclamation and avenues for God to guide the gospel into the heart of the Roman world.'[62]

24-25 *Several days later Felix came with his wife Drusilla, who was Jewish.*[63] It is unlikely that this was a prison visit, since Luke mentions that Felix *sent for (metepempsato) Paul and listened to him.* Perhaps Felix *came (paragenomenos)* to a particular place in the praetorium and called for Paul to be brought before him again. *Drusilla,* who had previously been married to Azizus, king of Emesa, was the youngest daughter of Herod Agrippa I (cf. 12:1) and sister of Herod Agrippa II (cf. 25:13). Josephus (*Ant.* 20.141-44) records that Felix wooed Drusilla away from Azizus, thus causing her to 'transgress the laws of her forefathers' through adultery. Although the Herods were not fully Jewish, they sought to maintain 'a façade of Jewishness'.[64] Given the aggressive opposition of Agrippa I to Christianity in Acts 12, it is fascinating to see both his daughter and son engaging with Paul and his teaching more openly in Acts 24 and 26. The formal trial before Felix did not afford Paul the opportunity to speak about *faith in Christ Jesus,* but privately he did not hesitate to develop this theme with the governor and his wife. 'Paul changes tack from shrewdly defending his honor as a devout Jew to boldly proclaiming the gospel; in other words, he switches from apologist to prophet.'[65]

It is significant that Luke first reports Paul proclaiming Jesus as the promised *Christ* or Messiah of Israel and calling upon this Gentile and his Jewish wife to believe in him. Although some manuscripts have the shorter reading 'faith in Christ', the longer reading is well attested.[66] Putting the title 'Christ' before the personal name 'Jesus' makes it clear that the messiahship of Jesus was being asserted. Since Paul goes on to talk about *righteousness, self-control and the judgment to come,* it seems likely that faith in Christ here is 'related to salvation (cf. 16:31) and thus to the forgiveness of sins'.[67] Such an explicitly biblical presentation of the gospel to a Gentile was presumably made possible because of Felix's existing knowledge of 'the Way' (v. 22) and Drusilla's Jewish connection. The fol-

---

62. Skinner, *Locating Paul,* 138.

63. There is a gloss to vv. 24 and 27 in some MSS, allowing for a more significant role for Drusilla in the governor's dealing with Paul. Cf. 24:27 note.

64. Barrett 1998, 1113.

65. Spencer 1997, 221.

66. Barrett 1998, 1113-14 discusses three variants in v. 24. The most significant is the omission of 'Jesus' from the expression 'faith in Christ Jesus' in some significant MSS. A shorter reading is normally preferred by textual critics as being the most original, and Barrett says, 'It is hard to see any reason why the name should have been omitted, easy to see why it might have been added'.

67. Barrett 1998, 1115. Contrast the way Johnson 1992, 419, interprets Paul's approach here.

lowing expressions suggest the need for repentance, which was another significant plank in Paul's regular appeal to Jews and Gentiles (cf. 20:21; 26:20). Genuine faith in Christ involves a change of allegiance and therefore a change in behaviour and priorities. Paul presented this challenge in terms that were particularly applicable to Felix and Drusilla. Elsewhere, Luke uses the word *righteousness* or 'justice' (NRSV; for *dikaiosynē*) in connection with both human behaviour (10:35; 13:10) and divine judgment (17:31). In the present context, it most likely refers to the former, rather than to God's righteousness in judgment or salvation (contrast Rom. 3:5, 21-26). The term *self-control (enkrateia)* is not a Lukan one, though Paul himself uses it to describe a fruit of the Spirit (Gal. 5:23), and employs cognate words with reference to self-discipline or mastery over pleasures, passions, and ungodly ways (1 Cor. 7:9; 9:25; Tit. 1:8; cf. 2 Pet. 1:6).[68] '"Justice" and "self-control" may be mentioned to indicate qualities particularly required of Felix and other rulers when they are measured in the judgment. Felix's desire for a bribe and favoritism in judgment (24:26-27) can be understood as indications of his lack of these qualities.'[69] Having proclaimed Jesus as the promised saviour-king, Paul challenged Felix and Drusilla at a personal, moral level concerning their readiness to face *the judgment to come,* and thus their need for faith in Christ. Although there is a parallel with Paul's proclamation of God's judgment to pagans in 17:31 *(krinein),* the gospel presentation to Felix and Drusilla involved no denunciation of idolatry, but rather a vigorous appeal to their consciences to recognise their guilt before God, and their consequent need to respond with *faith in Christ Jesus.* With a few brief phrases, Luke has illustrated how the gospel was presented and applied to the specific situation of a Gentile ruler and his Jewish wife. Paul's courageous example also functions in the narrative as 'encouragement to other witnesses to present their message even to high officials'.[70]

After this, *Felix was afraid and said, 'That's enough for now! You may leave.'* He puts off making a personal decision about Christ, even as he puts off making a decision about Paul the prisoner! His concluding response *('When I find it convenient, I will send for you')* is more than a polite dismissal, since Luke records further conversations between them (v. 26).[71] However, the governor's mixed motives are immediately highlighted.

26 Felix's mercenary interest *(he was hoping that Paul would offer him a bribe)* shows his fallibility as a human being and as an administrator of Ro-

---

68. Cf. W. Grundman, *TDNT* 2:339-42.

69. Tannehill 1990, 302. R. Cassidy, *Society and Politics in the Acts of the Apostles* (Maryknoll: Orbis, 1987), 105-6, notes how Felix's shortcomings are articulated in vv. 25-27, demonstrating not only his personal moral failure but also the way Roman justice is undermined by an unjust administrator.

70. Tannehill 1990, 302.

71. Bruce 1990, 483, translates *kairon de metalabōn* 'and when I have a spare moment' (TNIV *when I find it convenient*).

man justice.[72] This was blatantly expressed *at the same time (hama)* that he
was promising to send for Paul and hear more of his message. The practice
of seeking bribes from prisoners was illegal for Roman authorities, though
it continued to take place.[73] Luke does not tell us how the governor concluded that Paul might be able to pay a bribe or how he conveyed the suggestion to him. It is possible that Felix was impressed by the news that Paul
had brought a considerable monetary gift to Jerusalem (v. 17) and hoped
that some of Paul's friends (v. 23) might be able to secure money for his release. Doubtless this made Paul feel all the more need to challenge the governor about righteousness, self-control, and the judgment to come! Tannehill views vv. 22-27 as 'a tragic plot in miniature, beginning with attraction
to a great good, moving to a point of crisis, ending with tragic failure. Felix,
even more clearly than Lysias, emerges as a "round" character capable of
attracting our interest for his own sake.'[74] Cassidy emphasizes the negative
things that are said about Felix at the end of this chapter and concludes that
'such a report clearly does not portray an impartial Roman governor'.[75] Yet,
even without any encouragement from Paul that a bribe might be forth-
coming, the governor *sent for him frequently and talked with him.* Felix is presented as a confused and divided man, with some understanding of the
great issues at stake, but unwilling to take the steps required of him by the
challenge of Paul's gospel. His conversations with Paul continued for *two
years,* until his procuratorship came to an end.[76]

27 There is some uncertainty about the date of Felix's departure
from office. He was sent to Judea in AD 52 (cf. 23:30-31 note) and, according
to two different versions of Eusebius's *Chronicle,* he was replaced by Festus
either in 54 or in 56.[77] However, evidence concerning a change of coinage in
Judea for Nero's fifth year suggests to some scholars that Felix departed for
Rome in 58 and Festus arrived in 59.[78] Violence broke out between Gentiles
and Jews in Caesarea, and Felix sided with the Gentiles. Strong Jewish protests were sent to Rome, and he was soon removed from office (Josephus,

72. Some later MSS, followed by the Received Text, add *hopōs lysē auton* ('so that he
should release him'). So KJV and NKJV.
73. Barrett 1998, 1116, notes the prohibition of the practice in *Lex Julia de Repetundis* of
59 BC, contained in *Digest* 48.11. He also notes the accusation against a later procurator,
Albinus, reported by Josephus, *War* 2.273; *Ant.* 20.215.
74. Tannehill 1990, 303, responding to the presentation of contradictory aspects of the
portrait of Felix by Haenchen 1971.
75. Cassidy, *Society and Politics,* 106.
76. Bruce 1990, 484, rightly argues that the genitive absolute *dietias plērōtheisēs* ('when
a two-year interval was completed') means that 'Paul had been in custody two years when
the change of governors took place'. The expression is unlikely to mean that Felix was removed after two years in office since the evidence discussed in connection with 24:27 suggests a governorship of at least three years.
77. The later date is based on Jerome's version of Eusebius's *Chronicle,* which Barrett
1998, 1117-18, argues is more trustworthy than the Armenian version of the source.
78. Cf. Bruce 1990, 484; Witherington 1998, 716.

War 2.13.7; *Ant.* 20.182). Little is known of Felix's successor, *Porcius Festus*. Josephus (*War* 2.271) tells us that he 'proceeded to attack the principal plague of the country; he captured large numbers of the brigands and put not a few to death.' Josephus also records how he tolerated the building of a wall in the temple at Jerusalem, designed to prevent Agrippa from observing the sacrifices (*Ant.* 20.182-200). He died in office in AD 60 and was succeeded by Albinus.[79] So his administration was 'not marked by the excesses of his predecessor and successors, although vigorous actions continued to be taken against insurgents'.[80]

The impending arrival of a new governor could have a been a suitable time for Felix to release Paul, especially since the Jews had not succeeded in bringing witnesses forward to advance the case against him. *But because Felix wanted to grant a favour to the Jews,*[81] *he left Paul in prison*. Just as the Jewish authorities needed Felix to enforce certain judgments, so Felix needed them 'to help maintain order in Judea and give favourable reports of his administration to the emperor'.[82] So political expediency triumphed over justice for Paul in this situation. However, a few manuscripts offer a different reason for leaving Paul where he was: 'but Paul he kept in prison on account of Drusilla'. This corresponds with an expansion of v. 24 ('Felix came with his wife Drusilla, who was a Jewess, *who asked to see Paul and hear the word. Wishing therefore to satisfy her,* he summoned Paul').[83] In both cases, the additions, which are late and poorly attested, are designed to ascribe to Drusilla a more significant role in the governor's dealing with Paul. Although it is unlikely to be what Luke wrote, this variant is consistent with what we know about Drusilla. As a professing Jew, she may well have had a guilty conscience about her divorce from Azizus and remarriage to a pagan governor (cf. 24:23-24 note). Perhaps also she had a sneaking suspicion that Paul was a genuine prophet, whose words needed to be heeded.

In Acts 25, Paul not only defends himself but 'makes an exemplary case for why Christianity is a threat neither to Rome nor to any state'.[84] At the same time, he bears witness before his Jewish accusers and Gentile cap-

---

79. Witherington 1998, 717-18, dates Festus's assumption of office in AD 59-60 and his death in 61 or 62.

80. Bruce 1990, 484.

81. The expression *charita katatithesthai* means 'to lay up a store of gratitude', hence 'to grant or do someone a favour' (BDAG). Cf. 25:3, 9.

82. Spencer 1997, 221. Luke's account is therefore consistent with what we know of the deteriorating situation in Judea at the time. The way Felix dealt with insurgents alienated more moderate Jews and led to further rebellion (cf. 23:33 note). His desire to do a favour to the Jews with respect to Paul could have been a significant bridge-building exercise in this context.

83. Translation of Metzger, *Textual Commentary*, 435. This variant is found in the minuscules 614 and 2147, and in the margin of one Syriac MS.

84. Bock 2007, 697. Bock discusses the way Christian beliefs and practices can benefit a state, 'unless an ideological or religious agenda blinds it'.

tors to the beliefs that determine his life and ministry. He is a model of clarity, insight, and wisdom as he seeks to persuade his opponents about the real issues at stake in his situation and in the plan of God for Israel and the nations.

INTRODUCTION TO ACTS 25

The Caesarean section of Luke's narrative (Acts 24–26) marks 'a pivotal stage in the progress of Paul the prisoner from Jerusalem to Rome.'[1] Paul appears before two Roman governors, Felix and Festus, and an appointed 'king of the Jews', Agrippa. There are parallels with the situation of Jesus in Luke 23, especially concerning the role of Roman and Jewish officials in the trials, though there are obvious differences in the outcome for Paul.[2] The Jews of Jerusalem continue to seek Paul's demise, but 'the prospect of new opportunity in Rome also arises, as Paul registers a formal appeal to the emperor's tribunal (25:10-12, 21; 26:32)'.[3]

Acts 25 differs from the surrounding chapters in having only a brief summary of Paul's defence (v. 8), with a brief allusion to the fact that he included a reference to Jesus and his resurrection (v. 19). Gaventa observes that there are four scenes in the chapter (vv. 1-5, Festus in Jerusalem with the Jewish leaders; vv. 6-12, Paul before Festus in Caesarea; vv. 13-22, Festus confers with Agrippa and Bernice; vv. 23-27, Paul comes before all three, preparatory to making his next defence speech). 'In two of these scenes, Paul himself appears, and in two others he becomes the subject of conversation as people ponder what should be done with him.'[4] However, there is a case for combining the first two scenes under a single heading, since Luke tells the story as the authoritative narrator in vv. 1-12, but in the next two sections he has Festus reporting the same events to Agrippa from his perspective (vv. 13-22, 23-27). Festus's account often seeks to 'make his own handling of Paul's case look better than it was',[5] though his speeches also fill out the details for the reader. In the final scene, Paul is placed before 'a first century "show trial" that is part entertainment for the guests, part a subtle political maneuver'.[6] Overall, Festus emerges as a figure like

---

1. Spencer 1997, 217.

2. Barrett 1998, 1122-23, responds to the view that Acts 25–26 is a purely Lukan composition designed to show parallels between the trial of Paul and that of Jesus.

3. Spencer 1997, 217.

4. Gaventa 2003, 331.

5. Tannehill 1990, 311. Tannehill, 310, observes that where a character's interpretation of events differs from that of a reliable narrator, the unreliability or bias of the character is displayed, without the need for overt commentary. This has previously been shown with reference to Lysias's letter (23:25-30 note).

6. Johnson 1992, 428. The hearing before Agrippa is not presented as a formal trial in terms of the requirements of Roman law.

Felix, who is compromised as an administrator of Roman justice because of his concern to grant a favour to Paul's accusers.

Theologically, the theme that is implicit in this chapter is the gracious providence of God, fulfilling his purpose for Paul by protecting him from injustice and making it possible for him to be transported to Rome. Paul may appear to be 'the passive pawn of characters and events outside his control'.[7] However, as in the book of Esther, God is the hidden actor who influences all the events on the stage of history, as human beings play their part in the drama that unfolds. Indeed, if the glorified Lord Jesus is 'the Lord' who assures Paul of his destiny in 23:11, we may say that the one who called Paul to his service in the first place continues to provide opportunities for his name to be proclaimed 'to the Gentiles and their kings and to the people of Israel' (9:15). 'Paul can be so bold within his setting because of his confidence in God's promises and ability.'[8]

H. Appearing before Festus (25:1-12)

Festus first appears in this narrative as a just administrator, who will not be swayed by the demands of Paul's opponents. However, he is soon described as 'wishing to do the Jews a favour' (v. 9). Paul's awareness of this change in the governor's attitude moves him to speak boldly about the justice that is due to him and to appeal to Caesar. In view of the Lord's promise that Paul 'must also testify in Rome' (23:11), his appeal to Caesar is not just a legal manoeuvre but a way of advancing God's purpose for his life and ministry. This part of the narrative concludes with Paul as the dominant or leading character. Festus emerges as weak and compromised.

1. Festus Meets Paul's Accusers (25:1-5)

1-3 The new governor began his work energetically. *Three days after arriving in the province, Festus went up from Caesarea to Jerusalem,* which was his second capital city.[9] There, an impressive delegation from the Sanhedrin, consisting of the chief priests and Jewish leaders, *appeared before him and presented the charges against Paul (enephanisan autō kata tou Paulou,* 'laid information before him against Paul'; cf. 23:15; 24:1). Dissatisfied with the way Felix had dealt with their previous approach, they took the opportu-

---

7. Johnson 1992, 422.

8. M. L. Skinner, *Locating Paul: Places of Custody as Narrative Settings in Acts 21–28,* SBLAB 13 (Atlanta: SBL, 2003), 144.

9. For details about Porcius Festus, cf. 24:27 note. Barrett 1998, 1123, considers the possibility that *epibas tē eparcheia* means 'having entered upon his provincial office' (supplying *exousia* after the adjective *eparcheia*), but concludes that 'having arrived in the provincial region' (supplying *chōra*) is more likely.

nity to influence his successor and *requested Festus, as a favour to them, to have Paul transferred to Jerusalem.*[10] Noting the use of *charin (favour)* here and in v. 9 (cf. 24:27, *charita*), Tannehill observes that 'the possibility of Roman authorities granting a favor to Paul's powerful opponents plays an important role in developments after Felix established the precedent in 24:27'.[11] Their motive for this seemingly innocent request was that *they were preparing an ambush (enedran) to kill him along the way.* Such language recalls the previous plot to assassinate Paul (23:12-15), using an *ambush* (23:16, *enedran;* 23:21, *enedreuein*). However, this time the plot is attributed to the leadership in Jerusalem rather than to an unnamed group of conspirators. Their request implies that they considered it unlikely that they would win the case by following the normal judicial procedures in Caesarea. Witherington observes that 'it is a measure of the importance the Jewish officials placed on this matter that they not only confronted Festus with this matter as soon as he came to town but also were willing to go to such lengths to eliminate the Paul problem'.[12]

4-5 Festus, however *(ho men oun Phēstos)*, who was not initially moved by their request, behaved with 'a proper responsibility towards his prisoner'.[13] He was doubtless aware of the previous plot against Paul and the swift and decisive action of Lysias in delivering him to safety in Caesarea (23:12-25). Desiring to uphold Roman justice, Festus declares, *'Paul is being held at Caesarea, and I myself am going there soon'.* He calls for those who are *leaders* among the Jews *(hoi en hymin dynatoi,* 'those who are powerful among you')* to accompany him,[14] perhaps seeking to minimise the number of antagonists, to avoid any further public disturbances about Paul (cf. 21:27-36; 22:22-23; 23:10, 12-15). Festus then shows appropriate legal caution in suggesting that *'if the man has done anything wrong (atopon,* 'out of place', 'improper'; cf. 28:6; Lk. 23:41; 2 Thes. 3:2), *they can press charges against him there'.*

2. Paul Appeals to Caesar (25:6-12)

6-7 The new governor spent only *eight or ten days* with the Jews in Jerusalem before he returned to Caesarea. *The next day* he convened the

---

10. The imperfect tense of the verb *parekaloun* (v. 2, *requested*) suggests that the Jews made several approaches to Festus or continued to request Paul's transfer to Jerusalem.

11. Tannehill 1990, 305.

12. Witherington 1998, 720. Witherington, 718-19, discusses the political situation in which Festus had to operate, showing how believable Luke's record is at this point.

13. Witherington 1998, 720.

14. The language changes from indirect to direct speech in v. 5. Barrett 1998, 1125, gives examples of *dynatoi* being used to mean 'eminent men'. The whole expression *(hoi en hymin dynatoi)* appears to restrict the number of those invited to accompany Festus to Caesarea. Hence, TNIV *(some of your leaders).*

court (*kathisas epi tou bēmatos,* 'he sat down in the place of judgment'; NRSV, ESV, 'he took his seat on the tribunal'), in order to try Paul.[15] The word *bēma* means 'seat' and comes to stand for the place where judgment takes place (cf. also vv. 10, 17; 18:12). Then, seeking to deal with the request of the Jews in his own way, he *ordered that Paul be brought before him.* Luke uses technical language to signify the beginning of formal proceedings against Paul. His accusers were *the Jews who had come down from Jerusalem* with Festus, according to his instruction. They stood around Paul and *brought many serious charges against him.* Luke does not consider it necessary to detail the charges, having already set forth the arguments of Tertullus in 24:5-6. But he does emphasize that *they could not prove them.*[16] Marshall observes that the case was now two years old (24:27), making it difficult 'to secure eye-witnesses to specific accusations, and so the Jews must have had to be content with generalities'.[17]

8 In view of the previous account of Paul's trial before Felix (24:10-21), Luke only gives a brief outline of his *defence*[18] before Festus. He appears to reply one by one to the charges brought against him, saying, '*I have done nothing wrong* (*hēmarton,* 'offended') *against the Jewish law or against the temple or against Caesar'.* Paul denies both the religious and the sociopolitical aspects of the formal charge presented by Tertullus (24:5-6), which was a development of the original accusation of Paul's opponents in Jerusalem (21:28). 'Luke no doubt feels that he has by now presented the legal material in sufficient detail, and moves rapidly on to the great dramatic dénoument in v. 11.'[19] Paul's appeal to Caesar is both a surprising development in the story and a central theme in the narrative to follow (vv. 11, 21, 25-27; 26:32). In his previous defence, Paul made it clear that he had not abandoned the *law* or the prophets, but interpreted them in terms of the eschatological hope of a general resurrection and final judgment (24:14-16). From what Festus says in 25:19, it is clear that Paul specifically proclaimed the fulfillment of Israel's hope in the resurrection of Jesus.[20] The most com-

15. Bruce 1990, 487, comments that sitting on the judgment seat was 'a necessary formality so that his decision might have legal effect'. Cf. 18:12, 16; Mt. 27:19; Jn. 9:13; Josephus, *War* 2.172, 301; 3.532.

16. The imperfect *ischyon* in most MSS suggests 'continuous but unsuccessful attempts to prove' (Barrett 1998, 1126). The aorist *ischysan,* in Papyrus 74 and in the original of א, is not widely attested and is less likely to be what Luke wrote. In the context, it would have to be read as a summary aorist (Barrett suggests the meaning 'all they said did not amount to proof').

17. Marshall 1980, 384.

18. The verb *apologeisthai* is used here as a technical term for making a defence speech. The cognate noun *apologia* is used in 22:1.

19. Barrett 1998, 1126.

20. Paul's mention of this before a Roman court is not surprising when it is remembered that he experienced God's call to proclaim Jesus as glorified saviour to Jews and Gentiles alike (22:15, 21). Skinner, *Locating Paul,* 144, says that Paul 'does not evangelize his audience in this brief scene', but it is clear that he did not hesitate to assert the central gospel claim about Jesus and his resurrection.

prehensive explanation of the way Paul saw the Scriptures being fulfilled is in 26:16-23. There he insists that he taught nothing but 'what the prophets and Moses said would come to pass' (v. 22). With regard to the *temple,* he continued to participate in its ritual (at least to some extent) rather than using it as a place for disputing with anyone or stirring up a crowd (24:11-12, 17-18). Although he expounded a theology of worship that was 'according to the Way', and focused on the glorified Jesus rather than the temple, he saw this as consistent with scriptural teaching about the messianic era (24:14-16, 21). Charges about bringing Gentiles into the temple and violating its sacredness (24:6; cf. 21:27-29) could not be substantiated (24:18-19). With regard to the charge of offending against *Caesar,* Paul insisted that he was a loyal citizen of the Roman Empire and not a political rebel or deliberate troublemaker (21:38-39; 22:25-29; 24:12-13). On this basis, he was about to appeal for his case to be transferred to Rome.

9   Festus now responds to the request made by the Jews in v. 3, wishing to do them *a favour (charin).* Like Felix, Festus refuses to give a verdict, adopting the same prevaricating policy of leaving Paul in prison, as a favour to his accusers (24:27). Tannehill rightly observes that 'Roman justice is being undermined by political calculations. For its own purposes Rome needs to placate a powerful pressure group.'[21] But why would the governor change his mind in just a few days? Tannehill suggests that Festus's first response (v. 3) was that of 'a political novice not yet aware of who holds power and what their interests are', who quickly learns about 'the high priests, their importance to Rome, and the strength of their conviction that Paul should be tried in Jerusalem'.[22] So when he asks Paul, *'Are you willing to go up to Jerusalem and stand trial before me there on these charges?'* this is his way of making a concession towards Paul's opponents. Since he had come to the conclusion that there was no charge of a political nature to be answered (cf. vv. 18-19, 25), Festus presumably felt that the religious question could best be resolved in Jerusalem, where the offence against the temple was alleged to have taken place (cf. v. 20). Whatever his motivation, his desire to preserve the peace and give Paul a fair trial (vv. 4-5) was not completely abandoned. The words *before me (ep' emou)* emphasize that Festus would officiate at any future trial and not abandon Paul to the jurisdiction of the Jews.[23]

21. Tannehill 1990, 306. Noting the narrator's repeated use of *charis (favour)* in relation to the Roman governor (25:3, 9; cf. 24:27, *charita*), and the use of the cognate verb *charizomai (hand over)* in the speeches of Paul (25:11) and Festus (25:16), Tannehill argues that favouritism has become 'a major factor in the course of events'. Cf. R. Cassidy, *Society and Politics in the Acts of the Apostles* (Maryknoll: Orbis, 1987), 107-9; Witherington 1998, 719-20.

22. Tannehill 1990, 306-7. Discusses the difficulties which Haenchen 1971, 669-70, has with the narrative, suggesting that Haenchen fails to take seriously 'the indications that Festus is a biased judge and recognized as such by Paul'.

23. So Barrett 1998, 1127, argues against H. W. Tajra, *The Trial of St. Paul: A Juridical Exegesis of the Second Half of Acts,* WUNT 2, no. 35 (Tübingen: Mohr [Siebeck], 1989), 141-42, who proposes that the expression here means only 'in my presence'. Barrett reviews and cri-

10-11 Paul vigorously opposes the governor's suggestion, apparently suspecting its political motivation. He insists that he is in the proper court: '*I am now standing before Caesar's court, where I ought to be tried*'.[24] As in v. 6, *bēma* ('seat') stands for the place where judgment takes place or, perhaps more generally here, it refers to 'the judicial institution that makes use of the place'.[25] Paul means that only Caesar or his representative has the right to try this case, not the Jews! He does not expect Festus to delve more deeply into theological matters, but to maintain justice with respect to the case that has already been presented. In terms of strict legality, 'the Jews are his accusers and therefore cannot act as judges of the truth of his claim'.[26] Festus, however, can decide because of the evidence he has already heard (*'I have not done any wrong to the Jews, as you yourself know very well'*). Paul acknowledges that if he has 'done wrong' (*adikō*, responding to *ēdikēsa* in the preceding sentence) and is *'guilty of doing anything deserving death'*, he will not *'refuse to die'*.[27] But if the charges brought against him by the Jews are untrue, he insists that *'no one has the right to hand me over to them'* (*charisasthai* ['give up as favour'], echoing the language of *favour* [*charis*] in v. 9). Paul will not allow himself to be made 'a diplomatic gift to the Jews.'[28] For this reason, he goes over the governor's head and appeals to Caesar.

This was not an application to a higher court to have the sentence of a lower court changed, but the process called *provocatio*, which was 'an appeal before trial to a higher court which would then take the whole case, trial, verdict, and sentence out of the lower court'.[29] In the first century AD, only Roman citizens could make such an appeal to the emperor. Even to be acquitted by the governor and to be set free in Judea would have been dangerous for Paul, given the plot against him (v. 3). But the case needed to be

---

tiques several views that have been taken about this verse. It is difficult to be certain about the intention of Festus, but from a literary point of view Luke does not present his suggestion as being either wrongly motivated or an abandonment of his concerns in vv. 4-5.

24. Barrett 1998, 1128-29, points out that the periphrastic perfect (*hestōs eimi*) in this context adds great emphasis. Barrett notes that there are two variant readings which make the affirmation even more emphatic, but concedes that the most numerous and ancient support is found for the reading *hestōs eimi hou* ('I am now standing where').

25. Barrett 1998, 1129.

26. Barrett 1998, 1129.

27. Barrett 1998, 1130, points out that the verb *paraitoumai* can mean 'to refuse, to decline, to avert by entreaty'. If Paul can be found guilty, he indicates that he will not seek to 'buy off the appropriate penalty'. Bruce 1990, 488, translates, 'I do not beg myself off from death'.

28. Skinner, *Locating Paul*, 142, following Barrett 1998, 1120, 1130, who translates *me charisasthai* 'make a present of me.'

29. Barrett 1998, 1131. Cf. Tacitus, *Ann.* 6.5.2; A. N. Sherwin-White, *Roman Society and Roman Law in the New Testament* (Oxford: Clarendon, 1963), 68-70; Tajra, *Trial*, 144-47. The emperor at this time was Nero (AD 54-68), who was not yet guilty of the sort of injustices for which he later became famous. Witherington 1998, 726, therefore concludes that Paul 'might well hope for better things in Rome than he could get at the hands of a Felix or a Festus'. Witherington, 724-26, discusses the appeal system at some length.

transferred to Rome because political expediency was overtaking justice for Paul. Moreover, appealing to Caesar would enable him to visit the capital as planned (19:21). The Lord's words to Paul in the vision recorded in 23:11 were 'you must *(dei)* also testify in Rome'. As noted in connection with that verse, it is most likely the risen Jesus who addresses Paul, since 'the Lord' refers to testifying 'about me'. Tannehill concludes that 'by his own decision Paul can help to fulfill the Lord's purpose that he bear witness in the centers of power, including Rome'.[30] Bruce more expansively suggests that Paul made his appeal to Caesar 'not only for the sake of his personal safety but also from a desire to win recognition for the Gentile churches as *collegia licita* in their own right and, perhaps more than anything else, because of the incomparable opportunity of preaching the gospel which the hearing of his appeal would give him (cf. Eph. 6:19f.; Phil. 1:19f.; 2 Tim. 4:17?)'.[31]

12 *After Festus had conferred with his council,* following established custom, he made his own decision and declared: *'You have appealed to Caesar. To Caesar you will go!'*[32] It is not clear why the governor felt it necessary to consult with his council on this occasion. Since Paul was a Roman citizen, Festus was bound to respond to his request and send him to Rome.[33] Perhaps he sought advice about the way to report the case to Caesar, given the unusual nature of the proceedings and the lack of any hard evidence against Paul (cf. 25:26-27). It would not look good to have such a case poorly handled in the province and then referred to the emperor.

3. Festus Consults Agrippa (25:13-22)

This transitional narrative prepares for the next significant section, where Paul appears before Agrippa and gives his longest and theologically most explicit defence speech (25:23–26:32). We have no way of knowing how Luke became aware of the details of the conversation between Festus and Agrippa. The narrative has an important function with respect to Luke's presentation of Festus, but that does not mean that it is a Lukan fabrication, as some have argued.[34] The conversation may not have been completely

---

30. Tannehill 1990, 308. Tannehill thinks that Paul acts to make bearing witness to Caesar possible, 'whether it improves his chances of acquittal or not'.

31. Bruce 1990, 490.

32. Cf. Tajra, *Trial*, 148-49. Barrett 1998, 1131, gives examples of Gk. *symboulion* ('council') being used with reference to the Lat. *consilium* of a Roman magistrate or governor.

33. Cf. Sherwin-White, *Roman Law*, 63-64. The governor could not disallow the appeal under the *Lex Iulia de Vi Publica* (passed in the time of Augustus). Cf. *Digest* 48.6, 7 (Ulpian); *Sententiae Pauli* 5.26.1, 2. Johnson 1992, 422, seems to be unaware of this evidence, suggesting that Festus 'could probably have ignored Paul's appeal with no one the wiser'.

34. Witherington 1998, 728, suggests that 'Luke followed the historical convention of making the persons say what they were likely to have said on the occasion', but he also con-

private, and a court official may have been Luke's source.[35] The problem
with arguing that Luke deduced what was said from the resultant actions
of Festus and Agrippa is that Luke has Festus expand on his assessment of
Paul and the conduct of his case in a way that is not reflected in subsequent
verses. 'Comparison of this public image with the narrator's previous account of Festus' actions and motives enriches the characterization of
Festus.'[36] He speaks in a way that is 'decidedly biased in his own self-
interest',[37] yet there are aspects of this account which do not contradict the
narrator's report in vv. 1-12 and which therefore function to expand the
reader's understanding of what had happened.

13 *A few days later King Agrippa and Bernice arrived at Caesarea.* Herod
Agrippa II (AD 27-100) was the last ruler in the Herodian line. His father
was Herod Agrippa I, whose antagonism towards the church in Jerusalem
was described in Acts 12. His grandfather was Herod the Great (cf. Mt. 2:1-
23). He was educated in Rome at the court of Claudius and remained there
until he was allowed to take charge of the region ruled by his uncle, Herod
of Chalcis, in AD 50 or 52.[38] The emperor had considered giving Agrippa
charge of his father's kingdom when he died in 44, but was dissuaded because of Agrippa's youth. When he conferred on him his uncle's kingdom,
which was in Lebanon, he also gave him responsibility for the temple in Jerusalem, which included the appointment of the high priest (Josephus, *Ant.*
20.222-23). By the time Agrippa met Paul, his rule had been extended to include regions that formerly comprised his father's kingdom, although he
was required to exchange Chalcis for these other territories. *Bernice* was actually Agrippa's oldest sister, Drusilla being another (cf. 24:24 note). She
had been married to his uncle, Herod of Chalcis, and had given him two
sons. After his death in AD 48, she lived with Agrippa II in what appeared
to be an incestuous relationship (Josephus, *Ant.* 20.145-47; Juvenal, *Satire*
5.156-60). Josephus (*Ant.* 20.146) records that in 63 she married Polemon,
King of Cilicia, in an attempt to overcome the scandal, but soon returned to

siders the possibility that Luke had an informant. Cf. Marshall 1980, 386; Williams 1985,
1990, 410. Longenecker 1981, 547.

35. Cf. Larkin 1995, 348-49 (footnote on 25:13-22; 26:31-32); Witherington 1998, 728
note 397.

36. Tannehill 1990, 309. Tannehill, 310, discusses the narrative technique whereby a
character's interpretation of events differs from that of a reliable narrator, thus showing the
unreliability or bias of the character. This was previously demonstrated in 23:25-30, in the
case of Lysias.

37. Cassidy, *Society and Politics*, 111. Barrett 1998, 1139, considers that 'Luke can only
have guessed at the contents of any discussion between Agrippa and Felix', though he
thinks that Luke's guess is 'one creditable to Festus'. Barrett does not notice the bias in
Luke's presentation of the governor at this point.

38. Bruce 1990, 490, argues that Claudius gave Agrippa the kingdom of Chalcis in AD
50. Barrett 1998, 1134-35, refers to the debate about the dating of Agrippa's rule and suggests that it was not until after 52 that he took charge of Chalcis. Although there is some evidence that Agrippa II died in AD 100, Barrett dates his death in 92 or 93.

Agrippa.[39] So, despite their interest in Paul's case and their apparent objectivity about his innocence (26:30-32), this compromised couple must have been as disturbed as Felix was to hear Paul's testimony and to be challenged by his gospel (cf. 24:24-25; 26:24-29).

Luke tells us that on this occasion Agrippa and Bernice came *to pay their respects to Festus.*[40] Witherington suggests that this visit was intended as an official welcome to Festus: 'it was quite natural for Agrippa as ruler of the neighboring territory to come to pay his respects to the new Judean governor, especially since Agrippa was a supporter of Rome and interested in Roman affairs'.[41] Whether or not Agrippa or Festus took the initiative, Festus saw the opportunity presented by this visit to seek the help of one who had a knowledge of Jewish affairs and who was respected by the emperor.

14-16 *Since they were spending many days there, Festus discussed Paul's case with the king.* Luke gives an imprecise note of the time that Festus and Agrippa spent together *(many days)*, while indicating that it was an extended encounter. Luke dwells on the details of their exchange, even though it does not advance Paul's situation in any way.[42] He has Festus repeat some aspects of the preceding narrative and add new information, to highlight the realities of the case from his personal perspective. Thus, Festus recalls the imprisonment of Paul by Felix and the approach made to him by *'the chief priests and the elders of the Jews'*, when he first visited Jerusalem as governor (vv. 1-3). Festus mentions nothing of the plot against Paul — which was presumably unknown to him — but reveals for the first time that, when they brought charges against Paul, they asked *'that he be condemned'* (*aitoumenoi kat' autou katadikēn*, 'they were asking for a sentence of condemnation against him').[43] Although he does not say as much, his next statement presupposes the request for Paul to be transferred into Jewish hands for punishment, without further trial (*'I told them that it is not the Roman custom to hand over anyone before they have faced their accusers and have had an opportunity to defend themselves against their charges'*). This way of putting things explains the governor's insistence that the Jewish leaders come to Caesarea to present their case against Paul in a properly conducted

39. Cf. C. J. Hemer, *The Book of Acts in the Setting of Hellenistic History*, ed. C. Gempf, WUNT 49 (Tübingen: Mohr Siebeck, 1989; repr. Winona Lake: Eisenbrauns, 1990), 173-74. At the end of the Jewish war, she became mistress to the conqueror Titus, and went to Rome to live with him there (Suetonius, *Titus* 7; Tacitus, *Hist.* 2.81). When he became emperor in AD 79, Titus would not see her again, and she returned to Palestine.

40. TNIV has rightly understood the aorist participle *aspasamenoi* to express purpose here (*to pay their respects*; NRSV 'to welcome'). ESV simply takes the participle to express coincident action, translating it, 'and greeted'. Cf. Barrett 1998, 1135-36.

41. Witherington 1998, 727.

42. Note the discussion above about the way Luke possibly became informed about the details of this conversation (pp. 650-51).

43. The noun *katadikē* in v. 15 'probably has its juridical sense of condemnation (cf. Plutarch, *Coriolanus* 20.4; Josephus, *War* 4.5.2)', as Witherington 1998, 730, suggests.

trial (vv. 4-5). He gives the impression that he has been 'strongly committed to Roman standards of justice'.[44] Yet his desire to do the Jews a favour (v. 9), making him unwilling to release Paul because of the lack of evidence against him, calls this into question. Festus clearly 'did not have the same commitment to justice when it came to the verdict'.[45]

17-19 The governor's insistence that he *'did not delay the case, but convened the court the next day and ordered the man to be brought in'*, is somewhat self-serving in highlighting the urgency of his response. But he expresses genuine surprise that *'when his accusers got up to speak, they did not charge him with any of the crimes I had expected'*. Tertullus had previously suggested that there was a sociopolitical dimension to Paul's ministry (24:5-8), warranting a trial before the Roman governor. This must have been on record as part of the prosecution's case. The Jewish leaders' request for Paul to be condemned (25:15) seemed to confirm this. On this occasion, however, there was no *charge (oudemian aitian)* or 'proof',[46] requiring punishment under Roman law. Going further than the narrator did in vv. 7-8, Festus reveals that the accusations raised against Paul were actually theological: the Jewish leaders had *'some points of dispute about their own religion and about a dead man named Jesus who Paul claimed was alive'*. The expression *tēs idias deisidaimonias* is rightly translated *their own religion,* though some take it negatively to mean 'their own superstition' (cf. 17:22 note). A decision on this matter depends on the way we envisage Festus relating to Agrippa at this point.[47] In Luke's account of the trials before the Sanhedrin (23:6-8) and before Felix (24:12-21), Paul had highlighted the theme of resurrection, without specifically claiming that *Jesus* had risen from the dead. However, at least in the trial before Festus, he appears to have claimed that Jesus was the one in whom the resurrection hope of Israel was to be fulfilled (cf. 26:23). Here the governor gives 'a masterful "outsider" characterization of the central Christian claim: that one who was dead *(tethnēkotos)* is now being declared to be living *(zēn)'*.[48] If, however, Festus perceived that the debate was theological, not demanding a trial before the secular authorities, why did he not say so earlier and acquit Paul?[49] This clearly exposes his po-

---

44. Tannehill 1990, 311. Johnson 1992, 426, gives evidence for this Roman *ethos* requiring certain processes of law for justice.

45. Tannehill 1990, 311.

46. Tannehill 1990, 312 note 11, suggests that *aitian* here may refer not to the charge or accusation but 'to a reason for punishment under the law (roughly equivalent to the proof of a charge), as in Acts 13:28; 28:18; John 18:38; 19:4, 6'.

47. Bruce 1990, 492, argues that 'the more derogatory sense would be out of place here, since Agrippa was a very distinguished Jew'. However, Witherington 1998, 730, follows Johnson 1992, 426, in suggesting that Festus 'might have seen Agrippa as a Hellenized Jew and an outsider to such religious disputes and so spoke in a negative way'. Festus certainly seems to be distancing himself and Agrippa from these matters, though it hardly seems likely that he would treat Judaism as a superstition in this context.

48. Johnson 1992, 426.

49. So Tannehill 1990, 311.

litical compromise with the Jews and his failure to act justly according to Roman standards.

20-22 Festus now reveals that it was because he was *'at a loss how to investigate such matters'* that he asked Paul *'if he would be willing to go to Jerusalem and stand trial there on these charges'*. The implication is that such a purely religious matter could best be solved in Jerusalem. However, since Paul's accusers had not been able to prove the capital charge made against him (v. 7), this was not a fair proposal. Even if he was *at a loss how to investigate such matters*, why should he expose Paul to further danger in Jerusalem?[50] Why should this Roman citizen not be granted immediate acquittal and release from prison? Festus hides the fact that he was actually 'wishing to do the Jews a favour' (v. 9). He says nothing of Paul's protest and argument for justice (vv. 10-11), simply noting that he *'made his appeal to be held over for the Emperor's decision'* (eis tēn tou Sebastou diagnōsin, 'for His Majesty's examination and decision').[51] The story is brought up to date with the information that Paul has been held as a prisoner before being sent to Caesar. The reason for the delay and for consulting Agrippa is given in vv. 26-27. Meanwhile, Agrippa expresses his own desire to hear Paul (cf. Herod Antipas with Jesus in Luke 23:8) and is assured that this will happen on the next day.

I. Appearing before Agrippa (25:23–26:32)

The chapter division is unhelpful at this point, since 25:23-27 forms an introduction to Paul's extensive speech in Acts 26. Once more, Festus appears as a weak character, presenting himself as something of a victim in the situation. He declares Paul innocent of any crime deserving of death and implies that his appeal to Caesar was unnecessary, leaving Festus with an annoying problem. Against this background, Agrippa's encouragement for Paul to speak (26:1) sounds like an invitation to incriminate himself. Agrippa says very little, silently presiding over the proceedings, until Paul seeks to persuade him to be a Christian (26:26-29)![52] Despite his rejection of

50. Tannehill 1990, 313, suggests that Festus is possibly 'feigning ignorance in order to excuse his failure to acquit Paul'. But then he points out how quickly Gallio dismissed the Jewish case against Paul in 18:14-15, proposing that 'the difference may be due less to the differing competence of the two Roman administrators than to the realities of power. Gallio can afford to offend the Jews of Corinth, whereas there is a price to pay for offending the high priests and elders in Judea.'

51. Translation of Bruce 1990, 492-93, who notes that *Sebastos* is the equivalent of Lat. *Augustus* when used as a title of majesty. Cf. Witherington 1998, 731, for the history of its use.

52. Skinner, *Locating Paul*, 146-47, notes several reasons for arguing that Agrippa assumes charge of the proceedings. However, Agrippa works in conjunction with Festus on behalf of Caesar's interests. Agrippa does not represent in this scene 'purely Roman or purely Jewish interests and perspectives'. Agrippa stands as Paul does, 'within two worlds, Jewish and Roman'.

Paul's appeal, Agrippa echoes the judgment of Festus about Paul's innocence and declares that he could have been set free 'if he had not appealed to Caesar' (26:30-32). This apparently threatening situation for Paul turns out to be one in which he gives the most complete and public explanation of his calling and his message so far. As in previous contexts, Paul takes charge of the situation in order to give testimony to Christ (cf. Lk. 21:13).

1. Festus Initiates the Proceedings (25:23-27)

23 *The next day Agrippa and Bernice came with great pomp (phantasia,* 'spectacle', 'show') *and entered the audience room with the high-ranking military officers (chiliarchois,* 'with the tribunes'; cf. 21:31, 33) *and the prominent men of the city.*[53] Luke indicates that it was a grand occasion, with a glittering array of military and civic leaders present to hear Paul's defence. Johnson argues that what we read here 'does not in any way conflict with what we know of Palestinian politics in the first century'.[54] Indeed, he observes that,

> Agrippa and Bernice are made to play for Festus exactly the role taken by Herod in the trial of Jesus (Luke 23:6-12). For the Jewish king, there is the reward of political flattery and deference: the Romans recognize his importance! For the procurator, there is a sharing of responsibility: that's what friends are for (see Luke 23:12)! The trials of Paul therefore match in still another respect those of Jesus, *his* Lord.[55]

These influential people and their entourage gathered together in *the audience room (akroatērion),* probably in Herod's palace, which would have been a large space designed for any kind of public hearing or lecture.[56] Festus then initiated the proceedings, commanding that Paul be brought in. The contrast between the prisoner's clothes and condition and the ostentation of those gathered to hear him must have been stark.

24-27 Introducing Paul to Agrippa and all who were present, Festus exaggerated the political pressure he was under, stating that *'the whole Jewish community'* had petitioned him about Paul in Jerusalem and Caesarea, *'shouting that he ought not to live any longer'.*[57] At the same time,

---

53. Bruce 1990, 493, notes that 'there were at Caesarea five auxiliary cohorts, each of which would be commanded by a military tribune (Josephus, *Ant.* 19.365)'.

54. Johnson 1992, 428, citing Josephus, *Ant.* 16.30; 17.93; *War* 1.620 for evidence of two similar occasions. Skinner, *Locating Paul*, 147, agrees that 'Agrippa's magnificent entrance presents him as the height of political power in Palestine'.

55. Johnson 1992, 428-29.

56. Cf. Barrett 1998, 1145. Bruce 1990, 493, notes that Lat. *auditorium* is used in *Digest* 4.4.18.1 for a room in which the emperor heard trials. However, the meeting in Acts 25:23–26:32 is not really a formal trial.

57. Witherington 1998, 732, argues that *plēthos (multitude)* could refer to 'the whole as-

he acknowledged Paul's innocence (*'I found he had done nothing deserving of death'*).[58] This is the second such declaration (23:29), and there will be a third (26:31), 'so that Paul (like Jesus) will three times be exonerated by Roman justice (compare Luke 23:4, 15, 22)'.[59] Tannehill observes that 'Roman officials are quite willing to recognize Paul's innocence when they can do so cheaply, that is, when it has no effect on Paul's legal status and no political consequences. They speak of Paul's innocence as Paul passes out of their jurisdiction and they are rid of the political problem that Paul poses (see 23:29; 25:25; 26:31-32).'[60] Festus further presents himself as a victim in connection with Paul's unexpected *'appeal to the Emperor'*. He intends to send Paul to Rome, but this leaves him with a serious practical problem. He has *'nothing definite (asphales, 'certain'; cf. 21:34; 22:30) to write to His Majesty (tō kyriō)*[61] *about him'* and needs the help of King Agrippa and his court, so that as a result of this *'investigation'* he may have something to write.[62] As noted previously, Agrippa's knowledge of Judaism and his good standing in Rome would have been helpful in compiling such a report. Festus apparently fears that, without a reasonable report on Paul, his own competence as a judge and provincial administrator will be called into question. Here, however, that threat is expressed in a very restrained fashion (*'I think it is unreasonable to send a prisoner on to Rome without specifying the charges against him'*).

Tannehill's conclusion to this section of Luke's narrative is very helpful. He notes similarities in the way both Felix and Festus are presented, showing favouritism to the Jews in dealing with Paul's case and depriving the prisoner of justice. He continues:

> The narrator's characterization of the Roman governors contributes to a portrait of Paul as one caught in a web of self-interested maneuvers by people who vie for support within the political jungle. However,

---

sembly of Jews, referring to a specific gathered group of them, in this case the legal representatives of the nation'. Cf. Johnson 1992, 427. However, Festus appears to be exaggerating the seriousness of the situation to excite sympathy for his position, and so the TNIV rendering is appropriate.

58. Bruce 1990, 494, offers a translation of the much-expanded version of vv. 24-25 in the Western text.

59. Johnson 1992, 427.

60. Tannehill 1990, 308. Tannehill 313, further notes that 'Festus prefers to magnify the responsibility of the Jewish people while presenting himself as a judge who retains his independence in the midst of such pressure'.

61. This title for the emperor ('the master' or 'the lord') is introduced without explanation, Luke clearly expecting his readers to know whom he was talking about. Bruce 1990, 494-95, observes the way in which the title *ho Sebastos* (v. 25) was applied more frequently to emperors as time went by.

62. Barrett 1998, 1147, notes the duty of sending such a report, as mentioned in *Digest* 49.6.1. Witherington 1998, 734 note 438, suggests that *anakriseōs (investigation)* is being used here in the technical sense of 'preliminary investigation', since we are not dealing with another trial.

Paul is not just a helpless victim. As opportunity comes, he continues to bear witness to his Lord. Although Paul continues to be denied justice and freedom, the saving purpose of God still has use for this resourceful and faithful prisoner.[63]

INTRODUCTION TO ACTS 26

As noted previously, the chapter division is unhelpful at this point, since 25:23-27 forms the introduction to Paul's extensive speech in Acts 26. Paul had appealed to Caesar, making it necessary for Festus to seek the advice of King Agrippa about what he should write to the emperor when sending the prisoner to Rome. Agrippa takes charge of the proceedings, inviting Paul to speak, though Festus soon interrupts with the charge that Paul is going out of his mind (26:24).[1] The king remains silent until Paul seeks to persuade him to become a Christian (26:26-29), and then echoes the judgment of Festus about Paul's case (26:30-32; cf. 25:25). So Agrippa works in conjunction with Festus, neither representing '*purely* Roman or *purely* Jewish interests and perspectives'.[2]

Agrippa is presented as having a sufficient knowledge of Jewish customs and controversies (v. 3) to be able to understand what is in dispute, and an awareness of the way Christianity developed from its Jewish roots (v. 26). Moreover, as Tannehill observes, 'his knowledge is not that of an outsider with a merely professional interest in Judaism. He believes the prophets (26:27); therefore, the fulfillment of the prophetic hope is a matter of importance to him. Paul can use the language of the insider with Agrippa.'[3] Before this judge, Paul can present a more theologically explicit and lengthy defence. Two main themes are linked together. First, there is a clear statement on 'what Paul himself regards as the main issue of the trial, the one that he has repeatedly put forward since 23:6 and that Festus acknowledged in 25:19 — the issue of resurrection and the Jewish hope.'[4] In terms of Luke's overall purpose, this helps to clarify the rela-

---

63. Tannehill 1990, 314-15.

1. Haenchen 1971, 690-91, is sceptical about the historical value of Acts 26. He takes it to refer to a formal legal investigation, but then comments that 'there remains a trial without prosecutor or witnesses; only the defendant speaks'. He fails to acknowledge the literary and legal context in which Paul's speech is set.

2. M. L. Skinner, *Locating Paul: Places of Custody as Narrative Settings in Acts 21-28*, SBLAB 13 (Atlanta: SBL, 2003), 147. The nature of Agrippa's client kingship blurred these distinctions for him.

3. Tannehill 1990, 315, notes that Paul can refer to 'the people' (26:17, 23), while he speaks only of 'this nation' or 'my nation' with Felix (24:10, 17). Paul uses the Jewish term 'Satan' (26:18), and seems to include Agrippa in the 'you' of v. 8.

4. Tannehill 1990, 316. Repeated emphasis on the resurrection hope in previous speeches points to the need for this fuller exposition. Tannehill observes that the speech be-

tionship between Christianity and Judaism. Secondly, Paul's speech 'serves as a climactic review and interpretation of his mission. The whole narrative of Paul's ministry — and even earlier parts of Luke-Acts — is newly illuminated by this review.'[5] This defence speech incorporates and develops elements from the immediately preceding chapters, but its function is broader. It picks up themes from earlier in Luke's work, to demonstrate 'Paul's place in the unfolding purpose of God',[6] thus advancing another of Luke's aims in writing Acts. In particular, Paul likens his call and commission to that of various OT prophets (26:16-18), which helps to clarify his relationship with Jesus and the apostles in the fulfillment of God's plan of salvation.

At first glance, Paul's address to the Ephesian elders (20:18-35) appears to climax Luke's presentation of Paul's missionary activity, with subsequent chapters describing his various trials and tribulations as a prisoner. However, as already noted, the speech in Acts 26 is also climactic and reflects in significant ways on what the risen Lord was accomplishing through the ministry of Paul, even as he addressed his captors.[7] Tannehill suggests that the speech changes in v. 22 from what is technically a defence (*apologeisthai*, vv. 1, 2, 24), in which Paul is informally on trial (v. 6, *hestēka krinomenos*, 'I stand on trial'), to an act of missionary witness (v. 22, *hestēka martyromenos*, 'I stand bearing witness'). 'Paul continues his mission before our eyes as his review of his past message becomes present proclamation, ending with a missionary appeal to King Agrippa.'[8] As such, the speech functions like the one in 20:18-35, to provide Luke's readers with an important theological reflection on the nature of gospel ministry.

2. Paul's Defence (26:1-23)

Paul's defence is explicitly made 'against all the accusations of the Jews' (v. 2), though his accusers do not actually seem to have been present on this occasion. As in 22:1-21, his defence takes the form of an autobiography, with expanded comments on the significance of his calling to proclaim salvation to Jews and Gentiles alike. This information is eventually used to explain why his ministry has provoked such opposition from certain Jews

---

fore Agrippa is therefore 'a moment of climax and revelation'. Johnson 1992, 440-41, describes the speech as 'Christianity's first real *apologia* before the sophisticated Greek world', rightly noting that it does not 'transmute the messianic movement into a philosophy', but affirms the very features which were problematic to the educated Greek world.

5. Tannehill 1990, 316.
6. Tannehill 1990, 316.
7. Gaventa 2003, 338, describes this scene as 'a second dramatic climax in Acts' (the first being the conversion of Cornelius in 10:1–11:18) and says that 'the remainder of Acts constitutes the denouement, working out the implications of this scene.' But I am not persuaded that the structure of Acts is a simple as Gaventa, 55-56, suggests.
8. Tannehill 1990, 316.

(26:19-23). At the same time, as in 23:6; 24:15, 21, Paul makes it clear that he is on trial because of the Jewish hope of resurrection and its fulfillment in Christ (26:6-8, 23; cf. 25:19). He begins with an affirmation of his Jewishness and a claim that the resurrection hope is a critical factor in his debate with Judaism. His direct address to Agrippa in vv. 2, 7, 13, and 19 shows the extent to which he is a personally appealing to the king.

a. His Jewish Credentials (26:1-11)

1-3 When Agrippa gave Paul permission to speak for himself, he stretched out his hand (*ekteinas tēn cheira*), using the traditional rhetorical gesture of one assuming 'the pose of an orator (cf. Apuleius, *Meta.* 2.21)',[9] and began his *defence* (*apelogeito* in v. 1 is an inceptive imperfect). The same verb ('make a defence') is used again in vv. 2 and 24 (cf. 19:33; 24:10; 25:8; the noun *apologia* is used in 22:1; 25:16; 1 Pet. 3:15). Although not formally on trial, Paul took the opportunity to respond to *'the accusations of the Jews'* and to explain the reason for his ministry.[10] For details about Agrippa II and his reign see 25:13 note. Addressing the king directly, Paul begins with a brief *captatio benevolentiae* (cf. 24:2-4, 10): '*I consider myself fortunate to stand before you today as I make my defence against all the accusations of the Jews*'. As well as Agrippa, an august assembly of military and civic authorities was present to hear what was said (25:23): 'a grand gallery for a grand finale'.[11] But Paul's appeal was directly to the king, asking him to listen patiently on the basis of his knowledge of Judaism (*'especially so because you are well acquainted with all the Jewish customs and controversies'*).[12] Since Paul was bound to appear before Caesar, he must have shared the concern of Festus to have a proper interpretation of the case prepared and sent with him (25:12, 21, 25-27). However, the speech turns out to be defensive in the wider sense of explaining to all present why he spoke and acted as he did, both before and after his encounter with the risen Christ. From a strictly ju-

---

9. Witherington 1998, 738. Bruce 1990, 496, notes that *kataseisō tē cheiri* in 13:16; 21:40 (cf. 12:17) means something different, signifying 'an appeal for a quiet hearing'. The Western text 'heightens the solemnity and prophetic character of Paul's discourse by adding, "confident and having received the encouragement of the Holy Spirit . . ."' (Johnson 1992, 431).

10. Witherington 1998, 737-38, discusses the formal structure of Paul's defence and shows how certain linguistic features suggest Paul's excellence in rhetorical presentation on this occasion.

11. Spencer 1997, 224. However, Spencer notes that 'in the context of the larger Lukan narrative, the scenario of a double-trial before the Roman governor of Judea and the Herodian client-king also hints at a more precarious situation for the prisoner'. Cf. Lk. 23:1-25.

12. Although scholars debate the extent to which Agrippa lived as a Jew, the claim that he was well aware of the customs and the various disputes of the parties within Judaism simply highlights his competence to deal with the issues in comparison with Festus (cf. 25:18-20). Cf. Witherington 1998, 739.

dicial point of view, this would have been inadequate and largely irrelevant to the Roman authorities.[13] In the final analysis, his speech actually becomes evangelistic in intent (vv. 26-29).

4-6 The defence proper begins with a clear marker in the Greek (*men oun*, 'so then' or 'now', not translated by EVV). Paul first asserts what was known about him by '*all the Jewish people*' (*pantes hoi Ioudaioi*) concerning his life since childhood. TNIV has taken '*in my own country*' (*en tō ethnei mou*) to refer to the early period in Tarsus and '*in Jerusalem*' (*en te Hierosolymois*) to refer to the next stage of his life (cf. 22:3). However, Paul uses *ethnos* with reference to the 'nation' or 'people' of Israel elsewhere (24:17; 28:19), and the Greek syntax in 26:4 implies that '*in Jerusalem* should be included within the wider *in my nation*'.[14] Paul claims to have had a good reputation among his people '*for a long time*', and speaks quite comfortably to Agrippa about *our religion* (v. 5; cf. '*our ancestors*', v. 6; '*our twelve tribes*', v. 7). However, he claims a more specific identity with the Pharisees when he says '*I conformed to the strictest sect* (*kata tēn akribestatēn hairesin*) *of our religion, living as a Pharisee*' (cf. 22:3, *kata akribeian*; 23:6-7; Josephus, *Life* 191). Paul uses the term *sect* positively with respect to this Jewish party (cf. 5:17; 15:5; 24:14), whereas Tertullus used it negatively (24:5; cf. 28:22), to suggest that Christianity was a dangerous breakaway movement. The word for *religion* here (*thrēskeia*) is also more neutral than the one used by Festus with reference to Judaism (25:19 note, *deisidaimonia*).[15] Paul's association with the Pharisees may have been taken by those unfamiliar with the parties in Judaism to mean membership in 'a type of philosophical school'.[16] But his identification with the Pharisees is an important preparation for the claim that follows: '*And now it is because of my hope in what God has promised our fathers that I am on trial today*'.[17] It is soon explained that this *hope* concerns the

---

13. Cf. H. W. Tajra, *The Trial of St. Paul: A Juridical Exegesis of the Second Half of Acts*, WUNT 2, no. 35 (Tübingen: Mohr [Siebeck], 1989), 163. Bruce 1990, 496, asserts that this speech may best claim to be Paul's *apologia pro vita sua*. Witherington 1998, 736, contends that 'Paul is playing the part of a witness in his own defense, rather than defendant fending off charges'.

14. Barrett 1998, 1151, arguing against N. Turner, *Grammatical Insights into the New Testament* (Edinburgh: Clark, 1965), 84-85. Cf. Bruce 1990, 497. This reading of 26:4 suggests that Paul's life had been lived from his early years in Jerusalem, but it does not exclude the possibility that he had begun his education in Tarsus (22:3).

15. The noun *thrēskeia* is used of Christianity in Jas. 1:27 (contrast 1:26), but in Col. 2:18 it is used with reference to false worship. Barrett 1998, 1152, thinks the word may have been chosen here to portray Judaism and especially Pharisaism unfavourably. But his argument does not acknowledge the contrast with 25:19.

16. J. C. Lentz Jr., *Luke's Portrait of Paul*, SNTSMS 77 (Cambridge: Cambridge University, 1993), 53; Spencer 1997, 226. Josephus claimed a similar pedigree for himself when writing for the Roman aristocracy (*Ant.* 13.288, 297-98, 401-6; 17.41-46; *Life* 191).

17. Tannehill 1990, 318, notes that the words *and now* (v. 6) emphasize 'the continuity between his present faithfulness to this hope and his past origin and life as a Pharisee'. The expression *hestēka krinomenos* ('I stand on trial') is in an emphatic position in the sentence. Strictly speaking, Paul was not on trial, though, as Barrett 1998, 1152, says, 'it must have

resurrection from the dead (v. 8). The implication is that his fellow Pharisees were being inconsistent in opposing this aspect of his teaching. Doubtless they were, but their objections were also related to Paul's further claim that the Scriptures pointed to the Messiah as 'the first to rise from the dead', that Jesus of Nazareth was the promised saviour-king, and that his message of light would be brought 'to his own people and to the Gentiles' (v. 23). Many opposed Paul's teaching about the resurrection of Jesus and his offer of salvation to Gentiles on the same basis as Jews.

Some scholars are sceptical about the authenticity of Paul's attempt to present the Christian hope as identical with the hope of Israel (cf. 23:6; 24:15-16; 26:6-7; 28:20). Haenchen, for example, thinks Luke has invented this line of argument to assert continuity with Judaism through Paul's speeches, seeking to gain tolerance for Christianity from the Roman government.[18] A related concern is the extent to which the hope of resurrection was actually as important for early Judaism as Paul implies in his speeches. But Tannehill argues that the theme of resurrection, 'whether understood metaphorically or realistically, is closely connected in Old Testament–Jewish tradition with the hopes of Israel as a people'.[19] Most obviously, the restoration of Israel is being portrayed in Hosea 6:1-2; Ezekiel 37:11-14; Isaiah 25:8; 26:19; Daniel 12:1-2 in resurrection terms. More broadly, the renewed Davidic kingdom promised to Israel in the Scriptures is viewed as eternal and free from earthly corruption (e.g., Is. 9:6-7; 11:1-12; Jer. 23:5-6; Ezk. 37:24-28). It is against this background that Paul's sermon in Pisidian Antioch should be understood. There he proclaims Jesus' resurrection as the fulfillment of the promise given to Israel concerning a saviour-king (13:23, 32-37), basing his argument on texts such as Psalm 2:7; Isaiah 55:3; and Psalm 16:10. Paul indicates that 'Jesus is established as reigning Messiah through resurrection and his reign is characterized by resurrection life'.[20] The hope of which he speaks in 26:6-7 is thus 'not merely a hope for individual life after death but a hope for the Jewish people, to be realized through resurrection'.[21] Of course, resurrection becomes a promise for believing Gentiles to embrace as well (cf. 17:18; 20:32), which may be where Paul is heading with his argument in vv. 8 and 23. Surprisingly, however, his main concern in the speeches in Acts 23–26

---

seemed like it, and it was natural for Luke to describe it so'. Cf. 26:22 (*hestēka martyromenos*, 'I stand bearing witness').

18. Haenchen 1971, 691-94.

19. Tannehill 1990, 319, following K. Haacker, 'Das Bekenntnis des Paulus zur Hoffnung Israels nach der Apostelgeschichte des Lukas', *NTS* 31 (1985), 443-48. Haacker presents a six-point critique of Haenchen's approach to the four passages in Acts. He then goes on to show how certain OT texts portray the future of Israel in terms of resurrection and comments on the way these were understood in Jewish tradition.

20. Tannehill 1990, 319.

21. Tannehill 1990, 320. Tannehill demonstrates important linguistic parallels between Paul's first speech in Acts 13 and his last speech in Acts 26. For example, the promise realized in the resurrection of Jesus (13:32-33) is the same promise as in 26:6-8.

is to establish the resurrection of Jesus as the means by which the hope of
Israel is fulfilled.

7-8 The irony of this rejection of Paul and his gospel is highlighted
by emphasizing 'the passionate intensity of Jewish hope':[22] Paul claims that
the resurrection from the dead is *'the promise our twelve tribes are hoping to see
fulfilled as they earnestly serve God day and night'*. This national hope (cf.
24:15-16; 26:6; 28:20) was clearly not shared by all of Paul's contemporaries
(cf. 4:1-2; 23:6-8), though the OT texts cited above in connection with v. 6
clearly portray Israel's future in resurrection terms. Perhaps the reference
to *our twelve tribes* (*to dōdekaphylon hēmōn*, 'out twelve-tribe unit')[23] implies
an ideal Israel, comprising all true Israelites across time and scattered
among the nations. Ezekiel 37:15-28 certainly envisages a reunification of
the tribes of Israel when the Lord resurrects his people and brings them under the eternal rule of his servant David. As Paul sees it, believing Jews are
hoping 'to attain' (NRSV, ESV, for *katantēsai*; TNIV *to see fulfilled*) this promise *as they earnestly serve God day and night*.[24] The term for divine service
found in 24:14 *(latreuō)* is used again *(latreuon)*, but applied here to the traditional Jewish pattern of faithful obedience to God's commandments. The
expression *day and night* may have special reference to regular times of
prayer in association with the temple sacrifices (cf. Lk. 2:37; Acts 3:1 note).[25]
Earnestly (en ekteneia) implies a moral and spiritual zeal that is motivated by
the hope of resurrection, with no criticism of Judaism implied. However,
Paul goes on to show that Israel's hope has been realized in the suffering
and resurrection of the Messiah (v. 23). This explains why Paul now serves
God as 'a follower of the Way' (24:14) and continually challenges other
Jews to acknowledge the importance of Jesus and what happened to him
for the fulfillment of Israel's destiny.

Paul reiterates to Agrippa that *'it is because of this hope that the Jews are
accusing me'* (cf. v. 6). Tannehill notes how 'this passage contributes to a presentation of the story of Israel that emphasizes the fulfillment of its great
hope and then depicts a tragic turn away from this fulfillment. This story
line stretches from the beginning of Luke to the end of Acts.'[26] Paul's rhe-

---

22. Tannehill 1990, 318. Tannehill continues: 'this is tragic irony because the deepest
desire of the Jewish people, which rightly belongs to them by promise, is being rejected by
many of them'.

23. The adjective is used in *Sib. Or.* 2:171; 3:249, and the substantive in *1 Clem.* 55:6 (cf.
31:4). Bruce 1990, 498, notes other references to the twelve tribes in Mt. 19:28 par.; Lk. 22:30;
Jas. 1:1; Rev. 7:4-8; 21:12; *Test. Jud.* 25:1-3a; *Test. Ben.* 9:2, and says that 'such language expresses the totality of Israel, whether in an ethnic, religious, or eschatological sense'.

24. Barrett 1998, 1142, translates this complex verse more literally: '(the promise) to
which our twelve-tribe people, zealously worshipping (God) night and day, hope to attain'.

25. Cf. Bruce 1990, 498.

26. Tannehill 1990, 318. Tannehill, 319, continues: 'The rejection of Paul, the proclaimer of resurrection hope, has much to do with rejection of the risen Messiah. The
Christological issue is not being ignored, but it is placed in the context of the hope that Paul
and his accusers share, so that they may understand what is at stake.'

torical question at this point (*'Why should any of you [par' hymin] consider it incredible that God raises the dead?'*) is introduced abruptly in the Greek, without a connective. It comes across as a general challenge to sceptical Jews on the basis of scriptural teaching. However, Paul is probably also appealing to Gentiles in the audience (cf. 17:32), saying in effect, 'Once one admits there is an all-powerful God, why should anyone find the idea of resurrection incredible?'[27] As such, it is a preliminary to challenging Festus, Agrippa, and others personally about Jesus and the resurrection (vv. 25-29).

9-11 Paul resumes the narrative from v. 5 with the emphatic expression *egō men oun edoxa hemautō* (NRSV 'Indeed, I myself was convinced'; TNIV *'I too was convinced'*).[28] As a convinced Pharisee, he reasoned that he ought to do *'all that was possible to oppose the name of Jesus of Nazareth'*. Paul felt bound by a certain necessity *(dein)* to act as he did. Opposition to *the name of Jesus* must have included challenging what was proclaimed about him as well as attacking those who believed in him.[29] Paul goes on to accentuate the cruel thoroughness of his persecution of Christians, beginning *in Jerusalem*. Here he claims to have acted generally *'on the authority of the chief priests'*, though in 9:1-2 Luke refers only to such authorisation for the persecution of Christians in Damascus. Paul's involvement in the process of persecution across the region was comprehensive: he *'put many of the Lord's people (tōn hagiōn, 'the saints') in prison'*, and seeking to have them *'put to death'*, he cast his *'vote against them'* (*katēnenka psēphon*, [lit.] 'I cast my pebble against [them]'). The last expression may imply that Paul had a formal role in the process by which the Sanhedrin imposed the death penalty on Christians. However, Paul is nowhere else described as a member of the Sanhedrin, but is simply pictured as approving of the death of Stephen (7:58; 8:1; 22:20), 'perhaps with the implication that he was an *agent provocateur*'.[30] The less formal translation 'I gave my approval' (KJV 'I gave my voice against them') may therefore be more appropriate. Paul's testimony here also implies that believers other than Stephen and James were put to

27. Witherington 1998, 741. Against Barrett 1998, 1153-54, there is no need to believe that this verse has been misplaced. It is a digression that foreshadows the argument in vv. 22-23 and conveys Paul's concern to move beyond a defence of his own position and apply the issue of resurrection to his audience.

28. Luke marks a transition in the speech with another use of *men oun* ('so then' or 'now', as in v. 4). Barrett 1998, 1154, rightly opposes the view that v. 9 seeks to answer the rhetorical question in v. 8. Bruce 1990, 499, explains the link with v. 8 with this paraphrase: 'Pharisee though I was, and thus a believer in the resurrection from the dead, I yet judged it incredible in this particular instance (the resurrection of Jesus), and thought it my duty to oppose such a heresy'.

29. Cf. Witherington 1998, 741.

30. Johnson 1992, 434. J. Jeremias, *Jerusalem in the Time of Jesus: An Investigation into Economic and Social Conditions during the New Testament Period* (ET, London: SCM, 1969), 255 note 34, suggests that Paul's voting for the death penalty in such a context implies that he was an 'ordained scribe'. But Barrett 1998, 1155, is more cautious and, with Bruce 1990, 500, says the case cannot be proven since the expression 'cast my vote against them' could be used officially or unofficially. Cf. Witherington 1998, 741-42.

death.[31] His zeal for Pharisaic Judaism is further illustrated by the fact that he travelled extensively *'from one synagogue to another to have them punished'*. Although 8:3 speaks of his attack on Christian households in Jerusalem, 9:1-2 indicates that an attack on Christians in synagogues took place in Damascus. The evidence of 26:11 is that Christian Jews frequented synagogues elsewhere as well. Paul's aim in exposing their presence in the synagogues was *'to force them to blaspheme'*. The imperfect tense of the verb *ēnankazon* is correctly read by TNIV as conative (*'I tried to force them'*), meaning that he regularly tried but was unsuccessful (contrast KJV's 'compelled them to blaspheme'). From a Christian point of view, *to blaspheme* must have meant denying Christ in some way.[32] But perhaps Paul tried to get Christians to say things about Jesus that were considered blasphemous from a Jewish perspective and so worthy of punishment. Paul concludes this part of his story with the claim that, 'being exceedingly mad against them' *(perisōs te emmainomenos autois)*, he 'persecuted them even to foreign cities' *(ediōkon heōs kai eis tas exō poleis;* cf. 22:4-5).[33] Spencer suggests that Paul's audience of powerful Herodian and Roman officials would have been sympathetic to such violent ways in the enforcing of their own interests. 'Paul is speaking their language here — but only to subvert it. For ultimately Paul admits that his cruel and zealous pursuit of the early disciples sprang not from sober concerns for justice, but from "maniacal" *(emmainomai)* paroxysms of rage (26:11).'[34]

b. His Calling and Mission (26:12-23)

Paul recounts his call by the risen Christ, explaining his change from being a persecutor of Christians to being a vigorous protagonist of their beliefs (cf. 22:6-16). At the same time, he expands on the nature of his mission, emphasizing certain themes such as turning people from darkness to light, and from the power of Satan to God, so that they may receive forgiveness of sins and a place among the Messiah's holy people (26:16-18). Such turning to God involves genuine repentance (v. 20) and a belief that the Scriptures foretold the need for the Messiah to suffer and be the first to rise from the dead, to bring the message of hope to Israel and to the Gentiles (vv. 22-23). These themes appear early in Luke's Gospel (1:16, 77-79; 2:30-32; 3:3, 6,

---

31. Against Marshall 1980, 393, there is no reason to doubt this. Luke elsewhere gives hints of a wider phenomenon of events that he illustrates only in a limited way (e.g., 'signs and wonders').

32. 1 Cor. 12:3 *(anathema Iēsous,* 'Jesus be cursed') may reveal one way in which Christians were challenged to blaspheme. Cf. Pliny, *Ep.* 10.96.5.

33. TNIV (*'I was so obsessed with persecuting them that I even hunted them down in foreign cities'*) fails to bring out the sense of madness implied by the verb *emmainesthai*. This is important because the same verb is used in v. 25 in Paul's denial of the charge of madness by Festus. Paul was exhibiting madness in his persecuting days but not in his defence and proclamation of the Christian gospel! So NRSV and ESV.

34. Spencer 1997, 227.

8), in the commissioning scenes in Luke 24:46-47; Acts 1:8, and in the sermons of Peter and Paul in Acts.[35] With such literary and theological echoes, Luke confirms Paul's key role in bringing the gospel with all its promised blessings both to Israel and to the Gentiles. This passage also provides a theological analysis of what happens whenever the risen Christ is proclaimed and he uses this to draw people to himself. As such, these verses provide another perspective on what has been happening as 'the word' has grown and multiplied (cf. 6:7; 12:24; 19:20). They also offer the reader the encouragement that the same thing may happen wherever the gospel is faithfully proclaimed.

12-14 Paul begins to describe his encounter with the heavenly Lord by noting that it took place *'on one of these journeys'* (v. 12, *en hois*), when he was *'going to Damascus with the authority and commission of the chief priests'.*[36] His intention was to persecute and destroy, but the risen Christ had another plan! *'About noon'* (*hēmeras mesēs*; cf. 22:6, *peri mesēmbrian*), he tells Agrippa, *'as I was on the road, I saw a light from heaven, brighter than the sun, blazing around me and my companions'.*[37] As noted in connection with 9:1-19 and 22:6-15, there are differences among the three accounts of this event, some more significant than others. For example, in 9:7 Luke records that Paul's companions 'stood there speechless; they heard the sound (*akouontes tēs phōnēs*) but did not see anyone'. Here, however, Paul says, *'we all fell to the ground'* (cf. 22:7, 'I fell to the ground'), and 22:9 informs us that those who were with him 'did not understand the voice' *(tēn phōnēn ouk ēkousan)* of the one who was speaking. In all three accounts Paul recalls hearing a voice saying, '*"Saul, Saul, why do you persecute me?"'* But only here does he note that it was *'in Aramaic'* (*tē Hebraidi dialektō*, 'in the Hebrew language'; cf. 21:40; 22:2), possibly to explain the Lord's use of the name *Saul* to these Gentiles who know him as Paul. The following expression ('*"It is hard for you to kick against the goads"'*) also occurs only here. A goad was a sharp-pointed stick used to move animals in a particular direction. The image of kicking against the goads is found elsewhere in ancient literature, and Bruce observes that it is 'the kind of saying that might be current in any agricultural community'.[38] Such imagery expresses not only the intense strug-

---

35. Cf. Tannehill 1990, 317.

36. The phrase *en hois* could be taken temporally (cf. Lk. 12:1) — 'whereupon' (KJV), 'while thus occupied' (NKJV), *on one of these journeys* (TNIV) — or circumstantially (cf. 24:18) — 'with this in mind' (NRSV),'in this connection' (ESV). Cf. D. B. Wallace, *Greek Grammar beyond the Basics: An Exegetical Syntax of the New Testament* (Grand Rapids: Zondervan, 1996), 342.

37. The brightness of the light from heaven is described in progressively more vivid terms in 9:3; 22:6; 26:13. These differences highlight the supernatural, overwhelming nature of the light — 'from heaven', 'about noon', 'brighter than the sun' — with the most vivid being this personal recollection before Agrippa. However, Paul's blinding by the light is not mentioned in the third account. See Tannehill 1990, 324, on the way the light is understood in this speech as a positive metaphor.

38. Bruce 1990, 501. Cf. Pindar, *Pythians* 2.94-96; Aeschylus, *Agamemnon* 1624; Euripi-

gle Paul experienced before turning to Christ but also the overwhelming
power of the Lord to draw him to himself and transform his situation. This
is not a reference to Paul's guilty conscience, but a way of speaking about
the Lord 'prodding him in another direction which he had no choice but to
follow — the path of proclaiming this same Jesus he had been attacking'.[39]
Perhaps the saying was included in this particular account as a warning to
Agrippa and others present. 'Paul's plan to exterminate the church was
doomed to fail because he was "kicking against" the irresistible purpose of
God.'[40] By implication, the opposition of Jewish and Roman officials to
Christianity could not ultimately succeed.

15-16 This version of the encounter continues to emphasize what
was heard and what was said. Paul asked, '"*Who are you, Lord?*"', and the
Lord replied, '"*I am Jesus, whom you are persecuting*"'. At this point, the three
narratives of Paul's call and commissioning converge, but then they diverge significantly. In 9:6 there follows the simple command to get up and
go into the city, where he will be told what to do next. In 9:14-15 we learn of
what the Lord said to Ananias and must assume that this message was
passed on to Paul in due course. In 22:10 the same instruction about going
into Damascus is given, and the words of Ananias to Paul are then given in
22:14-15, including the explicit promise that Paul will be Christ's '"*witness*"' to all people of what he has seen and heard. In Acts 26 the same sequence of events is presented briefly, without mention of Ananias. Although the role of Ananias is important in the narrator's account in Acts
9:10-19; 22:12-16, his function as a witness to the reality of Paul's transformation and as a mouthpiece for the divine will is not relevant to the testimony before Agrippa. Furthermore, Paul makes no mention here of the
need to go into Damascus, but reports what '*the Lord*' himself said to him
on the road. In the light of preceding accounts, we may understand that the
message was actually mediated to Paul by Ananias, but the stress here is on
the mandate of the risen Lord himself. This abbreviation and simplification
of the story 'helps Paul to move swiftly and effectively from the encounter
with the Lord to the call as witness and the fulfillment of this call'.[41]

---

des, *Bacchae* 794-95; Terence, *Phormio* 1.2.27. Witherington 1998, 743, thinks that proposed
parallels from Jewish literature (*Ps. Sol.* 16:4; Philo, *On the Decalogue* 87) are less convincing.
There is no reason why a common proverbial expression could not have been employed by
the risen Lord as a way of describing the resistance Paul had been offering to the divine will.

39. Spencer 1997, 227. Bruce 1990, 501, similarly insists that the 'goads' were not 'the
prickings of an uneasy conscience over his persecuting activity but the new forces which
were impelling him in the opposite direction to that which he had hitherto pursued'.

40. Spencer 1997, 227.

41. Tannehill 1990, 321. Tannehill observes that this reformulation of the account 'carries a certain risk that some hearers or readers will doubt the accuracy of his account'. However, he concludes that Luke was not concerned about this risk and 'preferred to exercise
some freedom in presenting Paul's speech'. Indeed, 'the statement of Paul's commission in
vv. 16-18 is so closely connected with scriptural themes and previous statements of the
Lord's purpose in Acts itself that it is not likely to be suspect'.

The Lord's command to '"*get up and stand on your feet*"' recalls the commissioning of Ezekiel (Ezk. 2:1-3), after he had seen visions of God and fallen to the ground. Further echoes of OT prophetic calls will be noted in connection with vv. 17 and 18. Paul is then told that the risen Jesus appeared to him to '"*appoint*"' him (*procheirizomai*, as in Acts 3:20; 22:14) '"*as a servant and as a witness*"' (v. 16, *hypereten kai martyra*). Luke uses a similar expression at the beginning of his two-volume work to describe his sources (Lk. 1:2, *hoi ap' arches autoptai kai hyperetia . . . tou logou*, 'those who from the first were eyewitnesses and servants of the word'). The language in Acts 26:16 identifies Paul with such people but also highlights his distinctive role in the purpose of God, as a personal assistant to the risen Lord Jesus (*hypereten*; cf. John Mark's role in relation to Paul and Barnabas in 13:5). The great opponent of Christ (vv. 9-11) is now invited to become an 'instrument of his will'.[42] His farewell message to the Ephesian elders (20:19-35) describes what this meant for him in practical terms, using the related terms *douleuon* (v. 19, 'serving' the Lord) and *hyperetesan* (v. 34, 'supplied' my own needs and the needs of others). This service involved faithful, sacrificial ministry to believers and unbelievers, in the face of opposition, persecution, and various deprivations. In this respect he was a model for other 'ministers of the word'. However, Paul's role as *a witness* (*martys*, as in 22:15) suggests that he shared something of the distinct function and authority of the Twelve in testifying to the resurrection of Jesus and its implications (cf. 1:8, 22; 2:32; 3:15; 5:32; 10:39, 41; 13:31).[43] This is emphasized by the full expression '"*a witness of what you have seen*"', pointing to the Damascus road encounter (cf. 1 Cor. 9:1-2; 15:8-9). But the additional words '"*and will see of me*"' anticipate further revelations of the Lord's will and manifestations of his power to advance the mission he has given to Paul (e.g., 16:6-10, 25-34; 18:9-11; 27:23-25).[44] We know from the progression of Luke's narrative that such further revelations specifically enabled Paul to testify 'to the Lord's power to sustain witnesses under threat'.[45]

---

42. K. H. Rengstorf, *TDNT* 8:530-44, notes the different ways that various terms for 'servant' are used in Greek literature. Paul's willingness is stressed in v. 19, and the nature of his task is signified by the next term (v. 16, *kai martyra*, 'and witness'), which is probably exegetical, defining his service more closely.

43. Others in Acts are described as witnesses in the normal, technical sense of those who bring evidence to a court (6:13) or observe an event (7:58). Stephen is also identified as a witness of Jesus in 22:20, who loses his life for his faithful testimony. In the last reference, the term could have the developed sense of 'martyr' (TNIV), which later became so common in Christian literature. Cf. H. Strathmann, *TDNT* 4:474-508.

44. TNIV reflects the fact that the word *me* in 26:16 is omitted after *hōn te eides* (*what you have seen*) in a number of reliable MSS. This shorter version could be considered the original on the ground of being the harder reading. However, NRSV and ESV read *me* and take the whole construction (*hōn te eides me hōn te ophthēsomai soi*) to mean '[witness] to the things in which you have seen me and to those in which I will appear to you'. Cf. Barrett 1998, 1159-60.

45. Tannehill 1990, 323.

17-18   What Paul will see of Jesus in the future is specifically related
to a promise of deliverance: '*"I will rescue you from your own people and from
the Gentiles"*'. Preaching to Jews as well as to Gentiles would be Paul's way
of participating in the inclusive mission of the risen Lord (v. 23 note). This
would involve rejection and persecution from both groups, but especially
from his *own people*. The message conveyed to Ananias by the risen Jesus
contained the warning that Paul would suffer for the sake of his ministry
'to the Gentiles and their kings and to the people of Israel', without an explicit promise of deliverance (9:15-16).[46] Here the words *I will rescue you*
(*exairoumenos se*) seem to echo what was said to Jeremiah when he was
called to be a prophet (Jer. 1:8; cf. Acts 18:9-10 note). We have already
noted a possible allusion to Ezekiel 2:1-3 in v. 16. Further allusions to prophetic callings follow with the words '*"I am sending you* (*exapostellō se*; cf.
Jer. 1:7; Ezk. 2:3) *to them to open their eyes and turn them from darkness to
light"*' (cf. Is. 42:6-7, 16; 49:6). In various ways, Paul's call and commission
is likened to that of great canonical prophets in the exilic period, but the
Isaianic allusions in vv. 16-18 are particularly significant. Luke makes it
clear that Jesus fulfills the Servant's role (cf. Lk. 4:18-19; 22:37; Acts 3:13-
15, 26), but shares aspects of that role with his chosen representatives (cf.
Acts 1:8; 13:46-47). So what is said in Acts 26:16-18 'not only suggests the
continuity of Paul's mission with the scriptural prophets but also with the
mission of Jesus announced in the Nazareth synagogue'.[47] Luke thus confirms Paul's key role in the divine plan, which began to be fulfilled with
the coming of John the Baptist and then Jesus, to bring salvation to Israel
and to the Gentiles.

As well as rescuing him from danger, the risen Lord promises Paul
that he will work positively through his ministry to accomplish great
things. When Paul preaches the gospel in the power of the Spirit, he will be
enabled '*"to open their eyes and turn them from darkness to light, and from the
power of Satan to God"*'. These words provide us with an important theological reflection on what has been taking place in Luke's account so far.[48] We
find no actual mention of Paul challenging people to turn *from darkness to
light*, though his ministry in Acts has had that effect in various ways. Moreover, Paul uses similar language himself in Colossians 1:12-14 to describe
what God does in bringing people to himself through the work of Christ. In
this particular narrative (contrast 9:17-18; 22:11-13), the divine light 'does
not blind but enables sight and represents salvation'.[49] Paul sees the light of

---

46. It could be argued that deliverance was implied by the promise of continuing testimony to Christ 'to the Gentiles and their kings and to the people of Israel' (9:14).

47. Tannehill 1990, 323.

48. Cf. C. Stenschke, 'The Need for Salvation', in I. H. Marshall and D. G. Peterson
(eds.), *Witness to the Gospel: The Theology of Acts* (Grand Rapids/Cambridge: Eerdmans,
1998), 125-44.

49. Tannehill 1990, 324. Tannehill concludes that the triple reference to light in vv. 13,
18, and 23, together with the references to seeing and to opening eyes in vv. 16 and 18, 'turn

Christ (v. 13) in order to bring that light to others (vv. 18, 23; cf. 2 Cor. 4:1-6). There are certainly hints that he makes it possible for people to turn from the power or authority *(exousia)* of Satan to God (e.g., 13:6-12; 16:16-18; 19:13-20). Turning is closely linked to repentance (v. 20, *metanoein kai epistrephein*, 'repent and turn'). Both terms describe a regular aspect of Paul's preaching (14:15; 17:30; 20:21; 26:20; cf. 1 Thes. 1:9-10). Spiritual enlightenment and liberation from Satan's dominion require repentance in the sense of turning away from every alternative source of illumination and control to seek a genuine relationship with God. Such a relationship is then described in terms of its outcome: *'"so that they may receive forgiveness of sins and a place among those who are sanctified by faith in me"'* (en tois hēgias-menois pistei tē eis eme).[50] The language of sanctification is used in a covenantal and corporate sense, both here and in 20:32, where Paul indicates that 'the word of grace' is able to give you 'an inheritance among all those who are sanctified' *(en tois hēgiasmenois pasin)*. In both contexts, the perfect passive participle emphasizes that sanctification is a state or condition granted by God rather than a process of becoming holy (cf. 1 Cor. 1:2, *hēgiasmenois en Christō Iēsou*, 'sanctified in Christ Jesus').[51] Here it is linked with the *forgiveness of sins* on God's part and *faith* in Christ on our part (cf. 20:21; 24:24, where the Lord Jesus is also specifically the object of faith). Its outcome is a share in the eternal destiny of God's people, which contextually means a share in the resurrection from the dead (26:6-8, 23). If, in fact, it is 'the word of God' which accomplishes such things (cf. 6:7; 12:24; 19:20), the commission given to Paul in v. 18 must have application to others engaged in gospel ministry. When the gospel is faithfully proclaimed in the manner that Paul does, we may expect the risen Lord to bring spiritual enlightenment *(to open their eyes)* and genuine conversion *(to turn them from darkness to light, and from the power of Satan to God)*, enabling people to share in the benefits of his saving work *(so that they may receive forgiveness of sins and a place among those who are sanctified by faith in me)*.

19-21 Paul now addresses King Agrippa with the form of speech called 'litotes', where a modest statement (*'I was not disobedient to the vision*

---

light and sight into major unifying images in the speech'. As in Lk. 1:77-79; 2:30-32; Acts 13:47, the Isaianic link between light and salvation is exploited.

50. Barrett 1998, 1159-60, notes that there are three infinitives in v. 18 after *I am sending you* (v. 17) indicating purpose: 'to open' *(anoixai)*, 'to turn' *(tou epistrepsai)*, 'to receive' *(tou labein)*. The second clause is probably dependent on the first, indicating that the reason for opening their eyes is that they may turn. The absence of any connecting particle before the third infinitive suggests to Barrett that the third clause indicates what follows from conversion, namely the forgiveness of sins. However, he warns that it would be 'mistaken to read out of this verse a rigid sequence of elements in the process of conversion'.

51. Cf. D. G. Peterson, *Possessed by God: A New Testament Theology of Sanctification and Holiness* (Leicester: Apollos; Grand Rapids: Eerdmans, 1995), 1-92 (esp. 55-58). Tannehill 1990, 325, suggests that sanctification by faith in 26:18 recalls the argument of Peter in 15:9 about the Gentiles having their hearts cleansed by faith and thereby coming to share in the salvation promised to Israel (15:11).

from heaven') is used for the sake of emphasis: in truth, 'Paul was wholeheartedly obedient'.[52] Witherington rightly observes that the word *vision*
(optasia) here 'should not be seen as a reference to a purely subjective and
internal experience, as is shown by the stress in vv. 13-14 on the objectivity
of the occurrence, but rather one that originated from heaven but pene-
trated the inner being of Paul in a way that was not true of his companions'.[53] The account of his commission (vv. 16-18) is then followed by a report of how he carried out that commission. Fulfillment is highlighted by
'the repetition of theme words that bind the Lord's commission and Paul's
obedient response closely together (cf. "witness", "bearing witness", vv. 16,
22; "rescuing", "help from God", vv. 17, 22; "the people and the Gentiles",
vv. 17, 23; "turn . . . to God", vv. 18, 20; "light", vv. 18, 23)'.[54] Paul recalls the
geographical scope of his mission, *'first to those in Damascus'* (cf. 9:20-25),
'then to those in Jerusalem' (cf. 9:26-30) *'and in all Judea, and then to the*
Gentiles'.[55] He indicates that he conveyed the same message to all, declaring
(apēngellon, 'reporting', 'announcing', 'proclaiming') *'that they should repent*
and turn to God and demonstrate their repentance by their deeds' (cf. 20:21).
Challenged to preach repentance for the forgiveness of sins and a share in
the messianic salvation (v. 18 note), Paul was as serious as John the Baptist
in calling for *deeds* to demonstrate the genuineness of repentance (cf. Lk.
3:8; Acts 20:21). He understood conversion 'not only in terms of forgiveness
and faith, but also in terms of a full ethical transformation'.[56] Jewish missionaries might have said as much in their approach to Gentiles, but Paul
was calling for the same response from Jews as well. When he mentions
that certain Jews seized him in the temple courts and tried to kill him (v. 21;

52. Barrett 1998, 1162. Cf. 12:18; 15:2; 19:11, 23, 24; 20:12; 21:39; 26:26; 27:20; 28:2, for
other examples of this mode of speech.

53. Witherington 1998, 746. He argues that in Luke-Acts the term *orama* is used for
'vision' in the more subjective sense (Acts 9:10-11; 10:3, 17, 19; 11:5; 12:9; 16:9-10; 18:9) and
that *optasia* has more the meaning of 'heavenly appearance' (cf. Lk. 1:22; 24:23). Cf. Larkin
1995, 361.

54. Tannehill 1990, 325.

55. Since Acts does not record a ministry of Paul *in all Judea* following his ministry in
Jerusalem and preceding his ministry to the Gentiles, Tannehill 1990, 325-26, suggests that
the pattern in the Lord's commission to his first witnesses (1:8) 'proves to be more important than the details in the previous narrative of Paul's actions'. In other words, there is a
somewhat artificial attempt to show the similarity between Paul and the Twelve at this
point. However, Witherington 1998, 746, argues that the apparently intrusive expression
pasan te tēn chōran tēs Ioudaias (in all Judea) could be 'an accusative of extent referring to all
Paul's subsequent witnessing activity throughout the Judean region' (cf. 15:3-4; 18:22; 21:7-
16). Cf. Barrett 1998, 1163-64.

56. Spencer 1997, 227. Spencer, 227-28, observes that Paul's accusers had failed to appreciate that he 'reached out to the Gentiles not to flout the Jewish law or temple, but to *con-*
vert the Gentiles to a new way of life befitting the restored holy people of God'. Bruce 1990,
503, observes that the language of repentance is not used in Paul's earliest letters (though cf.
1 Thes. 1:9-10), but he clearly looked for a life of holiness and love as evidence of genuine
faith (cf. Gal. 5:22-23; 2 Cor. 13:5-7).

cf. 21:27-29; 24:5-8), he explains that this happened because of his preaching ministry (v. 21, *heneka toutōn*, 'because of these things'; TNIV *'that is why'*), which effectively put Gentiles 'on the same level as Israelites as potential heirs of salvation'.[57]

22-23 Paul concludes his speech with an important theological inference (*oun*, 'therefore', 'so') that is relevant to his present situation: *'God has helped me to this very day, so I stand here and testify to small and great alike'.* 'At this point the report of past witness turns into present proclamation.'[58] When Paul recalls how God has *helped* him in the past, he implies that the promise of rescue in v. 17 has been fulfilled. With God's help, he has also been able to testify to an audience like the present one, covering such a wide social spectrum *(to small and great alike)*. His testimony contains *'nothing beyond what the prophets and Moses said would happen'*, agreeing with the predictions of Scripture specifically related to the Messiah (cf. 2:14-36; 3:12-26 [Peter]; 13:16-41, 47; 24:14; 28:23 [Paul]). Paul's gospel summary in these verses begins with the assertion that the Scriptures have been fulfilled in the person and work of Jesus. The Greek syntax makes it clear that two specific predictions had to be fulfilled to provide salvation for Israel and the Gentiles. The first is that *'the Messiah would suffer'* (*ei pathētos ho Christos*) and the second is that, as *'the first to rise from the dead' (ei prōtos ex anastaseōs nekrōn)*, he *'would bring the message of light to his own people and to the Gentiles'.*[59] In Paul's letters, Christ is described as the 'firstfruits of those who have fallen asleep' (1 Cor. 15:20, 23) and the 'firstborn' of a large family of people brought to life by God (Rom. 8:29; Col. 1:18). Here the special point is made that the Messiah can *bring the message of light to his own people and to the Gentiles* because of his resurrection. By implication, he forms his own people by means of such proclamation. In Luke 24:44-48, there is a similar sequence of suffering, resurrection, and proclamation, with reference to the fulfillment of Scripture. However, in Luke 24:47 the proclama-

---

57. Barrett 1998, 1164. The charge that he had profaned the temple (21:27-28) had presumably lapsed because of a lack of evidence. However, as Bruce 1990, 503, notes, 'the real ground of those Asian Jews' hostility to him lay back in the years of his ministry at Ephesus (cf. 20:19)'.

58. Tannehill 1990, 317. Barrett 1998, 1143, translates *epikourias oun tychōn tēs apo tou theou* in 26:22 quite literally, to bring out the sense that Paul has been utterly dependent on God's aid ('so, having obtained the help that comes from God'). Barrett also suggests that the perfect tense of *hestēka* should be taken in the context to mean 'I have taken my stand and here I am'.

59. Tannehill 1990, 326 note 40, argues that 'comparison with Lk. 24:26 suggests that the conditional constructions express a divine necessity, steps in the divine plan that the Messiah must fulfill, like the *edei* ('it was necessary') of Luke 24:26'. Bruce 1990, 504, contends that the two clauses beginning with *ei* 'may be regarded as headings from a collection of messianic *testimonia*'. Witherington 1998, 747-48, noting the use of *ei* in Acts 26:8, argues that 'the translation "if" better conveys the sense that these are the points to be proved', though he allows that 'that' is a possible rendering. Barrett 1998, 1165-66, argues for the latter, which is the translation of KJV, NKJV, NRSV, ESV, TNIV. *pathētos* (only here in the NT) means 'liable to suffering' (Barrett, 1166).

tion is in the Messiah's name, whereas here it is the risen Messiah himself who proclaims *light to his own people and to the Gentiles.* This is consistent with the notion first implied in Acts 1:1-2 — that the risen Lord would continue to work through his disciples to fulfil his saving plan — and conveyed in various other ways throughout the narrative (e.g., 3:16; 4:9-12, 29-31, 9:5-6, 10-16, 31; 11:21; 16:6-10).[60] The mission is first and foremost the Lord's, but Paul is making the point that the Lord made him 'a part of the mission given to the first witnesses'.[61] Thus, in response to the original charge that his ministry is illegitimate and destructive of true Judaism (24:5-8; 25:8), Paul ultimately insists that it is scripturally based and God-given, a privileged share in the Messiah's own mission of salvation to Israel and the nations.

3. Paul's Personal Appeal and the Outcome (26:24-32)

Paul's claim to be divinely called to a worldwide mission based on the Jewish Scriptures, focussing on the implications of Jesus' death and resurrection, proves too much for Festus to believe (though 25:19 indicates that this was not all new to him). The governor's interruption moves Paul to make a more personal and passionate appeal to Agrippa as a nominal Jew. This is done in such a way as to challenge Jews and others who are still open to being persuaded from the Scriptures about the truth of the gospel. Indeed, Paul prays that all who are listening to him might become Christians. At this point in the account, personal defence turns to evangelism.[62] Luke again presents Paul as a bold evangelist, who takes every opportunity to proclaim Christ. In particular, Luke indicates through Paul's testimony that the mission to persuade Jews that their hope is fulfilled in Jesus and his resurrection must continue.

24-25 *At this point Festus interrupted Paul's defence* (*apologoumenou;* cf. vv. 1-2). Although Paul was not on trial in a formal sense, Festus was preparing a report on his case to be sent to the imperial court in Rome. The prisoner's claim that a crucified and rejected Messiah had commissioned him to bring people from every nation to repentance and faith did not strike the governor as being appropriate evidence. Indeed, with a

---

60. Spencer 1997, 228, observes that 'Jesus not only commissions Paul as a witness to his resurrection; he continues to participate with him in this witness'.

61. Tannehill 1990, 327. Tannehill rightly points out that in Luke 24 and Acts 26 'we find a consistent view of mission that controls the understanding of Jesus, his first witnesses in Jerusalem, and Paul. This mission, like the death and resurrection of the Messiah, is grounded in Scripture, which discloses God's purpose of carrying salvation, including repentance and release of sins, to all people'.

62. Gaventa 2003, 348, rightly observes that 'the only real defence available to Paul and the church as a whole is that of proclamation. Responding to charges might relieve Paul from his imprisonment, but it would not constitute obedience.'

loud voice he accused Paul of being in the grip of 'mania' — '*You are out of your mind (mainē), Paul*' — attributing this to Paul's excessive learning: '*Your great learning is driving you insane*' *(eis manian)*. The expression *your great learning* is a rendering of *ta polla grammata*, which literally means 'your many letters' or 'your many books'. Festus possibly refers to the Jewish Scriptures just mentioned (v. 22) 'as the source of Paul's madness',[63] but *your great learning* is a possible translation. Bruce claims that such a charge was not necessarily offensive, noting Plato's declaration that, without *mania*, no one could be a true poet (*Phaedr.* 245A), but concludes that 'anything in the nature of inspiration could not be treated seriously by a matter-of-fact Roman judge'.[64] However, Paul has already declared that he was truly 'maniacal' when expressing uncontrolled rage against the early disciples (v. 11, *emmainomenos autois*, 'being mad against them'), which suggests that the terminology may be used in a similarly negative sense in vv. 24-25. With due deference ('*most excellent Felix*'), Paul denies that he is *insane*, claiming that his whole approach is completely rational ('*What I am saying is true and reasonable*'). In contrast with his pre-Christian behaviour, his words 'set forth truth, and they are controlled by sober judgement'.[65]

26 Bringing Agrippa into the conversation, Paul asserts that the king has more knowledge than Festus does of the way Christianity emerged on the stage of world history ('*The king is familiar with these things*').[66] Christianity cannot simply be dismissed as the product of one man's madness! Agrippa II was born in AD 27/28 and remained in Rome until 50 or later, but he maintained a continuing interest in what was taking place in Jewish affairs (cf. Josephus, *War* 2.344-407). There is therefore 'no reason why he should not have heard of the origins of Christianity, especially if Christians were felt to be a disturbing factor in Jewish life'.[67] Paul believes he can '*speak freely*'[68] to Agrippa about *these things (toutōn)*, mean-

63. Tannehill 1990, 327. However, Barrett 1998, 1167, gives a number of examples in Greek literature of *grammata* meaning 'learning' in the more general sense (cf. Jn. 7:15; *Letter of Aristeas* 121; Plato, *Apol.* 26D). So also BDAG.

64. Bruce 1990, 505. Barrett 1998, 1167, feels that this rather flattering interpretation of Paul's 'philosophic' madness is not suitable to the context, since Paul goes on to rebut the charge. However, even if Festus meant philosophic madness, Paul's insistence that his testimony was true and reasonable makes sense. Tajra, *Trial*, 169, notes that in Roman law (cf. *Digest* 48.4.7) the defendant's mental state was supposed to be taken into account.

65. Barrett 1998, 1168, argues that the first genitive is objective and the second subjective. Johnson 1992, 439, suggests that the expression *alētheias kai sōphrosynēs rhēmata* could be read as a hendiadys ('words of sober truth'). Although the verb *apophthengomai* is used in 2:4, 14, with reference to inspired speech, here it refers to Paul's rational defence.

66. NRSV and ESV translate the litotes *lanthanein auton ti toutōn* literally: 'none of these things has escaped his notice'. TNIV (*the king is familiar with these things*) brings out the positive sense implied by this pattern of speech (cf. v. 19 note).

67. Barrett 1998, 1168-69.

68. The verb *parrēsiazomenos* (*speak freely*; ESV 'speak boldly') is also used in Acts 9:27, 28; 13:46; 14:3; 18:26; 19:8; Eph. 6:20; 1 Thes. 2:2. The related noun *parrēsia* ('boldness, confi-

ing the death and resurrection of Jesus and his bringing of the message of
light to Israel and the nations (v. 23). Such boldness comes from being convinced that nothing of what he proclaims has escaped the king's notice, *'because it was not done in a corner'*. Paul uses a stereotypical expression *(en
gōnia, in a corner)* to emphasize that 'Christianity is neither secret nor subversive'.[69] Haenchen rightly observes that 'these words light up Luke's presentation in Acts from beginning to end'.[70] Here we have a claim about the
public nature of the evidence available for Agrippa and others to consider.
Luke has illustrated the widespread testimony of Christians to Jews and
Gentiles throughout the Roman Empire, and the conversion of many from
various cultures and ranks of society. Christianity is 'not an inconspicuous
event any longer, but a factor in world history', and Christians are 'preparing themselves — Paul is the model! — to step out of their corner into the
world of history and culture.'[71]

27 Paul then asks Agrippa a question *('Do you believe the prophets?')*,
which he immediately answers for himself *('I know you do')*. At this point in
the narrative, Agrippa's role shifts from being an authority who can help
Paul to being one who needs help himself to recognize the fulfillment of Israel's hopes in Jesus and his resurrection. Although a Gentile, Agrippa
'could on occasion represent himself as a Jew in spirit, and had certain
rights in the Temple and in the appointment of the high priest'.[72] Paul asserts that Agrippa has a belief in *the prophets* that is basis enough for believing the gospel. Agrippa thus represents 'all those who know and believe
the prophets and are not yet hardened against the gospel, that is, Jews and
God-fearers who might still be reached in spite of the bitter Jewish opposition that first caused Paul's imprisonment and then resisted his release'.[73]
Paul the passionate evangelist is once more presented as a model for Luke's
readers (cf. 20:18-35). They too must not give up offering the gospel to Jews,
individually and collectively, no matter what response they have received
in the past. That appeal can begin with the challenge to *believe the prophets*
and to consider whether the events proclaimed in the gospel fulfil what the
prophets predicted.

---

dence') is found in 2:29; 4:13, 29, 31; 28:31. Luke indicates that such bold speech is made possible by the Holy Spirit.

69. Johnson 1992, 439. Bruce 1990, 505, describes the expression *en gōnia* as 'another
classical tag' (cf. v. 14 note). This proverbial idiom is also found in Plato, *Gorg.* 485D;
Epictetus, *Diss.* 2.12.17; Terence, *Adelphoe* 5.2.10; Plutarch, *On Curiosity* 516B, and other references. Cf. A. Malherbe, *Paul and the Popular Philosophers* (Minneapolis: Fortress, 1989), 147-63.

70. Haenchen 1971, 691.
71. Haenchen 1971, 692.
72. Barrett 1998, 1169.
73. Tannehill 1990, 316-17. Tannehill, 328-29, rightly opposes the view of Haenchen
1971, 693, that Luke no longer hoped for the conversion of the Jews and that the historical
detail in Acts 26 was only relevant to Paul's context, not that of Luke's readers. Tannehill argues that Paul before Agrippa has, in part, the same exemplary function as he has in the
speech to the Ephesian elders.

28 *Then Agrippa said to Paul, 'Do you think that in such a short time you can persuade me to be a Christian (en oligō me peitheis Christianon poiēsai)?'* The text here presents a number of difficulties. Firstly, there is the question of whether *en oligō* means 'in a short time', 'in a few words', or 'in a small measure'. Paul's adaptation of the same expression in Acts 26:29 *(en oligō kai en megalō)* must parallel in some way what Agrippa means in v. 28. Barrett holds that *en megalō* in v. 29 excludes the possibility of a time reference. He takes *en oligō* in v. 28 to mean 'with little trouble', and *oligō kai en megalō* in v. 29 to mean 'with little trouble or much'. [74] This is certainly a possible reading, though TNIV *('short time or long')*, ESV ('whether short or long'), and NRSV ('whether quickly or not') all understand the expression in v. 29 to be a time reference and render the shorter expression in v. 28 accordingly. Witherington believes that the rhetorical context rather implies the meaning 'with so few (or brief) arguments'.[75] KJV and NKJV translate *en oligō*, 'almost', in v. 28 and have the tortuous rendering 'both almost, and altogether as I am' in v. 29, but this cannot be supported by any linguistic parallel.[76] Secondly, there is the problem of the variant *genesthai* ('be, become', as in v. 29), which makes good sense (so also KJV, NRSV, ESV), but which is a later reading, not as widely attested as the harder *poiēsai* ('make').[77] Thirdly, there is the difficulty of understanding what is intended by *Christianon poiēsai*. Noting the way the LXX of 1 Kings 21:7 (3 Kdms. 20:7) uses the expression *poieis basilea* to mean 'play the king', some have argued that Agrippa means 'to act the Christian'.[78] However, despite the parallels adduced, there is not enough evidence to conclude that an established Greek idiom is being used in that way here. In fact, Paul's positive response in v. 29 suggests that he understood Agrippa to be talking about being 'made' a Christian, not about 'playing' the Christian.[79] Either a ques-

---

74. Barrett 1998, 1170. Barrett argues that we should understand the dative noun *ponō* ('with trouble, effort') to be implied in both verses. Cf. NEB, 'You think it will not take much to make me a Christian'; NJB, 'A little more, and your arguments would make a Christian of me'.

75. Witherington 1998, 751. Witherington continues: 'the complaint has to do with the fact that Paul has not really offered fully developed proofs, but only mentioned some of the elements of proof in his *narratio* and what follows it'. P. Harlé, 'Un "private-joke" de Paul dans le livre des Actes (xxxvi.28-29)', *NTS* 24 (1977-78), 527-33, argues that v. 29 should be read in the light of v. 22 *(mikrō te kai megalō, to small and great)* and so translated, 'whether small or great (in social stature)'.

76. Cf. Longenecker 1982, 554-55; Marshall 1980, 400 note 1; Barrett 1998, 1170. In Eph. 3:3 the same expression is translated 'in [a] few words' by KJV and NRSV, but ESV and TNIV have 'briefly'.

77. Barrett 1998, 1169-70, discusses several variants in the MSS of v. 28. Cf. Metzger, *Textual Commentary*, 439.

78. Haenchen 1971, 689; Bruce 1990, 506; Johnson 1992, 439-40; NRSV mg.; ESV mg. Cf. Barrett 1998, 1171, for a fuller discussion of this possibility.

79. Cf. Harlé, 'Private-joke', 527-33. An interesting parallel use of the verb could be Mt. 23:15, 'to make a single proselyte' (*poiēsai hena prosēlyton;* TNIV 'to win a single convert').

tion or a statement could be intended in v. 28. In my judgment, the meaning is either, 'Are you trying to convince me that in a short time you have made me a Christian?', or 'You are trying to convince me that in a short time you have made me a Christian!'[80] The term *Christian* appears here, as in 11:26, on the lips of an unbeliever (cf. Tacitus, *Ann.* 15.44; Pliny, *Ep.* 10.96-97; Lucian, *Alex.* 25.38), not as a term of contempt but as a way of differentiating the followers of Christ from Jews and pagans.

29 Agrippa may have been expressing surprise or cynicism with his question, or it could be a light-hearted attempt to 'get out of the logical trap in which he is in danger of being caught'.[81] Whatever the intention, Paul will not let him off the hook. Using the optative form of the verb *'pray'* *(euxaimēn)*, he expresses an earnest desire that he knows may be distasteful to his listener.[82] He picks up Agrippa's phrase and adapts it *(en oligō kai en megalō)* for rhetorical effect. Whatever noun supplement is understood with *en oligōi* in v. 28 must also be understood here. A time reference is certainly possible in both cases, and so TNIV *('short time or long')* is a valid rendering of the Greek.[83] Paul expresses his desire to Agrippa in very personal terms: *'that not only you but all who are listening to me today may become what I am, except for these chains'*. In so doing, he consciously widens his appeal to everyone present. Previously, he acknowledged that many in his audience might be sceptical about talk of resurrection from the dead (v. 8). However, just as in Athens he preached about 'Jesus and the resurrection' to Jews and Gentiles alike (17:18), so now he addresses all together. His *chains* are a reminder that his bold appeal is being made as a prisoner for this belief.

30-32 *The king rose, and with him the governor and Bernice and those sitting with them.*[84] Once again we are faced with the evidence of a private conversation without being told of Luke's source: it was *after they left the room* that they began speaking to one another (cf. 25:13-22 note). From a narrative perspective, these concluding verses reaffirm the innocence of Paul *('This man is not doing anything that deserves death or imprisonment')*. 'Like Jesus, who was declared innocent three times by the Roman authority Pontius Pilate (Luke 23:4, 14, 22) with the agreement of the Tetrarch Herod (23:15), so is Paul three times declared innocent of the charges against him

---

80. Cf. Larkin 1995, 365, note on 26:28. In either rendering, the present tense of the verb *peitheis* is understood in a conative sense ('trying to convince') and the infinitive *poiēsai* is read as a perfective aorist ('to have made').

81. Marshall 1980, 400. Cf. Bruce 1990, 506.

82. Cf. Johnson 1992, 440. To convey the sense of polite indefiniteness intended, the whole expression *(euxaimēn an tō theō)* could be better translated 'I might pray to God' or 'I wish to God'. S. E. Porter, *Idioms of the Greek New Testament* (2nd ed.; Sheffield: Sheffield Academic 1994), 59-60, notes the deliberative (potential) use of the optative mood here.

83. Barrett 1998, 1172, notes the unexpected use of *kai* in the expression *en oligō kai en megalō*, but gives evidence for this connective being employed to express an alternative (e.g., Acts 10:14, *koinon kai akatharton*, 'common or unclean').

84. Barrett 1998, 1172-73, gives evidence for the verb *synkathēmenoi (sitting with)* being specifically used of those who sit as assessors in a court.

by Roman authorities with the agreement of a representative of the Herodian family.'[85] At the same time, Agrippa joins Festus in acknowledging the impossibility of releasing Paul (*'This man could have been set free if he had not appealed to Caesar'*). Both officials are 'willing to declare Paul innocent after they have been conveniently relieved of responsibility for his case and can escape the political problems that freeing him might cause'.[86] But Sherwin-White also observes that 'to have acquitted him despite the appeal would have been to offend both the emperor and the province'.[87] The case had been unproven since the trial before Felix (24:1-21; cf. 25:7-8). Yet we know that Paul's appeal to Caesar was necessary to deliver him from impending disaster at the hands of his opponents in Jerusalem (25:9-11). We are thus about to see how remarkably he was transported to Rome, to begin another phase of his ministry as a prisoner of the Empire.

In Acts 26, Paul's distinctive role in the plan and purpose of God is highlighted once more. The Christophany on the road to Damascus enabled him to be a witness to the risen Jesus and an authorised interpreter of his life and ministry, somewhat like the Twelve. Moreover, scriptural allusions suggest Paul's likeness to certain OT prophets, with a particular commission to fulfill the Isaianic Servant's role: opening blind eyes, turning people from darkness to light and from the power of Satan to God, and enabling them to share in the messianic salvation made possible by Jesus. Nevertheless, as a faithful bearer of the word of God and as one who endures considerable suffering for the sake of that word, Paul also functions as a model for ministry and mission in the ongoing life of the people of God (as in 20:18-35). Luke has progressively demonstrated the progress of the word, as proclaimed by various characters in the narrative. In a range of speeches, he has also shown how the message was expressed and applied in different contexts. Here he gives a theological perspective on how the word changes lives and grows the church. This encourages readers to believe that similar blessings may follow, wherever the word is faithfully proclaimed and personal testimony is given to the Lord's grace and power.[88]

---

85. Johnson 1992, 440.
86. Tannehill 1990, 329.
87. A. N. Sherwin-White, *Roman Society and Roman Law in the New Testament* (Oxford: Clarendon, 1963), 65. He argues that it was not a question of law for Festus, 'but of the relation between the emperor and his subordinates, and of the element of "prestige", on which the supremacy of the Princeps so largely depended'.
88. Bock 2007, 724-25, considers the link between personal testimony and persuasive evangelism.

J. Journeying to Rome (27:1–28:15)

The final chapters of Acts provide further reflections on Paul's relations to both Jews and Gentiles. 'The problem of the Jews receives the climactic position as the final major scene. The voyage indicates that the narrator is also reflecting on Paul's relation to the large gentile world unaffected by Judaism. Both aspects of the narrative suggest the situation that Paul will leave behind.'[1] Paul's good relations with Gentiles throughout this whole journey sequence (27:1–28:16), and their receptivity to him, prepare for the affirmation that 'God's salvation has been sent to the Gentiles, and they will listen!' (28:28). Paul is once more presented as a prophetic figure, whose words and deeds testify to the power and grace of God, even in strange and difficult circumstances. In certain respects, he is also a model disciple who trusts God in testing situations and points others to the saving power of his Master. With the concluding assurance that Paul's ministry in Rome continued 'with all boldness and without hindrance' (28:31), readers are encouraged to reflect on the implications of these two chapters for the ongoing life of the church. Yet Luke's portrait of Paul is not guaranteeing a mission without problems. 'He himself remains a prisoner of the Romans, and the portrait of the natives of Malta shows that they have far to go in understanding and accepting central affirmations of Christian preaching. With Jews and God-fearers there is a foundation on which the missionary may build.'[2]

The various accounts of Paul's sea voyages in Acts suggest that he covered some three thousand miles in the nearly three decades of his ministry.[3] As an experienced sea traveller he knew the dangers of shipwreck and of being adrift at sea (2 Cor. 11:25). However, the extensive narrative in Acts 27 indicates a situation of unprecedented seriousness and of amazing deliverance. It is 'one of the most vivid pieces of descriptive narrative in the whole book, or indeed in the whole NT'.[4] Some have argued that this elaborate account is fictitious, following the pattern of ancient Hellenistic novels or romances, even though such tales were also common in Greek historical works.[5] Following the conventions of Greek historiography, Luke employs

---

1. Tannehill 1990, 342.
2. Tannehill 1990, 342.
3. So Witherington 1998, 754, following Haenchen 1971, 702-3.
4. Bruce 1990, 508.
5. See R. I. Pervo, *Profit with Delight: The Literary Genre of the Acts of the Apostles* (Philadelphia: Fortress, 1987), 51, for the argument that Luke was livening up his material as the composers of fiction did. But Johnson 1992, 451-52, notes the extent to which such tales can be found in Greek historical works. S. M. Praeder, 'Acts 27:1–28:16: Sea Voyages in Ancient Literature and the Theology of Luke-Acts', *CBQ* 46 (1984), 705, argues that 'travelogues, forecasts, and concerns for safety are not limited to any one literary genre. Storm scenes and speeches in storm scenes are characteristic of Greek and Latin epics but are not confined to them.' Pervo 136, categorises Acts as a 'historical novel', but S. E. Porter, *Paul in Acts* (Peabody: Hendrickson, 2001), a reprint of *The Paul of Acts: Essays in Literary Criticism, Rhetoric,*

a more classical linguistic style, and displays 'a Greek (and decidedly non-Jewish) love of sea travel and tales about such travel'.[6] This lengthy narrative was included, not simply for dramatic effect, but to teach something further about divine providence and Paul's role within God's plan for the nations. Luke's fundamental aim was to recount 'the *actual* events of a rough sea journey and shipwreck in a manner which helpfully addresses what would have been their troubling theological implications to a reader who knows a Paul of distressing experiences and mixed reputation'.[7] After several chapters recounting accusations, trials, and imprisonments, Luke demonstrates God's special care for Paul and all who travel with him. Once again, Paul's calling to be a servant and a witness of the risen Lord Jesus is confirmed (cf. 26:16). But that is not all that can be said about the significance of this narrative.

In the sea voyage from Philippi to Jerusalem (20:6–21:16), the main interest was Paul's giving and receiving of ministry from Christians along the way. Paul also meets believers in the course of this last journey (27:3; 28:14-15), but most of the narrative is about his engagement with unbelieving Gentiles — the centurion named Julius, the soldiers, the sailors, the rest of the ship's company, and the people of Malta. Paul appears in Acts 22–26 as 'an isolated and restricted, even if somewhat valuable, political prisoner', but in Acts 27–28, 'although technically remaining a prisoner and defendant, Paul re-establishes his role as a *dynamic prophet and servant* in the mold of Jesus'.[8] The theme of salvation predominates throughout, specifically with reference to being rescued from storm and sea.[9] Paul himself is also delivered from death by snakebite on Malta (28:3-6), and then heals the father of the chief official of that island and

---

and Theology, WUNT 115 (Tübingen: Mohr, 1999), 15-19, rightly criticises Pervo for creating a literary genre unparalleled by the ancient texts.

6. Witherington 1998, 756. Witherington agrees that 'Luke as a rhetorical historian had some interest in giving his audience pleasure as well as information'. But he rightly judges this to be a secondary concern and 'not the one that determined the genre of the work'. Witherington, 757-58, has several convincing arguments against the view of Haenchen 1971, 710-11, that Luke inserted a few Pauline snippets into a preexisting narrative. Cf. Bruce 1990, 508-9. Barrett 1998, 1178-80, concludes his examination of various critical approaches to the narrative by saying that some of the details of the chapter are 'more credible than some of the objections'.

7. B. Rapske, 'Acts, Travel, and Shipwreck', in D. W. J. Gill and C. Gempf (eds.), *The Book of Acts in Its First-Century Setting*, Vol. 2: *Graeco-Roman Setting* (Grand Rapids: Eerdmans; Carlisle: Paternoster, 1994), 46. Rapske, 43-47, is commenting on the view of G. B. Miles and G. Trompf, 'Luke and Antiphon: The Theology of Acts 27–28 in the Light of Pagan Beliefs about Divine Retribution, Pollution, and Shipwreck', *HTR* 69 (1976), 264, that the escape of all 276 passengers amounts to a 'divine confirmation of Paul's innocence'.

8. Spencer 1997, 230.

9. The verbs *sōzō* (27:20, 31) and *diasōzō* (27:43, 44; 28:1, 4) are used in conjunction with the noun *sōtēria* (27:34). Tannehill 1990, 336, notes that 'the rapid repetition of the same word in 27:43, 44; 28:1 is a particular sign of emphasis'. Such terminology is common in ancient sea-voyage literature.

many others who come to be cured (28:7-10). The language of salvation is used in similar ways in the OT. Faithful Israelites learned to depend on God for salvation from sickness, danger, and death (e.g., Pss. 69–71, 86, 88). In times of national disaster they recognized that God 'brings salvation on the earth' (Ps. 74:12), especially for his covenant people (e.g., Pss. 78–80, 85). Like the psalmists, Paul bears testimony to the saving power of God, though he addresses his challenge to Gentiles. Such deliverance points to the salvation offered through the gospel, though Paul does not get an opportunity to declare that within the narrative of this journey to Rome.[10]

1. From Caesarea to Malta (27:1-44)

Paul emerges as the key figure in this lengthy narrative. Spencer proposes that 'with this voyage to Rome, it is almost as if he embarks on another missionary expedition'.[11] This may be observed in three ways. First, instead of being an isolated prisoner, Paul is accompanied by others — prisoners, soldiers, sailors, and, notably again, fellow Christians (Aristarchus and Luke at least, vv. 1-2) — and is encouraged by believers along the way (v. 3; cf. 28:14-15). Secondly, Paul regains his authority as the crisis develops: 'in a striking reversal of roles, the centurion and the entire crew essentially come under Paul's command as the storm hits'.[12] Thirdly, as prophet and servant of God, he becomes a source of salvation for others because of an angelic revelation which he receives and applies to the situation (vv. 21-26, 31-32, 33-38). Based on the promise that 'God has graciously given you the lives of all who sail with you' (v. 24), Paul encourages the ship's company to trust in his God for deliverance. The narrative is not an allegory of personal redemption, illustrating what it means to be brought from darkness to light, and rescued from divine judgment. But it does portray human beings in a desperate situation, in need of God's help, and shows the importance of believing his word and relying on his power for deliverance. Moreover, it demonstrates the opportunity that the believer has in such a situation to draw attention to the character of God and to encourage unbelievers to turn to him for mercy. For some people, this might be the first step towards trusting God for salvation in the ultimate sense. In terms of Luke's concern about the gospel's progress among the nations, 'the insistence that all the ship's company must be saved echoes the promise that "all flesh will see the salvation of God" in Luke 3:6'.[13]

10. Witherington 1998, 767, 772-73, is unnecessarily sceptical about the theological implications of Luke's use of the terminology of salvation in this passage.
11. Spencer 1997, 230. Spencer, 231-32, notes that the transformation in Paul's status from political prisoner back to dynamic missionary is 'appropriately staged in an extraordinary, *liminal setting*'. By this he means that temporally and spatially the context is extraordinary, difficult, and turbulent.
12. Spencer 1997, 231.
13. Tannehill 1990, 337. Spencer 1997, 231, observes that 'instead of simply testifying

a. Sailing into Danger (27:1-20)

1 The majority text is vague about who initiated the voyage *(hōs de ekrithē, when it was decided)*, but the Western text characteristically states the obvious ('so then the governor decided to send him to Caesar').[14] Luke resumes the first person plural style in sections of this narrative (27:1-8, 12, 15-20, 27-29, 37; 28:1-2, 7, 10-16). 'We are not told where Luke had been since the last occurrence of the "we" form of narration (21:18), but it is often supposed that he stayed in Palestine, and even that he used this time in searching out information for the composition of his Gospel and the earlier parts of Acts; this is plausible, but beyond proof.'[15] The 'we' passages in this chapter mostly refer to the whole ship's company (e.g., *when it was decided that we would sail for Italy)*, and do not simply include the author and his fellow Christians (which is the pattern in 16:10-17; 20:5-15; 21:1-18; 28:14-16). But Luke continues to use this method of expression to highlight his own participation in the drama, not simply because it was the conventional approach in records of sea voyages.[16] He particularly wanted to make it clear that he shared the struggles and joys of that final journey to Rome with Paul. The prisoners *were handed over to a centurion named Julius, who belonged to the Imperial Regiment (speirēs Sebastēs,* 'Augustan Cohort', NRSV, ESV). This cohort is likely to have been part of the army of Syria and Judea, located in Batanea (Bashan) in the Transjordan, under Herod Agrippa II.[17] Like Claudius Lysias

---

to his personal belief in the hope of resurrection, as he did throughout his trials, Paul now provides tangible, life-giving aid to many others in a desperate situation where "all hope of our being saved was at last abandoned" (27:20)'.

14. Cf. Metzger, *Textual Commentary*, 439-40, for the complete Western paraphrase of vv. 1-2.

15. Marshall 1980, 403.

16. Cf. C. J. Hemer, 'First Person Narrative in Acts 27-28', *TynB* 36 (1985), 79-109, against V. K. Robbins, 'By Land and by Sea: The We-Passages and Ancient Sea Voyages', in C. H. Talbert (ed.), *Perspectives in Luke-Acts* (Edinburgh: Clark, 1978), 215-42. Porter, *Paul in Acts*, 10-46, argues that the author used a previously written, continuous, and independent 'we' source throughout Acts. He acknowledges that Lk. 1:1-4 could point to a firsthand witness but says that this cannot be determined with certainty. Some explanation must be given for the distinctive literary features of these passages and anomalies in the way they are integrated into the text of Acts. Porter, 47-66, goes on to argue that the 'we' source presented a picture of Paul that was appealing to the author but different in perspective from his own. However, Porter seems to be unnecessarily sceptical about the possibility that the author used his own eyewitness narrative. Cf. I. H. Marshall, *The Acts of the Apostles*, NTG (Sheffield: JSOT, 1992), 84-91; Witherington 1998, 480-86.

17. Witherington 1998, 758-59, following C. J. Hemer, *The Book of Acts in the Setting of Hellenistic History*, ed. C. Gempf, WUNT 49 (Tübingen: Mohr Siebeck, 1989; repr. Winona Lake: Eisenbrauns, 1990), 132-33 and note 96. Bruce 1990, 511, argues that *Sebastē* was a title of honour equivalent to *Augusta*, which was frequently bestowed upon troops. It should 'probably not be associated with the city of Sebaste, as though this were one of the cohorts of *Sebasteni*, mentioned by Josephus (*War* 2.52, 58, 63, 74, 236, etc.).'. Cf. B. Rapske, *The Book of Acts in Its First-Century Setting*, Vol. 3: *The Book of Acts and Paul in Roman Custody* (Grand Rapids: Eerdmans; Carlisle: Paternoster, 1994), 268-69; Barrett 1998, 1181.

in Acts 21–23, *Julius* is introduced as a named Roman official, who begins to take Paul's advice (vv. 31-32) and to care for him (vv. 42-43). The name 'Julius' suggests that 'one of his forbears acquired his freedom (and citizenship) during the reign of either Julius Caesar or Augustus'.[18] Since Claudius had prohibited the use of the simple *nomen* to all but Roman citizens, the name 'Julius' on its own suggests that he was an older man who possessed Roman citizenship. The sharing of Roman citizenship doubtless formed a basis for the respect shown to Paul by Julius.

2   In addition to Luke, at least one other believer accompanied Paul and the rest of the prisoners: *Aristarchus, a Macedonian from Thessalonica,* is named as being *with us*.[19] The reunion of believers with Paul for a sea voyage recalls the beginning of the missionary journey in 16:10-12 and the journey to Jerusalem in 20:1–21:16. As a prisoner in that culture, Paul might well have inspired the shame and revulsion of his associates and many others. But Luke consistently shows how 'Christian co-workers stand by the prisoner-missionary rather than taking the easier and safer route of slipping away from him. Luke and Aristarchus "cover" Paul with what status they have and show solidarity with him as he goes to Rome.'[20] The travellers *boarded a ship from Adramyttium* — (modern Edremit) a city north of Pergamum, in the region of Mysia — *about to sail for ports along the coast of the province of Asia.* Since there were no dedicated passenger vessels at that time, the centurion appears to have requisitioned a trading boat for the transport of his soldiers and prisoners (cf. 27:6; 28:11).[21] It was apparently working its way home along the southern and western coasts of Asia Minor. On a privately owned vessel, Luke and Aristarchus could have booked their own separate passages, so as to accompany Paul. In due course, they all *put out to sea.*

3   *The next day* the ship landed *at Sidon,* on the Phoenician coast, some 69 nautical miles (128 km.) north of Caesarea.[22] The relationship between *Julius* and *Paul,* which ultimately contributes to the rescue of every-

---

18. Witherington 1998, 759. Cf. Rapske, *Roman Custody,* 269-70. Rapske concludes that 'there could hardly be a better choice for supervising the transport of Paul and the others to Rome than a high ranking auxiliary soldier who also possessed citizenship'.

19. Aristarchus is mentioned at the end of the verse in a genitive absolute clause, which distinguishes him from 'Paul and certain other prisoners' (v. 1) and implies that he was a free man at this stage. In Acts 20:4 he is identified along with Secundus as one of the Macedonians who accompanied Paul on his final, fateful journey to Jerusalem (cf. also 19:29). In Col. 4:10 he is a fellow prisoner with Paul, presumably in Rome (cf. Phlm. 24, where he is a fellow worker along with Luke).

20. Rapske, *Roman Custody,* 434-35.

21. Witherington 1998, 760, observes that there was no state fleet responsible for transporting prisoners, nor was there a state merchant fleet. A Roman soldier could requisition a ship and other forms of transport for imperial purpose. Cf. Rapske, 'Travel', 18-21; *Roman Custody,* 272-73.

22. Cf. Marshall 1980, 404. I am taking these as U.K. nautical miles when converting distances to kilometres.

one on the ship, begins on a note of *kindness (philanthrōpōs te ho Ioulios tō Paulō chrēsamenos*, 'Julius treated Paul in a kindly way'). In practical terms, this involved allowing Paul *to go to his friends so they might provide for his needs.* Julius respected this unusual prisoner, though he doubtless sent a soldier to guard him when he was away from the ship. Unnamed Christians in Sidon were allowed to show hospitality to Paul as he began his arduous journey to Rome. We have no knowledge of the way the gospel reached Sidon, though it could well have been a result of the outreach mentioned in 11:19. The word *friends (philous)* suggests that Paul had visited Sidon previously (cf. 15:3) and had established good relationships with the believers there. It seems unlikely that the designation *friends* is a technical term for 'the Christians' (as possibly in 3 Jn. 15). In the last stages of the journey, Luke records the *kindness* of pagans on the island of Malta in showing hospitality to Paul and his fellow travellers (28:2 [*philanthrōpian*]; 28:7 [*philophronōs*, 'in a friendly manner']) before he is welcomed into the arms of caring Christians once more (28:14-15). Kindness is a virtue commended in Hellenistic literature as a way of being truly human or civilized (cf. Plato, *Euthyphro* 3D; Plutarch, *Oracles at Delphi* 16; Philo, *On Special Laws* 2.141).[23] *Philanthrōpia* is literally love for humanity. In Acts 27–28 it is demonstrated by Christians and pagans alike. Luke's implicit message is that Christians fulfill the best aspirations of human society in their care for one another (cf. 2:42-47 note).

4-6 Luke gives the first indication of any difficulty with the weather (cf. vv. 7-8, 9, 13-20) when he records, *From there we put out to sea again and passed to the lee of Cyprus because the winds were against us.* Late in the season, winds from the west and northwest made it necessary to sail on the eastern side of the island.[24] *When we had sailed across the open sea off the coast of Cilicia and Pamphylia, we landed at Myra in Lycia.* The site of *Myra* is now known as Kocademre ('Old Demre').[25] This was the southernmost part of Asia, almost due north of Alexandria, where ships on their way to Rome would often make a stopover. Luke notes that it was *there the centurion found an Alexandrian ship sailing for Italy and put us on board.* From v. 38 this appears to have been a grain ship. 'Egypt was an indispensable source of supply for Rome, providing a third of the corn used in the year.'[26] Although such ships were privately owned, they operated under state control when they were

23. Cf. Johnson 1992, 445. Elsewhere in the NT *philanthrōpia* is found in Titus 3:4, where it describes the love of God for humanity expressed in the saving work of Jesus Christ.

24. So L. Smith, *The Voyage and Shipwreck of St. Paul* (London, 1848; 4th ed. 1880), 67-68.

25. Bruce 1990, 513. Some Western MSS add that this journey took fifteen days. However, Metzger, *Textual Commentary*, 440, says, 'Neither the general character of the witnesses that include the longer reading, nor the variations of location where it appears in the text, inspire confidence in its originality'. Barrett 1998, 1184, suggests that the words were added by 'someone who knew the area at a time when the text of Acts could be handled freely'.

26. Barrett 1998, 1185.

contracted to bring grain to Rome. This was the second ship requisitioned by the centurion for the transport of his party (cf. v. 2 note).[27]

7-8 One long sentence in Greek runs through these two verses, giving a sense of increasing problems with the weather and creating a certain narrative tension.[28] The new ship *made slow headway for many days and had difficulty arriving off Cnidus*, which was at the end of the peninsula forming the southwest tip of Asia Minor, across from the island of Rhodes. This was a seaport regularly used by ships travelling from Alexandria (Thucydides, *Hist.* 8.24.35). When the strong northwest wind did not allow the ship to enter this port, Luke records, *we sailed to the lee of Crete, opposite Salmone* (the cape at the northeastern end of Crete). Once again, the weather made it necessary for the ship to hug the seaboard of a large island (cf. v. 4). The aim was to continue westwards on the southern side of Crete. Even so, *we moved along the coast with difficulty and came to a place called Fair Havens, near the town of Lasea. Fair Havens* was probably the site of modern Kal(o)i Limenes. This small bay is 5-6 nautical miles (8-9 km.) east of Cape Matala, 'at which point the coast curves to the north and is no longer sheltered'.[29] *Fair Havens* was actually *unsuitable to winter in* (v. 12), since 'it stands open to nearly half the compass'.[30] It may have offered immediate shelter, but it did not commend itself to the sailors for a longer stay.

9-10 Luke shows an accurate knowledge of seasonal conditions in the Mediterranean and the implications for travel, observing that *much time had been lost, and sailing had already become dangerous because by now it was after the Day of Atonement (dia to kai tēn nēsteian ēdē parelēlythenai,* 'because even the Fast had already passed'). There was only one fast prescribed in the Jewish calendar, and so TNIV has fairly translated *tēn nēsteian* ('the fast') as *the Day of Atonement.* The author clearly thought that those he was addressing were sufficiently influenced by a Jewish ethos to make sense of this way of reckoning time.[31] Because the Jewish calendar was a lunar one, the fast associated with *the Day of Atonement* (on the tenth day of the month Tishri) fell at a different time each year, either in the latter part of September or early October (cf. Josephus, *Ant.* 14.66; 18.94; *m. Menaḥ.* 11.9). Ac-

27. Bruce 1990, 511-12, 513, suggests that Julius may have been a member of the corps of *frumentarii* — centurions responsible for the safe transportation of grain *(frumentum)* to the capital. But Rapske, *Roman Custody,* 274, considers this to be doubtful.

28. Barrett 1998, 1185-86, examines the structure of this complex sentence carefully.

29. Marshall 1980, 405. Marshall notes that the modern site is '12 miles (18 km.) east of Cape Matala'. But 12 nautical miles is 19 km., and Witherington 1998, 762, following Longenecker 1981, 559, locates the bay 'about five miles east of Cape Matala'; Bruce 1990, 514, locates it 'two leagues east of Cape Matala', which is six nautical miles.

30. Bruce 1990, 514. Barrett 1998, 1187, describes this port as 'sheltered on the west, open to the east', giving protection from northerly and westerly winds.

31. Other references to the Jewish calendar can be found at 1:12; 2:1; 12:4; 18:21; 20:6, 16. This suggests that the intended readers are Christians, who either have a synagogue background or are in continuing dialogue with Jews. Such a conclusion is confirmed by the exegesis of Acts 28:17-31.

cording to the Roman writer Vegetius (*De Re Militari* 4.39), the dangerous season began after 15 September, and sailing ceased for the winter from 11 November to 10 March. Luke's allusion gives us a clue about the most likely date of this journey to Rome. If he was following the most widely known Jewish calendar, 'this day fell on October 5 in the year AD 59, but not nearly that late in the years immediately before 59 in the period from 57 to 62'.[32] The *kai* ('even'), which is not translated by TNIV, implies a particularly late date for the fast that year: 'not only had the dangerous time for sailing begun: even the fast was now past'.[33] Paul's first assessment of the situation was not dependent on a divine revelation (as in vv. 21-25), but appears to have been based on his own wisdom and experience as a traveller.[34] His intervention can be further explained in terms of his status on the ship: 'though under guard, and not free, he was in a sense a privileged person, who must be delivered to the Emperor'.[35] He 'advised' them (*parēnei*; TNIV *warned*), '*Men, I can see that our voyage is going to be disastrous and bring great loss to ship and cargo, and to our own lives also*'. Since 'Paul has repeatedly been portrayed as a perceptive and reliable person',[36] readers are encouraged to take this warning seriously. However, 'it is a measure of Luke's honesty and accuracy that he reports this advice in full, for in fact when the craft does sail on there is no loss of life, and Paul himself says God informed him that this would be the case (cf. vv. 21-24)'.[37] In short, there is a later adjustment to Paul's view of the situation when he receives explicit divine revelation in vv. 21-25.

11-12 *But the centurion, instead of listening to what Paul said, followed the advice of the pilot (tō kybernētē) and of the owner of the ship (kai tō nauklērō).*[38]

---

32. Witherington 1998, 762, following Bruce 1990, 289, 515. Bruce argues from the time indications in the passage about the length of the journey that AD 59 is most likely to have been the year. Marshall 1980, 406, agrees but notes that, after three months in Malta, they must have sailed for Italy at the end of January or the beginning of February the next year. On this reckoning, they would have been sailing again well before March 10, when Vegetius considered it safe to sail again. If Luke was following a Syrian Jewish calendar, the Day of Atonement would have been as late as 28 October in 59. This would mean a later start for their sailing in the following spring.

33. Bruce 1990, 515.

34. So also Bruce 1990, 515; Barrett 1998, 1189; Witherington 1998, 763. Marshall 1980, 406-7, suggests that 'the fact that Paul speaks with certainty of disaster rather than merely of the possibility may support the supposition of divine guidance behind his statement'. But Paul simply uses the emphatic language of someone who perceives the real danger in the situation.

35. Barrett 1998, 1187. Marshall 1980, 407, suggests that Paul could have addressed the whole ship's company (as he apparently does in v. 21), or had a less formal conversation with the centurion and the officers of the ship.

36. Tannehill 1990, 331.

37. Witherington 1998, 763. Cf. Barrett 1998, 1189-90, on the unexpected use of *hybris* to mean 'damage' (TNIV *disastrous*).

38. The first of these terms could refer to the pilot or to the captain of a ship (cf. Plutarch, *Mor.* 807B). If the owner *(ho nauklēros)* was the captain, the first term should be ren-

'Julius may have treated Paul well previously, but he is not yet ready to trust Paul's judgment.'[39] Perhaps *the pilot* and *the owner of the ship* had economic and personal reasons for wishing to keep going. Emperor Claudius (41-54) offered a bounty to shipowners willing to sail in the dangerous season to bring extra grain to Rome. A recompense was also promised for any loss or damage to ships (cf. Suetonius, *Claud*. 18.2). These incentives, which remained operative under Nero (54-68), were designed to cope with famine in the capital and forestall insurrections.[40] However, such matters are not mentioned by Luke, who simply resumes the narrative from v. 8 with the recollection *since the harbour was unsuitable to winter in*. The latter is a genitive absolute construction in Greek, providing the explanation for the decision of the majority *that we should sail on, hoping to reach Phoenix and winter there*. Although this destination is identified as *a harbour in Crete, facing both southwest and northwest*, there is some debate about its exact location. It is probably to be identified with modern Phineka, which is about 40 miles (74 km.) up the coast. It faces west and offers the sort of protection they were seeking.[41] But the ship failed to reach this haven and was driven wildly off course.

13-14   In the account of the storm and shipwreck which occupies the rest of the chapter, there are echoes of Homer's *Odyssey* and later such works, in language and content. 'As a whole, however, the passage falls short of the formulas for literary or rhetorical storm scenes.'[42] This suggests that Luke's eyewitness account was written up on the basis of literary models in ancient literature, without those models distorting the facts.[43] On this epic journey, *a gentle south wind began to blow*, favouring a westerly voyage and confirming for the crew the decision to dismiss Paul's warning. The captain and crew *saw their opportunity; so they weighed anchor and sailed along the shore of Crete*. It was only a short distance to Cape Matala, and then an-

---

dered 'pilot' or 'helmsman' (so most EVV). KJV has taken both terms to refer to the same person ('the master and the owner of the ship'). Barrett 1998, 1175, 1190, translates 'the captain and the owner', taking the first term to refer to the nautical director and the second to the financial.

39. Tannehill 1990, 331. Praeder, 'Sea Voyages', 690, observes that, in other ancient stories of storm and shipwreck, 'as a rule, forecasters of storm and shipwreck find no more favor with fellow sailors, passengers or officers than Paul finds'. Witherington 1998, 763, argues that 'it is understandable that a Roman might not take the advice of a Jew about the future, for Romans trusted divination more than Eastern prophecies or the advice of Eastern sages'. But, if Paul's words in v. 10 are offered as the 'commonsense advice of a seasoned traveler', the reasons for rejecting them may be otherwise.

40. Cf. Witherington 1998, 763-64; Rapske, 'Travel', 22-43.

41. For details regarding this place, cf. Bruce 1990, 516-17; Witherington 1998, 764; Barrett 1998, 1192-93.

42. Praeder, 'Sea Voyages', 689. Bruce 1990, 508, contends that Homer 'set the fashion in which stories of storm at sea and shipwreck continued to be told long after his day'. Witherington 1998, 764, lists some of the parallels with Homer.

43. Cf. M. Dibelius, *Studies in the Acts of the Apostles*, ed. H. Greeven, trans. M. Ling (London: SCM, 1956), 7-8, followed by Witherington 1998, 765.

other 36 miles or so (58 km.) around to Phoenix, where they hoped to spend the winter (v. 12). However, *before very long, a wind of hurricane force, called the 'Northeaster,' swept down from the island* (*kat' autēs,* 'from it'). This *wind of hurricane force* (*anemos typhōnikos*) notoriously came down from Mt. Ida, creating very dangerous conditions for ships at sea.[44] The earliest MSS, attested by Alexandrian and Western witnesses, identify it with the hybrid term *Eurakylōn (Northeaster),* combining the Greek word for the east wind (*Euros*) with the Latin word for the north wind (*Aquilo*). But later MSS have various spellings of the term *Euroklydōn,* which means either 'rough water' or 'southeaster'. The latter found its way into the Received Text and hence into KJV and NKJV. Although no use of *Eurakylōn* has been detected elsewhere in Greek writings or inscriptions, the Latin equivalent *Euroaquilo* has been found on a piece of pavement with indications of it being a wind from the north-northeast.[45]

15-17   So powerful was this 'Northeaster' that *the ship was caught by the storm and could not head into the wind* (*antophthalmein tō anemō,* 'face the wind eye to eye'),[46] *so we gave way to it and were driven along.* Ancient ships could not head into the wind as modern sailing boats can, and so they were carried before the wind some 23 miles (37 km.) southwest. As they passed *to the lee of a small island called Cauda* (modern Gk. *Gaudos;* Ital. *Gozzo*),[47] Luke says, *we were hardly able to make the lifeboat secure.* He uses the first person plural again to refer to the sailors (and goes on to refer to them in the third person, *so the men had hoisted it aboard*). But the rhetorical effect of the first-person usage is to portray the event from the perspective of all who were affected by it, including himself. The lifeboat, which was normally towed from the stern, could have damaged the ship and been itself destroyed by the force of the waves. Step by step, Luke reveals the desperate moves made to try and preserve the ship and get it back on course. The sailors also *passed ropes under the ship itself to hold it together* (*boētheiais echrōnto hypozōnnyntes to ploion,* 'they used helps to undergird the ship'). This possibly involved the technique called 'frapping', which means passing ropes under the ship to strengthen it. But they could also have braced the ship by

44. Bruce 1990, 518, notes that the adjective *typhōnikos* (from which English derives 'typhoon') refers to 'the whirling motion of the clouds and sea caused by the meeting of opposing currents of air'. Such winds were thought to come from *Typhōn,* the father of the winds. Cf. Rapske, 'Travel', 38-39; Barrett 1998, 1194.

45. Cf. Bruce 1990, 518; Witherington 1998, 765. Given the geography of the situation, *Euroklydōn* is surely a mistake. For example, 'the fact that they were driven past (Cauda) is sufficient proof that the wind was a northeaster' (Bruce, 519). This is still the most feared wind in the region and is now called *gregale* or *grigal.*

46. Witherington 1998, 765, follows Smith, *Voyage,* 98 note 2, in relating this expression to the practice of painting an eye on each side of the bow of a ship. Metzger, *Textual Commentary,* 440, notes that some Western MSS expand this text to read 'we gave way to [the wind] *which was blowing, and having furled the sails* we were driven'.

47. The variant *Klauda* is found in some MSS and is also attested by some ancient authors, hence KJV and NKJV. Cf. Metzger, *Textual Commentary,* 440-41.

tying ropes around the hull or transversely across the deck.[48] Part of their
concern would have been the movement of cargo in the storm and the fact
that grain when wet can swell dramatically and split the planks of a ship.[49]
Despite these practical steps, the sailors *were afraid they would run aground
on the sandbars of Syrtis* (*eis tēn Syrtin*, 'on the Syrtis'). This last expression
refers to the shoals and sandbars at the Gulf of Sidra, off the coast of Libya.
Since this was about 400 nautical miles (740 km.) from Cauda, we are given
a further indication of the strength of the wind and its potential to carry
them a long way off course. To prevent this, *they lowered the sea anchor*
(*skeuos*, 'gear', could alternatively refer to a sail that was lowered; cf. Jon.
1:5 LXX; Acts 10:11),[50] *and let the ship be driven along.* A drift anchor on a
rope astern would offer resistance every time the ship plunged from the
crest of a wave and slow down their running before the wind.

18-20   Nevertheless, Luke recalls, *we took such a violent battering from
the storm that the next day they began to throw the cargo overboard.* The crew did
not yet jettison all the grain (v. 38), since the transport of wheat would have
been the main purpose of the journey and the livelihood of the ship's
owner depended on it.[51] With no change in their situation, *on the third day,
they threw the ship's tackle* (*tēn skeuēn tou ploiou*) *overboard with their own
hands.* As with *skeuos* in v. 17, there is uncertainty about what exactly is
meant here (cf. Jon. 1:5). Smith conjectured that this could have been the
main yard: 'an immense spar, probably as long as the ship, which would require the united effort of passengers and crew to launch overboard'.[52]
Whatever it was, there would be less possible control over the ship once the
storm abated (vv. 30, 32, and 40 indicate that some tackle was left). The expression *with their own hands* (*autocheires*) highlights the desperate nature of
this action: the tackle was not washed overboard but was deliberately
thrown away by the sailors. *When neither sun nor stars appeared for many
days,* they would have been ignorant of their position and lost at sea. This
was a truly frightening situation for sailors and passengers alike. Since *the
storm continued raging,* Luke concludes, *we finally gave up all hope of being
saved.* For the first time in this narrative, the terminology of salvation
(*sōzesthai*, 'to be saved'; cf. vv. 31, 34, 43, 44; 28:1, 4) is introduced. The aban-

<hr/>

48. Cf. Bruce 1990, 518-20; Witherington 1998, 766; Barrett 1998, 1196. Marshall 1980,
409, points out that 'undergirders' were part of the equipment of Greek warships. These
were ropes or cables long enough to go right around the ship longitudinally. But no independent evidence has been found for the use of such equipment on trading ships.

49. Cf. Rapske, 'Travel', 34-35.

50. Bruce 1990, 520, lists three possible ways in which 'lowering the gear' (*chalasantes
to skeuos*) could be understood, but considers that 'dropping a floating anchor' is the most
likely meaning in the context. Cf. Barrett 1998, 1197.

51. Rapske, 'Travel', 32, thinks that the evidence points to a relatively small grain carrier. The crew would first have lightened the ship 'by jettisoning the topmost cargo (possibly located above decks?)'.

52. Smith, *Voyage*, 116. Marshall 1980, 408, notes that the foresail must have been left
in place or it would have been impossible to steer.

donment of *all hope of being saved* is the preliminary to Paul's prophetic word (vv. 21-26), which gives hope of salvation from death, but not from shipwreck.

b. Trusting God's Word (27:21-38)

21-22 *After they had gone a long time without food,* Paul stood up before them and intervened a second time (cf. v. 10). In ancient stories of storm and shipwreck, 'the usual place for such speeches is at a high point in the storm and a low point in the fortunes of the sea travelers'.[53] However, 'in those speeches the message is about the danger of the situation and preparation for impending doom. Here the message is one of hope in the midst of despair.'[54] Their going without food was presumably because of seasickness or anxiety, and the difficulty of preparing a meal under such circumstances. After a rebuke for not having taken his previous warning seriously (*'Men, you should have taken my advice not to sail from Crete; then you would have spared yourselves this damage and loss'*), Paul's message is surprisingly upbeat.[55] It comes immediately after Luke's confession, *we finally gave up all hope of being saved* (v. 20). *'But now'* (*ta nyn* is emphatic) Paul is able to offer them positive encouragement. Twice he urges them *'to keep up your courage'* (v. 22, *hymas euthymein*; v. 25, *euthymeite*). The first reason for this exhortation is the promise that *'not one of you will be lost; only the ship will be destroyed'* (*apobolē gar psychēs oudemia estai ex hymōn plēn tou ploiou,* 'for there will be no loss of life of any of you, but only of the ship').

23-26 The basis of Paul's promise is a revelation that he then recounts, beginning with an acknowledgement of its divine source: *'Last night an angel of the God whose I am and whom I serve* (*latreuō,* as in 24:14; 26:7) *stood beside me and said'.* Note that it is an angel, rather than the ascended Lord Jesus, who addresses Paul here (contrast 18:9-10; 23:11). This angelic revelation confirms the personal word of the Lord Jesus to Paul in 23:11 and expands on its implications to include all who accompany him on the boat.[56] Like Jonah, he confesses his devotion to the God whom they do not ac-

---

53. Praeder, 'Sea Voyages', 696.

54. Witherington 1998, 767. Witherington, 768, argues that the lack of conformity in function and message to the speeches noted by Praeder suggests that this one is not simply a literary creation by Luke.

55. Although Paul is portrayed as a prophet who receives divine revelations, he is also shown to be 'a man of like passions with ourselves, not above saying "I told you so!"' (Bruce 1990, 521). However, his rebuke is restrained and leads into the positive encouragement that follows.

56. Other characters in Acts encounter angels in 5:19; 8:26; 10:3; 12:7, 23. Since angelic appearances are rare in the narrative, they are significant moments of divine revelation and action. In comparison, the personal revelations of the ascended Lord to Paul stand out as being even more special, and unique to him. The Holy Spirit is the source of Paul's determination in 19:21; 20:22-23. Rapske, *Roman Custody,* 359, blurs the distinction between Christ and the angels.

knowledge (Jon. 1:9). Unlike Jonah, he is not seeking to escape from the implications of his service to God! Paul is no 'divine man' but the servant of one who alone can bear the title *God*.[57] The message was to Paul personally (*"Do not be afraid, Paul. You must stand trial before Caesar"*), confirming what was said in 23:11, but adding the explicit promise of a *trial before Caesar*. Personal assurance was accompanied by a promise concerning everyone else on board (*"and God has graciously given you the lives of all who sail with you"*). The language here (v. 24, *kecharistai soi, has graciously given you*) suggests a granting in response to prayer for the safekeeping of all.[58] The implication is that Paul has been asking for deliverance on behalf of the whole ship's company (like Abraham interceding for the people of Sodom in Genesis 18:23-33). On the basis of this promise (v. 25, *dio, so*), Paul repeats the exhortation *'keep up your courage'*, and supports this with the affirmation *'for I have faith in God that it will happen just as he told me'*. The challenge to trust God is based on the assertion that 'God is as good as his word'.[59] Paul concludes his speech with a prediction: *'we must run aground on some island'*. Bruce takes this as a statement of faith: 'the sailors knew that they had missed Sicily and could not hope that the ship would hold out for the 200 miles that had to be covered before they struck the African coast near Carthage (Tunisia). If they had no hope of a landfall on Sicily, Malta was the next best hope (though Paul would probably not have known this) — but it was a slender hope indeed.'[60] However, it is more likely that the expression *we must (dei hēmas)* refers to the divine plan, which Paul now discloses, without specifying the precise place where they will *run aground*. In this mostly unbelieving company, Paul functions as a prophet, by praying, predicting (cf. 11:27-28; 21:10-11), and exhorting (cf. 15:32). He does not appear to have any effect on the situation until he further encourages them by his words and actions in vv. 31-38 (v. 36, *euthymoi, encouraged*). At this point, he emerges as the character through whom God will achieve the rescue and preservation of all present. Gentile readers may also have concluded from this divine revelation and subsequent events that Paul was innocent in God's eyes of the charges against him and that he would ultimately be vindicated and released.[61]

27-29   The rest of the chapter demonstrates the fulfillment of Paul's prophecy. *On the fourteenth night,* Luke continues, *we were still being driven across the Adriatic Sea (en tō Adria, 'on the Adria').* We know from ancient

57. Barrett 1998, 1200-1201, notes the unusual word order in Greek, which gives prominence to the relative clauses describing Paul's relationship with God (*hou eimi [egō], hō kai latreuō,* 'whose I am and whom I serve').

58. Tannehill, 332-33, observes that 'this announcement is a key to understanding the rest of the episode, for it determines what must happen, and the acts of sailors, soldiers, and Paul are to be judged in the light of it. From this point on, no method of escape is acceptable that doesn't include all.'

59. Witherington 1998, 770.
60. Bruce 1990, 522.
61. Cf. Witherington 1998, 769-70.

sources that the whole sea as far south as Sicily, Crete, and west as far as Malta, could be described as part of the Adriatic.[62] So there is no ground for inferring that the ship was driven up into the Adriatic Gulf, which encompasses what is called the Adriatic Sea today. 'Thirteen or fourteen days would be almost exactly the time required to reach Malta from Cauda (476.6 miles) under the conditions described.'[63] *About midnight the sailors sensed they were approaching land (prosagein tina autois chōran, 'a certain land was approaching them').*[64] Arriving at Malta, and possibly entering what is now called St. Paul's Bay from the east, they would have passed within a quarter of a mile of the point of Koura and could have heard the breakers on the shore.[65] *They took soundings and found that the water was a hundred and twenty feet (forty metres) deep.* This depth (20 fathoms) corresponds to the sounding a ship would take when passing Koura.[66] *A short time later they took soundings again and found it was ninety feet (thirty metres) deep.* Even in the dark, they could thus measure the rapid approach of land. *Fearing that we would be dashed against the rocks, they dropped four anchors from the stern and prayed for daylight.* These anchors were intended to reduce their speed. 'Casting them from the stern was an unusual procedure, but advantageous in the circumstances; for had they anchored by the bow the ship would have swung around from the wind, whereas now the prow kept pointing to the shore.'[67] When these pagan sailors *prayed for daylight,* they were asking their gods to preserve them until they could evaluate their position and decide how to rescue themselves.

62. Cf. Ptolemy, *Geography* 3.4.1; 3.15.1; 3.17.1; Hemer, *Book of Acts,* 146 note 129; Bruce 1990, 522; Barrett 1998, 1202. Against Bruce, 522, and NRSV, Barrett contends that *diapheromenōn* means 'tossed about' (TNIV *being driven*) rather than 'drifting'.

63. Bruce 1990, 522, following Smith, *Voyage,* 124-28. This distance is 767 km. Rapske, 'Travel', 36-43, responds to arguments in favour of other locations and says the evidence points best to Malta as the island where they landed.

64. This expression, which is read by Papyrus 74 A C P and the corrected version of ℵ, makes sense as 'a matter of relative motion, and it is not without precedent' (Barrett 1998, 1202). There are several variants, including *prosachein* in the original of B, which is also reflected in some Old Latin MSS. This verb could indicate that the land was 'resounding' and refer to the sound of breakers on the rocks. Bruce describes it as 'very attractive', even though poorly attested. Cf. Marshall 1980, 411 note 1. Witherington 1998, 771 note 81, concludes that it is a secondary emendation. Either reading could have given rise to the other variants and be counted as the original. The original of ℵ is *proagagein,* which Barrett, 1203, says 'might be taken to mean that land was ahead of them, but it is hard to understand why anyone should express himself in this way'.

65. Bruce 1990, 522-23, following Smith, *Voyage,* 121. Cf. Rapske, 'Travel', 36-43.

66. Bruce 1990, 523, following Smith, *Voyage,* 131-32. Smith estimates about half an hour before the next sounding of fifteen fathoms would be reached. The verb *bolisantes (they took soundings)* literally means 'they swung the lead'. Witherington 1998, 771, notes that lead weights on long cords would have hollow spots filled with grease or tallow, which would pick up debris from the bottom of the sea. The length of line would then indicate depth.

67. Bruce 1990, 523. Witherington 1998, 771, notes that 'ancient ships were very much the same shape in the bow and stern, and so nothing in their form made one end or the other more advantageous for anchoring'.

30-32 The true danger of the situation is revealed by the fact that, *in an attempt to escape from the ship, the sailors let the lifeboat down into the sea, pretending they were going to lower some anchors from the bow.* To stop the ship from being struck broadside by the waves, *anchors from the bow* could be dropped by sailors in small boat. But these men were so worried about preserving their own lives that they were prepared to abandon ship. In truth, it would probably have been suicidal to head for the shore in such conditions.[68] The centurion and the soldiers finally began to take notice of Paul when he said to them, *'Unless these men stay with the ship, you cannot be saved.'* This was practical wisdom — not a new revelation — consistent with God's promise to save all who sailed with him (v. 24). If a significant number of sailors left the ship, they would all perish. Commenting on the interplay of human activity and God's will in this context, Tannehill observes, 'human actions that work toward the rescue of all are acceptable contributions to the realization of God's purpose, but actions that seek the safety of one's own group while abandoning others will block this purpose until corrected'.[69] In this tense context, even the response of the soldiers was rash and illconsidered. When they *cut the ropes that held the lifeboat and let it fall away*, they made it impossible for everyone to get ashore in small groupings on this craft. This action ultimately contributed to the loss of the ship, since it soon became necessary to beach it.

33-34 *Just before dawn* (achri de hou hēmera ēmellen ginesthai, 'until day was about to break') *Paul urged (parekalei) them all to eat.* His calm demeanour reflected a persistent trust in the promise about their impending deliverance (v. 24).[70] He began by reminding the whole ship's company of the stress they had been under, saying, *'For the last fourteen days, you have been in constant suspense and have gone without food — you haven't eaten anything'.*[71] Then he urged (parakalō) them *'to take some food'*, arguing, *'You need it to survive'* (touto gar pros tēs hymeteras sōtērias hyparchei, 'for this is for your welfare').[72] As in v. 31, his advice is a further application of the divine promise

68. Cf. Marshall 1980, 412. Tannehill 1990, 334, responds to the scepticism of Haenchen 1971, 706, 710, about the sailors' intentions in 27:30-31. Barrett 1998, 1205, also positively evaluates Luke's record, noting that it is a description of panic. Metzger, *Textual Commentary*, 441, discusses the Western additions to v. 29.

69. Tannehill 1990, 338. Tannehill argues that 'the implied author's interest in such a narrative could arise from concern about the role of a Christian minority in Roman society. . . . The possibility of salvation in the social and political sphere depends on Christians and non-Christians being willing to follow the lead of Paul, Julius, and the sailors, when they are acting for the good of all.'

70. This is more likely to be Luke's narrative intention than the portrayal of Paul as 'a true philosopher' (Witherington 1998, 772).

71. Barrett 1998, 1176, 1207, draws attention to the strange construction *tessareskaidekatēn sēmeron hēmeran prosdokōntes*, which he translates, 'Today, you are looking to the fourteenth day'. This presumes that nights on this journey were counted before days. TNIV renders this *for the last fourteen days, you have been in constant suspense* (ESV 'Today is the fourteenth day that you have continued in suspense').

72. Spencer 1997, 233-34, is worried about 'the sudden availability of food', and sug-

previously given (v. 24), expressed now in the assurance, *'Not one of you will lose a single hair from his head'*. Paul applies a biblical maxim to the situation in which they found themselves.[73] Eating was a contribution they could all make to their own practical welfare *(sōtērias)*. Luke introduced the cognate verb in v. 19 *(sōzesthai* 'to be saved') in a narrative containing several such terms (vv. 31, 43, 44; 28:1, 4). The focus in each case is on personal safety and well-being. In the context of the divine promise, eating would be a particular expression of confidence in God's provision for their future as well as an act of self-preservation.

35-36 *After he said this, he took some bread and gave thanks to God in front of them all. Then he broke it and began to eat.*[74] Paul initiated a meal in Jewish fashion (cf. 2:42, 46; 20:7, 11), giving thanks to God *in front of them all*. Doubtless this prayer included thanks for the deliverance experienced so far and for the prospect of rescue to come. Giving thanks for food and protection in this fashion was another brief moment of public testimony to the living God, such as in his preaching to the pagans in Lystra (14:15-17) and his prophetic ministry in 27:21-26. Some have seen this 'eucharistic' action as instituting a meal with even greater significance: 'the meal shared between Paul and his shipmates constitutes them as a community under God's protection'.[75] But this was no 'Lord's Supper', as in 1 Corinthians 11:17-34; since it had no Christological focus, there was no cup of wine, and it was not a fellowship of believers.[76] Tannehill reads too much sacramental significance into the situation when he argues that Paul allows the people in the ship 'to participate in a prefiguration of the Christian Lord's Supper as preparation for later discipleship'.[77] As far as language goes, 'this is

---

gests that the ship's company may have been fasting while praying. But Gaventa 2003, 353, is closer to the mark when she proposes that the storm may have 'induced seasickness and made food preparation difficult', and that v. 20 also suggests a lack of motivation: 'those without hope have no reason to seek the sustenance of food'.

73. This could be a deliberate echo of the sayings of Jesus in Lk. 12:7; 21:18, though these were directed to persecuted disciples. But the LXX records several promises about no hair of the head being harmed (1 Sa. 14:45; 2 Sa. 14:11; 1 Ki. 1:52).

74. Some Western MSS add that 'he gave also to us' *(epididous kai hēmin)*, but this appears to be secondary and unnecessary. Cf. Metzger, *Textual Commentary*, 441-42.

75. C. T. McMahan, 'Meals as Type-Scenes in the Gospel of Luke', Ph.D diss., Southern Baptist Theological Seminary (1987), 258, cited by Tannehill 1990, 336. McMahan 260, says this meal is like the Lord's Supper in serving 'to constitute the covenant community and to anticipate the promised salvation'.

76. Cf. Marshall 1980, 413-14; Praeder, 'Sea Voyages', 699; Witherington 1998, 772-73; Gaventa 2003, 355. Bruce 1990, 525, argues that it was an ordinary meal for the majority, but 'to those with Eucharistic intention it was a valid eucharist'. However, even this interpretation goes beyond the evidence of the text.

77. Tannehill, 335. He draws parallels with Jesus' feeding the multitude (Lk. 9:16-17) — but acknowledges that Paul does not feed the ship's company — and with the Last Supper (Lk. 22:19) and the meal at Emmaus (Lk. 24:30). The common factor here is simply the action of breaking a loaf with the hands and saying grace to initiate a meal together. Cf. J. Behm, *TDNT* 3:728-30.

more "eucharistic" than any other passage in Acts', but 'these terms and allusions are all such as are rooted in ordinary Jewish practice — a meal began with the blessing of God and the breaking of bread'.[78] Paul's action was fundamentally an encouragement for this needy group of soldiers, sailors and voyagers to eat (*They were all encouraged and ate some food themselves*) and to be grateful to God in the process.

37-38 Luke then records the number of those who were involved (*altogether there were 276 of us on board*), indicating that Paul was dealing with a large company of people.[79] The first person plural (*we*) in v. 27 changes to the third person plural (*they*) in vv. 28-44, with a brief reference to *us* in v. 37 (*ēmetha*, 'we were', as in most EVV). This gives the impression that Paul's ministry of encouragement was essentially to the unbelieving soldiers and sailors who were in charge of the situation. Paul inspired them to act decisively and courageously for the benefit of all. The result was that *when they had eaten as much as they wanted, they lightened the ship by throwing the grain into the sea*. This action would have given the ship a better chance of passing over the shoals — without its cargo weighing it down — and being safely beached. Thus, 'Paul's gratitude and trust are infectious. The others take heart and eat, showing the first signs that they too believe in the promise'.[80]

c. Experiencing God's Deliverance (27:39-44)

39-41 *When daylight came, they did not recognize the land, but they saw a bay* (*kolpon de tina*, 'a certain cove') *with a sandy beach*.[81] *There they decided to run the ship aground if they could*.[82] Three actions were necessary to achieve this goal. First, they had to cut away the anchors (*Cutting loose the anchors, they left them in the sea*). Then, *at the same time*, they 'unleashed the lashings

---

78. Barrett 1998, 1208-9. Barrett critiques a range of 'eucharistic' interpretations of this passage and rightly concludes that they 'fail because they assume something like the clear developed distinction between an "ordinary" meal and a "sacramental" or "eucharistic" meal, between bread and eucharistic bread' (1210).

79. 'There is no improbability in the large number (which included the soldiers under the centurion's command): the ship on which Josephus was bound for Rome in AD 63 had about 600 on board' (Bruce 1990, 526). Cf. Josephus, *Life* 15. No symbolic significance in the number should be sought. Metzger, *Textual Commentary*, 442, discusses variations in the statement of the number in various texts.

80. Tannehill 1990, 336. Rapske, 'Travel', 32-33, considers the mention of 276 significant here. All those on board could have aided the crew in jettisoning what remained of the cargo (cf. v. 18).

81. The word *kolpos* means 'bosom' or 'bay' (cf. R. Meyer, *TDNT* 3:824-26). Bruce 1990, 526, discusses the possible location of this beach in St Paul's Bay, on the northeast coast of Malta.

82. The best-attested reading is *exōsai*, which Bruce 1990, 526-27, declares to be 'the more natural expression for running a ship ashore (as, e.g., in Thuc. *Hist.* 2.90.5)'. However, the original of Codex B and some other MSS have *eksōsai* ('to get out safely'). Metzger, *Textual Commentary*, 442, suggests that the latter arose from an error in hearing.

of the steering paddles' *(anentes tas zeuktērias tōn pēdaliōn, untied the ropes that held the rudders).*[83] Finally, to accelerate their progress, *they hoisted the foresail to the wind and made for the beach.* 'Though ultimately ill-fated, the ship was nevertheless driven to land in a readied and controlled manner.'[84] Unfortunately, they were frustrated by coming 'into a place between two seas' *(eis topon dithalasson;* cf. KJV, NKJV). Although this has been taken to refer to the narrow channel between Salmonetta Island and the mainland of Malta,[85] the word *dithalasson* can also refer to 'a feature of land that creates "two seas," that is, a sandbar (Dio Chrysostom, *Disc.* 5.9; cf. Strabo, *Geog.* 1.1.8; 2.5.22)'.[86] On this basis, TNIV fairly translates, *The ship struck a sandbar* (NRSV, ESV 'striking a reef') *and ran aground (epekeilan).* At the entrance of St. Paul's Bay, 'there is a shoal, now sunk below its level in ancient times, which could well be where the vessel ran aground'.[87] Despite the best efforts of the sailors to preserve the ship and those who sailed in it, *the bow stuck fast and would not move, and the stern was broken to pieces by the pounding of the surf.*[88] That made it necessary for all to swim to shore.

42-44 Attention now turns to *the soldiers,* who saw what was coming and *planned to kill the prisoners to prevent any of them from swimming away and escaping.* 'The soldiers, like the sailors, forget in the crisis that God's promise is for all, and they plan to save themselves by eliminating others.'[89] It is also possible that they were concerned to avoid punishment for allowing any prisoners to escape (cf. 16:27). Luke portrays the fallibility of professional sailors and soldiers in the face of danger, while Paul remains calm and trusting. 'While the soldiers had heard Paul address them on several occasions during the voyage and even followed his directions, they seem not to have been impressed by him as the centurion was.'[90] Julius wanted *to spare Paul's life (diasōsai ton Paulon,* 'to save Paul') *and kept them from carrying out their plan.* The centurion's trust in Paul and his admiration for him seem to have developed during the journey. 'Paul is a benefactor of the others on this voyage, but he is also benefited.'[91] Indeed, all the prisoners were pre-

---

83. The translation of Bruce 1990, 527, who observes that 'in ancient ships steering paddles served as rudders'.

84. Rapske, 'Travel', 34. Barrett 1998, 1212, suggests that 'the crew had given up any thought of steering the ship; the wind would drive it where they wished to go'. But Bock 2007, 741, notes that the foresail would allow them to steer.

85. So Smith, *Voyage,* 143-47, followed by Bruce 1990, 527.

86. Witherington 1998, 774. Witherington argues that the shoal called 'St Paul's Bank' would have been much more substantial than it is today. Cf. Barrett 1998, 1212-13.

87. Marshall 1980, 414.

88. The Alexandrian witnesses A and B omit the words *tōn kymatōn* ('of the waves', TNIV *of the surf*), though the longer reading is found in Papyrus 74 C P and other MSS (the corrector of a has included these words). Although it is likely that the shorter version has been expanded by copyists, it is also possible that the Alexandrian MSS deleted the extra words in the interests of brevity. Cf. Metzger, *Textual Commentary,* 442.

89. Tannehill 1990, 339.

90. Rapske, *Roman Custody,* 271.

91. Tannehill 1990, 339.

served because the centurion wished to save Paul, and so *he ordered those who could swim to jump overboard first and get to land. The rest were to get there on planks or on pieces of the ship.*[92] This part of Luke's travel narrative finishes with a further reference to salvation: *In this way everyone reached land safely (houtōs egeneto pantas diasōthēnai epi tēn gēn).* The theme is immediately picked up again in the following section (28:1, 4). As noted previously, with this word usage (vv. 20, 31, 34) Luke wants to convey the idea that God saved Paul and all who were with him from perishing, in fulfilment of the promise given in v. 24. In various ways, the whole narrative (27:1–28:16) points to God as Creator and Saviour, and to Paul as his prophet or representative.[93]

ADDITIONAL NOTE: SALVATION TEMPORAL AND ETERNAL

Tannehill argues that 'the voyage narrative presents a more comprehensive vision of God's saving work, which is not limited to those who hear and accept the gospel. The mission continues within the context of this vision.'[94] However, he moves beyond the evidence when he suggests that 'this section of Acts represents a new boldness of hope that anticipates salvation (in some sense) for every individual of a pluralistic community and views persons such as Paul as mediators of this promise'.[95] Christians may indeed bring benefit to a community that arises from, or is incidental to, the preaching of the gospel. Those who know the saving purpose of God should be seeking to express his character and will in all that they say and do. They should be encouraging unbelievers to turn to God for deliverance and help in a whole range of everyday situations. They should be seeking the peace and prosperity of the people among whom they live (cf. Je. 29:4-7), the righting of wrongs, and deeds that glorify God (cf. 1 Pet. 2:11-17). This may include deliverance from injustice or poverty, rescue from social or political structures impeding the genuine welfare of citizens, and physical or emotional healing. While such a ministry may point to the restora-

---

92. It is possible that *epi tinōn tōn apo tou ploiou* ('on some of the [things] from the ship') could mean 'on some of the [people] from the ship', meaning that some were carried on the backs of those who could swim. Cf. Haenchen 1971, 708; Bruce 1990, 528; Barrett 1998, 1215. Two groups are distinguished in the Greek *(hous men . . . hous de)*, which makes this latter interpretation a more likely option. But EVV generally translate 'on pieces of the ship'.

93. Barrett 1998, 1214, suggests that the intensive form of the verb *(diasōzein)*, which is used in 27:43, 44; 28:1, 4, may mean 'coming safely *through water*'. He also suggests that Luke may have used this form of the verb to 'distinguish rescue from shipwreck from being saved in a Christian, religious sense'. Agreeing with this, one can still argue that there is a pattern of salvation in this chapter which points readers to the gospel promise and the need to trust in God for ultimate deliverance.

94. Tannehill 1990, 337.

95. Tannehill 1990, 338.

tion of all things promised in Scripture and made possible by the death and resurrection of the Lord Jesus (cf. 3:16, 21), Luke does not imply 'a universalism that includes every creature in God's ultimate salvation'.[96] Salvation from disease, danger, or sudden death may be a means used by God to bring people to believe the gospel and receive its benefits. But salvation in temporal matters is not to be confused with or equated with the forgiveness of sins, the gift of the Holy Spirit, and eternal life, which Luke consistently shows to be the essence of the messianic deliverance.[97]

INTRODUCTION TO ACTS 28

In this final chapter, Paul is presented in a series of encounters with pagans (vv. 1-10), Christians (vv. 14-15), and Jews (vv. 17-28). To some extent these encounters are reminiscent of previous ones, thus forming a summary conclusion to Luke's portrait of Paul. The focus in the first segment (vv. 1-10) is 'not on missionary preaching but on the generally positive way Paul was being received in the pagan world, perhaps as a signal to Luke's audience that such cooperation and kindness were still possible when this document was written'.[1] Although it is possible that others from the ship were entertained along with Paul and his companions in Puteoli (v. 14), the focus in this next segment (vv. 14-15) is on the generous welcome given to Paul by Christians in Italy. They may have known of Paul only by reputation, but they were unstinting in their practical expressions of care for him. Once Luke has established the nature of Paul's confinement in Rome (v. 16), he devotes most of the rest of the chapter to the subject of Paul's ministry to Jews in the imperial capital (vv. 17-28). The pattern of response is much the same as in previous contexts, with some showing increasing interest in what he has to say, while others resist his message, leading to disagreement and division. This elicits Paul's final scriptural quotation and declaration about salvation being sent to the Gentiles (vv. 25-28). But Luke's editorial conclusion (vv. 30-31) indicates Paul's continuing openness to minister to all who came to him — Jews and Gentiles — and suggests the need for this pattern of ministry to be endorsed and pursued by the readers.

96. Tannehill 1990, 338. The promise in Luke 3:6 relates to people of every nation and kind, but within the context of Luke's total presentation of the theme of salvation, not to every individual without exception. Indeed, as Tannehill, 337, notes, 'the reference to "as many as were ordained to eternal life" in Acts 13:48 suggests that there are some who are not ordained to eternal life'.

97. Cf. THE THEOLOGY OF ACTS: IV. SALVATION (pp. 65-70) for further reflection on this topic.

1. Witherington 1998, 782. This would have been a significant message in view of the antagonism and mistreatment experienced by Paul in certain previous encounters with pagans (e.g., 16:19-24; 19:23-41).

2. From Malta to Rome (28:1-15)

The inhabitants of Malta are described as 'barbarians' (vv. 2, 4), with a superstitious approach to life (vv. 4-6), but they show unusual kindness towards the strangers from the shipwreck (v. 2). In this context, they witness
a sign of Paul's special relationship with God, though they mistakenly
identify him as a god himself (vv. 3-6). A second scene in Malta begins with
another reference to kindly treatment, expressed again by way of hospitality (v. 7). In this case it is the chief official or 'first man' of the island who
cares for them all. Paul acts in kindness to this man by healing his father,
which leads to a series of healings for the islanders more generally (vv. 8-9).
The segment ends with a reference to the many 'honours' shown to Paul
and his friends and a note about the provision for all their needs (v. 10).
'The language of benefaction pervades this entire story, and what we see is
a reciprocity relationship set up between Publius and the islanders on one
hand and Paul and his fellow travellers on the other.'[2] There is no reference
to any conversions, and the focus of the story is on 'cooperative relationships between Christians and non-Christians, to the benefit of all'.[3] However, it is hard to imagine Paul failing to preach in this place. In the final
stages of the journey to Rome (vv. 11-16), Paul is met by Christians in various places, and is notably escorted by believers from the capital on the last
stage of the journey. Luke wishes to stress the warm acceptance and support of Christians in these western regions, even though Paul has not travelled this way before.

a. Hospitality from Pagans (28:1-10)

1 The expression *once safely on shore* (*diasōthentes*, 'having been
saved') forms a deliberate verbal link with 27:44 (cf. 28:4).[4] The voyagers
were safe, but they did not know where they were (27:39) until they *found
out* (*epegnōmen*) from the local inhabitants — or 'recognized' for themselves[5]
— *that the island was called Malta (Melitē)*. There has been some debate about
whether the island in question was *Malta* (Sicula Melita), or Mljet (Melita
Illyrica) off the Dalmatian coast, but the evidence points strongly to the former location.[6] Malta is only 18 miles long (29 km.) and 8 miles wide (13 km.),

---

2. Witherington 1998, 776.

3. Tannehill 1990, 340. Tannehill observes that 'although Paul is being unjustly held
as a prisoner, the narrative undermines any tendency for Christians to regard the world in
general as hostile and evil'.

4. Barrett 1998, 1216, translates even more literally, 'having got safely through'.

5. Barrett 1998, 1219, contends that this is the most natural rendering of the verb.
However, it is hard to reconcile this with the clear statement in 27:39 that they did not recognize the land. What changed for them? NRSV and ESV have 'learned'; NKJV 'found out'.

6. The textual evidence is strongly in favour of *Malta (Melitē)*, though there are several
variants in the MSS, including *Melitēnē* in the original of Codex B and some versions. Bruce

and is situated about 58 miles (93 km.) south of Sicily and 180 miles (290 km.) northeast of Africa.

2 Luke actually calls these *islanders* 'barbarians' (vv. 2, 4, *barbaroi;* NRSV, NKJV 'natives'), since Greek was not their first language and they were uncultured from a Greco-Roman perspective (cf. Rom. 1:14; 1 Cor. 14:11; Col. 3:11). They had been colonized by the Phoenicians about 1000 BC, 'apparently from their base in Africa',[7] and so their native tongue was a Punic or Carthaginian dialect. But Malta had been a Roman island since 218 BC, and inscriptions from the first century AD reveal that Greek and Latin were also spoken by some of the inhabitants. It might have been expected that such people would be hostile to strangers, but Luke records that they *showed us unusual kindness* (*ou tēn tychousan philanthrōpian,* [litotes] 'no ordinary kindness'). Indeed, this friendly attitude recalls the treatment of Paul by the Roman centurion Julius (27:3, *philanthrōpōs;* TNIV 'in kindness'), and it is demonstrated again by Publius (28:7, *philophronōs,* 'kindly' [TNIV *generous*]). On both occasions at Malta, kindness was expressed in the form of hospitality. In the first instance, *they built a fire and welcomed (proselabonto) us all because it was raining and cold.*[8]

3 As Paul helped to build this fire and *gathered a pile of brushwood,* he was suddenly in mortal danger again, as *a viper (echidna), driven out by the heat, fastened itself on his hand.* There are no poisonous snakes in Malta today, though there may well have been in Paul's time.[9] Barrett thinks that 'Luke plainly regards this as a miracle' and that he therefore understood the word *echidna* in its proper sense.[10] But it is not at all clear that Luke shared the perspective of the locals reflected in the following verses. Vipers tend to bite and withdraw rather than fastening on victims. It therefore seems more likely that it was a snake that resembled *a viper (echidna),* but that it could cling and bite without doing harm.[11] If this is so, then Luke is using the term loosely.

1990, 530, and Metzger, *Textual Commentary,* 443, hold that the latter arose through dittography. The suggestion that the island was Mljet arose from a more narrow and later understanding of the boundaries of the Adriatic Sea (cf. 27:27 note). The issue is fully discussed by C. J. Hemer, 'Euraquilo and Melita', *JTS* n.s. 26 (1975), 100-111. Cf. Barrett 1998, 1219-20.

7. Witherington 1998, 776. The term 'barbarian' is 'onomatopoetic and seems to have originated from the sound that the Greeks thought they heard when non-Greeks (those who lived beyond or mostly untouched by the influence of Greco-Roman culture) spoke to them, namely, "bar, bar, bar" ' (Witherington, 776 n. 113).

8. Bruce 1990, 531, suggests that the variant *prosanelambanon* in the original of ℵ and some later MSS gives 'the more satisfactory sense "they refreshed us all"'. But this is not as well attested as *proselabonto (welcomed).*

9. Marshall 1980, 416, rightly observes that 'the people would not have thought the snake was poisonous if there were no poisonous snakes on the island'.

10. Barrett 1998, 1222. Bruce 1990, 532, rightly believes that Luke distances himself from the thinking of the *barbaroi* in vv. 4-6.

11. Bruce 1990, 531, suggests that it might have been either *Coronella austriaca* or *Coronella leopardinus.* Australian readers will be amused to recall that the name *echidna* is now given to their harmless spiny anteater!

4-5 *When the islanders saw the snake hanging from his hand,* they were quite convinced (*pantōs,* 'no doubt') that he was a criminal (*'This man must be a murderer'*). Theologically, they considered that divine *'Justice' (hē Dikē)* was avenging herself on Paul for his misdeeds, saying, *'for though he escaped from the sea (diasōthenta,* 'was saved from'; cf. 27:44; 28:1), *Justice has not allowed him to live'.*[12] Since a sea voyage was viewed in Hellenistic literature as 'a prime opportunity for the gods to bring retribution upon the guilty, one could argue that a safe voyage was a sign of innocence'.[13] If Paul's survival offered confusing evidence, death by snakebite would confirm that he was truly being pursued by *Justice.* However, they were surprised to see that Paul *shook the snake off into the fire and suffered no ill effects.*

6 The tenses in Luke's account are very revealing at this point — conveying the drama of the situation — as the islanders changed their minds about Paul. They were attentively 'waiting for' (*prosedokōn,* imperfect indicative; TNIV *expected*) Paul 'to begin' (*mellein,* present infinitive) *to swell up* (*pimprasthai,* present infinitive) or *suddenly fall dead* (*katapiptein aphnō nekron,* present infinitive).[14] Their theological convictions and experience of snakebite and its consequences made them very sceptical about his prospects. *But after waiting a long time* (*prosdokōntōn,* present participle) *and seeing* (*theōrountōn,* present participle) *nothing unusual happen to him, they changed their minds* (*metabalomenoi,* aorist participle) *and* 'began to say' (*elegon,* imperfect indicative) *he was a god.*[15] When Paul and Barnabas were mistaken for gods in Lystra, they reacted quite negatively, but also took the opportunity to preach about the Creator God (14:11-18). Why not here? Tannehill argues that 'the voyage to Rome is concerned not with missionary preaching but with cooperative relationships that are possible between Christianity and pagan society. In this context pagans are allowed to be pagans.'[16] But this is a superficial reading of the text. Even in the previous

12. Witherington 1998, 778-79, cites Hesiod, *Work and Days* 239, 256; Plutarch, *Mor.* 161F, to support the conclusion that *hē Dikē* was the Greek goddess of justice, the virgin daughter of Zeus. 'She kept watch over injustices on the earth and reported them to her father, who dispensed final justice. The Phoenicians also had a god or demigod called Justice (*Sydyk*), and presumably Luke is simply using the equivalent Greek term.' Cf. Barrett 1998, 1223.

13. Tannehill 1990, 341, following D. Ladouceur, 'Hellenistic Preconceptions of Shipwreck and Pollution as a Concept for Acts 27–28', *HTR* 73 (1980), 435-49.

14. Bruce 1990, 532, notes that the word translated *swell up (pimprasthai)* was the usual medical word for inflammation. The cognate *prēnēs* ('swelling') is found in 1:18. The expression *atopon (unusual)* in 28:6 could also be used to describe something fatal. Contra Bruce and Witherington 1998, 779 note 129, Barrett 1998, 1224, contends that these terms were used too widely to be regarded as strictly medical expressions.

15. Cf. Barrett 1998, 1223-24, for comments on textual variants and grammatical peculiarities in this verse.

16. Tannehill 1990, 341. Tannehill 342, repeats this conclusion in a different way: 'Paul makes no attempt to gain conversions among these friendly people, but their open attitude is encouraging for a future mission'. This is building a lot on the silence of the narrative about Paul's preaching.

chapter, Paul twice uses the situation to testify to the grace and power of
the one true God (27:21-26, 33-36). It would be inconsistent with the picture
painted there — let alone earlier in Acts — to assume that he said nothing
to honour God in Malta.[17] Given the length of stay (v. 11, *three months*), it is
inconceivable that he did not preach Christ in some way! Luke sometimes
offers brief narratives in succession to longer ones, where it is natural to assume that Paul was saying similar things to those previous recorded (e.g.,
14:1-7; 17:10-12; 19:8-10). As this travel narrative moves to its climax, the
development of friendly relationships with pagans should not be taken to
exclude the possibility of evangelism.

7 *There was an estate nearby* (*en de tois peri ton topon ekeinon hypērchen*
chōria, 'in the district around that place there was an estate')[18] *that belonged*
to Publius, the chief official of the island. The expression 'the first [man] of the
island' (*tō prōtō* [dative of possession] *tēs nēsou*) could describe the Roman
governor or a local native officer who represented the regional procurator
in the administration of the island.[19] However, it is also possible that the
description refers to the most wealthy and leading citizen of the island.[20]
Luke identifies him with the Greek equivalent of the Roman name *Publius*
(*onomati Popliō*). This man had probably received the gift of Roman citizenship because of his position or his public benefactions.[21] *He welcomed us to*
his home and showed us generous hospitality for three days (*hos anadexamenos*
hēmas treis hēmeras philophronōs exenisen, 'who received us and for three
days kindly showed hospitality'). The language is emphatic here since
exenisen means 'entertained as a guest' and the adverb *philophronōs* stresses
that he did this 'in a friendly manner' (BAGD). Some have assumed that
the first-person plural language here no longer refers to the whole ship's
company (as it does in vv. 1-2 and the previous chapter), but that it applies
to Paul and his companions alone. Nevertheless, it is possible that all were
included in this hospitality, and that after *three days*, 'the burden of housing
and feeding Julius, his soldiers and the prisoners would probably have
fallen to various members of the community'.[22]

17. Cf. Spencer 1997, 235.

18. Translation of Bruce 1990, 532. Barrett 1998, 1224, believes that the noun that
should be supplied with *en de tois* is *chōriois* (estates'), so that the meaning is 'among the estates surrounding that place were estates belonging to . . .'.

19. Cf. Barrett 1998, 1224-25.

20. Cf. Johnson 1992, 462; Witherington 1998, 779. C. J. Hemer, 'First Person Narrative
in Acts 27–28', *TynB* 36 (1985), 100, notes the use of the expression *prōtos Meliataiōn* ('first of
the Maltese') on an inscription in Malta and thinks that the context, which speaks of architectural and statuary works, may refer to someone who was '"first" to perform benefactions
of the kind listed'.

21. It was unusual for a Roman official to be referred to by his praenomen alone.
Bruce 1990, 533, suggests that 'Luke, a Greek, has little time for the technicalities of Roman
nomenclature', and compares the pattern of the Greek historian Polybius. It is also possible
that this is the way Luke heard the peasantry on the estate describe their master.

22. B. Rapske, *The Book of Acts in Its First-Century Setting*, Vol. 3: *The Book of Acts and*

8-9 The experience of such hospitality provided Paul with the opportunity to demonstrate the grace of God towards this family of unbelievers. Luke is showing how the giving and receiving of acts of kindness built bridges for the gospel with good-living pagans. Now follows a healing story that is reminiscent of the account of Jesus' ministry in Capernaum in Luke 4:38-40. In both cases, the relative of the healer's host is healed and this blessing is then extended to others. The father of Publius was *ill in bed, suffering from fever and dysentery*. The plural (*pyretois*, 'with fevers') could imply 'attacks of intermittent fever',[23] and the combination with *dysentery* (*dysenteriō*) suggests that it was 'Malta fever' — known since the nineteenth century to be caused by a microbe in goat's milk. *Paul went in to see him and, after prayer, placed his hands on him and healed him.* Prayer with the laying on of hands for healing occurs only here in Acts, though the combination is used for commissioning in 6:6; 13:3 (cf. 9:12, 17 for the laying on of hands for healing without any mention of prayer), and prayer may be assumed in 8:18-19; 19:6. Prayer is especially mentioned here to show Paul's reliance on God and perhaps to differentiate him from portrayals of 'the divine man' in popular Greco-Roman literature. The contrast with Jesus in the Gospel story is also instructive: 'Jesus does not pray to a higher power for the cure but rather rebukes the fever on the basis of his own power'.[24] *When this had happened, the rest of those on the island who were ill came and were cured.* The glorified Lord Jesus thus continued his work of healing through Paul, in far distant places.

10 When Luke says that *they honoured us in many ways (pollais timais etimēsan hēmas*, 'they honoured us with many honours'), some have taken this to refer to monetary payments, especially related to the medical context.[25] A consequence of this reading would be the conclusion that *us* more narrowly refers to Paul and his Christian companions, because they were responsible for the healings. However, Luke uses the term *timē* for 'money' quite generally in 4:34; 5:2-3; 7:16; 19:19. The close connection between these gifts and the material provisions for their journey *(and when we were ready to sail, they furnished us with the supplies we needed)* suggests a more general reference to the care shown by the islanders for the whole company of travellers.[26] Of course, the healings were a particular stimulation for the

---

Paul in Roman Custody (Grand Rapids: Eerdmans; Carlisle: Paternoster, 1994), 273. This seems to be the implication of v. 10, but Barrett 1998, 1225, takes the beneficiaries to be Paul and his companions alone in vv. 7-10, and makes no comment about how the others fared. Rapske rightly has regard for the historical evidence regarding the responsibility of the centurion and of local citizens with reference to such travellers.

23. Bruce 1990, 533, who goes on to describe the character of 'Malta fever'.
24. Witherington 1998, 780.
25. Cf. Bruce 1990, 533, noting 1 Tim. 5:17; Sir. 38:1; Cicero, *Fam.* 16.9.3.
26. Cf. Rapske, *Roman Custody*, 273. Witherington 1998, 780, follows Johnson 1992, 463, in suggesting that this is a sign that Paul shared the gospel in Malta and that these gifts were travelling funds from grateful converts. But this seems to be reading too much into the text and the use of the quite general term for money employed by Luke.

generosity of the locals in this context. Paul's healing activity brought blessing to many, including his travel companions, who were supplied by the islanders with everything they needed *(ta pros tas chreias)* for the next stage of their journey.

b. Hospitality from Christians (28:11-15)

11 *After three months we put out to sea in a ship that had wintered in the island.* Much discussion has taken place about the timing of this departure, since it appears to be too soon for safe travel. The previous vessel — the second one requisitioned by the centurion (27:6) — went to sea in the unsafe period, possibly in early October (cf. 27:9 note), and there were at least two weeks of further sailing before the shipwreck (27:27). If the third ship left Malta *three months* later, it must have been late January or early February, when the winter was hardly over. Rapske summarizes the various solutions that have been offered to account for this and points to contemporary evidence which shows the extent to which adventurous transporters were willing to go to make more money.[27] Avarice caused many to risk lives and vessels with such ventures. The vessel is described as *an Alexandrian ship*, suggesting that Julius requisitioned another grain carrier (cf. 27:4-6 note), which had failed to complete its journey to Italy because of the winter weather. This time the ship was marked *with the figurehead of the twin gods (parasēmō Dioskourois,* 'having as its figurehead the Heavenly Twins').[28] TNIV rightly adds that their names were *Castor and Pollux,* though the Greek text is not so specific. These so-called sons of Zeus were regarded as the deities responsible for ensuring the smooth sailing of ships (Epictetus, *Disc.* 2.18.29; Lucian, *Navigium* 9). 'Their constellation (Gemini) was a sign of good fortune in a storm (Horace, *Od.* 1.3.2; 3.29.64).'[29] 'Implied readers can only smirk at such a reference in the present narrative, since it has become abundantly clear that Paul's security has everything to do with the benevolence of his God and nothing to do with the whims of pagan deities, whether *Dikē* ("Justice", 28:4) or *Dioskyri* ("Twin Brothers").'[30]

---

27. B. Rapske, 'Acts, Travel, and Shipwreck', in D. W. J. Gill and C. Gempf (eds.), *The Book of Acts in Its First-Century Setting,* Vol. 2: *Graeco-Roman Setting* (Grand Rapids: Eerdmans; Carlisle: Paternoster, 1994), 24-29. As noted in connection with 27:9-10, according to Vegetius, *De Re Militari* 4.39, March 10 was the beginning of the safe sailing period. However, Witherington 1998, 781, notes that in Pliny, *Nat. Hist.* 2.47, the beginning of the sailing season was said to be when the west winds began to blow, on or about February 8. Bruce 1990, 534, says that 'in practice the state of the weather would determine the date'. Furthermore, the extra incentives offered by the Emperor might be sufficient to encourage a trading ship to sail this early.

28. The translation of Bruce 1990, 534, who notes a parallel form of dedication in an inscription from Crete, dated around AD 110. The adjective *parasēmos* means 'marked' or 'identified'.

29. Bruce 1990, 534.

30. Spencer 1997, 236.

12-13 The rest of the sea journey is recounted briefly. After a journey of about 90 nautical miles (167 km.), they *put in at Syracuse* — the chief
city of Sicily, with two harbours on the east coast — *and stayed there three
days.* From there, they *set sail (perielontes* is rendered 'cutting loose' in
27:40),[31] and — after sailing another 70 miles (130 km.) — *arrived at
Rhegium* (modern Reggio di Calabria). This was 'a Greek colony in the toe
of Italy, about six or seven miles across the strait from Messana (Messina)
in Sicily'.[32] The harbour of Rhegium was a significant destination because
of its position on the strait. *The next day (meta mian hēmeran,* 'after one day')
the south wind came up — exactly what was needed for sailing up the west
coast of Italy — *and on the following day (deuteraioi,* 'on the second day') *we
reached Puteoli.* This was good time for a journey of about 175 nautical
miles (324 km.). *Puteoli* (modern Pozzuoli in the Bay of Naples) was
'founded by Ioanians, taken by the Romans in the Second Punic War, and
made a Roman sea colony in 194 BC'.[33] People travelling to Rome often
landed there and made the rest of the journey by road (Cicero, *Pro Plancio*
26[65]; Josephus, *Ant.* 17.328; 18.248). The cargo was probably taken further to Portus, the new harbour built by Claudius at Ostia, by the mouth of
the Tiber (Seneca, *Ep. Mor.* 77.1).

14 *There we found some brothers who invited us to spend a week with them.*
'In such a seaport it is not surprising that Christians were to be found, as also
around this time at Pompei and Herculaneum.'[34] But Luke tells us nothing
about the human agents responsible for the growth of this church. Under
normal circumstances, 'responsibility for transport and billeting arrangements for the company of prisoners and military escorts would have fallen to
the centurion and it is virtually certain that he did this by means of requisi-

31. The participle *perielontes* may provide an abridgment of the full expression in
27:40 *(tas ankyras perielontes)*, meaning 'cutting loose the anchors', hence NRSV 'weighing
anchor' and TNIV *set sail.* This is the original reading of א and B and Ψ, together with some
Coptic MSS. However, uncertainty as to its meaning appears to have given rise to a number
of variants. The best attested of these *(perielthontes)* means 'sailing around' or 'tacking'
(hence KJV, NKJV, ESV). This is witnessed by Papyrus 74, the corrector of א, Codex A, some
minuscules, and the Received Text. Metzger, *Textual Commentary,* 443, notes that *perielontes*
could have arisen because of the falling out of the letter *q* from *perielthontes* in copying.
However, Metzger, Bruce 1990, 535; and Barrett 1998, 1229, feel on balance that the harder
reading *perielontes* is more likely to have been the original.

32. Bruce 1990, 535.

33. Barrett 1998, 1229. A. D. Clarke, 'Rome and Italy', in Gill and Gempf, *Graeco-
Roman Setting,* 478-81, gives further historical and geographical detail about the various
places in Italy visited by Paul on this journey.

34. Bruce 1990, 535. Witherington 1998, 784, notes that there had been a Jewish community in Puteoli for some time (cf. Josephus, *War* 2.104; *Ant.* 17.328), where travelling
Christians may have first planted the gospel. But he disputes the idea that *brothers* could refer to Jews rather than to Christians in this context. C. J. Hemer, *The Book of Acts in the Setting
of Hellenistic History,* ed. C. Gempf, WUNT 49 (Tübingen: Mohr Siebeck, 1989; repr. Winona
Lake: Eisenbrauns, 1990), 155-56, evaluates the evidence for Christians being in the wider
region at this time.

tion (Acts 27:2, 6; 28:7, 10f.)'.[35] But the offering of hospitality by a Christian community to at least some of the travellers could have been a welcome alternative to be seized upon by Julius. In vv. 14-16 the first person plural seems to refer more narrowly to Paul and his companions, but it is not inconceivable that the Christians of Puteoli took care of the whole ship's company, just as the people of Malta seemed to have done (v. 10). The Greek makes it clear that the invitation came from the *brothers* (*pareklēthēmen par' autois epimeinai*, 'we were encouraged by them to stay'), but Julius must have given his permission (as in 27:3).[36] The road out of Puteoli towards Rome was 'rough and flinty, making significant demands upon its travellers.'[37] A longer rest stop after a difficult sea voyage and before attempting the journey to Rome (about 130 miles, 209 km.) made a lot of sense for the whole party. It was in this way *(kai houtōs, and so)* that they finally *came to Rome.*[38]

15 *The brothers there had heard that we were coming, and they travelled as far as the Forum of Appius and the Three Taverns to meet us. The Forum of Appius* was a marketplace about 43 Roman miles (65 km.) south of the city on the Appian Way, and *the Three Taverns* was a collection of shops or huts about 33 Roman miles (50 km.) from the city on the same road.[39] This suggests that two separate groups of *brothers* came from Rome to meet Paul and his companions in these places and to accompany him into the city. Luke says literally that they had heard 'about our affairs' *(ta peri hēmōn)*, probably meaning that they heard from Christians in Puteoli about their arrival and projected journey to Rome (hence TNIV's *that we were coming*). Paul had written to the Roman believers about three years previously, telling them about his longing to visit them and his desire to gain their support for another stage of his missionary outreach (Rom. 1:11-15; 15:23-29).[40] But now he was coming to them under very different circumstances.

35. Rapske, 'Travel', 18. Rapske, *Roman Custody*, 272-76, deals with objections by modern commentators to Luke's narrative at this point. The expression *there we found (heurontes)* does not necessarily mean that Paul or Luke and Aristarchus actively sought out these believers and made the arrangements. The longer stop in Puteoli can be explained in terms of the arrangements that the centurion would have to make for the last stage of the journey to Rome. Cf. Witherington 1998, 786.

36. Some MSS have *epimeinantes* ('having stayed') instead of *epimeinai* ('to stay'), suggesting that Paul and his friends 'were encouraged, having stayed with them seven days'. Barrett 1998, 1230, says that 'this alleviates the difficulty of the prisoners' being invited as if they were free men', but it appears to be a secondary reading.

37. Rapske, 'Travel', 20. Rapske, *Roman Custody*, 274-76, discusses more fully the difficulties for the centurion in arranging transport and billeting on this road for his group of 'non-priority' travellers.

38. Marshall 1980, 419, translates, 'and in this way we made our journey to Rome'. Barrett 1998, 1230, and Witherington 1998, 786-87, both endorse this anticipatory understanding of *kai houtōs* (cf. 1:11; 13:34).

39. Cf. Hemer, *Book of Acts*, 156; Barrett 1998, 1231.

40. For a consideration of how Christianity was established in Rome before Paul arrived, see E. A. Judge and G. S. R. Thomas, 'The Origins of the Church at Rome: A New Solution?' *RTR* 25 (1966), 81-94; F. F. Bruce, *New Testament History* (2nd ed.; London/New

At the sight of these people Paul thanked God and was encouraged. He was doubtless thankful for every kindness shown to him by fellow believers along the way, but he was especially encouraged by this welcome. They were 'preparing him to face his final ordeal in Rome "with courage"'.[41] Even as a prisoner, he was being afforded something like his own triumphal entry into the capital! Everyone travelling with him must have been astonished by this turnout of his supporters. From a narrative perspective, Luke has revealed enough of the positive relationship between Paul and the Roman Christians to devote his last section to the subject of Paul's ministry to Jews in the city. This is Luke's focus because 'the question of Jews and Gentiles in relation to the gospel is one of the dominant themes of the book'.[42]

K. Paul's Ministry in the Imperial Capital (28:16-31)

'The final scene of a narrative is an opportunity to clarify central aspects of plot and characterization in the preceding story and to make a final, lasting impression on the readers. The fact that the narrator has chosen to end the work with a scene that focuses on Paul's encounter with Jews shows how extraordinarily important the issues of this encounter are to the narrator.'[43] The preceding narrative (27:1–28:15), with its emphasis on the friendly responses of various Gentiles to Paul and the encouragement of Christians along the way (27:3; 28:14-15), contrasts with the response of many Jews in Rome (28:24). Paul challenges this Jewish community with a significant quotation from Scripture and reminds them that God's salvation has already been sent to the Gentiles (28:25-28). Although rejected by many of his own people, restricted by imprisonment, and awaiting further trial by the Romans, Paul nevertheless welcomes all who come to him, proclaiming the kingdom of God and teaching about the Lord Jesus Christ (28:30-31). This involves continuing ministry to any Jew or Gentile who is ready to listen. There is thus both a tragic and a triumphant aspect to the ending of Acts, though the narrative can also be described as open.[44]

York: Doubleday, 1971), 279-83, 373-89. Clarke, 'Rome and Italy', 469-71, ponders the Claudian Edict mentioned in Acts 18:2 and its relevance for this subject.

    41. Spencer 1997, 236.

    42. Marshall 1980, 420. Marshall rightly opposes the view that Luke is trying to get these Roman Christians out of the way so that Paul appears like a pioneer missionary in the city.

    43. Tannehill 1990, 344. D. W. Palmer, 'Mission to Jews and to Gentiles in the Last Episode of Acts', *RTR* 52 (1993), 62, notes the number of references to the Jews, or things associated with Judaism in this passage, and agrees about its climactic and thematic importance for Luke. Against P. W. Walaskay, *'And so we came to Rome': The Political Perspective of St. Luke*, SNTSMS 49 (Cambridge: Cambridge University, 1983), the final scenes in Acts do not support the theory that Luke is essentially writing a defence of the Roman authorities for Christian readers. Luke is focussed, as Paul is, on the issue of Israel's unbelief.

    44. Although Tannehill 1990, 348, says that Acts ends on a tragic note, he later de-

Three scenes unfold, 'each opening with key disclosures of spatial, temporal and social settings'.[45] Spatially, each episode (vv. 16-22, 23-29, 30-31) occurs in Paul's private quarters, where he is under house arrest. Although this is not strictly a house church, he does conduct 'a thriving house-based mission here similar to that carried out in other cities'.[46] Temporally, the first encounter with local Jews takes place three days after his arrival (v. 17), and the second intensive day of debate (v. 23, 'on a certain day . . . from morning till evening') appears to be soon after the first. However, the time reference for the final scene (v. 30, 'for two whole years') indicates a prolonged, extensive, and less urgent approach. Engaging with the Jews of Rome as a community was clearly a priority for Paul — as in other mission contexts — but an early hardening of the heart by many was the signal for him to minister to Jews on a more individual basis. Socially, the 'contours of Paul's mission in Rome also expand progressively', as 'various audiences of increasing magnitude gather at Paul's residence, beginning with local Jewish leaders, followed by "great numbers" of Jewish people and, finally, "all" types of seekers, both Jew and Gentile'.[47] Theologically, 'the hope of Israel' is the key idea in the first scene (v. 20), 'explaining about the kingdom of God' and persuading them about Jesus 'from the Law of Moses and from the Prophets' in the second scene (v. 23), and proclaiming the kingdom of God and teaching about the Lord Jesus in the third (v. 31). These are all different ways of presenting the same gospel, particularly with reference to those from a synagogue background. 'In the heart of the global mundane empire ruled by Caesar, Paul heralds the universal messianic kingdom of God.'[48] Within this kingdom, salvation is extended to all who hear and believe the gospel about the Lord Jesus Christ.

1. Reporting to the Jewish Leaders (28:16-22)

Luke first establishes the spatial context in which the three scenes of ministry in 28:16-31 will take place. Paul continues to be a prisoner of the Roman government, closely guarded by a single soldier, but with freedom to welcome various people to his quarters for discussion and teaching (v. 16). What follows in this first scene is effectively 'a summary of the preceding

---

scribes it as open, and explores more fully what that signifies for readers (355-57). Witherington 1998, 804, suggests that it is a mixed conclusion, 'one part triumph, with the gospel being proclaimed unhindered in the capital, but also one part great tragedy, with many Jews, indeed the majority of the Jewish people and its leadership, rejecting the gospel which was intended for them first and foremost'.

45. Spencer 1997, 237.

46. Spencer 1997, 237. Spencer notes that Paul conducts this ministry as host, rather than as a guest, in the homes of others now.

47. Spencer 1997, 237-38. I have modified Spencer's headings for the three scenes in 28:16-31.

48. Spencer 1997, 238.

trial narrative and imprisonment speeches in Acts 22–26'.[49] The narrator uses Paul's address to the Jewish leaders to highlight the things he most wants readers to remember from what has gone before. Paul claims to have done nothing against the people of Israel or against their customs (28:17; cf. 24:11-15; 25:8, 10). He further claims that the Roman authorities recognized that he was innocent of any crime deserving imprisonment or death (28:18; cf. 23:29; 25:25; 26:31). When he appealed to Caesar, he had no intention of bringing an accusation against his own nation (28:19). Indeed, he claims that his mission and imprisonment are 'acts of loyalty to Israel',[50] saying 'it is because of the hope of Israel that I am bound with this chain' (28:20; cf. 23:6; 24:15, 21; 26:6-8). The Jewish leaders conclude this meeting with the acknowledgement that they have received no bad report about Paul from Judea. Nevertheless, they want to hear more of his teaching, since 'people everywhere are talking against this sect' (28:21-22).

16 Luke specifically includes himself in the narrative for the last time *(when we got to Rome)*, as he turns once more to focus on Paul and his situation. Colossians 4:10-14 and Philemon 23–24 indicate that Luke remained in Rome, as a friend and co-worker, while Paul was in prison.[51] The majority text says that *Paul was allowed to live by himself, with a soldier to guard him*. Some Western manuscripts expand this to read, 'the centurion delivered the prisoners to the captain of the guard; but Paul was allowed to live by himself . . .'.[52] This longer reading, which passed into the Byzantine or Received Text and hence to KJV and NKJV, is late, and is not sufficiently well attested to indicate that it is what Luke wrote. 'Nevertheless, it may reflect accurate information, as there is no plausible reason why a scribe would invent such an idea.'[53] Witherington notes three possible people who could be identified as 'the captain of the guard' *(stratopedarch)*, and concludes that it may have been the Praetorian Prefect, Afranius Burrus. He was officially responsible for all prisoners coming from the provinces to be tried by Caesar in the period AD 51 to 62 (cf. Pliny, *Ep.* 10.57.2). However, the Praetorian Prefect may have been 'too exalted an officer of state to take formal delivery of a prisoner like Paul'.[54] Perhaps it was rather the head administrator of the *officium* of the Praetorian guard and the subordinate of Afranius Burrus the prefect.[55] Most importantly, 'if Burrus himself, or even his immediate subordinate with his approval, had treated Paul with this

49. Tannehill 1990, 344. So also Palmer, 'Mission', 62-63.

50. Tannehill 1990, 345.

51. H. W. Tajra, *The Martyrdom of St. Paul: Historical and Judicial Contexts, Traditions and Legends*, WUNT 2, no. 67 (Tübingen: Mohr [Siebeck], 1994), 51-72, carefully examines the Captivity Epistles for further details about Paul's custody in Rome.

52. Translation of Metzger, *Textual Commentary*, 443.

53. Witherington 1998, 788.

54. Bruce 1990, 537.

55. Cf. A. N. Sherwin-White, *Roman Society and Roman Law in the New Testament* (Oxford: Clarendon, 1963), 109-12; Tajra, *Martyrdom*, 42-43; Rapske, *Roman Custody*, 174-77.

sort of leniency, it strongly suggests that Paul was not thought to be any serious threat to Rome or the committer of any heinous crime punishable by Roman law'.[56] Even the shorter reading found in NRSV, ESV, and TNIV indicates that Paul was under the most relaxed form of detention. He was not in a prison or in a military camp, but was allowed *to live by himself (menein kath' heauton)*.[57] His accommodation is later described as 'rented' (v. 30), and it is clear that inquirers or co-workers and friends could easily visit him there (vv. 17, 23, 30; cf. Phil. 2:19-30; 4:19).[58] Instead of being under the control of a centurion and troop of soldiers, he was now being guarded by a single, ordinary *soldier (stratiōtēs)*. Two was the customary number of guards for *custodia militaris (Digest* 48.3.14; cf. Acts 12:6). This duty would have been rotated in the cohort, which explains why Paul could write to the Philippians about it becoming known throughout 'the whole Praetorian Guard' that his imprisonment was for Christ (Phil. 1:13). Chained by the wrist to his guard (v. 20), Paul doubtless took the opportunity to testify about the Lord Jesus to each one. Social status may partly account for this form of house arrest but, as already noted, another rationale may be found in 'the weakness of the case against Paul as indicated in the documentation sent with him to Rome'.[59]

17-18 Only a short time after his arrival in Rome *(three days later)*, Paul *called together the local Jewish leaders (tous ontas tōn Ioudaiōn prōtous*, 'those who were first among the Jews'; cf. 25:2). He took the initiative with these leaders because he wanted to forestall any opposition or antagonism that might have followed him from other places. But it is also clear from vv. 20, 23 that he wanted to preach the gospel to the Jewish community before embarking on a wider ministry. This does not mean that Paul was the first person to bring the gospel to them. Visitors from Rome, both Jews and proselytes, were present in Jerusalem on the Day of Pentecost (2:10). It is likely that some of them, or later Jewish converts from various places in the Empire, brought the gospel to Rome at an early date (v. 22 could include Jews in the capital already 'talking against this sect', as a local phenomenon).[60] Nev-

---

56. Witherington 1998, 788.

57. Rapske, *Roman Custody*, 177, notes that the expression here 'is properly rendered "by himself", "privately", or even "in his own quarters", and can hardly be taken to designate solitary confinement'. Tajra, *Martyrdom*, 43-44, uses Roman records to describe the nature and purpose of such custody *(custodia militaris)*.

58. Some Western MSS add to the end of the verse that he lived 'outside the barracks'. Witherington 1998, 789 note 26, suggests that if Paul was living at his own expense, as v. 30 suggests, 'this likely means that he was practicing his trade, in which case he may have lived in the region of Rome where tanners and leatherworkers lived. The Praetorian Guard of course could assume duties in various places in the city.' Cf. Tajra, *Martyrdom*, 44-46.

59. Rapske, *Roman Custody*, 183. The letters sent by Festus with Paul's appeal to the Emperor would doubtless have included the judgment that he was not guilty of any significant crime under Roman law. Cf. Witherington, 1998, 790-92.

60. Tajra, *Martyrdom*, 76-77, argues that Christianity reached Rome at the end of Tiberius's reign (which extended to AD 37) through the agency of the Jewish Dispersion.

ertheless, Paul was a figure of some importance in the Christian movement, whose arrival in the city must have caused some concern to the Jewish leaders.[61] Gathering them together first, Paul was seeking a way to reach the substantial number of Jews who lived in the city. Estimates vary from twenty thousand to fifty thousand Jews in Rome at this time.[62] Inscriptional evidence suggests that there were at least eleven synagogues by AD 60, but 'no central organization oversaw the various synagogues'.[63] Even though the Jews mostly lived together, 'on the other side of the Tiber', in the area known as Trastevere (Philo, *On the Embassy to Gaius* 155-57), they must have been a difficult community to reach in any unified way. Roman sources imply that the Jews were not a particularly wealthy group in the city.[64]

As noted above, the address which follows recollects speeches of defence and associated narratives in Acts 22–26. Those earlier speeches often included a theological element, and that is the case here too, since Paul concludes his appeal with a reference to 'the hope of Israel' (v. 20). Throughout the 'legal' section of Acts, Paul has been arguing that 'the main bone of contention between himself and other Jews was theological and not political'.[65] When they had assembled, Paul addressed them as fellow Jews (*andres adelphoi*, 'my brothers', as in 2:29; 22:1) and recounted his recent history from a personal point of view (the pronoun *egō* ['I'] is used emphatically at the beginning of the address). His opponents may have questioned the claim to *'have done nothing against our people or against the customs of our ancestors'*, but

61. Since there were already Christians in Rome (28:14-15), and Paul's letter to the Romans could be identifying tensions between believers from Jewish and Gentile backgrounds (Rom. 14:1–15:13), it seems likely that Christianity had had some impact on Judaism in the capital before Paul's visit. However, the Jews were large in numbers, and the impact may have been only marginal. Paul's consistent approach in the cities and towns of the Empire was first to address the community of Jews, to win leaders and people as a religious and social entity. As indicated in the following notes, the size of the Jewish population, the diversity of synagogues, and the lack of any central organization would have made this a particularly difficult task in Rome.

62. Clarke, 'Rome and Italy', 466, follows the majority view that 'by the time of the early empire there were probably some 40,000 to 50,000 Jews resident in Rome'. Witherington, 795, however, thinks that 20,000 in the time of Nero may be a fair estimate, due to the earlier expulsion of Jews under Claudius.

63. Witherington 1998, 794. Clarke, 'Rome and Italy', 466; Rapske, *Roman Custody*, 180, cite evidence for 'at least eleven' synagogues. The lack of organization and less visible approach of the Jews in Rome may have been due to several factors. After the expulsion by Claudius in AD 49, those who drifted back to the city doubtless desired to keep a low profile. Some Romans were sympathetic to them, and some even converted to Judaism. But this made other Romans antagonistic to the Jews.

64. Cf. H. W. Tajra, *The Trial of St. Paul: A Juridical Exegesis of the Second Half of Acts*, WUNT 2, no. 35 (Tübingen: Mohr [Siebeck], 1989), 182-83. Witherington 1998, 795, concludes that 'the Jews of Rome, in light of their recent history in Rome during Claudius's reign and their general socioeconomic status, were unlikely to go after Paul even if privately many may have hoped he would be found guilty'.

65. Cf. Witherington 1998, 796. Witherington classifies this penultimate Pauline speech-summary as another example of forensic rhetoric.

the context implies 'nothing worthy of being arrested and handed over to the Romans' (cf. 24:12-21; 25:8).[66] A parallel between Paul's experience and that of Jesus is suggested by the phrase *'handed over' (paredothēn eis tas cheiras,* 'delivered into the hands), which recalls Jesus' predictions about his own arrest and trials (Lk. 9:44; 18:32; cf. 24:7).[67] Again, when Paul says, *'they examined me (anakrinantes) and wanted to release me (apolysai me), because I was not guilty of any crime deserving death',* there are links with Luke's passion narrative and the judgment of Pilate about Jesus (Lk. 23:14-16, 18). 'The echoes of Jesus' trial reinforce the portrait of Paul as a true follower of Jesus in facing the same sort of rejection and suffering, a portrait that has been clearly emerging since 21:11.'[68] Although no Roman official expresses a desire to *release* Paul, they certainly state that he is *not guilty of any crime deserving death* (23:29; 25:25; 26:31) and, on two occasions, add that he is not worthy of imprisonment (23:29; 26:31). It is reasonable to assume that such judgments made his Jewish accusers fearful that Paul would indeed be released.

19-20 Hence, *'the Jews objected'* — as they did when Pilate declared his intention to release Jesus (Lk. 23:18).[69] Thus the ultimate blame for Paul's present situation is placed on the authorities from Jerusalem, who were not prepared to treat him fairly. However, Paul simplifies the account when he says, *'so I was compelled to appeal to Caesar'.*[70] Felix actually delayed Paul's release because he hoped the Jews would offer him a bribe (24:26) and, later, because he wanted to grant a favour to the Jews (24:27). Festus, who also wanted to do the Jews a favour, proposed sending Paul back to Jerusalem for a further trial (25:9), and it was this that finally provoked Paul to appeal to Caesar (25:10-11). The account is clearly abbreviated at this point. Then

---

66. Bruce 1990, 538, observes that 'on his own testimony, he did indeed live like a law-abiding Jew when he was in Jewish company but he did not adhere to his ancestral customs when he found himself among Gentiles'. It was his practice of living and teaching among the Gentiles, allowing them to become Christians without being yoked to the Jewish law, that caused so much controversy in Jewish circles.

67. Witherington 1998, 797, acknowledges that the report here may have been influenced by the passion predications about Jesus. However, he also suggests that if we translate the text more literally ('from Jerusalem I was delivered into the hands of the Romans'), Paul is not stating who handed him over but is thinking about the transfer of jurisdiction from Jerusalem to Caesarea, 'at which point he was placed into the hands of the ultimate Roman authority in that region'. Cf. Marshall 1980, 422.

68. Tannehill 1990, 346.

69. Some Western MSS expand v. 19, adding after 'the Jews objected' the words 'and crying out, "Away with our enemy"'. At the end of the verse, an even larger group of MSS continue with the words 'but that I might deliver my soul from death'. Cf. Metzger, *Textual Commentary,* 444; Barrett 1998, 1239. However, these late and only narrowly attested readings are clearly secondary.

70. The genitive absolute construction *antilegontōn de tōn 'Ioudaiōn* ('when/because the Jews objected') describes the attendant circumstances in which Paul made his appeal to Caesar. Tannehill, 345-46, overstates the case when he argues that the desire to show parallels with the experience of Jesus has distorted the record here.

Paul introduces a novel argument, claiming, *'I certainly did not intend to bring any charge against my own people'*. This suggests that he might have pursued a countersuit against his countrymen in a Roman court of law, 'perhaps charging that his opponents were guilty of malicious prosecution'.[71] Such a move could have had serious consequences for Jews in the imperial capital and elsewhere. Concluding his argument, Paul insists that the events and behaviour he has recounted are the presenting reason *(dia tautēn oun tēn aitian, 'for this reason')* for asking to see the Jewish leaders and talking with them.[72] But there is also a more fundamental reason which he now discloses. TNIV leaves out the connective *gar* ('for'), which is important in the flow of the argument. For, Paul concludes, *'it is because of the hope of Israel that I am bound with this chain'*. He wants to expound the gospel to them and show how the resurrection hope of Israel has been fulfilled in the person and work of the Messiah Jesus (cf. 23:6; 24:15, 21; 26:6-8). Even after all the opposition he has received, he still believes that there is a hope for Israel (cf. Rom. 11:26-29) and wishes to explain that he is a prisoner because he has been seeking to proclaim the realisation of God's end-time promises to Jews in every place. As in previous defence speeches, he is thus claiming to be a faithful Jew. But more than this, he is a prophet in chains: 'the messenger who proclaims the fulfillment of Israel's hope should be honoured by Israel. Instead, Paul wears a chain because of his faithfulness to Israel's hope. This means suffering for Paul. It is an even greater tragedy for Israel.'[73]

21-22 The Jewish leaders responded to Paul's argument by first saying, *'We have not received any letters from Judea concerning you'*. Letters may not have arrived because of the difficulties of winter travel. More significantly, however, the Sanhedrin may have decided to drop the charges against Paul. Since he was a Roman citizen, 'noncitizen Jews from Jerusalem would understandably not stand a good chance of proving a case against Paul, especially in view of the recorded views of the procurators of Palestine on this subject'.[74] The Jerusalem authorities had not even at-

---

71. Rapske, *Roman Custody,* 189. Rapske continues, 'Whatever the specific charge, the statement must surely presuppose the general strength of Paul's own case and the weakness of his opponents' case, but also more specifically that Pauline countercharges were capable of proof on the strength of the facts and the witness of available Roman documents'.

72. Witherington 1998, 798, suggests that the singular form of the expression here refers back primarily to the possibility of a charge against the Jews for wrongful prosecution. Paul wanted to clear the air with the Roman Jews and make his defence to them in private. He had no intention of taking any of his own people to court! Barrett 1998, 1240, argues that the expression has a wider reference.

73. Tannehill 1990, 345. Marshall 1980, 423, adds that 'this was surely something that demanded the attention of the Jews, since their religion was legally permitted by the Romans'. If Paul was on trial for proclaiming 'the hope of Israel', that could be the beginning of further political difficulties for Jews in the Empire.

74. Witherington 1998, 799. Tajra, *Martyrdom,* 73, argues that, if the Jews from Jerusalem had pursued the case, they would doubtless have solicited 'the active help of the Roman Jewish community which enjoyed marked influence in the imperial court'. Understandably, however, they would not have wished to become entangled in such a weak case.

tempted to solicit the support of the Roman Jews in any prosecution of Paul. Moreover, the Jewish leaders affirmed, *'none of the brothers who have come from there has reported or said anything bad about you'*. Negative reports about Christianity had reached them (*'people everywhere are talking against this sect'*), though they had not yet heard any specific criticism of Paul coming from Jerusalem. Some commentators have regarded this as unlikely, considering the lapse of time since Paul's arrest in Jerusalem.[75] But there was no particular reason to send news about him until he had appealed to Caesar. He then reached the capital quite rapidly for that season of the year, making it difficult for others to arrive before him and spread negative reports.[76] The Jewish leaders therefore expressed a willingness to hear Paul's *'views'*, and placed no obstacle in the way of large numbers of their community assembling to hear more from him (v. 23).[77] As well as this theological interest, they had a concern about the social and political implications of *'this sect'* (*hairesis* is used of Sadducees in 5:17; Pharisees in 15:5; 26:5; Christians in 24:5, 14; 28:22) which had recently arisen and caused division among Jews. The claim that *people everywhere* are *talking against this sect* could certainly include Jews in Rome who had come into contact with Christians, either in the city itself or elsewhere.[78]

2. Responding to Jewish Rejection (28:23-28[29])

Something of the irony of Paul's situation — expressed so graphically with the image of being in chains for the hope of Israel (v. 20) — is carried over into this next section and is 'forcefully expressed through the quotation from Isaiah'.[79] Here we find one of the longest biblical quotations in Acts, and the only major one since 15:16-18.[80] It begins with an unusual statement about the divine authority of the prophet's message (v. 25) and offers a powerful challenge to unbelievers in Paul's audience by applying the Holy Spirit's words to their situation (vv. 26-27; cf. 7:51-53). A further challenge comes with the reminder that God has already sent his salvation to

---

75. Cf. Barrett 1998, 1241-42.

76. Cf. Bruce 1990, 539; Witherington 1998, 799.

77. Gaventa 2003, 365, rightly observes that 'here the issue is not Paul's observance or nonobservance of the law (cf. 21:28; 24:5-6), or Paul's posture towards his own people, but the gospel'.

78. This partly meets the challenge of Barrett 1998, 1242, about the possible interaction between Jews and Christians at the time when Claudius expelled the Jews from Rome. However, scholars are by no means convinced that the evidence of Suetonius points to anything more than Jewish in-fighting as the cause of the expulsion (cf. 18:2 note)

79. Tannehill 1990, 345.

80. There are twenty-five biblical quotations up to and including 15:16-18, and only two in the rest of Acts (Ex. 22:28 is cited by Paul in 23:5). Most of these are in speeches to Jewish audiences. Palmer, 'Mission', 65-66, notes that Luke has been sparing in his use of quotations since 13:47, and this gives added weight to the final citation in 28:26-27.

the Gentiles, followed by the assurance 'and they will listen' (v. 28). There is deliberate irony in the original prophecy that Paul exploits here when he indicates that Gentiles will 'hear' *(akousontai),* even if Jews will not (v. 27, *mēpote . . . akousōsin,* 'lest they hear'). There are certain parallels with Paul's experience with the Jews of Pisidian Antioch in this segment. In both narratives, the initial response is positive or neutral (13:42; 28:22), but the second encounter brings opposition and resistance (13:44-45; 28:22-24). In both contexts, there is climactically a quotation from Isaiah (13:47; 28:26-27). The first stresses the divine mandate to take the gospel to the Gentiles, and the second emphasizes 'the rejection of God's message (and messenger)'.[81] The difference between these two narrative conclusions has provoked much discussion about the particular significance of the second (cf. v. 28 note).

23-24 *They arranged to meet Paul on a certain day* — stressing their own initiative in arranging a further encounter — *and came in even larger numbers to the place where he was staying (eis tēn xenian,* 'into the guestroom', 'to the lodging').[82] Although Paul could not go to the synagogue, he could address a representative Jewish assembly *(pleiones,* 'more' than in vv. 17-22)[83] in some appropriate space in his own rented accommodation (cf. v. 30 note). Rapske considers the options available for someone staying in an apartment in one of the many tenement buildings in ancient Rome and concludes that, if an atrium existed in his building, this could have been used by Paul for larger meetings with visitors. TNIV does not adequately convey the structure of the clauses that follow. The main indicative verb *exetitheto* literally means 'he expounded' to them (so KJV, ESV; NRSV 'he explained the matter to them'), and the following two participles express the content and intention of his exposition. First, *he witnessed (diamartyromenos,* 'testifying') *to them about the kingdom of God,* thus fulfilling the prediction in 23:11. Second, *he tried to persuade* (TNIV reads the present participle *peithōn* ['persuading'] in a conative sense) *them about Jesus* (the same verb is used with connotations of successful persuasion at 17:4; 19:26; 26:28). These two themes — *the kingdom of God* and *Jesus* — are interwoven at various points throughout Acts (1:3; 8:12; 20:24-25; 28:31). As in previous encounters with Jewish audiences, Paul's argument for believing in Jesus was taken *from the Law of Moses and from the Prophets* (cf. 13:16-41; 17:2-3). By implication, it was an argument about the fulfillment of Scripture in the person and work of Jesus. The expression *from morning till evening* comes at the end of v. 23, indicating a whole day of intensive testimony and discus-

---

81. Witherington 1998, 800, following Polhill, 541.

82. In the older classical sense, *xenia* means 'hospitality', but it came to be used for a 'place of hospitality', such as a guest room or lodging. With a definite article, but without a personal pronoun, the word here most naturally picks up the place indication from v. 16. Cf. G. Stählin, *TDNT* 5:19 and note 137; Rapske, *Roman Custody,* 179-80. The terminology is similarly used in Philemon 22; Philo, *On the Life of Moses* 2.33; Josephus, *Ant.* 1.200; 5.147.

83. *Pleiones* could be taken in a comparative sense, as in TNIV, or in an elative sense, 'in considerable numbers'. Cf. Barrett 1998, 1243.

sion. Two different responses are then indicated in v. 24 (*hoi men . . . hoi de, some . . . others*; cf. 17:32). As in other contexts where Paul addressed Jewish communities, *some were convinced* (the imperfect *epeithonto* could be taken to mean that they were 'in the process of being convinced') *by what he said, but others would not believe* (the imperfect *ēpistoun* here will mean 'continued not to believe').[84]

25-26 *They disagreed among themselves* — reflecting the division between belief and unbelief described in v. 24 — *and began to leave after Paul had made this final statement.*[85] A substantial quotation from Isaiah 6:9-10 is introduced, with a strong statement about its divine inspiration.[86] *'The Holy Spirit'* is identified as the author of this scripture (cf. 1:16; 4:25), though the human agent is also named *('through Isaiah the prophet').*[87] The Spirit is said to have spoken 'well' (NRSV, ESV 'was right in saying'; TNIV *'spoke the truth'*) to the people of Isaiah's time. Use of the adverb *kalōs* ('well') suggests that what was truly spoken in the past has continuing relevance (cf. Mt. 15:7; Mk. 7:6, 9). If those to whom the Spirit spoke through the prophet were *'ancestors'* (*tous pateras hymōn*, 'your fathers') of the Roman Jews,[88] the implication is 'like fathers, like children'.[89] The rejection of Isaiah and his message in the eighth century BC was followed by the rejection of Jesus and his message (cf. the same text in Mt. 13:14-15; Mk. 4:12; Lk. 8:9-10; Jn. 12:39-40). Paul then shared with other Christian preachers in the rejection of Jesus by his own people. 'Both prophet and people are caught in a tragic situation, for the prophet is commanded to speak to a people that cannot understand, a seemingly hopeless task. Paul assumes this prophetic task.'[90]

84. Against Marshall 1980, 424, although there is no mention of baptism or explicit turning to Christ here, use of the verb *peithō* (contrasted with *apisteuō*) suggests genuine belief or persuasion on the part of some. Cf. 14:1-2 (*pisteusai* ['to believe'] is contrasted with *apeithēsantes*, which in the context means 'not persuaded'); 17:4 (where *epeisthēsan* ['were persuaded'] clearly means that they believed); 19:9 (where *ēpeithoun* means 'refused to believe').

85. The genitive absolute construction with the aorist tense *eipontos tou Paulou* ('when Paul spoke') may convey the sense that Paul spoke this way as a final challenge, as they began to depart. Cf. Palmer, 'Mission', 65 note 4. Barrett 1998, 1244, insists that the participle refers to something said before they departed.

86. Cf. note 80 above for details about the distribution of biblical citations in Acts.

87. In 1:16; 4:25; 28:25, where the human author is named in each case, Luke reflects the view about the inspiration of Scripture found in 2 Pet. 1:21, that prophets 'moved by the Holy Spirit spoke from God'. In each context, the implication is also that the Spirit continues to speak to the new situation to which the Scripture is applied.

88. The Byzantine or Received Text has *tous pateras hēmōn* ('our fathers'), hence KJV and NKJV. However, the more ancient and more widely attested reading is *tous pateras hymōn* ('your fathers'), as in most EVV. Apart from the external evidence, Metzger, *Textual Commentary*, 444, observes that 'the tone and contents of the speech, conveying censure and rejection', point to the likelihood of the latter being the original.

89. Marshall 1980, 424. Like Stephen in 7:51-53, Paul implies a long-term pattern of Jewish resistance to the ministry of the Holy Spirit through the prophets.

90. Tannehill 1990, 348. Paul's prophetic calling has been indicated in previous chapters by the application of OT texts to his situation: Ezk. 33:4 in Acts 18:6; Je. 1:7-8 in 18:9-10; Is. 42:6-7; Je. 1:7-8; Ezk. 2:1, 3 in 26:16-18.

But Isaiah was given to understand that a remnant would believe and survive the coming judgment (Is. 6:13; 10:20), and Luke's narrative suggests the same for the Jews in Rome. It is important to notice that vv. 24 and 30 frame the citation, the first indicating some positive Jewish response and the second Paul's persistence in ministry to *all* who came to him.[91] As is usual in Luke-Acts, the citation is a modified version of the LXX text. God's challenge to Isaiah is introduced with the words, '"*Go to this people and say*"' (*poreuthēti pros ton laon touton kai eipon*).[92] This is not included in any other NT citation of Isaiah 6:9, suggesting that Paul saw himself fulfilling a similar calling (cf. 9:15-16, with the accompanying warning of suffering). The ironic challenge is that the people will never understand or respond appropriately: '"*You will be ever hearing but never understanding; you will be ever seeing but never perceiving*"'. They will 'indeed hear' (*akoē akousete*, 'with hearing you will hear'), but they will 'never understand' (*ou mē synēte*); they will 'certainly see' (*blepontes blepsete*, 'seeing you will see'), but will 'never perceive' (*ou mē idēte*).[93] Isaiah taught with a simplicity and clarity that made his message relatively easy to understand and believe. But the Lord revealed to him in advance that his people would be unwilling to receive and act upon his message. Jesus and Paul similarly proclaimed a message that many of their contemporaries did not wish to receive.

27 The reason for this is revealed in the diagnosis that follows:[94] '"*for this people's heart has become calloused* (*epachynthē*, 'hardened'); *they hardly hear with their ears* (*tois ōsin bareōs ēkousan*), *and they have closed their eyes*"' (*tous ophthalmous autōn ekammysan*). Paul's gospel did not deafen or blind people to the truth: 'it is because the people have grown obtuse that

91. Witherington 1998, 803, observes that 'the citation must be interpreted in light of the forensic context, which involves the rhetoric not only of defense but here also of attack due to the rejection of the gospel'. But before and after the quotation there are indications that some Jews remained open to persuasion. This is a more nuanced approach than that of Pao, which is critiqued in note 98 below.

92. This is slightly different from LXX, which has *poreuthēti kai eipon tō laō toutō* ('Go and say to this people'). The modification in Acts 28:26 appears to be influenced by the wording in Is. 6:8. Against Palmer, 'Mission', 66, this modification does not appear to give 'a more missionary tone to the command'. Rather, it emphasizes that the people to be addressed are God's people, Israel and not the nations.

93. In the Hebrew of Is. 6:9, there are two commands (*šimʿû šāmôaʿ wᵉʾal-tābînû ûrᵉʾû rāʾô wᵉʾal-tēḏāʿû*), translated in EVV, 'keep on hearing, but do not understand; keep on seeing, but do not perceive'. In the LXX, there are two future indicatives, with a cognate dative (*akoē*) and cognate participle (*blepontes*) used to represent the intensification of the Hebrew infinitive absolute, followed by two emphatic negative futures (the strongest form of denial possible). The Hebrew presents a harsher rhetorical form, but both versions blame Israel for the estrangement from God. Cf. Barrett 1998, 1245; D. Pao, *Acts and the Isaianic New Exodus*, WUNT 2, no. 130 (Tübingen: Mohr [Siebeck], 2000; repr. Grand Rapids: Baker Academic, 2000), 102-3.

94. The connective *gar* ('for') in Is. 6:10 LXX makes it clear that the prophet is proceeding to explain the reason for the predicted lack of response to his message. The Hebrew text continues in a more taunting mode, with a series of imperatives implying that the prophet is instrumental in causing or furthering this hardness by continuing to preach.

they do not perceive in the message about Jesus the realization of their own most authentic "hope".[95] Humility and repentance were required — in Isaiah's time, in Jesus' time, and in Paul's — involving a radical reorienting of thinking and behaviour towards God. The ironical conclusion to the oracle assumes that this will not happen. It is expressed in a negative purpose clause: '"*otherwise* (*mēpote*, 'lest', with four of the following verbs in the subjunctive) *they might see with their eyes, hear with their ears, understand with their hearts and turn*"'. In this form of rhetoric, although God's desire is that they might see, hear, understand, and turn, it is expressed negatively as a mocking challenge. It is like trying to persuade people to action by saying, 'You would never do that, would you!' The climactic statement is then unexpectedly in the future indicative (*kai iasomai autous*, 'and I shall heal them', '"*and I would heal them*"'). A change in the mood of the verb appears to highlight the hope of salvation,[96] which is here expressed in terms of divine healing for those who understand with their hearts and turn. Although some have argued otherwise, this Scripture is not used to write off the possibility of further ministry to Jews, either in Paul's time or subsequently.[97] This final statement about Jewish lack of response to the gospel is certainly pessimistic, and in marked contrast with the jubilant expectations in the early chapters of Luke's Gospel (e.g., 2:30-32; 3:4-6). But even there, intimations of division in Israel and rejection of the Messiah are found (Lk. 2:34-35).[98] Tannehill observes that, 'although the Jewish community, operating as a social entity controlled by its leadership, is blind and deaf, there are still those within it who are open to the Christian message. This openness appears through the text's description of the Jewish reaction as less completely negative than we might expect.'[99] However, if Paul was seeking a recognition by the Jewish community as a whole that Jesus is the fulfillment of the Jewish hope, 'the presence of significant opposition shows that this is not going to happen. Previous scenes have shown that the opposition of some can make preaching to the Jewish assembly impossible. Paul's closing statement in 28:25-28 is a response to this hard fact.'[100]

95. Johnson 1992, 476. Against Barrett 1998, 1245, who says that 'the built-in failure of the message is the content of it'.

96. It is true that the future indicative is sometimes used in Hellenistic Greek as an alternative for the subjunctive, but the change in this sequence of verbs appears to be rhetorically significant, and not merely stylistic. Witherington 1998, 804-5, wants to translate *mēpote* as 'perhaps', to give a more hopeful sense. But this does not fit so well with the mocking challenge of the oracle.

97. Cf. note 105 below.

98. Pao, *New Exodus*, 105-9, speaks of 'a dramatic reversal of the original Isaianic scheme': judgment-salvation has become salvation-judgment in Luke-Acts. But this is a simplistic reading of Isaiah and Luke-Acts. In each of these books there is an intermingling of teaching about salvation and judgment, not a simple progression of ideas in one direction or another.

99. Tannehill 1990, 347.

100. Tannehill 1990, 347.

28   Paul's prophetic challenge concludes with a statement and a promise: *'Therefore I want you to know that God's salvation has been sent to the Gentiles, and they will listen!'* As in 2:14; 4:10; 13:38, the expression *gnōston estō* ('let it be known', *I want you to know*) introduces an important declaration or revelation. The statement employs the aorist tense, used perfectively *(apestalē)*: God's salvation *has been sent.*[101] Although Paul told Jews and God-fearers in Pisidian Antioch, 'it is to us that this message of salvation has been sent' (13:26, *exapestalē*), the subsequent narrative showed a remarkable extension of this salvation *to the Gentiles,* in accordance with God's ancient promise (cf. 13:46-47). Preaching to Jews continued wherever possible, but Paul took the message to Gentiles whenever Jews rejected it and made it impossible for him to preach in their synagogues.[102] Paul here proclaims the sending of salvation to the Gentiles as an accomplished, historical fact. The attached promise is expressed emphatically *(autoi kai akousontai):* 'they indeed will hear'.[103] This contrasts with Israel's failure to hear (the same verb is used three times in vv. 26-27) with understanding. Mission to Gentiles is presented both as a past fact and as 'a future success'.[104] Even as many Gentiles have already heard and believed (e.g., 13:48; 19:10), in the same way, many will continue to respond. Paul is not specifically warning the Jews about divine judgment for rejecting the message (as in 13:40-41), but about continuing in hard-hearted unbelief and missing out on the salvation or 'healing' promised by God. The effect, however, is the same, for to miss out on God's salvation is to perish under his judgment. Again, Paul's aim here is not to justify the Gentile mission, or to make a final and categorical declaration about turning from ministry to Jews.[105] He

101. The Greek actually reads *touto to sōtērion tou theou* ('this salvation of God', NRSV, ESV), with the demonstrative *touto* ('this') presumably alluding to the prospect of divine healing for Israel at the end of the citation in 28:27. Marshall 1980, 425, fails to notice the perfective use of the aorist here and says that 'the message of salvation is now going to the Gentiles' (emphasis removed).

102. Pao, *New Exodus,* rightly argues from 13:46; 18:6; 28:28 that 'one cannot deny that a connection between the response of the Jews and the mission to the Gentiles is present in the narrative of Acts'. This represents 'a surprising move beyond the Isaianic vision', in which Israel is restored and then the Gentiles are saved. But the pattern of reaching out to Jews first and then going to Gentiles and any Jews who will listen continues in Paul's Roman ministry, and the text gives us no indication that the pattern should cease.

103. The personal pronoun *autoi* ('they') is in the emphatic position, followed by the conjunction *kai* used adverbially ('indeed'), and the verb is in the future tense. K. Litwak, 'One or Two Views of Judaism: Paul in Acts 28 and Romans 11 on Jewish Unbelief', *TynB* 57 (2006), 237-38, argues that Luke's normal pattern of using adverbial *kai* puts the emphasis on the verb rather than on the preceding pronoun, giving the sense, 'they also will *hear*'. But he ignores the implied contrast with v. 27, and the implication that Israel collectively will not hear, but Gentiles will hear and understand and be saved. There is more to this contrast than simply 'to the Jews first and then to the Gentiles'.

104. Palmer, 'Mission', 71.

105. Some have noted the sequence of rejection by Jews and turning to Gentiles in 13:46; 18:6, and have concluded that 28:28 signals a final and absolute turning in this way. Cf. J. T. Sanders, *The Jews in Luke-Acts* (London, SCM, 1987), 388-89; J. B. Tyson (ed.), *Luke-*

does not say 'we now turn to the Gentiles', as in 13:46, but talks about the past action of God as the basis for believing that many Gentiles will continue to be converted. 'What is contrasted is not the missions (to Jews or Gentiles) but the different audiences' responses to the one mission.'[106] As in Romans 10:19-21; 11:11-14, Paul is seeking to make the Jews jealous and provoke them to find in Jesus the hope of Israel fulfilled (28:20).[107] His final words recall Simeon's paraphrase of Isaiah's promises in Luke 2:30-32 ('my eyes have seen your salvation, which you have prepared in the sight of all nations: a light to lighten the Gentiles, and the glory of your people Israel'). They also recall John the Baptist's use of Isaiah's words in Luke 3:6 ('all people will see God's salvation').[108] Both Gospel texts speak about Jews and Gentiles seeing the salvation of God. But the Jews of Rome have failed to see — because they have closed their eyes — and to hear — because they have closed their ears — and their hearts are hardened. The chief emphasis at this point is on 'the unsolved problem of Jewish rejection',[109] though the reception of the gospel by Gentiles is clearly expected to continue.

[29] Readers of KJV and NKJV will discover an extra verse, which is not replicated in other English translations: 'And when he had said these words, the Jews departed, and had great reasoning among themselves'. Certain Western texts (represented by 383 614, some Old Latin, Vulgate, and Syriac MSS) added these words, which were then adopted by the Byzantine text. However, this reading is late and not widely attested, being absent from the earliest Greek manuscripts and some of the versions. It clearly represents what must have taken place, especially in view of the di-

---

Acts and the Jewish People: Eight Critical Perspectives (Minneapolis: Augsburg, 1988), 102-23. Palmer, 'Mission', 67-68, argues against this. Marshall 1980, 421, believes that the final picture which is presented to the reader is of Paul's last appeal to the Jews and his acceptance of a call to the Gentiles. But this is a misreading of the text in its context. When Marshall concludes that in principle the church is 'free to ignore the Jews, at least for the time being (Lk. 21:24), and go to the Gentiles', he is missing the point of 28:30-31.

106. Larkin 1995, 391. Witherington 1998, 806, agrees and adds that 'this salvation' is the one promised to Jews and Gentiles at the beginning of Luke's Gospel. The idea of one mission, to the Jew first but also to Gentiles, is also made plain in many ways throughout Luke's work, and this is not abandoned at the end. Cf. Bock 2007, 756-57.

107. Cf. Tannehill 1990, 348; Palmer, 'Mission', 71; Litwak, 'Judaism', 240-41. Litwak goes on to compare Paul's teaching in Romans 11 about his ministry to Gentiles provoking unbelieving Jews to emulate Gentile believers in Jesus.

108. Apart from Eph. 6:17, the rare neuter form of the noun *salvation (to sōtērion)* is found in the NT only in Lk. 2:30; 3:6; Acts 28:28. This suggests a deliberate literary and theological echo of the earlier texts by Luke. Tannehill 1990, 349-50, notes that there are also intimations of rejection in Lk. 2:34, which are picked up in Acts 4:14; 13:45; 28:19, 22, with the use of the same verb (*antilegō*, 'speak against').

109. Tannehill 1990, 349. Tannehill 353, concludes that Acts offers no solution to the problem of Jewish unbelief, 'except the patient and persistent preaching of the gospel in hope that the situation will change'. He goes on to develop more parallels between the ending of Acts and the beginning, and shows how 'multiple connections with key aspects of the earlier story bring the narrative to appropriate closure through circularity and parallelism' (355).

vision and disagreement noted in vv. 24-25, but it is unlikely to be what Luke wrote. 'The addition was probably made because of the abrupt transition from ver. 28 to ver. 30.'[110]

3. Welcoming All with the Gospel (28:30-31)

A piling up of familiar terms signals both a continuation of previous patterns of ministry for Paul and a clear narrative closure. Elsewhere, his turning to the Gentiles did not mean a total abandonment of ministry to Jews. Once rejected by the synagogue, he continued to encounter Jews on an individual basis, in various ways (cf. 13:46-52; 18:7-8; 19:8-10). The following verses suggest that the same thing happened in Rome. Luke emphasizes that he welcomed *all* who came to see him (v. 30), recalling the promises of salvation for Israel and the Gentiles in the early chapters of his Gospel. Paul's gospel message is once more described in a way that would make it particularly relevant to Jews or God-fearers, with whom he could speak directly about an expectation of the kingdom of God and Jesus as the promised Messiah (v. 31; cf. v. 23). Here there are important verbal links with the teaching of Jesus and Peter at the beginning of Acts, and with Paul's earlier pattern of preaching to Jewish audiences. There were different ways in which Paul sought to persuade Gentiles who had not come under the influence of biblical teaching (cf. 14:15-17; 17:22-31; 24:24-25), though the aim was ultimately to bring them also to an understanding of Jesus' resurrection and heavenly rule. If the ending of Acts implies an ongoing Pauline ministry to both Jews and Gentiles, the challenge for Christian readers is to consider how that pattern might be followed in their own situation and time.[111]

30 *For two whole years Paul stayed there in his own rented house and welcomed all who came to see him.* The period in view is probably from about AD 60 to 62. A full period of twenty-four months is implied by the expression *dietian holēn* (*two whole years*). A similar period (*dietias*, 'two years') is mentioned in 24:27, in connection with his imprisonment in Caesarea under Felix. The whole period of his captivity was thus more than four years. The expression translated *in his own rented house* (*en idiō misthōmati*) is rendered by some 'on his own earnings', 'at his own expense' (NRSV, ESV), putting the focus on Paul's personal responsibility for the cost of accommodation.[112] But it is also possible that the reference is to the type of dwelling (TNIV, KJV,

---

110. Metzger, *Textual Commentary*, 444.

111. Contrast Marshall 1980, 421, who holds that the message of 28:28-31 is that the church is 'free to ignore the Jews, at least for the time being (Lk. 21:24), and go to the Gentiles'.

112. Cf. Bruce 1990, 542. After an extensive survey, D. L. Mealand, 'The Close of Acts and Its Hellenistic Greek Vocabulary', *NTS* 36 (1990), 584-87, concludes that it is a technical legal term for expense in paying rent.

NKJV). Although there is no clear precedent for using the word *misthōma* in the latter sense, the usual terms for house or dwelling would not be sufficient to indicate rental status.[113] Only the privileged and aristocratic few could afford to purchase or rent private houses, and so it is likely that Paul lived in a room or rooms in one of the many thousands of tenement buildings in Rome.[114] If Paul's house arrest continued only *for two whole* years, what happened after that? It is likely that his accusers never appeared and so the charges against him were dropped. Although there was no formal statute of limitations, after which a charge would automatically be dismissed, Roman law acknowledged that if an accuser has 'given up when an appeal has been lodged, he will be indulgently regarded as not having carried through his accusation' (*Digest* 38.14.8).[115] Furthermore, 'the *imperium* of the emperor was such that he could choose to show clemency and dismiss various cases, especially when the charges were not being actively pursued'.[116] Early Christian tradition indicates that Paul was released and had another period of public ministry — reaching 'the limits of the West' (*1 Clem.* 5:5-7) — before being re-arrested and condemned to death by decapitation.[117] In the fourth century AD, the historian Eusebius (*Hist. Eccl.* 2.22.1-7) summarized the tradition and wrote that 'after defending himself the Apostle was again sent on the ministry of preaching, and coming a second time to the same city suffered martyrdom under Nero'. This implies some sort of trial in about AD 62, but then release, presumably because of lack of evidence or a failure of the prosecutors to appear. Eusebius went on to insist that 'Paul's martyrdom was not accomplished during the sojourn in Rome which Luke describes'. Although the patristic tradition mostly locates Paul's martyrdom in the last year of Nero's reign (AD 68), Tajra convincingly argues that 'Paul's re-arrest, trial, condemnation and martyrdom are more likely than not to have occurred before the great fire of 64 A.D.'[118]

113. Cf. Rapske, *Roman Custody*, 178-79, followed by Witherington 1998, 813. Thus, vv. 16, 23, and 30 will all be speaking about Paul's accommodation in different ways.

114. Rapske, *Roman Custody*, 228. Rapske goes on to describe what this accommodation may have provided.

115. Cf. S. G. Wilson, *The Gentiles and the Gentile Mission in Luke-Acts*, SNTSMS 23 (Cambridge: Cambridge University, 1973), 233-38; Hemer, *Book of Acts*, 383-87, 398; Barrett 1998, 1251-52, for further reflections on what this time reference may signify.

116. Witherington 1998, 792. Witherington, 790-92, includes the evidence of 28:19, 21 in his argument that Paul was released after two years. Tajra, *Martyrdom*, 12-15, describes the nature of the Emperor's *imperium* and how it was exercised by Nero.

117. Tajra, *Martyrdom*, 118-97, extensively examines the subject of Paul's martyrdom in Christian apocryphal and patristic literature. Tajra 108-17, concedes that the phrase 'the limits of the West' could refer to Italy, but goes on to argue from the tradition that it means Spain.

118. Tajra, *Martyrdom*, 31. Tajra thinks that the later date became part of Christian tradition for theological reasons, 'designed to put Paul's martyrdom in a close relationship with the *coup d'état* which overthrew Nero: that ruler's fall from power and subsequent death being considered as divine punishment for his ordering the killing of the two Apostles Peter and Paul'.

Paul's message is summarized for the last time in distinctly Jewish terms (v. 31, *he proclaimed the kingdom of God and taught about the Lord Jesus Christ*). These themes were also highlighted in Luke's earlier description of the ministry to Jews in Rome (v. 23). This suggests that Jews were among those who came to see Paul in v. 30, and that he did not adapt his message for a purely Gentile audience after the rejection portrayed in vv. 24-27. The scope of *all* should not be restricted to either Jews or Gentiles, but should be seen as deliberately universal at this point in the narrative.[119] It recalls the prophecies in Luke 2:30-32; 3:6, which predict that the messianic salvation will be enjoyed by Jews and Gentiles together, and suggests a fulfillment of those expectations. Moreover, although Rome was hardly 'the ends of the earth' (1:8, alluding to Is. 49:6), Paul's ministry in the imperial capital is certainly portrayed as a significant step in the advancement of the apostolic witness to dispersed Israel and the nations.

31 No distinction should be made here between preaching (*kēryssōn*) and teaching (*didaskōn*), since *the kingdom of God* and the messiahship of Jesus are not two separate agendas but one (cf. v. 23 note). Luke is employing a form of parallelism to make this clear. Paul's concern was to proclaim 'the realization of God's reign through the enthronement of Jesus at God's right hand as royal Messiah'.[120] Consistently throughout Acts, evangelism has been shown to involve an announcement of gospel claims, arguments from Scripture, and persuasion to repent and believe — preaching, teaching, and exhorting constituting a single act of communication. In Paul's preaching, there is an echo of Peter's message in 2:36, that the ascended Jesus is 'both Lord and Christ'. Furthermore, *the kingdom of God* has been mentioned at key points throughout Acts (1:3; 8:12; 14:22; 19:8; 20:25; 28:23) as a shorthand way of describing God's rule over sin, death, and everything that hinders his saving purpose for humanity. A significant inclusion is therefore formed between the beginning and end of Acts by the use of these terms. There are clearly also links back to Paul's preaching about the messiahship of Jesus in Acts 13. 'At the end of Acts Paul is presented as faithfully continuing the message that he and Peter preached to the Jews in the major sermons near the beginning of the narratives about their ministries.'[121] However, the issue is not simply the restoration of 'the kingdom to Israel' (1:6) through the raising of the Messiah. Paul proclaims 'a message of universalism that rivals the claims of the emperor, not endorses or builds upon the latter's claims. The kingdom of Jesus is not seen as a subset of the Roman Empire that fits nicely and quietly into that Empire without requiring any fundamental transvalu-

---

119. Against Palmer, 'Mission', 71, Gentiles should not be excluded from this number. Against Marshall 1980, 425, 427, Jews should not be excluded from Paul's audience. Gaventa 2003, 370, rightly concludes that 'if the speech of chapter 26 is climactic, then its insistence on Jesus as proclaimer of light for all people is not negated by this troubling conclusion'.

120. Tannehill 1990, 352.
121. Tannehill 1990, 352.

ation of values.'[122] There have been indications of this at various points throughout Acts. Readers are meant to contemplate the religious, social, and political consequences of the gospel message for citizens of the imperial capital. The expression *with all boldness (meta pasēs parrēsias,* 'with all freedom of speech') recalls previous use of such terminology for open gospel communication (2:29; 4:13, 29, 31; 9:27-28; 13:46; 14:3; 18:26; 19:8; 26:26).[123] It suggests the inward enabling of the Spirit to speak the truth, whatever the outward opposition or physical circumstances. *Without hindrance (akōlytōs)* is a legal term, indicating that there were no official impediments or restraints to this preaching and teaching, despite the house arrest.[124] In this way, Paul remained faithful to his calling, which was to bear witness to both Jews and Gentiles (9:15; 22:15; 26:16-18, 23), and, by implication, he completed the task given to him by the Lord Jesus (20:21-24).

Epilogue

In one respect, this is a surprising conclusion to Luke's second volume. Pious scribes in earlier centuries added extra words to some manuscripts.[125] Pious commentators have been discussing possible sequels or reasons for the incompleteness of Luke's narrative ever since![126] There are two related issues to consider: what might have happened to Paul when the two years of house arrest were concluded, and why did Luke end his narrative as he did? From a narrative point of view, the second is easier to answer than the first. 'If Acts is biography, it would seem clearly to be an unfinished work, for the audience is left suspended in midair, waiting to hear about the fate of the hero of the last half of the book.'[127] Witherington rightly argues that 'it makes much better sense if Acts is some sort of historical work, meant to chronicle not the life and death of Paul but the rise and spread of the gospel and of the social and religious movement to which the gospel gave birth'.[128]

122. Witherington 1998, 812.

123. Tajra, *Martyrdom*, 48-50, outlines the juridical, political, and spiritual implications of this expression.

124. Cf. Bruce 1990, 543; Barrett 1998, 1253. R. Cassidy, *Society and Politics in the Acts of the Apostles* (Maryknoll: Orbis, 1987), 134 note 37, links the expression *without hindrance* to the preceding one *(with all boldness)* and takes it as a further indication of his attitude ('unhindered in spirit, undaunted'), but this neglects the evidence for *akōlytōs* being constantly used in legal documents with reference to outward hindrance or impediment. Cf. Rapske, *Roman Custody*, 182.

125. Some Latin and Syriac texts added the words 'that this is Jesus the Son of God, through whom the whole world is to be judged'. Several Greek witnesses conclude the book with 'Amen', indicating a liturgical use of the text. Cf. Metzger, *Textual Commentary*, 445.

126. Barrett 1998, 1249-50, outlines several approaches with objections. Cf. Wilson, *Gentiles*, 233-36; Bock 2007, 757-60.

127. Witherington 1998, 808.

128. Witherington 1998, 809. Witherington goes on to draw an interesting parallel with the open ending of 2 Kings.

This is the focus of Acts 28, and it is consistent with various editorial indicators throughout the book concerning the growth of the word (6:7; 12:24; 19:20) and the expansion of the church through the preaching of the gospel (9:31; 16:5; 19:8-10). Acts 28:31 is effectively the summary conclusion to the final panel of the narrative which began at 19:21 (cf. INTRODUCTION TO ACTS: IV.B. Structure, pp. 32-36). Acts gives priority to the progress of the word, though there is clearly also interest in the human characters who are the 'servants of the word' (Lk. 1:2). Johnson is therefore right to conclude that 'what Luke was defending he has successfully concluded: God's fidelity to his people and to his own word'.[129] In the narrative of Acts, Peter, Paul, Stephen, and Philip have their own unique function in salvation history, but in certain ways they also function as models of faithful discipleship for others. Many others are involved in the growth of the word as divine agents. Some, such as Barnabas, Silas, and Mark, are named; others are not (e.g., 8:4; 11:19-21). By implication, the conclusion of Acts challenges readers to consider how they themselves will continue the story of the gospel's progress.[130] Acts 27–28 therefore have a theological and pastoral agenda. They highlight again the importance of persisting in ministry to Gentiles and Jews — whatever the indifference or hostility — using the variety of approaches that Luke has illustrated. They suggest that the ascended Lord is still working through his Spirit to empower his gospel agents to proclaim and teach *with all boldness* and — as the situation permits — *without hindrance.* 'Preachers may be persecuted, imprisoned, even killed, but the word of God is not bound.'[131]

For all that, we may still ask whether there are sufficient indications in the text of Acts to make any conclusions about Paul's subsequent history. A trial before Caesar was clearly predicted in 27:24, and it seems reasonable to suggest that this finally took place. Otherwise, we must conclude that Luke recorded a divine promise which was not fulfilled.[132] Tannehill also argues that we should assume such a trial 'because the major obstacles of the threatened return to Jerusalem (25:3, 9) and the storm at sea have been

---

129. Johnson 1992, 476.

130. Tannehill 1990, 356, rightly concludes that 'the ending of Acts invites retrospective consideration of the preceding narrative in light of the factors just mentioned'. In other words, 28:30-31, following on from vv. 25-28, provide a hermeneutical key for interpreting chapters 27–28 as a whole. Gaventa 2003, 370, says that 'the sense that the story is not finished summons readers to supply the ending themselves'. Cf. B. S. Rosner, 'The Progress of the Word', in I. H. Marshall and D. Peterson (eds.), *Witness to the Gospel: The Theology of Acts* (Grand Rapids/Cambridge: Eerdmans, 1998), 229-33.

131. Barrett 1998, 1246.

132. This would be out of character with the extensive use of the promise-fulfilment motif in Luke-Acts, as articulated in D. G. Peterson, 'The Motif of Fulfilment and the Purpose of Luke-Acts', in B. W. Winter and A. D. Clarke (eds.), *The Book of Acts in Its First-Century Setting*, Vol. 1: *Ancient Literary Setting* (Grand Rapids: Eerdmans; Carlisle: Paternoster 1993), 83-104. Rapske, *Roman Custody*, 191, and Witherington 1998, 788-93, consider the possibility that Paul never faced trial or conviction.

overcome and no further obstacles are apparent'.[133] He further suggests that previous narratives provide the basis for anticipating the outcome of Paul's trial: 'we have noted the inclination of high Roman officials to follow political expediency rather than the requirement of justice'.[134] Paul's death may also be foreshadowed in his farewell speech to the Ephesian elders (20:24-25, 37-38). Tannehill finally proposes that 'something happened after the two years mentioned in 28:30; it was probably not release and continued work'.[135] However, if there is any truth in the evidence of early Christian tradition (noted in connection with v. 30), the trial that finally condemned Paul to death came later. There could have been an appearance in Caesar's court after the period of house arrest, releasing him for ministry on a wider scale. Tannehill's helpful attempt to find indicators in the text of Acts about the final outcome for Paul need not be set against the patristic tradition.

133. Tannehill 1990, 355. He also adds that we have a good idea of Paul's conduct at this trial from his past conduct during trials.
134. Tannehill 1990, 355.
135. Tannehill 1990, 356.

Index of Subjects

Aaron, 259
Abraham, 247-50
Achaia, 526-27, 543, 552-57
Achan, 209
Acts: ancient literary models, 8-13; authorship, 1-4; and biblical histories, 13-15; as biography, 11-12; conclusion, 720-25; date, 4-5; editorial techniques, 42-49; genre, 5-15; as historical monograph, 8-10; as historical novel, 13; historicity, 23-25; literary approaches to, 39-42; and the Pauline letters, 18-19; purpose, 36-39; sources, 16-19; structure, 32-36; textual matters, 49-52; as theological history, 26-27; unity of Luke and, 6-8. *See also* Fulfillment; Rhetoric; Speeches; 'We' sections
Adramyttium, 682
Adriatic Sea, 690-91
Aeneas, 319-21
Agabus, 17, 357-58, 580-82
Agrippa. *See* Herod Agrippa I; Herod Agrippa II
Alexander (Ephesian Jew), 548-50
Alexandria, Alexandrians, 239, 525
Amphipolis, 477
Ananias (of Damascus), 306-11, 600-603
Ananias (high priest), 613-15, 630
Ananias and Sapphira, 207-13
Angel(s): appears to Cornelius, 327-28, 345; appears to Paul at sea, 689-90; at the ascension, 115-16; directs Philip, 292-93; face of, 243; and the giving of the law, 258, 265; Peter's, 365-66; Pharisees and, 618; rescues apostles

from prison, 218-19, 364-65; strikes down Herod, 369-70
Annas (high priest), 189
Antioch (in Syria), 234, 350-59, 416-17, 419-22, 440-42, 446-49, 521-22
Antioch (in Pisidia), 383-400, 411, 413
Antipatris, 625
Antonia Fortress, 590-91, 607, 621-22, 625
Apollonia, 477
Apollos, 523-27, 528
Apostles: arrested, 188-96, 216-28; commissioned by Jesus, 103-13; commissioning the Seven, 235; devoted to prayer and ministry of the word, 232-34; and elders in Jerusalem, 422-24, 436-37, 452; escape from prison, 218-19; leadership, 185-203; names, 117; Paul and Barnabas as, 404-5, 408-9; as prophetic successors of Jesus, 170, 186; replacing Judas, 119-29; succession, 126, 235; teaching, 160, 185-96, 219-20, 228; testifying to the resurrection, 205; visiting Samaria, 285-90; as witnesses, 104-5, 196
Apostolic Decree. *See* Idolatry; Jerusalem Council
Aquila, 507-10, 519-27
Arabia, 312, 314-15
Aramaic, 593, 665
Areopagus. *See* Paul, at the Areopagus
Aretas, 314-15
Aristarchus, 547, 550, 682
Artemis, 529, 543-51
Ascension. *See* Jesus: ascension

Index of Authors

Index of Scripture References

Index of Extrabiblical Literature